The Arnold Anthology of
POST-COLONIAL
LITERATURES
in English

The Arnold Anthology of

POST-COLONIAL LITERATURES

in English

Edited by
JOHN THIEME
Professor of New Literatures in English,
University of Hull, UK

EDITORIAL BOARD
Bruce Bennett
Shirley Chew
Jean-Pierre Durix
Michael Gilkes
Coral Ann Howells
G. D. Killam
Meenakshi Mukherjee
Rajiva Wijesinha
Nana Wilson-Tagoe

A member of the Hodder Headline Group
LONDON • NEW YORK • SYDNEY • AUCKLAND

First published in Great Britain in 1996 by
Arnold, a member of the Hodder Headline Group
338 Euston Road, London NW1 3BH
175 Fifth Avenue, New York, NY10010

Distributed exclusively in the USA by
St Martin's Press Inc.,
175 Fifth Avenue,
New York, NY10010

British Library Cataloguing in Publication Data
A catalogue record for this book is available from the British Library

Library of Congress Cataloging-in-Publication Data
The Arnold Anthology of Post-colonial Literatures in English / edited
by John Thieme
    p.   cm.
Includes bibliographical references and index.
1. Commonwealth literature (English).   2. Commonwealth countries–
–Literature collections.   3. English literature——Foreign countries.
4. Decolonization——Literary collections   5. English
literature——20th century.   I. Thieme, John.
PR9085.A7   1996
820.8'09171241——dc20   95-53843

ISBN 0 340 64620 9 (Pb)
ISBN 0 340 64619 5 (Hb)

Composition in 9½/11½ Berling by Anneset, Weston-super-Mare, Avon
Printed and bound in Great Britain by Mackays of Chatham plc, Kent

Contents

PART III: CANADA

PART IV: CARIBBEAN —————————

PART V: NEW ZEALAND AND SOUTH PACIFIC

PART VI: SOUTH ASIA

INDIA

SRI LANKA

BANGLADESH

PAKISTAN

PART VII: SOUTH-EAST ASIA ———

MALAYSIA

SINGAPORE

PART VIII: TRANS-CULTURAL WRITING

Acknowledgements

The editor and publishers would like to thank the following for permission to use copyright material in this book:

Chinua Achebe: Selection from *Arrow of God*, by Chinua Achebe, published by William Heinemann. Copyright © 1964, 1974 by Chinua Achebe. Reprinted by permission of the author and William Heinemann Ltd. Selection from *Hopes and Impediments*, by Chinua Achebe. Copyright © 1988 by Chinua Achebe. Reprinted by permission of the author. Selection from *Anthills of the Savannah*, by Chinua Achebe. Copyright © 1987 by Chinua Achebe. Reprinted by permission of the author.

John Agard: 'Mek Four', by John Agard. Copyright © 1990 by John Agard. Reprinted by permission of Serpent's Tail, London.

Ama Ata Aidoo: 'The Message', by Ama Ata Aidoo. Copyright © 1970 Ama Ata Aidoo. Reprinted by permission of the author. 'Motherhood and the Numbers Game', by Ama Ata Aidoo. Copyright © 1992 by Ama Ata Aidoo. Reprinted by permission of Dangaroo Press.

Meena Alexander: 'House of a Thousand Doors', from *House of a Thousand Doors*, by Meena Alexander (Washington DC, Three Continents Press, 1988). Copyright © 1988 by Meena Alexander. Reprinted by permission of the author.

Agha Shahid Ali: 'Postcard from Kashmir' and 'A Wrong Turn', from *The Half-Inch Himalayas*, by Agha Shahid Ali (Wesleyan University Press, 1987). Copyright © 1987 by Agha Shahid Ali. Reprinted by permission of University Press of New England.

Ahmed Ali: Selection from *Twilight in Delhi*, by Ahmed Ali. Reprinted by permission of the Estate of Ahmed Ali.

Mulk Raj Anand: Selection from *Untouchable*, by Mulk Raj Anand. Copyright © 1970 Mulk Raj Anand. Reprinted by permission of The Bodley Head.

Jean Arasanayagam: 'Passages', by Jean Arasanayagam, from *Reddened Water Flows Clear*, 1991. Copyright © by Jean Arasanayagam. Reprinted by permission of Forest Books.

Jeannette C. Armstrong: 'This Is a Story' by Jeannette C. Armstrong. Reprinted by permission of the author.

Margaret Atwood: 'Progressive Insanities of a Pioneer', from *The Animals in That Country*, by Margaret Atwood. Copyright © 1968 by Oxford University Press Canada. Reprinted by permission of Oxford University Press Canada. Selection from *Survival*, by Margaret Atwood. Copyright © 1972 by Margaret Atwood. Reprinted by permission of the Canadian Publishers, McClelland & Stewart, Toronto. 'The Age of Lead', from *Wilderness Tips*, by Margaret Atwood. Copyright © 1991 by O. W. Toad Ltd. Reprinted by permission of Curtis Brown Ltd, on behalf of Margaret Atwood, Doubleday, a division of Bantam Doubleday Dell Publishing Group, Inc., and the Canadian Publishers, McClelland & Stewart, Toronto. 'Morning in the Burned House', by Margaret Atwood, from *Morning in the Burned House*. Copyright © 1995 Margaret Atwood. Reprinted by permission of Curtis Brown Ltd, London, on behalf of Margaret Atwood, the Canadian Publishers, McClelland & Stewart, Toronto and Houghton Mifflin Company. All rights reserved.

Murray Bail: 'The Drover's Wife', by Murray Bail. Copyright © 1975, 1986 Murray Bail. Reprinted by permission of the author. 'The Drover's Wife' by Russell Drysdale. Copyright © 1945 by the Estate of Russell Drysdale. Reproduced by permission of the Estate of Russell Drysdale and the National Gallery of Australia.

James Baxter: 'On the Death of Her Body', 'Jerusalem Sonnets, I', and 'The Ikons', by James K. Baxter, from *Selected Poems*, ed. J. E. Weir. Copyright © 1982 Oxford University Press. Reprinted by permission of Oxford University Press.

Louise Bennett: 'Colonisation in Reverse' and 'Dear Departed Federation', by Louise Bennett. Copyright © 1966 by Louise Bennett. Reprinted by permission of Sangster's Book Stores Ltd.

Sujata Bhatt: 'A Different History', by Sujata Bhatt. Copyright © 1988 Carcanet. Reprinted from *Brunizem* by permission of Carcanet Press Ltd.

Earle Birney: 'Bushed', from *The Poems of Earle Birney*, by Earle Birney. Copyright © 1969 by Earle Birney. Reprinted by permission of the Estate of Earle Birney and the Canadian Publishers, McClelland & Stewart, Toronto. 'Mappemounde', from *The Poems of Earle Birney*, by Earle Birney. Reprinted by permission of the Estate of Earle Birney and the Canadian Publishers, McClelland & Stewart, Toronto.

Valerie Bloom: 'Language Barrier', from *Touch Mi, Tell Mi*, by Valerie Bloom (Bogle-L'Ouverture Press). Copyright © 1983 by Valerie Bloom. Reprinted by permission of the author.

George Bowering: 'Grandfather' by George Bowering. Reprinted by permission of the author.

Edward Kamau Brathwaite: 'Ananse' and 'Negus', from *Arrivants*, by Edward Kamau Brathwaite (1973). Reprinted by permission of Oxford University Press. Selection from *History of the Voice*, by Edward Kamau Brathwaite. New Beacon Books, 1984. Copyright © 1984 Edward Kamau Brathwaite. Reprinted by permission of New Beacon Books Ltd.

Jean 'Binta' Breeze: 'Spring Cleaning', by Jean 'Binta' Breeze. Copyright © 1992 by Jean 'Binta' Breeze. Reprinted by permission of Virago.

Erna Brodber: Selection from *Jane and Louisa Will Soon Come Home*, by Erna Brodber, New Beacon Books, 1980. Copyright © 1980 Erna Brodber. Reprinted by permission of New Beacon Books Ltd.

Bonnie Burnard: 'Music Lessons', reprinted from *Women of Influence*, by Bonnie Burnard, first published by Coteau Books, Canada, 1988. Copyright © 1988 Bonnie Burnard. Reprinted by permission of the author, Coteau Books and The Women's Press Ltd.

Peter Carey: 'Do You Love Me?', by Peter Carey, from *War Crimes*, University of Queensland Press, St Lucia, 1979. Copyright © 1979 by Peter Carey. Reprinted by permission of the author c/o Rogers, Coleridge & White Ltd, 20 Powis Mews, London W11 1JN, and University of Queensland Press.

George Elliott Clarke: 'How Exile Melts to One Hundred Roses', from *Whylah Falls*, by George Elliott Clarke, published by Polestar Press Ltd, 1011 Commercial Dr. Vancouver, Canada V5L 3X1. Copyright © 1990 by George Elliott Clarke. Reprinted by permission of Polestar Book Publishers.

J. M. Coetzee: Selection from *Foe*, by J. M. Coetzee. Copyright © 1986 by J. M. Coetzee. Reprinted by permission of Martin Secker & Warburg Ltd, and Viking Penguin, a division of Penguin Books USA Inc.

Rienzi Crusz: 'Roots', by Rienzi Crusz. Reprinted from *A Time for Loving* by Rienzi Crusz (Toronto: TSAR Publications, 1986), by permission of the Publishers.

Allen Curnow: 'House and Land' and 'Landfall in Unknown Seas', from *A Small Room with Large Windows: Selected Poems*, by Allen Curnow (1962). Copyright © 1962 Allen Curnow. Reprinted by permission of Oxford University Press.

Fred D'Aguiar: 'Letter from Mama Dot', from *Mama Dot*, by Fred D'Aguiar. Copyright © 1985 by Fred D'Aguiar. Reprinted by permission of Chatto.

David Dabydeen: 'Two Cultures', by David Dabydeen. Copyright © 1984 by David Dabydeen. Reprinted by permission of the author.

Tsitsi Dangarembga: Selection from *Nervous Conditions*, by Tsitsi Dangarembga, first published in 1988 by The Women's Press Ltd, 34 Great Sutton Street, London EC1V 0DX. Copyright © 1988 by Tsitsi Dangarembga. Reprinted by permission of The Women's Press Ltd.

Keki Daruwalla: 'Death of a Bird', by Keki N. Daruwalla, from *Ten Twentieth-Century Indian Poets*, ed. R. Parthasarathy. Reprinted by permission of Oxford University Press.

Kamala Das: 'An Introduction', by Kamala Das. Copyright © 1973 by Orient Longman Ltd. Reprinted by permission of the author.

Robertson Davies: Selections from *Fifth Business*, by Robertson Davies. Copyright © 1970 by Robertson Davies. Reprinted by permission of the author.

Jack Davis: Selection from *Kullark*, by Jack Davis, published by Currency Press, Sydney. Copyright ©1982 Jack Davis. Reprinted by permission of the Publishers.

Bruce Dawe: 'Life-Cycle', from *An Eye for a Tooth*, by Bruce Dawe. Reprinted by permission of Longman Australia. 'Homecoming', from *Beyond the Subdivisions*, by Bruce Dawe. Copyright © 1969 Bruce Dawe. Reprinted by permission of Longman Australia.

Eunice De Souza: 'Marriages Are Made', and 'Women in Dutch Paintings', from *Ways of Belonging*, by Eunice De Souza. Copyright © 1990 Eunice De Souza. Reprinted by permission of Polygon.

Richard De Zoysa: 'Apocalypse Soon', by Richard De Zoysa. Reprinted from *An Anthology of Contemporary Sri Lankan Poetry in English*, ed. Rajiva Wijesinha, by permission of The British Council, Sri Lanka.

Anita Desai: Selection from *In Custody*, by Anita Desai. Copyright © 1984 Anita Desai. Reprinted by permission of the author c/o Rogers, Coleridge & White Ltd, 20 Powis Mews, London W11 1JN.

Robert Drewe: 'Stingray', by Robert Drewe. Copyright © 1983 by Robert Drewe. Reprinted by permission of Pan Macmillan Australia Pty Ltd, and Hickson Associates on behalf of the author.

Zee Edgell: Selection from *Beka Lamb*, by Zee Edgell. Copyright © 1982 by Zee Edgell. Reprinted by permission of Heinemann Publishers (Oxford) Ltd.

Ee Tiang Hong: 'Heeren Street, Malacca', and 'Arrival', by Ee Tiang Hong. Copyright © 1976 by Ee Tiang Hong. Reprinted by permission of Mrs Ee Peck Lian.

Buchi Emecheta: Selection from *The Joys of Motherhood*, by Buchi Emecheta. Copyright © 1979 Buchi Emecheta. Reprinted by permission of the author.

Nissim Ezekiel: 'Background, Casually' and 'The Patriot', by Nissim Ezekiel, from *Collected Poems 1952–1988*, by Nissim Ezekiel. Copyright © 1989 Oxford University Press. Reprinted by permission of Oxford University Press, India.

A. R. D. Fairburn: 'Imperial' and 'Tapu', by A. R. D. Fairburn. Copyright © Estate of A.R.D. Fairburn. Reprinted by permission of Richards Literary Agency, Auckland.

Lloyd Fernando: Selection from *Scorpion Orchid*, by Lloyd Fernando. Copyright © 1992 by Times Editions Pte Ltd. Reprinted by permission of the author, and Times Publishing Ltd.

Patrick Fernando: 'The Fisherman Mourned by His Wife', by Patrick Fernando, from *Modern Sri Lankan Poetry*, D.C.R.A. Goonetilleke (ed.), 1987. Reprinted by permission of Sri Satguru Publications, a division of Indian Books Centre.

Timothy Findley: Selection from 'Lemonade', from *Dinner Along the Amazon*, by Timothy Findley. Copyright © 1984 by Pebble Productions Inc. Reprinted by permission of Penguin Books Canada Ltd.

Janet Frame: Selection from *Faces in the Water*, by Janet Frame, first published by The Women's Press Ltd, 1980, 34 Great Sutton Street, London EC1V 0DX. Copyright © 1961, 1982 by Janet Frame. Reprinted by permission of The Women's Press Ltd and George Braziller, Inc.

Miles Franklin: Selection from *My Brilliant Career*, by Miles Franklin. Reprinted by permission of HarperCollins Publishers.

Athol Fugard, John Kani and Winston Ntshona: Selection from *Sizwe Bansi is Dead* from *Statements*, by Athol Fugard, John Kani and Winston Ntshona. Copyright © 1973 and 1974 Athol Fugard, John Kani, and Winston Ntshona. Reprinted by permission of Oxford University Press.

Helen Garner: 'The Life of Art', by Helen Garner. Copyright © 1985 Helen Garner. Reprinted from *Postcards from Surfers* published by Bloomsbury in London, 1988. Reprinted by permission of Bloomsbury and Penguin Books Australia Ltd.

Zulfikar Ghose: 'This Landscape, These People'. Copyright © 1964 by Zulfikar Ghose. First published in *The Loss of India* (Routledge & Kegan Paul, London). 'The Attack on Sialkot', by Zulfikar Ghose. Copyright © 1967 by Zulfikar Ghose. First published in *Jets from Orange* (Macmillan, London). Reprinted by permission of the author.

Amitav Ghosh: Selections from *The Shadow Lines*, by Amitav Ghosh. Copyright © 1988 by Amitav Ghosh. Reprinted by permission of Wylie, Aitken & Stone Inc.

Michael Gilkes: Selections from 'Prospero's Island', by Michael Gilkes. Reprinted by permission of the author.

Mary Gilmore: 'Old Botany Bay', by Mary Gilmore, from *The Singing Tree*. Reprinted by permission of HarperCollins Publishers.

Lorna Goodison: 'I Am Becoming My Mother', from *I Am Becoming My Mother*, by Lorna Goodison, New Beacon Books, 1986. Reprinted by permission of New Beacon Books Ltd.

Yasmine Gooneratne: 'Big Match, 1983' and 'This Language, This Woman', by Yasmine Gooneratne. Reprinted by permission of the author. 'Bharat Changes His Image' from *A Change of Skies* by Yasmine Gooneratne. Copyright © 1991 by Yasmine Gooneratne. Reprinted by permission of the author and Pan Macmillan Australia Pty Ltd.

Nadine Gordimer: 'Six Feet of the Country', by Nadine Gordimer. Copyright © 1956 by Nadine Gordimer. Included in *Six Feet of the Country* by Nadine Gordimer (Jonathan Cape, 1975) and *Selected Stories* by Nadine Gordimer (Viking Penguin). Reprinted by permission of Jonathan Cape, and Viking Penguin, a division of Penguin Books USA Inc.

Patricia Grace: Selection from *Potiki*, by Patricia Grace, first published in 1987 by The Women's Press Ltd, 34 Great Sutton Street, London EC1V 0DX. Copyright © 1986 Patricia Grace. Reprinted by permission of Penguin Books (New Zealand) Ltd.

Kate Grenville: Selections from *Joan Makes History*, by Kate Grenville, published by Heinemann. Copyright © 1988 by Kate Grenville. Reprinted by permission of the author.

Abdulrazak Gurnah: Selection from *Paradise*, by Abdulrazak Gurnah (Hamish Hamilton, 1994). Copyright © 1994 by Abdulrazak Gurnah. Reprinted by permission of the author c/o Rogers, Coleridge & White Ltd, 20 Powis Mews, London W11 1JN, and Hamish Hamilton Ltd.

Kaiser Haq: 'A Myth Reworked', from *A Little Ado* by Kaiser Haq. Copyright © 1978 Kaiser Haq. Reprinted by permission of the author.

Githa Hariharan: 'The Remains of the Feast', by Githa Hariharan. Copyright ©1993 by Githa Hariharan. Reprinted by permission of the author.

Wilson Harris: Selection from *Palace of the Peacock*, by Wilson Harris. Copyright ©1960 by Wilson Harris. Reprinted by permission of Faber & Faber Ltd. Selection from 'Tradition and the West Indian Novel', from *Tradition, the Writer and Society*, by Wilson Harris, New Beacon Books, 1967. Copyright © 1967 by Wilson Harris. Reprinted by permission of New Beacon Books Ltd.

Gwen Harwood: 'Suburban Sonnet', from *Poems Vol II*, by Gwen Harwood. Copyright © 1975

Gwen Harwood. Reprinted by permission of HarperCollins Publishers.

Alamgir Hashmi: 'So What If I Live in a House Made by Idiots?' and 'Inland' from *Inland and Other Poems* (Islamabad, Gulmohar Press, 1988). Copyright © 1988 by Alamgir Hashmi. Reprinted by permission of the author.

Epeli Hau'ofa: 'The Seventh and Other Days', from *Tales of the Tikongs*, by Epeli Hau'ofa. Copyright © Epeli Hau'ofa. Reprinted by permission of Longman Paul Ltd.

Bessie Head: Selection from *A Question of Power*, by Bessie Head. Copyright © 1974 Bessie Head. Reprinted by permission of John Johnson Ltd on behalf of the Estate of Bessie Head.

Dorothy Hewett: Selection from 'Testament', by Dorothy Hewett. Copyright © 1968 Dorothy Hewett. Reprinted from *Windmill Country* by permission of the author, and *Overland*, Australia.

A. D. Hope: 'Australia', from *Selected Poems*, by A. D. Hope. Reprinted by permission of HarperCollins Publishers.

Attia Hosain: 'Gossamer Thread', by Attia Hosain. Copyright © 1953 by Attia Hosain. Reprinted by permission of Virago.

Keri Hulme: Selection from *The Bone People*, by Keri Hulme. Copyright © 1983 Keri Hulme. Reprinted by permission of Hodder Moa Beckett Publishers Ltd, and Picador.

Witi Ihimaera: 'The Whale', by Witi Ihimaera. Reprinted by permission of the author and Reed Publishing (NZ) Ltd. 'This Life is Weary', by Witi Ihimaera. Copyright © 1989 by Witi Ihimaera. Reprinted by permission of Penguin Books (New Zealand) Ltd.

C. L. R. James: Selection from *Beyond a Boundary*, by C. L. R. James. Copyright © 1969 by C. L. R. James. Reprinted by permission of Stanley Paul Publishers and Curtis Brown Ltd, London, on behalf of C. L. R. James.

Barbara Jefferis: 'The Drover's Wife' by Barbara Jefferis. Copyright © by Barbara Jefferis. Reprinted by permission of the author.

Philip Jeyaretnam: 'Making Coffee', by Philip Jeyaretnam. Copyright © 1993 Philip Jeyaretnam. Reprinted by permission of the author. Also by Philip Jeyaretnam: *First Loves* (Times Editions Ltd, 1987), *Raffles Place Ragtime* (Times Editions Ltd, 1988), and *Abraham's Promise* (Times Editions Ltd, 1995; The University of Hawai'i Press, 1995).

Ruth Prawer Jhabvala: 'Myself in India', from *An Experience of India*, by Ruth Prawer Jhabvala. Copyright © Ruth Prawer Jhabvala. Reprinted by permission of A. M. Heath on behalf of the author.

Nick Joaquin: Selection from *The Woman Who Had Two Navels*, by Nick Joaquin. Copyright © 1972 by Solidaridad Publishing House. Reprinted by permission of the author, and Solidaridad Publishing House.

Linton Kwesi Johnson: 'Doun de Road', by Linton Kwesi Johnson. Copyright © 1975 by Linton Kwesi Johnson. Reprinted by permission of the author.

Jamaica Kincaid: 'In the Night', by Jamaica Kincaid. Copyright © 1978, 1983 by Jamaica Kincaid. Reprinted by permission of Farrar, Straus & Giroux, Inc., and *The New Yorker*.

Thomas King: 'The One about Coyote Going West', by Thomas King from *One Good Story, That One*, copyright © 1993 by Dead Dog Cafe Productions Inc. Published in Canada by HarperCollins Publishers Ltd.

Joy Kogawa: Selection from *Obasan*, by Joy Kogawa, published by Lester and Orpen Dennys. Copyright © 1981 by Joy Kogawa. Reprinted by permission of Lester and Orpen Dennys, Toronto, Ontario.

Robert Kroetsch: 'Stone Hammer Poem', from *The Stone Hammer Poems 1960–1975*, by Robert Kroetsch (Oolichan Books, 1975). Copyright © 1975 by Robert Kroetsch. Reprinted by permission of the author. Selection from 'The Moment of the Discovery of America Continues', by Robert Kroetsch. Copyright © 1989 by Robert Kroetsch. Reprinted by permission of Sterling Lord Associates (Canada) Ltd.

George Lamming: Selection from *In the Castle of My Skin*, by George Lamming. Reprinted by permission of the author. Selection from *The Pleasures of Exile*, by George Lamming. Copyright © 1960, 1984 by George Lamming. Reprinted by permission of the author.

Evelyn Lau: Selection from 'Mercy' from *Fresh Girls and Other Stories*, by Evelyn Lau. Copyright © 1993 by Evelyn Lau. Published in Canada by HarperCollins Publishers Ltd, in the United States by Hyperion, and in the UK by Minerva. Reprinted by permission of Mandarin.

Margaret Laurence: Selection from *The Diviners*, by Margaret Laurence. Copyright © 1974 by Margaret Laurence. Reprinted by permission of the Canadian Publishers, McClelland & Stewart, Toronto, and A. P. Watt Ltd on behalf of New End, Inc.

Ray Lawler: Selection from *Summer of the Seventeenth Doll*, by Ray Lawler, published by Currency Press, Sydney. Copyright © 1957 Ray Lawler. Reprinted by permission of the Publishers.

Lee Kok Liang: 'Five Fingers', from *The Mutes of the Sun and Other Stories* by Lee Kok Liang. Copyright © 1964 by the Estate of Lee Kok Liang. Reprinted by permission of the Estate of Lee Kok Liang.

Lee Tzu Pheng: 'Excluding Byzantium', by Lee Tzu Pheng. Copyright © 1993 by Lee Tzu Pheng. Reprinted by permission of the author.

Shirley Geok-lin Lim: 'Christmas in Exile' and ' On Reading Coleridge's Poem', from *Crossing the Peninsula*, by Shirley Geok-lin Lim (Heinemann Writing in Asia Series, Kuala Lumpur, 1980). Copyright © 1980 by Shirley Lim. Reprinted by permission of the author.

Earl Lovelace: Selection from *The Dragon Can't Dance*, by Earl Lovelace. Copyright © 1979 by Earl Lovelace. Reprinted by permission of André Deutsch Ltd.

James McAuley: 'Terra Australis', by James McAuley from *Collected Poems*, by James McAuley. Copyright © 1988 Estate of James McAuley. Reprinted by permission of HarperCollins Publishers.

Gwendolyn MacEwen: Selection from *Terror and Erebus*, from *Afterworlds* by Gwendolyn MacEwen. Copyright © 1993 the Estate of Gwendolyn MacEwen. Reprinted by permission of the Gwendolyn MacEwen Estate, and the Canadian Publishers, McClelland & Stewart, Toronto.

Hugh MacLennan: Selection from *Barometer Rising*, by Hugh MacLennan. Copyright © 1941, 1958 by Hugh MacLennan. Reprinted by permission of Blanche C. Gregory Inc., on behalf of the Estate of Hugh MacLennan.

Alistair MacLeod: 'As Birds Bring Forth the Sun', from *The Lost Salt Gift of Blood*, by Alistair MacLeod. Copyright © 1988 by Ontario Review Press. Reprinted by permission of Jonathan Cape, and the Canadian Publishers, McClelland & Stewart, Toronto.

Jayanta Mahapatra: 'Grandfather', from *Selected Poems* by Jayanta Mahapatra. Reprinted by permission of Oxford University Press.

Jamal Mahjoub: Selection from *Navigation of a Rainmaker*, by Jamal Mahjoub. Copyright © 1989 by Jamal Mahjoub. Reprinted by permission of Heinemann Publishers (Oxford) Ltd.

Roger Mais: Selection from *Brother Man*, from *The Three Novels of Roger Mais*. Reprinted by permission of Jonathan Cape.

David Malouf: Selection from *Remembering Babylon*, by David Malouf. Copyright © 1993 David Malouf. Reprinted by permission of the author c/o Rogers, Coleridge & White Ltd, 20 Powis Mews, London W11 1JN and Chatto.

Eli Mandel: ' "Grandfather's Painting": David Thauberger', by Eli Mandel, originally published in *Life Sentence* by Eli Mandel, Victoria, B.C., Press Porcépic, 1981, p. 27. Copyright © 1981 Press Porcépic. Reprinted by permission of Beach Holme Publishing Ltd.

Bill Manhire: Selection from 'South Pacific', by Bill Manhire. Copyright © 1990 Bill Manhire. Reprinted by permission of the author and Carcanet Press Ltd.

K. S. Maniam: Selection from *The Return*, by K. S. Maniam. Copyright © 1981, 1993 K. S. Maniam. Reprinted by permission of the author.

Daphne Marlatt: Selection from *Ana Historic*, by Daphne Marlatt. Copyright © 1988 Daphne Marlatt. Reprinted from *Ana Historic* with the permission of Coach House Press. 'Arriving at Shared Ground Through Difference' by Daphne Marlatt. Copyright © 1990 by Daphne Marlatt. Reprinted from *Language in Her Eye*, with the permission of Coach House Press.

R. A. K. Mason: 'On the Swag', by R. A. K. Mason. Copyright © 1962 R. A. K. Mason. Reprinted by permission of Richards Literary Agency, Auckland.

The Mighty Sparrow (Slinger Francisco): 'Dan is the Man in the Van', by The Mighty Sparrow. Reprinted by permission of Sparrow Music Company. The copyright work 'Dan is the Man in the Van' is specifically excluded from any blanket photocopying arrangements.

Rohinton Mistry: 'Squatter', from *Tales from the Firozsha Baag*, by Rohinton Mistry. Copyright © 1987 Rohinton Mistry. Reprinted by permission of Faber & Faber Ltd, London, and the Canadian Publishers, McClelland & Stewart, Toronto.

Mohamad Bin Haji Salleh: 'Do Not Say', by Mohamad Bin Haji Salleh. Copyright © Singapore University Press Pte Ltd. Reprinted by permission of Singapore University Press (Pte) Ltd.

Frank Moorhouse: 'The Drover's Wife', from *Room Service*, by Frank Moorhouse. Copyright © 1987 by Frank Moorhouse. Reprinted by permission of Penguin Books Australia Ltd.

Dom Moraes: 'Sinbad', from *Collected Poems*, by Dom Moraes. Copyright © 1957, 1960, 1965, 1987 Dom Moraes. Reprinted by permission of the author and Penguin Books India Pvt Ltd.

Sally Morgan: 'A Black Grandmother', from *My Place*, by Sally Morgan. Copyright © 1987 by Sally Jane Morgan. Reprinted by permission of Virago, Henry Holt and Co., Inc., and Fremantle Arts Centre Press.

Mervyn Morris: 'The Pond' and 'Narcissus', from *The Pond*, by Mervyn Morris, New Beacon Books, 1973. Copyright © 1973 Mervyn Morris. Reprinted by permission of New Beacon Books Ltd.

Mudrooroo Narogin (Colin Johnson): 'They Give Jacky Rights', by Mudrooroo Narogin, from *Inside Black Australia: An Anthology of Aboriginal Poetry*, ed. Kevin Gilbert. Reprinted by permission of Penguin Books Australia Ltd.

Bharati Mukherjee: 'Loose Ends', from *The Middleman and Other Stories*, by Bharati Mukherjee. Copyright © 1988 by Bharati Mukherjee. Reprinted by permission of the author, Penguin Books Canada Ltd and Virago.

Alice Munro: 'Epilogue: The Photographer', from *Lives of Girls and Women*, by Alice Munro. Copyright © 1971 by Alice Munro. Published by McGraw-Hill Ryerson Ltd. Reprinted by permission of the Virginia Barber Literary Agency. All rights reserved.

Les Murray: 'Blood' and 'Quintets for Robert Morley,' by Les Murray. Copyright © 1965, 1969, 1972, 1974, 1977, 1982 by Les A. Murray. Reprinted by permission of Margaret Connolly & Associates Pty Ltd, on behalf of the author.

Mbulelo Mzamane: 'My Cousin Comes to Jo'burg', by Mbulelo Mzamane. Copyright © 1980 by Mbulelo Mzamane. Reprinted by permission of Shelley Power Literary Agency Ltd.

V. S. Naipaul: 'Man-Man', from *Miguel Street*, by V. S. Naipaul (Penguin Books 1971, first published by André Deutsch). Copyright © 1959 by V. S. Naipaul. Reprinted by permission of Penguin Books Ltd, and Aitken, Stone & Wylie Ltd on behalf of the author. Selection from *A House for Mr Biswas*, by V. S. Naipaul (Penguin Books 1969, first published by André Deutsch). Copyright © 1961, 1969 by V .S. Naipaul. Reprinted by permission of Penguin Books Ltd, and Aitken, Stone & Wylie Ltd on behalf of the author. Selection from *A Way in the World*, by V. S. Naipaul. Copyright © 1994 by V. S. Naipaul. Reprinted by permission of Aitken, Stone & Wylie Ltd on behalf of the author.

R. K. Narayan: Selection from *The Man-Eater of Malgudi*, by R. K. Narayan. Copyright © 1961 R. K. Narayan. Reprinted by permission of William Heinemann Ltd, and the Wallace Literary Agency, Inc.

Lauretta Ngcobo: Selection from *And They Didn't Die*, by Lauretta Ngcobo. Copyright © 1990 by Lauretta Ngcobo. Reprinted by permission of Virago, and Shelley Power Literary Agency Ltd.

Ngugi wa Thiong'o: Selection from *Decolonising the Mind: The Politics of Language in African Literature*, by Ngugi wa Thiong'o. Copyright © 1981, 1982, 1984 and 1986 Ngugi wa Thiong'o. Reprinted by permission of James Currey Publishers, London. Selection from *A Grain of Wheat*, by Ngugi wa Thiong'o. Copyright © 1967 Ngugi wa Thiong'o. Reprinted by permission of Heinemann Publishers (Oxford) Ltd.

Grace Nichols: 'One Continent/To Another', from *i is a long memoried woman*, by Grace Nichols. Copyright © 1983, 1995 Karnak House. Reprinted by permission of the Publishers.

Bernard O'Dowd: 'Australia', from *Collected Poems*, by Bernard O'Dowd. Reprinted by permission of Thomas C. Lothian Pty Ltd, Australia, on behalf of the Estate of Bernard O'Dowd.

Christopher Okigbo: 'Siren Limits', by Christopher Okigbo. Copyright © 1964 Christopher Okigbo. Reprinted by permission of Heinemann Publishers (Oxford) Ltd.

Okot p'Bitek: 'My Name Blew Like a Horn Among the Payira', from *Song of Lawino and Song of Ocol*, by Okot p'Bitek. Copyright ©1966, 1967 The Estate of Okot p'Bitek. Reprinted by permission of Heinemann Publishers (Oxford) Ltd.

Ben Okri: 'Incidents at the Shrine', by Ben Okri. Copyright © 1986 Ben Okri. Reprinted by permission of the author.

Michael Ondaatje: Selection from *Running in the Family*, by Michael Ondaatje. Copyright © 1982 by Michael Ondaatje. Reprinted by permission of the author and W. W. Norton & Company Inc. Selection from *In the Skin of a Lion*, by Michael Ondaatje. Copyright © 1987 by Michael Ondaatje. Reprinted by permission of the author, Alfred A. Knopf Inc., and the Canadian Publishers, McClelland & Stewart, Toronto.

Oodgeroo Noonuccal (Kath Walker): 'We Are Going', by Oodgeroo of the tribe Noonuccal (formerly known as Kath Walker), from *My People*, 3rd edition, 1990, published by Jacaranda Press. Reprinted by permission of the publishers.

Niyi Osundare: 'Harvestcall', by Niyi Osundare, from *The Eye of the Earth*, Heinemann Educational Books (Nigeria) Ltd. Reprinted by permission of Heinemann Educational Books (Nigeria) Ltd.

M. Nourbese Philip: 'She Tries Her Tongue: Her Silence Softly Breaks', from *She Tries Her Tongue: Her Silence Softly Breaks*, by M. Nourbese Philip, first published in 1995 by The Women's Press Ltd., 34 Great Sutton Street, London EC1V 0DX. Reprinted by permission of the author, and The Women's Press Ltd.

Caryl Phillips: Selections from *Crossing the River*, by Caryl Phillips, published by Bloomsbury in London, 1991. Copyright © 1992 Caryl Phillips. Reprinted by permission of Bloomsbury and Alfred A. Knopf Inc.

Peter Porter: 'Phar Lap in the Melbourne Museum', from *Collected Poems*, by Peter Porter. Copyright © 1983 by Peter Porter. Reprinted by permission of Oxford University Press.

E. J. Pratt: Selection from 'Brébeuf and His Brethren', by E. J. Pratt, from *E. J. Pratt Complete Poems Part 1*, eds Sandra Djwa and R. G. Moyles, University of Toronto Press Inc. Copyright © 1989 by University of Toronto Press. Reprinted by permission of University of Toronto Press Inc.

Al Purdy: 'Elegy for a Grandfather' and 'Roblin's Mills', from *The Collected Poems of Al Purdy*, by Al Purdy. Copyright © 1978 by Al Purdy. Reprinted by permission of the Canadian Publishers, McClelland & Stewart, Toronto.

Raja Rao: Selection from *Kanthapura*, by Raja Rao. Copyright © Raj Rao. Reprinted by permission of Oxford University Press.

A. K. Ramanujan: 'Small-Scale Reflections on a Great House', by A. K. Ramanujan, from *Ten*

Twentieth-Century Indian Poets, ed. R. Parthasarathy. Reprinted by permission of Oxford University Press.

Anne Ranasinghe: 'At What Dark Point', by Anne Ranasinghe. Copyright © 1991 Anne Ranasinghe. Reprinted by permission of the author.

James Reaney: 'Maps', by James Reaney. Copyright © 1972 Reaney. Reprinted by permission of Cultural Support Services Inc., Toronto, on behalf of the author who may be contacted through Cultural Support Services Inc., Toronto, Canada at tel: (416) 962-6200, fax (416) 962-6201.

Victor Stafford Reid: Selections from *New Day* by Victor Stafford Reid. Copyright © 1949 by Alfred A. Knopf, Inc. Reprinted by permission of the publisher and the estate of Victor Stafford Reid.

Jean Rhys: 'The Day They Burned the Books', from *Tigers Are Better Looking*, by Jean Rhys (Penguin Books 1972, first published by André Deutsch). Copyright © 1960 by Jean Rhys. 'I Used to Live Here Once', from *Sleep It Off Lady*, by Jean Rhys (Penguin Books 1979, first published by André Deutsch). Copyright © 1976 by Jean Rhys. Reprinted by permission of Penguin Books Ltd, and the Wallace Literary Agency, Inc. These stories also appear in *The Collected Short Stories* by Jean Rhys, published by W.W. Norton & Company, Inc.

Henry Handel Richardson: Selection from 'Australia Felix', by Henry Handel Richardson. Reprinted by permission of William Heinemann Ltd.

Sinclair Ross: Selection from *As for Me and My House*, by Sinclair Ross. Copyright © 1941 by Sinclair Ross, copyright © Canada, 1957 by Sinclair Ross. Reprinted by permission of the Canadian Publishers, McClelland & Stewart, Toronto.

Salman Rushdie: Selections from *Midnight's Children*, by Salman Rushdie. Copyright © 1981 by Salman Rushdie. Reprinted by permission of Jonathan Cape and London Management, on behalf of the author. Extracts from the *Koran*, translated by N. J. Dawood (Penguin Classics 1956, 4th rev. edn 1974). Copyright © 1956, 1959 by N. J. Dawood. Reprinted by permission of Penguin Books Ltd. Selection from 'Imaginary Homelands', from *Imaginary Homelands: Essays and Criticism 1981–1991*, by Salman Rushdie (Granta, 1991). Copyright © 1982 Salman Rushdie. Reprinted by permission of Penguin Books Ltd.

Nayantara Sahgal: 'Martand', by Nayantara Sahgal. Reprinted by permission of London Magazine Ltd.

Frank Sargeson: 'I've Lost My Pal' by Frank Sargeson, from *The Stories of Frank Sargeson*. Copyright © 1964, 1973, 1982 Frank Sargeson. Reprinted by permission of Longman Paul Ltd.

Shyam Selvadurai: Selection from *Funny Boy*, by Shyam Selvadurai. Copyright © 1994 by Shyam Selvadurai. Reprinted by permission of the Canadian Publishers, McClelland & Stewart, Toronto, William Morrow & Company, Inc., and Jonathan Cape.

Samuel Selvon: Selection from *The Lonely Londoners*, by Samuel Selvon. Copyright © 1972 Samuel Selvon. Reprinted by permission of Mrs Althea Selvon. 'Working the Transport', by Samuel Selvon. Reprinted by permission of Mrs Althea Selvon.

Olive Senior: 'Summer Lightning', from *Summer Lightning and Other Stories*, by Olive Senior. Copyright © 1986 Longman Group Ltd. Reprinted by permission of Longman Group Ltd.

Vikram Seth: Selection from *A Suitable Boy*, by Vikram Seth. Reprinted by permission of Phoenix House.

Alan Seymour: Selections from *The One Day of the Year*, by Alan Seymour. Copyright © 1962 by Alan Seymour. Reprinted by permission of HarperCollins Publishers.

Bapsi Sidhwa: Selections from *Ice-Candy-Man*, by Bapsi Sidhwa. Copyright © 1988 Bapsi Sidhwa. Reprinted by permission of William Heinemann Ltd, and the Peters Fraser & Dunlop Group Ltd.

Kenneth Slessor: 'South Country' and 'The Night-Ride', from *Collected Poems*, by Kenneth Slessor. Reprinted by permission of HarperCollins Publishers.

Elizabeth Smart: Selection from *By Grand Central Station I Sat Down and Wept*, by Elizabeth Smart. Copyright © 1966 by Elizabeth Smart. Reprinted by permission of HarperCollins Publishers.

S. P. Somtow: Selection from *Jasmine Nights*, by S. P. Somtow. Copyright © 1994 Somtow Sucharitkul. Reprinted by permission of Artellus Ltd.

Wole Soyinka: 'Abiku', from *Idanre & Other Poems*, by Wole Soyinka, published by Methuen, London. Copyright © 1967 by Wole Soyinka. Reprinted by permission of Hill and Wang, a division of Farrar, Straus & Giroux, Inc, and Methuen London. Selection from *The Lion and the Jewel*, from *Collected Plays 2*, by Wole Soyinka. Copyright © 1963, 1964, 1967, 1971, 1973, 1974 Wole Soyinka. Reprinted by permission of Oxford University Press.

Christina Stead: 'The Schoolboy's Tale: Day of Wrath', by Christina Stead, from *The Salzburg Tales*, Virago Press, Ltd, Editions Tom Thompson. Copyright © 1994 by the Estate of Christina Stead. Reprinted by permission of the Estate of Christina Stead, c/o Joan Daves Agency as agent for the proprietor.

Subramani: 'Marigolds', by Subramani. Copyright © 1988 Subramani. Reprinted by permission of Three Continents Press Inc.

Susan Swan: Selection from *The Biggest Modern Woman of the World*, by Susan Swan, published by Lester Orpen & Dennys. Copyright © 1983 by Susan Swan. Reprinted by permission of McIntosh and Otis, Inc., and Lester Orpen & Dennys.

Audrey Thomas: Selection from *Intertidal Life*, by Audrey Thomas. Copyright © 1984 by Audrey Thomas. Reprinted by permission of Stoddart Publishing Co. Ltd, Don Mills, Ontario.

Edwin Thumboo: 'Gods Can Die', by Edwin Thumboo. Copyright © Singapore University Press Pte Ltd. Reprinted by permission of Singapore University Press (Pte) Ltd.

John Tranter: Selection from 'The False Atlas', by John Tranter. Copyright © 1979 by John Tranter. All rights reserved. Reprinted by permission of the author.

Amos Tutuola: 'In the Bush of Ghosts', from *My Life in the Bush of Ghosts*, by Amos Tutuola. Reprinted by permission of Faber & Faber Ltd, and Grove/Atlantic, Inc.

Hone Tuwhare: 'Speak to Me, Brother', by Hone Tuwhare. Copyright © 1972 Hone Tuwhare. Reprinted by permission of the author.

Aritha van Herk: Selection from *No Fixed Address*, by Aritha van Herk. Copyright © 1986 by Aritha van Herk. Originally published by McClelland & Stewart. Reprinted by permission of Virginia Barber Literary Agency. All rights reserved.

M. G. Vassanji: 'Leaving', by M. G. Vassanji, from *Uhuru Street*. Reprinted by permission of Heinemann Publishers (Oxford) Ltd.

Derek Walcott: 'Ruins of a Great House', from *Collected Poems 1948–1984*, by Derek Walcott. Copyright © 1986 by Derek Walcott. Reprinted by permission of Farrar, Straus & Giroux, Inc., and Faber & Faber Ltd. Selection from *Dream on Monkey Mountain and Other Plays*, by Derek Walcott. Copyright © 1970 by Derek Walcott. Reprinted by permission of Farrar, Straus & Giroux, Inc. Selections from 'The Muse of History', by Derek Walcott, in Orde Coombs, ed., *Is Massa Day Dead?* (Anchor Press/Doubleday, Garden City, New York, 1974), pp. 1–8 and pp. 16–18. Copyright © 1974 by Doubleday, a division of Bantam Doubleday Dell Publishing Group, Inc. Reprinted by permission of Doubleday, a division of Bantam Doubleday Dell Publishing Group, Inc. Selection from *Omeros*, by Derek Walcott. Copyright © 1990 by Derek Walcott. Reprinted by permission of Farrar, Straus & Giroux, Inc., and Faber & Faber Ltd.

Phyllis Webb: 'Marvell's Garden', by Phyllis Webb. Reprinted by permission of the author.

Albert Wendt: 'A Resurrection' by Albert Wendt. Copyright © Albert Wendt. Reprinted by permission of the author. 'Towards a New Oceania', in Paul Sharrad, ed., *Readings in Pacific Literature* (Wollongong, New Literatures Research Centre, 1993), pp. 9–19. Reprinted by permission of the author and the New Literatures Research Centre.

Patrick White: 'The Prodigal Son', from *Patrick White Speaks*, by Patrick White. Copyright © 1989 Patrick White. Reprinted by permission of Jonathan Cape, and Barbara Mobbs on behalf of the Estate of Patrick White. Selection from *The Tree of Man*, by Patrick White. Copyright © 1956 Patrick White. Reprinted by permission of Barbara Mobbs on behalf of the Estate of Patrick White.

Rudy Wiebe: 'Where Is the Voice Coming From?', by Rudy Wiebe from *River of Stone: Fictions and Memories*, copyright © 1995 by Jackpine House Ltd. Published in Canada by Knopf Canada. Reprinted by permission of the Bukowski Agency.

Punyakante Wijenaike: Selection from *Giraya*, by Punyakante Wijenaike. Copyright © 1971 by Punyakante Wijenaike. Reprinted by permission of the author.

Rajiva Wijesinha: Selection from *Days of Despair*, by Rajiva Wijesinha (second novel of a trilogy; *Acts of Faith*, published by Navrang, New Delhi, 1985, was the first). Copyright © 1989 by Rajiva Wijesinha. Reprinted by permission of the author.

Lakdasa Wikkramasinha: 'Don't Talk to Me about Matisse', by Lakdasa Wikkramasinha. Copyright © 1988 by The British Council Sri Lanka. Reprinted from *An Anthology of Contemporary Sri Lankan Poetry in English*, ed. Rajiva Wijesinha, by permission of The British Council, Sri Lanka.

Denis Williams: Selection from *Other Leopards*, by Denis Williams. Copyright © 1963 by Denis Williams. Reprinted by permission of Hutchinson.

David Williamson: Selection from *The Club*, by David Williamson, published by Currency Press, Sydney. Copyright © 1978 by David Williamson. Reprinted by permission of the Publishers.

Tim Winton: 'Neighbours', from *Scission*, by Tim Winton. Copyright © 1985 by Tim Winton. Reprinted by permission of Penguin Books Australia Ltd.

Wong Phui Nam: 'Prospect in Spring', by Wong Phui Nam. Copyright © Singapore University Press Pte Ltd. Reprinted by permission of Singapore University Press (Pte) Ltd.

Judith Wright: 'Train Journey', from *Collected Poems*, by Judith Wright. Copyright © 1963 Judith Wright. Reprinted by permission of HarperCollins Publishers.

To the best of our knowledge all copyright holders of material reproduced in this book have been traced. Any rights not acknowledged here will be noted in subsequent printings if notice is given to the publisher.

Introduction

Recent decades have seen major changes in critical practice and assumptions about the terrain of literary studies and perhaps the most significant curricular development of the last thirty years has been the emergence of university courses in the anglophone literatures of countries other than Britain and the United States. This anthology endeavours to provide student (and other) readers with an extensive cross-section of writing from the 'new' anglophone literatures to illustrate their consanguinities and differences and their richness and variety. It also shows the extent to which they interrogate Eurocentric conceptions of culture and in so doing implicitly question the former canonical orthodoxies of 'English Studies'. In the last decade in particular there has been a major growth of interest in such literatures, as the field hitherto variously known as 'Commonwealth Literature', 'New Literatures in English' and 'World Literature in English' has been reinvented and reinvigorated as 'Post-Colonial Literature'. While the term 'post-colonial' and the conceptual assumptions usually contained within it (resistance to, or at least movement beyond, colonial agendas) have been crucial to the expansion of interest in the area, it is a problematic one – for reasons that are discussed in the next paragraph – and it is also debatable whether the field it demarcates should be constituted as a unified body of study. Nevertheless 'post-colonial' has become the most widely accepted descriptive shorthand for referring to this group of literatures which contain much of the finest writing being produced in the contemporary world.

In their seminal study, *The Empire Writes Back: Theory and Practice in Post-Colonial Literatures* (1989), Bill Ashcroft, Gareth Griffiths and Helen Tiffin use the term post-colonial to refer to 'all the culture affected by the imperial process from the moment of colonization to the present day', arguing that 'there is a continuity of preoccupations throughout the historical process initiated by European imperial aggression'.[1] This usage is clearly not unproblematic since it departs from the way in which historians and sociologists most commonly employ the term, that is to refer to the period *after* colonialism, the post-*independence* period of formerly colonized countries. A third possible usage of 'post-colonial' associates it with writing and other forms of cultural production which display an oppositional attitude towards colonialism, which are to a greater or lesser degree *anti*-colonial

1 Bill Ashcroft, Gareth Griffiths and Helen Tiffin, *The Empire Writes Back: Theory and Practice in Post-Colonial Literatures* (London and New York: Routledge, 1989), p. 2.

in orientation. Such a usage makes it possible to refer to texts produced in the colonial period as 'post-colonial' and discriminates between those that contest colonialism and those that exist in a complicitous relationship with it. Often, of course, writers are oblivious of the extent to which their works engage in such positioning and the borderline between contestation and complicity is in any case at best thinly drawn. Consequently it is perhaps more satisfactory to view the term 'post-colonial' as describing a continuum of experience, in which colonialism is perceived as an agency of disturbance, unsettling both the pre-existing 'Aboriginal' or 'Native' discourses of the cultures it penetrates *and* the English (or European) discourses it brings with it.

This can be seen in the work of Australian writers so different from one another that at first sight it is tempting simply to see their discursive procedure as involving a polar opposition. In 'A Mid-Summer Noon in the Australian Forest', the nineteenth-century poet Charles Harpur may seem to be writing from a 'colonial' standpoint, since the poem appears to be displacing an English poetic vocabulary into an 'alien' context: words such as 'vermeil-crusted', 'rill', 'bower' and 'slumbrous' are used to describe the Australian scene and moment. However, Harpur generates considerable discursive tension by using these signifiers to depict his 'new' environment and what the poem's practice actually does is to foreground the act of linguistic transplantation in which it is engaging. The redeployment of a Romantic poetic idiom in a different landscape context becomes the subject of the poem and it is impossible to ignore the negotiations that are taking place. The interaction of language and context decolonizes the idiom as much as it colonizes the landscape. Representing what might initially appear to be an opposite extreme, the contemporary Aboriginal playwright Jack Davis directly confronts the issue of the dispossession of his people through the employment of dramatic structures, which both thematically and formally contest white Australian versions of history. In his play *Kullark* Davis draws on numerous elements from the culture of the Nyoongah people of South West Australia, among them oral storytelling, pictorial representation, music, dance and mime. The play offers a historical pageant of scenes dramatizing key moments in the last 150 years of Western Australian history (the period since European settlement) from an Aboriginal perspective and Davis focuses on episodes that demonstrate the injustices suffered by the Nyoongah. So *Kullark* is clearly 'post-colonial' in the third of the senses mentioned above since, as revisionist historiography, it adopts an overtly adversarial attitude towards the colonial project. Yet the play is also the product of a hybridized, 'post-colonial' interaction of cultures: it both shows its contemporary urban Aboriginal characters living lives that are inextricably interlinked with and yet divorced from 'mainstream' Australian society *and* it employs an eclectic *mélange* of influences. In addition to the Aboriginal elements already noted, it draws on Western forms as diverse as British folk tunes, country-and-western music and European watercolour painting. So these two very different writers can both be seen to exist in a continuum of post-colonial hybridized experience, even if as embodiments of settler and colonized Aboriginal subjectivity, they come close to representing opposite ends of a spectrum. Neither finally exists in an undisturbed, culturally 'pure' world; both in their very different ways are products of the post-colonial encounter; both use hybridized Englishes.

The hybridization of cultures has been seen, by writers such as Salman Rushdie and cultural theorists such as Homi Bhabha,[2] as a central aspect of the post-colonial experience and indeed of culture more generally (see below). Such thinking poses a major challenge to many of the assumptions implicit in earlier conceptions of the territory of literary study, particularly the notion that literatures should be studied in terms of the historical evolution of national traditions, traditions often conceived of in essentialist terms. Putting it simply, if one replaces national paradigms by a post-colonial model in which 'purity' is seen to be a fiction and hybridity and cultural pluralism all-pervasive, then areas once conceived of as marginal (Europe's 'others') paradoxically, but not surprisingly, become central. Arguably this explains much of the current popularity of post-colonial studies. To borrow Louise Bennett's phrase, a process of 'colonization in reverse'[3] occurs, as post-colonial theoretical practice invades the metropolis and begins to dismantle the monocultural assumptions that have characterized much of the thinking of Western societies and, as a by-product, monocultural models of literary study. Unfortunately such reverse colonization is not without its own problems. One of the consequences of the popularity of 'hybridization' theory has been a tendency (at odds with the practice of a theorist such as Bhabha) to dehistoricize and dislocate writing from the temporal, geographical and linguistic factors which have produced it in favour of an abstract, globally conceived notion of hybridity which obscures the specificities of particular cultural situations; and this is perhaps the most powerful argument against the constitution of the 'post-colonial' as a single field.

In its selections and the ancillary material accompanying them, this anthology has attempted to mediate between these two positions. On the one hand it includes as broad and diverse a range of writing as possible and foregrounds the migrant, hybridized, constantly shifting aspects of cultures; at the same time, without implying a reductive Marxist materialism, it aims to emphasize the discursive specifics of particular texts through the use of annotations and by locating most of the selections in national or regional sections. There are seven such sections: African, Australian, Canadian, Caribbean, New Zealand and South Pacific, South Asian and South-East Asian. In many cases 'connections' are suggested between writing from different areas and a final 'Trans-Cultural' section acknowledges the impossibility of confining migrant writing within the strait-jacket of national or regional labels. In short, the anthology moves between the twin contexts of

2 See particularly Salman Rushdie, *Imaginary Homelands: Essays and Criticism, 1981–1991* (London: Granta, 1991); and Homi Bhabha, *The Location of Culture* (London and New York: Routledge, 1994). 3 Bennett's poem is included in the anthology as the first selection in the Trans-Cultural section.

national/regional specifics and trans-cultural migration; and finally *all* of the
writing included can be seen to exist in *both* contexts. Writers such as V.S.
Naipaul, Yasmine Gooneratne, Sam Selvon and Daphne Marlatt appear in
the Trans-Cultural section as well as one of the national/regional sections,
but more generally a dialogue between specific locality and migration informs
all the constituent parts of the anthology. Thus, in the African section the
work of writers such as Chinua Achebe, Wole Soyinka and Ama Ata Aidoo
illustrates the, often ambiguous, interaction of Western and traditional social
and discursive codes; and in the Canadian section, the impact of Aboriginal
cultures is seen not only in the work of Native writers, but also in the
responses of writers as different from one another as Major John Richardson,
Emily Carr, Rudy Wiebe and Robert Kroetsch to Native peoples. In the former case, the use of ancestral oral storytelling conventions by Thomas King
and Jeannette C. Armstrong blends with more contemporary narrative practices; in the case of writers such as Wiebe and Kroetsch the interpolation of
Native elements disrupts Western linear progressions. More generally, all
the texts included in the anthology can be seen to exist at the interface
of different literary and cultural traditions, traditions which are themselves
usually hybridized; and in this sense they are *all* ultimately trans-cultural.
While this is a particular facet of 'post-colonial' writing, again it is one which
can be seen to reflect back on metropolitan discourses and such a perspective offers the possibility of dismantling previously maintained, hierarchized
notions of centrality.

To return to the issue of terminology: the present anthology follows the
authors of *The Empire Writes Back* in using the term 'post-colonial' to denote
all the culture of the post-*colonization* period and the literatures are referred
to in the plural to indicate their multiplicity and diversity. The selections
range from material published in the early days of anglophone settler colonies
to writing produced in post-independence Africa and Asia at a time when
colonialism might seem to be a dead letter, a phenomenon of the historical
past of little or no significance in the present. In the latter contexts, there
is often an objection to any term incorporating the word 'colonial', since this
is seen to perpetuate the legacy of an era that most of those in now-inde-
pendent countries would prefer to consign to oblivion. So it is hardly surprising that calling the new anglophone literatures 'post-colonial' frequently
raises hackles in such quarters. Is it, for example, appropriate to relate
contemporary Indo-Anglian writing to the experience of colonialism when
it draws on a multiplicity of influences, many of them much older than
British colonialism? As the novelist and political journalist Nayantara Sahgal
puts it:

> First we were colonials, and now we seem to be post-colonials. So is 'colonial'
> the new Anno Domini from which events are to be everlastingly measured? My
> own awareness as a writer reaches back to x-thousand B.C., at the very end of
> which measureless time the British came, and stayed, and left. And now they're

gone, and their residue is simply one more layer added to the layer upon layer of Indian consciousness. Just one more.[4]

Equally, is it appropriate to see contemporary New Zealand writing through post-colonial blinkers, when it is increasingly rooted in or related to Maori discourses? Is it appropriate to term Canadian literature post-colonial, when its engagements with extra-national forces are dominated by those with its powerful neighbour south of the forty-ninth parallel?

The answer to these questions must surely be 'no' if the terms 'colonialism' and 'post-colonialism' seem to suggest a prescriptive and restrictive repertory of common concerns for the various literatures. Perhaps, though, it should be a cautious 'yes', if one takes the issue of language usage into account and reserves the term for writing in European languages and related forms, such as the Creoles of the Caribbean region. All the work included here is in this category, since it is in a form of 'English', whether its relationship to 'Standard' is complicitous or adversarial and however tenuous and uneasy the link proves to be. Ashcroft, Griffiths and Tiffin are quick to point out that there are many anglophone languages being used in post-colonial contexts and employ a democratic lower-case 'e' to differentiate post-colonial 'englishes' from Standard.[5] Again, the continuum model is helpful. Most of the languages of regions such as the Caribbean and South Pacific are classified as Creole linguistic continua, but applying such a classification more generally and suggesting that all (post-colonial) languages operate as continua opens up the possibility of a babel-like plurality of voices within what are usually conceived of as unitary language-systems.

So anglophone language forms provide a link between 'post-colonial literatures in English'. If this suggests that the various literatures are all transplanted offshoots from the same common stock, it quickly needs to be added that over the centuries the degree of cultural cross-pollination which has taken place has created new hybridized species that bear little or no resemblance to the supposed parent plant, which is increasingly regarded as an irrelevance in post-colonial contexts, as the Caribbean engages in dialogue with Africa, Canada with Australia and the Indian diaspora with its 'Mother Country'. And this situation is very reasonably described by the term 'post-colonial'. Contemporary world Englishes have roots in British colonialism, but today cultural traffic tends to bypass England.

Several of the texts included in the anthology specifically address the issue of language. In *The Backwoods of Canada*, the settler-woman Catherine Parr Traill explains her difficulty in finding names for North American plants; in the Foreword to *Kanthapura* Raja Rao discusses the problem he has in rendering the 'spirit' of his Indian experience in English; in *Decolonising the Mind* Ngugi wa Thiong'o argues against the use of 'Afro-English' and explains why he has turned to writing in Gikuyu; in *History of the Voice* (Edward) Kamau Brathwaite says that despite a basically English lexis, the anglophone

---

4 Nayantara Sahgal, 'The Schizophrenic Imagination', in *From Commonwealth to Post-Colonial*, ed. Anna Rutherford (Aarhus: Dangaroo, 1992), p. 30. 5 *The Empire Writes Back*, p. 8.

languages of the Caribbean owe more to African retentions and coins the term 'Nation Language'. Similarly, in his calypso 'Dan is the Man in the Van', The Mighty Sparrow playfully attacks the English educational curriculum that operated in the Caribbean during his youth, claiming that it was only his illiteracy that enabled him to escape comparatively unscathed from such an upbringing; and his use of the form of the calypso effectively embodies his preference for the oral over the scribal. The contexts in which Englishes are used in post-colonial societies are, of course, extremely varied, but nevertheless provide some common ground which has consequences for cultural contiguities more generally. The use of a form of English, however it is conceived, links all the selections in this anthology and provides them with a common post-colonial heritage, diverse though this is.

The anthology includes work by acknowledged major writers, but also a considerable body of writing by less well-known figures. Inevitably anthologies play their part in canon-formation, but the endeavour here has been less to provide a definitive array of big names than to provide a multiplicity of texts that are all stimulating and exciting in themselves. This has been the main principle of selection. Some pieces have been chosen because they complement other selections (thus there are three poems about Canadian grandfather figures, four Australian 'Drover's Wife' stories and three tales of Caribbean mock-crucifixions) but just as nothing has been included because it is by a particular author, nothing is here for purely thematic reasons. Some major figures have been excluded, while others are represented by multiple extracts, particularly when, as is the case with writers such as Margaret Atwood and Derek Walcott, their work spans more than one genre. The anthology reflects the generic diversity of post-colonial writing and its tendency to subvert or elide distinctions between classic genres. It is, however, a collection of work by creative writers and does not include pieces by academic cultural theorists unless, like Albert Wendt or Robert Kroetsch, they happen to be creative practitioners as well. It aims to redress a recent shift of attention away from the literatures themselves and towards theory. Necessary though this has been, since work in the field previously suffered seriously from under-theorization, the corrective provided by the explosion in post-colonial theory now threatens to tilt the balance in the opposite direction. In the title of an often-quoted essay, Gayatri Chakravorty Spivak asks the question 'Can the Subaltern Speak?'[6] The present anthology takes the view that writers are in danger of becoming the new subalterns of post-colonial studies and consequently endeavours to remedy this by offering the most extensive selection of anglophone post-colonial *writing* yet to have appeared in a single volume.[7]

6 Gayatri Chakravorty Spivak, 'Can the Subaltern Speak?', in Cary Nelson and Lawrence Grossberg, eds., *Marxism and the Interpretation of Culture* (London: Macmillan, 1988). 7 Two recent anthologies make a considerable body of post-colonial *theory* available: Patrick Williams and Laura Chrisman, eds., *Colonial Discourse and Post-Colonial Theory* (Hemel Hempstead: Harvester Wheatsheaf, 1993); and Bill Ashcroft, Gareth Griffiths and Helen Tiffin, eds., *The Post-Colonial Studies Reader* (London and New York: Routledge, 1995).

To allow for the inclusion of as much literature as possible, ancillary material has been kept to a minimum. Passages extracted from novels and plays are prefaced by brief contextualizing paragraphs, which explain their significance in the works from which they are taken. References which are likely to be unfamiliar to student readers from cultures different from that of the selection itself are annotated, a practice which accords with the anthology's aim of locating texts in terms of the cultural and linguistic specifics that inform them. And most of the selections are followed by a brief list of possible reading 'connections', a pointer towards other works with which they have something in common or can be contrasted. These connections are prefaced by the symbol '§' and a keyword or phrase in italics suggests the nature of the possible link(s). Where the 'connecting' works are in another section of the anthology, the abbreviations Af (Africa), Aus (Australia), Can (Canada), Carib (Caribbean), NZSP (New Zealand and South Pacific), SA (South Asia), SEA (South-East Asia) and TransC (Trans-Cultural writing) are used to indicate where they appear; works with no such reference preceding them are to be found in the same section of the anthology.

The connections are designed to suggest possible routes through the book, other than the historical progressions through national/regional areas provided by the sequential ordering of the material. In some cases the connection being made will be immediately obvious. Thus the stories entitled 'The Drover's Wife' by Murray Bail, Frank Moorhouse and Barbara Jefferis all respond to Henry Lawson's original 1892 sketch with this title, one of the best-known of Australian stories, while also engaging in a dialogue with one another and with a 1945 painting by the artist Russell Drysdale. Similarly, the poems about grandfathers by Al Purdy, Eli Mandel and George Bowering in the Canadian section, with their shared preoccupation with male ancestry, form another obvious grouping, but in this case readers are also directed towards Robert Kroetsch's 'Stone Hammer Poem', which has similar concerns but in addition investigates issues of origins in other ways, and towards Jayanta Mahapatra's 'Grandfather' poem, which reflects on the very different social world of nineteenth-century Orissa. Turning to Kroetsch's poem, there are onward pointers to three other Canadian works concerned with origins; turning to Mahapatra's poem, the route map leads to a poem – Zulfikar Ghose's 'The Attack on Sialkot' – in the Trans-Cultural section, which also engages with troubled South Asian ancestry. The aim of the suggested connections is not so much to provide neat correspondences as to draw attention to *possible* thematic and other links which will allow readers to piece together their own comparisons and contrasts.

Several preoccupations recur in multiple contexts in the anthology and among those that loom large are ancestry, Aboriginality, revisionist historiography, mappings, landscape and language, oral and scribal traditions, responses to 'European' texts (and the related area of counter-discourse), gender mythologies, 'discovery' and settlement, nationalisms, multiculturalism, migration and cultural schizophrenia. Again all of these concerns relate to the disturbances occasioned by colonialism, but are far from being its peculiar prerogative. Personal and public history, geography, language, literary and cultural traditions, constructions and disruptions of notions of the nation (today usually seen to be products of Western post-Enlightenment thought),[8] cultural diversity and psychic identity are clearly all areas that have assumed particular importance as a result of colonialism, but have consequences that stretch beyond its tentacles.

For those who prefer not to read sideways, the anthology also offers the possibility of approaching its material in terms of linear developments. Its basic organization focuses attention on the historical development of particular literatures and the degree to which they are products of the transculturalism engendered by colonialism and more recently by globalism. The ordering of the material in each section is loosely chronological, but a strict temporal progression based on authors' birth dates has been avoided in favour of an approach which attempts to indicate when writers or texts first made their mark. Thus a writer such as Jack Davis, who was first published in later life, appears with his younger contemporaries. Similarly the 'Drover's Wife' stories by Murray Bail, Frank Moorhouse and Barbara Jefferis are grouped together and printed in the order in which they were published, making it possible to trace the narrative and thematic progression of the collective story which they form together with Lawson's sketch and Drysdale's painting. Using the anthology to trace historical developments will probably be most rewarding with regard to the Australian, Canadian, Caribbean and New Zealand and South Pacific sections. The diversity of the other regions will render such an approach less useful, though it remains viable, particularly within national or regional sub-sections such as India or West Africa. At the same time, approaches which follow the historical continuities within particular literatures can still through the connections listings explore parallels in other post-colonial literatures. The final Trans-Cultural section opens up possibilities for comparative readings of texts about migration and cultural interaction more generally and this in turn reflects back on the importance of these concerns in the other seven sections.

This anthology would not have been possible without the help of the nine advisory editors whose expertise informs the particular national and regional sections: Bruce Bennett, Shirley Chew, Jean-Pierre Durix, Michael Gilkes, Coral Ann Howells, G.D. Killam, Meenakshi Mukherjee, Rajiva Wijesinha and Nana Wilson Tagoe. In addition to suggesting many of the selections which appear in the anthology, they gave invaluable advice on annotations and other matters, such as writers' birth dates. It is something of a cliché in contexts like this for a general editor to claim the blame for any flaws or weaknesses in the final text and to praise other contributors unstintingly. In

8 See Benedict Anderson, *Imagined Communities: Reflections on the Origin and Spread of Nationalism* (London and New York: Verso, 1983); and Homi Bhabha, ed., *Nation and Narration* (London and New York: Routledge, 1990).

this instance, however, it seems absolutely essential to reiterate this cliché, since I am confident that any 'howlers' that have crept into the book are of my own making.

A book like this needed to be a collaborative effort and in addition to the main advisers for the anthology, numerous other people – among them students, academics, literary agents, publishers, a diplomat and in some cases the authors themselves – gave assistance of one kind or another. Among those whom the editor particularly wishes to thank are Jean Arasanayagam, Loes Baker, Alan Bower, George Elliott Clarke, Arnold Davidson, Abdulrazak Gurnah, Bernard Hickey, Robin Howells, Bénédicte Ledent, Bernth Lindfors, Leloba Molema, Mbulelo Mzamane, Mahlomola Ntoane, Walter Perera, Shelley Power, Gaele Sobott-Mogwe, Kit Stead, Barbara Thieme, Kathleen Thieme, Kathleen Williamson, Sarah Welsh, Bruce Woodcock and Derek Wright. I am also very grateful to the staff of the Brynmor Jones Library of the University of Hull and the Austrian Institute in London for the help they provided. Finally, the vision of Christopher Wheeler of Arnold made the volume possible and he proved a particularly sympathetic and meticulous editor when it came to dealing with the minutiae of such a large-scale project, as did Marianne Kirby who coordinated the seemingly endless production process with speed, patience and attention to detail; and Jonathan Reeve worked wonders in securing permissions from all parts of the world with remarkable alacrity and unfailing good humour.

John Thieme

Part I

AFRICA

West Africa

AMOS TUTUOLA (1920–)

From My Life in the Bush of Ghosts

My Life in the Bush of Ghosts describes the extraordinary journey of a boy who enters the bush when he is 7 years old and after numerous adventures re-emerges 24 years later. His journey is as much a psychic as a physical voyage and in the second section of the novel, extracted here, he chooses a ghost who represents the African side of his personality in preference to ghosts who personify imported values. Tutuola's narrative technique draws on Yoruba tale-telling traditions, but when his work first appeared it received more critical acclaim in the West than in Nigeria. With the passage of time its style can be seen to have affinities with such writers as Wole Soyinka and Ben Okri, offering what could be viewed as a a distinctively West African form of magic realism.

At the same time as I entered into the bush I could not stop in one place as the noises of the guns were driving me farther and farther until I travelled about sixteen miles away from the road on which my brother left me. After I had travelled sixteen miles and was still running further for the fearful noises, I did not know the time that I entered into a dreadful bush which is called the 'Bush of Ghosts', because I was very young to understand the meaning of 'bad' and 'good'. This 'Bush of Ghosts' was so dreadful so that no superior earthly person ever entered it.

But as the noises of the enemies' guns drove me very far until I entered into the 'Bush of Ghosts' unnoticed, because I was too young to know that it was a dreadful bush or it was banned to be entered by any earthly person, so that immediately I entered it I stopped and ate both fruits which my brother gave me before we left each other, because I was very hungry before I reached there. After I ate it then I started to wander about in this bush both day and night until I reached a rising ground which was almost covered with thick bush and weeds which made the place very dark both day and night. Every part of this small hill was very clean as if somebody was sweeping it. But as I was very tired of roaming about before I reached there, so I bent down to see the hill clearly, because my aim was to sleep there. Yet I could not see it clearly as I bent down, but when I had lain down flatly then I saw clearly that it had an entrance with which to enter into it.

The entrance resembled the door of a house and it had a portico which was sparkling as if it was polished with brasso at all moments. The portico was also made of golden plate. But as I was too young to know 'bad' and 'good' I thought that it was an old man's house who was expelled from a town for an offence, then I entered it and went inside it until I reached a junction of three passages which each led to a room as there were three rooms.

One of these rooms had golden surroundings, the second had silverish surroundings and the third had copperish. But as I stood at the junction of these passages with confusion three kinds of sweet smells were rushing out to me from each of these three rooms, but as I was hungry and also starving before I entered into this hole, so I began to sniff the best smell so that I might enter the right room at once from which the best sweet smell was rushing out. Of course as I stood on this junction I noticed through my nose that the smell which was rushing out of the room which had golden surroundings was just as if the inhabitant of it was baking bread and roasting fowl, and when I sniffed again the smell of the room which had copperish surroundings was just as if the inhabitant of that was cooking rice, potatoes and other African food with very sweet soup, and then the room which had silverish surroundings was just as if the inhabitant was frying yam, roasting fowl and baking cakes. But I thought in my mind to go direct to the room from which the smell of the African food was rushing out to me, as I prefer my native food most. But I did not know that all that I was thinking in mind was going to the hearing of the inhabitants of these three rooms, so at the same moment that I wanted to move my body to go to the room from which the smell of the African's food was rushing to me (the room which had copperish surroundings) there I saw that these three rooms which had no doors and windows opened unexpectedly and three kinds of ghosts peeped at me, every one of them pointed his finger to me to come to him.

These ghosts were so old and weary that it is hard to believe that they were living creatures. Then I stood at this junction with my right foot which I dangled with fear and looking at them. But as I was looking at each of them surprisingly I noticed that the inhabitant of the room which had golden surroundings was a golden ghost in appearance, then the second room which had copperish surroundings was a copperish ghost and also the third was a silverish ghost.

As every one of them pointed his finger to me to come to him I preferred most to go direct to the copperish-ghost from whose room the smell of African's food was rushing out to me, but when the golden ghost saw my movement which showed that I wanted to go to the copperish-ghost, so at the same time he lighted the golden flood of light all over my body to persuade me not to go to the copperish-ghost, as every one of them wanted me to be his servant. So as he lighted the flood of golden light on my body and when I looked at myself I thought that I became gold as it was shining on my body, so at this time I preferred most to go to him because of his golden light. But as I moved forward a little bit to go to him then the copperish-ghost lighted the flood of his own copperish light on my body too, which persuaded me again to go to the golden-ghost as my body was changing to every colour that copper has, and my body was then so bright so that I was unable to touch it. And again as I preferred this copperish light more than the golden-light then I started to go to him, but at this stage I was prevented again to go to him by the silverish-light which shone on to my body at that moment unexpectedly. This silverish-light was as bright as snow so that it transparented every part of my body and it was this day I knew the number of the bones of my body. But immediately I started to count them these three ghosts shone the three kinds of their lights on my body at the same time in such a way that I could not move to and fro because of these lights. But as these three old ghosts shone their lights on me at the same time so I began to move round as a wheel at this junction, as I appreciated these lights as the same.

But as I was staggering about on this junction for about half an hour because of these lights, the copperish-ghost was wiser than the rest, he quenched his own copperish-light from my body, so at this time I had a little chance to go to the rest. Of course, when the golden-ghost saw that I could not run two races at a blow successfully, so he quenched his own light too from my body, and at this time I had chance to run a single race to the silverish-ghost. But when I nearly reached his room then the copperish-ghost and the golden-ghost were lighting their lights on me as signals and at the same moment the silverish-ghost joined them to use his own light as signal to me as well, because I was disturbed by the other two ghosts. Then I stopped again and looking at every one of them how he was shining his own lights on me at two or three seconds' interval as signal.

Although I appreciated or recognized these lights as the same, but I appreciated one thing more which is food, and this food is my native food which was cooked by the copperish-ghost, but as I was very hungry so I entered into his room, and when he saw that it was his room I entered he was exceedingly glad so that he gave me the food which was the same colour with copper. But as every one of these three old ghosts wanted me to be his servant, so that the other two ghosts who were the golden-ghost and the silverish-ghost did not like me to be servant for the copperish-ghost who gave me the food that I preferred most, and both entered into the room of the copperish-ghost, all of them started to argue. At last all of them held me tightly in such a way that I could not breathe in or out. But as they held me with argument for about three hours, so when I was nearly cut into three as they were pulling me about in the room I started to cry louder so that all the ghosts and ghostesses of that area came to their house and within twenty minutes this house could not contain the ghosts who heard information and came to settle the misunderstanding. But when they came and met them how they were pulling me about in the room with much argument then they told them to leave me and they left me at once.

After that all the ghosts who came to settle the matter arranged these three old ghosts in a single line and then they told me to choose one of them for myself to be my master so that there would be no more misunderstanding between themselves. So I stood before them and looking at every one of them with my heart which was throbbing hastily to the hearing of all of them, in such a way that the whole of the ghosts who came to settle the matter rushed to me to listen well to what my heart was saying. But as these wonderful creatures understood what my heart was saying they warned me not to choose any one of them with my mouth, because they thought it would speak partiality against one of these three ghosts, as my heart was throbbing repeatedly as if a telegraphist is sending messages by telegraph.

As a matter of fact my heart first told me to choose the silverish-ghost who stood at the extreme right and if to say I would choose by mouth I would only choose the copperish-ghost who had the African's food and that was partiality, and it was at this time I noticed carefully all the ghosts who came to settle the matter that many of them had no hands and some had no fingers, some had no feet and arms but jumped instead of walking. Some had heads without eyes and ears, but I was very surprised to see them walking about both day and night without missing their way and also it was this day I had ever seen ghosts without clothes on their bodies and they were not ashamed of their nakedness.

Uncountable numbers of them stood before me and looked at me as dolls with great surprise as they had no heads or eyes. But as they forced me to choose the silverish-ghost as he was the ghost that my heart throbbed out to their hearing to choose, when I chose him, he was exceedingly glad and ran to me, then he took me on his shoulder and then to his room. But still the other two were not satisfied with the judgement of the settlers and both ran to his room and started to fight again. This fight was so fearful and serious that all the creatures in that bush with big trees stood still on the same place that they were, even breezes could not blow at this time and these three old ghosts were still fighting on fiercely until a fearful ghost who was almost covered with all kinds of insects which represented his clothes entered their house when hearing their noises from a long distance.

§ *Interior journey* Okri; Carib: Harris (1), Williams

CHINUA ACHEBE (1930–)

1: *From* Arrow of God

Like Achebe's first novel *Things Fall Apart, Arrow of God* is a historical novel set in and around an Ibo village, in this case in the 1920s. Ezeulu, the priest, names the days for his people's two main festivals, the Feasts of the Pumpkin Leaves and the New Yam. During the course of the action he defies colonial authority, is imprisoned and as a result fails to eat two yams which, he claims, renders him unable to announce the date of the New Yam feast and the harvest that accompanies it. In addition to suggesting the disruption brought about by the colonial presence, the novel poses complex questions about Ezeulu's motivation. The opening chapter, included here, demonstrates his questioning attitude to his role as priest, as he asks whether he genuinely has power or is merely a custodian.

This was the third nightfall since he began to look for signs of the new moon. He knew it would come today but he always began his watch three days early because he must not take a risk. In this season of the year his task was not too difficult; he did not have to peer and search the sky as he might do when the rains came. Then the new moon sometimes hid itself for days behind rain clouds so that when it finally came out it was already half-grown. And while it played its game the Chief Priest sat up every evening waiting.

His *obi*[1] was built differently from other men's huts. There was the usual, long threshold in front but also a shorter one on the right as you entered. The eaves on this additional entrance were cut back so that sitting on the floor Ezeulu could watch that part of the sky where the moon had its door. It was getting darker and he constantly blinked to clear his eyes of the water that formed from gazing so intently.

Ezeulu did not like to think that his sight was no longer as good as it used to be and that some day he would have to rely on someone else's eyes as his grandfather had done when his sight failed. Of course he had lived to such a great age that his blindness became like an ornament on him. If Ezeulu lived to be so old he too would accept such a loss. But for the present he was as good as any young man, or better because young men were no longer what they used to be. There was one game Ezeulu never tired of playing on them. Whenever they shook hands with him he tensed his arm and put all his power into the grip, and being unprepared for it they winced and recoiled with pain.

The moon he saw that day was as thin as an orphan fed grudgingly by a cruel foster-mother. He peered more closely to make sure he was not deceived by a feather of cloud. At the same time he reached nervously for his *ogene*.[2] It was the same at every new moon. He was now an old man but the fear of the new moon which he felt as a little boy still hovered round him. It was true that when he became Chief Priest of Ulu the fear was often overpowered by the joy of his high office; but it was not killed. It lay on the ground in the grip of the joy.

He beat his *ogene*: gome, gome, gome, gome . . . and immediately children's voices took up the news on all sides. *Onwa atuo!* . . . *onwa atuo!* . . . *onwa atuo!* . . .[3] He put the stick back into the iron gong and leaned it on the wall.

The little children in his compound joined the rest in welcoming the moon. Obiageli's tiny voice stood out like a small *ogene* among drums and flutes. He could also make out the voice of his youngest son, Nwafo. The women too were in the open, talking.

'Moon,' said the senior wife, Matefi, 'may your face meeting mine bring good fortune.'

'Where is it?' asked Ugoye, the younger wife. 'I don't see it. Or am I blind?'

'Don't you see beyond the top of the ukwa tree? Not there. Follow my finger.'

'Oho, I see it. Moon, may your face meeting mine bring good fortune. But how is it sitting? I don't like its posture.'

---

1 Living quarters of the head of an Ibo family.   2 Bell-shaped metal gong.   3 'The moon is up'.

'Why?' asked Matefi.

'I think it sits awkwardly – like an evil moon.'

'No,' said Matefi. 'A bad moon does not leave anyone in doubt. Like the one under which Okuata died. Its legs were up in the air. '

'Does the moon kill people?' asked Obiageli, tugging at her mother's cloth.

'What have I done to this child? Do you want to strip me naked?'

'I said does the moon kill people?'

'It kills little girls,' said Nwafo, her brother.

'I did not ask you, ant-hill nose.'

'You will soon cry, long throat.'

The moon kills little boys

The moon kills ant-hill nose

The moon kills little boys . . . Obiageli turned everything into a song.

Ezeulu went into his barn and took down one yam from the bamboo platform built specially for the twelve sacred yams. There were eight left. He knew there would be eight; nevertheless he counted them carefully. He had already eaten three and had the fourth in his hand. He checked the remaining ones again and went back to his *obi*, shutting the door of the barn carefully after him.

His log fire was smouldering. He reached for a few sticks of firewood stacked in the corner, set them carefully on the fire and placed the yam, like a sacrifice, on top.

As he waited for it to roast he planned the coming event in his mind. It was Oye. Tomorrow would be Afo and the next day Nkwo,[4] the day of the great market. The festival of the Pumpkin Leaves would fall on the third Nkwo from that day. Tomorrow he would send for his assistants and tell them to announce the day to the six villages of Umuaro.

Whenever Ezeulu considered the immensity of his power over the year and the crops and, therefore, over the people he wondered if it was real. It was true he named the day for the feast of the Pumpkin Leaves and for the New Yam feast; but he did not choose it. He was merely a watchman. His power was no more than the power of a child over a goat that was said to be his. As long as the goat was alive it could be his; he would find it food and take care of it. But the day it was slaughtered he would know soon enough who the real owner was. No! the Chief Priest of Ulu[5] was more than that, must be more than that. If he should refuse to name the day there would be no festival – no planting and no reaping. But could he refuse? No Chief Priest had ever refused. So it could not be done. He would not dare.

Ezeulu was stung to anger by this as though his enemy had spoken it.

'Take away that word *dare*,' he replied to this enemy. 'Yes, I say, take it away. No man in all Umuaro can stand up and say that I dare not. The woman who will bear the man who will say it has not been born yet.'

But this rebuke brought only momentary satisfaction. His mind never con-

---

4 Days of the week. 5 Most powerful of the deities of Umuaro.

tent with shallow satisfactions crept again to the brinks of knowing. What kind of power was it if it would never be used? Better to say that it was not there, that it was no more than the power in the anus of a proud dog who sought to put out a furnace with his puny fart . . . He turned the yam with a stick.

His youngest son, Nwafo, now came into the *obi*, saluted Ezeulu by name and took his favourite position on the mud-bed at the far end, close to the shorter threshold. Although he was still only a child it looked as though the deity had already marked him out as his future Chief Priest. Even before he had learnt to speak more than a few words he had been strongly drawn to the god's ritual. It could almost be said that he already knew more about it than even the eldest. Nevertheless no one would be so rash as to say openly that Ulu would do this or do that. When the time came that Ezeulu was no longer found in his place Ulu might choose the least likely of his sons to succeed him. It had happened before.

Ezeulu attended the yam very closely, rolling it over with the stick again and again. His eldest son, Edogo, came in from his own hut.

'Ezeulu!' be saluted.

'E-e-i!'

Edogo passed through the hut into the inner compound to his sister Akueke's temporary home.

'Go and call Edogo,' said Ezeulu to Nwafo.

The two came back and sat down on the mud-bed. Ezeulu turned his yam once before before he spoke.

'Did I ever tell you anything about carving a deity?'

Edogo did not reply. Ezeulu looked in his direction but did not see him clearly because that part of the *obi* was in darkness. Edogo on his part saw his father's face lit up by the fire on which he was roasting the sacred yam.

'Is Edogo not there?'

'I am here.'

'I said what did I tell you about carving the image of gods? Perhaps you did not hear my first question; perhaps I spoke with water in my mouth.'

'You told me to avoid it.'

'I told you that, did I? What is this story I hear then – that you are carving an *alusi*[6] for a man of Umuagu?'

'Who told you?'

'Who told me? Is it true or not is what I want to know, not who told me.'

'I want to know who told you because I don't think he can tell the difference between the face of a deity and the face of a Mask.'

'I see. You may go, my son. And if you like you may carve all the gods in Umuaro. If you hear me asking you about it again take my name and give it to a dog.'

'What I am carving for the man of Umuagu is not . . .'

'It is not me you are talking to. I have finished with you.'

Nwafo tried in vain to make sense out of these words. When his father's

6 Spirit.

temper cooled he would ask. Then his sister, Obiageli, came in from the inner compound, saluted Ezeulu and made to sit on the mud-bed.

'Have you finished preparing the bitter-leaf?' asked Nwafo.

'Don't you know how to prepare bitter-leaf? Or are your fingers broken?'

'Keep quiet there, you two.' Ezeulu rolled the yam out of the fire with the stick and quickly felt it between his thumb and first finger, and was satisfied. He brought down a two-edged knife from the rafters and began to scrape off the coat of black on the roast yam. His hands were covered in soot when he had finished, and he clapped them together a few times to get them clean again. His wooden bowl was near at hand and he cut the yam into it and waited for it to cool.

When he began eating Obiageli started to sing quietly to herself. She should have known by now that her father never gave out even the smallest crumbs of the yam he ate without palm oil at every new moon. But she never ceased hoping.

He ate in silence. He had moved away from the fire and now sat with his back against the wall, looking outwards. As was usual with him on these occasions his mind seemed to be fixed on distant thoughts. Now and again he drank from a calabash of cold water which Nwafo had brought for him. As he took the last piece Obiageli returned to her mother's hut. Nwafo put away the wooden bowl and the calabash and stuck the knife again between two rafters.

Ezeulu rose from his goatskin and moved to the household shrine on a flat board behind the central dwarf wall at the entrance. His *ikenga*,[7] about as tall as a man's forearm, its animal horn as long as the rest of its human body jostled with faceless *okposi*[8] of the ancestors black with the blood of sacrifice, and his short personal staff of *ofo*.[9] Nwafo's eyes picked out the special *okposi* which belonged to him. It had been carved for him because of the convulsions he used to have at night. They told him to call it Namesake, and he did. Gradually the convulsions had left him.

Ezeulu took the *ofo* staff from the others and sat in front of the shrine, not astride in a man's fashion but with his legs stretched in front of him to one side of the shrine, like a woman. He held one end of the short staff in his right hand and with the other end hit the earth to punctuate his prayer:

Ulu, I thank you for making me see another new moon. May I see it again and again. This household may it be healthy and prosperous. As this is the moon of planting may the six villages plant with profit. May we escape danger in the farm – the bite of a snake or the sting of the scorpion, the mighty one of the scrubland. May we not cut our shinbone with the matchet or the hoe. And let our wives bear male children. May we increase in numbers at the next counting of the villages so that we shall sacrifice to you a cow, not a chicken as we did after the last New Yam feast. May children put their fathers into the earth and not fathers their children. May good meet the face of every man and every woman. Let it come to the land of the riverain folk and to the land of the forest peoples.

---

7 Household god. 8 Carved deity, associated with an ancestor. 9 Staff.

He put the *ofo* back among the *ikenga* and the *okposi*, wiped his mouth with the back of his hand and returned to his place. Every time he prayed for Umuaro bitterness rose into his mouth, a great smouldering anger for the division which had come to the six villages and which his enemies sought to lay on his head. And for what reason? Because he had spoken the truth before the white man. But how could a man who held the holy staff of Ulu know that a thing was a lie and speak it? How could he fail to tell the story as he had heard it from his own father? Even the white man, Wintabota,[10] understood, though he came from a land no one knew. He had called Ezeulu the only witness of truth. That was what riled his enemies – that the white man whose father or mother no one knew should come to tell them the truth they knew but hated to hear. It was an augury of the world's ruin.

The voices of women returning from the stream broke into Ezeulu's thoughts. He could not see them because of the darkness outside. The new moon having shown itself had retired again. But the night bore marks of its visit. The darkness was not impenetrable as it had been lately, but open and airy like a forest from which the undergrowth had been cut. As the women called out 'Ezeulu' one after another he saw their vague forms and returned their greeting. They left the *obi* to their right and went into the inner compound through the only other entrance – a high, carved door in the red, earth walls.

'Are these not the people I saw going to the stream before the sun went down?'

'Yes,' said Nwafo. 'They went to Nwangene.'

'I see.' Ezeulu had forgotten temporarily that the nearer stream, Ota, had been abandoned since the oracle announced yesterday that the enormous boulder resting on two other rocks at its source was about to fall and would take a softer pillow for its head. Until the *alusi* who owned the stream and whose name it bore had been placated no one would go near it.

Still, Ezeulu thought, he would speak his mind to whoever brought him a late supper tonight. If they knew they had to go to Nwangene they should have set out earlier. He was tired of having his meal sent to him when other men had eaten and forgotten.

Obika's great, manly voice rose louder and louder into the night air as he approached home. Even his whistling carried farther than some men's voices. He sang and whistled alternately.

'Obika is returning,' said Nwafo.

'The night bird is early coming home today,' said Ezeulu, at the same time.

'One day soon he will see Eru again,' said Nwafo, referring to the apparition Obika had once seen at night. The story had been told so often that Nwafo imagined he was there.

'This time it will be Idemili or Ogwugwu,' said Ezeulu with a smile, and Nwafo was full of happiness.

---

10 The English name 'Winterbottom'.

About three years ago Obika had rushed into the *obi* one night and flung himself at his father shivering with terror. It was a dark night and rain was preparing to fall. Thunder rumbled with a deep, liquid voice and flash answered flash.

'What is it, my son?' Ezeulu asked again and again, but Obika trembled and said nothing.

'What is it, Obika?' asked his mother, Matefi, who had run into the *obi* and was now shaking worse than her son.

'Keep quiet there,' said Ezeulu. 'What did you see, Obika?'

When he had cooled a little Obika began to tell his father what he had seen at a flash of lightning near the ugili tree between their village, Umuachala, and Umunneora. As soon as he had mentioned the place Ezeulu had known what it was.

'What happened when you saw It?'

'I knew it was a spirit; my head swelled.'

'Did he not turn into the Bush That Ruined Little Birds? On the left?'

His father's confidence revived Obika. He nodded and Ezeulu nodded twice. The other women were now ranged round the door.

'What did he look like?'

'Taller than any man I know.' He swallowed a lump. 'His skin was very light . . . like . . . like . . .'

'Was he dressed like a poor man or was it like a man of great wealth?'

'He was dressed like a wealthy man. He had an eagle's feather in his red cap.'

His teeth began to knock together again.

'Hold yourself together. You are not a woman. Had he an elephant tusk?'

'Yes. He carried a big tusk across his shoulder.'

The rain had now begun to fall, at first in big drops that sounded like pebbles on the thatch.

'There is no cause to be afraid, my son. You have seen Eru, the Magnificent, the One that gives wealth to those who find favour with him. People sometimes see him at that place in this kind of weather. Perhaps he was returning home from a visit to Idemili or the other deities. Eru only harms those who swear falsely before his shrine.' Ezeulu was carried away by his praise of the god of wealth. The way he spoke one would have thought he was the proud priest of Eru rather than Ulu who stood above Eru and all the other deities. 'When he likes a man wealth flows like a river into his house; his yams grow as big as human beings, his goats produce threes and his hens hatch nines.'

§ *Tradition and change* Achebe (3), Soyinka (2), Emecheta, Aidoo, Okot

2: *From* What Has Literature Got to Do with It?

. . . The universal creative rondo revolves on people and stories. *People create stories create people*; or rather, *stories create people create stories*. Was it stories first and then people, or the other way round? Most creation myths would seem to suggest the antecedence of stories – a scenario in which the story was already unfolding in the cosmos before, and even as a result of which, man came into being. Take this remarkable Fulani[1] creation story:

> In the beginning there was a huge drop of milk. Then the milk created stone; the stone created fire; the fire created water; the water created air.
>
> Then Doondari came and took the five elements and moulded them into man. But man was proud. Then Doondari created blindness and blindness defeated man . . .

A fabulously rich story, it proceeds in stark successions of creation and defeat to man's death through hubris, and then to a final happy twist of redemption when death itself, having inherited man's arrogance, causes Doondari to descend a third time as Gueno the eternal one, to defeat death.

So important have such stories been to mankind that they are not restricted to accounts of initial creation but will be found following human societies as they recreate themselves through vicissitudes of their history, validating their social organizations, their political systems, their moral attitudes and religious beliefs, even their prejudices. Such stories serve the purpose of consolidating whatever gains a people or their leaders have made or imagine they have made in their existential journey through the world; but they also serve to sanction change when it can no longer be denied. At such critical moments new versions of old stories or entirely fresh ones tend to be brought into being to mediate the changes and sometimes to consecrate opportunistic defections into more honourable rites of passage.

One of the paradoxes of Igbo political systems is the absence of kings on the one hand, and on the other the presence in the language and folklore of a whole range of words for 'king' an d all the paraphernalia of royalty. In the Igbo town of Ogidi where I grew up I have found two explanatory myths offered for the absence of kings. One account has it that once upon a time the title of king did exist in the community but that it gradually fell out of use because of the rigorous condition it placed on the aspirant, requiring him to settle the debt owed by every man and every woman in the kingdom.

The second account has it that there was indeed a king, who held the people in such utter contempt that one day when he had a ritual kola-nut[2] to break for them he cracked it between his teeth. So the people, who did not fancy eating kola-nut coated with the king's saliva, dethroned him and have remained republican ever since.

These are perhaps no more than fragmentary makeshift accounts though not entirely lacking in allegorical interest. There is, for instance, a certain philosophical appropriateness to the point that a man who would be king over his fellows should in return be prepared personally to guarantee their solvency.

---

1 Muslim people of West Africa, scattered throughout the area from Senegal to Cameroon.   2 A mild stimulant and traditional symbol of friendship.

Be that as it may, those two interesting fragments of republican propaganda played their part in keeping kings' noses out of the affairs of Ogidi for as long as memory could go until the community, along with the rest of Nigeria, lost political initiative to the British at the inception of colonial rule. Thereafter a new dynasty of kings rose to power in Ogidi with the connivance of the British administration, thus rendering those mythical explanations of republicanism obsolete. Except perhaps that they may have left a salutary, moderating residue in the psyche of the new rulers and those they ruled.

I shall now, with your indulgence, present two brief parables from precolonial Nigeria which are short enough for the present purpose but also complex enough to warrant my classifying them as literature. I chose these two particularly because they stand at the opposite ends of the political spectrum.

Once upon a time, all the animals were summoned to a meeting. As they converged on the public square early in the morning one of them, the fowl, was spotted by his neighbours going in the opposite direction. They said to him, 'How is it that you are going away from the public square? Did you not hear the town crier's summons last night?'

'I did hear it,' said the fowl, 'and I should certainly have gone to the meeting if a certain personal matter had not cropped up which I must attend to. I am truly sorry, but I hope you will make my sincere apologies to the meeting. Tell them that though absent in body I will be there with you in spirit in all your deliberations. Needless to say that whatever you decide will receive my whole-hearted support.'

The question before the assembled animals was what to do in the face of a new threat posed by man's frequent slaughtering of animals to placate his gods. After a stormy but surprisingly brief debate it was decided to present to man one of their number as his regular sacrificial animal if he would leave the rest in peace. And it was agreed without a division that the fowl should be offered to man to mediate between him and his gods. And it has been so ever since.

The second story goes like this:

One day a snake was riding his horse coiled up, as was his fashion, in the saddle. As he came down the road he met the toad walking by the roadside.

'Excuse me, sir,' said the toad, 'but that's not the way to ride a horse.'

'Really? Can you show me the right way, then?' asked the snake.

'With pleasure, if you will be good enough to step down a moment.'

The snake slid down the side of his horse and the toad jumped with alacrity into the saddle, sat bolt upright and galloped most elegantly up and down the road. 'That's how to ride a horse,' he said at the end of his excellent demonstration.

'Very good,' said the snake, 'very good indeed; you may now come down.'

The toad jumped down and the snake slid up the side of his horse back into the saddle and coiled himself up as before. Then he said to the toad, 'Knowing is good, but having is better. What good does fine horsemanship do to a fellow without a horse?' And then he rode away in his accustomed manner.

On the face of it those are just two charming animal stories to put a smile on the face or, if we are fortunate and have a generous audience, even a laugh in the throat. But beneath that admittedly important purpose of giving delight there lies a deep and very serious intent. Indeed what we have before us are political and ideological statements of the utmost consequence revealing more about the societies that made and sustained them, and by which, in the reciprocal rondo of creativity, they were made and sustained, revealing far more than any number of political-science monographs could possibly ever tell us. We could literally spend hours analysing each story and discovering new significances all the time. Right now, however, we can take only a cursory look.

Consider the story of the delinquent fowl. Quite clearly it is a warning, a cautionary tale, about the danger to which citizens of small-scale democratic systems may be exposed when they neglect the cardinal duty of active participation in the political process. In such systems a man who neglects to lick his lips, as a certain proverb cautions us, will be asking the harmattan[3] to lick them for him. It did for the fowl with a vengeance!

The second story is, if you will permit a rather predictable cliché, a horse of a different colour altogether. The snake is an aristocrat in a class society in which status and its symbols are not earned but ascribed. The toad is a commoner whose knowledge and expertise garnered through personal effort count for nothing beside the merit which belongs to the snake by some unspecified right such as birth or wealth. No amount of brightness or ability on the part of the toad is going to alter the position ordained for him. The few but potent words left with him by the snake embody a stern, utilitarian view of education which would tie the acquisition of skills to the availability of scope for their practice.

I have chosen those two little examples from Nigeria's vast and varied treasury of oral literature to show how such stories can combine in a most admirable manner the aesthetic qualities of a successful work of imagination with those homiletic virtues demanded of active definers and custodians of society's values.

But we must not see the the role of literature only in terms of providing latent support for things as they are, for it does also offer the kinetic energy necessary for social transition and change. If we tend to dwell more on stability it is only because society itself does aspire to, and indeed requires, longer periods of rest than of turmoil. But literature is also deeply concerned with change. That little fragment about the king who insulted his subjects by breaking their kola-nut in his mouth is a clear incitement to rebellion. But even more illuminating in this connection because of its subtlety is the story of the snake and the toad which at first sight may appear to uphold privilege but at another level of signification does in fact contain the seeds of revolution, the portents of the dissolution of an incompetent oligarchy. The brilliant makers of that story, by denying sympathetic attractiveness to the snake, are expos-

---

3 Dry, dusty wind from the Sahara, which usually blows from December to February.

ing him in the fullness of time to the harsh tenets of a revolutionary justice.

I think I have now set a wide-ranging enough background to attempt an answer to the rhetorical question: What has literature got to do with it?

In the first place, what does 'it' stand for? Is it something concrete like increasing the GNP or something metaphysical like the it which is the object of the quest in Gabriel Okara's novel, *The Voice*?

I should say that my 'it' begins with concrete aspirations like economic growth, health for all, education which actually educates, etc., etc., but soon reveals an umbilical link with a metaphysical search for abiding values. In other words I am saying that development or modernization is not merely, or even primarily, a question of having lots of money to spend or blueprints drawn up by the best experts available; it is in a critical sense a question of the mind and the will. And I am saying that the mind and the will belong first and foremost to the domain of stories. In the beginning was the Word, or the Mind, as an alternative rendering has it. It was the Word or the Mind that began the story of creation.

So it is with the creation of human societies. And what Nigeria is aiming to do is nothing less than the creation of a new place and a new people. And she needs must have the creative energy of stories to initiate and sustain that work.

Our ancestors created their different polities with myths embodying their varying perceptions of reality. Every people everywhere did the same. The Jews had their Old Testament on account of which early Islam honoured them as the people of the Book. The following passage appears in a brilliant essay in *Publications of the Modern Language Association of America*:

> The ideals that Homer portrayed in Achilles, Hector and Ulysses played a large role in the formation of the Greek character. Likewise when the Anglo-Saxons huddled around their hearth fires, stories of heroes like Beowulf helped define them as a people, through articulating their values and defining their goals in relation to the cold, alien world around them.[4]

In the essay from which I took that passage the authors set out to demonstrate in detail the potentiality of literature to reform the self in a manner analogous to the processes of psychoanalysis: eliciting deep or unconsciously held primary values and then bringing conscious reflection or competing values to bear on them. The authors underscore the interesting point made by Roy Schafer that psychoanalysis itself is an essay into story-telling. People who go through psychoanalysis tell the analyst about themselves and others in the past and present. In making interpretations the competent analyst reorganizes and retells these stories in such a way that the problematic and incoherent, self-consciously told at the beginning of the analysis, is sorted out to the benefit and sanity of the client.

It would be impossible and indeed inappropriate to pursue this percep-

---

4 M.W. Alcorn and M. Bracher, 'Literature, Psychoanalysis and the Reformation of the Self', *PMLA* (May 1985), p. 350 [adapted from author's note].

tive and tremendously important analogy between literature and psychoanalysis any further here, but I must quote its concluding sentence:

> . . . if as Kohut, Meissner and others suggest the self has an inherent teleology
> for growth and cohesion, then literature can have an important and profound
> positive effect as well, functioning as a kind of bountiful, nourishing matrix for
> a healthy, developing psyche.[5]

This is putting into scientific language what our ancestors had known all
along and reminds one of the common man who, on being told the meaning of 'prose', exclaimed: 'Look at that! So I have been speaking prose all
my life without knowing it.'

The matter is really quite simple. Literature, whether handed down by
word of mouth or in print, gives us a second handle on reality; enabling us
to encounter in the safe, manageable dimensions of make-believe the very
same threats to integrity that may assail the psyche in real life; and at the
same time providing through the self-discovery which it imparts a veritable
weapon for coping with these threats whether they are found within problematic and incoherent selves or in the world around us. What better preparation can a people desire as they begin their journey into the strange,
revolutionary world of modernization?

§ *Oral storytelling* Achebe (3); Can: King, Armstrong; Carib: Lamming (1),
Brodber; *Politics and social responsibility* SA: Wikkramasinha

3: *From* Anthills of the Savannah

Published two decades after Achebe's previous four novels (in 1987), *Anthills of the
Savannah* explores the troubled post-independence political situation in a fictional
West African state and the position of its elite class, whose education increasingly
isolates it from the people. In this central passage Ikem Osodi, a poet and editor,
meets a delegation from his own region of Abazon in the country's capital. The narrative mode of the novel is complex and varied, negotiating between traditional and
contemporary influences. Here in imagistic language reminiscent of Achebe's earlier
village novels, which attempt to render Ibo tale-telling traditions and proverbial lore
in English, the elder who is spokesperson for the delegation stresses the importance
of storytelling.

. . . 'Let me ask a question. How do we salute our fellows when we come
in and see them massed in assembly so huge we cannot hope to greet them
one by one, to call each man by his title? Do we not say: To everyone his
due? Have you thought what a wise practice our fathers fashioned out of
those simple words? To every man his own! To each his chosen title! We
can all see how that handful of words can save us from the ache of four
hundred handshakes and the headache of remembering a like multitude of
praise-names. But it does not end there. It is saying to us: Every man has

---

5 *Ibid.*, p. 352 [author's note].

what is his; do not bypass him to enter his compound . . .

'It is also like this (for what is true comes in different robes) . . . Long before sunrise in the planting or harvesting season; at that time when sleep binds us with a sweetness more than honey itself the bush-fowl will suddenly startle the farmer with her scream: o-o-i! o-o-i! o-o-i! in the stillness and chill of the grassland. I ask you, does the farmer jump up at once with heavy eyes and prepare for the fields or does he scream back to the bush-fowl: *Shut up! Who told you the time? You have never hoed a cassava ridge in your life nor planted one seed of millet.* No! If he is a farmer who means to prosper he will not challenge the bush-fowl; he will not dispute her battle-cry; he will get up and obey.

'Have you thought about that? I tell you it is the way the Almighty has divided the work of the world. Everyone and his own! The bush-fowl, her work; and the farmer, his.

'To some of us the Owner of the World has apportioned the gift to tell their fellows that the time to get up has finally come. To others He gives the eagerness to rise when they hear the call; to rise with racing blood and put on their garbs of war and go to the boundary of their town to engage the invading enemy boldly in battle. And then there are those others whose part is to wait and when the struggle is ended, to take over and recount its story.

'The sounding of the battle-drum is important; the fierce waging of the war itself is important; and the telling of the story afterwards – each is important in its own way. I tell you there is not one of them we could do without. But if you ask me which of them takes the eagle-feather I will say boldly: the story. Do you hear me? Now, when I was younger, if you had asked me the same question I would have replied without a pause: the battle. But age gives to a man some things with the right hand even as it takes away others with the left. The torrent of an old man's water may no longer smash into the bole of the roadside tree a full stride away as it once did but fall around his feet like a woman's; but in return the eye of his mind is given wing to fly away beyond the familiar sights of the homestead . . .

'So why do I say that the story is chief among his fellows? The same reason I think that our people sometimes will give the name Nkolika to their daughters – Recalling-Is-Greatest. Why? Because it is only the story can continue beyond the war and the warrior. It is the story that outlives the sound of war-drums and the exploits of brave fighters. It is the story, not the others, that saves our progeny from blundering like blind beggars into the spikes of the cactus fence. The story is our escort; without it, we are blind. Does the blind man own his escort? No, neither do we the story; rather it is the story that owns us and directs us. It is the thing that makes us different from cattle; it is the mark on the face that sets one people apart from their neighbours.'

The footfalls of waiters padding about the cemented courtyard rose to a new prominence in the profound silence.

'So the arrogant fool who sits astride the story as though it were a bowl of foo-foo[1] set before him by his wife understands little about the world.

The story will roll him into a ball, dip him in the soup and swallow him first. I tell you he is like the puppy who swings himself around and farts into a blazing fire with the aim to put it out. can he? No, the story is ever-lasting . . . Like fire, when it is not blazing it is smouldering under its own ashes or sleeping and resting inside its flint-house.

'When we are young and without experience we all imagine that the story of the land is easy, that every one of us can get up and tell it. But that is not so. True, we all have our little scraps of tale bubbling in us. But what we tell is like the middle of a mighty boa which a foolish forester mistakes for a tree trunk and settles upon to take his snuff . . . Yes, we lay into our little tale with wild eyes and a vigorous tongue. Then, one day Agwu comes along and knocks it out of our mouth and our jaw out of shape for our audacity and hands over the story to a man of his choice . . . Agwu does not call a meeting to choose his seers and diviners and artists; Agwu, the god of healers; Agwu, brother to Madness! But though born from the same womb he and Madness were not created by the same *chi*.[2] Agwu is the right hand a man extends to his fellows; Madness, the forbidden hand. Madness unleashes and rides his man roughly into the wild savannah. Agwu possesses his own just as securely but has him corralled to serve the compound. Agwu picks his disciple, rings his eye with white chalk and dips his tongue, will-ing or not, in the brew of prophecy; and right away the man will speak and put head and tail back to the severed trunk of our tale. This miracle-man will amaze us because he may be a fellow of little account, not the bold warrior we all expect nor even the war-drummer. But in his new-found utter-ance our struggle will stand reincarnated before us. He is the liar who can sit under his thatch and see the moon hanging in the sky outside. Without stirring from his stool he can tell you how commodities are selling in a dis-tant market-place. His chalked eye will see every blow in a battle he never fought. So fully is he owned by the telling that sometimes – especially when he looks around him and finds no age-mate to challenge the claim – he will turn the marks left on him by the chicken-pox and yaws he suffered in child-hood into bullet scars . . . yes, scars from that day *our men* pounded *their men* like palmfruit in the heavy mortar of iroko!'

The tense air was broken suddenly by loud laughter. The old man himself smiled with benign mischief.

'But the lies of those possessed by Agwu are lies that do no harm to any-one. They float on the top of story like the white bubbling at the pot-mouth of new palm-wine. The true juice of the tree lies coiled up inside, waiting to strike . . .

'I don't know why my tongue is crackling away tonight like a clay-bowl of *ukwa* seeds toasting over the fire; why I feel like a man who has been helped to lower a heavy load from off his head; and he straightens his neck again and shakes the ache from it. Yes, my children, I feel light-headed like one who has completed all his tasks and is gay and free to go. But I don't

---

1 Dough made from plantains. 2 Personal god.

want to leave thinking that any of you is being pushed away from his proper work, from the work his creator arranged with him before he set out for the world . . .'

He stopped speaking. The silence was so complete that one could hear him gnashing his teeth. Ikem realized that other people, habitués of the Harmoney Hotel, drinking their beer at single tables in different parts of the courtyard, had also fallen under this old man's spell and now had their eyes trained on him.

'When we were told two years ago that we should vote for the Big Chief to rule for ever and all kinds of people we had never seen before came running in and out of our villages asking us to say yes I told my people: we have Osodi in Bassa.³ If he comes home and tells us that we should say yes we will do so because he is there as our eye and ear. I said: if what these strange people are telling us is true, Osodi will come or he will write in his paper and our sons will read it and know that it is true. But he did not come to tell us and he did not write it in his paper. So we knew that cunning had entered that talk.

'There was another thing that showed me there was deception in the talk. The people who were running in and out and telling us to say yes came one day and told us that the Big Chief himself did not want to rule for ever but that he was being forced. Who is forcing him? I asked. The people, they replied. That means us? I asked, and their eyes shifted from side to side. And I knew finally that cunning had entered the matter. And I thanked them and they left. I called my people and said to them: The Big Chief doesn't want to rule for ever because he is sensible. Even when a man marries a woman he does not marry her for ever. One day one of them will die and the marriage will end. So my people and I said No.'

There was a huge applause, not only from the tables where the Abazon people sat but from other tables as well.

'But that was not the end. More shifting-eyes people came and said: Because you said no to the Big Chief he is very angry and has ordered all the water bore-holes they are digging in your area to be closed so that you will know what it means to offend the sun. You will suffer so much that in your next reincarnation you will need no one to tell you to say yes whether the matter is clear to you or not.'

'God will not agree,' replied many voices.

'So we came to Bassa to say our own yes and perhaps the work on our bore-holes will start again and we will not all perish from the anger of the sun. We did not know before but we know now that yes does not cause trouble. We do not fully understand the ways of today yet but we are learning. A dancing masquerade in my town used to say: it is true I do not hear English but when they say *Catch am* nobody tells me to take myself off as fast as I can.'

There was loud laughter from all parts of the courtyard, some of the people savouring the joke by repeating it to themselves or to their neighbours and laughing all over again.

---

3 Capital of the novel's fictional state.

'So we are ready to learn new things and mend our old, useless ways. If you cross the Great River to marry a wife you must be ready for the risk of night journey by canoe ... I don't know whether the people we have come to see will listen to our cry for water or not. Sometime ago we were told that the Big Chief himself was planning to visit our villages and see our suffering. Then we were told again that he was not coming because he had just remembered that we had said no to him two years ago. So we said, if he will not come, let us go and visit him instead in his house. It is proper that a beggar should visit a king. When a rich man is sick a beggar goes to visit him and say sorry. When the beggar is sick, he waits to recover and then goes to tell the rich man that he has been sick. It is the place of the poor man to make a visit to the rich man who holds the yam and the knife.'

'That is indeed the world,' replied the audience.

'Whether our coming to the Big Chief 's compound will do any good or not we cannot say. We did not see him face to face because he was talking to another Big Chief like himself who is visiting from another country. But we can go back to our people and tell them that we have struggled for them with what remaining strength we have ... Once upon a time the leopard who had been trying for a long time to catch the tortoise finally chanced upon him on a solitary road. *Aha*, he said; *at long last! Prepare to die.* And the tortoise said: *Can I ask one favour before you kill me?* The leopard saw no harm in that and agreed. *Give me a few moments to prepare my mind,* the tortoise said. Again the leopard saw no harm in that and granted it. But instead of standing still as the leopard had expected the tortoise went into strange action on the road, scratching with hands and feet and throwing sand furiously in all directions. *Why are you doing that?* asked the puzzled leopard. The tortoise replied: *Because even after I am dead I would want anyone passing by this spot to say, yes, a fellow and his match struggled here.*

'My people, that is all we are doing now. Struggling. Perhaps to no purpose except that those who come after us will be able to say: *True, our fathers were defeated but they tried.*'

§ *Oral storytelling* Achebe (2); Can: King, Armstrong; Carib: Brodber; *Tradition and change* Achebe (1), Soyinka (2), Emecheta, Aidoo, Okot

CHRISTOPHER OKIGBO (1932–67)

Siren Limits

I
Suddenly becoming talkative
like weaverbird

---

2 **weaverbird**: small sparrow-type bird.

Summoned at offside of
    dream remembered

5   Between sleep and waking,
I hang up my egg-shells
To you of palm grove,
Upon whose bamboo towers

Hang, dripping with yesterupwine,
10   A tiger mask and nude spear . . .

Queen of the damp half light,
I have had my cleansing,
Emigrant with air-borne nose,
The he-goat-on-heat.

II
15   For he was a shrub among the poplars,
Needing more roots
More sap to grow to sunlight,
Thirsting for sunlight,

A low growth among the forest.

20   Into the soul
The selves extended their branches,
Into the moments of each living hour,
Feeling for audience

Straining thin among the echoes;

25   And out of the solitude
Voice and soul with selves unite,
Riding the echoes,

Horsemen of the apocalypse;

And crowned with one self
30   The name displays its foliage,
Hanging low

A green cloud above the forest.

III
Banks of reed.
Mountains of broken bottles.

35   *& the mortar is not yet dry* . . .

Silent the footfall,

Soft as cat's paw,
Sandalled in velvet in fur,

So we must go, eve-mist on shoulders,
40   Sun's dust of combat,
With brand burning out at hand-end.

& the mortar is not yet dry . . .

Then we must sing, tongue-tied,
Without name or audience,
45   Making harmony among the branches.

And this is the crisis point,
The twilight moment between
    sleep and waking;
And voice that is reborn transpires,
50   Not thro' pores in the flesh,
    but the soul's back-bone.

Hurry on down –
    Thro' the high-arched gate –
Hurry on down
55   little stream to the lake;

Hurry on down –
    Thro' the cinder market
Hurry on down
    in the wake of the dream;

60   Hurry on down –
    To rockpoint of Cable,

To pull by the rope
    the big white elephant . . .

& the mortar is not yet dry
65   *& the mortar is not yet dry;*

And the dream wakes
    the voice fades
In the damp half light
    like a shadow,

70   Not leaving a mark.

---

61 Cable: Cable Point at Asaba, a sacred waterfront with rocky promontory, and terminal point of a traditional quinquennial pilgrimage [author's note].

IV

An image insists
From flag pole of the heart;
Her image distracts
With the cruelty of the rose . . .

75   Oblong-headed lioness –
No shield is proof against her –
Wound me, O sea-weed
Face, blinded like strong-room –

Distances of her armpit-fragrance
80   Turn chloroform enough for my patience –

When you have finished
& done up my stitches,
Wake me near the altar,
& this poem will be finished . . .

WOLE SOYINKA (1934 –)

1: Abiku

Wanderer child. It is the same child who dies and returns again and again to plague the mother – Yoruba belief.

In vain your bangles cast
Charmed circles at my feet
I am Abiku, calling for the first
And the repeated time.

5   Must I weep for goats and cowries
For palm oil and the sprinkled ash?
Yams do not sprout in amulets
To earth Abiku's limbs.

So when the snail is burnt in his shell,
10   Whet the heated fragment, brand me.
Deep on the breast – you must know him
When Abiku calls again.

I am the squirrel teeth, cracked
The riddle of the palm; remember

---

3 The 'abiku' is a spirit-child caught in a cycle of early death and rebirth.

15   This, and dig me deeper still into
       The god's swollen foot.

       Once and the repeated time, ageless
       Though I puke, and when you pour
       Libations, each finger points me near
20   The way I came, where

       The ground is wet with mourning
       White dew suckles flesh-birds
       Evening befriends the spider, trapping
       Flies in wine-froth;

25   Night, and Abiku sucks the oil
       From lamps. Mothers! I'll be the
       Suppliant snake coiled on the doorstep
       Yours the killing cry.

       The ripest fruit was saddest;
30   Where I crept, the warmth was cloying.
       In silence of webs, Abiku moans, shaping
       Mounds from the yolk.

§ *Death and rebirth* Carib: Harris

2: *From* The Lion and the Jewel

In The Lion and the Jewel Sidi, a 'village belle' whose beauty has recently been made famous by magazine photographs, is courted by the schoolteacher Lakunle and Baroka, the village 'Bale', or chief. Lakunle is a travesty of Western 'progress'; Baroka, an ageing trickster who has so far successfully resisted Western inroads into his world and preserved his position as a 'lion' with a harem of wives. Here, in the second of the play's three scenes, Sidi is wary of overtures received from Baroka through his head wife Sadiku. Later in the scene Baroka says that he has become impotent, a claim that is belied in the final scene where he seduces Sidi, who will now become his favourite wife. The play's classically simple structure evinces a clear preference for traditional Yoruba codes of manliness, though the self-serving Baroka is hardly an exemplary embodiment of such values.

Noon

[*A road by the market. Enter* Sidi, *happily engrossed in the pictures of herself in the magazine.* Lakunle *follows one or two paces behind carrying a bundle of firewood which* Sidi *has set out to obtain. They are met in the centre by* Sadiku, *who has entered from the opposite side.* Sadiku *is an old woman, with a shawl over her head.*]

Sadiku Fortune is with me. I was going to your house to see you.

Sidi [*startled out of her occupation.*] What! Oh, it is you, Sadiku.

Sadiku The Lion sent me. He wishes you well.

Sidi Thank him for me.
[*Then excitedly.*]
Have you seen these?
Have you seen these images of me
Wrought by the man from the capital city?
Have you felt the gloss? [*Caresses the page.*]
Smoother by far than the parrot's breast.

Sadiku I have. I saw them as soon as the city man came . . . . Sidi,
I bring a message from my lord. [*Jerks her head at* Lakunle.]
Shall we draw aside a little?

Sidi Him? Pay no more heed to that
Than you would a eunuch.

Sadiku Then, in as few words as it takes to tell, Baroka wants you
for a wife.

Lakunle [*bounds forward, dropping the wood.*]
What! The greedy dog!
Insatiate camel of a foolish, doting race;
Is he at his tricks again?

Sidi Be quiet, 'Kunle. You get so tiresome.
The message is for me, not you.

Lakunle [*down on his knees at once. Covers* Sidi's *hands with
kisses.*]
My Ruth, my Rachel, Esther, Bathsheba
Thou sum of fabled perfections
From Genesis to the Revelations
Listen not to the voice of this infidel . . . .

Sidi [*snatches her hand away.*]
Now that's your other game;
Giving me funny names you pick up
In your wretched books.
My name is Sidi. And now, let me be.
My name is Sidi, and I am beautiful.
The stranger took my beauty
And placed it in my hands.
Here, here it is. I need no funny names
To tell me of my fame.
Loveliness beyond the jewels of a throne –
That is what he said.

Sadiku [*gleefully.*] Well, will you be Baroka's own jewel? Will you be his sweetest princess, soothing him on weary nights? What answer shall I give my lord?

Sidi [*wags her finger playfully at the woman.*]
Ha ha. Sadiku of the honey tongue.
Sadiku, head of the Lion's wives.
You'll make no prey of Sidi with your wooing tongue
Not this Sidi whose fame has spread to Lagos
And beyond the seas.
[Lakunle *beams with satisfaction and rises.*]

Sadiku Sidi, have you considered what a life of bliss awaits you? Baroka swears to take no other wife after you. Do you know what it is to be the Bale's last wife? I'll tell you. When he dies – and that should not be long; even the Lion has to die sometime – well, when he does, it means that you will have the honour of being the senior wife of the new Bale. And just think, until Baroka dies, you shall be his favourite. No living in the outhouses for you, my girl. Your place will always be in the palace; first as the latest bride, and afterwards, as the head of the new harem . . . . It is a rich life, Sidi. I know. I have been in that position for forty-one years.

Sidi You waste your breath.
Why did Baroka not request my hand
Before the stranger
Brought his book of images?
Why did the Lion not bestow his gift
Before my face was lauded to the world?
Can you not see? Because he sees my worth
Increased and multiplied above his own;
Because he can already hear
The ballad-makers and their songs
In praise of Sidi, the incomparable,
While the Lion is forgotten.
He seeks to have me as his property
Where I must fade beneath his jealous hold.
Ah, Sadiku,
The school-man here has taught me certain things
And my images have taught me all the rest.
Baroka merely seeks to raise his manhood
Above my beauty.
He seeks new fame
As the one man who has possessed
The jewel of Ilujinle!

Sadiku [*shocked, bewildered, incapable of making any sense of* Sidi's *words.*] But Sidi, are you well? Such nonsense never passed your lips before. Did you not sound strange, even in your own hearing? [*Rushes suddenly at* Lakunle.] Is this your doing, you popinjay?[1] Have you driven the poor girl mad at last? Such rubbish . . . I will beat your head for this!

Lakunle [*retreating in panic.*] Keep away from me, old hag.

Sidi Sadiku, let him be.
Tell your lord that I can read his mind,
That I will none of him.
Look – judge for yourself.
[*Opens the magazine and points out the pictures.*]
He's old. I never knew till now,
He was that old . . .
[*During the rest of her speech,* Sidi *runs her hand over the surface of the relevant part of the photographs, tracing the contours with her fingers.*]
. . . To think I took
No notice of my velvet skin.
How smooth it is!
And no man ever thought
To praise the fulness of my breasts. . . .

Lakunle [*laden with guilt and full of apology.*]
Well, Sidi, I did think . . .
But somehow it was not the proper thing.

Sidi [*ignores the interruption.*]
See I hold them to the warm caress
[*Unconsciously pushes out her chest.*]
Of a desire-filled sun.
[*Smiles mischievously.*]
There's a deceitful message in my eyes
Beckoning insatiate men to certain doom.
And teeth that flash the sign of happiness,
Strong and evenly, beaming full of life.
Be just, Sadiku,
Compare my image and your lord's –
An age of difference!
See how the water glistens on my face
Like the dew-moistened leaves on a Harmattan[2] morning
But he – his face is like a leather piece
Torn rudely from the saddle of his horse,
[Sadiku *gasps.*]

---

1 Parrot; conceited person, fop (arch.).　　　2 Dry, dusty wind from the Sahara.

Sprinkled with the musty ashes
From a pipe that is long over-smoked.
And this goat-like tuft
Which I once thought was manly;
It is like scattered twists of grass –
Not even green –
But charred and lifeless, as after a forest fire!
Sadiku, I am young and brimming; he is spent.
I am the twinkle of a jewel
But he is the hind quarters of a lion!

Sadiku [*recovering at last from helpless amazement.*] May Sango[3]
restore your wits. For most surely some angry god has taken possession of you. [*Turns around and walks away. Stops again as she
remembers something else.*] Your ranting put this clean out of my
head. My lord says that if you would not be his wife, would you
at least come to supper at his house tonight. There is a small feast
in your honour. He wishes to tell you how happy he is that the
great capital city has done so much honour to a daught of Ilujinle.
You have brought great fame to your people.

Sidi Ho ho! Do you think that I was only born
Yesterday?
The tales of Baroka's little suppers,
I know all.
Tell your lord that Sidi does not sup with
Married men.

Sadiku They are lies, lies. You must not believe everything you
hear. Sidi, would I deceive you? I swear to you . . .

Sidi Can you deny that
Every woman who has supped with him one night,
Becomes his wife or concubine the next?

Lakunle Is it for nothing he is called the Fox?

Sadiku [*advancing on him.*] You keep out of this, or so Sango be
my witness . . .

Lakunle [*retreats just a little, but continues to talk.*]
His wiliness is known even in the larger towns.
Did you never hear
Of how he foiled the Public Works attempt
To build the railway through Ilujinle.

Sadiku Nobody knows the truth of that. It is all hearsay.

Sidi I love hearsays. Lakunle, tell me all.

---

3 Yoruba god of thunder and war, of power and kinetic energy.

Lakunle Did you not know it? Well sit down and listen.
My father told me, before he died. And few men
Know of this trick – oh he's a die-hard rogue
Sworn against our progress . . . yes . . . it was . . . somewhere here
The track should have been laid just along
The outskirts. Well, the workers came, in fact
It was prisoners who were brought to do
The harder part . . . to break the jungle's back . . .
[*Enter the prisoners, guarded by two warders. A white surveyor examines his map (khaki helmet, spats, etc.) The foreman runs up with his camp stool, table etc., erects the umbrella over him and unpacks the usual box of bush comforts – soda siphon, whisky bottle, and geometric sandwiches. His map consulted, he directs the sweat team to where to work. They begin felling, matchet swinging, log dragging, all to the rhythm of the work gang's metal percussion (rod on gong or rude triangle, etc.). The two performers are also the song leaders and the others fill the chorus. 'N'ijo itoro', 'Amuda el 'ebe l'aiya', 'Gbe je on'ipa' etc.*]

Lakunle They marked the route with stakes, ate
Through the jungle and began the tracks. Trade,
Progress, adventure, success, civilization,
Fame, international conspicuousity . . . it was
All within the grasp of Ilujinle . . .
[*The wrestler enters, stands horrified at the sight and flees. Returns later with the Bale himself who soon assesses the situation. They disappear. The work continues, the surveyor occupies himself with the flywhisk and whisky. Shortly after, a bull-roarer is heard. The prisoners falter a little, pick up again. The bull-roarer continues on its way, nearer and farther, moving in circles, so that it appears to come from all round them. The foreman is the first to break and then the rest is chaos. Sole survivor of the rout is the surveyor who is too surprised to move.*

Baroka *enters a few minutes later accompanied by some attendants and preceded by a young girl bearing a calabash bowl. The surveyor, angry and threatening, is prevailed upon to open his gift. From it he reveals a wad of pound notes and kola nuts. Mutual understanding is established. The surveyor frowns heavily, rubs his chin, and consults his map. Re-examines the contents of the bowl, shakes his head.* Baroka *adds more money, and a coop of hens. A goat follows, and more money. This time 'truth' dawns on him at last, he has made a mistake. The track really should go the other way. What an unfortunate error, discovered just in time! No, no, no possibly of a mistake this time, the track should be much further away. In fact (scooping up the soil) the earth is most unsuitable, couldn't possibly support the weight of a railway engine. A gourd of palm wine is brought to seal*] *the agreement and a cola-nut is broken.*[4] Baroka's *men help the surveyor pack and they leave with their arms round each other followed by the surveyor's booty.*]

Lakunle [*as the last of the procession disappears, shakes his fist at them, stamping on the ground.*]
Voluptuous beast! He loves this life too well
To bear to part from it. And motor roads
And railways would do just that, forcing
Civilization at his door. He foresaw it
And he barred the gates, securing fast
His dogs and horses, his wives and all his
Concubines . . . ah, yes . . . all those concubines.
Baroka has such a selective eye, none suits him
But the best. . . .
[*His eyes truly light up. Sidi and Sadiku snigger, tip-toe offstage.*]
. . . Yes, one must grant him that.
Ah, I sometimes wish I led his kind of life.
Such luscious bosoms make his nightly pillow.
I am sure he keeps a time-table just as
I do at school. Only way to ensure fair play.
He must be healthy to keep going as he does.
I don't know what the women see in him. His eyes
Are small and always red with wine. He must
Possess some secret. . . . No! I do not envy him!
Just the one woman for me. Alone I stand
For progress, with Sidi my chosen soul-mate, the one
Woman of my life. . . . Sidi! Sidi where are you?
[*Rushes out after them, returns to fetch the discarded firewood and runs out again.*]

[*Baroka in bed, naked except for baggy trousers, calf-length. It is a rich bedroom covered in animal skins and rugs. Weapons round the wall. Also a strange machine, a most peculiar contraption with a long lever. Kneeling beside the bed is Baroka's current Favourite, engaged in plucking the hairs from his armpit. She does this by first massaging the spot around the selected air very gently with her forefinger. Then, with hardly a break, she pull out the hair between her finger and the thumb with a sudden sharp movement. Baroka twitches slightly with each pull. Then an aspirated 'A-ah', and a look of complete beatitude spreads all over his face.*]

Favourite Do I improve my lord?

Baroka You are still somewhat over-gentle with the pull

---

4 Symbol of friendship.

As if you feared to hurt the panther of the trees.
Be sharp and sweet
Like the swift sting of a vicious wasp
For there the pleasure lies – the cooling aftermath.

Favourite I'll learn, my lord.

Baroka You have not time, my dear.
Tonight I hope to take another wife.
And the honour of this task, you know,
Belongs by right to my latest choice.
But – A-ah – Now that was sharp.
It had in it the scorpion's sudden sting
Without its poison.
It was an angry pull; you tried to hurt
For I had made you wrathful with my boast.
But now your anger flows in my blood stream.
How sweet it is! A-ah! That was sweeter still.
I think perhaps that I shall let you stay,
The sole out-puller of my sweat-bathed hairs.
Ach!
[*Sits up suddenly and rubs the sore point angrily.*]
Now that had far more pain than pleasure
Vengeful creature, you did not caress
The area of extraction long enough!
[*Enter Sadiku. She goes down on her knees at once and bows her head into her lap.*]
Aha! Here comes Sadiku
Do you bring some balm,
To soothe the smart of my misused armpit?
Away, you enemy!
[*Exit the* Favourite.]

Sadiku My lord . . .

Baroka You have my leave to speak.
What did she say?

Sadiku She will not my lord. I did my best, but she will have none of you.

Baroka It follows the pattern – a firm refusal
At the start. Why will she not?

Sadiku That is the strange part of it. She says you're much too old. If you ask me, I think that she is really off her head. All this excitement of the books has been too much for her.

Baroka [*springs to his feet.*]
She says . . . That I am old

That I am much too old? Did a slight
Unripened girl say this of me?

Sadiku My lord, I heard the incredible words with my ears, and
I thought the world was mad.

Baroka But is it possible, Sadiku? Is this right?
Did I not, at the festival of Rain,
Defeat the men in the log-tossing match?
Do I not still with the most fearless ones,
Hunt the leopard and the boa at night
And save the farmers' goats from further harm?
And does she say I'm old?
Did I not, to announce the Harmattan,
Climb to the top of the silk-cotton tree,
Break the first pod, and scatter tasselled seeds
To the four winds – and this but yesterday?
Do any of my wives report
A failing in my manliness?
The strongest of them all
Still wearies long before the Lion does!
And so would she, had I the briefest chance
To teach this unfledged birdling
That lacks the wisdom to embrace
The rich mustiness of age . . . if I could once . . .
Come hither, soothe me, Sadiku
For I am wroth at heart.
[*Lies back on the bed, staring up as before.* Sadiku *takes her place at
the foot of the bed and begins to tickle the soles of his feet.* Baroka
*turns to the left suddenly, reaches down the side, and comes up with
a copy of the magazine. Opens it and begins to study the pictures. He
heaves a long sigh.*]
That is good, Sadiku, very good.
[*He begins to compare some pictures in the book, obviously his own
and Sidi's. Flings the book away suddenly and stares at the ceiling
for a second or two. Then, unsmiling.*]
Perhaps it is as well, Sadiku.

Sadiku My lord, what did you say?

Baroka Yes, faithful one, I say it is as well.
The scorn, the laughter and the jeers
Would have been bitter
Had she consented and my purpose failed,
I would have sunk with shame.

Sadiku My lord, I do not understand.

Baroka The time has come when I can fool myself

No more. I am no man, Sadiku. My manhood
Ended near a week ago.

Sadiku The gods forbid.

Baroka I wanted Sidi because I still hoped –
A foolish thought I know, but still – I hoped
That, with a virgin young and hot within,
My failing strength would rise and save my pride.
[Sadiku *begins to moan.*]
A waste of hope. I knew it even then.
But it's a human failing never to accept
The worst; and so I pandered to my vanity.
When manhood must, it ends.
The well of living, tapped beyond its depth,
Dries up, and mocks the wastrel in the end.
I am withered and unsapped, the joy
Of ballad-mongers, the aged butt
Of youth's ribaldry.

Sadiku [*tearfully.*] The gods must have mercy yet.

Baroka [*as if suddenly aware of her presence, starts up.*]
I have told this to no one but you,
Who are my eldest, my most faithful wife.
But if you dare parade my shame before the world . . .
[Sadiku *shakes her head in protest and begins to stroke the soles of
his feet with renewed tenderness.* Baroka *sighs and falls back slowly.*]
How irritable I have grown of late
Such doubts to harbour of your loyalty . . .
But this disaster is too much for one
Checked thus as I upon the prime of youth.
That rains that blessed me from my birth
Number a meagre sixty-two;
While my grandfather, that man of teak,
Fathered two sons, late on sixty-five.
But Okiki, my father, beat them all
Producing female twins at sixty-seven.
Why then must I, descendant of these lions
Forswear my wives at a youthful sixty-two
My veins of life run dry, my manhood gone!
[*His voice goes drowsy;* Sadiku *sighs and moans and caresses his feet.
His face lights up suddenly with rapture.*]
Sango bear witness! These weary feet
Have felt the loving hands of much design
In women.
My soles have felt the scratch of harsh,
Gravelled hands.

They have borne the heaviness of clumsy,
Gorilla paws.
And I have known the tease of tiny,
Dainty hands,
Toy-like hands that tantalized
My eager senses,
Promised of thrills to come
Remaining
Unfulfilled because the fingers
Were too frail,
The touch too light and faint to pierce
The incredible thickness of my soles.
But thou Sadiku, thy plain unadorned hands
Encase a sweet sensuality which age
Will not destroy. A-ah,
Oyayi! Beyond a doubt Sadiku,
Thou art the queen of them all.
[*Falls asleep.*]

§ *Tradition and change* Achebe (1, 3), Emecheta, Aidoo, Okot

BUCHI EMECHETA (1944 –)

From The Joys of Motherhood

Nnu Ego, the heroine of The Joys of Motherhood, is an Ibo woman victimized by her culture's attitudes to motherhood, which deem a childless woman a failure. She leaves her village and moves to Lagos where she fares little better. Here, in the fifth chapter, her fellow-villager Nwakusor comes across her in Lagos, just after her newly-born child by her second husband has died and she is contemplating suicide. Nwakusor remembers her as the daughter of the village's proud chief Agbadi and is shocked to see her in her present predicament. Like much of the novel, the chapter interlinks a comparison of urban and rural value-systems with its critique of gender codes.

Nwakusor was returning home from working all night on the ship that docked along the marina in Lagos. He was an Ibo of medium height and slight build, and though it was difficult to determine his age from looking at him, with the knowledge that he had been a docker for ten years one could have guessed that he was between his mid-thirties and the age of forty. He was now noticeably tired; his eyes were bloodshot, his feet heavy. But he had one consolation: he was going home to catch up with some sleep before the evening shift. He did not wish to look beyond his quiet rest and cooling bath. With such sweet thoughts in his mind, he climbed on to his rickety bicycle, black with age, and faced the formidable task of setting it to work its way up the hill to Ebute Metta, where he lived with his sad-eyed wife.

He laboured painfully from the island to the mainland. The weather was damp and so dewy that all shapes seemed indistinct. Even the graceful palm trees and coconut palms that guarded the shores of Lagos like faithful sentries were vague this morning. Looking across the lagoon, Nwakusor could see mist rising from the bluey waters and melting into the moving clouds. To think that in a few hours this very place would be steaming from direct heat! By the time he got home, in any case, his wife Ato would be ready to go to her fish stall in Oyingbo market. It was not that he wished to avoid her, it was just that he was not in any mood to listen to her inconsequential prattling.

The Lagos bridge was restricted on both sides by intricate iron uprights, painted red and with spear-shaped points, and a narrow tarred road wound itself between these fence-like iron works. Near Tabalogun, it was necessary for Nwakusor to cycle from the wider road to the narrow part of the bridge joining the island to the mainland.

Still full of thoughts of his bed, and puffing away ominously at the same time, he was jolted into the present by angry shouts and screams.

'If you wish to die, why do you want me to be your killer, eh?'

Nwakusor looked up to see a kia-kia bus swerving dangerously to his left in order to avoid hitting him. As usual at that time in the morning, the ordinary buses were almost impossible to get, so all varieties of private vehicles cashed in on the high demand. They were dubbed with the name 'kia-kia bus', meaning literally 'quick quick bus', for the advantage of this kind of transport was that once loaded it would never stop until it reached the island, and several trips could be made each morning, while the bus owned by the white man's company would go from stop to stop, slogging slowly like a duck up and down the Lagos bridge. The quicker the owners of these minibuses went, the more money they would collect, for clerk and messengers working on the island preferred to go by them, even though a full kia-kia bus meant six to ten passengers hanging on at each window, another dozen or so by the door, some even clinging to the roof. It was one of these buses that was now almost knocking Nwakusor down.

The shouting driver, like Nwakusor, was sweating in the morning mist. This mini-bus seemed to be exceptionally tightly packed and, looking at the driver, one could not be blamed for thinking that it was his own physical energy that was propelling the vehicle along and not the power produced by any kind of petrol. The man was gasping breathlessly. He had swerved so dramatically that some of the passengers hanging outside the bus had to jump down to save themselves from injury. There were screams and the squeaking of brakes. Nwakusor realised that he had had a narrow escape from death. Instinctively like the precariously hanging passengers, his feet sought solid ground. He stood there breathless and confused. He looked about him wildly while his mind began to register the extent of the danger he had been in a minute before.

'Well?' thundered the driver, looking offended and demanding an apology. He shook an angry fist in the air at the same time. 'If you don't know what to say, at least take your ancient bundle of old iron off the road. I still want to make use of my life. Next time you are looking for a killer, please, in the name of Allah, take yourself somewhere else. Please move out of my way.'

Nwakusor, who was too shocked to protest, did as he was told, picking up his ancient bike from where it had fallen, twisted but still workable, and his shrivelled and shaky self with it. 'I am sorry,' he said, ignoring the laughing passengers who by now had recovered from their shock and were cheering the driver's uncouth language. Nwakusor would have replied in like manner, but he was too shaken to want to play the game of abuse. Moreover, his Yoruba was not good enough; he would lose such a contest. So he decided to be apologetic, seeing that it was all his fault. And he was tired; the driver saw this, and stopped his verbal fight.

'I am sorry, driver, I have been working all night, and my mind is still asleep, believe me.'

The driver smiled widely at this. It was not every morning that drivers were treated politely, and in fact one of the tools of their trade was their ability to reduce anybody to tears with pointed tongue. Still, he would not deny his passengers the joy of seeing him win once more.

'The life is yours, man. But next time you're tired of it, stay out of the road and out of my way. You can strangle yourself in your room. It's less spectacular, but at least wouldn't put an innocent man in trouble.' With that, he careered round a sharp corner, roaring his bus and its loudmouthed passengers towards the island.

Nwakusor, judging from the way his legs still shook, knew it would be better to walk, even though he could have manipulated the bicycle back into action. Only the front wheel was a little bent and he could have straightened that out had he the inclination. People who did not know what had happened passed him and wondered whether he was mad, to be simply rolling his cycle along the sidewalk, taking up so much space, when he could be riding it, arriving at his destination sooner and saving himself the effort of having to say 'sorry, sorry' to everyone he collided with. It was getting busy on the pavements siding Carter Bridge at this time of the morning. He knew that people tended to prejudge others without knowing the reasons for their unorthodox behaviour, but he did not have the time to go about justifying his actions. As long as he did not hurt anybody, and he arrived home safely, he did not much care what other people were thinking.

As the sun came out it infused a kind of energy into Nwakusor's exhausted body. He even began to accept that being alive on a day like this was a privilege, and he told himself to start enjoying it. He was like someone who had a valuable gift and who for a long time had not appreciated its value: it was only when the gift was about to be taken away from him that he realised what he had been taking for granted. He became appreciative. But it was a private appreciation. If he were to stop any of these hurrying people and tell them of it, they would think that he had suddenly taken leave of his senses. Indeed, he did not appear all that sane, in his dirty work clothes, wheeling an antiquated machine, and smiling benignly at vacancy.

He was debating with himself whether it was not about time he remounted, when he saw a crowd on the other side of the bridge. It was a group of early workers, market women and labourers on their way to the Ebute Ero market, all babbling in a kind of excitement. Their voices were tense and feverish, tinged with awe, like those of people watching a human sacrifice, he thought; not that he had ever seen such a sacrifice, but he had heard of people who had witnessed such an uncommon sight. They were all talking nervously, yet they stood away from a person whom Nwakusor could not make out. Was it a man or a woman? He peered in between the traffic and deduced that the person looked more like a woman.

She was not old; in fact, judging from her straight back and agile body, she must be rather young. But she was behaving in a curious way, almost as if she was doing some sort of acrobatic dance. Nwakusor wanted to look at closer quarters. He blasted the unceasing traffic, but his eyes never left the scene. He was extra careful after the shock he had earlier, not wishing to be knocked down just because he was going to look at a woman who was either mad or doing some kind of juju dance for her god. He was going to take his time. One shouldn't be near death twice on the same morning.

His impatience was far from diminished as he saw from where he stood what the woman was actually trying to do. She was trying to jump into the lagoon! 'Good Lord,' Nwakusor thought, 'look at me jubilant for being given another opportunity to live longer, and see this foolish woman eager to end her own life when her Maker is not yet ready for her. How uneven the whole business of living is . . . Oh, blast this traffic!' One would have thought that the unending business was being staged to tantalise him. Soon there was a little gap, and he ran, bicycle and all, across the road.

As he approached the other side, there was a roar from the crowd as the woman floored a man who was trying to wrestle with her and free her from the railings which she was climbing in order to facilitate her leap to death. To be floored by an opponent in wrestling meant defeat, but to be laid flat by a woman was more than a defeat, it was a humiliation. The crowd, while eager to be at their places of work, appreciated this free entertainment, though none of them wanted the woman to achieve her suicidal aim, not when they were there anyway. No one wanted to start the day with such an incident on their conscience. Another man tore himself from the crowd in an attempt to save her, but though the woman did not floor this one, she fought fiercely and expertly, so that both of them were panting, and the fear of everybody was that the man might give in and say, 'After all, it's her life.' However a thing like that is not permitted in Nigeria; you are simply not allowed to commit suicide in peace, because everyone is responsible for the other person. Foreigners may call us a nation of busybodies, but to us, an individual's life belongs to the community and not just to him or her. So a person has no right to take it while another member of the community looks on. He must interfere, he must stop it happening.

It was while watching the fight and the way she was warding off her opponent that Nwakusor realised that this woman whose face was still hidden from him was not a Yoruba woman. She was from his village, where women were taught to wrestle like men, to learn the art of self-defence. She turned her face in the struggle and Nwakusor saw Nnu Ego, unbelievable though it was. It took him less than a second to pinch himself and rub his hands over his face to convince himself that he was not dreaming. As if he needed a double reassurance, he shouted hoarsely:

'Nnu Ego! Nnu Ego, the child of Agbadi's love, Nnu Ego! What are you doing? What are you trying to do?'

She stopped abruptly in her fight. She looked up at the bystanders, her eyes roaming over their heads and not on their faces. She was shocked. Someone in this crowd knew who she was! She had bargained on the fact that Lagos was such a big place, with people of so many different races and backgrounds that it was very unlikely that anyone would know her. She had known she would probably be opposed by some pedestrians on the bridge, but she had calculated that she would arrive there before it got too busy. She was wrong. Though it was still misty and a little dampness lingered from the night before, yet the morning had a dazzling brightness from the young sun which drew people from their sleeping places and on to the open road.

Nnu Ego's hesitation gave Nwakusor the chance he needed. He had not made a mistake. It was Nnaife's wife, all right. Acting instinctively, he threw his cherished antiquated machine to one side where it crashed with a pathetic jangle of old pieces of rusty metal. Like an agile cat, pouncing on an unsuspecting mouse, he rolled himself almost into a round shape and leapt towards Nnu Ego. They both fell on the cemented ground. Nwakusor's grazed knee started to bleed immediately. Nnu Ego got up quickly, trying to tear herself away like a lunatic, but now there were more people willing to help Nwakusor. The first man who had tried unsuccessfully to restrain her undaunted came forward again and held her tightly by the wrist.

Nwakusor, breathing heavily, gasped in Ibo, 'What are you trying to do to your husband, your father, your people and your son who is only a few weeks old? You want to kill yourself, eh? Who is going to look after your baby for you? You are shaming your womanhood, shaming your motherhood.'

For the first time since Nnu Ego had seen her child there on the mat, tears of shock and frustration flowed down her cheeks. Who was going to give her the energy to tell the world that she had once been a mother, but had failed? How would people understand that she had wanted so desperately to be a woman like everybody else, but had now failed again? *Oh, God, I wish these people, though they mean well, had simply let me be.* Her heart was pounding in pain, and bitterness welled from the same heart into her mouth. She tried several times to talk, but her voice produced no sound.

She could only shake her head negatively at Nwakusor's angry tirade, trying to tell him that he was wrong.

Another Ibo woman, carrying a large basket of yams on her way to the market, was not satisfied with Nwakusor's verbal chastisement. She stepped forward and slapped Nnu Ego on one side of her face, adding, 'You mean you have a baby at home yet you come here disgracing the man who paid for you to be brought into this town? I don't know what our people are becoming; as soon as they step near the coast they think they own themselves and forget the tradition of our fathers.'

So angry was this woman that she had put all her energy into the slap and its sting went home, momentarily blinding Nnu Ego.

Then Nnu Ego cried, put so much force into the use of her voice that the sound broke through, and it sounded roughly like that of a man:

'But I am not a woman any more! I am not a mother any more. The child is there, dead on the mat. My *chi*[1] has taken him away from me. I only want to go in there and meet her . . .'

It was then that people understood the reason for her irrational behaviour. Even some of the men had tears of pity in their eyes. Pieces of advice and consolation poured from people she had never seen before and would never see again. Many took the time to tell her their own stories. Even the woman who had slapped her told her that out of six pregnancies she only had two children alive, yet she was still living. She reminded Nnu Ego that she was still very young, and said that once babies started coming, they came in great numbers.

'She is not mad after all,' the woman took it upon herself to inform the crowd in her imperfect Yoruba. 'She has only just lost the child that told the world that she is not barren.'

And they all agreed that a woman without a child for her husband was a failed woman. It was left to Nwakusor, who had saved a life, to lead Nnu Ego home safely to her husband Nnaife.

§ *Motherhood* Aidoo (2), Ngcobo; Carib: Goodison; *Tradition and change* Achebe (1, 3), Soyinka (2), Aidoo, Okot

---

1 Personal god.

NIYI OSUNDARE (1947–)

Harvestcall

(*To be chanted to lively* bata* *music*)

I

This is Iyanfoworogi
where, garnished in green
pounded yam rested its feted arms
on the back of stooping stakes.
5 This is Iyanfoworogi
where valiant heaps cracked, finally,
from the unquenchable zeal of fattening yams.

This is Iyanfoworogi
where yams, ripe and randy,
10 waged a noisy war against the knife;
here where, subdued by fire,
efuru provoked mouthful clamour
from the combat of hungry wood:
    the pestle fights the mortar
15   the mortar fights the pestle
    a dough of contention smooths down
    the rugged anger of hunger.

Here where yam wore the crown
in the reign of swollen roots
20 amid a retinue of vines and royal leaves;
between insistent sky and yielding earth,
the sun mellowed planting pageants
into harvest march,
a fiery pestle in his ripening hand.

25 This is Iyanfoworogi
where a tempting yam sauntered
out of the selling tray
and the marketplace became a mob
of instant suitors.

---

* bata: drums, used to salute gods.   12 *efuru:* the king of yams [author's note].

II

30 And this Oke Eniju
where coy cobs rocked lustily
in the loin of swaying stalks.
Once here in May
a tasselled joy robed the field
35 like hemless green.
Once here in May
the sky was a riot of pollen grains
and ivory mills waited (im)patiently
for the browning of grey tassels.

40 And when June had finally grabbed the year
by her narrow waist
corn cobs flashed their milky teeth
in disrobing kitchens.
Plenty's season announced its coming
45 and the humming mill at dawn
suddenly became the village heart.

III

(Finally) Ogbese Odo
where cotton pods, lips duly parted
by December's sun,
50 draped busy farmsteads
in a harvest of smiles.
Here a blooming loom curtailed
the tiger claws of the harmattan
and earth's wardrobe lent a garb
55 to every season.

IV

(*Music lowers in tempo, becoming solemn*)
But where *are* they?
Where are they gone:
aroso, geregede, otiili, pakala
which beckoned lustily to the reaping basket
60 Where are they
the yam pyramids which challenged the sun
in busy barns
Where are they
the pumpkins which caressed earthbreast
65 like mammary burdens

---

53 harmattan: dry, dusty wind from the Sahara.   **58 aroso...**: all four are types of beans. [author's note]

Where are they
the pods which sweetened harvest air
with the clutter of dispersing seeds?
Where are they? Where are they gone?

70   Uncountable seeds lie sleeping
in the womb of earth
uncountable seeds
awaiting the quickening tap
of our waking finger.

75   With our earth so warm
How can our hearth be so cold?

§ Yams *importance in culture* Achebe (1)

BEN OKRI (1959 –)

Incidents at the Shrine

Anderson had been waiting for something to fall on him. His anxiety was such that for the first time in several years he went late to work. It was just his luck that the Head of Department had chosen that day for an impromptu inspection. When he got to the museum he saw that his metal chair had been removed from its customary place. The little stool on which he rested his feet after running endless errands was also gone. His official messenger's uniform had been taken off the hook. He went to the main office and was told by one of the clerks that he had been sacked, and that the supervisor was not available. Anderson started to protest, but the clerk got up and pushed him out of the office.

He went aimlessly down the corridors of the Department of Antiquities. He stumbled past the visitors to the museum. He wandered amongst the hibiscus and bougainvillea. He didn't look at the ancestral stoneworks in the museum field. Then he went home, dazed, confused by objects, convinced that he saw many fingers pointing at him. He went down streets he had never seen in his life and he momentarily forgot where his compound was.

When he got home he found that he was trembling. He was hungry. He hadn't eaten that morning and the cupboard was empty of food. He couldn't stop thinking about the loss of his job. Anderson had suspected for some time that the supervisor had been planning to give his job to a distant relation. That was the reason why the supervisor was always berating him on the slightest pretext. Seven years in the city had begun to make Anderson feel powerless because he didn't belong to the important societies, and didn't have influential relatives. He spent the afternoon thinking about his condition in the world. He fell asleep and dreamt about his dead parents.

He woke up feeling bitter. It was late in the afternoon and he was hungry. He got out of bed and went to the market to get some beef and tripe for a pot of stew. Anderson slid through the noise of revving motors and shouting traders. He came to the goatsellers. The goats stood untethered in a small corral. As Anderson went past he had a queer feeling that the goats were staring at him. When he stopped and looked at them the animals panicked. They kicked and fought backwards. Anderson hurried on till he found himself at the meat stalls.

The air was full of flies and the stench was overpowering. He felt ill. There were intestines and bones in heaps on the floor. He was haggling the price of tripe when he heard confused howls from the section where they sold generators and videos. The meat-seller had just slapped the tripe down on the table and was telling him to go somewhere else for the price he offered, when the fire burst out with an explosion. Flames poured over the stalls. Waves of screaming people rushed in Anderson's direction. He saw the fire flowing behind them, he saw black smoke. He started to run before the people reached him.

He heard voices all around him. Dry palm fronds crackled in the air. Anderson ducked under the bare eaves of a stall, tripped over a fishmonger's basin of writhing eels, and fell into a mound of snailshells. He struggled back up. He ran past the fortune-tellers and the amulet traders. He was shouldering his way through the bamboo poles of the lace-sellers when it struck him with amazing clarity that the fire was intent upon him because he had no power to protect himself. And soon the fire was everywhere. Suddenly, from the midst of voices in the smoke, Anderson heard someone calling his names. Not just the one name, the ordinary one which made things easier in the city – Anderson; he heard all the others as well, even the ones he had forgotten: Jeremiah, Ofuegbu, Nutcracker, Azzi. He was so astonished that when he cut himself, by brushing his thigh against two rusted nails, he did not know how profusely he bled till he cleared out into the safety of the main road. When he got home he was still bleeding. When the bleeding ceased, he felt that an alien influence had insinuated itself into his body, and an illness took over.

He became so ill that most of the money he had saved in all the years of humiliation and sweat went into the hands of the quack chemists of the area. They bandaged his wound. They gave him tetanus injections with curved syringes. They gave him pills in squat, silvery bottles. Anderson was reduced to creeping about the compound, from room to toilet and back again, as though he were terrified of daylight. And then, three days into the illness, with the taste of alum stale in his mouth, he caught a glimpse of himself in the mirror. He saw the gaunt face of a complete stranger. Two days later, when he felt he had recovered sufficiently, Anderson packed his box and fled home to his village.

The Image-maker

Anderson hadn't been home for a long time. When the lorry driver dropped him at the village junction, the first things he noticed were the ferocity of the heat and the humid smell of rotting vegetation. He went down the dirt track that led to the village. A pack of dogs followed him for a short while and then disappeared. Cowhorns and the beating of drums sounded from the forest. He saw masks, eaten by insects, along the grass verge.

He was sweating when he got to the obeche tree[1] where, during the war, soldiers had shot a woman thought to be a spy. Passing the well which used to mark the village boundary, he became aware of three rough forms running after him. They had flaming red eyes and they shouted his names.

'Anderson! Ofuegbu!'

He broke into a run. They bounded after him.

'Ofuegbu! Anderson!'

In his fear he ran so hard that his box flew open. Scattered behind him were his clothes, his medicines, and the modest gifts he had brought to show his people that he wasn't entirely a small man in the world. He discarded the box and sped on without looking back. Swirls of dust came towards him. And when he emerged from the dust, he saw the village.

It was sunset. Anderson didn't stop running till he was safely in the village. He went on till he came to the pool office with the signboard that read: MR ABAS AND CO. LICENSED COLLECTOR. Outside the office, a man sat in a depressed cane chair. His eyes stared divergently at the road and he snored gently. Anderson stood panting. He wanted to ask directions to his uncle's place, but he didn't want to wake the owner of the pool office.

Anderson wasn't sure when the man woke up, for suddenly he said: 'Why do you have to run into our village like a madman?'

Anderson struggled for words. He was sweating.

'You disturb my eyes when you come running into our village like that.'

Anderson wiped his face. He was confused. He started to apologize, but the man looked him over once, and fell back into sleep, with his eyes still open. Anderson wasn't sure what to do. He was thirsty. With sweat dribbling down his face, Anderson tramped on through the village.

Things had changed since he'd been away. The buildings had lost their individual colours to that of the dust. Houses had moved several yards from where they used to be. Roads ran diagonally to how he remembered them. He felt he had arrived in a place he had almost never known.

Exhausted, Anderson sat on a bench outside the market. The roadside was full of ants. The heat mists made him sleepy. The market behind him was empty, but deep within it he heard celebrations and arguments. He listened to alien voices and languages from the farthest reaches of the world. Anderson fell asleep on the bench and dreamt that he was being carried

---

1 Tree yielding light-coloured timber.

through the village by the ants. He woke to find himself inside the pool office. His legs itched.

The man whom he had last seen sitting in the cane chair, was now behind the counter. He was mixing a potion of local gin and herbs. There was someone else in the office: a stocky man with a large forehead and a hardened face.

He stared at Anderson and then said: 'Have you slept enough?'

Anderson nodded. The man behind the counter came round with a tumbler full of herbal mixtures.

Almost forcing the drink down Anderson's throat, he said: 'Drink it down. Fast!'

Anderson drank most of the mixture in one gulp. It was very bitter and bile rushed up in his mouth.

'Swallow it down!'

Anderson swallowed. His head cleared a little and his legs stopped itching.

The man who had given him the drink said: 'Good.' Then he pointed to the other man and said: 'That's your uncle. Our Image-maker. Don't you remember him?'

Anderson stared at the Image-maker's face. The lights shifted. The face was elusively familiar. Anderson had to subtract seven years from the awesome starkness of the Image-maker's features before he could recognize his own uncle.

Anderson said: 'My uncle, you have changed!'

'Yes, my son, and so have you,' his uncle said.

'I'm so happy to see you,' said Anderson.

Smiling, his uncle moved into the light at the doorway. Anderson saw that his left arm was shrivelled.

'We've been expecting you,' his uncle said.

Anderson didn't know what to say. He looked from one to the other. Then suddenly he recognized Mr Abas, who used to take him fishing down the village stream.

'Mr Abas! It's you!'

'Of course it's me. Who did you think I was?'

Anderson stood up.

'Greetings, my elders. Forgive me. So much has changed.'

His uncle touched him benevolently on the shoulder and said: 'That's all right. Now, let's go.'

Anderson persisted with his greeting. Then he began to apologize for his bad memory. He told them that he had been pursued at the village boundary.

'They were strange people. They pursued me like a common criminal.'

The Image-maker said: 'Come on. Move. We don't speak of strange things in our village. We have no strange things here. Now, let's go.'

Mr Abas went outside and sat in his sunken cane chair. The Image-maker led Anderson out of the office.

They walked through the dry heat. The chanting of worshippers came from the forest. Drums and jangling bells sounded faintly in the somnolent air.

'The village is different,' Anderson said.

The Image-maker was silent.

'What has happened here?'

'Don't ask questions. In our village we will provide you with answers before it is necessary to ask questions,' the Image-maker said with some irritation.

Anderson kept quiet. As they went down the village Anderson kept looking at the Image-maker: the more he looked, the more raw and godlike the Image-maker seemed. It was as though he had achieved an independence from human agencies. He looked as if he had been cast in rock, and left to the wilds.

'The more you look, the less you see,' the Image-maker said.

It sounded, to Anderson, like a cue. They had broken into a path. Ahead of them were irregular rows of soapstone monoliths. Embossed with abstract representations of the human figure, the monoliths ranged from the babies of their breed to the abnormally large ones. There were lit candles and varied offerings in front of them. There were frangipani and iroko trees[2] in their midst. There were also red-painted poles which had burst into flower.

His uncle said: 'The images were originally decorated with pearls, lapis lazuli, amethysts and magic glass which twinkled wonderful philosophies. But the pale ones from across the seas came and stole them. This was whispered to me in a dream.'

Anderson gazed at the oddly elegant monoliths and said: 'You resemble the gods you worship.'

His uncle gripped him suddenly.

'We don't speak of resemblances in our village, you hear?'

Anderson nodded. His uncle relaxed his grip. They moved on.

After a while his uncle said: 'The world is the shrine and the shrine is the world. Everything must have a centre. When you talk rubbish, bad things fly into your mouth.'

They passed a cluster of huts. Suddenly the Image-maker bustled forward. They had arrived at the main entrance to a circular clay shrinehouse. The Image-maker went to the niche and brought out a piece of native chalk, a tumbler and a bottle of herbs. He made a mash which he smeared across Anderson's forehead. On a nail above the door, there was a bell which the Image-maker rang three times.

A voice called from within the hut.

The Image-maker sprayed himself forth in a list of his incredible names and titles. Then he requested permission to bring to the shrine an afflicted 'son of the soil'.

---

2 Trees of genus *Chlorophora*.

The voices asked if the 'son of the soil' was ready to come in.

The Image-maker was silent.

A confusion of drums, bells, cowhorns, came suddenly from within. Anderson fainted.

Then the Image-maker said to the voices: 'He is ready to enter!'

They came out and found that Anderson was light. They bundled him into the shrinehouse and laid him on a bed of congealed palm oil.

The Image

When Anderson came to he could smell burning candles, sweat and incense. Before him was the master Image, a hallucinatory warrior monolith decorated in its original splendour of precious stones and twinkling glass. At its base were roots, kola nuts and feathers. When Anderson gazed at the master Image he heard voices that were not spoken and he felt drowsiness come over him.

Candles burned in the mist of blue incense. A small crowd of worshippers danced and wove Anderson's names in songs. Down the corridors he could hear other supplicants crying out in prayer for their heart's desires, for their afflictions and problems. They prayed like people who are ill and who are never sure of recovering. It occurred to Anderson that it must be a cruel world to demand such intensity of prayer.

Anderson tried to get up from the bed, but couldn't. The master Image seemed to look upon him with a grotesque face. The ministrants closed in around him. They praised the master Image in songs. The Image-maker gave a sudden instruction and the ministrants rushed to Anderson. They spread out their multiplicity of arms and embraced Anderson in their hard compassions. But when they touched Anderson he screamed and shouted in hysteria. The ministrants embraced him with their remorseless arms and carried him through the corridors and out into the night. They rushed him past the monoliths outside. They took him past creeks and waterholes. When they came to a blooming frangipani tree, they dumped him on the ground. Then they retreated with flutters of their smocks, and disappeared as though the darkness were made of their own substance.

Anderson heard whispers in the forest. He heard things falling among the branches. Then he heard footsteps that seemed for ever approaching. He soon saw that it was Mr Abas. He carried a bucket in one hand and a lamp in the other. He dropped the bucket near Anderson.

'Bathe of it,' Mr Abas said, and returned the way he had come.

Anderson washed himself with the treated water. When he finished the attendants came and brought him fresh clothes. Then they led him back to the shrinehouse.

The Image-maker was waiting for him. Bustling with urgency, his bad arm moving restlessly like the special instrument of his functions, the Image-maker grabbed Anderson and led him to an alcove.

He made Anderson sit in front of a door. There was a hole greased with palm oil at the bottom of the door. The Image-maker shouted an instruction and the attendants came upon Anderson and held him face down. They pushed him towards the hole; they forced his head and shoulders through it.

In the pain Anderson heard the Image-maker say: 'Tell us what you see!'

Anderson couldn't see anything. All he could feel was the grinding pain. Then he saw a towering tree. There was a door on the tree trunk. Then he saw a thick blue pall. A woman emerged from the pall. She was painted over in native chalk. She had bangles all the way up her arms. Her stomach and waist were covered in beads.

'I see a woman,' he cried.

Several voices asked: 'Do you know her?'

'No.'

'Is she following you?'

'I don't know.'

'Is she dead?'

'I don't know.'

'Is she dead?'

'No!'

There was the merriment of tinkling bells.

'What is she doing?'

She had come to the tree and opened the door. Anderson suffered a fresh agony. She opened a second door and tried the third one, but it didn't open. She tried again and when it gave way with a crash Anderson finally came through – but he lost consciousness.

Afterwards, they fed him substantially. Then he was allowed the freedom to move round the village and visit some of his relations. In the morning the Image-maker sent for him. The attendants made him sit on a cowhide mat and they shaved off his hair. They lit red and green candles and made music around him. Then the Image-maker proceeded with the extraction of impurities from his body. He rubbed herbal juices into Anderson's shoulder. He bit into the flesh and pulled out a rusted little padlock which he spat into an enamel bowl. He inspected the padlock. After he had washed out his mouth, he bit into Anderson's shoulder again and pulled out a crooked needle. He continued like this till he had pulled out a piece of broken glass, a twisted nail, a cowrie, and a small key. There was some agitation as to whether the key would fit the padlock, but it didn't.

When the Image-maker had finished he picked up the bowl, jangled the objects, and said: 'All these things, where do they come from? Who sent them into you?'

Anderson couldn't say anything.

The Image-maker went on to cut light razor strokes on Anderson's arm and he rubbed protective herbs into the bleeding marks. He washed his hands and went out of the alcove. He came back with a pouch, which he gave to Anderson with precise instructions of its usage.

Then he said: 'You are going back to the city tomorrow. Go to your place of work, collect the money they are owing you, and look for another job. You will have no trouble. You understand?'

Anderson nodded.

'Now, listen. One day I went deep into the forest because my arm hurt. I injured it working in a factory. For three days I was in the forest praying to our ancestors. I ate leaves and fishes. On the fourth day I forgot how I came there. I was lost and everything was new to me. On the fifth day I found the Images. They were hidden amongst the trees and tall grasses. Snakes and tortoises were all around. My pain stopped. When I found my way back and told the elders of the village what I had seen they did not believe me. The Images had been talked about in the village for a long time but no one had actually seen them. That is why they made me the Image-maker.'

He paused, then continued.

'Every year, around this time, spirits from all over the world come to our village. They meet at the marketplace and have heated discussions about everything under the sun. Sometimes they gather round our Images outside. On some evenings there are purple mists round the iroko tree. At night we listen to all the languages, all the philosophies, of the world. You must come home now and again. This is where you derive power. You hear?'

Anderson nodded. He hadn't heard most of what was said. He had been staring at the objects in the enamel bowl.

The Image-eaters

Anderson ate little through the ceremonies that followed the purification of his body. After all the dancing and feasting to the music of cowhorns and tinkling bells, they made him lie down before the master Image. Then the strangest voice he had ever heard thundered the entire shrinehouse with its full volume.

'ANDERSON! OFUEGBU! YOU ARE A SMALL MAN. YOU CANNOT RUN FROM YOUR FUTURE. GOVERNMENTS CANNOT EXIST WITHOUT YOU. ALL THE DISASTERS OF THE WORLD REST ON YOU AND HAVE YOUR NAME. THIS IS YOUR POWER.'

The ministrants gave thanks and wept for joy.

Anderson spent the night in the presence of the master Image. He dreamt that he was dying of hunger and that there was nothing left in the world to eat. When Anderson ate of the master Image he was surprised at its sweetness. He was surprised also that the Image replenished itself.

In the morning Anderson's stomach was bloated with an imponderable weight. Shortly before his departure the Image-maker came to him and suggested that he contribute to the shrine fund. When Anderson made his donation, the Image-maker gave his blessing. The ministrants prayed for him and sang of his destiny.

Anderson had just enough money to get him back to the city. When he was ready to leave, Anderson felt a new heaviness come upon him. He thanked his uncle for everything and made his way through the village.

He stopped at the pool office. Mr Abas was in his sunken cane chair, his eyes pursuing their separate lines of vision. Anderson wasn't sure if Mr Abas was asleep.

He said: 'I'm leaving now.'

'Leaving us to our hunger, are you?'

'There is hunger where I am going,' Anderson said.

Mr Abas smiled and said: 'Keep your heart pure. Have courage. Suffering cannot kill us. And travel well.'

'Thank you.'

Mr Abas nodded and soon began to snore. Anderson went on towards the junction.

As he walked through the heated gravity of the village Anderson felt like an old man. He felt that his face had stiffened. He had crossed the rubber plantation, had crossed the boundary, and was approaching the junction, when the rough forms with blazing eyes fell upon him. He fought them off. He lashed out with his stiffened hands and legs. They could easily have torn him to pieces, because their ferocity was greater than his. There was a moment in which he saw himself dead. But they suddenly stopped and stared at him. Then they pawed him, as though he had become allied with them in some way. When they melted back into the heat mists, Anderson experienced the new simplicity of his life, and continued with his journey.

§ *Interior journey* Tutuola; Carib: Harris (1)

AMA ATA AIDOO (1942 –)

1: The Message

'Look here my sister, it should not be said but they say they opened her up.'

'They opened her up?'

'Yes, opened her up.'

'And the baby removed?'

'Yes, the baby removed.'

'Yes, the baby removed.'

'I say . . .'

'They do not say, my sister.'

'Have you heard it?'

'What?'

'This and this and that . . .'

'A-a-ah! that is it . . .'

'*Meewuo!*'

'They don't say *meewuo* . . .'

'And how is she?'

'Am I not here with you? Do I know the highway which leads to Cape Coast?'

'Hmmm . . .'

'And anyway how can she live? What is it like even giving birth with a stomach which is whole . . . eh? . . . I am asking you. And if you are always standing on the brink of death who go to war with a stomach that is whole, then how would she do whose stomach is open to the winds?'

'Oh, *poo*, pity . . .'

'I say . . .'

My little bundle, come. You and I are going to Cape Coast today.

I am taking one of her own cloths with me, just in case. These people on the coast do not know how to do a thing and I am not going to have anybody mishandling my child's body. I hope they give it to me. Horrible things I have heard done to people's bodies. Cutting them up and using them for instructions. Whereas even murderers still have decent burials.

I see Mensima coming. . . . And there is Nkama too . . . and Adwoa Meenu. . . . Now they are coming to . . . '*poo* pity' me. Witches, witches, witches . . . they have picked mine up while theirs prosper around them, children, grandchildren and great-grandchildren – theirs shoot up like mushrooms.

'Esi, we have heard of your misfortune . . .'

'That our little lady's womb has been opened up . . .'

'And her baby removed . . .'

Thank you very much.

'Has she lived through it?'

I do not know.

'Esi, bring her here, back home whatever happens.'

Yoo, thank you. If the government's people allow it, I shall bring her home.

'And have you got ready your things?'

Yes. . . . No.

I cannot even think well.

It feels so noisy in my head. . . . Oh my little child. . . . I am wasting time. . . . And so I am going . . .

Yes, to Cape Coast.

No, I do not know anyone there now but do you think no one would show me the way to this big hospital . . . if I asked around?

Hmmm . . . it's me has ended up like this. I was thinking that everything was alright now. . . . *Yoo*. And thank you too. Shut the door for me when you are leaving. You may stay too long outside if you wait for me, so go home and be about your business. I will let you know when I bring her in.

'Maami Amfoa, where are you going?'

My daughter, I am going to Cape Coast.

'And what is our old mother going to do with such swift steps? Is it serious?'

My daughter, it is very serious.

'Mother, may God go with you.'

Yoo, my daughter.

'Eno, and what calls at this hour of the day?'

They want me in Cape Coast.

'Does my friend want to go and see how much the city has changed since we went there to meet the new Wesleyan Chairman, twenty years ago?'

My sister, do you think I have knees to go parading on the streets of Cape Coast?

'Is it heavy?'

Yes, very heavy indeed. They have opened up my grandchild at the hospital, *hi, hi, hi.* . . .

'Eno *due, due, due* . . . I did not know. May God go with you. . . .'

Thank you. *Yaa.*

'O, the world!'

'It's her grandchild. The only daughter of her only son. Do you remember Kojo Amisa who went to sodja and fell in the great war, overseas?'

'Yes, it's his daughter. . . .'

. . . O, *poo*, pity.

'Kobina, run to the street, tell Draba Anan to wait for Nana Amfoa.'

'. . . Draba Anan, Draba, my mother says I must come and tell you to wait for Nana Amfoa.'

'And where is she?'

'There she comes.'

'Just look at how she hops like a bird . . . does she think we are going to be here all day? And anyway we are full already . . .'

O, you drivers!

'What have drivers done?'

'And do you think it shows respect when you speak in this way? It is only that things have not gone right; but she could, at least have been your mother. . . .'

'But what have I said? I have not insulted her. I just think that only Youth must be permitted to see Cape Coast, the town of the Dear and Expensive. . . .'

'And do you think she is going on a peaceful journey? The only daughter of her only son has been opened up and her baby removed from her womb.'

O . . . God.

O

O

O

Poo, pity.

'Me . . . *poo* – pity, I am right about our modern wives. I always say they are useless as compared with our mothers.'

'You drivers!'

'Now what have your modern wives done?'

'Am I not right what I always say about them?'

'You go and watch them in the big towns. All so thin and dry as sticks – you can literally blow them away with your breath. No decent flesh anywhere. Wooden chairs groan when they meet with their hard exteriors.'

'O you drivers . . . .'

'But of course all drivers . . . .'

'What have I done? Don't all my male passengers agree with me? These modern girls. . . . Now here is one who cannot even have a baby in a decent way. But must have the baby removed from her stomach. *Tchiaa*!'

'What . . .'

'Here is the old woman.'

'Whose grandchild . . . ?'

'Yes.'

'Nana,[1] I hear you are coming to Cape Coast with us.'

Yes my master.

'We nearly left you behind but we heard it was you and that it is a heavy journey you are making.'

Yes my master . . . thank you my master.

'Push up please . . . push up. Won't you push up? Why do you all sit looking at me with such eyes as if I was a block of wood?'

'It is not that there is nowhere to push up to. Five fat women should go on that seat, but look at you!'

'And our own grandmother here is none too plump herself . . . . Nana, if they won't push, come to the front seat with me.'

'. . . *Hei*, scholar, go to the back . . . .'

'. . . And do not scowl on me. I know your sort too well. Something tells me you do not have any job at all. As for that suit you are wearing and looking so grand in, you hired or borrowed it . . . .'

'Oh you drivers!'

Oh you drivers . . .

The scholar who read this tengram thing, said it was made about three days ago. My lady's husband sent it . . . . Three days . . . . God – that is too long ago. Have they buried her . . . where? Or did they cut her up . . . I should not think about it . . . or something will happen to me. Eleven or twelve . . . Efua Panyin, Okuma, Kwame Gyasi and who else? But they should not have left me here. Sometimes . . . ah, I hate this nausea. But it is this smell of petrol. Now I have remembered I never could travel in a lorry. I always was so sick. But now I hope at least that will not happen. These young people will think it is because I am old and they will laugh. At least if I knew the child of my child was alive, it would have been good. And the little things she sent me . . . . Sometimes some people like Mensima and Nkansa make me feel as if I had been a barren woman instead of only one with whom infant-mortality pledged friendship . . .

I will give her that set of earrings, bracelet and chain which Odwumfo Ata made for me. It is the most beautiful and the most expensive thing I have . . . . It does not hurt me to think that I am going to die very soon and have them and their children gloating over my things. After all what did

---

1 Term of respect for elder; grandmother.

they swallow my children for? It does not hurt me at all. If I had been someone else, I would have given them all away before I died. But it does not
matter. They can share their own curse. Now, that is the end of me and my
roots. . . . Eternal death has worked like a warrior rat, with diabolical sense
of duty, to gnaw my bottom. Everything is finished now. The vacant lot is
swept and the scraps of old sugar-cane pulp, dry sticks and bunches of hair
burnt . . . how it reeks, the smoke!

'O, Nana do not weep . . .'

'Is the old woman weeping?'

'If the only child of your only child died, won't you weep?'

'Why do you ask me? Did I know her grandchild is dead?'

'Where have you been, not in this lorry? Where were your ears when we
were discussing it?'

'I do not go putting my mouth in other people's affairs . . .'

'So what?'

'So go and die.'

'*Hei, hei*, it is prohibited to quarrel in my lorry.'

'Draba, here is me, sitting quiet and this lady of muscles and bones being
cheeky to me.'

'Look, I can beat you.'

'Beat me . . . beat me . . . let's see.'

'*Hei*, you are not civilised, eh?'

'Keep quiet and let us think, both of you, or I will put you down.'

'Nana, do not weep. There is God above.'

Thank you my master.

'But we are in Cape Coast already.'

Meewuo! My God, hold me tight or something will happen to me.

My master, I will come down here.

'O Nana, I thought you said you were going to the hospital . . . . We are
not there yet.'

I am saying maybe I will get down here and ask my way around.

'Nana, you do not know these people, eh? They are very impudent here.
They have no use for old age. So they do not respect it. Sit down, I will
take you there.'

Are you going there, my master?

'No, but I will take you there.'

Ah, my master, your old mother thanks you. Do not shed a tear when
you hear of my death . . . my master, your old mother thanks you.

I hear there is somewhere where they keep corpses until their owners
claim them . . . if she has been buried, then I must find her husband . . . Esi
Amfoa, what did I come to do under this sky? I have buried all my children and now I am going to bury my only grandchild!

'Nana we are there.'

Is this the hospital?

'Yes, Nana. What is your child's name?'

Esi Amfoa. Her father named her after me.

'Do you know her European name?'

No, my master.

'What shall we do?'

'. . . *Ei* lady, Lady Nurse, we are looking for somebody.'

'You are looking for somebody and can you read? If you cannot, you must ask someone what the rules in the hospital are. You can only come and visit people at three o'clock.'

Lady, please. She was my only grandchild . . .

'Who? And anyway, it is none of our business.'

'Nana, you must be patient . . . and not cry . . .'

'Old woman, why are you crying, it is not allowed here. No one must make any noise . . .'

My lady, I am sorry but she was all I had.

'Who? Oh, are you the old woman who is looking for somebody?'

Yes.

'Who is he?'

She was my granddaughter – the only child of my only son.

'I mean, what was her name?'

Esi Amfoa.

'Esi Amfoa . . . Esi Amfoa. I am sorry, we do not have anyone whom they call like that here.'

Is that it?

'Nana, I told you they may know only her European name here.'

My master, what shall we do then?

'What is she ill with?'

She came here to have a child . . .

'. . . And they say, they opened her stomach and removed the baby.'

'Oh . . . oh, I see.'

My Lord, hold me tight so that nothing will happen to me now.

'I see. It is the Caesarean case.'

'Nurse, you know her?'

And when I take her back, Anona Ebusuafo will say that I did not wait for them to come with me . . .

'Yes. Are you her brother?'

'No. I am only the driver who brought the old woman.'

'Did she bring all her clan?'

'No. She came alone.'

'Strange thing for a villager to do.'

I hope they have not cut her up already.

'Did she bring a whole bag full of cassava and plantain and kenkey?'

'No. She has only her little bundle.'

'Follow me. But you must not make any noise. This is not the hour for coming here . . .'

My master, does she know her?

'Yes.'

I hear it is very cold where they put them . . .

It was feeding time for new babies. When old Esi Amfoa saw young Esi Amfoa, the latter was all neat and nice. White sheets and all. She did not see the beautiful stitches under the sheets. 'This woman is a tough bundle,' Dr. Gyamfi had declared after the identical twins had been removed, the last stitches had been threaded off and Mary Koomson, alias Esi Amfoa, had come to.

The old woman somersaulted into the room and lay groaning, not screaming, by the bed. For was not her last pot broken? So they lay them in state even in hospitals and not always cut them up for instruction?

The Nursing Sister was furious. Young Esi Amfoa spoke. And this time old Esi Amfoa wept loud and hard – wept all her tears.

Scrappy nurse-under-training, Jessy Treeson, second-generation-Cape-Coaster-her-grandmother-still-remembered-at-Egyaa No. 7 said, 'As for these villagers,' and giggled.

Draba Anan looked hard at Jessy Treeson, looked hard at her, all of her: her starched uniform, apron and cap . . . and then dismissed them all. . . . 'Such a cassava stick . . . but maybe I will break my toe if I kicked at her buttocks,' he thought.

And by the bed the old woman was trying hard to rise and look at the only pot which had refused to get broken.

§ *Tradition and change* Achebe (1, 3), Emecheta, Soyinka, Okot

2: Motherhood and the Numbers Game

'Now
that I am suffering so much,
I know I am truly a mother,'

said
5 Egyeifi to the other screaming
woman.

2 painfully hoarse voices
still managing to bellow like
cows in an abattoir;
10 4 veins swollen to
sizes larger than the
2 necks they stood on.

'meda w'ase
meda w'ase
15 meda w'ase . . .

13–19 Meda w'ase . . . maawo: the Fantse words of which the first three lines of the poem are a translation, prefaced by three 'thank yous' [adapted from author's note].

osiande,
ama meehu de,
saana moso
maawo!'

20   I always marvelled at the
non-logic
of it all,

and even managed
the educated lady's dainty grin
25   the day
they told me that in all the
20 years I was away,
my mother never slept a wink!

The woman who spoke
30   – my mother's friend –
stared straight into my eyes
bespectacled already
as, it seems,
all eyes must be
35   20/20 visioned or not, when
folks turn 40 at the very least.

So
at 2 in the morning
I lie here in the dark
40   more sharp-eyed than
the cat my totem:

anxious
angry
sleepless –

45   blissfully anxious
happily angry and
nervously fulfilled

that

I
50   too
am
a mother!

§ *Motherhood* Emecheta, Ngcobo; Carib: Goodison

East Africa

OKOT P'BITEK (1931–82)

From Song of Lawino

Okot p'Bitek's poetry mainly derives from traditional songs of the Acoli people and when *Song of Lawino* first appeared (in 1966) it was hailed as the first major African poem in English to show no trace of European influences. While this may be an over-statement, the poem is nonetheless heavily dependent on traditional songs of praise and abuse. Lawino complains that she has been badly treated by her more educated husband and has been forced to share his favours with his Westernized girlfriend. Okot followed this poem with *Song of Ocol*, her husband's reply, and taken together the two poems may be read as a debate about the future of a society torn between traditional and modern attitudes to gender relationships. In the section included here Lawino contrasts Ocol's former love for her with his present neglect.

I was made chief of girls
Because I was lively,
I was bright,
I was not clumsy or untidy
5   I was not dull,
I was not heavy and slow.

I did not grow up a fool
I am not cold
I am not shy
10   My skin is smooth
It still shines smoothly in the moonlight.

When Ocol was wooing me
My breasts were erect.
And they shook
15   As I walked briskly,
And as I walked
I threw my long neck
This way and that way
Like the flower of the *lyonno* lily
20   Waving in a gentle breeze.

And my brothers called me *Nya-Dyang*
For my breasts shook
And beckoned the cattle,
And they sang silently:

25   *Father prepare the kraal,*
      Father prepare the kraal,
      The cattle are coming.

      I was the Leader of the girls
      And my name blew
30   Like a horn
      Among the Payira.
      And I played on my bow harp
      And praised my love.

      Ocol, my husband,
35   My friend,
      What are you talking?
      You saw me when I was young.
      In my mother's house
      This man crawled on the floor!
40   The son of the Bull wept
      For me with tears,
      Like a hungry child
      Whose mother has stayed long
      In the simsim field!

45   Every night he came
      To my father's homestead,
      He never missed one night
      Even after he had been beaten
      By my brothers.

50   You loved my giraffe-tail bangles,
      My father bought them for me
      From the Hills in the East.

      The roof of my mother's house
      Was beautifully laced
55   With elephant grass;
      My father built it
      With the skill of the Acoli.

---

21 *Nya-Dyang:* Cattle-daughter; one who brings
cattle through her dowry.
44 simsim: vegetable-oil grain.

31 Payira: territorial group inhabiting a central
position in Acoliland.
57 Acoli: people of northern Uganda and southernmost Sudan.

You admired my sister's
Colourful ten-stringed lion beads;
60 My mother threaded them
And arranged them with care.

You trembled
When you saw the tattoos
On my breasts
65 And the tattoos below my belly button;
And you were very fond
Of the gap in my teeth!
My man, what are you talking?
My clansmen, I ask you:
70 What has become of my husband?
Is he suffering from boils?
Is it ripe now?
Should they open it
So that the pus may flow out?

75 I was chief of youths
Because of my good manners,
Because my waist was soft.
I sang sweetly
When I was grinding millet
80 Or on the way to the well,
Nobody's voice was sweeter than mine!
And in the arena
I sang the solos
Loud and clear
85 Like the *ogilo* bird
At sunset.

Now, Ocol says
I am a mere dog
A puppy,
90 A little puppy
Suffering from skin diseases.

Ocol says
He does not love me any more
Because I cannot play the guitar
95 And I do not like their stupid dance,
Because I despise the songs
They play at the ballroom dance
And I do not follow the steps of foreign songs

On the gramophone records.
100 And I cannot tune the radio
Because I do not hear
Swahili or Luganda.

What is all this?

My husband refuses
105 To listen to me,
He refuses to give me a chance.
My husband has blocked up my path completely.

He has put up a road block
But has not told me why.
110 He just shouts
Like house-flies
Settling on top of excrement
When disturbed!

My husband says
115 He no longer wants a woman
With a gap in her teeth,
He is in love
With a woman
Whose teeth fill her mouth completely
120 Like the teeth of war-captives and slaves.

Like beggars
You take up white men's adornments,
Like slaves or war captives
You take up white men's ways.
125 Didn't the Acoli have adornments?
Didn't Black People have their ways?

Like drunken men
You stagger to white men's games,
You stagger to white men's amusements.

130 Is *lawala* not a game?
Is *cooro* not a game?
Didn't your people have amusements?
Like halfwits
You turn to white men's dances,
135 You turn to musical instruments of foreigners
As if you have no dances;
As if you have no instruments!

---

130 *lawala*: a hunting game.   131 *cooro*: a board game.

And you cannot sing one song
You cannot sing a solo
140   In the arena.
You cannot beat rhythm on the half-gourd
Or shake the rattle-gourd
To the rhythm of the *orak* dance!
And there is not a single *bwola* song
145   That you can dance,
You do not play the drum
Or do the mock-fight;
At the funeral dance
Or at the war dance
150   You cannot wield the shield!

And so you turn
To the dances of white people,
Ignorance and shame provoke you
To turn to foreign things!

155   Perhaps you are covering up
Your bony hips and chest
And the large scar on your thigh
And the scabies on your buttocks;

You are hiding
160   Under the blanket suit
Your sick stomach
That has swollen up
Like that of a pregnant goat.

And the dark glasses
165   Shield the rotting skin around your eyes
From the house-flies,
And cover up
The husks of the exploded eye balls.

§ *Tradition and change* Achebe (1, 3), Soyinka (2), Emecheta, Aidoo

---

143 *orak*: informal dance of the Acoli.   144 *bwola*: Acoli chieftain's dance and the songs associated with it.

NGUGI WA THIONG'O (1938 –)

1: *From* A Grain of Wheat

Like much of Ngugi's early fiction, *A Grain of Wheat* deals with the impact of public events on individual lives, particularly the effect that the Mau Mau freedom struggle had on ordinary Kenyans. Set during the days leading up to Uhuru (Independence), the novel employs a complex flashback technique, which gradually reveals the sequences of events that have determined the characters' present situations and poses questions about the nature of heroism and betrayal. The first chapter, included here, is typical of the way that the early sections of the novel create a sense of mystery about the characters' lives.

Mugo felt nervous. He was lying on his back and looking at the roof. Sooty locks hung from the fern and grass thatch and all pointed at his heart. A clear drop of water was delicately suspended above him. The drop fattened and grew dirtier as it absorbed grains of soot. Then it started drawing towards him. He tried to shut his eyes. They would not close. He tried to move his head: it was firmly chained to the bed-frame. The drop grew larger and larger as it drew closer and closer to his eyes. He wanted to cover his eyes with his palms; but his hands, his feet, everything refused to obey his will. In despair, Mugo gathered himself for a final heave and woke up. Now he lay under the blanket and remained unsettled fearing, as in the dream, that a drop of cold water would suddenly pierce his eyes. The blanket was hard and worn out; its bristles pricked his face, his neck, in fact all the unclothed parts of his body. He did not know whether to jump out or not; the bed was warm and the sun had not yet appeared. Dawn diffused through cracks in the wall into the hut. Mugo tried a game he always played whenever he had lost sleep in the middle of the night or early morning. In total, or hazy darkness most objects lose their edges, one shape merging with another. The game consisted in trying to make out the various objects in the room. This morning, however, Mugo found it difficult to concentrate. He knew that it was only a dream: yet he kept on chilling at the thought of a cold drop falling into his eyes. One, two, three; he pulled the blanket away from his body. He washed his face and lit the fire. In a corner, he discovered a small amount of maize-flour in a bag among the utensils. He put this in a sufuria[1] on the fire, added water and stirred it with a wooden spoon. He liked porridge in the morning. But whenever he took it, he remembered the half-cooked porridge he ate in detention. How time drags, everything repeats itself, Mugo thought; the day ahead would be just like yesterday and the day before.

He took a jembe[2] and a panga[3] to repeat the daily pattern his life had now fallen into since he left Maguita, his last detention camp. To reach his new strip of shamba[4] which lay the other side of Thabai, Mugo had to walk

---

1 Metal cooking-pot. 2 Hoe. 3 Machete. 4 (Plot of) land.

through the dusty village streets. And as usual Mugo found that some women had risen before him, that some were already returning from the river, their frail backs arched double with water-barrels, in time to prepare tea or porridge for their husbands and children. The sun was now up: shadows of trees and huts and men were thin and long on the ground.

'How is it with you, this morning?' Warui called out to him, emerging from one of the huts.

'It is well.' And as usual Mugo would have gone on, but Warui seemed anxious to talk.

'Attacking the ground early?'

'Yes.'

'That's what I always say. Go to it when the ground is soft. Let the sun find you already there and it'll not be a match for you. But if it reaches the shamba before you – hm.'

Warui, a village elder, wore a new blanket which sharply relieved his wrinkled face and the grey tufts of hair on his head and on his pointed chin. It was he who had given Mugo the present strip of land on which to grow a little food. His own piece had been confiscated by the government while he was in detention. Though Warui liked talking, he had come to respect Mugo's reticence. But today he looked at Mugo with new interest, curiosity even.

'Like Kenyatta is telling us,' he went on, 'these are days of Uhuru na Kazi.'[5] He paused and ejected a jet of saliva on to the hedge. Mugo stood embarrassed by this encounter. 'And how is your hut, ready for Uhuru?' continued Warui.

'Oh, it's all right,' Mugo said and excused himself. As he moved on through the village, he tried to puzzle out Warui's last question.

Thabai was a big village. When built, it had combined a number of ridges: Thabai, Kamandura, Kihingo, and parts of Weru. And even in 1963, it had not changed much from the day in 1955 when the grass-thatched roofs and mud-walls were hastily collected together, while the whiteman's sword hung dangerously above people's necks to protect them from their brethren in the forest. Some huts had crumbled; a few had been pulled down. Yet the village maintained an unbroken orderliness; from a distance it appeared a huge mass of grass from which smoke rose to the sky as from a burnt sacrifice.

Mugo walked, his head slightly bowed, staring at the ground as if ashamed of looking about him. He was re-living the encounter with Warui when suddenly he heard someone shout his name. He started, stopped, and stared at Githua, who was hobbling towards him on crutches. When he reached Mugo he stood to attention, lifted his torn hat, and cried out:

'In the name of blackman's freedom, I salute you.' Then he bowed several times in comic deference.

'Is it – is it well with you?' Mugo asked, not knowing how to react. By this time two or three children had collected and were laughing at Githua's antics. Githua did not answer at once. His shirt was torn, its collar gleamed

5 Freedom and work.

black with dirt. His left trouser leg was folded and fixed with a pin to cover the stump. Rather unexpectedly he gripped Mugo by the hand:

'How are you man! How are you man! Glad to see you going to the shamba early. Uhuru na Kazi. Ha! Ha! Ha! Even on Sundays. I tell you before the Emergency, I was like you; before the whiteman did this to me with bullets, I could work with both hands, man. It makes my heart dance with delight to see your spirit. Uhuru na Kazi. Chief, I salute you.'

Mugo tried to pull out his hand. His heart beat and he could not find the words. The laughter from the children increased his agitation. Githua's voice suddenly changed:

'The Emergency destroyed us,' he said in a tearful voice and abruptly went away. Mugo hurried on, conscious of the man's eyes behind him. Three women coming from the river stopped when they saw him. One of them shouted something, but Mugo did not answer or look at them. He raised dust like a man on the run. Yet he only walked asking himself questions: What's wrong with me today? Why are people suddenly looking at me with curiosity? Is there shit on my legs?

Soon he was near the end of the main street where the old woman lived. Nobody knew her age: she had always been there, a familiar part of the old and the new village. In the old village she lived with an only son who was deaf and dumb. Gitogo, for that was the son's name, spoke with his hands often accompanied with animal guttural noises. He was handsome, strongly built, a favourite at the Old Rung'ei centre where young men spent their time talking the day away. Occasionally the men went on errands for the shop-owners and earned a few coins 'for the pockets only, just to keep the trousers warm', as some carelessly remarked. They laughed and said the coins would call others (man! their relatives) in due time.

Gitogo worked in eating houses, meat shops, often lifting and carrying heavy loads avoided by others. He loved displaying his well-built muscles. Whispers current in Rung'ei and Thabai said that many a young woman had felt the weight of those limbs. In the evenings Gitogo bought food – a pound of sugar, or a pound of meat – and took them home to his mother, who brightened up, her face becoming youthful amidst the many wrinkles. What a son, what a man, people would say, touched by the tenderness of the deaf and dumb one to his mother.

One day people in Thabai and Rung'ei woke up to find themselves ringed round with black and white soldiers carrying guns, and tanks last seen on the road during Churchill's war with Hitler. Gunfire smoked in the sky, people held their stomachs. Some men locked themselves in latrines; others hid among the sacks of sugar and beans in the shops. Yet others tried to sneak out of the town towards the forest, only to find that all roads to freedom were blocked. People were being collected into the town-square, the market place, for screening. Gitogo ran to a shop, jumped over the counter, and almost fell on to the shopkeeper whom he found cowering amongst the empty bags. He gesticulated, made puzzled noises, furtively looked and pointed at the soldiers. The shopkeeper in stupid terror stared back blankly at Gitogo. Gitogo suddenly remembered his aged mother sitting alone in the hut. His mind's eye vividly saw scenes of wicked deeds and blood. He rushed out through the back door, and jumped over a fence into the fields, now agitated by the insecurity to which his mother lay exposed. Urgency, home, mother: the images flashed through his mind. His muscles alone would protect her. He did not see that a whiteman, in a bush jacket, lay camouflaged in a small wood. 'Halt!' the whiteman shouted. Gitogo continued running. Something hit him at the back. He raised his arms in the air. He fell on his stomach. Apparently the bullet had touched his heart. The soldier left his place. Another Mau Mau terrorist had been shot dead.

When the old woman heard the news she merely said: My God. Those who were present said that she did not weep. Or even ask how her son had met his death.

After leaving the detention camp Mugo had several times seen the old woman outside her hut. And every time he felt agitated as if the woman recognized him. She had a small face grooved with wrinkles. Her eyes were small but occasionally flashed with life. Otherwise they looked dead. She wore beads around her elbows, several copper chains around her neck, and cowrie-like tins around the ankles. When she moved she made jingling noises like a belled goat. It was her eyes that most disturbed Mugo. He always felt naked, seen. One day he spoke to her. But she only looked at him and then turned her face away. Mugo felt rejected, yet her loneliness struck a chord of pity in him. He wanted to help her. This feeling warmed him inside. He bought some sugar, maize-flour and a bundle of firewood at one of the Kabui shops. In the evening he went to the woman's place. The hut was dark inside. The room was bare, and a cold wind whistled in through the gaping holes in the wall. She slept on the floor, near the fireplace. Mugo remembered how he too used to sleep on the floor in his aunt's hut, sharing the fireplace with goats and sheep. He often crept and crouched near the goats for warmth. In the morning he found his face and clothes covered with ashes, his hands and feet smeared with the goats' droppings. In the end he had become hardened to the goats' smell. Amidst these thoughts, Mugo felt the woman fix him with her eyes, which glinted with recognition. Suddenly he shivered at the thought that the woman might touch him. He ran out, revolted. Perhaps there was something fateful in his contact with this old woman.

Today this thought was uppermost in his mind, as he again felt another desire to enter the hut and talk to her. There was a bond between her and him, perhaps because she, like him, lived alone. At the door he faltered, his resolution wavered, broke, and he found himself hurrying away, fearing that she would call him back with mad laughter.

In the shamba, he felt hollow. There were no crops on the land and what with the dried-up weeds, gakaraku,[6] micege,[7] mikengeria,[8] bangi[9] – and the sun, the country appeared sick and dull. The jembe seemed heavier than usual; the unfinished part of the shamba looked too big for his unwilling muscles.

---

6 A piece of wood.   7 A prickly plant.   8 A plant fed to goats.   9 Indian hemp.

He dug a little, and feeling the desire to pass water, walked to a hedge near the path; why had Warui, Githua and the women behaved that way towards him? He found his bladder had pressed him into false urgency. A few drops trickled down and he watched them as if each drop fascinated him. Two young women, dressed for church, passed near, saw a big man playing with his thing and giggled. Mugo felt foolish and dragged himself back to his work.

He raised the jembe, let it fall into the soil; lifted it and again brought it down. The ground felt soft as if there were mole-tunnels immediately below the surface. He could hear the soil, dry and hollow, tumble down. Dust flew into the sky, enveloped him, then settled into his hair and clothes. Once a grain of dust went into his left eye. He quickly dropped the jembe in anger and rubbed his eye which smarted with pain as water tossed out from both eyes. He sat down: where was the fascination he used to find in the soil before the Emergency?

Mugo's father and mother had died poor, leaving him, an only child in the hands of a distant aunt. Waitherero was a widow with six married daughters. When drunk, she would come home and remind Mugo of this fact.

'Female slime,' she would say, exposing her toothless gums; she would fix Mugo with a fierce glance, as if he and God had conspired against her. 'They don't even come to see me – Do you laugh, you – what's your penis worth? Oh God, see what an ungrateful wretch is left on my hands. You would have followed your father to the grave, but for me. Remember that and stop laughing.'

Another day she would complain that her money was missing.

'I didn't steal it,' Mugo retorted, withdrawing.

'There is only you and me in this house. I could not have stolen it. So who could have taken it?'

'I am not a thief!'

'Are you saying that I am telling lies? The money was here, you saw me bury it under this post. See the way he looks, he creeps behind the goats.'

She was a small woman who always complained that people were after her life; they had put broken bottles and frogs into her stomach; they wanted to put poison in her food or drink.

And yet she always went out to look for more beer. She would pester men from her husband's rika till they gave her a drink. One day she came back very drunk.

'That man Warui – he hates to see me eat and breathe – that sly – smile – he – creeps – coughs – like you – you – go and join him—'

And she tried to imitate Warui's cough; but in the attempt lurched forward and fell; all her beer and filth lay on the floor. Mugo cowered among the goats hoping and fearing she had died. In the morning she forced Mugo to pour soil on the filth. The acrid smell hit him. Disgust choked him so that he could not speak or cry. The world had conspired against him, first to deprive him of his father and mother, and then to make him dependent on an ageing harridan.

The more feeble she became, the more she hated him. Whatever he did or made, she would deride his efforts. So Mugo was haunted by the image of his own inadequacy. She had a way of getting at him, a question maybe, about his clothes, his face, or hands that made all his pride tumble down. He pretended to ignore her opinions, but how could he shut his eyes to her oblique smiles and looks?

His one desire was to kill his aunt.

One evening the mad thought possessed him. He raged within. Tonight Waitherero was sober. He would not use an axe or a panga. He would get her by the neck, strangle her with his naked hands. Give me the strength; give me the strength, God. He watched her struggle, like a fly in a spider's hands; her muffled groans and cries for mercy reached his ears. He would press harder, make her feel the power in his man's hands. Blood rushed to his finger-tips, he was breathless, acutely fascinated by the audacity and daring of his own action.

'Why are you staring at me so?' Waitherero asked, and laughed in her throat. 'I always say you are a strange one, the kind that would murder their own mother, eh?'

He winced. Her seeing into him was painful.

Waitherero suddenly died of age and over-drinking. For the first time since their marriage, her daughters came to the hut, pretended they did not see Mugo, and buried her without questions or tears. They returned to their homes. And then, strangely, Mugo missed his aunt. Whom could he now call a relation? He wanted somebody, anybody, who would use the claims of kinship to do him ill or good. Either one or the other as long as he was not left alone, an outsider.

He turned to the soil. He would labour, sweat, and through success and wealth, force society to recognise him. There was, for him, then, solace in the very act of breaking the soil: to bury seeds and watch the green leaves heave and thrust themselves out of the ground, to tend the plants to ripeness and then harvest, these were all part of the world he had created for himself and which formed the background against which his dreams soared to the sky. But then Kihika had come into his life.

Mugo went home earlier than usual. He had not done much work, yet he was weary. He walked like a man who knows he is followed or watched, yet does not want to reveal this awareness by his gait or behaviour. In the evening he heard footsteps outside. Who could his visitor be? He opened the door. Suddenly the all-day mixture of feelings distilled into fear and animosity. Warui, the elder, led the group. Standing beside him was Wambui, one of the women from the river. She now smiled, exposing a missing line of teeth in her lower jaw. The third man was Gikonyo, who had married Kihika's sister.

'Come inside,' he called in a voice that could hardly hide his agitation. He excused himself and went towards the latrine. Run away from all these men . . . I no longer care . . . I no longer care. He entered the pit lavatory and lowered his trousers to his knees: his thoughts buzzed around flashing images of his visitors seated in the hut. Several times he tried to force something out into the smelling pit. Failing, he pulled up his trousers, but still he felt better for the effort. He went back to the visitors and only now remembered that he had not greeted them.

'We are only voices sent to you from the Party,' Gikonyo said after Mugo had shaken hands all round.

'The Party?'

'Voices from the Movement!' Wambui and Warui murmured together.

§ *Politics and private lives* Achebe (2, 3), Gordimer, Coetzee; SA: Selvadurai; SEA: Ee Tiang Hong (2)

2: *From* Decolonising the Mind

. . . I was born into a large peasant family: father, four wives and about twenty-eight children. I also belonged, as we all did in those days, to a wider extended family and to the community as a whole.

We spoke Gĩkũyũ as we worked in the fields. We spoke Gĩkũyũ in and outside the home. I can vividly recall those evenings of story-telling around the fireside. It was mostly the grown-ups telling the children but everybody was interested and involved. We children would re-tell the stories the following day to other children who worked in the fields picking the pyrethrum flowers,[1] tea-leaves or coffee beans of our European and African landlords.

The stories, with mostly animals as the main characters, were all told in Gĩkũyũ. Hare, being small, weak but full of innovative wit and cunning, was our hero. We identified with him as he struggled against the brutes of prey like lion, leopard, hyena. His victories were our victories and we learnt that the apparently weak can outwit the strong. We followed the animals in their struggle against hostile nature – drought, rain, sun, wind – a confrontation often forcing them to search for forms of co-operation. But we were also interested in their struggles amongst themselves, and particularly between the beasts and the victims of prey. These twin struggles, against nature and other animals, reflected real-life struggles in the human world.

Not that we neglected stories with human beings as the main characters. There were two types of characters in such human-centred narratives: the species of truly human beings with qualities of courage, kindness, mercy, hatred of evil, concern for others; and a man-eat-man two-mouthed species with qualities of greed, selfishness, individualism and hatred of what was good for the larger co-operative community. Co-operation as the ultimate good in a community was a constant theme. It could unite human beings with animals against ogres and beasts of prey, as in the story of

---

1 Chrysanthemum with finely divided leaves.

how dove, after being fed with castor-oil seeds, was sent to fetch a smith working far away from home and whose pregnant wife was being threatened by these man-eating two-mouthed ogres.

There were good and bad story-tellers. A good one could tell the same story over and over again, and it would always be fresh to us, the listeners. He or she could tell a story told by someone else and make it more alive and dramatic. The differences really were in the use of words and images and the inflexion of voices to effect different tones.

We therefore learnt to value words for their meaning and nuances. Language was not a mere string of words. It had a suggestive power well beyond the immediate and lexical meaning. Our appreciation of the suggestive magical power of language was reinforced by the games we played with words through riddles, proverbs, transpositions of syllables, or through nonsensical but musically arranged words. So we learnt the music of our language on top of the content. The language, through images and symbols, gave us a view of the world, but it had a beauty of its own. The home and the field were then our pre-primary school but what is important, for this discussion, is that the language of our evening teach-ins, and the language of our immediate and wider community, and the language of our work in the fields were one.

And then I went to school, a colonial school, and this harmony was broken. The language of my education was no longer the language of my culture. I first went to Kamaandura, missionary run, and then to another called Maanguuũ run by nationalists grouped around the Gĩkũyũ Independent and Karinga Schools Association. Our language of education was still Gĩkũyũ. The very first time I was ever given an ovation for my writing was over a composition in Gĩkũyũ. So for my first four years there was still harmony between the language of my formal education and that of the Limuru peasant community.

It was after the declaration of a state of emergency over Kenya in 1952 that all the schools run by patriotic nationalists were taken over by the colonial regime and were placed under District Education Boards chaired by Englishmen. English became the language of my formal education. In Kenya, English became more than a language: it was *the* language, and all the others had to bow before it in deference.

Thus one of the most humiliating experiences was to be caught speaking Gĩkũyũ in the vicinity of the school. The culprit was given corporal punishment – three to five strokes of the cane on bare buttocks – or was made to carry a metal plate around the neck with inscriptions such as I AM STUPID or I AM A DONKEY. Sometimes the culprits were fined money they could hardly afford. And how did the teachers catch the culprits? A button was initially given to one pupil who was supposed to hand it over to whoever was caught speaking his mother tongue. Whoever had the button at the end of the day would sing who had given it to him and the ensuing process would bring out all the culprits of the day. Thus children were turned into witch-hunters and in the process were being taught the lucrative value of being a traitor to one's immediate community.

The attitude to English was the exact opposite: any achievement in spoken or written English was highly rewarded; prizes, prestige, applause; the ticket to higher realms. English became the measure of intelligence and ability in the arts, the sciences, and all the other branches of learning. English became *the* main determinant of a child's progress up the ladder of formal education.

As you may know, the colonial system of education in addition to its apartheid racial demarcation had the structure of a pyramid: a broad primary base; a narrowing secondary middle, and an even narrower university apex. Selections from primary into secondary were through an examination, in my time called Kenya African Preliminary Examination, in which one had to pass six subjects ranging from Maths to Nature Study and Kiswahili. All the papers were written in English. Nobody could pass the exam who failed the English language paper no matter how brilliantly he had done in the other subjects. I remember one boy in my class of 1954 who had distinctions in all subjects except English, which he had failed. He was made to fail the entire exam. He went on to become a turn boy in a bus company. I who had only passes but a credit in English got a place at the Alliance High School, one of the most elitist institutions for Africans in colonial Kenya. The requirements for a place at the University, Makerere University College, were broadly the same: nobody could go on to wear the undergraduate red gown, no matter how brilliantly they had performed in all the other subjects unless they had a credit – not even a simple pass! – in English. Thus the most coveted place in the pyramid and in the System was only available to the holder of an English language credit card. English was the official vehicle and the magic formula to colonial elitedom.

Literary education was now determined by the dominant language while also reinforcing that dominance. Orature (oral literature) in Kenyan languages stopped. In primary school I now read simplified Dickens and Stevenson alongside Rider Haggard. Jim Hawkins, Oliver Twist, Tom Brown – not Hare, Leopard and Lion – were now my daily companions in the world of imagination. In secondary school, Scott and G. B. Shaw vied with more Rider Haggard, John Buchan, Alan Paton, Captain W. E. Johns. At Makerere I read English: from Chaucer to T. S. Eliot with a touch of Graham Greene.

Thus language and literature were taking us further and further from ourselves to other selves, from our world to other worlds. . . .

I started writing in Gĩkũyũ language in 1977 after seventeen years of involvement in Afro-European literature, in my case Afro-English literature. It was then that I collaborated with Ngũgĩ wa Mĩriĩ in the drafting of the playscript, *Ngaahika Ndeenda* (the English translation was *I Will Marry When I Want*). I have since published a novel in Gĩkũyũ, *Caitaani Mũtharabainĩ* (English translation: *Devil on the Cross*) and completed a musical drama, Maitũ Njugĩra, (English translation: *Mother Sing for Me*); three books for children, *Njamba Nene na Mbaathi i Mathagu*, *Bathitoora ya Njamba Nene*, *Njamba Nene na Cibũ Kĩng'ang'i*, as well as another novel manuscript: *Matigari Ma Njirũũngi*. Wherever I have gone, particularly in Europe, I have been confronted with the question: why are you now writing in Gĩkũyũ? Why do you now write in an African language? In some academic quarters I have been confronted with the rebuke, 'Why have you abandoned us?' It was almost as if, in choosing to write in Gĩkũyũ, I was doing something abnormal. But Gĩkũyũ is my mother tongue! The very fact that what common sense dictates in the literary practice of other cultures is being questioned in an African writer is a measure of how far imperialism has distorted the view of African realities. It has turned reality upside down: the abnormal is viewed as normal and the normal is viewed as abnormal. Africa actually enriches Europe: but Africa is made to believe that it needs Europe to rescue it from poverty. Africa's natural and human resources continue to develop Europe and America: but Africa is made to feel grateful for aid from the same quarters that still sit on the back of the continent. Africa even produces intellectuals who now rationalise this upside-down way of looking at Africa.

I believe that my writing in Gĩkũyũ language, a Kenyan language, an African language, is part and parcel of the anti-imperialist struggles of Kenyan and African peoples. In schools and universities our Kenyan languages – that is the languages of the many nationalities which make up Kenya – were associated with negative qualities of backwardness, underdevelopment, humiliation and punishment. We who went through that school system were meant to graduate with a hatred of the people and the culture and the values of the language of our daily humiliation and punishment. I do not want to see Kenyan children growing up in that imperialist-imposed tradition of contempt for the tools of communication developed by their communities and their history. I want them to transcend colonial alienation.

Colonial alienation takes two interlinked forms: an active (or passive) distancing of oneself from the reality around; and an active (or passive) identification with that which is most external to one's environment. It starts with a deliberate disassociation of the language of conceptualisation, of thinking, of formal education, of mental development, from the language of daily interaction in the home and in the community. It is like separating the mind from the body so that they are occupying two unrelated linguistic spheres in the same person. On a larger social scale it is like producing a society of bodiless heads and headless bodies.

So I would like to contribute towards the restoration of the harmony between all the aspects and divisions of language so as to restore the Kenyan child to his environment, understand it fully so as to be in a position to change it for his collective good. I would like to see Kenya peoples' mother-tongues (our national languages!) carry a literature reflecting not only the rhythms of a child's spoken expression, but also his struggle with nature and his social nature. With that harmony between himself, his language and his environment as his starting point, he can learn other languages and even enjoy the positive humanistic, democratic and revolutionary elements in other people's literatures and cultures without any complexes about his own language, his own self, his environment. The all-Kenya national language (i.e. Kiswahili); the other national languages (i.e. the languages of the nationalities like Luo, Gĩkũyũ, Maasai, Luhya, Kallenjin, Kamba, Mijikenda, Somali, Galla, Turkana, Arabic-speaking people, etc.); other African languages like Hausa, Wolof, Yoruba, Ibo, Zulu, Nyanja, Lingala, Kimbundu; and foreign languages – that is foreign to Africa – like English, French, German, Russian, Chinese, Japanese, Portuguese, Spanish will fall into their proper perspective in the lives of Kenyan children.

§ *Oral storytelling* Achebe (2, 3); Carib: Lamming (1), Brodber; *Colonial education* Dangarembga; Carib: Sparrow; *Language usage* Carib: Brathwaite (3)

M. G. VASSANJI (1950–)

Leaving

Kichwele Street was now Uhuru[1] Street. My two sisters had completed school and got married and Mother missed them sometimes. Mehroon, after a succession of wooers, had settled for a former opening batsman of our school team and was in town. Razia was a wealthy housewife in Tanga, the coastal town north of Dar.[2] Firoz dropped out in his last year at school, and everyone said that it was a wonder he had reached that far. He was assistant bookkeeper at Oriental Emporium, and brought home stationery sometimes.

Mother had placed her hopes on the youngest two of us, Aloo and me, and she didn't want us distracted by the chores that always needed doing around the store. One evening she secured for the last time the half a dozen assorted padlocks on the sturdy panelled doors and sold the store. This was exactly one week after the wedding party had driven off with a tearful Razia, leaving behind a distraught mother in the stirred-up dust of Uhuru Street.

We moved to the residential area of Upanga. After the bustle of Uhuru Street, our new neighbourhood seemed quiet. Instead of the racket of buses, bicycles and cars on the road, we now heard the croaking of frogs and the chirping of insects. Nights were haunting, lonely and desolate and took some getting used to. Upanga Road emptied after seven in the evening and the side-streets became pitch dark, with no illumination. Much of the area was as yet uninhabited and behind the housing developments there were overgrown bushes, large, scary baobab trees,[3] and mango and coconut groves.

---

1 Independence.   2 Dar-es-Salaam.   3 Thick-trunked trees with large fruit and edible pulp.

Sometimes in the evenings, when Mother felt sad, Aloo and I would play two-three-five with her, a variation of whist for three people. I had entered the University by then and came back at weekends. Aloo was in his last year at school. He had turned out to be exceptionally bright in his studies – more so than we realised.

That year Mr Datoo, a former teacher from our school who was also a former student, returned from America for a visit. Mr Datoo had been a favourite with the boys. When he came he received a tumultuous welcome. For the next few days he toured the town like the Pied Piper followed by a horde of adulating students, one of whom was Aloo.

The exciting event inspired in Aloo the hope that not only might he be admitted to an American university, but he could also win a scholarship to go there. Throughout the rest of the year, therefore, he wrote to numerous universities, culling their names from books at the USIS,[4] often simply at random or even only by the sounds of their names.

Mother's response to all these efforts was to humour him. She would smile. 'Your uncles in America will pay thousands of shillings just to send you to college,' she would say. Evidently she felt he was wasting his time, but he would never be able to say that he did not have all the support she could give him.

Responses to his enquiries started coming within weeks and a handful of them were guardedly encouraging. Gradually Aloo found out which were the better places, and which among them the truly famous. Soon a few catalogues arrived, all looking impressive. It seemed that the more involved he became with the application process, the more tantalising was the prospect of going to an American university. Even the famous places did not discourage him. He learnt of subjects he had never heard of before: genetics, cosmology, artificial intelligence: a whole universe was out there waiting for him if only he could reach it. He was not sure if he could, if he was good enough. He suffered periods of intense hope and hopeless despair.

Of course, Aloo was entitled to a place at the local university. At the end of the year, when the selections were announced in the papers, his name was on the list. But some bureaucratic hand, probably also corrupt, dealt out a future prospect for him that came as a shock. He had applied to study medicine, he was given a place in agriculture. An agricultural officer in a rural district somewhere was not what he wanted to become however patriotic he felt. He had never left the city except to go to the national parks once on a school trip.

When Aloo received a letter from the California Institute of Technology offering him a place with a scholarship, he was stupefied at first. He read and reread the letter, not believing what it seemed to be saying, afraid that he might be reading something into it. He asked me to read it for him. When he was convinced there was no possibility of a mistake he became elated.

---

4 US Information Service.

'The hell I'll do agriculture!' he grinned.

But first he had to contend with Mother.

Mother was incredulous. 'Go, go,' she said, 'don't you eat my head, don't tease me!'

'But it's true!' he protested. 'They're giving me a scholarship!'

We were at the table – the three of us – and had just poured tea from the thermos. Mother sitting across from me stared at her saucer for a while, then she looked up.

'Is it true?' she asked me.

'Yes, it's true,' I said. 'All he needs is to take 400 dollars pocket money with him.'

'How many shillings would that make?' she asked.

'About three thousand.'

'And how are we going to raise this three thousand shillings? Have you bought a lottery? And what about the ticket? Are they going to send you a ticket too?'

As she said this Aloo's prospects seemed to get dimmer. She was right, it was not a little money that he needed.

'Can't we raise a loan?' he asked. 'I'll work there. Yes, I'll work as a waiter. A waiter! – I know you can do it, I'll send the money back!'

'You may have uncles in America who would help you,' Mother told him, 'but no one here will.'

Aloo's shoulders sagged and he sat there toying with his cup, close to tears. Mother sat drinking from her saucer and frowning. The evening light came in from the window behind me and gave a glint to her spectacles. Finally she set her saucer down. She was angry.

'And why do you want to go away, so far from us? Is this what I raised you for – so you could leave me to go away to a foreign place? Won't you miss us, where you want to go? Do we mean so little to you? If something happens . . .'

Aloo was crying. A tear fell into his cup, his nose was running. 'So many kids go and return, and nothing happens to them . . . Why did you mislead me, then? Why did you let me apply if you didn't want me to go . . . why did you raise my hopes if only to dash them?' He raised his voice to her, the first time I saw him do it, and he was shaking.

He did not bring up the question again and he prepared himself for the agricultural college, waiting for the term to begin. At home he would slump on the sofa putting away a novel a day.

If the unknown bureaucrat at the Ministry of Education had been less arbitrary, Aloo would not have been so broken and Mother would not have felt compelled to try and do something for him.

A few days later, on a Sunday morning, she looked up from her sewing machine and said to the two of us: 'Let's go and show this letter to Mr Velji. He is experienced in these matters. Let's take his advice.'

Mr Velji was a former administrator of our school. He had a large egg-shaped head and a small compact body. With his large forehead and big black spectacles he looked the caricature of the archetypal wise man. He also had the bearing of one. The three of us were settled in his sitting-room chairs staring about us and waiting expectantly when he walked in stiffly, like a toy soldier, to welcome us.

'How are you, sister?' he said. 'What can I do for you?'

Aloo and I stood up respectfully as he sat down.

'We have come to you for advice . . .' Mother began.

'Speak, then,' he said jovially and sat back, joining his hands behind his head.

She began by giving him her history. She told him which family she was born in, which she had married into, how she had raised her kids when our father died. Common relations were discovered between our families. 'Now this one here,' she pointed at me, 'goes to university here, and *that* one wants to go to America. Show him the documents,' she commanded Aloo.

As if with an effort, Aloo pushed himself out of the sofa and slowly made his way to place the documents in Mr Velji's hands. Before he looked at them Mr Velji asked Aloo his result in the final exam.

At Aloo's answer, his eyes widened. 'Henh?' he said, 'All A's?'

'Yes,' replied Aloo, a little too meekly.

Mr Velji flipped the papers one by one, cursorily at first. Then he went over them more carefully. He looked at the long visa form with the carbon copies neatly bound behind the original; he read over the friendly letter from the Foreign Student Adviser; he was charmed by the letters of invitation from the fraternities. Finally he looked up, a little humbled.

'The boy is right,' he said. 'The university is good, and they are giving him a bursary. I congratulate you.'

'But what should I do?' asked Mother anxiously. 'What is your advice? Tell us what we should do.'

'Well,' said Mr Velji, 'it would be good for his education.' He raised his hand to clear his throat. Then he said, a little slowly: 'But if you send him, you will lose your son.

'It's a far place, America,' he concluded, wiping his hands briskly at the finished business. 'Now what will you have – tea? orange squash?'

His wife appeared magically to take orders.

'All the rich kids go every year and they are not lost,' muttered Aloo bitterly as we walked back home. Mother was silent.

That night she was at the sewing machine and Aloo was on the couch, reading. The radio was turned low and through the open front door a gentle breeze blew in to cool the sitting room. I was standing at the door. The banana tree and its offspring rustled outside, a car zoomed on the road, throwing shadows on neighbouring houses. A couple out for a stroll, murmuring, came into sight over the uneven hedge; groups of boys or girls chattered before dispersing for the night. The intermittent buzz of an electric motor escaped from mother's sewing machine. It was a little darker where she sat at the other end of the room from us.

Presently she looked up and said a little nonchalantly, 'At least show me what this university looks like – bring that book, will you?'

Mother had never seen the catalogue. She had always dismissed it, had never shown the least bit of curiosity about the place Aloo wanted so badly to visit. Now the three of us crowded around the glossy pages, pausing at pictures of the neoclassic façades and domes, columns towering over humans, students rushing about in a dither of activity, classes held on lush lawns in ample shade. It all looked so awesome and yet inviting.

'It's something, isn't it?' whispered Aloo, hardly able to hold back his excitement. 'They teach hundreds of courses there,' he said. 'They send rockets into space . . . to other worlds . . . to the moon – '

'If you go away to the moon, my son, what will become of me?' she said humorously, her eyes gleaming as she looked up at us.

Aloo went back to his book and Mother to her sewing.

A little later I looked up and saw Mother deep in thought, brooding, and as she often did at such times she was picking her chin absent-mindedly. It was, I think, the first time I saw her as a person and not only as our mother. I thought of what she must be going through in her mind, what she had gone through in bringing us up. She had been thirty-three when Father died, and she had refused several offers of marriage because they would all have entailed one thing: sending us all to the 'boarding' – the orphanage. Pictures of her before his death showed her smiling and in full bloom: plump but not excessively fat, hair puffed fashionably, wearing high heels and make-up. There was one picture, posed at a studio, which Father had had touched up and enhanced, which now hung beside his. In it she stood against a black background, holding a book stylishly, the nylon pachedi painted a light green, the folds falling gracefully down, the borders decorated with sequins. I had never seen her like that. All I had seen of her was the stern face getting sterner with time as the lines set permanently and the hair thinned, the body turned squat, the voice thickened.

I recalled how Aloo and I would take turns sleeping with her at night on her big bed; how she would squeeze me in her chubby arms, drawing me up closer to her breast until I could hardly breathe – and I would control myself and hope she would soon release me and let me breathe.

She looked at me looking at her and said, not to me, 'Promise me . . . promise me that if I let you go, you will not marry a white woman.'

'Oh Mother, you know I won't!' said Aloo.

'And promise me that you will not smoke or drink.'

'You know I promise!' He was close to tears.

Aloo's first letter came a week after he left, from London where he'd stopped over to see a former classmate. It flowed over with excitement. 'How can I describe it,' he wrote, 'the sight from the plane . . . mile upon mile of carefully tilled fields, the earth divided into neat green squares . . . even the mountains are clean and civilised. And London . . . oh London! It seemed that it would never end . . . blocks and blocks of houses, squares, parks, monuments . . . could any city be larger? How many of our Dar es Salaams would fit here, in this one gorgeous city . . . ?'

A bird flapping its wings: Mr Velji nodding wisely in his chair, Mother staring into the distance.

§ *Migration* TransC: Gooneratne, Mistry

ABDULRAZAK GURNAH (1948–)

From Paradise

At the beginning of *Paradise* the 11-year-old Yusuf leaves his home and family when he is taken to the coast by his 'Uncle' Aziz, an affluent and powerful trader. Subsequently he discovers that he has been given to Aziz to pay off his father's debts. On the coast he works in Aziz's store; later he accompanies him on a trading expedition into the interior. *Paradise* is a coming-of-age novel which also reflects the changes in a society brought about by colonialism and offers a vivid dramatization of the encounter between values of the Islamic coast and the interior. The passages included here are from the early part of the novel.

The boy first. His name was Yusuf, and he left his home suddenly during his twelfth year. He remembered it was the season of drought, when every day was the same as the last. Unexpected flowers bloomed and died. Strange insects scuttled from under rocks and writhed to their deaths in the burning light. The sun made distant trees tremble in the air and made the houses shudder and heave for breath. Clouds of dust puffed up at every tramping footfall and a hard-edged stillness lay over the daylight hours. Precise moments like that came back of the season . . . .

His Uncle Aziz also came to visit them at that time. His visits were brief and far between, usually accompanied by a crowd of travellers and porters and musicians. He stopped with them on the long journeys he made from the ocean to the mountains, to the lakes and forests, and across the dry plains and the bare rocky hills of the interior. His expeditions were often accompanied by drums and tamburis[1] and horns and siwa,[2] and when his train marched into town animals stampeded and evacuated themselves, and children ran out of control. Uncle Aziz gave off a strange and unusual odour, a mixture of hide and perfume, and gums and spices, and another less definable smell which made Yusuf think of danger. His habitual dress was a thin, flowing kanzu[3] of

---

1 Long-necked lutes.   2 Type of horn.   3 Male outer garment.

fine cotton and a small crocheted cap pushed back on his head. With his refined airs and his polite, impassive manner, he looked more like a man on a late afternoon stroll or a worshipper on the way to evening prayers than a merchant who had picked his way past bushes of thorn and nests of vipers spitting poison. Even in the heat of arrival, amid the chaos and disorder of tumbled packs, surrounded by tired and noisy porters, and watchful, sharp-clawed traders, Uncle Aziz managed to look calm and at ease. On this visit he had come alone.

Yusuf always enjoyed his visits. His father said they brought honour on them because he was such a rich and renowned merchant – *tajiri mkubwa* – but that was not all, welcome though honour always was. Uncle Aziz gave him, without fail, a ten anna piece every time he stopped with them. Nothing was required of him but that he should present himself at the appropriate time. Uncle Aziz looked out for him, smiled and gave him the coin. Yusuf felt he wanted to smile too every time the moment arrived, but he stopped himself because he guessed that it would be wrong for him to do so. Yusuf marvelled at Uncle Aziz's luminous skin and his mysterious smell. Even after his departure, his perfume lingered for days.

By the third day of his visit, it was obvious that Uncle Aziz's departure was at hand. There was unusual activity in the kitchen, and the unmistakable, mingled aromas of a feast. Sweet frying spices, simmering coconut sauce, yeasty buns and flat bread, baking biscuits and boiling meat. Yusuf made sure not to be too far away from the house all day, in case his mother needed help preparing the dishes or wanted an opinion on one of them. He knew she valued his opinion on such matters. Or she might forget to stir a sauce, or miss the moment when the hot oil is trembling just enough for the vegetables to be added. It was a tricky business, for while he wanted to be able to keep an eye on the kitchen, he did not want his mother to see him loafing on the lookout. She would then be sure to send him on endless errands, which is bad enough in itself, but it might also cause him to miss saying goodbye to Uncle Aziz. It was always at the moment of departure that the ten anna piece changed hands, when Uncle Aziz would offer his hand to be kissed and stroke the back of Yusuf's head as he bent over it. Then with practised ease he would slip the coin into Yusuf's hand.

His father was usually at work until soon after noon. Yusuf guessed that he would be bringing Uncle Aziz with him when he came, so there was plenty of time to kill. His father's business was running a hotel. This was the latest in a line of businesses with which he had attempted to make his fortune and his name. When he was in the mood he told them stories at home of other schemes which he had thought would prosper, making them sound ridiculous and hilarious. Or Yusuf heard him complain of how his life had gone wrong, and everything he had tried had failed. The hotel, which was an eating house with four clean beds in an upstairs room, was in the small town of Kawa, where they had been living for over four years. Before that they had lived in the south, in another small town in a farming district where his father had kept a store. Yusuf remembered a green hill and distant shadows of mountains, and an old man who sat on a stool on the pavement at the storefront, embroidering caps with silk thread. They came to Kawa because it had become a boom town when the Germans had used it as a depot for the railway line they were building to the highlands of the interior. But the boom passed quickly, and the trains now only stopped to take on wood and water. On his last journey, Uncle Aziz had used the line to Kawa before cutting to the west on foot. On his next expedition, he said, he would go as far as he could up the line before taking a north-western or north-eastern route. There was still good trade to be done in either of those places, he said. Sometimes Yusuf heard his father say that the whole town was going to Hell.

The train to the coast left in the early evening, and Yusuf thought Uncle Aziz would be on it. He guessed from something in his manner that Uncle Aziz was on his way home. But you could never be sure with people, and it might turn out that he would take the up-train to the mountains, which left in mid-afternoon. Yusuf was ready for either outcome . . . .

Uncle Aziz spent the afternoon in the guest room, having a siesta. To Yusuf it seemed an aggravating delay. His father too had retreated into his room, as he did every day after his meal. Yusuf could not understand why people wanted to sleep in the afternoon, as if it was a law they had to obey. They called it resting, and sometimes even his mother did it, disappearing into their room and drawing the curtain. When he tried it once or twice, he became so bored that he feared he would never be able to get up again. On the second occasion he thought this was what death would be like, lying awake in bed but unable to move, like punishment.

While Uncle Aziz slept, Yusuf was required to clear up in the kitchen and yard. This was unavoidable if he was to have any say in the disposal of the leftovers. Surprisingly, his mother left him on his own while she went to speak with his father. Usually she supervised strictly, separating real leftovers from what would serve another meal. He inflicted as much damage as he could on the food, cleared and saved what was possible, scrubbed and washed the pots, swept the yard, then went to sit on guard in the shade by the back door, sighing about the burdens he had to carry.

When his mother asked him what he was doing, he replied that he was resting. He tried not to say it pompously, but it came out like that, making his mother smile. She reached suddenly for him, hugging him and lifting him up while he kicked furiously to be released. He hated to be treated like a baby, she knew that. His feet sought the dignity of the bare earth yard as he wriggled with restrained fury. It was because he was small for his age that she was always doing it – picking him up, pinching his cheeks, giving him hugs and slobbery kisses – and then laughing at him as if he was a child. He was already twelve. To his amazement she did not let him go this time. Usually she released him as soon as his struggles became furious, smacking his fleeing bottom as he ran. Now she held him, squeezing him to her steeping softness, saying nothing and not laughing. The back of her bodice was still wet with sweat, and her body reeked of smoke and exhaustion. He stopped struggling after a moment and let his mother hold him to her.

That was his first foreboding. When he saw the tears in his mother's eyes his heart leapt with terror. He had never seen his mother do that before. He had seen her wailing at a neighbour's bereavement as if everything was spinning out of control, and had heard her imploring the mercy of the Almighty on the living, her face sodden with entreaty, but he had never seen these silent tears. He thought something had happened with his father, that he had spoken harshly to her. Perhaps the food was not good enough for Uncle Aziz . . . .

His father came out to look for him. He had only just woken from his siesta and his eyes were still red with sleep. His left cheek was inflamed, perhaps where he had lain on it. He lifted a corner of his undershirt and scratched his belly, while his other hand stroked the shadowy stubble on his chin. His beard grew quickly and he usually shaved every afternoon after his sleep. He smiled at Yusuf and his smile grew to a broad grin. Yusuf was still sitting by the back door where his mother had left him. Now his father came to squat down beside him. Yusuf guessed that his father was trying to look unconcerned, and he was made nervous.

'Would you like to go on a little trip, little octopus?' his father asked him, pulling him nearer his masculine sweat. Yusuf felt the weight of the arm on his shoulder, and resisted the pressure to bury his face in his father's torso. He was too old for that kind of thing. His eyes darted to his father's face, to read the meaning of what he was saying. His father chuckled, crushing him against his body for a moment. 'Don't look so happy about it,' he said.

'When?' Yusuf asked, gently wriggling himself free.

'Today,' his father said, raising his voice cheerfully and then grinning through a small yawn, trying to look untroubled. 'Right now.'

Yusuf stood up on tiptoe and flexed his knees. He felt a momentary urge to go to the toilet, and stared anxiously at his father, waiting for the rest of it. 'Where am I going? What about Uncle Aziz?' Yusuf asked. The sudden damp fear he had felt was quelled by the thought of the ten anna. He couldn't go anywhere until he had collected his ten anna piece.

'You'll be going with Uncle Aziz,' his father said, and then gave him a small, bitter smile. He did that when Yusuf said something foolish to him. Yusuf waited, but his father said no more. After a moment his father laughed and made a lunge for him. Yusuf rushed out of the way and laughed too. 'You'll go on the train,' his father said. 'All the way to the coast. You love trains, don't you? You'll enjoy yourself all the way to the sea.' Yusuf waited for his father to say more, and could not think why he did not like the prospect of this journey. In the end, his father slapped him on the thigh and told him to go and see his mother about packing a few things.

When the time came to leave it hardly seemed real. He said goodbye to his mother at the front door of the house and followed his father and Uncle Aziz to the station. His mother did not hug and kiss him, or shed tears over him. He had been afraid she would. Later, Yusuf could not remember what his mother did or said, but he remembered that she looked ill or dazed, leaning exhaustedly against the doorpost. When he thought of the moment of his departure, the picture that came to mind was the shimmering road on which they walked and the men ahead of him. In front of all of them staggered the porter carrying Uncle Aziz's luggage on his shoulders. Yusuf was allowed to carry his own little bundle: two pairs of shorts, a kanzu which was still new from last Idd,[4] a shirt, a copy of the Koran, and his mother's old rosary. She had wrapped all but the rosary in an old shawl, then pulled the ends into a thick knot. Smilingly, she had pushed a cane through the knot so that Yusuf could carry his bundle over his shoulder, the way the porters did. The brownstone rosary she had pressed on him last, secretively.

It never occurred to him, not even for one brief moment, that he might be gone from his parents for a long time, or that he might never see them again. It never occurred to him to ask when he would be returning. He never thought to ask why he was accompanying Uncle Aziz on his journey, or why the business had to be arranged so suddenly. At the station Yusuf saw that in addition to the yellow flag with the angry black bird, there was another flag with a silver-edged black cross on it. They flew that one when the chief German officers were travelling on the train. His father bent down to him and shook his hand. He spoke to him at some length, his eyes watering in the end. Afterwards Yusuf could not remember what was said to him, but God came into it.

The train had been moving for a while before the novelty of it began to wear off for Yusuf, and then the thought that he had left home became irresistible. He thought of his mother's easy laughter, and began to cry. Uncle Aziz was on the bench beside him, and Yusuf looked guiltily at him, but he had dozed off, wedging himself between the bench and the luggage. After a few moments, Yusuf knew that the tears were no longer coming, but he was reluctant to lose the feeling of sadness. He wiped his tears away and began to study his uncle. He was to have many opportunities for doing so, but this was the first time since he had known his uncle that he could look him full in the face. Uncle Aziz had taken his cap off once they boarded the train, and Yusuf was surprised by how harsh he looked. Without the cap, his face looked more squat and out of proportion. As he lay back dozing silently, the gracious manners which caught the eye were absent. He still smelt very fine. Yusuf had always liked that about him. That and his thin, flowing kanzus and silk-embroidered caps. When he entered a room, his presence wafted in like something separate from the person, announcing excess and prosperity and daring. Now as he leaned back against the luggage, a small rounded pot-belly protruded under his chest. Yusuf had not noticed that before. As he watched he saw the belly rise and fall with his breathing, and once he saw a ripple of movement across it.

His leather money pouches were belted round his groin as usual, looping over his hip-bones and meeting in a thonged buckle over the join of his

---

4 Muslim festival.

thighs like a kind of armour. Yusuf had never seen the money belt unattached to him, even while he slept in the afternoon. He remembered the silver rupee he had hidden in the crevice at the base of a wall, and trembled at the thought that it would be discovered and his guilt would be proclaimed.

The train was noisy. Dust and smoke blew in through the open windows, and with them came the smell of fire and charred meat. On their right, the land they travelled across was flat plain with long shadows in the gathering dusk. Scattered farms and homesteads hugged the surface, clinging to the hurtling earth. On the other side were lumpy silhouettes of mountains whose crowns flared with haloes as they caught the setting sun. The train made no haste, lurching and grumbling as it struggled to the coast. At times it slowed nearly to a halt, moving almost imperceptibly and then suddenly lurching forward with high-pitched protests coming from the wheels. Yusuf did not remember the train stopping at any stations on the way, but he knew later it must have done. He shared the food which his mother had prepared for Uncle Aziz: maandazi,[5] boiled meat and beans. His uncle unwrapped the food with practised care, muttering bismillah[6] and smiling slightly, then with his palm half open in a gesture of welcome he invited Yusuf to the food. His uncle looked kindly on him as he ate, and smiled at him to see his long looks.

He could not sleep. The ribs of the bench dug deep into his body and kept him awake. At best he dozed, or lay half awake, nagged by the need to relieve himself. When he opened his eyes in the middle of the night, the sight of the half-full, dimmed carriage made him want to cry out. The darkness outside was a measureless void, and he feared that the train was too deep in it to be able to return safely. He tried to concentrate on the noise of the wheels, but their rhythm was eccentric and only served to distract him and keep him awake. He dreamt that his mother was a one-eyed dog he had once seen crushed under the wheels of a train. Later he dreamt that he saw his cowardice glimmering in moonlight, covered in the slime of its afterbirth. He knew it was his cowardice because someone standing in the shadows told him so, and he himself saw it breathing.

They arrived at their destination the following morning, and Uncle Aziz shepherded Yusuf calmly and firmly through the shouting crowds of traders inside and outside the station. He did not speak to Yusuf as they walked through the streets, which were littered with the remains of recent celebrations. There were palm-fronds still tied to doorposts and shaped into arches. Crushed garlands of marigolds and jasmine lay broken on the paths, and darkening fruit-peelings littered the road. A porter was carrying their luggage ahead of them, sweating and grunting in the mid-morning heat. Yusuf had been forced to give up his little bundle. 'Let the porter carry it,' Uncle Aziz had said, pointing to the grinning man who was standing lopsidedly over the rest of the luggage. The porter hopped and jumped as he

---

5 Bun.   6 'In the name of Allah'.

walked, taking the weight off a bad hip. The surface of the road was very
hot, and Yusuf, whose feet were unprotected, wished that he too could hop,
but he knew without being told that Uncle Aziz would not wish this. From
the way he was greeted in the streets, Yusuf understood that his uncle was
an eminent man. The porter shouted for people to make way – 'Let the
seyyid[7] pass, waungwana'[8] – and even though he was such a ragged and ill-
looking man, no one contested with him. Now and then he glanced round
with his lopsided grin, and Yusuf began to think that the porter knew something dangerous which he had no idea of.

Uncle Aziz's house was a long, low building towards the edge of town.
It stood some yards from the road and in front of it was a large clearing
ringed with trees. There were small neems,[9] coconut palms, a sufi[10] and a
huge mango tree at a corner of the yard. There were also other trees which
Yusuf did not recognize. In the shade of the mango tree a handful of people were already sitting, so early in the day. Beside the house ran a long
crenellated white wall, above which Yusuf glimpsed crowns of trees and
palms. The men under the mango tree stood up as they approached, raising their arms and calling out greetings.

They were met by a young man called Khalil who came rushing out of the
shop at the front of the bungalow with garrulous cries of welcome. He kissed
Uncle Aziz's hand reverently, and would have kissed it again and again if Uncle
Aziz had not pulled his hand away in the end. He said something irritably,
and Khalil stood silently in front of him, his hands clasped together as he
struggled to restrain himself from reaching for Uncle Aziz's hand. They
exchanged greetings and news in Arabic while Yusuf looked on. Khalil was
about seventeen or eighteen, thin and nervous looking, with the beginnings
of hair on his lip. Yusuf knew he was mentioned in the conversation, for Khalil
turned to look at him and nodded excitedly. Uncle Aziz walked away towards
the side of the house where Yusuf saw an open doorway in the long white-
washed wall. He caught a glimpse of the garden through the doorway, and
thought he saw fruit trees and flowering bushes and a glint of water. When
he started to follow, his uncle, without turning round, extended the palm of
his hand from his body and held it stiffly out as he walked away. Yusuf had
never seen the gesture before, but he felt its rebuke and knew it meant he
was not to follow. He looked at Khalil and found him appraising him with a
large smile. He beckoned Yusuf and turned to walk back to the shop. Yusuf
picked up the bundle with the stick, which the porter had left behind when
he took Uncle Aziz's luggage inside, and followed Khalil. He had already lost
the brownstone rosary, had left it on the train. Three old men were sitting on
a bench on the terrace in front of the shop, and their gaze calmly followed
Yusuf as he ducked under the counter flap and into the shop.

'This is my little brother, who has come to work for us,' Khalil told the
customers. 'He looks so small and feeble because he's just come from the

---

7 Gentleman.   8 Term used by people of coast to describe the free and civilized.   9 Trees whose leaf and
bark are used for medicinal purposes.   10 Kapok tree.

wild lands, back there behind the hills. They only have cassava and weeds to eat there. That's why he looks like living death. Hey, kifa urongo![11] Look at the poor boy. Look at his feeble arms and his long looks. But we'll fill him up with fish and sweetmeats and honey, and in no time he'll be plump enough for one of your daughters. Greet the customers, little boy. Give them a big smile.'

In the first few days everyone smiled at him, except Uncle Aziz, whom Yusuf saw only once or twice in a day. People hurried towards Uncle Aziz as he walked past, to kiss his hand if he would let them or bow their greetings a deferential yard or two away if he appeared unapproachable. He was impassive in the face of the grovelling salutes and prayers, and when he had listened long enough not to seem discourteous, he continued on his way, slipping a handful of coins to the most abject of his courtiers.

§ *Childhood discovery* Carib: Lamming, Edgell, Senior, Kincaid; Can: Munro, Findley, Burnard; SA: Selvadurai, Sidhwa; SEA: Maniam

---

11 A plant which curls up, as if dying.

Southern Africa

NADINE GORDIMER (1923–)

Six Feet of the Country

My wife and I are not real farmers – not even Lerice, really. We bought our place, ten miles out of Johannesburg on one of the main roads, to change something in ourselves, I suppose; you seem to rattle about so much within a marriage like ours. You long to hear nothing but a deep satisfying silence when you sound a marriage. The farm hasn't managed that for us, of course, but it has done other things, unexpected, illogical. Lerice, who I thought would retire there in Chekhovian sadness for a month or two, and then leave the place to the servants while she tried yet again to get a part she wanted and become the actress she would like to be, has sunk into the business of running the farm with all the serious intensity with which she once imbued the shadows in a playwright's mind. I should have given it up long ago if it had not been for her. Her hands, once small and plain and well-kept – she was not the sort of actress who wears red paint and diamond rings – are hard as a dog's pads.

I, of course, am there only in the evenings and at weekends. I am a partner in a travel agency which is flourishing – needs to be, as I tell Lerice, in order to carry the farm. Still, though I know we can't afford it, and though the sweetish smell of the fowls Lerice breeds sickens me, so that I avoid going past their runs, the farm is beautiful in a way I had almost forgotten – especially on a Sunday morning when I get up and go out into the paddock and see not the palm trees and fishpond and imitation-stone bird bath of the suburbs but white ducks on the dam, the lucerne field brilliant as window-dresser's grass, and the little, stocky, mean-eyed bull, lustful but bored, having his face tenderly licked by one of his ladies. Lerice comes out with her hair uncombed, in her hand a stick dripping with cattle dip. She will stand and look dreamily for a moment, the way she would pretend to look sometimes in those plays. 'They'll mate tomorrow,' she will say. 'This is their second day. Look how she loves him, my little Napoleon.' So that when people come to see us on Sunday afternoon, I am likely to hear myself saying as I pour out the drinks, 'When I drive back home from the city every day past those rows of suburban houses, I wonder how the devil we ever did stand it . . . Would you care to look around?' And there I am, taking some pretty girl and her young husband stumbling down to our riverbank, the girl catching her stockings on the mealie-stooks[1] and stepping over cow turds humming with jewel-green flies while she says, '. . . the *tensions* of the damned city. And you're near enough to get into town to a show, too! I think it's wonderful. Why, you've got it both ways!'

And for a moment I accept the triumph as if I *had* managed it – the impossibility that I've been trying for all my life: just as if the truth was that you could get it 'both ways', instead of finding yourself with not even one way or the other but a third, one you have not provided for at all.

But even in our saner moments, when I find Lerice's earthy enthusiasms just as irritating as I once found her histrionical ones, and she finds what she calls my 'jealousy' of her capacity for enthusiasm as big a proof of my inadequacy for her as a mate as ever it was, we do believe that we have at least honestly escaped those tensions peculiar to the city about which our visitors speak. When Johannesburg people speak of 'tension', they don't mean hurrying people in crowded streets, the struggle for money, or the general competitive character of city life. They mean the guns under the white men's pillows and the burglar bars on the white men's windows. They mean those strange moments on city pavements when a black man won't stand aside for a white man.

Out in the country, even ten miles out, life is better than that. In the country, there is a lingering remnant of the pre-transitional stage; our relationship with the blacks is almost feudal. Wrong, I suppose, obsolete, but more comfortable all around. We have no burglar bars, no gun. Lerice's farm boys have their wives and their piccanins living with them on the land. They brew their sour beer without the fear of police raids. In fact, we've always rather prided ourselves that the poor devils have nothing much to fear, being with us; Lerice even keeps an eye on their children, with all the competence of a woman who has never had a child of her own, and she certainly doctors them all – children and adults – like babies whenever they happen to be sick.

It was because of this that we were not particularly startled one night last winter when the boy Albert came knocking at our window long after we had gone to bed. I wasn't in our bed but sleeping in the little dressing-room-cum-linen-room next door, because Lerice had annoyed me and I didn't want to find myself softening towards her simply because of the sweet smell of the talcum powder on her flesh after her bath. She came and woke me up. 'Albert says one of the boys is very sick,' she said. 'I think you'd better go down and see. He wouldn't get us up at this hour for nothing.'

'What time is it?'

'What does it matter?' Lerice is maddeningly logical.

I got up awkwardly as she watched me – how is it I always feel a fool when I have deserted her bed? After all, I know from the way she never looks at me when she talks to me at breakfast next day that she is hurt and

---

1 Maize sheaves.

humiliated at my not wanting her – and I went out, clumsy with sleep.

'Which of the boys is it?' I asked Albert as we followed the dance of my torch.

'He's too sick. Very sick,' he said.

'But who? Franz?' I remembered Franz had had a bad cough for the past week.

Albert did not answer; he had given me the path, and was walking along beside me in the tall dead grass. When the light of the torch caught his face, I saw that he looked acutely embarrassed. 'What's this all about?' I said.

He lowered his head under the glance of the light, 'It's not me, baas. I don't know. Petrus he send me.'

Irritated, I hurried him along to the huts. And there, on Petrus's iron bed-stead, with its brick stilts, was a young man, dead. On his forehead there was still a light, cold sweat; his body was warm. The boys stood around as they do in the kitchen when it is discovered that someone has broken a dish – uncooperative, silent. Somebody's wife hung about in the shadows, her hands wrung together under her apron.

I had not seen a dead man since the war. This was very different. I felt like the others – extraneous, useless. 'What was the matter?' I asked.

The woman patted at her chest and shook her head to indicate the painful impossibility of breathing.

He must have died of pneumonia.

I turned to Petrus. 'Who was this boy? What was he doing here?' The light of a candle on the floor showed that Petrus was weeping. He followed me out the door.

When we were outside, in the dark, I waited for him to speak. But he didn't. 'Now, come on, Petrus, you must tell me who this boy was. Was he a friend of yours?'

'He's my brother, baas. He came from Rhodesia to look for work.'

The story startled Lerice and me a little. The young boy had walked down from Rhodesia to look for work in Johannesburg, had caught a chill from sleeping out along the way and had lain ill in his brother Petrus's hut since his arrival three days before. Our boys had been frightened to ask us for help for him because we had never been intended ever to know of his presence. Rhodesian natives are barred from entering the Union unless they have a permit; the young man was an illegal immigrant. No doubt our boys had managed the whole thing successfully several times before; a number of relatives must have walked the seven or eight hundred miles from poverty to the paradise of zoot suits, police raids and black slum townships that is their *Egoli*, City of Gold – the African name for Johannesburg. It was merely a matter of getting such a man to lie low on our farm until a job could be found with someone who would be glad to take the risk of prosecution for employing an illegal immigrant in exchange for the services of someone as yet untainted by the city.

Well, this was one who would never get up again.

'You would think they would have felt they could tell *us*,' said Lerice next morning. 'Once the man was ill. You would have thought at least –' When she is getting intense over something, she has a way of standing in the middle of a room as people do when they are shortly to leave on a journey, looking searchingly about her at the most familiar objects as if she had never seen them before. I had noticed that in Petrus's presence in the kitchen, earlier, she had had the air of being almost offended with him, almost hurt.

In any case, I really haven't the time or inclination any more to go into everything in our life that I know Lerice, from those alarmed and pressing eyes of hers, would like us to go into. She is the kind of woman who doesn't mind if she looks plain, or odd; I don't suppose she would even care if she knew how strange she looks when her whole face is out of proportion with urgent uncertainty. I said, 'Now I'm the one who'll have to do all the dirty work, I suppose.'

She was still staring at me, trying me out with those eyes – wasting her time, if she only knew.

'I'll have to notify the health authorities,' I said calmly. 'They can't just cart him off and bury him. After all, we don't really know what he died of.'

She simply stood there, as if she had given up – simply ceased to see me at all.

I don't know when I've been so irritated. 'It might have been something contagious,' I said. 'God knows.' There was no answer.

I am not enamoured of holding conversations with myself. I went out to shout to one of the boys to open the garage and get the car ready for my morning drive to town.

As I had expected, it turned out to be quite a business. I had to notify the police as well as the health authorities, and answer a lot of tedious questions: How was it I was ignorant of the boy's presence? If I did not supervise my native quarters, how did I know that that sort of thing didn't go on all the time? And when I flared up and told them that so long as my natives did their work, I didn't think it my right or concern to poke my nose into their private lives, I got from the coarse, dull-witted police sergeant one of those looks that came not from any thinking process going on in the brain but from that faculty common to all who are possessed by the master-race theory – a look of insanely inane certainty. He grinned at me with a mixture of scorn and delight at my stupidity.

Then I had to explain to Petrus why the health authorities had to take away the body for a post-mortem – and, in fact, what a post-mortem was. When I telephoned the health department some days later to find out the result, I was told that the cause of death was, as we had thought, pneumonia, and that the body had been suitably disposed of. I went out to where Petrus was mixing a mash for the fowls and told him that it was all right, there would be no trouble; his brother had died from that pain in his chest. Petrus put down the paraffin tin and said, 'When can we go to fetch him, baas?'

'To fetch him?'

'Will the baas please ask them when we must come?'

I went back inside and called Lerice, all over the house. She came down the stairs from the spare bedrooms, and I said, '*Now* what am I going to do? When I told Petrus, he just asked calmly when they could go and fetch the body. They think they're going to bury him themselves.'

'Well, go back and tell him,' said Lerice. 'You must tell him. Why didn't you tell him then?'

When I found Petrus again, he looked up politely. 'Look, Petrus,' I said. 'You can't go to fetch your brother. They've done it already – they've *buried* him, you understand?'

'Where?' he said slowly, dully, as if he thought that perhaps he was getting this wrong.

'You see, he was a stranger. They knew he wasn't from here, and they didn't know he had some of his people here so they thought they must bury him.' It was difficult to make a pauper's grave sound like a privilege.

'Please, baas, the baas must ask them.' But he did not mean that he wanted to know the burial place. He simply ignored the incomprehensibile machinery I told him had set to work on his dead brother; he wanted the brother back.

'But, Petrus,' I said, 'how can I? Your brother is buried already. I can't ask them now.'

'Oh, baas!' he said. He stood with his bran-smeared hands uncurled at his sides, one corner of his mouth twitching.

'Good God, Petrus, they won't listen to me! They can't, anyway. I'm sorry, but I can't do it. You understand?'

He just kept on looking at me, out of his knowledge that white men have everything, can do anything; if they don't, it is because they won't.

And then, at dinner, Lerice started. 'You could at least phone,' she said.

'Christ, what d'you think I am? Am I supposed to bring the dead back to life?'

But I could not exaggerate my way out of this ridiculous responsibility that had been thrust on me. 'Phone them up,' she went on. 'And at least you'll be able to tell him you've done it and they've explained that it's impossible.'

She disappeared somewhere into the kitchen quarters after coffee. A little later she came back to tell me, 'The old father's coming down from Rhodesia to be at the funeral. He's got a permit and he's already on his way.'

Unfortunately, it was not impossible to get the body back. The authorities said that it was somewhat irregular, but that since the hygiene conditions had been fulfilled, they could not refuse permission for exhumation. I found out that, with the undertaker's charges, it would cost twenty pounds. Ah, I thought, that settles it. On five pounds a month, Petrus won't have twenty pounds – and just as well, since it couldn't do the dead any good. Certainly I should not offer it to him myself. Twenty pounds – or anything else within reason, for that matter – I would have spent without grudging it on doctors or medicines that might have helped the boy when he was alive. Once he was dead, I had no intention of encouraging Petrus to throw away, on a gesture, more than he spent to clothe his whole family in a year.

When I told him, in the kitchen that night, he said, 'Twenty pounds?'

I said, 'Yes, that's right, twenty pounds.'

For a moment, I had the feeling, from the look on his face, that he was calculating. But when he spoke again I thought I must have imagined it. 'We must pay twenty pounds!' he said in the faraway voice in which a person speaks of something so unattainable it does not bear thinking about.

'All right, Petrus,' I said, and went back to the living room.

The next morning before I went to town, Petrus asked to see me. 'Please, baas,' he said, awkwardly, handling me a bundle of notes. They're so seldom on the giving rather than the receiving side, poor devils, they don't really know how to hand money to a white man. There it was, the twenty pounds, in ones and halves, some creased and folded until they were soft as dirty rags, others smooth and fairly new – Franz's money, I suppose, and Albert's, and Dora the cook's and Jacob the gardener's, and God knows who else's besides, from all the farms and small holdings round about. I took it in irritation more than in astonishment, really – irritation at the waste, the uselessness of this sacrifice by people so poor. Just like the poor everywhere, I thought, who stint themselves the decencies of life in order to ensure themselves the decencies of death. So incomprehensible to people like Lerice and me, who regard life as something to be spent extravagantly and, if we think about death at all, regard it as the final bankruptcy.

The farm hands don't work on Saturday afternoon anyway, so it was a good day for the funeral. Petrus and his father had borrowed our donkey-cart to fetch the coffin from the city, where, Petrus told Lerice on their return, everything was 'nice' – the coffin waiting for them, already sealed up to save them from what must have been a rather unpleasant sight after two weeks' interment. (It had taken all that time for the authorities and the undertaker to make the final arrangements for moving the body.) All morning, the coffin lay in Petrus's hut, awaiting the trip to the little old burial ground, just outside the eastern boundary of our farm, that was a relic of the days when this was a real farming district rather than a fashionable rural estate. It was pure chance that I happened to be down there near the fence when the procession came past; once again Lerice had forgotten her promise to me and had made the house uninhabitable on a Saturday afternoon. I had come home and been infuriated to find her in a pair of filthy old slacks and with her hair uncombed since the night before, having all the varnish scraped from the living-room floor, if you please. So I had taken my No. 8 iron and gone off to practise my approach shots. In my annoyance, I had forgotten about the funeral, and was reminded only when I saw the procession coming up the path along the outside of the fence towards me; from where I was standing, you can see the grave quite clearly, and that day the sun glinted on bits of broken pottery, a lopsided homemade cross, and jam-jars brown with rainwater and dead flowers.

I felt a little awkward, and did not know whether to go on hitting my golf ball or stop at least until the whole gathering was decently past. The donkey-cart creaks and screeches with every revolution of the wheels, and it came along in a slow, halting fashion somewhow peculiarly suited to the two donkeys who drew it, their little potbellies rubbed and rough, their heads sunk between the shafts, and their ears flattened back with an air submissive and downcast; peculiarly suited, too, to the group of men and women who came along slowly behind. The patient ass. Watching, I thought, you can see now why the creature became a Biblical symbol. Then the procession drew level with me and stopped, so I had to put down my club. The coffin was taken down off the cart – it was a shiny, yellow-varnished wood, like cheap furniture – and the donkeys twitched their ears against the flies. Petrus, Franz, Albert and the old father from Rhodesia hoisted it on their shoulders and the procession moved on, on foot. It was really a very awkward moment. I stood there rather foolishly at the fence, quite still, and slowly they filed past, not looking up, the four men bent beneath the shiny wooden box, and the straggling troop of mourners. All of them were servants or neighbours' servants whom I knew as casual easygoing gossipers about our lands or kitchen. I heard the old man's breathing.

I had just bent to pick up my club again when there was a sort of jar in the flowing solemnity of their processional mood; I felt it at once, like a wave of heat along the air, or one of those sudden currents of cold catching at your legs in a placid stream. The old man's voice was muttering something; the people had stopped, confused, and they bumped into one another, some pressing to go on, others hissing them to be still. I could see that they were embarrassed, but they could not ignore the voice; it was much the way that the mumblings of a prophet, though not clear at first, arrest the mind. The corner of the coffin the old man carried was sagging at an angle; he seemed to be trying to get out from under the weight of it. Now Petrus expostulated with him.

The little boy who had been left to watch the donkeys dropped the reins and ran to see. I don't know why – unless it was for the same reason people crowd around someone who has fainted in a cinema – but I parted the wires of the fence and went through, after him.

Petrus lifted his eyes to me – to anybody – with distress and horror. The old man from Rhodesia had let go of the coffin entirely, and the three others, unable to support it on their own, had laid it on the ground, in the pathway. Already there was a film of dust lightly wavering up its shiny sides. I did not understand what the old man was saying; I hesitated to interfere. But now the whole seething group turned on my silence. The old man himself came over to me, with his hands outspread and shaking, and spoke directly to me, saying something that I could tell from the tone, without understanding the words, was shocking and extraordinary.

'What is it, Petrus? What's wrong?' I appealed.

Petrus threw up hs hands, bowed his head in a series of hysterical shakes, then thrust his face up at me suddenly. 'He says, "My son was not so heavy." '

Silence. I could hear the old man breathing; he kept his mouth a little open, as old people do.

'My son was young and thin,' he said at last, in English.

Again silence. Then babble broke out. The old man thundered against everybody; his teeth were yellowed and few, and he had one of those fine, grizzled, sweeping moustaches one doesn't often see nowadays, which must have been grown in emulation of early Empire-builders. It seemed to frame all his utterances with a special validity. He shocked the assemby; they thought he was mad, but they had to listen to him. With his own hands he began to prise the lid off the coffin and three of the men came forward to help him. Then he sat down on the ground; very old, very weak and unable to speak, he merely lifted a trembling hand towards what was there. He abdicated, he handed it over to them; he was no good any more.

They crowded round to look (and so did I), and now they forgot the nature of this surprise and the occasion of grief to which it belonged, and for a few minutes were carried up in the astonishment of the surprise itself. They gasped and flared noisily with excitement. I even noticed the little boy who had held the donkeys jumping up and down, almost weeping with rage because the backs of the grownups crowded him out of his view.

In the coffin was someone no one had seen before: a heavily built, rather light-skinned native with a neatly stitched scar on his forehead – perhaps from a blow in a brawl that had also dealt him some other, slower-working injury that had killed him.

I wrangled with the authorities for a week over that body. I had the feeling that they were shocked, in a laconic fashion, by their own mistake, but that in the confusion of their anonymous dead they were helpless to put it right. They said to me, 'We are trying to find out,' and 'We are still making inquiries.' It was as if at any moment they might conduct me into their mortuary and say, 'There! Lift up the sheets; look for him – your poultry boy's brother. There are so many black faces – surely one will do?'

And every evening when I got home, Petrus was waiting in the kitchen. 'Well, they're trying. They're still looking. The baas is seeing to it for you, Petrus,' I would tell him. 'God, half the time I should be in the office I'm driving around the back end of the town chasing after this affair,' I added aside, to Lerice, one night.

She and Petrus both kept their eyes turned on me as I spoke, and, oddly, for those moments they looked exactly alike, though it sounds impossible: my wife, with her high, white forehead and her attenuated Englishwoman's body, and the poultry boy, with his horny bare feet below khaki trousers tied at the knee with string and the peculiar rankness of his nervous sweat coming from his skin.

'What makes you so indignant, so determined about this now?' said Lerice suddenly.

I stared at her. 'It's a matter of principle. Why should they get away with a swindle? It's time these officials had a jolt from someone who'll bother to take the trouble.'

She said, 'Oh.' And as Petrus slowly opened the kitchen door to leave, sensing that the talk had gone beyond him, she turned away, too.

I continued to pass on assurances to Petrus every evening, but although what I said was the same, every evening it sounded weaker. At last, it became clear that we would never get Petrus's brother back, because nobody really knew where he was. Somewhere in a graveyard as uniform as a housing scheme, somewhere under a number that didn't belong to him, or in the medical school, perhaps, laboriously reduced to layers of muscle and strings of nerve? Goodness knows. He had no identity in this world anyway.

It was only then, and in a voice of shame, that Petrus asked me to try and get the money back.

'From the way he asks, you'd think he was robbing his dead brother,' I said to Lerice later. But as I've said, Lerice had got so intense about this business that she couldn't even appreciate a little ironic smile.

I tried to get the money; Lerice tried. We both telephoned and wrote and argued, but nothing came of it. It appeared that the main expense had been the undertaker, and after all he had done his job. So the whole thing was a complete waste, even more of a waste for the poor devils than I had thought it would be.

The old man from Rhodesia was about Lerice's father's size, so she gave him one of her father's old suits, and he went back home rather better off, for the winter, than he had come.

§ *Life under apartheid* Fugard, Ngcobo, Mzamane

ATHOL FUGARD (1932–) with JOHN KANI and WINSTON NTSHONA

From Sizwe Bansi is Dead

Sizwe Bansi is Dead is an 'Open Space' play, conceived by Athol Fugard in conjunction with John Kani and Winston Ntshona, the actors who first played the parts in this two-hander. Sizwe Bansi is a black South African who takes over the passbook of a dead man in order to secure work, a vivid symbol of how apartheid dehumanized people to the extent that they became constructions of documents. Prior to his first appearance, a very different character, the photographer Styles, occupies the stage alone. He is a perfect foil to the hesitant Sizwe, a city entrepreneur who lives by his wits and, as can be seen in this monologue from the early part of the play, defies stereotyping through his capacity to play multiple roles.

> . . . *Styles* [*reading*] 'The Mass Murderer! Doom!'
> [*Smile of recognition.*] 'For fleas . . . Doom. Flies . . . Doom.
> Bedbugs . . . Doom. For cockroaches and other household pests.

The household insecticide . . . Doom.' Useful stuff. Remember, Styles? *Ja*.

[*To the audience*.] After all that time at Ford I sat down one day. I said to myself:

'Styles, you're a bloody monkey, boy!'

'What do you mean?'

'You're a monkey, man.'

'Go to hell!'

'Come on, Styles, you're a monkey, man, and you know it. Run up and down the whole bloody day! Your life doesn't belong to you. You've sold it. For what, Styles? Gold wrist-watch in twenty-five years time when they sign you off because you're too old for anything any more?'

I was right. I took a good look at my life. What did I see? A bloody circus monkey! Selling most of his time on this earth to another man. Out of every twenty-four hours I could only properly call mine the six when I was sleeping. What the hell is the use of that? Think about it, friend. Wake up in the morning, half-past six, out of the pyjamas and into the bath-tub, put on your shirt with one hand, socks with the other, realize you got your shoes on the wrong bloody feet, and all the time the seconds are passing and if you don't hurry up you'll miss the bus . . . . 'Get the lunch, dear. I'm late. My lunch, please, darling!' . . . then the children come in . . . 'Daddy, can I have this? Daddy, I want money for that.' 'Go to your mother. I haven't got time. Look after the children, please, sweetheart!!' . . . grab your lunch . . . 'Bye Bye!!' and then run like I-don't know-what for the bus stop. You call that living? I went back to myself for another chat:

'Suppose you're right. What then?'

'Try something else.'

'Like what?'

Silly question to ask. I knew what I was going to say. Photographer! It was my hobby in those days. I used to pick up a few cents on the side taking cards at parties, weddings, big occasions. But when it came to telling my wife and parents that I wanted to turn professional . . . ! !

My father was the worst.

'You call that work ? Click-click with a camera. Are you mad ?' I tried to explain. 'Daddy, if I could stand on my own two feet and not be somebody else's tool, I'd have some respect for myself. I'd be a man.'

'What do you mean? Aren't you one already? You're circumcised, you've got a wife . . . .'

Talk about the generation gap!

Anyway I thought: To hell with them. I'm trying it.

It was the Christmas shutdown, so I had lots of time to look around for a studio. My friend Dhlamini at the Funeral Parlour told me about a vacant room next door. He encouraged me. I remember his words. 'Grab your chance, Styles. Grab it before somebody in my line puts you in a box and closes the lid.' I applied for permission to use the room as a studio. After some time the first letter back:

'Your application has been received and is being considered.' A month later: 'The matter is receiving the serious consideration of the Board.' Another month: 'Your application is now on the director's table.' I nearly gave up, friends. But one day, a knock at the door – the postman – I had to sign for a registered letter. 'We are pleased to inform you . . . .'

[Styles *has a good laugh.*]

I ran all the way to the Administration Offices, grabbed the key, ran all the way back to Red Location, unlocked the door, and walked in!

What I found sobered me up a little bit. Window panes were all broken; big hole in the roof, cobwebs in the corners. I didn't let that put me off though. Said to myself: 'This is your chance, Styles. Grab it.' Some kids helped me clean it out. The dust! *Yo!* When the broom walked in the Sahara Desert walked out! But at the end of that day it was reasonably clean. I stood here in the middle of the floor, straight! You know what that means? To stand straight in a place of your own? To be your own . . . General Foreman, Mr 'Baas', Line Supervisor – the lot! I was tall, six foot six and doing my own inspection of the plant.

So I'm standing there – here – feeling big and what do I see on the walls? Cockroaches. *Ja,* cockroaches . . . in *my* place. I don't mean those little things that run all over the place when you pull out the kitchen drawer. I'm talking about the big bastards, the paratroopers as we call them. I didn't like them. I'm not afraid of them but I just don't like them! All over. On the floors, the walls. I heard the one on the wall say: 'What's going on? Who opened the door?' The one on the floor answered: 'Relax. He won't last. This place is condemned.' That's when I thought: Doom.

Out of here and into the Chinaman's shop. 'Good day, sir. I've got a problem. Cockroaches.'

The Chinaman didn't even think, man, he just said: 'Doom!' I said: 'Certainly.' He said: 'Doom, seventy-five cents a tin.' Paid him for two and went back. *Yo!* You should have seen me! Two-tin Charlie!

[*His two tins at the ready, forefingers on the press-buttons,* Styles *gives us a graphic re-enactment of what happened. There is a brief respite to 'reload' – shake the tins – and tie a handkerchief around his nose after which he returns to the fight.* Styles *eventually backs through the imaginary door, still firing, and closes it. Spins the tins and puts them into their holsters.*]

I went home to sleep. *I* went to sleep. Not them [*the cockroaches*]. What do you think happened he re? General meeting under the floorboards. All the bloody survivors. The old professor addressed them: 'Brothers, we face a problem of serious pollution . . . contamination! The menace appears to be called Doom. I have recommended a general inoculation of the whole community. Everybody in line, please. [*Inoculation proceeds.*] Next . . . next . . . next. . . .' While poor old Styles is smiling in his sleep! Next morning I walked in . . . . [*He stops abruptly.*] . . . What's this? Cockroach walking on the floor? Another one on the ceiling? Not a damn! Doom did it yesterday. Doom does it today. [*Whips out the two tins and goes in fighting. This time, however, it is not long before they peter out.*] Pssssssssss . . . pssssss . . . pssss . . . pss [*a last desperate shake, but he barely manages to get out a squirt*].

Pss.

No bloody good! The old bastard on the floor just waved his feelers in the air as if he was enjoying air-conditioning. .

I went next door to Dhlamini and told him about my problem. He laughed. 'Doom? You're wasting your time, Styles. You want to solve your problem, get a cat. What do you think a cat lives on in the township? Milk? If there's any the baby gets it. Meat? When the family sees it only once a week? Mice? The little boys got rid of them years ago. Insects, man, township cats are insect-eaters. Here. . . .'

He gave me a little cat. I'm . . . I'm not too fond of cats normally. This one was called Blackie . . . I wasn't too fond of that name either. But . . . Kitsy! Kitsy! Kitsy . . . little Blackie followed me back to the studio.

The next morning when I walked in what do you think I saw? Wings. I smiled. Because one thing I do know is that no cockroach can take his wings off. He's dead!

[*Proud gesture taking in the whole of his studio.*]

So here it is!

[*To his name-board.*]

'Styles Photographic Studio. Reference Books; Passports; Weddings; Engagements; Birthday Parties and Parties. Proprietor: Styles.'

When you look at this, what do you see? Just another photographic studio? Where people come because they've lost their Reference Book and need a photo for the new one? That I sit them down, set up the camera . . . 'No expression, please.' . . . click-click . . . 'Come back tomorrow, please' . . . and then kick them out and wait for the next ? No, friend. It's more than just that. This is a strong-room of dreams. The dreamers? My people. The simple people, who you never find mentioned in the history books, who never get statues erected to them, or monuments commemorating their great deeds. People who would be forgotten, and their dreams with them, if it wasn't for Styles. That's what I do, friends. Put down, in my way, on paper the dreams and hopes of my people so that even their children's children will remember a man . . . 'This was our Grandfather' . . . and say his name. Walk into the houses of New Brighton and on the walls you'll find hanging the story of the people the writers of the big books forget about.

[*To his display-board.*]

This one [*a photograph*] walked in here one morning. I was just passing the time. Midweek. Business is always slow then. Anyway, a knock at the door. Yes! I must explain something. I get two types of knock here. When I hear . . . [*knocks solemnly on the table*] . . . I don't even look up, man. 'Funeral parlour is next door.' But when I hear . . . [*energetic rap on the table . . . he laughs*] . . . that's *my* sound, and I shout 'Come in!'

In walked a chap, full of smiles, little parcel under his arm. I can still see him, man!

[Styles *acts both roles*.]

'Mr Styles?'

I said: 'Come in!'

'Mr Styles, I've come to take a snap, Mr Styles.'

I said: 'Sit down! Sit down, my friend!'

'No, Mr Styles. I want to take the snap standing. [*Barely containing his suppressed excitement and happiness*] Mr Styles, take the card, please!'

I said: 'Certainly, friend.'

Something you mustn't do is interfere with a man's dream. If he wants to do it standing, let him stand. If he wants to sit, let him sit. Do exactly what they want! Sometimes they come in here, all smart in a suit, then off comes the jacket and shoes and socks . . . [*adopts a boxer's stance*] . . . 'Take it, Mr Styles. Take it!' And I take it. No questions! Start asking stupid questions and you destroy that dream. Anyway, this chap I'm telling you about . . . [*laughing warmly as he remembers*] . . . I've seen a lot of smiles in my business, friends, but that one gets first prize. I set up my camera, and just as I was ready to go . . . 'Wait, wait, Mr Styles! I want you to take the card with this.' Out of his parcel came a long piece of white paper . . . looked like some sort of document . . . he held it in front of him. [Styles *demonstrates*.] For once I didn't have to say, 'Smile!' Just: 'Hold it!' . . . and, click, . . . finished. I asked him what the document was.

'You see, Mr Styles, I'm forty-eight years old. I work twenty-two years for the municipality and the foreman kept on saying to me if I want promotion to Boss-boy I must try to better my

education. I didn't write well, Mr Styles. So I took a course with
the Damelin Correspondence College. Seven years, Mr Styles! And
at last I made it. Here it is. Standard Six Certificate, School
Leaving, Third Class! I made it, Mr Styles. I made it. But I'm not
finished. I'm going to take up for the Junior Certificate, then
Matric . . . and you watch, Mr Styles. One day I walk out of my
house, graduate, self-made! Bye-bye, Mr Styles,' . . . and he walked
out of here happy man, self-made.
[*Back to his display-board; another photograph.*]
My best. Family Card. You know the Family Card? Good for business. Lot of people and they all want copies.
One Saturday morning. Suddenly a hell of a noise outside in the
street. I thought: What's going on now? Next thing that door burst
open and in they came! First the little ones, then the five- and six-
year-olds. . . . I didn't know what was going on, man! Stupid children, coming to mess up my place. I was still trying to chase them
out when the bigger boys and girls came through the door. Then
it clicked. Family Card!
[*Changing his manner abruptly.*]
'Come in! Come in!'
[*Ushering a crowd of people into his studio.*]
. . . now the young men and women were coming in, then the
mothers and fathers, uncles and aunties . . . the eldest son, a
mature man, and finally . . .
[*Shaking his head with admiration at the memory.*]
the Old Man, the Grandfather! [*The 'old man' walks slowly and
with dignity into the studio and sits down in the chair.*]
I looked at him. His grey hair was a sign of wisdom. His face,
weather-beaten and lined with experience. Looking at it was like
paging the volume of his history, written by himself. He was a living symbol of Life, of all it means and does to a man. I adored
him. He sat there – halfsmiling, halfserious – as if he had already
seen the end of his road.
The eldest son said to me: 'Mr Styles, this is my father, my mother,
my brothers and sisters, their wives and husbands, our children.
Twenty-seven of us, Mr Styles. We have come to take a card. My
father . . . ,' he pointed to the old man, '. . . my father always
wanted it.'
I said: 'Certainly. Leave the rest to me.' I went to work.
[*Another graphic re-enactment of the scene as he describes it.*]
The old lady here, the eldest son there. Then the other one, with
the other one. On this side I did something with the daughters,
aunties, and one bachelor brother. Then in front of it all the eight-
to-twelves, standing, in front of them the four-to-sevens, kneeling,
and finally right on the floor everything that was left, sitting. Jesus,

it was hard work, but finally I had them all sorted out and I went behind the camera.

[*Behind his camera.*]

Just starting to focus . . .

[*Imaginary child in front of the lens; Styles chases the child back to the family group.*]

'. . . Sit down! Sit down!'

Back to the camera, start to focus again. . . . Not One of Them Was Smiling! I tried the old trick. 'Say cheese, please.' At first they just looked at me. 'Come on! Cheese!' The children were the first to pick it up.

[*Child's voice.*] 'Cheese. Cheese. Cheese.' Then the ones a little bit bigger – 'Cheese' – then the next lot – 'Cheese' – the uncles and aunties – 'Cheese' – and finally the old man himself – Cheese'! I thought the roof was going off, man! People outside in the street came and looked through the window. They joined in: 'Cheese.' When I looked again the mourners from the funeral parlour were there wiping away their tears and saying 'Cheese'. Pressed my little button and there it was – New Brighton's smile, twenty-seven variations. Don't you believe those bloody fools who make out we don't know how to smile!

Anyway, you should have seen me then. Moved the bachelor this side, sister-in-laws that side. Put the eldest son behind the old man. Reorganized the children. . . . [*Back behind his camera.*] 'Once again, please! Cheese!' Back to work . . . old man and old woman together, daughters behind them, sons on the side. Those that were kneeling now standing, those that were standing, now kneeling. . . . Ten times, friends! Each one different!

[*An exhausted* Styles *collapses in a chair.*]

When they walked out finally I almost said Never Again! A week later the eldest son came back for the cards. I had them ready. The moment he walked through that door I could see he was in trouble. He said to me: 'Mr Styles, we almost didn't make it. My father died two days after the card. He will never see it.' 'Come on,' I said. 'You're a man. One day or the other everyone of us must go home. Here. . . .' I grabbed the cards. 'Here. Look at your father and thank God for the time he was given on this earth.' We went through them together. He looked at them in silence. After the third one, the tear went slowly down his cheek.

But at the same time . . . I was watching him carefully . . . something started to happen as he saw his father there with himself, his brothers and sisters, and all the little grandchildren. He began to smile. 'That's it, brother,' I said. 'Smile! Smile at your father. Smile at the world.'

When he left, I thought of him going back to his little house somewhere in New Brighton, filled that day with the little mothers in black because a man had died. I saw my cards passing from hand to hand. I saw hands wipe away tears, and then the first timid little smiles.

You must understand one thing. We own nothing except ourselves. This world and its laws, allows us nothing, except ourselves. There is nothing we can leave behind when we die, except the memory of ourselves. I know what I'm talking about, friends – I had a father, and he died.

§ *Life under apartheid* Gordimer, Ngcobo, Mzamane; *Countryman come to town* Mzamane

LAURETTA NGCOBO (1931–)

From And They Didn't Die

And They Didn't Die describes life in a deprived rural community in South Africa and illustrates the destruction of African family life under apartheid. The opening chapter, included here, shows the community's resistance to white officialdom and the separation, necessitated by economic forces, that threatens the protagonist Jezile's marriage.

The dipping tank was empty. The dip mixture lay green, drying in trickles and splashes on the grey clay soil. A lone white man stood planted like a spear in the earth of Sigageni. Mr Pienaar, the dipping officer the only white person whose duties brought him regularly to the black reserve of Sigageni – the only one who was thought to know the pulse of the people. Yet, he knew that he did not understand anything about the place or its people or its problems. Anger and loathing raced inside Mr Pienaar, pounding through his veins.

'How could they? How *could* they?' He heard himself growl. There was not a herdboy in sight and no cattle for miles around. And this was a Thursday, a dipping day. For the fourth successive week the women of Sigageni had emptied the tank in spite of the threats.

'Senseless, unthinking creatures!' he hissed looking at his feet. He raised his voice and threw his head back as he shouted again. 'Senseless, unthinking creatures!' And he stamped hard on his right foot. Then he slowly walked around in circles, in an attempt to stay his rage. What more was he to report to the authorities at Ixopo; he had assured them that it was nothing serious – childish pranks perhaps or some lunatic wandering free – anything but an act of rebellion on the part of these unpredictable creatures. He wanted nothing to tamper with his job; he didn't want trouble. 'What do dipping tanks have to do with clinics and doctors and starving children; what have they to do with schools and beer halls?' Sitting on a rock he continued to muse, 'The government is doing everything for them, and they deliberately wreck it – they accept nothing that is done for their own good, no appreciation, no understanding at all – how can anyone teach them to think!' Then he saw them. A group of about seven women approaching nonchalantly, with hoes slung over their shoulders. They were going to pass him by as though they had not seen him. He could hear the rhythmic muffled sound of the earth under their measured steps. The women looked away from the slippery contents of the tank spewed everywhere around it. He stood up quickly, flushed and furious at the sight of them. He could have stopped them, but he did not – he went on cursing inside. 'These women, this strange breed of womanhood, thin and ragged and not like women at all – they think they rule the world, they spill men's beers, they herd cattle, they plough fields, they run this community. That's what it is; that's why this defiance – they've lost respect for manhood, for all authority, but they haven't got the sense to do it properly. In the absence of their husbands they've lost the need for men, if nobody stops them, they're going to ruin this country. In spite of what others think, it is these women we have got to deal with, not those far away men in the cities.' He paced up and down. Then he wheeled round to look at their retreating backs. A few strides and he was behind the wheel of his fifteen-year-old car – it rattled and bellowed and shook and he drove straight at them, following them from behind, if only to filch away the apparent calm. And he succeeded. They screamed and scattered in spite of themselves. He sped off at a grinding speed, with a cloud of dust shielding his car up and beyond the hill, to his world – the world of roads and safety. He was determined that the people of Sigageni should be brought to their senses, if only to safeguard his job.

The women's screams and the screeching car wheels brought out a number of people from their midday meal. In the ensuing hubbub they called out the name of MaMapanga and gathered around her.

'MaMapanga, MaMapanga, it's worked, it's working, they're getting scared! You were right, you were right.'

Jezile, one of the very young women, became the centre of the excitement. They shouted and shook her hand and danced in a medley. She had suggested the whole idea at one of the Thursday prayer meetings.

'There goes god,' they shouted.

'There he is in his dust cloud.'

'He's gone to call the army – they'll be back in hordes today.'

'Let them do their worst, let them find the culprit.' And so went on the many voices. One last voice was Jezile's.

'Let them come, then perhaps they'll listen to what we have to say – we must tell them – ' Jezile did not finish, and in the excitement, no one noticed that she had not. Nor did they notice what had passed between her and MaBiyela, her mother-in-law. It was nothing more than a cautionary look and one or two barbed words in Jezile's ear. Jezile raised a phlegmy cough and turned silently towards her house. So ended the celebration prematurely but it did not destroy the sense of victory all around. In a community that knew very few victories the feeling lasted quite some time.

But for Jezile it was over. Mortified and angry she went straight home and flung the kitchen door wide open. The ashes lay white and cold in the brazier from the previous night. She slammed the door to shut out the voices of the other women. She sat down and stuffed her apron into her mouth to stifle a scream and allowed herself a good cry.

No one really knew how deeply affected Jezile was by her failure to have a baby. Up until she got married she had believed that one night with a man was enough to make her pregnant; Siyalo had left a week after the wedding and she had soon discovered that she was not pregnant. She would now have to wait another long year for him to come back home on leave from Durban – a whole long year of waiting before she could gamble another chance. She had recognised then that it was a game of chance. A couple of months after Siyalo had left home MaBiyela, his mother, had confronted her with the question that Jezile had seen forming on her lips several times before:

'Is there anything yet?'

'Anything?'

MaBiyela had fixed her eyes below Jezile's waist and had repeated, 'Anything?' Jezile had stared back at her mother-in-law and had shook her head silently. That almost silent exchange was to mark the nature of their relationship for a long time. That day Jezile had cried and cried. The episode was the start of a relentless persecution. MaBiyela would not stop. She talked about children, she talked about childless women and she wondered aloud often, to all and sundry, what would happen if Jezile was barren, for Siyalo, an only son, simply had to have children. The year was long and anxious and as it drew to a close Jezile began to twitch with anxiety – if only she could tune and time her body this time; her heart was filled with anticipation and renewed hope.

When Siyalo came home there never was so much love between two people in a hurry to squander the year's store in a couple of weeks. It bubbled like a spring and filled their house with noisy chatter and their silences with meaning. Given a chance they could have spent every moment of the first few days together, piecing broken intervals into one memorable stretch of time. But by the end of the first week there were frequent interruptions from different people. They were teased for consuming each other like that; they were gently but firmly pulled apart. MaBiyela turned up at their door three or four times a day. At first the young couple thought it was understandable, for she too had missed her son while he was away. But what became remarkable was the regularity with which she found chores for Jezile to do; duties that would take her away from Siyalo for hours. Soon other members of the family came to 'take Siyalo out' – 'other people had missed him, too, while he was away'. If their love hadn't been so all-enveloping she would have entertained a little bitterness at this social conspiracy. But the nights were too full to give room, even a little way, to petty interferences. As things were, she mildly wondered when social custom would alter to suit the new industrial practices.

Time flew by like a whirlwind. She was left cradling a feeling of expectancy and joy. There was even a defiant look in her eye when she encountered MaBiyela's searching eyes. But a few weeks later Jezile knew that nothing she had done had bent nature her way. She was not pregnant. She wept for days and she could not look anyone in the eyes. She fled back to Luve to be with her mother for several weeks. She was engulfed with a sense of failure. It took her weeks to write back to Siyalo, to break the news of their disappointment. The year ahead was very long. Nothing her mother said to comfort her could give her hope. She spent hours before her mother's bruised mirror scanning her shape – the scourge of barrenness. How to hold it in your hand – was it some tangible predisposition, some frailty, some constitutional failure, where was it – had Siyalo lied to her when he had said she was full and round, ripe, complete and bursting with womanhood. Siyalo wrote back, a letter full of reassurances – next time they would not fail – they needed more time together – no need for a doctor yet – he knew for certain she was not barren – he felt it each time they were together – nature takes its course – nature takes its time – before long he would arrange for her to come to him in the city. That whole year was agony and it discoloured all those wonderful feelings she had had when he first left. Anxiety is a corroding feeling; and couples living apart cannot escape anxiety.

That year MaBiyela had the upper hand. She did not say much, except once, a couple of months after Jezile's return from Luve. She chose her moment well, and in her most caustic voice she asked, 'Is there anything to tell us MaMapanga?' A gripe caught Jezile in the abdomen and once more all she could manage was to shake her head in silence and walk away.

Socially, Jezile began to keep a low profile, and even in political matters she became silent, which slowed things down quite a lot at Sigageni. She spent more time with her childhood friend, Zenzile, who was married to that good-for-nothing Mthebe. For a while their friendship had cooled off, for seeing Zenzile who, in the six years of marriage, had four children was painful for Jezile. Each time Mthebe came home from leave he found a new baby, and he left another growing, ready to find on his next visit. But, Zenzile was a captive in her house, with children who whimpered and hung around her skirts. Everything around was drab and Zenzile looked haggard and despondent. On occasion Jezile wondered if her friend was not somehow to blame for her own decline, but she would chide away this thought as soon as it intruded out of loyalty to her friend. She visited Zenzile regularly, at least once a week, to take her the current gossip of the community, to help her around the house – in short, to cheer up her friend for old times' sake. She washed the children when she could, fed them, put them to sleep, but tried not to wonder at the dried-up tears, or their thin withered legs. She needed Zenzile and her tumble-down family life. She needed to get away from her life as a water carrier, a wood gatherer, a road mender, from her life in the fields, ploughing, sowing, weeding and reaping. She hated running after cows that invariably broke through fences. It was a hard, unremitting life, which left her unfulfilled. So she looked forward to those days when she could manage a visit to Zenzile where all she could do was glaze over her friend's predicament. From this daze of superficiality she was jolted upright one day by the news that one of Zenzile's children had died suddenly. One of the ones she had washed just two days earlier – she could not even remember its name. She was there, helping with the funeral arrangements; she stayed with Zenzile for many days after. When the others tailed off to go back to their families, she had no reason to hurry back. She hung on and kept her friend company.

Jezile came back each night and helped to cook, wash the children and slowly to cheer her friend. She came to love the children – the more she knew them and played with them, the more she missed not having her own children. Zenzile was utterly disillusioned on the one hand and Jezile was full of hope and promise on the other. They differed heatedly. Jezile did not see motherhood as a bind, a fulfilment of other people's expectations of her. All she knew was that she needed children to love, to secure her, to help her with some jobs that threatened to break her life. She saw far into the future; she would bring them up healthy and strong, which was to her Zenzile's greatest failure. She would love them and present them a perfect gift to Siyalo. Above all, they would fulfil her life and save her from social torment.

When things had slowly returned to normal for Zenzile, Jezile went back to her routine and waited. The year was long. Essentially, life constituted long periods of waiting; all that the women of Sigageni ever did was wait. Then one day she got a letter from Siyalo. Her heart raced as always, and she read it greedily. But then she let it fall from her hands on to the table. She stared at the letter without seeing it. She could not believe it – wild apprehension stung her – in two weeks' time he would be home. And that's when her next period was due – the 15th of December, that's when he was due home . . . it couldn't be! It was obvious, she wouldn't make it again this time. She spun round and round, babbling to herself, 'Just why, just why did he always choose the wrong date? Why couldn't he plan the time of his leave in advance with her? He said it all depended on his employer; but what did his employer know about her, or her body or their need for a baby? How could he plan their life without them? Surely Siyalo must have a say about his leave. There must be a way I can intervene; I must influence things somehow. It is all about me; it is not true that I'm barren . . . it is just not true . . . I need time . . . I've never had a proper chance . . . chance, chance, chance . . . malignant fate is always against me. And that woman, she'll have a field day – she's so happy to call me barren; it's as if it didn't concern her son as well – as though she wished him as much pain as she inflicts on me. Perhaps she wants him to leave me for someone else. I wait a whole year for his leave – to clinch that trick of nature – conception. What is it? Why is it so completely out of my control; why is it that something that affects my whole life should be outside of me. Have I ever had any power to influence anything in my life? Once I swore that if Siyalo married me he would have changed the course of my life for ever; that I would long for nothing and would fall into the pattern of what was expected of me accordingly. Now this.' She leapt to the mirror as though the problem was sitting on her body like a mole. She whisked her dress up in one movement, right above her rounded breasts. For the hundredth time she looked at her shape critically, caressed her breasts and turned round to look at the body that had let her down each time.

On the night of the fourteenth, the day before Siyalo arrived she lay awake curled up in bed and waiting. She felt cold. When the fifteenth finally crept slowly through the cracks of the ill-fitting door she woke up and stretched. She could actually feel her body snap and creak, so tight was the tension that gripped her. She felt she would not even be able to smile at Siyalo without her face seizing up altogether. She had a hot bath to relax her body, to ease it for the welcome. She was half-way through her ablution when she heard the high-pitched laughter of her youngest sister-in-law Simo and her cousin-in-law Jabu. Their excitement quivered in the air. She knew how happy they were. This was a yearly celebration – if waiting was hard for adults, children did not know it – they lived in anticipation – to see fathers and uncles and brothers come and go. They lived for the festivities at the time of home-coming and the dreams filled the emptiness in between. Jezile tried to smile for their sake, but it was hard to whip her sluggish heart even to a pretence of joy. It was hard to recall and will herself into the passionate anticipation of his first return from the city exactly two years before. She felt completely alienated from the young woman she had been, and a complete stranger to the girl that accompanied him on his first tour after their marriage – just three years before. There had been so much hope between them then, on that dawn when she first saw him off. So many hopes had died. He too had faltered on a few promises. He no longer wrote her letters every week, his letters were much shorter than before and less amusing. Then there had been that time when he hadn't written at all for two whole months. What had he been up to? Had he really been ill? The thought of their love cheered her up a little. She chided herself, for, in the two weeks of waiting, since his letter she had morbidly dwelt on their aborted hopes and not once on their great love for each other. Perhaps, in the final analysis, nothing else mattered. If babies would not come, all the more reason why she should give him greater love.

An hour later, at the bus stop, she sat waiting, more cheerful than she had felt for several days. They saw the bus two miles away, winding its way down the hills, now behind them, now appearing. As it drew nearer her heart bit violently and perfidious joy filled her whole body and she trembled at the thought that he might not be inside the bus; what if he had missed the bus. She shared the tense, silent anticipation with the girls as the bus came hurtling on as though it had no reason to stop. But it did, and she saw him first as he stood up. He was home; he had come back to her; he had left the city attractions for her. She flushed all over; beads of perspiration on her forehead and a hot flood somewhere deep in her loins. She burst into tears and people thought they were tears of joy. Siyalo held her hand;

the magic was gone. He knew they were not tears of joy.

The days that followed were marred, full of empty talk when there were people around and flatulent silences when they were on their own. They had waited for eleven and a half months for this holiday and all it had brought was disappointment. At first Siyalo was determined to retrieve the happy times that they had had in the past. He knew he needed wholesome home-brewed love to anchor his heart in the long months of loneliness ahead in the city. But try as he might there was a sag in the middle, a hollowness that nothing would fill. He knew that this time their marriage could not survive the long separation and the inevitable taunts that she would receive. Other men did it – they resisted the city and came back to their wives, but they had children. For the first time he admitted to himself that they needed a child to hold their marriage together.

§ *Life under apartheid* Gordimer, Fugard, Mzamane; *Motherhood*: Emecheta, Aidoo (2)

MBULELO MZAMANE (1948–)

My Cousin Comes to Jo'burg

Township kids are incredibly good at tracing a man's origin. They can usually tell by his speech and deportment. They seldom pounce upon the swaggerer who crosses a busy intersection without pausing, even before the traffic lights turn green. But they'll not hesitate to taunt the man they hear humming a tribal ditty instead of whistling a jazz tune.

My cousin, Jola, comes from Tsolo in the Transkei. He has the stature of an adult gorilla and walks with his arms flung far out and his hands curving in, like a cowboy ready to draw. He has a protruding chest which seems to lead him wherever he goes. Overall, he gives the impression of a well-constructed tower. He can carry both our rubbish bins, full, with the ease and dignity of an educated man carrying a newspaper. His is not the delicate walking-cane amble of office workers who walk for relaxation, but the easy gait of one to whom walking is as customary as it is necessary.

He's been in the city for years now. But there was a time when he was as green and raw as a cabbage.

One day Mzal' uJola went to buy some cold drink. Shops are usually where street urchins 'rank', so they spotted him at a distance, carrying an empty family-size bottle.

'Where can I refill this bottle, *makwedini?*'

The boys laughed derisively at being called pickaninnies. Did he think he could lick them all, single-handed?

'He thinks we get cold drink from a tap?' one asked facetiously.

'Just because he's used to getting milk freely from a cow,' added another. They laughed.

Mzal' uJola was more surprised than annoyed by this unexpected outburst from boys who should have been looking after cattle in the veld. He left them and walked up to an elderly woman carrying a child on her back, who directed him to Mzimba's Native Eating Bazaar.

He came out of the shop with a bottle of raspberry. This again sent the boys into peals of laughter – red and green are favourites with country folk where people of the city will buy Fanta or Coke.

The boys had decided on a scheme to harass him. They stood in his path and pretended not to notice him. When he changed direction, they shifted to be directly in line with him.

His anger was mounting. He charged straight for the centre like an uncompromising rhino.

The boys found courage in numbers and stood their ground.

His eyes met those of the boy in the middle. The boy returned his stare. Mzal' uJola headed straight for him.

'Move out of my way, wena,'[1] he said to the boy in the middle.

He was now dangerously close. Mouths stood agape as the contest assumed the form of a duel. He'd picked on the boss of the gang – feared, begrudged and, if the truth be told, hated by the rest.

The boss's bravado melted. He moved aside. The rest broke rank and Mzal' uJola passed.

My father once hitchhiked from Natalspruit because his car had been stolen there while he was visiting a friend's house.

'But couldn't they approach you decently and borrow the car if they needed it that badly?' Mzal' uJola asked.

We all gaped.

The phone rang. It was the police. The car had been found abandoned near New Market in Alberton. Except for a broken side-window the car didn't appear damaged in any way.

'I can't understand the mentality of a man who takes another's car, or even a horse that belongs to another, only to dump it elsewhere,' Mzal' uJola said.

My younger brother, Soso, once offered to take Mzal' uJola to the movies. They were showing Richard Widmark in *Street With No Name*,[2] a great favourite with township audiences. Most of us had seen the film twice or three times before but we didn't mind seeing it again.

We had a transistor radio of which Mzal' uJola was inordinately fond. He played it even when we were listening to the radiogram. Its batteries were replaced daily. No matter how many times I told him to switch it off before going to bed, I always had to reach under his pillow and kill the music

---

1 You. 2 1948 crime thriller directed by William Keighley.

myself. He would never learn, that one. I remember threatening to break it once when he switched it on as I was listening to the news, and wondering if I could teach him how to use the earphones. I believe he even carried that transistor radio with him to the toilet.

In the evening we went to the movies. Nobody saw him hide the transistor under his overcoat.

The film offered plenty of action. But the dialogue was even more captivating. Most of us knew stretches of it off by heart, but we wanted to hear it all the same.

'There's only one guy who's the brains of this outfit, and that's me.'

'All these barbarians are under my command.'

'No shooting till I say so.'

'Friends, Romans, countrymen, lend me your ears . . .'

Suddenly a roaring noise from Mzal' uJola's overcoat. It was Lloyd Price's hit song, 'Personality'.

I dug my elbows into his ribs but only met with layers of cloth.

There was an uproar of hisses, catcalls and invective from the audience.

'Switch off that blerry gramophone.'

'Who's that f . . . . m . . . . ?'

'What are you up to?' Soso asked.

'Switch off that thing,' I whispered through clenched teeth.

He fumbled with the radio. I grabbed it and promptly switched it off.

'*Mzala*, please give it to me. I was going to insert the thing of the ear,' he said.

'Don't give it to him,' Soso said. '*Ufun' ukusibethisa ngabantu?*[3] *Hoekom het ek die spy hier gebring?*'[4]

I kept the transistor. At the end of the film, not long before the lights came on, I walked out to wait for them outside. I didn't care to be identified with a chap who played a radio during a film show.

My father had several outstations, mostly on the mines. At Crown Mines there were several migrant labourers who came from Tsolo. My father knew many of these men, whom he introduced to Mzal' uJola. When he went to Crown Mines he always took Mzal' uJola with him. Among the old friends Mzal' uJola met were Hlubi and Mbele, his former classmates – they'd all left school after standard four.

During weekends Hlubi and Mbele sometimes visited Mzal' uJola, too, and took him to their favourite shebeens in the township where they drank *mbhambha*.[5] But on most occasions it was my father who drove Mzal' uJola to Crown Mines, till he had learnt the way back home, more or less.

One Sunday they went to Crown Mines, as usual. Mzal' uJola asked my father to leave him behind. It was the first time he'd ever made such a request and so my father was worried. Hlubi and Mbele promised to take

---

3 Would you like to see us beaten up?   4 Why did I bring the spy here?   5 Deadly alcoholic concoction.

care of him and my father reluctantly left, alone. They remained drinking *mbhambha* until it was time for Mzal' uJola to return home. There was really no problem because the bus would drop him almost on our doorstep. They accompanied him to the bus stop and pointed out the right bus to him.

Darkness was fast descending. Heavy smoke hung over the township like a canopy. In the bus Mzal' uJola had to keep his face glued to the misty window to be able to see outside. The bus was packed to capacity and Mzal' uJola was seated at the back. A group of Zionists returning from a baptismal retreat sang lustily and danced spiritedly along the length of the bus. When Mzal' uJola recognised the bus stop nearest home the bus was already moving off. He edged his way to the front, over cursing folk's corns, through layers of human flesh, mostly feminine, until he reached the door. But by this time the bus had passed another stop so that he got off two stages beyond his intended alighting point.

To reach home he had to go through the shopping centre. Near the shops he heard someone saying, 'There's that Xhosa *mampara*,'[6] but he took no notice. He began to sing softly to himself '*Ulo Thixo Omkhulu*', a traditional hymn of praise.

A brick whizzed through the air, another found its mark. Mzal' uJola held his ribs in pain but walked on. He could hear the swift tread of footsteps retreating in the opposite direction.

Soso, coming from the shops, overheard a group of jubilant boys talking about how they had fixed that Xhosa *mampara*, but paid little attention. When he got home he found Mzal' uJola massaging his ribs in the privacy of the bathroom and asked him what had happened.

'Shh . . . *Mzala*.' He pulled Soso into the bathroom and shut the door. 'Don't tell anybody. I bumped into a brick.'

'Did you get beaten up by a group of boys near the shops?'

'How did you know?'

'I met a group of boys talking about someone they'd just fixed.'

'*Mzala* wam', if you know them, just take me to where I may lay my hands on them.'

'Hey, *ndoda*,[7] I haven't as yet grown tired of eating sorghum[8] in this world.'

Around this time Mzal' uJola struck up a few significant acquaintances, significant because they were later to turn into valuable allies. The first was Jikida, a sly man who could make his way out of a hungry crocodile's mouth with ease, a man of infinite resources and vast experience. He'd been a constable once, just in order to establish contacts with the police force. He also served two terms as a member of the township advisory board, during which period he made a small fortune by charging people who came to consult

---

6 Fool; idiot.   7 Man.   8 Tropical cereal grass.

him, as though he were a lawyer. At the time when Mzal' uJola got to know him he described himself as a herbalist and a landlord.

Jikida came to our house to see my father on some business. He found my father out and decided to wait for him for a while. While he waited he began to chat with Mzal' uJola.

'D'you also stay here,' he asked.

'Yes,' Mzal' uJola replied. 'This is my uncle's place.'

'Have we met before?'

'No. I came here last Christmas.'

'*Liphi ikhaya?*'[9]

'In the Transkei.'

'What part?'

It turned out Jikida was very familiar with Mzal' uJola's part of the Transkei, having himself trained at St. Cuthbert's as a carpenter. He'd originally come from Cofimvaba more than twenty years before. His wife still lived there and occasionally came to Johannesburg 'to fetch a child.'

'You should visit me some day to see what we do in this land,' Jikida said.

'What do you do for a living?' Mzal' uJola asked.

'I'm what you might call a herbalist.'

'Oh! You're just the man that might help. I've a pain here that's causing me sleepless nights.' He pointed at his ribs.

'I know just the right ointment for you. Got it during my last visit to the zoo. There's nothing more potent than the waste matter from some of these strong, wild animals.'

A definite appointment was fixed.

Thereafter Jikida's house became Mzal' uJola's second home.

It was at Jikida's that Mzal' uJola met his first girlfriend, one of Jikida's tenants. Jikida occupied a four-roomed municipality house and rented three of the rooms to different families. He meddled with the feminine members of his tenancy more than was appreciated by their male counterparts. It was the unavailability of alternative accommodation which kept them at Jikida's.

Mzal' uJola's woman – her husband was actually a nightwatchman in town – was stout in a pleasantly feminine way and bowlegged. Her breasts were two watermelons and her buttocks gave an equally succulent and corpulent impression. Her dresses sat loosely on her like an eiderdown on a double bed.

Mzal' uJola slept out for the first time during this period, something which became a habit with him and drew an endless volley of curses from my mother.

'The first thing you'll learn here,' she said, 'is to choose your friends with greater circumspection. You'll find that out the day you and that Jikida of yours land in prison. I know of everything that goes on at that den of iniquity. Yours won't be the first corpse to be found in that yard.'

---

9 Where do you come from?

Although in slightly milder terms, my father also expressed his disapproval of Mzal' uJola's association with Jikida.

'One other thing,' my father added, 'you shouldn't move about the township so much. We're still trying to get you a pass. Don't spoil your chances at this stage. '

'One of these days he'll see for himself,' my mother said. 'He'll bump into Mawulawula and his police gang. Let him continue roaming the streets.'

It didn't happen as my mother had predicted. For one thing he wasn't roaming the streets but was actually in our yard, leaning against the gate and watching traffic, when a few policemen on bicycles stopped just opposite our house.

'Can you lend us some matches, *mfowethu?*'[10] one of them asked.

'I don't smoke but I think I can get it for you from the house.' He disappeared into the house and came back with a box of matches.

The policemen remained on their bicycles in the street so that Mzal' uJola had to walk up to them to give them matches.

'Do you stay here?' asked the policeman who'd sent him for matches.

'Yes.'

'But I don't know you.'

'Let him produce his pass to prove it,' another policeman suggested.

'Where's your pass?'

'It's not here.'

'We can pull him in for failing to produce,' said the one with the bright ideas.

Mzal' uJola's trousers were now doing the jitterbug.

Another policeman put his bicycle down and approached Mzal' uJola with handcuffs. But before he could fasten them a second group of policemen appeared round the corner.

'*Wenzeni?*'[11] one of them asked.

'He hasn't got a pass, *sajeni,*'[12] the policeman with the handcuffs answered.

'Wait a minute, I think I've seen this chap before. Aren't you *mfundisi's*[13] nephew?'

Mzal' uJola nodded.

'That's right, leave him alone chaps. He's our *mfundisi's* nephew. Recently arrived from the Transkei?'

Mzal' uJola again nodded.

'*Pasop,*'[14] the policeman with the handcuffs said. 'You must thank your stars for Sergeant Mawulawula's timely intervention. We don't want vagrants in this location.'

The other policeman gave him back the box of matches. They cycled away.

Mzal' uJola could never forget Sergeant Mawulawula. The longer he

---

10 Brother. 11 What's happening? 12 Sergeant. 13 Priest's. 14 Watch out.

remained in our township the more his admiration for him increased. The sergeant was essentially a man of the world.

It was days before Mzal' uJola could summon enough courage to venture out of our yard. But even then he travelled with my father to Crown Mines.

Hlubi and Mbele had good news for him. They'd been talking to their foreman, a most understanding white man. There was a job he could get which didn't require him to carry a pass. They discussed the matter with my father who agreed that Mzal' uJola should take up the job.

Mzal' uJola thus started work on the mines as a compound cleaner. He stayed there and only came home over the weekend.

When he eventually got a pass he left his job at the mines and went to work as a hotel cleaner. He was later promoted to cook.

His pass gave him a sense of space. He refused to be confined to any one job, so that in his many years in the city he's worked as a doctor, a painter, a priest and a prophet.

He's been arrested and deported to the Transkei several times. Once the police managed to guard him as far as Bloemfontein. He came back to Johannesburg on a goods train.

These experiences have revealed rather more to Mzal' uJola than a landscape shows to a bat's eyes. *'Uvulekile manje,'*[15] as everybody acknowledges: he's as wide-awake as an owl. He has remained in the township, where his wits have sharpened with exposure to the vicissitudes of life. What's more, he's lived so long under the shadow of the vagrancy laws, the Influx Control regulations and the rest that he has come to consider such hazards as a shield and an umbrella. I also happen to know that the twenty-third psalm is his personal favourite. He lives, as township folk never fail to point out, by *'Nkosi Sikelela'.*[16]

§ *Life under apartheid* Gordimer, Fugard, Ngcobo; *Countryman come to town* Fugard

J. M. COETZEE (1940–)

From Foe

Foe is one of a number of post-colonial texts which 'write back' to a canonical English text, in this case Defoe's *Robinson Crusoe*. Susan Barton, an Englishwoman, who is on the island with 'Cruso' (as he is called here) and a mute, tongueless Friday in the first part of the novel, subsequently comes to London with Friday, and begs the author Daniel Foe to write her story. He envisages it differently from her (and also from the

---

15 You've been tipped off now. 16 'God bless . . .'; opening words of the South African National Anthem, first adopted in 1923 as the African National Congress anthem.

text of *Robinson Crusoe*). At the same time other Defoe narratives, particularly *Roxana* – like the protagonist of this novel, Susan has a lost daughter –, vie for space in *Foe* and ultimately the obliqueness of all the parallels disrupts the possibility of reading the novel as a neat reversal of Defoe's classic allegory of imperialism. In this passage, the opening of the second section, Susan gives an account of her first days in London.

April 15th

'We are now settled in lodgings in Clock Lane off Long Acre. I go by the name Mrs Cruso, which you should bear in mind. I have a room on the second floor. Friday has a bed in the cellar, where I bring him his meals. By no means could I have abandoned him on the island. Nevertheless, a great city is no place for him. His confusion and distress when I conducted him through the streets this last Saturday wrenched my heartstrings.

'Our lodging is together five shillings a week. Whatever you send I shall be grateful for.

'I have set down the history of our time on the island as well as I can, and enclose it herewith. It is a sorry, limping affair (the history, not the time itself) – "the next day," its refrain goes, "the next day . . . the next day" – but you will know how to set it right.

'You will wonder how I came to choose you, given that a week ago I did not so much as know your name. I admit, when I first laid eyes on you I thought you were a lawyer or a man from the Exchange. But then one of my fellow-servants told me you were Mr Foe the author who had heard many confessions and were reputed a very secret man. It was raining (do you remember?); you paused on the step to fasten your cloak, and I came out too and shut the door behind me. "If I may be so bold, sir," I said (those were the words, bold words). You looked me up and down but did not reply, and I thought to myself: What art is there to hearing confessions? – the spider has as much art, that watches and waits. "If I may have a moment of your time: I am seeking a new situation." "So are we all seeking a new situation," you replied. "But I have a man to care for, a Negro man who can never find a situation, since he has lost his tongue," I said – "I hoped that you might have place for me, and for him too, in your establishment." My hair was wet by now, I had not even a shawl. Rain dripped from the brim of your hat. "I am in employ here, but am used to better things," I pursued – "You have not heard a story before like mine. I am new-returned from far-off parts. I have been a castaway on a desert island. And there I was the companion of a singular man." I smiled, not at you but at what I was about to say. "I am a figure of fortune, Mr Foe. I am the good fortune we are always hoping for."

'Was it effrontery to say that? Was it effrontery to smile? Was it the effrontery that aroused your interest?'

April 20th

'Thank you for the three guineas. I have bought Friday a drayer's woollen jerkin, also woollen hose. If there is underlinen you can spare, I should welcome it. He wears clothes without murmur, though he will not yet wear shoes.

'Can you not take us into your house? Why do you keep me apart? Can you not take me in as your close servant, and Friday as your gardener?

'I climb the staircase (it is a tall house, tall and airy, with many flights of stairs) and tap at the door. You are sitting at a table with your back to me, a rug over your knees, your feet in pantoufles,[1] gazing out over the fields, thinking, stroking your chin with your pen, waiting for me to set down the tray and withdraw. On the tray are a glassful of hot water into which I have squeezed a citron, and two slices of buttered toast. You call it your first breakfast.

'The room is barely furnished. The truth is, it is not a room but a part of the attic to which you remove yourself for the sake of silence. The table and chair stand on a platform of boards before the window. From the door of the attic to this platform, boards are laid to form a narrow walk-way. Otherwise there are only the ceiling-boards, on which one treads at one's peril, and the rafters, and overhead the grey rooftiles. Dust lies thick on the floor; when the wind gusts under the eaves there are flurries in the dust, and from the corners moaning noises. There are mice too. Before you go downstairs you must shut your papers away to preserve them from the mice. In the mornings you brush mouse-droppings from the table.

'There is a ripple in the window-pane. Moving your head, you can make the ripple travel over the cows grazing in the pasture, over the ploughed land beyond, over the line of poplars, and up into the sky.

'I think of you as a steersman steering the great hulk of the house through the nights and days, peering ahead for signs of storm.

'Your papers are kept in a chest beside the table. The story of Cruso's island will go there page by page as you write it, to lie with a heap of other papers: a census of the beggars of London, bills of mortality from the time of the great plague, accounts of travels in the border country, reports of strange and surprising apparitions, records of the wool trade, a memorial of the life and opinions of Dickory Cronke (who is he?); also books of voyages to the New World, memoirs of captivity among the Moors, chronicles of the wars in the Low Countries, confessions of notorious lawbreakers, and a multitude of castaway narratives,[2] most of them, I would guess, riddled with lies.

'When I was on the island I longed only to be elsewhere, or, in the word I then used, to be saved. But now a longing stirs in me I never thought I would feel. I close my eyes and my soul takes leave of me, flying over the

---

1 Slippers or loose shoes. 2 Sources for several of Defoe's works, including *A Journal of the Plague Year* (1722), *A Tour through the Whole Island of Great Britain* (1724–7), *Captain Singleton* (1720), *Robinson Crusoe* (1719) and *Moll Flanders* (1722).

houses and streets, the woods and pastures, back to our old home, Cruso's and mine. You will not understand this longing, after all I have said of the tedium of our life there. Perhaps I should have written more about the pleasure I took in walking barefoot in the cool sand of the compound, more about the birds, the little birds of many varieties whose names I never knew, whom I called sparrows for want of a better name. Who but Cruso, who is no more, could truly tell you Cruso's story? I should have said less about him, more about myself. How, to begin with, did my daughter come to be lost, and how, following her, did I reach Bahia? How did I survive among strangers those two long years? Did I live only in a rooming-house, as I have said? Was Bahia an island in the ocean of the Brazilian forest, and my room a lonely island in Bahia? Who was the captain whose fate it became to drift forever in the southernmost seas, clothed in ice? I brought back not a feather, not a thimbleful of sand, from Cruso's island. All I have is my sandals. When I reflect on my story I seem to exist only as the one who came, the one who witnessed, the one who longed to be gone: a being without substance, a ghost beside the true body of Cruso. Is that the fate of all storytellers? Yet I was as much a body as Cruso. I ate and drank, I woke and slept, I longed. The island was Cruso's (yet by what right? by the law of islands? is there such a law?), but I lived there too, I was no bird of passage, no gannet or albatross, to circle the island once and dip a wing and then fly on over the boundless ocean. Return to me the substance I have lost, Mr Foe: that is my entreaty. For though my story gives the truth, it does not give the substance of the truth (I see that clearly, we need not pretend it is otherwise). To tell the truth in all its substance you must have quiet, and a comfortable chair away from all distraction, and a window to stare through; and then the knack of seeing waves when there are fields before your eyes, and of feeling the tropic sun when it is cold; and at your fingertips the words with which to capture the vision before it fades. I have none of these, while you have all.'

April 21st

'In my letter yesterday I may have seemed to mock the art of writing. I ask your pardon, I was unjust. Believe me, there are times when, as I think of you labouring in your attic to bring life to your thieves and courtesans and grenadiers, my heart aches with pity and I long only to be of service. I think of you (forgive me the figure) as a beast of burden, and your house as a great wagon you are condemned to haul, a wagon full of tables and chairs and wardrobes, and on top of these a wife (I do not even know whether you have a wife!) and ungrateful children and idle servants and cats and dogs, all eating your victuals, burning your coal, yawning and laughing, careless of your toil. In the early mornings, lying in my warm bed, I seem to hear the shuffle of your footsteps as, draped in a rug, you climb the stairs to your attic. You seat yourself, your breathing is heavy, you light the lamp, you pinch your eyes shut and begin to grope your way back to where you were last night, through the dark and cold, through the rain, over fields where sheep lie huddled together, over forests, over the seas, to Flanders or wherever it is that your captains and grenadiers must now too begin to stir and set about the next day in their lives, while from the corners of the attic the mice stare at you, twitching their whiskers. Even on Sundays the work proceeds, as though whole regiments of foot would sink into everlasting sleep were they not roused daily and sent into action. In the throes of a chill you plod on, wrapped in scarves, blowing your nose, hawking, spitting. Sometimes you are so weary that the candlelight swims before your eyes. You lay your head on your arms and in a moment are asleep, a black stripe across the paper where the pen slips from your grasp. Your mouth sags open, you snore softly, you smell (forgive me a second time) like an old man. How I wish it were in my power to help you, Mr Foe! Closing my eyes, I gather my strength and send out a vision of the island to hang before you like a substantial body, with birds and fleas and fish of all hues and lizards basking in the sun, flicking out their black tongues, and rocks covered in barnacles, and rain drumming on the roof-fronds, and wind, unceasing wind: so that it will be there for you to draw on whenever you have need.'

April 25th

'You asked how it was that Cruso did not save a single musket from the wreck; why a man so fearful of cannibals should have neglected to arm himself.

'Cruso never showed me where the wreck lay, but it is my conviction that it lay, and lies still, in the deep water below the cliffs in the north of the island. At the height of the storm Cruso leapt overboard with the youthful Friday at his side, and other shipmates too, it may be; but they two alone were saved, by a great wave that caught them up and bore them ashore. Now I ask: Who can keep powder dry in the belly of a wave? Furthermore: Why should a man endeavour to save a musket when he barely hopes to save his own life? As for cannibals, I am not persuaded, despite Cruso's fears, that there are cannibals in those oceans. You may with right reply that, as we do not expect to see sharks dancing in the waves, so we should not expect to see cannibals dancing on the strand; that cannibals belong to the night as sharks belong to the depths. All I say is: What I saw, I wrote. I saw no cannibals; and if they came after nightfall and fled before the dawn, they left no footprint behind.

'I dreamed last night of Cruso's death, and woke with tears coursing down my cheeks. So I lay a long while, the grief not lifting from my heart. Then I went downstairs to our little courtyard off Clock Lane. It was not yet light; the sky was clear. Under these same tranquil stars, I thought, floats the island where we lived; and on that island is a hut, and in that hut a bed of soft grass which perhaps still bears the imprint, fainter every day, of my body. Day by day the wind picks at the roof and the weeds creep across the terraces. In a year, in ten years, there will be nothing left standing but a circle of sticks to mark the place where the hut stood, and of the terraces only the walls. And of the walls they will say, These are cannibal walls, the ruins of a cannibal city, from the golden age of the cannibals. For who will believe they were built by one man and a slave, in the hope that one day a seafarer would come with a sack of corn for them to sow?

'You remarked it would have been better had Cruso rescued not only musket and powder and ball, but a carpenter's chest as well, and built himself a boat. I do not wish to be captious, but we lived on an island so buffeted by the wind that there was not a tree did not grow twisted and bent. We might have built a raft, a crooked kind of raft, but never a boat.

'You asked also after Cruso's apeskin clothes. Alas, these were taken from our cabin and tossed overboard by ignorant sailors. If you so desire, I will make sketches of us as we were on the island, wearing the clothes we wore.

'The sailor's blouse and pantaloons I wore on board ship I have given to Friday. Moreover he has his jerkin and his watch-coat. His cellar gives on to the yard, so he is free to wander as he pleases. But he rarely goes abroad, being too fearful. How he fills his time I do not know, for the cellar is bare save for his cot and the coal-bin and some broken sticks of furniture.

'Yet the story that there is a cannibal in Clock Lane has plainly got about, for yesterday I found three boys at the cellar door peering in on Friday. I chased them off, after which they took up their stand at the end of the lane, chanting the words: "Cannibal Friday, have you ate your mam today?"

'Friday grows old before his time, like a dog locked up all its life. I too, from living with an old man and sleeping in his bed, have grown old. There are times when I think of myself as a widow. If there was a wife left behind in Brazil, she and I would be sisters now, of a kind.

'I have the use of the scullery two mornings of the week, and am turning Friday into a laundryman; for otherwise idleness will destroy him. I set him before the sink dressed in his sailor clothes, his feet bare as ever on the cold floor (he will not wear shoes). "Watch me, Friday!" I say, and begin to soap a petticoat (soap must be introduced to him, there was no soap in his life before, on the island we used ash or sand), and rub it on the washing-board. "Now *do*, Friday!" I say, and stand aside. *Watch* and *Do*: those are my two principal words for Friday, and with them I accomplish much. It is a terrible fall, I know, from the freedom of the island where he could roam all day, and hunt birds' eggs, and spear fish, when the terraces did not call. But surely it is better to learn useful tasks than to lie alone in a cellar all day, thinking I know not what thoughts?

'Cruso would not teach him because, he said, Friday had no need of words. But Cruso erred. Life on the island, before my coming, would have been less tedious had he taught Friday to understand his meanings, and devised ways by which Friday could express his own meanings, as for example by gesturing with his hands or by setting out pebbles in shapes standing for words. Then Cruso might have spoken to Friday after his manner, and Friday responded after his, and many an empty hour been whiled away. For I cannot believe that the life Friday led before he fell into Cruso's hands was bereft of interest, though he was but a child. I would give much to hear the truth of how he was captured by the slave-traders and lost his tongue.

'He is become a great lover of oatmeal, gobbling down as much porridge in a day as would feed a dozen Scotsmen. From eating too much and lying abed he is growing stupid. Seeing him with his belly tight as a drum and his thin shanks and his listless air, you would not believe he was the same man who brief months ago stood poised on the rocks, the seaspray dancing about him, the sunlight glancing on his limbs, his spear raised, ready in an instant to strike a fish.

'While he works I teach him the names of things. I hold up a spoon and say "Spoon, Friday!" and give the spoon into his hand. Then I say "Spoon!" and hold out my hand to receive the spoon; hoping thus that in time the word *Spoon* will echo in his mind willy-nilly whenever his eye falls on a spoon.

'What I fear most is that after years of speechlessness the very notion of speech may be lost to him. When I take the spoon from his hand (but is it truly a spoon to him, or a mere thing? – I do not know), and say *Spoon*, how can I be sure he does not think I am chattering to myself as a magpie or an ape does, for the pleasure of hearing the noise I make, and feeling the play of my tongue, as he himself used to find pleasure in playing his flute? And whereas one may take a dull child and twist his arm or pinch his ear till at last he repeats after us, *Spoon*, what can I do with Friday? "Spoon, Friday!" I say; "Fork! Knife!" I think of the root of his tongue closed behind those heavy lips like a toad in eternal winter, and I shiver. "Broom, Friday!" I say, and make motions of sweeping, and press the broom into his hand.

'Or I bring a book to the scullery. "This is a book, Friday," I say. "In it is a story written by the renowned Mr Foe. You do not know the gentleman, but at this very moment he is engaged in writing another story, which is your story, and your master's, and mine. Mr Foe has not met you, but he knows of you, from what I have told him, using words. That is part of the magic of words. Through the medium of words I have given Mr Foe the particulars of you and Mr Cruso and of my year on the island and the years you and Mr Cruso spent there alone, as far as I can supply them; and all these particulars Mr Foe is weaving into a story which will make us famous throughout the land, and rich too. There will be no more need for you to live in a cellar. You will have money with which to buy your way to Africa or Brazil, as the desire moves you, bearing fine gifts, and be reunited with your parents, if they remember you, and marry at last and have children, sons and daughters. And I will give you your own copy of our book, bound in leather, to take with you. I will show you how to trace your name in it, page after page, so that your children may see that their father is known in all parts of the world where books are read. Is writing not a fine thing, Friday? Are you not filled with joy to know that you will live forever, after a manner?"

'Having introduced you thus, I open your book and read from it to Friday. "This is the story of Mrs Veal,[3] another humble person whom Mr Foe has

---

3 Alluding to Defoe's first notable work of fiction, 'A True Relation of the Apparition of One Mrs Veal' (1706), a version of a current ghost-story.

made famous in the course of his writing," I say. "Alas, we shall never meet Mrs Veal, for she has passed away; and as to her friend Mrs Barfield, she lives in Canterbury, a city some distance to the south of us on this island where we find ourselves, named Britain; I doubt we shall ever go there."

'Through all my chatter Friday labours away at the washing-board. I expect no sign that he has understood. It is enough to hope that if I make the air around him thick with words, memories will be reborn in him which died under Cruso's rule, and with them the recognition that to live in silence is to live like the whales, great castles of flesh floating leagues apart one from another, or like the spiders, sitting each alone at the heart of his web, which to him is the entire world. Friday may have lost his tongue but he has not lost his ears – that is what I say to myself. Through his ears Friday may yet take in the wealth stored in stories and so learn that the world is not, as the island seemed to teach him, a barren and a silent place (is that the secret meaning of the word story, do you think: a storing-place of memories?).

'I watch his toes curl on the floorboards or the cobblestones and know that he craves the softness of earth under his feet. How I wish there were a garden I could take him to! Could he and I not visit your garden in Stoke Newington? We should be as quiet as ghosts. "Spade, Friday!" I should whisper, offering the spade to his hand; and then: "Dig!" – which is a word his master taught him – "Turn over the soil, pile up the weeds for burning. Feel the spade. Is it not a fine, sharp tool? It is an English spade, made in an English smithy."

'So, watching his hand grip the spade, watching his eyes, I seek the first sign that he comprehends what I am attempting: not to have the beds cleared (I am sure you have your own gardener), not even to save him from idleness, or for the sake of his health to bring him out of the dankness of his cellar, but to build a bridge of words over which, when one day it is grown sturdy enough, he may cross to the time before Cruso, the time before he lost his tongue, when he lived immersed in the prattle of words as unthinking as a fish in water; from where he may by steps return, as far as he is able, to the world of words in which you, Mr Foe, and I, and other people live.

'Or I bring out your shears and show him their use. "Here in England," I say, "it is our custom to grow hedges to mark the limits of our property. Doubtless that would not be possible in the forests of Africa. But here we grow hedges, and then cut them straight, so that our gardens shall be neatly marked out." I lop at the hedge till it becomes clear to Friday what I am doing: not cutting a passage through your hedge, not cutting down your hedge, but cutting one side of it straight. "Now, Friday, take the shears," I say: "Cut!"; and Friday takes the shears and cuts in a clean line, as I know he is capable of doing, for his digging is impeccable.

'I tell myself I talk to Friday to educate him out of darkness and silence. But is that the truth? There are times when benevolence deserts me and I use words only as the shortest way to subject him to my will. At such times I understand why Cruso preferred not to disturb his muteness. I understand, that is to say, why a man will choose to be a slaveowner. Do you think less of me for this confession?'

§ *Responses to European texts* Carib: Lamming (2), Walcott (4), Gilkes; SEA: Lim, Lee Tzu Pheng, Somtow

BESSIE HEAD (1937–86)

From A Question of Power

A Question of Power offers a vision of schizophrenia from the inside. The 'coloured' protagonist, Elizabeth, offspring of a white South African woman and a stable-boy (the novel hints that apartheid may have caused her condition), has moved to Botswana where she hopes to find mental stability. Most of the novel is the creation of Elizabeth's tortured imagination and characters such as 'Dan' and 'Sello', though they have counterparts in the real world, are products of her paranoid fantasies. The opening, included here, establishes the main details of Elizabeth's situation. More conventionally written than most of what follows, it nevertheless provides an introduction to the novel's vivid method of representing 'madness'; and its suggestion that relief can only come from the abnegation of 'power', a path which Elizabeth associates with Asian religions.

It seemed almost incidental that he was African. So vast had his inner perceptions grown over the years that he preferred an identification with mankind to an identification with a particular environment. And yet, as an African, he seemed to have made one of the most perfect statements: 'I am just anyone'. It was as though his soul was a jigsaw; one more piece being put into place. How often was a learner dependent on his society for his soul-evolution? But then how often was a society at fault and conclusions were drawn, at the end of each life in opposition to the social trends. It wasn't as though his society were not evil too, but nowhere else could he have acquired the kind of humility which made him feel, within, totally unimportant, totally free from his own personal poisons – pride and arrogance and egoism of the soul. It had always been like this, for him – a hunger after the things of the soul, in which other preoccupations were submerged; they were intuitions mostly of what is right, but the confirmation was so strong this time that a quiet and permanent joy filled his heart. A man might laugh at intense suffering only if the evil which tortured him became irrelevant and if obsessive love, which was also one of his evils, became irrelevant too. Had it? Again, he could only apply intuition. Everything felt right with him. A barrier of solitude and bleak, arid barrenness of soul had broken down. He loved each particle of earth around him, the everyday event of sunrise, the people and animals of the village of Motabeng; perhaps his love included the whole universe. He said to himself that evening: 'I might have died before I found this freedom of heart.' That was another perfect statement, to him – love was freedom of heart.

The man's name was Sello. A woman in the village of Motabeng paralleled his inner development. Most of what applied to Sello applied to her, because they were twin souls with closely-linked destinies and the same capacity to submerge other preoccupations in a pursuit after the things of the soul. It was an insane pursuit this time. It did not bear comparing with the lofty statements of mankind's great teachers. Hidden in all their realizations were indistinct statements about evil. They never personified it, in vivid detail, within themselves. What they did say, vaguely, was that it was advisable to overcome one's passions as the source of all evil. It was harder to disclose the subtle balances of powers between people – how easy it was for people with soft shuffling, loosely-knit personalities to be preyed upon by dominant, powerful persons. The woman had at first possessed the arrogance of innocence, and had grown over a period of four years to despise the man Sello. He had freely disclosed some unpleasant and horrific details about his inner life, which damned him as a monumental sinner in her eyes. But once her relationship with the man, Dan Molomo, could be looked at with clear, hard eyes, she had turned again to Sello and held out her hands and said: 'Thank you! Oh God, thank you for the lever out of hell!' He said something in reply like: 'You see, you are just the same'. It seemed as though, now, she spent hours and hours undoing the links which bound her to Dan, whereas at one time it had been a fierce, forever relationship with wonderful music and fantastic thrills and sensations. If Dan hadn't been such a hard spitter (he spat with glorious contempt at things he dominated) she might have permanently made excuses for the other side of his song. As it was, she said: 'I might have died under the illusion that I loved him'.

The woman's name was Elizabeth. Unlike Sello and Elizabeth, the man Dan did not hold conversations with death. Only he did not look so pretty these days, and he was an extremely pretty man. It was arguable whom he wanted to destroy most, Elizabeth or Sello. The three of them had shared the strange journey into hell and kept close emotional tabs on each other. There seemed to be a mutual agreement in the beginning that an examination of inner hells was meant to end all hells forever. The pivot of the examination was Elizabeth. Both men flung unpleasant details at her in sustained ferocity. She had no time to examine her own hell. Suddenly, in one sharp, short leap to freedom, she called it Dan. He was taken off guard. He had been standing in front of her, his pants down, as usual, flaying his powerful penis in the air and saying: 'Look, I'm going to show you how I sleep with B . . . She has a womb I can't forget. When I go with a woman I go for one hour. You can't do that. You haven't got a vagina. . . .' He was going on like that when she had landed, after four years of it, on unvolcanic ground. She was shaking her head slowly, befuddled by the tablets prescribed for a mental breakdown, when suddenly Sello said something: 'Love isn't like that. Love is two people mutually feeding each other, not one living on the soul of the other, like

a ghoul.' These were the first words that sank into her pain-torn consciousness after a long interval of contemptuous hatred of Sello. First she repeated
the words over and over. Next, she threw the tablets out of the window. In
the early morning, she sped down a dusty road, greeting any passer-by with
an exuberant shout of joy. So infectious was her happiness that they responded
with spontaneous smiles. The panic-stricken Dan pulled up his pants too late.
He said: 'Look, I'm uplifted, I'm changed.' She no longer heard.

When Elizabeth looked back she could see that the whole story had its
beginnings with Sello. The course and direction of it did not remain in his
hands for long. It was taken over by Dan, first as a subtle, unseen shadow
in the background, later as a wild display of wreckage and destruction.
Admittedly, it had taken her a year of slow, painful thought to say at the
end of it: 'Phew! What a load of rubbish!' Dan understood the mechanics
of power. From his gestures, he clearly thought he had a wilting puppet in
his hands. Once sure of that, he never cared a damn what he thought and
did. Was it a deliberate ruse to arouse him to a total exposure? Because after
she came back from the mental hospital he dropped any pose he had formally had of the great romantic lover and protector, and said: 'You are now
going to have eight love affairs. You are going to be so loose your legs are
going to go like this.' And he moved his large, splaying hands with lewd gestures in her face. Nothing happened. He tried another prophecy: 'You are
going to commit suicide at a quarter to one tomorrow.' She nearly did,
except that her small boy had asked her to buy him a football and he came
down the road with a gang of eager friends. They set up a football pitch
outside the house. Her son was so eager to impress everyone that he kept
on kicking the football too high in the air and falling flat on his back. She
spent the whole afternoon at the window watching him, he was so comi-
cal. So Dan tried another prophecy. He said: 'I have the power to take the
life of your son. He will be dead in two days.' The next morning her son
awoke with a high fever. Panic stricken, she rushed him to hospital. The
doctor said: 'Oh, he'll be all right in a few days. You'll be more careful in
future about the sores he gets when he falls down. This one on his knee has
festered badly and is the cause of the fever.' The prophecies became worse
and worse. Naked women were prancing wildly in front of her and there
was Dan, gyrating his awful penis like mad. She swallowed six bottles of
beer and six sleeping tablets to induce a blackout. She had a clear sensation
of living right inside a stinking toilet; she was so broken, so shattered, she
hadn't even the energy to raise one hand. How had she fallen in there? How
had she fallen so low? It was a state below animal, below living and so dark
and forlorn no loneliness and misery could be its equivalent. She half raised
herself from the bed, intending to make a cup of tea, when Sello said quite
loudly: 'I've never seen such savage cruelty'. She turned her head towards
the chair where he had always sat, was it three years or four years, a ghostly,
persistent commentator on all her thoughts, perceptions and experiences.
Then he added: 'Love isn't like that. Love is two people mutually feeding
each other . . . .'

The nightmare was over. Dan was not over. He had not yet told the whole of mankind about his ambitions, like Hitler and Napoleon, to rule the world. He had told half the story to Elizabeth. But who was she? Again she turned for her answers to Sello. She would never have earned a second glance from a man like Dan. She was not his type – Miss Glamour, Miss Beauty Queen, Miss Legs, Miss Buttocks (he said there were seventy-one of them) were all his. What concerned her was Sello and his relationship to Sello. It was Sello and what he saw in people. First, he had introduced his own soul, so softly like a heaven of completeness and perfection. Elizabeth had put tentative questions to many people, testing her sanity against theirs.

'What would you do one day if you saw someone who looked like God?' she had asked.

'Oh,' the person she spoke to had replied. 'I should love the person, but the love would be of a special quality.'

'So you think it's quite all right to start an argument from God downwards?' she asked.

'Of course you can,' he said, smiling.

Of course you can, he'd said. He was a young IVS[1] volunteer from England. He was not African, and an argument had been worked out, in Elizabeth's mind, in an entirely African way. Perhaps in India they would have started the argument from the Superman and his accompaniment of prophecies. Nothing else need be said. In fact, they might even be hostile to any criticisms of their Gods or Supermen. If there had been a Sello in India, would the poor of India have had the courage to challenge him? Types like Sello were always Brahmins[2] or Rama[3] there.

One might propose an argument then, with the barriers of the normal, conventional and sane all broken down, like a swimmer taking a rough journey on wild seas. It was in Botswana where, mentally, the normal and the abnormal blended completely in Elizabeth's mind. It was mangeable to a certain point because of Elizabeth's background and the freedom and flexibility with which she had brought herself up. Was the story of her mother sheer accident or design? It seemed to add to her temperament and capacity to endure the excruciating. They had kept the story of her real mother shrouded in secrecy until she was thirteen. She had loved another woman as her mother, who was also part African, part English, like Elizabeth. She had been paid to care for Elizabeth, but on the death of her husband she resorted to selling beer as a means of livelihood. It was during the war, and the beer-house mainly catered for soldiers off duty. They came along with their prostitutes and there was an awful roar and commotion going on all day. Though Elizabeth loved the woman, she was secretly relieved to be taken away from the beer-house and sent to a mission school, as hours and hours of her childhood had been spent sitting under a lamp-post near her house, crying because everyone was drunk and there was no food, no one to think about children.

---

1 International Voluntary Service.   2 Members of the highest caste of Hindus, traditionally priests or scribes.
3 Hero of the Sanskrit epic, the *Ramayana*; seventh avatar of the god Vishnu.

The principal of the mission school was a tall, thin, gaunt, incredibly cruel woman. She was the last, possibly, of the kind who had heard 'the call' from Jesus and come out to save the heathen. Their calls seemed to make them very bitter at the end of it, and their professed love for Jesus never awakened love and compassion in their hearts. As soon as Elizabeth arrived at the mission school, she was called to one side by the principal and given the most astounding information. She said:

'We have a full docket on you. You must be very careful. Your mother was insane. If you're not careful you'll get insane just like your mother. Your mother was a white woman. They had to lock her up, as she was having a child by the stable boy, who was a native.'

Elizabeth started to cry, through sheer nervous shock. The details of life and oppression in South Africa had hardly taken form in her mind. The information was almost meaningless to her. She had always thought of herself as the child of the woman who had been paid to care for her. Seeing her tears, the gaunt missionary unbent a little, in her version of tenderness.

'There now,' she said. 'Don't cry. Your mother was a good woman who thought about you.' She stopped and rummaged among the papers, then read: 'Please set aside some money for my child's education. . . .'

It was a letter written by Elizabeth's mother from a mental hospital in South Africa. Still, she could not relate it to herself in any way. She really belonged emotionally to her foster-mother, and the story was an imposition on her life. Not so for the missionary. She lived on the alert for Elizabeth's insanity. Once Elizabeth struck a child during a quarrel, and the missionary ordered:

'Isolate her from the other children for a week.'

The other children soon noticed something unusual about Elizabeth's isolation periods. They could fight and scratch and bite each other, but if she did likewise she was locked up. They took to kicking at her with deliberate malice as she sat in a corner reading a book. None of the prefects would listen to her side of the story.

'Come on,' they said. 'The principal said you must be locked up.'

At the time, she had merely hated the principal with a black, deep bitter rage. But later, when she became aware of subconscious appeals to share love, to share suffering, she wondered if the persecution had been so much the outcome of the principal's twisted version of life as the silent appeal of her dead mother:

'Now you know. Do you think I can bear the stigma of insanity alone? Share it with me.'

Seven years later, when she had become a primary-school teacher, she returned to the small town where her foster-mother lived and said: 'Tell me about my mother.'

The foster-mother looked at Elizabeth for some time, then abruptly burst into tears.

'It's such a sad story,' she said. 'It caused so much trouble and the family was frightened by the behaviour of the grandmother. My husband worked on the child welfare committee, and your case came up again and again. First they received you from the mental hospital and sent you to a nursing-home. A day later you were returned because you did not look white. They sent you to a Boer family. A week later you were returned. The woman on the committee said: "What can we do with this child? Its mother is white." My husband came home that night and asked me to take you. I agreed. The next thing was, the family came down in a car from Johannesburg on their way to the racecourse in Durban. The brother of your mother came in. He was very angry and said: "We want to wash our hands of this business. We want to forget it, but the old lady insists on seeing the child. We had to please her. We are going to leave her here for a while and pick her up later." The old lady came down every time they entered horses in the races. She was the only one who wanted to see your mother and you. When you were six years old we heard that you mother had suddenly killed herself in the mental home. The grandmother brought all her toys and dolls to you.'

It was such a beautiful story, the story of the grandmother, her defiance, her insistence on filial ties in a country where people were not people at all. The last thing Elizabeth did in that small town where she had been born was to walk to the mental hospital and stare at it. There was a very high wall surrounding the building, and the atmosphere was so silent there hardly seemed to be people alive behind it. People had named the building the Red House because its roof was painted red. As a small child she had often walked past it. It was on the same road that led to the bird sanctuary, the favourite playground of all the children of the town. She remembered saying: 'Now we are passing the Red House,' never dreaming that her own life was so closely linked to its life. She seemed to have that element of the sudden, the startling, the explosive detail in her destiny and, for a long time, an abounding sense of humour to go with it.

For a few years she quietly lived on the edge of South Africa's life. It was interesting. She spent some time living with Asian families, where she learnt about India and its philosophies, and some time with a German woman from whom she learned about Hitler and the Jews and the Second World War. A year before her marriage she tentatively joined a political party. It was banned two days later, and in the state of emergency which was declared she was searched along with thousands of other people, briefly arrested for having a letter about the banned party in her handbag, and involved in a court case which bewildered the judge: 'Why did you bring this letter to court?' he said severely to the policeman in charge of the case. 'Can't you read English? The two people involved in the writing of this letter are extremely critical of the behaviour of people belonging to the banned party. They are not furthering the aims of communism.' It might have been the court case which eventually made her a stateless person in Botswana.

She married a gangster just out of jail. He said he had thought deeply about life while in prison. What really made her talk to him was that he said he was interested in Buddhism, and she knew a little about it from her friendships with Asian people. It seemed perfectly all right, a week later, to marry someone interested in philosophies, especially those of India. A month later a next-door neighbour approached her and said: 'You have a strange husband. Susie was standing outside the door and called to him. He walked straight in and they went to bed. He's been doing this nearly every day now with Susie. I also once greeted him and he said: "How about a kiss?" And I said: "Bugger off." What made you marry that thing?'

Women were always complaining of being molested by her husband. Then there was also a white man who was his boy-friend. After a year she picked up the small boy and walked out of the house, never to return. She read a newspaper advertisement about teachers being needed in Botswana. She was forced to take out an exit permit, which, like her marriage, held the 'never to return' clause. She did not care. She hated the country. In spite of her inability to like or to understand political ideologies, she had also lived the back-breaking life of all black people in South Africa. It was like living with permanent nervous tension, because you did not know why white people there had to go out of their way to hate you or loathe you. They were just born that way, hating people, and a black man or woman was just born to be hated. There wasn't any kind of social evolution beyond that, there wasn't any lift to the heart, just this vehement vicious struggle between two sets of people with different looks; and, like Dan's brand of torture, it was something that could go on and on and on. Once you stared the important power-maniac in the face you saw that he never saw people, humanity, compassion, tenderness. It was as though he had a total blank spot and only saw his own power, his influence, his self. It was not a creative function. It was death. What did they gain, the power people, while they lived off other people's souls like vultures? Did they seem to themselves to be most supreme, most God-like, most wonderful, most cherished? Elizabeth felt that some of the answers lay in her experiences in Botswana. That they were uncovered through an entirely abnormal relationship with two men might not be so much due to her dubious sanity as to the strangeness of the men themselves.

§ *Competing ancestries* Carib: Rhys (2), Walcott (2), Williams, Brodber; *Women and 'madness'* NZSP: Frame

TSITSI DANGAREMBGA (1960 –)

From Nervous Conditions

Taking Sartre's remark 'The condition of native is a nervous condition' (from the Preface to Fanon's *The Wretched of the Earth*) as its epigraph, Dangarembga's novel demonstrates the injurious psychological effects of colonialism, extending Fanon's critique to embody a feminist viewpoint. Here the protagonist Tambu, allowed an elite education when her brother Nhamo dies, describes how she first came to the house of her benefactor, the family patriarch Babamukuru. At this point she idolizes

Babamukuru; later she changes her view and this is anticipated in the way in which Tambu, the more mature narrator, relates the episode. The text contains several complex studies of women in what was then Rhodesian society, among them Maiguru, Babamukuru's educated but submissive wife, and Nyasha, his daughter whose 'nervous condition' leads to a serious eating disorder.

. . . It was painted white. This was one of the less beautiful aspects of that house, one of the less sensible aspects too. There seemed to be no good reason for wasting time and effort, to say nothing of paint, on painting the cheerful red brick that I had seen elsewhere on the mission as we drove up to Babamukuru's house this clinical, antiseptic white. Naturally, though, there was a reason. I found out from Nyasha, who knew all sorts of things, or glued together facts for herself when knowledge was lacking, that this particular house, the headmaster's house, had been built in the early days of the mission. She said that was around the turn of the nineteenth century at a time when the missionaries believed that only white houses were cool enough to be comfortably lived in. Diligently this belief was translated into action. White houses sprang up all over the mission. All those white houses must have been very uninspiring for people whose function was to inspire. Besides, natives were said to respond to colour, so after a while the missionaries began to believe that houses would not overheat, even when they were not painted white, as long as pastel shades were used. They began to paint their houses cream, pale pink, pale blue, pale green. Nyasha liked to embellish this point. 'Imagine,' she used to say, 'how *pretty* it must have looked. All those pinks and blues gleaming away among the white. It must have been so sweet, so very appealing.'

Later, much later, as late as the time that I came to the mission, there was a lot of construction going on. Houses had to be built to shelter the new crop of educated Africans that had been sown in so many Sub A and Sub B night-school classes and was now being abundantly reaped as old boys returned to the mission to contribute by becoming teachers in their turn. Possibly because there was no time for finesse, possibly because the aim was to shelter as many people as quickly as possible, these houses that accommodated the returning teachers remained dark and ruddy.

Nyasha taught me this history with a mischievous glint in her eye. I was like a vacuum then, taking in everything, storing it all in its original state for future inspection. Today I am content that this little paragraph of history as written by Nyasha makes a good story, as likely if not more so than the chapters those very same missionaries were dishing out to us in those mission schools.

At the time that I arrived at the mission, missionaries were living in white houses and in the pale painted houses, but not in the red brick ones. My uncle was the only African living in a white house. We were all very proud of this fact. No, that is not quite right. We were all proud, except Nyasha, who had an egalitarian nature and had taken seriously the lessons about oppression and discrimination that she had learnt first-hand in England.

As the car slowed down to turn into the drive, the pace of my life increased. I packed a lot of living into the few minutes that it took to creep up the drive to the garage. First was the elation from realising that the elegant house ahead of me was indeed my uncle's. Then there was a disappointment. There was a building almost as long as the house if not as high, so that it could very well have been a little house itself and I thought I had made a mistake. I thought I was not going to live in a mansion after all and my spirits went plunging down. But even then there were plenty of things to be happy about. The smooth, stoneless drive ran between squat, robust conifers on one side and a blaze of canna lilies[1] burning scarlet and amber on the other. Plants like that had belonged to the cities. They had belonged to the pages of my language reader, to the yards of Ben and Betty's uncle in town. Now, having seen it for myself because of my Babamukuru's kindness, I too could think of planting things for merrier reasons than the chore of keeping breath in the body. I wrote it down in my head: I would ask Maiguru for some bulbs and plant a bed of those gay lilies on the homestead. In front of the house. Our home would answer well to being cheered up by such lively flowers. Bright and cheery, they had been planted for joy. What a strange idea that was. It was a liberation, the first of many that followed from my transition to the mission.

Then I discovered that Nhamo had not been lying. Babamukuru was indeed a man of consequence however you measured him. The old building that had disappointed me turned out to be a garage. It was built to shelter cars, not people! And this garage sheltered two cars. Not one, but two cars. Nhamo's chorus sang in my head and now it sounded ominous. Its phrases told me something I did not want to know, that my Babamukuru was not the person I had thought he was. He was wealthier than I had thought possible. He was educated beyond books. And he had done it alone. He had pushed up from under the weight of the white man with no strong relative to help him. How had he done it? Having done it, what had he become? A deep valley cracked open. There was no bridge; at the bottom, spiked crags as sharp as spears. I felt separated forever from my uncle.

It all became very depressing and confusing. At first I had been disappointed because I thought the garage was Babamukuru's house. Now I was worried because it wasn't. For the first time I caught sight of endings to my flight from the homestead that were not all happy. I scolded myself severely for having dared this far in the first place. Hadn't I known, I asked myself, that Babamukuru was a big-hearted man? That didn't make me anything special. Or even deserving. I didn't have anything to do with my uncle's kindness. He would have taken in any poor, needy relative, and to prove it I was only here because my brother had died.

Had I really thought, I continued callously, that these other-wordly relations of mine could live with anyone as ignorant and dirty as myself? I, who

---

1 Plant with bright yellow, red or orange flowers and ornamental leaves.

was so ignorant that I had not been able to read the signs in their clothes which dared not deteriorate or grow too tight in spite of their well-fleshed bodies, or in the accents of their speech, which were poised and smooth and dropped like foreign gemstones from their tongues. All these signs stated very matter-of-factly that we were not of a kind. I deserved to suffer, I threatened myself, for having been too proud to see that Babamukuru could only be so charitable to our branch of the family because we were so low. He was kind because of the difference.

With a sigh I slid into a swamp of self-pity. My finely tuned survival system set off its alarm at once, warning me to avoid that trap, but I was lost. I could see no path of escape except the one that led back to the homestead. But that, I knew, would do me no good because I was burning up with wanting to escape from there. I did make an effort to improve my state of mind. I scolded myself strongly for not appreciating Babamukuru's concern for my family and me. I tried to call up my courage by imagining the fine grades I would make, which was what mattered, why I had come to the mission in the first place. I must have been much more frightened by the strangeness and awesomeness of my new position than I knew, because none of these tactics worked. I climbed out of the car much less hopefully than I had climbed into it, and followed Babamukuru uneasily as he walked towards the house.

A huge, hairy hound appeared in front of me from nowhere. It leapt out of thin air and scared me to death. Its black lips wrinkled up to show piercing incisors spiking out of gums that were even blacker than its lips. Its ears flattened themselves so far back on its head that its eyes stretched upwards in a demonic squint. Its sudden appearance made it seem all the more sinister. I could not help it. I yelped, which annoyed the beast and set it barking to summon its pink-eyed companion. That albino hound was even more unsettling. Everything about it was either pink or white. So pink were its gums that it took very little for my unhappy mind to conjure up blood and have it seep through the animal's skin to stain its pale teeth red. I was in a bad state or else I would have noticed the chains that bound them to their kennel and the fence that enclosed them in their pen. To me they were loose, ferocious guardians of the gates to this kingdom, this kingdom that I should not have been entering. Their lust for my blood was justified: they knew I did not belong.

Anna came to my rescue. 'If they were loose,' she called cheerfully, coming round the back of the house to greet me, 'they would have chewed you to pieces by now. Welcome, Tambu, welcome. It's good to see you again. That's why they are tied, these dogs. They aren't dogs to play about with, these.'

Tied . . . Tied . . . Ah, yes, they were tied! Perspective restored itself. I saw the chains and the fence. My knees calcified again, speech returned. I laughed nervously and tried to tell Anna how silly I had been not to realise that I was safe, but one did not need to do much talking when Anna was around. 'What about luggage? Where is it?' she chattered on. 'But sometimes they aren't tied – just think! – because they go off and we can't find them. When that happens, ha-a!, you don't catch me outside, not even to hang the laundry. But it's good you have come. I've been thinking of you. Enter, enter,' she invited pleasantly, holding the back door open for me.

I was not half-way through the door before Nyasha was on me with a big hug, which I understood, and a kiss on both cheeks, which I did not. She was excited to see me, she was pleased she said. I was surprised to see her in such high spirits, pleasantly surprised, since this was not the cousin I had been steeling myself to meet. Believing my words, I hugged her back and told her that I too had been looking forward to her company.

Nyasha had a lot to say, during which time Anna disappeared to tell Maiguru that I had arrived. Nyasha was baking a cake, she said, for her brother, who was going back to his boarding school next day. The cake was ready to go into the oven, the weather was hot: the cake would rise in the mixing-bowl and flop in the baking-tin if it was not put to bake immediately. Anna would show me where to go. Nyasha disappeared back into the kitchen, taking with her some of the security that had settled on me with her warm welcome. I grew disapproving again of my cousin's bad manners and hoped that she would not carry on like that, because in the few minutes of our conversation I had seen that here at the mission at least I might have my old friend back.

She was very busy, dextrously greasing and flouring a cake tin and pouring in the batter. Not wanting to impose I busied myself with inspecting the kitchen. It looked very sophisticated to me at the time. But looking back, I remember that the cooker had only three plates, none of which was a ring; that the kettle was not electric; that the refrigerator was a bulky paraffin-powered affair. The linoleum was old, its blue and white pattern fading to patches of red where the paint had worn off and patches of black where feet had scuffed up the old flooring at its seams and water had dripped from hands and vegetables and crockery to create a stubborn black scum. The kitchen window was not curtained; a pane of glass was missing. This missing pane caused many problems because through the hole a draught blew, mischievously lowering temperatures in the oven so that buns and cakes were never quite light unless you could close the kitchen door and stop anybody from opening it, blocking the draught in its path. The broken window, the draught and its consequences were particularly annoying to Maiguru.

'It surprises me!' she used to mutter whenever she battled with oven temperatures. 'You'd think people would find time to fix windows in their own homes. Yet they don't. Ts! It surprises me.'

Later, as experience sharpened my perception of such things, I saw too that the colours were not co-ordinated. The green and pink walls – it was the fashion to have one wall a different colour from the others – contrasted harshly with each other and with the lino. It pleased me, though, to see that the kitchen was clean. What dirt could be removed from the lino was removed regularly by thorough scrubbing with a strong ammonia cleaner, which was efficient but chapped your hands much more roughly than ash dissolved in water from Nyamarira ever did. The enamel of the cooker and the plastic of the fridge, although not shining, were white, and the kitchen sink gleamed greyly. This lack of brilliance was due, I discovered years later when television came to the mission, to the use of scouring powders which, though they sterilised 99 per cent of a household, were harsh and scratched fine surfaces. When I found this out, I realised that Maiguru, who had watched television in England, must have known about the dulling effects of these scourers and about the brilliance that could be achieved by using the more gentle alternatives. By that time I knew something about budgets as well, notably their inelasticity. It dawned on me then that Maiguru's dull sink was not a consequence of slovenliness, as the advertisers would have had us believe, but a necessity.

Anna came back with the news that Maiguru was resting. She would be with me in the time that it took to get out of bed and dressed. She would show me to the living-room, where I was to wait for my aunt.

Hoping that it was not illness that had put my aunt in bed at that time of the day, I followed Anna to the living-room, where I made myself comfortable on a sofa. It was impossible not to notice that this sofa was twice as long and deep and soft as the one in the house at home. I took stock of my surroundings, noting the type, texture and shape of the furniture, its colours and its arrangement. My education had already begun, and it was with a pragmatic eye that I surveyed Maiguru's sitting-room: I would own a home like this one day; I would need to know how to furnish it.

Since I had entered my uncle's house through the back door, and so had moved up a gradient of glamour from the kitchen, through the dining-room to the living-room, I did not benefit from the full impact of the elegance of that living-room, with its fitted carpet of deep, green pile, tastefully mottled with brown and gold, and chosen to match the pale green walls (one slightly lighter than the other three according to the fashion). The heavy gold curtains flowing voluptuously to the floor, the four-piece lounge suite upholstered in glowing brown velvet, the lamps with their tasselled shades, the sleek bookcases full of leather-bound and hard-covered volumes of erudition, lost a little, but only a very little, of their effect.

Had I entered from the driveway, through the verandah and the front door, as visitors whom it was necessary to impress would enter, the taste and muted elegance of that room would have taken my breath away. As it was, having seen the kitchen, and the dining-room, which was much smarter than the kitchen, with shiny new linoleum covering every square inch of floor and so expertly laid that the seams between the strips were practically invisible, I was a little better prepared for what came next. This was not altogether a bad thing, because the full force of that opulent living-room would have been too much for me. I remember feeling slightly intimidated by the dining-room, with its large, oval table spacious enough to seat eight people taking up the centre of the room. That table, its shape and size, had a lot of say about the amount, the calorie content, the complement of vitamins and minerals, the relative proportions of fat, carbohydrate and protein of the food that would be consumed at it. No one who ate from such a table could fail to grow fat and healthy. Pushed up against a window, and there were several windows flanked by plain, sensible sun-filters and sombre, blue cotton curtains, was a display cabinet. Glossy and dark as the table, it displayed on greenish glass shelves the daintiest, most delicate china I had ever seen – fine, translucent cups and saucers, teapots and jugs and bowls, all covered in roses. Pink on white, gold on white, red on white. Roses. Old English, Tea, Old Country. Roses. These tea-sets looked so delicate it was obvious they would disintegrate the minute you so much as poured the tea into a cup or weighted a plate down with a bun. No wonder they had been shut away. I fervently hoped I would not be expected to eat or drink from them. I was relieved to find out in due course that everyone was a bit afraid of those charmingly expensive and fragile tea-sets, so they were only ever admired and shown off to guests.

If I was daunted by Maiguru's dainty porcelain cups, the living-room, as I have said, would have finished me off had I not been inoculated by the gradient I have talked of, although calling it a glamour gradient is not really the right way to describe it. This increase in comfort from kitchen to living-room was a common feature of all the teachers' houses at the mission. It had more to do with means and priorities than taste. Babamukuru's taste was excellent, so that where he could afford to indulge it, the results were striking. The opulence of his living-room was very strong stuff, overwhelming to someone who had first crawled and then toddled and finally walked over dung floors. Comfortable it was, but overwhelming nevertheless. Some strategy had to be devised to prevent all this splendour from distracting me in the way that my brother had been distracted. Usually in such dire straits I used my thinking strategy. I was very proud of my thinking strategy. It was meant to put me above the irrational levels of my character and enable me to proceed from pure, rational premises. Today, though, it did not work.

Every corner of Babamukuru's house – every shiny surface, every soft contour and fold – whispered its own insistent message of comfort and ease and rest so tantalisingly, so seductively, that to pay any attention to it, to think about it at all, would have been my downfall. The only alternative was to ignore it. I remained as aloof and unimpressed as possible.

This was not easy, because my aunt took a long time to come from her bedroom. I put this interval to good use in building up my defences. I had only to think of my mother, with Netsai and Rambanai superimposed in the background, to remember why and how I had come to be at the mission. And having seen how easily it could happen, I judged my brother less harshly. Instead, I became more aware of how necessary it was to remain steadfast. Then, to make sure that I was not being soft and sentimental in revising my opinion of Nhamo, I had to survey my surroundings again to see whether they really were potent enough to have had such a devastating effect on him, thus exposing myself again to all the possible consequences. I triumphed. I was not seduced.

You might think that there was no real danger. You might think that, after all, these were only rooms decorated with the sort of accessories that the local interpretations of British interior-decor magazines were describing as standard, and nothing threatening in that. But really the situation was not so simple. Although I was vague at the time and could not have described my circumstances so aptly, the real situation was this: Babamukuru was God, therefore I had arrived in Heaven. I was in danger of becoming an angel, or at the very least a saint, and forgetting how ordinary humans existed – from minute to minute and from hand to mouth. The absence of dirt was proof of the other-wordly nature of my new home. I knew, had known all my life, that living was dirty and I had been disappointed by the fact. I had often helped my mother to resurface the kitchen floor with dung. I knew, for instance, that rooms where people slept exuded peculiarly human smells just as the goat pen smelt goaty and the cattle kraal[2] bovine. It was common knowledge among the younger girls at school that the older girls menstruated into sundry old rags which they washed and reused and washed again. I knew, too, that the fact of menstruation was a shamefully unclean secret that should not be allowed to contaminate immaculate male ears by indiscreet reference to this type of dirt in their presence. Yet at a glance it was difficult to perceive dirt in Maiguru's house. After a while, as the novelty wore off, you began to see that the antiseptic sterility that my aunt and uncle strove for could not be attained beyond an illusory level because the buses that passed through the mission, according to an almost regular schedule, rolled up a storm of fine red dust which perversely settled in corners and on surfaces of rooms and armchairs and bookshelves. When the dust was obvious it was removed, but enough of it always remained invisibly to creep up your nose and give you hay fever, thus restoring your sense of proportion by reminding you that this was not heaven. Sneezing and wiping my nose on the back of my hand, I became confident that I would not go the same way as my brother.

§ *Childhood* Gurnah; Carib: Edgell, Senior; *Colonial education* Ngugi (2); Carib: Sparrow; *Women's colonization* Head; Carib: Brodber, Nichols, Breeze

---

2 Enclosure.

North Africa

JAMAL MAHJOUB (1960–)

From Navigation of a Rainmaker

Navigation of a Rainmaker confronts the harsher realities of contemporary life in North Africa from the perspective of its part-British, part-Sudanese protagonist, Tanner. Tanner goes to Khartoum on a personal odyssey, but finds himself caught up in the suffering, occasioned by famine and war, that is all around him. Like Lionel Froad, the hero of Denis Williams's *Other Leopards*, he travels south into the desert heartland and the novel moves uncompromisingly towards a tragic climax. Here in the opening chapter, Mahjoub establishes the mood of the whole novel, as he shows an age-old way of life threatened by both natural and technological forces.

In a place such as this: where the wind turns on silent stone, where, if you pause for a moment in that instant of turmoil when the dawn sweeps the cold night back into the stagnant stars, you can smell the emptiness that lingers here. It waits for the sullen heat of day to arrive. Gently the sun comes creeping over the edge of the blue earth. The horizon is a line of red slashed into the cobalt sky, still sad and hollow from the night before. The elusive stars vanish slowly into the monochromatic semi-arch of a halo that announces the sun. As it steals into the melting blue, so the light changes: burning from red to a furious incandescent white. So the silent dawn air is replaced once again by a layer of pure heat that hangs over the sand like a blanket.

The old man watched the sun rise, just as he did every morning. He enjoyed being alone at this time of day, finding comfort in the habit just as he found peace in the solitude. Today, though, he found himself praying that nature would not follow its course, hoping that somehow the habit could be broken. As he looked down from the low outcrop the desert began to come to life; the sand began to shimmer and shift in its tracks and the wind hummed through the thorn bushes, making them rustle with delight.

The desert is a broken place where the wind and the sand and the stars live. Anything else is no longer welcome. The desert has seasons just like any other part of the world. Further to the west of the place where the old man watched the day beginning, the rains had come and turned the land green and the ground would soon be dotted with bush and wild trees. The wells would fill with water so that everyone could drink their fill; life could go on. The old man had seen drought before. In his sixty years of nomadic life he had seen waterholes dry up like a bone, waterholes that people swore would never dry out and which no one could remember having dried out before. The desert was full of surprises; the rains pleased themselves. Some years it didn't please them to come and who could argue with that? Perhaps only Allah. The old man knew this land, he understood the way it breathed. He could feel the steady beat of its heart through the soles of his feet worn hard by the rocks and the sand. He and his family were on their way south and in all his life had had never seen so many abandoned camps; the whole country was on the move. The rains were very late – even the deepest holes had run dry. It had been a big mistake to be caught this far north. The old man knew that they would have to travel as fast as they could to the more populated areas, to the water pipes and the towns.

Picking up his wooden staff polished smooth by years of use, the old man turned away from the sunrise towards the camp. There were already signs of movement from the *damar* – smoke was beginning to rise in curling wraiths from a small fire. He started down the rocky ground towards the shelter. His leather sandals slapped against his hard feet, his legs – frail-looking but sinewy and strong like coiled springs – bending with the movement.

The tents were set facing east in the hard, gravel-covered ground. The old man went to each of the three tents in turn and called out to the occupants while standing in the doorway with his back to the entrance. They were his family, all these people: his wife and children, her sister and her husband, their children. When he'd roused them he went back to join his brother-in-law who stood by the fire fanning the flames with a piece of cardboard.

The procession got under way with the usual bustle of activity, though every day, thought the old man, it seemed to take longer. They were tired, all of them. Finally the march started. The old man walked at the front, leading the first camel which carried his wife and her belongings. They were heading south and east on a path which they rarely used. Each well they had come to was dry. Everyone they met told the same story. The land was drying up, shrivelling like a leaf in front of their eyes. They carried on from one place to the next, but it was always the same story.

The old man and his family stopped at midday. The camels could go for maybe ten days without water but there was no point in exhausting them by driving them too hard. There was a good chance, with this continued hard walking, that they would go lame. The travellers couldn't stop for a day, and they couldn't afford one of the animals going lame. That was the last thing they wanted now. They constructed a shelter and sat down to rest a little before the cool of late afternoon when, said the old man, they would do another hour's walking before stopping for the night.

He leaned back with his head on his arm and closed his eyes. Just then a Mig jet roared low overhead, the screech of the jet engines jolting him awake. In an instant the camp was filled with the excited chatter of the children as they pointed at the black dot disappearing into the sun.

Behind them a dust-storm began to gather.

§ *Sudanese journeying* Carib: Williams

Part II

AUSTRALIA

CHARLES HARPUR (1813–68)

A Mid-Summer Noon in the Australian Forest

Not a bird disturbs the air,
There is quiet everywhere;
Over plains and over woods
What a mighty stillness broods.

5   Even the grasshoppers keep
Where the coolest shadows sleep;
Even the busy ants are found
Resting in their pebbled mound;
Even the locust clingeth now
10 In silence to the barky bough:
And over hills and over plains
Quiet, vast and slumbrous, reigns.

Only there's a drowsy humming
From yon warm lagoon slow coming:
15 'Tis the dragon-hornet – see!
All bedaubed resplendently
With yellow on a tawny ground –
Each rich spot nor square nor round,
But rudely heart-shaped, as it were
20 The blurred and hasty impress there,
Of a vermeil-crusted seal
Dusted o'er with golden meal:
Only there's a droning where
Yon bright beetle gleams the air –
25 Gleams it in its droning flight
With a slanting track of light,
Till rising in the sunshine higher,
Its shards flame out like gems on fire.

Every other thing is still,
30 Save the ever wakeful rill,
Whose cool murmur only throws
A cooler comfort round Repose;
Or some ripple in the sea
Of leafy boughs, where, lazily,
35 Tired Summer, in her forest bower
Turning with the noontide hour,
Heaves a slumbrous breath, ere she
Once more slumbers peacefully.

---

21 **vermeil**: vermilion (poetic).   28 **shards**: wing-cases.

O 'tis easeful here to lie
40   Hidden from Noon's scorching eye,
In this grassy cool recess
Musing thus of Quietness.

§ *Landscape and language* Clarke; Can: Traill

MARCUS CLARKE (1846–81)

Preface to Poems of the Late Adam Lindsay Gordon

The poems of Gordon have an interest beyond the mere personal one which his friends attach to his name. Written, as they were, at odd times and leisure moments of a stirring and adventurous life, it is not to be wondered at if they are unequal or unfinished. The astonishment of those who knew the man, and can gauge the capacity of this city to foster poetic instinct, is, that such work was ever produced here at all. Intensely nervous, and feeling much of that shame at the exercise of the higher intelligence which besets those who are known to be renowned in field sports, Gordon produced his poems shyly, scribbled them on scraps of paper, and sent them anonymously to magazines. It was not until he discovered one morning that everybody knew a couplet or two of 'How we Beat the Favourite' that he consented to forego his anonymity and appear in the unsuspected character of a versemaker. The success of his republished 'collected' poems gave him courage, and the unreserved praise which greeted *Bush Ballads* should have urged him to forget or to conquer those evil promptings which, unhappily, brought about his untimely death.[1]

Adam Lindsay Gordon was the son of an officer in the English army, and was educated at Woolwich, in order that he might follow the profession of his family. At the time when he was a cadet there was no sign of either of the two great wars which were about to call forth the strength of English arms, and, like many other men of his day, he quitted his prospects of service, and emigrated. He went to South Australia and started as a sheep farmer. His efforts were attended with failure. He lost his capital, and, owning nothing but a love for horsemanship and a head full of Browning and Shelley, plunged into the varied life which gold-mining, 'overlanding,'[2] and cattle-driving affords. From this experience he emerged to light in Melbourne as the best amateur steeplechase rider in the colonies. The victory he won for Major Baker in 1868, when he rode Babbler for the Cup Steeplechase, made him popular, and the almost simultaneous publication of his last volume of poems gave him welcome entrance to the houses of all who had

---

1 See end of paragraph 2.   2 Droving or going a long distance overland.

pretensions to literary taste. The reputation of the book spread to England, and Major Whyte-Melville did not disdain to place the lines of the dashing Australian author at the head of his own dashing descriptions of sporting scenery. Unhappily, the melancholy which Gordon's friends had with pain observed increased daily, and in the full flood of his success, with congratulations pouring upon him from every side, he was found dead in the heather near his home with a bullet from his own rifle in his brain.

I do not purpose to criticize the volumes which these few lines of preface introduce to the reader. The influence of Browning and of Swinburne upon the writer's taste is plain. There is plainly visible also, however, a keen sense for natural beauty and a manly admiration for healthy living. If in 'Ashtaroth' and 'Bellona' we recognize the swing of a familiar metre, in such poems as the 'Sick Stockrider' we perceive the genuine poetic instinct united to a very clear perception of the loveliness of duty and of labour.

> 'Twas merry in the glowing morn, among the gleaming grass,
>> To wander as we've wandered many a mile,
> And blow the cool tobacco cloud, and watch the white wreaths pass,
>> Sitting loosely in the saddle all the while;
> 'Twas merry 'mid the blackwoods, when we spied the station roofs,
>> To wheel the wild scrub cattle at the yard,
> With a running fire of stockwhips, and a fiery run of hoofs,
>> Oh! the hardest day was never then too hard!
>
> Aye! we had a glorious gallop after 'Starlight' and his gang,
>> When they bolted from Sylvester's on the flat;
> How the sun-dried reed-beds crackled, how the flint-strewn ranges rang
>> To the strokes of 'Mountaineer' and 'Acrobat';
> Hard behind them in the timber, harder still across the heath,
>> Close behind them through the tea-tree scrub we dash'd;
> And the golden-tinted fern leaves, how they rustled underneath!
>> And the honeysuckle osiers, how they crash'd!

This is genuine. There is no 'poetic evolution from the depths of internal consciousness' here. The writer has ridden his ride as well as written it.

The student of these unpretending volumes will be repaid for his labour. He will find in them something very like the beginnings of a national school of Australian poetry. In historic Europe, where every rood of ground is hallowed in legend and in song, the least imaginative can find food for sad and sweet reflection. When strolling at noon down an English country lane, lounging at sunset by some ruined chapel on the margin of an Irish lake, or watching the mists of morning unveil Ben Lomond, we feel all the charm which springs from association with the past. Soothed, saddened, and cheered by turns, we partake of the varied moods which belong not so much to ourselves as to the dead men who, in old days, sung, suffered, or conquered in the scenes which we survey. But this our native or adopted land has no past, no story. No poet speaks to us. Do we need a poet to interpret

Nature's teachings, we must look into our own hearts, if perchance we may find a poet there.

What is the dominant note of Australian scenery? That which is the dominant note of Edgar Allan Poe's poetry – Weird Melancholy. A poem like 'L'Allegro'[3] could never be written by an Australian. It is too airy, too sweet, too freshly happy. The Australian mountain forests are funereal, secret, stern. Their solitude is desolation. They seem to stifle, in their black gorges, a story of sullen despair. No tender sentiment is nourished in their shade. In other lands the dying year is mourned, the falling leaves drop lightly on his bier. In the Australian forests no leaves fall. The savage winds shout among the rock clefts. From the melancholy gum strips of white bark hang and rustle. The very animal life of these frowning hills is either grotesque or ghostly. Great grey kangaroos hop noiselessly over the coarse grass. Flights of white cockatoos stream out, shrieking like evil souls. The sun suddenly sinks, and the mopokes[4] burst out into horrible peals of semi-human laughter. The natives aver that, when night comes, from out the bottomless depth of some lagoon the Bunyip[5] rises, and, in form like monstrous sea-calf, drags his loathsome length from out the ooze. From a corner of the silent forest rises a dismal chant, and around a fire dance natives painted like skeletons. All is fear-inspiring and gloomy. No bright fancies are linked with the memories of the mountains. Hopeless explorers have named them out of their sufferings – Mount Misery, Mount Dreadful, Mount Despair. As when among sylvan scenes in places

> Made green with the running of rivers,
> And gracious with temperate air,

the soul is soothed and satisfied, so, placed before the frightful grandeur of these barren hills, it drinks in their sentiment of defiant ferocity, and is steeped in bitterness.

Australia has rightly been named the Land of the Dawning. Wrapped in the mist of early morning, her history looms vague and gigantic. The lonely horseman riding between the moonlight and the day sees vast shadows creeping across the shelterless and silent plains, hears strange noises in the primeval forest, where flourishes a vegetation long dead in other lands, and feels, despite his fortune, that the trim utilitarian civilization which bred him shrinks into insignificance beside the contemptuous grandeur of forest and ranges coeval with an age in which European scientists have cradled his own race.

There is a poem in every form of tree or flower, but the poetry which lives in the trees and flowers of Australia differs from those of other countries. Europe is the home of knightly songs, of bright deeds and clear morning thought. Asia sinks beneath the weighty recollections of her past magnificence, as the Suttee sinks, jewel-burdened, upon the corpse of dead

---

3 'The happy man'; early poem by Milton.   4 A type of small brown owl.   5 A fabulous monster of swamps, lagoons and billabongs in Aboriginal mythology.

grandeur, destructive even in its death. America swiftly hurries on her way, rapid, glittering, insatiable even as one of her own giant waterfalls. From the jungles of Africa, and the creeper-tangled groves of the islands of the South, arise, from the glowing hearts of a thousand flowers, heavy and intoxicating odours – the Upas[6]-poison which dwells in barbaric sensuality. In Australia alone is to be found the Grotesque, the Weird, the strange scribblings of nature learning how to write. Some see no beauty in our trees without shade, our flowers without perfume, our birds who cannot fly, and our beasts who have not yet learned to walk on all fours. But the dweller in the wilderness acknowledges the subtle charm of this fantastic land of monstrosities. He becomes familiar with the beauty of loneliness. Whispered to by the myriad tongues of the wilderness, he learns the language of the barren and the uncouth, and can read the hieroglyphs of haggard gum-trees, blown into odd shapes, distorted with fierce hot winds, or cramped with cold nights, when the Southern Cross freezes in a cloudless sky of icy blue. The phantasmagoria of that wild dreamland termed the Bush interprets itself, and the Poet of our desolation begins to comprehend why free Esau loved his heritage of desert sand better than all the bountiful richness of Egypt.[7]

§ *Landscape and language* Harpur; Can: Traill

ADAM LINDSAY GORDON (1833–70)

The Sick Stockrider

> Hold hard, Ned! Lift me down once more, and lay me in
>   the shade.
>   Old man, you've had your work cut out to guide
> Both horses, and to hold me in the saddle when I sway'd,
>   All through the hot, slow, sleepy, silent ride.
> 5   The dawn at 'Moorabinda' was a mist rack dull and dense,
>   The sunrise was a sullen, sluggish lamp;
>   I was dozing in the gateway at Arbuthnot's bound'ry fence,
>   I was dreaming on the Limestone cattle camp.
> We crossed the creek at Carricksford, and sharply through
>   the haze,
> 10   And suddenly the sun shot flaming forth;
>   To southward lay 'Katâwa', with the sandpeaks all ablaze,
>   And the flush'd fields of Glen Lomond lay to north.
> Now westward winds the bridle path that leads to
>   Lindisfarm,

6 Javanese tree with poisonous sap. 7 See *Genesis*, xxv ff.

And yonder looms the double-headed Bluff;
15 From the far side of the first hill, when the skies are clear
      and calm,
    You can see Sylvester's woolshed fair enough.
    Five miles we used to call it from our homestead to the
      place
    Where the big tree spans the roadway like an arch;
    'Twas here we ran the dingo down that gave us such a
      chase
20   Eight years ago – or was it nine? – last March.

    'Twas merry in the glowing morn, among the gleaming
      grass,
    To wander as we've wandered many a mile,
    And blow the cool tobacco cloud, and watch the white
      wreaths pass,
    Sitting loosely in the saddle all the while.
25 'Twas merry 'mid the blackwoods, when we spied the
      station roofs,
    To wheel the wild scrub cattle at the yard,
    With a running fire of stockwhips and a fiery run of hoofs;
    Oh! the hardest day was never then too hard!

    Aye! we had a glorious gallop after 'Starlight' and his
      gang,
30   When they bolted from Sylvester's on the flat;
    How the sun-dried reed-beds crackled, how the flint-strewn
      ranges rang
    To the strokes of 'Mountaineer' and 'Acrobat'.
    Hard behind them in the timber, harder still across the
      heath,
    Close beside them through the tea-tree scrub we dash'd;
35 And the golden-tinted fern leaves, how they rustled
      underneath!
    And the honeysuckle osiers, how they crash'd!

    We led the hunt throughout, Ned, on the chestnut and the
      grey,
    And the troopers were three hundred yards behind,
    While we emptied our six-shooters on the bushrangers at
      bay,
40   In the creek with stunted box-tree for a blind!
    There you grappled with the leader, man to man and
      horse to horse,

---

39 bushrangers: outlaws living in bush.

And you roll'd together when the chestnut rear'd;
He blazed away and missed you in that shallow water-
  course –
A narrow shave – his powder singed your beard!
45 In these hours when life is ebbing, how those days when
  life was young
Come back to us; how clearly I recall
Even the yarns Jack Hall invented, and the songs Jem
  Roper sung;
And where are now Jem Roper and Jack Hall?
Aye! nearly all our comrades of the old colonial school,
50 Our ancient boon companions, Ned, are gone;
Hard livers for the most part, somewhat reckless as a rule,
  It seems that you and I are left alone.

There was Hughes, who got in trouble through that
  business with the cards,
  It matters little what became of him;
55 But a steer ripp'd up MacPherson in the Cooraminta
  yards,
  And Sullivan was drown'd at Sink-or-swim.

And Mostyn – poor Frank Mostyn – died at last a fearful
  wreck,
  In 'the horrors', at the Upper Wandinong;
And Carisbrooke, the rider, at the Horsefall broke his neck,
60 Faith! the wonder was he saved his neck so long!
Ah! those days and nights we squander'd at the Logans'
  in the glen –
The Logans, man and wife, have long been dead.
Elsie's tallest girl seems taller than your little Elsie then;
  And Ethel is a woman grown and wed.

65 I've had my share of pastime, and I've done my share of
  toil,
  And life is short – the longest life a span;
I care not now to tarry for the corn or for the oil,
  Or for the wine that maketh glad the heart of man.
For good undone and gifts misspent and resolutions vain,
70 'Tis somewhat late to trouble. This I know –
I should live the same life over, if I had to live again;
  And the chances are I go where most men go.

---

58 'the horrors': fit of depression, especially as in *delirium tremens*.

The deep blue skies wax dusky, and the tall green trees
    grow dim,
    The sward beneath me seems to heave and fall;
75   And sickly, smoky shadows through the sleepy sunlight
    swim,
    And on the very sun's face weave their pall.
Let me slumber in the hollow where the wattle blossoms
    wave,
    With never stone or rail to fence my bed;
Should the sturdy station children pull the bush flowers on
    my grave,
80   I may chance to hear them romping overhead.

§ *Bush ballads* Paterson; *Mateship* Lawler, Seymour; NZSP: Sargeson;
National/male mythologies Lawson (1, 2), Paterson, Lawler, Seymour, Drewe

HENRY KENDALL (1839–82)

The Last of His Tribe

He crouches, and buries his face on his knees,
    And hides in the dark of his hair;
For he cannot look up to the storm-smitten trees,
    Or think of the loneliness there:
5   Of the loss and the loneliness there.

The wallaroos grope through the tufts of the grass,
    And turn to their covers for fear;
But he sits in the ashes and lets them pass
    Where the boomerangs sleep with the spear:
10   With the nullah, the sling, and the spear.

Uloola, behold him! The thunder that breaks
    On the tops of the rocks with the rain,
And the wind which drives up with the salt of the lakes,
    Have made him a hunter again:
15   A hunter and fisher again.

For his eyes have been full with a smouldering thought;
    But he dreams of the hunts of yore,

---

74 sward: turf; expanse of short grass.   **77 wattle**: Australian acacia.
6 wallaroos: large, brownish-black kangaroos.   **10 nullah**: hardwood club.

And of foes that he sought, and of fights that he fought
With those who will battle no more:
20   Who will go to the battle no more.

It is well that the water which tumbles and fills
Goes moaning and moaning along;
For an echo rolls out from the sides of the hills,
And he starts at a wonderful song:
25   At the sounds of a wonderful song.

And he sees, through the rents of the scattering fogs,
The corroboree warlike and grim,
And the lubra who sat by the fire on the logs,
To watch, like a mourner, for him:
30   Like a mother and mourner, for him.

Will he go in his sleep from these desolate lands,
Like a chief, to the rest of his race,
With the honey-voiced woman who beckons, and stands.
And gleams like a Dream in his face –
35   Like a marvellous Dream in his face?

§ *Elegies for Aboriginality* Oodgeroo; Can: Armstrong; NZSP: Hyde, Ihimaera
(1)

A. B. 'BANJO' PATERSON (1864 –1941)

The Man from Snowy River

There was movement at the station, for the word had
    passed around
That the colt from old Regret had got away,
And had joined the wild bush horses – he was worth a
    thousand pound,
So all the cracks had gathered to the fray.
5 All the tried and noted riders from the stations near and
    far
Had mustered at the homestead overnight,
For the bushmen love hard riding where the wild bush
    horses are,
And the stock-horse snuffs the battle with delight.

---

27 **corroboree**: Aboriginal ceremonial dance.   28 **lubra**: Aboriginal woman.

There was Harrison, who made his pile when Pardon won
    the cup,
10   The old man with his hair as white as snow;
But few could ride beside him when his blood was fairly
    up –
    He would go wherever horse and man could go.
And Clancy of the Overflow came down to lend a hand,
    No better horseman ever held the reins;
15   For never horse could throw him while the saddle-girths
    would stand –
    He learnt to ride while droving on the plains.

And one was there, a stripling on a small and weedy beast;
    He was something like a racehorse undersized,
With a touch of Timor pony – three parts thoroughbred
    at least –
20   And such as are by mountain horsemen prized.
He was hard and tough and wiry – just the sort that won't
    say die –
    There was courage in his quick impatient tread;
And he bore the badge of gameness in his bright and fiery
    eye,
    And the proud and lofty carriage of his head.

25   But still so slight and weedy, one would doubt his power
    to stay,
    And the old man said, 'That horse will never do
For a long and tiring gallop – lad, you'd better stop away,
    Those hills are far too rough for such as you.'
So he waited, sad and wistful – only Clancy stood his
    friend –
30   'I think we ought to let him come,' he said;
'I warrant he'll be with us when he's wanted at the end,
    For both his horse and he are mountain bred.

'He hails from Snowy River, up by Kosciusko's side,
    Where the hills are twice as steep and twice as rough;
35   Where a horse's hoofs strike firelight from the flint stones
    every stride,
    The man that holds his own is good enough.
And the Snowy River riders on the mountains make their
    home.
    Where the river runs those giant hills between;

---

33 Kosciusko: Australia's highest mountain (2,229 m./7,316 ft.) in South-East New South Wales.

I have seen full many horsemen since I first commenced to
    roam,
40   But nowhere yet such horsemen have I seen.'

So he went; they found the horses by the big mimosa
    clump,
They raced away towards the mountain's brow,
And the old man gave his orders, 'Boys, go at them from
    the jump,
No use to try for fancy riding now.
45   And, Clancy, you must wheel them, try and wheel them to
    the right.
Ride boldly, lad, and never fear the spills,
For never yet was rider that could keep the mob in sight,
If once they gain the shelter of those hills.'

So Clancy rode to wheel them – he was racing on the
    wing
50   Where the best and boldest riders take their place,
And he raced his stock-horse past them, and he made the
    ranges ring
With the stockwhip, as he met them face to face.
Then they halted for a moment, while he swung the
    dreaded lash,
But they saw their well-loved mountain full in view,
55   And they charged beneath the stockwhip with a sharp and
    sudden dash,
And off into the mountain scrub they flew.

Then fast the horsemen followed, where the gorges deep
    and black
Resounded to the thunder of their tread,
And the stockwhips woke the echoes, and they fiercely
    answered back
60   From cliffs and crags that beetled overhead.
And upward, ever upward, the wild horses held their way,
Where mountain ash and kurrajong grew wide;
And the old man muttered fiercely, 'We may bid the mob
    good day,
No man can hold them down the other side.'
65   When they reached the mountain's summit, even Clancy
    took a pull –
It well might make the boldest hold their breath;

---

62 kurrajong: tree with tough inner bark.

The wild hop scrub grew thickly, and the hidden ground
    was full
  Of wombat holes, and any slip was death.
But the man from Snowy River let the pony have his head,
70   And he swung his stockwhip round and gave a cheer,
And he raced him down the mountain like a torrent down
    its bed,
  While the others stood and watched in very fear.

He sent the flint-stones flying, but the pony kept his feet,
  He cleared the fallen timber in his stride,
75 And the man from Snowy River never shifted in his seat –
  It was grand to see that mountain horseman ride.
Through the stringy barks and saplings, on the rough and
    broken ground,
  Down the hillside at a racing pace he went;
And he never drew the bridle till he landed safe and sound
80 At the bottom of that terrible descent.

He was right among the horses as they climbed the farther
    hill,
  And the watchers on the mountain, standing mute,
Saw him ply the stockwhip fiercely; he was right among
    them still,
  As he raced across the clearing in pursuit.
85 Then they lost him for a moment, where two mountain
    gullies met
  In the ranges – but a final glimpse reveals
On a dim and distant hillside the wild horses racing yet,
  With the man from Snowy River at their heels.

And he ran them single-handed till their sides were white
    with foam;
90 He followed like a bloodhound on their track,
Till they halted, cowed and beaten; then he turned their
    heads for home,
  And alone and unassisted brought them back.
But his hardy mountain pony he could scarcely raise a trot,
  He was blood from hip to shoulder from the spur;
95 But his pluck was still undaunted, and his courage fiery hot,
  For never yet was mountain horse a cur.

And down by Kosciusko, where the pine-clad ridges raise
  Their torn and rugged battlements on high,

---

77 **stringy barks**: eucalyptus with tough, fibrous bark.

Where the air is clear as crystal, and the white stars fairly
    blaze
100   At midnight in the cold and frosty sky,
And where around the Overflow the reed-beds sweep and
    sway
To the breezes, and the rolling plains are wide,
The Man from Snowy River is a household word today,
And the stockmen tell the story of his ride.

§ *Bush ballads* Gordon; *Mateship* Gordon; Lawler, Seymour; NZSP:
Sargeson; *National/male mythologies* Lawson (1, 2), Lawler, Seymour, Drewe

HENRY LAWSON (1867–1922)

1: The Drover's Wife

The two-roomed house is built of round timber, slabs and stringbark,[1] and
floored with split slabs. A big bark kitchen standing at one end is larger than
the house itself, veranda included.

Bush all round – bush with no horizon, for the country is flat. No ranges
in the distance. The bush consists of stunted, rotten native apple-trees. No
undergrowth. Nothing to relieve the eye save the darker green of a few she-
oaks[2] which are sighing above the narrow, almost waterless creek. Nineteen
miles to the nearest sign of civilization – a shanty on the main road.

The drover, an ex-squatter, is away with sheep. His wife and children are
left here alone.

Four ragged, dried-up-looking children are playing about the house.
Suddenly one of them yells: 'Snake! Mother, here's a snake!'

The gaunt, sun-browned bushwoman dashes from the kitchen, snatches
her baby from the ground, holds it on her left hip, and reaches for a stick.

'Where is it?'

'Here! gone into the woodheap!' yells the eldest boy – a sharp-faced
urchin of eleven. 'Stop there, mother! I'll have him. Stand back! I'll have
the beggar!'

'Tommy, come here, or you'll be bit. Come here at once when I tell you,
you little wretch!'

The youngster comes reluctantly, carrying a stick bigger than himself. Then
he yells, triumphantly:

'There it goes – under the house!' and darts away with club uplifted. At
the same time the big, black, yellow-eyed dog-of-all-breeds, who has shown
the wildest interest in the proceedings, breaks his chain and rushes after that
snake. He is a moment late, however, and his nose reaches the crack in the

---

1 Eucalyptus. 2 Australian casuarina.

slabs just as the end of its tail disappears. Almost at the same moment the boy's club comes down and skins the aforesaid nose. Alligator takes small notice of this, and proceeds to undermine the building; but he is subdued after a struggle and chained up. They cannot afford to lose him.

The drover's wife makes the children stand together near the dog-house while she watches for the snake. She gets two small dishes of milk, and sets them down near the wall to tempt it to come out; but an hour goes by and it does not show itself.

It is near sunset, and a thunderstorm is coming. The children must be brought inside. She will not take them into the house, for she knows the snake is there, and may at any moment come up through a crack in the rough slab floor: so she carries several armfuls of firewood into the kitchen, and then takes the children there. The kitchen has no floor – or, rather, an earthen one – called a 'ground floor' in this part of the bush. There is a large, roughly-made table in the centre of the place. She brings the children in, and makes them get on this table. They are two boys and two girls – mere babies. She gives them some supper, and then, before it gets dark, she goes into the house, and snatches up some pillows and bedclothes – expecting to see or lay her hand on the snake any minute. She makes a bed on the kitchen table for the children, and sits down beside it to watch all night.

She has an eye on the corner, and a green sapling club laid in readiness on the dresser by her side; also her sewing basket and a copy of the *Young Ladies' Journal*. She has brought the dog into the room.

Tommy turns in, under protest, but says he'll lie awake all night and smash that blinded snake.

His mother asks him how many times she has told him not to swear.

He has his club with him under the bedclothes, and Jacky protests:

'Mummy! Tommy's skinnin' me alive wif his club. Make him take it out.'

Tommy: 'Shet up, you little —! D'yer want to be bit with the snake?'

Jacky shuts up.

'If yer bit,' says Tommy, after a pause, 'you'll swell up, an' smell, an' turn red an' green an' blue all over till yer bust. Won't he, mother?'

'Now then, don't frighten the child. Go to sleep,' she says.

The two younger children go to sleep, and now and then Jacky complains of being 'skeezed'. More room is made for him. Presently Tommy says:

'Mother! listen to them (adjective) little possums. I'd like to screw their blanky necks.'

And Jacky protests drowsily.

'But they don't hurt us, the little blanks!'

Mother: 'There, I told you you'd teach Jacky to swear.' But the remark makes her smile. Jacky goes to sleep.

Presently Tommy asks:

'Mother! Do you think they'll ever extricate the (adjective) kangaroo?'

'Lord! How am I to know, child? Go to sleep.'

'Will you wake me if the snake comes out?'

'Yes. Go to sleep.'

Near midnight. The children are all asleep and she sits there still, sewing and reading by turns. From time to time she glances round the floor and wall-plate, and whenever she hears a noise she reaches for the stick. The thunderstorm comes on, and the wind, rushing through the cracks in the slab wall, threatens to blow out her candle. She places it on a sheltered part of the dresser and fixes up a newspaper to protect it. At every flash of lightning the cracks between the slabs gleam like polished silver. The thunder rolls, and the rain comes down in torrents.

Alligator lies at full length on the floor, with his eyes turned towards the partition. She knows by this that the snake is there. There are large cracks in that wall opening under the floor of the dwelling-house.

She is not a coward, but recent events have shaken her nerves. A little son of her brother-in-law was lately bitten by a snake, and died. Besides, she has not heard from her husband for six months, and is anxious about him.

He was a drover, and started squatting here when they were married. The drought of 18— ruined him. He had to sacrifice the remnant of his flock and go droving again. He intends to move his family into the nearest town when he comes back, and, in the meantime, his brother, who keeps a shanty on the main road, comes over about once a month with provisions. The wife has still a couple of cows, one horse, and a few sheep. The brother-in-law kills one of the latter occasionally, gives her what she needs of it, and takes the rest in return for other provisions.

She is used to being left alone. She once lived like this for eighteen months. As a girl she built the usual castles in the air; but all her girlish hopes and aspirations have long been dead. She finds all the excitement and recreation she needs in the *Young Ladies' Journal*, and – Heaven help her! – takes a pleasure in the fashion-plates.

Her husband is an Australian, and so is she. He is careless, but a good enough husband. If he had the means he would take her to the city and keep her there like a princess. They are used to being apart, or at least she is. 'No use fretting,' she says. He may forget sometimes that he is married; but if he has a good cheque when he comes back he will give most of it to her. When he had money he took her to the city several times – hired a railway sleeping compartment, and put up at the best hotels. He also bought her a buggy, but they had to sacrifice that along with the rest.

The last two children were born in the bush – one while her husband was bringing a drunken doctor, by force, to attend to her. She was alone on this occasion, and very weak. She had been ill with a fever. She prayed to God to send her assistance. God sent Black Mary – the 'whitest' gin[3] in all the land. Or, at least, God sent King Jimmy first, and he sent Black Mary. He put his black face round the door-post, took in the situation at a glance, and said cheerfully: 'All right, missus – I bring my old woman, she down alonga creek.'

---

3 Aborigine.

One of the children died while she was here alone. She rode nineteen miles for assistance, carrying the dead child.

It must be near one or two o'clock. The fire is burning low. Alligator lies with his head resting on his paws, and watches the wall. He is not a very beautiful dog, and the light shows numerous old wounds where the hair will not grow. He is afraid of nothing on the face of the earth or under it. He will tackle a bullock as readily as he will tackle a flea. He hates all other dogs – except kangaroo-dogs – and has a marked dislike to friends or relations of the family. They seldom call, however. He sometimes makes friends with strangers. He hates snakes and has killed many, but he will be bitten some day and die; most snake-dogs end that way.

Now and then the bushwoman lays down her work and watches, and listens, and thinks. She thinks of things in her own life, for there is little else to think about.

The rain will make the grass grow, and this reminds her how she fought a bushfire once while her husband was away. The grass was long, and very dry, and the fire threatened to burn her out. She put on an old pair of her husband's trousers and beat out the flames with a green bough, till great drops of sooty perspiration stood out on her forehead and ran in streaks down her blackened arms. The sight of his mother in trousers greatly amused Tommy, who worked like a little hero by her side, but the terrified baby howled lustily for his 'mummy'. The fire would have mastered her but for four excited bushmen who arrived in the nick of time. It was a mixed-up affair all round; when she went to take up the baby he screamed and struggled convulsively, thinking it was a 'blackman'; and Alligator, trusting more to the child's sense than his own instinct, charged furiously, and (being old and slightly deaf) did not in his excitement at first recognize his mistress's voice, but continued to hang on to the moleskins until choked off by Tommy with a saddle-strap. The dog's sorrow for his blunder, and his anxiety to let it be known that it was all a mistake, was as evident as his ragged tail and twelve-inch grin could make it. It was a glorious time for the boys; a day to look back to, and talk about, and laugh over for many years.

She thinks how she fought a flood during her husband's absence. She stood for hours in the drenching downpour, and dug an overflow gutter to save the dam across the creek. But she could not save it. There are things that a bushwoman cannot do. Next morning the dam was broken, and her heart was nearly broken too, for she thought how her husband would feel when he came home and saw the result of years of labour swept away. She cried then.

She also fought the pleuro-pneumonia – dosed and bled the few remaining cattle, and wept again when her two best cows died.

Again, she fought a mad bullock that beseiged the house for a day. She made bullets and fired at him through the cracks in the slabs with an old shot-gun. He was dead in the morning. She skinned him and got seventeen-

and-sixpence for the hide.

She also fights the crows and eagles that have designs on her chickens. Her plan of campaign is very original. The children cry 'Crows, mother!' and she rushes out and aims a broomstick at the birds as though it were a gun, and says 'Bung!' The crows leave in a hurry; they are cunning, but a woman's cunning is greater.

Occasionally a bushman in the horrors[4] or a villainous-looking sun-downer,[5] comes and nearly scares the life out of her. She generally tells the suspicious-looking stranger that her husband and two sons are at work below the dam, or over at the yard, for he always cunningly inquires for the boss.

Only last week a gallows-faced swagman[6] – having satisifed himself that there were no men on the place – threw his swag down on the veranda, and demanded tucker.[7] She gave him something to eat; then he expressed his intention of staying for the night. It was sundown then. She got a batten from the sofa, loosened the dog, and confronted the stranger, holding the batten in one hand and the dog's collar with the other. 'Now you go!' she said. He looked at her and at the dog, said 'All right, mum,' in a cringing tone, and left. She was a determined-looking woman, and Alligator's yellow eyes glared unpleasantly – besides, the dog's chawing-up apparatus greatly resembled that of the reptile he was named after.

She has few pleasures to think of as she sits here alone by the fire, on guard against a snake. All days are much the same to her; but on Sunday afternoon she dresses herself, tidies the children, smartens up baby, and goes for a lonely walk along the bush-track, pushing an old perambulator in front of her. She does this every Sunday. She takes as much care to make herself and the children look smart as she would if she were going to do the block in the city. There is nothing to see, however, and not a soul to meet. You might walk twenty miles along this track without being able to fix a point in your mind, unless you are a bushman. This is because of the everlasting, maddening sameness of the stunted trees – that monotony which makes a man long to break away and travel as far as trains can go, and sail as far as ship can sail – and further.

But this bushwoman is used to the loneliness of it. As a girl-wife she hated it, and now she would feel strange away from it.

She is glad when her husband returns, but she does not gush or make a fuss about it. She gets him something good to eat, and tidies up the children.

She seems contented with her lot. She loves her children, but has no time to show it. She seems harsh to them. Her surroundings are not favourable to the development of the 'womanly' or sentimental side of nature.

It must be near morning now; but the clock is in the dwelling-house. Her candle is nearly done; she forgot that she was out of candles. Some more wood must be got to keep the fire up, and so she shuts the dog inside and

---

4 *Delirium tremens.*   5 Tramp who times arrival at a settlement for the evening.   6 Tramp or itinerant with bundle of possessions.   7 Food.

hurries round to the woodheap. The rain has cleared off. She seizes a stick, pulls it out, and – crash! the whole pile collapses.

Yesterday she bargained with a stray blackfellow to bring her some wood, and while he was at work she went in search of a missing cow. She was absent an hour or so, and the native black made good use of his time. On her return she was so astonished to see a good heap of wood by the chimney that she gave him an extra fig of tobacco, and praised him for not being lazy. He thanked her, and left with head erect and chest well out. He was the last of his tribe and a King; but he had built that woodheap hollow.

She is hurt now, and tears spring to her eyes as she sits down again by the table. She takes up a handkerchief to wipe the tears away, but pokes her eyes with her bare fingers instead. The handkerchief is full of holes, and she finds that she has put her thumb through one, and her forefinger through another.

This makes her laugh, to the surprise of the dog. She has a keen, very keen, sense of the ridiculous; and some time or other she will amuse bushmen with the story.

She had been amused before like that. One day she sat down 'to have a good cry', as she said – and the old cat rubbed against her dress and 'cried too'. Then she had to laugh.

It must be near daylight now. The room is very close and hot because of the fire. Alligator still watches the wall from time to time. Suddenly he becomes greatly interested; he draws himself a few inches nearer the partition, and a thrill runs through his body. The hair on the back of his neck begins to bristle, and the battle-light is in his yellow eyes. She knows what this means, and lays her hand on the stick. The lower end of one of the partition slabs has a large crack on both sides. An evil pair of small bright bead-like eyes glisten at one of these holes. The snake – a black one – comes slowly out, about a foot, and moves its head up and down. The dog lies still, and the woman sits as one fascinated. The snake comes out a foot further. She lifts her stick, and the reptile, as though suddenly aware of danger, sticks his head in through the crack on the other side of the slab, and hurries to get his tail round after him. Alligator springs, and his jaws come together with a snap. He misses, for his nose is large, and the snake's body close down in the angle formed by the slabs and the floor. He snaps again as the tail comes round. He has the snake now, and tugs it out eighteen inches. Thud, thud, comes the woman's club on the ground. Alligator pulls again. Thud, thud. Alligator gives another pull and he has the snake out – a black brute, five feet long. The head rises to dart about, but the dog has the enemy close to the neck. He is a big, heavy dog, but quick as a terrier. He shakes the snake as though he felt the original curse in common with mankind. The eldest boy wakes up, seizes his stick, and tries to get out of bed, but his mother forces him back with a grip of iron. Thud, thud – the snake's back is broken in several places. Thud, thud – its head is crushed, and Alligator's nose skinned again.

She lifts the mangled reptile on the point of her stick, carries it to the fire, and throws it in; then piles on the wood and watches the snake burn. The boy and dog watch too. She lays her hand on the dog's head, and all the fierce, angry light dies out of his yellow eyes. The younger children are quieted, and presently go to sleep. The dirty-legged boy stands for a moment in his shirt, watching the fire. Presently he looks up at her, sees the tears in her eyes, and, throwing his arms round her neck, exclaims:

'Mother, I won't never go drovin'; blast me if I do!'

And she hugs him to her worn-out breast and kisses him; and they sit thus together while the sickly daylight breaks over the bush.

§ *'Drover's Wife' stories* Bail, Moorhouse, Jefferis; *Women and the bush* Baynton, Franklin, Bail, Jefferis

2: Middleton's Rouseabout

Tall and freckled and sandy,
    Face of a country lout;
This was the picture of Andy,
    Middleton's Rouseabout.

5   Type of a coming nation
    In the land of cattle and sheep;
Worked on Middleton's station,
    Pound a week and his keep;

On Middleton's wide dominions
10   Plied the stockwhip and shears;
Hadn't any opinions,
    Hadn't any 'idears'.

Swiftly the years went over,
    Liquor and drought prevailed;
15   Middleton went as a drover
    After his station had failed.

Type of a careless nation,
    Men who are soon played out,
Middleton was: – and his station
20   Was bought by the Rouseabout.

---

4 Rouseabout: station-hand; labourer.

Flourishing beard and sandy,
   Tall and solid and stout;
This is the picture of Andy,
   Middleton's Rouseabout.

25   Now on his own dominions
   Works with his overseers;
Hasn't any opinions,
   Hasn't any idears.

§ *National/male mythologies* Gordon, Lawson (1), Paterson, Lawler, Seymour, Williamson, Drewe

MARY GILMORE (1864–1962)

Old Botany Bay

'I'm old
Botany Bay;
Stiff in the joints,
Little to say.

5   I am he
Who paved the way,
That you might walk
At your ease to-day;

I was the conscript
10   Sent to hell
To make in the desert
The living well;

I bore the heat,
I blazed the track –
15   Furrowed and bloody
Upon my back.

I split the rock;
I felled the tree:
The nation was –
20   Because of me!'

---

2 Botany Bay: site of the first landing in Australia of Captain Cook, 29 April 1770; widely used in the nineteenth century as a metonym for the penal colony of New South Wales.

> Old Botany Bay
> Taking the sun
> From day to day . . .
> Shame on the mouth
> 25   That would deny
> The knotted hands
> That set us high!

§ *Poems about 'Australia'* O'Dowd, Hope, McAuley

BERNARD O'DOWD (1866–1953)

Australia

Last sea-thing dredged by sailor Time from Space,
Are you a drift Sargasso, where the West
In halcyon calm rebuilds her fatal nest?
Or Delos of a coming Sun-God's race?
5   Are you for Light, and trimmed, with oil in place,
Or but a Will o' Wisp on marshy quest?
A new demesne for Mammon to infest?
Or lurks millennial Eden 'neath your face?

The cenotaphs of species dead elsewhere
10   That in your limits leap and swim and fly,
Or trail uncanny harp-strings from your trees,
Mix omens with the auguries that dare
To plant the Cross upon your forehead sky,
A virgin helpmate Ocean at your knees.

§ *Poems about 'Australia'* Gilmore, Hope, McAuley

---

2 **Sargasso**: seaweed forming island-like masses especially in the Sargasso sea of the North Atlantic.
4 **Delos:** Aegean island; supposedly raised from the sea as a floating island and containing a temple to Apollo, the Sun God.

3 **halcyon:** in classical mythology, the kingfisher bird was said to breed in a floating nest during a charmed period of calm.

'STEELE RUDD' (ARTHUR HOEY DAVIS) (1868–1935)

Starting the Selection[1]

This extract is the opening chapter of *On Our Selection*, the first of 'Rudd'/Davis's four books about the Rudd family. It established his reputation as a humorist, whose comic mode encompassed a kindly irony and broad farce. As well as being comic, his fiction documents the harshness of the lives of the impoverished selectors, who attempted to cultivate inhospitable tracts of land.

It's twenty years ago now since we settled on the Creek. Twenty years! I remember well the day we came from Stanthorpe, on Jerome's dray – eight of us, and all the things – beds, tubs, a bucket, the two cedar chairs with the pine bottoms and backs that Dad put in them, some pintpots and old Crib. It was a scorching hot day, too – talk about thirst! At every creek we came to we drank till it stopped running.

Dad didn't travel up with us: he had gone some months before, to put up the house and dig the water-hole. It was a slabbed house, with shingled roof, and space enough for two rooms, but the partition wasn't up. The floor was earth, but Dad had a mixture of sand and fresh cow-dung with which he used to keep it level. About once every month he would put it on, and everyone had to keep outside that day till it was dry. There were no locks on the doors. Pegs were put in to keep them fast at night, and the slabs were not very close together, for we could easily see anybody coming on horseback by looking through them. Joe and I used to play at counting the stars through the cracks in the roof.

The day after we arrived Dad took Mother and us out to see the paddock and the flat on the other side of the gully that he was going to clear for cultivation. There was no fence round the paddock, but he pointed out on a tree the surveyor's marks showing the boundary of our ground. It must have been fine land, the way Dad talked about it. There was very valuable timber on it, too, so he said; and he showed us a place among some rocks on a ridge where he was sure gold would be found, but we weren't to say anything about it. Joe and I went back that evening and turned over every stone on the ridge, but we didn't find any gold.

No mistake, it was a real wilderness – nothing but trees, goannas, dead timber, and bears; and the nearest house, Dwyer's, was three miles away. I often wonder how the women stood it the first few years, and I can remember how Mother, when she was alone, used to sit on a log where the lane is now and cry for hours. Lonely! It *was* lonely.

Dad soon talked about clearing a couple of acres and putting in corn – all of us did, in fact – till the work commenced. It was a delightful topic

---

1 Portion of land.

before we started, but in two weeks the clusters of fires that illuminated the whooping bush in the night, and the crash upon crash of the big trees as they fell, had lost all their poetry.

We toiled and toiled clearing those four acres, where the haystacks are now standing, till every tree and sapling that had grown there was down. We thought then the worst was over – but how little we knew of clearing land! Dad was never tired of calculating and telling us how much the crop would fetch if the ground could only be got ready in time to put it in; so we laboured the harder.

With our combined male and female forces and the aid of a sapling lever we rolled the thundering big logs together in the face of hell's own fires, and when there were no logs to roll it was tramp, tramp the day through, gathering armfuls of sticks, while the clothes clung to our backs with a muddy perspiration. Sometimes Dan and Dave would sit in the shade beside the billy[2] of water and gaze at the small patch that had taken so long to do, then they would turn hopelessly to what was before them and ask Dad (who would never take a spell) what was the use of thinking of ever getting such a place cleared. And when Dave wanted to know why Dad didn't take up a place on the plain, where there were no trees to grub[3] and plenty of water, Dad would cough as if something was sticking in his throat, and then curse terribly about the squatters[4] and political jobbery.[5] He would soon cool down, though, and get hopeful again.

'Look at the Dwyers,' he'd say. 'From ten acres of wheat they got seventy pounds last year, besides feed for the fowls. They've got corn in now, and there's only the two of them.'

It wasn't only burning off! Whenever there was a short drought the water-hole was sure to run dry. Then we had to take turns to carry water from the springs – about two miles. We had no draught-horse,[6] and even if we had had one there was neither water-cask, trolly, nor dray. So we humped it – and talk about a drag! By the time you returned, if you hadn't drained the bucket, in spite of the big drink you'd take before leaving the springs, more than half would certainly be spilt through the vessel bumping against your leg every time you stumbled in the long grass. Somehow, none of us liked carrying water. We would sooner keep the fires going all day without dinner than do a trip to the springs.

One hot, thirsty day it was Joe's turn with the bucket, and he managed to get back without spilling very much. We were all pleased because there was enough left after the tea had been made to give us each a drink. Dinner was nearly over. Dan had finished and was taking it easy on the sofa when Joe said, 'I say, Dad, what's a nater-dog like?'

Dad told him. 'Yellow, sharp ears and bushy tail.'

'Those muster bin some then that I seen – I don't know 'bout the bushy tail – all the hair had comed off.'

---

2 Cylindrical tin, mainly used for boiling. 3 Clear away. 4 Settlers, on unclaimed land. 5 Corruption.
6 Horse for drawing cart, etc.

'Where'd y' see them, Joe?' we asked.

'Down 'n the springs floating about – dead.'

Then everyone seemed to think hard and look at the tea. *I* didn't want any more. Dan jumped off the sofa and went outside; and Dad looked after Mother.

At last the four acres – except for the biggest of the ironbark-trees[7] and about fifty stumps – were pretty well cleared. Then came a problem that couldn't be worked out on a draught-board. I have already said that we hadn't any draught-horses. Indeed, the only thing on the selection like a horse was an old 'tuppy'[8] mare that Dad used to straddle. The date of her foaling went farther back than Dad's, I believe, and she was shaped something like an alderman. We found her one day in about eighteen inches of mud, with both eyes picked out by the crows, and her hide bearing evidence that a feathery tribe had made a roost of her carcass. Plainly, there was no chance of breaking up the ground with her help. And we had no plough. How, then, was the corn to be put in? That was the question.

Dan and Dave sat outside in the corner of the chimney, both scratching the ground with a chip and not saying anything. Dad and Mother sat inside talking it over. Sometimes Dad would get up and walk round the room shaking his head, then he would kick old Crib for lying under the table. At last Mother struck something which brightened him up, and he called Dave.

'Catch Topsy and –' he paused because he remembered the old mare was dead.

'Run over and ask Mr Dwyer to lend me three hoes.'

Dave went. Dwyer lent the hoes, and the problem was solved. That was how we started.

§ *Settling the land* Lawson (1), Baynton, White (2); Can: Traill

BARBARA BAYNTON (1857–1929)

The Chosen Vessel

She laid the stick and her baby on the grass while she untied the rope that tethered the calf. The length of the rope separated them. The cow was near the calf, and both were lying down. Feed along the creek was plentiful, and every day she found a fresh place to tether it, since tether it she must, for if she did not, it would stray with the cow out on the plain. She had plenty of time to go after it, but then there was baby; and if the cow turned on her out on the plain, and she with baby – she had been a town girl and was afraid of the cow, but she did not want the cow to know it. She used to run at first when it bellowed its protest against the penning up of its calf.

---

7 Species of eucalyptus with thick bark. 8 Worthless horse.

This satisfied the cow, also the calf, but the woman's husband was angry, and called her – the noun was cur. It was he who forced her to run and meet the advancing cow, brandishing a stick, and uttering threatening words till the enemy turned and ran. 'That's the way!' the man said, laughing at her white face. In many things he was worse than the cow, and she wondered if the same rule would apply to the man, but she was not one to provoke skirmishes even with the cow.

It was early for the calf to go 'to bed' – nearly an hour earlier than usual; but she had felt so restless all day. Partly because it was Monday, and the end of the week that would bring her and baby the companionship of its father, was so far off. He was a shearer, and had gone to his shed before daylight that morning. Fifteen miles as the crow flies separated them.

There was a track in front of the house, for it had once been a wine shanty, and a few travellers passed along at intervals. She was not afraid of horsemen; but swagmen,[1] going to, or worse, coming from the dismal, drunken little township, a day's journey beyond, terrified her. One had called at the house today, and asked for tucker.[2]

Ah! that was why she had penned up the calf so early! She feared more from the look of his eyes, and the gleam of his teeth, as he watched her newly awakened baby beat its impatient fists upon her covered breasts, than from the knife that was sheathed in the belt at his waist.

She had given him bread and meat. Her husband, she told him, was sick. She always said that when she was alone, and a swagman came, and she had gone in from the kitchen to the bedroom, and asked questions and replied to them in the best man's voice she could assume. Then he had asked to go into the kitchen to boil his billy,[3] but she gave him tea, and he drank it on the wood-heap. He had walked round and round the house, and there were cracks in some places, and after the last time he had asked for tobacco. She had none to give him, and he had grinned, because there was a broken clay pipe near the wood-heap where he stood, and if there were a man inside, there ought to have been tobacco. Then he asked for money, but women in the bush never have money.

At last he had gone, and she, watching through the cracks, saw him when about a quarter of a mile away, turn and look back at the house. He had stood so for some moments with a pretence of fixing his swag,[4] and then, apparently satisfied, moved to the left towards the creek. The creek made a bow round the house, and when he came to it she lost sight of him. Hours after, watching intently for signs of smoke, she saw the man's dog chasing some sheep that had gone to the creek for water, and saw it slink back suddenly, as if the man had called it.

More than once she thought of taking her baby and going to her husband. But in the past, when she had dared to speak of the dangers to which her loneliness exposed her, he had taunted and sneered at her. She need not

---

1 Tramps; itinerants. 2 Food. 3 Cylindrical boiling tin. 4 Bundle of possessions.

flatter herself, he had coarsely told her, that anybody would want to run away with her.

Long before nightfall she placed food on the kitchen table, and beside it laid the big brooch that had been her mother's. It was the only thing of value that she had. And she left the kitchen door wide open.

The doors inside she securely fastened. Beside the bolt in the back one she drove in the steel and scissors; against it she piled the table and the stools. Underneath the lock of the front door she forced the handle of the spade, and the blade between the cracks in the flooring boards. Then the prop-stick, cut into lengths, held the top, as the spade held the middle. The windows were little more than port-holes; she had nothing to fear through them.

She ate a few mouthfuls of food and drank a cup of milk. But she lighted no fire, and when night came, no candle, but crept with her baby to bed.

What woke her? The wonder was that she had slept – she had not meant to. But she was young, very young. Perhaps the shrinking of the galvanized roof – yet hardly, since that was so usual. Something had set her heart beating wildly; but she lay quite still, only she put her arm over her baby. Then she had both round it, and she prayed, 'Little baby, little baby, don't wake!'

The moon's rays shone on the front of the house, and she saw one of the open cracks, quite close to where she lay, darken with a shadow. Then a protesting growl reached her; and she could fancy she heard the man turn hastily. She plainly heard the thud of something striking the dog's ribs, and the long flying strides of the animal as it howled and ran. Still watching, she saw the shadow darken every crack along the wall. She knew by the sounds that the man was trying every standpoint that might help him to see in; but how much he saw she could not tell. She thought of many things she might do to deceive him into the idea that she was not alone. But the sound of her voice would wake baby, and she dreaded that as though it were the only danger that threatened her. So she prayed, 'Little baby, don't wake, don't cry!'

Stealthily the man crept about. She knew he had his boots off, because of the vibration that his feet caused as he walked along the veranda to gauge the width of the little window in her room, and the resistance of the front door.

Then he went to the other end, and the uncertainty of what he was doing became unendurable. She had felt safer, far safer, while he was close, and she could watch and listen. She felt she must watch, but the great fear of wakening baby again assailed her. She suddenly recalled that one of the slabs on that side of the house had shrunk in length as well as in width, and had once fallen out. It was held in position only by a wedge of wood underneath. What if he should discover that! The uncertainty increased her terror. She prayed as she gently raised herself with her little one in her arms, held tightly to her breast.

She thought of the knife, and shielded her child's body with her hands and arms. Even its little feet she covered with its white gown, and baby never murmured – it liked to be held so. Noiselessly she crossed to the other side, and stood where she could see and hear, but not be seen. He was trying every slab, and was very near to that with the wedge under it. Then she saw him find it; and heard the sound of the knife as bit by bit he began to cut away the wooden support.

She waited motionless, with her baby pressed tightly to her, though she knew that in another few minutes this man with the cruel eyes, lascivious mouth, and gleaming knife, would enter. One side of the slab tilted; he had only to cut away the remaining little end, when the slab, unless he held it, would fall outside.

She heard his jerked breathing as it kept time with the cuts of the knife, and the brush of his clothes as he rubbed the wall in his movements, for she was so still and quiet, that she did not even tremble. She knew when he ceased, and wondered why. She stood well concealed; she knew he could not see her, and that he would not fear if he did, yet she heard him move cautiously away. Perhaps he expected the slab to fall. Still his motive puzzled her, and she moved even closer, and bent her body the better to listen. Ah! what sound was that? 'Listen! Listen!' she bade her heart – her heart that had kept so still, but now bounded with tumultuous throbs that dulled her ears. Nearer and nearer came the sounds, till the welcome thud of a horse's hoof rang out clearly.

'Oh, God! oh, God! oh, God!' she cried, for they were very close before she could make sure. She turned to the door, and with her baby in her arms tore frantically at its bolts and bars.

Out she darted at last, and running madly along, saw the horseman beyond her in the distance. She called to him in Christ's name, in her babe's name, still flying like the wind with the speed that deadly peril gives. But the distance grew greater and greater between them, and when she reached the creek her prayers turned to wild shrieks, for there crouched the man she feared, with outstretched arms that caught her as she fell. She knew he was offering terms if she ceased to struggle and cry for help, though louder and louder did she cry for it, but it was only when the man's hand gripped her throat, that the cry of 'Murder' came from her lips. And when she ceased, the startled curlews took up the awful sound, and flew shrieking over the horseman's head.

'By God!' said the boundary rider,[5] 'it's been a dingo right enough! Eight killed up here, and there's more down in the creek – a ewe and a lamb, I'll bet; and the lamb's alive!' And he shut out the sky with his hand, and watched the crows that were circling round and round, nearing the earth one moment, and the next shooting skywards. By that he knew the lamb must be alive; even a dingo will spare a lamb sometimes.

Yes, the lamb was alive, and after the manner of lambs of its kind did not know its mother when the light came. It had sucked the still warm breasts, and laid its little head on her bosom, and slept till the morn. Then, when

---

5 Rider round sheep station, attending to perimeter fences etc.

it looked at the swollen disfigured face, it wept and would have crept away, but for the hand that still clutched its little gown. Sleep was nodding its golden head and swaying its small body, and the crows were close, so close, to the mother's wide-open eyes, when the boundary rider galloped down.

'Jesus Christ!' he said, covering his eyes. He told afterwards how the little child held out its arms to him, and how he was forced to cut its gown that the dead hand held.

It was election time, and as usual the priest had selected a candidate. His choice was so obviously in the interests of the squatter, that Peter Hennessey's reason, for once in his life, had over-ridden superstition, and he had dared promise his vote to another. Yet he was uneasy, and every time he woke in the night (and it was often) he heard the murmur of his mother's voice. It came through the partition, or under the door. If through the partition, he knew she was praying in her bed; but when the sounds came under the door, she was on her knees before the little altar in the corner that enshrined the statue of the Blessed Virgin and Child. 'Mary, Mother of Christ! save my son! Save him!' prayed she in the dairy as she strained and set the evening's milking. 'Sweet Mary! for the love of Christ, save him!' The grief in her old face made the morning meal so bitter, that to avoid her he came late to his dinner. It made him so cowardly, that he could not say goodbye to her, and when night fell on the eve of the election day, he rode off secretly.

He had thirty miles to ride to the township to record his vote. He cantered briskly along the great stretch of plain that had nothing but stunted cottonbush to play shadow to the full moon, which glorified a sky of earliest spring. The bruised incense of the flowering clover rose up to him, and the glory of the night appealed vaguely to his imagination, but he was preoccupied with his present act of revolt.

Vividly he saw his mother's agony when she would find him gone. At that moment, he felt sure, she was praying.

'Mary! Mother of Christ!' He repeated the invocation, half unconsciously. And suddenly, out of the stillness, came Christ's name to him – called loudly – in despairing accents.

'For Christ's sake! Christ's sake! Christ's sake!' called the voice. Good Catholic that he had been, he crossed himself before he dared to look back. Gliding across a ghostly patch of pipe-clay, he saw a white-robed figure with a babe clasped to her bosom.

All the superstitious awe of his race and religion swayed his brain. The moonlight on the gleaming clay was a 'heavenly light' to him, and he knew the white figure not for flesh and blood, but for the Virgin and Child of his mother's prayers. Then, good Catholic that once more he was, he put spurs to his horse's sides and galloped madly away.

His mother's prayers were answered.

Hennessey was the first to record his vote – for the priest's candidate. Then he sought the priest at home, but found that he was out rallying the voters. Still, under the influence of his blessed vision, Hennessey would not go near the public-houses, but wandered about the outskirts of the town for hours, keeping apart from the townspeople, and fasting as penance. He was subdued and mildly ecstatic, feeling as a repentant chastened child, who awaits only the kiss of peace.

And at last, as he stood in the graveyard crossing himself with reverent awe, he heard in the gathering twilight the roar of many voices crying the name of the victor at the election. It was well with the priest.

Again Hennessey sought him. He sat at home, the housekeeper said, and led him into the dimly-lighted study. His seat was immediately opposite a large picture, and as the housekeeper turned up the lamp, once more the face of the Madonna and Child looked down on him, but this time silently, peacefully. The half-parted lips of the Virgin were smiling with compassionate tenderness; her eyes seemed to beam with the forgiveness of an earthly mother for her erring but beloved child.

He fell on his knees in adoration. Transfixed, the wondering priest stood, for, mingled with the adoration, 'My Lord and my God!' was the exaltation, 'And hast Thou chosen me?'

'What is it, Peter?' said the priest.

'Father,' he answered reverently, and with loosened tongue he poured forth the story of his vision.

'Great God!' shouted the priest, 'and you did not stop to save her! Have you not heard?'

Many miles further down the creek a man kept throwing an old cap into a waterhole. The dog would bring it out and lay it on the opposite side to where the man stood, but would not allow the man to catch him, though it was only to wash the blood of the sheep from his mouth and throat, for the sight of blood made the man tremble.

§ *Women and the bush* Lawson (1), Franklin, Bail, Jefferis

MILES FRANKLIN (1879–1954)

From My Brilliant Career

In the Introduction to *My Brilliant Career*, the 16-year-old narrator–protagonist Sybylla Melvin appears to be offering an Australian alternative to the Victorian novel – she claims to be writing 'a real yarn' not a 'romance' – but the work is more hybridized than this suggests and is not without its descriptions of the 'beautiful sunsets' that she rejects here. It is also poised between the primarily male nationalist tradition of earlier Australian writers such as Lawson (who wrote the Preface) and Paterson and strong, if inconsistently developed, feminist leanings. Chapter 5 illustrates Sybylla's ambivalent attitude towards the defining site of the bush and her aspirations towards a more cultured life. Written while Franklin was still in her teens, the novel is above all a classic study of adolescence.

Introduction

Possum Gully, near Goulburn,
N.S. Wales, Australia, 1st March, 1899

MY DEAR FELLOW AUSTRALIANS,

Just a few lines to tell you that this story is all about myself – for no other purpose do I write it.

I make no apologies for being egotistical. In this particular I attempt an improvement on other autobiographies. Other autobiographies weary one with excuses for their egotism. What matters it to you if I am egotistical? What matters it to you though it should matter that I am egotistical?

This is not a romance – I have too often faced the music of life to the tune of hardship to waste time in snivelling and gushing over fancies and dreams; neither is it a novel, but simply a yarn – a *real* yarn. Oh! as real, as really real – provided life itself is anything beyong a heartless little chimera – it is as real in its weariness and bitter heartache as the tall gum-trees, among which I first saw the light, are real in their stateliness and substantiality.

My sphere in life is not congenial to me. Oh, how I hate this living death which has swallowed all my teens, which is greedily devouring my youth, which will sap my prime, and in which my old age, if I am cursed with any, will be worn away! As my life creeps on for ever through the long toil-laden days with its agonizing monotony, narrowness, and absolute uncongeniality, how my spirit frets and champs its unbreakable fetters – all in vain!

Special Notice

You can drive into this story head first as it were. Do not fear encountering such trash as descriptions of beautiful sunsets and whisperings of wind. We (999 out of every 1000) can see nought in sunsets save as signs and tokens whether we may expect rain on the morrow or the contrary, so we will leave such vain and foolish imagining to those poets and painters – poor fools! Let us rejoice that we are not of their temperament!

Better be born a slave than a poet, better be born a black, better be born a cripple! For a poet must be companionless – alone! *fearfully* alone in the midst of his fellows whom he loves. Alone because his soul is as far above common mortals as common mortals are above monkeys.

There is no plot in this story, because there has been none in my life or in any other life which has come under my notice. I am one of a class, the individuals of which have not time for plots in their life, but have all they can do to get their work done without indulging in such a luxury . . .

Chapter 5: Disjointed Sketches and Grumbles

It was my duty to 'rare the poddies'.[1] This is the most godless occupation in which it has been my lot to engage. I did a great amount of thinking while feeding them – for, by the way, I am afflicted with the power of thought, which is a heavy curse. The less a person thinks and inquires regarding the why and the wherefore and the justice of things, when dragging along through life, the happier it is for him, and doubly, trebly so, for her.

Poor little calves! Slaves to the greed of man! Bereft of the mothers with which Nature has provided them, and compelled to exist on milk from the separator, often thick, sour, and icy cold.

Besides the milking I did, before I went to school every morning, for which I had to prepare myself and the younger children, and to which we had to walk two miles, I had to feed thirty calves and wash the breakfast dishes. On returning from school in the afternoon, often in a state of exhaustion from walking in the blazing sun, I had the same duties over again, and in addition boots to clean and home lessons to prepare for the morrow. I had to relinquish my piano practice for want of time.

Ah, those short, short nights of rest and long, long days of toil! It seems to me that dairying means slavery in the hands of poor people who cannot afford hired labour. I am not writing of dairy-farming, the genteel and artistic profession as eulogized in leading articles of agricultural newspapers and as taught in agricultural colleges. I am depicting practical dairying as I have lived it, and seen it lived, by dozens of families around me.

It takes a great deal of work to produce even one pound of butter fit for market. At the time I mention it was 3d. and 4d. per lb., so it was much work and small pay. It was slaving and delving from morning till night – Sundays, week-days, and holidays, all alike were work-days to us.

Hard graft is a great leveller. Household drudgery, woodcutting, milking, and gardening soon roughen the hands and dim the outside polish. When the body is wearied with much toil the desire to cultivate the mind, or the cultivation it has already received, is gradually wiped out. Thus it was with my parents. They had dropped from swelldom to peasantism. They were among and of the peasantry. None of their former acquaintances came without their circle now, for the iron ungodly hand of class distinction has settled surely down upon Australian society – Australia's democracy is only a tradition of the past.

I say naught against the lower life. The peasantry are the bulwarks of every nation. The life of a peasant is, to a peasant who is a peasant with a peasant's soul, when times are good and when seasons smile, a grand life. It is honest, clean, and wholesome. But the life of a peasant to me is purgatory. Those around me worked from morning till night and then enjoyed their well-earned sleep. They had but two states of existence – work and sleep.

---

1 Rear the hand-fed calves.

There was a third part in me which cried out to be fed. I longed for the arts. Music was a passion with me. I borrowed every book in the neighbourhood and stole hours from rest to read them. This told upon me and made my physical burdens harder for me than for other children of my years around me. That third was the strongest part of me. In it I lived a dream-life with writers, artists, and musicians. Hope, sweet, cruel, delusive Hope, whispered in my ear that life was long with much by and by, and in that by and by my dream-life would be real. So on I went with that gleaming lake in the distance beckoning me to come and sail on its silver waters, and Inexperience, conceited, blind Inexperience, failing to show the impassable pit between it and me.

To return to the dairying.

Old and young alike we earned our scant livelihood by the heavy sweat of our brows. Still, we *did* gain an honest living. We were not ashamed to look day in the face, and fought our way against all odds with the stubborn independence of our British ancestors. But when 1894 went out without rain, and '95, hot, dry, pitiless '95, succeeded it, there came a time when it was impossible to make a living.

The scorching furnace-breath winds shrivelled every blade of grass, dust and the moan of starving stock filled the air, vegetables became a thing of the past. The calves I had reared died one by one, and the cows followed in their footsteps.

I had left school then, and my mother and father and I spent the days in lifting our cows. When our strength proved inadequate, the help of the neighbours had to be called in, and father would give his services in return. Only a few of our more well-to-do neighbours had been able to send their stock away, or had any better place to which to transfer them. The majority of them were in as tight a plight as ourselves. This cow-lifting became quite a trade, the whole day being spent in it and in discussing the bad prospect ahead if the drought continued.

Many an extra line of care furrowed the brows of the disheartened bushmen then. Not only was their living taken from them by the drought, but there is nothing more heartrending than to have poor beasts, especially dairy cows, so familiar, valued, and loved, pleading for food day after day in their piteous dumb way when one has it not to give.

We shore ourselves of all but the bare necessaries of life, but even they for a family of ten are considerable, and it was a mighty tussle to get both ends within cover of meeting. We felt the full force of the heavy hand of poverty – the most stinging kind of poverty too, that which still holds up its head and keeps an outside appearance. Far more grinding is this than the poverty inherited from generations which is not ashamed of itself, and has not as an accompaniment the wounded pride and humiliation which attacked us.

Some there are who argue that poverty does not mean unhappiness. Let those try what it is to be destitute of even one companionable friend, what it means to be forced to exist in an alien sphere of society, what it is like to be unable to afford a stamp to write to a friend; let them long as passionately as I have longed for reading and music, and be unable to procure it because of poverty; let poverty force them into doing work against which every fibre of their being revolts, as it has forced me, and then see if their lives will be happy.

My school life had been dull and uneventful. The one incident of any note had been the day that the teacher, better known as old Harris, 'stood up' to the inspector. The latter was a precise, collar-and-cuffs sort of little man. He gave one the impression of having all his ideas on the subjects he thought worthy of attention carefully culled and packed in his brain-pan, and neatly labelled, so that he might without fluster pounce upon any of them at a moment's warning. He was gentlemanly and respectable, and discharged his duties punctiliously in a manner reflecting credit on himself and his position, but, comparing the mind of a philanthropist to the Murrumbidgee[2] in breadth, his, in comparison, might be likened to the flow of a bucket of water in a dray-rut.

On the day in question – a precious hot one it was – he had finished examining us in most subjects, and was looking at our copy-books. He looked up from them, ahemed! and fastidiously straightened his waistcoat.

'Mr Harris!'

'Yes, sir.'

'Comparisons are odious, but, unfortuantely, I am forced to draw one now.'

'Yes, sir.'

'This writing is much inferior to that of town scholars. It is very shaky and irregular. Also, I notice that the children seem stupid and dull. I don't like putting it so plainly, but, in fact, ah, they seem to be possessed with the proverbial stupidity of country people. How do you account for this?'

Poor old Harris! In spite of his drunken habits and inability to properly discharge his duties, he had a warm heart and much fellowshiply humanity in him. He understood and loved his pupils, and would not have aspersions cast upon them. Besides, the nip he had taken to brace himself to meet the inspector had been two or three, and they robbed him of the discretion which otherwise might have kept him silent.

'Si-r-r-r, I can and will account for it. Look you at every one of those children. Every one, right down to this little tot,' indicating a little girl of five, 'has to milk and work hard before and after school, besides walk on an average two miles to and from school in this infernal heat. Most of the elder boys and girls milk on an average fourteen cows morning and evening. You try that treatment for a week or two, my fine gentleman, and then see if your fist doesn't ache and shake so that you can't write at all. See if you won't look a trifle dozy. Stupidity of country people be hanged! If you had to work from morning till night in the heat and dust, and get precious little for it too, I bet you wouldn't have much time to scrape your finger-nails,

---

2 Major river of New South Wales, approx. 1,690 km. (1,050 miles) in length.

read science notes, and look smart.' Here he took off his coat and shaped up to his superior.

The inspector drew back in consternation.

'Mr Harris, you forget yourself!'

At this juncture they went outside together. What happened there we never knew. That is all we heard of the matter except the numerous garbled accounts which we carried home that afternoon.

A Drought Idyll

'Sybylla, what are you doing? Where is your mother?'

'I'm ironing. Mother's down at the fowl-house seeing after some chickens. What do you want?'

It was my father who addressed me. Time, 2 o'clock p.m. Thermometer hung in the shade of the veranda registering 105½ degrees.

'I see Blackshaw coming across the flat. Call your mother. You bring the leg-ropes – I've got the dog-leg. Come at once; we'll give the cows another lift. Poor devils – might as well knock 'em on the head at once, but there might be rain next moon. This drought can't last for ever.'

I called mother, got the leg ropes, and set off, pulling my sunbonnet closely over my face to protect my eyes from the dust which was driving from the west in blinding clouds. The dog-leg to which father had referred was three poles about eight or ten feet long, strapped together so they could be stood up. It was an arrangement father had devised to facilitate our labour in lifting the cows. A fourth and longer pole was placed across the fork formed by the three, and to one end of this were tied a couple of leg-ropes, after being placed round the beast, one beneath the flank and one around the girth. On the other end of this pole we would put our weight while one man would lift with the tail and another with the horns. New-chum cows would sulk, and we would have great work with them; but those used to the performance would help themselves, and up they'd go as nice as a daisy. The only art needed was to draw the pole back quickly before the cows could move, or the leg-ropes would pull them over again.

On this afternoon we had six cows to lift. We struggled manfully, and got five on their feet, and then proceeded to where the last one was lying, back downwards, on a shadeless stony spot on the side of a hill. The men slewed her round by the tail, while mother and I fixed the dog-leg and adjusted the ropes. We got the cow up, but the poor beast was so weak and knocked about that she immediately fell down again. We resolved to let her have a few minutes' spell before making another attempt at lifting. There was not a blade of grass to be seen, and the ground was too dusty to sit on. We were too overdone to make more than one-worded utterances, so waited silently in the blazing sun, closing our eyes against the dust.

Weariness! Weariness!

A few light wind-smitten clouds made wan streaks across the white sky, haggard with the fierce relentless glare of the afternoon sun. Weariness was written across my mother's delicate careworn features, and found expression in my father's knitted brows and dusty face. Blackshaw was weary, and said so, as he wiped the dust, made mud with perspiration, off his cheeks. I was weary – my limbs ached with the heat and work. The poor beast stretched at our feet was weary. All nature was weary, and seemed to sing a dirge to that effect in the furnace-breath wind which roared among the trees on the low ranges at our back and smote the parched and thirsty ground. All were weary, all but the sun. He seemed to glory in his power, relentless and untiring, as he swung boldly in the sky, triumphantly leering down upon his helpless victims.

Weariness! Weariness!

This was life – my life – my career, my brilliant career! I was fifteen – fifteen! A few fleeting hours and I would be old as those around me. I looked at them as they stood there, weary, and turning down the other side of the hill of life. When young, no doubt they had hoped for, and dreamed of, better things – had even known them. But here they were. This had been their life; this was their career. It was, and in all probability would be, mine too. My life – my career – my brilliant career!

Weariness! Weariness!

The summer sun danced on. Summer is fiendish, and life is a curse, I said in my heart. What a great dull hard rock the world was! On it were a few barren narrow ledges, and on these, by exerting ourselves so that the force wears off our finger-nails, it allows us to hang for a year or two, and then hurls us off into outer darkness and oblivion, perhaps to endure worse torture than this.

The poor beast moaned. The lifting had strained her, and there were patches of hide worn off her the size of breakfast-plates, sore and most harrowing to look upon.

It takes great suffering to wring a moan from the patience of a cow. I turned my head away, and with the impatience and one-sided reasoning common to fifteen, asked God what He meant by this. It is well enough to heap suffering on human beings, seeing it is supposed to be merely a probation for a better world, but animals – poor, innocent animals – why are they tortured so?

'Come now, we'll lift her once more,' said my father. At it we went again; it is surprising what weight there is in the poorest cow. With great struggling we got her to her feet once more, and were careful this time to hold her till she got steady on her legs. Father and mother at the tail and Blackshaw and I at the horns, we marched her home and gave her a bran mash. Then we turned to our work in the house while the men sat and smoked and spat on the veranda, discussing the drought for an hour, at the end of which time they went to help someone else with their stock. I made up the fire and we continued our ironing, which had been interrupted some hours before. It was hot unpleasant work on such a day. We were forced to keep the doors and windows closed on account of the wind and dust. We were hot and tired, and our feet ached so that we could scarcely stand on them.

Weariness! Weariness!
Summer is fiendish and life is a curse, I said in my heart.
Day after day the drought continued. Now and again there would be a
few days of the raging wind before mentioned, which carried the dry grass
off the paddocks and piled it against the fences, darkened the air with dust,
and seemed to promise rain, but ever it dispersed whence it came, taking
with it the few clouds it had gathered up; and for weeks and weeks at a
stretch, from horizon to horizon, was never a speck to mar the cruel dazzling brilliance of the metal sky,
Weariness! Weariness!
I said the one thing many times but, ah, it was a weary thing which took
much repetition that familiarity might wear away a little of its bitterness!

§ *Women and the bush* Lawson (1), Franklin; Can: Traill; *Changing roles of
women* Harwood, Garner, Grenville; Can: Marlatt

'HENRY HANDEL RICHARDSON' (ETHEL FLORENCE LINDESAY ROBERTSON) (1870–1946)

Proem to Australia Felix

Australia Felix is the first volume of Richardson's *Fortunes of Richard Mahony* trilogy,
a work which is both an exploration of numerous aspects of nineteenth-century colonial life and an early masterpiece about the psychology of migrancy. Set on the Victoria
goldfields, the Proem to *Australia Felix* anticipates the whole trilogy: its vividly realized naturalistic detail and stress on the sense of psychological exile felt by Long Jim
typify the mixture of elements that gives the trilogy its distinctive vision. Subsequently
the main character, Dr Richard Mahony, feels a similar sense of alienation in Australia,
but proves equally ill at ease amid the snobbery and mean-spiritedness he finds in
England.

In a shaft on the Gravel Pits, a man had been buried alive. At work in a
deep wet hole, he had recklessly omitted to slab the walls of a drive; uprights
and tailors yielded under the lateral pressure, and the rotten earth collapsed,
bringing down the roof in its train. The digger fell forward on his face, his
ribs jammed across his pick, his arms pinned to his sides, nose and mouth
pressed into the sticky mud as into a mask; and over his defenceless body,
with a roar that burst his ear-drums, broke stupendous masses of earth.

His mates at the windlass went staggering back from the belch of violently discharged air: it tore the wind-sail to strips, sent stones and gravel
flying, loosened planks and props. Their shouts drawing no response, the
younger and nimbler of the two – he was a mere boy, for all his amazing

growth of beard – put his foot in the bucket and went down on the rope, kicking off the sides of the shaft with his free foot. A group of diggers, gathering round the pit-head, waited for the tug at the rope. It was quick in coming; and the lad was hauled to the surface. No hope: both drives had fallen in; the bottom of the shaft was blocked. The crowd melted with a 'Poor Bill – God rest his soul!' or with a silent shrug. Such accidents were not infrequent; each man might thank his stars it was not he who lay cooling down below. And so, since no more washdirt would be raised from this hole, the party that worked it made off for the nearest grog-shop, to wet their throats to the memory of the dead, and to discuss future plans.

All but one: a lean and haggard-looking man of some five and forty, who was known to his comrades as Long Jim. On hearing his mate's report he had sunk heavily down on a log, and there he sat, a pannikin of raw spirit in his hand, the tears coursing ruts down cheeks scabby with yellow mud, his eyes glassy as marbles with those that had still to fall.

He wept, not for the dead man, but for himself. This accident was the last link in a chain of ill-luck that had been forging ever since he first followed the diggings. He only needed to put his hand to a thing, and luck deserted it. In all the sinkings he had been connected with, he had not once caught his pick in a nugget or got the run of the gutter; the 'bottoms' had always proved barren, drives been exhausted without his raising the colour. At the present claim he and his mates had toiled for months, overcoming one difficulty after another. The slabbing, for instance, had cost them infinite trouble; it was roughly done, too, and, even after the pins were in, great flakes of earth would come tumbling down from between the joints, on one occasion nearly knocking silly the man who was below. Then, before they had slabbed a depth of three times nine, they had got into water, and in this they worked for the next sixty feet. They were barely rid of it, when the two adjoining claims were abandoned, and in came the flood again – this time they had to fly for their lives before it, so rapid was its rise. Not the strongest man could stand in this ice-cold water for more than three days on end – the bark slabs stank in it, too, like the skins in a tanner's yard – and they had been forced to quit work till it subsided. He and another man had gone to the hills, to hew trees for more slabs; the rest to the grog-shop. From there, when it was feasible to make a fresh start, they had to be dragged, some blind drunk, the rest blind stupid from their booze. That had been the hardest job of any: keeping the party together. They had only been eight in all – a hand-to-mouth number for a deep wet hole. Then, one had died of dysentery, contracted from working constantly in water up to his middle; another had been nabbed in a man-hunt and clapped into the 'logs.' And finally, but a day or two back, the three men who completed the nightshift had deserted for a new 'rush' to the Avoca. Now, his pal had gone, too. There was nothing left for him, Long Jim, to do, but to take his dish and turn fossicker[1]; or even to aim

---

1 Search for gold in rejected workings.

no higher than washing over the tailings[2] rejected by the fossicker.

At the thought his tears flowed anew. He cursed the day on which he had first set foot on Ballarat.

'It's 'ell for white men – 'ell, that's what it is!'

' 'Ere, 'ave another drink, matey, and fergit yer bloody troubles.'

His re-filled pannikin drained, he grew warmer round the heart; and sang the praises of his former life. He had been a lamplighter in the old country, and for many years had known no more arduous task than that of tramping round certain streets three times daily, ladder on shoulder, bitch at heel, to attend the little flames that helped to dispel the London dark. And he might have jogged on at this up to three score years and ten, had he never lent an ear to the tales that were being told of a wonderful country, where, for the mere act of stooping, and with your naked hand, you could pick up a fortune from the ground. Might the rogues who had spread these lies be damned to all eternity! Then, he had swallowed them only too willingly; and, leaving the old woman wringing her hands, had taken every farthing of his savings and set sail for Australia. That was close on three years ago. For all he knew, his wife might be dead and buried by this time; or sitting in the almshouse. She could not write, and only in the early days had an occasional newspaper reached him, on which, alongside the Queen's head, she had put the mark they had agreed on, to show that she was still alive. He would probably never see her again, but would end his days where he was. Well, they wouldn't be many; this was not a place that made old bones. And, as he sat, worked on by grief and liquor, he was seized by a desperate homesickness for the old country. Why had he ever been fool enough to leave it? He shut his eyes, and all the well-known sights and sounds of the familiar streets came back to him. He saw himself on his rounds of a winter's afternoon, when each lamp had a halo in the foggy air; heard the pit-pat of his four-footer behind him, the bump of the ladder against the prong of the lamp-post. His friend the policeman's glazed stovepipe shone out at the corner; from the distance came the tinkle of the muffin-man's bell, the cries of the buy-a-brooms. He remembered the glowing charcoal in the stoves of the chestnut and potato sellers; the appetising smell of the cooked-fish shops; the fragrant steam of the hot, dark coffee at the twopenny stall, when he had turned shivering out of bed; he sighed for the lights and jollity of the 'Hare and Hounds' on a Saturday night. He would never see anything of the kind again. No; here, under bare blue skies, out of which the sun frizzled you alive; here, where it couldn't rain without at once being a flood; where the very winds blew contrarily, hot from the north and bitter-chill from the south; where, no matter how great the heat by day, the night would as likely as not be nipping cold: here he was doomed to end his life, and to end it, for all the yellow sunshine, more hopelessly knotted and gnarled with rheumatism than if, dawn after dawn, he had gone out in a cutting north-easter, or groped his way through the grey fog-mists sent up

2 Inferior part of ore.

by grey Thames.

Thus he sat and brooded, all the hatred of the unwilling exile for the land that gives him house-room burning in his breast.

Who the man was, who now lay deep in a grave that fitted him as a glove fits the hand, careless of the pass to which he had brought his mate; who this really was, Long Jim knew no more than the rest. Young Bill had never spoken out. They had chummed together on the seventy-odd-mile tramp from Melbourne; had boiled a common billy[3] and slept side by side in rain-soaked blankets, under the scanty hair of a she-oak.[4] That was in the days of the first great stampede to the goldfields, when the embryo seaports were as empty as though they were plague-ridden, and every man who had the use of his legs was on the wide bush-track, bound for the north. It was better to be two than one in this medley of bullock-teams, lorries, carts and pack-horses, of dog-teams, wheelbarrows and swagmen,[5] where the air rang with oaths, shouts and hammering hoofs, with whip-cracking and bullock-prodding; in the hurly-burly of thieves, bushrangers and foreigners, of drunken convicts and deserting sailors, of slit-eyed Chinese and apt-handed Lascars,[6] of expirees[7] and ticket-of-leave[8] men, of Jews, Turks and other infidels. Long Jim, himself stunned by it all: by the pother of landing and of finding a roof to cover him; by the ruinous price of bare necessaries; by the length of this unheard-of walk that lay before his town-bred feet: Long Jim had gladly accepted the young man's company on the road. Originally, for no more than this; at heart he distrusted Young Bill, because of his fine-gentleman airs, and intended shaking the lad off as soon as they reached the diggings. There, a man must, for safety's sake, be alone, when he stooped to pick up his fortune. But at first sight of the strange, wild scene that met his eyes he hastily changed his mind. And so the two of them had stuck together; and he had never had cause to regret it. For all his lily-white hands and finical[9] speech Young Bill had worked like a nigger, standing by his mate through the latter's disasters; had worked till the ladyish hands were horny with warts and corns, and this, though he was doubled up with dysentery in the hot season, and racked by winter cramps. But the life had proved too hard for him, all the same. During the previous summer he had begun to drink – steadily, with the dogged persistence that was in him – and since then his work had gone downhill. His sudden death had only been a hastening-on of the inevitable. Staggering home to the tent after nightfall he would have been sure, sooner or later, to fall into a dry shicer[10] and break his neck, or into a wet one and be drowned.

On the surface of the Gravel Pits his fate was already forgotten. The rude activity of a gold-diggings in full swing had closed over the incident, swallowed it up.

Under a sky so pure and luminous that it seemed like a thinly drawn veil

---

3 Cylindrical boiling tin.   4 Australian casuarina.   5 Travellers carrying possessions (usually in a blanket roll).
6 Indian sailors.   7 Ex-convicts; those whose sentence has expired.   8 System allowing convicts leave to work prior to finishing their sentence; a kind of probation.   9 Over-precise; finicky.   10 A mining claim that proves unproductive.

of blueness, which ought to have been transparent, stretched what, from a short way off, resembled a desert of pale clay. No patch of green offered rest to the eye; not a tree, hardly a stunted bush had been left standing, either on the bottom of the vast shallow basin itself, or on the several hillocks that dotted it and formed its sides. Even the most prominent of these, the Black Hill, which jutted out on the Flat like a gigantic tumulus, had been stripped of its dense timber, feverishly disembowelled, and was now become a bald protuberance strewn with gravel and clay. The whole scene had that strange, repellent ugliness that goes with breaking up and throwing into disorder what has been sanctified as final, and belongs, in particular, to the wanton disturbing of earth's gracious, green-spread crust. In the pre-golden era this wide valley, lying open to sun and wind, had been a lovely grassland, ringed by a circlet of wooded hills; beyond these, by a belt of virgin forest. A limpid river and more than one creek had meandered across its face; water was to be found there even in the driest summer. She-oaks and peppermints[11] had given shade to the flocks of the early settlers; wattles had bloomed their brief delirious yellow passion against the grey-green foliage of the gums. Now, all that was left of the original 'pleasant resting-place' and its pristine beauty were the ancient volcanic cones of Warrenheip and Buninyong. These, too far off to supply wood for firing or slabbing, still stood green and timbered, and looked down upon the havoc that had been made of the fair, pastoral lands.

Seen nearer at hand, the dun-coloured desert resolved itself into uncountable pimpling clay and mud-heaps, of divers shade and varying sizes: some consisted of but a few bucketfuls of mullock,[12] others were taller than the tallest man. There were also hundreds of rain-soaked, mud-bespattered tents, sheds and awnings; wind-sails, which fell, funnel-like, from a kind of gallows into the shafts they ventilated; flags fluttering on high posts in front of stores. The many human figures that went to and fro were hardly to be distinguished from the ground they trod. They were coated with earth, clay-clad in ochre and gamboge.[13] Their faces were daubed with clauber;[14] it matted great beards, and entangled the coarse hairs on chests and brawny arms. Where, here and there, a blue jumper had kept a tinge of blueness, it was so besmeared with yellow that it might have been expected to turn green. The gauze neck-veils that hung from the brims of wide-awakes or cabbage-trees were become still little lattices of caked clay.

There was water everywhere. From the spurs and gullies round about, the autumn rains had poured freely down on the Flat; river and creeks had been over their banks; and such narrow ground-space as remained between the thick-sown tents, the myriads of holes that abutted one on another, jealous of every inch of space, had become a trough of mud. Water meandered over this mud, or carved its soft way in channels; it lay about in puddles, thick and dark as coffee-grounds; it filled abandoned shallow holes to the brim.

---

11 Type of eucalyptus, yielding peppermint oil. 12 Refuse from which gold has been extracted. 13 Gum-resin yellow. 14 Paste used to cover cracks in leather.

From this scene rose a blurred hum of sound; rose and as it were remained stationary above it – like a smoke-cloud, which no wind comes to drive away. Gradually, though, the ear made out, in the conglomerate of noise, a host of separate noises infinitely multiplied: the sharp tick-tick of surface-picks, the dull thud of shovels, their muffled echoes from the depths below. There was also the continuous squeak and groan of windlasses; the bump of the mullock emptied from the bucket; the trundle of wheelbarrows, pushed along a plank from the shaft's mouth to the nearest pool; the dump of the dart on the heap for washing. Along the banks of a creek, hundreds of cradles rattled and grated; the noise of the spades, chopping the gravel into the puddling-tubs or the Long Toms, was like the scrunch of shingle under waves. The fierce yelping of the dogs chained to the flag-posts of stores, mongrels which yapped at friend and foe alike, supplied a note of earsplitting discord.

But except for this it was a wholly mechanical din. Human brains directed operations, human hands carried them out, but the sound of the human voice was, for the most part, lacking. The diggers were a sombre, preoccupied race, little given to lip-work. Even the 'shepherds,' who, in waiting to see if their neighbours struck the lead, beguiled the time with euchre and 'lambskinnet,'[15] played moodily, their mouths glued to their pipe-stems; they were tail-on-end to fling down the cards for pick and shovel. The great majority, ant-like in their indefatigable busyness, neither turned a head nor looked up: backs were bent, eyes fixed, in a hard scrutiny of cradle or tin-dish: it was the earth that held them, the familiar, homely earth, whose common fate it is to be trodden heedlessly underfoot. Here, it was the loadstone that drew all men's thoughts. And it took toll of their bodies in odd, exhausting forms of labour, which were swift to weed out the unfit.

The men at the windlasses spat into their horny palms and bent to the crank: they paused only to pass the back of a hand over a sweaty forehead, or to drain a nose between two fingers. The barrow-drivers shoved their loads, the bones of their forearms standing out like ribs. Beside the pools, the puddlers chopped with their shovels; some even stood in the tubs, and worked the earth with their feet, as wine-pressers trample grapes. The cradlers, eternally rocking with one hand, held a long stick in the other with which to break up any clods a careless puddler might have deposited in the hopper.[16] Behind these came the great army of fossickers, washers of surface-dirt, equipped with knives and tin-dishes, and content if they could wash out half-a-pennyweight to the dish. At their heels still others, who treated the tailings they threw away. And among these last was a sprinkling of women, more than one with an infant sucking at her breast. Withdrawn into a group for themselves worked a body of Chinese, in loose blue blouses, flapping blue leg-bags and huge conical straw hats. They, too, fossicked and re-washed, using extravagant quantities of water.

Thus the pale-eyed multitude worried the surface, and, at the risk and

---

15 Card games.   16 Inverted pyramid through which ore is passed.

cost of their lives, probed the depths. Now that deep sinking was in vogue, gold-digging no longer served as a play-game for the gentleman and the amateur; the greater number of those who toiled at it were work-tried, seasoned men. And yet, although it had now sunk to the level of any other arduous and uncertain occupation, and the magic prizes of the early days were seldom found, something of the old, romantic glamour still clung to this most famous gold-field, dazzling the eyes and confounding the judgment. Elsewhere, the horse was in use at the puddling-trough, and machines for crushing quartz were under discussion. But the Ballarat digger resisted the introduction of machinery, fearing the capitalist machinery would bring in its train. He remained the dreamer, the jealous individualist; he hovered for ever on the brink of a stupendous discovery.

This dream it was, of vast wealth got without exertion, which had decoyed the strange, motley crowd, in which peers and churchmen rubbed shoulders with the scum of Norfolk Island,[17] to exile in this outlandish region. And the intention of all alike had been: to snatch a golden fortune from the earth and then, hey, presto! for the old world again. But they were reckoning without their host: only too many of those who entered the country went out no more. They became prisoners to the soil. The fabulous riches of which they had heard tell amounted, at best, to a few thousands of pounds: what folly to depart with so little, when mother earth still teemed! Those who drew blanks nursed an unquenchable hope, and laboured all their days like navvies, for a navvy's wage. Others again, broken in health or disheartened, could only turn to an easier handiwork. There were also men who, as soon as fortune smiled on them, dropped their tools and ran to squander the work of months in a wild debauch; and they invariably returned, tail down, to prove their luck anew. And, yet again, there were those who, having once seen the metal in the raw: in dust, fine as that brushed from a butterfly's wing; in heavy, chubby nuggets; or, more exquisite still, as the daffodil-yellow veining of bluish-white quartz: these were gripped in the subtlest way of all. A passion for the gold itself awoke in them an almost sensual craving to touch and possess; and the glitter of a few specks at the bottom of pan or cradle came, in time, to mean more to them than 'home,' or wife, or child.

Such were the fates of those who succumbed to the 'unholy hunger.' It was like a form of revenge taken on them, for their loveless schemes of robbing and fleeing; a revenge contrived by the ancient, barbaric country they had so lightly invaded. Now, she held them captive – without chains; ensorcelled – without witchcraft; and, lying stretched like some primeval monster in the sun, her breasts freely bared, she watched, with a malignant eye, the efforts made by these puny mortals to tear their lips away.

§ *Landscape and language* Harpur, Clarke; *Types of settlement* Rudd, White (2); Can: Traill

---

17 Island approx. 1,500 km. east north-east of Sydney; in early nineteenth century penal settlement, to which most serious criminals were sent.

KENNETH SLESSOR (1901–71)

1: South Country

    After the whey-faced anonymity
    Of river-gums and scribbly-gums and bush,
    After the rubbing and the hit of brush,
    You come to the South Country

5   As if the argument of trees were done,
    The doubts and quarrelling, the plots and pains,
    All ended by these clear and gliding planes
    Like an abrupt solution.

    And over the flat earth of empty farms
10   The monstrous continent of air floats back
    Coloured with rotting sunlight and the black,
    Bruised flesh of thunderstorms:

    Air arched, enormous, pounding the bony ridge,
    Ditches and hutches, with a drench of light,
15   So huge, from such infinities of height,
    You walk on the sky's beach

    While even the dwindled hills are small and bare,
    As if, rebellious, buried, pitiful,
    Something below pushed up a knob of skull,
20   Feeling its way to air.

§ *Representations of landscape* Lawson (1), Richardson, Wright, Hope, White (2)

2: The Night Ride

    Gas flaring on the yellow platform; voices running up and
      down;
    Milk-tins in cold dented silver; half-awake I stare,
    Pull up the blind, blink out – all sounds are drugged;
    The slow blowing of passengers asleep;
5   Engines yawning; water in heavy drips;
    Black, sinister travellers, lumbering up the station,
    One moment in the window, hooked over bags;
    Hurrying, unknown faces – boxes with strange labels –
    All groping clumsily to mysterious ends,
10   Out of the gaslight, dragged by private Fates.

Their echoes die. The dark train shakes and plunges;
Bells cry out; the night-ride starts again.
Soon I shall look out into nothing but blackness,
Pale, windy fields. The old roar and knock of the rails
15 Melts in dull fury. Pull down the blind. Sleep. Sleep.
Nothing but grey, rushing rivers of bush outside.
Gaslight and milk-cans. Of Rapptown I recall nothing else.

§ *Train journey* Wright

A. D. HOPE (1907–)

Australia

A Nation of trees, drab green and desolate grey
In the field uniform of modern wars,
Darkens her hills, those endless, outstretched paws
Of Sphinx demolished or stone lion worn away.

5   They call her a young country, but they lie:
She is the last of lands, the emptiest,
A woman beyond her change of life, a breast
Still tender but without the womb is dry.

Without songs, architecture, history:
10   The emotions and supersitions of younger lands,
Her rivers of water drown among inland sands,
The river of her immense stupidity

Floods her monotonous tribes from Cairns to Perth.
In them at last the ultimate men arrive
15   Whose boast is not: 'we live' but 'we survive',
A type who will inhabit the dying earth.

And her five cities, like five teeming sores,
Each drains her: a vast parasite robber-state
Where second-hand Europeans pullulate
20   Timidly on the edge of alien shores.

Yet there are some like me turn gladly home
From the lush jungle of modern thought, to find
The Arabian desert of the human mind,
Hoping, if still from the deserts the prophets come,

---

13 **Cairns/Perth**: cities representing opposite ends of Australia: in the north-east and south-west respectively.

25 Such savage and scarlet as no green hills dare
Springs in that waste, some spirit which escapes
The learned doubt, the chatter of cultured apes
Which is called civilization over there.

§ *Poems about 'Australia'*: Gilmore, O'Dowd, McAuley; *Representations of landscape* Lawson (1), Richardson, Slessor (1), Wright

JAMES MCAULEY (1917–76)

Terra Australis*

Voyage within you, on the fabled ocean,
And you will find that Southern Continent,
Quiros' vision – his hidalgo heart
And mythical Australia, where reside
5 All things in their imagined counterpart.

It is your land of similes: the wattle
Scatters its pollen on the doubting heart;
The flowers are wide-awake; the air gives ease.
There you come home; the magpies call you Jack
10 And whistle like larrikins at you from the trees.

There too the angophora preaches on the hillsides
With the gestures of Moses; and the white cockatoo,
Perched on his limbs, screams with demoniac pain;
And who shall say on what errand the insolent emu
15 Walks between morning and night on the edge of the plain?

But northward in valleys of the fiery Goat
Where the sun like a centaur vertically shoots
His raging arrows with unerring aim,
Stand the ecstatic solitary pyres
20 Of unknown lovers, featureless with flame.

§ *Poems about 'Australia'* Gilmore, O'Dowd, Hope; *Antipodean 'discovery'* NZSP: Curnow (2); *Interior journey* Af: Tutuola, Okri; Carib: Harris

---

* Latin phrase meaning 'the South Land', used in Europe from ancient times to refer to the notion of an 'undiscovered' southern continent; here suggestive of 'Australia' as an imaginative possibility.
3 hidalgo: gentleman.
10 larrikins: street rowdies; hooligans.
16 fiery Goat: presumably the Tropic of Capricorn

3 Quiros: Capt. Pedro Fernandez de Quiros (1563–1614), Portuguese explorer who attempted to found the New Jerusalem in the South Seas.
6 wattle: Australian acacia.
11 angophora: tree with vase-like fruits of family Myrtacae, found on east mainland of Australia; also known as 'apple tree'.

CHRISTINA STEAD (1902–83)

The Schoolboy's Tale: Day of Wrath

Do the mountains wear black for the death of a bee in the old world? Not so in the new. Perhaps Ardennes[1] wept over the 'unreturning brave,' but I saw death ride naked on a tropic shore and his breath never darkened the water nor brushed the sky: nature's children drowned, curdled the water with their blood, while she painted her cheeks, wreathed in smiles, and the hills sparkled with jollity by the pacific sea.

I lived in Avallon, a waterside village in a seaport. A woman in the district was divorced for adultery. Her husband was a cabinet minister, a rich man, coarse, luxurious and tyrannical. Public opinion was bitter against his wife because she had left his house and gone to live with her lover, and it was proved that because they were poor, she had slept with her two children nightly in her lover's bed. The children had to appear in court and give this evidence. The father renounced these children, who he declared were not of his blood, and he left all three in great poverty: this was not condemned, for a woman who forsakes wealth for poverty is obviously poor-spirited, and beneath commiseration: even the poor despise her.

The son was ten years old, the daughter fourteen. I knew her, her name was Viola. She was pretty, but thin, with long black hair, and rather smart with her tongue. Certainly she suffered in such an honest city, where the 'Decameron' is forbidden, and England's colonial history is expurgated for the school books.

I saw her mother once, a pretty, dark, sweet woman, who ventured timidly into the ladies' cabin on the ferry, and looked quickly but without expectation of greeting at the female faces decorating the walls. When I raised my hat to her she smiled with pleasure, but with indulgence also: she knew I pitied her, but she regarded us all very calmly from another world. The ladies were indignant that she continued to live in our district. 'She should have at least the delicacy to go where she is not known,' said my maiden aunt. Society, great beast of tender skin, blind, with elephant ears, felt indignant, lashed its little tail and got hot round the rump. It required a sacrifice, and when Jumbo wants something the gods themselves obey.

One Wednesday afternoon, the four o'clock ferry, which carried the schoolchildren home from town, was struck amidships by an ocean liner and sank immediately, carrying down more than fifty souls. Thirty children were drowned, and all those who died were from our village of Avallon. I went down to catch the four-thirty ferry and saw the stretchers with bodies brought in already by the rescuers. All the way home, with my books on the seat, I watched the lustrous tide flow in, bearing planks, seats, lifebuoys and splintered wood up into the bays and rivers. Eddies of soot and oil floated past. In a few minutes we reached the spot where the ferry lay with

---

1 Alluding to the heavy fighting in this part of Belgium in World War I.

her passengers, and I felt paralysed with a strange and almost voluptuous cramp, and my spirit being wound out of me like a djinn out of a pot. We went dead slow, with our flag at half-mast, and there was a silence on the boat. I thought of those people sitting below, almost living, with a glow on their cheeks still through the green gloom of the deep-water channel: they seemed a company that had gone apart for some conclave. I believed my two young sisters were there, waiting for me with open eyes, and wanted to dive in, but I could not move. When we neared home I saw my little brother running and jumping on our lawn, so I was reassured.

After a few days, when the last rumours and hopes had died out, and the whole village was in mourning, in the lovely weather, only one piece of fantasy remained: Viola alone had not been found. She must have been carried away, or been lost in the deeper mud of the bottom; the ferry itself had moved several hundred feet. It seemed to my mother and aunt that this was the 'judgment of God'; though for what mortal sins the other bereaved women had been punished, no one thought to conjecture.

At the end of a week Viola was found on one end of the wreck, standing upright, uninjured, her right foot simply entangled in a rope. The founts of pity at this word broke their seals and jetted in each breast, and everyone that night had before his eye the image of Viola standing in the green gloom for a week, upright, looking for the rescuers, astonished that they did not come for her, perhaps with a lively word on her lips at their slowness, and then, prisoned by her poor weak foot, decaying, but with her arms still floating up; a watermaiden tangled in a lily-root, and not able to reach the surface. I cried and thought how she died in that attitude to ask pity.

In fact, it turned out that way; or at least, if the church and justice were not moved, for they should be above the frailties of flesh and blood, the women began to lament on her mother's account, to say she was well punished and one could even pity her. The beast was appeased, as in ancient days, by the sacrifice of a virgin.

PATRICK WHITE (1912–90)

1: The Prodigal Son

This is by way of being an answer to Alister Kershaw's recent article *The Last Expatriate*,[1] but as I cannot hope to equal the slash and dash of Kershaw's journalistic weapons, I shall not attempt to answer him point by point. In any case, the reasons why anybody is an expatriate, or why another chooses to return home, are such personal ones that the question can only be answered in a personal way.

At the age of 46 I have spent just on twenty of those years overseas.

---

1 Published in *Australian Letters* in 1958, when 'The Prodigal Son' also appeared.

During the last ten, I have hardly stirred from the six acres of 'Dogwoods', Castle Hill.[2] It sounds odd, and is perhaps worth trying to explain.

Brought up to believe in the maxim: Only the British can be right, I did accept this during the earlier part of my life. Ironed out in an English public school and finished off at King's, Cambridge, it was not until 1939, after wandering by myself through most of Western Europe, and finally most of the United States, that I began to grow up and think my own thoughts. The War did the rest. What had seemed a brilliant, intellectual, highly desirable existence, became distressingly parasitic and pointless. There is nothing like a rain of bombs to start one trying to assess one's own achievement. Sitting at night in his London bed-sitting room during the first months of the Blitz, this chromium-plated Australian with two fairly successful novels to his credit came to the conclusion that his achievement was practically nil. Perhaps significantly, he was reading at that time Eyre's *Journal*.[3] Perhaps also he had the wind up; certainly he reached rather often for the bottle of Calvados in the wardrobe. Anyway, he experienced those first sensations of rootlessness which Alister Kershaw has deplored and explained as the 'desire to nuzzle once more at the benevolent teats of the mother country'.

All through the War in the Middle East there persisted a longing to return to the scenes of childhood, which is, after all, the purest well from which the creative artist draws. Aggravated further by the terrible nostalgia of the desert landscapes, this desire was almost quenched by the year I spent stationed in Greece, where perfection presents itself on every hand, not only the perfection of antiquity, but that of nature, and the warmth of human relationships expressed in daily living. Why didn't I stay in Greece? I was tempted to. Perhaps it was the realisation that even the most genuine resident Hellenophile accepts automatically the vaguely comic role of Levantine beachcomber. He does not belong, the natives seem to say, not without affection; it is sad for him, but he is nothing. While the Hellenophile continues humbly to hope.

So I did not stay in my elective Greece. Demobilisation in England left me with the alternative of remaining in what I then felt to be an actual and spiritual graveyard, with the prospect of ceasing to be an artist and turning instead into that most sterile of beings, a London intellectual, or of returning home, to the stimulus of time remembered. Quite honestly, the thought of a full belly influenced me as well, after toying with the soft, sweet awfulness of horsemeat stew in the London restaurants that I could afford. So I came home. I bought a farm at Castle Hill, and with a Greek friend and partner, Manoly Lascaris, started to grow flowers and vegetables, and to breed Schnauzers and Saanen goats.

The first years I was content with these activities, and to soak myself in landscape. If anybody mentioned Writing, I would reply: 'Oh, one day, perhaps'. But I had no real intention of giving the matter sufficient thought.

---

2 On the outskirts of Sydney. 3 Edward John Eyre's *Journal* (1845) describes his 1840–1 journey of exploration into central Australia from Adelaide and onward around the Great Australian Bight to King George Sound in Western Australia.

The Aunt's Story, written immediately after the War, before returning to Australia, had succeeded with overseas critics, failed as usual with the local ones, remained half-read, it was obvious from the state of the pages in the lending libraries. Nothing seemed important, beyond living and eating, with a roof of one's own over one's head.

Then, suddenly, I began to grow discontented. Perhaps, in spite of Australian critics, writing novels was the only thing I could do with any degree of success; even my half-failures were some justification of an otherwise meaningless life. Returning sentimentally to a country I had left in my youth, what had I really found? Was there anything to prevent me packing my bag and leaving like Alister Kershaw and so many other artists? Bitterly I had to admit, no. In all directions stretched the Great Australian Emptiness, in which the mind is the least of possessions, in which the rich man is the important man, in which the schoolmaster and the journalist rule what intellectual roost there is, in which beautiful youths and girls stare at life through blind blue eyes, in which human teeth fall like autumn leaves, the buttocks of cars grow hourly glassier, food means cake and steak, muscles prevail, and the march of material ugliness does not raise a quiver from the average nerves.

It was the exaltation of the 'average' that made me panic most, and in this frame of mind, in spite of myself, I began to conceive another novel. Because the void I had to fill was so immense, I wanted to try to suggest in this book every possible aspect of life, through the lives of an ordinary man and woman. But at the same time I wanted to discover the extraordinary behind the ordinary, the mystery and the poetry which alone could make bearable the lives of such people, and incidentally, my own life since my return.

So I began to write *The Tree of Man*. How it was received by the more important Australian critics is now ancient history. Afterwards I wrote *Voss*, possibly conceived during the early days of the Blitz, when I sat reading Eyre's *Journal* in a London bed-sitting room. Nourished by months spent trapesing backwards and forwards across the Egyptian and Cyrenaican deserts, influenced by the arch-megalomaniac of the day, the idea finally matured after reading contemporary accounts of Leichhardt's expeditions[4] and A. H. Chisholm's *Strange New World* on returning to Australia.

It would be irrelevant to discuss here the literary aspects of the novel. More important are those intentions of the author which have pleased some readers without their knowing exactly why, and helped to increase the rage of those who have found the book meaningless. Always something of a frustrated painter, and a composer *manqué*, I wanted to give my book the textures of music, the sensuousness of paint, to convey through the theme and characters of *Voss* what Delacroix and Blake might have seen, what Mahler and Liszt might have heard. Above all I was determined to prove that the

---

4 Ludwig Leichhardt, who disappeared without trace on his third expedition into the Australian interior in 1848, is generally seen as an inspiration for White's protagonist in *Voss* (1957).

Australian novel is not necessarily the dreary, dun-coloured offspring of journalistic realism. On the whole, the world has been convinced, only here, at the present moment, the dingoes are howling unmercifully.

What, then, have been the rewards of this returned expatriate? I remember when, in the flush of success after my first novel, an old and wise Australian journalist called Guy Innes came to interview me in my London flat. He asked me whether I wanted to go back. I had just 'arrived'; who was I to want to go back? 'Ah, but when you do,' he persisted, 'the colours will come flooding back onto your palette.' This gentle criticism of my first novel only occurred to me as such in recent years. But I think perhaps Guy Innes has been right.

So, amongst the rewards, there is refreshed landscape which even in its shabbier, remembered version has always made a background to my life. The worlds of plants and music may never have revealed themselves had I sat talking brilliantly to Alister Kershaw over a Pernod on the Left Bank. Possibly all art flowers more readily in silence. Certainly the state of simplicity and humility is the only desirable one for artist or for man. While to reach it may be impossible, to attempt to do so is imperative. Stripped of almost everything that I had considered desirable and necessary, I began to try. Writing, which had meant the practice of an art by a polished mind in civilised surroundings, became a struggle to create completely fresh forms out of the rocks and sticks of words. I began to see things for the first time. Even the boredom and frustration presented avenues for endless exploration; even the ugliness, the bags and iron of Australian life, acquired a meaning. As for the cat's cradle of human intercourse, this was necessarily simplified, often bungled, sometimes touching. Its very tentativeness can be reward. There is always the possibility that the book lent, the record played, may lead to communication between human beings. There is the possibility that one may be helping to people a barely inhabited country with a race possessed of understanding.

These, then, are some of the reasons why an expatriate has stayed, in the face of those disappointments which follow inevitably upon his return. Abstract and unconvincing, the Alister Kershaws will probably answer, but such reasons, as I have already suggested, are a personal matter. More concrete, and most rewarding of all, are the many letters I have received from unknown Australians, for whom my writing seems to have opened a window. To me, the letters alone are reason enough for staying.

§ White (2)

2: *From* The Tree of Man

Covering a period extending from the 1880s to the 1930s, *The Tree of Man* has been descrbed as an Australian epic. Its account of how Stan Parker and his wife Amy clear and farm a piece of land in the bush brings a visionary perspective to one of the classic themes of Australian fiction. In 'The Prodigal Son' (see above) White speaks of his attempt in *The Tree of Man* 'to discover the extraordinary behind the ordinary, the mystery and the poetry which alone could make bearable the lives of [ordinary] people'. The passage included here is the opening chapter of the novel.

A cart drove between the two big stringybarks[1] and stopped. These were the dominant trees in that part of the bush, rising above the involved scrub with the simplicity of true grandeur. So the cart stopped, grazing the hairy side of a tree, and the horse, shaggy and stolid as the tree, sighed and took root.

The man who sat in the cart got down. He rubbed his hands together, because already it was cold, a curdle of cold cloud in a pale sky, and copper in the west. On the air you could smell the frost. As the man rubbed his hands, the friction of cold skin intensified the coldness of the air and the solitude of that place. Birds looked from twigs, and the eyes of animals were drawn to what was happening. The man lifting a bundle from a cart. A dog lifting his leg on an anthill. The lip drooping on the sweaty horse.

Then the man took an axe and struck at the side of a hairy tree, more to hear the sound than for any other reason. And the sound was cold and loud. The man struck at the tree, and struck, till several white chips had fallen. He looked at the scar in the side of the tree. The silence was immense. It was the first time anything like this had happened in that part of the bush.

More quickly then, as if deliberately breaking with a dream, he took the harness from the horse, leaving a black pattern of sweat. He hobbled the strong fetlocks of the cobby[2] little horse and stuck the nosebag on his bald face. The man made a lean-to with bags and a few saplings. He built a fire. He sighed at last, because the lighting of his small fire had kindled in him the first warmth of content. Of being somewhere. That particular part of the bush had been made his by the entwining fire. It licked at and swallowed the loneliness.

By this time also the red dog had come and sat at the fire, near, though not beside the man, who was not intimate with his animals. He did not touch or address them. It was enough for them to be there, at a decent distance. So the dog sat. His face had grown sharp with attention, and with a longing for food, for the tucker[3] box that had not yet been lifted from the cart. So the sharp dog looked. Hunger had caused him to place his paws delicately. His yellow eyes consumed the man in the interval before meat.

---

1 Eucalyptus trees. 2 Short-legged; thickset. 3 Food.

The man was a young man. Life had not yet operated on his face. He was good to look at; also, it would seem, good. Because he had nothing to hide, he did perhaps appear to have forfeited a little of his strength. But that is the irony of honesty.

All around, the bush was disappearing. In that light of late evening, under the white sky, the black limbs of trees, the black and brooding scrub, were being folded into one. Only the fire held out. And inside the circle of its light the man's face was unconcerned as he rubbed tobacco in the palms of his hard hands, a square of tinkling paper stuck to his lower lip.

The dog whistled through his pointed nose. In the light of the fire the bristles of his muzzle glistened. As he watched for an end to this interminable act.

Still there it was, with the smoke coming out.

The man got up. He dusted his hands. He began to take down the tucker box.

How the dog trembled then.

There was the sound of tin plate, tea on tin, the dead thump of flour. Somewhere water ran. Birds babbled, settling themselves on a roost. The young horse, bright amongst his forelock, and the young and hungry dog were there, watching the young man. There was a unity of eyes and firelight.

The gilded man was cutting from a lump of meat. It made the dog cavort like a mad, reddish horse. The man was throwing to the dog, while pretending, according to his nature, not to do so. The dog gulped at the chunks of fatty meat, the collar working forward on his neck, the eyes popping in his head. The man ate, swallowing with some ugliness, swallowing to get it down, he was alone, and afterwards swilling the hot, metallic tea, almost to get it finished with. But warmth came. Now he felt good. He smelled the long, slow scent of chaff slavered in the nosebag by the munching horse. He smelled the smell of green wood burning. He propped his head against the damp collar discarded by the horse. And the cavern of fire was enormous, labyrinthine, that received the man. He branched and flamed, glowed and increased, and was suddenly extinguished in the little puffs of smoke and tired thoughts.

The name of this man was Stan Parker.

While he was still unborn his mother had thought she would like to call him Ebenezer, but he was spared this because his father, an obscene man, with hair on his stomach, had laughed. So the mother thought no more about it. She was a humourless and rather frightened woman. When the time came she called her boy Stanley, which was, after all, a respectable sort of a name. She remembered also the explorer, of whom she had read.

The boy's mother had read a lot, through frail gold-rimmed spectacles, which did not so much frame her watery blue eyes as give them an unprotected look. She had begun to read in the beginning as a protection from the frightening and unpleasant things. She continued because, apart from the story, literature brought with it a kind of gentility for which she craved.

Then she became a teacher. All this before she married. The woman's name was Noakes. And she remembered hearing her own mother, talking of things that had happened at Home, tell of a Noakes who had married the chaplain to a lord.

The woman herself did no such thing. By some mistake or fascination, she had married Ned Parker, the blacksmith at Willow Creek, who got drunk regular, and once had answered a question in a sermon, and who could twist a piece of iron into a true lover's knot. This was not genteel, but at least she was protected by a presence of brawn. So Miss Noakes had become Mrs Parker, became also, in a way, more frightened than before.

'Stan,' said his mother once, 'you must promise to love God, and never to touch a drop.'

'Yes,' said the boy, for he had had experience of neither, and the sun was in his eyes.

In the drowsy bosom of the fire that he had made the young man remembered his parents and his mother's God, who was a pale-blue gentleness. He had tried to see her God, in actual feature, but he had not. Now, Lord, he had said, lying with his eyes open in the dark. Sometimes he would hear his father, swearing and belching, the other side of the door.

His father did not deny God. On the contrary. He was the blacksmith, and had looked into the fire. He smote the anvil, and the sparks flew. All fiery on his own strength, deaf with the music of metal, and superior to the stench of burned hoof, there was no question. Once, from the bottom of a ditch, on his way home, after rum, he had even spoken to God, and caught at the wing of a protesting angel, before passing out.

The God of Parker the father, the boy saw, was essentially a fiery God, a gusty God, who appeared between belches, accusing with a horny finger. He was a God of the Prophets. And, if anything, this was the God that the boy himself suspected and feared rather than his mother's gentleness. Anyway, in the beginning. At Willow Creek, God bent the trees till they streamed in the wind like beards, He rained upon the tin roofs till even elders grew thoughtful, and smaller, and yellower, by the light of smoking lamps, and He cut the throat of old Joe Skinner, who was nothing to deserve it, not that anyone knew of, he was a decent old cuss, who liked to feed birds with crusts of bread.

This was one of the things, the young man remembered, his mother had not attempted to explain. 'It is one of those things that happen,' she said.

So the mother looked upset and turned away. There were many things to which she did not have the answers. For this reason she did not go much with the other women, who knew, most of them, most things, and if they didn't, it wasn't worth knowing. So the mother of Stan Parker was alone. She continued to read, the Tennyson with brass hasps and the violets pressed inside, the spotted Shakespeare that had been in a flood, and the collection of catalogues, annuals, recipe books, and a cyclopaedia and gazetteer that composed her distinguished and protective reading. She read, and she practised neatness, as if she might tidy things up that way; only time and moth destroyed her efforts, and the souls of human beings, which will burst out of any box they are put inside.

There was the young man her son, for instance, who now lay with his head on a horse's collar, beside his bit of a fire, the son had thrown off the lid. He had sprung out, without unpleasantness, he was what you would call a good lad, good to his mother and all that, but somehow a separate being. Ah, she had said, he will be a teacher, or a preacher, he will teach the words of the poets and God. With her respect for these, she suspected, in all twilight and good faith, that they might be interpreted. But to the son, who had read the play of *Hamlet* in his mother's Shakespeare, and of the Old Testament those passages in which men emerged from words, reading by day to the buzz of fly or at night while puddle cracked, there seemed no question of interpretation. Anyway, not yet.

He was no interpreter. He shifted beside his fire at the suggestion that he might have been. He was nothing much. He was a man. So far he had succeeded in filling his belly. So far, mystery was not his personal concern, doubts were still faint echoes. Certainly he had seen the sea, and the hurly-burly of it did hollow out of him a cave of wonderment and discontent. So also the words of songs floating in the dust and pepper trees of a country town at dusk do become personal. And once some woman, some whore, neither young nor pretty, had pressed her face against a windowpane and stared out, and Stan Parker had remembered her face because he shared the distance from which he eyes had looked.

But the fire was dying, he saw, with such cold thoughts. He shivered, and leaned forward, and raked at the fragments of red fire, so that they shot up into the night on a fresh lease. His place in the present was warm enough. On the fringe of firelight stood the young horse, his knees bent, trailing from his head the nosebag, now empty and forgotten. The red dog, who had been lying with his nose on his paws, crawled forward on his belly and nuzzled and licked at the wrist of the man, who pushed him away on principle. The dog sighed at the touch. And the man too was reassured of his own presence.

Night had settled on the small cocoon of light, threatening to crush it. The cold air flowing sluiced the branches of trees, surged through the standing trunks, and lay coldly mounting in the gully. Rocks groaned with cold. In the saucers that pocked the face of stone, water tightened and cracked.

A frosty, bloody hole, complained the man, from out of the half-sleep in which he had become involved, and twitched the bags tighter round his body.

But he knew also there was nothing to be done. He knew that where his cart had stopped, he would stop. There was nothing to be done. He would make the best of this cell in which he had been locked. How much of will, how much of fate, entered into this it was difficult to say. Or perhaps fate is will. Anyway, Stan Parker was pretty stubborn.

He was neither a preacher nor a teacher, as his mother had hoped he might still become, almost up to the moment when they put her under the yellow grass at the bend in Willow Creek. He had tried his hand at this and that. He had driven a mob of skeleton sheep, and a mob of chafing, satin cattle; he had sunk a well in solid rock, and built a house, and killed a pig; he had weighed out the sugar in a country store, and cobbled shoes, and ground knives. But he had not continued to do any of these things for long, because he knew that it was not intended.

'There goes young Stan,' people said, pulling down their mouths and blowing the air through their noses, because, they felt, here was somebody assailable.

Because they had looked through the doorway and seen him, as a little boy, blowing the bellows for his father, there, they felt, he shall stay put.

To stay put was, in fact, just what the young man Stanley Parker himself desired; but where, and how? In the streets of towns the open windows, on the dusty roads the rooted trees, filled him with the melancholy longing for permanence. But not yet. It was a struggle between two desires. As the little boy, holding the musical horseshoes for his father, blowing the bellows, or scraping up the grey parings of hoof and the shapely yellow mounds of manure, he had already experienced the unhappiness of these desires. Ah, here, the sun said, and the persistent flies, is the peace of permanence; all these shapes are known, act opens out of act, the days are continuous. It was hard certainly in the light of that steady fire not to interpret all fire. Besides, he had an affection for his belching and hairy father, and quite sincerely cried when the blacksmith finally died of the rum bottle and a stroke.

Then, more than at any time, the nostalgia of permanence and the fiend of motion fought inside the boy, right there at the moment when his life was ending and beginning.

'At least you will be a comfort to your mother, Stan,' said Mrs Parker, her nose grown thin and pink, not so much from grief as from remembering many of those incidents which had pained her in a world that is not nice.

The boy looked at her in horror, not understanding altogether what she implied, but knowing for certain he could not be what she expected.

Already the walls of their wooden house were being folded back. The pepper tree invaded his pillow, and the dust of the road was at his feet. One morning early, while the dew was still cold outside his boots, he got up and left, in search, if he had known it, of permanence. And so he went and came for several years, getting nothing much beyond his muscles, scabs on his hands, and on his face the first lines.

'Why, Stan, you are a man now,' said his mother once, when he walked in across the creaking board in the doorway of their house at Willow Creek and caught her going through the things in a drawer.

It was as if she had come out of herself for the first time in years, to take surprised notice.

And he was surprised too, for his manhood did not feel exactly different.

They were both awkward for a while.

Then Stan Parker knew by his mother's shoulders and the gristle in her neck that she would die soon. There was, too, a smell of old letters in the room.

She began to talk of money in the bank. 'And there's that land that was your father's, in the hills back from here, I don't just know the name, I don't think it ever had one, people always called it Parker's when they spoke. Well, there is this land. Your father did not think much of it. The land was always uncleared. Scrubby, he said. Though the soil is good in patches. When the country opens up it will perhaps be worth a little. The railway is a wonderful invention, and, of course, assistance to the landowner. So keep this property, Stan,' she said, 'it's safe.'

Mrs Parker's voice had been scrubbed clean of the emotions. It was bare and very dull.

But the young man's breath thickened, his heart tolled against his ribs – was it for a liberation or imprisonment? He did not know. Only that this scrubby, anonymous land was about to become his, and that his life was taking shape for the first time.

'Yes, Mother,' he said. As always when she spoke of matters of importance. And turned away to hide his certainty.

Not long after that she died, and he touched her cold hands, and buried her, and went away.

Some people said that young Stan Parker had no feelings, but it was just that he had not known her very well.

Nobody took much notice when the young man left for good, in a cart that he had bought from Alby Veitch, with a shaggy sort of a brumby[4] horse. As the wheels of the cart moved over the melting ruts and screaming fowls made way, only a face or two, released from the beating of a mat or kneading of dough, remarked that young Stan was on the move. Soon there would be no reason to remember Parkers in that place. Because the present prevails.

Stan Parker drove on, through mud and over stones, towards those hills in which his land lay. All that day they rattled and bumped, the sides of the sturdy horse grown sleeker in sweat. Under the cart a red dog lolloped loosely along. His pink tongue, enormous with distance, swept the ground.

So they reached their destination, and ate, and slept, and in the morning of frost, beside the ashes of a fire, were faced with the prospect of leading some kind of life. Of making that life purposeful. Of opposing silence and rock and tree. It does not seem possible in a world of frost.

That world was still imprisoned, just as the intentions were, coldly, sulkily. Grass that is sometimes flesh beneath the teeth would have splintered now, sharp as glass. Rocks that might have contracted physically had grown in hostility during the night. The air drank at the warm bodies of birds to swallow them in flight.

But no bird fell.

Instead, they continued to chafe the silence. And the young man, after

---

4 Wild; unbroken.

sighing a good deal, and turning in his bags, in which the crumbs of chaff still tickled and a flea or two kept him company, flung himself into the morning. There was no other way.

But to scrape the ash, but to hew with the whole body as well as axe the grey hunks of fallen wood, but to stamp the blood to life, and the ground thawing took life too, the long ribbons of grass bending and moving as the sun released, the rocks settling into peace of recovered sun, the glug and tumble of water slowly at first, heard again somewhere, the sun climbing ever, with towards it smoke thin but certain that the man made.

A little bird with straight-up tail flickered and took the crumb that lay at the man's feet.

The man's jaws took shape upon the crusts of stale bread. His jaws that were well shaped, strong, with a bristling of sun about the chin. This was gold.

Down through him wound the long ribbon of warm tea. He felt glad.

As the day increased, Stan Parker emerged and, after going here and there, simply looking at what was his, began to tear the bush apart. His first tree fell through the white silence with a volley of leaves. This was clean enough. But there was also the meaner warfare of the scrub, deadly in technique and omnipresence, that would come up from behind and leave warning on the flesh in messages of blood. For the man had stripped down to his dark and wrinkled pants. Above this indecency his golden body writhed, not in pain, but with a fury of impatience. Anaesthetized by the future, he felt neither whips nor actual wounds. He worked on, and the sun dried his blood.

Many days passed in this way, the man clearing his land. The muscular horse, shaking his untouched forelock, tautened the chain traces and made logs move. The man hewed and burned. Sometimes, possessed by his daemon of purpose, the ribs seemed to flow beneath his skin. Sometimes his ordinarily moist and thoughtful mouth grew rigid, fixed in the white scales of thirst. But he burned and hewed. At night he lay on the heap of sacks and leaves, on the now soft and tranquil earth, and abandoned the bones of his body. The logs of sleep lay dead heavy.

There in the scarred bush, that had not yet accepted its changed face, the man soon began to build a house, or shack. He brought the slabs he had shaped for logs. Slowly. He piled his matchsticks. So the days were piled too. Seasons were closing and opening on the clearing in which the man was at work. If days fanned the fury in him, months soothed, so that time, as it passed, was both shaping and dissolving, in one.

But the house was being built amongst the stumps, that in time had ceased to bleed. It was more the symbol of a house. Its prim, slab walls fulfilled necessity. There were windows to let the light into the oblong room, there was a tin chimney, shaped like a matchbox, through which the smoke came at last. Finally he stuck on a veranda. It was too low, rather a frowning addition, but which did not forbid. Seen through the trees, it was a plain but honest house that the man had built.

If there had been neighbours, it would have been a comfort to see the smoke occur regularly in the matchbox-chimney. But there were no neigh-bours. Only sometimes, if you listened on the stiller days, you might hear the sound of an axe, like the throb of your own heart, in the blue distance. Only very distant. Or more distantly, a cock. Or imagination. It was too far.

Sometimes the man would drive off into that distance in his high cart. Then the clearing was full of the whinge and yelping of the red dog, left chained to a veranda post. Till in time the silence grew, and his yellow eyes watched it. Or a parrot flurried the blue air. Or a mouse glistened on the dirt floor of the house. The abandoned dog was at the service of silence at last. He was no longer attached, even by his chain, to the blunt house of the man's making.

The man always brought back things in his cart. He brought a scratched table and chairs, with mahogany lumps in the proper places. He brought an iron bed, big and noisy, of which the bars had been bent a bit by kids shov-ing their heads between. And he brought all those necessities, like flour, and a bottle of pain killer, and pickled meat, and kerosene, and seed potatoes, and a packet of needles, and oaten chaff for the shaggy horse, and the tea and sugar that trickled from their bags, so that you crunched across them, almost always, on the hardened floor.

The dog's collar almost carved off his neck when the man came, and there was always the joy and excitement and the smell of brought things.

Then, once, when the man had been gone some time, longer than nor-mal perhaps, he brought with him a woman, who sat beside him in the cart, holding the board and her flat hat. When she had got down, the dog, loosed from his chain, craned forward, still uncertain of his freedom, on trembling toes, in silence, and smelled the hem of her skirt.

§ White (1); *Settling the land* Lawson (1), Rudd, Baynton; Can: Traill; *Representations of landscape* Lawson (1), Richardson, Wright, Hope

JUDITH WRIGHT (1915–)

Train Journey

Glassed with cold sleep and dazzled by the moon,
out of the confused hammering dark of the train
I looked and saw under the moon's cold sheet
your delicate dry breasts, country that built my heart;

5   and the small trees on their uncoloured slope
like poetry moved, articulate and sharp
and purposeful under the great dry flight of air,
under the crosswise currents of wind and star.

Clench down your strength, box-tree and ironbark.
10 Break with your violent root the virgin rock.
Draw from the flying dark its breath of dew
till the unliving come to life in you.

Be over the blind rock a skin of sense,
under the barren height of a slender dance . . .

15 I woke and saw the dark small trees that burn
suddenly into flowers more lovely than the white moon.

§ *Representations of landscape* Hope, Lawson (1), Richardson, Slessor (1);
Train journey Slessor (2)

RAY LAWLER (1921–)

From Summer of the Seventeenth Doll

Summer of the Seventeenth Doll has been viewed as a breakthrough in the establishment of a vernacular Australian stage tradition. For sixteen years, two Queensland
cane-cutters, Roo and Barney, have come south to spend their lay-off period with two
Melbourne bar-maids, Olive and Nancy. Now, in the seventeenth summer, Nancy has
broken the sequence by marrying a city man and it is hoped that the widowed Pearl
can replace her. Emma is Olive's mother; 'Bubba' the young woman next door, whom
the two men continue to treat as a child. Viewed as an allegory about the changing
nature of Australian society, the play suggests the difficulty of sustaining older bush
mythologies in an increasingly urbanized present. In this extract Roo and Barney arrive
in 1953 – for the seventeenth summer.

> . . . [*Meanwhile, offstage, the taxi has drawn up in front of the house
> and has sounded a merry 'Om diddly om pom' on the horn. As* Olive
> *moves towards the front door we hear excited voices*].
> **Roo** [*off*] Hey, wake up in there.
> **Barney** [*off*] You little trimmer,[1] Emma, you little beauty. [Barney
> *moves easily up onto the verandah, carrying* Emma *over his shoul-
> der,* Emma *shrieking with laughter and pretended anger, beating at
> him with aged fists. As* Olive *opens the door,* Barney *yells.*]
> Hey, missus, where's your rubbish heap? Got some old sugar gone
> dry.
> [*Laughing,* Olive *stands aside and they rock into the house, coming*

---

1 Trouncer; person excellent in some respect.

*into prominence in the archway. Roo enters onto front verandah,
Olive moves into his arms and they kiss long and warmly. Pearl is
regarding Barney's antics with Emma in a restrained apprehension
which she hopes looks like amusement, when Barney focuses her for
the first time. He slaps Emma's rear and lets her slide down onto the
sofa.*]

Here, here, stop all this, you wicked old thing, you oughta have
more sense, playin' up like that in front of visitors.

Emma [*pummelling him*] It was you – you started it.

Barney [*holding her off, his eyes on Pearl*] That's enough, cut it out
now or I really will toss you out with the rubbish – look at the
lady watching you.

Emma [*screwing round*] Oh, her! She's the one I was tellin' you
about.

Barney Is she? Well, you nip out and give 'em a hand with the
bags then.

[*He puts her to one side and moves down on Pearl, but Emma stands
her ground. She is a wizened, life-battered wisp of a woman nearly
seventy, with no illusions about humanity, expecting the worst from
it, and generally crowing with cynical delight when her expectations
are fulfilled. Her eye, as she watches this meeting, is definitely
satirical.* Barney *swaggers down, and* Pearl *stands in front of the fireplace, self-consciously formal. He pauses before her with a wide boyish grin.*]

'Lo. S'pose they've told you about me, have they? I'm Barney.

Pearl [*stammering*] Yes. Olive did mention – I'm Mrs
Cunningham. How d'yer do.

[*She offers her hand awkwardly and he takes it, not shaking it, but
holding it gently as if to feel its weight.*]

Barney I'm pretty good. How's yerself?

[*He puts his other hand on top of hers, and, still grinning broadly,
forces her to meet his eyes.* Barney *owes most of his success in love to
this natural technique: he has an overwhelming weakness for women,
and makes them recognise it. Previous mention of him as a little man
is not quite correct. He is short certainly, but not much below medium
height, and solidly built. Probably his constant association with the
bigger* Roo *emphasises his lack of inches. His matter is assertive, confident and impudently bright, perhaps a little overdone as a defiance
to his forty years and the beginning of a pot belly. He has a returned
soldiers' badge in his lapel.* Pearl *tries to carry off her embarrassment
lightly*].

Pearl Oh, you know, a bit hot.

[Emma *gives a cackle of laughter and skitters off towards the kitchen,
passing* Olive *who, after her close silent meeting on the verandah with*
Roo, *is returning to the front room. Meanwhile* Roo *has gone offstage
and shortly reappears with two suitcases*].

Barney [*calling after* Emma] Cut out the rough stuff now.

Olive [*embracing* Barney] What's the matter with the old girl?

Barney [*giggling*] Phenyle decay, I think. It's getting her down.

Olive [*moving into the room*] I suppose you two have met by now, uh?

Barney Well, we've got as far as Barney and Mrs Cunningham.

Olive Ah, Pearl it is. Don't let us have any of that Mister and Missus stuff. Pearl!

Barney Pearl! [*Smiling, then swinging jovially up to* Olive] And how about you? Not down at Swanston Street to see us in.

[*He slaps his hands together suggestively and she fends him off.*]

Olive Cut it out now – didn't want to have you two meetin' at the Airways 'mong a lot of people, that's all.

Barney What – was you frightened I'd go off like a jet or somethin'?

[*He turnes and winks at* Pearl, *who smiles feebly in return.*]

Olive We'd have brought you down pretty quick if you had. Where's Roo? Come on, Roo. . .

[*He detaches himself from the arch against which he has been leaning, and* Olive *goes up to take him lovingly by the arm and steers him down.*]

I want you to meet a friend of mine. Pearl Cunningham, Roo Webber.

Pearl [*shaking hands*] How d'yer do.

Roo Pleased to meet yer.

[Roo *smiles slowly at her, and* Pearl *relaxes a little. He is a man's man with a streak of gentleness, a mixture that invites confidence. Tall, forty-one years of age, hair tinged with grey, a rather battered face with a well-cut mouth. Recent experiences have etched a faint line of bewilderment between his eyes, but his manner seems free and easygoing. Both men are deeply tanned, a strong contrast to the white fleshiness of the woman.*]

Mrs Cunningham, is it?

Olive [*quickly*] Yes, she's a widow.

Roo [*understandingly*] Ah.

[Barney *sees the walking-sticks on the mantelpiece and grabs one in a sudden burst of high spirits.*]

Barney Hey, look at this, willya? Where is she? Where's that Bubba?

Olive Home.

Barney [*heading for the windows*] What's she doing at home? She oughta be in here.

[*He pulls open the windows and steps onto the back verandah*]

Olive She's coming in after.

[Olive *makes to arrest* Barney *but* Roo *holds her.*]

Barney [*cupping his hands and yelling*] Buubbaa, what are yer hiding for? Reckon we're gunna lam[2] into you with a walkin' stick or something?

Bubba [*off, distant and laughing*] Take a bigger man than you, Mr Ibbot.

[Roo *joins* Barney *on the verandah as* Olive *guides* Pearl *soothingly to the sofa.* Olive *and* Roo *speak together.*]

Olive Don't worry, they'll calm down in a minute.

Roo [*yelling to* Bubba] What about me, then?

[Bubba *laughs in the distance.*]

How're you goin', Bub?

Bubba [*off*] Fine.

Olive [*coming to the French windows*] Hey, cut it out, you two, it's Sunday. Come inside, you'll see her after.

[Olive *takes* Barney's *arm to draw him into the room.*]

Roo [*calling in farewell*] Don't you be too long comin' in, now.

Bubba [*off*] I won't.

[*Inside the room,* Barney *sweeps* Olive *off her feet, twirls her around, cuddles his cheek next to hers and speaks expressively.*]

Barney Ah, my favourite barmaid.

Olive You'd better not let Pearl hear you say that.

Barney [*delightedly*] Don't tell me she's. . . .

Olive [*nodding*] Same pub – same bar!

Barney [*jubilantly moving in to sit by* Pearl *on the sofa*] Whacko! That makes it just like old times.

[Pearl *wriggles uneasily,* Emma *rushes into the room, furious.*]

Emma Thieves! Dirty thieves! Pinchin' an old woman's food while her back's turned.

Barney Hullo, what's biting Emma?

Emma Vinegar, that's what's biting me. Who's been at my vinegar?

Olive I took a tiny little skerrick[3] to put in a salad.

Emma [*fiercely*] A whole half-bottle, that's how much a skerrick it was. Robbing your own mother. Whose house do you think this is, anyway?

Olive I pay the rates and taxes –

Emma Never mind that, I own it, and things in it is private. I've told you before to keep away from my cupboard.

Olive That makes us quits then. I told you to keep away from the Airways.

Emma The community singin' was out early, else I wouldn't 'ave gone near the place. And you oughta be damned glad I did go, or these larrikins[4] wouldn't be here . . .

Barney [*covering up*] Hold your horses, Emma, you dunno what

---

2 Hit.   **3** Very small bit.   **4** Street rowdies; hooligans.

you're talking about.

Emma Don't I just?

Roo Kickin' up a fuss about a bit of vinegar. You got enough to buy a new bottle, didn't yer?

Emma [*scornfully*] Two quid, two lousy fiddlies, a fortune! [*To her daughter*] I'm drummin' you for the last time, you touch my cupboard again and I'm off down to Russell Street. . . .

[Barney, Roo *and* Olive *join in a chorus; it is evidently a well-known threat.*]

Barney
Olive } Just as fast as me legs can carry me.
Roo

Emma [*terribly*] Yez'll be laughing the other side your face once the johns[5] git after yer.

[*She stumps out. Barney calls after her.*]

Barney What do you need vinegar for anyway, you wicked old thing, you're sour enough now.

[*There is a general laugh.* Emma's *entrance has dissipated a lot of strangeness.*]

Roo Better get the bags out of the way, I s'pose.

[*He moves towards the arch.* Olive *interposes quickly.*]

Olive Just your own, then. Don't take Barney's up.

Barney Why? What's the matter with mine?

Olive You're big and ugly enough to carry 'em yourself.

[Roo *laughs shortly, picks up one of the cases and exits upstairs.* Barney *meanwhile threatens* Olive *playfully.*]

Barney Oh, I can see I'm gunna have to take you in hand, they been lettin' yer run wild.

Olive Yeah, stout and oysters. [*Moving to the mantelpiece*] Here, I've got a telegram for you. Came yesterday.

Barney [*taking it*] For me? [*Eyeing it off*] Wonder what's wrong?

Olive It'll be inside.

[*He begins to open it reluctantly.* Olive *crosses to* Pearl *and speaks with a broad hint in her voice.*]

Pearl, go out and rescue that salad from the old girl, will you? She's just as likely to tip it down the gulley trap.

Pearl [*thankfully*] Yes. She might, too.

[Pearl *exits discreetly.* Barney *reading the telegram, speaks with bravado.*]

Barney Whadya know – it's from Nancy.

Olive [*tightly*] I guessed it would be.

Barney [*reading*] Up there Cazaly,[6] lots of love, Nance. [*Folding the slip*] Where's she living now?

---

5 The police.   6 A phrase which originated from the high leaps (to catch the ball) of a famous Australian Rules footballer, Roy Cazaly, and which has passed into the Australian language more generally.

Olive Never you mind, you leave her alone.

Barney Just wanted to say hello.

Olive Yes, we all know your sort of hello. You had your chance with Nancy.

Barney What'd you bet I couldn't get her back?

Olive It wouldn't do you a scrap of good. Not in this place, anyway. The day she got married I swore I'd never have the two of you here together again no matter what happened. Pearl's the one you've got to concentrate on.

Barney [*turning away easily*] Ah, Pearl'll be all right.

Olive Will she? Don't you be too sure of that. Fact, she's got her bags piled up by the stairs, 'n' if she doesn't take to you by tomorrow morning she's shifting out.

Barney Why? What's the matter?

Olive She's not too shook on the whole thing. Doesn't understand it, for one thing; then she's got a daughter, kid of eighteen. Livin' with relations at present, but it makes Pearl nervous, she's scared of putting her foot wrong. Then when I wised her up about your handful of errors, that made her more nervous still –

Barney [*astounded*] Don't tell me she's jibbin' at her age?

Olive Oh, it's not for herself. She just doesn't think you've done the right thing.

Barney [*indignantly*] What the hell does she know about it? Did you tell her how regular I've been, coughin' up every week?

Olive Yes, but she says it's not the money, it's the principle.

Barney [*disgusted*] Oh, one of them, is she?

Olive No, she ain't, she's a very decent sort. 'Matter of fact, I think she's got some idea of reforming you.

Barney Yes? Well, that's been tried before today, too.

Olive She's got this kid, Vera, and I'd say she was lookin' for some sort of nest for the pair of 'em.

Barney With me? [*As she nods*] Well, what a thing to let a bloke in for!

Olive You don't have to do anything about it if you don't want to, not even talk to her. But I'm warnin' you, you pass her up for any of those painted crows of yours, don't think you can bring 'em home here to live.

Barney Looks like Pearl or nothin' then, eh? [*Expansively*] Righto, I'll have a word with her after. She'll be jake.[7]

Olive Pretty sure of yourself, aren't yer?

Barney [*winking*] My oath.

Olive Don't kid yourself, Barney. It won't be any walk-over.

---

7 All right.

Barney No? Well, now I'll tell you something. You've got a bit of a battle ahead of you, too.
[*She looks questioningly at him. He speaks on a quieter note.*] You heard what Emma said, 'bout if it hadn't been for her we wouldn't be here? 'S true.
Olive [*disbelieving*] Aah . . .
Barney I'm telling yer, when you weren't down at the terminal, for a minute or two Roo was talkin' about tryin' to get in some joint he knows at North Melbourne –
Olive [*staring*] Lots of times I haven't been down to meet yez. Saturdays . . .
Barney He wasn't mad at yer not being there. It's nothing like that.
Olive What then?
Barney [*hesitating*] He's broke.
Olive Roo?
Barney I had to buy his ticket down.
Olive [*incredulous*] But how can he be broke? Before he even gets here?
Barney [*sighing*] You dunno what a bloody awful season it's been, everythin' went wrong. Worse we've ever had, I reckon.
Olive Couldn't you get work?
Barney [*scornfully*] Oh it wasn't that, the work was there, any amount of it. It was just plain bad luck.
[*She makes a move towards the archway.*]
Now don't go runnin' up to him, he's chockablock, you'd better hear it from me.
[*She hesitates, then returns.*]
Olive [*flatly*] What happened?
Barney Well, first set off, Roo, the silly cow, strains his back – There's no need to throw a fit, nothin' serious, nearly better. But it slowed him down all through the season, see. [*Frankly putting his cards on the table*] Roo's a pretty hard man, y'know, on the job. Got no use for anyone can't pull their weight; and bein' able to pick and choose almost, 'coz everyone knows he's one of the best gangers[8] there is, gen'rally he gets a champion bunch together. But he's gotta be hard doin' it sometimes. [*Facing her*] This year he got the boys to turn off Tony Moreno. You must've heard us talk of Tony, real character, everyone likes him, but anyway Roo thought he was gettin' too slow. Instead he takes on a big young bloke we'd heard a lot about, name of Johnnie Dowd. Cracked up to be as fast as lightnin'.
Olive Was he?

---

8 Foremen (of gang).

Barney Yeah. Not as good as Roo, when he's fit, mind yer, but he could run rings round the best of us. And this time he even made Roo look a bit sick.

Olive Did Roo know?

Barney Well, that's the point. He's fast at both loadin' and cuttin', this Dowdie, and got a head on him, just the same as Roo, and it's not often you get fellers like that. The boys noticed it and they started pickin', telling Roo he'd have to watch out or they'd have a new ganger. Didn't mean nothin' by it, just jokin', but Roo takes it up the wrong way. Instead of pointin' out that he had a bad back, he puts himself to work by this Dowd – gunna show him up, see. Well, that's just what he shouldna done, the kid towelled him up proper. I never seen Roo git so mad, in no time at all he'd made it a running fight between 'em . . .

Olive The damned fool!

Barney That's what I told him. Calm down, I says, what's it matter . . .

Olive [*exasperated*] And with a busted back, how the hell could he win?

Barney [*shrugging*] I dunno. Reckons he's twice as good as everyone else, I s'pose. Anyway, 'bout two months ago, flamin' hot day it was, gettin' near knock-off time, they had a blue.[9]

Olive Bad?

Barney Pretty bad. I was right on the spot when it happened. Started off over nothing. They was workin' side by side, and when Dowdie finishes the strip he looks back to see how far behind Roo was. Well, right at that moment Roo's knees went. Never seen anythin' like it, they just buckled under him and there he was, down on the ground. This strikes Dowd as bein' funny, see, and he starts to laugh. Well, that did it. Roo went for him and it was on, cane knives and the lot. Took six of us to separate 'em, could've been murder, I reckon. Course the boys all blamed Roo for it, so he did his block again, packed up his gear and walked off. [*After an uncomfortable pause*] I didn't see him after that till I picked him up at Brisbane a week ago.

Olive You didn't go with him?

Barney No.

Olive Why not?

Barney [*disturbed*] I dunno. It was all messed up. You know what Roo's always been to me, a sort of little tin god. I've never seen him in the wrong before.

Olive He's been wrong plenty of times.

Barney [*strongly*] Not to me he hasn't. Not even in the – War.

Olive Well, go on. What happened?

---

9 Argument.

Barney Nothin'. He went off and I stayed. Then, like I said, I picked him up in Brisbane a week ago. By then he hardly had a razoo.[10]

Olive What was it – booze?

Barney Yeah. Been hitting it pretty heavy. We didn't talk much about it, I think he's got a spite on me for not walkin' out with him. But honest, the way I felt at the time, I just couldn't –

[*She is staring accusingly at him, and he escapes her eyes with a twisted shrug.*]

Apart from that, I needed the money. And of course I had to put me foot in it all over again by tellin' him how they made Dowdie ganger in his place, and what a bottling[11] job he done.

[*Unperceived by either of them,* Roo *moves downstairs to stand in the entrance.*]

Well, you gotta give him credit, for a kid he made a very smart fist of it. . .

Roo [*crudely*] Yeah. And have you told her 'bout the big booze-up he threw when yez all got back to Cairns?

[Barney *looks at him and then turns away, ashamed.*]

Barney Bein' sarcastic won't get you anywhere.

Roo Blabber-gutsing doesn't take you far, either.

Olive It's not his fault. I asked him. [*Addressing* Barney] Better take your cases up.

[*He moves toward the arch and she adds hastily, remembering.*]

Oh, you're in the little back room for tonight.

[Barney *grins wryly, with a flash of his former spirits.*]

Barney Is it as bad as that?

[*She nods and he carries on to pick up his bag and exit upstairs. There is an embarrassed pause.*]

Roo If I know him when he opens his big trap, I don't s'pose he's left much to tell.

Olive [*on edge*] One or two things. Where you was thinkin' of going in North Melbourne, for instance?

Roo [*shrugging irritably*] Aah, who the hell cares about that?

Olive Me, for one. I'd like to know what's around there you can't get here.

Roo [*sulkily*] I got a kind of cousin, used to keep a grocery shop. Bloke named Wallace.

Olive Well, that's lovely, that is. After seventeen years, the first time there's trouble, that's who you go to, bloke named Wallace in a grocery shop.

Roo [*turning on her angrily*] Olive, I'm broke. D'yer understand? Flat, stoney, stinkin' broke!

Olive [*shrilly*] Yeah, and I'd care a lot for that, wouldn't I? That's

---

10 No money at all.   11 Fine; excellent.

how I've always met you, standin' on the front verandah with a cash register, looking like a – like a bloody –
[*She breaks off, overcome by sudden gasping tears, gropes for a hand-kerchief. Roo is troubled and comes from behind to take her in his arms, drawing her to him with the gentle ease of long familiarity.*]
Roo [*humbly*] Olive, I wasn't thinkin'. Aw, c'mon, hon, you know I didn't mean that.
Olive [*muffled*] Fellers like you – yer ought to be kicked.
Roo I was lookin' for something to make it easy.
Olive [*twisting in his arms to face him*] What's wrong with me? I'm, workin', ain't I?
Roo [*stubbornly*] I won't bludge[12] on you.
Olive [*tearfully*] You can lay off here just as you always have, and – and I can –
Roo [*finally*] I won't bludge. I'll get a job or somethin'.
Olive A job?
Roo Well, something or other, we'll think about it tomorrow. Now stop your crying and let's forget it. It'll work out all right. You pleased to see me?
Olive [*hoarsely*] If you hadna come I would have gone looking for you with a razor.
[*They hold each other in a long kiss.*]
Roo You know what we both need, don't yer? A nice long beer to cool us down . . .
[*Olive draws away from him, giggling, her spirits already swinging back on the upsurge.*]
Olive I've already had some. Me and Pearl was in the middle of cracking a bottle when you got here. [*Fishing it out from under the table and holding it aloft*] Look, we hid it so you wouldn't know.
Roo Well, what a pair of clowns you are!
[*Suddenly it seems very funny, and they roar with laughter. She rushes up to the arch. He crosses to the sideboard, turns on the radio, which presently plays gay infectious music.*]
C'mon, my tongue's hanging out after that long plane trip.
Olive [*calling upstairs*] Up there, Cazaly – come on down – the party's on –
Roo Get 'em all in . . .
Olive [*calling towards the kitchen*] Pearl, don't be all night with that salad. I told him . . .
Pearl [*off*] Be right with you.
[*Barney comes downstairs with an armful of presents, among them the seventeenth doll. He sneaks past Olive to enter the room and hands the doll to Roo, who quickly hides it behind his back.*]
Olive Come on, Emma, Roo's poured you a beer.

---

12 Live off.

> *Emma* [*off, her voice raised in mechanical fury*] Wouldn't soil me lips.
> [*Laughing,* Olive *comes back from the kitchen entrance.* Pearl *enters bearing a large bowl of salad, followed by* Emma. *When* Olive *is at archway* Roo *holds high the gift.*]
> *Roo* Here you are – the seventeenth doll!
> [*She gives a cry of sheer happiness and rushes down into his encircling arms.* Barney *is standing by, watching with a grin. Music reaches a peak. Blackout.*]

§ *Post-war Australian drama* Seymour, Williamson; *National/male mythologies* Lawson (2), Paterson, Seymour, Williamson, Drewe

ALAN SEYMOUR (1927–)

From The One Day of the Year

The One Day of the Year dramatizes changing attitudes to Australian mythologies by focusing on generational conflicts. The 'one day' in question is Anzac Day (25 April), a public holiday commemorating the first landing of the soldiers of the Australian and New Zealand Army Corps at Gallipoli in 1915, as well as an occasion for celebrating traditional Australian values such as mateship. The shorter of the two extracts included here (from the opening) illustrates the chauvinistic Australianness of the main protagonist, Alf Cook; the longer extract (from Act II) his growing realization that his university-educated son Hughie does not share his 'digger' values. Like Lawler's *Doll*, the play was extremely popular and helped to foster a vernacular Australian stage tradition.

> *Alf* I'm a bloody Australian and I'll always stand up for bloody Australia. That's what I felt like sayin' to him, bloody Pommy,[1] you can't say anything to 'em, they still think they own the bloody earth, well, they don't own the bloody earth. The place is full of 'em. Isn't it? Wacka! Isn't it?
> *Wacka* Yes, Alf.
> *Alf* The place is full of 'em. Poms and I-ties. Bloody I-ties. Wherever y'look. New Au-bloody-stralians. Jabber, jabber, jabber. The country ain't what it used to be, is it? Is it?
> *Wacka* No, Alf.
> *Alf* 'E gets in the lift, 'e says 'Seven'. Like that. Not please, thank you, or kiss me foot. Just 'Seven'. I get'm all day, jumped-up little clerks, think they're God Almighty, well, they're not God Almighty,

---

1 British person (usually derogatory).

I know'm, I take'm up and down all day, you think I'm not sick of that lift. Well, it won't be for that long, I'll show 'em, won't be that long now. You see when I get my new job. Did I tell you about my new job? I'll be right when I get my new job. None of this up and down, up and down all day. [*He drinks.*] 'E says 'Seven'. I says: 'Wotcher say?' 'E looks me up and down as if I'm a lumpa dirt, his nose wrinkles up, he dunno he's doin' it but I seen it. I seen it so I says, more polite like, layin' it on only he don't see I'm havin' a go at him, I says Beg yr pardon, sir, did you say Seven or Second? I wish I had a quid for every time I've had to ask that in the last thirteen years. And he says, 'I said Seven, old man.' Gawd, when they start old man-n' me . . . Bloody Poms. I thought of a few things I could've said but there was a dame in the lift, she was eight months gone if she was a day. I thought what I'd say'd make you drop that colt right 'ere and it'd be me who'd have to deliver it, wouldn't be the first time neither. You dunno what it's like, shut up in that thing, it's like a bloody cage, being polite to every no-hoper every day, all day, holdin' yr horses when they tread on yr foot or ask silly bloody questions or bloody near insult you in front of the mob, they give me the dries,[2] they do, they give me the screamin' – [*by now almost beside himself*] I'm as good a man as them, who says I'm not? Who says I'm not? . . .

Anzac Day. Behind the house the sky is dark. It is before dawn. A light is on in the kitchen. Mum, *in her dressing-gown, is getting a cup of tea.* Alf, *dressed in an old but neat blue suit, comes out of bedroom at rear, crosses lounge switching on light, and goes to door of* Hughie's *bedroom. He knocks gently on door. His manner when he calls to* Hughie *is unsure.*

Alf Err – er – wakey, wakey. Rise and shine. [*Louder*] Hughie! Er – Hughie! [*Listens.*] Come on, matey, 'Urry up.

[Alf *hurries back across lounge, switches off light, switches it on again immediately and glares at a television set sitting in downstage corner facing up into room. Grunts, snaps light off again, goes into kitchen.*]

[*Grins at* Dot.] Got that cuppa tea ready, Mother?

Mum No. I bin bakin' a cake. [*Hands him cup.*]

Alf [*taking it*] Wouldn't be surprised what you did. Gawd, that kid can sleep. [*He sits, starts putting new lace into shoe.*] Why do your laces always snap when y'r runnin' late? They never go when y'got all day to fix it, only when y'r runnin' late. [*Laughs.*] That's life, ay, Dot? [*He looks towards* Hughie's *room, listens, the smile momentarily vanishing and a certain tension returning.*] [*Calls*] Ay, Hughie!

---

2 'The dry horrors'; *delirium tremens.*

Mum You make a fool of y'self over that boy.

Alf Oh get out.

Mum Y'give in to him. One minute you can't say enough about him, next thing you're all over him like a rash.

Alf [*smiles*] Don't pick me, Mother. [*Sits, sugars tea.*] Not today. [*Grins happily.*] It's the old diggers'[3] day today.

[ALF *suddenly looks around restlessly.*]

Knew there was someth'n wrong. No Wacka.

Mum [*nods*] Mmm. Funny without Wack.

Alf [*a bit piqued*] Never thought I'd see that you know. Wack not gettin' up to go to the Dawn Service. Not marchin' either.

Mum Y'know 'is leg nearly went on 'im last year. It was me made him promise he wouldn't do marchin' again. Standin' on his feet all that time with that leg.

Alf You c'n be 'ard, Dot. Where's yr sentiment?

Mum I face up to things. Not like you.

Alf It's not the same without old Wack.

Mum Lots of old blokes are droppin' out of it. Y' can't expect 'em to go on forever.

Alf He's not that old. Lot of 'em older than him still march.

Mum On a gammy leg? He'll be with y'in spirit, if that cheers you up. We'll be watchin' – in comfort.

Alf Comfort. I dunno what this country's coming to. If I ever thought I'd see the day when people'd think of their own comfort on Anzac Day –

Mum Well, I'm not sorry. It was Wacka's idea and it was a very nice thought hiring the television.

Alf *Television.*

Mum Don't you go 'im. If he gets 'ere before you go, don't you go 'im.

Alf Television.

Mum I noticed you looked at it last night.

Alf Bloody cowboys and Indians. Bang, bang, bang – had a headache all night. I'll give 'im television.

Mum You leave him alone. It was his idea and he's gunna enjoy it. [*Laughs*] Best idea Wacka's had since we knew him.

Alf Only one.

Mum His landlady'll be wild he didn't put it in there.

Alf I wouldn't care where he put it, he could shove it up his jumper for mine. [*Jumps up, drinks down last of tea.*] Well, while you two sit back like Lord and Lady Muck the two patriotic members of the family'll be there – in person. [*Yells*] Hughie!

[*The slightest pause.*]

---

3 Australian (and New Zealand) soldiers, from their experience in the Gallipoli campaign in World War I; earlier goldminers.

Mum [*softly*] Hughie won't be goin' to no march.

Alf Hughie's never missed a Dawn Service yet and he always come and watched me march after. What are y'talkin' about? Where's my medals? Hughie!

[*He marches across darkened lounge and raps on* Hughie's *door.*] C'm'on, matey. Nearly dinnertime. We'll never get there. [*A pause.*] Hughie!

Hughie [*voice muffled, drowsy, from dark bedroom*] What do you want?

Alf Y'know the mob they get in Martin Place – if we don't get goin' we'll be stuck up the back. Come on, hurry it up.

Hughie I'm not going.

Alf Come on, son, we haven't got that much – [*Then he registers.*] What did you say? [Hughie *doesn't answer.* Alf *suddenly rages*] What did you say?

[Alf *throws the door open, switches on the light.* Hughie, *in pyjamas, rolls over, props himself up on one elbow. They look at each other in silence.*]

Hughie I'm not going.

Alf You get up out of bed or I'll –

Hughie I'm tired.

[*He reaches up, switches off light switch near bed. Out of the dark comes* Alf's *roar of rage. He flings out of the room, slamming the door. And charges across the lounge into the bedroom at rear.*]

[Mum *has heard it all from kitchen, now goes into lounge. She is about to switch on light when* Alf *comes charging out of bedroom. He is viciously jabbing his long-service medals into his coat and almost collides with her in centre of room. She grabs him by shoulders, steadies him. They stand still facing each other.*]

[*Light spills across the room from open door of kitchen and their bedroom.*]

Mum Alf –

Alf Who does 'e think he is?

Mum Gimme those. [*She takes medals from him and pins them carefully.*] You want them to look right, don't you?

Alf What's the matter with the lot of yz? What's come-overyer?

Mum Now . . .

Alf Well . . . Gawd . . .

Mum Don't get y'self worked up, love.

Alf Well, you know what day this is. This day used to mean someth'n' once. [*She opens her mouth to speak.*] Don't shut me up, I'm not ashamed of it. I'm proud to be a bloody Australian. If it wasn't for men like my old man this country'd never bin heard of. They put Australia on the map they did, the Anzacs did. An' bloody died doin' it. Well, even a snotty-nosed little kid oughta be proud of that. What's happened to him. Why isn't he?

Mum Don't you go using this as an excuse for one of your –
Alf [*quietly*] One of my what?
Mum You know what.
Alf I don't need no excuse today. It's my day, see.
Mum [*as he moves towards door*] What time'll y'be home?
Alf When I get here.
Mum Alf –
Alf You know I never know what time I'll get home on Anzac Day.
Mum And what d'you think you're gunna get up to?
Alf I'm gunna celebrate this day the way I always celebrated this day. That's all. [*He shoots one glance towards* Hughie's *room.*] Little runt.
[*He goes out quickly.*]
[*A pause.* Mum *walks back to kitchen, switches off light. Stands thoughtfully in lounge. Crosses, stands outside* Hughie's *room.*]
Mum [*quietly*] Hughie. [*A pause.*] You're not asleep.
Hughie [*quietly*] What do you want?
Mum [*after a pause*] Do you want me to get you a cup of tea?
Hughie [*softening a little*]: No thanks, Mum.
Mum All right. [*She is about to move away.*]
Hughie I thought you were going to go off at me.
Mum Hughie, what's the good in goin' off at you? [*Slight break before she manages to say it.*] Y'don't see things the same as us any more and that's that. I knew you wouldn't go with him. Y'might've give 'im a bit of warning, that's all.
Hughie I'm sorry. How did you know?
Mum I didn't come down in the last shower.
Hughie Why didn't you tell him then, Mum? You could have softened the blow.
Mum You fight your own battles. I'm not buyin' into any arguments. I get enough of 'em around here.
Hughie Mum . . . [*He stops.*]
Mum What?
Hughie Nothing.
Mum Go to sleep. I'm going back to bed. [*She goes towards bedroom.*] Wacka can let himself in.
[*She goes into bedroom, shuts door. Its light goes out. General lighting fades momentarily to suggest a passing of time.*]
[*Light fades in again, held down very softly. The sky behind the house has traces of pink through it. Very gradually it begins to lighten.*]
[*In* Hughie's *bedroom some slight movement. He lights a cigarette, lies back, hand behind head. Then he flicks radio on. Its small light glows softly in dark.*]
[*Steps are heard approaching. The front door opens,* Wacka *is silhouetted against light from sky spilling through door. He comes in,*

*leaving door open to give himself some light. Crosses to lounge
windows, quietly pulls up blinds. Dawn light comes in. He looks
around, moves quietly back to door.*]
[*He is about to close it but a sudden quickening of light all through
the sky stops him. He takes a step outside, looks up at the sky. It is
dawn. He stands very still as though listening for something.*]
[*Wacka turns, comes back to door. Stands another second or two then
shrugs, laughs quietly to himself. But still he stands, looking out and
up. There is absolute silence.*]
Wacka [*to himself, so quietly it can hardly be heard*] It was now.
[*He stands still, remembering.*]
[*And out of the silence comes, soft and distant, the sound of a trum-
pet playing 'The Last Post'.*]
[*Wacka stands as though paralysed. As it plays through, the bedroom
door opens and Mum stands there without putting on the light. She
is fussily wrapping gown about her but the sound stops her. She sees
Wacka's face, the dawn gradually lighting it, and she does not move.
They both stand listening. The last notes die away.*]
[*For a moment neither one moves.*]
[*Shakes his head, comes back to earth.*] Where'd that come from?
Mum Hughie's room, I think. [*Hughie switches the radio off.*] He
must've put the wiless on to hear the service.
Wacka Didn't 'e go?
[*Mum shakes her head, stares across towards his room, her usually
set expression about to break into a grudging smile.*]
Mum Funny kid. [*Snaps out of it.*] Waste of time tryin' to sleep.
May as well stay up now. I'll get you a cuppa tea.
[*They go towards kitchen.*]
[*Lights fade.*]

§ *Post-War Australian Drama* Lawler, Williamson; *Attitudes to war* Dawe (2);
National/male mythologies Lawson (2), Paterson, Lawler, Williamson, Drewe

OODERGOO NOONUCCAL (KATH WALKER) (1920–93)

We Are Going

They came in to the little town
A semi-naked band subdued and silent,
All that remained of their tribe.
They came here to the place of their old bora ground

---

4 **bora ground**: sacred ceremonial grounds of Aborigines.

5 Where now the many white men hurry about like ants.
Notice of estate agent reads: 'Rubbish May Be Tipped Here'.
Now it half covers the traces of the old bora ring.
They sit and are confused, they cannot say their thoughts:
'We are as strangers here now, but the white tribe are the strangers.
10 We belong here, we are of the old ways.
We are the corroboree and the bora ground,
We are the old sacred ceremonies, the laws of the elders.
We are the wonder tales of Dream Time, the tribal legends told.
We are the past, the hunts and the laughing games, the wandering camp fires.
15 We are the lightning-bolt over Gaphembah Hill
Quick and terrible,
And the Thunderer after him, that loud fellow.
We are the quiet daybreak paling the dark lagoon.
We are the shadow-ghosts creeping back as the camp fires burn low.
20 We are nature and the past, all the old ways
Gone now and scattered.
The scrubs are gone, the hunting and the laughter.
The eagle is gone, the emu and the kangaroo are gone from this place.
The bora ring is gone.
25 The corroboree is gone.
And we are going.'

§ *Elegies for Aboriginality* Kendall; NZSP: Hyde, Ihimaera (1); *Aboriginality more generally* Mudrooroo, Davis; Can: Wiebe, King, Armstrong

GWEN HARWOOD (1920–)

Suburban Sonnet

She practises a fugue, though it can matter
to no one now if she plays well or not.
Beside her on the floor two children chatter,
then scream and fight. She hushes them. A pot
5 boils over. As she rushes to the stove
too late, a wave of nausea overpowers
subject and counter-subject. Zest and love

---

11 **corroboree**: Aboriginal ceremonial dance. 13 **Dream Time**: the period of Creation and the origin of myths, simultaneously present in all periods.

drain out with soapy water as she scours
the crusted milk. Her veins ache. Once she played
10 for Rubinstein, who yawned. The children caper
round a sprung mousetrap where a mouse lies dead.
When the soft corpse won't move they seem afraid.
She comforts them; and wraps it in a paper
featuring: *Tasty dishes from stale bread.*

§ *Suburban life* Lawler, Winton; *Changing roles of women* Baynton, Franklin,
Garner, Grenville; Can: Thomas, Marlatt

PETER PORTER (1929–)

Phar Lap* in the Melbourne Museum

A masterpiece of the taxidermist's art,
Australia's top patrician stares
Gravely ahead at crowded emptiness.
As if alive, the lustre of dead hairs,
5   Lozenged liquid eyes, black nostrils
Gently flared, otter-satin coat declares
That death cannot visit in this thin perfection.

The democratic hero full of guile,
Noble, handsome, gentle Houyhnhnm
10 (In both Paddock and St Leger difference is
Lost in the welter of money) – to see him win
Men sold farms, rode miles in floods,
Stole money, locked up wives, somehow got in:
First away, he led the field and easily won.

15 It was his simple excellence to be best.
Tough men owned him, the minds beset
By stakes, bookies' doubles, crooked jocks.
He soon became a byword, public asset,
A horse with a nation's soul upon his back –
20 Australia's Ark of the Covenant, set
Before the people, perfect, loved like God.

---

10 Rubinstein: Arthur Rubinstein (1887–1982), Polish–American pianist.
9 Houyhnhnm: virtuous, anthropomorphic horse inhabitant of the utopia in the fourth part of Swift's *Gulliver's Travels.*

*Legendary Australian race-horse, foaled in New Zealand in 1926; won 36 races, including the 1930 Melbourne Cup, before dying in mysterious circumstances in California in 1932.

And like God to be betrayed by friends.
Sent to America, he died of poisoned food.
In Australia children cried to hear the news
25　(This Prince of Orange knew no bad or good).
It was, as people knew, a plot of life:
To live in strength, to excel and die too soon,
So they drained his body and they stuffed his skin.

Twenty years later on Sunday afternoons
30　You still can't see him for the rubbing crowds.
He shares with Bradman and Ned Kelly some
Of the dirty jokes you still can't say out loud.
It is Australian innocence to love
The naturally excessive and be proud
35　Of a thoroughbred bay gelding who ran fast.

§ *Sporting Mythologies* Dawe (1), Williamson; Carib: James

LES MURRAY (1938–)

1: Blood

Pig-crowds in successive, screaming pens
we still to greedy drinking, trough by trough,
tusk-heavy boars, fat mud-beslabbered sows:
Gahn, let him drink, you slut, you've had enough!

5　Laughing and grave by turns, in milky boots,
we stand and yarn, and whet our butcher's knife,
sling cobs of corn – hey, careful of his nuts!
It's made you cruel, all that smart city life.

In paper spills, we roll coarse, sweet tobacco.
10　That's him down there, the one we'll have to catch,
that little Berkshire with the pointy ears.
I call him Georgie. Here, you got a match?

The shadow of a cloud moves down the ridge,
on summer hills, a patch of autumn light.
15　My cousin sheathes in dirt his priestly knife.
They say pigs see the wind. You think that's right?

---

31 **Bradman/Kelly**: both culture heroes in the Australian popular imagination; Donald Bradman was the most successful batsman in cricketing history; Ned Kelly a legendary nineteenth-century bushranger.

I couldn't say. It sounds like a fair motto.
There are some poets – Right, he's finished now.
Melon-sized and muscular, with shrieks
20   the pig is seized and bundled anyhow

his twisting strength permits, then sternly held.
My cousin tests his knife, sights for the heart
and sinks the blade with one long, even push.
A wild scream bursts as knife and victim part

25   and hits the showering heavens as our beast
flees straight downfield, choked in his pumping gush
that feeds the earth, and drags him to his knees –
Bleed, Georgie, pump! And with a long-legged rush

my cousin is beside the thing he killed
30   and pommels it, and lifts it to the sun:
I should have knocked him out, poor little bloke.
It gets the blood out if you let them run.

We hold the dangling meat. Wet on its chest
the narrow cut, the tulip of slow blood.
35   We better go. We've got to scald him next.
Looking at me, my cousin shakes his head.

What's up, old son? You butchered things before . . .
it's made you squeamish, all that city life.
Sly gentleness regards me, and I smile:
40   You're wrong, you know. I'll go and fetch the knife.

I walk back up the trail of crowding flies,
back to the knife which pours deep blood, and frees
sun, fence and hill, each to its holy place.
Strong in my valleys, I may walk at ease.

45   A world I thought sky-lost by leaning ships
in the depth of our life – I'm in that world once more.
Looking down, we praise for its firm flesh
the creature killed according to the Law.

2: Quintets for Robert Morley*

Is it possible that hyper-
ventilating up Parnassus
I have neglected to pay tribute
to the Stone Age aristocracy?
5   I refer to the fat.

We were probably the earliest
civilized, and civilizing, humans,
the first to win the leisure,
sweet boredom, life-enhancing sprawl
10   that require style.

Tribesfolk spared us and cared for us
for good reasons. Our reasons.
As age's counterfeits, forerunners of the city
we survived, and multiplied. Out of self-defence
15   we invented the Self.

It's likely we also invented some of love,
much of fertility (see the Willensdorf Venus)
parts of theology (divine feasting, Unmoved Movers)
likewise complexity, stateliness, the ox-cart
20   and self-deprecation.

Not that the lists of pugnacity are bare
of stout fellows. Ask a Sumo.
Warriors taunt us still, and fear us:
in heroic war, we are apt to be the specialists
25   and the generals.

But we do better in peacetime. For ourselves
we would spare the earth. We were the first moderns
after all, being like the Common Man
disqualified from tragedy. Accessible to shame, though,
30   subtler than the tall.

we make reasonable rulers.
Never trust a lean meritocracy
nor the leader who has been lean;

---

* Portly British film actor (1908–92).
17 **Willensdorf Venus**: c. 25,000-year-old, 11 cm.
high limestone figure, found in Willensdorf, Austria;
symbol of fertility.

2 **Parnassus**: mountain in Greece, close to Delphi; the
home of the Muses.

only the lifelong big have the knack of wedding
35   greatness with balance.

Never wholly trust the fat man
who lurks in the lean achiever
and in the defeated, yearning to get out.
He has not been through our initiations,
40   he lacks the light feet.

Our having life abundantly
is equivocal, Robert, in hot climates
where the hungry watch us. I lack the light step then.
How many of us, I wonder, walk those streets
45   in terrible disguise?

So much climbing, on a spherical world;
had Newton not been a mere beginner at gravity
he might have asked how the apple got up there
in the first place. And so might have discerned
50   an ampler physics.

§ *Size* Can: Swan

BRUCE DAWE (1930–)

1: Life-Cycle

When children are born in Victoria
they are wrapped in the club-colours, laid in beribboned cots,
having already begun a lifetime's barracking.

Carn, they cry, Carn . . . feebly at first
5   while parents playfully tussle with them
for possession of a rusk: Ah, he's a little Tiger! (And they
    are . . .)

Hoisted shoulder-high at their first League game
they are like innocent monsters who have been years
    swimming
towards the daylight's roaring empyrean

---

2 **club-colours**: of Australian Rules football clubs.   9 **empyrean**: the highest heaven.

10 Until, now, hearts shrapnelled with rapture,
they break surface and are forever lost,
their minds rippling out like streamers

In the pure flood of sound, they are scarfed with light, a
     voice
like the voice of God booms from the stands
15 Ooohh you bludger and the covenant is sealed.

Hot pies and potato-crisps they will eat,
they will forswear the Demons, cling to the Saints
and behold their team going up the ladder into Heaven,

And the tides of life will be the tides of the home-team's
     fortunes
20 – the reckless proposal after the one-point win,
the wedding and honeymoon after the grand-final . . .

They will not grow old as those from more northern States
     grow old,
for them it will always be three-quarter-time
with the scores level and the wind advantage in the final
     term,

25 That passion persisting, like a race-memory, through the
     welter of seasons,
enabling old-timers by boundary-fences to dream of resurgent
     lions
and centaur-figures from the past to replenish continually the
     present,

So that mythology may be perpetually renewed
and Chicken Smallhorn return like the maize-god
30 in a thousand shapes, the dancers changing

But the dance forever the same – the elderly still
loyally crying Carn . . . Carn . . . (if feebly) unto the very end,
Having seen in the six-foot recruit from Eaglehawk their hope
     of salvation.

§ *Sporting mythologies* Porter, Williamson; Carib: James

---

15 bludger: idler; scrounger (often affectionate).   **17 Demons/Saints**: club nicknames.

2: Homecoming

All day, day after day, they're bringing them home,
they're picking them up, those they can find, and bringing
    them home,
they're bringing them in, piled on the hulls of Grants, in
    trucks, in convoys,
they're zipping them up in green plastic bags,
5   they're tagging them now in Saigon, in the mortuary coolness
they're giving them names, they're rolling them out of
the deep-freeze lockers – on the tarmac at Tan Son Nhut
the noble jets are whining like hounds,
they are bringing them home
10   – curly-heads, kinky-hairs, crew-cuts, balding non-coms
– they're high, now, high and higher, over the land, the
    steaming *chow mein*,
their shadows are tracing the blue curve of the Pacific
with sorrowful quick fingers, heading south, heading east,
home, home, home – and the coasts swing upward, the old
    ridiculous curvatures
15   of earth, the knuckled hills, the mangrove-swamps, the desert
    emptiness . . .
in their sterile housing they tilt towards these like skiers
– taxiing in, on the long runways, the howl of their home-
    coming rises
surrounding them like their last moments (the mash, the
    splendour)
then fading at length as they move
20   on to small towns where dogs in the frozen sunset
raise muzzles in mute salute,
and on to cities in whose wide web of suburbs
telegrams tremble like leaves from a wintering tree
and the spider grief swings in his bitter geometry
25   – they're bringing them home, now, too late, too early.

§ *Attitudes to war* Seymour

DOROTHY HEWETT (1923–)

From Testament

     ... These have I lost, being too much beloved,
     And having for their virtue only this –
     That I have loved them.
     That cold white wanton with the stiff-necked pride
5   Of centuries of narrow-minded squires,
     Migrating to a strange, dark brutal country,
     Where you met the convicts shackled on the roads,
     And the hangman's rope cast shadows on the soil.
     Sitting astride their horses, their two feet
10   Clamped coldly in the mud marsh;
     Giving birth to sons; all with the dignity of Englishmen.
     They carefully translated their whole way
     And pride of living to a hangman's land,
     Ploughed the dark soil, wrenched order from its chaos,
15   Its sullen, hostile hatred of their hands,
     Subdued it, mixed their coldness with its hunger,
     Never gave up, or ceased to plough and sow,
     Because it was their only living passion,
     These cold-eyed men with honor in their hearts:
20   The passion for the land, to feel the soil
     Ache through their thin loins, it was like
     Another man's hunger for a wanton woman:
     Building their red board churches in the clearing,
     Puritanical among the ringbarked gum trees,
25   Standing like a witches' sabbath on the sky;
     Leading the flock, sending their thin, dark daughters
     Home to England for their education;
     Treating the sad-eyed blacks with kind contempt;
     Shipping their piano, portraits, rugs, from England;
30   Building their English houses by the rivers; and yet
     All mad-eyed, lonely men with strange misgivings.
     Your heritage, my love, these forefathers,
     Who sit with white skulls nodding in the grass,
     Holding you with their stiff-necked principles,
35   As if they were a council of old men
     Crouching like stumps against the reddened sky ...

§ *Ancestry/settlement*: Harpur, Clarke; Can: Traill, Kroetsch

DAVID WILLIAMSON (1942–)

From The Club

The 'club' of Williamson's title is an Australian Rules football club, but the play is more concerned with behind-the-scenes power struggles than the sport itself. The action takes place in the symbolic arena of the club's committee room, prior to a meeting. In this extract (from the end of the first act and beginning of the second), Geoff, the club's recently signed new star player, who is considered not to have been pulling his weight, talks to Laurie, the coach, and Jock, the former president. As in similar passages in *Summer of the Seventeenth Doll* and *The One Day of the Year*, these exchanges reveal generational differences, with Geoff interrogating the values on which the club has been founded.

. . . *Laurie* You've read the morning papers, I suppose?

Geoff Yep.

Laurie The Committee are meeting in just over an hour to decide whether they're going to accept my resignation. I think they're going to ask me to reconsider it but it's hardly worth my while if you're going to keep defying me.

Geoff So what are we supposed to do? Kiss and make up?

Laurie I don't want you to defy me in front of the players again.

Geoff I don't want to be told to do push-ups again.

Laurie If you break discipline you do push-ups. Everyone does.

Geoff I don't.

Laurie Nobody else objects to push-ups.

Geoff That's because most of them have got ear to ear bone.

Laurie I see. You've done a few subjects at University so you're out of our class.

Geoff If you like doing push-ups I must be.

Laurie All right. Point taken. You don't like push-ups, but it goes deeper than that, doesn't it? Why are you playing so badly?

Geoff I'm doing my best.

Laurie No you're not. You played two good games at the start of the year, you went to pieces in your third game and you've got progressively worse ever since.

Geoff I've lost form.

Laurie It's more than that. You're not even trying. Is it just that you object to me personally or is there some other reason?

Geoff I've lost form. That's all.

Laurie Look, I know there's some degree of antagonism from the other players. You came to the Club with a big reputation and a lot of money so there's bound to be, but it's not going to help matters if you lay down and stop trying.

Geoff You're reading too much into it. I've lost form.

Laurie It's more than that. Last week you stood down on the forward line staring into the crowd for over a minute. The ball came and you let it go right past you. Look, level with me, Geoff. That's more than being out of form. What's going on?

Geoff All right. If you really want to know, what's going on is that I'm sick to death of football and I couldn't care less if I never played another game in my life. It's all a lot of macho-competitive bullshit. You chase a lump of pigskin around a muddy ground as if your bloody life depended on it and when you get it you kick it to buggery and go chasing it again. Football shits me.

Laurie I wish you'd let us know your attitude to the game before we paid ninety thousand dollars for you.

Geoff If you think you can buy me like a lump of meat then you'd better think again.

Laurie You took our money with your eyes open, Geoff. Don't you think you owe us something?

Geoff If you're stupid enough to offer me that sort of money I'll take it, but all you've bought is my presence out on an oval for two hours every Saturday afternoon.

Laurie We thought we were buying a lot more than that.

Geoff Took your money? It was practically thrown at me. You weren't there at that final sign-up session?

[Geoff *shakes his head ruefully.*]

It was a joke. There were three of my guys on one side of the table and Gerry, Jock and Ted on the other. Jock was looking at me, and I'm not joking, as if I was a giant pork chop. He was almost salivating. I felt sure that any moment he'd bring out a little hammer and test whether my reflexes are as good as they're cracked up to be. I couldn't believe that those three goons were for real. By the time we'd got ourselves through the pleasantries I was getting pretty crapped off and I decided to make myself a bit difficult, so when they shoved the form in front of me to sign, I read it through four times, put down the pen, shook my head and said I wanted more money. I didn't really expect to get any more – I just wanted to establish myself as something more than a tailor's dummy – but it was marvellous. All hell broke loose. Your guys called my guys cheats, Jock thumped our President on the snout, and Gerry sat there stirring his coffee with a retractable biro. I was just about to burst out laughing when I looked across and there was Ted Parker sitting in the middle of all this pandemonium, his face as white as a sheet, scribbling frantically in his cheque book. 'Ten thousand,' he yelled. 'I'll go an extra ten thousand, but that's my limit.' Everyone had a ball.

Laurie Are you still living with that girl?

Geoff Susy? Yes. Why? Do you think she's a corrupting influence?

Laurie She didn't seem very interested in your football career when I met her.

Geoff She's not.

Laurie She thinks it's macho-competitive bullshit too?

Geoff You can't exactly blame her, when it gets to the point where we start coming to blows behind the lockers.

Laurie How's your jaw?

Geoff Still sore. How's your gut?

Laurie Likewise.

Geoff Push-ups are one thing but slugging me into submission just isn't on.

Laurie I know. I'm sorry. I love football and I love this Club and it's a bit hard for me to understand someone who holds both of them in contempt.

Geoff Love the Club? Jock, Ted and Gerry?

Laurie The Club's not Jock, Ted and Gerry. It's nearly a hundred years of history.

Geoff Yeah. Well I missed the history and copped Jock, Ted and Gerry. Honestly, what's an old fool like Jock doing in a position of power?

Laurie He was a great player, and whether he deserved to or not he won four premierships when he was our coach.

Geoff Didn't he deserve to win them?

Laurie We're not here to talk about Jock.

Geoff Was he a bad coach?

Laurie Yes.

Geoff How come he got those premierships then?

Laurie [*irritated*] He got them in his first six years, in the days when the best talent in the country was fighting to get a purple and gold guernsey.[1] By the time I took over all of that had long finished.

Geoff Someone told me that you were responsible for getting him the sack.

Laurie I thought he was coaching disgracefully and I did some lobbying. I'll admit that to anyone. He dosed himself up with whisky before the '67 Grand Final and halfway through the last quarter he took Benny McPhee out of the centre where he was really firing and put him at full forward, where he was never sighted. It cost us the premiership. Why are you so interested in Jock?

Geoff I'm not. It just amuses me to see you guys sticking around in this Club for years, having your little power battles, cutting each

---

1 Football jersey.

others throats and filling up your lives with petty nonsense. So
Jock was a bad coach and you lost a premiership. What does it
matter? It's not important.

Laurie I might be old fashioned but it seems important to me to
step in and do something when a great Club's going downhill
because of incompetent coaching.

Geoff I don't want to play the devil's advocate but you've done
some pretty bad coaching yourself lately.

Laurie Such as?

Geoff Such as not shifting Danny off Wilson last week. He was
getting thrashed.

Laurie I know.

Geoff Wilson was leaving him for dead.

Laurie [*irritably*] I know.

Geoff Then why didn't you shift him?

Laurie Because he was desperate to keep trying. He's never been
that badly beaten before. I know it was the wrong thing to do but
Danny's been the backbone of my team for eight years and I felt
I owed him something. Besides, I doubt whether there's anyone
in the team who could've done any better.

Geoff I could beat Wilson.

Laurie You? You were down the other end of the ground staring
into the crowd!

Geoff I could beat him.

Laurie [*angrily*] I'm getting pretty bloody fed up with your arrogance, Geoff. You've been paid a fortune and you won't even try;
and when I try and talk to you about it you give me a lecture
about how petty my life is, and to cap it all off you nonchalantly
tell me you could beat Wilson when in the last five weeks you've
hardly got a kick. I was watching you carefully last week and you
couldn't even outrun Butcher Malone.

Geoff I was stoned.

Laurie Drunk?

Geoff Stoned.

Laurie Marihuana?

Geoff Hash.

Laurie Why?

Geoff Because it feels fantastic. Five minutes after you smoke it
your head lifts right off your shoulders. I wasn't looking out into
the crowd, incidentally, I was watching a seagull. Not just an ordinary seagull. It was the prince of seagulls, dazzling me with blasts
of pure white everytime its wings caught the sun. The roar of the
crowd paid homage to its grace and beauty. You ought to try some,
Laurie. It alters your whole perspective on things.

Laurie Are you stoned now?

Geoff [*nods*] I had a smoke before I came.

Laurie Are you addicted?

Geoff You don't get addicted to hash, Laurie. Hey, did you see me fly for the ball in the second quarter? I was so far up over the pack I felt like Achilles chasing the golden orb.

Laurie Jesus, Geoff. How am I supposed to deal with this ?

Geoff Just don't ask me to do push-ups.

[Jock *pokes his head through the right door. He is smiling affably.*]

Jock Sorted things out yet?

Geoff Not quite.

Jock Would you like me to have a talk to the lad, Laurie? Sometimes a fresh viewpoint can help in these sort of situations.

Laurie [*irritated*] No.

Jock Just give me a few minutes, Laurie. I've got something I want to say to him.

[Laurie *gets up, looking at* Jock *in an irritated way, and leaves through the left door.*]

He's got it in for you, I'm afraid, Geoff. Not to worry. We'll sort it out. You did some nice things last week. Not one of your best games but you did some nice things. Glorious mark you took in the second quarter. You just seemed to go up and up.

Geoff I felt like Achilles.

Jock Who's he?

Geoff A Greek guy who could really jump.

Jock (nods) Some of our new Australians could be champions if they'd stop playing soccer and assimilate. Why did Butcher Malone take a swing at you when you hit the deck? Did you give him an elbow in the gut?

Geoff No, I blew him a kiss.

Jock That's good. That's subtle. I was a bit more direct in my day, although I did have a little trick that used to throw 'em out of their stride, come to think of it. You know those times when you're half a yard behind your man and he's going for the ball and there doesn't seem any way you can stop him?

[Geoff *nods.*]

Jock Well, the thing in your favour is that everyone, including the umpire, is looking at the ball, right?

Geoff Right.

Jock Right. Well as soon as your man leaves the ground, get your thumb and ram it up his arse. Works every time.

Geoff Sounds effective.

Jock It's a beauty. Wait here while I have a piss.

[*As* Jock *moves to the door he notices that* Geoff *has taken out a pouch of tobacco. He stops.*]

Jock Roll your own?

Geoff Mmm.

Jock I used to roll my own.

Geoff Would you like me to roll you one?

Jock Yeah. Thanks. I'll be back in a minute and we'll have a nice quiet smoke and a little chat.

[Geoff *nods his head as* Jock *goes out the door. He looks in his back pocket and takes out a tin. He looks at the door through which* Jock *has gone, looks at the tin, nods his head and smiles. Blackout and house lights up.*]

Interval

[Jock *re-enters. A minute or two of stage time has elapsed.* Geoff *has rolled two cigarettes. He smokes one and hands the other to* Jock.]

Jock [*coughing*] Hope you don't smoke too many of these?

Geoff Eh?

Jock Makes you short of breath. How many do you have a day?

Geoff Three or four.

Jock Ah, that's no problem. (*Inhaling*) Quite strong. You get a bit used to having it filtered. Laurie's a bit worried about your form lately. I think you're playing well but Laurie thinks you could do better. I do too. I don't think you're playing as badly as Laurie thinks you are but I think you could do better. What do you think?

Geoff I think I could too.

Jock Good lad. Puts me in a bit of a spot if you're down on form because I was the bugger that stuck me neck out and said we had to get you. The first time I saw you play I knew you were a freak. One in a million. I still think I'm right. Nothing's worrying you is it?

Geoff No.

Jock No problems with women?

Geoff No.

Jock Don't screw too many or you'll get the jack.[2]

[*There is a pause.*]

I get the feeling something is worrying you, Geoff.

Geoff You could be right.

Jock I've got an instinct about problems. Do you want to talk about it?

Geoff I don't know whether I can.

Jock It won't get any further than this room if you do. You know that.

Geoff Thanks.

Jock Have you been able to talk about it to Laurie?

---

2 Venereal disease.

[Geoff *shakes his head.* Jock *looks pleased.*]
Yeah. It's hard to talk heart to heart with Laurie. He lacks that little human touch. When I was coach I used to spend hours with my men – joking, chatting, horseing around – but Laurie's a bit stand-offish. Not really one of the boys, don't you think? Bit remote.
Geoff Well he hasn't told me too many jokes.
Jock That's right. No sense of humour. None at all. Bit of a fanatic don't you think?
Geoff He lives for football.
Jock Right. I used to take the boys up to a country race meeting sometimes in the middle of the week to break the tension and we'd have a few beers and a laugh and it was great. But Laurie would never come. He'd stay back and train by himself in the middle of the oval for hours and hours. Bloody fanatic even then. Do the players *really* like him?
Geoff They seem to.
Jock I can't understand that. He seems too stand-offish. I was one of the boys when I was coach and they'd do anything for me. Of course you'll hear some stories that my men weren't fit but that's all bullshit. I didn't make a god of fitness and overtrain my men like Laurie; but they were fit, and if you hear any stories that my discipline was lax and that I played favourites, don't believe that either. If someone didn't do what I told 'em I tore strips off them whether they were my drinking mates or not. Laurie started all those stories. He's always had it in for me. From the minute he joined the Club he's made it his business to rewrite the Club's history with him as its biggest shining star. He was obsessed with beating my record of two hundred and eighty two games. Absolutely obsessed. He had a bad groin injury and a dicey hamstring and he was in agony every time he went out onto the field but there was no stopping him.
Geoff He didn't beat it though, did he?
Jock No, he tripped over little Rabbit Rutherford coming out of a pack and did his cartilages with three games to go, and I can't say I was sorry; in fact to tell you the truth, I laughed me bloody head off. No, I'll make no bones about it. I've got no love for Laurie. Not after the way he took over as coach. I know the style of game had changed and I was making a few mistakes – I was brought up on a different brand of football, not this modern play on, killer instinct, steamroller, win at all costs stuff – and if anyone had have put it to me straight and open that I was getting a bit past it I probably would've agreed and stepped down like a man. But that's not Laurie's style. He went around to the members of the Committee behind my back and told them I was drunk during the '67 Grand Final. I had a cold and I had a few sips of

whisky, but I wasn't drunk. He'd had his eye on the job for years.
He just waited till I made one little mistake and went in for the
kill. He'll keep. He's going to get his. He promised that Committee
the world and he hasn't won them one premiership. Not one
bloody premiership and I've won four. I don't wonder that you're
having trouble with him Geoff and I don't blame you at all because
you've got real ability and you can see through him. He can't command the respect of anyone of real ability and he never will. What
we need around here is a man of authority who can command,
because these days it's fear that wins you premierships, Geoff, I'm
afraid. These days the game is so bloody tough that you've got
to get your players so scared of making a mistake that they go
out there and play the game in a state of fucking terror. Fear's
what wins you premierships and Laurie couldn't scare a field
mouse.
[*There is a pause.*]
Yes, I can understand why you can't discuss anything with Laurie
and I just wanted you to know that I'm on side. What's your
problem?

Geoff It's a bit difficult to know where to begin. It *is* to do with
women.

Jock Usually is. Are you going with anyone in particular?

Geoff No.

Jock What about that tall sheila[3] I saw you with at the Club ball?

Geoff She's just a friend.

Jock Jesus, I'll tell you what. I wish I had a few friends like that.
I don't mind admitting, Geoff, I was having a bit of a perve.[4]
Did she know you could see straight through that thing she was
wearing?

Geoff I think that was the idea.

Jock Marvellous looker, Geoff. Couldn't keep my eyes off her.

Geoff She's a beautiful girl.

Jock So what's your problem?

Geoff It's so bloody embarrassing.

Jock Get it off your chest.

Geoff You'll keep it absolutely secret, Jock. It'd destroy me if it
ever got out.

Jock It won't get past this room, lad.

Geoff It's not that I'm not attracted to women, Jock. I am.
Desperately attracted. But when it gets to the vital . . .
[*pause.*]

Jock Can't you get your act together?

[Geoff *shakes his head morosely.*]
Hell.

---

3 Woman. 4 Voyeuristic look.

Geoff For Christ's sake keep that to yourself, Jock.

Jock Maybe you're training too hard. I could never get it up on Saturday night after a match. Have you – er – always had – er – this sort of problem?

Geoff No. At one stage of my life I had no problem at all.

Jock Mind you, you're not the only one. There was an article in the Sunday paper that said that the young men of the nation were being swept by an epidemic of impotence. Woman has become the hunter and man the hunted. Bloody unnatural.

Geoff I don't think it's that.

Jock Have you seen a doctor?

Geoff Yes. There's nothing wrong with me physically. It's up here. [Geoff *taps his head.*]

Jock Yeah, well I'm a bit suspicious of these psychological explanations. Nothing up there [*tapping his head*] could've stopped my old trooper rising to the occasion. Are you sure you're not training too hard?

Geoff It's not that. It's my family.

Jock Your family?

Geoff They've screwed me up. In more ways than one.

Jock Yeah?

Geoff You don't mind me telling you this, Jock?

Jock No, not at all.

Geoff It gets pretty sordid.

Jock Fire away.

Geoff It won't get past this room?

Jock Certainly won't.

Geoff Have I ever talked to you about my sister?

Jock No. I didn't know you had one.

Geoff I don't speak about her very often. She was in a serious car accident the night before her eighteenth birthday. I was only fourteen.

Jock Badly hurt?

Geoff Very. Both legs were amputated above the knee.

Jock Hell.

Geoff It would've been tragic for anyone – but for someone as young and beautiful as Gabrielle it was shattering. She wasn't just beautiful either, Jock; she was intelligent, warm, cheerful, popular – she had everything going for her. We tried to keep a stiff lip but I was distraught and so were my parents. Every time I looked at her I had to turn my head away so that she wouldn't see me cry, because the last thing she wanted was pity. I just can't tell you how brave she was, Jock. Don't be sad, she'd say. I'm still alive and I've still got my family. I mean Jesus, is that courage, Jock? Is it?

Jock That's courage.

Geoff One night I heard her crying in the dark in the next room and it became too much for me to bear – is this all too much for you, Jock?

Jock No, no, go on.

Geoff You're looking a bit pale.

Jock No, no. It's just that the tobacco's stronger than I'm used to. Go on.

Geoff So I went and lay beside her and held her in my arms and we cried together. For hours. Every night after that I'd comfort her in the same way and we'd lie together crying in the dark, then one night . . . I'm sorry Jock, I shouldn't inflict this story on anyone. You're looking as white as a sheet.

Jock It's the tobacco. Honest.

Geoff Are you sure it's not getting too heavy?

Jock No. Go on.

Geoff Well, without either of us knowing quite how or why, we became lovers.

Jock Jesus.

Geoff We knew what we were doing was wrong. The surprising thing was that we didn't care. It all seemed so right. Can you understand that, Jock? It was wrong but it was right. Can you understand that?

Jock No legs?

Geoff It sounds sordid but it wasn't. I loved her, Jock.

Jock How long did this go on?

Geoff Not long. One night when Dad was away on one of his many business trips the light was suddenly switched on and there was my mother.

Jock Hell.

Geoff Can you imagine how we felt? Can you imagine how she felt? I can still see her standing there. Still young, and still beautiful in a flowing silk negligee and with a look of utter shock on her face. There was nothing she could say to us and there was nothing we could say to her. She turned off the light and went back to her room and we clung together listening to her sobbing. Finally I couldn't stand it any longer. I picked up my sister and carried her to Mother's room and we all clung together crying like lost souls in the dark. Gradually as the night wore on . . . this is too much for you, isn't it, Jock?

Jock No, really.

Geoff It gets worse.

Jock Go on.

Geoff Again, I've no idea quite how and why but my mother and I became lovers too.

Jock Hell.

Geoff Three nights later my father arrived home early from a conference . . .

Jock Hell.

Geoff He looked at the three of us and said just one thing. 'You've killed me, son.' Three days later he shot himself. I've been impotent ever since.

Jock No bloody wonder.

Geoff It's got so bad that every time I run out onto the ground I feel as if everyone's whispering to each other about me. I just can't concentrate on the game.

[Jock *frowns and takes another puff of his cigarette. He looks at the photos on the walls, blinks his eyes and looks at them again.*]

Jock I'm going to have to lay it on the line I'm afraid, Geoff. It wasn't right to get involved with your sister or your mother and I can't pretend I'm not disgusted, but the Club must not suffer because you happen to have no moral bloody sense. The thing in our favour is that no one knows about it, so thinking that anyone's whispering about you is nonsense and you just better get out there and start playing.

[Jock *turns, looks at the photos again and frowns.*]

That bloody tobacco's made my eyes go funny. I'll swear I saw those photos move. Quite frankly I had my doubts about paying eighty thousand for a Protestant – if a good Catholic lad so much as even thought of screwing his handicapped sister he'd still be down on his hands and knees yelling Hail Marys – but the damage is done. I held out for you and I'm the one that's going to be crucified if any of this ever comes out. I've got all kinds of enemies around this place and most of 'em are up there on that wall.

[Jock *looks at a particular photo.*]

Look at that frown on Jimmy McPhee. Look at all of them just itching to sit in judgement.

[Jock *turns back to* Geoff.]

This is worrying, Geoff. Extremely worrying. They know that I was the one responsible for getting you. The word gets around.

[Jock *turns again to the photo of McPhee.*]

Wipe that bloody frown off your face, McPhee.

§ *Post-war Australian drama/male mythologies* Lawler, Seymour; *Sporting mythologies* Dawe (1), Porter; Carib: James

PETER CAREY (1943–)

'Do You Love Me?'

1 The Role of the Cartographers

Perhaps a few words about the role of the Cartographers in our present society are warranted.

To begin with one must understand the nature of the yearly census, a manifestation of our desire to know, always, exactly where we stand. The census, originally a count of the population, has gradually extended until it has become a total inventory of the contents of the nation, a mammoth task which is continuing all the time – no sooner has one census been announced than work on another begins.

The results of the census play an important part in our national life and have, for many years, been the pivot point for the yearly 'Festival of the Corn' (an ancient festival, related to the wealth of the earth).

We have a passion for lists. And nowhere is this more clearly illustrated than in the Festival of the Corn which takes place in midsummer, the weather always being fine and warm. On the night of the festival, the householders move their goods and possessions, all furniture, electrical goods, clothing, rugs, kitchen utensils, bathrobes, slippers, cushions, lawnmowers, curtains, doorstops, heirlooms, cameras, and anything else that can be moved into the street so that the census officials may the more easily check the inventory of each household.

The Festival of the Corn is, however, much more than a clerical affair. And, the day over and the night come, the householders invite each other to view their possessions which they refer to, on this night, as gifts. It is like nothing more than a wedding feast – there is much cooking, all sorts of traditional dishes, fine wines, strong liquors, music is played loudly in quiet neighbourhoods, strangers copulate with strangers, men dance together, and maidens in yellow robes distribute small barley sugar corncobs to young and old alike.

And in all this the role of the Cartographers is perhaps the most important, for our people crave, more than anything else, to know the extent of the nation, to know, exactly, the shape of the coastline, to hear what land may have been lost to the sea, to know what has been reclaimed and what is still in doubt. If the Cartographers' report is good the Festival of the Corn will be a good festival. If the report is bad, one can always sense, for all the dancing and drinking, a feeling of nervousness and apprehension in the revellers, a certain desperation. In the year of a bad Cartographers' report there will always be fights and, occasionally, some property will be stolen as citizens attempt to compensate themselves for their sense of loss.

Because of the importance of their job the Cartographers have become an elite – well-paid, admired, envied, and having no small opinion of themselves. It is said by some that they are over-proud, immoral, vain and footloose, and it is perhaps the last charge (by necessity true) that brings about the others. For the Cartographers spend their years travelling up and down the coast, along the great rivers, traversing great mountains and vast deserts. They travel in small parties of three, four, sometimes five, making their own time, working as they please, because eventually it is their own responsibility to see that their team's task is completed in time.

My father, a Cartographer himself, often told me stories about himself or his colleagues and the adventures they had in the wilderness.

There were other stories, however, that always remained in my mind and, as a child, caused me considerable anxiety. These were the stories of the nether regions and I doubt if they were known outside a very small circle of Cartographers and government officials. As a child in a house frequented by Cartographers, I often heard these tales which invariably made me cling closely to my mother's skirts.

It appears that for some time certain regions of the country had become less and less real and these regions were regarded fearfully even by the Cartographers, who prided themselves on their courage. The regions in question were invariably uninhabited, unused for agriculture or industry. There were certain sections of the Halverson Ranges, vast stretches of the Greater Desert, and long pieces of coastline which had begun to slowly disappear like the image on an improperly fixed photograph.

It was because of these nebulous areas that the Fischerscope was introduced. The Fischerscope is not unlike radar in its principle and is able to detect the presence of any object, no matter how dematerialized or insubstantial. In this way the Cartographers were still able to map the questionable parts of the nether regions. To have returned with blanks on the maps would have created such public anxiety that no one dared think what it might do to the stability of our society. I now have reason to believe that certain areas of the country disappeared so completely that even the Fischerscope could not detect them and the Cartographers, acting under political pressure, used old maps to fake-in the missing sections. If my theory is grounded in fact, and I am sure it is, it would explain my father's cynicism about the Festival of the Corn.

2 The Archetypal Cartographer

My father was in his fifties but he had kept himself in good shape. His skin was brown and his muscles still firm. He was a tall man with a thick head of grey hair, a slightly less grey moustache and a long aquiline nose. Sitting on a horse he looked as proud and cruel as Genghis Khan. Lying on the beach clad only in bathers and sunglasses he still managed to retain his authoritative air.

Beside him I always felt as if I had betrayed him. I was slightly built, more like my mother.

It was the day before the festival and we lay on the beach, my father, my mother, my girlfriend and I. As was usual in these circumstances my father addressed all his remarks to Karen. He never considered the members of his own family worth talking to. I always had the uncomfortable feeling that he was flirting with my girlfriends and I never knew what to do about it.

People were lying in groups up and down the beach. Near us a family of five were playing with a large beach ball.

'Look at those fools,' my father said to Karen.

'Why are they fools?' Karen asked.

'They're fools,' said my father. 'They were born fools and they'll die fools. Tomorrow they'll dance in the streets and drink too much.'

'So.' said Karen triumphantly, in the manner of one who has become privy to secret information. It will be a good Cartographers' report?'

My father roared with laugher.

Karen looked hurt and pouted. 'Am I a fool?'

'No,' my father said, 'you're really quite splendid.'

3 The Most Famous Festival

The festival, as it turned out, was the greatest disaster in living memory.

The Cartographers' report was excellent, the weather was fine, but somewhere something had gone wrong.

The news was confusing. The television said that, in spite of the good report, various items had been stolen very early in the night. Later there was a news flash to say that a large house had completely disappeared in Howie Street.

Later still we looked out the window to see a huge band of people carrying lighted torches. There was a lot of shouting. The same image, exactly, was on the television and a reporter was explaining that bands of vigilantes were out looking for thieves.

My father stood at the window, a martini in his hand, and watched the vigilantes set alight a house opposite.

My mother wanted to know what we should do.

'Come and watch the fools,' my father said, 'they're incredible.'

4 The I.C.I. Incident

The next day the I.C.I. building disappeared in front of a crowd of two thousand people. It took two hours. The crowd stood silently as the great steel and glass structure slowly faded before them.

The staff who were evacuated looked pale and shaken. The caretaker who was amongst the last to leave looked almost translucent. In the days that followed he made some name for himself as a mystic, claiming that he had been able to see other worlds, layer upon layer, through the fabric of the here and now.

5 Behaviour when Confronted with Dematerialization

The anger of our people when confronted with acts of theft has always been legendary and was certainly highlighted by the incidents which occurred on the night of the festival.

But the fury exhibited on this famous night could not compare with the intensity of emotion displayed by those who witnessed the earliest scenes of dematerialization.

The silent crowd who watched the I.C.I. building erupted into hysteria when they realized that it had finally gone and wasn't likely to come back.

It was like some monstrous theft for which punishment must be meted out.

They stormed into the Shell building next door and smashed desks and ripped down office partitions. Reporters who attended the scene were rarely impartial observers, but one of the cooler-headed members of the press remarked on the great number of weeping men and women who hurled typewriters from windows and scattered files through crowds of frightened office workers.

Five days later they displayed similar anger when the Shell building itself disappeared.

6 Behaviour of Those Dematerializing

The first reports of dematerializing people were not generally believed and were suppressed by the media. But these things were soon common knowledge and few families were untouched by them. Such incidents were obviously not all the same but in many victims there was a tendency to exhibit extreme aggression towards those around them. Murders and assaults committed by these unfortunates were not uncommon and in most cases they exhibited an almost unbelievable rage, as if they were the victims of a shocking betrayal.

My friend James Bray was once stopped in the street by a very beautiful woman who clawed and scratched at his face and said: 'You did this to me you bastard, you did this to me.'

He had never seen her before but he confessed that, in some irrational way, he felt responsible and didn't defend himself. Fortunately she disappeared before she could do him much damage.

7 Some Theories that Arose at the Time

1 The world is merely a dream dreamt by god who is waking after a long sleep. When he is properly awake the world will disappear completely. When the world disappears we will disappear with it and be happy.

2 The world has become sensitive to light. In the same way that prolonged use of say penicillin can suddenly result in a dangerous allergy, prolonged exposure of the world to the sun has made it sensitive to light.

The advocates of this theory could be seen bustling through the city crowds in their long, hooded black robes.

3 The fact that the world is disappearing has been caused by the sloppy work of the Cartographers and census-takers. Those who filled out their census forms incorrectly would lose those items they had neglected to describe. People overlooked in the census by impatient officials would also disappear. A strong pressure group demanded that a new census be taken quickly before matters got worse.

8 My Father's Theory

The world, according to my father, was exactly like the human body and had its own defence mechanisms with which it defended itself against anything that either threatened it or was unnecessary to it. The I.C.I. building and the I.C.I. company had obviously constituted some threat to the world or had simply been irrelevant. That's why it had disappeared and not because some damn fool god was waking up and rubbing his eyes.

'I don't believe in god,' my father said. 'Humanity is god. Humanity is the only god I know. If humanity doesn't need something it will disappear. People who are not loved will disappear. Everything that is not loved will disappear from the face of the earth. We only exist through the love of others and that's what it's all about.'

9 A Contradiction

'Look at those fools,' my father said, 'they wouldn't know if they were up themselves.'

10 An Unpleasant Scene

The world at this time was full of unpleasant and disturbing scenes. One that I recall vividly took place in the middle of the city on a hot, sultry Tuesday afternoon. It was about one-thirty and I was waiting for Karen by the post office when a man of forty or so ran past me. He was dematerializing rapidly. Everybody seemed to be deliberately looking the other way, which seemed to me to make him dematerialize faster. I stared at him hard, hoping that I could do something to keep him there until help arrived. I tried to love him, because I believed in my father's theory. I thought, I must love that man. But his face irritated me. It is not so easy to love a stranger and I'm ashamed to say that he had the small mouth and close-together eyes that I have always disliked in a person. I tried to love him but I'm afraid I failed.

While I watched he tried to hail taxi after taxi. But the taxi drivers were only too well aware of what was happening and had no wish to spend their time driving a passenger who, at any moment, might cease to exist. They looked the other way or put up their NOT FOR HIRE signs.

Finally he managed to waylay a taxi at some traffic lights. By this time he was so insubstantial that I could see right through him. He was beginning to shout. A terrible thin noise, but penetrating none the less. He tried to open the cab door, but the driver had already locked it. I could hear the man's voice, high and piercing: 'I want to go home.' He repeated it over and over again. 'I want to go home to my wife.'

The taxi drove off when the lights changed. There was a lull in the traffic. People had fled the corner and left it deserted and it was I alone who saw the man finally disappear.

I felt sick.

Karen arrived five minutes later and found me pale and shaken. 'Are you all right?' she said.

'Do you love me?' I said.

11 The Nether Regions

My father had an irritating way of explaining things to me I already understood, refusing to stop no matter how much I said 'I know' or 'You told me before.'

Thus he expounded on the significance of the nether regions, adopting the tone of a lecturer speaking to a class of particularly backward children.

'As you know,' he said, 'the nether regions were amongst the first to disappear and this in itself is significant. These regions, I'm sure you know, are seldom visited by men and only then by people like me whose sole job is to make sure that they're still there. We had no use for these areas, these deserts, swamps, and coastlines which is why, of course, they disappeared. They were merely possessions of ours and if they had any use at all it was as symbols for our poets, writers and film-makers. They were used as symbols of alienation, lovelessness, loneliness, uselessness and so on. Do you get what I mean?'

'Yes,' I said, 'I get what you mean.'

'But do you?' My father insisted. 'But do you really, I wonder.' He examined me seriously, musing on the possibilities of my understanding him. 'How old are you?'

'Twenty,' I said.

'I knew, of course,' he said. 'Do you understand the significance of the nether regions?'

I sighed, a little too loudly and my father narrowed his eyes. Quickly I said: 'They are like everything else. They're like the cities. The cities are deserts where people are alone and lonely. They don't love one another.'

'Don't love one another,' intoned my father, also sighing. 'We no longer love one another. When we realize that we need one another we will stop disappearing. This is a lesson to us. A hard lesson, but, I hope, an effective one.'

My father continued to speak, but I watched him without listening. After a few minutes he stopped abruptly: 'Are you listening to me?' he said. I was surprised to detect real concern in his voice. He looked at me questioningly. 'I've always looked after you,' he said, 'ever since you were little.'

12 The Cartographers' Fall

I don't know when it was that I noticed that my father had become depressed. It probably happened quite gradually without either my mother or me noticing it.

Even when I did become aware of it I attributed it to a woman. My father had a number of lovers and his moods usually reflected the success or failure of these relationships.

But I know now that he had heard already of Hurst and Jamov, the first two Cartographers to disappear. The news was suppressed for several weeks and then, somehow or other, leaked to the press. Certainly the Cartographers had enemies amongst the civil servants who regarded them as over-proud and overpaid, and it was probably from one of these civil servants that the press heard the news.

When the news finally broke I understood my father's depression and felt sorry for him.

I didn't know how to help him. I wanted, badly, to make him happy. I had never ever been able to give him anything or do anything for him that he couldn't do better himself. Now I wanted to help him, to show him I understood.

I found him sitting in front of the television one night when I returned from my office and I sat quietly beside him. He seemed more kindly now and he placed his hand on my knee and patted it.

I sat there for a while, overcome with the new warmth of this relationship and then, unable to contain my emotion any more, I blurted out: 'You could change your job.'

My father stiffened and sat bolt upright. The pressure of his hand on my knee increased until I yelped with pain, and still he held on, hurting me terribly.

'You are a fool,' he said, 'you wouldn't know if you were up yourself.'

Through the pain in my leg, I felt the intensity of my father's fear.

13 Why the World Needs Cartographers

My father woke me at 3 a.m. to tell me why the world needed Cartographers. He smelled of whisky and seemed, once again, to be very gentle.

'The world needs Cartographers,' he said softly, 'because if they didn't have Cartographers the fools wouldn't know where they were. They wouldn't know if they were up themselves if they didn't have a Cartographer to tell them what's happening. The world needs Cartographers,' my father said, 'it fucking well needs Cartographers.'

14 One Final Scene

Let me describe a final scene to you: I am sitting on the sofa my father brought home when I was five years old. I am watching television. My father is sitting in a leather armchair that once belonged to his father and which has always been exclusively his. My mother is sitting in the dining alcove with her cards spread across the table, playing one more interminable game of patience.

I glance casually across at my father to see if he is doing anything more than stare into space, and notice, with a terrible shock, that he is showing the first signs of dematerializing.

'What are you staring at?' My father, in fact, has been staring at me.

'Nothing.'

'Well, don't.'

Nervously I return my eyes to the inanity of the television. I don't know what to do. Should I tell my father that he is dematerializing? If I don't tell him will he notice? I feel I should do something but I can feel, already, the anger in his voice. His anger is nothing new. But this is possibly the beginning of a tide of uncontrollable rage. If he knows he is dematerializing, he will think I don't love him. He will blame me. He will attack me. Old as he is, he is still considerably stronger than I am and he could hurt me badly. I stare determinedly at the television and feel my father's eyes on me.

I try to feel love for my father, I try very, very hard.

I attempt to remember how I felt about him when I was little, in the days when he was still occasionally tender towards me.

But it's no good.

Because I can only remember how he has hit me, hurt me, humiliated me and flirted with my girlfriends. I realize, with a flush of panic and guilt, that I don't love him. In spite of which I say: 'I love you.'

My mother looks up sharply from her cards and lets out a surprised cry.

I turn to my father. He has almost disappeared. I can see the leather of the chair through his stomach.

I don't know whether it is my unconvincing declaration of love or my mother's exclamation that makes my father laugh. For whatever reason, he begins to laugh uncontrollably: 'You bloody fools,' he gasps, 'I wish you could see the looks on your bloody silly faces.'

And then he is gone.

My mother looks across at me nervously, a card still in her hand. 'Do you love me?' she asks.

§ *Cartographies* Tranter; Can: Birney (2), Reaney; SA: Ghosh; TransC: Ondaatje (1)

JOHN TRANTER (1943–)

From The False Atlas

1

The atlas is related to the globe
    which it represents
like an uncle representing his niece
    to whom he is related
5   but when you look at the atlas
    you begin to think.
Why is it flat? is the first thing
    to worry you. Never mind,
that has worried generations
10   of cartographers
or 'mappies' as they're known
    in Portsmouth
where the 'mappie' thing began.
    Yes, flat,
15 in many variations called
    'projections'.
In fact, being flat, the atlas
    is totally unlike the world
and yet it's very similar and I
20   love it and think it's crazy

2

even those faint colours like 'mauve'
    which is sexually exciting
to those who have a 'thing' for mauve.
    I've been around
25 and believe me, I've yet to come across
    a 'mauve' country
yet there they are, in the atlas –
    Ethiopia, Bengal
and Spanish Guinea – all 'mauve'.
30   In real life
there are Red countries, lots of them,
    reeking of Communism.
Now that's a funny thing: Russia
    looks green, or yellow,
35 and look at Portugal –
    is that 'blue'? 'Cerise'?
The British Empire
    has gone from the atlas

3
but its red memory will never fade.
40   Later on
much later, in fact, about ten years
               later
I go loony trying to work out the atlas
               and rush out and buy
45   a drink. It's an 'iced coffee'

4
I think you'd like it

5
give it a try
          the atlas, I mean, though
it's a very unimpressive thing, much
50   smaller
than the thing it represents, necessarily
          a faint and shrunken shadow
of the world, it's like a globe
          run over by a truck
55   if you need a comparison
          but how else
do you fit a globe on your bookshelf?
          Run out, quick
get a truck
60   Hyacinth honey

6
The qualities of the atlas
          are about the same as your brain:
a uniform temperature, no ice,
          smooth, folded a hundred times
65   and multi-layered. Now that I think about it
          the atlas has less and less in common
with its niece, who is now 'lonely'
          weeping, deprived
of a sympathetic relationship

7
70   no more nuncles

8
On page twenty-seven
          we have China
pressed flat against Japan

now that's a funny thing
75   and yet it seems
     'natural'
how freaky, you remark
     all those Chinamen and
all those Japanese!
80   A quick look at the distribution
graph at the back of the atlas
     puts their combined population
at about a thousand million
     Jesus

9
85   The atlas is capable of very little
     change; no growth
and so an atlas can only decay
     when it then becomes
part of the real world
90   at last

10
In the atlas
     people
or the idea of people
     (that's all you get in the atlas)
95   are designated by their cities
     'He's a Londoner'
nation-states, political
     divisions
'She's a Yugoslavian Communist'
100   that's not fair
she's not really Yugoslavian

11
     just Un-American.
What about Abyssinia? What about
     Malaya? None of these
105   exists, in the atlas. What about
     Babylon? Gone,
all gone; nobody put them in the atlas,
     nobody cares.
I think I'm beginning to get
110   a little angry
okay, tear up the atlas
     as if that'll do any good.
What about the shrunken countries,

the climates that can't operate?
115   What about the methane atmosphere,
            the Jovian Kingdom,
      the countries that don't exist?
            What about the nerve graph?
      What about the anatomical chart?
120   What about the map of the brain? . . .

§ *Cartographies* Carey; Can: Birney (2), Reaney; SA: Ghosh; TransC: Ondaatje (1)

MURRAY BAIL (1941–)

The Drover's Wife

Russell Drysdale, Australia 1912–1981, *The Drovers' Wife*, 1945, oil on canvas, 51.3 x 61.3 cm. A gift to the people of Australia from Mr and Mrs Benno Schmidt of New York City and Esperance, Western Australia, 1986. Collection: National Gallery of Australia, Canberra.

---

116 Jovian: of or like the planet Jupiter.

There has perhaps been a mistake – but of no great importance – made in the denomination of this picture. The woman depicted is not 'The Drover's Wife'. She is my wife. We have not seen each other now . . . it must be getting on thirty years. This portrait was painted shortly after she left – and had joined him. Notice she has very conveniently hidden her wedding hand. It is a canvas 20 x 24 inches, signed 1/r 'Russell Drysdale'.[1]

I say 'shortly after' because she has our small suitcase – Drysdale has made it look like a shopping bag – and she is wearing the sandshoes she normally wore to the beach. Besides, it is dated 1945.

It is Hazel all right.

How much can you tell by a face? That a woman has left a husband and two children? Here, I think the artist has fallen down (though how was he to know?). He has Hazel with a resigned helpless expression – as if it was all my fault. Or, as if she had been a country woman all her ruddy life.

Otherwise the likeness is fair enough.

Hazel was large-boned. Our last argument I remember concerned her weight. She weighed – I have the figures – 12 st 4 lbs. And she wasn't exactly tall. I see that she put it back on almost immediately. It doesn't take long. See her legs.

She had a small, pretty face, I'll give her that. I was always surprised by her eyes. How solemn they were. The painting shows that. Overall, a gentle face, one that other women liked. How long it must have lasted up in the drought conditions is anybody's guess.

A drover! Why a drover? It has come as a shock to me.

'I am just going round the corner,' she wrote, characteristically. It was a piece of butcher's paper left on the table.

Then, and this sounded odd at the time: 'Your tea's in the oven. Don't give Trev any carrots.'

Now that sounded as if she wouldn't be back, but after puzzling over it, I dismissed it.

And I think that is what hurt me most. No 'Dear' at the top, not even 'Gordon'. No 'love' at the bottom. Hazel left without so much as a good-bye. We could have talked it over.

Adelaide is a small town. People soon got to know. They . . . shied away. I was left alone to bring up Trevor and Kay. It took a long time – years – before, if asked, I could say: 'She vamoosed. I haven't got a clue to where.'

Fancy coming across her in a painting, one reproduced in colour at that. I suppose in a way that makes Hazel famous.

The picture gives little away though. It is the outback – but where exactly? South Australia? It could easily be Queensland, West Australia, the Northern Territory. We don't know. You could never find that spot.

He is bending over (feeding?) the horse, so it is around dusk. This is borne out by the length of Hazel's shadow. It is probably in the region of 5 p.m. Probably still over the hundred mark. What a place to spend the night. The

---

1 Drysdale is one of Australia's best-known artists and is noted for his paintings of outback life.

silence would have already begun.

Hazel looks unhappy. I can see she is having second thoughts. All right, it was soon after she had left me; but she is standing away, in the foreground, as though they're not speaking. See that? Distance = doubts. They've had an argument.

Of course, I want to know all about him. I don't even know his name. In Drysdale's picture he is a silhouette. A completely black figure. He could have been an Aborigine; by the late forties I understand some were employed as drovers.

But I rejected that.

I took a magnifying glass. I wanted to see the expression on his face. What colour is his hair? Magnified, he is nothing but brush strokes. A real mystery man.

It is my opinion, however, that he is a small character. See his size in relation to the horse, to the wheels of the cart. Either that, or it is a ruddy big horse.

It begins to fall into place.

I had an argument with our youngest, Kay, the other day. Both she and Trevor sometimes visit me. I might add, she hasn't married and has her mother's general build. She was blaming me, said people said mum was a good sort.

Right. I nodded.

'Then why did she scoot?'

'Your mother,' I said thinking quickly, 'had a silly streak.'

If looks could kill!

I searched around – 'She liked to paddle in water!'

Kay gave a nasty laugh, 'What? You're the limit. You really are. '

Of course, I hadn't explained properly. And I didn't even know then she had gone off with a drover.

Hazel was basically shy, even with me: quiet, generally non-committal. At the same time, I can imagine her allowing herself to be painted so soon after running off without leaving even a phone number or forwarding address. It fits. It sounds funny, but it does.

This silly streak. Heavy snow covered Mt Barker for the first time and we took the Austin up on the Sunday. From a visual point of view it was certainly remarkable. Our gum trees and stringy barks[2] somehow do not go with the white stuff, not even the old Ghost Gum. I mentioned this to Hazel but she just ran into it and began chucking snowballs at me. People were laughing. Then she fell in up to her knees, squawking like a schoolgirl. I didn't mean to speak harshly, but I went up to her, 'Come on, don't be stupid. Get up.' She went very quiet. She didn't speak for hours.

Kay of course wouldn't remember that.

With the benefit of hindsight, and looking at this portrait by Drysdale, I can see Hazel had a soft side. I think I let her clumsiness get me down. The

---

2 Eucalyptus trees.

sight of sweat patches under her arms, for example, somehow put me in a bad mood. It irritated me the way she chopped wood. I think she enjoyed chopping wood. There was the time I caught her lugging into the house the ice for the ice chest – this is just after the war. The ice man didn't seem to notice; he was following, working out his change. It somehow made her less attractive in my eyes, I don't know why. And then of course she killed that snake down at the beach shack we took one Christmas. I happened to lift the lid of the incinerator – a black brute, its head bashed in. 'It was under the house,' she explained.

It was a two-roomed shack, bare floorboards. It had a primus stove, and an asbestos toilet down the back. Hazel didn't mind. Quite the contrary; when it came time to leave she was downcast. I had to be at town for work.

The picture reminds me. It was around then Hazel took to wearing just a slip around the house. And bare feet. The dress in the picture looks like a slip. She even used to burn rubbish in it down the back.

I don't know.

'Hello, missus!' I used to say, entering the kitchen. Not perfect perhaps, especially by today's standards, but that is my way of showing affection. I think Hazel understood. Sometimes I could see she was touched.

I mention that to illustrate our marriage was not all nit-picking and argument. When I realized she had gone I sat for nights in the lounge with the lights out. I am a dentist. You can't have shaking hands and be a dentist. The word passed around. Only now, touch wood, has the practice picked up to any extent.

Does this explain at all why she left?

Not really.

To return to the picture. Drysdale has left out the flies. No doubt he didn't want Hazel waving her hand, or them crawling over her face. Nevertheless, this is a serious omission. It is altering the truth for the sake of a pretty picture, or 'composition'. I've been up around there – and there are hundreds of flies. Not necessarily germ carriers, 'bush flies' I think these are called; and they drive you mad. Hazel of course accepted everything without a song and dance. She didn't mind the heat, or the flies.

It was a camping holiday. We had one of those striped beach tents shaped like a bell. I thought at the time it would prove handy – visible from the air – if we got lost. Now that is a point. Although I will never forget the colours and the assortment of rocks I saw up there I have no desire to return, none. I realized one night. Standing a few yards from the tent, the cavernous sky and the silence all round suddenly made me shudder. I felt lost. It defied logic. And during the day the bush, which is small and prickly, offered no help (I was going to say 'sympathy'). It was stinking hot.

Yet Hazel was in her element, so much so she seemed to take no interest in the surroundings. She acted as if she were part of it. I felt ourselves moving apart, as if I didn't belong there, especially with her. I felt left out. My mistake was to believe it was a passing phase, almost a form of indolence on her part.

An unfortunate incident didn't help. We were looking for a camp site. 'Not yet. No, not there,' I kept saying – mainly to myself, for Hazel let me go on, barely saying a word. At last I found a spot. A tree showed in the dark. We bedded down. Past midnight we were woken by a terrifying noise and lights. The children all began to cry. I had pitched camp alongside the Adelaide–Port Augusta railway line.

Twenty or thirty miles north of Port Augusta I turned back. I had to. We seemed to be losing our senses. We actually met a drover somewhere around there. He was off on the side making tea. When I asked where were his sheep, or the cattle he gave a wave of his hand. For some reason this amused Hazel. She squatted down. I can still see her expression, silly girl.

The man didn't say much. He did offer tea though. 'Come on,' said Hazel, smiling up at me.

Hazel and her silly streak – she knew I wanted to get back. The drover, a diplomat, poked at the fire with a stick.

I said: 'You can if you want. I'll be in the car.'

That is all.

I recall the drover as a thin head in a khaki hat, not talkative, with dusty boots. He is indistinct. Is it him? I don't know. Hazel – it is Hazel and the rotten landscape that dominate everything.

§ *'Drover's Wife' stories* Lawson (1), Moorhouse, Jefferis; *Women and the bush* Lawson (1), Baynton, Franklin, Jefferis

FRANK MOORHOUSE (1938–)

The Drover's Wife

Memo Editor :

Chief, I picked this paper up while hanging out at the Conference on Commonwealth Writing in Milan. This Italian student, Franco Casamaggiore, seems to be onto something. As far as I know it's a scoop, me being the only press around. I'd go with it as the cover story if I were you. This study of Australian culture is a big deal here in Europe – twenty six universities have courses on Australian writing. I'm hanging out angling for a professorship or something like that. This Casamaggiore has got a few of his facts wrong, but the subs can pick those up. Great stuff, eh! He could do for the Merino what Blainey[1] did for Asians. (The inspired Suzanne Kiernan helped me with the translation.)

---

1 Geoffrey Blainey, economic and social historian, best known for his book *The Tyranny of Distance* (1966).

Conference Paper by Franco Casamaggiore

The writing of a story called *The Drover's Wife* by Henry Lawson in 1893,[2] the painting of a picture called *The Drover's Wife* by Russell Drysdale in 1945, and the writing of another story by the same name in 1975, by Murray Bail, draws our attention to what I will argue in this paper, is an elaborate example of a national culture joke, an 'insider joke' for those who live in that country – in this example, the country of Australia. Each of these works has the status of an Australian classic and each of these works, I will show, contains a joking wink in the direction of the Australian people which they understand but which non-Australians do not. The joke draws on the colloquial Australian humour surrounding the idea of a drover's 'wife'.

First, a few notations of background for those who are unfamiliar with Australian folklore and the occupation of a drover, which is corruption of the word 'driver'. The drover or driver of sheep literally drove the sheep to market. The sheep, because of health regulations governing strictly the towns and cities of Australia, were kept many kilometres inland from the sea-market towns. The sheep had then to be 'driven' by the driver or drover from inland to the towns, often many thousands of kilometres, taking many months. I am told that this practice has ceased and the sheep are now housed in the cities in high-rise pens.

The method of driving the sheep was that each sheep individually was placed in a wicker basket on the backs of bullock-drawn wagons known as the woollen wagons. This preserved the sheep in good condition for the market. These bullocks, it is said, could pull the sheep to the coast without human guidance, if needed, being able, of course, to smell the sea. But the sheep had to be fed and the drover or driver would give water and seed to the sheep during the journey. The wagon in the Drysdale painting is horse-drawn, denoting a poorer peasant-class of drover. The wagon in the painting would probably hold a thousand sheep in wicker baskets.

Now the length of the journey and the harshness of conditions precluded the presence of women and the historical fact is that for a century or more there were no women in this pioneering country. This, understandably, led men to seek other solace in this strange new country. Australian historians acknowledge the closeness of men under this condition of pioneering and have described it as mateship, or a pledging of unspoken alliance between two men, a marriage with vows unspoken.

Quite naturally too, with the drover or driver, a close and special relationship grew between him and his charges who became an object for emotional and physical drives, but this remains unacknowledged by historians for reasons of national shame, but is widely acknowledged by the folk culture of Australia. And now acknowledged by art. Interspecies reciprocity. Hence the joke implicit in the use by two writers and a painter of the title *The Drover's Wife* and the entry of this unacceptable historical truth from

---

2 Lawson's story first appeared in the Sydney *Bulletin* in 1892, not 1893.

the oral culture to high culture via coded humour and until this paper (which I modestly consider a breakthrough study) absent from academic purview.

I elicited the first inklings of this from answers received to questions asked of Australian visitors to Italia about the sheep droving. First, I should explain. Unfortunately, I am a poor student living in a humble two-room tugurio. It is a necessity for me to work in the bar of the Hotel Principe e Savoia in Milano and for a time before that, in the Gritti Palace Hotel Venezia. If the authorities would provide more funds for education in this country maybe Italia would regain its rightful place at the forefront of world culture. But I wander from my point. This experience in the bar work gave me the opportunity on many occasions to talk and question visiting Australians, although almost always men.

There is an Australian humour of the coarse peasant type not unknown in Italia. Without becoming involved in these details it is necessary for me to document some of the information harvested from contact with the Australian, not having been to the country at first-hand – thanks to the insufficiency of funds from the educational authorities in Italia – however, my brother Giovanni is living there in Adelaide, but is not any help in such matters, knowing nothing of the droving or culture and knowing only of the price of things and the Holden automobile. Knowing nothing of things of the spirit. You are wrong, Giovanni.

Yes, but to continue. A rubber shoe or boot used when hunting in wet weather called the gun boot was used by the drovers or drivers and found to be a natural love aid while at the same time a symbol used in a gesture of voluntary submission by the drover before his charge.

The boots were placed on the hind legs of the favoured sheep. The drover would be shoeless like the sheep and the sheep would 'wear the boots' (cf. 'wearing pants' in marriage). The toe of the boots would be turned towards the drover who would stand on the toes of the boot thus holding the loved sheep close to him in embrace. These details suffice.

According to my Australian informants the sheep often formed an emotional attachment to the drover who reciprocated. But the journey to the coast had its inherent romantic tragedy. The long journey and shared hardship, shared shelter, the kilometres of companionship, daily took them closer to the tragic conclusion with the inevitable death of the loved one through the workings of capitalist market forces. But also the return of the drover's natural drives to his own species as he re-entered the world of people. And the limited vision of the anti-life Church.

'Why not dogs?' comes the question. Close questioning of my Australian sources suggests that dogs as bed companions was characteristic of the Aboriginal and thus for reasons of racial prejudice considered beneath the Australian white man. The sheep from Europe was a link with the homelands from whence he had migrated and further, I speculate, that the maternal bulk of the merino sheep, with its woolly coat and large soft eyes, its comforting bleat, offered more feminine solace than the lean dog with fleas.

Again, on this and other matters, Giovanni is of no assistance being concerned only with his Holden automobile and the soccer football. The unimaginative reaction of the educational authorities for research funding for this project indicts our whole system of education in this country.

Returning now to the art works under study. In Henry Lawson's story the woman character lives out her life *as if she were a sheep*. She is not given a name – in English animal husbandry it is customary to give cows names (from botany) and domestic pets are named, but not sheep. The scholar Keith Thomas says that a shepherd however, could recognise his sheep by their faces. She is penned up in her outback fold, unable to go anywhere. Her routines of the day resemble closely the life of a sheep and it can be taken that this is a literary transformation for the sake of propriety. She tells in the story how she was taken to the city a few times in a 'compartment', as is the sheep. In the absence of her drover husband she is looked after by a dog, as is a sheep. The climax of the Henry Lawson story is the 'killing of the snake' which needs no Doctor Freud, being the expression of a savage and guilt-ridden male detumescence (in Australia the male genitalia is referred to in folklore, as the 'one-eyed trouser snake'. The Australian folk language is much richer than its European counterpart, which is in state of decay). I am told that to this day, Australian men are forever killing the snake. The drover is absent from the story, a point to be taken up later.

In the Drysdale painting (1945) oddly and fascinatingly, there are no sheep. Then we realise uneasily that it is as if they have been swept up into a single image overwhelming the foreground – the second drover's 'wife'. This unusually shaped woman is, on second glance, in the form of a sheep, a merino sheep, the painter having given her the same maternal physical bulk as the merino. Her shadow forms the shape of a sheep. Again, the drover is all but absent. He is a background smudge. The snake, you ask? In the trees we find the serpents. They writhe before our eyes.

Murray Bail is a modern Australian long removed from the days of pioneering and droving. However, his biography reveals that his father was a drover, but our discipline requires us to disregard this fact when considering his work of art. In his contemporary story he pays homage both to the Drysdale painting and the Lawson story. In the Bail story the woman is referred to as having one defining characteristic, what author Bail calls a 'silly streak'. This is a characteristic traditionally ascribed to sheep (cf. 'woolly minded'). The woman figure in this Bail story, or precisely the 'sheep figure', wanders in a motiveless way; strays, as it were; away from the city and her dentist husband. Curious it is to note that she flees the man whose work it is to care for the teeth which are the instrument used to eat the sheep, and for the sheep, symbol of death. Recall: the journey from the inland paradise in the protection of a loving drover to the destination of death: the city and the slaughterhouse and finally the teeth of the hungry city. In the Bail story the woman goes from the arms of her natural predator, the one who cares for the predator's teeth – the dentist – into the arms of the natural protector, the drover or driver. The Bail story reverses the tragedy and turns it to romantic comedy. Again, the drover himself is absent from the story. The Bail story also has a 'killing of the snake'.

So, in all three works of High Art under discussion we have three women clearly substituting (for reasons of propriety) for sheep, but coded in such a way as to lead us, through the term 'drover's wife' back into the folk culture and its joke. And we note that in the three works there is *no drover*. This is a reversal of situation, an inside-out-truth, for we know historically that *there was a drover* but there was historically *no wife*, not in any acceptable conventional sense.

The question comes, given that the drover has a thousand sheep in his care, how did the drover choose, from that thousand, just one mate? This question, intriguing and bizarre at the same time, was put to my Australian sources. Repeatedly I also ask Giovanni to ask the other men at GMH factory, but he has a head that is too full of materialism to concern himself with exploration of the mythology of this new culture.

How was the sheep chosen? But as in all matters of the human emotion the answer comes blindingly plain. It was explained to me that it is very much like being in a crowded lift, or in a prison, or on board a ship. In a situation of confinement it is instinctive for people to single out one another from the herd. There is communication by eye, an eye-mating, the search for firstly, mate, and then community. The same it is with sheep, my Australian sources tell me (thanks to educational authorities of Italia I have no chance to research this first hand). In the absence of human contact the eyes wander across species, the eyes meet, the eyes and ewes (that is English language pun).

Yes, and the question comes, was I being fooled about by these Australian visitors and their peasant humour after they had drunk perhaps too much? Was I being 'taken in' as they, the Australians say. I ask in return – were the Australian visitors telling more than they knew or wanted to tell? The joking is a form of truth telling, a way of confession. They were also by joking with my questions, trying to make me look away from my enquiry. To joke away something that was too painfully serious. But they were also telling me what they did not wish me to know as outsider, for the confession is precisely this, and brings relief. They experience an undefined relief from their joking about such matters – that is, the relief of confession. I let them joke at me for it was the joke to which I listened not them. This is the manoeuvre of the national joke, the telling and the not telling at the same time. So yes, I was being 'taken in' by my Australian sources – 'taken in' to the secret. Taken in to their confidence. We are told that humour has within it the three dialogues.

The dialogue between the teller and the listener, where the teller is seeking approval and giving a gift at the same time. The dialogue between the teller's unconscious mind and his voice, to which the teller cannot always listen. The dialogue between the joker, teller, and the racial memory which is embodied in the language and the type of joke the teller chooses to tell, the well of humour from which the joker must draw his bucket of laughter. Humour is the underground route that taboo material – or material of national shame – must travel, and it is the costume it must wear.

Today such relations between sheep and men are, of course, rare in Australia. However, the racial memory of those stranger and more primitive days – days closer, can we say, to nature and a state of grace – still lingers. It is present in a number of ways. As illustrated, it is present in the elaborate cultural joke of High Art. The art which winks. It is there in the peasant humour of the male Australian, the joke which confesses. It is present, I would argue (here I work from photographs and cinema), in the weekly ritual called 'mowing the lawn'. On one afternoon of the weekend the Australian male takes off grass from his suburban garden which in earlier times would have been fodder for the sheep – this is an urban 'hay-making ritual', Australian city man's last connection with agriculture. But, alas, his sheep is gone, and the grass, the hay, is burned, to a memory of an association all but forgotten. Finally, I am told that there is an Australian national artefact – the sheepskin with wool attached. It is used often as a seat cover in the automobile. That today the driver or drover of a car sits (or lies) with sheep, as it were, under him while driving not a flock of sheep but a family in a modern auto. It gives comfort through racial memory far exceeding the need for warmth in that temperate land. The car sheepskin covering is an emotional trophy from the sexual underworld of the Australian past. The artefact which remembers.

Naturally, all this is still not an open subject for academic explicitness in Australia and it is only here in Italia where such candour can be enjoyed with our perspective of centuries – and our knowledge of such things. But I say, Australia – be not ashamed of that which is bizarre, seek not always the genteel. Remember that we, the older cultures, have myths which also acknowledge such happenings of interspecies reciprocity (cf. Jason and Search for Golden Fleece). See in these happenings the beginnings of you own mythology. See it as an affirmation of the beautiful truth – that we share the planet with animals and we are partners, therefore in its destiny.

So, in Lawson, Drysdale and Bail, we see how High Art in this new culture, admits a message of unspeakable truth (albeit, in a coded and guilty way), this being the ploy of all great national cultures.

Thus is the magic of the imagination.

§ *'Drover's Wife' stories* Lawson (1), Bail, Jefferis

BARBARA JEFFERIS (1917–)

The Drover's Wife

It ought to be set straight. All very well for them to spin yarns and make jokes but nobody has written any sense about me. Nobody has even given me a name except one and he got it wrong and said I was called Hazel. The drover's wife, the doctor's wife, the butcher's wife. You wouldn't think of all the countries the one where women are the fewest would be the one where they don't exist, where men'll say 'the missus' sooner than give a name. Small wonder the Eyetalian got his facts wrong and said there weren't any women in the country for the first 100 years. I had to laugh. I don't know why; it isn't funny when you think about it.

I better say first who I am. I'm 46 years old. I have four children, all of them boys. My womb has fallen, so've most of my teeth, but I've got a straight back and a good head of hair and I can match anyone on a hard day's work. I know 73 poems off by heart and I'm not afraid of the dark.

I was born somewhere on the stock route between Tibooburra and Broken Hill; nobody ever told me exactly where.

My father was a drover. Times there was no stock to be moved he dug dams or went fencing – hard grafting for very little money. He died quietly one night by his campfire without saying a word to anyone. I was 12.

We weren't on the road with him. We had a shack out of Nyngan – my mother, my two brothers, my sister Bessie and me. Ma was a hard-handed woman. I never saw her after I cleared out with the dentist but sometimes still I dream I run into her. I'm glad to wake up.

The boys cleared out together as soon as the first was old enough. We never did hear what became of them. We had a few acres and three cows and some pigs and fowls. We made do. It wasn't much of a life. Ma took up with a shearer when I was 14 and *she* cleared out for six months. It was better there without her than with her. Then they both came back and the next thing was Bessie ran off with a Bananalander.[1] I'd like to see old Bess again; I really would, but she was never much for writing letters so there wasn't anything I could do, not knowing where she was. She's 49 now if she's alive.

That left me stuck there two years with them, like a bandicoot[2] on a burnt ridge. I gave as good as I got but I took the first chance that offered to get out of it.

Now, it's a matter of what each of them had to say – answering it. Take them as they came. Mr Lawson first. He didn't mean me any harm, far from it. But men can only see women as being heroines when they do something a decent man would do for them if he happened to be around, like killing

---

1 Queenslander. 2 Small marsupial animal.

a snake or an injured calf, or hauling a rotting sheep carcass out of the well.

He was a nice little bloke, Mr Lawson. No bother to anyone, quiet, deaf, drank too much. Every man I've had to do with from my own dad down to the drover drank too much on occasions, but very little was too much for Mr Lawson and it didn't seem to make him happier any longer than the time it took to get it down his gullet. He was a good listener – the best I ever knew in those dry times when there wasn't much listening going begging for ones like me who'd spend weeks talking to the flies on the wall. And he really listened. You could tell because he'd ask things, wanting more.

So I told him a lot. Talked too much – must've – because some of it he took and turned into that story about the snake, as though what I'd really told him wasn't true or wasn't fit. His snake story was true enough. Nobody, man or woman, goes to sleep with a black snake under a floor that's got gaps in it in a room that's full of children. Yes, I watched; yes, I had a candle going and a green sapling close at hand and Alligator in with me because he was a champion snake-dog all his life till a big brown brute got him down at the dam. Mr Lawson made it a great and terrible night. It wasn't. I've spent great and terrible nights.

Like the one I told him about. Joe was droving and the baby was 10 months old the time it happened. He was the one Mr Lawson mentioned that I had without anyone with me, only the old black woman, Mary. I was into my time and Tommy and Billy both in the cot together and me blind silly with the pain and the fear of what'd happen to them if I died, which can happen. And her ugly face came in at the doorway. I screamed, and that set the two kids screaming. Next thing I knew she had her hands on me, and she knew what she was doing.

Only time I worried was when she went off down the cow-yard with a bucket to get some milk for the kids. I thought she mightn't come back, being who she was. It made me feel a bit different about the blacks and Reg was as fine a body as the others had been, and fatter.

Until he was 10 months old. One moment he was as bonny as usual, the next he was screaming and going into a fit. I got the tub and the hot water the way I'd been told but had never needed before. It was no good. I got the dog in and threw the tub of water on the fire and banged the door and left the kids yelling in the dark hut with only Alligator to mind them.

He took another fit in my arms while I was catching Roley, and another on the ground while I was saddling up. Then I don't know how many more there were. Roley wasn't a fast horse but he was a stayer and we would have made the 19 miles in an hour and a half. We'd gone maybe 10 miles, perhaps 11, when the baby had another fit and right at the height of it everything stopped. I knew he'd gone.

I got down, holding him, and lay down with him behind some bushes. I don't know how long I was there. When I do remember again there was enough light, starlight I suppose, to see Roley, off a hundred yards grazing. I was lucky he'd been trained not to light out for home.

But I wasn't thinking of home. I could only think of the baby. I was hugging him, crying and talking, kissing him, closing his eyelids and then opening them up again, trying to push my tit into his mouth. You do strange things when you're by yourself at a death. I must have been there a long time. He began to get cold. I put him inside my clothes and caught Roley and went home.

The dog got up when I opened the door, but the boys were asleep with their arms round each other. It was near dawn. I got the spade and went out. It took me a long time to dig deep enough, being a dry year and my head full of strange fears out of things I'd read about vampires and wolves' claws digging him up. It was when I had finished and was making it all tidy that I suddenly felt the pains, and there was no mistaking what they were. I could have gone back, but what was the point? The kids would have woke and asked about their brother. All I could do was what the black gins[3] do – scrape a hole in the ground and squat over it, waiting for what was to come to come. I would have given Roley and his saddle and bridle then for a sight of Black Mary, but there was nothing there but small trees and the dry ground and the grey light that said it was nearly sun-up.

It hurt me a lot for a little thing no bigger than a small peach with the stone out of it. I covered it up and went back, gathering sticks on the way, knowing I'd have a wet stove to work at before I could boil the kettle and start the day. But later, when I had the fire going and the children were fed and playing round the woodheap, what with the sadness and no sleep and the sick fancies I had about wolves and that, I went back and scratched the soil off the hole and took the thing back with me and lifted the lid of the stove and dropped it into the heart of the fire. I don't know why I did it.

That was the story I told Mr Lawson a long time afterwards, or at least the parts of it that were all right to tell to a man. Funny the way he was more taken by a snake story, the sort that happens to everyone two or three times in a year. But that was the thing about him. Nervous. A nervous man who could never write about things as they really were but only about how they would have seemed to be if he'd been what he would have liked to be.

Gloomy, that, but I wanted to tell it just to show how wrong they are when they write about us. They don't understand the strength women have got – won't see it, because they think it takes away from them. Not that I'm gloomy much, far from it. Wasn't it the dentist said I had a silly streak? Well, fair enough, if that's his name for someone who laughs a lot and can see the funny side.

Mr Lawson could laugh himself when he felt at his ease and had half a pint of tanglefoot[4] under his belt, but it's a funny thing about humorous men – they don't go much on other people's jokes, only liking to work them over into something funnier for themselves.

He said another thing that wasn't right; he said 'As a girl she built . . . the usual air-castles, but all her girlish hopes and aspirations are dead. She finds

---

3 Aboriginal women. 4 'Colonial tangle'; beer.

all the excitement and recreation she needs in the *Young Ladies' Journal*, and, Heaven help her, takes a pleasure in the fashion-plates.'

Who says they're dead? Who thinks that hopes and aspirations have anything much to do with expectations? Even the hardest times don't stop your fancies, don't stop a woman being broody, trying to hatch out stones like an old hen we had when I was a kid. And times haven't all been hard, not by a long chalk.

Hardest thing of all for women is that everything they do is for un-doing. It's not like sinking fence-posts or putting up a shed. *They'll* last, maybe 50 years if they don't get burnt. But the work a woman does hardly lasts a minute – if it's not mouths today its moths or mould tomorrow, and the whole lot's got to be done over again. You have to laugh sometimes at the way your hard work goes down people's throats or under their dirty boots. Either that, or lash out with the copper stick. Best to laugh if you can and get on with it.

Another thing: didn't he notice the hut was papered floor to roof with pages from the Bushman's Bible?[5] Perhaps he thought I put them up and never looked at them again. I put them up for two reasons – they were all pieces that were worth keeping to read again, and because they were the best thing I had for teaching the boys something a bit better than the simple rubbish out of school readers. Well, for three reasons, the third being that the walls looked better covered than bare.

If he'd looked he would have seen one of his own *Bulletin* stories. There was *Telling Mrs Baker* stuck right along under the shelf we kept the plates on. His idea of a good woman – a fool who'd believe anything she was told even when the truth was plain in front of her face. But I had it up there for the words, and the beautiful way he had of using them.

That's something I got from my dad. He had a way with words and a great belief in them. He used to say, 'No one knows what's coming after you die, or if anything's coming at all. Best you can do is stuff your head with words and poems and things to think about, just in case that's all you're going to have to keep you happy for ever and ever.' Well, he's gone now, so he knows what the answer is. It makes me laugh to think of him up there somewhere, spouting out all those verses from the *Bulletin*, loud-voiced.

Come to think of it, if you count hymns I know a lot more than 73 poems. Some of them must be by poets. Only a poet could have thought of 'blinded sight'. It doesn't make any sense but it's beautiful enough for me to think of it six times a day. And the one that says 'Before the hills in order stood.' I like that. I suppose it's because all around here it's so flat and there's no hills to make you lift up your eyes. I suppose the best thing you could take with you when you die is some words you've put together yourself into a poem. But you try it; it's not as easy as it looks.

I wish they had more poems from women. I don't mean I like them just

---

5 A nickname for the Sydney *Bulletin*, in which Lawson's story first appeared and which played a central role in the making of the 'Australian Legend'.

because they're women's poems, but some of them really get into the heart of things. Everyone says Mrs Browning but for me they're like men's poems, written on ruled lines. Christina Rossetti – there's a name. I wonder if it's made up, like The Banjo[6] and The Breaker[7] and Ironbark[8] and the rest of them. Not that she's in the *Bulletin*, but I bought a fourpenny *Goblin Market* once in Sydney. Something to think about in the next world, if my dad's right. And I know some others of hers, too. 'Sing no sad songs for me.' That's a fine poem, sad and funny too, if it means what I think it does.

The next one was Mr Drysdale. He did no harm, except to my vanity, which I wouldn't have if all my hopes and aspirations were dead. He knew the place, give him his due. He didn't sit down in George Street and try to imagine it. You can smell the dust and the ants squashed under your feet, and you can hear the crows when you look at it, even though they're not there. He made me into a black dress over a big belly. And the feet! Could have been size 11. And a soft look like butter wouldn't melt to my face. But he knew it; he knew how the ground reaches up into you.

Then there was Murray Bail. I never remember seeing him, though he may have called himself something different then. He doesn't sound like one from our part of the country – more like a cow cocky,[9] from the river areas. He must've known the dentist, but don't think much of the company he keeps.

He never could tell the truth. He'd never come right out and tell an honest lie, just say enough to give the wrong idea and then never a word to put it right. Like him saying about me, 'How can you tell by a face? That a woman has left a husband and two children.' I'd left a husband, all right, and *his* children, which is a different thing. Isn't anything a woman can do blacker than leaving her own kids, and that's what he was trying to make you believe.

He was a dirty man, the dentist – I didn't like him. I could tell what the night would be like by the way he came home. If his patients had been men, he'd come home wanting his tea. If they'd been women he'd come home with spit in the corners of his mouth and some of the things he wanted, in the dark with the blinds down, would've fetched him a bullet if he'd been an animal wanting them in the farmyard. Should've known, since that's the way I met him, over a rotten tooth that had to come out. Should have had more sense.

People said I'd never last, shut up in a backyard in a town. He had these two kids, poor little buggers. I was 16. Did what I could for them, them having no mother and him what he was. There were times I thought he was more than a bit mad – forever looking out to see who was looking in. He was very ignorant for all he had letters after his name and a brass plate. He couldn't read more than half a page of a book without getting bored and coming on words that were too big for him. I never knew him read

---

6 A. B. 'Banjo' Paterson.   7 Harry Harbord Morant (1864?–1902), known as 'The Breaker' because of his skill as a rider and horse-breaker; controversially executed by firing squad during the Boer War; minor poet.
8 G. H. Gibson (1864–1921), balladist.   9 Small farmer.

anything much except for the racing pages in the paper and the labels on bottles, to see whether they'd thought up a better germ-killer than the one before.

All my life I never knew anyone who worried so much about germs. He was frightened of flies the way most people are of crocodiles, and a bit of fruit that hadn't been washed or a moth falling into his soup would give him something to talk about for half an hour. He says I was quiet. Well, I was while I was with him. Day to day things are for doing, not talking about, and he had nothing else.

He couldn't abide to see me chop wood or dig a hole to bury a bit of rubbish or a runover dog from the street. He'd do it himself in his good clothes and his white shirt with the sleeves rolled up and his chin stuck up on his starched collar like a sick calf trying to look over a paling fence. Poor job he'd make of it. I never knew him ever put on old clothes for a bit of hard yakka.[10] Too afraid people would see him and think he was used to it.

That he was no bushman you could tell from the stupid thing he said, when he used a magnifying glass on Mr Drysdale's picture to see if he could tell who it was I'd gone off with. He says, 'It's my opinion, however, that he's a small character. See his size in relation to the horse, to the wheels of the cart. Either that, or it's a ruddy big horse.' Any fool could see there were two horses, and that the waggon had a centre pole, not shafts. But that was him – couldn't see what didn't interest him.

That holiday he talks about, up over Port Augusta, that was a disaster. It was supposed to be for me. He never for a moment stopped grousing – the heat, the flies, the dust, the snakes, the flies, the blacks, the cattle, the flies. Frightened. His kids liked it though. He says we only saw the drover once, boiling up on one side of the track. Gordon wanted to know where his cattle were. The drover just waved his arm, gave a grin. He was half-miling them and the grin meant the half-mile had got stretched and they'd be eating someone's good grass four days or more before anyone could cut the travelling brands out from those that belonged to the place.

We'd seen him five days before, a few miles up, and that day too I'd had a mug of tea from his billy[11] with Gordon wandering off, too afraid of germs and the look of the thing. We didn't say much – just enough for him to know the two kids weren't mine and me to know he'd make it into Adelaide in a month with the cattle. It was how he looked – I knew he'd find me.

It's no surprise the dentist can't understand it. He could never see what it was about the country, so dry that days you could sit looking at it and your mouth would melt for the thought of a peach, maybe, or a tomato. He couldn't understand you could give up a board floor and a bit of carpet and some wax fruit under a glass bell for a shack with no floor at all in the kitchen and water that had to be carried half a mile when the tank ran dry. Lonely at times, yes, but it's quiet, and that's something.

There's more to a man than trimmed nails and a dark suit, and I'd rather

---

10 Work.   11 Cylindrical boiling tin.

have beer fumes breathed in my face than fancy pink mouth-wash.

He's never going to understand it, how I could find the drover superior. Put it down to my silly streak if you like, but we could *laugh*. We used to laugh over something or nothing, it didn't matter; just laughing because we felt good, because our skins liked each other, and our hair and teeth. Laughter doesn't last for ever any more than hair or teeth. But what I'm saying, when it all boils down and you've stopped laughing, he was a good man. Still is, even though his back's gone. And anyway, there are our kids, and bringing them up to know there are two or three more things in the world than how to break a horse and bring down a tree without smashing your fences.

Another thing he said, how a dentist can't afford to have shaky hands and how after I left him he sat for nights in the lounge with the lights out. Heart-rending, that is. Makes me laugh. The lights out and the blinds down too, I'll be bound, so's nobody passing could see the bottle on the table. There's nothing better than rot-gut to give you a shaky hand next day, particularly if you're not eating right, and he'd never learnt to do for himself the way men learn in the bush. Truth is I worried about those kids of his when I'd left. Kay'd have been all right, but young Kev was a picky little kid, had a weak stomach.

After him, I thought I'd done with them talking about me, but then this Eyetie bloke. Dirty-minded. Hard to tell whether he'd had his leg pulled or is trying to pull ours. I'll thank him all the same not to call me a sheep. You have to laugh, though. He's fallen for one of those stories they tell, round the fire. Voices carry a long way at night. I've heard worse than that. You can tell he's a foreigner by the words he uses, like 'interspecies reciprocity.' I had to first look it up and then sit and puzzle it out to mean taking a poke at a sheep. Any backblocker[12] would have come right out with it, in four letters.

But once you've puzzled it out all you've got is the old story about someone off on his own having to do with a sheep or a pig or a cow. Only when they tell it here it's not a drover, not one of their mates, it's a half-mad manager or some rotten overseer. I don't say it never happened; they say everything you can think of happened somewhere or some time. So they say. But it's not the drovers' way. I don't have to spell it out, do I, more than that he can count on his five fingers?

It's funny to think this Eyetie chap, Franco Casamaggiore, isn't really different from any of the rest of them. Truth is there are many sorts of men, all the same; only one sort of women, all different. We could be a lot fonder of them if only they'd admit how scared they are. Having their sex on the outside leads to a lot of boasting and worrying.

A lot of them cover it up by telling yarns. With our men it's some trollopy girl or a flash barmaid they took up with. With the Eyetalians it's animals. Same difference with the Greeks. It's rams with golden fleeces or it's

---

12 Resident of a region (or block of land) remote from settled areas.

white bulls or it's swans having their way with young girls. Our fellows don't go as far as that but often enough they talk about women as though they were animals – 'She's in pup,' they'll say, or 'She's running round Bourke like a slut on heat,' or 'Got to get home to the missus, she's due to drop her foal any minute.' Reason's plain enough; these are things you can own, use, brand – better or worse, batter or curse.

I'll say that for the drover; he doesn't talk about me as though I've got four legs and he doesn't think the way to praise a woman is to say she thinks like a man, acts like a man. Perhaps it's why I'm still with him, after so long. That, and the kids.

Worst thing ever happened to me was the day the baby died, losing two of them at once. And never knowing what it was I lost. Mary's black face came in at the door about a week later. I asked her about the thing I'd put in the fire. 'Inside . . . little man . . . all curled up,' she said. I'd never thought to look.

That started me dreaming. Dreams all mixed up with *Goblin Market* – golden head and long neck, dimples and pink nails. Laura like a leaping flame. One may lead a horse to water, 20 cannot make him drink. I would have called her Laura. More sensible to have called her Lizzie, for the sober sister. Put it down to my silly streak, if you like, but I would have called her Laura, and hoped she'd have some wildness and wisdom, like Miss C. Rossetti. I suppose I dreamed that dream 20 times before I wore it out. Oh well, dreams go by opposites, they say. Chances are it would have been another boy.

What I meant was to tell not so much about me and the drover and the dentist and the rest of them but about how women have a history, too, and about how the Bushman's Bible and the other papers only tell how half the world lives. You ought to be able to put it down in two words, or 12, so people could remember. Women have a different history. Someone ought to write it down. We're not sheep or shadows, or silly saints the way Mr Lawson would have. There's more to us. More to me than any of them have written, if it comes to that.

The dentist was right about one thing, though. I'm not the drover's wife. Or only in the eyes of God if he's got any, if he's not another one with blinded sight.

§ '*Drover's Wife*' stories Lawson (1), Bail, Moorhouse; *Women and the bush* Lawson (1), Baynton, Franklin, Bail

MUDROOROO NAROGIN (COLIN JOHNSON) (1938–)

They Give Jacky Rights

They give Jacky rights,
Like the tiger snake gives rights to its prey:
They give Jacky rights,
Like the rifle sights on its victim.
5 They give Jacky rights,
Like they give rights to the unborn baby,
Ripped from the womb by its uncaring mother.

They give Jacky the right to die,
The right to consent to mining on his land.
10 They give Jacky the right to watch
His sacred dreaming place become a hole –
His soul dies, his ancestors cry;
His soul dies, his ancestors cry:
They give Jacky his rights –
15 A hole in the ground!

Justice for all, Jacky kneels and prays;
Justice for all, they dig holes in his earth;
Justice for all, they give him his rights –
A flagon of cheap wine to dull his pain,
20 And his woman has to sell herself for that.
Justice for all, they give him his rights –
A hole in the ground to hide his mistrust and fear.
What can Jacky do, but struggle on and on:
The spirits of his Dreaming keep him strong!

§ *Aboriginal dispossession* Kendall, Oodgeroo, Davis; Can: Wiebe, Armstrong;
NZSP: Ihimaera (1)

JACK DAVIS (1917–)

From Kullark

Written for the Western Australia sesquicentennial 'celebrations' in 1979 to convey
the Aboriginal point of view, *Kullark* ('Home') offers a pageant-like account of the

---

1 **Jacky**: generic name for an Aborigine, usually derogatory. 11 **dreaming**: communing with ancestral archetypes and the shared repository of Aboriginal spirituality.

dispossession of the local Nyoongah Aborigines during the last 150 years. The play alternates between naturalistic scenes set in the present and expressionist scenes sketching in key episodes from the past. It draws on a broad range of Aboriginal and European oral and scribal genres and an equally wide repertory of pictorial and musical forms. The first three scenes illustrate this mixture of elements, suggesting that while Aboriginal culture should continue to draw on ancestral traditions, it is inevitiably discursively hybridized in contemporary social contexts.

Act I Scene 1

February 1979. Morning. A kitchen in the Yorlah *household, somewhere in the South West of Western Australia. A radio is blaring out the local commercial station.*

Rosie *enters, clearing up the bottles of the night before.* Alec *enters clearly suffering from the night before. He yawns, stretches and scratches himself.*

Alec What's for breakfast?
Rosie Well it ain't 'am and eggs.
[Alec *turns the radio off, picks up the paper and sits down.* Rosie *turns the radio on again.*]
Alec Turn that flamin' radio down, will ya?
Rosie [*turning it off*] Crook[1] head, eh?
Alec [*flipping through the newspaper*] Watcha done with the flamin' racing page?
Rosie I never touched it.
[Alec *finds the page, takes it out, thumps it and squares it off methodically.*]
Alec Gawd, will ya look at that, Star Pixie, fifty to one. If it wasn't for that long-winded missionary bloke ravin' on yesterday I woulda won two hundred bucks.
Rosie You never won two hundred bucks in your life.
Alec Anyway, who was that bloke?
Rosie Aw, he's somethin' to do with the *Nyoongah*[2] Church.
Alec That weren't no funeral service. More like a flamin' sermon.
Rosie Anyway, he meant well, and it don't hurt to shake *Nyoongahs* up about livin' or dyin'.
Alec Look, he spoke for three quarters of an hour at the church and three quarters of an hour at the graveside, and that's what I call playin' on people's feelin's.
Rosie But that's his job. That's what 'e's there for.
Alec Ah, all 'e was tryin' to do was frighten people inta goin' to 'is church.
Rosie When you're dyin' you'll be glad of a man like 'im.

---

1 Sick. 2 Aborigines of S.W. Australia.

Alec [*laughing*] You know, 'e can't lose, it's like an each way bet: If 'e can't get ya to 'is church that don't matter, 'e'll still get to 'eaven 'cause 'e tried. It's even better than an each way bet, cause 'e bets on the whole bloody field.

Rosie [*reproachfully*] Alex Yorlah, I'm sure I know where you're going when your time comes.

Alec But what I said's true.

[*He points vaguely upwards.*]

'E's just a bookie's clerk, and 'im up there, 'e's sort of in charge of like the T.A.B.[3] in the sky.

[*Pause.* Rosie *continues the dishes,* Alec *pencils in his selections.*]

Rosie It's a pity you don't take more notice of people like 'im.

Alec Who d'yer mean? [*Derisively*] That missionary bloke?

Rosie Yeah, I do.

Alec A good tomater in the face would've done 'im the world of good.

[*His head goes back into the paper.* Rosie *pours* Alec *a cup of tea in a chipped enamel mug and turns the radio down.*]

The only good thing about funerals is ya get to see people ya ain't seen for a long time.

Rosie Yeah, I saw Auntie Peg and Uncle Eli there, I ain't seen them fa years.

Alec They still livin' down Gnowangerup, on the reserve?

Rosie Yeah, they're still there with Libby and Joe and all the kids.

Alec Gawd, how can they bring a family up in that cold bloody dump?

Rosie Well, at least it's their 'ome, not like this place 'ere. We could be kicked out any time.

Alec Old Tony can't do that. Our rent's paid up.

Rosie That ain't the point. If mobs of *Nyoongahs* keep comin' round here we'll be in trouble, that's for sure.

Alec They can'd do that. *Wetjalas*[4] have their friends visitin' 'em so we can do the same.

Rosie No we can't. *Wetjalas* look at us as bein' different and we can't get away with things the way they do.

Alec Look, if I wanta 'ave my friends 'round 'ere for a drink no ding lan'lord's gonna stop me, that's for sure.

Rosie Yeah, y'all had to come back here after the funeral and get drunk. You ain't got no shame.

Alec Well, it's better than cryin' and moaning', ain't it? That won't bring the old fella back. Poor old bloke. Auntie Peg reckons 'e'd 'ave been well over a'undred.

Rosie Oh, he wouldn't 'ave been that old, would 'e?

Alec Well 'e used to tell us when we was kids back at Moore River

---

3 Totalizator Agency Board; 'the Tote'.   4 White people.

'ow 'e was brought up shepherdin' sheep before any fences was put up. An' that wasn't yesterday.

Rosie Yeah, 'e was always tellin' yarns about them old *Nyoongahs*.

Alec Yeah.

[*He sighs and his eyes light up. The radio fades to a quiet Country and Western ballad.*]

Yeah, I remember one he told us. We was at Moore River sittin' round the fire cooking *gilgies*[5] in the ashes. How'd it go? You know the one about Ol' Wahrdung an' Koolbahrdi?

Rosie Oh yeah. I ain't heard that one in years.

Alec [*animatedly*] Oh yeah, yeah. Now the magpie and the crow was brothers, and they both 'ad beautiful white feathers, and they were always arguin' about which one was the most beautiful. Anyway one day they decided to fly up into the sky and fight it out. So Wahrdung, that's the crow, and Koolbahrdi, that's the magpie, they flew into the air, and they fought and they fought, round and round, *nunbuly bukuly*,[6] up and down. Anyway, they didn't know they was gettin' closer an' closer to the ground, then all of a sudden, *tyoppul*,[7] they fell straight into this pool of black sticky mud. Well Koolbahrdi, 'e was the first to get out, and he took off into the sky half covered in mud, and poor ol' Wahrdung 'e was the last to get out, and when 'e flew up into the sky 'e was black all over.

[*They both laugh warmly. The radio stops, and they fall still and silent. A long pause. Rosie sighs.*]

Rosie Yeah, hearin' that story again, whenever I see a crow or a magpie it'll always remind me of that ol' fella.

[Rosie *weeps quietly.* Alec *gazes into his tea. Didgeridoo music crashes in.* Alec *and* Rosie *exit.*]

Scene 2

Yagan *enters in ceremonial paint. He chants and dances.*

Yagan *Woolah!*[8]
You came, Warrgul,[9]
With a flash of fire and a thunder roar,
And as you came
You flung the earth up to the sky,
You formed the mountain ranges
And the undulating plains.
You made a home for me
On Kargattup and Karta Koomba,[10]

---

5 Small crustaceans. 6 Round and round. 7 Plop. 8 A shout of praise. 9 Rainbow serpent, creative spirit of the Nyoongah people. 10 Mt. Eliza, highest point of the area round the Swan River in S.W. Australia and a sacred site.

Kargattup and Karta Koomba.
You made the *beeyol beeyol*,[11]
The wide clear river,
As you travelled onward to the sea.
And as you went into the sunset
Two rocks[12] you left to mark your passing,
To tell of your returning
And our affinity.
You gave me kangaroo and emu for my middens,
Feathers for corroboree at night,
The swan, the duck and other birds you gave me,
And the waters teemed with fish a-shimmering bright.
You gave me laws and legends
To protect me,
And sacred places hidden in the hills.
Then, oh *wirilo, wirilo*,[13]
The *jungara*[14] came across the deep blue waters
To rend my soul, to decimate and kill.
[Yagan *exits*.]

Scene 3

*The music cuts abruptly to a rollicking folk tune. Charles Fraser, a
well dressed botanist carrying a shovel and butterfly net enters through
a revolving screen, revealing a watercolour of the Swan River in 1827.
This picture cuts the Rainbow Serpent near the tail.*

Fraser [*calling*] Captain Stirling, look. More fresh water, right on
the surface this time.
[Captain James Stirling *enters*.]
Stirling Good, good. Fresh water, rich soil, pleasant climate, all
the natural attractions of New South Wales.
Fraser Sir, shouldn't we be getting back to the boat?
Stirling Mr Fraser, a British colony would stand a better chance
of prospering here on the Swan River than anywhere in the world.
Fraser But, sir, it'll soon be dark.
Stirling Just a bit further, Mr Fraser! Come on man!
[Yagan, Mitjitjiroo *and* Moyarahn *enter, clad in kangaroo skin capes.
The men carry spears, the woman a* wahna.][15]
Fraser Look sir, savages.
Yagan Tjinahng baalah bok ['Look at their clothing'.]
Fraser Do you think they're hostile, sir?

---

11 River. 12 Rottnest and Garden islands, off the coast of S.W. Australia. 13 Cry of grief derived from the
sound of the curlew. 14 Returned dead. 15 Digging stick.

Moyarahn *Gnung wayarning, wayarning.* ['I am frightened.']
Stirling Just curious, I think, but don't make any sudden move.
Mitjitjiroo *Baalup dahdahrup wilgeeul.* ['They are painted white.']
Fraser Our guns are back in the boat, sir.
Stirling Try not to talk, Mr Fraser.
Moyarahn *Baal tjennuk tjennuk nyinning.* ['They are devils, devils.']
Mitjitjiroo *Baalup wahnging gnullarah.* ['They are talking to us.']
Yagan [*raising his spear*] *Gitjul! Gitjul!* ['Spear! Spear!']
Mitjitjiroo [*holding him back*] *Yuart, yuart, yuart!* ['No, no, no.']
[Stirling *and* Fraser *shrink back at the sight of the spear. Finally* Stirling *advances cautiously.*]
Stirling It's all right, Mr Fraser. I've handled such a situation before.
Mitjitjiroo [*to* Stirling] *Gneean noonuk?* ['Who are you?']
[*To* Yagan] *Gneean baal?* ['Who is he?']
Stirling [*slapping his chest*] Captain Stirling . . . Stir-ling.
[*He extends his hand in a friendly gesture.* Yagan *and* Moyarahn *are reticent but* Mitjitjiroo *advances. Instead of shaking* Stirling's *hand he rubs it vigorously, to see if the colour will come off. Astounded, he runs back to the others.*]
Mitjitjiroo *Tjinung, baalup, marp dardarah dardarah.* ['See his skin is white, white.']
Moyarahn *Allewah, gnurrlah yuarl kooking.* ['Look out, come let us go.'] *Mitja baal warramut.* ['They are very bad.']
[Stirling *draws back towards* Fraser.]
Stirling Have we got anything we can give them?
Fraser My butterfly net?
Stirling I don't think they would attach much value to that. No, something colourful. Your coat and trousers.
Fraser I beg your pardon, sir?
Stirling Take your coat and trousers off, Mr Fraser.
[Fraser *does so.*]
Fraser Sir, is this really necessary?
[Fraser *folds his trousers neatly.* Stirling *offers them to* Mitjitjiroo. *With* Stirling's *help,* Mitjitjiroo *dons the coat, but hands the trousers to* Yagan, *who tries to put them on as a coat.* Stirling *moves to help* Yagan, *but he raises his spear.* Stirling *retreats again. They begin to enjoy their new clothes.*]
Moyarahn [*screaming*] *Allewah, allewah!* ['Look out, look out!'] *Kynya, kynya, nitjuk. Warrah bok, warrah bok.* ['Shame, shame, this clothing is bad.']
[*Didgeridoo music and clapsticks fade in.*]
Baal warramut, warramut. ['They are bad, bad.'] *Yuarl gnullarah kooliny. Yuarl gnullarah kooliny. Yuarl, yuarl, yuarl.* ['Come, let us go. Come, let us go. Come, come, come.']

[*The music builds to a climax and stops abruptly as* Moyarahn '*puts mobyrne' (i.e. casts a death wish) on* Stirling *and* Fraser. *She marks the ground in front of them with her* wahna, *and gestures to the sky. The Aborigines then exit.*]

Fraser [*terrified*] Can we go back to the boat now, sir?

Stirling That, Mr Fraser, would be an excellent idea.

[Fraser *exits hurriedly.*]

[*There is a drum roll,* Stirling *addressed the audience as if they were attending a meeting in England.*]

The natives are fascinated by the colour of our skin, believing it to be painted white, but care must be taken in all dealings with them, for they are vengeful and capricious and will not hesitate to resort to offensive weapons. The intention I adopted, therefore, in dealing with the natives, was to avoid all possible means of quarrel with them, and the necessity consequent thereon of rendering them hostile to future settlers in revenge for the severe measures we should be obliged to take, if put to our defence. I am happy to say in this plan I was not disappointed.

[Stirling *exits through the revolving screen, returning the Rainbow Serpent painting to its original form.*]

§ *Aboriginal dispossession* Oodgeroo, Mudrooroo; Can: Wiebe, Armstrong; NZSP: Ihimaera (1); *Alternative histories* Grenville; Carib: Reid, Walcott (3)

HELEN GARNER (1942–)

The Life of Art

My friend and I went walking the dog in the cemetery. It was a Melbourne autumn: mild breezes, soft air, gentle sun. The dog trotted in front of us between the graves. I had a pair of scissors in my pocket in case we came across a rose bush on a forgotten tomb.

'I don't like roses,' said my friend. 'I despise them for having thorns.'

The dog entered a patch of ivy and posed there. We pranced past the Elvis Presley memorial.

'What would you like to have written on your grave,' said my friend, 'as a tribute?'

I thought for a long time. Then I said, '*Owner of two hundred pairs of boots.*'

When we had recovered, my friend pointed out a headstone which said, *She lived only for others.* 'Poor thing,' said my friend. 'On my grave I want you to write, *She lived only for herself.*'

We went stumbling along the overgrown paths.

My friend and I had known each other for twenty years, but we had never lived in the same house. She came back from Europe at the perfect moment to take over a room in the house I rented. It became empty because the man – but that's another story.

My friend has certain beliefs which I have always secretly categorised as *batty*. Sometimes I have thought, 'My friend is what used to be called "a dizzy dame".' My friend believes in reincarnation: not that this in itself is unacceptable to me. Sometimes she would write me long letters from wherever she was in the world, letters in her lovely, graceful, sweeping hand, full of tales from one or other of her previous lives, tales to explain her psychological make-up and behaviour in her present incarnation. My eye would fly along the lines, sped by embarrassment.

My friend is a painter.

When I first met my friend she was engaged. She was wearing an antique sapphire ring and Italian boots. Next time I saw her, in Myers, her hand was bare. I never asked. We were students then. We went dancing in a club in South Yarra. The boys in the band were students too. We fancied them, but at twenty-two we felt ourselves to be older women, already fading, almost predatory. We read *The Roman Spring of Mrs Stone*[1]. This was in 1965; before feminism.

My friend came off the plane with her suitcase. 'Have you ever noticed,' she said, 'how Australian men, even in their forties, dress like small boys? They wear shorts and thongs and little stripey T-shirts.'

A cat was asleep under a bush in our back yard each morning when we opened the door. We took him in. My friend and I fought over whose lap he would lie in while we watched TV.

My friend is tone deaf. But she once sang *Blue Moon*, verses and chorus, in a talking, tuneless voice in the back of a car going up the Punt Road hill and down again and over the river, travelling north; and she did not care.

My friend lived as a student in a house near the university. Her bed was right under the window in the front room downstairs. One afternoon her father came to visit. He tapped on the door. When no-one answered he looked through the window. What he saw caused him to stagger back into the fence. It was a kind of heart attack, my friend said.

My friend went walking in the afternoons near our house. She came out of lanes behind armfuls of greenery. She found vases in my dusty cupboards. The arrangements she made with the leaves were stylish and generous-handed.

---

1 1950 novel by Tennessee Williams.

Before either of us married, I went to my friend's house to help her paint the bathroom. The paint was orange, and so was the cotton dress I was wearing. She laughed because all she could see of me when I stood in the bathroom were my limbs and my head. Later, when it got dark, we sat at her kitchen table and she rolled a joint. It was the first dope I had ever seen or smoked. I was afraid that a detective might look through the kitchen window. I could not understand why my friend did not pull the curtain across. We walked up to Genevieve in the warm night and ate two bowls of spaghetti. It seemed to me that I could feel every strand.

My friend's father died when she was in a distant country.
'So now,' she said to me, 'I know what grief is.'
'What is it?' I said.
'Sometimes,' said my friend, 'it is what you expect. And sometimes it is nothing more than bad temper.'
When my friend's father died, his affairs were not in order and he had no money.

My friend was the first person I ever saw break the taboo against wearing striped and floral patterns together. She stood on the steps of the Shrine of Remembrance and held a black umbrella over her head. This was in the 1960s.

My friend came back from Europe and found a job. On the days when she was not painting theatre sets for money she went to her cold and dirty studio in the city and painted for the other thing, whatever that is. She wore cheap shoes and pinned her hair into a roll on her neck.

My friend babysat, as a student, for a well-known woman in her forties who worked at night.
'What is she like?' I said.
'She took me upstairs,' said my friend, 'and showed me her bedroom. It was full of flowers. We stood at the door looking in. She said, "Sex is not a problem for me."'

When the person . . . the man whose room my friend had taken came to dinner, my friend and he would talk for hours after everyone else had left the table about different modes of perception and understanding. My friend spoke slowly, in long, convoluted sentences and mixed metaphors, and often laughed. The man, a scientist, spoke in a light, rapid voice, but he sat still. They seemed to listen to each other.
'I don't mean a god in the Christian sense,' said my friend.
'It is egotism,' said the man, 'that makes people want their lives to have meaning beyond themselves.'

My friend and I worked one summer in the men's underwear department of a big store in Footscray. We wore our little cotton dresses, our blue sandals. We were happy there, selling, wrapping, running up and down the ladder, dinging the register, going to the park for lunch with the boys from the shop. *I* was happy. The youngest boy looked at us and sighed and said, 'I don't know which one of youse I love the most.' One day my friend was serving a thin-faced woman at the specials box. There was a cry. I looked up. My friend was dashing for the door. She was sobbing. We all stood still, in attitudes of drama. The woman spread her hands. She spoke to the frozen shop at large.

'I never said a thing,' she said. 'It's got nothing to do with *me*.'

I left my customer and ran after my friend. She was halfway down the street, looking in a shop window. She had stopped crying. She began to tell me about . . . but it doesn't matter now. This was in the 1960s; before feminism.

My friend came home from her studio some nights in a calm bliss. 'What we need,' she said, 'are those moments of abandon, when the real stuff runs down our arm without obstruction.'

My friend cut lemons into chunks and dropped them into the water jug when there was no money for wine.

My friend came out of the surgery. I ran to take her arm but she pushed past me and bent over the gutter. I gave her my hanky. Through the open sides of the tram the summer wind blew freely. We stood up and held on to the leather straps. 'I can't sit down,' said my friend. 'He put a great bolt of gauze up me.' This was in the 1960s; before feminism. The tram rolled past the deep gardens. My friend was smiling.

My friend and her husband came to visit me and my husband. We heard their car and looked out the upstairs window. We could hear his voice haranguing her, and hers raised in sobs and wails. I ran down to open the door. They were standing on the mat, looking ordinary. We went to Royal Park and flew a kite that her husband had made. The nickname he had for her was one he had picked up from her father. They both loved her, of course. This was in the 1960s.

My friend was lonely.

My friend sold some of her paintings. I went to look at them in her studio before they were taken away. The smell of the oil paint was a shock to me: a smell I would have thought of as masculine. This was in the 1980s; after feminism. The paintings were big. I did not 'understand' them; but then again perhaps I did, for they made me feel like fainting, her weird plants and creatures streaming back towards a source of irresistible yellow light.

'When happiness comes,' said my friend, 'it's so thick and smooth and uneventful, it's like nothing at all.'

My friend picked up a fresh chicken at the market. 'Oh,' she said. 'Feel this.' I took it from her. Its flesh was pimpled and tender, and moved on its bones like the flesh of a very young baby.

I went into my friend's room while she was out. On the wall was stuck a sheet of paper on which she had written: 'Henry James to a friend in trouble: "throw yourself on the *alternative* life . . . which is what I mean by the life of art, and which religiously invoked and handsomely understood, je vous le garantis, never fails the sincere invoker – sees him through everything, and reveals to him the secrets of and for doing so." '

I was sick. My friend served me pretty snacks at sensitive intervals. I sat up on my pillows and strummed softly the five chords I had learnt on my ukulele. My friend sat on the edge of a chair, with her bony hands folded round a cup, and talked. She uttered great streams of words. Her gaze skimmed my shoulder and vanished into the clouds outside the window. She was like a machine made to talk on and on forever. She talked about how much money she would have to spend on paint and stretchers, about the lightness, the optimism, the femaleness of her work, about what she was going to paint next, about how much tougher and more violent her pictures would have to be in order to attract proper attention from critics, about what the men in her field were doing now, about how she must find this out before she began her next lot of pictures.

'Listen,' I said. 'You don't have to think about any of that. Your work is terrific.'

'My work is terrific,' said my friend on a high note, 'but *I'm not*.' Her mouth fell down her chin and opened. She began to sob. 'I'm forty,' said my friend, 'and I've got *no money*.'

I played the chords G, A and C.

'I'm lonely,' said my friend. Tears were running down her cheeks. Her mouth was too low in her face. 'I want a man.'

'You could have one,' I said.

'I don't want just any man,' said my friend. 'And I don't want a boy. I want a man who's not going to think my ideas are crazy. I want a man who'll see the part of me that no-one ever sees. I want a man who'll look after me and love me. I want a grown-up.'

I thought, If I could play better, I could turn what she has just said into a song.

'Women like us,' I said to my friend, 'don't have men like that. Why should *you* expect to find a man like that?'

'Why shouldn't I?' said my friend.

'Because men won't do those things for women like us. We've done something to ourselves so that men won't do it. Well – there are men who will.

But we despise them.'
  My friend stopped crying.
  I played the ukulele. My friend drank from the cup.

§ *Changing roles of women* Baynton, Franklin, Harwood, Grenville; Can: Thomas, Marlatt, van Herk

ROBERT DREWE (1943–)

Stingray

Something miraculous happens, thinks David, when you dive into the surf at Bondi after a bad summer's day. Today had been humid and grim, full of sticky tension since this morning when he'd spilled black coffee down the crotch of his new Italian cotton suit. He'd had professional and private troubles, general malaise and misery pounding behind his eyes as he drove home to his flat. He was still bruised from his marriage dissolution, abraded from the ending of a love affair and all the way up William Street the car radio news had elaborated on a pop star's heroin and tequila overdose. Then in New South Head Road it warned that child prostitution was rife and economic depression imminent. Markets tumbled and kids sold themselves. Only the coffee stain on his trousers and his awareness of his own body smell prevented him from stopping at the Lord Dudley and sinking many drinks. Instead, a mild brainwave struck him – he'd have a swim.

The electric cleansing of the surf is astonishing, the cold effervescing over the head and trunk and limbs. And the internal results are a greater wonder. At once the spirits lift. There is a grateful pleasure in the last hour of softer December daylight. The brain sharpens. The body is charged with agility and grubby lethargy swept away.

David swims vigorously beyond the breakers until he is the farthest swimmer out. He feels he could swim forever. He swims onto a big wave, surfs it to the beach. In the crystal evening ocean he even gambols. He is anticipating another arched wave, striking out before it through a small patch of floating weed, when there is an explosion of pain in his right hand.

David stands in chest-deep water shaking his hand in surprise. He's half-aware of a creature camouflaged in the weed scraps and wavelets, on the defensive and aimed at his chest. As he flails away from it into clear water it vanishes. Immediately it seems as if it had never existed and that his demonstration of stunned agony is an affectation, like the exaggerated protestations of a child. But the hand he holds out of the sea is bleeding freely from the little finger and swelling even as he stumbles ashore.

Pain speeds quickly to deeper levels, and then expands. Bleeding from a small jagged hole between the joints, the finger balloons to the size of a thumb, then to a taut, blotchy sausage. Even so, the pain is out of

proportion to the minor nature of the wound. This sensation belongs to a
bloody, heaving stump. Dripping water and blood, David trudges up the
beach, up the steps of the bathing pavilion, to the first-aid room, where the
beach inspector washes and nonchalantly probes the wound with a lancet.
'Lots of stingrays out there at the moment,' he volunteers.

The point of the knife seems to touch a nerve. It's all he can do not to
cry out. 'Is that what it was?' he asks. His voice sounds like someone speaking on the telephone, mechanical and breathless. The beach inspector shrugs.
'I can't find any spine in it. ' He gives a final jab of the lancet to make sure.

'Shouldn't you warn the swimmers?' David suggests, making a conscious
effort to sound normal. He wants to see signs erected, warning whistles
blown. He's beginning to shiver and notices that he has covered the floor
of the beach inspector's room with sand and water and a dozen or so drops
of blood. He feels ruffled and awry; glancing down he sees one of his balls
has come out of his bathers in the panic; he adjusts himself with his good
hand.

The beach inspector is dabbing mercurichrome on his wounded finger.
On *his* hand a blue tattooed shark swims sinuously among the wrist hairs
and veins. He shrugs again. 'Stingrays're pretty shy unless you tread on them.'

'Not so shy!'

The beach inspector screws the top back on his mercurichrome bottle.
'I'd get up to the hospital if I were you,' he suggests laconically. 'You never
know.'

By instinct David drives home, left-handed, his pulsating right hand
hooked over the wheel. Impossibly, the pain worsens. In Bondi Road he is
struck by the word POISON. He is poisoned. This country is world champion in the venomous creatures' department. The box jellyfish. Funnel-web
spiders. Stonefish. The tiny blue-ringed octopus, carrying enough venom to
paralyse ten grown men. The land and sea abound with evil stingers. It suddenly occurs to him he might be about to die. The randomness and lack of
moment are right. Venom is coursing through his body. Stopped at the Bondi
Road and Oxford Street lights, he waits in the car for progressive paralysis.
Is it the breathing or the heart that stops? In the evening traffic he is scared
but oddly calm, to the extent of noting the strong smell of frangipani in
Edgecliff Road. He knows that trivia fills the mind at the end: his mother's
last words to him were, 'Your baked beans are on the stove.' Baked beans
and frangipani scent, not exactly grave and pivotal last thoughts.

It would be ironic for such a beach lover to die from the sea. David has
known people killed by the sea, three or four, drowned mostly in yachting
accidents over the years. He certainly has a respectful attitude to the sea –
as a young lifesaver he even saved a handful of drowning swimmers himself.
Thinking back, he has never heard of anyone dying from a stingray sting,
unless the shock touched off a cardiac arrest. This knowledge gives small
comfort as a new spasm of pain shoots up his arm.

He gets the car home, parks loosely against the kerb and carries his hand
inside. He circles the small living room holding his hand. Left-handed, he

pours himself a brandy and drinks a mouthful, then, wondering whether it is wise to mix poison and alcohol, pours the brandy down the sink. The hand throbs now with a power all its own and the agitation it causes prevents him even from sitting down. The hand dominates the room; it seems to fill the whole flat. He wishes to relinquish responsibility for it as he has done for much of his past life.

Living alone suddenly acquires a new meaning. Expiring privately on the beige living-room carpet from a stingray sting would be too conducive to mordant dinner-party wit. He considers phoning Angela, his former wife. He imagines himself announcing, 'Sorry to bother you. A stingray stung me,' and her turning to her new friend Gordon, a hand over the mouthpiece, their gins and tonics arrested, saying, 'Now he's been stung by a stingray!' (He never could leave well enough alone.)

She would hurry over, of course. She was cool in a crisis. Gordon would hold the fort. Gordon was adept at holding the fort, perhaps because it wasn't Gordon's fort. This did not stop Gordon from making proprietorial gestures, sitting him down in his old chair and pouring him convivial drinks in his old glasses, when he dropped the children off.

'He's wonderful with the kids,' she'd said, driving a barb into David's heart.

He doesn't phone.

He is becoming distracted and decides to telephone Victoria, of whom he is fond. She has mentioned recently at lunch that her present relationship is in its terminal stage and he feels that a stingray mercy dash may not be beyond her.

'Christ Almighty,' she says. 'Don't move. Sit down or something.' In ten minutes she is running up his stairs, panicking at the door with tousled hair and no make-up, and ushering him into her Volkswagen.

The casualty ward at St Vincent's is crowded with victims of the city summer night. Lacerated drunks rant along the corridors. Young addicts are rushed in, comatose, attached to oxygen. Under questioning, pale concussees try to guess what day it is and count backwards from one hundred.

'Please don't wait around for me,' David tells Victoria, painfully filling in forms about next of kin. He can barely print. He can't remember his brother Max's address.

'I'll wait,' she insists.

As he and his hand are led into the hospital's inner recesses he glances back at Victoria, rumpled and out of kilter, perched on the edge of a waiting-room chair. Their parting seems suddenly quietly dramatic, moving, curiously cinematic. From beneath her ruffled spaniel's hairstyle she smiles anxiously, reflecting this telepathic mood. Rubberised black curtains close behind him.

Among the sea of street and household injuries David's finger is a medical curiosity. A young Malaysian doctor with acned cheeks informs him, 'We'll play it by the book.' Self-consciously squatting on a narrow bed in an open cubicle, his shoulder blades and buttocks exposed traditionally in a green hospital gown, David is not necessarily relieved.

It was never him in hospitals. It was usually women – having babies, miscarriages, assorted gynaecological conditions which owed something to his participation. They always wanted him present. Alone with his unique sting he understands. He lies back holding his own hand.

They inoculate him against tetanus, take his blood pressure, pulse and temperature readings and a urine sample. They wash and dress the finger and apply a bandage tourniquet to his forearm. 'We want to keep an eye on you,' says the Malaysian doctor. Around his cubicle the raving of grazed drunks continues. He hears a nurse's voice say, 'It's no use, we'll have to put the straps on.' A man howls often and mournfully for 'Nora'. In answer to a nurse's shouted question a concussed woman suggests it is the month of August.

'Close,' says the nurse.

'March?' says the woman.

David calls for a nurse and asks whether Victoria is still in the waiting room. 'Please tell her to go home.' A moment later she peers through his curtains, enters, sits on the edge of the bed and holds his good hand.

'You look vulnerable,' she tells him, touching his bare back.

'So do you, actually.'

'I came out in a hurry.'

Amid some commotion four medical staff now wheel an unconscious young woman into the cubicle in front. The staff try to bring her round but the girl, dark-haired and with even, small features, seems to be fighting consciousness. All at once she threshes and moans and tosses her naked body against its restraining straps. 'Hilary! Hilary!' the nurses shout. 'Come on, Hilary. Be a good girl!'

'What are you still doing here?' David asks Victoria. 'It's getting late.'

'I want to wait.'

'I'm all right. I'm under observation.'

'Do shut up.'

Hilary is given the stomach-pump. The staff attach her to oxygen and various intravenous drips, all the time yelling and laughing in strained cameraderie. Hilary is one of them, their age. Immediately David sees Helena [his daughter] in five, ten years time, her straight hair, her suddenly longer, womanly limbs, her emotional problems. His pulse beneath the tourniquet throbs almost audibly. 'Hilary! Hilary! Do you know where you are?' the nurses sing. His fault.

He and Victoria are silent in sight of this drama. Though the pain doesn't let up he thinks he is getting used to it and feels slightly ridiculous being here.

'Nora, I want Nora,' howls the man.

David wants nothing more at this instant than for Hilary to recover.

A violent commotion comes from the girl's cubicle. Suddenly it is jammed with doctors, nurses and orderlies. The Malaysian doctor is wrestling her, so are two sisters and a nurse. Everyone is loudly swearing and grunting, her bed is shaking, metal clangs and instruments fall to the floor.

'God!' cries David.

They are forcing something down Hilary's throat and mixed up in her gagging and moaning is a cry of outrage and ferocity.

Victoria's hand is squeezing his good one with great pressure. The howling man is muffled by the tumult from the cubicle opposite, now jammed with what seems like the complete hospital staff. Hilary begins to gag again, vomits, and all the staff exclaim and curse angrily. Then they start to laugh. They are all covered in black liquid, the emetic they had forced into her stomach. Hilary has vomited up her pills.

At 2.00 a.m. they release him. Victoria drives him home and keeps him under observation for the rest of the night.

Though the pain lessens next day, six months later the tip of his finger is still numb, the nerve-endings damaged. Victoria, early in their living together, produces one evening a copy of *Venomous Creatures of Australia*, reading which it becomes clear to David that his attacker was most likely a butterfly cod, a small brown fish which looks like a weed.

'They're actually very poisonous,' she says generously. 'People are thought to have died.'

'Let's keep it a stingray,' he says.

§ *Changing male mythologies* Lawson (2), Lawler, Seymour, Williamson; *Move from bush to beach as key Australian site* Gordon, Lawson (1), Paterson

SALLY MORGAN (1951–)

A Black Grandmother

In *My Place*, her autobiography about growing up in the north-west of Australia, Sally Morgan describes her gradual discovery of her Aboriginal origins. In this central chapter she becomes aware of her grandmother's Aboriginality and this leads to her asking questions about her own ethnic identity.

On the fourteenth of February, 1966, Australia's currency changed from pounds, shillings and pence, to dollars and cents. According to Mum and Nan, it was a step backwards in our history. 'There's no money like the old money', Nan maintained, and Mum agreed. They had both been shocked when they heard that our new money would not have as much silver in it as the old two-shilling, one-shilling, sixpence and threepence. They influenced my views to such an extent that, when we were given a free choice for our creative writing essay at school, I wrote a long paper on how the country was going to rack and ruin because we were changing our money.

'It'll go bad, Glad', said Nan one night, 'you wait and see. You can't make money like that, it'll turn green.'

Then I noticed that Nan had a jar on the shelf in the kitchen with a handful of two-shilling pieces in it. Towards the end of the week, the jar was overflowing with sixpences, threepences, one-shilling and two-shilling pieces. I could contain my curiosity no longer.

'What are you saving up for, Nan?'

'Nothin'! Don't you touch any of that money!'

I cornered Mum in the bath. 'Okay Mum, why is Nan hoarding all that money? You're supposed to hand it over to the bank and get new money.'

'Don't you say anything to anyone about that money, Sally.'

'Why not?'

'Look, that money's going to be valuable one day, we're saving it for you kids. When it's worth a lot, we'll sell it and you kids can have what we make. You might need it by then.'

I went back in the kitchen and said to Nan, 'Mum told me what you're up to. I think it's crazy.'

'Hmph! We don't care what you think, you'll be glad of it in a few years' time. Now you listen, if anyone from the government comes round asking for money, you tell them we gave all ours to the bank. If they pester you about the old money, you just say you don't know nothin'. You tell 'em we haven't got money like that in this house.'

'Nan', I half laughed, 'no one from the govenrment is gunna come round and do that!'

'Ooh, don't you believe it. You don't know what the government's like, you're too young. You'll find out one day what they can do to people. You never trust anybody who works for the government, you dunno what they say about you behind your back. You mark my words, Sally.'

I was often puzzled by the way Mum and Nan approached anyone in authority, it was as if they were frightened. I knew that couldn't be the reason, why on earth would anyone be frightened of the government?

Apart from Art and English, I failed nearly everything else in the second term of my third year in high school. And Mum was disgusted with my seven per cent for Geometry and Trigonometry.

'You've got your Junior, soon. How on earth do you expect to pass that?'

'I don't care whether I pass or not. Why don't you let me leave school?'

'You'll leave school over my dead body!'

'What's the point in all this education if I'm going to spend the rest of my life drawing and painting?'

'You are not going to spend the rest of your life doing that, there's no future in it. Artists only make money after they're dead and gone.'

'Suits me.'

I gave up arguing and retreated to my room. Mum never took my ambition to be an artist seriously. Not that she didn't encourage me to draw. Once when I was bored, she had let me paint pictures all over the asbestos sheets that covered in our back verandah. Nan had thought it was real good: 'Better than getting the housing to do it.'

I sighed. Nan believed in my drawings.

The following weekend, my Aunty Judy came to lunch. She was a friend of Mum's. Her family, the Drake-Brockmans, and ours had known each other for years. 'Sally, I want to have a talk with you about your future', she said quietly, after we'd finished dessert.

I glared at Mum.

'You know you can't be an artist. They don't get anywhere in this world. You shouldn't worry your mother like that. She wants you to stay at school and finish your Leaving. You can give up all idea of Art School because it's just not on!'

I was absolutely furious. Not because of anything Aunty Judy had said, but because Mum had the nerve to get someone from outside the family to speak to me. Mum walked around looking guilty for the rest of the afternoon.

It wasn't only Mum and Aunty Judy, it was my Art teacher at school, as well. He held up one of my drawings in front of the class one day and pointed out everything wrong with it. There was no perspective, I was the only one with no horizon line. My people were flat and floating. You had to turn it on the side to see what half the picture was about. On and on he went. By the end of ten minutes, the whole class was laughing and I felt very small. I always believed that drawing was my only talent, now I knew I was no good at that, either.

The thought of that horrible day made me want to cry. I was glad I was in my room and on my own, because I suddenly felt tears rushing to my eyes and spilling down my cheeks. I decided then to give up drawing. I was sick of banging my head against a brick wall. I got together my collection of drawings and paintings, sneaked down to the back of the yard, and burnt them.

When Mum and Nan found out what I'd done, they were horrified. 'All those beautiful pictures', Nan moaned, 'gone for ever'. Mum just glared at me. I knew she felt she couldn't say too much, after all, she was partly responsible for driving me to it.

It took about a month for Mum and I to make up. She insisted that if I did my Junior, she wouldn't necessarily make me go on to my Leaving. I, like a fool, believed her.

Towards the end of the school year, I arrived home early one day to find Nan sitting at the kitchen table, crying. I froze in the doorway, I'd never seen her cry before.

'Nan . . . what's wrong?'

'Nothin'!'

'Then what are you crying for?'

She lifted up her arm and thumped her clenched fist hard on the kitchen table. 'You bloody kids don't want me, you want a bloody white grandmother, I'm black. Do you hear, black, black, black!' With that, Nan pushed back her chair and hurried out to her room. I continued to stand in the doorway, I could feel the strap of my heavy school-bag cutting into my shoulder, but I was too stunned to remove it.

For the first time in my fifteen years, I was conscious of Nan's colouring. She was right, she wasn't white. Well, I thought logically, if she wasn't white, then neither were we. What did that make us, what did that make me? I had never thought of myself as being black before.

That night, as Jill and I were lying quietly in our beds, looking at a poster of John, Paul, George and Ringo, I said, 'Jill . . . did you know Nan was black?'

'Course I did.'

'I didn't, I just found out.'

'I know you didn't. You're really dumb, sometimes. God, you reckon I'm gullible, some things you just don't see.'

'Oh . . .'

'You know we're not Indian, don't you?' Jill mumbled.

'Mum said we're Indian.'

'Look at Nan, does she look Indian?'

'I've never really thought about how she looks. Maybe she comes from some Indian tribe we don't know about.'

'Ha! That'll be the day! You know what we are, don't you?'

'No, what?'

'Boongs, we're Boongs!' I could see Jill was unhappy with the idea.

It took a few mintues before I summoned up enough courage to say. 'What's a Boong?'

'A Boong. You know, Aboriginal. God, of all things, we're Aboriginal!'

'Oh.' I suddenly understood. There was a great deal of social stigma attached to being Aboriginal at our school.

'I can't believe you've never heard the word Boong', she muttered in disgust. 'Haven't you ever listened to the kids at school? If they want to run you down, they say, "Aah, ya just a Boong". Honestly, Sally, you live the whole of your life in a daze!'

Jill was right, I did live in a world of my own. She was much more attuned to our social environment. It was important for her to be accepted at school, because she enjoyed being there. All I wanted to do was stay home.

'You know, Jill', I said after a while, 'if we are Boongs, and I don't know if we are or not, but if we are, there's nothing we can do about it, so we might as well just accept it.'

'Accept it? Can you tell me one good thing about being an Abo?'

'Well, I don't know much about them', I answered. 'They like animals, don't they? We like animals.'

'A lot of people like animals, Sally. Haven't you heard of the RSPCA?'

'Of course I have! But don't Abos feel close to the earth and all that stuff?'

'God, I don't know. All I know is none of my friends like them. You know, I've been trying to convince Lee for two years that we're Indian.' Lee was

Jill's best friend and her opinions were very important. Lee loved Nan, so I didn't see that it mattered.

'You know Susan?' Jill said, interrupting my thoughts. 'Her mother said she doesn't want her mixing with you because you're a bad influence. She reckons all Abos are a bad influence.'

'Aaah, I don't care about Susan, never liked her much anyway.'

'You still don't understand, do you', Jill groaned in disbelief. 'It's a terrible thing to be Aboriginal. Nobody wants to know you, not just Susan. You can be Indian, Dutch, Italian, anything, but not Aboriginal! I suppose it's all right for someone like you, you don't care what people think. You don't need anyone, but I do!' Jill pulled her rugs over her head and pretended she'd gone to sleep. I think she was crying, but I had too much new information to think about to try and comfort her. Besides, what could I say?

Nan's outburst over her colouring and Jill's assertion that we were Aboriginal heralded a new phase in my relationship with my mother. I began to pester her incessantly about our background. Mum was a hard nut to crack and consistently denied Jill's assertion. She even told me that Nan had come out on a boat from India in the early days. In fact, she was so convincing I began to wonder if Jill was right after all.

When I wasn't pestering Mum, I was busy pestering Nan. To my surprise, I discovered that Nan had a real short fuse when it come to talking about the past. Whenever I attempted to question her, she either lost her temper and began to accuse me of all sorts of things, or she locked herself in her room and wouldn't emerge until it was time for Mum to come home from work. It was a conspiracy.

One night, Mum came into my room and sat on the end of my bed. She had her This Is Serious look on her face. With an unusual amount of firmness in her voice, she said quietly, 'Sally, I want to talk to you'.

I lowered my *Archie* comic. 'What is it?'

'I think you know, don't act dumb with me. You're not to bother Nan any more. She's not as young as she used to be and your questions are making her sick. She never knows when you're going to try and trick her. There's no point in digging up the past, some things are better left buried. Do you understand what I'm saying? You're to leave her alone.'

'Okay Mum', I replied glibly, 'but on one condition.'

'What's that?'

'You answer one question for me?'

'What is it?' Poor Mum, she was a trusting soul.

'Are we Aboriginal?'

Mum snorted in anger and stormed out. Jill chuckled from her bed. 'I don't know why you keep it up. Why keep pestering them? I think it's better not to know for sure, that way you don't have to face up to it.'

'I keep pestering them because I want to know the truth, and I want to hear it from Mum's own lips.'

'It's a lost cause, they'll never tell you.'

'I'll crack 'em one day.'

Jill shrugged good-naturedly and went back to reading her *True Romance* magazine.

I settled back onto my mattress and began to think about the past. Were we Aboriginal? I sighed and closed my eyes. A mental picture flashed vividly before me. I was a little girl again, and Nan and I were squatting in the sand near the back steps.

'This is a track, Sally. See how they go.' I watched, entranced, as she made the pattern of a kangaroo. 'Now, this is a goanna and here are emu tracks. You see, they all different. You got to know all of them if you want to catch tucker.'

'That's real good, Nan.'

'You want me to draw you a picture, Sal?' she said as she picked up a stick.

'Okay.'

'These are men, you see, three men. They are very quiet, they're hunting. Here are kangaroos, they're listening, waiting. They'll take off if they know you're coming.' Nan wiped the sand picture out with her hand. 'It's your turn now', she said, 'you draw something'. I grasped the stick eagerly. 'This is Jill and this is me. We're going down the swamp.' I drew some trees and bushes.

I opened my eyes, and, just as suddenly, the picture vanished. Had I remembered something important? I didn't know. That was the trouble, I knew nothing about Aboriginal people. I was clutching at straws.

It wasn't long before I was too caught up in my preparations for my Junior examinations to bother too much about where we'd come from. At that time, the Junior exam was the first major one in high school, and, to a large extent, it determined your future. If you failed, you automatically left school and looked for a job. If you passed, it was generally accepted that you would do another two years' study and aim at entrance to university.

Mum was keen on me doing well, so I decided that, for her, I'd make the effort and try and pass subjects I'd previously failed. For the first time in my school life, I actually sat up late, studying my textbooks. It was hard work, but Mum encouraged me by bringing in cups of tea and cake or toast and jam.

After each examination, she'd ask me anxiously how I'd gone. My reply was always, 'Okay'. I never really knew. Sometimes, I thought I'd done all right, but then I reasoned that all I needed was a hard marker and I might fail. I didn't want to get Mum's hopes up.

Much to the surprise of the whole family, I passed every subject, even scoring close to the distinction mark in English and Art. Mum was elated.

'Now, aren't you pleased? I knew you could do it. Mr Buddee was right about you.'

Good old Mr Buddee. I didn't know whether to curse or thank him. Now that I had passed my Junior, I sensed that there was no hope of Mum allowing me to leave school. I should have deliberately failed, I thought. Then, she wouldn't have had any choice. Actually, I had considered doing just that, but, for some reason, I couldn't bring myself to do it. I guess it was my pride again. . . .

§ *Aboriginal identity* Oodgeroo, Mudrooroo, Davis; *Competing ancestries* Carib: Walcott (2), Williams, Brodber; SEA: Joaquin

KATE GRENVILLE (1950–)

From Joan Makes History

Grenville's Joan is a female Kilroy, a protagonist who has been present at all the key moments in Australian history; her 'making history' provides a revisionist feminist perspective on the Australian past. Born at the moment of Australian Federation, Joan is, like Rushdie's Saleem Sinai (in *Midnight's Children*), a personification of her nation. The two sections included here are the beginning of Grenville's novel.

Prologue

In the beginning was nothing much. Vague things swirled and whirled, impulses grouped and dissolved, light came and went. It was a fluke, or a leap of faith: but there it was all at once, the first atom, and everything else was just a matter of time.

Imagine the stars burning their hearts out in brand-new galaxies! Imagine the time when bundles of hot gas decided to draw together and be Mars or Earth! Imagine the first rain sizzling down on the first hot rocks; and starting the business of the land and the sea! What aeons of racket there were, of magma[1] squirting up and lava gushing out: what tumult as the globe heated, froze, cracked, drowned: as rock wore away to sand that ebbed and flowed on the floors of warm seas. What convulsions there were, as the bottom of the sea became the top of a surprised mountain steaming in the sun and melting away again, until at last it formed the shapes of Africa and Iceland and the Great South Land!

Imagine dew forming, sun scorching, winds whipping: lichen grasping the side of a rock: grass sprouting and dying, small flowers holding their faces up to the sun. Imagine saplings thickening, putting forth leaves and dropping them off: imagine them swelling at last beyond the strength of the roots and crashing back down to the ground, and from their ruin new trees springing.

Consider the extravagant excess of nature, providing every different bit of earth with its particular kind of life: with Pale Prickly Moses, with the Leafless Milkwort, with the Spoonleaf Sundew: with the Gregarious Stick Insect, with

---

1 Semi-molten stratum of matter from which igneous rock is formed.

the Sugar Ant, with the Small Green-Banded Blue Butterfly, with the Pie-Dish Beetle, with the Yellow Monday Cicada and the Shining Swift Moth: with the Yellow-Bellied Black Snake, the Sulphur-Crested White Cockatoo, the Frill-Necked Lizard: with the Crest-Tailed Pouched Mouse as well as the Flat-Headed Pouched Mouse: what an unnecessary prodigality of supply!

Imagine, too, those formless jellies from which they say we come: something – what was it? – made them desire history, clustering together and becoming particular: *You be skin, I will be legs.* What a journey it was, from the trilobite, the graptolite,[2] the pterygotus,[3] to the pterodactyl, the brontosaurus, the tyrannosaurus rex! Things with teeth where their ears should have been, things with four mouths and seven feet, things with eggs the size of houses and tongues as long as tree-trunks!

They trundled and hopped, slithered and leaped, swam, flapped and waddled, and after them came the humans who left footprints in the dust. So many births: imagine them, born every second of every day, year after year: now, and now, and now, and now, just now there are three, four, five new humans in the world, I cannot speak quickly enough to outstrip them. They are pink, brown, or yellow, angry or solemn, arching in a midwife's hands or staring around in a knowing way: bursting forth with a roar, or being lifted astonished out of cut flesh. They suck blindly at nipples, they whimper or crow, they lie in possum-skin rugs or a proud father's arms. Imagine them in their millions, all driven by the same few urgent promptings: to suck, to grasp, to kick, and at last to smile, and with that smile to begin their public life.

So many lives! Being explorers or prisoners of the Crown, hairdressers or tree-choppers, washerwomen or judges, ladies of leisure or bareback riders, photographers or mothers or mayoresses.

I, Joan, have been all these things. I am known to my unimaginative friends simply as Joan, born when this century was new, and now a wife, a mother, and a grandmother: Joan who has cooked dinners, washed socks and swept floors while history happened elsewhere. What my friends do not know is that I am also every woman who has ever drawn breath: there has been a Joan cooking, washing and sweeping through every event of history, although she has not been mentioned in the books until now.

Allow me to introduce myself: Joan, a woman as plain as a plate, and devoid of bust, a grandmother you would pass on the street without a glance. Allow me also to acquaint you with a small selection of those other Joans, those who made the history of this land.

I will begin in the beginning, with myself.

Joan

My conception: it was not night, no, Europeans have no shame and do not trouble to wait until dark for lust. It was the middle of a hot afternoon in the first year of the century,[4] with the sun blazing down outside on planks

2 Prehistoric marine creature. 3 Prehistoric winged creature. 4 Australia was united as a Federation on 1 January 1901.

steaming and adding their salt dampness to air that was already too thick to breathe. It was afternoon, and the rhythm of a thin woman and a thick balding man was attuned, after so many months, to the restless rocking and shifting of the boat under the mattress – oh, that mattress and its manifold rustlings! – on which they coupled.

This was a ship built for the transport of many in cheapness rather than of a few in luxury. It was a mean and cramped ship, a ship of tiny airless cabins with peeling walls, cracked ceilings, and dripping pipes in the corners that conveyed other people's plumbing with a rush and rattle late at night.

Those seedy cabins had occasionally heard the roiling and difficult syllables, the guttural hawkings and strange sibilances of some of Europe's lesser-known languages, and had echoed even more to the ingenious obscenities and sly rude wit of many folk from Lambeth, Bow and Cheapside. They had echoed to the sighs of gentlewomen in reduced circumstances, weeping into embroidered lawn and hankering for home: weeping, but knowing that their chance of husband and hearth, livelihood and life worth living would not be found in the genteel squalor of some seedy out-of-season Brighton boarding house, but here, in this savage new land that wanted everyone: carpenters, cooks, governesses, dentists and hopefuls of no defined skill.

In many languages, the voyagers squeezed into their cabins had spoken of hope, of futures, of the blank sheet of new possibilities waiting for them. They had left behind the squalor of cities so old the very cockroaches were descended from those that had been crushed beneath the buckled feet of Goethe and Shakespeare: they had come with a few plates or bits of embroidered garments, leather-bound books with silverfish in the endpapers, or an engraving or two of Tower Bridge or the Danube, with a pair of candlesticks or their grandfather's chased silver double hunter, with their love of dumplings and pale ale, with their heads full of things in dark forests and wolves on cold plains, or of the way the Thames looked on a spring morning at Wapping: with all this useless baggage they had come, bursting with hope, to the Antipodes for a new life in a new land.

And what a land! Here, they had been told, the sun rose on the wrong side of the sky, stones lay upside down and the trees grew so thick together you could walk for miles along their crests. Now, on this glassy afternoon, their tiresome ship was passing between the headlands that were the gates to that new life, and all those weary folk were gesticulating at the foreign gum trees and asking their hearts what the future held.

My coming into existence was the main thing that made that day so special, but I am a person of magnanimous turn of mind, not one to hog the stage of history. Up on deck those muddles of mixed people gaped at their first sight of their future, but down below in their cabin, my thin woman and her brown-eyed man celebrated their new life in the way they loved to celebrate anything at all, or nothing in particular.

That balding man whispered in an oily language to that thin woman under him: *Darling*, he whispered, and caressed the bit of cheek beside her mouth, that favourite bit of his wife's face. *Darling, we have arrived,* he said, and for the last time they heard the mattress rustle and creak under them, and the pipes in the corner mocking them. It was an episode appropriate to such a significant moment: while my father groaned and my mother wept with the storms of pleasure he gave her, a vigorous questing tadpole was nosing into the skin of a ripe egg waiting to be courted, and in that moment's electric interchange, I, Joan, had my beginning.

Those two humans who had come together with lewd and effortful noises to conceive me, who were they, making history in a sound of sighs? Well, there was a thin woman, and a man chunky like a block of chopped wood, and balding so the dome of his cranium was egglike. The thin woman was thin by nature, not design, was in fact not in any way a woman of design, her long face, with its tanned-looking skin, having only its own features for adornment. She was a woman of narrow mobile lips with fine creases at their corners from years of finding things funny. When she smiled or laughed, gold glittered in that mouth, for back in the country they had left behind, that tiny country of werewolves and vampires, the father of the thin woman spent his days peering at molars, and loved nothing better than a bit of fine work on a gold inlay.

And the balding man, who was he? Just another stocky man in a lumpy cheap suit, with his father's signet ring on his little finger. He had always had a way of clutching at the handle of his heavy leather briefcase that had made the thin woman love him, there was such determination, and such innocent hope and purpose in that grip. In the briefcase, she had learned, was not much: a clean handkerchief, a notebook for great thoughts as they occurred, and a few bits of paper relating to enterprises that flickered and smouldered but never caught fire.

My love for you is hunger, he had whispered to the thin woman on the dentist's slippery couch, which during the day was the place where anxious folk squirmed and waited with their toothaches. *My love for you is hope. What is your thinking about a new life in a new land?* The thin woman loved this man in his suit that bulged and buckled, had loved him for a year or more, and had long ago decided that this was the man she wished to spend her life with. She was impatient with dentists and their cautions, their painstaking days fiddling with the endless decaying molars of folk stiff with the apprehension of pain, and was even willing to undergo the rigours of being foreign, and go to a new land on the bottom of the earth, to be with this man. He was a man of wit, a man given in a mild way to the extravagant gesture, and he was a man of intense brown eyes and a mouth that made most things plausible, but it was for none of this that the thin woman loved him. It was for his adoration of her that she loved him, knowing she would never again meet with a love like his.

My pink-scalped father panted, then, and groaned with the pain of adoring his wife, that no amount of penetrating her flesh could assuage, and while he panted and history was being made in the interior of a thin woman, other kinds of history were also being made.

In the new land they were approaching, men with frockcoats and small knowing eyes spoke of the birth of a nation, and thought with satisfaction of their fertile acres and the cash in their strongboxes. These were starchier folk, not eaters of garlic or wearers of rustic embroidery, they were folk who had never had to confront jellied eel, or the bailiff on an empty stomach. They were folk made uneasy by gesticulation and suspicious of too much hope: they were men in frockcoats and side-whiskers that hid the shape of their faces, they were women with heavy cheeks made bland by privilege.

The birth of a nation, the men brayed, from their mouths concealed under heavy moustaches that smelled of mutton. *Our debt to the mother country*, they intoned, and turned up their small eyes piously. They thought, or said they thought, that this was the moment at which this barbarous land was entering into its glory after a long and squalid beginning. In their folly they thought that was history. But the real history of that moment was known only to myself, where something as real as a human was being made.

No book has yet recorded that event, though whole forests have been sacrificed to all those men with their frockcoats and to princes burdened with frogging. The books are strangely silent on all that matters, so here I am to put them right: watch, and you will see history being made in front of your eyes.

§ *Changing roles of women* Baynton, Franklin, Harwood, Garner; Can: Marlatt; *Alternative histories* Jefferis; Can: Wiebe; Carib: Reid, Walcott (3); SA: Rushdie

TIM WINTON (1960–)

Neighbours

When they first moved in, the young couple were wary of the neighbourhood. The street was full of European migrants. It made the newly-weds feel like sojourners in a foreign land. Next door on the left lived a Macedonian family. On the right, a widower from Poland.

The newly-weds' house was small, but its high ceilings and paned windows gave it the feel of an elegant cottage. From his study window, the young man could see out over the rooftops and used-car yards the Moreton Bay figs in the park where they walked their dog. The neighbours seemed cautious about the dog, a docile, moulting collie.

The young man and woman had lived all their lives in the expansive outer suburbs where good neighbours were seldom seen and never heard. The sounds of spitting and washing and daybreak watering came as a shock. The Macedonian family shouted, ranted, screamed. It took six months for the newcomers to comprehend the fact that their neighbours were not murdering each other, merely talking. The old Polish man spent most of his day hammering nails into wood only to pull them out again. His yard was stacked with salvaged lumber. He added to it, but he did not build with it.

Relations were uncomfortable for many months. The Macedonians raised eyebrows at the late hour at which the newcomers rose in the mornings. The young man sensed their disapproval at his staying home to write his thesis while his wife worked. He watched in disgust as the little boy next door urinated in the street. He once saw him spraying the cat from the back step. The child's head was shaved regularly, he assumed, in order to make his hair grow thick. The little boy stood at the fence with only his cobalt eyes showing; it made the young man nervous.

In the autumn, the young couple cleared rubbish from their backyard and turned and manured the soil under the open and measured gaze of the neighbours. They planted leeks, onions, cabbage, brussels sprouts and broad beans and this caused the neighbours to come to the fence and offer advice about spacing, hilling, mulching. The young man resented the interference, but he took careful note of what was said. His wife was bold enough to run a hand over the child's stubble and the big woman with black eyes and butcher's arms gave her a bagful of garlic cloves to plant.

Not long after, the young man and woman built a henhouse. The neighbours watched it fall down. The Polish widower slid through the fence uninvited and rebuilt it for them. They could not understand a word he said.

As autumn merged into winter and the vermilion sunsets were followed by sudden, dark dusks touched with the smell of woodsmoke and the sound of roosters crowing day's end, the young couple found themselves smiling back at the neighbours. They offered heads of cabbage and took gifts of grappa and firewood. The young man worked steadily at his thesis on the development of the twentieth century novel. He cooked dinners for his wife and listened to her stories of eccentric patients and hospital incompetence. In the street they no longer walked with their eyes lowered. They felt superior and proud when their parents came to visit and to cast shocked glances across the fence.

In the winter they kept ducks, big, silent muscovies that stood about in the rain growing fat. In the spring the Macedonian family showed them how to slaughter and to pluck and to dress. They all sat around on blocks and upturned buckets and told barely-understood stories – the men butchering, the women plucking, as was demanded. In the haze of down and steam and fractured dialogue, the young man and woman felt intoxicated. The cat toyed with severed heads. The child pulled the cat's tail. The newcomers found themselves shouting.

But they had not planned on a pregnancy. It stunned them to be made parents so early. Their friends did not have children until several years after being married – if at all. The young woman arranged for maternity leave. The young man ploughed on with his thesis on the twentieth century novel.

The Polish widower began to build. In the late spring dawns, he sank posts and poured cement and began to use his wood. The young couple turned in their bed, cursed him behind his back. The young husband, at times, suspected that the widower was deliberately antagonizing them. The young wife threw up in the mornings. Hay fever began to wear him down.

Before long the young couple realized that the whole neighbourhood knew of the pregnancy. People smiled tirelessly at them. The man in the deli gave her small presents of chocolates and him packets of cigarettes that he stored at home, not being a smoker. In the summer, Italian women began to offer names. Greek women stopped the young woman in the street, pulled her skirt up and felt her belly, telling her it was bound to be a boy. By late summer the woman next door had knitted the baby a suit, complete with booties and beanie. The young woman felt flattered, claustrophobic, grateful, peeved.

By late summer, the Polish widower next door had almost finished his two-car garage. The young man could not believe that a man without a car would do such a thing, and one evening as he was considering making a complaint about the noise, the Polish man came over with barrowfuls of woodscraps for their fire.

Labour came abruptly. The young man abandoned the twentieth century novel for the telephone. His wife began to black the stove. The midwife came and helped her finish the job while he ran about making statements that sounded like queries. His wife hoisted her belly about the house, supervising his movements. Going outside for more wood, he saw, in the last light of the day, the faces at each fence. He counted twelve faces. The Macedonian family waved and called out what sounded like their best wishes.

As the night deepened, the young woman dozed between contractions, sometimes walking, sometimes shouting. She had a hot bath and began to eat ice and demand liverwurst. Her belly rose, uterus flexing downward. Her sweat sparkled, the gossamer highlit by movement and firelight. The night grew older. The midwife crooned. The young man rubbed his wife's back, fed her ice and rubbed her lips with oil.

And then came the pushing. He caressed and stared and tried not to shout. The floor trembled as the young woman bore down in a squat. He felt the power of her, the sophistication of her. She strained. Her face mottled. She kept at it, push after push, assaulting some unseen barrier, until suddenly it was smashed and she was through. It took his wind away to see the look on the baby's face as it was suddenly passed up to the breast. It had one eye on him. It found the nipple. It trailed cord and vernix smears and its mother's own sweat. She gasped and covered the tiny buttocks with a hand. A boy, she said. For a second, the child lost the nipple and began to cry. The young man heard shouting outside. He went to the back door. On the Macedonian side of the fence, a small queue of bleary faces looked up, cheering, and the young man began to weep. The twentieth century novel had not prepared him for this.

§ *Suburban life* Lawler, Harwood; *Migrants in Australia* Drewe; TransC: Gooneratne

DAVID MALOUF (1934–)

From Remembering Babylon

The central subject of *Remembering Babylon* is the impact that Jemmy Fairley, an 'Englishman' who returns to white society after living for many years among Aborigines, and the inhabitants of a small nineteenth-century Queensland settlement have on one another. The novel questions numerous dividing-lines between supposedly discrete areas of experience, among them civilization and savagery, superiority and inferiority, rationality and sensuality and subject and object. Here, at the very beginning, Jemmy is established in the role that he will occupy throughout: that of a man on the fence between two cultures, a liminal, transcultural figure whose arrival challenges the fiction of commonality of outlook and purpose on which the settlers' lives have hitherto been based.

One day in the middle of the nineteenth century, when settlement in Queensland had advanced little more than halfway up the coast, three children were playing at the edge of a paddock when they saw something extraordinary. They were two little girls in patched gingham and a boy, their cousin, in short pants and braces, all three barefooted farm children not easily scared.

They had little opportunity for play but had been engaged for the past hour in a game of the boy's devising: the paddock, all clay-packed stones and ant trails, was a forest in Russia – they were hunters on the track of wolves.

The boy had elaborated this scrap of make-believe out of a story in the fourth grade Reader; he was lost in it. Cold air burned his nostrils, snow squeaked underfoot; the gun he carried, a good-sized stick, hung heavy on his arm. But the girls, especially Janet, who was older than he was and half a head taller, were bored. They had no experience of snow, and wolves did not interest them. They complained and dawdled and he had to exert all his gift for fantasy, his will too, which was stubborn, to keep them in the game.

They had a blue kelpie with them. He bounced along with his tongue lolling, excited by the boy's solemn concentration but puzzled too that he could get no sense of what they were after: the idea of wolf had not been transmitted to him. He danced around the little party, sometimes in front, sometimes to the side, sniffing close to the earth, raising his moist eyes in hope of instruction, and every now and then, since he was young and easily distracted, bounding away after the clippered insects that sprang up as they approached, or a grasshopper that rose with a ponderous whirring and rolled sideways from his jaws. Then suddenly he did get the scent. With a yelp of pure delight he shot off in the direction of their boundary fence, and the children, all three, turned away to see what he had found.

Lachlan Beattie felt the snow melt at his feet. He heard a faint far-off rushing, like wind rolling down a tunnel, and it took him a moment to understand that it was coming from inside him.

In the intense heat that made everything you looked at warp and glare, a fragment of ti-tree[1] swamp, some bit of the land over there that was forbidden to them, had detached itself from the band of grey that made up the far side of the swamp, and in a shape more like a watery, heat-struck mirage than a thing of substance, elongated and airily indistinct, was bowling, leaping, flying towards them.

A black! That was the boy's first thought. We're being raided by blacks. After so many false alarms it had come.

The two little girls stood spellbound. They had given a gasp, one sharp intake of breath, then forgotten to breathe out. The boy too was struck but had begun to recover. Though he was very pale about the mouth, he did what his manhood required him to do. Holding fast to the stick, he stepped resolutely in front.

But it wasn't a raid, there was just one of them; and the thing, as far as he could make it out through the sweat in his eyes and its flamelike flickering, was not even, maybe, human. The stick-like legs, all knobbed at the joints, suggested a wounded waterbird, a brolga,[2] or a human that in the manner of the tales they told one another, all spells and curses, had been *changed* into a bird, but only halfway, and now, neither one thing nor the other, was hopping and flapping towards them out of a world over there, beyond the no-man's-land of the swamp, that was the abode of everything savage and fearsome, and since it lay so far beyond experience, not just their own but their parents' too, of nightmare rumours, superstitions and all that belonged to Absolute Dark.

A bit of blue rag was at its middle from which sleeves hung down. They swung and signalled. But the sticks of arms above its head were also signalling, or beating off flies, or licks of invisible flame. Ah, that was it. It was a scarecrow that had somehow caught the spark of life, got down from its pole, and now, in a raggedy, rough-headed way, was stumbling about over the blazing earth, its leathery face scorched black, but with hair, they saw, as it bore down upon them, as sun-bleached and pale-straw coloured as their own.

Whatever it was, it was the boy's intention to confront it. Very sturdy and purposeful, two paces in front of his cousins, though it might have been a hundred yards in the tremendous isolation he felt, and with a belief in the power of the weapon he held that he knew was impossible and might not endure, he pushed the stick into his shoulder and took his stance.

The creature, almost upon them now and with Flash at its heels, came to a halt, gave a kind of squawk, and leaping up onto the top rail of the fence, hung there, its arms outflung as if preparing for flight. Then the ragged mouth gapped.

'Do not shoot,' it shouted. 'I am a B-b-british object!'

---

1 Tea-tree; shrub yielding tea. 2 Species of crane.

It was a white man, though there was no way you could have known it from his look. He had the mangy, half-starved look of a black, and when, with a cry, he lost his grip on the rail and came tumbling at their feet, the smell of one too, like dead swamp-water; and must have been as astonished as they were by the words that had jumped out of his mouth because he could find no more of them. He gaped, grinned, rubbed his side, winced, cast his eyes about in a hopeless way, and when he found speech again it was a complaint, against himself perhaps, in some whining blackfeller's lingo.

The boy was incensed. The idea of a language he did not know scared him. He thought that if he allowed the man to go on using it, he would see how weak they were and get the advantage of them. He jerked the stick in the direction of the man's heart. 'Stop that,' he yelled. 'Just steik yur mooth.'

The man, responding to the truculence of the boy's tone, began to crawl about with his nose in the dust. The boy relaxed – That's better, he thought – and even Flash, seeing now that the fellow was prepared to be docile, stopped yapping and began to tongue the stranger's knees.

The man was not keen on it. With a childish whimper he began to hop about, trying to shake the dog off. Lachlan, disturbed and a little disgusted by this display of unmanliness but eager to show that he could be a generous victor, as well as a stern one, called Flash off. 'Ge on wi' ye,' he told the fellow in as gruff a voice as he could manage, and soon had his prisoner going, but at a hobbling gait – one of his legs was shorter than the other. He ordered his cousins to keep back, and in the glow of his new-found mastery they let themselves be led.

After a time the man began to grunt, then to gabble as if in protest, but when Lachlan put the stick into his spine, moved on faster, producing sounds of such eager submissiveness that the boy's heart swelled. He had a powerful sense of the springing of his torso from the roots of his belly. He had known nothing like this! He was bringing a prisoner in. Armed with nothing, too, but his own presumptuous daring and the power of make-believe.

So the little procession made its way to where the girls' father was ringbarking[3] in the gully below their hut.

An hour later news of the affair had spread all through the settlement. A crowd had gathered to see this specimen of – of what? What was he?

They stood in the heat, which was overpowering at this time of the day, and stared.

Distractions were unusual up here; even the Syrian pedlar did not trouble to come so far. They were isolated, at the end of the line.

Apart from their scattered holdings, the largest of which was forty acres, there was nothing to the settlement but a store and post office of unpainted

---

3 Killing trees by cutting a ring around trunk; preparing land by so doing.

weatherboard, with a verandah and a dog in front of it that was permanently asleep but if kicked would shift itself, walk five steps, then flop.

Opposite the store was a corrugated iron shack, a shanty-pub, unlicensed as yet, with hitching posts and a hollowed log that served as a trough.

The area between, the open space where they now stood, was part of a road perhaps, since horses and carts went back and forth upon it, and women in sunbonnets, and barefoot youths who, with nothing to do in the evening, came to sit with their feet up on the rails of the verandah and tell raw jokes, practise their spitting, and flick cigarette butts with a hiss into the trough. It was not yet a street, and had no name.

The nearest named place, Bowen, was twelve miles off, but the twelve miles meant that they were only lightly connected to it, and even more lightly to what *it* was connected to: the figure in an official uniform who had given it his name and the Crown he represented, which held them all, a whole continent, in its grip.

'He's an ugly-lookin' bloke, aren't you, eh? Faugh! Don't 'e stink, but!'

'Dumb. I reckon 'e's dumb.'

'No he's no'! He spoke t' me. Don't shoot, he said, didn' ye, eh? Don't shoot! Don't shoot!'

The man, recognising the words as his own, showed his blackened teeth, which were ground down to the stumps, and did a little lopsided dance, then looked foolish.

'Don't shoot,' the boy repeated, and held the stick up to his shoulder. One of the smaller children laughed.

'Ah'm the wan he kens,'[4] the boy repeated. He was determined to keep hold of the bit of glory he had won. 'Don't you, eh? Eh? Ah'm the wan.' With a boisterous persistence that kept him very nearly breathless, he scampered off to collar newcomers, but always dashed back to be at the man's side, at the centre of their gaze.

For a moment back there, seeing himself as these grown-ups might see him, a mere kid, a twelve-year-old and small for his age, he had felt a wave of anxiety at how shaky his power might be. But he'd recovered – all his recoveries were like this, as quick as the fits of despondency he fell into – and was fired once more with the excitement of the thing. The air crackled around him. He shone. Over and over, in words that each time he repeated them made him see the event, and himself too, in a light more vivid, more startling, he told how it had happened: how the fellow had come flying at the fence 'as if an airmy o' fiends were aifter him', and when he leapt up onto the rail, his words.

The words were what mattered most to the boy. By changing the stick he held into what his gesture had claimed for it, they had changed him too, and he did not want, now, to change back. So long as he kept talking, he thought, and the others listened, he would not.

---

4 Knows.

Janet McIvor, who had also been there and seen all that occurred, though no one seemed interested in her version, was surprised that he was allowed to get away with it; their father wasn't always so easy. But he and their mother seemed as gawpingly awe-struck as the rest. Neither of them had made the least move to bring him down.

The fact was that the event itself, which was so unusual and unexpected, had made the boy, since he claimed so large a part in it, as strange almost to their customary view of him as the half-caste or runaway. Something impressive and mysterious set the two figures, Lachlan Beattie as much as the straw-topped half-naked savage, in a dimension where they appeared unreachable. So the boy simply had his way till his aunt, who had never seen him in such a state, darting this way and that like an actor on a stage, out of a fear that he might be about to explode under her very eyes, told him for heaven's sake to cool down, and his uncle, woken as if from a dream, stepped in and took a hand to him.

He looked about him, open-eyed at last, rubbed the side of his head where his uncle's hand had come down, and was again just a wiry twelve-year-old. The runaway, who might, they now thought, be some sort of simpleton, was alarmed at this outburst and began to moan.

'Me and Meg found him, just as much as Lachlan,' Janet McIvor put in, seizing her opportunity, but no one paid heed. 'And anyway, it was Flash.'

'Oh for heaven's sake, lassie,' her mother told her, 'dinnae you start.'

Meanwhile the man stood waiting. For what?

For one of them to start something.

But where *could* you start with an odd, unsettled fellow who, beyond what the boy Lachlan had heard him shout, had not a word you could make sense of in the English tongue; a pathetic, muddy-eyed, misshapen fellow, all fidgets, who seemed amazed by them – as if *they* were the curiosities here – and kept laughing and blinking.

He was a man who had suffered a good deal of damage. There were scorch marks on his chest and arms where he had rolled into a camp fire, and signs that he had, at one time or another, taken a fair bit of knocking about. One of his eyebrows was missing. Strange how unimportant eyebrows can be, so long as there are two of them. It gave his face a smudged appearance. He had the baffled, half-expectant look of a mongrel that has been often whipped but still turns to the world, out of some fund of foolish expectancy, as a source of scraps as well as torments.

His joints were swollen and one leg was shorter than the other and a little twisted. When he got excited he jerked about as if he was being worked by strings, one or two of which had snapped. He screwed his face up, grinned, looked interested, then, in a lapse of courage or concentration, went mute and glanced about as if he did not know, suddenly, how he had got there or where he was.

The country he had broken out of was all unknown to them. Even in full sunlight it was impenetrable dark.

To the north, beginning with the last fenced paddock, lay swamp country, bird-haunted marshes; then, where the great spine of the Dividing Range rose in ridges and shoals of mist, rainforest broken by sluggish streams.

The land to the south was also unknown. Settlement up here proceeded in frog-leaps from one little coastal place to the next. Between lay tracts of country that no white man had ever entered. It was disturbing, that: to have unknown country behind you as well as in front. When the hissing of the lamp died out the hut sank into silence. A child's murmuring out of sleep might keep it human for a moment, or a rustling of straw; but what you were left with when the last sleeper settled was the illimitable night, where it lay close over the land. You lay listening to the crash of animals through its underbrush, the crack, like a snapped bone, of a ringbarked tree out in a paddock, then its muffled fall; or some other, unidentifiable sound, louder, further off, that was an event in the land's history, no part of yours. The sense then of being submerged, of being hidden away in the depths of the country, but also lost, was very strong.

In all their lives till they came here, they had never ventured, most of them, out of sight or earshot of a village steeple that, as they stooped to carry stooks and lean them one against the other, was always there when they looked up, breaking the horizon beyond the crest of a rise or across open fields.

Out here the very ground under their feet was strange. It had never been ploughed. You had to learn all over again how to deal with weather: drenching downpours when in moments all the topsoil you had exposed went liquid and all the dry little creek-beds in the vicinity ran wild; cyclones that could wrench whole trees up by their roots and send a shed too lightly anchored sailing clear through the air with all its corrugated iron sheets collapsing inward and slicing and singing in the wind. And all around, before and behind, worse than weather and the deepest night, natives, tribes of wandering myalls[5] who, in their traipsing this way and that all over the map, were forever encroaching on boundaries that could be insisted on by daylight – a good shotgun saw to that – but in the dark hours, when you no longer stood there as a living marker with all the glow of the white man's authority about you, reverted to being a creek-bed or ridge of granite like any other, and gave no indication that six hundred miles away, in the Lands Office in Brisbane, this bit of country had a name set against it on a numbered document, and a line drawn that was empowered with all the authority of the Law.

Most unnerving of all was the knowledge that, just three years back, the very patch of earth you were standing on had itself been on the other side of things, part of the unknown, and might still, for all your coming and going over it, and the sweat you had poured into its acre or two of ploughed earth, have the last of mystery upon it, in jungle brakes between paddocks and ferny places out of the sun. Good reason, that, for stripping it, as soon as you could manage, of every vestige of the native; for ringbarking and

---

5 Aborigines.

clearing and reducing it to what would make it, at last, just a bit like home.

It was from this standpoint that the little crowd of settlers, drawn together in such an unusual manner at this time of day, faced the black white man the children had brought in.

§ *Borderline protagonists* Morgan; Carib: Williams; SA: Ghosh; *Attitudes to Aboriginality* Kendall, Davis, Mudrooroo, Morgan

Part III

CANADA

FRANCES BROOKE (1724–89)

From The History of Emily Montague

Although written by an Englishwoman (who lived for five years in Quebec City), *The History of Emily Montague* is generally regarded as the first 'Canadian' novel since it contrasts Old and New World manners and explores some of the central tensions in Canadian settler life. The extract included here, Letter 36, is typical of the way in which Brooke adaptes the themes and conventions of the popular eighteenth-century genre of the epistolary novel, widely used by Samuel Richardson and his French counterparts for explorations of sentimental courtship and sexuality, to discuss differences in the way love affairs are conducted in England, continental Europe and North America.

To John Temple, Esq; Pall Mall

QUEBEC, OCT. 14: I am this moment arrived from a ramble down the river; but, a ship being just going, must acknowlege your last.

You make me happy in telling me my dear Lady H— has given my place in her heart to so honest a fellow as Jack Willmott; and I sincerely wish the ladies always chose their favourites as well.

I should be very unreasonable indeed to expect constancy at almost four thousand miles distance, especially when the prospect of my return is so very uncertain.

My voyage ought undoubtedly to be considered as an abdication: I am to all intents and purposes dead in law as a lover; and the lady has a right to consider her heart as vacant, and to proceed to a new election.

I claim no more than a share in her esteem and remembrance, which I dare say I shall never want.

That I have amused myself a little in the dowager way, I am very far from denying; but you will observe, it was less from taste than the principle of doing as little mischief as possible in my few excursions to the world of gallantry. A little deviation from the exact rule of right we men all allow ourselves in love affairs; but I was willing to keep as near it as I could. Married women are, on my principles, forbidden fruit; I abhor the seduction of innocence; I am too delicate, and (with all my modesty) too vain, to be pleased with venal beauty: what was I then to do, with a heart too active to be absolutely at rest, and which had not met with its counterpart? Widows were, I thought, fair prey, as being sufficiently experienced to take care of themselves.

I have said married women are, on my principles, forbidden fruit: I should have explained myself; I mean in England, for my ideas on this head change as soon as I land at Calais.

Such is the amazing force of local prejudice, that I do not recollect having ever made love to an English married woman, or a French unmarried one. Marriages in France being made by the parents, and therefore generally without inclination on either side, gallantry seems to be a tacit condition, though not absolutely expressed in the contract.

But to return to my plan: I think it an excellent one; and would recommend it to all those young men about town, who, like me, find in their hearts the necessity of loving, before they meet with an object capable of fixing them for life.

By the way, I think the widows ought to raise a statue to my honour, for having done my *possible* to prove that, for the sake of decorum, morals and order, they ought to have all the men to themselves.

I have this moment your letter from Rutland. Do you know I am almost angry? Your ideas of love are narrow and pedantic; custom has done enough to make the life of one half of our species tasteless; but you would reduce them to a state of still greater insipidity than even that to which our tyranny has doomed them.

You would limit the pleasure of loving and being beloved, and the charming power of pleasing, to three or four years only in the life of that sex which is peculiarly formed to feel tenderness; women are born with more lively affections than men, which are still more softened by education: to deny them the privilege of being amiable, the only privilege we allow them, as long as nature continues them so, is such a mixture of cruelty and false taste as I should never have suspected you of, notwithstanding your partiality for unripened beauty.

As to myself, I persist in my opinion, that women are most charming when they join the attractions of the mind to those of the person, when they feel the passion they inspire; or rather, that they are never charming till then.

A woman in the first bloom of youth resembles a tree in blossom, when mature in fruit; but a woman who retains the charms of her person till her understanding is in its full perfection, is like those trees in happier climes, which produce blossoms and fruit together.

You will scarce believe, Jack, that I have lived a week *tête à tête*, in the midst of a wood, with just the woman I have been describing; a widow extremely my taste, *mature*, five or six years more so than you say I require, lively, sensible, handsome, without saying one civil thing to her; yet nothing can be more certain.

I could give you powerful reasons for my insensibility; but you are a traitor to love, and therefore have no right to be in any of his secrets.

I will excuse your visits to my sister; as well as I love you myself, I have a thousand reasons for chusing she should not be acquainted with you.

What you say in regard to my mother, gives me pain; I will never take back my little gift to her; and I cannot live in England on my present income, though it enables me to live *en prince* in Canada.

Adieu! I have not time to say more. I have stole this half-hour from the loveliest woman breathing, whom I am going to visit; surely you are infinitely obliged to me. To lessen the obligation, however, my calash[1] is not yet come to the door.

Adieu once more.

Yours,
ED. RIVERS

§ *Adaptation of European codes* Richardson; Aus: Harpur

MAJOR JOHN RICHARDSON (1796–1852)

From Wacousta

Wacousta is a historical romance in the tradition of Scott and Fenimore Cooper. Its complex and often melodramatic plot engages with many of the central debates of early (and subsequent) Canadian writing, among them the relative merits of garrison and wilderness, 'civilisation' and 'savagery', male and female. Here, in Chapter 7, Captain de Haldimar leaves the fort where his father is governor to spy on an 'Indian' council of war. His guide is Oucanasta, a young Ottawa woman whose life he has previously saved. During this night journey in border territory de Haldimar's Old World beliefs are challenged, particularly when he is persuaded to wear Oucanasta's mocassins to protect his feet, thus questioning European ideas of male chivalry and also other hierarchical notions, such as the superiority of white to Native and military boots to mocassins.

. . . Meanwhile, Captain de Haldimar and his guide trod the mazes of the forest, with an expedition that proved the latter to be well acquainted with its bearings. On quitting the bomb-proof, she had struck into a narrow winding path, less seen than felt in the deep gloom pervading the wood, and with light steps bounded over obstacles that lay strewed in their course, emitting scarcely more sound than would have been produced by the slimy crawl of its native rattlesnake. Not so, however, with the less experienced tread of her companion. Wanting the pliancy of movement given to it by the light mocassin, the booted foot of the young officer, despite of all his precaution, fell heavily to the ground, producing such a rustling among the dried leaves, that, had an Indian ear been lurking any where around, his approach must inevitably have been betrayed. More than once, too, neglecting to follow the injunction of his companion, who moved in a stooping posture, with her head bent over her chest, his hat was caught in the closely matted

---

1 Light, low-wheeled carriage with removable hood.

branches, and fell sullenly and heavily to the earth, evidently much to the discomfiture of his guide.

At length they stood on the verge of a dark and precipitous ravine, the abrupt sides of which were studded with underwood, so completely interwoven, that all passage appeared impracticable. What, however, seemed an insurmountable obstacle, proved, in reality, an inestimable advantage; for it was by clinging to this, in imitation of the example set him by his companion, the young officer was prevented from rolling into an abyss, the depth of which was lost in the profound obscurity that pervaded the scene. Through the bed of this dark dell rolled a narrow stream, so imperceptible to the eye in the 'living darkness,' and so noiseless in its course, that it was not until warned by his companion he stood on the very brink of it, Captain de Haldimar was made sensible of its existence. Both cleared it at a single bound, in which the activity of the female was not the least conspicuous, and, clambering up the opposite steep, secured their footing, by the aid of the same underwood that had assisted them in their descent.

On gaining the other summit, which was not done without detaching several loose stones from their sandy bed, they again fell into the path, which had been lost sight of in traversing the ravine. They had proceeded along this about half a mile, when the female suddenly stopped, and pointing to a dim and lurid atmosphere that now began to show itself between the thin foliage, whispered that in the opening beyond stood the encampment of the Indians. She then seated herself on the trunk of a fallen tree, that lay at the side of the almost invisible path they had hitherto pursued, and motioning to her companion to unboot himself, proceeded to unlace the fastenings of her mocassins.

'The foot of the Saganaw must fall like the night dew on the prairie,' she observed: 'the ear of the red skin is quicker than the lightning, and he will know that a pale face is near, if he hear but his tread upon a blade of grass.'

Gallantry in the civilised man is a sentiment that never wholly abandons him; and in whatever clime he may be thrown, or under whatever circumstances he may be placed – be it called forth by white or by blackamoor – it is certain to influence his conduct: it is a refinement, of that instinctive deference to the weaker sex, which nature has implanted in him for the wisest of purposes; and which, while it tends to exalt those to whom its influence is extended, fails not to reflect a corresponding lustre on himself.

The young officer had, at the first suggestion of his guide, divested himself of his boots, prepared to perform the remainder of the journey merely in his stockings, but his companion now threw herself on her knees before him, and, without further ceremony, proceeded to draw over his foot one of the mocassins she had just relinquished.

'The feet of the Saganaw are soft as those of a young child,' she remarked, in a voice of commiseration; 'but the mocassins of Oucanasta shall protect them from the thorns of the forest.'

This was too un-European – too much reversing the established order of things, to be borne patiently. As if he had felt the dignity of his manhood offended by the proposal, the officer drew his foot hastily back, declaring, as he sprang from the log, he did not care for the thorns, and could not think of depriving a female, who must be much more sensible of pain than himself.

Oucanasta, however, was not to be outdone in politeness. She calmly reseated herself on the log, drew her right foot over her left knee, caught one of the hands of her companion, and placing it upon the naked sole, desired him to feel how impervious to attack of every description was that indurated portion of the lower limb.

This practical argument was not without its weight, and had more effect in deciding the officer than a volume of remonstrance. Most men love to render tribute to a delicate and pretty foot. Some, indeed, go so far as to connect every thing feminine with these qualities, and to believe that nothing can be feminine without them. For our parts, we confess, that, although no enemies to a pretty foot, it is by no means a *sine qua non* in our estimate of female perfection; being in no way disposed, where the head and heart are gems, to undervalue these in consideration of any deficiency in the heels. Captain de Haldimar probably thought otherwise; for when he had passed his unwilling hand over the foot of Oucanasta, which, whatever her face might have been, was certainly any thing but delicate, and encountered numerous ragged excrescences and raspy callosities[1] that set all symmetry at defiance, a wonderful revolution came over his feelings; and, secretly determining the mocassins would be equally well placed on his own feet, he no longer offered any opposition.

§ *Adaptation of European codes* Brooke; Aus: Harpur; *Response to Native cultures* Carr, Kroetsch, Wiebe; *Garrison and bush* Atwood (1, 2)

CATHARINE PARR TRAILL (1802–99)

From The Backwoods of Canada

Like her sister, Susanna Moodie (author of *Roughing It in the Bush*), the English-born Catharine Parr Traill (née Strickland) migrated to Canada, settling near Lakefield, Ontario in 1832. Her best-known book *The Backwoods of Canada* is a classic of Canadian settler writing. It shows her pragmatism and resilience in adapting to her new environment and her fascination with the local flora and fauna. The chapter included here is notable not only for its account of building a log-house, but also for its reflections on the problem of naming species hitherto unfamiliar to her.

---

1 Hard lumps of skin.

Lake House, April 18, 1833
But it is time that I should give you some account of our log-house, into which we moved a few days before Christmas. Many unlooked-for delays having hindered its completion before that time, I began to think it would never be habitable.

The first misfortune that happened was the loss of a fine yoke of oxen that were purchased to draw in the house-logs, that is, the logs for raising the walls of the house. Not regarding the bush as pleasant as their former master's cleared pastures, or perhaps foreseeing some hard work to come, early one morning they took into their heads to ford the lake at the head of the rapids, and march off, leaving no trace of their route excepting their footing at the water's edge. After many days spent in vain search for them, the work was at a stand, and for one month they were gone, and we began to give up all expectation of hearing any news of them. At last we learned they were some twenty miles off, in a distant township, having made their way through bush and swamp, creek and lake, back to their former owner, with an instinct that supplied to them the want of roads and compass.

Oxen have been known to traverse a tract of wild country to a distance of thirty or forty miles going in a direct line for their former haunts by unknown paths, where memory could not avail them. In the dog we consider it is scent as well as memory that guides him to his far-off home – but how is this conduct of the oxen to be accounted for? They returned home through the mazes of interminable forest, where man, with all his reason and knowledge, would have been bewildered and lost.

It was the latter end of October before even the walls of our house were up. To effect this we called 'a bee.'[1] Sixteen of our neighbours cheerfully obeyed our summons; and though the day was far from favourable, so faithfully did our hive perform their tasks, that by night the outer walls were raised.

The work went merrily on with the help of plenty of Canadian nectar (whiskey), the honey that our *bees* are solaced with. Some huge joints of salt pork, a peck of potatoes, with a rice-pudding, and a loaf as big as an enormous Cheshire cheese, formed the feast that was to regale them during the raising. This was spread out in the shanty, in a *very rural style*. In short, we laughed, and called it a *picnic in the backwoods*; and rude as was the fare, I can assure you, great was the satisfaction expressed by all the guests of every degree, our 'bee' being considered as very well conducted. In spite of the difference of rank among those that assisted at the bee, the greatest possible harmony prevailed, and the party separated well pleased with the day's work and entertainment.

The following day I went to survey the newly raised edifice, but was sorely puzzled, as it presented very little appearance of a house. It was merely an oblong square of logs raised one above the other, with open spaces between

---

1 A cooperative gathering of neighbours, usually for work purposes and often followed by a party.

every row of logs. The spaces for the doors and windows were not then sawn out, and the rafters were not up. In short, it looked a very queer sort of a place, and I returned home a little disappointed, and wondering that my husband should be so well pleased with the progress that had been made. A day or two after this I again visited it. The *sleepers* were laid to support the floors, and the places for the doors and windows cut out of the solid timbers, so that it had not quite so much the look of a bird-cage as before.

After the roof was shingled, we were again at a stand, as no boards could be procured nearer than Peterborough, a long day's journey through horrible roads. At that time no saw-mill was in progress; now there is a fine one building within a little distance of us. Our flooring-boards were all to be sawn by hand, and it was some time before any one could be found to perform this necessary work, and that at high wages – six-and-sixpence per day. Well, the boards were at length down, but of course of unseasoned timber: this was unavoidable; so as they could not be planed we were obliged to put up with their rough, unsightly appearance, for no better were to be had. I began to recall to mind the observation of the old gentleman with whom we travelled from Cobourg to Rice Lake. We console ourselves with the prospect that by next summer the boards will all be seasoned, and then the house is to be turned topsy-turvy by having the floors all relaid, jointed, and smoothed.

The next misfortune that happened was that the mixture of clay and lime that was to plaster the inside and outside of the house between the chinks of the logs was one night frozen to stone. Just as the work was about half completed, the frost suddenly setting in, put a stop to our proceeding for some time, as the frozen plaster yielded neither to fire nor to hot water, the latter freezing before it had any effect on the mass, and rather making bad worse. Then the workman that was hewing the inside walls to smooth them wounded himself with the broad axe, and was unable to resume his work for some time . . . .

Every man in this country is his own glazier; this you will laugh at: but if he does not wish to see and feel the discomfort of broken panes, he must learn to put them in his windows with his own hands. Workmen are not easily to be had in the backwoods when you want them, and it would be preposterous to hire a man at high wages to make two days' journey to and from the nearest town to mend your windows. Boxes of glass of several different sizes are to be bought at a very cheap rate in the stores. My husband employed himself by glazing the windows of the house preparatory to their being put in . . . .

But while I have been recounting these remarks, I have wandered far from my original subject, and left my poor log-house quite in an unfinished state. At last I was told it was in a habitable condition, and I was soon engaged in all the bustle and fatigue attendant on removing our household goods. We received all the assistance we required from S—, who is ever ready and willing to help us. He laughed, and called it a *'moving bee'*; I said it was a 'fixing bee'; and my husband said it was a 'settling bee.' I know we were unsettled enough till it was over. What a den of desolation is a small house, or any house under such circumstances. The idea of chaos must have been taken from a removal or a settling to rights, for I suppose the ancients had their *flitting*, as the Scotch call it, as well as the moderns.

Various were the valuable articles of crockeryware that perished in their short but rough journey through the woods. Peace to their manes. I had a good helper in my Irish maid, who soon roused up famous fires and set the house in order.

We have now got quite comfortably settled, and I shall give you a description of our little dwelling. The part finished is only a portion of the original plan; the rest must be added next spring, or fall, as cirumstances may suit.

A nice small sitting-room with a store closet, a kitchen, pantry, and bed-chamber form the ground floor; there is a good upper floor that will make three sleeping-rooms.

'What a nut-shell!' I think I hear you exclaim. So it is at present; but we purpose adding a handsome frame front as soon as we can get boards from the mill, which will give us another parlour, long hall, and good spare bed-room. The windows and glass door of our present sitting-room command pleasant lake-views to the west and south. When the house is completed we shall have a verandah in front and at the south side, which forms an agreeable addition in the summer, being used as a sort of outer room, in which we can dine, and have the advantage of cool air, protected from the glare of the sunbeams. The Canadians call these verandahs 'stoups'. Few houses, either log or frame, are without them. The pillars look extremely pretty, wreathed with the luxuriant hop-vine, mixed with the scarlet creeper and '*morning glory*,' (the American name for the most splendid of major con-volvuluses.) These stoups are really a considerable ornament, as they conceal in a great measure the rough logs, and break the barn-like form of the buildings.

Our parlour is warmed by a handsome Franklin stove[2] with brass gallery and fender. Our furniture consists of a brass-railed sofa, which serves upon occasion for a bed; Canadian painted chairs; a stained pine table; green and white muslin curtains; and a handsome Indian mat which covers the floor. One side of the room is filled up with our books. Some large maps and a few good prints nearly conceal the rough walls, and form the decoration of our little dwelling. Our bed-chamber is furnished with equal simplicity. We do not, however, lack comfort in our humble home; and though it is not exactly such as we could wish, it is as good as, under existing circumstances, we could expect to obtain.

I am anxiously looking forward to the spring, that I may get a garden laid out in front of the house; as I mean to cultivate some of the native fruits and flowers, which, I am sure, will improve greatly by culture. The strawberries that grow wild in our pastures, woods, and clearings, are of two

---

2 Free-standing stove for heating room, named after its American inventor.

varieties, and bear abundantly. They make excellent preserves, and I mean to introduce beds of them into my garden. There is a pretty little wooded islet on our lake, that is called Strawberry Island, another Raspberry Island; they abound in a variety of fruits – wild grapes, raspberries, strawberries, black and red currants, a wild gooseberry, and a beautiful little trailing plant that bears white flowers like the raspberry and a darkish purple fruit consisting of a few grains of a pleasant brisk acid, somewhat like in flavour to our dewberry, only not quite so sweet. The leaves of this plant are of a bright light green, in shape like the raspberry, to which it bears in some respect so great a resemblance (though it is not shrubby or thorny) that I have called it the 'trailing raspberry.'

I suppose our scientific botanists in Britain would consider me very impertinent in bestowing names on the flowers and plants I meet with in these wild woods: I can only say, I am glad to discover the Canadian or even the Indian names if I can, and where they fail I consider myself free to become their floral godmother, and give them names of my own choosing.

Among our wild fruits we have plums, which, in some townships, are very fine and abundant; these make admirable preserves, especially when boiled in maple molasses, as is done by the American housewives. Wild cherries, also a sort called choke berries, from their peculiar astringent qualities, high and low-bush cranberries, blackberries, which are brought by the squaws in birch baskets – all these are found on the plains and beaver meadows. The low-bush cranberries are brought in great quantities by the Indians to the towns and villages. They form a standing preserve on the tea-tables in most of the settlers' houses; but for richness of flavour, and for beauty of appearance, I admire the high-bush cranberries; these are little sought after, on account of the large flat seeds, which prevent them from being used as a jam; the jelly, however, is delightful, both in colour and flavour.

The bush on which this cranberry grows resembles the guelder rose. The blossoms are pure white, and grow in loose umbels;[3] they are very ornamental, when in bloom, to the woods and swamps skirting the lakes. The berries are rather of a long oval, and of a brilliant scarlet, and when just touched by the frosts are semi-transparent, and look like pendent bunches of scarlet grapes.

I was tempted one fine frosty afternoon to take a walk with my husband on the ice, which I was assured was perfectly safe. I must confess for the first-half mile I felt very timid, especially when the ice is so transparent tht you may see every little pebble or weed at the bottom of the water. Sometimes the ice was thick and white, and quite opaque. As we kept within a little distance of the shore, I was struck by the appearance of some splendid red berries on the leafless bushes that hung over the margin of the lake, and soon recognized them to be the aforesaid high-bush cranberries. My husband soon stripped the boughs of their tempting treasure, and I, delighted with my prize, hastened home, and boiled the fruit with some sugar to eat

---

3 Flower clusters in which stalks spring from a common centre.

at tea with our cakes. I never ate anything more delicious than they proved; the more so perhaps from having been so long without tasting fruit of any kind, with the exception of preserves, during our journey, and at Peterborough.

Soon after this I made another excursion on the ice, but it was not in quite so sound a state. We nevertheless walked on for about three-quarters of a mile. We were overtaken on our return by S— with a handsleigh, which is a sort of barrow, such as porters use, without sides, and instead of a wheel, is fixed on wooden runners, which you can drag over the snow and ice with the greatest ease, if ever so heavily laden. S— insisted that he would draw me home over the ice like a Lapland lady on a sledge. I was soon seated in state, and in another minute felt myself impelled forward with a velocity that nearly took away my breath. By the time we reached the shore I was in a glow from head to foot . . . .

§ *Landscape and language*: Aus: Harpur, Clarke; *Women and the bush* Aus: Baynton, Franklin; *Settling the land* Atwood (1); Aus: Rudd, White (2)

SARA JEANNETTE DUNCAN (1861–1922)

From The Imperialist

The Imperialist is another Canadian novel built around the conventions of the novel of courtship (cf. *The History of Emily Montague*). It is, however, arguably more notable for its representation of small-town Canadian life. Duncan's Elgin (based on Brantford, Ontario) is, as the passage included here indicates, a microcosm of the country, a quintessential Canadian small town which prefigures Stephen Leacock's Mariposa, Margaret Laurence's Manawaka, Alice Munro's Jubilee and Robertson Davies's Deptford.

The office of Messrs Fulke, Warner, & Murchison was in Market Street, exactly over Scott's drug store. Scott, with his globular blue and red and green vessels in the window and his soda-water fountain inside, was on the ground floor; the passage leading upstairs separated him from Mickie, boots and shoes; and beyond Mickie, Elgin's leading tobacconist shared his place of business with a barber. The last two contributed most to the gaiety of Market Street: the barber with the ribanded pole, which stuck out at an angle; the tobacconist with a nobly featured squaw in chocolate effigy, who held her draperies under her chin with one hand and outstretched a packet of cigars with the other.

The passage staircase between Scott's and Mickie's had a hardened look, and bore witness to the habit of expectoration; ladies, going up to Dr Simmons, held their skirts up and the corners of their mouths down. Dr Simmons was the dentist: you turned to the right. The passage itself turned to the left, and after passing two doors bearing the law firm's designation in black letters on ground glass, it conducted you with abruptness to the office of a bicycle agent, and left you there. For greater emphasis the name of the firm of Messrs Fulke, Warner, & Murchison was painted on the windows also; it could be seen from any part of the market square, which lay, with the town hall in the middle, immediately below. During four days in the week the market square was empty. Odds and ends of straw and paper blew about it; an occasional pedestrian crossed it diagonally for the short cut to the post-office; the town hall rose in the middle, and defied you to take your mind off the ugliness of municipal institutions. On the other days it was a scene of activity. Farmers' wagons, with the shafts turned in, were ranged round three sides of it; on a big day they would form into parallel lanes and cut the square into sections as well. The produce of all Fox County filled the wagons, varying agreeably as the year went round. Bags of potatoes leaned against the sidewalk, apples brimmed in bushel measures, ducks dropped their twisted necks over the cart wheels; the town hall, in this play of colour, stood redeemed. The produce was mostly left to the women to sell. On the fourth side of the square loads of hay and cordwood demanded the master mind, but small matters of fruit, vegetables, and poultry submitted to feminine judgement. The men 'unhitched,' and went away on their own business; it was the wives you accosted, as they sat in the middle, with their knees drawn up and their skirts tucked close, vigilant in rusty bonnets, if you wished to buy. Among them circulated the housewives of Elgin, pricing and comparing and acquiring; you could see it all from Dr Simmons's window, sitting in his chair that screwed up and down. There was a little difficulty always about getting things home; only very ordinary people carried their own marketing. Trifling articles, like eggs or radishes, might be smuggled into a brown wicker basket with covers, but it did not consort with elegance to 'trapes' home with anything that looked inconvenient or had legs sticking out of it. So that arrangements of mutual obligation had to be made: the good women from whom Mrs Jones had bought her tomatoes would take charge of the spring chickens Mrs Jones had bought from another good woman just as soon as not, and deliver them at Mrs Jones's residence, as under any circumstances she was 'going round that way.'

It was a scene of activity but not of excitement, or in any sense of joy. The matter was too hard an importance; it made too much difference on both sides whether potatoes were twelve or fifteen cents a peck. The dealers were laconic and the buyers anxious; country neighbours exchanged the time of day, but under the pressure of affairs. Now and then a lady of Elgin stopped to gossip with another; the countrywomen looked on, curious, grim, and a little contemptuous of so much demonstration and so many words. Life on an Elgin market day was a serious presentment even when the sun shone, and at times when it rained or snowed the æsthetic seemed a wholly unjustifiable point of view. It was not misery, it was even a difficult kind of prosperity, but the margin was small and the struggle plain. Plain, too, it was that here was no enterprise of yesterday, no fresh broken ground of dramatic promise, but a narrow inheritance of the opportunity to live which generations had grasped before. There were bones in the village graveyards of Fox County to father all these sharp features; Elgin market square, indeed, was the biography of Fox County and, in little, the history of the whole Province. The heart of it was there, the enduring heart of the new country already old in acquiescence. It was the deep root of the race in the land, twisted and unlovely, but holding the promise of all. Something like that Lorne Murchison felt about it as he stood for a moment in the passage I have mentioned and looked across the road. The spectacle never failed to cheer him; he was uniformly in gayer spirits, better satisfied with life and more consciously equal to what he had to do, on days when the square was full than on days when it was empty. This morning he had an elation of his own; it touched everything with more vivid reality. The familiar picture stirred a joy in him in tune with his private happiness; its undernote came to him with a pang as keen. The sense of kinship surged in his heart; these were his people, this his lot as well as theirs. For the first time he saw it in detachment. Till now he had regarded it with the friendly eyes of a participator who looked no further. Today he did look further: the whole world invited his eyes, offering him a great piece of luck to look through. The opportunity was in his hand which, if he could seize and hold, would lift and carry him on. He was as much aware of its potential significance as anyone could be, and what leapt in his veins till he could have laughed aloud was the splendid conviction of resource. Already in the door of the passage he had achieved, from that point he looked at the scene before him with an impulse of loyalty and devotion. A tenderness seized him for the farmers of Fox County, a throb of enthusiasm for the idea they represented, which had become for him suddenly moving and pictorial. At that moment his country came subjectively into his possession; great and helpless it came into his inheritance as it comes into the inheritance of every man who can take it, by deed of imagination and energy and love. He held this microcosm of it, as one might say, in his hand and looked at it ardently; then he took his way across the road.

§ *Small town* Leacock, Ross, Davies, Munro

BLISS CARMAN (1861–1929)

Low Tide on Grand Pré*

> The sun goes down, and over all
> These barren reaches by the tide
> Such unelusive glories fall,

---

* Village in Nova Scotia, from which Acadians were deported in 1755 (see next note).

5   I almost dream they yet will bide
           Until the coming of the tide.

           And yet I know that not for us,
              By any ecstasy of dream,
           He lingers to keep luminous
              A little while the grievous stream,
10   Which frets, uncomforted of dream –

           A grievous stream, that to and fro
              Athrough the fields of Acadie
           Goes wandering, as if to know
              Why one beloved face should be
15   So long from home and Acadie.

           Was it a year or lives ago
              We took the grasses in our hands,
           And caught the summer flying low
              Over the waving meadow lands,
20   And held it there between our hands?

           The while the river at our feet –
              A drowsy inland meadow stream –
           At set of sun the after-heat
              Made running gold, and in the gleam
25   We freed our birch upon the stream.

§ *Maritimes* MacLennan, MacLeod

STEPHEN LEACOCK (1869–1944)

From Sunshine Sketches of a Little Town

Traditionally regarded as one of Canada's best-loved books, *Sunshine Sketches of a Little Town* is a collection of interlinked short stories about 'Mariposa' (based on Orillia, Ontario where Leacock had a summer home). This extract from the beginning of the first sketch, 'The Hostelry of Mr Smith', typifies the text's ambivalent attitude – an attitude which blends nostalgia and social satire, sentimentality and irony – to its quintessential small Canadian town and those who live there.

---

12 **Acadie**: Acadia; primarily francophone colony in lands now forming S.E. part of Québec, eastern Maine, New Brunswick and Prince Edward Island. Between 1755 and 1763 more than three-quarters of the Acadian population were deported by the British, because of their insistence on remaining neutral in the struggle between England and France.

I don't know whether you know Mariposa.[1] If not, it is of no consequence, for if you know Canada at all, you are probably well acquainted with a dozen towns just like it.

There it lies in the sunlight, sloping up from the little lake that spreads out at the foot of the hillside on which the town is built. There is a wharf beside the lake, and lying alongside of it a steamer that is tied to the wharf with two ropes of about the same size as they use on the Lusitania. The steamer goes nowhere in particular, for the lake is landlocked and there is no navigation for the Mariposa Belle except to 'run trips' on the first of July and the Queen's Birthday, and to take excursions of the Knights of Pythias and the Sons of Temperance to and from the Local Option Townships.

In point of geography the lake is called Lake Wissanotti and the river running out of it the Ossawippi just as the main street of Mariposa is called Missinaba Street and the county Missinaba County. But these names do not really matter. Nobody uses them. People simply speak of the 'lake' and the 'river' and the 'main street,' much in the same way as they always call the Continental Hotel, 'Pete Robinson's' and the Pharmaceutical Hall, 'Eliot's Drug Store.' But I suppose this is just the same in every one else's town as in mine, so I need lay no stress on it.

The town, I say, has one broad street that runs up from the lake, commonly called the Main Street. There is no doubt about its width. When Mariposa was laid out there was none of that shortsightedness which is seen in the cramped dimensions of Wall Street and Piccadilly. Missinaba Street is so wide that if you were to roll Jeff Thorpe's barber shop over on its face it wouldn't reach halfway across. Up and down the Main Street are telegraph poles of cedar of colossal thickness, standing at a variety of angles and carrying rather more wires than are commonly seen at a transatlantic cable station.

On the Main Street itself are a number of buildings of extraordinary importance – Smith's Hotel and the Continental and Mariposa House, and the two banks (the Commercial and the Exchange), to say nothing of McCarthy's Block (erected in 1878), and Glover's Hardware Store with the Oddfellows'[2] Hall above it. Then on the 'cross' street that intersects Missinaba Street at the main corner there is the Post Office and the Fire Hall and the Young Men's Christian Association and the office of the Mariposa Newspacket – in fact, to the eye of discernment a perfect jostle of public institutions comparable only to Threadneedle Street or Lower Broadway. On all the side streets there are maple trees and broad sidewalks, trim gardens with upright calla lilies,[3] houses with verandahs, which are here and there being replaced by residences with piazzas.

To the careless eye the scene on the Main Street of a summer afternoon is one of deep and unbroken peace. The empty street sleeps in the sunshine.

---

1 The main street of Orillia is Mississauga Street and the newspaper *The Packet and Times.* 2 A fraternity, cf. masons. 3 Arum lilies.

There is a horse and buggy tied to the hitching post in front of Glover's hardware store. There is, usually and commonly, the burly figure of Mr. Smith, proprietor of Smith's Hotel, standing in his chequered waistcoat on the steps of his hostelry, and perhaps, further up the street, Lawyer Macartney going for his afternoon mail, or the Rev. Mr. Drone, the Rural Dean of the Church of England Church, going home to get his fishing rod after a mothers' auxiliary meeting.

But this quiet is mere appearance. In reality, and to those who know it, the place is a perfect hive of activity. Why, at Netley's butcher shop (established in 1882) there are no less than four men working on the sausage machines in the basement; at the Newspacket office there are as many more job-printing; there is a long distance telephone with four distracting girls on high stools wearing steel caps and talking incessantly; in the offices in McCarthy's Block are dentists and lawyers, with their coats off, ready to work at any moment; and from the big planing factory down beside the lake where the railroad siding is, you may hear all through the hours of the summer afternoon the long-drawn music of the running saw.

Busy – well, I should think so! Ask any of its inhabitants if Mariposa isn't a busy, hustling, thriving town. Ask Mullins, the manager of the Exchange Bank, who comes hustling over to his office from the Mariposa House every day at 10:30 and has scarcely time all morning to go out and take a drink with the manager of the Commercial; or ask – well, for the matter of that, ask any of them if they ever knew a more rushing go-ahead town than Mariposa.

Of course if you come to the place fresh from New York, you are deceived. Your standard of vision is all astray. You do think the place is quiet. You do imagine that Mr. Smith is asleep merely because he closes his eyes as he stands. But live in Mariposa for six months or a year and then you will begin to understand it better; the buildings get higher and higher; the Mariposa House grows more and more luxurious; McCarthy's Block towers to the sky; the 'buses roar and hum to the station; the trains shriek; the traffic multiplies; the people move faster and faster; a dense crowd swirls to and fro in the post-office and the five and ten cent store – and amusements! well, now! lacrosse, baseball, excursions, dances, the Firemen's Ball every winter and the Catholic picnic every summer! and music – the town band in the park every Wednesday evening, and the Oddfellows' brass band on the street every other Friday; the Mariposa Quartette, the Salvation Army – why, after a few months' residence you begin to realize that the place is a mere mad round of gaiety.

In point of population, if one must come down to figures the Canadian census puts the numbers every time at something round five thousand. But it is very generally understood in Mariposa that the census is largely the outcome of malicious jealousy. It is usual that after the census the editor of the Mariposa Newspacket makes a careful re-estimate (based on the data of relative non-payment of subscriptions), and brings the population up to 6,000. After that the Mariposa Times-Herald makes an estimate that runs the figures up to 6,500. Then Mr. Gingham, the undertaker, who collects the vital statistics for the provincial government, makes an estimate from the number of what he calls the 'demised' as compared with the less interesting persons who are still alive, and brings the population to 7,000. After that somebody else works it out that it's 7,500; then the man behind the bar of the Mariposa House offers to bet the whole room that there are 9,000 people in Mariposa. That settles it, and the population is well on the way to 10,000, when down swoops the federal census taker on his next round and the town has to begin all over again.

Still, it's a thriving town and there is no doubt of it. Even the transcontinental railways, as any townsman will tell you, run through Mariposa. It is true that the trains mostly go through at night and don't stop. But in the wakeful silence of the summer night you may hear the long whistle of the through train for the west as it tears through Mariposa, rattling over the switches and past the semaphores and ending in a long, sullen roar as it takes the trestle bridge over the Ossawippi. Or, better still, on a winter evening about eight o'clock you will see the long row of the Pullmans and diners of the night express going north to the mining country, the windows flashing with brilliant light, and within them a vista of cut glass and snow-white table linen, smiling negroes and millionaires with napkins at their chins whirling past in the driving snowstorm.

I can tell you the people of Mariposa are proud of the trains, even if they don't stop! The joy of being on the main line lifts the Mariposa people above the level of their neighbours in such places as Tecumseh and Nichols Corners into the cosmopolitan atmosphere of through traffic and the larger life. Of course, they have their own train, too – the Mariposa Local, made up right there in the station yard, and running south to the city a hundred miles away. That, of course, is a real train, with a box stove on end in the passenger car, fed with cordwood upside down, and with seventeen flat cars of pine lumber set between the passenger car and the locomotive so as to give the train its full impact when shunting.

Outside of Mariposa there are farms that begin well but get thinner and meaner as you go on, and end sooner or later in bush and swamp and the rock of the north country. And beyond that again, as the background of it all, though it's far away, you are somehow aware of the great pine woods of the lumber country reaching endlessly into the north.

Not that the little town is always gay or always bright in the sunshine. There never was such a place for changing its character with the season. Dark enough and dull it seems of a winter night, the wooden sidewalks creaking with the frost, and the lights burning dim behind the shop windows. In olden times the lights were coal oil lamps; now, of course, they are, or are supposed to be, electricity – brought from the power house on the lower Ossawippi nineteen miles away. But, somehow, though it starts off as electricity from the Ossawippi rapids, by the time it gets to Mariposa and filters into the little bulbs behind the frosty windows of the shops, it has turned into coal oil again, as yellow and bleared as ever.

After the winter, the snow melts and the ice goes out of the lake, the sun shines high and the shanty-men come down from the lumber woods and lie round drunk on the sidewalk outside of Smith's hotel – and that's spring time. Mariposa is then a fierce, dangerous lumber town, calculated to terrorize the soul of a newcomer who does not understand that this also is only an appearance and that presently the rough-looking shanty-men will change their clothes and turn back again into farmers.

Then the sun shines warmer and the maple trees come out and Lawyer Macartney puts on his tennis trousers, and that's summer time. The little town changes to a sort of summer resort. There are visitors up from the city. Every one of the seven cottages along the lake is full. The Mariposa Belle churns the waters of the Wissanotti into foam as she sails out from the wharf, in a cloud of flags, the band playing and the daughters and sisters of the Knights of Pythias dancing gaily on the deck.

That changes too. The days shorten. The visitors disappear. The goldenrod beside the meadow droops and withers on its stem. The maples blaze in glory and die. The evening closes dark and chill, and in the gloom of the main corner of Mariposa the Salvation Army around a naphtha lamp lift up the confession of their sins – and that is autumn. Thus the year runs its round, moving and changing in Mariposa, much as it does in other places.

§ *Small town* Duncan, Ross, Davies, Munro

EMILY CARR (1871–1945)

From Klee Wyck

Klee Wyck describes the beginnings of Emily Carr's life-long engagement with the culture of the Native peoples of Canada's west coast, an interest subsequently displayed in both her writing and her paintings. The opening chapter gives an account of her first journey to the village of Ucluelet on the west coast of Vancouver Island and tells how she acquired her nickname 'Klee Wyck'.

The lady Missionaries expected me. They sent an enormous Irishman in a tiny canoe to meet the steamer. We got to the Ucluelet wharf soon after dawn. Everything was big and cold and strange to me, a fifteen-year-old school girl. I was the only soul on the wharf. The Irishman did not have any trouble deciding which was I.

It was low tide, so there was a long, sickening ladder with slimy rungs to climb down to get to the canoe. The man's big laugh and the tippiness of the canoe were even more frightening than the ladder. The paddle in his great arms rushed the canoe through the waves.

We came to Toxis, which was the Indian name for the Mission House. It stood just above hightide water. The sea was in front of it and the forest behind.

The house was of wood, unpainted. There were no blinds or curtains. It looked, as we paddled up to it, as if it were stuffed with black. When the canoe stuck in the mud, the big Irishman picked me up in his arms and set me down on the doorstep.

The Missionaries were at the door. Smells of cooking fish jumped out past them. People lived on fish at Ucluelet.

Both the Missionaries were dignified, but the Greater Missionary had the most dignity. They had long noses straddled by spectacles, thin lips, mild eyes, and wore straight, dark dresses buttoned to the chin.

There was only two of everything in the kitchen, so I had to sit on a box, drink from a bowl and eat my food out of a tin pie-dish.

After breakfast came a long prayer. Outside the kitchen window, just a few feet away at the edge of the forest, stood a grand balsam pine tree. It was very tall and straight.

The Missionaries' 'trespasses' jumped me back from the pine tree to the Lord's Prayer just in time to 'Amen'. We got up from our knees to find the house full of Indians. They had come to look at me.

I felt so young and empty standing there before the Indians and the two grave Missionaries! The Chief, old Hipi, was held to be a reader of faces. He perched himself on the top of the Missionaries' drug cupboard; his brown fists clutched the edge of it, his elbows taut and shoulders hunched. His crumpled shoes hung loose as if they dangled from strings and had no feet in them. The stare of his eyes searched me right through. Suddenly they were done; he lifted them above me to the window, uttered several terse sentences in Chinook, jumped off the cupboard and strode back to the village.

I was half afraid to ask the Missionary, 'What did he say?'

'Not much. Only that you had no fear, that you were not stuck up, and that you knew how to laugh.'

Toxis sat upon a long, slow lick of sand, but the beach of the Indian village was short and bit deep into the shoreline. Rocky points jutted out into the sea at either end of it.

Toxis and the village were a mile apart. The school house was half-way between the two and, like them, was pinched between sea and forest.

The school house called itself 'church house' on Sundays. It had a sharp roof, two windows on each side, a door in front, and a woodshed behind.

The school equipment consisted of a map of the world, a blackboard, a stove, crude desks and benches and, on a box behind the door, the pail of drinking-water and a tin dipper.

The Lesser Missionary went to school first and lit the fire. If the tide were high she had to go over the trail at the forest's edge. It was full of holes where high seas had undermined the big tree roots. Huge upturned stumps necessitated detours through hard-leafed sallal bushes and skunk cabbage bogs. The Lesser Missionary hated putting her feet on ground which she could not see, because it was so covered with growing green. She was glad when she came out of the dark forest and saw the unpainted school house. The Greater Missionary had no nerves and a long, slow stride. As she came over the trail she blew blasts on a cow's horn. She had an amazing wind, the blasts were stunning, but they failed to call the children to school, because no voice had ever suggested time or obligation to these Indian children. Then the Greater Missionary went to the village and hand-picked her scholars from the huts.

On my first morning in Ucluelet there was a full attendance at school because visitors were rare. After the Lord's Prayer the Missionaries duetted a hymn while the children stared at me.

When the Missionary put A, B, C on the board the children began squirming out of their desks and pattering down to the drinking bucket. The dipper registered each drink with a clank when they threw it back.

The door squeaked open and shut all the time, with a second's pause between opening and closing. Spitting on the floor was forbidden, so the children went out and spat off the porch. They had not yet mastered the use of the pocket handkerchief, so not a second elapsed between sniffs.

Education being well under way, I slipped out to see the village.

When I did not return after the second's time permitted for spitting, the children began to wriggle from the desks to the drinking bucket, then to the spitting step, looking for me. Once outside, their little bare feet never stopped till they had caught me up.

After that I was shut up tight at Toxis until school was well started; then I went to the village, careful to creep low when passing under the school windows.

On the point at either end of the bay crouched a huddle of houses – large, squat houses made of thick, hand-hewn cedar planks, pegged and slotted together. They had flat, square fronts. The side walls were made of driftwood. Bark and shakes, weighted with stones against the wind, were used for roofs. Every house stood separate from the next. Wind roared through narrow spaces between.

Houses and people were alike. Wind, rain, forest and sea had done the same things to both – both were soaked through and through with sunshine, too.

I was shy of the Indians at first. When I knocked at their doors and received no answer I entered their houses timidly, but I found a grunt of welcome was always waiting inside and that Indians did not knock before entering. Usually some old crone was squatted on the earth floor, weaving cedar fibre or tatters of old cloth into a mat, her claw-like fingers twining in and out, in and out, among the strands that were fastened to a crude frame of sticks. Papooses tumbled around her on the floor for she was papoose-minder as well as mat-maker.

Each of the large houses was the home of several families. The door and the smoke-hole were common to all, but each family had its own fire with its own things round it. That was their own home.

The interiors of the great houses were dim. Smoke teased your eyes and throat. The earth floors were not clean.

It amused the Indians to see me unfold my camp stool, and my sketch sack made them curious. When boats, trees, houses, appeared on the paper, jabbering interest closed me about. I could not understand their talk. One day, by grin and gesture, I got permission to sketch an old mat-maker. She nodded and I set to work. Suddenly a cat jumped in through the smoke-hole and leaped down from a rafter on to a pile of loose boxes. As the clatter of the topple ceased there was a bestial roar, a pile of mats and blankets burst upwards, and a man's head came out of them. He shouted and his black eyes snapped at me and the old woman's smile dried out.

'Klatawa' (Chinook for 'Go') she shouted, and I went. Later, the old wife called to me across the bay, but I would not heed her call.

'Why did you not reply when old Mrs. Wynook called you?' the Missionary asked.

'She was angry and drove me away.'

'She was calling, "Klee Wyck, come back, come back," when I heard her.'

'What does "Klee Wyck" mean?'

'I do not know.'

The mission house door creaked open and something looking like a bundle of tired rags tumbled on to the floor and groaned.

'Why, Mrs. Wynook,' exclaimed the Missionary, 'I thought you could not walk!'

The tired old woman leaned forward and began to stroke my skirt.

'What does Klee Wyck mean, Mrs. Wynook?' asked the Missionary.

Mrs. Wynook put her thumbs into the corners of her mouth and stretched them upwards. She pointed at me; there was a long, guttural jabber in Chinook between her and the Missionary. Finally the Missionary said, 'Klee Wyck is the Indians' name for you. It means "Laughing One".'

The old woman tried to make the Missionary believe that her husband thought it was I, not the cat, who had toppled the boxes and woke him, but the Missionary, scenting a lie, asked for 'straight talk'. Then Mrs. Wynook told how the old Indians thought the spirit of a person got caught in a picture of him, trapped there so that, after the person died, it had to stay in the picture.

'Tell her that I will not make any more pictures of the old people,' I said. It must have hurt the Indians dreadfully to have the things they had always believed trampled on and torn from their hugging. Down deep we all hug something. The great forest hugs its silence. The sea and the air hug the spilled cries of sea-birds. The forest hugs only silence; its birds and even its beasts are mute.

When night came down upon Ucluelet the Indian people folded themselves into their houses and slept.

At the Mission House candles were lit. After eating fish, and praying aloud, the Missionaries creaked up the bare stair, each carrying her own tin candlestick. I had a cot and scrambled quickly into it. Blindless and carpetless, it was a bleak bedroom even in summer.

The room was deathly still. Outside, the black forest was still, too, but with a vibrant stillness tense with life. From my bed I could look one storey higher into the balsam pine. Because of his closeness to me, the pine towered above his fellows, his top tapering to heaven.

Every day might have been a Sunday in the Indian village. At Toxis only the seventh day was the Sabbath. Then the Missionaries conducted service in the school house which had shifted its job to church as the cow's horn turned itself into a church bell for the day.

The Indian women with handkerchiefs on their heads, plaid shawls round their shoulders and full skirts billowing about their legs, waddled leisurely towards church. It was very hard for them to squeeze their bodies into the children's desks. They took two whole seats each, and even then the squeezing must have hurt.

Women sat on one side of the church. The very few men who came sat on the other. The Missionaries insisted that men come to church wearing trousers, and that their shirt tails must be tucked inside the trousers. So the Indian men stayed away.

'Our trespasses' had been dealt with and the hymn, which was generally pitched too high or too low, had at last hit square, when the door was swung violently back, slopping the drinking bucket. In the outside sunlight stood old Tanook, shirt tails flapping and legs bare. He entered, strode up the middle of the room and took the front seat.

Quick intakes of horror caught the breath of the women; the Greater Missionary held on to her note, the Lesser jumped an octave.

A woman in the back seat took off her shawl. From hand to hand it travelled under the desks to the top of the room, crossed the aisle and passed into the hand of Jimmy John, old Tanook's nephew, sitting with the men. Jimmy John squeezed from his seat and laid the shawl across his uncle's bare knees.

The Missionary's address rolled on in choppy Chinook, undertoned by a gentle voice from the back of the room which told Tanook in pure Indian words what he was to do.

With a defiant shake of his wild hair old Tanook got up; twisting the shawl about his middle he marched down the aisles, paused at the pail to take a loud drink, dashed back the dipper with a clank, and strode out.

The service was over, the people had gone, but a pink print figure sat on in the back seat. Her face was sunk down on her chest. She was waiting till all were away before she slunk home. It is considered more indecent for an Indian woman to go shawl-less than for an Indian man to go bare-legged. The woman's heroic gesture had saved her husband's dignity before the Missionaries but had shamed her before her own people.

The Greater Missionary patted the pink shoulder as she passed.

'Brave woman!' said the Greater Missionary, smiling.

One day I walked upon a strip of land that belonged to nothing.

The sea soaked it often enough to make it unpalatable to the forest. Roots of trees refused to thrive in its saltiness.

In this place belonging neither to sea nor to land I came upon an old man dressed in nothing but a brief shirt. He was sawing the limbs from a fallen tree. The swish of the sea tried to drown the purr of his saw. The purr of the saw tried to sneak back into the forest, but the forest threw it out again into the sea. Sea and forest were always at this game of toss with noises.

The fallen tree lay crosswise in this 'nothing's place'; it blocked my way. I sat down beside the sawing Indian and we had dumb talk, pointing to the sun and to the sea, the eagles in the air and the crows on the beach. Nodding and laughing together I sat and he sawed. The old man sawed as if aeons of time were before him, and as if all the years behind him had been leisurely and all the years in front of him would be equally so. There was strength still in his back and limbs but his teeth were all worn to the gums. The shock of hair that fell to his shoulders was grizzled. Life had sweetened the old man. He was luscious with time like the end berries of the strawberry season.

With a final grin, I got up and patted his arm – 'Goodbye!' He patted my hand. When he saw me turn to break through the forest so that I could round his great fallen tree, he ran and pulled me back, shaking his head and scolding me.

'Swaawa! Hiyu swaawa!' Swaawa were cougar: the forest was full of these great cats. The Indians forbade their children to go into the forest, not even into its edge. I was to them a child, ignorant about the wild things which they knew so well. In these things the Indian could speak with authority to white people.

§ *Responses to Aboriginal cultures* Richardson, Wiebe; Aus: Kendall, Malouf; NZSP: Fairburn (2), Hyde, Baxter (3)

E. J. PRATT (1882–1964)

From Brébeuf and His Brethren

One of the most significant of Canadian narrative poems, *Brébeuf and His Brethren* is a putative national epic. It describes the attempt by Jean de Brébeuf and a group of Jesuit priests to establish a mission near Georgian Bay in the seventeenth century. Among his other activities Brébeuf supervised the compilation of a Huron grammar and dictionary. He was killed in Huronia by invading Iroquois in 1649; and canonized in 1940. The passage included here describes both the physical and linguistic difficulties of establishing such a settlement.

> *July, 1626*
>
> Midsummer and the try again – Brébeuf,
> Daillon, de Nouë just arrived from France;
> Quebec up to Three Rivers; the routine
> Repeated; bargaining with the Indians,
> 5   Axes and beads against the maize and passage;
> The natives' protest when they saw Brébeuf,
> High as a totem-pole. What if he placed
> His foot upon the gunwale, suddenly
> Shifted an ounce of those two hundred pounds

10 Off centre at the rapids! They had visions
   Of bodies and bales gyrating round the rocks,
   Plunging like stumps and logs over the falls.
   The Hurons shook their heads: the bidding grew;
   Kettles and porcelain necklaces and knives,
15 Till with the last awl thrown upon the heap,
   The ratifying grunt came from the chief.
   Two Indians holding the canoe, Brébeuf,
   Barefooted, cassock pulled up to his knees,
   Planted one foot dead in the middle, then
20 The other, then slowly and ticklishly
   Adjusted to the physics of his range
   And width, he grasped both sides of the canoe,
   Lowered himself and softly murmuring
   An *Ave*, sat, immobile as a statue.
25 So the flotilla started – the same route
   Champlain and Le Caron eleven years
   Before had taken to avoid the swarm
   Of hostile Iroquois on the St. Lawrence.
   Eight hundred miles – along the Ottawa
30 Through the steep gorges where the river narrowed,
   Through calmer waters where the river widened,
   Skirting the island of the Allumettes,
   Thence to the Mattawa through lakes that led
   To the blue waters of the Nipissing,
35 And then southward a hundred tortuous miles
   Down the French River to the Huron shore.
   The record of that trip was for Brébeuf
   A memory several times to be re-lived;
   Of rocks and cataracts and portages,
40 Of feet cut by the river stones, of mud
   And stench, of boulders, logs and tangled growths,
   Of summer heat that made him long for night,
   And when he struck his bed of rock – mosquitoes
   That made him doubt if dawn would ever break.
45 'Twas thirty days to the Georgian Bay, then south
   One hundred miles threading the labyrinth
   Of islands till he reached the western shore
   That flanked the Bay of Penetanguishene.
   Soon joined by both his fellow priests he followed
50 The course of a small stream and reached Toanché,
   Where for three years he was to make his home
   And turn the first sod of the Jesuit mission.

---

26 **Champlain**: cartographer, explorer and governor of New France (i.e. francophone North America) in seventeenth century.

'Twas ploughing only – for eight years would pass
Before even the blades appeared. The priests
55 Knew well how barren was the task should signs,
Gestures and inarticulate sounds provide
The basis of the converse. And the speech
Was hard. De Noue set himself to school,
Unfalteringly as to his Breviary,
60 Through the long evenings of the fall and winter.
But as light never trickled through a sentence,
Either the Hurons' or his own, he left
With the spring's expedition to Quebec,
Where intermittendly for twenty years
65 He was to labour with the colonists,
Travelling between the outposts, and to die
Snow-blind, caught in the circles of his tracks
Between Three Rivers and Fort Richelieu.

Daillon migrated to the south and west
70 To the country of the Neutrals. There he spent
The winter, fruitless. Jealousies of trade
Awoke resentment, fostered calumnies,
Until the priest under a constant threat
That often issued in assault, returned
75 Against his own persuasion to Quebec.

Brébeuf was now alone. He bent his mind
To the great end. The efficacious rites
Were hinged as much on mental apprehensions
As on the disposition of the heart.
80 For that the first equipment was the speech.
He listened to the sounds and gave them letters,
Arranged their sequences, caught the inflections,
Extracted nouns from objects, verbs from actions
And regimented rebel moods and tenses.
85 He saw the way the chiefs harangued the clans,
The torrent of compounded words, the art
Concealed within the pause, the look, the gesture.
Lacking all labials, the open mouth
Performed a double service with the vowels
90 Directed like a battery at the hearers.
With what forebodings did he watch the spell
Cast on the sick by the Arendiwans:
The sorcery of the Huron rhetoric
Extorting bribes for cures, for guarantees
95 Against the failure of the crop or hunt!
The time would come when steel would clash on steel,

And many a battle be won or lost
With weapons from the armoury of words.
Three years of that apprenticeship had won
100   The praise of his Superior and no less
Evoked the admiration of Champlain.
That soldier, statesman, navigator, friend,
Who had combined the brain of Richelieu
With the red blood of Cartier and Magellan,
105   Was at this time reduced to his last keg
Of powder at the citadel. Blockade,
The piracy of Kirke on the Atlantic,
The English occupation of Quebec,
And famine, closed this chapter of the Mission.

§ *Settlement/exploration* Atwood (1, 2, 3), MacEwen, Marlatt; *National myth-making* MacLennan, Atwood (2); *Finding a language* Traill, Atwood (1)

SINCLAIR ROSS (1908–85)

From As for Me and My House

This passage is the opening of Ross's classic novel of Canadian Prairie life in the Depression years. Through the narrative medium of the journal of 'Mrs Bentley', the wife of the new minister of the fictional Saskatchewan town of Horizon, it contrasts the vast open spaces of the Prairie landscape with the claustrophobia and hypocrisy that Mrs Bentley finds in the small town with its 'false-fronted' stores. But the novel is about far more than this: it vividly portrays the difficulties of sustaining relationships and the personal frustrations and failings of its central characters and is particularly notable for its complex use of a narrator who is both sympathetic and unreliable.

Saturday Evening, April 8

Philip has thrown himself across the bed and fallen asleep, his clothes on still, one of his long legs dangling to the floor.

It's been a hard day on him, putting up stovepipes and opening crates, for the fourth time getting our old linoleum down. He hasn't the hands for it. I could use the pliers and hammer twice as well myself, with none of his mutterings or smashed-up fingers either, but in the parsonage, on calling days, it simply isn't done. In return for their thousand dollars a year they expect a genteel kind of piety, a well-bred Christianity that will serve as an

---

103 **Richelieu**: French cardinal and statesman; chief minister of Louis XIII.
104 **Magellan**: Portuguese navigator; discoverer of strait separating continental South America from Tierra del Fuego which bears his name.

104 **Cartier**: French navigator and explorer, who made three voyages to the St Lawrence River region between 1534 and 1542.

example to the little sons and daughters of the town. It was twelve years ago, in our first town, that I learned my lesson, one day when they caught me in the woodshed making kindling of a packing box. 'Surely this isn't necessary, Mrs. Bentley – your position in the community – and Mr. Bentley such a big, able-bodied man – '

So today I let him be the man about the house, and sat on a trunk among the litter serenely making curtains over for the double windows in the living-room. For we did have visitors today, even though it was only yesterday we arrived. Just casual calls to bid us welcome, size us up, and see how much we own. There was a portly Mrs. Wenderby who fingered my poor old curtains and said she had better ones in her rag bag I could have; and there was a gray-haired, sparrow-eyed Miss Twill who looked the piano up and down reprovingly, and all but said, 'If they were really Christians now they'd sell such vanities and put the money in the mission-box.'

She introduced herself as the choir leader, and in expiation of the piano the least I could do was consent to play the organ for her. All the musicians in the town, it seems, are a backsliding lot, who want strange new hymns that nobody knows at an ungodly pace that nobody can keep up with. In Miss Twill's choir they sing the old hymns, slowly.

It was about tomorrow's hymns that she came, and Philip, his nerves all ragged, and a smear of soot across his face, didn't make a particularly good impression.

'Any ones you like, Miss Twill,' he tried to be pleasant. 'I'm sure you'll make a better choice than I could anyway.' But with her lips thin she reproved him, 'Other ministers we've had have considered the musical part of the service rather important. Of course, if it doesn't matter to you whether the hymns are in keeping with the text or not – '

'You'll understand tomorrow when you hear his sermon,' I slipped in quickly. 'It's a special sermon – he always preaches it on his first Sunday. Any good old-fashioned gospel hymns will do. I think, though, he would like *The Church's One Foundation* to start off with.'

So we got rid of her at last, and steeled ourselves for the next one. Poor Philip – for almost twelve years now he's been preaching in these little prairie towns, but he still hasn't learned the proper technique for it. He still handicaps himself with a guilty feeling that he ought to mean everything he says. He hasn't learned yet to be bland.

He looks old and worn-out tonight; and as I stood over him a little while ago his face brought home to me how he shrinks from another town, how tired he is, and heartsick of it all. I ran my fingers through his hair, then stopped and kissed him. Lightly, for that is of all things what I mustn't do, let him ever suspect me of being sorry. He's a very adult, self-sufficient man, who can't bear to be fussed or worried over; and sometimes, broodless old woman that I am, I get impatient being just his wife, and start in trying to mother him too.

His sermon for tomorrow is spread out on the little table by the bed, the text that he always uses for his first Sunday. *As For Me and My House We Will Serve the Lord.*[1] It's a stalwart, four-square, Christian sermon. It nails his colors to the mast. It declares to the town his creed, lets them know what they may expect. The Word of God as revealed in Holy Writ – Christ Crucified – salvation through His Grace – those are the things that Philip stands for.

And as usual he's been drawing again. I turned over the top sheet, and sure enough on the back of it there was a little Main Street sketched. It's like all the rest, a single row of smug, false-fronted stores, a loiterer or two, in the distance the prairie again. And like all the rest there's something about it that hurts. False fronts ought to be laughed at, never understood or pitied. They're such outlandish things, the front of a store built up to look like a second storey. They ought always to be seen that way, pretentious, ridiculous, never as Philip sees them, stricken with a look of self-awareness and futility.

That's Philip, though, what I must recognize and acknowledge as the artist in him. Sermon and drawing together, they're a kind of symbol, a summing up. The small-town preacher and the artist – what he is and what he nearly was – the failure, the compromise, the going-on – it's all there – the discrepancy between the man and the little niche that holds him.

And that hurt too, made me slip away furtively and stand a minute looking at the dull bare walls, my shoulders drawn up round my ears to resist their cold damp stillness. And huddling there I wished for a son again, a son that I might give back a little of what I've taken from him, that I might at least believe I haven't altogether wasted him, only postponed to another generation his fulfillment. A foolish, sentimental wish that I ought to have outgrown years ago – that drove me outside at last, to stand on the doorstep shivering, my lips locked, a spatter of rain in my face.

It's an immense night out there, wheeling and windy. The lights on the street and in the houses are helpless against the black wetness, little unilluminating glints that might be painted on it. The town seems huddled together, cowering on a high, tiny perch, afraid to move lest it topple into the wind. Close to the parsonage is the church, black even against the darkness, towering ominously up through the night and merging with it. There's a soft steady swish of rain on the roof, and a gurgle of eaves-troughs running over. Above, in the high cold night, the wind goes swinging past, indifferent, liplessly mournful. It frightens me, makes me feel lost, dropped on this little perch of town and abandoned. I wish Philip would waken.

It's the disordered house and the bare walls that depress me. I keep looking at the leak in the ceiling, and the dark wet patch as it gradually seeps its way towards the wall. There's never been a leak before, Mrs. Finley told me this afternoon, reproach in her voice that set me fiddling with my apron like a little girl. 'Only last week we papered this room for you' – she's

---

1 *Joshua* xxiv 15.

President of the Ladies Aid, entrusted with the supervision of the parsonage – 'Only last week, and it's worse now than before we touched it. I don't
know when we'll be able to do the ceiling over for you. Couldn't your husband get up on the roof and put a few new shingles on?'

She met us at the train yesterday, officially, and took us home with her
for dinner. There's one at least in every town, austere, beyond reproach, a
little grim with the responsibilities of self-assumed leadership – inevitable as
broken sidewalks and rickety false fronts. She's an alert, thin-voiced, thin-
featured little woman, up to her eyes in the task of managing the town and
making it over in her own image. I'm afraid it may mean some changes for
Philip and me too, for there's a crusading steel in her eye to warn she brooks
no halfway measures. The deportment and mien of her own family bear witness to a potter's hand that never falters. Her husband, for instance, is an
appropriately meek little man, but you can't help feeling what an achievement is his meekness. It's like a tight wire cage drawn over him, and words
and gestures indicative of a more expansive past, keep squeezing through it
the same way that parts of the portly Mrs. Wenderby this afternoon kept
squeezing through the back and sides of Philip's study armchair. And her
twelve-year-old twins, George and Stanley, when they recited grace in unison their voices tolled with such sonority that Philip in his scripture reading after dinner sounded like a droney auctioneer. Philip at the table, I
noticed, kept watching them, his eyes critical and moody. He likes boys –
often, I think, plans the bringing-up and education of *his* boy. A fine, well-
tempered lad by now, strung just a little on the fine side, responsive to too
many overtones. For I know Philip, and he has a way of building in his own
image, too.

It was a good dinner though, and after breakfast on the train, of milk and
arrowroot we found it hard to keep our parson manners uppermost. They're
difficult things at the dinner table anyway, eating with a heartiness that com-
pliments your hostess, at the same time with a reluctance that attests your
absorption in the things of the spirit. Often we have lapses. Our fare at
home is usually on the plain side, and the formal dinner of a Main Street
hostess is invariably good. Good to an almost sacrificial degree. A kind of
rite, at which we preside as priest and priestess – an offering, not for us, but
through us, to the exacting small-town gods Propriety and Parity.

Mrs. Finley, for instance: she must have spent hours preparing for us,
cleaning her house, polishing her cut glass and silver – and if I know anything at all about Main Street economics she'll spend as many more hours
polishing her wits for ways and means to make ends meet till next allowance
day. Yet as President of the Ladies Aid, and first lady of the congregation,
she had to do the right thing by us – that was Propriety; and as Main Street
hostess she had to do it so well that no other hostess might ever invite us
to her home and do it better – that was Parity.

But just the same they're a worthy family, and Philip and I shall be deferential to them. Feeble as it is, we have a little technique. Philip will sometimes have them help pick out the hymns, and I'll ask Mrs. Finley about

arranging the furniture in our living-room; and in two or three weeks, when we're settled, our first social duty will be to return their dinner. Ours, of course, a simple, unpretentious meal, for of such must be the household of a minister of God.

§ *Small town* Duncan, Leacock, Davies, Munro; *Prairies* Kroetsch (1), Wiebe, van Herk

HUGH MacLENNAN (1907–90)

From Barometer Rising

This, the final chapter of *Barometer Rising* links its Nova Scotian characters' futures to that of Canada. It comes after the 1917 Halifax Explosion, when a French munitions ship blew up in the harbour, has helped to resolve the complications and tangled personal destinies of the plot. Penelope Wain (the name alludes to the waiting wife of *The Odyssey*) believed her cousin and lover, Neil Macrae, to have been killed in World War I. However, Neil has returned and now at the end of the novel is able to commit himself not only to Penelope and their daughter Jean, but also to Canada, which is seen as offering the embryonic possibility a 'new order' based on a synthesis of English and American values.

Monday night

Eight o'clock

It had stormed again over the week-end with rain and sleet, and then the blizzard had renewed itself and turned the atmosphere into a flux of dry snow drifting with a gentle motion out of the east. Now, for the first time in days, the night sky was clear. Everything was buried under shimmering snow so delicately clean that it seemed as though nature had conspired to conceal the misbegotten effects of human ingenuity. The peninsula of Halifax was a white shield curving upward under the sharp-edged stars. The patches of harbour visible where the streets ended at the foot of the hill shone like sections of a river moving in moonlight and flicked by a breeze.

Penny closed the house door behind her and followed Neil across the snow-filled sidewalk to a military truck parked with engine running on the slope of the hill. A soldier inside opened the door and they entered, Neil sitting next to the driver with his knees straddling the gears, Penny on the outside.

'You're sure you can get through to the train?' Neil said.

The soldier let in the clutch and the car slipped forward with a cushioned movement through the deep wool of the snow. 'The main street's pretty well beaten down now,' he said. 'We can try, anyway.'

The car surged down the hill in an uncanny silence and the rear wheels slithered widely as they swerved into the beaten level of Barrington Street. It would be almost impossible to return up that hill, Penny thought; and then she realized with a sense of shock that she had left home for the last time. The house would be there for years to come. Spring would revive the flowers in the garden, and by the Queen's Birthday[1] the creeper would have covered the stone wall, and by mid-June the cones of the chestnut blossoms would be nodding by the upper windows. But the familiar intimacy of the house would never return. Her father, the most untouchable man she had ever known, had been capriciously extinguished, and it was as though something profoundly improper had occurred without any adequate reason beyond the physical fact that two ships had met at a point where only one should have been.

She looked sideways as they passed one of the emergency street lights just installed, and saw Neil's profile clearly etched for a second; then it merged with the darkness again, and she was left with the impression of a man who seemed strange and unknown. The lines of his face were like sweeping arcs bound over an enormous spring of energy. They were tense and concentrated. She was tied to this man, and the realization made her shiver. She was a prisoner of his maleness because once she had wanted him and he had refused to forget it.

Turning, and seeing her eyes on him, he slipped his arm about her shoulder and pressed her closely against his side.

'Are you all right?'

'Yes,' she said.

'Seems funny, going out to the suburbs at a time like this. Prince's Lodge was just a few houses on the edge of the woods the last time I saw it.'

'I suppose it still is.'

'This youngster of Jim and Mary's – how old did you say she was?'

'Just about two years.' Penny waited for him to make some other comment, but none came. 'She can talk a little.'

'Is that remarkable at two?'

'Oh yes.'

She felt she must cry out if Neil said nothing more. He had not even asked why she was so anxious to go out to Prince's Lodge immediately after the storm, when it would have been reasonable to wait awhile or to send someone else to bring Jean into town. He had asked her no serious questions at all since that first afternoon when she had admitted him to the house. Now when he spoke to the soldier his voice sounded indifferent and practical.

'Is that the Shipyards down there?'

The soldier's reply came back carelessly. 'What's left of it. It gets worse farther north. You'll have to walk through a lot of junk to reach the train. That ship blew right into the middle of the railroad yard. It ain't pretty.'

The car bumped onward and the Shipyards slipped by in darkness on their

---

1 24 May also known as Victoria Day, Empire or Commonwealth Day; celebrated as a national holiday on the Monday before 25 May.

right. They drove slowly on through the darkened street, past scattered groups of tired men and women, past sleighs and slovens[2] dragging wearily to the south, and on their left was a dreadful area of emptiness with incongruous bulges projecting along the slope where a few days ago thouands of people had lived.

Neil's hand tightened on her shoulder. He looked down and she saw his teeth as he smiled and then felt his chin harsh on the line where her hair met her forehead.

'This is a good town,' he said. 'Professional soldiers could have been demoralized by a lot less than these people have taken.'

Everything he said seemed to frustrate her. 'Neil – ' she began.

'Yes, Penny.'

'Neil – did you ever think – '

Here in the jolting truck, crawling through the darkness along the slope of Fort Needham, she was no more capable of telling him about Jean than when she had been in the oppressive atmosphere of her own home, with patients filling the upstairs rooms and Roddie and Aunt Maria hanging on every scrap of conversation that passed between them.

'Are you sure you're all right?' His voice was anxious. 'Maybe we should go back? If the child has managed to get along all this time without us, another day or so won't make any difference.'

'No. No, let's go on. We've got to.'

She was in the current now. She had been in it ever since that night in Montreal, except that by synthetic action she had tried to pretend she was safe on dry land, safe with the accumulated weight of her environment to support her. She could see nothing clearly ahead. To force one's self on into the darkness to keep one's integrity as one moved – this was all that mattered because this was all there was left.

Neil's hand was hard against her upper arm. She tried to visualize something of the welter out of which he had preserved himself. She saw him trying to make himself a cog in the machine of the army. She saw him lying like a dead man alone on a patch of tormented earth. She heard the sound of his footsteps echoing bleakly as he wandered like a fugitive through strange cities in England.

Then she knew that it was inevitable for him and Jean and herself to go on together, even if they could do nothing better than preserve themselves blindly for a future she felt to be epitomized by the events of the past few days. She was too much of a scientist to forget that titanic forces once let loose are slow in coming to rest again. Did Neil have any idea what confronted him? By nature he would fight indefinitely to achieve a human significance in an age where the products of human ingenuity make mockery of the men who had created them. He would fight because nothing yet had been too big for his courage. And perhaps he would gain his significance, just as within the last few days he had achieved his dignity.

---

2 Low dray wagons (in Atlantic Canada).

She relaxed against his shoulder and tried to rest. Then out of the blackness enfolding the landscape they saw the glow of an engine's fire-box and the flickering of moving lanterns, and finally they came in view of a string of coaches with their lighted windows drawing a long line around a gentle curve.

'It's almost like a wrecked ship!'

'A train in the middle of all this!' Neil's voice was eager. 'When there are no trains to take people away from the messes they make – then you'll know the lights have gone out for sure.'

The truck came to a standstill and the soldier pointed down the embankment to the tracks. 'That's your way, sir. The path's been beaten down some since suppertime. I guess the lady'll make it easy enough.'

Neil thanked him and jumped to the ground after Penny. They made their way through a confusion of tracks, overturned and gutted box cars and uprooted sleepers. This yard had been almost totally destroyed, but the snow had buried the worst remnants of the carnage and the moon gave the scene a false peace. The greater constellations were only a little dimmed by the moon, and their lights were hard and clear; the Bear hung over the Basin, Orion at their backs was mounting toward its zenith.

Neil laughed suddenly. 'Remember the old tobogganning parties we used to have on the golk links? Do the kids still do it?'

'Oh, Neil!'

'What's the matter?'

'What a thing to think of now!'

'It's not that bad. Some things never change.'

'But people do. I've seen the war changing them all the time.'

'Maybe that's a good thing.' He pulled her strongly forward as she sank into a deep hole in the snow.

'Neil, I'm so tired. I can't think any more about what may happen now.'

'Yes, I know. Being tired is the worst part of things like this.'

They reached the train and he left her while he picked his way foward to find the conductor. Then he was back almost immediately. 'Standing room,' he said. 'We leave in a few minues. Let's wait here till they start.'

They stood at the rear of the train watching the opposite shore slope up from the black surface of the Narrows. Penny knew that in his own way he was trying to find means of assuring her that she was no longer alone.

He breathed deeply and smiled. 'This air – it smells so damned clean! God, it's good to be back! Over on the other side I sometimes thought I could smell the future, but as soon as I got to thinking about it I couldn't tell the future from the past. I wonder how many people realize how fast they're breaking up, over there? It's not a decline and fall. It's just one bloody smash.'

'Do you think we're much better here?'

'Better? I didn't mean that. But I'm damn well sure we're different. The trouble with us is, we've been taught to think we're pioneers. We ended that phase long ago, and now we don't know what we are. I tell you, if Canada ever gets to understand what her job in this world really is – well, unless she does, she'll never be a nation at all. She'll just have to look on the rest of the world committing suicide.'

Penny made no answer, but continued to stare into the darkness over the Narrows. Neil knew next to nothing of his own country. He had never been able to see how it was virtually owned by people like her father, the old men who were content to let it continue second-rate indefinitely, looting its wealth while they talked about its infinite opportunities. And meanwhile the ones like Neil, the generous ones who had believed the myth that this was a young man's country, were being killed like fools thousands of miles away in a foreign world.

The conductor came down the line swinging a lantern. 'You folks better get aboard,' he said. 'We're starting.'

Every car in the train was crowded. Some were ordinary day coaches, but the majority were old-fashioned colonist cars generally used to transport harvesters and settlers to the West at cheap rates. These had board seats padded with black letter and backs which could be lowered so that passengers could sleep flat with their clothes on and their heads on their kits. The backs of the seats were down now, and wounded lay on either side of the aisles. In each car there was a single nurse.

Neil drew Penny into the door of the rearmost coach and they stood just inside the corner by the drinking-water tank. The interior of the car was in half light and most of the prone forms seemed asleep.

'Neil – apart from the trouble you were in – why are you so glad to be back? What makes you think you'll find things so much better over here?'

There was a muffled blast from the locomotive's whistle; the engine passed a gentle shudder from coach to coach and the whole train began to move forward.

'A man has to think he hasn't got a country before he knows what having one means,' he said.

He looked down the car and saw the lines of quiet bodies sway gently with the train's motion. Why was he glad to be back? It was so much more than a man could ever put into words. It was more than the idea that he was young enough to see a great country move into its destiny. It was what he felt inside himself, as a Canadian who had lived both in the United States and England. Canada at present was called a nation only because a few laws had been passed and a railway line sent from one coast to the other. In returning home he knew that he was doing more than coming back to familiar surroundings. For better or worse he was entering the future, he was identifying himself with the still-hidden forces which were doomed to shape humanity as certainly as the tiny states of Europe had shaped the past. Canada was still hesitant, was still ham-strung by men with the mentality of Geoffrey Wain. But if there were enough Canadians like himself, half-American and half-English, then the day was inevitable when the halves would join and his country would become the central arch which united the new order.

The train swung through a long arc and he saw the bodies of the wounded slide gently to the right as the force of the curve pulled them. They were outside Halifax now, going around the foot of Richmond Bluff.

'How long does it take to get to Prince's Lodge?' he said.

'Ordinarily we'd be there in less than ten minutes.'

The statement tightened the muscles of her throat. She tried to look at Neil but was unable to keep her eyes on his. She felt his fingers on her wrist as he stood swaying with the train, and with the hundreds of wounded they surged on into the darkness of the continent, wheels clicking over the joints and the echo racketing back from the rock-face. In a few minutes the train slowed at Prince's Lodge.

They passed on the narrow, snow-banked platform and watched the lights of the coaches disappear around the next curve and heard the dying echoes of the whistle reverberating through the forest. A slight wind out of the north-west dragged down the gully of the track, bringing with it the fresh smell of balsam. There were no lights anywhere, but under the moon and stars the snow gleamed faintly out of the woods. Everything was utterly silent.

Suddenly Penny required his tenderness so greatly that it was as though all her life she had been starving for it. She wanted him to take her in his arms and hold her as he had done that unbelievable night in Montreal when nothing had existed but sounds in the darkness and the sense that each of them had been born for that moment. All this she wanted, but the habit of restraint, the cold control she had trained herself to acquire, was still unbreakable.

Neil made no effort to move up the road. He stood watching her, then came close and his fingers touched her hair where it escaped over her temples. He gave a sudden smile, and all strain vanished from his face.

'Wise Penelope! That's what Odysseus said to his wife when he got home. I don't think he ever told her he loved her. He probably knew the words would sound too small.'

Tears welled up in her eyes and receded without overflowing, and her fingers closed over his. He looked over her head to the patch of moonlight that broke and shivered in the centre of the Basin, and heard in the branches of the forest behind him the slight tremor of a rising wind.

§ *National myth-making* Pratt, Atwood (2); *Maritimes* Carman, MacLeod

ELIZABETH SMART (1913–86)

From By Grand Central Station I Sat Down and Wept

By Grand Central Station is a unique poetic celebration of immersion in 'love' – specifically a woman's passion for an older married writer, whose wife dies during the course of the narrative. The novel is set mainly in the United States, but in this extract the narrator/protagonist returns to Canada. Although something of an interlude from the main action, her account of coming home to a more 'reserved' Canadian world, 'waiting ... for history to be performed upon it', illustrates the text's sensual and impressionistic prose, its employment of a broad range of biblical and mythological allusions and its anguished celebration of the heroine's sexuality.

And so, returning to Canada through the fall sunshine, I look homeward now and melt, for though I am crowned and anointed with love and have obtained from life all I asked, what am I as I enter my parents' house but another prodigal daughter? I see their faces at which I shall never be free to look dispassionately. They gaze out of the window with eyes harassed by what they continually fear they see, like premature ghosts, straggling homeward over the plain.

And I, who have the world in my pocket, can bring them nothing to comfort their disappointment or reward their optimism, but supplicate again for the fatted calf which they killed so often before and so in vain. Parents' imaginations build frameworks out of their own hopes and regrets into which children seldom grow, but instead, contrary as trees, lean sideways out of the architecture, blown by a fatal wind their parents never envisaged.

But the old gold of the October trees, the stunted cedars, the horizons, the chilly gullies with their red willow whips, intoxicate me and confirm belief in what I have done, claiming me like an indisputable mother saying Whether or No, Whether or No, my darling. The great rocks rise up to insist on belief, since they remain though Babylon is fallen, being moulded, but never conquered, by time pouring from eternity. Can I expect less than sympathy from those who see such things when they draw aside their curtains in the mornings? Like Antæus,[1] when I am thrust against this earth, I bounce back recharged with hope. Every yellow or scarlet leaf hangs like a flag waving me on. The brown ones lie on the ground like a thousand thousand witnesses to the simplicity of truth.

So love may blind the expectations in my parents' eyes; or eloquence rise from my urgency and melt them too with ruth;[2] understanding may now stalk down Sparks Street[3] in every clerk, undoing wrongs begun before Wolfe;[4] or in Honey Dew cafés a kind look glance towards me as I open the door.

Asking no one's forgiveness for sins I refuse to recognize, why do I cry then to be returning homeward through a land I love like a lover? From a long way off those faces with their prayers like wounds peer out of the window, stiff with anxiety, but ready to welcome me with love. The sound of their steps pacing before the fireplace voices all the pain of the turning world.

---

1 A giant wrestler, son of Poseidon and Gaea, the earth; attacked by Hercules, he drew new strength whenever he touched the earth. 2 Pity (arch.). 3 In Ottawa. 4 British general, victor of the Battle of Québec, in which he was killed, in 1759.

O Absalom, Absalom,[5] melt, melt with ruth.

Coming from California, which is oblivious of regret, approaching November whips me with the passion of the dying year. And after the greed already hardening part of the American face into stone, I fancy I see kindness and gentleness looking out at me from train windows. Surely the porter carrying my bags has extracted a spiritual lesson from his hardship. Surely this acceptance of a mediocre role gives human dignity.

And over the fading wooden houses I sense the reminiscences of the pioneers' passion, and the determination of early statesmen who were mild but individual, and able to allude to Shakespeare while discussing politics under the elms. No great neon face has been superimposed over their minor but memorable history. Nor has the blood of the early settlers, spilt in feud and heroism, yet been bottled by a Coca-Cola firm and sold as ten-cent tradition.

The faces, the faded houses, the autumn air, everything is omens of promise to the prodigal. But leaning against the train window, drunk with the hope which anything so unbegun always instils, I remember my past returnings: keep that vision, I pray, pressing my forehead against the panes: the faces *are* kind; the people *have* reserve; the birds gather in groups to migrate, forecasting fatal change: remember, when your eyes shrivel aggrievedly because you notice the jealousy of those that stay at home, here is no underlining of an accidental picturesqueness, but a waiting, unself-conscious as the unborn's, for future history to be performed upon it.

Remember that although this initial intoxication disappears, yet these things in that hour moved you to tears, and made of an outward gaze through the dining-car window a plenitude not to be borne.

§ *Alternative identities for women* Thomas, Swan, Marlatt, van Herk, Lau

EARLE BIRNEY (1904–95)

1: Bushed

> He invented a rainbow but lightning struck it
> shattered it into the lake-lap of a mountain
> so big his mind slowed when he looked at it
>
> Yet he built a shack on the shore
> 5 learned to roast porcupine belly and
> wore the quills on his hatband

---

5 Son of David, whose death occasioned his father's lament alluded to here; see 2 Samuel xviii 33.

At first he was out with the dawn
whether it yellowed bright as wood-columbine
or was only a fuzzed moth in a flannel of storm
10 But he found the mountain was clearly alive
sent messages whizzing down every hot morning
boomed proclamations at noon and spread out
a white guard of goat
before falling asleep on its feet at sundown

15 When he tried his eyes on the lake ospreys
would fall like valkyries
choosing the cut-throat
He took then to waiting
till the night smoke rose from the boil of the sunset

20 But the moon carved unkown totems
out of the lakeshore
owls in the beardusky woods derided him
moosehorned cedars circled his swamps and tossed
their antlers up to the stars
25 then he knew   though the mountain slept the winds
were shaping its peak to an arrowhead
poised

And now he could only
bar himself in and wait
30 for the great flint to come singing into his heart

§ *Settler consciousness* Purdy (2), Atwood (1), Marlatt

2: Mappemounde

No not this old whalehall can whelm us,
shiptamed, gullgraced, soft to our glidings.
Harrows that mere more that squares our map.
See in its north where scribe has marked *mermen*,
5 shore-sneakers who croon, to the seafarer's girl,
next year's gleewords. East and west *nadders*,
flamefanged bale-twisters; their breath dries up tears,
chars in the breast-hoard the dear face-charm.

---

16 **valkyries**: Odin's handmaidens, who chose those to be killed in battle.
6 **nadders**: adders.

3 **mere more**: the poem draws on the conventions of Old English alliterative poetry, particularly elegies such as *The Wanderer* and *The Seafarer*.

Southward *Cetegrande*, that sly beast who sucks
10 in with whirlwind also the wanderer's pledges.
That sea is hight Time, it hems all hearts' landtrace.
Men say the redeless, reaching its bounds,
topple in maelstrom, tread back never.
Adread in that mere we drift to map's end.

§ *Cartographies* Reaney; Aus: Tranter; SA: Ghosh; TransC: Ondaatje (1)

JAMES REANEY (1926–)

Maps

Five miles up from Pork Street
The maps hang on the wall
Gray-green windows on the world
Before which the scholars stand
5 And hear the gasp and roll Atlantic
Above, like the cynosure of a Queen Anne's Lace Dance
The dark red island, Britain
Proud and proud.

O there are maps of Asia
10 Where warm winds blow
When outside the Janus-frost
Rules the bread-white snow.
A sultry coil of breeze,
And a blossom,
15 Clogged winds of
Cinnamon and amber.

Fat yellow China
and purple India,
Ceylon like a chocolate comfit
20 The rim and dim ghost of Europe
Where the colour has run out . . .

Whenever we sing
'In days of yore'
We think of the New World's crown.
25 The green Northwest with its quaint inlets.

---

9 *Cetegrande*: the great whale.
12 **redeless**: without counsel or advice (arch.).
11 **Janus**: January; the month of Janus.

11 **hight**: called (arch.).
6 **cynosure**: guiding star.

The brown Yukon.
Ungava Bay and Newfoundland
Pink fevered Saskatchewan
and purple Alberta.

§ *Cartographies* Birney (2); Aus: Tranter; SA: Ghosh; TransC: Ondaatje (1)

AL PURDY (1918–)

1: Elegy for a Grandfather

Well, he died I guess. They said he did.
His wide whalebone hips will make a prehistoric barrow
men of the future may find and perhaps may not:
where this man's relatives ducked their heads
5 in real and pretended sorrow
for the dearly beloved gone thank Christ to God,
after a bad century: a tough big-bellied Pharaoh,
with a deck of cards in his pocket and a Presbyterian grin –

Maybe he did die, but the boy didn't understand it;
10 the man knows now and the scandal never grows old
of a happy lumberjack who lived on rotten whiskey,
and died of sin and Quaker oats age 90 or so.
But all he was was too much for any man to be,
a life so full he couldn't include one more thing,
15 nor tell the same story twice if he'd wanted to,
and didn't and didn't –

Just the same he's dead. A sticky religious voice
folded his century sideways to get it out of sight,
and lowered him into the ground like someone still alive
20 who made other people uncomfortable:
barn raiser and backwoods farmer,
become an old man in a one-room apartment
over a drygoods store –
And earth takes him as it takes more beautiful things:
25 populations of whole countries,
museums and works of art,
and women with such a glow
it makes their background vanish
    they vanish too,

30   and Lesbos' singer in her sunny islands
       stopped when the sun went down –

       No, my grandfather was decidedly unbeautiful,
       250 pounds of scarred slag.
       And I've somehow become his memory,
35   taking on flesh and blood again
       the way he imagined me,
       floating among the pictures in his mind
       where his dead body is,
       laid deep in the earth –
40   and such a relayed picture perhaps
       outlives any work of art,
       survives among its alternatives.

§ *Grandfather/ancestor poems* Mandel, Bowering, Kroetsch (1); SA: Mahapatra

2: Roblin's Mills

       The wheels stopped
       and the murmur of voices
       behind the flume's tremble
       stopped
5   and the wind-high ships
       that sailed from Rednersville
       to the sunrise ports of Europe
       are delayed somewhere
       in a toddling breeze
10   The black millpond
       turns an unreflecting eye
       to look inward
       like an idiot child
       locked in the basement
15   when strangers come
       whizzing past on the highway
       above the dark green valley
       a hundred yards below
       The mill space is empty
20   even stones are gone
       where hands were shaken
       and walls enclosed laughter

---

30 Lesbos' singer: Sappho, Greek poetess probably born in the 7th century BC.

saved up and brought here
from the hot fields
25   where all stories
are rolled into one
And white dust floating
above the watery mumble
and bright human sounds
30   to shimmer among the pollen
where bees dance now
Of all these things
no outline remains
no shadow on the soft air
35   no bent place in the heat glimmer
where the heavy walls pressed
And some of those who vanished
lost children of the time
kept after school
40   left alone in a graveyard
who may not change
or ever grow six inches
in one hot summer
or turn where the great herons
45   graze the sky's low silver
– stand between the hours
in a rotting village
near the weed-grown eye
that looks into itself
50   deep in the black crystal
that holds and contains
the substance of shadows
manner and custom
              of the inarticulate
55   departures and morning rumours
gestures and almost touchings
announcements and arrivals
gossip of someone's marriage
when a girl or tired farm woman
60   whose body suddenly blushes
beneath a faded house dress
with white expressionless face
turns to her awkward husband
to remind him of something else
65   The black millpond
              holds them
movings and reachings and fragments
the gear and tackle of living

under the water eye
70   all things laid aside
        discarded
           forgotten
but they had their being once
and left a place to stand on

§ *Settler past* Traill, Birney (1), Atwood (1), Marlatt

ELI MANDEL (1922–)

'Grandfather's Painting': David Thauberger

Under David Thauberger's painting
showing his grandfather's house
and that giant horse standing above it,
the town of Holdfast, wheat fields,
5   church, elevators, and prairie grass
the TV set turned to a
Saturday Night Movie called 'Marathon Man'
looks very small and peculiar,
but the movie is about politics,
10   betrayal and South American Nazis: it has to do
with various kinds of torture,
the use of a dentist's drill,
for example, the tyranny of McCarthy
in America of the fifties, Jews,
15   their memory, camps, the White Angel,
specialist in teeth, skulls, and diamonds.
      You wouldn't believe how large the horse is
in Thauberger's painting above the TV set
and yet it only portrays a symbol of how his grandfather
20   ruled the land, the power by which the little town
was run, the motor of the little town called Holdfast
while beneath it the real powers that run us,
pictures, say, and how we know how to kill one another,
metaphors of murder, these are played out night
25   upon night and I watch them and watch the painting,

---

7 'Marathon Man': 1976 thriller, directed by John Schlesinger and starring Dustin Hoffman and Laurence Olivier.

13 McCarthy: US Senator from Wisconsin, who in the 1950s chaired Senate hearings into alleged Communism, which ruined many careers and are widely regarded as having constituted a witch-hunt.

no longer knowing whether I should write poetry,
especially poems about land, about Estevan,
or about why I came back to Regina, Saskatchewan,
this cold winter of 1979 or what I thought
30   I might find in a city of this kind to write of,
now that my father is dead for many years, and my mother,
and most of my friends are in the arts.
                            There are nights
cold enough to kill. They remind me of my boyhood,
how much I loved the winter on the prairies, never
35   believing it was deadly or that we fought to be alive here
though my fantasies were of war. That powerful animal,
this evening with the Marathon Man running,
running, I suddenly know David was right to paint him,
his grandfather. We stand over the land, fathers,
40   and over our homes and over each other.
We have terrible forces inside us: we can paint them,
green, acrylic, glitter: the form never lies.
The truth is in the long dead winters where we live.

§ *Grandfather/ancestor poems* Purdy (1), Bowering, Kroetsch (1); SA: Mahapatra

GEORGE BOWERING (1935–)

Grandfather

Grandfather
          Jabez Harry Bowering
strode across the Canadian prairie
hacking down trees
5   and building churches
delivering personal baptist sermons in them
leading Holy holy holy lord god almighty songs in them
red haired man squared off in the pulpit
reading Saul on the road to Damascus at them

10   Left home
             big walled Bristol town
at age eight
           to make a living
buried his stubby fingers in roots snarled earth

---

27 **Estevan:** Saskatchewan city; Mandel's birthplace.

15   for a suit of clothes and seven hundred gruelly meals a year
taking an anabaptist cane across the back every day
for four years till he was whipped out of England

    Twelve years old
                  and across the ocean alone
20   to apocalyptic Canada
                         Ontario of bone bending child labor
six years on the road to Damascus till his eyes were blinded
with the blast of Christ and he wandered west
to Brandon among wheat kings and heathen Saturday nights
25   young red haired Bristol boy shoveling coal
in the basement of Brandon college five in the morning

    Then built his first wooden church and married
a sick girl who bore two live children and died
leaving several pitiful letters and the Manitoba night
30   He moved west with another wife and built children and
        churches
Saskatchewan Alberta British Columbia Holy holy holy
lord god almighty
                    struck his labored bones with pain
35   and left him a postmaster prodding grandchildren with
        crutches
another dead wife and a glass bowl of photographs
and holy books unopened save the bible by the bed

    Till he died the day before his eighty fifth birthday
40   in a Catholic hospital of sheets white as his hair

§ *Grandfather/ancestor poems* Purdy (1), Mandel, Kroetsch (1); SA:
Mahapatra

MARGARET LAURENCE (1926–87)

From The Diviners

The fifth and final work in Laurence's 'Manawaka' sequence, *The Diviners* is both
technically more complex and thematically more diverse than the earlier novels in
the series. Its central figure, the author Morag Gunn, who narrates much of the book,
reviews her life in a mode which foregrounds the problems of historiographical writing, whether dealing with personal or public pasts. This section, the opening of the
novel, introduces several of its central themes, among them: the interpenetration of present and past ('The river flowed both ways . . .'), family albums, the

mother–daughter relationship and divining – an activity seen as analogous to both writing and, more generally, inventing versions of the past and ancestry.

The river flowed both ways. The current moved from north to south, but the wind usually came from the south, rippling the bronze-green water in the opposite direction. This apparently impossible contradiction, made apparent and possible, still fascinated Morag, even after the years of river-watching.

The dawn mist had lifted, and the morning air was filled with swallows, darting so low over the river that their wings sometimes brushed the water, then spiralling and pirouetting upward again. Morag watched, trying to avoid thought, but this ploy was not successful.

Pique had gone away. She must have left during the night. She had left a note on the kitchen table, which also served as Morag's desk, and had stuck the sheet of paper into the typewriter, where Morag would be certain to find it.

> Now please do not get all uptight, Ma. I can look after myself. Am going west. Alone, at least for now. If Gord phones, tell him I've drowned and gone floating down the river, crowned with algae and dead minnows, like Ophelia.

Well, you had to give the girl some marks for style of writing. Slightly derivative, perhaps, but let it pass. Oh jesus, it was not funny. Pique was eighteen. Only. Not dry behind the ears. Yes, she was, though. If only there hadn't been that other time when Pique took off, that really bad time. That wouldn't happen again, not like before. Morag was pretty sure it wouldn't. Not sure enough, probably.

I've got too damn much work in hand to fret over Pique. Lucky me. I've got my work to take my mind off my life. At forty-seven that's not such a terrible state of affairs. If I hadn't been a writer, I might've been a first-rate mess at this point. Don't knock the trade.

Morag read Pique's letter again, made coffee and sat looking out at the river, which was moving quietly, its surface wrinkled by the breeze, each crease of water outlined by the sun. Naturally, the river wasn't wrinkled or creased at all – wrong words, implying something unfluid like skin, something unenduring, prey to age. Left to itself, the river would probably go on like this, flowing deep, for another million or so years. That would not be allowed to happen. In bygone days, Morag had once believed that nothing could be worse than killing a person. Now she perceived river-slaying as something worse. No wonder the kids felt themselves to be children of the apocalypse.

No boats today. Yes, one. Royland was out, fishing for muskie.[1] Seventy-four years old this year, Royland. Eyesight terrible, but he was too stubborn to wear glasses. A marvel that he could go on working. Of course, his work did not depend upon eyesight. Some other kind of sight. A water diviner. Morag always felt she was about to learn something of great significance

---

1 Muskellunge; largest member of pike family, found in eastern North America.

from him, something which would explain everything. But things remained mysterious, his work, her own, the generations, the river.

Across the river, the clumps of willow bent silver-green down to the water, and behind them the great maples and oaks stirred a little, their giant dark green tranquility disturbed only slightly by the wind. There were more dead elms this year, dry bones, the grey skeletons of trees. Soon there would be no elms left.

The swallows dipped and spun over the water, a streaking of blue-black wings and bright breastfeathers. How could that colour be caught in words? A sort of rosy peach colour, but that sounded corny and was also inaccurate.

I used to think words could do anything. Magic. Sorcery. Even miracle. But no, only occasionally.

The house seemed too quiet. Dank. The kitchen had that sour milk and stale bread smell that Morag remembered from her childhood, and which she loathed. There was, however, no sour milk or stale bread here – it must be all in the head, emanating from the emptiness of the place. Until recently the house was full, not only Pique but A-Okay Smith and Maudie and their shifting but ever-large tribe. Morag, for the year when the Smiths lived here, had gone around torn between affection and rage – how could anyone be expected to work in such a madhouse, and here she was feeding them all, more or less, and no goddamn money would be coming in if she didn't get back to the typewriter. Now, of course, she wished some of them were here again. True, they only lived across the river, now that they had their own place, and visited often, so perhaps that was enough.

Something about Pique's going, apart from the actual departure itself, was unresolved in Morag's mind. The fact that Pique was going west? Yes. Morag was both glad and uncertain. What would Pique's father think, if he knew? Well, he wouldn't know and didn't have all that much right to judge anyway. Would Pique go to Manawaka? If she did, would she find anything there which would have meaning for her? Morag rose, searched the house, finally found what she was looking for.

These photographs from the past never agreed to get lost. Odd, because she had tried hard enough, over the years, to lose them, or thought she had. She had treated them carelessly, shoved them away in seldom-opened suitcases or in dresser drawers filled with discarded underwear, scorning to put them into anything as neat as an album. They were jammed any-old-how into an ancient tattered manilla envelope that Christie had given her once when she was a kid, and which said *McVitie & Pearl, Barristers & Solicitors, Manawaka, Manitoba.* Christie must have found it at the dump – the Nuisance Grounds, as they were known; what an incredible name, when you thought of the implications.

The thick brown paper stank a bit when Christie had handed it to her, faintly shitlike, faintly the sweetish ether smell of spoiled fruit. He said Morag could have it to keep her pictures in, and she had taken it, although despising it, because she did not have any other sturdy envelope for the few and valued snapshots she owned then. Not realizing that if she had chucked them out, then and there, her skull would prove an envelope quite sturdy enough to retain them.

I've kept them, of course, because something in me doesn't want to lose them, or perhaps doesn't dare. Perhaps they're my totems, or contain a portion of my spirit. Yeh, and perhaps they are exactly what they seem to be – a jumbled mess of old snapshots which I'll still be lugging along with me when I'm an old lady, clutching them as I enter or am shoved into the Salvation Army Old People's home or wherever it is that I'll find my death.

Morag put the pictures into chronological order. As though there were really any chronological order, or any order at all, if it came to that. She was not certain whether the people in the snapshots were legends she had once dreamed only, or were as real as anyone she now knew.

I keep the snapshots not for what they show but for what is hidden in them.

§ *Dialogues with past* Purdy (1, 2), Kroetsch (1, 2), Wiebe, Atwood (1), Marlatt

MARGARET ATWOOD (1939–)

1: Progressive Insanities of a Pioneer

I

He stood, a point
on a sheet of green paper
proclaiming himself the centre,

5   with no walls, no borders
anywhere; the sky no height
above him, totally un-
enclosed
and shouted:

Let me out!

II

10   He dug the soil in rows,
imposed himself with shovels
He asserted
into the furrows, I
am not random.

15   The ground
replied with aphorisms:

a tree-sprout, a nameless
weed, words
he couldn't understand.

III

20 The house pitched
the plot staked
in the middle of nowhere.

At night the mind
inside, in the middle
25 of nowhere.

The idea of an animal
patters across the roof.

In the darkness the fields
defend themselves with fences
30 in vain:
everything
is getting in.

IV

By daylight he resisted.
He said, disgusted
35 with the swamp's clamourings and the outbursts
of rocks,
This is not order
but the absence
of order.

40 He was wrong, the unanswering
forest implied:

It was
an ordered absence

V

For many years
45 he fished for a great vision,
dangling the hooks of sown
roots under the surface
of the shallow earth.

It was like
50 enticing whales with a bent
pin. Besides he thought

in that country
only the worms were biting.

VI
If he had known unstructured
55   space is a deluge
and stocked his log house-
boat with all the animals

even the wolves,

he might have floated.

60   But obstinate he
stated, The land is solid
and stamped,

watching his foot sink
down through stone
65   up to the knee.

VII
Things
refused to name themselves; refused
to let him name them.

The wolves hunted
70   outside.

On his beaches, his clearings,
by the surf of under-
growth breaking
at his feet, he foresaw
75   disintegration
                 and in the end
through eyes
made ragged by his
effort, the tension
80   between subject and object,

the green
vision, the unnamed
whale invaded.

§ *Settling the land/finding a language* Traill, Purdy (1, 2), Laurence, Atwood
(2), Marlatt; Aus: Lawson (1), Rudd, Baynton, White (2)

2: *From* Survival: A Thematic Guide to Canadian Literature

When it first appeared in 1972, *Survival* was widely viewed as a ground-breaking study of archetypal patterns in 'CanLit'. Over the years, its arguments have been disputed but, along with Northrop Frye's *The Bush Garden*, it remains a classic work of Canadian myth criticism. In this passage Atwood outlines her central thesis that the dominant symbol of the country's literature is survival and that its writing demonstrates a collective victim mentality.

I'd like to begin with a sweeping generalization and argue that every country or culture has a single unifying and informing symbol at its core. (Please don't take any of my oversimplifications as articles of dogma which allow of no exceptions; they are proposed simply to create vantage points from which the literature may be viewed.) The symbol, then – be it word, phrase, idea, image, or all of these – functions like a system of beliefs (it *is* a system of beliefs, though not always a formal one) which holds the country together and helps the people in it to co-operate for common ends. Possibly the symbol for America is The Frontier, a flexible idea that contains many elements dear to the American heart: it suggests a place that is *new*, where the old order can be discarded (as it was when America was instituted by a crop of disaffected Protestants, and later at the time of the Revolution); a line that is always expanding, taking in or 'conquering' ever-fresh virgin territory (be it The West, the rest of the world, outer space, Poverty or The Regions of the Mind); it holds out a hope, never fulfilled but always promised, of Utopia, the perfect human society. Most twentieth century American literature is about the gap between the promise and the actuality, between the imagined ideal Golden West or City Upon a Hill, the model for all the world postulated by the Puritans, and the actual squalid materialism, dotty small town, nasty city, or redneck-filled outback. Some Americans have even confused the actuality with the promise: in that case Heaven is a Hilton hotel with a coke machine in it.

The corresponding symbol for England is perhaps The Island, convenient for obvious reasons. In the seventeenth century a poet called Phineas Fletcher wrote a long poem called *The Purple Island*, which is based on an extended body-as-island metaphor, and, dreadful though the poem is, that's the kind of island I mean: island-as-body, self-contained, a Body Politic, evolving organically, with a hierarchical structure in which the King is the Head, the statesmen the hands, the peasants or farmers or workers the feet, and so on. The Englishman's home as his castle is the popular form of this symbol, the feudal castle being not only an insular structure but a self-contained microcosm of the entire Body Politic.

The central symbol for Canada – and this is based on numerous instances of its occurrence in both English and French Canadian literature – is undoubtedly Survival, *la Survivance*. Like the Frontier and The Island, it is a multi-faceted and adaptable idea. For early explorers and settlers, it meant bare survival in the face of 'hostile' elements and/or natives: carving out a place and a way of keeping alive. But the word can also suggest survival of a crisis or disaster, like a hurricane or a wreck, and many Canadian poems have this kind of survival as a theme; what you might call 'grim' survival as opposed to 'bare' survival. For French Canada after the English took over it became cultural survival, hanging on as a people, retaining a religion and a language under an alien government. And in English Canada now while the Americans are taking over it is acquiring a similar meaning. There is another use of the word as well: a survival can be a vestige of a vanished order which has managed to persist after its time is past, like a primitive reptile. This version crops up in Canadian thinking too, usually among those who believe that Canada is obsolete.

But the main idea is the first one: hanging on, staying alive. Canadians are forever taking the national pulse like doctors at a sickbed: the aim is not to see whether the patient will live well but simply whether he will live at all. Our central idea is one which generates, not the excitement and sense of adventure or danger which The Frontier holds out, not the smugness and/or sense of security, of everything in its place, which The Island can offer, but an almost intolerable anxiety. Our stories are likely to be tales not of those who made it but of those who made it back, from the awful experience – the North, the snow-storm, the sinking ship – that killed everyone else. The survivor has no triumph or victory but the fact of his survival; he has little after his ordeal that he did not have before, except gratitude for having escaped with his life.

A preoccupation with one's survival is necessarily also a preoccupation with the obstacles to that survival. In earlier writers these obstacles are external – the land, the climate, and so forth. In later writers the obstacles tend to become both harder to identify and more internal; they are no longer obstacles to physical survival but obstacles to what we may call spiritual survival, to life as anything more than a minimally human being. Sometimes fear of these obstacles becomes itself the obstacle, and a character is paralyzed by terror (either of what he thinks is threatening him from the outside, or of elements in his own nature that threaten him from within). It may even be life itself that he fears; and when life becomes a threat to life, you have a moderately vicious circle. If a man feels he can survive only by amputating himself, turning himself into a cripple or a eunuch, what price survival?

Just to give you a quick sample of what I'm talking about, here are a few capsule Canadian plots. Some contain attempts to survive which fail. Some contain bare survivals. Some contain crippled successes (the character does more than survive, but is mutilated in the process).

Pratt: *The Titanic*: Ship crashes into iceberg. Most passengers drown.
Pratt: *Brébeuf and His Brethren*: After crushing ordeals, priests survive briefly and are massacred by Indians.
Laurence: *The Stone Angel*: Old woman hangs on grimly to life and dies at the end.

Carrier: *Is It The Sun, Philibert?* Hero escapes incredible rural poverty and
           horrid urban conditions, almost makes it financially, dies when
           he wrecks his car.

Marlyn: *Under The Ribs of Death*: Hero amputates himself spiritually in
           order to make it financially, fails anyway.

Ross: *As For Me and My House*: Prairie minister who hates his job and
           has crippled himself artistically by sticking with it is offered a
           dubious chance of escape at the end.

Buckler: *The Mountain and the Valley*: Writer who has been unable to
           write has vision of possibility at the end but dies before he can
           implement it.

Gibson: *Communion*: Man who can no longer make human contact tries
           to save sick dog, fails, and is burned up at the end.

And just to round things out, we might add that the two English Canadian
feature films (apart from Allan King's documentaries) to have had much success so far, *Goin' Down the Road*[1] and *The Rowdyman*,[2] are both dramatizations of failure. The heroes survive, but just barely; they are born losers, and
their failure to do anything but keep alive has nothing to do with the
Maritime Provinces or 'regionalism.' It's pure Canadian, from sea to sea.

My sample plots are taken from both prose and poetry, and from regions
all across Canada; they span four decades, from the thirties to the early seventies. And they hint at another facet of Survivalism: at some point the failure to survive, or the failure to achieve anything beyond survival, becomes
not a necessity imposed by a hostile outside world but a choice made from
within. Pushed far enough, the obsession with surviving can become the will
not to survive.

Certainly Canadian authors spend a disproportionate amount of time making sure that their heroes die or fail. Much Canadian writing suggests that
failure is required because it is felt – consciously or unconsciously – to be
the only 'right' ending, the only thing that will support the characters' (or
their authors') view of the universe. When such endings are well-handled
and consistent with the whole book, one can't quarrel with them on aesthetic grounds. But when Canadian writers are writing clumsy or manipulated endings, they are much less likely to manipulate in a positive than they
are in a negative direction: that is, the author is less likely to produce a sudden inheritance from a rich old uncle or the surprising news that his hero
is really the son of a Count than he is to conjure up an unexpected natural
disaster or an out-of-control car, tree or minor character so that the protagonist may achieve a satisfactory *failure*. Why should this be so? Could it be
that Canadians have a will to lose which is as strong and pervasive as the
Americans' will to win?

It might be argued that, since most Canlit has been written in the

---

1 1970 film directed by Donald Shebib, following fortunes of two Nova Scotians in Toronto.   2 1971 film
directed by Peter Carter and filmed in Newfoundland.

twentieth century and since the twentieth century has produced a generally pessimistic or 'ironic' literature, Canada has simply been reflecting a trend. Also, though it's possible to write a short lyric poem about joy and glee, no novel of any length can exclude all but these elements. A novel about unalloyed happiness would have to be either very short or very boring. 'Once upon a time John and Mary lived happily ever after, The End.' Both of these arguments have some validity, but surely the Canadian gloom is more unrelieved than most and the death and failure toll out of proportion. Given a choice of the negative or positive aspects of any symbol – sea as life-giving Mother, sea as what your ship goes down in; tree as symbol of growth, tree as what falls on your head – Canadians show a marked preference for the negative.

You might decide at this point that most Canadian authors with any pretensions to seriousness are neurotic or morbid, and settle down instead for a good read with *Anne of Green Gables* (though it's about an orphan . . .) But if the coincidence intrigues you – so many writers in such a small country, and *all with the same neurosis* – then I will offer you a theory. Like any theory it won't explain everything, but it may give you some points of departure.

Let us suppose for the sake of argumment, that Canada as a whole is a victim, or an 'oppressed minority,' or 'exploited.' Let us suppose in short that Canada is a colony. A partial definition of a colony is that it is a place from which a profit is made, but *not by the people who live there*: the major profit from a colony is made in the centre of the empire. That's what colonies are for, to make money for the 'mother country,' and that's what – since the days of Rome and, more recently, of the Thirteen Colonies – they have always been for. Of course there are cultural side-effects which are often identified as 'the colonial mentality,' and it is these which are examined here; but the root cause of them is economic.

If Canada is a collective victim, it should pay some attention to the Basic Victim Positions. These are like the basic positions in ballet or the scales on the piano: they are primary, though all kinds of song-and-dance variations on them are possible.

The positions are the same whether you are a victimized country, a victimized minority group or a victimized individual. . . .

§ *National mythologies/mentalities* Richardson, Traill, Pratt, Purdy (2), Ross; Aus: Lawson (1, 2), Paterson; NZSP: Wendt (2), Manhire

3: The Age of Lead

The man has been buried for a hundred and fifty years. They dug a hole in the frozen gravel, deep into the permafrost, and put him down there so the wolves couldn't get to him. Or that is the speculation.

When they dug the hole the permafrost was exposed to the air, which was warmer. This made the permafrost melt. But it froze again after the man was covered up, so that when he was brought to the surface he was completely enclosed in ice. They took the lid off the coffin and it was like those maraschino cherries you used to freeze in ice-cube trays for fancy tropical drinks: a vague shape, looming through a solid cloud.

Then they melted the ice and he came to light. He is almost the same as when he was buried. The freezing water has pushed his lips away from his teeth into an astonished snarl, and he's a beige colour, like a gravy stain on linen, instead of pink, but everything is still there. He even has eyeballs, except that they aren't white but the light brown of milky tea. With these tea-stained eyes he regards Jane: an indecipherable gaze, innocent, ferocious, amazed, but contemplative, like a werewolf meditating, caught in a flash of lightning at the exact split second of his tumultuous change.

Jane doesn't watch very much television. She used to watch it more. She used to watch comedy series, in the evenings, and when she was a student at university she would watch afternoon soaps about hospitals and rich people, as a way of procrastinating. For a while, not so long ago, she would watch the evening news, taking in the disasters with her feet tucked up on the chesterfield, a throw rug over her legs, drinking a hot milk and rum to relax before bed. It was all a form of escape.

But what you can see on the television, at whatever time of day, is edging too close to her own life; though in her life, nothing stays put in those tidy compartments, comedy here, seedy romance and sentimental tears there, accidents and violent deaths in thirty-second clips they call *bites*, as if they were chocolate bars. In her life, everything is mixed together. *Laugh, I thought I'd die*, Vincent used to say, a very long time ago in a voice imitating the banality of mothers; and that's how it's getting to be. So when she flicks on the television these days, she flicks it off again soon enough. Even the commercials, with their surreal dailiness, are beginning to look sinister, to suggest meanings behind themselves, behind their facade of cleanliness, lusciousness, health, power, and speed.

Tonight she leaves the television on, because what she is seeing is so unlike what she usually sees. There is nothing sinister behind this image of the frozen man. It is entirely itself. *What you sees is what you gets*, as Vincent also used to say, crossing his eyes, baring his teeth at one side, pushing his nose into a horror-movie snout. Although it never was, with him.

The man they've dug up and melted was a young man. Or still is: it's difficult to know what tense should be applied to him, he is so insistently present. Despite the distortions caused by the ice and the emaciation of his illness, you can see his youthfulness, the absence of toughening, of wear. According to the dates painted carefully onto his nameplate, he was only twenty years old. His name was John Torrington. He was, or is, a sailor, a seaman. He wasn't an able-bodied seaman though; he was a petty officer, one of those marginally in command. Being in command has little to do with the ableness of the body.

He was one of the first to die. This is why he got a coffin and a metal nameplate, and a deep hole in the permafrost – because they still had the energy, and the piety, for such things, that early. There would have been a burial service read over him, and prayers. As time went on and became nebulous and things did not get better, they must have kept the energy for themselves; and also the prayers. The prayers would have ceased to be routine and become desperate, and then hopeless. The later dead ones got cairns of piled stones, and the much later ones not even that. They ended up as bones, and as the soles of boots and the occasional button, sprinkled over the frozen stony treeless relentless ground in a trail heading south. It was like the trails in fairy tales, of bread crumbs or seeds or white stones. But in this case nothing had sprouted or lit up in the moonlight, forming a miraculous pathway to life; no rescuers had followed. It took ten years before anyone knew even the barest beginnings of what had been happening to them.

All of them together were the Franklin Expedition. Jane has seldom paid much attention to history except when it has overlapped with her knowledge of antique furniture and real estate – '19th C. pine harvest table,' or 'Prime location Georgian centre hall, impeccable reno' – but she knows what the Franklin Expedition was. The two ships with their bad-luck names have been on stamps – the *Terror*, the *Erebus*. Also she took it in school, along with a lot of other doomed expeditions. Not many of those explorers seemed to have come out of it very well. They were always getting scurvy, or lost.

What the Franklin Expedition was looking for was the Northwest Passage, an open seaway across the top of the Arctic, so people, merchants, could get to India from England without going all the way around South America. They wanted to go that way because it would cost less and increase their profits. This was much less exotic than Marco Polo or the headwaters of the Nile; nevertheless, the idea of exploration appealed to her then: to get onto a boat and just go somewhere, somewhere mapless, off into the unknown. To launch yourself into fright; to find things out. There was something daring and noble about it, despite all of the losses and failures, or perhaps because of them. It was like having sex, in high school, in those days before the Pill, even if you took precautions. If you were a girl, that is. If you were a boy, for whom such a risk was fairly minimal, you had to do other things: things with weapons or large amounts of alcohol, or high-speed vehicles, which at her suburban Toronto high school, back then at the beginning of the sixties, meant switchblades, beer, and drag races down the main streets on Saturday nights.

Now, gazing at the television as the lozenge of ice gradually melts and the outline of the young sailor's body clears and sharpens, Jane remembers Vincent, sixteen and with more hair then, quirking one eyebrow and lifting his lip in a mock sneer and saying, 'Franklin, my dear, I don't give a damn.'[1]

---

1 Parodying Rhett Butler's remark to Scarlett O'Hara in *Gone with the Wind*: 'Frankly, my dear . . .'

He said it loud enough to be heard, but the history teacher ignored him, not knowing what else to do. It was hard for the teachers to keep Vincent in line, because he never seemed to be afraid of anything that might happen to him.

He was hollow-eyed even then; he frequently looked as if he'd been up all night. Even then he resembled a very young old man, or else a dissipated child. The dark circles under his eyes were the ancient part, but when he smiled he had lovely small white teeth, like the magazine ads for baby foods. He made fun of everything, and was adored. He wasn't adored the way other boys were adored, those boys with surly lower lips and greased hair and a studied air of smouldering menace. He was adored like a pet. Not a dog, but a cat. He went where he liked, and nobody owned him. Nobody called him Vince.

Strangely enough, Jane's mother approved of him. She didn't usually approve of the boys Jane went out with. Maybe she approved of him because it was obvious to her that no bad results would follow from Jane's going out with him: no heartaches, no heaviness, nothing burdensome. None of what she called *consequences*. Consequences: the weightiness of the body, the growing flesh hauled around like a bundle, the tiny frill-framed goblin head in the carriage. Babies and marriage, in that order. This was how she understood men and their furtive, fumbling, threatening desires, because Jane herself had been a consequence. She had been a mistake, she had been a war baby. She had been a crime that had needed to be paid for, over and over.

By the time she was sixteen, Jane had heard enough about this to last her several lifetimes. In her mother's account of the way things were, you were young briefly and then you fell. You plummeted downwards like an over-ripe apple and hit the ground with a squash; you fell, and everything about you fell too. You got fallen arches and a fallen womb, and your hair and teeth fell out. That's what having a baby did to you. It subjected you to the force of gravity.

This is how she remembers her mother, still: in terms of a pendulous, drooping, wilting motion. Her sagging breasts, the downturned lines around her mouth. Jane conjures her up: there she is, as usual, sitting at the kitchen table with a cup of cooling tea, exhausted after her job clerking at Eaton's department store, standing all day behind the jewellery counter with her bum stuffed into a girdle and her swelling feet crammed into the mandatory medium-heeled shoes, smiling her envious, disapproving smile at the spoiled customers who turned up their noses at pieces of glittering junk she herself could never afford to buy. Jane's mother sighs, picks at the canned spaghetti Jane has heated up for her. Silent words waft out of her like stale talcum powder: *What can you expect*, always a statement, never a question. Jane tries at this distance for pity, but comes up with none.

As for Jane's father, he'd run away from home when Jane was five, leaving her mother in the lurch. That's what her mother called it – 'running away from home' – as if he'd been an irresponsible child. Money arrived from time to time, but that was the sum total of his contribution to family life. Jane resented him for it, but she didn't blame him. Her mother inspired in almost everyone who encountered her a vicious desire for escape.

Jane and Vincent would sit out in the cramped backyard of Jane's house, which was one of the squinty-windowed little stuccoed wartime bungalows at the bottom of the hill. At the top of the hill were the richer houses, and the richer people: the girls who owned cashmere sweaters, at least one of them, instead of the Orlon and lambswool so familiar to Jane. Vincent lived about halfway up the hill. He still had a father, in theory.

They would sit against the back fence, near the spindly cosmos flowers[2] that passed for a garden, as far away from the house itself as they could get. They would drink gin, decanted by Vincent from his father's liquor hoard and smuggled in an old military pocket flask he'd picked up somewhere. They would imitate their mothers.

'I pinch and I scrape and I work my fingers to the bone, and what thanks do I get?' Vincent would say peevishly. 'No help from you, Sonny Boy. You're just like your father. Free as the birds, out all night, do as you like and you don't care one pin about anyone else's feelings. Now take out that garbage.'

'It's love that does it to you,' Jane would reply, in the resigned, ponderous voice of her mother. 'You wait and see, my girl. One of these days you'll come down off your devil-may-care high horse.' As Jane said this, and even though she was making fun, she could picture love, with a capital L, descending out of the sky towards her like a huge foot. Her mother's life had been a disaster, but in her own view an inevitable disaster, as in songs and movies. It was Love that was responsible, and in the face of Love, what could be done? Love was like a steamroller. There was no avoiding it, it went over you and you came out flat.

Jane's mother waited, fearfully and uttering warnings, but with a sort of gloating relish, for the same thing to happen to Jane. Every time Jane went out with a new boy her mother inspected him as a potential agent of downfall. She distrusted most of these boys; she distrusted their sulky, pulpy mouths, their eyes half-closed in the up-drifting smoke of their cigarettes, their slow, sauntering manner of walking, their clothing that was too tight, too full: too full of their bodies. They looked this way even when they weren't putting on the sulks and swaggers, when they were trying to appear bright-eyed and industrious and polite for Jane's mother's benefit, saying goodbye at the front door, dressed in their shirts and ties and their pressed heavy-date suits. They couldn't help the way they looked, the way they were. They were helpless; one kiss in a dark corner would reduce them to speechlessness; they were sleepwalkers in their own liquid bodies. Jane, on the other hand, was wide awake.

Jane and Vincent did not exactly go out together. Instead they made fun of going out. When the coast was clear and Jane's mother wasn't home, Vincent

---

2 Plant with dahlia-like blossoms.

would appear at the door with his face painted bright yellow, and Jane would put her bathrobe on back to front and they would order Chinese food and alarm the delivery boy and eat sitting cross-legged on the floor, clumsily, with chopsticks. Or Vincent would turn up in a threadbare thirty-year-old suit and a bowler hat and a cane, and Jane would rummage around in the cupboard for a discarded church-going hat of her mother's; with smashed cloth violets and a veil, and they would go downtown and walk around, making loud remarks about the passersby, pretending to be old, or poor, or crazy. It was thoughtless and in bad taste, which was what they both liked about it.

Vincent took Jane to the graduation formal, and they picked out her dress together at one of the second-hand clothing shops Vincent frequented, giggling at the shock and admiration they hoped to cause. They hesitated between a flame-red with falling-off sequins and a backless hip-hugging black with a plunge front, and chose the black, to go with Jane's hair. Vincent sent a poisonous-looking lime-green orchid, the colour of her eyes, he said, and Jane painted her eyelids and fingernails to match. Vincent wore white tie and tails, and a top hat, all frayed Sally-Ann[3] issue and ludicrously too large for him. They tangoed around the gymnasium, even though the music was not a tango, under the tissue-paper flowers, cutting a black swath through the sea of pastel tulle, unsmiling, projecting a corny sexual menace, Vincent with Jane's long pearl necklace clenched between his teeth.

The applause was mostly for him, because of the way he was adored. Though mostly by the girls, thinks Jane. But he seemed to be popular enough among the boys as well. Probably he told them dirty jokes, in the proverbial locker room. He knew enough of them.

As he dipped Jane backwards, he dropped the pearls and whispered in her ear, 'No belts, no pins, no pads, no chafing.' It was from an ad for tampons, but it was also their leitmotif. It was what they both wanted: freedom from the world of mothers, the world of precautions, the world of burdens and fate and heavy female constraints upon the flesh. They wanted a life without consequences. Until recently, they'd managed it.

The scientists have melted the entire length of the young sailor now, at least the upper layer of him. They've been pouring warm water over him, gently and patiently; they don't want to thaw him too abruptly. It's as if John Torrington is asleep and they don't want to startle him.

Now his feet have been revealed. They're bare, and white rather than beige; they look like the feet of someone who's been walking on a cold floor, on a winter day. That is the quality of the light that they reflect: winter sunlight, in early morning. There is something intensely painful to Jane about the absence of socks. They could have left him his socks. But maybe the others needed them. His big toes are tied together with a strip of cloth; the man talking says this was to keep the body tidily packaged for burial, but Jane is not convinced. His arms are tied to his body, his ankles are tied

---

3 Salvation Army.

together. You do that when you don't want a person walking around.

This part is almost too much for Jane; it is too reminiscent. She reaches for the channel switcher, but luckily the show (it is only a show, it's only another show) changes to two of the historical experts, analyzing the clothing. There's a close-up of John Torrington's shirt, a simple, high-collared, pin-striped white-and-blue cotton, with mother-of-pearl buttons. The stripes are a printed pattern, rather than a woven one; woven would have been more expensive. The trousers are grey linen. Ah, thinks Jane. Wardrobe. She feels better: this is something she knows about. She loves the solemnity, the reverence, with which the stripes and buttons are discussed. An interest in the clothing of the present is frivolity, an interest in the clothing of the past is archaeology; a point Vincent would have appreciated. After high school, Jane and Vincent both got scholarships to university, although Vincent had appeared to study less, and did better. That summer they did everything together. They got summer jobs at the same hamburger heaven, they went to movies together after work, although Vincent never paid for Jane. They still occasionally dressed up in old clothes and pretended to be a weird couple, but it no longer felt careless and filled with absurd invention. It was beginning to occur to them that they might conceivably end up looking like that.

In her first year at university Jane stopped going out with other boys: she needed a part-time job to help pay her way, and that and the schoolwork and Vincent took up all her time. She thought she might be in love with Vincent. She thought that maybe they should make love, to find out. She had never done such a thing, entirely; she had been too afraid of the untrustworthiness of men, of the gravity of love, too afraid of consequences. She thought, however, that she might trust Vincent.

But things didn't go that way. They held hands, but they didn't hug; they hugged, but they didn't pet; they kissed, but they didn't neck. Vincent liked looking at her, but he liked it so much he would never close his eyes. She would close hers and then open them, and there would be Vincent, his own eyes shining in the light from the streetlamp or the moon, peering at her inquisitively as if waiting to see what odd female thing she would do next, for his delighted amusement. Making love with Vincent did not seem altogether possible.

(Later, after she had flung herself into the current of opinion that had swollen to a river by the late sixties, she no longer said 'making love'; she said 'having sex.' But it amounted to the same thing. You had sex, and love got made out of it whether you liked it or not. You woke up in a bed or more likely on a mattress, with an arm around you, and found yourself wondering what it might be like to keep on doing it. At that point Jane would start looking at her watch. She had no intention of being left in any lurches. She would do the leaving herself. And she did.)

Jane and Vincent wandered off to different cities. They wrote each other postcards. Jane did this and that. She ran a co-op food store in Vancouver, did the financial stuff for a diminutive theatre in Montreal, acted as managing editor for a small publisher, ran the publicity for a dance company. She had a head for details and for adding up small sums – having to scrape her way through university had been instructive – and such jobs were often available if you didn't demand much money for doing them. Jane could see no reason to tie herself down, to make any sort of soul-stunting commitment, to anything or anyone. It was the early seventies; the old heavy women's world of girdles and precautions and consequences had been swept away. There were a lot of windows opening, a lot of doors: you could look in, then you could go in, then you could come out again.

She lived with several men, but in each of the apartments there were always cardboard boxes, belonging to her, that she never got around to unpacking; just as well, because it was that much easier to move out. When she got past thirty she decided it might be nice to have a child, some time, later. She tried to figure our a way of doing this without becoming a mother. Her own mother had moved to Florida, and sent rambling, grumbling letters, to which Jane did not often reply.

Jane moved back to Toronto, and found it ten times more interesting than when she'd left it. Vincent was already there. He'd come back from Europe, where he'd been studying film; he'd opened a design studio. He and Jane met for lunch, and it was the same: the same air of conspiracy between them, the same sense of their own potential for outrageousness. They might still have been sitting in Jane's garden, beside the cosmos flowers, drinking forbidden gin and making fun.

Jane found herself moving in Vincent's circles, or were they orbits? Vincent knew a great many people, people of all kinds; some were artists and some wanted to be, and some wanted to know the ones who were. Some had money to begin with, some made money; they all spent it. There was a lot more talk about money, these days, or among these people. Few of them knew how to manage it, and Jane found herself helping them out. She developed a small business among them, handling their money. She would gather it in, put it away safely for them, tell them what they could spend, dole out an allowance. She would note with interest the things they bought, filing their receipted bills: what furniture, what clothing, which *objets*. They were delighted with their money, enchanted with it. It was like milk and cookies for them, after school. Watching them play with their money, Jane felt responsible and indulgent, and a little matronly. She stored her own money carefully away, and eventually bought a townhouse with it.

All this time she was with Vincent, more or less. They'd tried being lovers but had not made a success of it. Vincent had gone along with this scheme because Jane had wanted it, but he was elusive, he would not make declarations. What worked with other men did not work with him: appeals to his protective instincts, pretences at jealousy, requests to remove stuck lids from jars. Sex with him was more like a musical workout. He couldn't take it seriously, and accused her of being too solemn about it. She thought he might be gay, but was afraid to ask him; she dreaded feeling irrelevant to him, excluded. It took them months to get back to normal.

He was older now, they both were. He had thinning temples and a widow's peak, and his bright inquisitive eyes had receded even farther into his head. What went on between them continued to look like a courtship, but was not one. He was always bringing her things: a new, peculiar food to eat, a new grotesquerie to see, a new piece of gossip, which he would present to her with a sense of occasion, like a flower. She in her turn appreciated him. It was like a yogic exercise, appreciating Vincent; it was like appreciating an anchovy, or a stone. He was not everyone's taste.

There's a black-and-white print on the television, then another: the nineteenth century's version of itself, in etchings. Sir John Franklin, older and fatter than Jane had supposed; the *Terror* and the *Erebus*, locked fast in the crush of the ice. In the high Arctic, a hundred and fifty years ago, it's the dead of winter. There is no sun at all, no moon; only the rustling northern lights, like electronic music, and the hard little stars.

What did they do for love, on such a ship, at such a time? Furtive solitary gropings, confused and mournful dreams, the sublimation of novels. The usual, among those who have become solitary.

Down in the hold, surrounded by the creaking of the wooden hull and the stale odours of men far too long enclosed, John Torrington lies dying. He must have known it; you can see it on his face. He turns toward Jane his tea-coloured look of puzzled reproach.

Who held his hand, who read to him, who brought him water? Who, if anyone, loved him? And what did they tell him about whatever it was that was killing him? Consumption, brain fever, Original Sin. All those Victorian reasons, which meant nothing and were the wrong ones. But they must have been comforting. If you are dying, you want to know why.

In the eighties, things started to slide. Toronto was not so much fun any more. There were too many people, too many poor people. You could see them begging on the streets, which were clogged with fumes and cars. The cheap artists' studios were torn down or converted to coy and upscale office space; the artists had migrated elsewhere. Whole streets were torn up or knocked down. The air was full of windblown grit.

People were dying. They were dying too early. One of Jane's clients, a man who owned an antique store, died almost overnight of bone cancer. Another, a woman who was an entertainment lawyer, was trying on a dress in a boutique and had a heart attack. She fell over and they called the ambulance, and she was dead on arrival. A theatrical producer died of AIDS, and a photographer; the lover of the photographer shot himself, either out of grief or because he knew he was next. A friend of a friend died of emphysema, another of viral pneumonia, another of hepatitis picked up on a tropical vacation, another of spinal meningitis. It was as if they had been weakened by some mysterious agent, a thing like a colourless gas, scentless and invisible, so that any germ that happened along could invade their bodies, take them over.

Jane began to notice news items of the kind she'd once skimmed over. Maple groves dying of acid rain, hormones in the beef, mercury in the fish, pesticides in the vegetables, poison sprayed on the fruit, God knows what in the drinking water. She subscribed to a bottled spring-water service and felt better for a few weeks, then read in the paper that it wouldn't do her much good, because whatever it was had been seeping into everything. Each time you took a breath, you breathed some of it in. She thought about moving out of the city, then read about toxic dumps, radioactive waste, concealed here and there in the countryside and masked by the lush, deceitful green of waving trees.

Vincent has been dead for less than a year. He was not put into the permafrost or frozen in ice. He went into the Necropolis, the only Toronto cemetery of whose general ambience he approved; he got flower bulbs planted on top of him, by Jane and others. Mostly by Jane. Right now John Torrington, recently thawed after a hundred and fifty years, probably looks better than Vincent.

A week before Vincent's forty-third birthday, Jane went to see him in the hospital. He was in for tests. Like fun he was. He was in for the unspeakable, the unknown. He was in for a mutated virus that didn't even have a name yet. It was creeping up his spine, and when it reached his brain it would kill him. It was not, as they said, responding to treatment. He was in for the duration.

It was white in his room, wintry. He lay packed in ice, for the pain. A white sheet wrapped him, his white thin feet poked out the bottom of it. They were so pale and cold. Jane took one look at him, laid out on ice like a salmon, and began to cry.

'Oh Vincent,' she said. 'What will I do without you?' This sounded awful. It sounded like Jane and Vincent making fun, of obsolete books, obsolete movies, their obsolete mothers. It also sounded selfish: here she was, worrying about herself and her future, when Vincent was the one who was sick. But it was true. There would be a lot less to do, altogether, without Vincent.

Vincent gazed up at her; the shadows under his eyes were cavernous. 'Lighten up,' he said, not very loudly, because he could not speak very loudly now. By this time she was sitting down, leaning forward; she was holding one of his hands. It was thin as the claw of a bird. 'Who says I'm going to die?' He spent a moment considering this, revised it. 'You're right,' he said. 'They got me. It was the Pod People from outer space. They said, "All I want is your poddy." '

Jane cried more. It was worse because he was trying to be funny. 'But what *is* it?' she said. 'Have they found out yet?'

Vincent smiled his ancient, jaunty smile, his smile of detachment, of amusement. There were his beautiful teeth, juvenile as ever. 'Who knows?' he said. 'It must have been something I ate.'

Jane sat with the tears running down her face. She felt desolate: left behind, stranded. Their mothers had finally caught up to them and been proven right. There were consequences after all; but they were the consequences to things you didn't even know you'd done.

The scientists are back on the screen. They are excited, their earnest mouths are twitching, you could almost call them joyful. They know why John Torrington died; they know, at last, why the Franklin Expedition went so terribly wrong. They've snipped off pieces of John Torrington, a fingernail, a lock of hair, they've run them through machines and come out with the answers.

There is a shot of an old tin can, pulled open to show the seam. It looks like a bomb casing. A finger points: it was the tin cans that did it, a new invention back then, a new technology, the ultimate defence against starvation and scurvy. The Franklin Expedition was excellently provisioned with tin cans, stuffed full of meat and soup and soldered together with lead. The whole expedition got lead-poisoning. Nobody knew it. Nobody could taste it. It invaded their bones, their lungs, their brains, weakening them and confusing their thinking, so that at the end those that had not yet died in the ships set out in an idiotic trek across the stony, icy ground, pulling a lifeboat laden down with toothbrushes, soap, handkerchiefs, and slippers, useless pieces of junk. When they were found ten years later, they were skeletons in tattered coats, lying where they'd collapsed. They'd been heading back towards the ships. It was what they'd been eating that had killed them.

Jane switches off the television and goes into her kitchen – all white, done over the year before last, the outmoded butcher-block counters from the seventies torn out and carted away – to make herself some hot milk and rum. Then she decides against it; she won't sleep anyway. Everything in here looks ownerless. Her toaster oven, so perfect for solo dining, her microwave for the vegetables, her espresso maker – they're sitting around waiting for her departure, for this evening or forever, in order to assume their final, real appearances of purposeless objects adrift in the physical world. They might as well be pieces of an exploded spaceship orbiting the moon.

She thinks about Vincent's apartment, so carefully arranged, filled with the beautiful or deliberately ugly possessions he once loved. She thinks about his closet, with its quirky particular outfits, empty now of his arms and legs. It has all been broken up now, sold, given away.

Increasingly the sidewalk that runs past her house is cluttered with plastic drinking cups, crumpled soft-drink cans, used take-out plates. She picks them up, clears them away, but they appear again overnight, like a trail left by an army on the march or by the fleeing residents of a city under bombardment, discarding the objects that were once thought essential but are now too heavy to carry.

§ *North-West Passage* MacEwen

4: Morning in the Burned House

In the burned house I am eating breakfast.
You understand: there is no house, there is no breakfast,
yet here I am.

The spoon which was melted scrapes against
5   the bowl which was melted also.
No one else is around.

Where have they gone to, brother and sister,
mother and father? Off along the shore,
perhaps. Their clothes are still on the hangers,

10   their dishes piled beside the sink,
which is beside the woodstove
with its grate and sooty kettle,

every detail clear,
tin cup and rippled mirror.
15   The day is bright and songless,

the lake is blue, the forest watchful.
In the east a bank of cloud
rises up silently like dark bread.

I can see the swirls in the oilcloth,
20   I can see the flaws in the glass,
those flares where the sun hits them.

I can't see my own arms and legs
or know if this is a trap or blessing,
finding myself back here, where everything

25   in this house has long been over,
kettle and mirror, spoon and bowl,
including my own body,

including the body I had then,
including the body I have now
30   as I sit at this morning table, alone and happy,

bare child's feet on the scorched floorboards
(I can almost see)
in my burning clothes, the thin green shorts

and grubby yellow T-shirt
35 holding my cindery, non-existent,
radiant flesh. Incandescent.

§ *Female body and Nature* Marlatt; *House as symbol* Carib: Naipaul (2), Walcott (1); SA: Ramanujan, Alexander, Wijenaike, Hashmi; Af: Dangerembga

GWENDOLYN MACEWEN (1941–87)

From Terror and Erebus

This is the opening of MacEwen's radio-play about the ill-fated Franklin Expedition to discover the North-West Passage, a subject that has attracted increasing attention in contemporary Canadian literature as writers have looked towards the North as the last wilderness and found in Franklin's quest a correlative for their own exploration of imaginative spaces outside society.

[*Roaring wind which fades out to Rasmussen*]

Rasmussen

King William Island . . . latitude unmentionable.
But I'm not the first here.
They preceded me, they marked the way with bones
White as the ice is, whiter maybe,
5   The white of death, of purity . . .

But it was almost a century ago
And sometimes I find their bodies
Like shattered compasses, like sciences
Gone mad, pointing in a hundred directions at once –
10 The last whirling graph of their agony.
How could they know what I now know,
A century later, my pockets stuffed with comfortable maps –
That this was, after all, an island,
That the ice can camouflage the straits
15 And drive men into false channels,
Drive men into white, sliding traps . . ?

How could they know, even stand back and see
The nature of the place they stood on,
When no man can, no man knows where he stands

20   Until he leaves his place, looks back and knows.
      Ah, Franklin! I would like to find you

      Now, your body spreadeagled like a star,
      A human constellation in the snow.
         The earth insists
25   There is but one geography, but then
      There is another still –
      The complex, crushed geography of men.
      You carried all maps within you;
      Land masses moved in relation to you –
30   As though you created the Passage
      By willing it to be.
         Ah, Franklin!
      To follow you one does not need geography.
      At least not totally, but more of that
35   Instrumental knowledge the bones have,
      Their limits, their measurings.
      The eye creates the horizon,
      The ear invents the wind,
      The hand reaching out from a parka sleeve
40   By touch demands that the touched thing be.

      [*Music and more wind sound effects, fade out*]

      Rasmussen

      So I've followed you here
      Like a dozen others, looking for relics of your ships, your men.
      Here to this awful monastery
         where you, where Crozier died,
45   and all the men with you died,
      Seeking a passage from imagination to reality,
      Seeking a passage from land to land by sea.

      Now in the arctic night
      I can almost suppose you did not die,
50   But are somewhere walking between
      The icons of ice, pensively like a priest,
      Wrapped in the cold holiness of snow, of your own memory . . .

      [*Music bridge to* Franklin, *wind sound effects*]

      Franklin

      I brought them here, a hundred and twenty-nine men,

Led them into this bottleneck,
55   This white asylum.
I chose the wrong channel and
The ice folded in around us,
Gnashing its jaws, folded in around us . . .

The ice clamps and will not open.
60   For a year it has not opened
Though we bash against it
Like lunatics at padded walls.

My ships, The Terror, The Erebus
Are learning the meanings of their names.
65   What madman christened them
The ships of Terror and of Hell?
In open sea they did four knots;
Here, they rot and cannot move at all.

Another winter in the ice,
70   The second one for us, folds in.
Latitude 70 N. November 25, 1846.
The sun has vanished.

[*Music, etc.* . . . .]

§ *North-West Passage* Atwood (3); *'Discovering' 'new' worlds* Atwood (3),
Thomas, King; Aus: McAuley; NZSP: Curnow

ROBERTSON DAVIES (1913–95)

From Fifth Business

These two extracts are from the opening of the first novel of Davies's 'Deptford Trilogy',
a complex sequence in which all the events are causally derived from the initial snowball episode. The narrator of *Fifth Business*, Dunstan Ramsay, is an elderly schoolteacher who reviews his earlier life in a confessional mode and often, as in the second
extract included here, adopts an ironic and distancing tone towards Deptford, the
small town where he grew up. In later life he involves himself with a 'world of wonders' (the title of the trilogy's third part), variously represented by myth, magic and
hagiography (saints' lives), all of which offer escape from 'Deptford' values, which he
views as narrow-minded and puritanical.

My lifelong involvement with Mrs Dempster began at 5.58 o'clock p.m. on
27 December 1908, at which time I was ten years and seven months old.

I am able to date the occasion with complete certainty because that afternoon I had been sledding with my lifelong friend and enemy Percy Boyd Staunton, and we had quarrelled, because his fine new Christmas sled would not go as fast as my old one. Snow was never heavy in our part of the world, but this Christmas it had been plentiful enough almost to cover the tallest spears of dried grass in the fields: in such snow his sled with its tall runners and foolish steering apparatus was clumsy and apt to stick, whereas my low-slung old affair would almost have slid on grass without snow.

The afternoon had been humiliating for him, and when Percy was humiliated he was vindictive. His parents were rich, his clothes were fine, and his mittens were of skin and came from a store in the city, whereas mine were knitted by my mother; it was manifestly wrong, therefore, that his splendid sled should not go faster than mine, and when such injustice showed itself Percy became cranky. He slighted my sled, scoffed at my mittens, and at last came right out and said that his father was better than my father. Instead of hitting him, which might have started a fight that could have ended in a draw or even a defeat for me, I said, all right, then, I would go home and he could have the field to himself. This was crafty of me, for I knew it was getting on for suppertime, and one of our home rules was that nobody, under any circumstances, was to be late for a meal. So I was keeping the home rule, while at the same time leaving Percy to himself.

As I walked back to the village he followed me, shouting fresh insults. When I walked, he taunted, I staggered like an old cow; my woollen cap was absurd beyond all belief; my backside was immense and wobbled when I walked; and more of the same sort, for his invention was not lively. I said nothing, because I knew that this spited him more than any retort, and that every time he shouted at me he lost face.

Our village was so small that you came on it at once; it lacked the dignity of outskirts. I darted up our street, putting on speed, for I had looked ostentatiously at my new Christmas dollar watch (Percy had a watch but was not let wear it because it was too good) and saw that it was 5.57; just time to get indoors, wash my hands in the noisy, splashy way my parents seemed to like, and be in my place at six, my head bent for grace. Percy was by this time hopping mad, and I knew I had spoiled his supper and probably his whole evening. Then the unforeseen took over.

Walking up the street ahead of me were the Reverend Amasa Dempster and his wife; he had her arm tucked in his and was leaning towards her in the protective way he had. I was familiar with this sight, for they always took a walk at this time, after dark and when most people were at supper, because Mrs Dempster was going to have a baby, and it was not the custom in our village for pregnant women to show themselves boldly in the streets – not if they had any position to keep up, and of course the Baptist minister's wife had a position. Percy had been throwing snowballs at me, from time to time, and I had ducked them all; I had a boy's sense of when a snowball was coming, and I knew Percy. I was sure that he would try to land one last, insulting snowball between my shoulders before I ducked into our house. I stepped briskly – not running, but not dawdling – in front of the Dempsters just as Percy threw, and the snowball hit Mrs Dempster on the back of the head. She gave a cry and, clinging to her husband, slipped to the ground; he might have caught her if he had not turned at once to see who had thrown the snowball.

I had meant to dart into our house, but I was unnerved by hearing Mrs Dempster; I had never heard an adult cry in pain before and the sound was terrible to me. Falling, she burst into nervous tears, and suddenly there she was, on the ground, with her husband kneeling beside her, holding her in his arms and speaking to her in terms of endearment that were strange and embarrassing to me; I had never heard married people – or any people – speak unashamedly loving words before. I knew that I was watching a 'scene', and my parents had always warned against scenes as very serious breaches of propriety. I stood gaping, and then Mr Dempster became conscious of me.

'Dunny,' he said – I did not know he knew my name – 'lend us your sleigh to get my wife home.'

I was contrite and guilty, for I knew that the snowball had been meant for me, but the Dempsters did not seem to think of that. He lifted his wife on my sled, which was not hard because she was a small, girlish woman, and as I pulled it towards their house he walked beside it, very awkwardly bent over her, supporting her and uttering soft endearment and encouragement, for she went on crying, like a child.

Their house was not far away – just around the corner, really – but by the time I had been there, and seen Mr Dempster take his wife inside, and found myself unwanted outside, it was a few minutes after six, and I was late for supper. But I pelted home (pausing only for a moment at the scene of the accident), washed my hands, slipped into my place at table, and made my excuse, looking straight into my mother's sternly interrogative eyes. I gave my story a slight historical bias, leaning firmly but not absurdly on my own role as the Good Samaritan. I suppressed any information or guesswork about where the snowball had come from, and to my relief my mother did not pursue that aspect of it. She was much more interested in Mrs Dempster, and when supper was over and the dishes washed she told my father she thought she would just step over to the Dempsters' and see if there was anything she could do.

On the face of it this was a curious decision of my mother's, for of course we were Presbyterians, and Mrs Dempster was the wife of the Baptist parson. Not that there was any ill-will among the denominations in our village, but it was understood that each looked after its own, unless a situation got too big, when outside help might be called in. But my mother was, in a modest way, a specialist in matters relating to pregnancy and childbirth; Dr McCausland had once paid her the great compliment of saying that 'Mrs Ramsay had her head screwed on straight'; she was ready to put this levelness of head at the service of almost anybody who needed it. And she had a tenderness, never obviously displayed, for poor, silly Mrs Dempster, who was not twenty-one yet and utterly unfit to be a preacher's wife.

So off she went, and I read my Christmas annual of the *Boy's Own Paper*, and my father read something that looked hard and had small print, and my older brother Willie read *The Cruise of the 'Cachalot'* , all of us sitting round the base-burner with our feet on the nickel guard, till half-past eight, and then we boys were sent to bed. I have never been quick to go to sleep, and I lay awake until the clock downstairs struck half-past nine, and shortly after that I heard my mother return. There was a stove-pipe in our house that came from the general living-room into the upstairs hall, and it was a fine conductor of sound. I crept out into the hall – Willie slept like a bear – put my ear as near to it as the heat permitted and heard my mother say:

'I've just come back for a few things. I'll probably be all night. Get me all the baby blankets out of the trunk, and then go right down to Ruckle's and make him get you a big roll of cotton wool from the store – the finest he has – and bring it to the Dempsters'. The doctor says if it isn't a big roll to get two.'

'You don't mean it's coming now?'

'Yes. Away early. Don't wait up for me.'

But of course he did wait up for her, and it was four in the morning when she came home, self-possessed and grim, as I could tell from her voice as I heard them talking before she returned to the Dempsters' – why, I did not know. And I lay awake too, feeling guilty and strange.

That was how Paul Dempster, whose reputation is doubtless familiar to you (though that was not the name under which he gained it), came to be born early on the morning of 28 December in 1908. . . .

Village life has been so extensively explored by movies and television during recent years that you may shrink from hearing more about it. I shall be as brief as I can, for it is not by piling up detail that I hope to achieve my picture, but by putting the emphasis where I think it belongs.

Once it was the fashion to represent villages as places inhabited by laughable, lovable simpletons, unspotted by the worldliness of city life, though occasionally shrewd in rural concerns. Later it was the popular thing to show villages as rotten with vice, and especially such sexual vice as Krafft-Ebing[1] might have been surprised to uncover in Vienna; incest, sodomy, bestiality, sadism, and masochism were supposed to rage behind the lace curtains and in the haylofts, while a rigid piety was professed in the streets. Our village never seemed to me to be like that. It was more varied in what it offered to the observer than people from bigger and more sophisticated places generally think, and if it had sins and follies and roughnesses, it also had much to show of virtue, dignity, and even of nobility.

It was called Deptford and lay on the Thames River about fifteen miles east of Pittstown, our county town and nearest big place. We had an official

---

1 Late nineteenth-century German physician and neurologist recognized in his own day as an authority on deviant sexual behaviour.

population of about five hundred, and the surrounding farms probably brought the district up to eight hundred souls. We had five churches: the Anglican, poor but believed to have some mysterious social supremacy; the Presbyterian, solvent and thought – chiefly by itself – to be intellectual; the Methodist, insolvent and fervent; the Baptist, insolvent and saved; the Roman Catholic, mysterious to most of us but clearly solvent, as it was frequently and, so we thought, quite needlessly repainted. We supported one lawyer, who was also the magistrate, and one banker in a private bank, as such things still existed at that time. We had two doctors: Dr McCausland who was reputed to be clever, and Dr Staunton, who was Percy's father and who was also clever, but in the realm of real estate – he was a great holder of mortgages and owned several farms. We had a dentist, a wretch without manual skill, whose wife underfed him, and who had positively the dirtiest professional premises I have ever seen; and a veterinarian who drank but could rise to an occasion. We had a canning factory, which operated noisily and feverishly when there was anything to can; also a sawmill and a few shops.

The village was dominated by a family called Athelstan, who had done well out of lumber early in the nineteenth century; they owned Deptford's only three-storey house, which stood by itself on the way to the cemetery; most of our houses were of wood, and some of them stood on piles, for the Thames had a trick of flooding. One of the remaining Athelstans lived across the street from us, a poor demented old woman who used from time to time to escape from her nurse-housekeeper and rush into the road, where she threw herself down, raising a cloud of dust like a hen having a dirt-bath, shouting loudly, 'Christian men, come and help me!' It usually took the housekeeper and at least one other person to pacify her; my mother often assisted in this way, but I could not do so for the old lady disliked me – I seemed to remind her of some false friend in the past. But I was interested in her madness and longed to talk with her, so I always rushed to the rescue when she made one of her breaks for liberty.

My family enjoyed a position of modest privilege, for my father was the owner and editor of the local weekly paper, *The Deptford Banner*. It was not a very prosperous enterprise, but with the job-printing plant it sustained us and we never wanted for anything. My father, as I learned later, never did a gross business of $5000 in any year that he owned it. He was not only publisher and editor, but chief mechanic and printer as well, helped by a melancholy youth called Jumper Saul and a girl called Nell Bullock. It was a good little paper, respected and hated as a proper local paper should be; the editorial comment, which my father composed directly on the typesetting machine, was read carefully every week. So we were, in a sense, the literary leaders of the community, and my father had a seat on the Library Board along with the magistrate.

Our household, then, was representative of the better sort of life in the village, and we thought well of ourselves. Some of this good opinion arose from being Scots; my father had come from Dumfries as a young man, but my mother's family had been three generations in Canada without having become a whit less Scots than when her grandparents left Inverness. The Scots, I believed until I was aged at least twenty-five, were the salt of the earth, for although this was never said in our household it was one of those accepted truths which do not need to he laboured. By far the majority of the Deptford people had come to Western Ontario from the south of England, so we were not surprised that they looked to us, the Ramsays, for common sense, prudence, and right opinions on virtually everything.

Cleanliness, for example. My mother was clean – oh, but she was clean! Our privy set the sanitary tone of the village. We depended on wells in Deptford, and water for all purposes was heated in a tank called a 'cistern' on the side of the kitchen range. Every house had a privy, and these ranked from dilapidated, noisome shacks to some quite smart edifices, of which our own was clearly among the best. There has been much hilarity about privies in the years since they became rarities, but they were not funny buildings, and if they were not to become disgraceful they needed a lot of care.

As well as this temple of hygiene we had a 'chemical closet' in the house, for use when someone was unwell; it was so capricious and smelly, however, that it merely added a new misery to illness and was rarely set going.

That is all that seems necessary to say about Deptford at present: any necessary additional matter will present itself as part of my narrative. We were serious people, missing nothing in our community and feeling ourselves in no way inferior to larger places. We did, however, look with pitying amusement on Bowles Corners, four miles distant and with a population of one hundred and fifty. To live in Bowles Corners, we felt, was to be rustic beyond redemption.

§ *Small town* Duncan, Leacock, Ross, Munro

PHYLLIS WEBB (1927–)

Marvell's Garden

> Marvell's garden, that place of solitude,
> is not where I'd choose to live
> yet is the fixed sundial
> that turns me round
> 5   unwillingly
> in a hot glade
> as closer, closer I come to contradiction
> to the shade green within the green shade.

---

8 **shade green . . . green shade**: like the sundial and time references, alluding to Marvell's poem, 'The Garden'.

The garden where Marvell scorned love's solicitude –
10   that dream – and played instead an arcane solitaire,
shuffling his thoughts like shadowy chance
across the shrubs of ecstasy,
and cast the myths away to flowering hours
as yes, his mind, that sea, caught at green
15   thoughts shadowing a green infinity.

And yet Marvell's garden was not Plato's
garden – and yet – he did care more for the form
of things than for the thing itself –
ideas and visions,
20   resemblances and echoes,
things seeming and being
not quite what they were.

That was his garden, a kind of attitude
struck out of an earth too carefully attended,
25   wanting to be left alone
And I don't blame him for that.
God knows, too many fences fence us out
and his garden closed in on Paradise.

On Paradise! When I think of his hymning
30   Puritans in the Bermudas, the bright oranges
lighting up that night! When I recall
his rustling tinsel hopes
beneath the cold decree of steel,
Oh, I have wept for some new convulsion
35   to tear together this world and his.

But then I saw his luminous plumèd Wings
prepared for flight,
and then I heard him singing glory
in a green tree,
40   and then I caught the vest he'd laid aside
all blest with fire.

And I have gone walking slowly in
his garden of necessity

29–31 Cf. Marvell's 'Bermudas'.   17–18 Cf. Plato's world of the Forms, ideal essences
located outside the everyday world.

leaving brothers, lovers, Christ
45 outside my walls
where they have wept without
and I within.

§ *Responses to European texts*: Af: Coetzee; Carib: Lamming (2), Walcott
(4); SEA: Lim (2), Lee Tzu Pheng, Somtow

ROBERT KROETSCH (1927–)

1: Stone Hammer Poem

1
This stone
become a hammer
of stone, this maul

is the colour
5 of bone (no,
bone is the colour
of this stone maul).
The rawhide loops
are gone, the
10 hand is gone, the
buffalo's skull
is gone;

the stone is
shaped like the skull
15 of a child.

2
This paperweight on my desk

where I begin
this poem   was

found in a wheatfield
20 lost (this hammer,
this poem).

Cut to a function,
this stone was
(the hand is   gone –

3

25 Grey, two-headed,
the pemmican maul

fell from the travois or
a boy playing   lost it in
the prairie wool or
30 the squaw   left it in
the brain of a buffalo or

It is a million
years older than
the hand that
35 chipped stone or
raised slough
water (or blood) or

4
This stone maul
was found.

40 In the field
my grandfather
thought
was his

my father
45 thought was his

5
It is a stone
old as the last
Ice Age, the
retreating/ the
50 recreating ice,
the retreating
buffalo, the
retreating Indians

(the saskatoons bloom
55 white (infrequently
the chokecherries the
highbush cranberries the
pincherries bloom

---

26 pemmican: Native American cake of dried meat mixed with melted fat.

60　white along the barbed
　　wire fence (the
　　pemmican　　winter

6
This stone maul
stopped a plow
long enough for one
65　*Gott im Himmel.*

The Blackfoot (the
Cree?) not

finding the maul
cursed.

70　?did he curse
　　?did he try to
　　go back
　　?what happened
　　I have to/ I want
75　to know (not know)
　　?WHAT HAPPENED

7
The poem
is the stone
chipped and hammered
80　until it is shaped
　　like the stone
　　hammer, the maul.

8
Now the field is
mine because
85　I gave it
　　(for a price)

to a young man
(with a growing son)
who did not

90　notice that the land
　　did not belong

---

65 *Gott im Himmel*: expletive: 'God in Heaven'.

to the Indian who
gave it to the Queen
(for a price) who
95   gave it to the CPR
(for a price) which
gave it to my grandfather
(for a price) who
gave it to my father
100   (50 bucks an acre
Gott im Himmel I cut
down all the trees I
picked up all the stones) who

gave it to his son
105   (who sold it)

9
This won't
surprise you.

My grandfather
lost the stone maul.

10
110   My father (retired)
grew raspberries
He dug in his potato patch.
He drank one glass of wine
each morning.
115   He was lonesome
for death.

He was lonesome for the
hot wind on his face, the smell
of horses, the distant
120   hum of a threshing machine,
the oilcan he carried, the weight
of a crescent wrench in his hind pocket.

He was lonesome for his absent
son and his daughters
125   for his wife, for his own
brothers and sisters and
his own mother and father.

---

95 **CPR**: Canadian Pacific Railway.

He found the stone maul
on a rockpile in the
130   north-west corner of what
he thought of
as his wheatfield.

He kept it (the
stone maul) on the railing
135   of the back porch in
a raspberry basket.

11
I keep it
on my desk
(the stone).

140   Sometimes I use it
in the (hot) wind
(to hold down paper)

smelling a little of cut
grass or maybe even of
145   ripening wheat or of
buffalo blood hot
in the dying sun.

Sometimes I write
my poems for that

150   stone hammer.

§ *Ancestor poems* Purdy (1), Mandel, Atwood (1), Bowering; *Origins*
Laurence, Wiebe, Marlatt

2: *From* The Moment of the Discovery of America Continues

I was a child – I don't know how old – when my parents took me to
Spring Lake, to a picnic. Spring Lake is a small, round lake, surrounded by
willows and poplars; it was the centre of the community that my mother
grew up in – in the parklands southeast of Edmonton, a few miles from
the valley of the Battle River. I was playing in a large, shallow depression
in the ground, a depression that somehow wasn't natural. My father came
by, looking for me. I asked about the place where I was playing. He said,

casually, that it was a buffalow wallow.

It's where buffalo rolled and scratched, he said. He could tell me a little more – the lake never went dry, he explained, the buffalo came here to drink.

What buffalo? I asked. Or wondered, if I didn't ask. I don't remember now. When? From where? . . . Even at that young age I was secure in the illusion that the land my parents and grandparents homesteaded had had no prior occupants, animal or human. Ours was the ultimate *tabula rasa*. We were truly innocent.

There was an older boy a mile from our farm who, as we kids liked to put it, knew everything. He was so smart a lot of people thought he'd become a priest. I remember that he could recite the names and dates of kings and prime ministers from whomever was thought to be first to the latest. I asked him about buffalo wallows. He'd never even heard of buffalo wallows. But more: he made considerable show of not caring that he hadn't heard. He was educated.

My sense of the gap between me and history was growing. History as I knew it did not account for the world I lived in. Present here in this landscape, I was taking my first lesson in the idea of absence.

There was, half a mile south from our farm, a ring of stones in the prairie grass. My dad and the hired men, strangely, plowed around it. One day, again when I was a child, I ran away from home; instead of going to a neighbour's house, where I could play, I went to that ring of stones . . . and again I began to wonder. I went back home and asked my mother about those stones. She had, then, never heard of a tipi[1] ring; she said the stones were magical. I suspect now that her notion of magical went back two or three generations to the forests of southern Germany, surviving the long transcription through Wisconsin and Minnesota to the District and then the Province of Alberta. The connection between the name and the named – the importance and the failure of that connection – is one of my obsessions.

I was that day on my way to embracing the model of archaeology, against that of history. The authorized history, the given definition of history, was betraying us on those prairies. A few years after I sat in that tipi ring and cried and then began to notice and then began to wonder, a gang of dam-builders from a Battle River site came by and picked up the stones, and my father broke the sod. If history betrayed us, we too betrayed it. I remember my father one night at supper, saying out of nowhere that he'd made a mistake, letting those men pick up those stones. For reasons he couldn't understand, he felt guilty. Where I had learned the idea of absence, I was beginning to learn the idea of trace. There is always something left behind. That is the essential paradox. Even abandonment gives us memory.

I had to tell a story. I responded to those discoveries of absence, to that invisibility, to that silence, by knowing I had to make up a story. Our story.

---

1 Conical, buffalo-skin house of Plains Indian.

How do you write in a new country?

Thirty years after the experiences that I have just now described, I wrote a series of poems called 'Old Man Stories'. I had discovered the literature of the Blackfoot – the stories they might well have told along the Battle River through the many generations when that river was a kind of boundary between the Blackfoot and the Cree. The Blackfoot trickster figure was (and still is) called Old Man. And those old stories are appropriate to the new Province of Alberta:

Old Man and Fox went out hunting. They might have starved to death except that Old Man spotted four buffalo bulls lying down by a slough.

He had an idea.

'My little brother,' he said to Fox, 'there's enough meat by this slough to see us through the winter. What we have to do is this: I will pluck all the hair off you except for a tuft at the end of your tail. You will seem so funny to the bulls, they will die laughing'.

Fox, try as he might, could not think of a better plan. So he let Old Man pluck him bare, except for a tuft at the end of his tail.

First the bulls stood up to look. Then they began to laugh. Then they fell down laughing. Even then they could not keep from looking at Fox; the more they looked, the more they laughed. One by one they died laughing.

'Little brother,' Old Man said, stepping out from behind a clump of red willow, 'you were very funny. I nearly died laughing myself.' And he began to butcher the dead bulls.

It was late in the afternoon. A wind was coming up from the north. A few snowflakes were beginning to fall. 'Let it snow,' Old Man said. He was working busily while Fox sat and watched. 'We can feast until spring.'

Fox made no reply. Old Man kept on talking. 'We can dance and sing all winter. We can sleep when the blizzard blows. Cheer up, little brother.'

Again Fox did not answer. This made Old Man very mad. He turned from where he was preparing the last pack of meat. He saw Fox sitting hunched and still and gave him a poke. 'Wake up, we're ready.'

Fox fell over. He was frozen clean through. . . .

How do you write in a new country?

Our inherited literature, the literature of our European past and of eastern North America, is emphatically the literature of a people who have not lived on prairies. We had, and still have, difficulty finding names for the elements and characteristics of this landscape. The human response to this landscape is so new and ill-defined and complex that our writers come back, uneasily but compulsively, to landscape writing. Like the homesteaders before us, we are compelled to adjust and invent, to remember and forget. We feel a profound ambiguity about the past – about both its contained stories and its modes of perception.

There are, first and always, the questions of form and language. For reasons that are not very clear, the prairies developed a tradition of fiction before developing a tradition of poetry. This seems to be contradictory to the cultural experience of most societies. I suspect it has to do with the nature of the experience – in one word, often hard (that's two words). And there was available, to record that harshness, the realistic mode of fiction.

But even as I say this I ask: Might it not be possible that we now look back on the experience as having been a harsh one because the realistic (or even naturalistic) mode of fiction pictured it so? What if the prairies had been settled – as much of the United States was in the nineteenth century – at a time when the Gothic model was easily available to novelists?

The effect of perceptual models on what we see is now the concern of social and literary critics (thanks to such books as Dick Harrison's *Unnamed Country*). I was living outside of Alberta (and outside of Canada) while writing most of my fiction and poetry. Perhaps for that reason I was constantly aware that we both, and at once, record and invent these new places called Alberta and Saskatchewan. That pattern of contraries, all the possibilities implied in *record* and *invent*, for me finds its focus in the model suggested by the phrase: a local pride. (The phrase is from Williams Carlos Williams – indeed those three words are the opening of his great poem *Paterson*, about Paterson, New Jersey: a local pride.) The feeling must come from an awareness of the authenticity of our own lives. People who feel invisible try to borrow visibility from those who are visible. To understand others is surely difficult. But to understand ourselves becomes impossible if we do not see images of ourselves in the mirror – be that mirror theatre or literature or historical writing. A local pride does not exclude the rest of the world, or other experiences; rather, it makes them possible. It creates an organizing centre. Or as Williams put it, more radically: the acquiring of a local pride enables us to create our own culture – 'by lifting an environment to expression'.

How do we lift an environment to expression? How do you write in a new country?

The great sub-text of prairie literature is our oral tradition. In the face of books, magazines, films, and TV programs that are so often someone else, we talk to each other by, literally, talking.

The visit is the great prairie cultural event. People go visiting, or they go to other events in order to visit. This accounts for the predominance of the beer parlour and the church in prairie fiction. In addition, we see fictional characters going to stampedes and country dances and summer resorts – those places where we talk ourselves into existence.

Oral history is not likely to go back more than two generations – to parents and grandparents. Beyond that little remains – with huge consequences for our sense of history. Within that time-framework exists an enormous prospect of fiction-making. Individuals in a lifetime become characters. Events become story, become folklore, edge towards the conditon of myth. Many of our best novels – the novels of Margaret Laurence and Rudy Wiebe especially – assert the primacy of the act of speech over the act of writing. The poetry of Andy Suknaski acknowledges a huge and continuing debt to the oral tradition. The sophisticated sound poetry of Stephen Scobie and Doug Barbour suggests that print is merely a kind of notation for speech, as a muscial score is for music.

A local pride leads us to a concern with myths of origin. Obviously, on the prairies, there has been an enormous interest in ethnic roots – that version of the myth of origin. But now, in our growing urban centres, there is a new kind of myth emerging. Again, for writers like Laurence or Wiebe, there is available to our imaginations a new set of ancestors: the native or Métis people,[2] Big Bear,[3] Riel,[4] the fictional Tonnerre family of *The Diviners*, Dumont.[5] And I would suggest that along with this comes the urban dream that our roots are just over the horizon, in the small towns and the rural communities of the prairies. This dream of origins is already evident in Laurence's work. It is already evident in a larger Canadian context – surely it is no accident that the classics of modern Canadian writing are set in rural areas: Sheila Watson's *The Double Hook* with its setting in the Cariboo Country, Ross's Saskatchewan, Ernest Buckler's Nova Scotia in his novel *The Mountain and the Valley*. The oral tradition, become a literary tradition, points us back to our own landscape, our recent ancestors, and the characteristic expressions and modes of our own speech.

It is a kind of archaeology that makes *this place*, with all its implications, available to us for literary purposes. We have not yet grasped the whole story; we have hints and guesses that slowly persuade us towards the recognition of larger patterns. Archaeology allows the fragmentary nature of the story, against the coerced unity of traditional history. Archaeology allows for discontinuity. It allows for layering. It allows for imaginative speculation.

I am aware that it is the great French historian Michel Foucault who has formalized our understanding of the appropriateness of the archaeological method. But the prairie writer understands that appropriateness in terms of the particulars of place: newspaper files, place names, shoe boxes full of old photographs, tall tales, diaries, journals, tipi rings, weather reports, business ledgers, voting records – even the wrong-headed histories written by eastern historians become, rather than narratives of the past, archaeological deposits.

For me, one of those deposits turned out to be an old seed catalogue. I

2 People of mixed Native and European (usually French) descent. 3 Cree chief (1825?–88), who resisted federal Canadian authority in late nineteenth century; central figure in Rudy Wiebe's *The Temptations of Big Bear* (1973). 4 Louis Riel (1844–85), Métis leader and key figure in North-West Rebellion; executed for treason; self-styled 'Prophet of the New World' widely regarded as a saviour of his people; central figure in Wiebe's novel *The Scorched Wood People* (1977); also discussed in Margaret Laurence's *The Diviners* (1974). 5 Gabriel Dumont (1837–1906), Métis leader.

found a 1917 catalogue in the Glenbow archives in 1975. I translated that seed catalogue into a poem called 'Seed Catalogue'. The archaeological discovery, if I might call it that, brought together for me the oral tradition and the dream of origins.

§ *Origins/Prairies* Laurence, Ross, Kroetsch (1), Wiebe; *Adamic experience* Carib: Walcott (3); *Trickster* King, Armstrong; Carib: Brodber

ALICE MUNRO (1931–)

The Photographer

'The Photographer' is the final story in Munro's *Lives of Girls and Women*, in which Del Jordan, the narrator, undergoes a series of adolescent initiations. The story also illustrates another of the main motifs of the volume, as Del discovers the interpenetration of the extraordinary and the ordinary, coming to realize that the small town in which she lives and its inhabitants are more multi-faceted than she has hitherto appreciated.

'This town is rife with suicides,' was one of the things my mother would say, and for a long time I carried this mysterious, dogmatic statement around with me, believing it to be true – that is, believing that Jubilee had many more suicides than other places, just as Porterfield had fights and drunks, that its suicides distinguished the town like the cupola on the Town Hall. Later on my attitude towards everything my mother said became one of skepticism and disdain, and I argued that there were, in fact, very few suicides in Jubilee, that certainly their number could not exceed the statistical average, and I would challenge my mother to name them. She would go methodically along the various streets of the town, in her mind, saying, '— hanged himself, while his wife and family were at church — went out of the room after breakfast and shot himself in the head –' but there were not really so many; I was probably closer to the truth than she was.

There were two suicides by drowning, if you counted Miss Farris my old teacher. The other one was Marion Sherriff, on whose family my mother, and others, would linger with a touch of pride, saying, 'Well, there is a family that has had its share of Tragedy!' One brother had died an alcoholic, one was in the asylum at Tupperton, and Marion had walked into the Wawanash River. People always said she *walked into* it, though in the case of Miss Farris they said she *threw herself into* it. Since nobody had seen either of them do it, the difference must have come from the difference in the women themselves, Miss Farris being impulsive and dramatic in all she did, and Marion Sherriff deliberate and take-your-time.

At least that was how she looked in her picture, which was hanging in the main hall of the high school, above the case containing the Marion A. Sherriff Girls Athletic Trophy, a silver cup taken out each year and presented to the best girl athlete in the school, then put back in, after having that girl's name engraved on it. In the picture Marion Sherriff was holding a tennis racket and wearing a white pleated skirt and a white sweater with two dark stripes around the V of the neck. She had her hair parted in the middle, pinned unbecomingly back from the temples; she was stocky and unsmiling.

'Pregnant, naturally,' Fern Dogherty used to say, and Naomi said, everybody said, except my mother.

'That was never established. Why blacken her name?'

'Some fellow got her in trouble and walked out on her,' said Fern positively. 'Otherwise why drown herself, a girl seventeen?'

A time came when all the books in the library in the Town Hall were not enough for me, I had to have my own. I saw that the only thing to do with my life was to write a novel. I picked on the Sherriff family to write it about; what had happened to them isolated them, splendidly, doomed them to fiction. I changed the family name from Sherriff to Halloway, and the dead father from a storekeeper to a judge. I knew from my reading that in the families of judges, as of great landowners, degeneracy and madness were things to be counted on. The mother I could keep just as she was, just as I used to see her in the days when I went to the Anglican Church, and she was always there, gaunt and superb, with her grand trumpeting supplications. I moved them out of their house, though, transported them from the mustard-colored stucco bungalow behind the *Herald-Advance* building, where they had always lived and where even now Mrs. Sherriff kept a tidy lawn and picked-clean flower beds, and into a house of my own invention, a towered brick house with long narrow windows and *porte cochère*[1] and a great deal of surrounding shrubbery perversely cut to look like roosters, dogs, and foxes.

Nobody knew about this novel. I had no need to tell anybody. I wrote out a few bits of it and put them away, but soon I saw that it was a mistake to try to write anything down; what I wrote down might flaw the beauty and wholeness of the novel in my mind.

I carried it – the idea of it – everywhere with me, as if it were one of those magic boxes a favored character gets hold of in a fairy story: touch it and his troubles disappear. I carried it along when Jerry Storey and I walked out on the railway tracks and he told me that some day, if the world lasted, newborn babies could be stimulated with waves of electricity and would be able to compose music like Beethoven's, or like Verdi's, whatever was wanted. He explained how people could have their intelligence and their talents and preferences and desires built into them, in judicious amounts; why not?

'Like *Brave New World*?' I asked him, and he said, what was that?

---

1 Structure extending from building entrance, where vehicles discharge passengers.

I told him, and he answered chastely, 'I don't know, I never read fiction.'

I just kept hold of the idea of the novel, and felt better; it seemed to make what he said unimportant even if true. He began to sing sentimental songs with a German accent and tried goose-stepping along the rails, falling off as I knew he would.

'Be-*lieff* me if all those en-dearing jung tcharms –'

In my novel I had got rid of the older brother, the alcoholic; three tragic destinies were too much even for a book, and certainly more than I could handle. The younger brother I saw as gentle and loving, with an offensive innocence about him; pink freckled face, defenseless fattish body. Bullied at school, unable to learn arithmetic or geography, he would be happy once a year, when he was allowed to ride round and round on the merry-go-round at the Kinsmen's Fair, beatifically smiling. (I got this of course from Frankie Hall, that grown idiot who used to live out on the Flats Road, and was dead by now; he was always let ride free, all day long, and would wave at people with a royal negligence, though he never acknowledged anybody at any other time.) Boys would taunt him about his sister, about – *Caroline*! Her name was Caroline. She came ready-made into my mind, taunting and secretive, blotting out altogether that pudgy Marion, the tennis player. Was she a witch? Was she a nymphomaniac? Nothing so simple!

She was wayward and light as a leaf, and she slipped along the streets of Jubilee as if she was trying to get through a crack in an invisible wall, sideways. She had long black hair. She bestowed her gifts capriciously on men – not on good-looking young men who thought they had a right to her, not on sullen high-school heroes, athletes, with habits of conquest written on their warm-blooded faces, but on middle-aged weary husbands, defeated salesmen passing through town, even, occasionally, on the deformed and mildly deranged. But her generosity mocked them, her *bittersweet flesh, the color of peeled almonds*, burned men down quickly and left a taste of death. She was the sacrifice, spread for sex on moldy uncomfortable tombstones, pushed against the cruel bark of trees, her frail body squashed into the mud and hen dirt of barnyards, supporting the killing weight of men, but it was she, more than they, who survived.

One day a man came to take photographs at the high school. She saw him first shrouded in his photographer's black cloth, a hump of gray-black, shabby cloth behind the tripod, the big eye, the black accordion pleating of the old-fashioned camera. When he came out, what did he look like? Black hair parted in the middle, combed back in two wings, dandruff, rather narrow chest and shoulders, and a pasty, flaky skin – and in spite of his look of scruffiness and ill health, a wicked fluid energy about him, a bright unpitying smile.

He had no name in the book. He was always called *The Photographer*. He drove around the country in a high square car whose top was of flapping black cloth. The pictures he took turned out to be unusual, even frightening. People saw that in his pictures they had aged twenty or thirty years. Middle-aged people saw in their own features the terrible, growing, inescapable likeness of their dead parents; young fresh girls and men showed what gaunt or dulled or stupid faces they would have when they were fifty. Brides looked pregnant, children adenoidal. So he was not a popular photographer, though cheap. However no one liked to refuse him business; everybody was afraid of him. Children dropped into the ditches when his car was coming along the road. But Caroline ran after him, she tramped the hot roads looking for him, she waited and waylaid him and offered herself to him without the tender contempt, indifferent readiness she showed to other men, but with straining eagerness and hope and cries. And one day (when she could already feel her womb swollen *like a hard yellow gourd in her belly*), she found the car overturned beside a bridge, overturned in a ditch beside a dry creek. It was empty. He was gone. That night she walked into the Wawanash River.

That was all. Except that after she died her poor brother, looking at the picture The Photographer had taken of his sister's high-school class, saw that in this picture *Caroline's eyes were white.*

I had not worked out all the implications of this myself, but felt they were varied and powerful.

For this novel I had changed Jubilee, too, or picked out some features of it and ignored others. It became an older, darker, more decaying town, full of unpainted board fences covered with tattered posters advertising circuses, fall fairs, elections that had long since come and gone. People in it were very thin, like Caroline, or fat as bubbles. Their speech was subtle and evasive and bizarrely stupid; their platitudes crackled with madness. The season was always the height of summer – white, brutal heat, dogs lying as if dead on the sidewalks, waves of air shuddering, jellylike, over the empty highway. (But how, then – for niggling considerations of fact would pop up, occasionally, to worry me – how then was there going to be enough water in the Wawanash River? Instead of moving, head bowed, moonlight-naked, acquiescent, into its depths, Caroline would have to lie down on her face as if she was drowning herself in the bathtub.)

All pictures. The reasons for things happening I seemed vaguely to know, but could not explain; I expected all that would come clear later. The main thing was that it seemed true to me, not real but true, as if I had discovered, not made up, such people and such a story, as if that town was lying close behind the one I walked through every day.

I did not pay much attention to the real Sherriffs, once I had transformed them for fictional purposes. Bobby Sherriff, the son who had been in the asylum, came home for a while – it seemed this was something that had happened before – and was to be seen walking around Jubilee chatting with people. I had been close enough to him to hear his soft, deferential, leisurely voice, I had observed that he always looked freshly barbered, talcumed, wore clothes of good quality, was short, stout, and walked with that carefree air of enjoyment affected by those who have nothing to do. I hardly connected him with my mad Halloway brother.

Jerry Storey and I coming back from our walks could see Jubilee so plainly, now the leaves were off the trees; it lay before us in a not very complicated pattern of streets named after battles and ladies and monarchs and pioneers. Once as we walked over the trestle a car full of people from our class at school passed underneath, hooting at us, and I did have a vision, as if from outside, of how strange this was – Jerry contemplating and welcoming a future that would annihilate Jubilee and life in it, and I myself planning secretly to turn it into black fable and tie it up in my novel, and the town, the people who really were the town, just hooting car horns – to mock anybody walking, not riding, on a Sunday afternoon – and never knowing what danger they were in from us.

Every morning, starting about the middle of July, the last summer I was in Jubilee, I would walk downtown between nine and ten o'clock. I would walk as far as the *Herald-Advance* building look in their front window, and walk home. I was waiting for the results of the departmental examinations which I had written in June. The results would come to us in the mail but they always came to the paper a day or so in advance, and were taped up in the front window. If they had not come in the morning mail, they would not come that day. Every morning when I saw that there was no sheet of paper in the window, nothing but the potato shaped like a pigeon that Pork Childs had dug up in his garden, and which sat on the windowsill waiting for the double squash and deformed carrot and enormous pumpkin which would surely join it later, I felt reprieved. I could be at peace for one more day. I knew I had done badly in those exams. I had been sabotaged by love, and it was not likely I would get the scholarship which for years I and everybody else had been counting on, to carry me away from Jubilee.

One morning after I had gone down to the *Herald-Advance* I walked past the Sherriffs' house instead of going back up the main street as I usually did, and Bobby Sherriff surprised me, standing by the gate, saying, 'Good morning.'

'Good morning.'

'Could I persuade you to step into my yard and try a piece of cake? Said the spider to the fly, eh?' His good manners were humble and, I thought, ironic. 'Mother went to Toronto on the six o'clock train so I thought well, I'm up anyway, why don't I try and bake a cake?'

He held the gate open. I did not know how to get out of it. I followed him up the steps.

'It's nice and cool on the porch here. Sit over here. Would you like a glass of lemonade? I'm an expert at making lemonade.'

So I sat on the porch of the Sherriffs' house, rather hoping that nobody would go by and see me, and Bobby Sherriff brought me a piece of cake on a small plate, with a proper cake fork, and an embroidered napkin. He went back inside and brought me a glass of lemonade with ice cubes, mint leaves, and a maraschino cherry. He apologized for not bringing both the cake and the lemonade at once, on a tray; he explained to me where the trays were in the cupboard, under a great pile of plates, so that it was difficult to get one out, and he would rather be sitting here with me, he said, than down on his knees poking around in some dark old cupboard. Then he apologized for the cake, saying he was not a great baker, it was just that he liked to try some recipe once in a while, and he did feel he shouldn't offer me a cake without icing, but he had never mastered the art of making icing, he relied on his mother for that, so here it was. He said he hoped I liked mint leaves in my lemonade – as if most people were very fussy about this, and you never could tell whether they would take it into their heads to throw the mint leaves out. He behaved as if it was a great act of courtesy, of unlooked-for graciousness on my part, to sit here, to eat and drink at all.

There was a strip of carpet on the porch floorboards, which were wide, had cracks between, and were painted gray. It looked like an old hall carpet, too worn for inside. There were two brown wicker chairs, with faded, lumpy cretonne cushions, which we were sitting on, and a round wicker table. On the table was something like a china mug, or vase, with no flowers in it, but a tiny red ensign, and a Union Jack. It was one of those souvenirs that had been sold when the king and queen visited Canada in 1939; there were their youthful, royal faces, shedding kind light, as at the front of the Grade Eight classroom in the public school. Such an object on the table did not mean that the Sherriffs were particularly patriotic. These souvenirs could be found in plenty of houses in Jubilee. That was just it. The ordinariness of everything brought me up short, made me remember. *This was the Sherriffs' house.* I could see a little bit of the hallway, brown and pink wallpaper, through the screen door. That was the doorway through which Marion had walked. Going to school. Going to play tennis. Going to the Wawanash River. Marion was Caroline. She was all I had had, to start with; her act and her secrecy. I had not even thought of that when I first entered the Sherriffs' yard, or while I sat waiting on the porch for Bobby to bring me my cake. I had not thought of my novel. I hardly ever did think of it, any more. I never said to myself that I had lost it, I believed that it was carefully stored away, to be brought out some time in the future. The truth was that some damage had been done to it that I knew could not be put right. Damage had been done; Caroline and the other Halloways and their town had lost authority; I had lost faith. But I did not want to think about that, and did not.

But now I remembered with surprise how I had made it, the whole mysterious and, as it turned out, unreliable structure rising from this house, the Sherriffs, a few poor facts, and everything that was not told.

'I know you,' said Bobby Sherriff shyly. 'Didn't you think I knew who you were? You're the girl who's going to university, on scholarships.'

'I haven't got them yet.'

'You're a clever girl.'

And what happened, I asked myself, to Marion? Not to Caroline. *What happened to Marion?* What happened to Bobby Sherriff when he had to stop baking cakes and go back to the asylum? Such questions persist, in spite of novels. It is a shock, when you have dealt so cunningly, powerfully, with reality, to come back and find it still there. Would Bobby Sherriff give me a clue now, to madness? Would he say, in his courteous conversational voice, 'Napoleon was my father'? Would he spit through a crack in the floorboards and say, 'I'm sending rain over the Gobi Desert'? Was that the sort of thing they did?

'You know I went to college. The University of Toronto. Trinity College. Yes.

'I didn't win any scholarships,' he went on in a minute, as if I had asked. 'I was an average student. Mother thought they might make a lawyer out of me. It was a sacrifice to send me. The Depression, you know how nobody had any money in the Depression. Now they seem to. Oh, yes. Since the war. They're all buying. Fergus Colby, you know, down at Colby Motors, he was showing me the list he's got, people putting their names down to get the new Oldsmobiles, new Chevrolets.

'When you go to college you must look after your diet. That is very important. Anybody at college tends to eat a lot of starchy food, because it is filling and cheap. I knew a girl who used to cook in her room, she lived on macaroni and bread. Macaroni and bread! I blame my own breakdown on the food I was eating. There was no nourishment for the brain. You have to nourish the brain if you want to use the brain. What's good for that are the B vitamins. Vitamin B1, vitamin B2, vitamin B12. You've heard of those, haven't you? You get them in unpolished rice, unrefined flour – am I boring you now?'

'No,' I said guiltily. 'No, no.'

'I must beg your pardon if I do. I get carried away on this subject, I know it. Because I think my own problems – all my own problems since my young days – are related to undernourishment. From studying so hard and not replenishing the brain. Of course I did not have a first-rate brain to begin with, I never claimed that.'

I kept watching him attentively so he would not ask me again if he was boring me. He wore a soft, well-pressed yellow sport shirt, open at the neck. His skin was pink. He did resemble, distantly, Caroline's brother that I had made him into. I could smell his shaving lotion. Odd to think that he shaved, that he had hair on his face like other men, and a penis in his pants. I imagined it curled up on itself, damp and tender. He smiled at me sweetly, reasonably talking; could he read what I was thinking? There must be some secret to madness, some gift about it, something I didn't know.

He was telling me how rats, even, refused to eat white flour, because of the bleach, the chemicals that were in it. I nodded, and past his head saw Mr. Fouks come out the back door of the *Herald-Advance* building, empty a wastebasket into an incinerator, and plod back in. That back wall had no windows in it; it had certain stains, chipped bricks, a long crack running down diagonally, starting a bit before the middle and ending up at the bottom corner next to the Chainway store.

At ten o'clock the banks would open, the Canadian Bank of Commerce and the Dominion Bank across the street. At twelve-thirty, a bus would go through the town, southbound from Owen Sound to London. If anybody wanted to get on it there would be a flag out in front of Haines' Restaurant.

Bobby Sherriff talked about rats and white flour. His sister's photographed face hung in the hall of the high school, close to the persistent hiss of the drinking fountain. Her face was stubborn, unrevealing, lowered so that shadows had settled in her eyes. People's lives, in Jubilee as elsewhere, were dull, simple, amazing, and unfathomable – deep caves paved with kitchen linoleum.

It did not occur to me then that one day I would be so greedy for Jubilee. Voracious and misguided as Uncle Craig out at Jenkin's Bend, writing his history, I would want to write things down.

I would try to make lists. A list of all the stores and businesses going up and down the main street and who owned them, a list of family names, names on the tombstones in the cemetery and any inscriptions underneath. A list of the titles of movies that played at the Lyceum Theatre from 1938 to 1950, roughly speaking. Names on the cenotaph (more for the First World War than for the Second). Names of the streets and the pattern they lay in.

The hope of accuracy we bring to such tasks is crazy, heartbreaking.

And no list could hold what I wanted, for what I wanted was every last thing, every layer of speech and thought, stroke of light on bark or walls, every smell, pothole, pain, crack, delusion, held still and held together – radiant, everlasting.

At present I did not look much at this town.

Bobby Sherriff spoke to me wistfully, relieving me of my fork, napkin, and empty plate.

'Believe me,' he said, 'I wish you luck in your life.'

Then he did the only special thing he ever did for me. With those things in his hands, he rose on his toes like a dancer, like a plump ballerina. This action, accompanied by his delicate smile, appeared to be a joke not shared with me so much as displayed for me, and it seemed also to have a concise meaning, a stylized meaning – to be a letter, or a whole word, in an alphabet I did not know.

People's wishes, and their other offerings, were what I took then naturally, a bit distractedly, as if they were never anything more than my due.

'Yes,' I said, instead of thank you.

§ *Small town* Duncan, Leacock, Davies; *Childhood discovery* Findley, Burnard; Carib: Lamming, Edgell, Senior; SA: Sidhwa; SEA: Maniam

RUDY WIEBE (1934–)

Where Is the Voice Coming From?

The problem is to make the story.

One difficulty of this making may have been excellently stated by Teilhard de Chardin.[1] 'We are continually inclined to isolate ourselves from the things and events which surround us . . . as though we were spectators, not elements, in what goes on.' Arnold Toynbee[2] does venture, 'For all that we know, Reality is the undifferentiated unity of the mystical experience,' but that need not here be considered. This story ended long ago; it is one of finite acts, of orders, or elemental feelings and reactions, of obvious legal restrictions and requirements.

Presumably all the parts of the story are themselves available. A difficulty is that they are, as always, available only in bits and pieces. Though the acts themselves seem quite clear, some written reports of the acts contradict each other. As if these acts were, at one time, too well-known; as if the original nodule of each particular fact had from somewhere received non-factual accretions; or even more, as if, since the basic facts were so clear perhaps there were a larger number of facts than any one reporter, or several, or even any reporter had ever attempted to record. About facts that are simply told by this mouth to that ear, of course, even less can be expected.

An affair seventy-five years old should acquire some of the shiny transparency of an old man's skin. It should.

Sometimes it would seem that it would be enough – perhaps more than enough – to hear the names only. The grandfather One Arrow; the mother Spotted Calf; the father Sounding Sky; the wife (wives rather, but only one of them seems to have a name, though their fathers are Napaise, Kapahoo, Old Dust, The Rump) – the one wife named, of all things, Pale Face; the cousin Going-Up-To-Sky; the brother-in-law (again, of all things) Dublin. The names of the police sound very much alike; they all begin with Constable or Corporal or Sergeant, but here and there an Inspector, then a Superintendent and eventually all the resonance of an Assistant Commissioner echoes down. More. Herself: Victoria, by the Grace of God etc., etc., QUEEN, defender of the Faith, etc., etc.; and witness 'Our Right Trusty and Right Well-beloved Cousin and Councillor the Right Honorable Sir John Campbell Hamilton-Gordon, Earl of Aberdeen; Viscount Formartine, Baron Haddo, Methlic, Tarves and Kellie in the Peerage of Scotland; Viscount Gordon of Aberdeen, County of Aberdeen in the Peerage of the United Kingdom; Baronet of Nova Scotia, Knight Grand Cross of Our Most Distinguished Order of Saint Michael and Saint George, etc., Governor General of Canada.' And of course himself: in the award proclamation named 'Jean-Baptiste' but otherwise known only as Almighty Voice.

---

1 French Jesuit mystic who died in 1955. 2 English economic historian.

But hearing cannot be enough; not even hearing all the thunder of A Proclamation: 'Now Hear ye that a reward of FIVE HUNDRED DOLLARS will be paid to any person or persons who will give such information as will lead ... (etc., etc.) this Twentieth day of April, in the year of Our Lord one thousand eight hundred and ninety-six, and the Fifty-ninth year of Our Reign ...' etc. and etc.

Such hearing cannot be enough. The first item to be seen is the piece of white bone. It is almost triangular, slightly convex – concave actually as it is positioned at this moment with its corners slightly raised – graduating from perhaps a strong eighth to a weak quarter of an inch in thickness, its scattered pore structure varying between larger and smaller on its perhaps polished, certainly shiny surface. Precision is difficult since the glass show-case is at least thirteen inches deep and therefore an eye cannot be brought as close as the minute inspection of such a small, though certainly quite adequate, sample of skull would normally require. Also, because of the position it cannot be determined whether the several hairs, well over a foot long, are still in some manner attached to it or not.

The seven-pounder cannon can be seen standing almost shyly between the showcase and the interior wall. Officially it is known as a gun, not a cannon, and clearly its bore is not large enough to admit a large man's fist. Even if it can be believed that this gun was used in the 1885 Rebellion and that on the evening of Saturday, May 29, 1897 (while the nine-pounder, now unidentified, was in the process of arriving with the police on the special train from Regina), seven shells (all that were available in Prince Albert at that time) from it were sent shrieking into the poplar bluffs as night fell, clearly such shelling could not and would not disembowel the whole earth. Its carriage is now nicely lacquered, the perhaps oak spokes of its petite wheels (little higher than a knee) have been recently scraped, puttied and varnished; the brilliant burnish of its brass breeching testifies with what meticulous care charmen and women have used nationally advertised cleaners and restorers.

Though it can also be seen, even a careless glance reveals that the same concern has not been expended on the one (of two) .44 calibre 1866 model Winchesters apparently found at the last in the pit with Almighty Voice. It is also preserved in a glass case; the number 1536735 is still, though barely, distinguishable on the brass cartridge section just below the brass saddle ring. However, perhaps because the case was imperfectly sealed at one time (though sealed enough not to warrant disturbance now), or because of simple neglect, the rifle is obviously spotted here and there with blotches of rust and the brass itself reveals discolorations almost like mildew. The rifle bore, the three long strands of hair themselves, actually bristle with clots of dust. It may be that this museum cannot afford to be as concerned as the other; conversely, the disfiguration may be something inherent in the items themselves.

The small building which was the police guardroom at Duck Lake, Saskatchewan Territory, in 1895 may also be seen. It had subsequently been moved from its original place and used to house small animals, chickens perhaps, or pigs – such as a woman might be expected to have under her responsibility. It is, of course, now perfectly empty, and clean so that the public may enter with no more discomfort than a bend under the doorway and a heavy encounter with disinfectant. The door-jamb has obviously been replaced; the bar network at one window is, however, said to be original; smooth still, very smooth. The logs inside have been smeared again and again with whitewash, perhaps paint, to an insistent point of identity-defying characterlessness. Within the small rectangular box of these logs not a sound can be heard from the streets of the, probably dead, town.

Hey Injun you'll get hung for stealing that steer
Hey Injun for killing that government cow you'll get three
weeks on the woodpile Hey Injun

The place named Kinistino seems to have disappeared from the map but the Minnechinass Hills have not. Whether they have ever been on a map is doubtful but they will, of course, not disappear from the landscape as long as the grass grows and the rivers run. Contrary to general report and belief, the Canadian prairies are rarely, if ever, flat and the Minnechinass (spelled five different ways and translated sometimes as 'The Outside Hill,' sometimes as 'Beautiful Bare Hills') are dissimilar from any other of the numberless hills that everywhere block out the prairie horizon. They are bare; poplars lie tattered along their tops, almost black against the straw-pale grass and sharp green against the grey soil of the plowing laid in half-mile rectangular blocks upon their western slopes. Poles holding various wires stick out of the fields, back down the bend of the valley; what was once a farmhouse is weathering into the cultivated earth. The poplar bluff where Almighty Voice made his stand has, of course, disappeared.

The policemen he shot and killed (not the ones he wounded, of course) are easily located. Six miles east, thirty-nine miles north in Prince Albert, the English Cemetery. Sergeant Colin Campbell Colebrook, North West Mounted Police Registration Number 605, lies presumably under a gravestone there. His name is seventeenth in a very long 'list of non-commissioned officers and men who have died in the service since the inception of the force.' The date is October 29, 1895, and the cause of death is anonymous: 'Shot by escaping Indian prisoner near Prince Albert.' At the foot of this grave are two others: Constable John R. Kerr, No. 3040, and Corporal C. H. S. Hockin, No. 3106. Their cause of death on May 28, 1897 is even more anonymous, but the place is relatively precise: 'Shot by Indians at Min-etch-inass Hills, Prince Albert District.'

The gravestone, if he has one, of the fourth man Almighty Voice killed is more difficult to locate. Mr. Ernest Grundy, postmaster at Duck Lake in 1897, apparently shut his window the afternoon of Friday, May 28, armed himself, rode east twenty miles, participated in the second charge into the bluff at about 6:30 p.m., and on the third sweep of that charge was shot dead at the edge of the pit. It would seem that he thereby contributed substantially not only to the Indians' bullet supply, but his clothing warmed them as well.

The burial place of Dublin and Going-Up-To-Sky is unknown, as is the grave of Almighty Voice. It is said that a Métis[3] named Henry Smith lifted the latter's body from the pit in the bluff and gave it to Spotted Calf. The place of burial is not, of course, of ultimate significance. A gravestone is always less evidence than a triangular piece of skull, provided it is large enough.

Whatever further evidence there is to be gathered may rest on pictures. There are, presumably, almost numberless pictures of the policemen in the case, but the only one with direct bearing is one of Sergeant Colebrook who apparently insisted on advancing to complete an arrest after being warned three times that if he took another step he would be shot. The picture must have been taken before he joined the force; it reveals him a large-eared young man, hair brush-cut and ascot tie, his eyelids slightly drooping, almost hooded under thick brows. Unfortunately a picture of Constable R. C. Dickson, into whose charge Almighty Voice was apparently committed in that guardroom and who after Colebrook's death was convicted of negligence, sentenced to two months hard labour and discharged, does not seem to be available.

There are no pictures to be found of either Dublin (killed early by rifle fire) or Going-Up-To-Sky (killed in the pit), the two teen-age boys who gave their ultimate fealty to Almighty Voice. There is, however, one said to be of Almighty Voice, Junior. He may have been born to Pale Face during the year, two hundred and twenty-one days that his father was a fugitive. In the picture he is kneeling before what could be a tent, he wears striped denim overalls and displays twin babies whose sex cannot be determined from the double-laced dark bonnets they wear. In the supposed picture of Spotted Calf and Sounding Sky, Sounding Sky stands slightly before his wife; he wears a white shirt and a striped blanket folded over his left shoulder in such a manner that the arm in which he cradles a long rifle cannot be seen. His head is thrown back; the rim of his hat appears as a black half-moon above eyes that are pressed shut in, as it were, profound concentration; above a mouth clenched thin in a downward curve. Spotted Calf wears a long dress, a sweater which could also be a man's dress coat, and a large fringed and embroidered shawl which would appear distinctly Dukhobor[4] in origin if the scroll patterns on it were more irregular. Her head is small and turned slightly towards her husband so as to reveal her right ear. There is what can only be called a quizzical expression on her crumpled face; it may be she does not understand what is happening and that she would have asked a question, perhaps of her husband, perhaps of the photographers, perhaps even of anyone, anywhere in the world if such questioning were possible for an Indian woman.

There is one final picture. That is one of Almighty Voice himself. At least it is purported to be of Almighty Voice himself. In the Royal Canadian

---

3 Person of mixed Native and European descent.   4 Russian dissenting sect, many of whose members migrated to Canada after experiencing persecution.

Mounted Police Museum on the Barracks Grounds just off Dewdney Avenue in Regina, Saskatchewan, it lies in the same showcase, as a matter of fact immediately beside that triangular piece of skull. Both are unequivocally labelled, and it must be assumed that a police force with a world-wide reputation would not label *such* evidence incorrectly. But here emerges an ultimate problem in making the story.

There are two official descriptions of Almighty Voice. The first reads: 'Height about five feet, ten inches, slight build, rather good looking, a sharp hooked nose with a remarkably flat point. Has a bullet scar on the left side of his face about 1½ inches long running from near corner of mouth towards ear. The scar cannot be noticed when his face is painted but otherwise is plain. Skin fair for an Indian.' The second description is on the Award Proclamation: 'About twenty-two years old, five feet ten inches in height, weight about eleven stone, slightly erect, neat small feet and hands; complexion inclined to be fair, wavey dark hair to shoulders, large dark eyes, broad forehead, sharp features and parrot nose with flat tip, scar on left cheek running from mouth towards ear, feminine appearance.'

So run the descriptions that were, presumably, to identify a well-known fugitive in so precise a manner that an informant could collect five hundred dollars – a considerable sum when a police constable earned between one and two dollars a day. The nexus of the problem appears when these supposed official descriptions are compared to the supposed official picture. The man in the picture is standing on a small rug. The fingers of his left hand touch a curved Victorian settee, behind him a photographer's backdrop of scrolled patterns merges to vaguely paradisiacal trees and perhaps a sky. The moccasins he wears make it impossible to deduce whether his feet are 'neat small.' He may be five feet, ten inches tall, may weigh eleven stone, he certainly is 'rather good looking' and, though it is a frontal view, it may be that the point of his long and flaring nose could be 'remarkably flat.' The photograph is slightly over-illuminated and so the unpainted complexion could be 'inclined to be fair'; however, nothing can be seen of a scar, the hair is not wavy and shoulder-length but hangs almost to the waist in two thick straight braids worked through with beads, fur, ribbons and cords. The right hand that holds the corner of the blanket-like coat in position is large and, even in the high illumination, heavily veined. The neck is concealed under coiled beads and the forehead seems more low than 'broad.'

Perhaps, somehow, these picture details could be reconciled with the official description if the face as a whole were not so devastating.

On a cloth-backed sheet two feet by two and one-half feet in size, under the Great Seal of the Lion and the Unicorn, dignified by the names of the Deputy of the Minister of Justice, the Secretary of State, the Queen herself and all the heaped detail of her 'Right Trusty and Right Well-beloved Cousin,' this description concludes: 'feminine appearance.' But the pictures: any face of history, any believed face that the world acknowledges as *man* – Socrates, Jesus, Attila, Genghis Khan, Mahatma Gandhi, Joseph Stalin – no believed face is more *man* than this face. The mouth, the nose, the clenched brows, the eyes – the eyes are large, yes, and dark, but even in this watered-down reproduction of unending reproductions of that original, a steady look into those eyes cannot be endured. It is a face like an axe.

It is now evident that the de Chardin statement quoted at the beginning has relevance only as it proves itself inadequate to explain what has happened. At the same time, the inadequacy of Aristotle's much more famous statement becomes evident: 'The true difference [between the historian and the poet] is that one relates what *has* happened, the other what *may* happen.' These statements cannot explain the storymaker's activity since, despite the most rigid application of impersonal investigation, the elements of the story have now run me aground. If ever I could, I can no longer pretend to objective, omnipotent disinterestedness. I am no longer *spectator* of what *has* happened or what *may* happen: I am become *element* in what is happening at this very moment.

For it is, of course, I myself who cannot endure the shadows on that paper which are those eyes. It is I who stand beside this broken veranda post where two corner shingles have been torn away, where barbed wire tangles the dead weeds on the edge of this field. The bluff that sheltered Almighty Voice and his two friends has not disappeared from the slope of the Minnechinass, no more than the sound of Constable Dickson's voice in that guardhouse is silent. The sound of his speaking is there even if it has never been recorded in an official report:

> hey injun you'll get
> hung for stealing that steer
> hey injun for killing that government
> cow you'll get three
> weeks on the woodpile hey injun

The unknown contradictory words about an unprovable act that move a boy to defiance, an implacable Cree warrior long after the three-hundred-and-fifty-year war is ended, a war already lost the day the Cree watch Cartier[5] hoist his guns ashore at Hochelaga and they begin the long retreat west; these words of incomprehension, of threatened incomprehensible law are there to be heard just as the unmoving tableau of the three-day siege is there to be seen on the slopes of the Minnechinass. Sounding Sky is somewhere not there, under arrest, but Spotted Calf stands on a shoulder of the Hills a little to the left, her arms upraised to the setting sun. Her mouth is open. A horse rears, riderless, above the scrub willow at the edge of the bluff, smoke puffs, screams tangle in rifle barrage, there are wounds, somewhere. The bluff is so green this spring, it will not burn and the ragged line of seven police and two civilians is staggering through, faces twisted in rage, terror, and rifles sputter. Nothing moves. There is no sound of frogs in the night; twenty-seven policemen and five civilians stand in cordon at thirty-yard

---

5 Sixteenth-century French navigator and explorer; one of the first European 'discoverers' of North America.

intervals and a body also lies in the shelter of a gully. Only a voice rises from the bluff:

> *We have fought well*
> *You have died like braves*
> *I have worked hard and am hungry*
> *Give me food*

but nothing moves. The bluff lies, a bright green island on the grassy slope surrounded by men hunched forward rigid over their long rifles, men clumped out of rifle-range, thirty-five men dressed as for fall hunting on a sharp spring day, a small gun positioned on a ridge above. A crow is falling out of the sky into the bluff, its feathers sprayed as by an explosion. The first gun and the second gun are in position, the beginning and end of the bristling surround of thirty-five Prince Albert Volunteers, thirteen civilians and fifty-six policemen in position relative to the bluff and relative to the unnumbered whites astride their horses, standing up in their carts, staring and pointing across the valley, in position relative to the bluff and the unnumbered Indians squatting silent along the higher ridges of the Hills, motionless mounds, faceless against the Sunday morning sunlight edging between and over them down along the tree tips, down into the shadows of the bluff. Nothing moves. Beside the second gun the red-coated officer has flung a handful of grass into the motionless air, almost to the rim of the red sun.

And there is a voice. It is an incredible voice that rises from among the young poplars ripped of their spring bark, from among the dead somewhere lying there, out of the arm-deep pit shorter than a man; a voice rises over the exploding smoke and thunder of guns that reel back in their positions, worked over, serviced by the grimed motionless men in bright coats and glinting buttons, a voice so high and clear, so unbelievably high and strong in its unending wordless cry.

The voice of 'Gitchie-Manitou Wayo' – interpreted as 'voice of the Great Spirit' – that is, The Almighty Voice. His death chant no less incredible in its beauty than in its incomprehensible happiness.

I say 'wordless cry' because that is the way it sounds to me. I could be more accurate if I had a reliable interpreter who would make a reliable interpretation. For I do not, of course, understand the Cree myself.

§ *Native dispossession* King, Armstrong; Aus: Oodgeroo, Mudrooroo, Davis; *Alternative histories* Aus: Davis; Carib: Reid, Walcott (3); SA: Rushdie

ALISTAIR MacLEOD (1936–)

As Birds Bring Forth the Sun

Once there was a family with a Highland name who lived beside the sea. And the man had a dog of which he was very fond. She was large and gray, a sort of staghound from another time. And if she jumped up to lick his face, which she loved to do, her paws would jolt against his shoulders with such force that she would come close to knocking him down and he would be forced to take two or three backward steps before he could regain his balance. And he himself was not a small man, being slightly over six feet and perhaps one hundred and eighty pounds.

She had been left, when a pup, at the family's gate in a small handmade box and no one knew where she had come from or that she would eventually grow to such a size. Once, while still a small pup, she had been run over by the steel wheel of a horse-drawn cart which was hauling kelp from the shore to be used as fertilizer. It was in October and the rain had been falling for some weeks and the ground was soft. When the wheel of the cart passed over her, it sunk her body into the wet earth as well as crushing some of her ribs; and apparently the silhouette of her small crushed body was visible in the earth after the man lifted her to his chest while she yelped and screamed. He ran his fingers along her broken bones, ignoring the blood and urine which fell upon his shirt, trying to soothe her bulging eyes and her scrabbling front paws and her desperately licking tongue.

The more practical members of his family, who had seen run-over dogs before, suggested that her neck be broken by his strong hands or that he grasp her by the hind legs and swing her head against a rock, thus putting an end to her misery. But he would not do it.

Instead, he fashioned a small box and lined it with woolen remnants from a sheep's fleece and one of his old and frayed shirts. He placed her within the box and placed the box behind the stove and then he warmed some milk in a small saucepan and sweetened it with sugar. And he held open her small and trembling jaws with his left hand while spooning in the sweetened milk with his right, ignoring the needle-like sharpness of her small teeth. She lay in the box most of the remaining fall and into the early winter, watching everything with her large brown eyes.

Although some members of the family complained about her presence and the odor from the box and the waste of time she involved, they gradually adjusted to her; and as the weeks passed by, it became evident that her ribs were knitting together in some form or other and that she was recovering with the resilience of the young. It also became evident that she would grow to a tremendous size, as she outgrew one box and then another and the gray hair began to feather from her huge front paws. In the spring she was outside almost all of the time and followed the man everywhere; and when she came inside during the following months, she had grown so large that she would no longer fit into her accustomed place behind the stove and was forced to lie beside it. She was never given a name but was referred to in Gaelic as *cù mòr glas*, the big gray dog.

By the time she came into her first heat, she had grown to a tremendous height, and although her signs and her odor attracted many panting and highly aroused suitors, none was big enough to mount her and the frenzy of their disappointment and the longing of her unfulfillment were more than the man could stand. He went, so the story goes, to a place where he knew there was a big dog. A dog not as big as she was, but still a big dog, and he brought him home with him. And at the proper time he took the *cù mòr glas* and the big dog down to the sea where he knew there was a hollow in the rock which appeared only at low tide. He took some sacking to provide footing for the male dog and he placed the *cù mòr glas* in the hollow of the rock and knelt beside her and steadied her with his left arm under her throat and helped position the male dog above her and guided his blood-engorged penis. He was a man used to working with the breeding of animals, with the guiding of rams and bulls and stallions and often with the funky smell of animal semen heavy on his large and gentle hands.

The winter that followed was a cold one and ice formed on the sea and frequent squalls and blizzards obliterated the offshore islands and caused the people to stay near their fires much of the time, mending clothes and nets and harness and waiting for the change in season. The *cù mòr glas* grew heavier and even more large until there was hardly room for her around the stove or even under the table. And then one morning, when it seemed that spring was about to break, she was gone.

The man and even his family, who had become more involved than they cared to admit, waited for her but she did not come. And as the frenzy of spring wore on, they busied themselves with readying their land and their fishing gear and all of the things that so desperately required their attention. And then they were into summer and fall and winter and another spring which saw the birth of the man and his wife's twelfth child. And then it was summer again.

That summer the man and two of his teenaged sons were pulling their herring nets about two miles offshore when the wind began to blow off the land and the water began to roughen. They became afraid that they could not make it safely back to shore, so they pulled in behind one of the offshore islands, knowing that they would be sheltered there and planning to outwait the storm. As the prow of their boat approached the gravelly shore, they heard a sound above them, and looking up they saw the *cù mòr glas* silhouetted on the brow of the hill which was the small island's highest point.

'M'eudal cù mòr glas' shouted the man in his happiness – *m'eudal* meaning something like dear or darling; and as he shouted, he jumped over the side of his boat into the waist-deep water, struggling for footing on the rolling gravel as he waded eagerly and awkwardly towards her and the shore. At the same time, the *cù mòr glas* came hurtling down towards him in a shower of small rocks dislodged by her feet; and just as he was emerging from the water, she met him as she used to, rearing up on her hind legs and placing her huge front paws on his shoulders while extending her eager tongue.

The weight and speed of her momentum met him as he tried to hold his balance on the sloping angle and the water rolling gravel beneath his feet, and he staggered backwards and lost his footing and fell beneath her force. And in that instant again, as the story goes, there appeared over the brow of the hill six more huge gray dogs hurtling down towards the gravelled strand. They had never seen him before; and seeing him stretched prone beneath their mother, they misunderstood, like so many armies, the intention of their leader.

They fell upon him in a fury, slashing his face and tearing aside his lower jaw and ripping out his throat, crazed with bloodlust or duty or perhaps starvation. The *cù mòr glas* turned on them in her own savagery, slashing and snarling and, it seemed, crazed by their mistake; driving them bloodied and yelping before her, back over the brow of the hill where they vanished from sight but could still be heard screaming in the distance. It all took perhaps little more than a minute.

The man's two sons, who were still in the boat and had witnessed it all, ran sobbing through the salt water to where their mauled and mangled father lay; but there was little they could do other than hold his warm and bloodied hands for a few brief moments. Although his eyes 'lived' for a small fraction of time, he could not speak to them because his face and throat had been torn away, and of course there was nothing they could do except to hold and be held tightly until that too slipped away and his eyes glazed over and they could no longer feel his hands holding theirs. The storm increased and they could not get home and so they were forced to spend the night huddled beside their father's body. They were afraid to try to carry the body to the rocking boat because he was so heavy and they were afraid that they might lose even what little of him remained and they were afraid also, huddled on the rocks, that the dogs might return. But they did not return at all and there was no sound from them, no sound at all, only the moaning of the wind and the washing of the water on the rocks.

In the morning they debated whether they should try to take his body with them or whether they should leave it and return in the company of older and wiser men. But they were afraid to leave it unattended and felt that the time needed to cover it with protective rocks would be better spent in trying to get across to their home shore. For a while they debated as to whether one should go in the boat and the other remain on the island, but each was afraid to be alone and so in the end they managed to drag and carry and almost float him towards the bobbing boat. They lay him face down and covered him with what clothes there were and set off across the still-rolling sea. Those who waited on the shore missed the large presence of the man within the boat and some of them waded into the water and others rowed out in skiffs, attempting to hear the tearful messages called out across the rolling waves.

The *cù mòr glas* and her six young dogs were never seen again, or perhaps I should say they were never seen again in the same way. After some
weeks, a group of men circled the island tentatively in their boats but they
saw no sign. They went again and then again but found nothing. A year
later, and grown much braver, they beached their boats and walked the island
carefully, looking into the small sea caves and the hollows at the base of the
wind-ripped trees, thinking perhaps that if they did not find the dogs, they
might at least find their whitened bones; but again they discovered nothing.

The *cù mòr glas*, though, was supposed to be sighted here and there for
a number of years. Seen on a hill in one region or silhouetted on a ridge in
another or loping across the valleys or glens in the early morning or the
shadowy evening. Always in the area of the half perceived. For a while she
became rather like the Loch Ness Monster or the Sasquatch[1] on a smaller
scale. Seen but not recorded. Seen when there were no cameras. Seen but
never taken.

The mystery of where she went became entangled with the mystery of
whence she came. There was increased speculation about the handmade box
in which she had been found and much theorizing as to the individual or
individuals who might have left it. People went to look for the box but could
not find it. It was felt she might have been part of a *buidseachd* or evil spell
cast on the man by some mysterious enemy. But no one could go much farther than that. All of his caring for her was recounted over and over again
and nobody missed any of the ironies.

What seemed literally known was that she had crossed the winter ice to
have her pups and had been unable to get back. No one could remember
ever seeing her swim; and in the early months at least, she could not have
taken her young pups with her.

The large and gentle man with the smell of animal semen often heavy on
his hands was my great-great-great-grandfather, and it may be argued that
he died because he was too good at breeding animals or that he cared too
much about their fulfillment and well-being. He was no longer there for his
own child of the spring who, in turn, became my great-great-grandfather,
and he was perhaps too much there in the memory of his older sons who
saw him fall beneath the ambiguous force of the *cù mòr glas*. The youngest
boy in the boat was haunted and tormented by the awfulness of what he
had seen. He would wake at night screaming that he had seen the *cù mòr
glas a' bhàis*, the big gray dog of death, and his screams filled the house and
the ears and minds of the listeners, bringing home again and again the consequences of their loss. One morning, after a night in which he saw the *cù
mòr glas a' bhàis* so vividly that his sheets were drenched with sweat, he
walked to the high cliff which faced the island and there he cut his throat
with a fish knife and fell into the sea.

The other brother lived to be forty, but, again so the story goes, he found
himself in a Glasgow pub one night, perhaps looking for answers, deep and

---

1 Mysterious ape-like creature said to inhabit remote areas in the Pacific North-West.

sodden with the whiskey which had become his anaesthetic. In the half darkness he saw a large, gray-haired man sitting by himself against the wall and mumbled something to him. Some say he saw the *cù mòr glas a' bhàis* or uttered the name. And perhaps the man heard the phrase through ears equally affected by drink and felt he was being called a dog or a son of a bitch or something of that nature. They rose to meet one another and struggled outside into the cobblestoned passageway behind the pub where, most improbably, there were supposed to be six other large, gray-haired men who beat him to death on the cobblestones, smashing his bloodied head into the stone again and again before vanishing and leaving him to die with his face turned to the sky. The *cù mòr glas a' bhàis* had come again, said his family, as they tried to piece the tale together.

This is how the *cù mòr glas a' bhàis* came into our lives, and it is obvious that all of this happened a long, long time ago. Yet with succeeding generations it seemed the specter had somehow come to stay and that it had become *ours* – not in the manner of an unwanted skeleton in the closet from a family's ancient past but more in the manner of something close to a genetic possibility. In the deaths of each generation, the gray dog was seen by some – by women who were to die in childbirth, by soldiers who went forth to the many wars but did not return, by those who went forth to feuds or dangerous love affairs, by those who answered mysterious midnight messages, by those who swerved on the highway to avoid the real or imagined gray dog and ended in masses of crumpled steel. And by one professional athlete who, in addition to his ritualized athletic superstitions, carried another fear or belief as well. Many of the man's descendants moved like careful hemophiliacs, fearing that they carried unwanted possibilities deep within them. And others, while they laughed, were like members of families in which there is a recurrence over the generations of repeated cancer or the diabetes which comes to those beyond middle age. The feeling of those who may say little to others but who may say often and quietly to themselves, 'It has not happened to me,' while adding always the cautionary 'yet.'

I am thinking all of this now as the October rain falls on the city of Toronto and the pleasant, white-clad nurses pad confidently in and out of my father's room. He lies quietly amidst the whiteness, his head and shoulders elevated so that he is in that hospital position of being neither quite prone nor yet sitting. His hair is white upon his pillow and he breathes softly and sometimes unevenly, although it is difficult ever to be sure.

My five gray-haired brothers and I take turns beside his bedside, holding his heavy hands in ours and feeling their response, hoping ambiguously that he will speak to us, although we know that it may tire him. And trying to read his life and ours into his eyes when they are open. He has been with us for a long time, well into our middle age. Unlike those boys in that boat of so long ago, we did not see him taken from us in our youth. And unlike their youngest brother who, in turn, became our great-great-grandfather, we did not grow into a world in which there was no father's touch. We have been lucky to have this large and gentle man so deep into our lives.

No one in this hospital has mentioned the *cù mòr glas a' bhàis*. Yet as my mother said ten years ago, before slipping into her own death as quietly as a grownup child who leaves or enters her parents' house in the early hours, 'It is hard to *not* know what you do know.'

Even those who are most skeptical, like my oldest brother who has driven here from Montreal, betray themselves by their nervous actions. 'I avoided the Greyhound bus stations in both Montreal and Toronto,' he smiled upon his arrival, and then added, 'Just in case.'

He did not realize how ill our father was and has smiled little since then. I watch him turning the diamond ring upon his finger, knowing that he hopes he will not hear the Gaelic phrase he knows too well. Not having the luxury, as he once said, of some who live in Montreal and are able to pretend they do not understand the 'other' language. You cannot *not* know what you do know.

Sitting here, taking turns holding the hands of the man who gave us life, we are afraid for him and for ourselves. We are afraid of what he may see and we are afraid to hear the phrase born of the vision. We are aware that it may become confused with what the doctors call 'the will to live' and we are aware that some beliefs are what others would dismiss as 'garbage.' We are aware that there are men who believe the earth is flat and that the birds bring forth the sun.

Bound here in our own peculiar mortality, we do not wish to see or see others see that which signifies life's demise. We do not want to hear the voice of our father, as did those other sons, calling down his own particular death upon him.

We would shut our eyes and plug our ears, even as we know such actions to be of no avail. Open still and fearful to the gray hair rising on our necks if and when we hear the scrabble of the paws and the scratching at the door.

§ *Maritimes* Carman, MacLennan

AUDREY THOMAS (1935–)

From Intertidal Life

Set on one of British Columbia's Gulf Islands, *Intertidal Life* is about the protagonist Alice's recovery from a broken marriage, her relationship with her adolescent daughter and the need she feels to write. Much of the narrative reviews her past and the web of relationships between men and women and women and women which has brought her to her present situation. This passage links a number of the novel's central concerns, as Alice appropriates traditionally male 'maritime images' – of navigation, exploration and discovery – to suggest the colonization experienced by women, argues against the gender ideology inscribed in romantic fiction and articulates the need for women to rename themselves.

. . . 'Women have been shanghaied,' Alice said, 'and now we are waking up and rubbing our eyes and murmuring "Where are we?" '

'What's the answer then?'

'Some kind of mutiny, I suppose. Unless we can talk the captain into letting us go.'

'But that's where your argument falls down,' Stella said. 'We don't want to be "let go." '

'True, o queen. No, we don't want to be let out at the nearest port or unceremoniously tossed overboard – although that's the fate awaiting a lot of us I think – what we really want is to be officers and captains ourselves. It's funny, since I've been reading all this history about the Spanish and the English and the Pacific I think more and more in maritime images. I'm like John Donne in his love poetry. Navigational instruments, new lands, maps, merchant ships. His language reflects what was going on around him in the outside world. I read about prizes and shipwrecks and plunder, strange instruments which measure the artificial horizon, about conquests and conventions, this whole male world of the age of exploration and I see that women are going to have to get out there and do the same thing.'

'Conquest and plunder?'

'Well no. No. We don't want to emulate the male with all his bad habits, now do we? What I mean is that what's happening to men and women today is just as exciting and terrifying as the discovery that the earth was round, not flat, or even that the earth was not the center of the universe but just part of a solar system. But we all need new maps, new instruments to try and fix our new positions, unless we think we're competent enough to try and steer by the stars.

'And to go on with my maritime theme, imperialism is over, for nations, for men. Do we really want somebody planting a flag on us and claiming us forever?' She laughed.

'I talk big, of course, but I guess that's maybe what in our hearts we still want. I was looking up "abandon" the other day and discovered it, literally, means "to set at liberty." I say Peter abandoned me, and mean "poor me," when maybe I should be feeling "he has set me free." '

Stella lit a cigarette. 'But what you really feel is that he has tossed you overboard.'

'Yes.'

'We all want one special relationship,' Trudl said. 'We're all looking for Prince Charming.'

'Yes,' Alice said, 'and we ought to be ashamed of ourselves.'

Trudl looked worried. 'Don't you think it's natural to want to be loved?'

'Absolutely,' Alice said. 'And to be loved deeply and intensely. But we can't make that our whole life, our whole reason for being. Women have *let* men define them, taken their *names* even, with marriage, just like a conquered or newly settled region, British Columbia, British Guiana, New Orleans, New Jersey, New France, New England, etcetera. I really understand all those African nations taking new names with their independence, names that relate to their racial history. Also the Afro-Americans, and the Indians.'

'But what could women change their names to?' Stella asked. 'Isn't it really as pretentious if we do that as all these hippie girls calling themselves Rosamund Apple or Johanna New Moon or whatever? I mean, we can take back our *maiden* names, such a quaint term, like "horsepower" or one of those isn't it, but they were given us, we didn't have any choice. Or about our first names.'

'Well, perhaps we have to change all our names,' Alice said, 'I don't know. Somehow one's first name doesn't seem as politically oppressive as one's married name. And yet I loved being "Mrs. Hoyle." Then everybody knew I was married, you see. I had status. I had an official lover and protector. You'd go to a party: "I'd like you to meet Peter and Alice Hoyle." A couple, a unit. I loved all that stuff.'

'I did too,' Trudl said, 'until I wanted to leave.'

'I never wanted that,' Stella said.

'Yes, but we all know you're the miraculous exception. And I'll bet you would've wanted it with Robert if you hadn't met him when he was already dying.'

'Maybe.'

'Are you going to go back to your maiden name?' Alice asked.

'Müller-Stach? That's quite a mouthful, isn't it? I don't know.'

'It would be nice if one could just be "Colette" or "Garbo." '

'I guess. I've actually been thinking of changing my name,' Alice said, 'but the children seem frightened by the idea.'

'Why?'

'I'm not sure, since they call me mom or mummy anyway.'

'What are you thinking of changing it to?'

'I don't know, that's the trouble. I like "Justine" but of course *that's* out. I hardly look a neurasthenic Jewess. I've been trying to think of something Irish but not sentimental. Nora, maybe, d'you like that?'

'No. Not really.'

'What about Suzanne?'

'Yes, that's pretty and a nice bilingual touch. But it doesn't suit me.'

'What about Christine?' said Trudl. Stella said, 'What about Pristeen?'

'Del-feen.'

'Vaseline.'

'I'm serious,' Alice said, laughing. 'I need help.'

'We're helping you.'

'Thanks a lot.'

§ *Women's colonization*: Atwood (4), Marlatt; Aus: Grenville; Carib: Brodber, Nichols; Af: Dangarembga

DAPHNE MARLATT (1942–)

From Ana Historic

In *Ana Historic* Annie, the wife of a history professor, discovers fragments of the life-story of Mrs Richards, a nineteenth-century schoolteacher living in the 'bush settlement' that was to become Vancouver. She begins imaginatively to reconstruct Mrs Richards's history and in so doing engages in a dialogue with a Victorian woman precursor which enables her to recover submerged elements of her own past. This extract from the early part of the novel, in which Annie addresses her own dead mother, is typical of the way the work suggests an opposition between (male) history and 'native' space, associated with the bush, animality and the female body.

. . . i want to talk to you. (now? now when it's too late?) i want to say something. tell you something about the bush and what you were afraid of, what i escaped to: anonymous territory where names faded to a tiny hubbub, lost in all that other noise – the soughing, sighing of bodies, the cracks and chirps, odd rustles, something like breath escaping, something inhuman i slipped through. in communion with trees, following the migratory routes of bugs, the pathways of water, the warning sounds of birds, i was native, i was the child who grew up with wolves, original lost girl, elusive, vanished from the world of men . . .

but you, a woman, walked with the possibility of being seen, ambushed in the sudden arms of bears or men. 'never go into the woods with a man,' you said, 'and don't go into the woods alone.'

we knew about bears. sometimes they would raid our garbage cans at night and the phones would ring all up and down the block, there's a bear at the Potts', keep the dogs and kids inside. excitement, peering through the windows out at streetlight pooling gravel. so they were real then? shambling shadows, garbage-eaters, only a little larger than the Newfoundland next door. but with something canny in them, resistant to attempts to scare them off, looking over their shoulders with contempt, four-footed men in shaggy suits intent on a meal.

'if a man talks to you on the street, don't answer him,' you said. 'but what if he wants directions? what if he wants a dime?' we asked. 'just keep walking,' you said. but we saw you fish for quarters when the men shambled up to you on the street outside department stores, we watched you in your trim black coat, well-tailored, your little hat, we watched you scrambling around in your purse for change, and it was true, you didn't say a word, though you did respond, awkward and flushed. when we asked if that's what you meant, you said it wasn't that.

skid row was a name we learned. rape was a word that was hidden from us. 'but what would he do?' 'bad things you wouldn't like.'

our bodies were ours as far as we knew and we knew what we liked, laughing exhausted and sweaty in our fort or wiping bloody knees with leaves and creek water. without history we squatted in needle droppings to pee, flung our bodies through the trees – we would have swung on vines if there had been any, as it was we swung on vine maples. always we imagined we were the first ones there, the first trespassers –

if you go down in the woods today you'd better go in disguise. it was bears' territory we entered, or cedars'. it was the land of skunk cabbage. it was not ours and no one human, no man preceded us.

§ *Women and 'native' space* Traill, Atwood (4), Thomas; Aus: Baynton, Bail, Jefferis

TIMOTHY FINDLEY (1930–)

From Lemonade

This is the begining of a long short story, in which a sensitive and lonely boy struggles to come to terms with his mother's self-destruction.

Every morning at seven o'clock Harper Dewey turned over and woke up. And every morning he would lie in his tumbled bed (for he slept without repose even at the age of eight) until it was seven-thirty, thinking his way back into his dreams, which were always of his father. At seven-thirty he would get out of bed and cross to his window where he would stand for a moment watching his dreams fade in the sunlight until there was nothing in the garden save the lilac and the high board fence.

And the birds.

Robins and starlings and sparrows flowed over the smooth lawn in great droves, turning it into the likeness of a market-place; and the raucous babble of their bargaining (of dealings in worms and beetles and flies) poured itself, like something distilled or dehydrated, from the jar of darkness into the morning air, which made it swell and burst. This enormous shout of birds at morning was always a delight to Harper Dewey.

Presently, over this sound, there would burst the first indication of an awakening household: Bertha Millroy's hymn.

Bertha Millroy was the maid – and a day, to Bertha, wasn't a day at all unless it began with a hymn and ended with a prayer.

She lived – Bertha – in the attic, in a small room directly above Harper's room and she sang her hymn from the window which opened over his head.

When it was finished she would say the same thing every morning – 'Amen' and 'Good morning Harper.' Then they would race each other to the landing on the stairs. Harper never cheated, although he could easily have been dressed long before Bertha if he had chosen to be, because he was always awake so much earlier than her. But this every morning race had never been specifically agreed upon and if Harper had ever said to Bertha at the window 'Let's race,' or if Bertha had ever said to Harper below her 'Beat you downstairs,' the whole procedure would have been off. Neither of them could remember when this habit had started – it just had.

Well, one morning early in the summer, (in fact it was hardly more than late spring), Harper and Bertha met on the stairs' landing – Bertha won – and after they had scanned the note they found there, they looked at each other and then quickly looked away. They descended to the first floor in their usual fashion – Harper going down the front stairs to collect the paper from the front porch – and Bertha going down the back stairs to light the stove and to bring in the milk.

This morning, Harper didn't open the paper, although he usually read the comics sitting on the porch step. Instead he returned inside, letting the screen door clap behind him and leaving the big oak and glass door open so that the air could come through, into the still house. He went straight out to the kitchen and sat down at the table, slipping the still folded paper onto the breakfast tray which was laid out for his mother.

In the kitchen, Bertha Millroy behaved in the same morose fashion, as though touched by the same hand. And indeed their mutual despondency was based upon a kindred misgiving. And Mrs Renalda Harper Dewey was the instigator of that misgiving.

Mrs Renalda Harper Dewey, widow of Harper Peter Dewey the First (killed in the battle for Caen, August 1944, the year after Harper P. Dewey the Second's birth) was a lady who lay in bed till nine o'clock every morning because of the night before. It used to be that she would lie abed until eight and then it became an occasional night before – but now the lie abed was until nine and had ceased to be occasional.

This morning there had been a note on the flat top of the balustrade on the landing. On the note were written the words 'Ten o'clock – thank you' in rather indistinct watery blue ink. 'Ten o'clock, thank you' and that was all.

Bertha put on the kettle.

'I don't want any tea,' said Harper Dewey.

'You don't drink morning tea because you want to, Master Harper Dewey,' said Bertha Millroy in her flat voice, 'you drink it to assist nature.'

The kettle boiled.

Bertha warmed the teapot.

They were silent.

Bertha threw out the water into the sink and put tea leaves in the pot.

The robins moved across the lawn outside the kitchen window.

Harper watched them.

Bertha poured boiling water over the tea leaves, turned off the stove and put the lid on the teapot. One, two, three, and sat down.

'Ten o'clock indeed,' she muttered – and then she poured tea into their cups.

One of the robins was listening to a worm under the dew. Harper watched. The robin's head was cocked to one side as it listened. Then it ran a few steps on tiptoe and caught the worm noise again – this time nearer to it. The robin waited. Harper waited – Bertha Millroy waited – and then the robin stabbed the ground with its beak – caught the worm and tossed it into the sunlight. Harper shivered.

'I don't want to assist nature,' he said, and he pushed his teacup away.

The thought of having to wait until ten o'clock to see his mother was unbearable to Harper. He had never had to wait that long on any other morning that he could remember.

There was a procedure – one which took place every day – which they followed, commencing with the preparation of Mrs Dewey's breakfast tray. Bertha would serve up the eggs into the plate and pour coffee into the silver thermos bottle and Harper would butter toast. Then Bertha would take the tray and Harper would take the paper and they would mount the stairs to the second floor. Outside his mother's door Harper had placed, long ago, a small chair with a cushion on it, where, at this stage of the procedure he would sit, while Bertha went into the bedroom to awaken his mother.

Then he would listen to all the sounds which came from his mother's room. First of all Bertha Millroy pulled the curtains after which, every morning, she would say, 'It's nine o'clock, Mrs Dewey,' (this morning she would say 'ten o'clock') – and Harper's beautiful mother would reply in a sleepy voice, 'Thank you Bertha, let me have my wrapper.'

After this he would count to himself the various stages of her awakening which he had trained his ear to recognize, although in his whole life he had never witnessed them.

First of all his mother rolled over from her side onto her back. Then there was the sound of Bertha mincing to the bedside. The sitting up came next. This was a combination of three sounds. The plumping of pillows, a slight voiceless sound which his mother uttered as she was helped into a sitting position (simultaneously there would be a grunt from Bertha) – and finally Bertha saying pleasantly 'There.'

After the sitting up came a pause. 'Now,' Bertha would inevitably say, 'here we are.' And she could be heard mincing across the room to where she'd lift the breakfast tray and mince back again to the bed, accompanied on the return journey by the tinkle of ice against the walls of the orange juice glass and sometimes a harsh clank when the coffee thermos hit the plate of eggs. 'Thank you' followed that and then silence.

Next, coffee being poured and the paper being opened and Bertha stepping to the dressing table to get the brush and then, sometimes but not always, a few listless strokes of the brush through his mother's hair.

Then Bertha would emerge from the room, somewhat triumphantly, and she would say as she appeared, 'Call if you want – don't if you don't,' and then she went downstairs.

At this juncture Harper's turn came.

'Good morning, mother.'

'Good morning, Harpie. You sit there like a good boy 'till I'm ready – then you can come in dear.'

'All right.'

He knew that he wasn't allowed inside until she'd gone into the bathroom and shut the door behind her, he knew this explicitly, but for some reason or other she felt she must tell him again and again every morning and so he let her.

After she had gone into the bathroom he would go into the bedroom and sit on the bed and look at the pictures in the paper and listen to the bath water running into the tub. Afterwards, when he heard the water running out of the tub he would go to the highboy[1] (it had been his father's) and open the middle drawer.

Inside the middle drawer there was always the Colt revolver lying on a white tea towel – and beside it lay two boxes of cartridges. But the Colt revolver held no interest for him at all. He knew what it was there for and he respected this, but aside from respect he felt nothing. It guarded a treasure, which lay under the white tea towel, contained in two boxes – one which had velveteen on the outside and another which was leather. These were his mother's jewel cases. This was the treasure.

Although Harper had no idea, had no conception of the value of these jewels he believed them to be the most beautiful objects he had ever seen. Actually their value was enormous (but Harper wouldn't have understood the meaning of value – he only understood that they were beautiful).

There were earrings and finger rings and necklaces and brooches. There were strings and strands of pearls and an emerald on a golden thread. There was an opal ring and a sapphire ring of such gigantic proportions that Harper wondered always how his mother ever wore it. And there was a diamond set in the midst of emeralds and yellow sapphires that truly dazzled the beholder with its radiance.

Every day, Mrs Renalda Harper Dewey wore either one piece or several pieces of this jewelry and Harper every day would take out the two boxes and stare at the contents trying to guess which piece or pieces she would choose. Very often he was right in his choice because he had a certain insight into the inflection of his mother's voice which she employed when she called to him in the hallway.

However – in the last two months this had become a source, not of pleasure to him but of anguish, for something was happening – an extreme mystery – which no one could explain to him no matter how often he asked about it. Certain of the smaller pieces of jewelry were disappearing.

---

1 Tall chest of drawers.

The first piece had disappeared over six months before, just after Christmas. It had been a small brooch of silver, studded with tiny diamonds. It was in the shape of a spider's web and the diamonds had represented dewdrops. Harper had been especially enamoured of this piece and when he found it gone he was panic-stricken and searched the entire room for it. But then his mother said to him: 'I sold it,' in a cold beautiful voice, and he was heartbroken. She said she'd sold it to finance a gift for her own mother. But she didn't tell him what the gift was and he had never heard his grandmother mention it.

Since then, other pieces had gone – none without immediate notice from his loving eye – but, as they went the cold beautiful voice delivered credible reasons as excuse – Granny's insurance – Mary Flannagan's wedding present – old Aunt Alice's silver anniversary – and more.

During the last two months there had been a marked increase in the loss which could not be ignored or brushed aside as more 'expenses for gifts.' And since it was two months since the first note, which read 'Nine o'clock please' had appeared on the landing, Harper Dewey with a sinking heart (but with a mind that could not prompt him to an exact reason) somehow, perhaps instinctively, put two and two together and made four.

As for Bertha Millroy, there was no mystery to her – whatever it was – she knew.

So that now, when there lay between their cups of tea – between their two pairs of moving hands which drummed with speculation on the kitchen table – a note, which read 'Ten o'clock, thank you,' their eyes could not meet and they could not voice their distress for they were filled with fear.

Bertha Millroy wondered just how Harper would discover and she said a word to God asking him 'not to make her do the telling . . .'

§ *Childhood discovery*: Munro, Burnard; Af: Gurnah; Carib: Lamming, Edgell, Senior, Kincaid; SA: Selvadurai, Sidhwa; SEA: Maniam, Somtow

THOMAS KING (1943–)

The One about Coyote Going West

This one is about Coyote. She was going west. Visiting her relations. That's what she said. You got to watch that one. Tricky one. Full of bad business. No, no, no, no, that one says. I'm just visiting.

Going to see Raven.[1]

Boy, I says. That's another tricky one.

Coyote comes by my place. She wag her tail. Make them happy noises.

---

1 Coyote and Raven are both culture-heroes who mediate between life and death and have simultaneously destructive and beneficial aspects in many Native mythologies. As this story suggests, Coyote is also a Creator-trickster figure.

Sit on my porch. Look around. With them teeth. With that smile. Coyote put her nose in my tea. My good tea. Get that nose out of my tea, I says.

I'm going to see my friends, she says. Tell those stories. Fix this world. Straighten it up.

Oh boy, pretty scary that, Coyote fix the world, again.

Sit down, I says. Eat some food. Hard work that fix up the world. Maybe you have a song. Maybe you have a good joke.

Sure, says Coyote. That one wink her ears. Lick her whiskers.

I tuck my feet under that chair. Got to hide my toes. Sometimes that tricky one leave her skin sit in that chair. Coyote skin. No Coyote. Sneak around. Bite them toes. Make you jump.

I been reading those books, she says.

You must be one smart Coyote, I says.

You bet, she says.

Maybe you got a good story for me, I says.

I been reading about that history, says Coyote. She tricks that nose back in my tea. All about who found us Indians.

Ho, I says. I like those old ones. Them ones are the best. You tell me your story, I says. Maybe some biscuits will visit us. Maybe some moose-meat stew come along, listen to your story.

Okay, she says and she sings her story song.

> Snow's on the-ground the snakes are asleep.
> Snow's on the ground my voice is strong.
> Snow's on the ground the snakes are asleep.
> Snow's on the ground my voice is strong.

She sings like that. With that tail, wagging. With that smile. Sitting there.

Maybe I tell you the one about Eric the Lucky[2] and the Vikings play hockey for the Old-timers, find us Indians in Newfoundland, she says.

Maybe I tell you the one about Christopher Cartier[3] looking for something good to eat. Find us Indians in a restaurant in Montreal.

Maybe I tell you the one about Jacques Columbus[3] come along that river, Indians waiting for him. We all wave and say, here we are, here we are.

Everyone knows those stories, I says. White man stories. Baby stories you got in your mouth.

No, no, no, no, says the Coyote. I read these ones in that old book.

Ho, I says. you are trying to bite my toes. Everyone knows who found us Indians. Eric the Lucky and that Christopher Cartier and that Jacques Columbus come along later. Those ones get lost. Float about. Walk around. Get mixed up. Ho, ho, ho, ho, those ones cry, we are lost. So we got to find them. Help them out. Feed them. Show them around.

Boy, I says. Bad mistake that one.

---

2 Suggestive of Eric 'the Red', Eirikr Thorvaldsson, fl.980–1000, allegedly the first European to 'discover' Greenland. His son, Leif Ericsson, reached 'Vinland', probably Nova Scotia. **3 Christopher Cartier ... Jacques Columbus** Mixing the names of Christopher Columbus and Jacques Cartier, early European 'discoverer' of eastern Canada.

You are very wise, grandmother, says Coyote, bring her eyes down. Like she is sleepy. Maybe you know who discovered Indians.

Sure, I says. Everyone knows that. It was Coyote. She was the one.

Oh, grandfather, that Coyote says. Tell me that story. I love those stories about that sneaky one. I don't think I know that story, she says.

All right, I says. Pay attention.

Coyote was heading west. That's how I always start this story. There was nothing else in this world. Just Coyote. She could see all the way, too. No mountains then. No rivers then. No forests then. Pretty flat then. So she starts to make things. So she starts to fix this world.

This is exciting, says Coyote, and she takes her nose out of my tea.

Yes, I says. Just the beginning, too. Coyote got a lot of things to make.

Tell me, grandmother, says Coyote. What does the clever one make first?

Well, I says. Maybe she makes that tree grows by the river. Maybe she makes that buffalo. Maybe she makes that mountain. Maybe she makes them clouds.

Maybe she makes that beautiful rainbow, says Coyote.

No, I says. She don't make that thing. Mink makes that.

Maybe she makes that beautiful moon, says Coyote.

No, I says. She don't do that either. Otter finds that moon in a pond later on.

Maybe she makes the oceans with that blue water, says Coyote.

No, I says. Oceans are already here. She don't do any of that. The first thing Coyote makes, I tell Coyote, is a mistake.

Boy, Coyote sit up straight. Them eyes pop open. That tail stop wagging. That one swallow that smile.

Big one, too, I says. Coyote is going west thinking of things to make. That one is trying to think of everything to make at once. So she don't see that hole. So she falls in that hole. Then those thoughts bump around. They run into each other. Those ones fall out of Coyote's ears. In that hole. Ho, that Coyote cries. I have fallen into a hole. I must have made a mistake. And she did.

So, there is that hole. And there is that Coyote in that hole. And there is that big mistake in that hole with Coyote. Ho, says that mistake. You must be Coyote.

That mistake is real big and that hole is small. Not much room. I don't want to tell you what that mistake looks like. First mistake in the world. Pretty scary. Boy, I can't look. I got to close my eyes. You better close your eyes, too, I tell Coyote.

Okay, I'll do that, she says, and she puts her hands over her eyes. But she don't fool me. I can see she's peeking.

Don't peek, I says.

Okay, she says. I won't do that.

Well, you know, that Coyote thinks about the hole. And she thinks about how she's going to get out of that hole. She thinks how she's going to get that big mistake back in her head.

Say, says that mistake. What is that you're thinking about?

I'm thinking of a song, says Coyote. I'm thinking of a song to make this hole bigger.

That's a good idea, says that mistake. Let me hear your hole song.

But that's not what Coyote sings. She sings a song to make the mistake smaller. But that mistake hears her. And that mistake grabs Coyote's nose. And that one pulls off her mouth so she can't sing. And that one jumps up and down on Coyote until she is flat. Then that one leaps out of that hole, wanders around looking for things to do.

Well, Coyote is feeling pretty bad, all flat her nice fur coat full of stomp holes. So she thinks hard, and she thinks about a healing song. And she tries to sing a healing song, but her mouth is in other places. So she thinks harder and tries to sing that song through her nose. But that nose don't make any sound, just drip a lot. She tries to sing that song out her ears, but those ears don't hear anything.

So, that silly one thinks real hard and tries to sing out her butt-hole. Pssst! Pssst! That is what that butt-hole says, and right away things don't smell so good in that hole. Pssst.

Boy, Coyote thinks. Something smells.

That Coyote lies there flat and practise and practise. Pretty soon, maybe two days, maybe one year, she teach that butt-hole to sing. That song. That healing song. So that butt-hole sings that song. And Coyote begins to feel better. And Coyote don't feel so flat anymore. Pssst! Pssst! Things still smell pretty bad, but Coyote is okay.

That one look around in that hole. Find her mouth. Put that mouth back. So, she says to that butt-hole. Okay, you can stop singing now. You can stop making them smells now. But, you know, that butt-hole is liking all that singing, and so that butt-hole keeps on singing.

Stop that, says Coyote. You going to stink up the whole world. But it don't. So Coyote jumps out of that hole and runs across the prairies real fast. But that butt-hole follows her. Pssst. Pssst. Coyote jumps into a lake, but that butt-hole don't drown. It just keeps on singing.

Hey, who is doing all that singing, someone says.

Yes, and who is making that bad smell, says another voice.

It must be Coyote, says a third voice.

Yes, says a fourth voice. I believe it is Coyote.

That Coyote sit in my chair, put her nose in my tea, say, I know who that voice is. It is that big mistake playing a trick. Nothing else is made yet.

No, I says. That mistake is doing other things.

Then those voices are spirits, says Coyote.

No, I says. Them voices belong to them ducks.

Coyote stand up on my chair. Hey, she says, where did them ducks come from?

Calm down, I says. This story is going to be okay. This story is doing just fine. This story knows where it is going. Sit down. Keep your skin on.

So.

Coyote look around, and she see them four ducks. In that lake. Ho, she says. Where did you ducks come from? I didn't make you yet.

Yes, says them ducks. We were waiting around, but you didn't come. So we got tired of waiting. So we did it ourselves.

I was in a hole, says Coyote.

Psst. Psst.

What's that noise, says them ducks. What's that bad smell?

Never mind, says Coyote. Maybe you've seen something go by. Maybe you can help me find something I lost. Maybe you can help me get it back.

Those ducks swim around and talk to themselves. Was it something awful to look at? Yes, says Coyote, it certainly was. Was it something with ugly fur? Yes, says Coyote, I think it had that, too. Was it something that made a lot of noise? ask them ducks. Yes, it was pretty noisy, says Coyote. Did it smell bad, them ducks want to know. Yes, says Coyote. I guess you ducks have seen my something.

Yes, says them ducks. It is right there behind you.

So that Coyote turn around, and there is nothing there.

It's still behind you, says those ducks.

So Coyote turn around again but she don't see anything.

Psst! Psst!

Boy, says those ducks. What a noise! What a smell! They say that, too. What an ugly thing with all that fur!

Never mind, says that Coyote, again. That is not what I'm looking for. I'm looking for something else.

Maybe you're looking for Indians, says those ducks.

Well, that Coyote is real surprised because she hasn't created Indians, either. Boy, says that one, mischief is everywhere. This world is getting bent.

All right.

So Coyote and those ducks are talking, and pretty soon they hear a noise. And pretty soon there is something coming. And those ducks says, oh, oh, oh, oh. They say that like they see trouble, but it is not trouble. What comes along is a river.

Hello, says that river. Nice day. Maybe you want to take a swim. But Coyote don't want to swim, and she looks at that river and she looks at that river again. Something's not right here, she says. Where are those rocks? Where are those rapids? What did you do with them waterfalls? How come you're so straight?

And Coyote is right. That river is nice and straight and smooth without any bumps or twists. It runs both ways, too, not like a modern river.

We got to fix this, says Coyote, and she does. She puts some rocks in that river, and she fixes it so it only runs one way. She puts a couple of waterfalls in and makes a bunch of rapids where things get shallow fast.

Coyote is tired with all this work, and those ducks are tired just watching. So that Coyote sits down. So she closes her eyes. So she puts her nose in her tail. So those ducks shout, wake up, wake up! Something big is heading this way! And they are right.

Mountain comes sliding along, whistling. Real happy mountain. Nice and round. This mountain is full of grapes and other good things to eat. Apples, peaches, cherries. Howdy-do, says that polite mountain, nice day for whistling.

Coyote looks at that mountain, and that one shakes her head. Oh, no, she says, this mountain is all wrong. How come you're so nice and round. Where are those craggy peaks? Where are all them cliffs? What happened to all that snow? Boy, we got to fix this thing, too. So she does.

Grandfather, grandfather, says that Coyote, sit in my chair, put her nose in my tea. Why is that Coyote changing all those good things?

That is a real sly one, ask me that question. I look at those eyes. Grab them ears. Squeeze that nose. Hey, let go my nose, that Coyote says.

Okay, I says. Coyote still in Coyote skin. I bet you know why Coyote change that happy river. Why she change that mountain sliding along whistling.

No, says that Coyote, look around my house, lick her lips, make them baby noises.

Maybe it's because she is mean, I says.

Oh, no, says Coyote. That one is sweet and kind.

Maybe it's because that one is not too smart.

Oh, no, says Coyote. That Coyote is very wise.

Maybe it's because she made a mistake.

Oh, no, says Coyote. She made one of those already.

All right, I says. Then Coyote must be doing the right thing. She must be fixing up the world so it is perfect.

Yes, says Coyote. That must be it. What does that brilliant one do next?

Everyone knows what Coyote does next, I says. Little babies know what Coyote does next.

Oh no, says Coyote. I have never heard this story. You are a wonderful storyteller. You tell me your good Coyote story.

Boy, you got to watch that one all the time. Hide them toes.

Well, I says. Coyote thinks about that river. And she thinks about that mountain. And she thinks somebody is fooling around. So she goes looking around. She goes looking for that one who is messing up the world.

She goes to the north, and there is nothing. She goes to the south, and there is nothing there, either. She goes to the east, and there is still nothing there. She goes to the west, and there is a pile of snow tires.

And there is some televisions. And there is some vacuum cleaners. And there is a bunch of pastel sheets. And there is an air humidifier. And there is a big mistake sitting on a portable gas barbecue reading a book. Big book. Department store catalogue.

Hello, says that mistake. Maybe you want a hydraulic jack.

No, says that Coyote. I don't want one of them. But she don't tell that mistake what she wants because she don't want to miss her mouth again. But when she thinks about being flat and full of stomp holes, that butt-hole wakes up and begins to sing. Pssst. Pssst.

What's that noise? says that big mistake.

I'm looking for Indians, says that Coyote, real quick. Have you seen any? What's that bad smell?

Never mind, says Coyote. Maybe you have some Indians around here.

I got some toaster ovens, says that mistake.

We don't need that stuff, says Coyote. You got to stop making all those things. You're going to fill up this world.

Maybe you want a computer with a colour monitor. That mistake keeps looking through that book and those things keep landing in piles all around Coyote.

Stop, stop, cries Coyote. Golf cart lands on her foot. Golf balls bounce off her head. You got to give me that book before the world gets lopsided.

These are good things, says that mistake. We need these things to make up the world. Indians are going to need this stuff.

We don't have any Indians, says Coyote.

And that mistake can see that that's right. Maybe we better make some Indians, says that mistake. So that one looks in that catalogue, but it don't have any Indians. And Coyote don't know how to do that, either. She has already made four things.

I've made four things already, she says. I got to have help.

We can help, says some voices and it is those ducks come swimming along. We can help you make Indians, says the white duck. Yes, we can do that, says the green duck. We have been thinking about this, says that blue duck. We have a plan, says the red duck.

Well, that Coyote don't know what to do. So she tells them ducks to go ahead because this story is pretty long and it's getting late and everyone wants to go home.

You still awake, I says to Coyote. You still here?

Oh yes, grandmother, says Coyote. What do those clever ducks do?

So I tell Coyote that those ducks lay some eggs. Ducks do that, you know. That white duck lay an egg, and it is blue. That red duck lay an egg, and it is green. That blue duck lay an egg, and it is red. That green duck lay an egg, and it is white.

Come on, says those ducks. We got to sing a song. We got to do a dance. So they do. Coyote and that big mistake and those four ducks dance around the eggs. So they dance and sing for a long time, and pretty soon Coyote gets hungry.

I know this dance, she says, but you got to close your eyes when you do it or nothing will happen. You got to close you eyes tight. Okay, says those ducks. We can do that. And they do. And that big mistake closes its eyes, too.

But Coyote, she don't close her eyes, and all of them start dancing again, and Coyote dances up close to that white duck, and she grabs that white duck by her neck.

When Coyote grabs that duck, that duck flaps her wings, and that big mistake hears the noise and opens them eyes. Say, says that big mistake, that's not the way the dance goes.

By golly, you're right, says Coyote, and she lets that duck go. I am getting it mixed up with another dance.

So they start to dance again. And Coyote is very hungry, and she grabs that blue duck, and she grabs his wings, too. But Coyote's stomach starts to make hungry noises, and that mistake opens them eyes and sees Coyote with the blue duck. Hey, says that mistake, you got yourself mixed up again.

That's right, says Coyote, and she drops that duck and straightens out that neck. It sure is good you're around to help me with this dance.

They all start that dance again, and, this time, Coyote grab the green duck real quick and tries to stuff it down that greedy throat, and there is nothing hanging out but them yellow duck feet. But those feet are flapping in Coyote's eyes, and she can't see where she is going, and she bumps into the big mistake and the mistake turns around to see what has happened.

Ho, says that big mistake, you can't see where you're going with them yellow duck feet flapping in your eyes, and that mistake pulls that green duck out of Coyote's throat. You could hurt yourself dancing like that.

You are one good friend, look after me like that, says Coyote.

Those ducks start to dance again, and Coyote dances with them, but that red duck says, we better dance with one eye open, so we can help Coyote with this dance. So they dance some more, and, then, those eggs begin to move around, and those eggs crack open. And if you look hard, you can see something inside those eggs.

I know, I know, says that Coyote, jump up and down on my chair, shake up my good tea. Indians come out of those eggs. I remember this story, now. Inside those eggs are the Indians Coyote's been looking for.

No, I says. you are one crazy Coyote. What comes out of those duck eggs are baby ducks. You better sit down, I says. You may fall and hurt yourself. You may spill my tea. You may fall on top of this story and make it flat.

Where are the Indians? says that Coyote. This story was about how Coyote found the Indians. Maybe the Indians are in the eggs with the baby ducks.

No, I says, nothing in those eggs but little ducks. Indians will be along in a while. Don't lose your skin.

So.

When those ducks see what has come out of the eggs, they says, boy, we didn't get that quite right. We better try that again. So they do. They lay them eggs. They dance that dance. They sing that song. Those eggs crack open and out comes some more baby ducks. They do this seven times and each time, they get more ducks.

By golly, says those four ducks. We got more ducks than we need. I guess we got to be the Indians. And so they do that. Before Coyote or that big mistake can mess things up, those four ducks turn into Indians, two women and two men. Good-looking Indians, too. They don't look at all like ducks anymore.

But those duck-Indians aren't too happy. They look at each other and they begin to cry. This is pretty disgusting, they says. All this ugly skin. All these bumpy bones. All this awful black hair. Where are our nice soft feathers? Where are our beautiful feet? What happened to our wonderful wings? It's probably all that Coyote's fault because she didn't do the dance right, and those four duck-Indians come over and stomp all over Coyote until she is flat like before. Then they leave. That big mistake leave, too. And that Coyote, she starts to think about a healing song.

Psst. Psst.

That's it, I says. It is done.

But what happens to Coyote, says Coyote. That wonderful one is still flat.

Some of these stories are flat, I says. That's what happens when you try to fix this world. This world is pretty good all by itself. Best to leave it alone. Stop messing around with it.

I better get going, says Coyote. I will tell Raven your good story. We going to fix this world for sure. We know how to do it now. We know how to do it right.

So, Coyote drinks my tea and that one leave. And I can't talk anymore because I got to watch the sky. Got to watch out for falling things that land in piles. When that Coyote's wandering around looking to fix things, nobody in this world is safe.

§ *Native peoples* Armstrong, Carr, Wiebe; Aus: Oodgeroo, Mudrooroo, Davis; NZSP: Ihimaera (1), Grace; *Trickster-figure* Kroetsch (2); Carib: Brodber

JEANNETTE C. ARMSTRONG (1948–)

This Is a Story

It came to me one morning early, when the morning star was up shining so big and bright, the way she does in the summers. It was during the women's gathering at Owl Rock. It was the same year that the Red Star came so close to the earth that it was mentioned in the papers.

I had been sitting up with the fire. One woman had to sit up with it at all times during the gathering. One friend had stayed up with me to help keep me awake. It had been cold and I was wrapped up in a Pendleton blanket. It was the second to last night of the gathering. I was getting very sleepy when George said, 'Tell me a story.' 'Okay,' I said. 'This story happened a long time ago. It's real.'

Kyoti[1] was coming up the river, from the great Columbia River up to the Okanagan River. Kyoti had come up through there before. One time before that I know of. That time Kyoti came up the Okanagan River which runs into the Columbia River. That was the time when Kyoti brought salmon to

---

1 Coyote.

the Okanagan. Everywhere Kyoti stopped at the Peoples' villages, salmon was left. It made everyone happy. It was a great gift. Kyoti did that a long time ago.

Now, after waking up from an unusually short nap, Kyoti was walking along upstream, wanting to visit with the People in the Okanagan. These were Kyoti's favourite people. Visiting them always meant a real feast with salmon. Kyoti was partial to salmon.

While walking along, Kyoti noticed a lot of new things. A lot of things changed since that last trip through here. There sure were a lot of Swallow people,[2] and they had houses everywhere, but Kyoti couldn't find any People, or even the villages of the People. Things looked very strange.

Eventually, Kyoti came to a huge thing across the river at Grand Coulee. It was so high it stretched all the way across the water and blocked it off. Kyoti stopped and looked at it for a while not having any idea what it might be. It didn't look good, whatever it was. Something was worrisome about it. Kyoti had thought of going up to the Kettle Falls to where the Salmon Chief stayed, but there didn't seem to be any way salmon could get past that thing, no matter how high they jumped. Kyoti was pretty hungry by then, not having seen any People. Just to make sure, Kyoti decided to go up the Okanagan River to where the People had been real happy to get the salmon brought to them.

It was a good thing Kyoti didn't go up to Kettle Falls anyway. Kyoti didn't know, yet, that all the People had moved away when the Falls had disappeared under the new lake behind Grand Coulee.

So Kyoti went back down the river and started up the Okanagan. Kyoti kept going along the river and, sure enough, what Kyoti was afraid of came true. There was another one of those things right there at Chief Joseph. But this time there were a couple of People fishing there. They were the first People Kyoti had seen anywhere along the river. They were directly below that huge thing that stretched way up and across the river.

So Kyoti went up to them and waited for a greeting and some show of respect. Like an invite to eat. After all Kyoti was respected in these parts. Kyoti had brought the salmon to these People.

Kyoti waited for a while but neither of the young men said anything. They just kept on fishing. Kyoti got tired waiting for them to speak first and said, 'How is the fishing?'

They both just looked at Kyoti, like they didn't understand.

Kyoti again spoke, slower and louder this time, 'Is the fishing good? I bet there are some big ones this time of year.'

One of them shrugged and tried to say in Swallow talk that they didn't know the language.

That was how Kyoti found out that they couldn't understand the language of the Okanagan People!

Kyoti couldn't figure that one out, but since Kyoti knew all the languages,

---

2 Whites.

Kyoti talked to them in Swallow talk. Kyoti asked them again how the fishing was.

They looked at Kyoti and one of them answered, 'We been here two days, nothing yet.'

Well Kyoti was pretty disappointed. Kyoti was hoping to eat a couple of salmon for lunch. Kyoti thought that maybe it wasn't a lost cause after all. People in their village might have food, maybe even salmon, since this was fishing season.

Kyoti waited around for a while and finally asked, 'Where are all the People?'

One of them answered by asking what Kyoti meant.

'Well, I would like to talk to your headman,' Kyoti said very seriously.

Actually Kyoti just wanted to eat. Kyoti was starving.

They both laughed. 'What headman. Hey, man, where'd you come from?' one of them asked.

Kyoti kinda got mad then and answered, 'I came walking up the river. I never saw any People. All I been seeing is those Swallows and they sure got lots of houses. Now you talk to me in their talk and laugh at me. I'm hungry and you don't even offer me anything to eat.'

Well that shamed them guys out. Even though they weren't quite sure of what Kyoti was talking about. One of them said, 'Cheeze, you coulda just said that in the first place. We're Indians. Come on, we'll go over to the house and feed you up.'

So that was how Kyoti got to Nespelum. Kyoti got to meet one old person there that talked right. All the rest of the People just kept talking Swallow talk. They used words in Swallow that didn't have a meaning that Kyoti could figure out.

What was the most surprising was that all the people lived in Swallow houses and ate Swallow food. A whole lot of things were pretty strange.

Kyoti had looked and looked for somebody who could talk in the People's language. Kyoti asked the one person who could talk proper, how this had all happened.

The person was a very old woman. Kyoti recognized her name and knew which family and village her People were from. She was from an old headman family.

She looked at Kyoti for quite a while and recognized Kyoti. Then she cried and cried for a long time. 'Kyoti,' she said, 'I never thought you was ever going to come back. Things haven't been good for quite a while now. I kept hoping you would show up. Them Swallows came. We don't know what happened. They did lots of things. They built that thing across the river again, like when they were Monster people and you broke their dams to bring the salmon up. I don't think it's made out of spit and clay like that other time, but it's made something like that. They did lots of other worse stuff. How come you never came back for a long time? Now look what happened.'

Kyoti was quiet for a while. 'Well I guess I went to sleep for a while. You know sometimes I oversleep a little,' Kyoti joked, trying to make her feel better.

Actually Kyoti was well known for oversleeping all the time. And actually Kyoti always used that as an excuse for being too late for something important.

But the old woman just kept crying. She kept on talking, saying, 'Nobody listens to me. Nobody knows you anymore. You better go up to Vernon, up there in the North Okanagan. Go see Tommy, he keeps telling people about you. Maybe he can tell you something about what happened.'

So Kyoti continued on up the river, stopping at each village. This time they were easy to find, now that Kyoti knew that the People had moved into Swallow homes. They were easy to find because they looked different than the way Swallows kept their houses. The People didn't seem to care to keep up the houses the way the Swallows worked at it, day in day out, non-stop until they dropped dead. That was no surprise. They weren't Swallows.

Kyoti tried to talk to some of the headmen. Kyoti would suggest something like, 'You should break them Swallow dams, and let the salmon come back. They know where to come, they never forget. I told them not to. You shouldn't eat that Swallow food. Look at all the sick People.'

Actually Kyoti himself was getting pretty sick and gaunt from eating stuff that didn't taste or look like food. Especially real food like fresh salmon.

But the headman would just shake his head and say, 'Get out of here, Kyoti. Your kind of talk is just bullshit. If you say them things People will get riled up and they might start to raise hell. They might even try to do something stupid like break the dams. Them Swallows get mad real easy. Besides, we'll just end up looking stupid. We gotta work with them now even if we don't exactly like what they do. We gotta survive. We gotta get money to buy food and other things. We gotta have jobs to live. That's how it is now, we can't go back to old times. We need them Swallows, they're smart. They know lots that we don't know about. They know how to live right. We just got to try harder to be like them. So get outta here. You're not real anyway. You're just a dream of the old People.'

They would say things like that even while they talked right face-to-face to Kyoti. Even when Kyoti was right there in front of them.

Kyoti would walk on feeling real bad. Kyoti had seen lots of People in really bad shape. They walked around with their minds hurt. They couldn't see or hear good anymore. Their bodies were poisoned. They didn't care much for living anymore. They thought they were Swallows, but couldn't figure out why the Swallows taunted and laughed at them. They couldn't seem to see how the Swallows stole anything they could pick up for their houses, how they took over any place and shitted all over it, not caring because they could just fly away to another place. They couldn't seem to see that the Swallows treated them just as they pleased without any respect.

Kyoti could see that them Swallows were still a Monster people. They were pretty tricky making themselves act like they were People but all the while, underneath, being really selfish Monsters that destroy People and things like rivers and mountains. Now Kyoti could see the reason for being awakened early. There was work to be done. It was time to change the Swallows from Monsters into something that didn't destroy things. Kyoti was Kyoti and that was the work Kyoti had to do.

Eventually Kyoti came to a place where a young one was sitting by the river. This young one greeted Kyoti properly in People talk. He looked at Kyoti's staff and asked politely, 'Who are you, old one? I know all the old People in the Okanagan. I haven't seen you before, but you look like somebody I must have known before.'

Kyoti sat down and then said, 'You look like somebody I once knew. An old chief. He was really a big important chief. He was so important that he took care of People all up and down the whole Okanagan. He never kept a single salmon for himself if somebody needed it. Me, I'm just a traveller. I move around a lot when I'm not sleeping. Never know where I'll be tomorrow. I'm looking for Tommy, I guess.'

The young man said, 'Tommy? The old man? Yeah you must mean him. Some of us call him our chief now. It was Tommy told my mom to make sure that I was to sit here and watch the river, every day during salmon-run time.

'You see he knows that I'm a chief of the Kettle Falls. I'm a Salmon Chief, but no salmon come up here now, and there is no falls there anymore. My great grandfather was the last Salmon Chief to see the salmon come up the river. The Swallows came after that. Now I wait here and watch the river, like my father and his father before him did. They died without seeing one salmon come up the river.

'I guess I will keep on waiting. I believe Tommy when he says that we got to not give up. Sometimes I think I will see them coming. Shining and in clean water. I close my eyes during salmon-run time, and I see them. Millions of salmon coming up the river. I see my People singing, all coming down to the river to be with me, to eat again what we were given to eat. But then I open my eyes and nothing is ever there. I'm so tired and so all alone here. Nobody else cares.'

So that was when Kyoti took out the shining rainbow ribbons and hung them on his staff.

Kyoti walked up to Tommy's door and said, 'Tommy, open the door. I have come to talk to you. I'm going to ask you to get the People together. The ones who can hear. Tell them that I am back. You know all of them. I am going to break the dams. I'm hungry and that young one at the river has waited long enough. All my children will eat salmon again.'

Kyoti shook the staff and the ground shook, too, as Tommy came out the door facing east. You shoulda seen Tommy's face, when he saw Kyoti and the rainbow ribbons hanging on the staff.

That story happened. I tell you that much. It's a powerful one. I tell it now because it's true.

Sometimes I think of that story and that morning at Owl Rock, when I see rainbow colours in the oil slicks along the river, during salmon-run time in the Okanagan, and I feel the ground shake ever so little.

§ *Native peoples* King, Carr, Wiebe; Aus: Oodgeroo, Mudrooroo, Davis; NZSP: Ihimaera (1), Grace; *Trickster-figure* King, Kroetsch (2); Carib: Brodber

BONNIE BURNARD (1943–)

Music Lessons

Most of us who grew up in that time, in that place, in that little subclass of well off girls in well off towns seem now to me interchangeable, like foundlings. We all grew around the same rules, the same expectations. Among the many things we did in my town, with a strangely limited variation in skill, was play the piano. We were all taught to play by Mrs. Summers, though I finished with her alone.

The osmosis which is at work among very young women, beginning always with the one who will tell, the one who will act out a scene for friends gathered round her in some flouncy bedroom, was at work among us. The substance of our minds, like the contents of our closets, was swapped and shared in a continuous, generous game. Perhaps, if we had lost our virginity at thirteen, I would have many elaborate scenes in my memory rather than one. Perhaps not. The osmosis thickened and slowed just as the loss of virginity accelerated. But we knew for a time, and were happy knowing, what the world held. I remember knowing what Mrs. Summers would do when I showed up for a lesson sporting my first bra. I remember knowing that when it was over I would be able to sit on the flouncy bed and say, *guess what*. My world and my comfort in it depended on the sharing of events. This is part of the silliness for which young girls are, cruelly, ridiculed.

What Mrs. Summers did was exactly as had been reported. She put her hand firmly on my shoulder and turned me under her gaze like a work of art. 'Sweet,' she said. 'Just sweet.' And I felt, as it had been guaranteed I would feel, dumb. The surprise was the kindness in her voice and in her hands. She was encouraging our adolescence when everyone else was extremely busy avoiding it. In her time, she said, girls had been bound tight and flat.

Mrs. Summers had, even into her sixties, elegant sculptured legs and wonderful carriage. She had the good shoulders and the deep full bosom of women who love and manage music. Though she played the organ in the Presbyterian church, she had no affiliation with any of our mothers or grandmothers. She was not a bridge player or a Daughter of the Empire.[1] She did

---

1 Member of the Imperial Order of Daughters of the Empire, founded in 1900 to support imperial ideals, but subsequently more concerned with community issues.

not quilt or make hats or gossip.

Her dark red brick house had a wide front porch and an oak door with three small, uncurtained windows. Before each lesson I would stretch up to those windows and watch her coming to the door. She walked erect, patting her hair to ensure that no grey blonde strands had escaped the chignon, straightening her gown; it was always a gown, full and rich with colour. And always, just before she put her hand to the knob, she prepared a smile. With the swing of the door came a rush of smells: furniture polish and perfume and smoke from the fire in the winter. And her voice, across the threshold, 'Elizabeth dear,' as if surprised, delighted.

The piano was a brilliant black, dustless always, with one framed picture sitting on top, of the two of them, Mrs. Summers and her husband, standing under a grapefruit tree, in the south. I could always feel Mr. Summers in the house when I took my lesson, though he never coughed or answered the phone. He was not seen in church either; if he liked music his taste did not run to hymns or to the plunkings of adolescent girls. They had no children, only a Scottie dog and a vegetable garden.

Each spring he could be seen painting the red front porch steps, alternately, so his wife's students could still get in to her. He would stand back beside his paint can, the brush in his hand and watch us leap up the steps, giving no instruction, trusting our good sense.

Within hours of his death, the doctor's wife let it be known that Mrs. Summers had found him slumped at the sweet pea fence. He had been tidying them, arranging them through the wire. People said he had only a few yards left to do, as if that signified injustice.

His funeral was a big one. He had been the hardware man and a councillor and years before he had bought the Scouts four big tents which were still in use. It was my first non-family funeral. I was determined to go, as were all my friends, because we wanted to see how Mrs. Summers would grieve.

She grieved at her usual place, at the organ. The front row of the church was filled with his people, brothers and nephews and nieces and a few strange children, but she did not take her place with them. She stayed at the organ throughout the service, playing the music or staring at it. I was smart enough to know that she was expressing something through the music but it was nothing I could recognize, nothing I had been exposed to in her living room. I knew only that the level of difficulty was beyond her audience, had likely been pulled up from her time as a young woman at the conservatory. Toward the end of the service she switched to the chimes, making herself heard throughout the town and into the countryside. I imagined a farmer, not far away, walking across a yard with a cream can in his hand, pausing, his movement stopped by the chimes. After the service the word 'appalled' moved through the circles of people standing on the sidewalk and on the grass. My friends and I were not appalled, we were thrilled.

It was assumed that lessons would stop for at least a while but Mrs. Summers put out a few phone calls and said no, there would be no interruption. As I took the steps up to my lesson a week later I wondered about them, wondered who would paint them. I decided I would. I would get my dad or my brother to help me or I would do it alone, in the spring, when I could be sure the memory of the painting wouldn't hurt her. I didn't tell my friends about this plan; they would have wanted to join me, to help. I wanted it to be a small thing, a quiet private thing.

I had checked with my mother about what to say to Mrs. Summers, not sure if I should say anything at all.

'Just keep it simple,' she said. 'Just say you are sorry.'

'How should I say it?' I asked.

'Well, are you sorry?' she asked. 'Did you like him?'

'Yes.'

'Then don't worry.' As usual her help, her preparation, her warning, was unadorned. It seemed inadequate when compared to the enriched and detailed advice of my friends, who had rehearsed their sympathy.

As Mrs. Summers approached the door I repeated under my breath, I'm sorry, I'm sorry. The smile she prepared was not the same as the old smiles. She opened the door and I said it aloud just at the moment she was saying my name. I didn't know if she'd heard me.

There was some concern about the vegetable garden that fall but she managed it. It was almost as well tended as it had been. My friends and I saw her when we were riding past on our way to school, stooped low in the varying greens of the garden, bright and undaunted in her yellow pedal pushers[2] and grey sweatshirt. She wore gloves to protect her hands.

The first change came a few weeks later, when the garden was finished. On the piano, beside the Florida picture, sat another, younger picture. She was not a bride, was something between a bride and a Florida woman, perhaps thirty. Mr. Summers was slim and grinning and turned away from her as if talking to someone just outside the camera's range.

The following week the picture I had been hoping for was there. She was a bride, though not in white, like my mother. She wore a tailored suit and a wrist corsage and spectator shoes, black and white or navy and white. Her left hand was held in such a way that her ring picked up the sunlight of the wedding day. He wore a suit with wide lapels and wide stripes and a felt hat tipped forward, on an angle across his face. His arm was wrapped around her waist, his hand flat on her stomach. I liked these pictures, liked their arrangement on the piano, facing me.

When the other pictures appeared on the opposite side of the piano, in grey cardboard frames, five of them, I forgot good manners and stared boldly. There were five men, all young. One leaned against the flank of a Clydesdale, his hands in the pockets of his draped pants. One knelt in a soldier's uniform beside a dog. Two others, though not alike, leaned in a shared pose against the hoods of large dark cars. And one of them, with the unmistakable jaw and the eyes I saw every day in the mirror, was my grandfather.

---

2 Women's sports trousers reaching to calf.

'Lovers,' she said. 'They're just my lovers, dear.'

She was not with any of them.

Word got out, of course. Lovers on the piano. It wasn't good. Soon music students were taking the longer walk across the tracks to the new high school teacher who, it was said, was just as qualified, if not quite so experienced.

I didn't take the longer walk. My mother was puzzled; I saw her on the phone, listening, and I knew she was puzzled but she shook her head. 'No,' she said. 'No. I won't be taking Elizabeth away from her.'

I didn't ask my mother why she insisted that I continue with Mrs. Summers and though it's too late now, I still wonder how the characters arranged themselves in her head that fall. My friends hounded me for a while about the lovers, about the possibility of deeper, darker things, eager for oddity at least, if not perversity. But something stopped me from acting out the small things I saw. I was not puffed up with knowledge, did not feel unique and envied; if they had sensed any of that they would have sliced my fingers off at the knuckles, ending my music lessons forever. I felt alone and terrified.

Mrs. Summers struck my hands with her crossword puzzle book just after Christmas. I remember the mantel was still draped in garlands and the reindeer stood precariously on the snow-covered mirror on the buffet. I hadn't practised much during the vacation; my pieces were weak. Perhaps, knowing I was the only student, I wanted to feel a bit of power over her. She was sorry immediately, or seemed to be, but the next week she rapped my back with her knuckles, telling me to sit up straight, sit erect. Her gowns were no longer starched and crisp, the chignon was gone. Her hair hung loose and coarse and long. Eventually she sat in the brocade chair by the window, leafing absently through old photograph albums while I played. This arrangement suited me but I knew I wouldn't pass my examination without her help. I wanted to play the piano well, perhaps thinking this would please her, in spite of everything.

I knew about winter by then, how it works on women. My father joked secretly about my mother's February moods, telling us not to take things to heart, that spring would bring her back to herself. I hoped spring would work for Mrs. Summers too.

But when it came, when the snow moved in dirty chunks down the street, carried by the run-off, things were worse. Mrs. Summers hadn't helped me at all; my mother seemed oblivious to my flounderings on the piano at home and my friends said they were far ahead of me. The day of my last lesson Mrs. Summers didn't prepare a smile at all and she looked back at me through those three small windows in the oak door. I was bent down unlacing my saddle shoes when I noticed the navy and white spectators from her wedding day. She lifted her dingy gown.

'Remember these?' she asked.

'Yes,' I answered.

She wheeled her back to me, going to the piano bench. 'Of course you don't,' she snapped. 'How could you?' She sat down and played for me, pieces I had not even imagined. She began to hiss at her blue-veined fingers as they missed their place, their time. When the half-hour was up she named a date for my examination. We both knew there was little chance I'd pass.

I could have told. I could have given the details to my mother and to my friends, who would have confided in their mothers. I could have lied myself into the glory of victimization. I'd done it before. But I was drawn to the hurt, to the chaos. There was an odd comfort in me. I wondered if I was making what my mother had once called a moral choice, a choice that would make my life easier, or harder.

The steps had always been blood red. I charged the paint and the brush to my father's account at the hardware store and I took our broom over with me and a rag I had soaked with the garden hose. I cleaned the steps and painted every other one, just as Mr. Summers had. She didn't come out that first day but on the second day I had just dropped everything and begun to wipe the steps again with my rag when the oak door swung open.

'Will you just go away?' she said. 'Just disappear.'

I held my ground, stood erect with the rag dripping at my side. She watched the tears, unstoppable, sliding down my cheeks. I didn't wipe them away or take the deep breath that brings pride back.

She came at me with her arms out and though there was no way to tell whether she was going to pound me or lean on me or hug me, I could not have run. Her hands were firm on my shoulders; the sound she made was loud and brutal and almost young.

§ *Childhood discovery* Munro, Findley; Af: Gurnah; Carib: Lamming, Edgell, Senior, Kincaid; SA: Selvadurai, Sidhwa; SEA: Maniam, Somtow

SUSAN SWAN (1945–)

From The Biggest Modern Woman of the World

The Biggest Modern Woman of the World is the fictional autobiography of Anna Haining Swan, a real-life nineteenth-century giantess from Nova Scotia, who may have been an ancestor of the author, Susan Swan. Anna Swan achieved celebrity status as an exhibit in the freaks collection of the showman P. T. Barnum's Museum of America in New York and the novel mixes a richly circumstantial account of her life with a varied showbusiness-like manner of presentation and a flair for magniloquent language. This can be seen here in the opening chapter, 'Spieling', which anticipates much of the subsequent action.

Do you know how a giantess grows? Overnight? Like the sumac bush? Or slowly, like a cedar of Lebanon?

I, Hominida Pina Pituitosa Majora, a warm-blooded, viviparous,[1] conifer-

---

1 Bringing forth young alive, not hatching through an egg.

ous giantess, grew as an elephant grows, expanding in pounds as I rose in inches. My body weight doubled and then tripled by the time I was four.

I did not grow straight up like an Eastern White Pine, the largest conifer in North-East America, although I sprang from a Nova Scotian floor and learned to consort with livewood throughout the world without losing my needles. The LIVING LUMBER GIRL who walked and talked and juggled the Pre-Cambrian Shield[2] (rocks to you, sir).

But I digress from my opener. I grew *out* and up as does the BLUE WHALE, LARGEST IN THE SEA, and the AFRICAN BUSH ELEPHANT, LARGEST ON LAND. The principle that weight varies as the cube of linear dimensions – that's the proper answer.

My resemblance to other babies was amazing, but my ecstatic face was a dead giveaway: I was a hyperendocrinal[3] nympha, with too much resin in the blood. The gummy elixir shot through my veins in uncontrolled quantities. Lifting up my tubby form, the juice propelled me HEAD FIRST past the unpainted stomach of the kitchen table, and aimed my crown of red curls at the top of the loft where chinks in the roof let daylight through in a sideways blare of light.

There was a sky-breaking crash! My head splintered the ceiling: it stuck through the shanty roof, higher than chimneys. My red-hot forehead, throbbing from the effort of growth, cooled in special breezes reserved for the forest's uppermost branches. That's how I, Anna Haining Swan, the INCREDIBLE KNOTSUCKING LUMBER LASS, confounded her first audience in 1846 in the land of the Blue-noses.[4] This maritime region is located on the eastern coast of the diverse and infinite Dominion of Canada and its inhabitants are called Blue-noses, not on account of the northern gales that nip their faces, but because of a superior brand of potato that is grown there, called Blue-nose.

Now I am in full voice . . . blowing my own horn . . . spieling the way I used to for P.T. Barnum, Queen Victoria, and all the normals who came to my performances after I grew up into an eight-foot giantess who toured North America and the Continent. This is my final appearance and I promise to tell all. What really happened to the BIGGEST MODERN WOMAN OF THE WORLD in a never-before-revealed autobiography which contains testimonials and documents by friends and associates (from their perspective) of a Victorian lady who refused to be inconsequential.

Yes, I was a GENUINE SHOW-BIZ CELEBRITY who found no forum modern enough to suit my talents and who has written this authentic account to entertain you the way I could not during my career as a professional giantess. A good performer has many spiels and I have three up my long sleeve to delight and astound:

1. my lecture at Barnum's museum

---

2 Canadian Shield.   3 With an excess of growth hormone produced by the anterior pituitary gland.   4 Nova Scotians.

2. what my hometown will say about me 100 years from now
3. the real time spiel

May I start with Barnum and work up? (It's the only direction I understand.)

Spiel No. 1: The American Museum, *Circa* 1863

Welcome, dear friends and visitors. I, Anna Haining Swan, am not a hoax. I am the FIRST GIANTESS to be presented at the American Museum and I stand 8'1" in my bare feet. My cloth boots, which you can't see because the canons of taste forbid it, are low to the ground. Mr. P.T. Barnum likes to say that if I left a slipper on the stairs of a palace, he would be hard pressed to find a prince to fit it. This is not as rude as it sounds: it is the sort of bragging I am accustomed to hearing from the GREAT SHOWMAN who will not hire or exhibit any giants unless the women are over seven feet and men higher than seven and a half.

You may be humbugged in other theatres where giants reinforce their height with small stilts or elevated shoes, high hats and platforms designed to pile illusion upon illusion. But not in the Grand Lecture Hall which holds authentic curiosities such as the ORIGINAL THIN MAN, the SWISS BELL RINGERS, the WONDERFUL ELIOPHOBUS FAMILY OF AFRICA whose albino physiognomy stuns the wondering audience, and Commodore Nutt, the SHORTEST OF MEN, whom you see before you, on my shoulder.

The Commodore and I are an excellent illustration of the way extremes meet in Mr. Barnum's showcase. But allow me to return to his remark about my shoe. He is quite wrong. You have only to look around this wonderful pavilion to find a few princes whose shoes I can't fill.

On the next dais, you will see Colonel Goshen, the PALESTINIAN GIANT, who is an object of admiration, not only on account of his immense height and frame, but also by reason of his manly beauty and delightful manners. He is a giant in every sense of the word.

I mention extraordinary men like the Colonel not because I am flirtatious by nature, but to show you that we of extreme height are not different from you of normal stature. We share normal interests – I do shell work and the Commodore plays polo and we are concerned with the business of making a living, which some of us do best by being ourselves. My manager, Judge Apollo Ingalls, is a man of your size, and he says Mr. Barnum's prodigies have an important part to play in the human drama. But who can say it is greater than your own contributions to the public weal?

As our society becomes standardized, it grows more difficult for giants and dwarfs to fit in. Our clothes must be specially made, and our shoes, which costs a great deal of money. I find eight-foot doorways too low, carriages, trains and depots too confining. I can't visit a theatre unless I sit in the back row so my head won't block the view and unless I can stretch my legs down the aisle.

The Commodore experiences these difficulties in reverse. Just as I must be cautious about ceiling fans, the Commodore avoids large dogs and cats that could menace his diminutive form. On the New Hampshire farm where he was raised, the Commodore was attacked by one of his father's turkeys, with unhappy consequences. When I was a child in New Annan, Nova Scotia, I could eat dinner with my family only if I sat on the floor. If I sat in a chair, my head would be too far above the heads of my siblings to allow me to converse.

I mention this, not to invoke pity, but to share with you the irritation the Commodore and I face in our daily lives. We do not feel a modicum of self-pity, since the accidents of our physical natures have made it possible for us to travel widely, to converse with royalty and celebrated personages and, in my case, to study and learn many fascinating things.

Those who have paid for the additional feature of our drawing-room exhibition are invited to stay and watch the Commodore and I perform Act 1, Scene VII, of *Macbeth*. The Commodore vacillates wonderfully as Macbeth while I have been complimented by Queen Victoria on my sympathetic portrait of a mother who claimed she could pluck a nipple from her infant's boneless gums and dash the child's brains out. The playlet is an example of Mr. Barnum's belief that amusement is the best way to eliminate ignorance and destroy barriers between the world of normal size and the one inhabited by the Commodore and myself.

This concludes my lecture, which is offered every afternoon and evening in the lecture hall for a 25¢ ticket. In Mr. Barnum's world of marvels, SCIENCE is the RINGLEADER, taming NATURE, who pours forth BOUNTY for all.

Apollo wrote my lecture, borrowing phrases from Barnum's handbills, and rehearsed me on our walk to work through Central Park. My manager had a loud voice. 'Send your voice over in a phaeton,'[5] Barnum liked to tell Apollo, who was called the AUSTRALIAN MOUTH at the museum.

Every morning, Apollo walked me past the Astor Hotel, where Yankees of fashion loitered, whispering to me under his breath to take small steps. Then his mouth yawned open and his voice assaulted the passers-by: 'THE ONLY GIANTESS IN THE WORLD LEAVES FOR LONDON TODAY TO VISIT THE QUEEN. DON'T MISS YOUR LAST CHANCE TO SEE THIS ASTOUNDING CURIOSITY. SHE'LL MEET YOU IN PERSON AND INSTRUCT YOU ON THE TOPIC OF GIGANTISM. THIS OLYMPIAN CINDERELLA IS A MARVEL YOU WILL NEVER FORGET.'

Spiel No. 2: Sunrise Trail Museum, Tatamagouche, *Circa* 1977

Have you heard the story of Annie Swan? One time more famous than the

---

5 Open, four-wheeled carriage.

other Maritime giant, McAskill. No. Ahm. Born in 1846, she was a charming girl, ah, eight feet tall with, ahm, a Mona Lisa look there. That smile, ahm. Hard to figure it. Now she joined P.T. Barnum's museum in 1862, toured the world, entertained royalty and married for love. Ahm, that's her shoe here. And the green basque, and here's her wedding portrait.

At fifteen years of age: take a good look at the pict. . . . at her father, ahm, the one with his hands folded across his chest. Her mother was 5'2" and her father, Alex Swan, couldn't have been more than, ahm, 5'6". At fifteen, she could look out the window above the door of her home. Let's see, she went and lived with relatives in Truro to go to teachers' college. A regular bookworm, you know. Ahm, she was unhappy, ah, there. Crowds followed her home from school. Then she went out and married the KENTUCKY GIANT in 1871 and settled in Ohio. She was the tallest woman in the world and she got her man. Ahm, strange to say, she died a day before she was 42 and her husband married a five-foot woman. That's ah – a great difference. And, ah, Annie and the KENTUCKY GIANT had giant babies. The two biggest babies in the world. But they both died. Ahm, this is, uh-huh, a dog churn. The dog, ahm, would get inside and run and run. Over there? A baby churn, ahm, same principle. And here's the – ah, Hubert Carruthers who lived down the road from Annie's family, though in her papers, you know, Annie always called him Hubert Belcourt. He was 3'10". Yeah, ahm, it's him in the donkey cart. He died at the age of 76 and them are his pants beside the cavalry trousers of Annie's husband, ahm, Martin Van Buren Bates.

The Real Time Spiel

It could be said of me that I'm preoccupied with scale, but I am not as concerned with body length as you might expect. I am more concerned with hand size. That's my standard of reference because experience has taught me there is a correlation between the size of the hand and the size of what makes a man a man. Besides, men's hands have helped to shape my life.

My own hand measures ten inches from the wrist to the tip of my middle finger. My index finger is six inches long and I have a span of one foot. No man except my childhood sweetheart has matched the length of my hand. You know what doctors say: big woman, big finger.

Angus had wider digits. The tufts of men's fingers are fleshier, *n'est-ce pas?* If we redefined the digit using Angus as a model, we could double our homes, children, our schools, banks . . . sorry. I see this would make us shrink, not grow. What could be worse for North America? Here I get into dangerous ground, tangling myself up like M.V.B. I mean Martin Van Buren Bates, the KENTUCKY GIANT, who shared my devotion to scale. Only Martin, the silly ogre, thought North Americans like us should boss the world because normals are too small and puny to know what's good for them.

I, *au contraire*, have always wanted to be a gallant giantess, a doer of good deeds, and I have spent my life searching for ways to put my size to best use.

Martin's hands were small for a giant's. They measured eight inches from wrist to tip, and his index finger was three and a quarter. Unlike Angus, Martin pampered his hands. He wore yellow kid gloves, which a reporter in the *Floyd County Times* (just north of Martin's Kentucky birthplace) said made his hands look like 'pressed hams.' He was flattering Martin, who enjoyed having himself described as a well-proportioned colossus.

Angus neglected his hands – as he did the rest of his imposing figure – and they hung like dejected children at his sides. A glimpse of them, dangling beneath his muslin cuffs, made a hollow clunk go off in my head. Immediately, I saw their companion image: my hands, beneath my trumpet-shaped sleeves, clasping a parasol of watered silk.

Ingalls' measurements were greater than Martin's, which was astonishing since Ingalls, my manager, was a shorter man. He was the normal fellow in my life and the only one with the name of a god. Very fanciful for an Australian whose grandparents were Essex convicts. Of course, Apollo and Martin had titles. They also shared an astrology sign, Scorpio, which they believed to be the sign of powerful men.

Apollo's literary ability showed itself in the titles 'Judge' and 'Captain' which he gave to himself and Martin respectively. It was customary to use military titles after the civil war in the U.S. But a real gentleman has no need to dress himself up: Apollo and Martin were not saluted thus by me.

Barnum's hands were surprisingly average.

The smallest fingers, no more than an inch, belonged to my childhood friend, Hubert Belcourt. When he was nice to me, I didn't want to remind him of the size of his hands, but during his pedantic moods, I wanted to shout to the Maritimes: HUBERT BELCOURT HAS THE SMALLEST HANDS IN THE CANADAS. His fingers were teenier than those of the Commodore or Tom Thumb, my theatrical colleagues.

And wait – in spite of family delicacy, I can't omit my father, whose fingers were a nice fit with my four-year-old mitt. By that time I realized I wasn't an extension of my mother's body and I considered my father a physical equivalent. (It is not the lot of young giants to be awed by parental dimensions.)

When I was twelve, my fingers enfolded my father's baby fist. His bantam size endeared him to me and set the precedent for my reaction to all human males. Their size makes them seem vulnerable and I confess that as a grown woman I can't meet a man smaller than myself – i.e., every man except Angus – without acting like a welcome wagon. I want to shout to all of them: SAMPLE ANNIE'S FREE EATS & TONICS! GUARANTEED TO MAKE YOU GROW.

I'm too big now to care what they say about me in Colchester County. Let small minds have their say. I know my preoccupation with size is unladylike, but at least it stops with hands and goes no farther. I truly do not care how tall men are or how broad. I don't even know how big I am. I stopped measuring the march of my head to the sky before my mother accepted Barnum's contract (which she redrafted herself so the Connecticut horse trader had to provide me with lessons in French and music as well as my salary of $1,000 a month). Why bother measuring? Clearly, I *am* large.

Barnum sent an agent up to Nova Scotia to see if I was authentic, a Quaker gentleman who measured me while I lay on the dirt floor of the shanty like a corpse. The agent scribbled notations in a book, but he didn't sing them out the way I had anticipated. Barnum is infamous for exaggerating the heights of his giants, and as he bills me at 8'1", I am definitely less.[6] In New Annan, my mother told friends I was 7'9" and privately hoped I would not top eight feet. I put my height at 7'11½". It's an educated guess.

§ *Alternative identities for women* Smart, Thomas, Marlatt, van Herk, Lau; *Size* Aus: Murray (2)

GEORGE ELLIOTT CLARKE (1960–)

How Exile Melts to One Hundred Roses

I climb to Whylah Falls because I thirst,
Hunger, for you, Shelley, and shake to touch
Your house that slides down Mount Eulah to fog –
The misery of the Sixhiboux River.
5 My five-winter exile now melts
To roses gorged where tears once hammered dirt.
I dream the poems I sent all smell of grass
And gold daisies sprouted in a tumbler,
While song cartwheels in air scrubbed deaf to threats
10 Of disaster, and fiddle-eights cry out
With crows, wedding memory with desire,
And I peer through pined distance to your home:
Pushkin drawls dirty songs, his banjo packed
With bluebells and mayflowers; plump Cora whoops,
15 Cackles, tells him to 'Keep a-strummin', man!'
Othello looses pants, spills into bed
With Liana, and their feet never touch
The floor until morning. Pushkin's voice twangs,
Then, smelling of plug tobacco, and staggered
20 By home-stilled rum, he winks out in Cora's lap.

---

6 According to *The Guinness Book of Records*, Anna Swan was 7ft 5½in.; she and Martin Van Buren Bates (7ft 2½ in) are listed as the tallest married couple on record.

1 **Whylah Falls**: a Nova Scotian village founded by loyalist African–Americans in 1783.

10 **fiddle-eights**: 'an invented word to describe the juxtaposed two circle shape of a fiddle' (George Elliott Clarke).

2 **Shelley**: like Pushkin and Othello, a resident of Whylah Falls in Clarke's poem.

I ramble home and find love's fleshed: mermaids
And drunk sailors kiss in the Sixhiboux;
Bearded, black saints, reeking of oil, comb fields
That plunge to poverty no budget soothes;
25   Reverend Langford hollers against silk
And money, devil booze and bingo chips,
And false communion between the sexes,
Then slinks to Liana once O is done.
Mrs. Belle Brooks gulps marijuana smoke,
30   Uncorks seventy-five years of gossip,
To preach scotch-breathed sermons of tinfoil-winged
Angels hauled from pines or pulled, naked,
From sties. Shelley, we wrest diamonds from coal,
Scrounge pears from grubs and stones, lest penury
35   Work filthy rags of our magnificence,
Or planners bulldoze our flowers into dirt.
   I love you, Sweets – your eyes black with sorrow,
Your Sphinx-like smile, your breasts like ripe apples!
I hurry home, weary of seeking love
40   In banks and trusts, lusting to clench you tight –
While night is wet with fire, the earthy taste
Of mushrooms black with dew, the ash of figs –
And sweat love until crows usher in dawn.
Shelley, I pick my steps out of the earth!

ARITHA VAN HERK (1954–)

From No Fixed Address

Sub-titled 'an amorous journey', *No Fixed Address* reverses the gender conventions of picaresque fiction. It describes the adventures of Arachne Manteia, an underwear saleswoman who travels through the Prairie provinces, peddling her wares and eluding the snares in which the various men she encounters endeavour to entrap her. 'Wild Woman' and 'Apprehended', taken from the latter part of the novel, show her as attuned to the Prairie landscape, but falling foul of the law when she is arrested for kidnapping. The offence in question relates to her having taken Josef, a Bosnian Serb immigrant now in his late eighties, away from the old people's home in which his family has recently placed him.

Wild Woman

They sink farther and farther into prairie that mirrors the landscape of their confusion, and the wind echoes their exchange. Arachne works in slowly advancing circles, a movement determined by coulees[1] and bluffs, the winding rivers they cross again and again. From Cadillac to Pambrun, Neidpath, Wymark, Chortitz, Blumenhof, back to Pontex, on to Kincaid, Lafleche, Gravelbourg, Kelstern, Vanguard, back to Gravelbourg, then Mossbank, Assiniboia, Rockglen, Willow Bunch (where he disappears and she finds him in the basement of the local museum, asleep on the Willow Bunch giant's bed), Bengough, Ogema, Ceylon, Minton. The Mercedes spins a froth of dust and gravel, the prairie folds itself around them, the sky blazes.

In Minton Arachne has to wait while Jack Ross serves customers.

'Wife's gone to Weyburn for the day,' he grumbles. 'Got a bad hip, and standing on this floor all day don't help.'

'Isn't the clinic in Estevan better?' Arachne is mentally reducing the size of his order. Without Jess, Jack settles for a dozen of everything. He doesn't like lengthy discussions of 'wimmin's stuff' and he always brightens when Arachne's samples are stowed in her car and he can tell her about the town's latest accident, death or fire.

'She goes to the chiropractor. Seems to help. But she's gone a whole day and I've got to manage.'

Arachne checks his old stock while he rings up a customer's order. She's making a notation when Josef pushes open the screen door and stumps inside. She left him sleeping in the car. She goes to him. 'Are you all right?' Jack is sure to notice, will say, She's done for now, taking her grandpa on the road with her. Ladies' will have to find another rep. She almost giggles. But the screen slams again and the pair who come in are as curious as she and Josef.

'What'll we get?' says the man.

The girl fairly spins in his radius. The man, sixty at least, holding a cane even, white-haired, a scarred face, laughs down at her with indulgent delight. She swirls around him, filling her arms.

'Bread. Cheese. Eggs. Coffee. Steak. Have you got matches?'

'Yes,' says the man, openly caressing her buttocks.

Josef and Arachne watch across a pyramid of cans, their mirror image free and pleasured, no inheritances, no legacies.

'Juice,' says the girl. 'I'm so thirsty in the middle of the night.'

'Chocolate,' says the man, and the girl throws her arms around him and kisses his cheek.

'And butter –'

'Yes, of course, don't forget the butter.'

They deposit everything in front of Jack's cash register.

'Oh, bacon! Where's the bacon?'

'I'll slice it right up,' says Jack drily. 'Side or back? Side's $2.29 a pound and back's $2.99.'

'Back,' says the girl, rubbing one leg against the man. 'Half a pound.'

'Do you know,' asks the man, 'where we can find a huge hill that's sup-

---

1 Ravines.

posed to have some effigy on it?' He fingers the girl's arm.

'What hill?' Jack moves the slicer back and forth.

'Some high bluff. Saskatchewan archives said it was around here. Supposed to have a human shape on it.'

'Don't know,' says Jack. 'I think you're better off going over Big Muddy way to Bengough.'

The girl is suddenly serious. 'Aren't there any high hills around here?'

'Could be,' Jack mumbles. 'They say there are but I've never seen any.'

The girl lifts a serious face to the man. 'Maybe we're looking in the wrong place.'

'We'll find it. We know it's there.' He gives Jack some bills and they bang out, each holding a bag in one hand, the other busy touching skin.

Arachne takes Josef's arm. 'Jack, what are they looking for?'

'A motel. There's one close to Bengough.'

'Come on.'

'There's miles of prairie to fool around in. They don't need to do it up there.'

'Where?'

'Wild Woman. Why are you so interested?' He looks from Arachne to Josef and back again. 'If you want to know, you go over to Big Beaver and ask old Dunc. You can find him in that Drop-in Centre. He knows.'

'All right. Now, what's your order?'

'Dozen of everything.'

On the oiled street Arachne opens the trunk and throws her sample boxes inside. The movie set seems to blink and then hunch itself lower on its props, bizarre lumber against the April sky.

They find him, old Dunc, sitting on a rungless wooden chair outside the door of a cinder-block hall watching two men pour the town's new sidewalks. 'You gotta go east, then south. Highest hill for miles around. Line rider used to sit up there, watch the border.' He chuckles. 'No Yanks in those days.' His eyelids, loose and sagged, cannot hold themselves open. Each lid is carefully anchored to his eyebrows with white bandage tape, as though he wants to prevent the narrowed, diminished vision of age, stay watchful. 'You can see everything. Up there.' He spits carefully onto the new cement. 'That other pair was going up there too.'

They are unprepared for the cone that springs over the last gravel rise. It looks a worn volcano planted there, looming into sky. Arachne searches for a road, finally finds a barbed-wire gate to a gravel pit. She cuts her hand forcing it open, then skirts the pit until the Mercedes is hidden behind the cliff. They pull on their coats, lock the car and climb. Arachne slowing herself to Josef's caned pace, silent, scrambling, they climb. Disappear, vanish into another element.

On the ridge the fierce wind thrusts at them. Arachne looks at the sky, at the circle of world below them, and begins to dance. Old Dunc was right; up here she can see everything, everything. It is a long way east she has circled and circled, finally come to this nipple of land on the breast of the world, immensely high and windswept. She spins, then stops and looks at Josef crouched over his cane, his spun hair torn, his face papery in the dust-flinging wind. She takes his hand and pulls him with her, down to one of the hill's folds, flanked against the nose of the cone.

And there they find the Wild Woman, her stone outline spread to infinite sky, to a prairie grassland's suggestion of paradise, a woman open-armed on the highest hill in that world. They trace her outline: arms, amulet, hair, teeth, skirt, breasts, feet. Arachne stands between her legs.

Her face speaks, the welcome gesture of arms, the amulet's adornment, the breasts' soft curves, immensely eloquent. Arachne's small shadow falls within the woman's shape, the stone-shaped woman. She stretches out inside the woman, lies within the stones on her back beneath that wheeling sky, arms outflung like the woman's, her head cushioned on a circle of breast. Josef stands between her legs, watching, then he stumps away.

The ridge is sheltered from the gusting wind; it is almost warm here. Arachne will never get tired of looking at the sky from within the woman's arms, but she finally rises and stares beyond the outline of rock to the horizon that wheels four dimensions around her. What secret burial she makes before she walks down the steep ridge to the car and the waiting old man is buried there.

Apprehended

When Arachne answers the door, it's the shoes she sees, highly polished black shoes that mirror her, distant and oblated. Her eyes travel from the cruel toes up the black pants and uniform coat to the square, clean-shaven face.

'Miss Manteia?'

'Yes.'

'You're under arrest. The charges are kidnapping, transportation out of the province and intent to extort. Come with us, please.'

§ *Alternative identities for women* Smart, Thomas, Marlatt, Swan, Lau; Aus: Garner, Grenville

EVELYN LAU (1971–)

From Fresh Girls

Set in Vancouver, *Fresh Girls* is a collection of short stories about young women whose sexual experiences and fantasies isolate them from society at large. This extract is the beginning of 'Mercy', a story which illustrates the volume's representation of the release offered by transgressive sexual behaviour.

It is your wife's fortieth birthday, and I am torturing you to the sounds of a tape of Dylan Thomas giving a poetry recital. His voice is theatrical, and at times it hovers at the edges of breaking into song. 'Do not go gentle into that good night . . . Rage, rage against the dying of the light . . . .' His words, charged with command, seem to pulse through my own body. Obediently I slip the spiked heel of my shoe into your mouth. You are watching me with confusion because I am drunk and balancing over your naked body takes more skill than you think. I don't want to fall on you with my weight and the stabbing silver of my bracelet, injuring you, making it impossible for you to meet your wife later in the evening for dinner down by the harbor where the white ships come in. She will chatter on about *The New York Review of Books*, literary magazines, publishers' conventions, and other things that bewilder you because you decided to make money in medicine instead of writing poetry. Neither of us knew when we made our respective choices that we might be equally unfulfilled. I do not want to hurt you, at least not clumsily, not out of drunkenness, not because the high arches of my feet prevent me from balancing in spike heels. I want it to mean something when I hurt you, I want each transgression to be a deliberate one that cuts both ways, something that neither of us will be able to blame on bottles of wine or the fact that when I am in this position, one foot balanced on your neck, there is nothing nearby to hold on to and the only thing stable is the floor which seems a long way off from up here.

I will not go gentle into you. The high heel of my shoe is in your mouth, and it is cutting the roof where the flesh is ridged and ticklish. You suck the heel as you would a phallus, and I wonder what you are tasting, what grotty remains of dust and dirt and sidewalk you are swallowing down the soft pinkness of your throat. Up here I can see you are going bald, the expanse of your forehead with your gray hair tossed backwards onto the carpet is wide and gleaming. With your eyes shut and your mouth working to please the point of my shoe, you could easily be an inflatable doll or a cartoon and I am able then to withdraw my heel as carefully as a penis and rake it in pink crescents across your cheek and down your chin.

In my sessions with you I search for the evil inside us that we share like kisses between our open mouths. The boundaries I once saw as steel fences in my mind turned out to be sodden wooden planks when I reached them, easily kicked down. Each act of pain became easier to inflict once the initial transgressions had been committed, and we had understood ourselves capable of surviving them. Once I even tried on myself the things I do to you. Whipping myself with a silver chain, I became fascinated by the stopped seconds of pain that opened my mouth and closed my eyes. Afterwards I was left looking down at my thighs where the circle of the chain I had snapped down my body had left a perfect imprint of itself, pink like a rubber stamp, like one of those playful rubber stamps with happy faces on them.

When the pain stopped, time moved again and I wondered if perhaps in our time together you felt this also, this stopping of time as it races past you now that you are middle-aged and some of your friends are already dead. Perhaps only the absorption of pain can distract you from the details of your daily life – the necessary hours at the office, the teenaged children demanding money for concerts and clothes, the golf lessons on weekend afternoons. All this leading you down the road of increasing age, minor illnesses, and death.

'Old age should burn and rave at close of day,' Thomas instructs sternly.

§ *Alternative identities for women* Smart, Thomas, Marlatt, Swan, van Herk

Part IV

CARIBBEAN

C. L. R. JAMES (1901–89)

From Beyond a Boundary

Beyond a Boundary is a classic of cricket literature which relates developments in the sport to changes in society at large. In this passage, James, one of the Caribbean's most versatile authors – he was a distinguished Marxist historian, social commentator, novelist and literary critic as well as a cricket writer – discusses the significance of the controversial 'body-line' tour of Australia by England in 1932–3 and sees the career of the Australian batsman Don Bradman, the most prolific scorer in cricketing history, as a product of its era.

. . . What has happened to the house built by Arnold,[1] Thomas Hughes[2] and W.G.?[3] The history of its decline is as fascinating (and as unexplored) as the history of its rise.

By 1887, when the *Badminton Book of Cricket* was published, cricket as a guardian of morals was at its best and most prosperous. That book is evidence sufficient. It was beautifully written and to this day is as entertaining and instructive as anything that has ever been published on the game. It had style, it had confidence. The writers had no doubt of what the status of a professional cricketer was and why it should be so. They could tell the Australians frankly that they didn't want them back for another five years: they were bored with the personnel of the England–Australia games, they wanted time to set the internal business of English cricket in order. The book is utterly free of cant. The one blatant moralism seems to have been tacked on to the end of a chapter as an afterthought. They had the thing itself and they did not need to sing, i.e. to cant about it. Ten years later, by the *Jubilee Book of Cricket*, 1897, the guardians were conscious of profane murmurings. Cricket, says a writer in the *Jubilee Book*, is very valuable, but he confesses that he finds it hard to explain why. Nevertheless, cricket as a cult was preserved intact up to 1913. Like the special interests which had made it their own, it received a violent shock from the war of 1914–18. Country house cricket was after 1918 but a shadow, the University match was barely holding its own, the long struggle of the amateur against extinction began. The game, however, was now part of the national life, it maintained its special connotations in the public schools, despite the sniping of the Waughs, the Graveses, the Sassoons.

The blow from which 'It isn't cricket' has never recovered came from within and it came in 1932. This was body-line.

J. H. Fingleton, the Australian journalist, has written an excellent and necessary book on the body-line controversy. He takes an historical view, but in the end he makes out the cause of body-line to be the phenomenal

---

1 Thomas Arnold (1795–1842), educator and historian who as headmaster of Rugby School made it a model for the English public school. 2 Thomas Hughes (1822–96), best known as the author of *Tom Brown's Schooldays* (1857), a novel about Rugby during Thomas Arnold's time.. 3 W. G. Grace.

batting of Bradman and the search of English selectors for means to over-throw him. I believe that there was more than that to body-line. And, more important, I believe that what body-line signified is still with us.

Body-line was not an incident, it was not an accident, it was not a tempo-rary aberration. It was the violence and ferocity of our age expressing itself in cricket. The time was the early thirties, the period in which the contempo-rary rejection of tradition, the contemporary disregard of means, the con-temporary callousness, were taking shape. The totalitarian dictators cultivated brutality of set purpose. By now all of us have supped full with horrors. Today cruelties and abominations which would have immeasurably shocked and per-manently distressed earlier ages are a commonplace. We must toughen our hides to live at all. We are now like Macbeth in his last stage:

'The time has been my senses would have cool'd
To hear a night-shriek, and my fell of hair
Would at a dismal treatise rouse and stir
As life were in't. I have supped full with horrors;
Direness, familiar to my slaughterous thoughts,
Cannot once start me.'[4]

It began in World War I. Exhaustion and a fictitious prosperity in the late twenties delayed its maturity. It came into its own in 1929. Cricket could no more resist than the other organizations and values of the nineteenth cen-tury were able to resist. That big cricket survived the initial shock at all is a testimony to its inherent decency and the deep roots it had sunk.

The violence of the cricket passions unloosed in the thirties is what strikes the observer today. There was no absolute necessity for Voce and Larwood to take the actions that they did on their return from Australia. Rather than submit to the opinions of a large majority, A. W. Carr preferred to go out of the game altogether. Jardine[5] seemed to be at war not with the Australian eleven but all Australia. The history books tell us that he carried his relent-lessness to India: there were no Bradmans in India. What objective neces-sity was there to introduce body-line into England after the Australian tour? Yet the attempt was made. Jardine soon went, never to return. Ponsford abandoned the game when he was only thirty-four. Sir Donald Bradman assures us that but for the intervention of the war, 1938 would have been his last visit to England, and he contemplated only one more season in Australia. He was younger than Ponsford. No balls had whizzed past his head for years. Yet he had had enough.

It is in Bradman's autobiography that we can today see conveniently the mentality of the time. The most remarkable page in that remarkable book is his account of his feelings after he had completed his hundredth century. He had played big cricket for nearly twenty years. In that time he had scored as no one had ever scored before. He had made his runs at the rate of fifty an hour. He had scored centuries and double centuries and treble centuries in cricket of the most demanding type. He had conquered bowlers and

4 *Macbeth*, v. 5. 10–15. 5 Captain of the English team on the body-line tour.

decided series. Yet what are his sentiments after he had made the hundredth run of the hundredth century? He felt it incumbent upon him, he says, to give the crowd which had so cheered his achievement some reward for its wonderful feelings towards him. He therefore proceeded to hit 71 runs in 45 minutes. This, he adds, is the way he would always wish to have batted if circumstances had permitted him. However, as circumstances did at last permit him the luxury, he classed 'that particular section of my innings as the most satisfying of my career'. In all the years that I have been reading books on cricket this remains the strangest statement that I have ever read, and one to which I frequently return; to it, and to the writer. If Sir Donald Bradman was able to play 'in the way I would always have loved to do had circumstances permitted' only after he had made one hundred centuries, we have to ask ourselves: What were these inhibiting circumstances?

This much at least is obvious. The game he had played between 1928 and 1947 was a game quite different from the one that had been played by Grace and Shrewsbury, Trumper and Ranjitsinhji, Hobbs and Rhodes, the game we had played in the West Indies. Grace, Ranjitsinhji, Trumper and their fellows who had played with them lost infinitely more matches and series than Sir Donald Bradman ever lost. They were painstaking men who gave all they had to cricket. Yet I cannot conceive of any of them thinking of batting in the way Sir Donald thought of it. He has been blamed for machine-like play. He has been blamed for the ruthlessness with which he piled up big scores. This is absurd. I have seen some of his greatest innings and I do not wish to see anything finer. George Headley has explained to me that people speak of Sir Donald's heavy scoring as if each and every great batsman was able to do the same, but refrained for aesthetic or chival- rous reasons which Sir Donald ignored. Speaking with authority, Headley is lost in admiration and even in wonder at the nervous stamina and concen- tration which Sir Donald displayed in making these mammoth scores so con- sistently over so long a period. In the autobiography Sir Donald maintains that he played cricket according to the rules as he saw them. There is no need to question this. Every page of his book shows that he has been deeply hurt by what he considers unfair criticism. Every accusation that I have ever heard made against him he has taken care to answer. The slightest wound still gives pain to this tough, relentless opponent. He is conscious of right- eousness. His sincerity is patent. He feels himself a victim, and a victim he is, but not of petty jealousies of individual men. The chronicles of the time (far more then than now), when re-read today in the light of after events, tell the story clearly enough. The 1930 Australian team which broke all pre- vious records took a little time to get going and was left in no doubt as to what spectators and pressmen thought.

By 1928, when he began, big cricket was already being played everywhere with the ruthlessness that Bradman is saddled with. He never knew any other kind of cricket. Ponsford and his triple and quadruple centuries had set the tone for Bradman. If Bradman made 974 runs in Tests in 1930 he had experienced when a boy of eighteen a far more merciless 905 from Hammond in the season of 1928–9. His gifts and his cricket personality matured at a time when the ethics, the morals, the personal impulses and desires of cricketers were quite different from those who had played the game in the decades that had preceded. Cricketers already mature when Bradman appeared might want to play like Bradman. They couldn't. They hadn't the outlook. They hadn't the temper. They had inhibitions Bradman never knew.

The new ones could learn. Hutton at the Oval in 1938 showed that he had learnt well. I have never had so painful an experience at any cricket match as when watching Hutton and Hardstaff together during the England innings of 903 for eight declared. Body-line may have vanished. Its temper remained. Other men had stood out above their fellows. W.G. had. But 1865 was not 1930. The spirit which Sir Donald Bradman could release only after a hundred centuries was present, I am sure, in every single one of the hundred centuries that W. G. Grace made, was always present in Trumper and Ranjitsinhji, Fry and Hobbs. That spirit was dead. If Hobbs had been born in 1910, or later, England would have bred another Bradman. Sir Donald first ran the cricket mile in under four minutes and unloosed the floodgates. Circumstances conspired to place the blame on him. I have gathered that even in Australia the attitude to him is ambivalent. They admire him, they are grateful to him, they love him, but they know that the disregard of the compulsions of everyday life, the chivalry that was always a part of the game, began to fade at the time he came into it. Sir Donald is not to blame. He was unfortunate in his place and time. The fact remains that he was in his own way as tough as Jardine.

This was the situation faced by 'It isn't cricket' in 1930. It was not only a Test series at stake. Everything that the temple stood for seemed threatened within and without. If Bradman continued his portentous career a way of life, a system of morals, faced the possibility of disgrace and defeat just at the particular time when more than ever it needed the stimulus of victory and prestige. The men who had made it their special preserve were threatened not only in cricket. They were threatened everywhere. As is usual in such cases, they fought back blindly and were driven into extravagance and immorality. The body-line upheaval shocked everyone and made the cricket world pull itself up and tread carefully. The spirit was not exorcized. The Oval match of 1938 was followed by the long-drawn-out siege in Durban. Luckily the war put an abrupt end to cricket as it was being played in the thirties. The relief was only temporary. Today the same relentlessness is abroad. Cricketers try to preserve the external decencies. The tradition is still strong. But instead of 'It isn't cricket', now one hears more frequently the cynical 'Why isn't it cricket?' Scarcely a tour but hits the headlines for some grave breach of propriety on and off the cricket field. The strategy of Test matches is the strategy of stalking the prey: you come out in the open to attack only when the victim is wounded. No holds are barred. Captains encourage their bowlers to waste time. Bowlers throw and drag. Wickets are shamelessly doctored. Series are lost or believed to be lost by doubtful decisions and immoral practices, and the victims nurse their wrath and return in kind. Writing in the *Cricketer* in the early twenties MacLaren said that in all his career he had known batsmen duck short balls only on two or three occasions. In the West Indies up to when I left in 1932 you took the short ball round to the leg-boundary (or you underwent repairs). Today statisticians and metaphysicians seek to impose a categorical imperative on the number of bumpers the fast bowler may bowl per over. To legislators for relief batsmen of all nations, like Cherubim and Seraphim, continually do cry.

A corps of cricket correspondents functions as an auxiliary arm of their side, but is ready to turn and rend it at the slightest opportunity. What little remains of 'It isn't cricket' is being finally stifled by the envy, the hatred, the malice and the uncharitableness, the shamelessness of the memoirs written by some of the cricketers themselves. Compared with these books, Sir Donald's ruthless autobiography of a dozen years ago now reads like a Victorian novel. How to blind one's eye to all this? Body-line was only a link in a chain. Modern society took a turn downwards in 1929 and 'It isn't cricket' is one of the casualties. There is no need to despair of cricket. Much, much more than cricket is at stake, in fact everything is at stake. If and when society regenerates itself, cricket will do the same. The Hambledon men built soundly. What Arnold, Hughes and W.G. brought is now indelibly a part of the national life and character, and plays its role, the farther it is away from the pressure of publicity. There it is safe. The values of cricket, like much that is now in eclipse, will go into the foundations of new moral and educational structures. But that they can be legislated to what they used to be is a vain hope which can only sour on the tongue and blear the eye. The owl of Minerva[6] flies only at dusk. And it cannot get much darker without becoming night impenetrable.

§ *Sport and society* Aus: Porter, Dawe (1), Williamson; SA: Gooneratne

LOUISE BENNETT (1919–)

Dear Departed Federation

> Dear Departed Federation,
> Referendum muderation
> Bounce you eena outa space
> Hope you fine a restin place.

---

6 Roman goddess of wisdom, the arts and trade.
1 Federation: the West Indian federation of   3 eena: into.
1958–61, which collapsed when Jamaica left after a
'no' vote in a referendum on the subject.

```
 5   Is a heavy blow we gi yuh
     An we know de fault noh fe yuh
     For we see you operate
     Over continent an state.
     But de heap o' boderation
10   Eena fe we lickle nation
     From de start o' yuh duration
     Meck we frighten an frustrate.
     A noh tief meck yuh departed
     A noh lie meck yuh departed
15   But a fearful meck we careful
     How we let yuh tru we gate.
     Fearful bout de big confusion
     Bout de final constitution
     An Jamaica contribution
20   All we spirit aggrivate.
     An we memba self-protection
     All we ears of preparation!
     Referendum Mutilation
     Quashie start to contemplate!
25   Beg yuh pardon Federation
     Fe de sudden separation
     If we sufferin' survive
     We acquaintance might revive.
     Dear Departed Federation
30   Beg you beg dem tarra nation
     Who done quarrel and unite
     Pray fe po' West Indies plight.
```

§ *Language usage* Reid, Sparrow, Brathwaite (3), Bloom, Agard, Breeze; *Federation* SEA: Fernando; Bennett also in TransC

JEAN RHYS (1890–1979)

1: The Day They Burned the Books

My friend Eddie was a small, thin boy. You could see the blue veins in his wrists and temples. People said that he had consumption and wasn't long for this world. I loved, but sometimes despised him.

His father, Mr Sawyer, was a strange man. Nobody could make out what he was doing in our part of the world at all. He was not a planter or a doctor or a lawyer or a banker. He didn't keep a store. He wasn't a school-

---

10 Eena fe we lickle: in our little..   **24 Quashie:** type-name for an ordinary Jamaican
30 tarra: that there.

master or a government official. He wasn't – that was the point – a gentleman. We had several resident romantics who had fallen in love with the
moon on the Caribees – they were all gentlemen and quite unlike Mr Sawyer
who hadn't an 'h' in his composition. Besides, he detested the moon and
everything else about the Caribbean and he didn't mind telling you so.

He was agent for a small steamship line which in those days linked up
Venezuela and Trinidad with the smaller islands, but he couldn't make much
out of that. He must have a private income, people decided, but they never
decided why he had chosen to settle in a place he didn't like and to marry
a coloured woman. Though a decent, respectable, nicely educated coloured
woman, mind you.

Mrs Sawyer must have been very pretty once but, what with one thing
and another, that was in days gone by.

When Mr Sawyer was drunk – this often happened – he used to be very
rude to her. She never answered him.

'Look at the nigger showing off,' he would say; and she would smile as if
she knew she ought to see the joke but couldn't. 'You damned, long-eyed
gloomy half-caste, you don't smell right,' he would say; and she never
answered, not even to whisper, 'You don't smell right to me, either.'

The story went that once they had ventured to give a dinner party and
that when the servant, Mildred, was bringing in coffee, he had pulled Mrs
Sawyer's hair. 'Not a wig, you see,' he bawled. Even then, if you can believe
it, Mrs Sawyer had laughed and tried to pretend that it was all part of the
joke, this mysterious, obscure, sacred English joke.

But Mildred told the other servants in the town that her eyes had gone
wicked, like a soucriant's[1] eyes, and that afterwards she had picked up some
of the hair he pulled out and put it in an envelope, and that Mr Sawyer
ought to look out (hair is obeah[2] as well as hands).

Of course, Mrs Sawyer had her compensations. They lived in a very pleasant house in Hill Street. The garden was large and they had a fine mango
tree, which bore prolifically. The fruit was small, round, very sweet and juicy
– a lovely, red-and-yellow colour when it was ripe. Perhaps it was one of
the compensations, I used to think.

Mr Sawyer built a room on to the back of this house. It was unpainted
inside and the wood smelt very sweet. Bookshelves lined the walls. Every
time the Royal Mail steamer came in it brought a package for him, and gradually the empty shelves filled.

Once I went there with Eddie to borrow *The Arabian Nights*. That was
on a Saturday afternoon, one of those hot, still afternoons when you felt
that everything had gone to sleep, even the water in the gutters. But Mrs
Sawyer was not asleep. She put her head in at the door and looked at us,
and I knew that she hated the room and hated the books.

It was Eddie with the pale blue eyes and straw-coloured hair – the living
image of his father, though often as silent as his mother – who first infected

---

1 Sorceress who flies by night, leaving her human skin behind, and sucks the blood of babies. 2 Magic.

me with doubts about 'home', meaning England. He would be so quiet when others who had never seen it – none of us had ever seen it – were talking about its delights, gesticulating freely as we talked – London, the beautiful, rosy-cheeked ladies, the theatres, the shops, the fog, the blazing coal fires in winter, the exotic food (whitebait eaten to the sound of violins), strawberries and cream – the word 'strawberries' always spoken with a guttural and throaty sound which we imagined to be the proper English pronunciation.

'I don't like strawberries,' Eddie said on one occasion.

'You *don't like* strawberries?'

'No, and I don't like daffodils either. Dad's always going on about them. He says they lick the flowers here into a cocked hat and I bet that's a lie.'

We were all too shocked to say, 'You don't know a thing about it.' We were so shocked that nobody spoke to him for the rest of the day. But I for one admired him. I also was tired of learning and reciting poems in praise of daffodils, and my relations with the few 'real' English boys and girls I had met were awkward. I had discovered that if I called myself English they would snub me haughtily: 'You're not English; you're a horrid colonial.' 'Well, I don't much want to be English,' I would say. 'It's much more fun to be French or Spanish or something like that – and, as a matter of fact, I am a bit.' Then I was too killingly funny, quite ridiculous. Not only a horrid colonial, but also ridiculous. Heads I win, tails you lose – that was the English. I had thought about all this, and thought hard, but I had never dared to tell anybody what I thought and I realized that Eddie had been very bold.

But he was bold, and stronger than you would think. For one thing, he never felt the heat; some coldness in his fair skin resisted it. He didn't burn red or brown, he didn't freckle much.

Hot days seemed to make him feel especially energetic. 'Now we'll run twice round the lawn and then you can pretend you're dying of thirst in the desert and that I'm an Arab chieftain bringing you water.'

'You must drink slowly,' he would say, 'for if you're very thirsty and you drink quickly you die.'

So I learnt the voluptuousness of drinking slowly when you are very thirsty – small mouthful by small mouthful, until the glass of pink, iced Coca-Cola was empty.

Just after my twelfth birthday Mr Sawyer died suddenly, and as Eddie's special friend I went to the funeral, wearing a new white dress. My straight hair was damped with sugar and water the night before and plaited into tight little plaits, so that it should be fluffy for the occasion.

When it was all over everybody said how nice Mrs Sawyer had looked, walking like a queen behind the coffin and crying her eyeballs out at the right moment, and wasn't Eddie a funny boy? He hadn't cried at all.

After this Eddie and I took possession of the room with the books. No one else ever entered it, except Mildred to sweep and dust in the mornings, and gradually the ghost of Mr Sawyer pulling Mrs Sawyer's hair faded though this took a little time. The blinds were always half-way down and going in out of the sun was like stepping into a pool of brown-green water. It was empty except for the bookshelves, a desk with a green baize top and a wicker rocking-chair.

'My room,' Eddie called it. 'My books,' he would say, 'my books.'

I don't know how long this lasted. I don't know whether it was weeks after Mr Sawyer's death or months after, that I see myself and Eddie in the room. But there we are and there, unexpectedly, are Mrs Sawyer and Mildred. Mrs Sawyer's mouth tight, her eyes pleased. She is pulling all the books out of the shelves and piling them into two heaps. The big, fat glossy ones – the good-looking ones, Mildred explains in a whisper – lie in one heap. *The Encyclopaedia Britannica, British Flowers, Birds and Beasts*, various histories, books with maps, Froude's *English in the West Indies*[3] and so on – they are going to be sold. The unimportant books, with paper covers or damaged covers or torn pages, lie in another heap. They are going to be burnt – yes, burnt.

Mildred's expression was extraordinary as she said that – half hugely delighted, half-shocked, even frightened. And as for Mrs Sawyer – well, I knew bad temper (I had often seen it), I knew rage, but this was hate. I recognized the difference at once and stared at her curiously. I edged closer to her so that I could see the titles of the books she was handling.

It was the poetry shelf. *Poems*, Lord Byron, *Poetical Works*, Milton, and so on. Vlung, vlung, vlung – all thrown into the heap that were to be sold. But a book by Christina Rossetti, though also bound in leather, went into the heap that was to be burnt, and by a flicker in Mrs Sawyer's eyes I knew that worse than men who wrote books were women who wrote books – infinitely worse. Men could be mercifully shot; women must be tortured.

Mrs Sawyer did not seem to notice that we were there, but she was breathing free and easy and her hands had got the rhythm of tearing and pitching. She looked beautiful, too – beautiful as the sky outside which was a very dark blue, or the mango tree, long sprays of brown and gold.

When Eddie said 'No', she did not even glance at him.

'No,' he said again in a high voice. 'Not that one. I was reading that one.'

She laughed and he rushed at her, his eyes starting out of his head, shrieking, 'Now I've got to hate you too. Now I hate you too.'

He snatched the book out of her hand and gave her a violent push. She fell into the rocking-chair.

Well, I wasn't going to be left out of all this, so I grabbed a book from the condemned pile and dived under Mildred's outstretched arm.

Then we were both in the garden. We ran along the path, bordered with crotons. We pelted down the path, though they did not follow us and we could hear Mildred laughing – kyah, kyah, kyah, kyah. As I ran I put the

---

3 James Anthony Froude's *The Bow of Ulysses or the English in the West Indies* (1888), a classic of Victorian imperialist writing which stirred up an adverse reaction in sections of the local population: see the Trinidadian J. J. Thomas's *Froudacity* (1888).

book I had taken into the loose front of my brown holland dress. It felt warm and alive.

When we got into the street we walked sedately, for we feared the black children's ridicule. I felt very happy, because I had saved this book and it was my book and I would read it from the beginning to the triumphant words 'The End'. But I was uneasy when I thought of Mrs Sawyer.

'What will she do?' I said.

'Nothing,' Eddie said. 'Not to me.'

He was white as a ghost in his sailor suit, a blue-white even in the setting sun, and his father's sneer was clamped on his face.

'But she'll tell your mother all sorts of lies about you,' he said. 'She's an awful liar. She can't make up a story to save her life, but she makes up lies about people all right.'

'My mother won't take any notice of her.' I said. Though I was not at all sure.

'Why not? Because she's . . . because she isn't white?'

Well, I knew the answer to that one. Whenever the subject was brought up – people's relations and whether they had a drop of coloured blood or whether they hadn't – my father would grow impatient and interrupt. 'Who's white?' he would say. 'Damned few.'

So I said, 'Who's white? Damned few.'

'You can go to the devil,' Eddie said. 'She's prettier than your mother. When she's asleep her mouth smiles and she has curling eyelashes and quantities and quantities and *quantities* of hair.'

'Yes,' I said truthfully. 'She's prettier than my mother.'

It was a red sunset that evening, a huge, sad, frightening sunset.

'Look, let's go back,' I said. 'If you're sure she won't be vexed with you, let's go back. It'll be dark soon.'

At his gate he asked me not to go. 'Don't go yet, don't go yet.'

We sat under the mango tree and I was holding his hand when he began to cry. Drops fell on my hand like the water from the dripstone in the filter in our yard. Then I began to cry too and when I felt my own tears on my hand I thought, 'Now perhaps we're married.'

'Yes, certainly, now we're married,' I thought. But I didn't say anything. I didn't say a thing until I was sure he had stopped. Then I asked, 'What's your book?'

'It's *Kim*,' he said. 'But it got torn. It starts at page twenty now. What's the one you took?'

'I don't know; it's too dark to see,' I said.

When I got home I rushed into my bedroom and locked the door because I knew that this book was the most important thing that had ever happened to me and I did not want anybody to be there when I looked at it.

But I was very disappointed, because it was in French and seemed dull. *Fort Comme La Mort*, it was called. . . .

§ *Competing ancestries* Rhys (2), Walcott (2), Williams, Brodber

2: I Used to Live Here Once

She was standing by the river looking at the stepping stones and remembering each one. There was the round unsteady stone, the pointed one, the flat one in the middle – the safe stone where you could stand and look round. The next wasn't so safe for when the river was full the water flowed over it and even when it showed dry it was slippery. But after that it was easy and soon she was standing on the other side.

The road was much wider that it used to be but the work had been done carelessly. The felled trees had not been cleared away and the bushes looked trampled. Yet it was the same road and she walked along feeling extraordinarily happy.

It was a fine day, a blue day. The only thing was that the sky had a glassy look that she didn't remember. That was the only word she could think of. Glassy. She turned the corner, saw that what had been the old pavé had been taken up, and there too the road was much wider, but it had the same unfinished look.

She came to the worn stone steps that led up to the house and her heart began to beat. The screw pine was gone, so was the mock summer house called the ajoupa, but the clove tree was still there and at the top of the steps the rough lawn stretched away, just as she remembered it. She stopped and looked towards the house that had been added to and painted white. It was strange to see a car standing in front of it.

There were two children under the big mango tree, a boy and a little girl, and she waved to them and called 'Hello' but they didn't answer her or turn their heads. Very fair children, as Europeans born in the West Indies so often are: as if the white blood is asserting itself against all odds.

The grass was yellow in the hot sunlight as she walked towards them. When she was quite close she called again, shyly: 'Hello.' Then, 'I used to live here once,' she said.

Still they didn't answer. When she said for the third time 'Hello' she was quite near them. Her arms went out instinctively with the longing to touch them.

It was the boy who turned. His grey eyes looked straight into hers. His expression didn't change. He said: 'Hasn't it gone cold all of a sudden. D'you notice? Let's go in.' 'Yes let's,' said the girl.

Her arms fell to her sides as she watched them running across the grass to the house. That was the first time she knew.

§ *Competing ancestries* Rhys (1), Walcott (2), Williams, Brodber

V. S. REID (1913–87)

From New Day

In *New Day* the narrator, 87-year-old John Campbell, looks back over his life and in so doing reviews Jamaican history between 1865, the year of the Morant Bay uprising, and 1944, when a new constitution that extended the franchise came into being. Notable for its use of a modified form of Jamaican Creole as the narrative mode, *New Day*, which appeared in 1949, prefigures several motifs that are prominent in Caribbean novels of the 1950s and 1960s, among them boyhood as a time of discovery, a revisionist perspective on history and a celebration of local landscape and customs. These two extracts are from the very beginning of the novel.

Tomorrow I will go with Garth to the city to hear King George's man proclaim from the square that now Jamaica-men will begin to govern themselves. Garth will stand on the high platform near the Governor and the Bishop and the Chief Justice, and many eyes will make four with his. Garth will stand proud and strong, for mighty things ha' gone into his conception.

Eh, but now I am restless tonight. Through the half-opened window near where I sit, night winds come down the Blue Mountains to me. Many scents come down on the wind, and I know them all. I know all the scents o' the shrubs up on the mountains. There are *cerosee*, mint, mountain jasmine, *ma raqui*, there are *peahba*[1] and sweet cedars. I know that the bitter *cerosee* will drive away fever, that *ma raqui* will heal any wounds – even wounds from musket balls.

I am restless tonight. There is a blue velvet case on the table side o' me, and my fingers caress this case. My fingers find the catch and press inwards, and six little gold studs wink at the light – the studs which Son-Son gave me.

Sundown this evening, Garth, who is Son-Son, came in from Morant Bay. Handing me the velvet case, he told me:

'In memory of the great-grand whom I didn't know. These will make a dandy granddaddy tomorrow.'

Aie – Garth remembers all the old things I ha' told him.

This restlessness will no' make me find my bed. You know how long I have sat here? Nine o'clock come, and gone, and first rooster crowed, and here I am sitting down.

I move my feet to find firmness on the polished *yacca*[2] floor. Find, I find it and get up without touching the chair arm. If Son-Son was here with me, he would laugh and say I grow younger every day. I step to the window and open it wide. But how good are the scents!

Clock is talking of the hour. Is what it the clock say now? Ten o'clock? Eh, you mean I ha' sat here till now?

---

1 Plants and shrubs used medicinally. 2 Tough wood, capable of being highly polished.

I can no' go to my bed now. I must wait until the Morant people come, for I ha' heard that they will come and sing mighty hymns under our window tonight. They will sing away the old time and sing in the new, for tomorrow the English Governor o' our island will proclaim that Jamaica has got a new constitution. Garth will be up there on the platform near the Governor and the Bishop and the Colonial Secretary and the Chief Justice, for all o' these know he will be leader of the new government after the General Elections. . . .[3]

But God O! Look what my eyes ha' lived to see!

Then, now! Pa John and Ma Tamah, father and mother o' sorrow – are you hearing? And my brethren, Emmanuel, David, Samuel, Ezekiel, Ruth, Naomi, are you hearing?

Are you a-hear, George William Gordon? And Paul Bogle,[4] Abram M'Laren, and the good Doctor Creary?

And you too, bloody Governor Eyre and your crow Provost-Marshal Ramsey, are you hearing wherever you are? Tell me, Bro' Zaccy O' Gilvie, are you a-listen of me tonight?

Then, now! All o' you Dead Hundreds who looked at the sun without blink in your eyes, you Dead Hundreds who fell to British redcoats' bullets and the swords o' the wild Maroons, the wild men o' the mountains; tell me, you Dead Hundreds o' Morant Bay, are you hearing that tomorrow is the day? And that sorrow and restlessness are here with my joy, for I am standing here alone?

Aie – me, John Campbell, youngest o' Pa John Campbell.

I turn back and look in at the room. Younder in another room Garth is asleep. Hard day it has been for him today, and the long, long tomorrow only hours away. Rest, he will rest now.

A good house, this. Well has my grand looked after me. There is thick mahogany in this room, much silver and glass talk to me o' prosperity, tells we ha' come a far way since 'Sixty-five.

I hear the singing now. Our Party people are coming to our house at Salt Savannah, marching with torchlight and mighty hymns. Make them come.

Bring your torchlights and your voices and put fire and music in the soul of an old man tonight!

For many years now bank the flame that was young John Campbell. If the Master plans that I turn this year my face to the wall and sleep, then Son-Son must make a head-cut to say:

BORN 1857. DIED 1944

---

3 Garth is loosely based on Norman Manley, who was later prime minister of Jamaica from 1953 to 1962.
4 **Paul Bogle ... Governor Eyre:** Historical figures, who played a leading role in the 1865 Morant Bay uprising in Jamaica.

Music is swelling in my ears as I go over to the east window. Our people are marching from the Bay, and now I can glimpse the torches carried by those taller ones. I listen good, and can hear the words. . . .

Onward, Christian Soldiers. . . .

Funny how my mind turns back and I can remember it well.

'Sixty-five, it was. October morning; sun-up is fire and blood, and fear walks with my family. Remember, I remember, that this was the tune Pa John told us to sing that time when we came down out of the mountains.

Hear my father: *Sing, family O! British redcoats do no' make war on Christians.*

But just the same time was when Davie came out of the bush so sudden that Zekiel and Naomi must cry out. Davie was nineteen years old that time, and tall nearly like my father. He has taken up Maroon[5] war style, with shrubs tied on all over his body, to fool the English redcoats. So, when we looked at him, we did no' know where Davis ended and the shrubs began.

Hear my bro' Davie to Father: *Do no' go down, Father. Stay up here in the mountains. Mr. Gordon and Deacon Bogle are hanging by their necks from the court-house steps.*

But how my father was stubborn! His head was tossing leader-bull fashion as he walked out in front of us.

Come behind me, Tamah, he said. *Sing after your mother, you pickneys.*

So, we went out of the mountains down into Baptism Valley, a-sing. . . .

Now they round the foot of the hill and come up to our house. Candlewood torches make our road as bright as day.

You know how you make candlewood shine? Go into the woodland and find a limb as big as your wrist and a half. Strip the bark partways down, and leave it hanging over your hand to keep off the sparks. Sharpen the point, then light it with a lucifer-match. And then how it will burn bright!

Under our windows they are now, many, many o' them. The song has changed and softer it is now. From their throat the song sobs, but with no sorrow in it. A plaintiveness like a January nightingale winging through the Cuna Cuna Pass, and yet with deepness and richness like cloud robes wrapping an evening sun.

There are children and full women and full men. There is me there, at the window, singing too; for good it is that a ripe man should have music in his soul. So soon they sing a hymn to the finish, so soon do they change. No time this is for quiet.

Edge up yourself sharp, Coney Mount tenor-man! Roll it out, big-bone bass-man from Cedar Valley! Roll it out, for the girls from Morant fishing beach must ha' something solid to pour molasses from their throats on. Sing, my people, for good this is.

And then the hymn is finished, and there is:

Hooray! Hooray! Bring out Garth Campbell! Bring out our Son-Son!

---

5 Escaped slaves (from early Spanish period of colonization), living in hills and mountains of Jamaica.

But tired Son-Son is, and there is tomorrow soon to come. So I shake my head and put finger to my lips and form like I am asleep. They know what I mean, and there is a long *sshh* to one another; so, although they meant it for quiet, the hush is loud as the *hooray*.

That time, then, they all laugh and nod at me so I must laugh too. Then, humming of the tune, there is *Abide with Me*.

God o' me! Hear my people sing! Is no' the Image and the Likeness this?

No sleep will come to me. Restless memories are rising inside me, bringing wetness to my eyes. But old men must no' cry. Cry, and is the end of the purpose, that, leaving just a waiting. But ripe men can no' forget their memories. Most of everything is behind, so little is in front; unless there is a son-son.

Then behind and in front will be the same distance, for a man can live in the son of a son.

Tomorrow after I ha' put on my shirt with the gold studs, Son-Son will knot my tie. Then I know down in the garden where a pretty rosebud is. I will fasten it in my buttonhole, and he will laugh and say: *Sheik*.

We must eat a good breakfast tomorrow. Newspapers say the ceremony to proclaim the new constitution will be short; but the city sun is much hotter than Morant sun, so a man must have heavy provender back o' his waist band. Tomorrow we must have *renta*[6] baked in coconut milk and new butter. We will eat i' with *ackee*[7] and codfish mince. We will wash down our *bammie*[8] with Blue Mountain coffee. Good I will feel when Garth leaves the table with heavy provender packing his insides.

Newspapers say Morant and Pedro Cays will be in the declaration o' the new constitution. I read o' Morant Cays,[9] and memories shake at me.

Memories are a-shake me tonight. Memories o' hot sand and mangrove bush and hunting-Maroons with naked swords. Of the boom of redcoats' muskets, the whistle o' whips, and the crack o' lashes; of a dozen men twitching on Provost Ramsey's gallows.

Memories o' Colonel Judas Hobbs of the Sixth Regiment o' Foot. Memories of Mr. Abram and his forty for forty. Memories of a high wind, and weakness coming to my bro's loins when his woman was no' with him. Memories o' two old men stumbling through dark-night to bring Davie's seed from a plague house.

Aie – I must no' be restless longer. Quiet, I will sit quiet, while they sing and make my mind walk back. I will talk a talk o' the years what ha' passed.

---

6 A variety of yam.   7 Fruit, resembling scrambled eggs when cooked.   8 Flat bread made from cassava. 9 Islands or reefs of coral, sand, etc.

Chapter 1

For three years now, no rain has come. Grass-piece and yam-vines are brown with dryness, cane leaves have not got much green to them. Thirst and hunger walk through our land, four hundred thousand people have no osnaburgs[10] to their backs.

For three years now, no rain has come and only the rich laugh deep.

It is the year 1865. For three years, there have been no croptimes in our fields. In America, brothers o' the North have just done warred with brothers o' the South, and so no clipper ships are riding the ocean to bring flour and codfish for our empty bellies.

No growth on the land, no ship on the sea – Lord O! But there is suffering!

For three years, Edward John Eyre has been a-sit in the Queen's House at St. Jago de la Vega parish as Governor of our island. With dryness on the land and a shipless ocean we turn to the man who stands for Missis Queen Victoria. Men ha' lost skin off their feet tramping with Petitions on the rocky roads to St. Jago. But always they are met with muskets and bayonets, and always they come home with foodless bellies but vexation curdling their bowels.

But now, badness is coming. From Westmoreland parish in the west to St. Thomas parish in the east, men are talking in secret under heavy cotton-tree roots.

Mr. George William Gordon and his friends in the House of Assembly ask for the recall o' John Eyre. Good pastors from their pulpits plead say we must be calm. Buckra[11] planters on great estates and pastors o' the Established Church say hooray for Governor Eyre, curse the Baptist pastors and laugh at the hunger of our people. For soon then, by-and-by, labour will be cheap. But at length and at last Westminster is hearing.

Rage and bitterness walk with Eyre's voice as he tells his Council of Doctor Underhill. Underhill is o' the Baptist faith and he has penned a letter to the Secretary of State for the Colonies telling him of our sufferings. Rage and bitterness walk with the voices of Eyre's Church of England clergymen as they deny that men are very hungry. And same time, now, they are calling with heavy voices for more and more tithes from the poor. And same time, now, the Established Church sends a note to the Queen; but still we wait in hope on Westminster.

Is the year it 1865, and pastors o' the Baptist faith stir again to help the poor. A Petition has gone by packet to the Queen, praying that starvation should no' take us. We wait in hope on Missis Queen.

But when the packet returns, and the *Queen's Advice* is taken to every village church and nailed to every constabulary station, and on market-day we gather around and read it with lips o' stiffness – *aie* bro'!

Then we know the Church of England has won the fight, the Baptist letter has no' been credited.

---

10 A thick, coarse cloth; formerly work clothes for slaves. 11 White.

Hear the QUEEN'S ADVICE:

THE MEANS OF SUPPORT OF THE LABOURING CLASSES DEPEND ON THEIR
LABOUR. HER MAJESTY WILL REGARD WITH INTEREST AND SATISFACTION
THEIR ADVANCEMENT THROUGH THEIR OWN MERITS AND EFFORTS.

Wait! plead good pastors from their pulpits, *Her Majesty has been wrongly
advised*!

Wait, says Mr. Gordon at his Underhill meetings, *we will take the case to
Whitehall ourselves*.

Wait? Paul Bogle asks at Stoney Gut, *Is war it, or peace, they want*?

It is the year 1865. June and July and August gone, and no rain comes
with October. Brown on our yam-vines, the earth a-crack with dryness, there
is no *osnaburg* to make clothing for our backs, four hundred thousand are
a-moan.

God O! – there are tears all over the land and only the rich laugh deep.

§   *Alternative histories* Walcott (3); Aus: Davis; Can: Wiebe; SA: Rushdie;
Language usage Bennett, Sparrow, Brathwaite (3), Bloom, Agard, Breeze

ROGER MAIS (1905–53)

From Brother Man

Like V. S. Reid, Roger Mais was a member of the 'Focus' group which helped to promote local literature and culture in Jamaica in the 1940s. *Brother Man* is set in a
deprived area of Kingston, but is not so much a naturalistic representation of 'slum'
life as a religious fable centred on the figure of a Christlike ex-Rastafarian, the epony-
mous Brother Man. It also offers a striking portrait of the interaction of individuals in
a community. The passages included here are from the early part of the novel and
illustrate its movement between the choric 'clack-clack' of the voices of 'people in
the lane' and scenes built around dialogues, usually between couples.

Chorus of People in the Lane

The tongues in the lane clack-clack almost continuously, going up and down
the full scale of human emotions, human folly, ignorance, suffering, vicious-
ness, magnanimity, weakness, greatness, littleness, insufficiency, frailty,
strength.

They clack on street corners, where the ice-shop hangs out a triangular
red flag, under the shadow of overhanging buildings that lean precariously,
teetering across the dingy chasm of the narrow lane.

Around the yam-seller's barrow, and the tripe-seller's basket, and the coal-
vendor's crazy push-cart drawn up against the seamy sidewalk, they clack,

interspersing the hawking and the bargaining, and what-goes-on in the casual, earnest, noisy, meaningless business of buying and selling; and where the mango-seller sets down her country-load.

They clack where the neighbours meet in the Chinese grocery shop on the corner, leaning elbows against the counter with its saltfish odour and the spilled rice grains and brown sugar grains, and amid the dustings of corn-meal and flour under the smirking two-faced scale, waiting for change.

– Mis' Brody's clubfootbwoy get run over . . .
– You hear wha' Bra'[1] Ambo say? Say we is gwine get nodder breeze-blow[2] dis year yet . . .
– Cho Missis, no mind Bra' Ambo, after him no eena Big Massa council . . .
– Coal-price gone up since todder day . . .
– Ee-ee Ma, him do an' get run over . . .
– Oonu[3] lissen hear wha' Bra' Ambo say . . .

Behind the pocked visage and the toothless grin, behind the wrinkled skin gathered and seamed around the lips and under the eyes, behind the façade of haltness and haleness and cursing and laughter, slander lurks in ambush to take the weakest and the hindmost, and the tongues clack upon every chance.

– Cordy's man get tek-up fo' ganga[4] . . .
– Bra' Man show de gospel way . . .
– Me-gal still wi' hold wid Bra' Ambo . . .
– Coal-price gone up since todder day . . .
– Lawd Jesus, po' Mis' Brody . . .
– No mind, God is over all . . .
– Hush yaw ma', you' mout'-lip favour . . .
– No God do dem t'ing de at all . . .

There are sad-faced old ones, and sleek-faced young ones, and all ways in between; and there are those with an accounting of troubles the same and equal to and over and beyond the ones they tell; and there are those too who have missed the accounting, ducking and dodging and putting by for another day; but all, all are involved in the same chapter of consequences, all are caught up between the covers of the same book of living; they look with shuddering over their shoulder past the image of their own secret terror, feeling the shadow of it over them in another's fate.

– Po' Cordy one fe mind de pickney[5] . . .
– Lissen good wha' Bra' Ambo say . . .
– Cho gwan wid you' Bra' Ambo . . .
– Bra' Man know de gospel way . . .
– Papacita beat up him gal las' night . . .
– Is a shame de way dem two de-live . . .
– Gal waan fo' him an' she get married . . .
– Hm! Papacita know what 'married' give . . .

Over washtubs in noisome yards where the drip-drip of the eternally

---

1 Brother. 2 Hurricane. 3 You (plural). 4 Possession of marijuana. 5 Child.

leaking standpipe makes waste in the sun-cracked green-slimed concrete cistern, and under the ackee tree or the custard-apple tree or the Spanish-guava tree or the Seville orange tree behind the lean-to pit-latrine in the yard, they clack-clack eternally telling their own hunger and haltness and lameness and nightness and negation, like flies buzzing an open unremitting sore, tasting again, renewing, and giving again, the wounds they have taken of the world.

    – Flyin' Saucer tek-in Mercedes . . .
    – Cho! A-swing her tail up an' down de street! . . .
    – How she-one manage ketch so-much sailor? . . .
    – Mus' be black-gal somet'ing sweet! . . .
    – Hear dem say-say Papacita de mek eye after Bra' Man gal . . .
    – Mek Bra' Man find out! . . .
    – Hm! jus' wait bwoy! . . .
    – Massa Jesus! gwine be hell! . . .

Night comes down and the tongues have not ceased to shuttle and to clatter, they still carry their burden of the tale of man's woes. It is their own story over that they tell in secret, overlaying it with the likeness of slander, licking their own ancient scrofulous sores. . . .

I, 5

Brother Man sat at his cobbler's bench before the open window looking out upon the lane. He worked quietly, efficiently, his head bowed over his last.

He was of medium height, medium build. The hair crisped and curled all about his head, around his mouth, over his chin. When he looked up from his work his eyes pinpointed the light, and you could see almost all of the pupils. He had a far-away, searching look, as though the intensity of his being came to focus in his eyes. Many looked away and were embarrassed before the quiet intensity of that gaze.

He had now, as he always did, an open Bible on the stool beside him. He was putting heels to a pair of slippers, and Minette sat on a lower stool, at his feet, blacking a pair of shoes.

Every now and then she stole a glance at him, and went back to blacking the shoes again.

From the yard next door they could hear voices of people, talking, laughing, quarrelling. Beyond they could hear the yam-vendor hawking down the lane.

Brother Man belonged to that cult known as the Ras Tafarites,[6] and some people said he was mad. Others again thought he was a holy man and a healer, and many came to him, secretly, because they feared gossip, to heal their sick, and for advice and encouragement when things were going wrong.

Sometimes when they heard other people abusing and traducing Brother Man, they stood up in his defence, the people whom he had helped in times

---

6 A local sect in West Kingston at the time when the novel was written; named after Emperor Haile Selassie of Ethiopia (Ras Tafari), whom Rastafarians believe was the incarnation of God.

of trouble and sickness, but at other times they thought better of it, because they feared what their neighbours might have to say about them behind their backs, lacking the courage of their convictions. Sometimes they forgot, some of these people, that he had helped and comforted them, and healed their wounds. Sometimes they secretly despised him that he cared so little for himself, and so much for others, that he would give what little he had to succour another whose need he thought greater than his.

Minette held up to the light the shoe she was polishing to see how it shone. She sighed and set it down on the floor beside her on a piece of old newspaper, and took up the other one.

From the yard next door came the sound of someone singing, 'Jesu, lover of my soul. . . .'

She said suddenly, 'What is love?'

Brother Man said, 'Eh? What you say, child?'

'Say what is love? Bra' Man,' she repeated.

She let the shoe rest on her lap and looked up into his face.

He looked at her, earnestly, as though weighing his answer, and presently she let her eyes fall. She took up the shoe from her lap, and started polishing it again.

'Love is everything,' he said, simply. 'It is what created the world. It is what made you an' me, child, brought us into this world.'

And somehow the words didn't sound banal, coming from him. He spoke with such simple directness that it seemed to give a new import to everything he said. It was as though the common words of everyday usage meant something more, coming from his lips, than they did in the casual giving and taking of change in conversation, the way it was with other folks.

'Why you ask? You love somebody, child?'

'Yes an' no. I love plenty-plenty people, but none like you.'

He looked at her gravely and said: 'Peace an' love.'

'Why you always say that?' she asked, half closing one eye, as though the better to study his face.

'It is the salutation. It is the way the brothers should greet each other. It is like sayin' good morning, howdydo. But it is more than that too, it is the affirmation of our faith, the Jesus-talk, what you call the way.'

She didn't understand a word of all this. It showed in her face.

'Did Jesus talk it that way, that what you mean, Bra' Man?'

He nodded his head, gravely. 'He give us that word, sister: peace an' love.'

A bird flew smack into the window glass with a dull thud. It fell to the ground outside with a faint cry, stunned with the impact.

Brother Man got up, with a murmured exclamation, went out through the door, and presently came back with the bird in his hand. It fluttered a little, scared, though scarcely conscious, almost dead. A single drop of blood congealing at the side of its beak glowed like a jewel against the dark grey-green of its feathers.

It was going to die, Minette knew it, and she had an instant of impatience and vexation with Brother Man for trying to bring it back, to make it live.

She didn't know why she felt this, only knew that it came up inside her, until she wanted to cry out at him, but it stopped in her throat.

She watched him as he stood there, holding the bird in his cupped hand, his head bowed over it.

'Don't trouble you'self over it, Bra' Man,' she said, 'it not goin' live.'

She came up and stood by his elbow, her body just touching his, and felt him move away instinctively, and as he did so she knew a sharp pang, savage and strong, and with a surge of exhilaration; but she could not have told what it was all about if somebody had asked her.

'Maybe,' he said, still holding the bird, and looking down at it.

It lay on its side now, and its eyes were shut in death.

'It's dead,' she said.

And she could scarcely hear his whisper, 'Yes.'

But he still held the little dead body cupped in his hand, as though he could not bear to part with it.

'What you goin' do with it?'

And she moved just that breathing space nearer, so that when she drew her breath in, long, the nipple of her breast rested against his arm an instant, and came away with respiration. He stood still, like someone lost in a trance, and as though he was not conscious of her presence.

'What you goin' do with it, Bra' Man?' she said again.

He went and sat down on his stool, let his hand rest on the bench, relaxed his fingers. He sat there looking at the dead bird a longish time, as though in truth he did not know what to do with it. He set it down on the bench, and took up his last again.

She came up, stood behind him, said almost fiercely: 'Why you don't throw it out into the street, what you keepin' it for?'

He looked up at her, and she met his gaze without flinching.

'What's troublin' you, me daughter?'

'Why you want to keep it before you? Why you don't throw it outside?'

'It is one of God's creatures, and it was alive a little while back, and now it is dead, an' it didn't do no harm. Let it rest there, eh?' he said.

And she felt rebuked.

She said: 'I am sorry.'

He put out his hand and touched her arm.

He said: 'Peace an' love.'

§ *Folk/Rastafarian experience* Brathwaite (2)

GEORGE LAMMING (1927–)

1: *From* In the Castle of My Skin

In the Castle of My Skin has been acclaimed as the finest of a group of Caribbean novels about boyhood, published in the 1950s and 1960s. On one level it is about a boy – nine years old at the outset and nineteen at the end – gradually growing up and losing his innocence, but his story is complemented by that of a village community's parallel loss of the sense of security it has hitherto enjoyed in the quasi-feudal world of late colonial Barbados. This passage from the middle part of the novel illustrates both the camaraderie between the narrator and his friends and how outside forces are upsetting the balance of the community. The novel employs multiple narrative modes, perhaps suggesting that polyphony (multi-voicedness) is necessary to encompass the discursive diversity of Caribbean experience. The passage illustrates its use of oral storytelling conventions.

. . . Bob did not return and we sat under the grape tree looking out across the sea. The sun went under cloud and we noticed how the shade of the sand deepened, and the sea in a level patch turn to dull grey. The sun surfaced the clouds and the light was everywhere once more. We looked at the sand and the sea and it seemed we could see the gradations of light, but one got the feeling the light had climbed from below the sand and the sea. A fisherman walked up the beach in our direction dragging a large fish net after him, and we watched him till he turned behind the lighthouse and was out of sight. The beach seemed empty but for us three sitting in a half-circle on the sand under the grape tree. We were silent.

' 'Tis always like this,' Trumper said suddenly, and we were startled by the fall of his voice on the air. It was as if someone had dropped a pebble on a pane of glass.

'What's always like what?' Boy Blue asked.

'I mean the way we is here,' Trumper said. ' 'Tis always like this at home. The way we is here. My mother over yonder in that corner, an' my father down there in that corner, an' me somewhere else. An' you get the feeling you know, that everything's all right. 'Cause of the way everybody sittin', just sittin' there, an' for the moment you feel nothin' ever change. Everything's all right, 'tis the same yesterday an' today an' tomorrow an' forever as they says in the Bible.'

'I know what you mean,' Boy Blue said. ' 'Tis always like that at home too. 'Specially when my sister ain't there, an' my grangran don't sneeze. There ain't no noise at all, an' I don't know for you, but I get the feelin' that I always this size, an' all I try to remember, I can't remember myself bigger or smaller than I is now.'

'As you say so,' Trumper said, 'you make me wonder if we ever was older than we is now.'

'How you mean?' Boy Blue asked.

'Well, they always say you get older,' Trumper said, 'but that's to come. That's something you don't know 'bout. You's fourteen this year, an' next time you'll be fifteen, an' then sixteen, an' so on an' so on; but you ain't ever fourteen an' then thirteen an' then twelve an' so on.'

'No,' Boy Blue said, 'you ain't ever that; although they say that after a certain age you start to get a child again, like Pa and Ma, for instance.'

'Once a man twice a chil',' Trumper said.

'That's what they say,' Boy Blue said, 'though I'd like to be one time a chil' an' two times a man. Is so hard on you when you've got to be a chil'.'

'You can't talk, for instance,' Trumper said.

'Nor you can' say what's in yuh mind,' Boy Blue said. 'An' when you ain't cryin', you quiet.'

' 'Tis true,' Trumper said. 'Sometimes I get frighten when I see my mother baby starin'. Seems he ain't seeing anything, an' yet he seeing something.'

'My mother baby can't see,' Boy Blue said, 'an' that is worse. He more than frightens me sometimes, 'cause the sort of look he carries on his face makes me feel he still seeing like cross-eye Botsie who when his face turns one way see everybody passin' the other way. Sometimes I put my head right down to his nose an' peep to see if I could spot his eyes under the lid.'

'You mustn't do that,' Trumper said. 'You'll frighten him.'

'But he can't see,' Boy Blue said.

'It don't matter,' Trumper said, 'you'll frighten him all the same.'

The waves had settled for a while and the wind, it seemed, had lodged in the trees. Nothing moved but the tide of the wave drifting gently to the shore. There was no one on the beach but us three sitting in a half-circle on the sand under the grape tree. Behind us was the soldiers' cemetery where the trees were thick, and the sound most arresting when the wind came. The broken wall covered with moss and vine veered in and out through the trees, and in the open spaces were the red signals: KEEP OFF. No one could go beyond the signals. Farther away behind the trees were the oil tanks from which the ships in the harbour drew their supplies of fuel.

On the other side was the lighthouse which climbed so many feet in the air. The top was like a glass-chimney which you brought down over the bed-room lamp that remained burning low all through the night. The bright red and green glass at the top was always burning in the sun. When the sun went down a new light came on from inside, and the panes never lost their brightness. We looked around at everything, and we started to get afraid of our own silence.

'Just like this as you wus sayin',' Boy Blue said. ' 'Tis always like this at home. Even when my mother an' father fight, it don't take long before it get like this again.'

'True,' Trumper said, 'an' when my mother beat me, she says all the time she hittin' me, let's have a little peace in the house, an' when I finished cryin' it seems the peace come. Just like this.'

' 'Tis the same with all of us,' Boy Blue said, 'except that p'raps the peace is more with some than with others. The peace is plenty with us, 'specially when my sister ain't at home. An' sometimes sittin' here or there or any-where for that matter, I feel that where I sittin' now I wus sittin' all the time, an' it seem I wus sittin' since I can remember myself. 'Tis as if time like the clock itself stop, an' everything you tell yourself is all right.'

'That said thing happen to me,' Trumper said. 'I wus sittin' under the cel-lar at home. I don't remember why I went under the cellar, p'raps I wus search-ing for eggs. But anyway, I wus there, under the cellar, an' it seem everything wus dark as everything always is under the cellar, an' it seem I wus all by myself there under the cellar, jus' looking at the dust and dirt an' rubbish under the cellar. It wus quiet, quiet, quiet, an' I wus just there all by myself just lookin' at nothing in particular, when suddenly somebody say something 'bout the weddings, an' I right away rush out from the cellar to hear what's wrong with the weddings, an' I hear the story 'bout the weddings, but all time it seem to me something gone. I had the feelin' that something, I don't exactly know what, but something wus gone. Seems to me sometimes it wus the cellar that disappear, but not the cellar I lookin' at as I listen to the story. 'Twas as if there was another cellar in that cellar, an' 'twas the other cellar which disappear.'

'That's happen to me too,' said Boy Blue, 'an' where you wus sittin' wus a worl' all by itself, an' then the something happen, an' that world come to an end, an' you got to get up an' go to the other world where the new something happen. It sound stupid, but 'tis true the way it happen.'

'Stupid or not it happen to me with the weddings,' Trumper said.

'Who get marry?' Boy Blue asked.

'Nobody get marry,' Trumper said.

'An' how you mean there wus weddings?' Boy Blue asked.

' 'Twus like this,' Trumper said. 'You know Jon who can pitch marbles so clean? He put down four marbles here, he stay there a mile away an' before you say Jack Robinson he scatter them all. Well, 'twus Jon. For a long time he wus living with Susie who live down the train line, an' Susie had two children for him, Po King an' Puss in Boots, Number one. It seem Jon join the Free for All Brethren an' get save; he says he turn to the Lord an' so on. Brother Bannister take him in an' try to make a hand of him. He wus comin' on good, good, good, an' it seem he start to make much of Brother Bannister daughter, Jen. He was *muching* up Jen plenty, but nobody say anything, cause they consider in the church that all who break bread is of the same family. An' Brother Bannister, for God knows what reason, give Jon all the rope he want. Poor Jon forget he wusn't always what he say he wus, an' he got real entangle with Jen an' before you say Jack Robinson he get her in trouble. Jen wus in the way, an' Brother Bannister call on Jon to marry Jen, an' say if he didn't come like a man an' bear his own burden like a Christian an' a man, what an' what he would do with him. There wus talk 'bout shootin' an' all that. Jon get frighten an' he go straight an' put the matter before Susie. He ask Susie what she think 'bout it. When all wus said an' done, 'twus she, Susie, who he had to think 'bout. Susie come right out an' ask him what he think Brother Bannister would do if he din't marry Jen, an' he say with his tongue between his teeth that Brother Bannister swear by the church he would shoot him. It seem there ain't no man in all Creighton's village more 'fraid to die than Jon, an' he put it to Susie that if Brother Bannister did shoot him as he say he would the children don't have no father. Susie din't like the sound of it. Seems he wus askin' her to let him marry Jen. But she won't hear a word of it, an' she put it to him that if he an' she, meanin' Susie, went an' get marry quiet, then he, Jon, could put it to Brother Bannister that it wus against the law to marry Jen, whatever her condition. An' after all, she Susie it wus, who had a rightful claim to him. But Jon couldn't get out of his mind that Brother Bannister wus goin' to shoot him if he didn't, as Brother Bannister say, bear his burden an' do his duty to Jen as a man an' a Christian, saved through the blood of the lamb. He put it to Susie that once he wus alive, everything would be all right, an' that nothing matter for the children sake, but that he be alive, 'cause if anything happen to him the children won't have no father no more. Susie refuse, an' she swear by her dead grangran that if it wus brought to her notice than Jon marry Jen she would poison his guts out. Poor Jon wus betwix' the devil an' the deep blue sea, as they say. On one hand Brother Bannister with a gun, an' on the other Susie with a bottle of arsenic. He tremble like a chil', an' say to Susie if that wus so, they had better go an' get marry quick an' quiet. But Jon wus like a feather in the wind that go now here and now there, an' he couldn't make up his mind 'cause he din't have a mind to make up. So when Brother Bannister approach him again, he put it to Brother Bannister that if anything wus goin' to happen between himself an' Jen they would have to do it quick an' quiet, 'cause Susie swear she'd poison him. Brother Bannister had to save his face from shame, 'cause of his position in the church, an' he says once Jen get marry, he din't care how it wus done, once there wus a ring before anything happen. Poor Jon had make the same promise to the two of them, an' with each he state the same condition, quick an' quiet. He wus like a feather in the wind, an' all 'cause he frighten to die. 'Tis a hell of a thing when you got to decide an' you ain't sure what you deciding between, an' worse when you ain't got nothin' to decide with. That wus Jon. No an' yes wus the same thing. An' when Jen say do so, he do so, an' when Susie say do so, he do so, an' the two so's din't add up to one so, not even up to the day of the weddings. I don't know if to call Jon a fool or a ass, you never knew what might have been happenin' in his min', but up to the day of the weddings he din't know which church to go to, 'cause he had sent Jen to one church an' Susie to another, an' on the same same day. On all sides everything wus quiet. Jen wus goin' to marry in her father church, quiet, quiet, an' Susie in the big church quiet, quiet, an' nobody wus takin' notice, 'cause when the priest in the big church read out the things you call banns, an' say there wus goin' to be a weddin' between Miss McCauley an' Mr. Trevelayn, it didn't make much sense to anybody. The names din't connect, 'cause in the village everybody know Susie as Susie an' Jon as Jon, an' to say Mr. McCauley and Miss Trevelayn wus like sayin' alias Jack an' Jill. It jus' didn't make no sense. An' that's jus' what happen. Susie went to one church an' Jen to another. An' the two of them wait for hours, an' Jon never turn up. He wusn't with Susie an' he wusn't with Jen. Then the talk get around. Somebody say they see a car in the churchyard for a damn long time an' went to see what happen. An' the news spread like wildfire, like wild bees who don't want to see the hive again. An' some went to tell Jen it wus Susie who wus goin' to marry with Jon, an' others went to tell Susie it wus Jen who wus goin' to marry with Jon. 'Twus a big, terrible mix-up. People bawl for murder when they hear, an' they turn out like if it wus a funeral to see the brides who din't make sure about the groom. Everybody start to wonder what could have happen. Some say this, an' some say that, but no matter what some say or not say, everybody start to refer to Jon as the cock in the yard. An' some say cocks wus gettin' scarce. What a scandal it wus, an' I hear things about cocks I never hear in all my born days. 'Twus a hell of a mix-up, an' I hope never to hear of such a thing again.'

'An' how they fin' Jon ?' Boy Blue asked.

'They din't fin' him,' Trumper said. 'The police search, an' Brother Bannister search, an' lots of others, an' they couldn't fin' him. Some say they saw him pitchin' jus' 'bout the time the wedding would be, an' some say probably he wus that sort of person, once he had a marble you couldn't get him to do anything else. Some say he went to the sea, an' some say this an' some say that, an' they went to look for him wherever they think he might be. Then there wus nearly a fight between Brother Bannister an' the priest, 'cause the priest tell Brother Bannister he wus a hypocrite, an' wus encouragin' the poor people to sin, an' Brother Bannister tell him back all he heard an' din't hear 'bout him. I never know there wus so much to tell 'bout the clergy, an' only God in heaven knows if it's all true, but we here on this earth can only hope it ain't true, the things I heard about the clergy. An' all that through Jon. They din't fin' him an' they never would have find him, 'cause he wus sittin' at the top of a mahogany tree in the cemetery. He had a good view of the two churches, an' so he says afterwards, he see when Jen go in, an' he see when Susie go in, an' he see when Jen come out an' he see when Susie come out, but he couldn't move 'cause he couldn't make up his mind, an' when everything wus said an' done he had to think 'bout his life. He stay there quiet as a mouse an' he see all the commotion, an' he hear all what they wus sayin' 'bout where he wus, an' he just look an' listen. An' when it turn dark, an' the tree wus steady as a lamp-post, an' you couldn't see nothin' but the light of the stars on the tombstones he climb down. Not before did he dare move. The graveyard wus quiet an' silent like nothin' he ever know before, an' he sit down betwixt two graves with a teeny-weeny bit of light on his shirt sleeve, an' wait. An' 'twus there 'twixt the graves that foreday mornin' catch him, lookin' up at the mahogany tree where he had sit all day the day before, turnin' his mind now this way, now that, like a fowl feather in the wind.'

§ *Childhood discovery* Edgell, Senior; SA: Sidhwa, Selvadurai; SEA: Maniam; *Oral storytelling* Selvon, Brathwaite (1); Brodber

2: *From* The Pleasures of Exile

The Pleasures of Exile is a non-fiction work about migration, primarily centred on the relationship between the *Tempest* archetypes of Prospero (colonizer) and Caliban (colonized), but also discussing the historical and contemporary significance of other characters in Shakespeare's play. Here, in the opening section, Lamming employs another, Afrocentric, model for Caribbean culture, in drawing on Haitian *vodun*.

> History is a nightmare from which I am trying to awake.[1]
>
> James Joyce

In the republic of Haiti – one corner of the Caribbean cradle – a native religion sometimes forces the official Law to negotiate with peasants who have retained a racial, and historic, desire to worship their original gods. We do not have to share their faith in order to see the universal significance of certain themes implicit in the particular ceremony of the Souls which I witnessed four years ago in the suburbs of Port-au-Prince.

The details of this ceremony are very elaborate; but the outline, the conscious style of intention, is quite simple. In our time it is even familiar. This drama between religion and the Law is important to my purpose; for it suggests parallels with William Shakespeare's play, *The Tempest*; and it is my intention to make use of *The Tempest* as a way of presenting a certain state of feeling which is the heritage of the exiled and colonial writer from the British Caribbean.

Naturally, I anticipate from various quarters the obvious charge of blasphemy; yet there are occasions when blasphemy must be seen as one privilege of the excluded Caliban. Such is this occasion, and I am determined to tell you why.

This ceremony of the Souls is regarded by the Haitian peasant as a solemn communion; for he hears, at first hand, the secrets of the Dead. The celebrants are mainly relatives of the deceased who, ever since their death, have been locked in Water. It is the duty of the Dead to return and offer, on this momentous night, a full and honest report on their past relations with the living. A wife may have to say why she refused love to her husband; a husband may have to say why he deprived his wife of their children's affection. It is the duty of the Dead to speak, since their release from that purgatory of Water cannot be realised until they have fulfilled the contract which this ceremony symbolises. The Dead need to speak if they are going to enter that eternity which will be their last and permanent Future. The living demand to hear whether there is any need for forgiveness, for redemption; whether, in fact, there may be any guide which may help them towards reforming their present condition. Different as they may be in their present state of existence, those alive and those now Dead – their ambitions point to a similar end. They are interested in their Future.

Through the medium of the Priest, the Dead speak of matters which it must have been difficult to raise before; and through the same medium, the living learn and understand what the Dead tongues have uttered. Revenge, guilt, redemption, and some future expectation make for an involvement which binds the Dead and the living together. The ceremony takes its course according to custom, and the result is, probably, always the same except in details. But it is precisely the details which may determine each future.

The official Law which, it seems, is never more than a temporary arrange-

---

1 Stephen Dedalus to Mr Deasy in the second section of Joyce's *Ulysses*; also used as the epigraph to Walcott's 'Muse of History'.

ment for our safety, has difficulty in applying its rules. This particular ceremony had been 'allowed.' But there are times when the Law decrees that there should be no Vodun[2] rites. The peasants find it difficult to obey. Fearful of being found in their wooden *tonelles*[3] they will perform their rites in the street. The ceremony is simple. You make certain *ververs*[4] in the dust, and wherever two or three are gathered together by the sign of the *ververs*, the gods are there. It is that sign, like a cross, which reminds them of their need. Then the Law arrives. The police arrive without warning; but no charge can be made. For the worshippers stand to welcome their protectors, the police, and in the same moment their feet have erased the signs of invocation which they had made in the dust. The god is not there, for his cross has gone. But the moment the police depart, the signatures will be made again; the god will return, and prayer will assume whatever needs those peasants whisper.

The Law can bring a charge of loitering, which is the privilege of Beggars and Kings, a way of life for both idle and unemployed. Like Prospero identified with his privilege, the Haitian peasant exercises a magic that vanishes and returns according to the contingencies of the moment.

But let's assume that a charge, other than loitering, is brought. Let's assume that there is a trial; that you are on trial for the very evidence which you have given; or worse still, for withholding the evidence which it is within your power to give. How can we proceed? In the widest and narrowest terms of reference? I shall state them.

We accept the fact of a trial. We realise that the Judge is late, and may, in fact, not even arrive before the accused escapes. The accused is there, but like an agent with his magic, he appears and disappears, and with each stage of evidence, he appears to change his role. We know that there must be a trial; for we have all offered to give evidence, some from rumour and others from facts.

Among us there is a witness who says that he cannot distinguish between rumour and fact. Sometimes he recognises fact, accepts it, exploits it, lives it until he discovers that its original author was cheating. Another time he confronts a rumour, investigates it, memorises it, stores it away as a reservation which must not be used against fact until his awareness changes, until he sees that the rumour was not altogether invalid; for it has given birth to new facts which demand that he liberate himself from his original knowledge, the knowledge of his original fact.

The case remains open. Each in his own way is conspiring with the other to postpone the hearing. But the trial goes on. It cannot be suspended while they are alive, for they are the trial, changing the roles of Judge and Jury, demanding to be prosecutor as well as chief witness for the defence.

Another witness arrives claiming extraordinary privileges. He wants to assume Prospero's privilege of magic, while arguing in his evidence that no

---

2 Afro-Caribbean folk-religion of Haiti, derived from Dahomey. 3 Conduit or space for a *vodun* ceremony, either marked out by *houngan* (priest) in sand; or as here temporary shelter. 4 Chalk marks made on ground at start of a *vodun* ceremony.

man has a right to use magic in his dealings with another. On the other hand he sees himself as Caliban while he argues that he is not the Caliban whom Prospero had in mind. This witness claims a double privilege. He thinks he is, in some way, a descendant of Prospero. He knows he is a direct descendant of Caliban. He claims to be the key witness in the trial; but his evidence will only be valid if the others can accept the context in which he will give it. For it is only by accepting this special context that his evidence can reveal its truth. What is the context which he proposes?

He says: I am chief witness for the prosecution, but I shall also enter the role of Prosecutor. I shall defend the accused in the light of my own evidence. I reserve the right to choose my own Jury to whom I shall interpret my own evidence since I know that evidence more intimately than any man alive. Who then is most qualified to be the Judge? For the Law itself, like the men involved, is in some doubt about the nature of this charge. The result may be capital punishment, and I shall be hangman, provided I do not have to use the apparatus that will put the accused to death. It is likely that the accused, when he is found and convicted and forgotten, may turn out to be innocent. That is unfortunate, for I am working on the fundamental belief that there are no degrees of innocence.

Involvement in crime, whether as witness, or an accomplice, makes innocence impossible. To be innocent is to be eternally dead. And this trial embraces only the living. Some may be corpses, but their evidence is the evidence of a corpse who has returned to make the unforgivable apology: 'Gentlemen I did not realise. Although I was there, although I took part, believe me, I did not realise! I was not aware!' The confession of unawareness is a confession of guilt. This corpse, dead as he may be, cannot be allowed to go free; for unawareness is the basic characteristic of the slave. Awareness is a minimum condition for attaining freedom.

'He is asking the impossible,' you say. Agreed. But it is the privilege of his imagination to do so.

'Is he God or What?' You ask the question in a way which implies a chosen denial of his answer. It is not the right spirit for just enquiry; so the question must remain open.

This book is based upon facts of experience, and it is intended as an introduction to a dialogue between you and me. I am the whole world of my accumulated emotional experience, vast areas of which probably remain unexplored. You are the other, according to your way of seeing me in relation to yourself. There will be no chairman. Magic is permissible. Indeed, any method of presentation may be used. There is one exception. Don't tell lies. From time to time, the truth may go into hiding; but don't tell lies.

We have met before. Four centuries separate our first meeting when Prospero was graced with the role of thief, merchant and man of God. Our hero was 'the right worshipfull and valiant knight sir John Haukins, sometimes treasurer of her Majesties navie Roial'; and it is his first Voyage in search of human merchandise.

'With this companie he put off and departed from the coast of England in the moneth of October 1562 and in his course touched first at Teneriffe, where he received friendly entertainment. From thence he passed to Sierra Leona, upon the coast of Guinea, which place by the people of the countrey is called Tagarin, where he stayed some good time, and got into his possession, *partly by the sworde, and partly by other meanes, to the number of 300 Negros at the least, besides other merchandises which that countrey yieldeth. With this praye he sayled over the Ocean sea unto the Iland of Hispaniola and arrived first at the port of Isabella.'*

The narrative is Hakluyt, but the italics are my way of pointing the triangular course of that tremendous Voyage which swept Caliban from his soil and introduced him to Heaven through the long wet hell of the Middle Passage.

'The 29 of this same moneth we departed with all our shippes from Sierra Leona, towardes the West Indies, and for the space of eighteen dayes, we were becalmed, having nowe and then contrary windes, and some Ternados, amongst the same calme, which happened to us very ill, beeing but reasonably watered, for so great a companie of Negros, and our selves, which pinched us all, and that which was worst, put us in such feare that many never thought to have reached to the Indies, without great death of Negros, and of themselves: *but the Almightie God, who never suffereth his elect to perish,* sent us the sixteenth of Februarie, the ordinary Brise, which is the Northwest winde, which never left us, till wee came to an Island of the Canybals, called Dominica.'

Now we know – although we cannot locate – the seeds of Prospero's eternal confidence. The slave whose skin suggests the savaged deformity of his nature becomes identical with the Carib Indian who feeds on human flesh. Carib Indian and African slave, both seen as the wild fruits of Nature, share equally that spirit of revolt which Prospero by sword or Language is determined to conquer.

'The Canybals of that Island, and also others adjacent are the most desperate warriers that are in the Indies, by the Spaniardes report, who are never able to conquer them, and they are molested by them not a little, when they are driven to water there in any of those Islands: of very late, not two moneths past, in the said Island, a Caravel being driven to water, was in the night sette upon by the inhabitants, who cutte their cable in the halser, whereby they were driven ashore, and so taken by them, and eaten.'

I cannot read *The Tempest* without recalling the adventure of those voyages reported by Hakluyt; and when I remember the voyages and the particular period in African history, I see *The Tempest* against the background of England's experiment in colonisation. Considering the range of Shakespeare's curiosity, and the fact that these matters were being feverishly discussed in England at the time, they would most certainly have been present in his mind. Indeed, they must have been part of the conscious stuff of his thinking. And it is Shakespeare's capacity for experience which leads me to feel that *The Tempest* was also prophetic of a political future which is our present. Moreover, the circumstances of my life, both as a colonial and exiled descendant of Caliban in the twentieth century, is an example of that prophecy.

It will not help to say that I am wrong in the parallels which I have set out to interpret; for I shall reply that my mistake, lived and deeply felt by millions of men like me – proves the positive value of error. It is a value which you must learn.

My subject is the migration of the West Indian writer, as colonial and exile, from his native kingdom, once inhabited by Caliban, to the tempestuous island of Prospero's and his language.

This book is a report on one man's way of seeing.

§ *Vodun* Brathwaite (2); *Responses to European texts* Walcott (4), Gilkes; Af: Coetzee; SEA: Lim (2), Lee Tzu Pheng, Somtow

SAM SELVON (1923–94)

From The Lonely Londoners

The Lonely Londoners is an episodic novel about the first generation of post-war Caribbean migrants to settle in Britain. In this brief passage from late on in the text, the central character Moses and his friend Galahad engage in a typical piece of 'old talk', reminiscing about life back in Trinidad. The juxtaposition of comic storytelling and a more reflective and sombre mood, occasioned by the 'loneliness' of the London situation, is typical of the novel.

. . . Moses laugh. 'You hear bout the time they nail Brackley to the cross?' he ask Galahad.

'No.'

'One Sunday morning they nail Brackley to the cross up on Calvary Hill. You know where that is? Up there behind the Dry River, as you going up Laventille.[1] Well it had a gang of wayside preachers, and Brackley join them, and he decide this morning to make things look real. So he tell them to nail him to the cross before they start to preach. Brackley stretch out there, and they drive nails between his fingers and tie up his hands with twine. Brackley look as if he really suffering. A test[2] went and get a bucket of cattle blood and throw it over him, and Brackley hang up there while the wayside preachers start to preach. The leader take out a white sheet and spread it on the ground, and three-four women stand up with hymnbook in their hand, and they singing and preaching. But them boys start to make rab. They begin with little pebbles, but they gradually increase to some big brick. Brick flying all by Brackley head until he start to bawl. "Take me down from here!" Brackley shout, "they didn't stone Christ on the cross!" And this time big

---

1 On the east side of Port of Spain. 2 Man.

macadam and rock flying all about in the air.'

Galahad laugh until tears come, and Moses suddenly sober up, as if it not right that in these hard times he and Galahad could sit there, belly full with pigeon, smoking cigarette, and talking bout them characters back home. As if Moses get a guilty feeling, and he watch Galahad with sorrow, thinking that he ain't have no work and the winter upon the city.

§ *Mock-crucifixions* Naipaul (1), Lovelace; *Oral storytelling* Lamming (1), Brathwaite (1), Brodber; Af: Achebe (2,3); Selvon also in TransC

V. S. NAIPAUL (1932–)

1: Man-man

Everybody in Miguel Street said that Man-man was mad, and so they left him alone. But I am not so sure now that he was mad, and I can think of many people much madder than Man-man ever was.

He didn't look mad. He was a man of medium height, thin; and he wasn't bad-looking either. He never stared at you the way I expected a mad man to do; and when you spoke to him you were sure of getting a very reasonable reply.

But he did have some curious habits.

He went up for every election, city council or legislative council, and then he stuck posters everywhere in the district. These posters were well printed. They just had the word 'Vote' and below that, Man-man's picture.

At every election he got exactly three votes. That I couldn't understand. Man-man voted for himself, but who were the other two?

I asked Hat.

Hat said, 'I really can't say, boy. Is a real mystery. Perhaps is two jokers. But they is funny sort of jokers if they do the same thing so many times. They must be mad just like he.'

And for a long time the thought of these two mad men who voted for Man-man haunted me. Every time I saw someone doing anything just a little bit odd, I wondered, 'Is he who vote for Man-man?'

At large in the city were these two men of mystery.

Man-man never worked. But he was never idle. He was hypnotised by the word, particularly the written word, and he would spend a whole day writing a single word.

One day I met Man-man at the corner of Miguel Street.

'Boy, where you going? ' Man-man asked.

'I going to school,' I said.

And Man-man, looking at me solemnly, said in a mocking way, 'So you goes to school, eh?'

I said automatically, 'Yes, I goes to school.' And I found that without intending it I had imitated Man-man's correct and very English accent.

That again was another mystery about Man-man. His accent. If you shut your eyes while he spoke, you would believe an Englishman – a good-class Englishman who wasn't particular about grammar – was talking to you.

Man-man said, as though speaking to himself, 'So the little man is going to school.'

Then he forgot me, and took out a long stick of chalk from his pocket and began writing on the pavement. He drew a very big s in outline and then filled it in, and then the c and the H and the o. But then he started making several o's, each smaller than the last, until he was writing in cursive, o after flowing o.

When I came home for lunch, he had got to French Street, and he was still writing o's, rubbing off mistakes with a rag.

In the afternoon he had gone round the block and was practically back in Miguel Street.

I went home, changed from my school-clothes into my home-clothes and went out to the street.

He was now half-way up Miguel Street.

He said, 'So the little man gone to school today?'

I said, 'Yes.'

He stood up and straightened his back.

Then he squatted again and drew the outline of a massive L and filled that in slowly and lovingly.

When it was finished, he stood up and said, 'You finish your work. I finish mine.'

Or it was like this. If you told Man-man you were going to the cricket, he would write CRICK and then concentrate on the E's until he saw you again.

One day Man-man went to the big café at the top of Miguel Street and began barking and growling at the customers on the stools as though he were a dog. The owner, a big Portuguese man with hairy hands, said, 'Man-man, get out of this shop before I tangle with you.'

Man-man just laughed.

They threw Man-man out.

Next day, the owner found that someone had entered his café during the night, and had left all the doors open. But nothing was missing.

Hat said, 'One thing you must never do is trouble Man-man. He remember everything.'

That night the café was entered again and the doors again left open.

The following night the café was entered and this time little blobs of excrement were left on the centre of every stool and on top of every table and at regular intervals along the counter.

The owner of the café was the laughing-stock of the street for several weeks, and it was only after a long time that people began going to the café again.

Hat said, 'Is just like I say. Boy, I don't like meddling with that man. These people really bad-mind, you know. God make them that way.'

It was things like this that made people leave Man-man alone. The only friend he had was a little mongrel dog, white with black spots on the ears. The dog was like Man-man in a way, too. It was a curious dog. It never barked, never looked at you, and if you looked at it, it looked away. It never made friends with any other dog, and if some dog tried either to get friendly or aggressive, Man-man's dog gave it a brief look of disdain and ambled away, without looking back.

Man-man loved his dog, and the dog loved Man-man. They were made for each other, and Man-man couldn't have made a living without his dog.

Man-man appeared to exercise a great control over the movements of his dog's bowels.

Hat said, 'That does really beat me. I can't make that one out.'

It all began in Miguel Street.

One morning, several women got up to find that the clothes they had left to bleach overnight had been sullied by the droppings of a dog. No one wanted to use the sheets and the shirts after that, and when Man-man called, everyone was willing to give him the dirty clothes.

Man-man used to sell these clothes.

Hat said, 'Is things like this that make me wonder whether the man really mad.'

From Miguel Street Man-man's activities spread, and all the people who had suffered from Man-man's dog were anxious to get other people to suffer the same thing.

We in Miguel Street became a little proud of him.

I don't know what it was that caused Man-man to turn good. Perhaps the death of his dog had something to do with it. The dog was run over by a car, and it gave, Hat said, just one short squeak, and then it was silent.

Man-man wandered about for days, looking dazed and lost.

He no longer wrote words on the pavement; no longer spoke to me or to any of the other boys in the street. He began talking to himself, clasping his hands and shaking as though he had ague.

Then one day he said he had seen God after having a bath.

This didn't surprise many of us. Seeing God was quite common in Port of Spain and, indeed, in Trinidad at that time. Ganesh Pundit, the mystic masseur from Fuente Grove,[1] had started it. He had seen God, too, and had published a little booklet called *What God Told Me*. Many rival mystics and not a few masseurs had announced the same thing, and I suppose it was natural that since God was in the area Man-man should see Him.

Man-man began preaching at the corner of Miguel Street, under the awning of Mary's shop. He did this every Saturday night. He let his beard grow and he dressed in a long white robe. He got a Bible and other holy things and stood in the white light of an acetylene lamp and preached. He was an impressive preacher, and he preached in a odd way. He made women cry, and he made people like Hat really worried.

---

1 Cf. Naipaul's first novel, *The Mystic Masseur* (1957).

He used to hold the Bible in his right hand and slap it with his left and say in his perfect English accent, 'I have been talking to God these few days, and what he tell me about you people wasn't really nice to hear. These days you hear all the politicians and them talking about making the island self-sufficient. You know what God tell me last night? Last night self, just after I finish eating? God say, "Man-man, come and have a look at these people." He show me husband eating wife and wife eating husband. He show me father eating son and mother eating daughter. He show me brother eating sister and sister eating brother. That is what these politicians and them mean by saying that the island going to become self-sufficient. But, brethren, it not too late now to turn to God.'

I used to get nightmares every Saturday night after hearing Man-man preach. But the odd thing was that the more he frightened people the more they came to hear him preach. And when the collection was made they gave him more than ever.

In the week-days he just walked about, in his white robe, and he begged for food. He said he had done what Jesus ordered and he had given away all his goods. With his long black beard and his bright deep eyes, you couldn't refuse him anything. He noticed me no longer, and never asked me, 'So you goes to school?'

The people in Miguel didn't know what to make of the change. They tried to comfort themselves by saying that Man-man was really mad, but, like me, I think they weren't sure that Man-man wasn't really right.

What happened afterwards wasn't really unexpected.

Man-man announced that he was a new Messiah.

Hat said one day, 'You ain't hear the latest?'

We said, 'What? '

'Is about Man-man. He say he going to be crucified one of these days.'

'Nobody go touch him,' Edward said. 'Everybody fraid of him now.'

Hat explained. 'No, it ain't that. He going to crucify hisself. One of these Fridays he going to Blue Basin and tie hisself to a cross and let people stone him.'

Somebody – Errol, I think – laughed, but finding that no one laughed with him, fell silent again.

But on top of our wonder and worry, we had this great pride in knowing that Man-man came from Miguel Street.

Little hand-written notices began appearing in the shops and cafés and on the gates of some houses, announcing Man-man's forthcoming crucifixion.

'They going to have a big crowd in Blue Basin,' Hat announced, and added with pride, 'and I hear they sending some police too.'

That day, early in the morning, before the shops opened and the trolley-buses began running in Ariapita Avenue, the big crowd assembled at the comer of Miguel Street. There were lots of men dressed in black and even more women dressed in white. They were singing hymns. There were also about twenty policemen, but they were not singing hymns.

When Man-man appeared, looking very thin and very holy, women cried and rushed to touch this gown. The police stood by, prepared to handle anything.

A van came with a great wooden cross.

Hat, looking unhappy in his serge suit, said, 'They tell me it make from match-wood. It ain't heavy. It light light.'

Edward said, in a snapping sort of way, 'That matter? Is the heart and the spirit that matter.'

Hat said, 'I ain't saying nothing.'

Some men began taking the cross from the van to give it to Man-man, but he stopped them. His English accent sounded impressive in the early morning. 'Not here. Leave it for Blue Basin.'

Hat was disappointed.

We walked to Blue Basin, the waterfall in the mountains to the northwest of Port of Spain, and we got there in two hours. Man-man began carrying the cross from the road, up the rocky path and then down to the Basin.

Some men put up the cross, and tied Man-man to it.

Man-man said, 'Stone me, brethren.'

The women wept and flung bits of sand and gravel at his feet.

Man-man groaned and said, 'Father, forgive them. They ain't know what they doing.' Then he screamed out, 'Stone me, brethren!'

A pebble the size of an egg struck him on the chest.

Man-man cried 'Stone, *stone*, STONE me, brethren! I forgive you.'

Edward said, 'The man really brave.'

People began flinging really big stones at Man-man, aiming at his face and chest.

Man-man looked hurt and surprised. He shouted, 'What the hell is this? What the hell you people think you doing? Look, get me down from this thing quick, let me down quick, and I go settle with that son of a bitch who pelt a stone at me.'

From where Edward and Hat and the rest of us stood, it sounded like a cry of agony.

A bigger stone struck Man-man; the women flung the sand and gravel at him.

We heard Man-man's shout, clear and loud, 'Cut this stupidness out. Cut it out, I tell you. I finish with this arseness, you hear.' And then he began cursing so loudly and coarsely that the people stopped in surprise.

The police took away Man-man.

The authorities kept him for observation. Then for good.

§ *Mock-crucifixions* Selvon, Lovelace; *Trickster-figure* Brathwaite (1), Brodber; Can: King, Armstrong

2: *From* A House for Mr Biswas

A House for Mr Biswas tells the life-story of Mr Biswas (a character based on Naipaul's own father), who dies prematurely at the age of forty-six. A minutely detailed tragi-comic account of an individual's life, the novel can also be read as an allegory of the experience of Hindus in the Caribbean and provides a vivid depiction of the attenu-ation of their culture. In this passage, from an early section of this long work, Mr Biswas is trapped into marrying one of the many daughters of the wealthy Tulsi fam-ily, in a scene which can be seen as a parody of a Hindu arranged marriage. The novel's various houses particularly lend themselves to allegorical interpretation and Hanuman House, with its backyard called 'Ceylon', is fairly clearly a bastion of old Indian values, fighting a losing battle in rural Trinidad.

... Among the tumbledown timber-and-corrugated-iron buildings in the High Street at Arwacas, Hanuman House stood like an alien white fortress. The concrete walls looked as thick as they were, and when the narrow doors of the Tulsi Store on the ground floor were closed the House became bulky, impregnable and blank. The side walls were windowless, and on the upper two floors the windows were mere slits in the façade. The balustrade which hedged the flat roof was crowned with a concrete statute of the benevolent monkey-god Hanuman. From the ground his whitewashed features could scarcely be distinguished and were, if anything, slightly sinister, for dust had settled on projections and the effect was that of a face lit up from below.

The Tulsis[1] had some reputation among Hindus as a pious, conservative, landowning family. Other communities, who knew nothing of the Tulsis, had heard about Pundit Tulsi, the founder of the family. He had been one of the first to be killed in a motorcar accident and was the subject of an irrever-ent and extremely popular song. To many outsiders he was therefore only a creature of fiction. Among Hindus there were other rumours about Pundit Tulsi, some romantic, some scurrilous. The fortune he had made in Trinidad had not come from labouring and it remained a mystery why he had emi-grated as a labourer. One or two emigrants, from criminal clans, had come to escape the law. One or two had come to escape the consequences of their families' participation in the Mutiny. Pundit Tulsi belonged to neither class. His family still flourished in India – letters arrived regularly – and it was known that he had been of higher standing than most of the Indians who had come to Trinidad, nearly all of whom, like Raghu, like Ajodha, had lost touch with their families and wouldn't have known in what province to find them. The deference paid Pundit Tulsi in his native district had followed him to Trinidad and now that he was dead attached to his family. Little was really known about this family; outsiders were admitted to Hanuman House only for certain religious celebrations.

Mr Biswas went to Hanuman House to paint signs for the Tulsi Store, after a protracted interview with a large, moustached, overpowering man

---

1 The *tulsi*, or basil, plant is used in some forms of Hindu *puja* (worship).

called Seth, Mrs Tulsi's brother-in-law. Seth had beaten down Mr Biswas's price and said that Mr Biswas was getting the job only because he was an Indian; he had beaten it down a little further and said that Mr Biswas could count himself lucky to be a Hindu; he had beaten it down yet further and said that signs were not really needed but were being commissioned from Mr Biswas only because he was a Brahmin.

The Tulsi Store was disappointing. The façade that promised such an amplitude of space concealed a building which was trapezoid in plan and not deep. There were no windows and light came only from the two narrow doors at the front and the single door at the back, which opened on to a covered courtyard. The walls, of uneven thickness, curved here and jutted there, and the shop abounded in awkward, empty, cob-webbed corners. Awkward, too, were the thick ugly coloumns, whose number dismayed Mr Biswas because he had undertaken, among other things, to paint signs on all of them.

He began by decorating the top of the back wall with an enormous sign. This he illustratred meaninglessly with a drawing of Punch, who appeared incongruously gay and roguish in the austere shop where goods were stored rather than displayed and the assistants were grave and unenthusiastic.

These assistants, he had learned with surprise, were all members of the House. He could not therefore let his eyes rove as freely as usual among the unmarried girls. So, as circumspectly as he could, he studied them while he worked, and decided that the most attractive was a girl of about sixteen, whom the others called Shama. She was of medium height, slender but firm, with fine features, and though he disliked her voice, he was enchanted by her smile. So enchanted, that after a few days he would very much have liked to do the low and possibly dangerous thing of talking to her. The presence of her sisters and brothers-in-law deterred him, as well as the unpredictable and forbidding appearances of Seth, dressed more like a plantation overseer than a store manager. Still, he stared at her with growing frankness. When she found him out he looked away, became very busy with his brushes and shaped his lips as though he were whistling softly. In fact he couldn't whistle; all he did was to expel air almost soundlessly through the lecherous gap in his top teeth.

When she had responded to his stares a few times he felt that a certain communion had been established between them; and, meeting Alec in Pagotes, where Alec was working in Ajodha's garage once again, as a mechanic and a painter of buses and signs, Mr Biswas said, 'I got a girl in Arwacas.'

Alec was congratulatory. 'Like I did say, these things come when you least expect them. What you was fussing so for?'

And a few days later Bhandat's eldest boy said, 'Mohun, I hear you got a girl at long last, man.' He was patronizing; it was well known that he was having an affair with a woman of another race by whom he had already had a child; he was proud both of the child and its illegitimacy.

The news of the girl at Arwacas spread and Mr Biswas enjoyed some glory at Pagotes until Bhandat's younger son, a prognathous, contemptuous boy, said, 'I feel you lying like hell, you know.'

When Mr Biswas went to Hanuman House the next day he had a note in his pocket, which he intended to give to Shama. She was busy all morning, but just before noon, when the store closed for lunch, there was a lull and her counter was free. He came down the ladder, whistling in his way. Unnecessarily, he began stacking and restacking his paint tins. Then, preoccupied and frowning, he walked about the store, looking for tins that were not there. He passed Shama's counter and, without looking at her, placed the note under a bolt of cloth. The note was crumpled and slightly dirty and looked ineffectual. But she saw it. She looked away and smiled. It was not a smile of complicity or pleasure; it was a smile that told Mr Biswas he had made a fool of himself. He felt exceedingly foolish, and wondered whether he shouldn't take back his note and abandon Shama at once.

While he hestitated a fat Negro woman went to Shama's counter and asked for flesh-coloured stockings, which were then enjoying some vogue in rural Trinidad.

Shama, still smiling, took down a box and held up a pair of black cotton stockings.

'Eh!' The woman's gasp could be heard throughout the shop. 'You playing with me? How the hell all-you get so fresh and conceited?' She began to curse. 'Playing with me!' She pulled boxes and bolts of cloth off the counter and hurled them to the floor and every time something crashed she shouted, 'Playing with me!' One of the Tulsi sons-in-law ran up to pacify her. She cuffed him back. 'Where the old lady?' she called, and screamed, 'Mai! Mai!' as though in great pain.

Shama had ceased to smile. Fright was plain on her face. Mr Biswas had no desire to comfort her. She looked so much like a child now that he only became more ashamed of the note. The bolt of cloth which concealed it had been thrown to the ground, and the note was exposed, caught at the end of the brass yard-stick that was screwed to the counter.

He moved towards the counter, but was driven back by the woman's fat flailing arms.

Then silence fell on the shop. The woman's arms became still. Through the back doorway, to the right of the counter, Mrs Tulsi appeared. She was as laden as Tara with jewellery; she lacked Tara's sprightliness but was statelier; her face, though not plump, was slack, as if unexercised.

Mr Biswas moved back to his tins and brushes.

'Yes, ma'am, I want to see you.' The woman was breathless with anger. 'I want to see you. I want you to beat that child, ma'am. I want you to beat that conceited, rude child of yours.'

'All right, miss. All right.' Mrs Tulsi pressed her thin lips together repeatedly. 'Tell me what happened.' She spoke English in a slow, precise way which surprised Mr Biswas and filled him with apprehension. She was now behind the counter and her fingers which, like her face were creased rather than wrinkled, rubbed along the brass yardstick. From time to time, while she listened, she pressed the corner of her veil over her moving lips.

Mr Biswas, now busily cleaning brushes, wiping them dry, and putting soap in the bristle to keep it supple, was sure that Mrs Tulsi was listening with only half a mind, that her eyes had been caught by the note: *I love you and I want to talk to you.*

Mrs Tulsi spoke some abuse to Shama in Hindi, the obscenity of which startled Mr Biswas. The woman looked pacified. Mrs Tulsi promised to look further into the matter and gave the woman a pair of flesh-coloured stockings free. The woman began to re-tell her story. Mrs Tulsi, treating the matter as closed, repeated that she was giving the stockings free. The woman went on unhurriedly to the end of the story. Then she walked slowly out of the shop, muttering, exaggeratedly swinging her large hips.

The note was in Mrs Tulsi's hand. She held it just above the counter, far from her eyes, and read it, patting her lips with her veil.

'Shama, that was a shameless thing to do.'

'I wasn't thinking, Mai,' Shama said, and burst into tears, like a girl about to be flogged.

Mr Biswas's disenchantment was complete.

Mrs Tulsi, holding her veil to her chin, nodded absently, still looking at the note.

Mr Biswas slunk out of the store. He went to Mrs Seeung's, a large café in the High Street, and ordered a sardine roll and a bottle of aerated water. The sardines were dry, the onion offended him, and the bread had a crust that cut the inside of his lips. He drew comfort only from the thought that he had not signed the note and could deny writing it.

When he went back to the store he was determined to pretend that nothing had happened, determined never to look at Shama again. Carefully he prepared his brushes and set to work. He was relieved that no one showed an interest in him; and more relieved to find that Shama was not in the store that afternoon. With a light heart he outlined Punch's dog on the irregular surface of the white washed column. Below the dog he ruled lines and sketched BARGAINS! BARGAINS! He painted the dog red, the first BARGAINS! black, the second blue. Moving a rung or two down the ladder he ruled more lines, and between these lines he detailed some of the bargains the Tulsi Store offered, in letters which he 'cut out', painting a section of the column red, leaving the letters cut out in the whitewash. Along the top and bottom of the red strip he left small circles of whitewash; these he gashed with one red stroke, to give the impression that a huge red placque had been screwed on to the pillar; it was one of Alec's devices. The work absorbed him all afternoon. Shama never appeared in the store, and for minutes he forgot about the morning's happenings.

Just before four, when the store closed and Mr Biswas stopped work, Seth came, looking as though he had spent the day in the fields. He wore muddy bluchers[2] and a stained khaki topee; in the pocket of his sweated khaki shirt

---

2 Type of boots, named after Prussian general in Napoleonic wars.

he carried a black notebook and an ivory cigarette holder. He went to Mr Biswas and said, in a tone of gruff authority, 'The old lady want to see you before you go.'

Mr Biswas resented the tone, and was disturbed that Seth had spoken to him in English. Saying nothing, he came down the ladder and washed out his brushes, doing his soundless whistling while Seth stood over him. The front doors were bolted and barred and the Tulsi Store became dark and warm and protected.

He followed Seth through the back door to the damp, gloomy courtyard, where he had never been. Here the Tulsi Store felt even smaller: looking back he saw life-size carvings of Hanuman, grotesquely coloured, on either side of the shop doorway. Across the courtyard there was a large, old, grey wooden house which he thought must be the original Tulsi house. He had never suspected its size from the store; and from the road it was almost hidden by the tall concrete building, to which it was connected by an unpainted, new-looking wooden bridge, which roofed the courtyard.

They climbed a short flight of cracked concrete steps into the hall of the wooden house. It was deserted. Seth left Mr Biswas, saying he had to go and wash. It was a spacious hall, smelling of smoke and old wood. The pale green paint had grown dim and dingy and the timbers revealed the ravages of woodlice which left wood looking so new where it was rotten. Then Mr Biswas had another surprise. Through the doorway at the far end he saw the kitchen. And the kitchen had mud walls. It was lower than the hall and appeared to be completely without light. The doorway gaped black; soot stained the wall about it and the ceiling just above; so that blackness seemed to fill the kitchen like a solid substance.

The most important piece of furniture in the hall was a long unvarnished pitchpine table, hard-grained and chipped. A hammock made from sugar-sacks hung across one corner of the room. An old sewing-machine, a baby-chair and a black biscuit-drum occupied another corner. Scattered about were a number of unrelated chairs, stools and benches, one of which, low and carved with rough ornamentation from a solid block of cyp wood, still had the saffron colour which told that it had been used at a wedding cere-mony. More elegant pieces – a dresser, a desk, a piano so buried among papers and baskets and other things that it was unlikely it was ever used – choked the staircase landing. On the other side of the hall there was a loft of curious construction. It was as if an enormous drawer had been pulled out of the top of the wall; the vacated space, dark and dusty, was crammed with all sorts of articles Mr Biswas couldn't distinguish.

He heard a creak on the staircase and saw a long white skirt and a long white petticoat dancing above silver-braceleted ankles. It was Mrs Tulsi. She moved slowly; he knew from her face that she had spent the afternoon in bed. Without acknowledging his presence she sat on a bench and, as if already tired, rested her jewelled arms on the table. He saw that in one smooth ringed hand she was holding the note.

'You wrote this?'

He did his best to look puzzled. He stared hard at the note and stretched a hand to take it. Mrs Tulsi pulled the note away and held it up.

'That? I didn't write that. Why should I want to write that?'

'I only thought so because somebody saw you put it down.'

The silence outside was broken. The tall gate in the corrugated iron fence at the side of the courtyard banged repeatedly, and the courtyard was filled with the shuffle and chatter of the children back from school. They passed to the side of the house, under the gallery formed by the projecting loft. A child was crying; another explained why; a woman shouted for silence. From the kitchen came sounds of activity. At once the house felt peopled and full.

Seth came back to the hall, his bluchers resounding on the floor. He had washed and was without his topee; his damp hair, streaked with grey, was combed flat. He sat down across the table from Mrs Tulsi and fitted a cigarette into his cigarette-holder.

'What?' Mrs Biswas said. 'Somebody saw me put *that* down?'

Seth laughed. 'Nothing to be ashamed about.' He clenched his lips over the cigarette holder and opened the corners of his mouth to laugh.

Mr Biswas was puzzled. It would have been more understandable if they had taken his word and asked him never to come to their house again.

'I believe I know your family,' Seth said.

In the gallery outside and in the kitchen there was now a continual commotion. A woman came out of the black doorway with a brass plate and a blue-rimmed enamel cup. She set them before Mrs Tulsi and, without a word, without looking right or left, hurried back to the blackness of the kitchen. The cup contained milky tea, the plate *roti*[3] and curried beans. Another woman brought similar food in an equally reverential way to Seth. Mr Biswas recognized both women as Shama's sisters; their dress and manner showed that they were married.

Mrs Tulsi, scooping up some beans with a shovel of *roti*, said to Seth, 'Better feed him?'

'Do you want to eat?' Seth spoke as though it would have been amusing if Mr Biswas did want to eat.

Mr Biswas disliked what he saw and shook his head.

'Pull up that chair and sit here,' Mrs Tulsi said and, barely raising her voice, called, 'C, bring a cup of tea for this person.'

'I know your family,' Seth repeated. 'Who's your father again?'

Mr Biswas evaded the question. 'I am the nephew of Ajodha. Pagotes.'

'Of course.' Expertly Seth ejected the cigarette from the holder to the floor and ground it with his bluchers, hissing smoke down from his nostrils and up from his mouth. 'I know Ajodha. Sold him some land. Dhanku's land,' he said, turning to Mrs Tulsi.

'O yes.' Mrs Tulsi continued to eat, lifting her armoured hand high above her plate.

C turned out to be the woman who had served Mrs Tulsi. She resembled

---

3 Bread.

Shama but was shorter and sturdier and her features were less fine. Her veil was pulled decorously over her forehead, but when she brought Mr Biswas his cup of tea she gave him a frank, unimpressed stare. He attempted to glare back but was too slow; she had already turned and was walking away briskly on light bare feet. He put the tall cup to his lips and took a slow, noisy draught, studying his reflection in the tea and wondering about Seth's position in the family.

He put the cup down when he heard someone else come into the hall. This was a tall, slender, smiling man dressed in white. His face was sunburnt and his hands were rough. Breathlessly, with many sighs, laughs and swallows, he reported to Seth on various animals. He seemed anxious to appear tired and anxious to please. Seth looked pleased. C came from the kitchen again and followed the man upstairs; he was obviously her husband.

Mr Biswas took another draught of tea, studied his reflection and wondered whether every couple had a room to themselves; he also wondered what sleeping arrangements were made for the children he heard shouting and squealing and being slapped (by mothers alone?) in the gallery outside, the children he saw peeping at him from the kitchen doorway before being dragged away by ringed hands.

'So you really do like the child?'

It was a moment or so before Mr Biswas, behind his cup, realized that Mrs Tulsi had addressed the question to him, and another moment before he knew who the child was.

He felt it would be graceless to say no. 'Yes,' he said, 'I like the child.'

Mrs Tulsi chewed and said nothing.

Seth said: 'I know Ajodha. You want me to go and see him?'

Incomprehension, surprise, then panic, overwhelmed Mr Biswas. 'The child,' he said desperately. 'What about the child?'

'What about her?' Seth said. 'She is a good child. A little bit of reading and writing even.'

'A little bit of reading and writing –' Mr Biswas echoed, trying to gain time.

Seth, chewing, his right hand working dexterously with *roti* and beans, made a dismissing gesture with his left hand. 'Just a little bit. So much. Nothing to worry about. In two or three years she might even forget.' And he gave a little laugh. He wore false teeth which clacked every time he chewed.

'The child –' Mr Biswas said.

Mrs Tulsi stared at him.

'I mean,' said Mrs Biswas, 'the child knows?'

'Nothing at all,' Seth said appeasingly.

'I mean,' said Mr Biswas, 'does the child like me?'

Mrs Tulsi looked as though she couldn't understand. Chewing, with lingering squelchy sounds, she raised Mr Biswas's note with her free hand and said, 'What's the matter? *You* don't like the child?'

'Yes,' Mr Biswas said helplessly. 'I like the child.'

'That is the main thing,' Seth said. 'We don't want to force you to do anything. Are we forcing you?'

Mr Biswas remained silent.

Seth gave another disparaging little laugh and poured tea into his mouth, holding the cup away from his lips, chewing and clacking between pours. 'Eh, boy, are we forcing you?'

'No,' Mr Biswas said. 'You are not forcing me.'

'All right, then. What's upsetting you?'

Mrs Tulsi smiled at Mr Biswas. 'The poor boy is shy. *I* know.'

'I am *not* shy and I am *not* upset,' Mr Biswas said, and the aggression in his voice so startled him that he continued softly. 'It's only that – well, it's only that I have no money to start thinking about getting married.'

Mrs Tulsi became as stern as he had seen her in the store that morning. 'Why did you write this then?' She waved the note.

'Ach! Don't worry with him,' Seth said. 'No money! Ajodha's family, and no money!'

Mr Biswas thought it would be useless to explain.

Mrs Tulsi became calmer. 'If your father was worried about money, he wouldn't have married at all.'

Seth nodded solemnly.

Mr Biswas was puzzled by her use of the words 'your father'. At first he had thought she was speaking to Seth alone, but then he saw that the statement had wider, alarming implications.

Faces of children and women peeped out from the kitchen doorway.

The world was too small, the Tulsi family too large. He felt trapped.

How often, in the years to come, at Hanuman House or in the house at Shorthills or in the house in Port of Spain, living in one room, with some of his children sleeping on the next bed, and Shama, the prankster, the server of black cotton stockings, sleeping downstairs with the other children, how often did Mr Biswas regret his weakness, his inarticulateness, that evening! How often did he try to make events appear grander, more planned and less absurd than they were!

And the most absurd feature of that evening was to come. When he had left Hanuman House and was cycling back to Pagotes, he actually felt elated! In the large, musty hall with the sooty kitchen at one end, the furniture-choked landing on one side, and the dark, cob-webbed loft on the other, he had been overpowered and frightened by Seth and Mrs Tulsi and all the Tulsi women and children; they were strange and had appeared too strong; he wanted nothing so much then as to be free of that house. But now the elation he felt was not that of relief. He felt he had been involved in large events. He felt he had achieved status.

His way lay along the County Road and the Eastern Main Road. Both were lined for stretches with houses that were ambitious, incomplete, unpainted, often skeletal, with wooden frames that had grown grey and mildewed while their owners lived in one or two imperfectly enclosed rooms.

Through unfinished partitions, patched up with box-boards, tin and canvas, the family clothing could be seen hanging on lengths of string stretched across the inhabited rooms like bunting; no beds were to be seen, only a table and chair perhaps, and many boxes. Twice a day he cycled past these houses, but that evening he saw them as for the first time. From such failure, which until only that morning awaited him, he had by one stroke made himself exempt.

And when that evening Alec asked in his friendly mocking way, 'How the girl, man?' Mr Biswas said happily, 'Well, I see the mother.'

Alec was stupefied. 'The mother? But what the hell you gone and put yourself in?'

All Mr Biswas's dread returned, but he said, 'Is all right. I got my eyes open. Good family, you know. Money. Acres and acres of land. No more sign-painting for me.'

Alec didn't look reassured. 'How you manage this so quick?'

'Well, I see this girl, you know. I see this girl and she was looking at me, and I was looking at she. So I give she a little of the old sweet talk and I see that she was liking me too. And, well, to cut a long story short, I ask to see the mother. Rich people, you know. Big house.'

But he was worried, and spent much time that evening wondering whether he should go back to Hanuman House. He began feeling that it was he who had acted, and was unwilling to believe that he had acted foolishly. And, after all, the girl was good-looking. And there would be a handsome dowry. Against this he could set only his fear, and a regret he could explain to no one: he would be losing romance forever, since there could be no romance at Hanuman House.

In the morning everything seemed so ordinary that both his fear and regret became unreal, and he saw no reason why he should behave unusually.

He went back to the Tulsi Store and painted a column.

He was invited to lunch in the hall, off lentils, spinach and a mound of rice on a brass plate. Flies buzzed on fresh food-stains all along the pitch-pine table. He disliked the food and disliked eating off brass plates. Mrs Tulsi, who was not eating herself, sat next to him, stared at his plate, brushed the flies away from it with one hand, and talked.

At one stage she directed his attention to a framed photograph on the wall below the loft. The photograph, blurred at the edges and in many other places, was of a moustached man in turban, jacket and dhoti, with beads around his neck, caste-marks on his forehead and an unfurled umbrella on the crook of his left arm. It was Pundit Tulsi.

'We never had a quarrel,' Mrs Tulsi said. 'Suppose I wanted to go to Port of Spain, and he didn't. You think we'd quarrel about a thing like that? No. We would sit down and talk it over, and he would say, "All right, let us go." Or I would say, "All right, we *won't* go." That's the way we were, you know.'

She had grown almost maudlin, and Mrs Biswas was trying to appear solemn while chewing. He chewed slowly and wondered whether he shouldn't stop altogether; but whenever he stopped eating Mrs Tulsi stopped talking.

'This house,' Mrs Tulsi said, blowing her nose, wiping her eyes with her veil and waving a hand in a fatigued way, 'this house – he built it with his own hands. Those walls aren't concrete, you know. Did you know that?'

Mr Biswas went on eating.

'They looked like concrete to you, didn't they?'

'Yes, they looked like concrete.'

'It looks like concrete to *everybody*. But everybody is wrong. Those walls are really made of clay bricks. Clay bricks,' she repeated, staring at Mr Biswas's plate and waiting for him to say something.

'Clay bricks!' he said. 'I would never have thought that.'

'Clay bricks. And he made every brick himself. Right here. In Ceylon.'

'Ceylon?'

'That is how we call the yard at the back. You haven't seen it? Nice piece of ground. Lots of flower trees. He was a great one for flowers, you know. We still have the brick-factory and everything there as well. There's a lot of people don't know about this house. Ceylon. You'd better start getting to know these names.' She laughed and Mr Biswas felt a little stab of fear. 'And then,' she went on, 'he was going to Port of Spain one day, to make arrangements to take us all back to India. Just for a trip, you know. And this car came and knocked him down, and he died. Died,' she repeated, and waited.

Mr Biswas swallowed hurriedly and said, 'That must have been a blow.'

'It was a blow. Only one daughter married. Two sons to educate. It was a blow. And we had no money, you know.'

This was news to Mr Biswas. He hid his perturbation by looking down at his brass plate and chewing hard.

'And Seth says, and I agree with him, that with the father dead, one shouldn't make too much fuss about marrying people off. You know' – she lifted her heavy braceleted arms and made a clumsy dancer's gesture which amused her a good deal – 'drums and dancing and big dowry. We don't believe in that. We leave that to people who want to show off. You know the sort of people. Dressed up to kill all the time. Yet go and see where they come out from. You know those houses in the County Road. Half built. No furniture. No, we are not like that. Then, all this fuss about getting married was more suitable for oldfashioned people like myself. Not for you. Do you think it matters how people get married?'

'Not really.'

'You remind me a little of *him*.'

He followed her gaze to other photographs of Pundit Tulsi on the wall. There was one of him flanked by potted palms against the sunset of a photographer's studio. In another photograph he stood, a small indistinct figure, under the arcade of Hanuman House, beyond the High Street that was empty except for a broken barrel which, because it was nearer the camera, stood out in clear detail. (How did they empty the street, Mr Biswas wondered. Perhaps it was a Sunday morning, or perhaps they had roped the populace off.) There was another photograph of him behind the balustrade. In every photograph he carried the unfurled umbrella.

'He would have liked you,' Mrs Tulsi said. 'He would have been proud to know that you were going to marry one of his daughters. He wouldn't have let things like your job or your money worry him. He always said that the only thing that mattered was the blood. I can just look at you and see that you come from good blood. A simple little ceremony at the registrar's office is all that you need.'

And Mr Biswas found that he had agreed.

§ *House as symbol* Walcott (1); SA: Ramanujan, Alexander, Wijenaike, Hashmi; *Hindu acculturation* NZSP: Subramani; SEA: Maniam; Naipaul also in TransC

DEREK WALCOTT (1930–)

1: Ruins of a Great House

> though our longest sun sets at right
> declensions* and makes but winter
> arches, it cannot be long before we
> lie down in darkness, and have our
> light in ashes . . .
>   BROWNE: *Urn Burial*

Stones only, the *disjecta membra* of this Great House,
Whose moth-like girls are mixed with candledust,
Remain to file the lizard's dragonish claws;
The mouths of those gate cherubs streaked with stain.
5   Axle and coachwheel silted under the muck
Of cattle droppings.

                    Three crows flap for the trees,
And settle, creaking the eucalyptus boughs.
A smell of dead limes quickens in the nose
10 The leprosy of Empire.

                    'Farewell, green fields'
                    'Farewell, ye happy groves!'

Marble as Greece, like Faulkner's south in stone,
Deciduous beauty prospered and is gone;
15 But where the lawn breaks in a rash of trees

---

* declensions: angular distance of sun north of Equator.
11–12 'Farewell . . . groves!': From Blake's 'Night'.
1 *disjecta membra*: 'scattered fragments' (from Horace).

A spade below dead leaves will ring the bone
Of some dead animal or human thing
Fallen from evil days, from evil times.

It seems that the original crops were limes
20 Grown in the silt that clogs the river's skirt;
The imperious rakes are gone, their bright girls gone,
The river flows, obliterating hurt.

I climbed a wall with the grill ironwork
Of exiled craftsmen, protecting that great house
25 From guilt, perhaps, but not from the worm's rent.
Nor from the padded cavalry of the mouse.
And when a wind shook in the limes I heard
What Kipling heard; the death of a great empire, the abuse
Of ignorance by Bible and by sword.

30 A green lawn, broken by low walls of stone
Dipped to the rivulet, and pacing, I thought next
Of men like Hawkins, Walter Raleigh, Drake,
Ancestral murderers and poets, more perplexed
In memory now by every ulcerous crime.
35 The world's green age then was a rotting lime
Whose stench became the charnel galleon's text.
The rot remains with us, the men are gone.
But, as dead ash is lifted in a wind,
That fans the blackening ember of the mind,
40 My eyes burned from the ashen prose of Donne.

Ablaze with rage, I thought
Some slave is rotting in this manorial lake,
And still the coal of my compassion fought:
That Albion too, was once
45 A colony like ours, 'Part of the continent, piece of the main'
Nook-shotten, rook o'er blown, deranged
By foaming channels, and the vain expense
Of bitter faction.

All in compassion ends
50 So differently from what the heart arranged:
'as well as if a manor of thy friend's . . .'

§ *House as symbol* Naipaul (2); Af: Dangarembga; Can: Atwood (4); SA:
Ramanujan, Alexander, Wijenaike, Hashmi

---

44 Albion: Britain (poetic).   45 'Part . . . main': Donne, *Devotions*, 17: from the
46 Nook-shotten: an exhausted corner (of the world?)   famous 'No man is an island . . .' passage.
51 'as . . . friend's . . .': Donne, ibid.

2: *From* Dream on Monkey Mountain

Imprisoned for drunkeness, the charcoal-burner Makak dreams of a White Goddess figure, a European Muse who instils in him a belief that he must be a redeemer of his race and lead them back to Africa. Acting under her spell, he performs messianic acts of healing, but eventually comes to realize that he is a 'king among shadows'. He beheads the Goddess and in so doing appears to liberate himself from Europe. Finally, he awakens and decides to go 'home': not to Africa, but to 'the green beginning of this world', a view which accords with Walcott's belief in the Adamic potential of the New World (cf. 'The Muse of History'). The play's use of St Lucian folk elements also promotes the case of a Caribbean aesthetic. Here in the Prologue, mime, dance and the call-and-response song of the Conteur all create a distinctively Caribbean ambience before the main action starts.

[*A spotlight warms the white disc of an African drum until it glows like the round moon above it. Below the moon is the stark silhouette of a volcanic mountain. Reversed, the moon becomes the sun. A dancer enters and sits astride the drum. From the opposite side of the stage a top-hatted, frock-coated figure with white gloves, his face halved by white make-up like the figure of* Baron Samedi,[1] *enters and crouches behind the dancer. As the lament begins, dancer and figure wave their arms slowly, sinuously, with a spidery motion. The figure rises during the lament and touches the disc of the moon. The drummer rises, dancing as if in slow motion, indicating, as their areas grow distinct, two prison cages on either side of the stage. In one cell, Tigre*[2] *and Souris,*[3] *two half-naked felons are squabbling. The figure strides off slowly, the Conteur*[4] *and Chorus, off-stage, increase the volume of their lament.*]

Conteur
Mooma, mooma,
Your son in de jail a'ready,
Your son in de jail a'ready,
Take a towel and
           band your belly.

Chorus
Mooma, mooma,
Your son in de jail a'ready,
Your son in de jail a'ready,
Take a towel and
           band your belly.

---

1 Haitian folklore figure of death, with a half-white, half-black face.   2 Tiger.   3 Mouse.   4 Storyteller.

Conteur
I pass by the police station,
Nobody to sign de bail bond.
Chorus
Mooma, don't cry,
Your son in de jail a'ready.
I pass by de police station,
Nobody to sign de bail bond.

Conteur
Forty days before the Carnival, Lord,
I dream I see my funeral.

Chorus
Mooma, mooma,
Your son in de jail a'ready,
Take a towel and band your belly.
[*The* Corporal, *in Sunday uniform, enters with* Makak, *an old Negro with a jute sack, and lets him into the next cell*]

Tigre
Forty days before the Carnival,
Lord, I dream I see me funeral . . .

Tigre and Souris
Mooma, don't cry, your son in de jail a'ready . . .

Tigre
Take a towel and band you' belly,
Mooma, don't cry, your son in de jail a'ready.
[Makak *sits on the cell cot, an old cloth around his shoulders*]

Souris
Shut up! Ay, Corporal. Who is dat?

Tigre
[*Singing*]
Momma, don't cry, your son in de jail a'ready.

Corporal
Dat, you mange-ridden habitual felon, is de King of Africa.

Tigre
[*Singing*]
Your son in de jail a'ready,
Your son in de jail a'ready . . .

Souris

Tigre, shut your trap. It have Majesty there.
[*The* Corporal *elaborately removes a notebook and gold pencil*]

Corporal

Now before I bring a specific charge against you, I will require
certain particulars . . .

Tigre, Souris and Corporal

You are required by law to supply me with certain data, for no
man is guilty except so proven, and I must warn you that anything you say may be held against you . . .

Corporal
[*Turning*] Look!

Souris

Don't tell him a damn thing! You have legal rights. Your lawyer!
Get your lawyer.

Tigre
[*Singing*]
I pass by de police station,
Nobody to sign de bail bond,
Mooma, don't cry . . .

Souris
[*Shrilly*] What he up for, Corporal? What you lock him up for?

Corporal

Drunk and disorderly! A old man like that! He was drunk and he
mash up Alcindor café.

Souris

And you going cage him here on a first offence? Old man, get a
lawyer and defend your name!
[*The* Corporal *bends down and removes a half-empty bottle of
rum from the bag, and a white mask with long black sisal hair*]

Corporal

I must itemize these objects! Can you identify them?

Souris

O God, O God, Tigre! The king got a bottle! [Souris *and*
Tigre *grope through the bars, howling, groaning*] O God, just one,

Corporal. My throat on fire. One for the boys. Here, just one swallow, Corp.

Tigre

Have mercy on two thieves fallen by the wayside. You call yourself a Catholic?

[*Inchoate, animal howling, leaping and pacing*]

Corporal

Animals, beasts, savages, cannibals, niggers, stop turning this place to a stinking zoo!

Souris

Zoo? Just because you capture some mountain gorilla?

[*The* Corporal *with his baton cracks* Souris's *extended wrist*]

Corporal

In the beginning was the ape, and the ape had no name, so God call him man. Now there were various tribes of the ape, it had gorilla, baboon, orang-outan, chimpanzee, the blue-arsed monkey and the marmoset, and God looked at his handiwork, and saw that it was good. For some of the apes had straighten their backbone, and start walking upright, but there was one tribe unfortunately that lingered behind, and that was the nigger. Now if you apes will behave like gentlemen, who knows what could happen? The bottle could go round, but first it behoves me, Corporal Lestrade, to perform my duty according to the rules of Her Majesty's Government, so don't interrupt. Please let me examine the Lion of Judah.[5] [*Goes towards* Makak] What is your name?

Tigre

[*Singing softly*]
Oh, when the roll
Is called up yonder,
When the roll
Is called up yonder,
When the roll
Is called up yonder,
When the roll is called up yonder,
I ain't going!

---

5 Name applied to Emperor Haile Selassie of Ethiopia, believed by Rastafarians to be God incarnate.

[Chorus: *When the roll . . .*]

[*Spoken*] And nobody else here going, you all too black, except possibly the Corporal. [*Pauses, points*] Look, is the full moon.

Corporal
[*As moonlight fills the cell*] Your name in full, occupation, status, income, ambition, domicile or place of residence, age, and last but not least, your race?

Souris
The man break my hand. The damn man break my hand.

Tigre
Well, you can't t'hief again.

Makak
Let me go home, my Corporal.

Souris
Ay, wait, Tigre, the king has spoken.

Tigre
What the king say?

Souris
He want to go home.

Corporal
Where is your home? Africa?

Makak
Sur Morne Macaque . . .[6]

Corporal
[*Infuriated*] English, English! For we are observing the principles and precepts of Roman law, and Roman law is English law. Let me repeat the query: Where is your home?
Makak
I live on Monkey Mountain, Corporal.

Corporal
What is your name?

---

6 On Monkey Mountain.

Makak
I forget.

Corporal
What is your race?

Makak
I am tired.

Corporal
What is your denominational affiliation?
[*Silence*]

Souris
[*Whispering*] *Ça qui religion-ous?*[7]

Makak
[*Smiling*] Cat'olique.

Corporal
I ask you, with all the patience of the law, what is or has been
your denominational affiliation?

Makak
Cat'olique.

Corporal
[*Revising notes*] You forget your name, your race is tired, your
denominational affiliation is Catholique, therefore, as the law, the
Roman law, had pity on our Blessed Saviour, by giving him, even
in extremis, a draught of vinegar, what, in your own language,
you would call *vinegre*, I shall give all and sunday here, including these two thieves, a handful of rum, before I press my
charge.

[Tigre *and* Souris *applaud loudly. The* Corporal *takes a swallow
from the bottle and passes it through the bars to* Tigre *and* Souris;
then, holding it in his hand, paces around Makak]

Tigre
How a man like that can know so much law? Could know so much
language? Is a born Q.C. Still every man entitle to his own defence.

Souris
The wig and gown, Corporal. Put on the wig and gown!

---

7 What religion are you?

Tigre
You have a sense of justice, put on the wig and gown.

Corporal
I can both accuse and defend this man.

Souris
The wig and gown, Lestrade. Let us hear English!

[*The* Corporal *strides off*]

Souris
[*Sings*]
Drill him, Constable, drill him,
Drill him, Constable, drill him,
Drill him, Constable, drill him.
He t'ief a bag of coals yesterday!

Chorus
[*Repeats*]
Drill him, Constable, drill him . . .

Souris
Drill him, Constable, drill him,
He mash up old Alcindor café!

[*The* Corporal, *isolated in a spot, with counsel's wig and gown, returns with four towels, two yellow, two red*]

Tigre
Order, order, order in de court.

[*A massive gong is sounded, and the* Corporal *gives the two prisoners the towels. They robe themselves like judges*]

Corporal
My noble judges. When this crime has been categorically examined by due process of law, and when the motive of the hereby accused by whereas and ad hoc shall be established without dychotomy, and long after we have perambulated through the labyrinthine bewilderment of the defendant's ignorance, let us hope, that justice, whom we all serve, will not only be done, but will appear, my lords, to have itself, been done . . . [*The* Judges *applaud*] Ignorance is no excuse. Ignorance of the law is no excuse. Ignorance of one's own ignorance is no excuse. This is

the prisoner. I will ask the prisoner to lift up his face. *Levez la
tête-ous!*[8]

[Makak *lifts up his head. The* Corporal *jerks it back savagely*]

Corporal
My lords, as you can see, this is a being without a mind, a will, a
name, a tribe of its own. I shall ask the prisoner to turn out his
hands. *Montrez-moi la main-ous!* [Makak *turns his palm outward*] I
will spare you the sound of that voice, which have come from a
cave of darkness, dripping with horror. These hands are the hands
of Esau, the fingers are like roots, the arteries as hard as twine,
and the palms are seamed with coal. But the animal, you observe,
is tamed and obedient. Walk round the cage! *Marchez! Marchez!*

[Makak *rises and walks round the bench, as the* Chorus *begins
to sing*]

Chorus
I don't know what to say this monkey won't do,
I don't know what to say this monkey won't do.

[*As the* Corporal, *like an animal tamer, cracks out his orders, the
choir of* Judges *keeps time, clapping*]

Corporal
About turn!

[Makak *turns around wearily*]

Chorus
Cause when I turn round, monkey turn around too,
I don't know what to say this monkey won't do.

Corporal
On your knees!

[Makak *drops to his knees,* Souris *shrieks with delight, then col-
lects his dignity*]
I kneel down, monkey kneel down too,
I don't know what to say this monkey won't do.
I praying, monkey praying too,
I don't know what the hell this monkey won't do.

---

8 Raise your head!

Corporal

Stand up! Sit down! Up on the bench! Sit down! Hands out! Hands in!

[Makak *does all this. The* Chorus *sings faster, and the* Judges *keep time*]

Chorus

Everything I say this monkey does do,
I don't know what to say this monkey won't do.
I sit down, monkey sit down too,
I don't know what to say this monkey won't do.

[Makak *sits wearily on the bench*]

Corporal

[*Holds up a palm*] The exercise, my lords, prove that the prisoner is capable of reflexes, of obeying orders, therefore of understanding justice. Sound body. Now the charge!

[*Drum roll*]

[*To the sound of martial drums*] His rightful name is unknown, yet on Saturday evening, July 25th, to wit tonight, at exactly three hours ago, to wit at 5:30 p.m., having tried to dispose of four bags of charcoal in the market of Quatre Chemin, to wit this place, my lords, in which aforesaid market your alias, to wit Makak, is well known to all and sunday, the prisoner, in a state of incomprehensible intoxication, from money or moneys accrued by the sale of self-said bags, is reputed to have entered the licenced alcoholic premises of one Felicien Alcindor, whom the prisoner described as an agent of the devil, the same Felicien Alcindor being known to all and sunday as a God-fearing, honest Catholic. [*He rests the bottle down*] When some intervention was attempted by those present, the prisoner than began to become vile and violent; he engaged in a blasphemous, obscene debate with the two other villagers, Hannibal Dolcis and Market Inspector Caiphas Joseph Pamphilion, describing in a foul, incomprehensible manner . . .

[*The* Judges *posture: Hear no evil. Hands to their ears*]

a dream which he claims to have experienced, a vile, ambitious, and obscene dream . . .

[*The* Judges *mime: See no evil. Hands to their faces in horror*] elaborating on the aforesaid dream with vile words and with a variety of sexual obscenities both in language and posture! Further, the prisoner, in defiance of Her Majesty's Government, urged the aforementioned villagers to join him in sedition and the defilement of the flag, and when all this was rightly received with civic laughter and pious horror . . .

[*The* Judges *mime: Speak no evil. Their hands to their mouths*]

the prisoner, in desperation and shame, began to wilfully damage the premises of the proprietor Felicien Alcindor, urging destruction on Church and State, claiming that he was the direct descendant of African kings, a healer of leprosy and the Saviour of his race.

[*Pause. Silence*]

You claimed that with the camera of your eye you had taken a photograph of God and all that you could see was blackness.

[*The* Judges *rise in horror*]

Blackness, my lords. What did the prisoner imply? That God was neither white nor black but nothing? That God was not white but black, that he had lost his faith? Or . . . or . . . what . . .

Makak
I am an old man. Send me home, Corporal. I suffer from madness. I does see things. Spirits does talk to me. All I have is my dreams and they don't trouble your soul.

Tigre
I can imagine your dreams. Masturbating in moonlight. Dreaming of women, cause you so damn ugly. You should walk on all fours.

Makak
Sirs, I does catch fits. I fall in a frenzy every full-moon night. I does be possessed. And after that, sir, I am not responsible. I responsible only to God who once speak to me in the form of a woman on Monkey Mountain. I am God's warrior.

[*The* Judges *laugh*]

Corporal
You are charged with certain things. Now let the prisoner make his deposition.

Makak

[*During this speech, the cage is raised out of sight*]

Sirs, I am sixty years old. I have live all my life
Like a wild beast in hiding. Without child, without wife.
People forget me like the mist on Monkey Mountain.
Is thirty years now I have look in no mirror,
Not a pool of cold water, when I must drink,
I stir my hands first, to break up my image.
I will tell you my dream. Sirs, make a white mist
In the mind; make that mist hang like cloth
From the dress of a woman, on prickles, on branches,
Make it rise from the earth, like the breath of the dead
On resurrection morning, and I walking through it
On my way to my charcoal pit on the mountain.
Make the web of the spider heavy with diamonds
And when my hand brush it, let the chain break.
I remember, in my mind, the cigale sawing,
Sawing, sawing wood before the woodcutter,
The drum of the bull-frog, the blackbird flute,
And this old man walking, ugly as sin,
In a confusion of vapour,
Till I feel I was God self, walking through cloud.
In the heaven on my mind. Then I hear this song.
Not the blackbird flute,
Not the bull-frog drum,
Not the whistling of parrots
As I brush through the branches, shaking the dew,
A man swimming through smoke,
And the bandage of fog unpeeling my eyes,
As I reach to this spot,
I see this woman singing
And my feet grow roots. I could move no more.
A million silver needles prickle my blood,
Like a rain of small fishes.
The snakes in my hair speak to one another,
The smoke mouth open, and I behold this woman,
The loveliest thing I see on this earth,
Like the moon walking along her own road.
[*During this, the apparition appears and withdraws*]

[*Flute music*]

Makak

You don't see her? Look, I see her! She standing right there. [*He points at nothing*] Like the moon had climbed down the steps of heaven, and was standing in front me.

Corporal

I can see nothing. [*To the* Judges] What do you see?

Judges

Nothing. Nothing.

Makak

Nothing? Look, there she is!

Tigre

Nothing at all. The old man mad.

Souris

[*Mocking*] Yes, I see it. I can see it. Is the face of the moon moving over the floor. Come to me, darling. [*He rolls over the cell floor groaning*]

Corporal

My lords, is this rage for whiteness that does drive niggers mad.

Makak

[*On his knees*]

Lady in heaven, is your old black warrior,
The king of Ashanti, Dahomey, Guinea,
Is this old cracked face you kiss in his sleep
Appear to my enemies, tell me what to do?
Put on my rage, the rage of the lion?

[*He rises slowly and assumes a warrior's stance. Drums build to a frenzy*]

Help poor crazy Makak, help Makak
To scatter his enemies, to slaughter those
That standing around him.
So, thy hosts shall be scattered,
And the hyena shall feed on their bones!

[*He falls*]

Sirs, when I hear that voice,
Singing so sweetly,
I feel my spine straighten,
My hand grow strong.
My blood was boiling
Like a brown river in flood,
And in that frenzy,
I let out a cry,
I charged the spears about me,
Grasses and branches,
I began to dance,
With the splendour of a lion,
Faster and faster,
Faster and faster,
Then, my body sink,
My bones betray me
And I fall on the forest floor,
Dead, on sweating grass,
And there, maybe, sirs,
Two other woodmen find me,
And take me up the track.
Sirs, if you please . . .

[*The two prisoners carry him*]

Corporal
Continue, continue, the virtue of the law is its infinite patience.
Continue . . .

[*The cells rise, the others withdraw.* Makak *lies alone in the hut*]

§ *Competing ancestries* Rhys (1,2), Harris, Williams, Brodber; *Caribbean as Eden* Walcott (3), Gilkes

3: *From* The Muse of History

History is a nightmare from which I am trying to awake.[1]

Joyce

The common experience of the New World, even for its patrician writers whose veneration of the Old is read as the idolatry of the mestizo,[2] is colonialism. They too are victims of tradition, but they remind us of our debt to

---

1 Remark made by Stephen Dedalus to Mr Deasy in the second section of *Ulysses*; also used as the epigraph to the Introduction to George Lamming's *The Pleasures of Exile*. 2 Mixed Spanish and Native American.

the great dead, that those who break a tradition first hold it in awe. They perversely encourage disfavor, but because their sense of the past is of a timeless, yet habitable, moment, the New World owes them more than it does those who wrestle with that past, for their veneration subtilizes an arrogance which is tougher than violent rejection. They know that by openly fighting tradition we perpetuate it, that revolutionary literature is a filial impulse, and that maturity is the assimilation of the features of every ancestor.

When these writers cunningly describe themselves as classicists and pretend an indifference to change, it is with an irony as true of the colonial anguish as the fury of the radical. If they appear to be phony aristocrats, it is because they have gone past the confrontation of history, that Medusa[3] of the New World.

These writers reject the idea of history as time for its original concept as myth, the partial recall of the race. For them history is fiction, subject to a fitful muse, memory. Their philosophy, based on a contempt for historic time, is revolutionary, for what they repeat to the New World is its simultaneity with the Old. Their vision of man is elemental, a being inhabited by presences, not a creature chained to his past. Yet the method by which we are taught the past, the progress from motive to event, is the same by which we read narrative fiction. In time every event becomes an exertion of memory and is thus subject to invention. The further the facts, the more history petrifies into myth. Thus, as we grow older as a race, we grow aware that history is written, that it is a kind of literature without morality, that in its actuaries the ego of the race is indissoluble and that everything depends on whether we write this fiction through the memory of hero or of victim.

In the New World servitude to the muse of history has produced a literature of recrimination and despair, a literature of revenge written by the descendants of slaves or a literature of remorse written by the descendants of masters. Because this literature serves historical truth, it yellows into polemic or evaporates in pathos. The truly tough aesthetic of the New World neither explains nor forgives history. It refuses to recognize it as a creative or culpable force. This shame and awe of history possess poets of the Third World who think of language as enslavement and who, in a rage for identity, respect only incoherence or nostalgia.

The great poets of the New World, from Whitman to Neruda, reject this sense of history. Their vision of man in the New World is Adamic. In their exuberance he is still capable of enormous wonder. Yet he had paid his accounts to Greece and Rome and walks in a world without monuments and ruins. They exhort him against the fearful magnet of older civilizations. Even in Borges, where the genius seems secretive, immured from change, it celebrates an elation which is vulgar and abrupt, the life of the

---

3 Chief of the Gorgons, who changed those who looked at her to stone.

plains given an instant archaism by the hieratic style. Violence is felt with the simultaneity of history. So the death of a gaucho does not merely repeat, but is, the death of Caesar. Fact evaporates into myth. This is not the jaded cynicism which sees nothing new under the sun, it is an elation which sees everything as renewed. Like Borges too, the poet St. John Perse[4] conducts us from the mythology of the past to the present without a tremor of adjustment. This is the revolutionary spirit at its deepest, it recalls the spirit to arms. In Perse there is the greatest width of elemental praise of winds, seas, rains. The revolutionary or cyclic vision is as deeply rooted as the patrician syntax. What Perse glorifies is not veneration but the perennial freedom; his hero remains the wanderer, the man who moves through the ruins of great civilizations with all his worldly goods by caravan or pack mule, the poet carrying entire cultures in his head, bitter perhaps, but unencumbered. His are poems of massive or solitary migrations through the elements. They are the same in spirit as the poems of Whitman or Neruda, for they seek spaces where praise of the earth is ancestral.

New World poets who see the 'classic style' as stasis must see it also as historical degradation, rejecting it as the language of the master. This self-torture arises when the poet also sees history as language, when he limits his memory to the suffering of the victim. Their admirable wish to honor the degraded ancestor limits their language to phonetic pain, the groan of suffering, the curse of revenge. The tone of the past becomes an unbearable burden, for they must abuse the master or hero in his own language, and this implies self-deceit. Their view of Caliban is of the enraged pupil. They cannot separate the rage of Caliban from the beauty of his speech when the speeches of Caliban are equal in their elemental power to those of his tutor. The language of the torturer mastered by the victim. This is viewed as servitude, not as victory.

But who in the New World does not have a horror of the past, whether his ancestor was torturer or victim? Who, in the depth of conscience, is not silently screaming for pardon or for revenge? The pulse of New World history is the racing pulse beat of fear, the tiring cycles of stupidity and greed. The tongues above our prayers utter the pain of entire races to the darkness of a Manichean God: *Dominus illuminatio mea*,[5] for what was brought to this New World under the guise of divine light, the light of the sword blade and the light of *dominus illuminatio mea*, was the same iridescent serpent brought by a contaminating Adam, the same tortured Christ exhibited with Christian exhaustion, but what was also brought in the seeded entrails of the slave was a new nothing, a darkness which intensified the old faith.

---

4 Pseudonym of Alexis Saint-Léger Léger (1887–1975), Caribbean-born French poet and diplomat; winner of 1960 Nobel Prize for Literature. 5 'The Lord is my illumination'.

In time the slave surrendered to amnesia. That amnesia is the true history of the New World. That is our inheritance, but to try and understand why this happened, to condemn or justify is also the method of history, and these explanations are always the same: This happened because of that, this was understandable because, and in days men were such. These recriminations exchanged, the contrition of the master replaces the vengeance of the slave, and here colonial literature is most pietistic, for it can accuse great art of feudalism and excuse poor art as suffering. To radical poets poetry seems the homage of resignation, an essential fatalism. But it is not the pressure of the past which torments great poets but the weight of the present:

> there are so many dead,
> and so many dikes the red sun breached,
> and so many heads battering hulls
> and so many hands that have closed over kisses
> and so many things that I want to forget.
>   (Neruda)

The sense of history in poets lives rawly along their nerves:

> My land without name, without America,
> equinoctial stamen, lance-like purple,
> your aroma rose through my roots
> into the cup I drained, into the most tenuous
> world not yet born in my mouth.
>   (Neruda)

It is this awe of the numinous, this elemental privilege of naming the new world which annihilates history in our great poets, an elation common to all of them, whether they are aligned by heritage to Crusoe and Prospero or to Friday and Caliban.[6] They reject ethnic ancestry for faith in elemental man. The vision, the 'democratic vista,' is not metaphorical, it is a social necessity. A political philosophy rooted in elation would have to accept belief in a second Adam, the re-creation of the entire order, from religion to the simplest domestic rituals. The myth of the noble savage would not be revived, for that myth never emanated from the savage but has always been the nostaliga of the Old World, its longing for innocence. The great poety of the New World does not pretend to such innocence, its vision is not naïve. Rather, like its fruits, its savor is a mixture of the acid and the sweet, the apples of its second Eden have the tartness of experience. In such poetry there is a bitter memory and it is the bitterness that dries last on the tongue. It is the acidulous that supplies its energy. The golden apples of this sun are shot with acid. The taste of Neruda is citric, the *Pomme de*

---

6 i.e. colonizer and colonized.

Cythère of Césaire[7] sets the teeth on edge, the savor of Perse is of salt fruit at the sea's edge, the sea grape, the 'fat-poke,' the sea almond.[8] For us in the archipelago the tribal memory is salted with the bitter memory of migration.

To such survivors, to all the decimated tribes of the New World who did not suffer extinction, their degraded arrival must be seen as the beginning, not the end of our history. The shipwrecks of Crusoe and of the crew in *The Tempest* are the end of an Old World. It should matter nothing to the New World if the Old is again determined to blow itself up, for an obsession with progress is not within the psyche of the recently enslaved. That is the bitter secret of the apple. The vision of progress is the rational madness of history seen as sequential time, of a dominated future. Its imagery is absurd. In the history books the discoverer sets a shod foot on virgin sand, kneels, and the savage also kneels from his bushes in awe. Such images are stamped on the colonial memory, such heresy as the world's becoming holy from Crusoe's footprint or the imprint of Columbus' knee. These blasphemous images fade, because these hieroglyphs of progress are basically comic. And if the idea of the New and the Old becomes increasingly absurd, what must happen to our sense of time, what else can happen to history itself, but that it too is becoming absurd? This is not existentialism. Adamic, elemental man cannot be existential. His first impulse is not self-indulgence but awe, and existentialism is simply the myth of the noble savage gone baroque. Such philosophies of freedom are born in cities. Existentialism is as much nostalgia as is Rousseau's sophisticated primitivism, as sick a recurrence in French thought as the isle of Cythera,[9] whether it is the tubercular, fevered imagery of Watteau or the same fever turned delirious in Rimbaud and Baudelaire. The poets of the 'new Aegean,' of the Isles of the Blest, the Fortunate Isles, of the remote Bermudas, of Prospero's isle, of Crusoe's Juan Fernandez, of Cythera, of all those rocks named like the beads of a chaplet, they know that the old vision of paradise wrecks here.

> I want to hear a song in which the rainbow breaks
> and the curlew alights among forgotten shores
> I want the liana creeping on the palm-tree
> (on the trunk of the present 'tis our stubborn future)
> I want the conquistador with unsealed armour
> lying down in death of perfumed flowers,
> the foam censing a sword gone rusty
> in the pure blue flight of slow wild cactuses
> (*Césaire*)

---

7 Aimé Césaire (b. 1913), Martiniquan poet and essayist who helped formulate concept of négritude.   8 cf. Walcott's own volume of poems, *Sea Grapes*.   9 Southernmost of Ionian islands, associated with Aphrodite and romantic imaginings.

But to most writers of the archipelago who contemplate only the ship-wreck, the New World offers not elation but cynicism, a despair at the vices of the Old which they feel must be repeated. Their malaise is an oceanic nostalgia for the older culture and a melancholy at the new, and this can go as deep as a rejection of the untamed landscape, a yearning for ruins. To such writers the death of civilizations is architectural, not spiritual, seeded in their memories is an imagery of vines ascending broken columns, of dead terraces, of Europe as a nourishing museum. They believe in the responsibility of tradition, but what they are in awe of is not tradition, which is alert, alive, simultaneous, but of history, and the same is true of the new magnifiers of Africa. For these their deepest loss is of the old gods, the fear that it is worship which has enslaved progress. Thus the humanism of politics replaces religion. They see such gods as part of the process of history, subjected like the tribe to cycles of achievement and despair. Because the Old World concept of God is anthropomorphic, the New World slave was forced to remake himself in His image, despite such phrases as 'God is light, and in Him is no darkness,' and at this point of intersecting faiths the enslaved poet and enslaved priest surrendered their power. But the tribe in bondage learned to fortify itself by cunning assim-ilation of the religion of the Old World. What seemed to be surrender was redemption. What seemed the loss of tradition was its renewal. What seemed the death of faith was its rebirth. . . .

Perse and Césaire, men of diametrically challenging backgrounds, racial opposites to use the language of politics, one patrician and conservative, the other proletarian and revolutionary, classic and romantic, Prospero and Caliban, all such opposites balance easily, but they balance on the axis of a shared sensibility, and this sensibility, with or deprived of the presence of a visible tradition, is the sensibility of waking to a New World. Perse sees in this New World vestiges of the old, of order and of hierarchy, Césaire sees in it evidence of past humiliations and the need for a new order, but the deeper truth is that both poets perceive this New World through mystery. Their language tempts us to endless quotation, there are moments when one hears both voices simultaneously, until the tone is one voice from these different men. If we think of one as poor and the other as privileged when we read their addresses to the New World, if we must see one as black and one as white, we are not only dividing this sensibil-ity by the process of the sociologist, but we are denying the range of either poet, the power of compassion and the power of fury. One is not making out a case for assimilation and for the common simplicity of all men, we are interested in their differences, openly, but what astonishes us in both poets is their elation, their staggering elation in possibility. And one is not talking of an ideal possible society, for you will find that only in the later work of Perse, a society which is inaccessible by its very grandeur, but of the elation in presences which exists in *Éloges* and in *Pour Fêter une Enfance*, the possibility of the individual Caribbean man, African, European, or

Asian in ancestry, the enormous, gently opening morning of his possibility, his body touched with dew, his nerves as subtilized to sensation as the mimosa, his memory, whether of grandeur or of pain, gradually erasing itself as recurrent drizzles cleanse the ancestral or tribal markings from the coral skull, the possibility of a man and his language waking to wonder here. As the language of Perse later becomes hammered and artificial, so does the rhetoric of Césaire move toward the heraldic, but their first great work is as deeply rooted and supple as a vine.

But these poems are in French. The fact that they have now begun to influence English poetry from the archipelago is significant because they are powerful works and all power attracts to itself, but their rhetoric is unmanageable for our minor 'revolutionary' poets who assume a grandeur without a language to create it, for these imitators see both poems through history, or through sociology; they are seduced by their subjects. Therefore there is now a brood of thin, querulous fledglings who steal fragments of Césaire for their own nests, and yet these fledglings will condemn Perse as a different animal, a white poet. These convulsions of bad poetry appear when the society is screaming for change.

Because we think of tradition as history, one group of anatomists claims that this tradition is wholly African and that its responses are alerted through the nostalgia of one race, but that group must allow the Asian and the Mediterranean the same fiction, and then the desolate terraces of Perse's epic memory will be as West Indian to the Middle Easterners among us as the kingdoms of the Guinea Coast are to Césaire or the poetry of China is to the Chinese grocer. If we can psychologize, divide, trace these degenerations easily, then we must accept the miracle of possibility which every poet demonstrates. The Caribbean sensibility is not marinated in the past. It is not exhausted. It is new. But it is its complexity, not its historically explained simplicities, which is new. Its traces of melancholy are the chemical survivals of the blood which remain after the slave's and the indentured worker's convalescence. It will survive the malaria of nostalgia and the delirium of revenge just as it survived its self-contempt.

Thus, while many critics of contemporary Commonwealth verse reject imitation, the basis of the tradition, for originality, the false basis of innovation, they represent eventually the old patronizing attitude adapted to contemporaneous politics, for their demand for naturalness, novelty, originality, or truth is again based on preconceptions of behavior. They project reflexes as anticipated as the exuberance, spontaneity, and refreshing dialect of the tribe. Certain performances are called for, including the fashionable incoherence of revolutionary anger, and everyone is again appeased, the masochist-critic by the required attack on his 'values,' the masochist-poet by the approval of his victim. Minstrel postures, in their beginnings, are hard to identify from private truths, but their familiarity soon establishes the old formulae of entertainment. Basically, the anger of the black is entertainment, or theater, if it makes an aesthetic out of anger, and this is no different in its 'naturalness' than the legendary joy or spontaneous laughter of the minstrel. It is still night-club and cabaret, professional fire-eating and dancing on broken bottles. The critic-tourist can only gasp at such naturalness. He wouldn't care to try it himself, really. We are back to Dr. Johnson's female preacher.[10]

§ *Alternative histories* Reid; Aus: Davis, Grenville; Can: Wiebe; SA: Rushdie; SEA: Fernando; *Caribbean as Eden* Walcott (2), Gilkes

4: *From* Omeros

Omeros is a book-length epic poem. While its title may suggest a dependence on Homer and *Omeros* has St Lucian characters with names such as Achille, Philoctete and Helen, Walcott maintains that his creations are of heroic stature in their own right, equivalents and not derivatives of their namesakes in the *Iliad*. The scope of the poem is, however, much broader than the story of the St Lucian fishermen who are at the centre of its action. It is also part-autobiography and a meditation on Caribbean and New World history and geography. In the sections included here the poet, himself a restless travelling Odysseus figure, journeys to the Old World and in so doing not only questions the positioning of the post-colonial subject, but also the historiographical and cartographical hegemonies initiated by 'Pope Alexander' and 'Greenwich'.

Book Five, Chapter XXXVII

I

I crossed my meridian. Rust terraces, olive trees,
the grey horns of a port. Then, from a cobbled corner
of this mud-caked settlement founded by Ulysses –

5   swifts, launched from the nesting sills of Ulissibona,
their cries modulated to 'Lisbon' as the Mediterranean
aged into the white Atlantic, their flight, in reverse,

repeating the X of an hourglass, every twitter an aeon
from which a horizon climbed in the upturned vase.
A church clock spun back its helm. Turtleback alleys

10   crawled from sea, not towards it, to resettle
in the courtyard under the olives, and a breeze
turned over the leaves to show their silvery metal.

---

10 'A woman's preaching is like a dog's walking on his hind legs. It is not done well; but you are surprised to find it done at all', Boswell, *Life of Johnson*, 31 July 1763.
4 swifts: symbols of transatlantic migration through-out *Omeros*.

Here, clouds read backwards, muffling the clash
of church bells in cotton. There, on an opposite wharf,
15   Sunday in a cream suit, with a grey horned moustache,

strolled past wooden crates, and the long-shadowed Sabbath
was no longer Lisbon but Port of Spain. There, time sifts
like grain from a jute sack under the crooning pigeons.

Sunday clicks open a gold watch, startling the swifts
20   from the opening eye of a tower, closes it, then slips the sun's
pendulum back into its fob, patting it with a nod.

Sunday strolls past a warehouse whose iron-ringed door
exhales an odor of coffee as a reek of salt cod
slithers through the railings. Sunday is a widower

25   in an ice-cream suit, and a straw with a mourning band,
an old Portugee leathery as Portugal, via Madeira,
with a stalled watch for a compass. When he rewinds its
    hand

it raises an uproad of docks, mulatto clerks cowed
by jets of abuse from wine-barrelled wholesalers,
30   winches and cranes, black drivers cursing black loaders,

and gold-manacled vendors teasing the Vincentian sailors
folded over the hulls. Then not a single word, as
Saturday went home at one, except from the pigeons

And a boy rattling his stick along the rusted staves
35   of a railing, its bars caging him as he runs.
After that arpeggio, Sunday hears his own footsteps,

making centuries recede, the ebbing market in slaves
and sugar declining below the horizon. Then Sunday stops
to hear schooners thudding on overlapping wharves.

II

40   Across the meridian, I try seeing the other side,
past rusty containers, waves like welts from the lash
in a light as clear as oil from the olive seed.

Once the world's green gourd was split like a calabash

by Pope Alexander's decree. Spices, vanilla
45   sweetened this wharf; the grain of swifts would scatter

in their unchanging pattern, their cries no shriller
than they are now over the past, or ours, for that matter,
if our roles were reversed, and the sand in one half

replicated the sand in the other. Now I had come
50   to a place I felt I had known, an antipodal wharf
where my forked shadow swayed to the same brass
      pendulum.

Yes, but not as one of those pilgrims whose veneration carried
the salt of their eyes up the grooves of a column
to the blue where forked swifts navigated. Far from it;
      instead,

55   I saw how my shadow detached itself from them
when it disembarked on the wharf through a golden haze
of corn from another coast. My throat was scarred

from a horizon that linked me to others, when our eyes
lowered to the cobbles that climbed to the castle yard,
60   when the coins of the olives showed us their sovereign's face.

My shadow had preceded me. How else could it recognize
that light to which it was attached, this port where Europe
rose with its terrors and terraces, slope after slope?

III

A bronze horseman halts at a wharf, his green-bronze
65   cloak flecked with white droppings, his wedged visor
shading the sockets' hyphenating horizons,

his stare fixed like a helm. We had no such erections
above our colonial wharves, our erogenous zones
were not drawn to power, our squares shrank the directions

70   of the Empire's plazas. Above us, no stallions paw
the sky's pavement to strike stars from the stones,
no sword is pointed to recapture the port of Genoa.

---

44 Pope Alexander's decree: Pope Alexander VI's decree which, at the end of the fifteenth century, divided
the New World between Portugal and Spain.

There the past is an infinite Sunday. It's hot, or it rains;
the sun lifts the sheets of the rain, and the gutters
75   run out. For those to whom history is the presence

of ruins, there is a green nothing. No bell tower utters
its flotilla of swallows memorizing an alphabet,
no cobbles crawl towards the sea. We think of the past

as better forgotten than fixed with stony regret.
80   Here, a castle in the olives rises over the tiered roofs
of crusted tile but, like the stone Don in the opera,

is the ghost of itself. Over the flagstones, hooves
clop down from the courtyard, stuttering pennons appear
from the mouths of arches, and the past dryly grieves

85   from the O's of a Roman aqueduct; silver cuirasses
flash in the reversible olives, their silvery leaves,
and twilight ripens the municipal canvases,

where, one knee folded, like a drinking deer, an admiral
with a grey horned moustache and foam collar proffers a gift
90   of plumed Indians and slaves. The wharves of Portugal

were empty as those of the islands. The slate pigeons lift
from the roof of a Levantine warehouse, the castle in the
        trees
is its own headstone. Yet, once, Alexander's meridian

gave half a gourd to Lisbon, the seeds of its races,
95   and half to Imperial Spain. Now Sunday afternoon passes
the empty cafés, their beads hanging like rosaries,

as shawled fado singers sob in turn to their mandolins
while a cobbled lane climbs like a tortoise, and tiredly raises
its head of a pope at the limp sails on washing lines.

Chapter XXXVIII

III

100   . . . Who decrees a great epoch? The meridian of Greenwich.
Who doles out our zeal, and in which way lies our
hope? In the cobbles of sinister Shoreditch,

---

81 **opera**: Mozart's *Don Giovanni*, cf. Walcott's play   85 **cuirasses**: breast-plate armour.
The Joker of Seville, a reworking of the Don Juan   97 **fado**: Portuguese folk-song.
legend.

in the widening rings of Big Ben's iron flower,
in the barges chained like our islands to the Thames.
105   Where is the alchemical corn and the light it yields?

Where, in which stones of the Abbey, are incised our names?
Who defines our delight? St. Martin-in-the-Fields.
After every Michaelmas, its piercing soprano steeple

defines our delight. Within whose palatable vault
110   will echo the Saints' litany of our island people?
St. Paul's salt shaker, when we are worth their salt.

Stand by the tilted crosses of well-quiet Glen-da-Lough.
Follow the rook's crook'd finger to the ivied grange.
As black as the rook is, it comes from a higher stock.

115   Who screams out our price? The crows of the Corn
      Exchange.
Where are the pleasant pastures? A green baize-table.
Who invests in our happiness? The Chartered Tour.

Who will teach us a history of which we too are capable?
The red double-decker's view of the Bloody Tower.
120   When are our brood, like the sparrows, a public nuisance?

When they screech at the sinuous swans on the Serpentine.
The swans are royally protected, but in whose hands
are the black crusts of our children? In the pointing sign

under the harps of the willows, to the litter of Margate Sands.
125   What has all this to do with the price of fish, our salary
tidally scanned with the bank-rate by waxworks tellers?

Where is the light of the world? In the National Gallery.
In Palladian Wren. In the City that can buy and sell us
the packets of tea stirred with our crystals of sweat.

130   Where is our sublunar peace? In that sickle sovereign
peeling the gilt from St. Paul's onion silhouette.
There is our lunar peace: in the glittering grain

of the coined estuary, our moonlit, immortal wheat,
its white sail cresting the gradual swell of the Downs,
135   startling the hare from the pillars on Salisbury Plain,

> sharpening the grimaces of thin-lipped market towns,
> whitewashing the walls of Brixton, darkening the grain
> when coal-shadows cross it. Dark future down darker street.

§ *Responses to European texts* Lamming (2), Gilkes; Af: Coetzee; SEA: Lim (2), Lee Tzu Pheng, Somtow

WILSON HARRIS (1921–)

§: *From* Palace of the Peacock

Written in a form which departs from social realism and what Harris has called the 'novel of persuasion' (see the next extract), *Palace of the Peacock* employs a dream-like technique to suggest the possibility of a metamorphosis of Caribbean subjectivity. The novel describes a journey into the Guyanese interior undertaken by a crew who retrace the voyage of an earlier dead crew. The journey is a primarily psychic experience and ends in arrival at the heartland of the palace of the peacock and a new, more integrated consciousness. The dividing-lines between past and present, waking reality and dream and blindness and sight collapse, as the text insists that dead, inert experience can be transformed. This is exemplified in the double protagonist of Donne (archetypal colonizer) and the 'I' dreamer, introduced here in the first two chapters.

1

A horseman appeared on the road coming at a breakneck stride. A shot rang out suddenly, near and yet far as if the wind had been stretched and torn and had started coiling and running in an instant. The horseman stiffened with a devil's smile, and the horse reared, grinning fiendishly and snapping at the reins. The horseman gave a bow to heaven like a hanging man to his executioner, and rolled from his saddle on to the ground.

The shot had pulled me up and stifled my own heart in heaven. I started walking suddenly and approached the man on the ground. His hair lay on his forehead. Someone was watching us from the trees and bushes that clustered the side of the road. Watching me as I bent down and looked at the man whose open eyes stared at the sky through his long hanging hair. The sun blinded and ruled my living sight but the dead man's eye remained open and obstinate and clear.

I dreamt I awoke with one dead seeing eye and one living closed eye. I put my dreaming feet on the ground in a room that oppressed me as though I stood in an operating theatre, or a maternity ward, or I felt suddenly, the glaring cell of a prisoner who had been sentenced to die. I arose with a violent giddiness and leaned on a huge rocking-chair. I remembered the first time I had entered this bare curious room; the house stood high and alone in the flat brooding countryside. I had felt the wind rocking me with the oldest uncertainty and desire in the world, the desire to govern or be governed, rule or be ruled for ever.

Someone rapped on the door of my cell and room. I started on seeing the dream-horseman, tall and spare and hard-looking as ever. 'Good morning,' he growled slapping a dead leg and limb. I greeted him as one greeting one's gaoler and ruler. And we looked through the window of the room together as though through his dead seeing material eye, rather than through my living closed spiritual eye, upon the primitive road and the savannahs dotted with sentinel trees and slowly moving animals.

His name was Donne, and it had always possessed a cruel glory for me. His wild exploits had governed my imagination from childhood. In the end he had been expelled from school.

He left me a year later to join a team of ranchers near the Brazil frontier and border country. I learnt then to fend for myself and he soon turned into a ghost, a million dreaming miles away from the sea-coast where we had lived.

'The woman still sleeping,' Donne growled, rapping on the ground hard with his leg again to rouse me from my inner contemplation and slumber.

'What woman?' I dreamed, roused to a half-waking sense of pleasure mingled with foreboding.

'Damnation,' Donne said in a fury, surveying a dozen cages in the yard, all open. The chickens spied us and they came half-running, half-flying, pecking still at each other piteously and murderously.

'Mariella,' Donne shouted. Then in a still more insistent angry voice – 'Mariella'.

I followed his eyes and realized he was addressing a little shack partly hidden in a clump of trees.

Someone was emerging from the shack and out of the trees. She was barefoot and she bent forward to feed the chickens. I saw the back of her knees and the fine beautiful grain of her flesh. Donne looked at her as at a larger and equally senseless creature whom he governed and ruled like a fowl.

I half-woke for the second or third time to the sound of insistent thumping and sobbing in the hall outside my door. I awoke and dressed quickly. Mariella stood in the hall, dishevelled as ever, beating her hand on my door.

'Quiet, quiet,' I said roughly, shrinking from her appearance. She shuddered and sobbed. 'He beat me,' she burst out at last. She lifted her dress to show me her legs. I stroked the firm beauty of her flesh and touched the ugly marks where she had been whipped. 'Look,' she said, and lifted her dress still higher. Her convulsive sobbing stopped when I touched her again.

A brilliant day. The sun smote me as I descended the steps. We walked to the curious high swinging gate like a waving symbol and warning taller than a hanging man whose toes almost touched the ground; the gate was as curious and arresting as the prison house we had left above and behind, standing on the tallest stilts in the world.

'Donne cruel and mad,' Mariella cried. She was staring hard at me. I turned away from her black hypnotic eyes as if I had been blinded by the sun, and saw inwardly in the haze of my blind eye a watching muse and phantom whose breath was on my lips.

She remained close to me and the fury of her voice was in the wind. I turned away and leaned heavily against the frail brilliant gallows-gate of the sky, looking down upon the very road where I had seen the wild horse, and the equally wild demon and horseman fall. Mariella had killed him.

I awoke in full and in earnest with the sun's blinding light and muse in my eye. My brother had just entered the room. I felt the enormous relief one experiences after a haze and a dream. 'You're still alive,' I cried involuntarily. 'I dreamt Mariella ambushed and shot you.' I started rubbing the vision from my eye. 'I've been here just a few days,' I spoke guardedly, 'and I don't know all the circumstances' – I raised myself on my elbow – 'but you are a devil with that woman. You're driving her mad.'

Donne's face clouded and cleared instantly. 'Dreamer,' he warned, giving me a light wooden tap on the shoulder, 'life here is tough. One has to be a devil to survive. I'm the last landlord. I tell you I fight everything in nature, flood, drought, chicken hawk, rat, beast and woman. I'm everything. Midwife, yes, doctor, yes, gaoler, judge, hangman, every blasted thing to the labouring people. Look man, look outside again. Primitive. Every boundary line is a myth. No-man's land, understand?'

'There are still labouring people about, you admit that.' I was at a loss for words and I stared blindly through the window at an invisible population.

'It's an old dream,' I plucked up the courage to express my inner thoughts.

'What is?'

'It started when we were at school, I imagine. Then you went away suddenly. It stopped then. I had a curious sense of hard-won freedom when you had gone. Then to my astonishment, long after, it came again. But this time with a new striking menace that flung you from your horse. You fell and died instantly, and yet you were the one who saw, and I was the one who was blind. Did I ever write and tell you' – I shrank from Donne's supercilious smile, and hastened to justify myself – 'that I am actually going blind in one eye?' I was gratified by his sudden startled expression.

'Blind?' he cried.

'My left eye has an incurable infection,' I declared. 'My right eye – which is actually sound – goes blind in my dream,' I felt foolishly distressed. 'Nothing kills *your* sight,' I added with musing envy. 'And your vision becomes,' I hastened to complete my story, 'your vision becomes the only remaining window on the world for me.'

I felt a mounting sense of distress.

'Mariella?' There was a curious edge of mockery and interest in Donne's voice.

'I never saw her before in my dream,' I said. I continued with a forced warmth – 'I am glad we are together again after so many years. I may be able to free myself of this – this –' 'I searched for a word – 'this obsession. After all it's childish.'

Donne flicked ash and tobacco upon the floor. I could see a certain calculation in his dead seeing eye. 'I had almost forgotten I had a brother like you,' he smiled matter-of-factly. 'It had passed from my mind – this dreaming twin responsibility you remember.' His voice expanded and a sinister under-current ran through his remarks – 'We belong to a short-lived family and people. It's so easy to succumb and die. It's the usual thing in this country as you well know.' He was smiling and indifferent. 'Our parents died early. They had a hard life. Tried to fight their way up out of an economic nightmare: farmers and hand-to-mouth business folk they were. They gave up the ghost before they had well started to live.' He stared at me significantly. 'I looked after you, son.' He gave me one of his ruthless taps. 'Father and Mother rolled into one for a while. I was a boy then. I had almost forgotten. Now I'm a man. I've learnt,' he waved his hands at the savannahs, 'to rule *this*. This is the ultimate. This is everlasting. One doesn't have to see deeper than that, does one?' He stared at me hard as death. 'Rule the land,' he said, 'while you still have a ghost of a chance. And you rule the world. Look at the sun.' His dead eye blinded mine. 'Look at the sun,' he cried in a stamping terrible voice.

2

The map of the savannahs was a dream. The names Brazil and Guiana were colonial conventions I had known from childhood. I clung to them now as to a curious necessary stone and footing, even in my dream, the ground I knew I must not relinquish. They were an actual stage, a presence, however mythical they seemed to the universal and the spiritual eye. They were as close to me as my ribs, the rivers and the flatland, the mountains and heartland I intimately saw. I could not help cherishing my symbolic map, and my bodily prejudice like a well-known room and house of superstition within which I dwelt. I saw this kingdom of man turned into a colony and battleground of spirit, a priceless tempting jewel I dreamed I possessed.

I pored over the map of the sun my brother had given me. The river of the savannahs wound its way far into the distance until it had forgotten the open land. The dense dreaming jungle and forest emerged. Mariella dwelt above the falls in the forest. I saw the rocks bristling in the legend of the river. On all sides the falling water boiled and hissed and roared. The rocks in the tide flashed their presentiment in the sun, everlasting courage and the other obscure spirits of creation. One's mind was a chaos of sensation, even pleasure, faced by imminent mortal danger. A white fury and foam churned and raced on the black tide that grew golden every now and then like the crystal memory of sugar. From every quarter a mindless stream came through the ominous rocks whose presence served to pit the mad foaming face. The boat shuddered in an anxious grip and in a living streaming hand that issued from the bowels of earth. We stood on the threshold of a precarious stand-still. The outboard engine and propeller still revolved and flashed with mental silent horror now that its roar had been drowned in other wilder unnatural voices whose violent din rose from beneath our feet in the waters. Donne gave a louder cry at last, human and incredible and clear, and the boat-crew sprang to divine attention. They seized every paddle and with immortal effort edged the vessel forward. Our bow pointed to a solid flat stone unbroken and clear, running far into the river's bank. It looked near and yet was as far from us as the blue sky from the earth. Sharp peaks and broken hillocks grew on its every side, save where we approached, and to lose our course or fail to keep our head signified a crashing stop with a rock boring and gaping open our bottom and side. Every man paddled and sweated and strained toward the stone and heaven in his heart. The bow-man sprang upon the hospitable ground at last followed by a nimble pair from the crew. Ropes were extended and we were drawn into a pond and still water between the whirling stream and the river's stone.

I felt an illogical disappointment and regret that we were temporarily out of danger. Like a shell after an ecstasy of roaring water and of fast rocks appearing to move and swim again, and yet still and bound as ever where the foam forced its way and seethed and curdled and rushed.

The crew[1] swarmed like upright spiders, half-naked, scrambling under a burden of cargo they were carrying ashore. First I picked and counted the da-Silva twins of Sorrow Hill, thin, long-legged, fair-skinned, of Portuguese extraction. Then I spotted old Schomburgh,[2] also of Sorrow Hill, agile and swift as a monkey for all his seasoned years. Donne prized Schomburgh as a bowman, the best in all the world his epitaph boasted and read. There was Vigilance, black-haired, Indian, sparkling and shrewd of eye, reading the river's mysterious book. Vigilance had recommended Carroll, his cousin, a thick-set young Negro boy gifted with his paddle as if it were a violin and a sword together in paradise. My eye fell on Cameron, brick-red face, slow feet, faster than a snake in the forest with his hands; and Jennings, the mechanic, young, solemn-featured, carved out of still wood it seemed, sweating still the dew of his tears, cursing and reproving his whirling engine and toy in the unearthly terrifying grip in the water. Lastly I counted Wishrop, assistant bowman and captain's understudy. Wishrop resembled Donne, especially when they stood side by side at the captain's paddle. I felt my heart come into my mouth with a sense of recognition and fear. Apart from this fleeting wishful resemblance it suddenly seemed to me I had never

---

1 Representative of most of the races of Guyana. 2 The name evokes Richard and Robert Schomburgk, nine-teenth-century naturalists who explored the interior of Guyana (then British Guiana) for the British and Prussian governments.

known Donne in the past – his face was a dead blank. I saw him now for the first faceless time as the captain and unnatural soul of heaven's dream; he was myself standing outside of me while I stood inside of him.

The crew began, all together, tugging and hauling the boat, and their sing-song cry rattled in my throat. They were as clear and matter-of-fact as the stone we had reached. It was the best crew any man could find in these parts to cross the falls towards the Mission where Mariella lived. The odd fact existed of course that their living names matched the names of a famous dead crew that had sunk in the rapids and been drowned to a man, leaving their names inscribed on Sorrow Hill which stood at the foot of the falls. But this in no way interfered with their lifelike appearance and spirit and energy. Such a dreaming coincidence we were beginning to learn to take in our stride. Trust Donne to rake up every ghost in his hanging world and house. Mariella was the obsession we must encounter at all costs, and we needed gifted souls in our crew. Donne smiled with a trace of mockery at my rank impatience. His smile suddenly changed. His face grew younger and brutal and impatient too. And innocent like a reflection of everlasting dreaming life.

The sun was high in the heavens. The river burned and flamed. The particular section, where we were, demanded hauling our vessel out of the water and along the bank until we had cleared an impassable fury and obstruction. The bright mist lifted a little from my mind's eye, and I saw with a thumping impossible heart I was reliving Donne's first innocent voyage and excursion into the interior country.[3] This was long before he had established himself in his brooding hanging house. Long before he had conquered and crushed the region he ruled, annihilating everyone and devouring himself in turn. I had been struck by a peculiar feeling of absence of living persons in the savannahs where he governed. I knew there were labouring people about but it had seemed that apart from his mistress – the woman Mariella – there was no one anywhere. Now she too had become an enigma; Donne could never hope to regain the affection and loyalty he had mastered in her in the early time when he had first seduced her above the doom of the river and the waterfall. Though he was the last to admit it, he was glad for a chance to return to that first muse and journey when Mariella had existed like a shaft of fantastical shapely dust in the sun, a fleshly shadow in his consciousness. This had vanished. And with his miraculous return to his heart's image and lust again, I saw – rising out of the grave of my blindness – the nucleus of that bodily crew of labouring men I had looked for in vain in his republic and kingdom. They had all come to me at last in a flash to fulfil one self-same early desire and need in all of us.

I knew I was dreaming no longer in the way I had been blind and dreaming before. My eye was open and clear as in the strength of youth. I stood

---

3 Suggestive of a more spiritual vision of the New World associated with early European visitors, but quickly tainted by materialist exploitation.

on my curious stone as upon the reality of an unchanging presence Donne had apprehended in a wild and cruel devouring way which had turned Mariella into a vulgar musing executioner. This vision and end I had dimly guessed at as a child, fascinated and repelled by his company as by the company of my sleeping life. How could I escape the enormous ancestral and twin fantasy of death-in-life and life-in-death? It was impossible to turn back now and leave the crew in the wild inverse stream of beginning to live again in a hot and mad pursuit in the midst of imprisoning land and water and ambushing forest and wood.

The crew – all of us to a man – toiled with the vessel to lift it from still water and whirlpool. At last it stood on the flat stone. We placed round logs of wood beneath it, and half-rolled, half-pushed, until its bow poked the bushy fringe on the bank. This was the signal for reconnoitre. A wild visionary prospect. The sun glowed upon a mass of vegetation that swarmed in crevices of rocky nature until the stone yielded and turned a green spongy carpet out of which emerged enormous trunks and trees from the hidden dark earth beneath and beyond the sun.

The solid wall of trees was filled with ancient blocks of shadow and with gleaming hinges of light. Wind rustled the leafy curtains through which masks of living beard dangled as low as the water and the sun. My living eye was stunned by inversions of the brilliancy and the gloom of the forest in a deception and hollow and socket. We had armed ourselves with prospecting knives and were clearing a line as near to the river as we could.

The voice of roaring water declined a little. We were skirting a high outcrop of rock that forced us into the bush. A sigh swept out of the gloom of the trees, unlike any human sound as a mask is unlike flesh and blood. The unearthly, half-gentle, half-shuddering whisper ran along the tips of graven leaves. Nothing appeared to stir. And then the whole forest quivered and sighed and shook with violent instantaneous relief in a throaty clamour of waters as we approached the river again.

We had finished our connection, and we began retracing our steps in the line to the starting point where our boat stood. I stopped for an instant overwhelmed by a renewed force of consciousness of the hot spirit and moving spell in the tropical undergrowth. Spider's web dangled in a shaft of sun, clothing my arms with subtle threads as I brushed upon it. The whispering trees spun their leaves to a sudden fall wherein the ground seemed to grow lighter in my mind and to move to meet them in the air. The carpet on which I stood had an uncertain place within splintered and timeless roots whose fibre was stone in the tremulous ground. I lowered my head a little, blind almost, and began forcing a new path into the trees away from the river's opening and side.

A brittle moss and carpet appeared underfoot, a dry pond and stream whose course and reflection and image had been stamped for ever like the breathless outline of a dreaming skeleton in the earth. The trees rose around me into upward flying limbs when I screwed my eyes to stare from underneath above. At last I lifted my head into a normal position. The heavy undergrowth had lightened. The forest rustled and rippled with a sigh and ubiquitous step. I stopped dead where I was, frightened for no reason whatever. The step near me stopped and stood still. I stared around me wildly, in surprise and terror, and my body grew faint and trembling as a woman's or a child's. I gave a loud ambushed cry which was no more than an echo of myself – a breaking and grotesque voice, man and boy, age and youth speaking together. I recovered myself from my dead faint supported by old Schomburgh, on one hand, and Carroll, the young Negro boy, on the other. I was speechless and ashamed that they had had to come searching for me, and had found me in such a state.

Schomburgh spoke in an old man's querulous, almost fearful voice, older than his fifty-odd seasoned years. Words came to him with grave difficulty. He had schooled himself into a condition of silent stoical fear that passed for rare courage. He had schooled himself to keep his own counsel, to fish in difficult waters, to bow or steer his vessel under the blinding sun and the cunning stars. He spoke now out of necessity, querulous, scratching the white unshaven growth on his chin.

'Is a risk everyman tekking in this bush,' he champed his mouth a little, rasping and coughing out of his lungs the old scarred broken words of his life. I thought of the sound a boat makes grating against a rock. 'Is a dead risk,' he said as he supported me. 'How you feeling son?' he had turned and was addressing me.

Carroll saw my difficulty and answered. 'Fine, fine,' he cried with a laugh. His voice was rich and musical and young. Schomburgh grinned, seasoned, apologetic, a little unhappy, seeing through the rich boyish mask. Carroll trembled a little. I felt his work-hardened hands, so accustomed to abnormal labour they always quivered with a muscular tension beyond their years; accustomed to making a tramp's bed in the bottom of a boat and upon the hard ground of the world's night. This toughness and strength and enduring sense of limb were a nervous bundle of longing.

'Fine, fine,' he cried again. And then his lively eyes began darting everywhere, seeking eagerly to forget himself and to distract his own thoughts. He pointed – 'You notice them tracks on the ground Uncle? Game plenty-plenty.'

Old Schomburgh scratched his bearded chin. 'How you feeling?' he rasped at me again like a man who stood by his duty.

'Fine, fine, right as rain Uncle,' Carroll cried and laughed. Old Schomburgh turned his seasoned apology and grin on Carroll – almost with disapproval I felt – 'How come you answer so quick-quick for another man? You think you know what mek a man tick? You can't even know you own self, Boy. You really think you can know he or me?' It was a long speech he had made. Carroll trembled, I thought, and faltered a little. But seeing the difficulty I still had in replying, he cried impulsively and naively taking words from my lips – 'He fine-fine Uncle, I tell you. I know –'

'Well why he so tongue-tied?

'He see something,' Carroll laughed good-naturedly and half-musingly, staring once again intently on the ground at the tracks he had discerned.

Schomburgh was a little startled. He rubbed away a bit of grey mucus from the corners of his eyes. His expression grew animal-sharp and strained to attention. Every word froze on his lips with the uncanny silence and patience of a fisherman whose obsession has grown into something more than a normal catch. He glared into my eye as if he peered into a stream and mirror, and he grumbled his oldest need and desire for reassurance and life. He caught himself at last looking secretive and ashamed that he had listened to what Carroll had said. I too started suddenly. I felt I must deny the vague suggestion – given as an excuse to justify my former appearance and stupefaction – that I had seen something. I was about to speak indignantly when I saw the old man's avid eye fixed shamefully on me, and felt Carroll's labouring hand tremble with the longing need of the hunter whose vision leads him; even when it turns faint in the sense of death. I stifled my words and leaned over the ground to confirm the musing footfall and image I had seen and heard in my mind in the immortal chase of love on the brittle earth.

§ *Competing ancestries* Rhys (1, 2), Walcott (2), Williams, Brodber; *Interior journeys* Af: Tutuola, Okri

2: *From* Tradition and the West Indian Novel

. . . What in my view is remarkable about the West Indian in depth is a sense of subtle links, the series of subtle and nebulous links which are latent within him, the latent ground of old and new personalities. This is a very difficult view to hold, I grant, because it is not a view which consolidates, which invests in any way in the consolidation of popular character. Rather it seeks to visualize a *fulfilment* of character. Something which is more extraordinary than one can easily imagine. And it is this possible revolution in the novel – *fulfilment* rather than *consolidation* – I would like first of all to look at in a prospective way because I feel it is profoundly consistent with the native tradition – the depth of inarticulate feeling and unrealized wells of emotion belonging to the whole West Indies.

The Potential of the Novel

The consolidation of character is, to a major extent, the preoccupation of most novelists who work in the twentieth century within the framework of the nineteenth-century novel. Indeed the nineteenth-century novel has exercised a very powerful influence on reader and writer alike in the contemporary world. And this is not surprising after all since the rise of the novel in its conventional and historical mould coincides in Europe with states of society which were involved in consolidating their class and other vested interests. As a result 'character' in the novel rests more or less on the self-sufficient individual – on elements of 'persuasion' (a refined or liberal persuasion at best in the spirit of the philosopher Whitehead)[1] rather than 'dialogue' or 'dialectic' in the profound and unpredictable sense of person which Martin Buber,[2] for example, evokes. The novel of persuasion rests on grounds of apparent common sense: a certain 'selection' is made by the writer, the selection of items, manners, uniform conversation, historical situations, etc, all lending themselves to build and present an individual span of life which yields self-conscious and fashionable judgements, self-conscious and fashionable moralities. The tension which emerges is the tension of individuals – great or small – on an accepted plane of society we are persuaded has an inevitable existence. There is an element of freedom in this method nevertheless, an apparent range of choices, but I believe myself that this freedom – in the convention which distinguishes it, however liberal this may appear – is an illusion. It is true of course that certain kinds of realism, impressive realism, and also a kind of fateful honesty distinguished and still distinguishes the novel of individual character especially where an element of great suffering arises and does a kind of spiritual violence to every 'given' conception. . . . I would like to break off here for a moment to say that the novel of the West Indies, the novel written by West Indians of the West Indies (or of other places for that matter), belongs – in the main – to the conventional mould. Which is not surprising at this stage since the novel which consolidates situations to depict protest or affirmation is consistent with most kinds of overriding advertisement and persuasion upon the writer for him to make national and political and social simplifications of experience in the world at large today. Therefore the West Indian novel – so-called – in the main – is inclined to suffer in depth (to lose in depth) and may be properly assessed in nearly every case in terms of surface tension and realism – as most novels are assessed today – in the perceptive range of choices which emerges, and above all in the way in which the author *persuades* you to ally yourself with situation and character. I shall return to this point and to a close look at the work of certain West Indian writers. . . . But at the moment I would like to pursue the subtler prospective thread I have raised to your attention. I believe it is becoming possible to see even now at this relatively early time that the ruling and popular convention, as such, is academic and provincial in the light of a genuine – and if I may use a much abused term – *native* tradition of depth.

Native and Phenomenal Environment

The native and phenomenal environment of the West Indies, as I see it, is broken into many stages in the way in which one surveys an existing river in its present bed while plotting at the same time ancient and abandoned, indeterminate courses the river once followed. When I speak of the West Indies I am thinking of overlapping contexts of Central and South America

---

1 British mathematician and logician, 1861–1947.   2 Jewish philosopher and theologian, 1878–1965.

as well. For the mainstream of the West Indies in my estimation possesses an enormous escarpment down which it falls, and I am thinking here of the European discovery of the New World and conquest of the ancient American civilizations which were themselves related by earlier and obscure levels of conquest. This escarpment seen from another angle possesses the features of a watershed, main or subsidiary, depending again on how one looks at it.

The environment of the Caribbean is steeped – as I said before – in such broken conceptions as well as misconceptions of the residue and meaning of conquest. No wonder in the jungles of Guiana and Brazil, for example, material structural witnesses may be obliterated or seem to exist in a terrible void of unreality. Let us look once again at the main distinction which for convenience one may describe as the divide pre-Columbian/post-Columbian. The question is – how can one begin to reconcile the broken parts of such an enormous heritage, especially when those broken parts appear very often like a grotesque series of adventures, volcanic in its precipitate effects as well as human in its vulnerable settlement? This distinction is a large, a very large one which obviously has to be broken down into numerous modern tributaries and other immigrant movements and distinctions so that the smallest area one envisages, island or village, prominent ridge or buried valley, flatland or heartland, is charged immediately with the openness of imagination, and the longest chain of sovereign territories one sees is ultimately no stronger than its weakest and most obscure connecting link.

Vision of Consciousness

It is in this light that one must seek to relate the existing pattern of each community to its variable past, and if I may point to the phenomenal divide again, the question which arises is how one can begin to let these parts act on each other in a manner which fulfils *in the person* the most nebulous instinct for a vocation of being and independent spirit within a massive landscape of apparent lifelessness which yields nevertheless the essential denigration and erosion of historical perspectives. This indeed is a peculiarly West Indian question, strange as it may appear to some, and in fact a question peculiar to every phenomenal society where minorities (frail in historical origin or present purpose) may exist, and where comparatively new immigrant and racial cells sometimes find themselves placed within a dangerous misconception and upon a reactionary treadmill. And it is right here – if one begins to envisage an expanding outward and inward creative significance for the novel – that the monument of consolidation breaks down and becomes the need for a vision of consciousness. And this vision of consciousness is the peculiar reality of language because the concept of language is one which continuously transforms inner and outer formal categories of experience, earlier and representative modes of speech itself, the still life resident in painting and sculpture as such, even music which one ceases to 'hear' – the peculiar reality of language provides a medium to *see* in consciousness the 'free' motion and to *hear* with consciousness the 'silent' flood of sound by a continuous inward revisionary and momentous logic of potent explosive images evoked in the mind. Such a capacity for language is a real and necessary one in a world where the inarticulate person is continuously frozen or legislated for in mass and a genuine experience of his distress, the instinct of distress, sinks into a void. The nightmare proportions of this are already becoming apparent throughout the world.

The point I want to make in regard to the West Indies is that the pursuit of a strange and subtle goal, melting pot, call it what you like, is the mainstream (though unacknowledged) tradition in the Americas. And the significance of this is akin to the European preoccupation with alchemy, with the growth of experimental science, the poetry of science as well as of explosive nature which is informed by a solution of images, agnostic humility and essential beauty, rather than vested interest in a fixed assumption and classification of things.

Let us look at the *individual* African slave. I say *individual* deliberately though this is an obviously absurd label to apply to the persons of slaves in their binding historical context. But since their arrival in the Americas bred a new and painful obscure isolation (which is difficult to penetrate in any other terms but a free conceptual imagination) one may perhaps dream to visualize the suffering and original grassroots of individuality. (In fact I believe this is one of the growing points of both alienation and feeling in modern West Indian literature.) He (the problematic slave) found himself spiritually alone since he worked side by side with others who spoke different dialects. The creative human consolation – if one dwells upon it meaningfully today – lies in the search for a kind of inward dialogue and space when one is deprived of a ready conversational tongue and hackneyed comfortable approach.

Irony

I would like to stress again the curious irony involved in this. To assume that the slave was an *individual* is historically absurd since the *individual* possesses certain distinguishing marks, education, status, background, morality, etc, while a slave – in the American context of which we are speaking, as in most situations I imagine – was like an animal put up for sale. (The same qualitative deprivation – though not in terms of absolute coercion – exists for the illiterate East Indian peasant, for example, in the twentieth century in the West Indies.) When therefore one speaks of an inarticulate body of men, confined on some historical plane, as possessing the grassroots of Western individuality one is creatively rejecting, as if it were an illusion, every given, total and self-sufficient situation and dwelling within a capacity for liberation, a capacity for mental and unpredictable pain which the human person endured *then* or endures now *in* or *for* any time or place. To develop the point further it is clear that one is rejecting the sovereign individual as such. For in spite of his emancipation he consolidates every advance by conditioning himself to function solely within his contemporary situation more or less as the slave appears bound still upon his historical and archaic plane. It is in this 'closed' sense that freedom becomes a progressive illusion and it is within the open capacity of the person – as distinct from the persuasive refinements of any social order – within the suffering and enduring mental capacity of the obscure person (which capacity one shares with both 'collective' slave and 'separate' individual in the past and in the future) that a scale emerges and continues indefinitely to emerge which makes it possible for one (whoever that *one* may be, today or tomorrow) to measure and abolish each given situation.

Scale

The use of the word 'scale' is important, a scale or a ladder, because bear in mind what we are saying is that the capacity of the person in terms of words and images is associated with a drama of living consciousness, a drama within which one responds not only to the overpowering and salient features of a plane of existence (which 'over-poweringness', after all, is often a kind of self-indulgent realism) but to the essence of life, to the instinctive grains of life which continue striving and working in the imagination for fulfilment, a visionary character of fulfilment. Such a fulfilment can never be intellectually imposed on the material; it can only be realized in experiment instinctive to the native life and passion of persons known and unknown in a structure of time and space.

Therefore it is clear that the change which is occurring slowly within the novel and the play and the poem is one which has been maturing slowly for centuries. Some of the most daring intimations exist in the works of modern writers, Proust, Joyce, Faulkner, and I would also venture to say in the peculiar style and energy of Australian novelists like Patrick White and Hal Porter, a French novelist like Claude Simon, an English/Canadian novelist like Malcolm Lowry and an African problematic writer like Tutuola. Lowry's novel *Under the Volcano* is set in Mexico where it achieves a tragic reversal of the material climate of our time, assisted by residual images, landscape as well as the melting pot of history, instinctive to the cultural environment of the Central and South Americas.

Let us apply our scale, for example, to the open myth of El Dorado. The religious and economic thirst for exploration was true of the Spanish conquistador, of the Portuguese, French, Dutch and English, of Raleigh, of Fawcett,[3] as it is true of the black modern pork-knocker[4] and the pork-knocker of all races. An instinctive idealism associated with this adventure was overpowered within individual and collective by enormous greed, cruelty and exploitation. In fact it would have been very difficult a century ago to present these exploits as other than a very material and degrading hunger for wealth spiced by a kind of self-righteous spirituality. It is diffi-

---

3 British economist and politician, 1833–84. 4 Gold prospector.

cult enough today within clouds of prejudice and nihilism; nevertheless the substance of this adventure, involving men of all races, past and present conditions, has begun to acquire a residual pattern of illuminating correspondences. El Dorado, City of Gold, City of God, grotesque, unique coincidence, another window within upon the Universe, another drunken boat, another ocean, another river; in terms of the novel the distribution of a frail moment of illuminating adjustments within a long succession and grotesque series of adventures, past and present, capable *now* of discovering themselves and continuing to discover themselves so that in one sense one relives and reverses the 'given' conditions of the past, freeing oneself from catastrophic idolatry and blindness to one's own historical and philosophical conceptions and misconceptions which may bind one within a statuesque present or a false future. Humility is all, says the poet, humility is endless.

§ *Form of Caribbean novel* Reid, Mais, Lamming (1), Naipaul (2), Harris (1), Williams, Brodber; TransC: Phillips

DENIS WILLIAMS (1923–90)

From Other Leopards

The Guyanese protagonist of *Other Leopards*, Lionel/Lobo Froad, is a character who feels he exists on the border between two worlds, which are variously Europe and Africa, Islam and Christianity, culture and nature. Froad is an archaeological draughtsman, working at a site in the Sudanic desert, terrain which is itself seen as 'mulatto', and while his profession might promise the resolution of his identity-crisis in a discovery of origins, the novel resists any such easy answer. In Chapter 1, included here, Froad is a man on a bridge; at the end he is up a tree. *Other Leopards* has been seen as an exploration of the Caribbean return to Africa – and it is the finest *novel* to have been written on this subject – but it is also about the 'mulatto' nature of the Caribbean situation and borderline subjectivity more generally.

Lionel. What sort of name is that! That's what my little sister thought way back smallboy in the Guianas twenty, thirty, a hundred thousand years ago; don't blame me I have no memory worth the name and it isn't important. Lionel! That's no proper kind of name for a man-child of three, so she thought, she a woman-child of one. So too, without much effort and a lot of help, she soon had everybody believing, myself and all. She called me Lobo, and Lobo I became, except that Lionel remained on my birth certificate and is set to plague me like a festering conscience for the rest of my days, look of it. I became Lobo and that's the whole trouble; I am a man, you see, plagued by these two names, and this is their history: Lionel, the who I was, dealing with Lobo, the who I continually felt I ought to become. And there you have it in a nutshell.

Now I'd better say where I was: Lionel embracing Lobo. On a bus, Kutam Bridge, Johkara, Africa. Sudanic belt of Africa. Not quite sub-Sahara, but then not quite desert; not Equatorial black, not Mediterranean white. Mulatto. Sudanic mulatto, you could call it. Ochre. Semi-scrub. Not desert, not sown. Different colour in the atlas (look it up, you'll see); different from the empty blowing spaces of the true Sahara. To the north, though, a few hundred miles outside the cities – outside Kutam, for instance – you do get the blowing spaces: bellied sand, violent hills, volcanic plains, black chasms like the tired creations of a god gone crazy. Here, by the way, a lot of my work continually took me. I am an archaeological draughtsman, you see, or rather at the time I was.

Standing on this bridge, then, or rather sitting in the broken-down Commer truck enclosed with expanded metal, covered with zinc sheeting, painted about nine different colours all primary, and called Public Transport. A Wednesday afternoon, latish. Though the hour was still early – only about twenty to five or so – in a little while the sun would plunge the river, suddenly, as always in Africa, and shatter the day to splinters, into a shower of singing stars.

That's where I was, and when; though the story doesn't begin anywhere near there. It began, way back, with those two names: the one on my birth certificate, on my black-Frank-Sinatra face; and the one I carried like a pregnant load waiting to be freed and to take itself with every despatch back to the swamps and forests and vaguely felt darknesses of my South American home. But I start with the incident on Kutam Bridge because it was then that for the first time I came to realize that I was really on some basic level uncommitted to either name!

All along, ever since I'd grown up, I'd been Lionel looking for Lobo. I'd felt I ought to become this chap, this *alter ego* of ancestral times that I was sure quietly slumbered behind the cultivated mask. Now on that afternoon I came consciously to sense the thing that has made this story: that not enviable state of being, the attitude of involuntary paralysis, that made them know me in Africa – the more intelligent, that is – as the Uncommitted African.

From the moment of realizing it, of course, I struggled against this thing; desperately. I didn't wish to be uncommitted; I wished to be committed, happy. Like everybody else. For why shouldn't a man, equipped as he is, be happy? That's what I wanted to know. It's why I had come out. But, then, that's the story . . . .

Everywhere I looked, people; more people than you could think about. All the way down to right down beneath the trees; then behind all the way back to back where the bridge curved round to Kutam North. And everyone standing. Up front I knew they were turning off, but near the bus, down towards the middle, they all stood still, nobody making much noise. Johkresi are quiet people, restrained; but they were waiting till they got up there, up to the top, to the main gate. It was when they got up there that the real bawling would begin.

Some kept tiptoeing and reaching up as though that could get them any-where; kept trying to see over the heads or between them, between the snowy turbans; trying to be up the top all the way from where they stood. Somebody said, 'W'Allahi, O brother, if this bus would only go!' Some-body else, 'If you stand, O my brothers, you can see the policemen, the jeeps. . . .' Many said: 'I can see the banners; I can see . . . Long live Noba! Colours, O brothers, like mirages over everybody's heads. I can see from here . . .'

I peered beyond the crowd and into the garden.

Maybe I won't get there in time; maybe I don't even wish to. At the last moment, though, I'll know.

Inside the garden the farrashene looked like snowmen melting in the desert sun; mute, detached like snowmen, like cheap toys: Turkish pan-taloons of crimson satin, tomato-coloured blouses, silky tarbooshes:[1] the real thing. And the askari:[2] askari white with white turbans, ceremonial; ordi-nary days camel-coloured khaki against Kutam ochre. Then the ladies: European ladies with breasts aggressively exposed. (Why only the European woman and the savage? Every other kind of man conceals his woman.) Muslim ladies none, never.

'*Zaghareet!*' somebody shouted, which was a kind of yodelling ululation, hysterical sounding.

On the podium the flags of Noba and of Johkara floated side by side. The *zaghareet* gathered force. The crowd began to shuffle forward slowly. The occasion of a visit of the state of Noba to the state of Johkara, Arab and African once more face to face.

The *zaghareet* soared like a Comet working up scream. The river looked as though there'd been a giant car smash with all the glass left splintered in the sun over to the ochre of Kutam West. Above it a pillar of cloud hung like the conclusion of a quarrel over everybody's heads. The lorries had raised that earlier, bringing people into town since before the dawn. I leaped off the bus.

But gained nothing by it, for I found I could hardly move. The heart of the crowd, white everywhere – a grey mass of white, for the sun was already leaving, and it was, anyway, now among the trees – stood still. Behind the standing heads the sun turned the pillar of cloud into a pillar of fire where, splintered to a million glittering fragments, the river bent past Kutam West.

The bus heaved alongside me as though borne on by the pressure of the crowd. Petrol-fumes, warm sweat, close stench; no escape. Tiptoeing, I could see the spot where the head of the crowd should have been turning off. But it wasn't; it was being forced back from the turning, made to go straight along the main road. Word came back: 'We're going straight on down the main road, they not letting us into the river walk.' Affronted, shoved from mouth to ear. 'They're turning us back, O brothers, keeping us off the river

---

1 Cape-like fez. 2 Soldiers.

walk.' Which ran past the main gates; where stood the parked motor-cars of the officials and the guests. 'So we won't be in the way of the motor-cars when the show's over.'

'I like that: in the way of the motor-cars! And who th'hell are the motor-cars, eh?'

Those who'd been waiting longest began being easily offended, aggressive, mustard-tempered. You could pick them out: different look from the others, from those who'd come later: possessive, strained to a pitch, ready to start crying or ripping somebody up least excuse. At the negative news some of these spilled off, cascaded down the embankment like water suddenly breaking a dam, and piled against the fence beyond reach of the policemen on horseback, in jeeps, on motor-cycles.

Up front unbroken mechanical howling, ragged cheering. After a while word came back:

'He's arrived, ai, they're coming. Two palace cars and the red Rolls-Royce. He's very black, O brothers, laughing, see? There! There under the leaves . . . on the river walk, they're here. . . .'

'Welcome, Noba, welcome, welcome!'

The band played in a less desultory fashion, even kicking up its hind legs now and then. Suddenly no one could see clearly enough, everyone trying to grow instantly taller; each feeling the next was getting more, getting in his way. Here and there a few sharp sudden rows, but no time, no time – men frantically trying to climb one another – they were here. . . .

'Six, seven, nine official cars, oh, lots of them; they're driving in, see, that's why they turned us off; they turned us off because they're driving in. They're letting those cars through now, you couldn't have a crowd up there; they had to turn us off the river walk because, look, they driving right in through the gates beneath the trees, see? There, isn't he *black*!'

'He's not wearing clothes, robes!'

A roar went up. The newly arrived guests fanned hurriedly across the lawn.

Now the procession moved – a mass of white gone grey at its limits – beneath the trees. The shrubs on the embankment came up sloping downwards. The *zaghareet* came faster, hotter, singed everybody's senses, and died echoing across the river. At the great tables the Prime Ministers, Arab and African, took their ease. The distinguished of Kutam, the leaders of the Moslem sects, the Roman Catholic, the Protestant, the Coptic bishops, all took their ease. The Mayor of Kutam mounted the podium for the welcome speech. The photographers followed, the interpreters, journalists, all easy. People craned for the real-life view that for years to come would lend authority to their patter.

The Mayor's felicitations went unheard, the crowd wanted the Noba Prime Minister. So badly that when he at last mounted the podium they wouldn't let him speak, merely topped up their delirium with ever-wilder shouting. It began to seem doubtful whether they'd allow him to speak at all, but, as I heard him placidly claim a few days later on the occasion of the Chief's garden party, he was far from worried.

'Far from worried man,' he boomed. 'You should see some of our crowds on the coast; got to mind your phrases I can tell you.' Mopping his forehead with powerful ripping movements. 'This crowd was bounded by the road and the river; it was nothing, nothing.' And he swept round, pinning me a moment with a suspicious bulldog glare. This part of the story, then, I put together from the fringes of the honoured little group that hung round the P.M. that afternoon at the Chief's party.

From the podium the P.M. faced the crowd. He faced, that is, from behind the microphones, the guests, but his attention was really on the crowd; on the cheers building up with uninterrupted mechanical unity. He held the mass with eyes waiting for his moment. Never resist at first; let it come up, let it flood to capacity, wave upon wave. Merely a question of timing. Let them expect something next; keep them that way. There is a moment of pause before the giant roller breaks; that saturated moment will bear you to the beach. You move in on the surge.

Ten, fifteen minutes the howling, darkness threatening. You look at a you crowd, see yourself multiplied a million times. A crowd is not it, or even they, it is I! The P.M. found his moment. He raised his arms above his head. First he took in the audience, then turned his face slowly right, left, let his glance pass over every man of them – each man must feel he's been observed, that I am no better than he; each woman must feel arresting, flattered.

Somebody said, '*W'Allahi*, O brother, just like one of us!'

Arms outstretched, he faced the crowd. He couldn't see their faces, but remember, he told himself, they do have faces. Speak as though you believe this.

The chants broke into a howl of delight embroidered with a pattern of clapping. Men are turning to their neighbours, the P.M. thought, nudging one another in the ribs. At this moment I am a Magnificent Idea; I am the Answer to a Million Frustrations; I am in the Flesh a Force! Each one waiting to make me his private possession, each standing assured behind an 'I told you so', a 'did you know', bewitched by the publicity photograph that went out like John the Baptist to herald the One Absolutely New. Now for the beach.

He watched the breakers. He lowered his arms, slowly. Beyond the fence a gradual hush fell with his falling arms, soft, like the retreating echo of a shattering explosion; a wash of falling sound.

'What a man, by Allah; a man !'

'You could call that magnetism, you know; that's what you call magnetism. This man knows his Africa.'

'People . . .' he boomed. Unforgettable voice, unforgettable resonance, coming from unexploited African places.

Call them people; not friends, Africans, nor countrymen; keep it abstract. Make no assumptions save only one: I am the Face of a Force. Bundle their emotions into that, let them take it home, take it down the years, outliving the kings of old Nile, the kings of old Axum, Candace, Queen of Sheba, what have you. . . .

He folded his arms. Impressive the silence; impressive his calm, his control.

'W'Allahi, O brother, a real thinker you can tell.'

'People of Africa, we have met today . . .' The voice rose, struck poise, hung for a moment waiting for the farthest echoes to return. This man didn't need a painted mask, as his father would have done, to achieve heroic size; didn't need medicine men and miracles and mirrors to dazzle and subdue; he had his microphones, his unique mind. The man surveyed the heaving breakers. 'We have met today . . .' briefest pause, 'in Freedom!'

The photographers rushed forward to preserve the image of an historic moment.

'Here the man talk, O brothers!'

The P.M.'s voice floated, 'In this land of ancient bondage, this land of our inheritance . . .' like wind over muted waves. But facts now, no more emotion, they're not fools; they'll forget the facts, the emotion they'll talk about for ever. It will cause them to invent their own facts, their own reading of the issue according to their needs, more credible than any. This is the way of history. Do not treat them like fools or children; emotion is all well and good, but hang it on to something, appeal to the snob in them. Even savages wish to be appealed to intellectually. Choose your beads. Facts, keep them sober.

Hearing him talk this way at the Chief's garden party I realized the fellow knew his stuff all right; you can't beat these politicians when they know their stuff. I was pleased though, now, to see that the thing wasn't developing into a tedious political affair. This P.M. knew better than that. 'The time, a new time, our time, has come . . .' Not much gesture, no flourish, cool. '. . . emergence of this African person carries with it responsibilities unique in the history of mankind . . .'

'Hear; oh, hear!'

'. . . being at the same time fraught with possibilities for a fuller definition of the species. People, this living moment can create the world!'

The interpreter was meticulous, pacing the voice like shadow after a flying car. 'Returning therefore from the realms of idealism, we sponsor among the races a situation in which Equality, Non-Aggression, Non-Interference, and Solidarity are inherent . . .'

Across the river, in Kutam West, a minaret pointed the sky like a malignant witness. The voice of the muezzin[3] floated across the water; hot Lybian wind lifted the Johkara sand.

'. . . the last of Empire, the dawn of responsibility; a balance in human affairs now for the first time possible. Not of course in a spirit of revenge, but possessing the future by being truly worthy of the present . . . !' And so on.

---

3 Muslim crier.

'We would be ill-advised, nevertheless, to put aside the great book of the past, however bitter its pages may sometimes read to us. We seek not grievance, but justice. Your neighbours in the Sudan, for instance, can they wisely forget the memories of Kitchener, of the Mahdi?[4] Indeed the question remains with us all: Kitchener or the Mahdi, as for centuries the West has struggled with that other, Pilate or Christ.'

Justice or Truth! Not bad. Quick vision through my mind of Kitchener 'digging up the lands of the blacks' as some Pharaoh, according to Hughie, had boasted in the inscriptions. What a man this P.M.! Did he perhaps recognize this parting of our mothers' legs by Crescent, by Cross?[5]

The reference was, however, unfortunate. The interpreter fumbled, embarrassed, over it. Kitchener or the Mahdi, Pilate or Christ! What did it mean? He wasn't sure, he dropped it. But the crowd (Kitchener, the Mahdi) they could easily see the challenge to humour, the appeal of the last laugh so dear to Arabs. The cheers were a long time dying down.

'Oh, hear!'

I began picking my way to the main gate. I heard, 'People of Africa, Africa will be free!'

Bit of a come-down that, I thought, but, still, a P.M. can't afford to take chances. Emotion, that's the real prince's garment of the illiterate. The rollers crashed and broke silence once more. The pillar of fire burned itself to ashes. The *zaghareet* ascended, hovered, and spiralled as though plotting a new course in the darkness. I pressed on to the main gate trying hard to feel – how shall I say? – this mystic union, this ineffable what's-it, this identity. I can never be reproached, God knows, for not trying.

§ *Competing ancestries* Rhys (1, 2), Walcott (2), Harris (1), Brodber; *African connections* Brathwaite (1, 2); Af: Mahjoub; *Borderline figure* Aus: Malouf

'THE MIGHTY SPARROW' (SLINGER FRANCISCO) (1935–)

Dan is the Man in the Van

I

According to the education you get when you small
You'll grow up with true ambition and respect from one an
    all
But in my days in school they teach me like a fool
The things they teach me I should be a block-headed mule.

---

4 Rival British and Islamic Sudanese leaders in late–nineteenth-century struggle for Khartoum.   **5** By Islam and Christianity.

5   Pussy has finished his work long ago
     And now he resting and thing
     Solomon Agundy was born on a Monday
     The Ass in the Lion skin
     Winkin Blinkin and Nod
10   Sail off in a wooden shoe
     How the Agouti lose he tail and Alligator trying to get
        monkey liver soup.

II
     The poems and the lessons they write and send from England
     Impress me they were trying to cultivate comedians
     Comic books made more sense
15   You know it was fictitious without pretence
     J.O. Cutteridge wanted to keep us in ignorance.

     Humpty Dumpty sat on a wall
     Humpty Dumpty did fall
     Goosey Goosey Gander
20   Where shall I wander
     Ding dong dell . . . Pussy in the well
     RIKKI . . . TIKKI TAVI.
     Rikki Tikki Tavi

III
     Well Cutteridge he was plenty times more advanced than
        them scientists
25   I ain't believe that no one man could write so much
        foolishness
     Aeroplane and rockets didn't come too soon
     Scientist used to make the grade in balloon
     This time Cutteridge done make a cow jump over the moon.

     Tom Tom the piper son
30   Stole the pig and away he ran
     Once there was a woman who lived in a shoe
     She had so many children she didn't know what to do

---

7 **Solomon . . . Monday**: from a nursery-rhyme, like many of the references in this calypso, which was one of those for which Sparrow, the most famous of post-war calypsonians, won the 1963 Calypso Monarch crown in Trinidad.
16 **Cutteridge**: an English Director of Education in Trinidad, who edited the six-volume *West Indian Readers* (1926–9), widely used in Caribbean schools in the late colonial period.

11 **'How . . . tail'**: a Trinidadian Anancy story; the agouti is a guinea-pig-like rodent.
23 **Rikki Tikki Tavi**: mongoose hero of story in Kipling's *Jungle Book*.

Dickery Dickery Dock
The mouse run up the Clock
35   The lion and the mouse
A woman pushing a cow up a ladder to eat grass on top a
    house.

IV
How I happen to get some education my friends I don't
    know
All they teach me is about Brer Rabbit and Rumplestilskin . . .
    O
They wanted to keep me down indeed
40   They tried their best but didn't succeed
You see I was dunce and up to now I can't read.

Peter Peter was a pumpkin eater
And the Lilliput people tie Gulliver
When I was sick and lay abed
45   I had two pillows at my head
I see the Goose that lay the golden egg
The Spider and the Fly
Morocoy with wings flying in the sky
They beat me like a dog to learn that in school
50   If me head was bright I woulda be a damn fool.

§ *Language usage* Bennett, Reid, Brathwaite (3), Bloom, Agard, Breeze;
Colonial education Af: Ngugi (2), Dangarembga

(EDWARD) KAMAU BRATHWAITE (1930–)

1: Ananse*

With a black snake's un-
winking eye
thinking thinking through glass
through quartz

5   quarries of stony water
with a doll's liquid gaze, crystal,

---

48 **Morocoy**: land turtle.
*Ananse: spiderman trickster figure of Akan origin, brought to the Caribbean by the slaves of the Middle Passage; hero of Caribbean children's stories from which Brathwaite reclaims him in this poem.

his brain green, a green chrysalis
storing leaves,

memories trunked up in a dark attic,
10 he stumps up the stares
of our windows, he stares, stares
he squats on the tips

of our language
black burr of conundrums
15 eye corner of ghosts, ancient histories;

he spins drum-
beats, silver skin
webs of sound
20 through the villages;

Tacky heard him
and L'Ouverture
all the hung-
ry dumb-bellied chieftains

25 who spat
their death into the ground:
Goave, Port-au-Prince, Half Moon Fort,
villages,

dead lobster-pot crews,
30 wire, red sea shells, coconut trees' hulls, nodding skulls,
black iron bells, clogged,
no glamour of noon on man-

grove shore.
Now the poor hang him up in the ceiling,
35 their brooms cannot reach his hushed corner
and he sits with the dust, desert's rainfall of soot,
plotting a new fall from heaven

threading
threading

12–13 he . . . language: Anansi (or Anancy – the
name is spelt in various ways) is often represented as
having a lisp.

21–22 Tacky . . . L'Ouverture: leaders of slave
rebellions: in Jamaica and Haiti respectively.

40 the moon
  moonlight stories

  his full mouth agape
  a black pot
  grinning
45 grinning

  round fire that boils in his belly
  walloboa wood words,
  eyes, fireflies, sparks,
  crashing coals' waterfalls,

50 grey ashes aroused,
  old men's ghosts,
  cinders,
  burnt memories' eyes in the hot hut,

  flesh
55 curling silver,
  revealing their shadows of meaning
  as the god stared down,

  black beating heart of him breathing
  breathing
60 consuming our wood
  and the words of our houses

  black iron-eye'd eater, the many-eye'd maker,
  creator,
  dry stony world-maker, word-breaker,
65 creator. . .

  In the yard the dog barks at the stranger.

§ *Trickster-figure* Naipaul (1), Brodber; Can: King, Armstrong; *African connections* Williams, Brathwaite (2)

---

62 iron-eye'd: punning on 'irony' and probably also the Rastafarian 'I an I' (for 'we').

2: Negus*

It
it
it
it is not

5   it
it
it
it is not

it is not
10   it is not
it is not enough
it is not enough to be free
of the red white and blue
of the drag, of the dragon

15   it is not
it is not
it is not enough
it is not enough to be free
of the whips, principalities and powers
20   where is your kingdom of the Word?

It
it
it
it is not

25   it
it
it
it is not

it is not
30   it is not
it is not enough
it is not enough to be free
of malarial fevers, fear of the hurricane,
fear of invasions, crops' drought, fire's
35   blisters upon the cane

---

*Negus: one of the titles of Haile Selassie, Emperor of Ethiopia, used by Rastafarians as a substitute for Jesus.

It is not enough
to tinkle to work on a bicycle bell
when hell
crackles and burns in the fourteen-inch screen of the Jap
40 of the Jap of the Japanese-constructed
United-Fruit-Company-imported
hard sell, tell tale tele-
vision set, rhinocerously knobbed, cancerously tubed

It is not
45 it is not
it is not enough
to be able to fly to Miami,
structure skyscrapers, excavate the moon-
scaped seashore sands to build hotels, casinos, sepulchres

50 It is not
it is not
it is not enough
it is not enough to be free
to bulldoze god's squatters from their tunes, from their relics
55 from their tombs of drums

It is not enough
to pray to Barclays bankers on the telephone
to Jesus Christ by short wave radio
to the United States marines by rattling your hip
60 bones

I
must be given words to shape my name
to the syllables of trees

I
65 must be given words to refashion futures
like a healer's hand

I
must be given words so that the bees
in my blood's buzzing brain of memory

70 will make flowers, will make flocks of birds,
will make sky, will make heaven,

the heaven open to the thunder-stone and the volcano and
   the unfolding land.
It is not
it is not
75 it is not enough
to be pause, to be hole
to be void, to be silent
to be semicolon, to be semicolony;

fling me the stone
80 that will confound the void
find me the rage
and I will raze the colony
fill me with words
and I will blind your God.

85 *Att*
    Att
    Attibon

    Attibon Legba
    Attibon Legba
90 *Ouvri bayi pou' moi*
    Ouvri bayi pou' moi . . .

§ *Folk/Rastafarian experience* Mais; *Vodun* Lamming

3: *From* History of the Voice

Sub-titled *The Development of Nation Language in Anglophone Caribbean Poetry*, *History of the Voice* was originally an 'electronic lecture' delivered at Harvard University in 1979. Its published form includes detailed footnotes providing references to the work of authors mentioned in the text. These have been omitted here because of space constraints.

It is *nation language* in the Caribbean that, in fact, largely ignores the pentameter. Nation language is the language which is influenced very strongly by the African model, the African aspect of our New World/Caribbean heritage. English it may be in terms of some of its lexical features. But in its contours, its rhythm and timbre, its sound explosions, it is not English, even though the words, as you hear them, might be English to a greater or lesser degree. And this brings us back to the question that some of you raised yes-

---

85–91 **Att . . . moi . . .**: an invocation to the Haitian god Legba, intercessor between humanity and the other gods, to open the way at the beginning of a *vodun* ceremony.

terday: can English be a revolutionary language? And the lovely answer that came back was: *it is not English that is the agent. It is not language, but people, who make revolutions.*

I think, however, that language does really have a role to play here, certainly in the Caribbean. But it is an English which is not the standard, imported, educated English, but that of the submerged, surrealist experience and sensibility, which has always been there and which is now increasingly coming to the surface and influencing the perception of contemporary Caribbean people. It is what I call, as I say, *nation language*. I use the term in contrast to *dialect*. The word 'dialect' has been bandied about for a long time, and it carries very pejorative overtones. Dialect is thought of as 'bad English'. Dialect is 'inferior English'. Dialect is the language used when you want to make fun of someone. Caricature speaks in dialect. Dialect has a long history coming from the plantation where people's dignity is distorted through their language and the descriptions which the dialect gave to them. Nation language, on the other hand, is the *submerged* area of that dialect which is much more closely allied to the African aspect of experience in the Caribbean. It may be in English: but often it is in an English which is like a howl, or a shout or a machine-gun or the wind or a wave. It is also like the blues. And sometimes it is English and African at the same time. I am going to give you some examples. But I should tell you that the reason I have to talk so much is that there has been very little written on this subject. I bring to you the notion of nation language but I can refer you to very little literature, to very few resources. I cannot refer you to what you call an 'Establishment'. I cannot really refer you to Authorities because there aren't any. One of our urgent tasks now is to try to create our own Authorities. But I will give you a few ideas of what people have tried to do.

The forerunner of all this was of course Dante Alighieri who at the beginning of the fourteenth century argued, in *De vulgari eloquentia* (1304), for the recognition of the (his own) Tuscan vernacular as the nation language to replace Latin as the most natural, complete and accessible means of verbal expression. And the movement was in fact successful throughout Europe with the establishment of national languages and literatures. But these very successful national languages then proceeded to ignore local European colonials such as Basque and Gaelic, for instance, and suppressed overseas colonials wherever they were heard. And it was not until Burns in the 18th century and Rothenberg, Trask, Vansina, Tedlock, Waley, Walton, Whallon, Jahn, Jones, Whiteley, Beckwith, Herskovits, and Ruth Finnegan, among many others in this century, that we have returned, at least, to the notion of oral literature. Although I don't need to remind you that oral literature is our oldest form of literature and that it continues richly throughout the world today. In the Caribbean, our novelists have always been conscious of these native resources, but the critics and academics have, as is kinda often the case, lagged far behind. Indeed, until 1970, there was a positive intellectual, almost social, hostility to the concept of 'dialect' as language. But there were some significant studies in linguistics: Beryl Loftman Bailey's

Jamaican creole syntax: a transformational approach (Cambridge 1966), F. G. Cassidy, *Jamaica talk* (Kingston 1961), Cassidy and R. B. LePage, *Dictionary of Jamaican English* (Cambridge 1967); and, still to come, Richard Allsopp's mind-blowing *Dictionary of Caribbean English*; three glossaries from Frank Collymore in Barbados, and A. J. Seymour and John R. Rickford of Guyana; plus studies on the African presence in Caribbean language by Mervyn Alleyne, Beverley Hall, and Maureen Warner Lewis. In addition, there has been work by Douglas Taylor and Cicely John, among others, on aspects of some of the Amerindian languages; and Dennis Craig, Laurence Carrington, Velma Pollard and several others, at the University of the West Indies' School of Education, on the structure of nation language and its psychosomosis in and for the classroom.

Few of the writers mentioned, however, have gone into nation language as it affects literature. They have set out its grammar, syntax, transformation, structure and all of those things. But they haven't really been able to make any contact between the nation language and its expression in our literature. Recently a French poet and novelist from Martinique, Edouard Glissant, had a very remarkable article in *Alcheringa*, a 'nation language' journal published at Boston University. The article was called 'Free and Forced Poetics', and in it, for the first time, I feel an effort to describe what nation language really means. For the author of the article it is the language of enslaved persons. For him, nation language is a strategy: the slave is forced to use a certain kind of language in order to disguise himself, to disguise his personality and to retain his culture. And he defines that language as a 'forced poetics' because it is a kind of prison language, if you want to call it that. And then we have another nation language poet, Bruce St John, from Barbados, who has written some informal introductions to his own work which describe the nature of the experiments that he is conducting and the kind of rules that he begins to perceive in the way that he uses his language. I myself have an article called 'Jazz and the West Indian novel', which appeared in a journal called *Bim* in the early 1960s, and there I attempt to show that very necessary connection to the understanding of nation language is between native musical structures and the native language. That music is, in fact, the surest threshold to the language which comes out of it.

In terms of more formal literary criticism, the pioneers have been H. P. Jacobs (1949) on V. S. Reid, Mervyn Morris (1964) on Louise Bennett and most of Gordon Rohlehr's work, beginning with 'Sparrow and the language of calypso' (1967).

And that is all we have to offer as Authority, which isn't very much, really. But, in fact, one characteristic of nation language is its orality. It is from 'the oral tradition'. And therefore you wouldn't really expect that large, encyclopedic body of learned comment on it that you would expect for a written language and literature.

Now I'd like to describe for you some of the characteristics of our nation language. First of all, it is from, as I've said, an oral tradition. The poetry, the culture itself, exists not in a dictionary but in the tradition of the spoken word. It is based as much on sound as it is on song. That is to say, the noise that it makes is part of the meaning, and if you ignore the noise (or what you would *think* of as noise, shall I say) then you lose part of the meaning. When it is written, you lose the sound or the noise, and therefore you lose part of the meaning. Which is, again, why I have to have a tape recorder for this presentation. I want you to get the sound of it, rather than the sight of it.

In order to break down the pentameter, we discovered an ancient form which was always there, the calypso. This is a form that I think nearly everyone knows about. It does not employ the iambic pentameter. It employs dactyls. It therefore mandates the use of the tongue in a certain way, the use of sound in a certain way. It is a model that we are moving naturally towards now. Compare

(IP)   To be or not to be, that is the question
(Kaiso) The stone had skidded arc'd and bloomed into islands
         Cuba San Domingo
         Jamaica Puerto Rico[1]

But not only is there a difference in syllabic or stress pattern, there is an important difference in shape of intonation. In the Shakespeare (IP above), the voice travels in a single forward plane towards the horizon of its end. In the kaiso, after the skimming movement of the first line, we have a distinct variation. The voice dips and deepens to describe an intervallic pattern. And then there are more ritual forms like *kumina*[2], like *shango*,[3] the religious forms, which I won't have time to go into here, but which begin to disclose the complexity that is possible with nation language.

The other thing about nation language is that it is part of what may be called total *expression*, a notion which is not unfamiliar to you because you are coming back to that kind of thing now. Reading is an isolated, individualistic expression. The oral tradition on the other hand demands not only the griot[4] but the audience to complete the community: the noise and sounds that the maker makes are responded to by the audience and are returned to him. Hence we have the creation of a continuum where meaning truly resides. And this *total expression* comes about because people be in the open air, because people live in conditions of poverty ('unhouselled') because they come from a historical experience where they had to rely on their very *breath* rather than on paraphernalia like books and museums and machines. They had to depend on *immanence*, the power within themselves, rather than the technology outside themselves.

§ *Nation language usage* Bennett, Reid, Selvon, Sparrow, Bloom, Agard, Breeze; TransC: Bennett, Selvon, Johnson, D'Aguiar, Dabydeen

---

1 From Brathwaite's poem 'Calypso'. 2 Ancestor worship cult. 3 Spirit-possession dance; from Yoruba god of thunder. 4 Tribal story-teller; oral repository of people's culture in West Africa.

MERVYN MORRIS (1937–)

1: The Pond

There was this pond in the village
and little boys, he heard till he was sick,
were not allowed too near,
Unfathomable pool, they said,
5 that swallowed men and animals just so;
and in its depth, old people said,
swam galliwasps and nameless horrors;
bright boys kept away.

Though drawn so hard by prohibitions,
10 the small boy, fixed in fear, kept off;
till one wet summer, grass growing lush,
paths muddy, slippery, he found himself
there at the fabled edge.

The brooding pond was dark.
15 Sudden, escaping cloud, the sun
came bright; and shimmering in guilt,
he saw his own face peering from the pool.

§ *Self-reflection* Morris (2)

2: Narcissus

They're lying; lying, all of them:
he never loved his shadow.
He saw it was another self
and tried to wring its neck.
5 Not love but murder on his mind,
he grappled with the other man
inside the lucid stream.

Only the surface broke.
Unblinking eyes
10 came swimming back in view.

---

7 **galliwasps**: a Caribbean lizard.

At last he knew
he never would
destroy that other self.
And knowing made him shrink.

15   He shrank into a yellow-bellied flower.

§ *Self-reflection* Morris (1)

MICHAEL GILKES (1933–)

From Prospero's Island

1. Ferdinand

Shipwrecked,
following the arrows
of a Sandpiper's track,
on foot, prince
5   Ferdinand, cosmic cartographer,
checking the beach
for footprints,
screws the island
to his telescopic eye,
10   sets down his gyroscope.
Stretching the taut ropes
of his back
he reads the dial of the sun.
Sudden rain puckers the sand
15   marking, in braille,
his reading down.

'To make a sea change
you must seek beneath the surface.
You must drown'.

20   Righting the spinning earth again
he stumbles on
watching worlds collide
in his mind's cyclotron.

---

23 **cyclotron**: apparatus for accelerating charged atomic particles revolving in a magnetic field.

2. Miranda

There on the beach,
all copper and cornsilk hair,
the eyes a blur of blue,
she might have been the girl
5   on the brochure
of this green, paradisal island.
But mind, her mind has mountains
where deep forests grow,
liana-hung:
10   another Eden where, as yet,
no bird has sung.

It calls to her in dreams.
She cannot go there yet.
There's too much needing
15   to be done
there, on the beach.
Each day, sand to be swept,
firewood to fetch:
The island's not the paradise
20   it seems.

Lately,
there have been storms
and hammering seas,
and she must run
25   to comfort Caliban
when he screams.

§ *Responses to European texts* Lamming (2), Walcott (4); Af: Coetzee; SEA: Lim (2), Lee Tzu Pheng, Somtow; *Caribbean as Eden* Walcott (3)

EARL LOVELACE (1935–)

From The Dragon Can't Dance

The Dragon Can't Dance is centred on the role played by Trinidad Carnival in the lives of the inhabitants of Calvary Hill, one of the poorer areas of Port of Spain. The novel asks whether Carnival culture offers a genuine possibility of transformation or whether it is simply licensed escapism. It is also about codes of manhood, again viewed in a double-edged manner – both fragile male bravura and a more dignified and sustaining life-style. The passage included here is the Prologue, which establishes the mood of excitement and possible release associated with Carnival and begins with a tale of a mock-crucifixion similar to those in *The Lonely Londoners* and *Miguel Street*.

The Hill

This is the hill tall above the city where Taffy, a man who say he is Christ, put himself up on a cross one burning midday and say to his followers: 'Crucify me! Let me die for my people. Stone me with stones as you stone Jesus, I will love you still.' And when they start to stone him in truth he get vex and start to cuss: 'Get me down! Get me down!' he say. 'Let every sinnerman bear his own blasted burden; who is I to die for people who ain't have sense enough to know that they can't pelt a man with big stones when so much little pebbles lying on the ground.'

This is the hill, Calvary Hill, where the sun set on starvation and rise on potholed roads, thrones for stray dogs that you could play banjo on their rib bones, holding garbage piled high like a cathedral spire, sparkling with flies buzzing like torpedoes; and if you want to pass from your yard to the road you have to be a high-jumper to jump over the gutter full up with dirty water, and hold your nose. Is noise whole day. Laughter is not laughter; it is a groan coming from the bosom of these houses – no – not houses, shacks that leap out of the red dirt and stone, thin like smoke, fragile like kite paper, balancing on their rickety pillars as broomsticks on the edge of a juggler's nose.

This is the hill, swelling and curling like a machauel snake from Observatory Street to the mango fields in the back of Morvant, its guts stretched to bursting with a thousand narrow streets and alleys and lanes and traces and holes, holding the people who come on the edge of this city to make it home.

This hill is it; and in it; in Alice Street, named for Princess Alice, the Queen's aunt – Alice – soft word on the lips, is a yard before which grows a governor plum tree that has battled its way up through the tough red dirt and stands now, its roots spread out like claws, gripping the earth, its leaves rust red and green, a bouquet in this desert place: a tree bearing fruit that never ripens for Miss Olive's seven, and the area's other children, lean and hard like whips, their wise yellowed eyes filled with malnutrition and too early knowing – innocence was in the womb – children imitating the grown-up laughter and the big-man pose of their elders, who survive here, holding their poverty as a possession, tending it stubbornly as Miss Cleothilda tends her flower garden, clasping it to their bosom as a pass-key whose function they only half-remembered now, and, grown rusty, they wore as jewellery, a charm, a charmed medallion whose magic invested them with a mysterious purity, made them the blue-bloods of a resistance lived by their ancestors all through slavery, carried on in their unceasing escape – as Maroons, as Runways, as Bush Negroes, as Rebels: and when they could not perform in space that escape that would take them away from the scene of their brutalization they took a stand in the very guts of the slave plantation, among tobacco and coffee and cotton and canes, asserting their humanness in the most wonderful acts of sabotage they could imagine and perform, making a religion of laziness and neglect and stupidity and waste: singing hosannahs for flood and hurricane and earthquake, praying for damage and pestilence: continuing it still after Emancipation, that emancipated them to a more profound idleness and waste when, refusing to be grist for the mill of the colonial machinery that kept on grinding in its belly people to spit out sugar and cocoa and copra, they turned up this hill to pitch camp here on the eyebrow of the enemy, to cultivate again with no less fervor the religion with its Trinity of Idleness, Laziness and Waste, so that now, one hundred and twenty-five years after Emancipation, Aldrick Prospect, an aristocrat in this tradition, not knowing where his next meal was coming from, would get up at midday from sleep, yawn, stretch, then start to think of where he might get something to eat, his brain working in the same smooth unhurried nonchalance with which he moved his feet, a slow, cruising crawl which he quickened only at Carnival.

Carnival

Carnival it is that springs this hill alive. Right after Christmas young men get off street corners where they had watched and waited, rubber-tipped sticks peeping out of their back pockets, killing time in dice games, watching the area high-school girls ripening, holding over them the promise of violence and the threat of abuse to keep them respectful, to discourage them from passing them by with that wonderful show of contempt such schoolgirls seem to be required to master to lift them above these slums and these 'hooligans', their brethren, standing at street corners, watching the road grow richer with traffic, the drains float down their filth, holding their backs pressed against the sides of shop buildings from dawn until the scream of police jeeps drive them sullenly on the run, to bring into their waiting a sense of dangerousness and adventure they are happy to embrace, since in these daily police raids they see as much an acknowledgement of their presence as an effort to wrench from them sovereignty of these streets. This moves them to strain all the harder to hold their poses on the walls, to keep alive their visibility and aliveness. And these walls to which they return as soon as the police have driven off, their ritual harassment complete, become more their territory, these walls on which they have scrawled their own names and that of their gangs, Marabuntas,[1] Apple-Jackers, Brimstone, Shane – hard names derived from the movies which on some nights they slip off the walls to see, Western movies of the gun talk and the quick draw and the slow crawl, smooth grand gestures which they imitate so exquisitely as though those gestures were their own borrowed to the movie stars for them to later reclaim as proper to their person, that person that leans against the wall, one foot drawn up to touch the thigh, the hat brim turned down, the eyelid half closed, the body held in that relaxed aliveness, like a deer, watching the world from under the street lamp whose bulb they dutifully shatter as soon as it is changed: that person savouring his rebellion as a ripe starch

---

1 Wasps.

mango, a matchstick fixed between his teeth at an angle that he alone could measure, and no one imitate.

With Carnival now, they troop off street corners, desert their battlefield and territory, and turn up the hill to the steelband tent to assemble before steel drums cut to various lengths and tuned and fashioned to give out the different tones – bass, alto, cello – instruments that had their beginnings in kerosene tins, biscuit drums, anything that could sound a note, anything that could ring; metal drums looted from roadsides, emptied of their garbage and pressed into service to celebrate the great war's end, and to accompany the calypsonian's instant song: It's your moustache we want, Hitler.

Now, the steelband tent will become a cathedral, and these young men priests. They will draw from back pockets those rubber-tipped sticks, which they had carried around all year, as the one link to the music that is their life, their soul, and touch them to the cracked faces of the drums. Hours, hours; days, days; for weeks they beat these drums, beat these drums, hammering out from them a cry, the cry, the sound, stroking them more gently than they will ever caress a woman; and then they have it. At last, they have it. They have the tune that will sing their person and their pose, that will soar over the hill, ring over the valley of shacks, and laugh the hard tears of their living when, for Carnival, they enter Port of Spain.

Calypso

Up on the hill with Carnival coming, radios go on full blast, trembling these shacks, booming out calypsos, the songs that announce in this season the new rhythms for people to walk in, rhythms that climb over the red dirt and stone, break-away rhythms that laugh through the groans of these sights, these smells, that swim through the bones of these enduring people so that they shout: Life! They cry: Hurrah! They drink a rum and say: Fuck it! They walk with a tall hot beauty between the garbage and dog shit, proclaiming life, exulting in the bare bones of their person and their skin.

Up on the hill with Carnival coming and calypso tunes swimming in the hair of these shacks, piercing their nostrils, everybody catches the spirit and these women with baskets and with their heads tied, these women winding daily down this hill on which no buses run, tramping down this asphalt lane slashed across this mountain's face, on their way, to Port of Spain city, to market, to work as a domestic, or to any other menial task they inherit because of their beauty; these women, in this season, bounce with that tall delicious softness of bosom and hip, their movements a dance, as if they were earth priestesses heralding a new spring.

The children dance too, coming home from school in the hot afternoon when the sun has cooked the castles of dog shit well, so that its fumes rise like incense proper to these streets. They dance, skipping along, singing calypsos whose words they know by heart already, swishing their skirt tails, moving their waists, laughing, their laughter scattering like shells into the hard flesh of the hill. Dance! There is dancing in the calypso. Dance! If the words mourn the death of a neighbour, the music insists that you dance; if it tells the troubles of a brother, the music says dance. Dance to the hurt! Dance! If you catching hell, dance, and the government don't care, dance! Your woman take your money and run away with another man, dance. Dance! Dance! Dance! It is in dancing that you ward off evil. Dancing is a chant that cuts off the power from the devil. Dance! Dance! Dance! Carnival brings this dancing to every crevice on this hill.

§ *Mock-crucifixions* Selvon, Naipaul (1); *Folk experience* Reid, Mais, Lamming (1), Brathwaite (1, 2)

ERNA BRODBER (1940–)

From Jane and Louisa Will Soon Come Home

Written in a fragmentary and anti-linear narrative form, *Jane and Louisa* explores the psychic dislocation experienced by Nellie, its mixed-race protagonist, who has been brainwashed to distrust 'black' sexuality. As the text's jigsaw of episodes set at different moments in time gradually comes together, the complex process of conditioning that she has undergone is revealed and she is able to break free of the protective but stultifying white 'kumbla' in which she has enshrouded herself. The novel takes its title from a children's ring-game and finally its apparent disjointedness can be seen to be underpinned by a cyclic structure. *Jane and Louisa* also moves away from Eurocentric scribal discourse through its use of a broad range of oral registers and genres, such as the Anansi story narrated here.

The Kumbla

A kumbla[1] is like a beach ball. It bounces with the sea but never goes down. It is indomitable. More so than the beach buoy. The sea never covers it; it never stoops to fight. It takes no orders from the sea but neither does it seek to limit it. The beach ball sets no measures on the sea, seeks not to guide swimmer or non-swimmers; it merely bounces as it will upon the sea, the sand or anywhere. Haughtily.

A kumbla has these properties. It bounces anywhere. Unlike the buoy, it is not tethered. It blows as the wind blows it, if the wind has enough strength to move it: it moves if it is kicked, if it is thrown, if it is nudged . . . if anyone has that much strength, that much energy or that much interest. It makes no demands of you, it cares not one whit for you.

But the kumbla is not just a beach ball. The kumbla is an egg shell, not a chicken's egg or a bird's egg shell. It is the egg of the August worm. It does not crack if it is hit. It is as pliable as sail cloth. Your kumbla will not

---

1 Apparently a neologism; a 'coubla' is a small calabash used for drinking.

open unless you rip its seams open. It is a round seamless calabash that protects you without caring.

Your kumbla is a parachute. You, only you, pull the cord to rip its seams. From the inside. For you. Your kumbla is a helicopter, a transparent umbrella, a glassy marble, a comic strip space ship. You can see both in and out. You hear them. They can hear you. They can touch you. You can touch them. But they cannot handle you. And inside is soft carpeted foam, like the womb and with an oxygen tent. Safe, protective time capsule. Fed simply by breathing!

They usually come in white.

Anancy[2] took his son Tucuma to fish in Dryhead's waters. He was taking a chance and Anancy knew it but he didn't intend to starve. Anancy took his son Tucuma to fish but having no skill on water, he rowed right into Dryhead's palace and Dryhead is the king of the water. Anancy went too far this time. He put himself in deep waters. But Anancy is a born liar, a spinner of fine white cocoons, a protector of his children. Not to worry, they'll survive. Anancy is a maker of finely crafted kumblas.

Peeny Wally was in the fishing expedition too but he abandoned them. He had asked Nancy certain questions and had learnt once more that Nancy's eyes couldn't see further than his children: – So is you and Tucuma one fish and is you and Tucuma one going to eat fish. Well me take my light and gone – And he went.

The river was dark. You should have seen it. Good for black hog and they had caught a great number but not good for making your way home when you can't row well, when you have no light and when you are nervous because you are poaching on another man's property. It was dark as mud which begins to assume a life of its own, to form glistening malarial rainbows of light, to give birth to fireflies. Wild cocoes, wild shot, rushes, bhang grass, kept it damp and outside of God's light. Nancy rowed and Tucuma rowed, following this firefly and that:

– Favour like we los' Father –

– Hush your mouth boy, your Father can los' you? –

Anancy rowed and Tucuma rowed.

– Don't follow no firefly boy. Look inside of yourself and row. Them will los' you. Them will put you out of your way. See what nearly happen little while?

And they rowed.

– But when you find out where you want to go, you watch for them other one what going there and you use their light. See what me do with Peeny Wally? Eh boy? Use his light and don't we have fish? Eh boy? Don't we have fish? Answer me boy. You ever see so much black hog and janga. Is just left fi wi get home and you know your father never let you down. Answer me boy. True or lie? –

---

2 Spiderman-trickster of Caribbean, particularly Jamaican folklore.

– True sah. –

– So we soon ketch home! Right boy? –

– Right sah. –

– Follow me boy. Now you see like how the night dark and the river like is pure mud, and you see like how them firefly out to fool we. Watch me boy. You see them light over there like is a firefly jamboree. Is there we going. To the king himself. Watch your father boy. Watch your father. Look deep inside yourself, use the senses God give you and learn. –

Firefly is a fire-kitty[3] beast. Jumping up and down all the time. He can give you plenty light but not for Heaven's sake would he stop long enough in one place to do a good job. Jumping up and down like a childish rubber ball, he wouldn't even stay quiet long enough to listen. Well! And an 's' don't mean anything to him at all. Singulars and plurals is the same thing to him for the man would just not listen. And Anancy knew that.

– Come firefly, take this chiles of mine and put him at store house. Things too bad with me. Can't feed myself much less fu go feed five six mouth. Put these chiles at store house man and Dryhead can do anything with them that he likes. He can eat them, he can put them to work. I just can't make it, I pass the point of caring. And I am going to tell him so. – Fire-kitty firefly see children, not child. Put children, not child in the store house and what is more make that report to Dryhead that Brer 'Nancy had come with all his children. Anancy could depend him, that firekitty one!

– Brother Dryhead, you hear my plight. You see how the drought mash me up? I broke, I los', I bow to you. You is King. I just can't make it, can't mek it at all. I bring the children them. All of them. Take them, eat them, work them, anything. I can't manage no more. I just can't make it Brother Dryhead. Things just too hard. Rather than tief, I bring them to you. For your mercy. I wouldn't beg you a thing for myself either, only a bed to rest on for the night.

– See here Brother Dryhead, I telling you. The pickney[4] them give me a hard time to carry them here you see. They know things is hard but we love we one another. You know that 'bout we. So you understand my sorrow. Turn over the boat and try to swim back home I tell you. And I have to get out there in the river and haul them back. So if you smell any fish or anything like that on me, is only that why. I tell you Sir, things hard and my boat, it not even so good. Them punch hole into it and make it worse, for them rather drown than leave them father and I have to take mud and stop it up so that we could get here . . . which reminds me. I going to have to beg you lend me a boat to get back home for my shame tree don't quite dry down yet and I can't force myself as well on you. I know I not asking anything too hard, for you is not like me. You is a big man. You know how to manage and you have plenty boat, can well afford to lend me one.

– I poor but I honest and have mind. I only asking for a bed for tonight and that you lend me a boat tomorrow morning and that through I so tired,

---

3 Over-energetic or fiery person. 4 Child.

you leave it till tomorrow morning before we talk business. Boy, Sir, my children, the children them dirty. Love them you know. Poor children but I have pride (And Nancy cried long eye water). I wouldn't want you to see my children them now. You shoulda see the condition. Maugre and weak but them have pride. Them didn't want to come but I couldn't watch them dead. Pride them have. Them have them father pride. Jump out of the boat. Rather dead than give stranger trouble. Mi poor children and them looking so dirty now. A morning I clean them up and hand them over to you one by one. –

Early next morning, Nancy wake Dryhead.
– Brother Dries. My head not too good you know. Is the pressure. Pressure dey⁵ pon mi bad man. Clean forget that your people don't have much use at day time. And I don't want keep your boat. I am a poor man but I honest. Many a man woulda see this as a chance to get something for nothing. I coulda sell this boat to my friend Peeny Wally. He have light better than any two of your men for you know his light steady. And is my friend and he needs a boat and he can buy one. But I could never do that. Rather dead first. Tell you what you do. Lend me one of the children so that he can row me over and take back your boat to you. The biggest one. Send Tucuma. He is the one that understand why I have to give them away. Fact is, me and him talk 'bout it like two big man and he agree so he will bring back the boat. And I beg you, don't eat him. You can't lose off of him. He can work. Now I am going to tidy up the rest of the children and count them off right before your eyes. –

Anancy takes Tucuma out of the store house while the fool-fool firefly who can't see well in the day, just bopping his eyes, seeing doubles and saying:
– Only one at a time. The King say one at a time. –
– See him there. Touch him. Don't you feel say that is only one? –
To Dryhead, big fat and resplendent in his court dress, Anancy says: – See him here Sir, Number one. –

You know how sometimes when you love somebody and you don't want the whole world to know how powerlessly in love you are, you sometimes manhandle him in public.

How at the times when your love makes you most vulnerable to attack from outsiders, you scream, kick and curse the loved one in company? Anancy spoke this kind of language and knew that Dryhead understood it. His vulnerability was supposedly under double attack: he had to expose his deep love for his children in public and had to watch himself give away the things that were dearest to his heart. So it was expected that he would revile them doubly cruelly at a time such as this. As soon as each supposed child appeared Anancy would shout at him contemptuously as he did at this one:

---

5 There.

– Your face favour . . . go eena kumbla –

To Dryhead and his court, this was a bad word that only a man so torn with grief could utter to his child. To Tucuma, it meant: find yourself a camouflage and get back into the store house.

– You face favour . . . go eena kumbla –

Tucuma follows his father's command, shrinks as if his father has insulted him, goes under the cellar as the guard would have him, changes his colour with mud, crawls out and around and back into the store house while Nancy grumbles in a loud voice:

– Time so hard. I try to show you children by reason. I do all the best I can. I tell you that I have to give you to Brother Dryhead. He is some of you godfather, he won't treat you no more badly than he has to, but you wouldn't even look smart and make him take a fancy to you. You children going to let me leave with a heavy heart (And Dryhead was so sorry for him) I wouldn't do this if I didn't know that is only starvation I have to give you. Guard see there, is only one I'm taking. Child straighten your shoulders and go long. Number two Brother Dryhead. This is the mother's favourite and it grieve me heart Sir to part with him. . . . Child try to look smart, fix up yourself, don't shame me . . . you face favour . . . go eena kumbla –

Tucuma follows the guard, slinks as if he has something to be ashamed of, changes his colour again, creeps out of the cellar and around to the back and into the store-room again in time for Brer Anancy's speech:

– Guard, you sorry for me. Don't it. Talk the truth. To see a man come down til him have to sell him own pickney. Feel here is only one. Chile take your father hand. It not going to be too bad. You will see. Just behave yourself. Brother Dryhead will love you just like a father. . . . See him here Brother Dryhead, number three. Chile remember what your father say. Dry up the eye-water man. Wipe off your face . . . you face favour . . . go eena kumbla. –

Tucuma follows the guard, slinks as if he is afraid, changes his colour and rushes back to the store-house. They do that five times. – See guard, is two here this time. But you go ask the King if he didn't say that I could take this big one here with me to row back over the boat. Hold on to him here. Not this one, the big one, the one on my right. This big one here is not to go under the cellar. You feel him up and measure him so that you will know that is only this said one that is leaving in the boat with me. . . . Son go back in the corner. Your father soon come for you –

Firefly have no hand so he can't feel nothing but he don't want Nancy to know what everybody else knows, so he blinks and would swear blind that he saw two children, took the measure of the bigger one and saw the other leaving through the door with Nancy. So Nancy took Tucuma to be counted by Dryhead for a fifth time:

– Last one Brother Dryhead. Remember you said that the big boy could come with me and carry back the boat. . . . Look Brother Dryhead straight in the eye child. Let him see that your father is poor and that you know that he has come up on hard times or else he would not be doing you this. Hold up your head man. Smile chile. You face face favour . . . go eena kumbla –

Tucuma does what he knows he has to do.

– Guard pass my son here. Let us make the last little trip that we will ever make together. God's willing, he will be a better man than me. Come Tucuma – And they left.

And remember the time when he spirited away all of his children, each into his own kumbla, outwitting the man-eating Tiger? Anancy crafts such finely woven white silk kumblas designed to protect for generations.

But the trouble with the kumbla is the getting out of the kumbla. It is a protective device. If you dwell too long in it, it makes you delicate. Makes you an albino: skin white but not by genes. Vision extra-sensitive to the sun and blurred without spectacles. Baba and Alice urged me out of mine. Weak, thin, tired like a breach baby. Now where are they?

§ *Oral storytelling* Lamming, Selvon; *Trickster-figure* Brathwaite (1); Can: King, Armstrong; *Women's colonization* Nichols, Breeze

ZEE EDGELL (1940–)

From Beka Lamb

Beka Lamb is important in the historical development of anglophone Caribbean fiction in more than one way: it was the first novel from Belize to receive international recognition and one of the region's earliest significant 'novels of girlhood'. While 'novels of boyhood' had been prominent in the Caribbean literary renaissance of the 1950s and 1960s, it was not until the 1980s that a similar cluster of novels about girlhood appeared. The novel interlinks events in Beka's immediate world and her response to them with the situation of her country at large, as can be seen in the second chapter included here. Race, religion, gender and colonialism are all explored in a text, which like Lamming's *In the Castle of My Skin* is as much about a society 'growing up' as a child doing so.

In her dream, barefooted old men, trousers rolled to their knees, were chaining off the bridge approaches, in front and behind her, to prevent people, trucks, cars, mules, carts and bicycles from delaying the five o'clock swinging of the bridge. Beka rushed along the aisle nearest the market desperate to reach Northside before the bridge swung to the middle of the creek to give waiting sailboats a passage from the sea to the creek. She screamed above the uproar,

'I'm coming! Please wait 'pon me, sa!'

It was too late. The bridge, shuddering beneath her feet, began turning slowly away from the shore. Back and forth along the narrow aisle she ran, stopping again and again to shout and beat on the high iron wall separating the main traffic line from the pedestrian aisle. But the rattle and creak of machinery, and the noise from both sides of the creek, prevented the operators behind the wall from hearing her voice.

Laughing uproariously, the crowd pressed against the barriers, pointed elongated fingers to where she now stood exhausted, clinging to the railing. She felt shrunken except for her head which had grown to the size of a large calabash. Bicycle bells rang continuously. The chain attendant shouted directions she couldn't hear. Drivers honked their horns, short beeps and then longer blasts like the sawmill whistle. Sailors standing on the decks of their boats stretched muscled brown arms upwards, calling.

'Jump, nigger gial, jump! We'll ketch you!'

Beka stared at the laughing faces below her, and at the whiskered catfishes nibbling at the filth floating on the surface of the water. Without warning, the bridge canted downwards propelling Beka into the waters and excrement of Haulover Creek . . .

The tapping of the adding machine woke her up. The shops were shuttered and barred for the night. It was after nine o'clock. A rain breeze was rising, and her heart thumped in her chest like a pestle pounding plantains. Slowly she got to her feet and stumbled into the house. The polished pinewood floor felt cool underfoot. Bill Lamb was at his desk under the attic stairs in the dining room. A tin of coffee anchored a stack of waybills on the table behind him. Beka leaned against the table rubbing one dusty foot against the other, watching her father tap out a long row of numbers. Finally she asked,

'Importing coffee from Guatemala now, Dad?'

'What do you mean by "now"? Belize has always traded with the Republics around here,' Bill Lamb answered, turning to peer at Beka over the top of his rimless glasses.

'But you said that since Guatemala wants to take over Belize, it was dangerous to have contact with them.'

'When did you hear me say such a thing?'

'That time you and Granny Ivy quarrelled about P.I.P. maybe getting money from Guatemala to help start the party.'

'There's an alligator under my bed! I said, bad as it is, the British brand of colonialism isn't the worst we could have. Our politicians are new to politics, and they'd better watch which countries they accept aid from including Guatemala. I didn't say a word about trading.'

'Can they take us over?'

'Who, Beka?'

'The Guatemantecans!'

'Britain and Guatemala signed that treaty, Beka. It's not really our quarrel, but how should I know? Look what happened to India after the last world war! Look at the mess in the Caribbean! After all that how can a few people here matter that much?'

'What happened in those places, Dad?'

'I am busy tonight, Beka. Several ships came in yesterday. Why don't you go to bed – it's late.'

'I just woke up, Daddy!' Beka said sitting down on a chair.

In the brief sketch of the colony Beka had studied at school, there was a drawing of two black men, bare to the waist, standing on either side of the spreading branches of a mahogany tree. One held an axe, the other, a saw. Beka had been told in history class, the year she failed first form, that the Latin words beneath the picture meant: 'Under the shade we flourish.'

Beka, who had never seen a mahogany tree in her life, examined the laughing senorita decorating the label of the coffee tin. The Lamb family was black, but it was not one of those that flourished under the shade of a mahogany tree. Beka couldn't think of many families that did nowadays except maybe shareholders of the British Lumber Company, who still owned much of the forests where the mahogany grew. Her family seemed to be doing all right, though, under Blanco's Import Commission Agency. People depended on condensed milk imported from abroad, as well as flour, rice, beans and many other basic commodities needed to sustain life. Moreover, Beka's Dad was too impatient a man, he said, to subject himself to the uncertainties of the mahogany tree scattered fewer than ten to an acre out in the bush.

'May I have some?' Beka asked.

'Some of what, Beka?'

'Dis here cawfee.'

'At this time of night? Gial, what is wrong with you of late?'

Her father's bloodshot eyes glared round at her. The electric light above his desk make his forehead shine. The workers at the bond shed near the sea called him 'Wild Bill' behind his back. But Granny Ivy said unless Daddy Bill got wild, the workers at the shed would let the boxes pile high in the warehouses, and then Daddy Bill would be in trouble. Of course, Granny Ivy always added, wages everywhere were so low, you couldn't blame them for stretching out the work or dropping a box now and then and splitting the goods amongst themselves, especially at Christmas time.

As if remembering that Beka had redeemed herself earlier that day, his eyes softened as he said,

'All right, Beka, one spoonful.'

Jumping up, Beka went into the kitchen and removed a pottery mug from a high shelf her mother reserved for the promotional gift items her Dad brought home from work. 'Drink Scotch Whisky' was fired in blue glaze across the front of the big mug. She filled it with water from the thermos, sweetening the scalding water with a generous amount of condensed milk from a tin in the grocery safe. Stirring the milk and water, Beka returned to the dining room. *The Bulletin* lay on the table next to the coffee tin. The headlines read: PRITCHAD, GLADSEN IMPRISONED TODAY MEETING AT

BATTLEFIELD TONIGHT. Restlessly, Beka flipped through the four pages. She was beginning to regret not going to the meeting with her Granny Ivy.

The door leading to the other part of the house was closed against the noise of the adding machine. She turned the knob. Her small brothers were asleep on cots drawn close together under a large square mosquito net. Passing them quietly, she tiptoed into her parents' room. Lilla lay on her stomach, peering through the blinds. Beka knew that her mother was worrying about her rose plants, and hoping it would rain once more before the dry season began. Two years earlier, all her bushes dried up in the drought. Miss Ivy and Lilla exchanged words because Granny Ivy felt that Lilla had no business 'going on so bad over rose bush when people out district watching corn and yams shrivel under the sun.'

When the rains finally came that drought year, Beka's Dad tried to persuade Lilla to concentrate on bougainvillea, crotons, and hibiscus. Plants like these grew easily and luxuriantly in the yard, but Lilla kept those trimmed back, and continued to struggle year after year in her attempt to cultivate roses like those she saw in magazines which arrived in the colony three months late from England.

'How are your eyes, Ma?' Beka whispered from the doorway. A small fan rattled as it whirled from left to right on the bedside table.

'Not too bad, Beka, and the headache is gone.'

'Do you want your headcloth wet with more bay rum?' Beka asked, going further into the room.

'All right.'

Beka took a green pint bottle off the table, sat on the edge of her Dad's bed, and began saturating the cloth her mother passed to her. The rummy smell burned Beka's nostrils making her eyes water. Lilla raised herself up on the pillow and Beka retied the cloth firmly around her head.

'Shall I switch off the fan? It's cooling down.'

'No, leave it on. And, Beka?'

'Yes, Mama?'

'Can you manage to pass the other two terms?'

'I'll try, but this last one was very hard.'

'Things won't always be as bad as it's been for you these last months. If you manage to finish school, your education will help you to reach a clearing.'

'Then what do I do?'

'There are more opportunities nowadays, man.'

'You think so, Mama?'

'I hope so, Beka.'

'I'll try then,' Beka said. 'Night, Ma.'

'Night, Beka pet. Leave the verandah door unlocked for your Gran but fasten the shutters upstairs – it will rain.'

In the dining-room once more, Beka quickly shovelled three heaped teaspoons of coffee into her mug of milky water and called,

'Night, Dad,' as she started to climb the stairs to the attic floor she shared with her Gran.

§ *Childhood discovery* Lamming, Kincaid, Senior; Af: Gurnah; Can: Munro, Findley, Burnard; SA: Selvadurai, Sidhwa SEA: Maniam

JAMAICA KINCAID (1949–)

In the Night

In the night, way into the middle of the night, when the night isn't divided like a sweet drink into little sips, when there is no just before midnight, midnight, or just after midnight, when the night is round in some places, flat in some places, and in some places like a deep hole, blue at the edge, black inside, the night-soil men come.

They come and go, walking on the damp ground in straw shoes. Their feet in the straw shoes make a scratchy sound. They say nothing.

The night-soil men can see a bird walking in trees. It isn't a bird. It is a woman who has removed her skin and is on her way to drink the blood of her secret enemies. It is a woman who has left her skin in a corner of a house made out of wood. It is a woman who is reasonable and admires honeybees in the hibiscus. It is a woman who, as a joke, brays like a donkey when he is thirsty.

There is the sound of a cricket, there is the sound of a church bell, there is the sound of this house creaking, that house creaking, and the other house creaking as they settle into the ground. There is the sound of a radio in the distance – a fisherman listening to merengue music. There is the sound of a man groaning in his sleep; there is the sound of a woman disgusted at the man groaning. There is the sound of the man stabbing the woman, the sound of her blood as it hits the floor, the sound of Mr. Straffee, the undertaker, taking her body away. There is the sound of her spirit back from the dead, looking at the man who used to groan; he is running a fever forever. There is the sound of a woman writing a letter; there is the sound of her pen nib on the white writing paper; there is the sound of the kerosene lamp dimming; there is the sound of her head aching.

The rain falls on the tin roofs, on the leaves in the trees, on the stones in the yard, on sand, on the ground. The night is wet in some places, warm in some places.

There is Mr. Gishard, standing under a cedar tree which is in full bloom, wearing that nice white suit, which is as fresh as the day he was buried in it. The white suit came from England in a brown package: 'To: Mr. John Gishard,' and so on and so on. Mr. Gishard is standing under the tree, wearing his nice suit and holding a glass full of rum in his hand – the same glass full of rum that he had in his hand shortly before he died – and looking at the house in which he used to live. The people who now live in the house walk through the door backward when they see Mr. Gishard standing under the tree, wearing his nice white suit. Mr. Gishard misses his accordion; you can tell by the way he keeps tapping his foot.

In my dream I can hear a baby being born. I can see its face, a pointy little face – so nice. I can see its hands – so nice, again. Its eyes are closed. It's breathing, the little baby. It's breathing. It's bleating, the little baby. It's bleating. The baby and I are now walking to pasture. The baby is eating green grass with its soft and pink lips. My mother is shaking me by the shoulders. My mother says, 'Little Miss, Little Miss.' I say to my mother, 'But it's still night.' My mother says, 'Yes, but you have wet your bed again.' And my mother, who is still young, and still beautiful, and still has pink lips, removes my wet nightgown, removes my wet sheets from my bed. My mother can change everything. In my dream I am in the night.

'What are the lights in the mountains?'

'The lights in the mountains? Oh, it's a jablesse.'[1]

'A jablesse! But why? What's a jablesse?'

'It's a person who can turn into anything. But you can tell they aren't real because of their eyes. Their eyes shine like lamps, so bright that you can't look. That's how you can tell it's a jablesse. They like to go up in the mountains and gallivant. Take good care when you see a beautiful woman. A jablesse always tries to look like a beautiful woman.'

No one has ever said to me, 'My father, a nightsoil man, is very nice and very kind. When he passes a dog, he gives a pat and not a kick. He likes all the parts of a fish but especially the head. He goes to church quite regularly and is always glad when the minister calls out, "A Mighty Fortress Is Our God," his favorite hymn. He would like to wear pink shirts and pink pants but knows that this color isn't very becoming to a man, so instead he wears navy blue and brown, colors he does not like at all. He met my mother on what masquerades as a bus around here, a long time ago, and he still likes to whistle. Once, while running to catch a bus, he fell and broke his ankle and had to spend a week in hospital. This made him miserable, but he cheered up quite a bit when he saw my mother and me, standing over his white cot, holding bunches of yellow roses and smiling down at him. Then he said, "Oh, my. Oh, my." What he likes to do most, my father the night-soil man, is to sit on a big stone under a mahogany tree and watch small children playing play-cricket while he eats the intestines of animals stuffed with blood and rice and drinks ginger beer. He has told me this many times: "My dear, what I like to do most," and so on. He is always reading botany books and knows a lot about rubber plantations and rubber trees; but this is an interest I can't explain, since the only rubber tree he has ever seen is a specially raised one in the botanic gardens. He sees to it that my

---

1 Diablesse or devil-woman.

school shoes fit comfortably. I love my father the night-soil man. My mother loves my father the night-soil man. Everybody loves him and waves to him whenever they see him. He is very handsome, you know, and I have seen women look at him twice. On special days he wears a brown felt hat, which he orders from England, and brown leather shoes, which he also orders from England. On ordinary days he goes barehead. When he calls me, I say, "Yes, sir." On my mother's birthday he always buys her some nice cloth for a new dress as a present. He makes us happy, my father the night-soil man, and has promised that one day he will take us to see something he has read about called the circus.'

In the night, the flowers close up and thicken. The hibiscus flowers, the flamboyant flowers, the bachelor's buttons, the irises, the marigolds, the whitehead-bush flowers, the lilies, the flowers on the daggerbush, the flowers on the turtleberry bush, the flowers on the soursop tree, the flowers on the sugar-apple tree, the flowers on the mango tree, the flowers on the guava tree, the flowers on the cedar tree, the flowers on the stinking-toe tree, the flowers on the dumps tree, the flowers on the papaw tree, the flowers everywhere close up and thicken. The flowers are vexed.

Someone is making a basket, someone is making a girl a dress or a boy a shirt, someone is making her husband a soup with cassava so that he can take it to the cane field tomorrow, someone is making his wife a beautiful mahogany chest, someone is sprinkling a colorless powder outside a closed door so that someone else's child will be stillborn, someone is praying that a bad child who is living prosperously abroad will be good and send a package filled with new clothes, someone is sleeping.

Now I am a girl, but one day I will marry a woman – a red-skin woman with black bramblebush hair and brown eyes, who wears skirts that are so big I can easily bury my head in them. I would like to marry this woman and live with her in a mud hut near the sea. In the mud hut will be two chairs and one table, a lamp that burns kerosene, a medicine chest, a pot, one bed, two pillows, two sheets, one looking glass, two cups, two saucers, two dinner plates, two forks, two drinking-water glasses, one china pot, two fishing strings, two straw hats to ward the hot sun off our heads, two trunks for things we have very little use for, one basket, one book of plain paper, one box filled with twelve crayons of different colors, one loaf of bread wrapped in a piece of brown paper, one coal pot, one picture of two women standing on a jetty, one picture of the same two women embracing, one picture of the same two women waving goodbye, one box of matches. Every day this red-skin woman and I will eat bread and milk for breakfast, hide in bushes and throw hardened cow dung at people we don't like, climb coconut trees, pick coconuts, eat and drink the food and water from the coconuts we have picked, throw stones in the sea, put on John Bull masks and frighten defenseless little children on their way home from school, go fishing and catch only our favorite fishes to roast and have for dinner, steal green figs to eat for dinner with the roast fish. Every day we would do this. Every night I would sing this woman a song; the words I don't know yet, but the tune is in my head. This woman I would like to marry knows many things, but to me she will only tell about things that would never dream of making me cry; and every night, over and over, she will tell me something that begins, 'Before you were born.' I will marry a woman like this, and every night, every night, I will be completely happy.

§ *Childhood discovery* Lamming, Edgell, Senior; Af: Gurnah; Can: Munro, Findley, Burnard; SA: Selvadurai, Sidhwa; SEA: Maniam

OLIVE SENIOR (1941–)

Summer Lightning

The man came to stay with them for a few weeks each year. For his 'nerves' they said. They always gave him the garden room. No one called it by that name but that was how the boy thought about it. This room by some architectural whimsy completely unbalanced the house. There on one side were three large bedrooms and a bathroom, in the middle the kitchen and the dining room and what the uncle called the living room and the aunt the parlour, and on the far side this one bedroom. Adjoining it was the side verandah where the full blue-seam crocus bags of pimento were sometimes stacked, where the uncle sat on Sundays when the travelling barber came to cut his hair, and where visitors who were not up to the standard of the front verandah were received, standing.

The room was the smallest in the house. It had no glass, no mirrors, just a bed, the uncle's desk, and ten green jalousies. In fact most of the house was painted green since the aunt thought it was a restful colour for the eyes. One of the doors led to the dining room, one to the side verandah, and the other down broken marble steps into a tangled and overgrown garden.

It was amazing that a room with so many openings could be so private. But it was. And it was the boy's secret room, a place where he could hide during thunderstorms. 'Lightning only strike liard,' Brother Justice had told him once, and since then he had lived in an agony of mid-afternoons when sheet lightning washed the house. 'Lightning is Jah[1] triple vision. Is like X-ray dat,' Bro. Justice also said. 'When Jah want to search I out Jah send the lightning to see right through I'. Brother Justice also told him that he would be safe from lightning only in a place where there was no glass at all since everybody knew that 'glass draw lightning,' glass and 'shiny instrument'. Brother Justice said that that was why he had no mirror in his hut, that and the fact that glass is an instrument of Babylon. Whenever lightning started to flash, Bro. Justice would put into his crocus bag his machete, the only

---

1 Jehovah or God (Rastafarian).

shiny instrument he possessed, for he kept the blade sharp. But then Bro. Justice knew everything, was right about everything, including the lightning.

Thus it came about that at the first sign of rain the boy would go into the garden room, slowly and in a certain order which he had worked out as most satisfying close all ten jalousies, lock the doors, and in darkness to which his eyes soon became accustomed, wait out the storm. No one troubled him for the thunder-storms usually coincided with the aunt and uncle's afternoon rest.

He was never lonely for he harboured many secret places inside him. It was as if when he closed the windows and doors, the doors of his mind flew open one after another, like living inside the heart of an opening flower.

He was enchanted by these places for they were located in another world, occupied different space, transcended dimensions. People and animals changed places at will, and he was the master of them all. Bro. Justice was the only actual living human being he knew who also moved in this world, and Bro. Justice he could never transform into anything but what he was. The aunt and uncle were excluded because he couldn't see them stiff and proper quite fitting into and accepting the mysteries of this world. At first his father and mother sometimes appeared but his memories of them got dimmer and dimmer and finally he saw them only as through the one winking and mysterious green eye in his uncle's box level which swam up and down in a fluid.

And this world was so satisfying that after a time even when there was no sign of rain he would still go into the room cool and shaded for there his uncle kept his desk, a goldmine of pigeonholes. Though he was forbidden to touch, he intimately knew its secrets: semi-precious stones from Panama and Costa Rica, unpolished lead weights, a small whetstone, and the box level with the green fluid in which reposed the eye, or so it seemed, that winked at him when he tilted it. There were bundles of string and rusty nails forgotten and still in tarpaper. There were oil cans and oil stains and grease and a great many papers tied with string that looked official and held no interest. And as long as he was alone in this room he was happy because he knew instinctively that if in the world he had nothing else, he was still rich because he had this space which allowed him to explore secret places inside him.

The old man had been coming for years; the boy was the newcomer to the house, the room had been 'his' for a short time only. At first he did not mind the man coming and occupying the room for he brought a welcome chaos to a too-ordered household. The boy thought he was, in a funny kind of way, nice, though his smile was crooked and at times his eyes glazed over and his mouth trembled and he mumbled to himself. He also did not appear to see too well and this the boy liked, for he could hide in the shadows and listen to the man's mumblings. The man also brought him presents. One was a tiny elephant carved in ivory. The man told him to always turn the elephant to face the door, for luck. This advice pleased him immensely and he planned to incorporate it into his door-closing window-shutting ritual when he reclaimed the room, although in a room with three doors facing in different directions he remained uncertain about which was 'the' door. Still, he believed that one day some secret signal would be given to indicate which door the elephant should face. For the moment, he turned it to face the corner.

For all his kindness though, the man had habits which were not pleasant. He smelled and it was not nice like the rusty nails or the grease of the desk. It was a damp mouldy smell like a dirty wet dog or a saddlecloth caught in the rain. At table his hands shook so much that the boy would watch in fascination as more often than not he missed his mouth and the carrots would sail across the aunt's highly polished rosewood and mahogany floor. At such times the boy did not laugh. He was fascinated by a certain precision which hovered over the old man's actions. He soon discovered that every movement by the man, even those which were obviously stupid, functioned along lines of scientific exactitude gone slightly askew. There was also an element of habitual action, almost of ritual in whatever the old man did, and it gave the boy a strong sense of identification.

Sometimes with invisible string the old man formed elaborate cat's cradles. He knew them by heart for the pattern never varied. These activities seemingly required from the man almost total concentration, his mouth slightly open. At other times he simply sat still with his hands interlaced in his lap while his thumbs chased endless circles round each other. It was something the boy admired and practised in secret until he sometimes found himself doing it effortlessly and thoughtlessly like the old man. The man also had lucid times, when he would sit on the front verandah talking late into the night with the uncle. And one night at least, the boy in bed the other side of the house thought he heard the sound of uncontrolled weeping coming from the garden room. But he was too scared to investigate and wondered afterwards if he had really heard it.

At first he thought that the old man was unaware of his presence. Then after a while he saw that the man noticed him in a sly kind of way – sometimes when his cat's cradles had reached elaborate perfection he would turn to the boy and give him a nod of triumph as if to say 'ha'. At other times the old man would pass a limp hand vaguely in his direction. The old man, however, never spoke directly to him.

The boy did not mind. To him the old man was such an object of fascination that he seemed not quite ordinarily human. Rather, the boy imagined that he was like a space traveller in baggy clothes cast adrift from his planet and flung wondrously upon the lonely country house.

So fascinated was he by the old man that he no longer visited Bro. Justice. At first when he thought of his neglect of Bro. Justice he was supremely self-conscious, for he knew that the old man had usurped Bro. Justice's place in his life and that Bro. Justice was in some unspoken way, angry.

When he had first come to the aunt and uncle's, Bro. Justice was the only person with whom he felt comfortable. In that big house with the perpetual smell of wax, the heavy mahogany furniture, the glass windows, he felt displaced, as if he had been plucked from one world which was small and snug and mistakenly placed into another which was like a suit many times too large and to which he could never have hopes of growing to a perfect fit. And in an unspoken way the aunt seemed to criticise him for his failure to grow quickly enough to flesh out the suit. The uncle was kindly in a vague manner; there were times when he even indulged the boy, for it was not his sister, after all, who had made the disastrous marriage.

Now the aunt's relationship with Bro. Justice was double-edged. The aunt both feared Bro. Justice and grudgingly respected him, as the bully does anyone who defies. For Bro. Justice was a Rastafarian and the only reason she tolerated him at all was that Bro. Justice's father had been with the uncle since his father's time, and Bro. Justice under his father's tutelage had in his turn developed into one of the best cattle men in the parish. He had also been the best man on the Pen[2] before he, according to the aunt, began to turn 'queer' with his beard and his matted hair and his Bible.

One night a passing Rastaman had stopped off at the barracks where the penmen lived. They viewed him first with alarm and then as a creature wondrous and strange for in those days Rastamen were a novelty. People had heard of this strange and dreaded group of men in the cities but the only ones ever seen in that part of the world were ones who would simply be passing through. It turned out that this one, Bro. Naptali, had worked as a penman on the property at one time, though now he had grown almost unrecognisable to all who had known him. For three days and three nights Bro. Naptali stayed with them, leaving at the crack of dawn as mysteriously as he had come. While the rest of the men had treated him as a figure of derision, Bro. Justice had been deeply moved by his words and his demeanour. After Bro. Naptali left, Bro. Justice pondered on his words long and deeply. Then suddenly one day he took off for no one knows where. He stayed away forty days and forty nights and suddenly, dramatically, reappeared as Bro. Justice.

Apart from his physical appearance, the thing that the aunt noticed and disliked most about Bro. Justice was the fact that in going away, he had lost that respect for them which had been inculcated in men like him for centuries, and which the aunt at least considered only her due. While the other workers continued to address her as 'maam' and 'mistress', Bro. Justice refused to address her at all. He had withdrawn himself from the life of the Pen, confining his contact with others only to his duties, and retreated to the bottom of the citrus grove where he erected a little hut. After a while, so deeply did he burrow himself into his new life, that even the aunt stopped questioning his right to his own existence.

At first she did not know what to do about the boy's relationship with Bro. Justice. But since she herself had no idea what to do to entertain or amuse a boy child of that age, she did not interfere in case she might become saddled with the responsibility. She was thus pleased in a vindictive way

---

2 Farm; plantation.

when the old man came to stay and, for the time being anyway, so attracted the child's attention that he seemed to have completely forgotten about the Rastafarian.

Now, just as the aunt thought, Bro. Justice was angry about the boy's desertion for he had been extremely pleased about the way in which the child could sit for hours listening to his discourses, and in a sense considered the boy a potential disciple. The child was also a novelty in Bro. Justice's life, for as he got deeper and deeper into his religion, he found himself more and more distanced from the people around him, until he sometimes felt as remote from them as the furthest star. The boy alone had been able to enter his world, questioning only its superficial manifestations. The boy did not ask for or take anything from this world. The boy simply was.

He was also angry at the boy's defection because, simply, he missed him. For once the boy was gone he again had to contend with his own loneliness. But he was also upset for another reason: he did not like the old man. In fact he feared and disliked the old man for a reason that shamed him deeply, something that had occurred while his father was still alive and he was a young boy about the Pen, and something which he never liked to think about. And ever after that he had always taken pains to keep out of the man's way whenever he came for his nerves.

He had been coming each year for his nerves as long as Bro. Justice could remember. In the early days though, nothing seemed too wrong with him, he was then a good-looking man, probably the uncle's age though now he looked twice as old. He would spend endless hours walking about the property aimlessly. The thing that Bro. Justice never liked to think about was this: it was the way the man used to watch him. Even in those days before he became religious, Bro. Justice felt instinctively that for one man to look at another man like that was sinful. As a youngster, Bro. Justice had the jobs around the yard – feeding the young calves, looking after the chickens, helping the aunt with her vegetable garden. He could not escape from the gaze of this man. Even when he was fully occupied with his chores he could feel the man watching him, would turn suddenly and there the man would be. He knew the man was not watching the chickens or what he was doing. He was watching *him*. And watching him the way he should be watching a woman. Bro. Justice went out of his way to avoid the man. Once the two of them coming in opposite directions approached the narrow gate which led to the backyard at the same time and as Bro. Justice shrunk into the narrow space to let him pass, the man had actually reached out and lightly touched his face. Bro. Justice instinctively drew away and the man did nothing else as he continued past but turn his head sideways and smile at him. The smile held a threat or a promise and Bro. Justice wanted to kill him. For years afterwards whenever the image of the man came to his mind the blood would fly to his head and he would want to annihilate that smile.

But that was really a long time ago. With the passing years, the man had seemed more frail, less assured, and even though he still walked over the property it was with the unsure steps of a spacewalker. And as he became more pathetic, Bro. Justice, remembering Job, softened towards him, although he still carefully maintained a distance. After a while he had even forgotten his earlier, even childish fear of the man for he had, after all, done him no harm. But now the man had come again; for his nerves, and the boy was also here, and this configuration disturbed Bro. Justice profoundly.

Bro. Justice was given to deep concentration counterbalanced by sudden and sometimes irrational action. Now, he reasoned deeply with himself on the subject. His reasoning did not help him. So distressed did he become that he took the unbelievable step of going to the aunt herself to plead with her please look after the little boy. But the aunt, immensely pleased that Bro. Justice had finally felt the need to approach her, took it as an occasion to lecture him about his appearance, his manners, his attitude, and in their double conversation which came to be conducted loudly and simultaneously, heard nothing of his mutterings of 'Sodom', 'sin', or the foolishness that is bound up in the heart of a child.

Indeed, when she afterwards remembered a few words of the conversation she dismissed them as part of Bro. Justice's jealousy at being supplanted in the eyes of the child, and she rejoiced at his discomfort. Bro. Justice could have called the child and seduced him back from the old man but he was too proud lest the boy think he could not continue life without him. So Bro. Justice ended up doing the only thing he could, and that was to attempt to keep the boy and the old man constantly under his eye. Whereas before he used to sit in his hut in the afternoons, he now took to sitting motionless underneath the house which rose on stilts at the back. His favourite perch was on a large smooth rock immediately beneath the garden room where he was hidden by the steps leading into the garden. He quietened his spirit by deciding that if ever the child should be in danger, Jehovah-Jah would give him a sign – any sign. In the meantime, his machete beside him, he pursued earnestly his reading of the Bible.

The boy and the old man had taken to spending a lot of time in the room where the old man would rest and the boy, when he thought the man was asleep, would try and recapture some of the magic of the room by rifling the pigeonholes. But there were times when all the life with which he had once imbued the objects in the room seemed drained from them by the old man and his mysterious 'nerves'. The boy did not know what nerves were except that they were alive and he could feel them pulsating in the room like telegraph wires. The hum occurred even when the old man was sleeping which he thought strange – until he discovered that frequently the man wasn't sleeping at all but was surreptitiously watching him beneath half-closed eyes. At first this made him feel strange and uncomfortable and he wished himself safe back in Bro. Justice's hut. But he did not leave the room. For one thing he was now ashamed to go back to Bro. Justice. Besides, something told him that if he once deserted, then even when the man left, he would never again in any shape or form be able to reclaim the room again.

So he continued to watch the man and to visit the room while he was there. But now he knew that the man was watching him, he grew more conscious of himself, and of the man. Sometimes sitting at the desk he would quickly turn toward the bed and feel triumphant if he caught the old man quickly closing his eyes. At other times when he was sure the man was sleeping because he could hear his thin snores, he would go and stand by the bed and look down on the unshaven face and try to summon up a feeling of power to counteract the nerves flowing through him. But when the old man was awake he kept a physical distance from him for over time he felt that the old man was gradually drawing him in towards him, probably by means of his mysterious nerves. And he sensed that the old man would one day draw close enough to touch him even as he feared that if this ever happened, everything – Bro. Justice, the room, the magic world, even the order of the aunt and uncle's life that he both loved and despised – would be lost to him forever and he too might thereafter be condemned to float wonderingly in time and space in a suit many times too large.

Then one afternoon as usual the old man was having his rest in the darkened room. The boy crept in and started to play with the objects in the uncle's desk, the semi-precious stones, the rusted nails, the official papers, and the box level. He played this game frequently: first he would try to get the eye in the box level perfectly in the centre and this was hard for the desk top sloped, and then he would try to project his mind deep into this eye so that he could reach through to the mysterious world he felt certain existed beyond. He was so engaged in this game that he did not hear the old man. Rather he first sensed his presence, then felt his breath. The boy jumped from the chair, setting the box level askew, for the old man standing so close to him was no longer looking coy or foolish. His hair was standing untidily from his head as always, his dirty merino collar rose above his shirt, and he smelled the same way, but his eyes were no longer weak and uncertain. They were firmly focussed on the boy and they held a command. All through his body the boy suddenly felt drained and weak. Through a film like that covering the eye of the spirit level he saw the man advance towards him.

He stepped backwards. his heart beating wildly, and on the window sill his hand encountered a tiny object – it was the ivory elephant. Instinctively, he turned it to face the door leading to the garden through which he felt any moment now would come Bro. Justice and his shiny machete, even though there was in the sky more than a hint of summer lightning. But his heart was pounding out a message so loudly that he knew no matter where Bro. Justice was, or the state of the weather, he was bound to receive it.

§ *Childhood discovery* Lamming, Edgell, Kincaid; Can: Munro, Findley, Burnard; SA: Sidhwa; SEA: Maniam; *Competing ancestries* Rhys (2), Brodber

LORNA GOODISON (1947–)

I Am Becoming My Mother

Yellow/brown woman
fingers smelling always of onions

My mother raises rare blooms
and waters them with tea
5   her birth waters sung like rivers
my mother is now me

My mother had a linen dress
the colour of the sky
and stored lace and damask
10   tablecloths
to pull shame out of her eye.

I am becoming my mother
brown/yellow woman
fingers smelling always of onions.

§ *Motherhood* Af: Emecheta: Aidoo (2)

JOHN AGARD (1949–)

Mek Four

Who seh West Indian creole
is not a language of love?
Well I tell you . . .

When me and she eye
5   mek four
negative vibration
walk out de door

when me and she eye
mek four
10 tenderness was a guest
that didn't need invitation

---

5 **mek four**: meet.

when me and she eye
mek four
the world was neither
15   more or less
but a moment of rightness

we tongue locked
in a syntax of yes

§ *Language usage* Bennett, Reid, Sparrow, Brathwaite (3), Bloom, Breeze; TransC: Johnson, D'Aguiar

VALERIE BLOOM (1956–)

Language Barrier

Jamaica language sweet yuh know bwoy,
An yuh know mi nebba notice i',
Till tarra day one foreign frien'
Come spen some time wid mi.

5   An den im call mi attention to
Some tings im sey soun' queer,
Like de way wi always sey 'koo yah'
When we really mean 'look here'.

Den annodda ting whey puzzle im,
10   Is how wi lub 'repeat' wise'f
For de ongle time im repeat a wud
Is when smaddy half deaf.

Todda day im a walk outa road
An when im a pass one gate,
15   Im see one bwoy a one winda,
An one nodda one outside a wait.

Im sey dem did look kine o' nice
Soh im ben a go sey howdy,
But im tap shart when de fus' bwoy sey
20   'A ready yuh ready aready?'

---

12 **smaddy**: somebody.

Den like sey dat ney quite enuff,
Fe po' likkle foreign Hugh,
Him hear de nedda bwoy halla out,
'A come mi come fe come wait fe yuh'.

25 An dat is nat all dat puzzle him,
Why wi run wi words togedda?
For when im expec' fe hear 'the other',
him hear dis one word, 'todda'.

Instead o' wi sey 'all of you'
30 Wi ongle sey unoo,
Him can dis remember sey
De wud fe 'screech owl' is 'patoo'.

As fe some expression him hear,
Im wouldn badda try meck dem out,
35 Like 'boonoonoonos,' 'chamba-chamba,'
An 'kibba up yuh mout'.

Him can hardly see de connection,
Between 'only' an 'dengey',
An im woulda like fe meet de smaddy
40 Who invent de wud 'preckey'.

Mi advise im no fe fret imself,
For de Spaniards do it to,
For when dem mean fe sey 'jackass',
Dem always sey 'burro'.

45 De French, Italian, Greek an Dutch,
Dem all guilty o' de crime
None a dem no chat im language,
Soh Hugh betta larn fe mime.

But sayin' dis an dat yuh know,
50 Some o' wi cyan eben undastan one anodda,
Eben doah wi all lib yah
An chat de same patois.

For from las' week mi a puzzle out,
Whey Joey coulda mean,

---

35 boonoonoonos: term of endearment: pretty, beautiful; also pleasant, nice.
36 kibba: cover.
51 lib yah: live here.

35 chamba-chamba: disfigured; tattered.
40 preckey: foolish or credulous person; clown; also used adjectivally.

When im teck im facey self soh ax
      Ef any o' im undapants clean.

§ *Language usage* Bennett, Reid, Sparrow, Brathwaite (3), Bloom, Agard,
Breeze; NZSP: Tuwhare; SEA: Mohamad Bin Haji Salleh; TransC: D'Aguiar

GRACE NICHOLS (1950–)

One Continent/To Another

      Child of the middle passage womb
      push
      daughter of a vengeful Chi
      she came
5   into the new world
      birth aching her pain
      from one continent/to another

      moaning

      her belly cry sounding the wind

10   and after fifty years
      she hasn't forgotten
      hasn't forgotten
      how she had lain there
      in her own blood
15   lain there in her own shit

      bleeding memories in the darkness

      how she stumbled onto the shore
      how the metals dragged her down
      how she thirsted . . . . .

20   But being born a woman
      she moved again
      knew it was the Black Beginning
      though everything said it was
      the end

---

55 facey: impudent, cheeky.
1 middle passage womb: Atlantic slave ship.   **3 Chi**: personal god.

25 And she went forth with others of her kind
to scythe the earth knowing that bondage
would not fall like poultice from the
children's forehead

But O she grieved for them
30 walking beadless
in another land

From the darkness within her
from the dimness of previous
incarnations
35   the Congo surfaced
so did Sierra Leone   and the
Gold Coast which she used to tread
searching the horizons for lost
moons
40 her jigida guarding the crevice
the soft wet forest
between her thighs

§ *Women's colonization* Brodber, Breeze; Af: Dangarembga; *Crossing the Middle Passage* Brathwaite (1, 2); TransC: Phillips

JEAN 'BINTA' BREEZE (1956–)

Spring Cleaning

de Lord is my shepherd
I shall not want

an she scraping
de las crumbs
5   aff de plate
knowing ants will feed

maketh me to lie down
in green pastures
leadeth me beside de still
10 waters
an she han washing clothes
spotless

1–2 de . . . want: *Psalm* xxiii, quoted throughout the poem.

lifting dem outa de water
drying she han careful slow
15 pon she apron

restoreth my soul

she mixing
sugar
water
20 lime
she filling she favourite jug
de one wid de cool palm pattern

yea though I walk
troo de valley of de
25 shadow of death

she opening de fridge
de cowl stapping her breath
for a motion

I will fear no evil

30 she put een wah she want
tek out wah she want
shut de door

for thou art wid me
they rod an they staff
35 dey comfort me

an she looking wid a far eye
pon de picture a de children
side a de almanac
pon de wall

40 surely goodness an mercy
shall follow me

she pick up de broom
an she sweeping

all de days of my life

45 an she sweeping

an I will dwell
in de house of de Lord

she sweeping out
sweeping
50 out

shake de broom
in de wind
dus fly
she beat it gains de fence
55 dus fly
she cup she han
unda de pipe
an she sprinkle water
roun she
60 stan up
hans akimbo

she watching
all de dark spirits
departing wid de dus

65 sunrise in er eyes

forever
an ever

§ *Language usage* Bennett, Reid, Sparrow, Brathwaite (3), Bloom, Agard;
Women's colonization Brodber, Nichols; Af: Dangarembga

Part V

NEW ZEALAND AND SOUTH PACIFIC

KATHERINE MANSFIELD (1888–1923)

The Garden Party

And after all the weather was ideal. They could not have had a more perfect day for a garden party if they had ordered it. Windless, warm, the sky without a cloud. Only the blue was veiled with a haze of light gold, as it is sometimes in early summer. The gardener had been up since dawn, mowing the lawns and sweeping them, until the grass and the dark flat rosettes where the daisy plants had been seemed to shine. As for the roses, you could not help feeling they understood that roses are the only flowers that impress people at garden parties; the only flowers that everybody is certain of knowing. Hundreds, yes, literally hundreds, had come out in a single night; the green bushes bowed down as though they had been visited by archangels.

Breakfast was not yet over before the men came to put up the marquee.

'Where do you want the marquee put, mother?'

'My dear child, it's no use asking me. I'm determined to leave everything to you children this year. Forget I am your mother. Treat me as an honoured guest.'

But Meg could not possibly go and supervise the men. She had washed her hair before breakfast, and she sat drinking her coffee in a green turban, with a dark wet curl stamped on each cheek. Jose, the butterfly, always came down in a silk petticoat and a kimono jacket.

'You'll have to go, Laura; you're the artistic one.'

Away Laura flew, still holding her piece of bread-and-butter. It's so delicious to have an excuse for eating out of doors, and besides, she loved having to arrange things; she always felt she could do it so much better than anybody else.

Four men in their shirt-sleeves stood grouped together on the garden path. They carried staves covered with rolls of canvas, and they had big tool-bags slung on their backs. They looked impressive. Laura wished now that she was not holding that piece of bread-and-butter, but there was nowhere to put it, and she couldn't possibly throw it away. She blushed and tried to look severe and even a little bit short-sighted as she came up to them.

'Good morning,' she said, copying her mother's voice. But that sounded so fearfully affected that she was ashamed, and stammered like a little girl, 'Oh – er – have you come – is it about the marquee?'

'That's right, miss,' said the tallest of the men, a lanky, freckled fellow, and he shifted his tool-bag, knocked back his straw hat and smiled down at her. 'That's about it.'

His smile was so easy, so friendly, that Laura recovered. What nice eyes he had, small, but such a dark blue! And now she looked at the others, they were smiling too. 'Cheer up, we won't bite,' their smile seemed to say. How very nice workmen were! And what a beautiful morning! She mustn't mention the morning; she must be business-like. The marquee.

'Well, what about the lily-lawn? Would that do?'

And she pointed to the lily-lawn with the hand that didn't hold the bread-and-butter. They turned, they stared in the direction. A little fat chap thrust out his under-lip, and the tall fellow frowned.

'I don't fancy it,' said he. 'Not conspicuous enough. You see, with a thing like a marquee,' and he turned to Laura in his easy way, 'you want to put it somewhere where it'll give you a bang slap in the eye, if you follow me.'

Laura's upbringing made her wonder for a moment whether it was quite respectful of a workman to talk to her of bangs slap in the eye. But she did quite follow him.

'A corner of the tennis-court,' she suggested. 'But the band's going to be in one corner.'

'H'm, going to have a band, are you?' said another of the workmen. He was pale. He had a haggard look as his dark eyes scanned the tennis-court. What was he thinking?

'Only a very small band,' said Laura gently. Perhaps he wouldn't mind so much if the band was quite small. But the tall fellow interrupted.

'Look here, miss, that's the place. Against those trees. Over there. That'll do fine.'

Against the karakas. Then the karaka-trees would be hidden. And they were so lovely, with their broad, gleaming leaves, and their clusters of yellow fruit. They were like trees you imagined growing on a desert island, proud, solitary, lifting their leaves and fruits to the sun in a kind of silent splendour. Must they be hidden by a marquee?

They must. Already the men had shouldered their staves and were making for the place. Only the tall fellow was left. He bent down, pinched a sprig of lavender, put his thumb and forefinger to his nose and snuffed up the smell. When Laura saw that gesture she forgot all about the karakas in her wonder at him caring for things like that – caring for the smell of lavender. How many men that she knew would have done such a thing. Oh, how extraordinarily nice workmen were, she thought. Why couldn't she have workmen for friends rather than the silly boys she danced with and who came to Sunday night supper? She would get on much better with men like these.

It's all the fault, she decided, as the tall fellow drew something on the back of an envelope, something that was to be looped up or left to hang, of these absurd class distinctions. Well, for her part, she didn't feel them. Not a bit, not an atom . . . And now there came the chock-chock of wooden hammers. Someone whistled, someone sang out, 'Are you right there, matey?' 'Matey!' The friendliness of it, the – the – Just to prove how happy she was, just to show the tall fellow how at home she felt, and how she despised stupid conventions, Laura took a big bite of her bread-and-butter as she stared at the little drawing. She felt just like a workgirl.

'Laura, Laura, where are you? Telephone, Laura!' a voice cried from the house.

'Coming!' Away she skimmed, over the lawn, up the path, up the steps, across the veranda, and into the porch. In the hall her father and Laurie were brushing their hats ready to go to the office.

'I say, Laura,' said Laurie very fast, 'you might just give a squiz at my coat before this afternoon. See if it wants pressing.'

'I will,' said she. Suddenly she couldn't stop herself. She ran at Laurie and gave him a small, quick squeeze. 'Oh, I do love parties, don't you?' gasped Laura.

'Ra-ther,' said Laurie's warm, boyish voice, and he squeezed his sister too, and gave her a gentle push. 'Dash off to the telephone, old girl. '

The telephone. 'Yes, yes; oh yes. Kitty? Good morning, dear. Come to lunch? Do, dear. Delighted of course. It will only be a very scratch meal – just the sandwich crusts and broken meringue-shells and what's left over. Yes, isn't it a perfect morning? Your white? Oh, I certainly should. One moment – hold the line. Mother's calling.' And Laura sat back. 'What, mother? Can't hear.'

Mrs Sheridan's voice floated down the stairs. 'Tell her to wear that sweet hat she had on last Sunday.'

'Mother says you're to wear that sweet hat you had on last Sunday. Good. One o'clock. Bye-bye.'

Laura put back the receiver, flung her arms over her head, took a deep breath, stretched and let them fall. 'Huh,' she sighed, and the moment after the sigh she sat up quickly. She was still, listening. All the doors in the house seemed to be open. The house was alive with soft, quick steps and running voices. The green baize door that led to the kitchen regions swung open and shut with a muffled thud. And now there came a long, chuckling absurd sound. It was the heavy piano being moved on its stiff castors. But the air! If you stopped to notice, was the air always like this? Little faint winds were playing chase in at the tops of the windows, out at the doors. And there were two tiny spots of sun, one on the inkpot, one on a silver photograph frame, playing too. Darling little spots. Especially the one on the inkpot lid. It was quite warm. A warm little silver star. She could have kissed it.

The front door bell pealed, and there sounded the rustle of Sadie's print skirt on the stairs. A man's voice murmured; Sadie answered, careless, 'I'm sure I don't know. Wait. I'll ask Mrs Sheridan.'

'What is it, Sadie?' Laura came into the hall.

'It's the florist, Miss Laura.'

It was, indeed. There, just inside the door, stood a wide, shallow tray full of pots of pink lilies. No other kind. Nothing but lilies – canna lilies, big pink flowers, wide open, radiant, almost frighteningly alive on bright crimson stems.

'O-oh, Sadie!' said Laura, and the sound was like a little moan. She crouched down as if to warm herself at that blaze of lilies; she felt they were in her fingers, on her lips, growing in her breast.

'It's some mistake,' she said faintly. 'Nobody ever ordered so many. Sadie, go and find mother.'

But at that moment Mrs Sheridan joined them.

'It's quite right,' she said calmly. 'Yes, I ordered them. Aren't they lovely?' She pressed Laura's arm. 'I was passing the shop yesterday, and I saw them in the window. And I suddenly thought for once in my life I shall have enough canna lilies. The garden party will be a good excuse.'

'But I thought you said you didn't mean to interfere,' said Laura. Sadie had gone. The florist's man was still outside at his van. She put her arm round her mother's neck and gently, very gently, she bit her mother's ear.

'My darling child, you wouldn't like a logical mother, would you? Don't do that. Here's the man.'

He carried more lilies still, another whole tray.

'Bank them up, just inside the door, on both sides of the porch, please,' said Mrs Sheridan. 'Don't you agree, Laura?'

'Oh, I *do*, mother.'

In the drawing-room Meg, Jose and good little Hans had at last succeeded in moving the piano.

'Now, if we put this chesterfield against the wall and move everything out of the room except the chairs, don't you think?'

'Quite.'

'Hans, move these tables into the smoking-room, and bring a sweeper to take these marks off the carpet and – one moment, Hans –' Jose loved giving orders to the servants, and they loved obeying her. She always made them feel they were taking part in some drama.'Tell mother and Miss Laura to come here at once.'

'Very good, Miss Jose.'

She turned to Meg. 'I want to hear what the piano sounds like, just in case I'm asked to sing this afternoon. Let's try over "This Life is Weary".'

Pom! Ta-ta-ta *Tee*-ta! The piano burst out so passionately that Jose's face changed. She clasped her hands. She looked mournfully and enigmatically at her mother and Laura as they came in.

> This Life is *Wee*-ary,
> A Tear – a Sigh.
> A Love that *Chan*-ges,
> This Life is Wee-ary,
> A Tear – a Sigh.
> A Love that *Chan*-ges,
> And then . . . Good-bye!

But at the word 'Goodbye', and although the piano sounded more desperate than ever, her face broke into a brilliant, dreadfully unsympathetic smile.

'Aren't I in good voice, mummy?' she beamed.

> This Life is *Wee*-ary,
> Hope comes to Die.
> A Dream – a *Wa*-kening.

But now Sadie interrupted them. 'What is it, Sadie?'

'If you please, m'm, cook says have you got the flags for the sandwiches?'

'The flags for the sandwiches, Sadie?' echoed Mrs Sheridan dreamily. And the children knew by her face that she hadn't got them. 'Let me see.' And she said to Sadie firmly, 'Tell cook I'll let her have them in ten minutes.'

Sadie went.

'Now, Laura,' said her mother quickly, 'come with me into the smoking-room. I've got the names somewhere on the back of an envelope. You'll have to write them out for me. Meg, go upstairs this minute and take that wet thing off your head. Jose, run and finish dressing this instant. Do you hear me, children, or shall I have to tell your father when he comes home tonight? And – and, Jose, pacify cook if you do go into the kitchen, will you? I'm terrified of her this morning.'

The envelope was found at last behind the dining-room clock, though how it had got there Mrs Sheridan could not imagine.

'One of you children must have stolen it out of my bag, because I remember vividly – cream-cheese and lemon-curd. Have you done that?'

'Yes.'

'Egg and –' Mrs Sheridan held the envelope away from her. 'It looks like mice. It can't be mice, can it?'

'Olive, pet,' said Laura, looking over her shoulder.

'Yes, of course, olive. What a horrible combination it sounds. Egg and olive.'

They were finished at last, and Laura took them off to the kitchen. She found Jose there pacifying the cook, who did not look at all terrifying.

'I have never seen such exquisite sandwiches,' said Jose's rapturous voice. 'How many kinds did you say there were, cook? Fifteen?'

'Fifteen, Miss Jose.'

'Well, cook, I congratulate you.'

Cook swept up crusts with the long sandwich knife and smiled broadly.

'Godber's has come,' announced Sadie, issuing out of the pantry. She had seen the man pass the window.

That meant the cream puffs had come. Godber's were famous for their cream puffs. Nobody ever thought of making them at home.

'Bring them in and put them on the table, my girl,' ordered cook.

Sadie brought them in and went back to the door. Of course Laura and Jose were far too grown-up to really care about such things. All the same, they couldn't help agreeing that the puffs looked very attractive. Very. Cook began arranging them, shaking off the extra icing sugar.

'Don't they carry one back to all one's parties?' said Laura.

'I suppose they do,' said practical Jose, who never liked to be carried back. 'They look beautifully light and feathery, I must say.'

'Have one each, my dears,' said cook in her comfortable voice. 'Yer ma won't know.'

Oh, impossible. Fancy cream puffs so soon after breakfast. The very idea made one shudder. All the same, two minutes later Jose and Laura were licking their fingers with that absorbed inward look that only comes from whipped cream.

'Let's go into the garden, out by the back way,' suggested Laura. 'I want to see how the men are getting on with the marquee. They're such awfully nice men.'

But the back door was blocked by cook, Sadie, Godber's man and Hans. Something had happened.

'Tuk-tuk-tuk,' clucked cook like an agitated hen. Sadie had her hand clapped to her cheek as though she had toothache. Hans's face was screwed up in the effort to understand. Only Godber's man seemed to be enjoying himself; it was his story.

'What's the matter? What's happened?'

'There's been a horrible accident,' said cook. 'A man killed.'

'A man killed! Where? How? When?'

But Godber's man wasn't going to have his story snatched from under his very nose.

'Know those little cottages just below here, miss?' Know them? Of course, she knew them. 'Well, there's a young chap living there, name of Scott, a carter. His horse shied at a traction-engine, corner of Hawke Street this morning, and he was thrown out on the back of his head. Killed.'

'Dead!' Laura stared at Godber's man.

'Dead when they picked him up,' said Godber's man with relish. 'They were taking the body home as I come up here.' And he said to the cook, 'He's left a wife and five little ones.'

'Jose, come here.' Laura caught hold of her sister's sleeve and dragged her through the kitchen to the other side of the green baize door. There she paused and leaned against it. 'Jose!' she said, horrified, 'however are we going to stop everything?'

'Stop everything, Laura!' cried Jose in astonishment. 'What do you mean?'

'Stop the garden party, of course.' Why did Jose pretend?

But Jose was still more amazed. 'Stop the garden party? My dear Laura, don't be so absurd. Of course we can't do anything of the kind. Nobody expects us to. Don't be so extravagant.'

'But we can't possibly have a garden party with a man dead just outside the front gate.'

That really was extravagant, for the little cottages were in a lane to themselves at the very bottom of a steep rise that led up to the house. A broad road ran between. True, they were far too near. They were the greatest possible eyesore, and they had no right to be in that neighbourhood at all. They were little mean dwellings painted a chocolate brown. In the garden patches there was nothing but cabbage stalks, sick hens and tomato canes. The very smoke coming out of their chimneys was poverty-stricken. Little rags and shreds of smoke, so unlike the great silvery plumes that uncurled from the Sheridans' chimneys. Washerwomen lived in the lane and sweeps and a cobbler, and a man whose housefront was studded all over with minute bird-cages. Children swarmed. When the Sheridans were little they were forbidden to set foot there because of the revolting language and of what they might catch. But since they were grown up, Laura and Laurie on their prowls sometimes walked through. It was disgusting and sordid. They came out with a shudder. But still one must go everywhere; one must see everything. So through they went.

'And just think of what the band would sound like to that poor woman,' said Laura.

'Oh, Laura!' Jose began to be seriously annoyed. 'If you're going to stop a band playing every time someone has an accident, you'll lead a very strenuous life. I'm every bit as sorry about it as you. I feel just as sympathetic.' Her eyes hardened. She looked at her sister just as she used to when they were little and fighting together. 'You won't bring a drunken workman back to life by being sentimental,' she said softly.

'Drunk! Who said he was drunk?' Laura turned furiously on Jose. She said just as they had used to say on those occasions, 'I'm going straight up to tell mother.'

'Do, dear,' cooed Jose.

'Mother, can I come into your room?' Laura turned the big glass doorknob.

'Of course, child. Why, what's the matter? What's given you such a colour?' And Mrs Sheridan turned round from her dressing-table. She was trying on a new hat.

'Mother, a man's been killed,' began Laura.

'*Not* in the garden?' interrupted her mother.

'No, no!'

'Oh, what a fright you gave me!' Mrs Sheridan sighed with relief, and took off the big hat and held it on her knees.

'But listen, mother,' said Laura. Breathless, half-choking, she told the dreadful story. 'Of course, we can't have our party, can we?' she pleaded. 'The band and everybody arriving. They'd hear us, mother; they're nearly neighbours!'

To Laura's astonishment her mother behaved just like Jose; it was harder to bear because she seemed amused. She refused to take Laura seriously.

'But, my dear child, use your common sense. It's only by accident we've heard of it. If someone had died there normally – and I can't understand how they keep alive in those poky little holes – we should still be having our party, shouldn't we?'

Laura had to say 'yes' to that, but she felt it was all wrong. She sat down on her mother's sofa and pinched the cushion frill.

'Mother, isn't it really terribly heartless of us?' she asked.

'Darling!' Mrs Sheridan got up and came over to her, carrying the hat. Before Laura could stop her she had popped it on. 'My child!' said her mother, 'the hat is yours. It's made for you. It's much too young for me. I have never seen you look such a picture. Look at yourself!' And she held up her hand-mirror.

'But, mother,' Laura began again. She couldn't look at herself; she turned aside.

This time Mrs Sheridan lost patience just as Jose had done.

'You are being very absurd, Laura,' she said coldly. 'People like that don't expect sacrifices from us. And it's not very sympathetic to spoil everybody's enjoyment as you're doing now.'

'I don't understand,' said Laura, and she walked quickly out of the room into her own bedroom. There, quite by chance, the first thing she saw was this charming girl in the mirror, in her black hat trimmed with gold daisies, and a long black velvet ribbon. Never had she imagined she could look like that. Is mother right? she thought. And now she hoped her mother was right. Am I being extravagant? Perhaps it was extravagant. Just for a moment she had another glimpse of that poor woman and those little children, and the body being carried into the house. But it all seemed blurred, unreal, like a picture in the newspaper. I'll remember it again after the party's over, she decided. And somehow that seemed quite the best plan . . .

Lunch was over by half past one. By half past two they were all ready for the fray. The green-coated band had arrived and was established in a corner of the tennis-court.

'My dear!' trilled Kitty Maitland, 'aren't they too like frogs for words? You ought to have arranged them round the pond with the conductor in the middle on a leaf.'

Laurie arrived and hailed them on his way to dress. At the sight of him Laura remembered the accident again. She wanted to tell him. If Laurie agreed with the others, then it was bound to be all right. And she followed him into the hall.

'Laurie!'

'Hallo!' He was half-way upstairs, but when he turned round and saw Laura he suddenly puffed out his cheeks and goggled his eyes at her. 'My word, Laura! You do look stunning,' said Laurie. 'What an absolutely topping hat!'

Laura said faintly 'Is it?' and smiled up at Laurie, and didn't tell him after all.

Soon after that people began coming in streams. The band struck up; the hired waiters ran from the house to the marquee. Wherever you looked there were couples strolling, bending to the flowers, greeting, moving on over the lawn. They were like bright birds that had alighted in the Sheridans' garden for this one afternoon, on their way to – where! Ah, what happiness it is to be with people who all are happy, to press hands, press cheeks, smile into eyes.

'Darling Laura, how well you look!'

'What a becoming hat, child!'

'Laura, you look quite Spanish. I've never seen you look so striking.'

And Laura, glowing, answered softly, 'Have you had tea? Won't you have an ice? The passion-fruit ices really are rather special.' She ran to her father and begged him. 'Daddy darling, can't the band have something to drink?'

And the perfect afternoon slowly ripened, slowly faded, slowly its petals closed.

'Never a more delightful garden-party ...' 'The greatest success...' 'Quite the most...'

Laura helped her mother with the goodbyes. They stood side by side in the porch till it was all over.

'All over, all over, thank heaven,' said Mrs Sheridan. 'Round up the others, Laura. Let's go and have some fresh coffee. I'm exhausted. Yes, it's been very successful. But oh, these parties, these parties! Why will you children insist on giving parties!' And they all of them sat down in the deserted marquee.

'Have a sandwich, daddy dear. I wrote the flag.'

'Thanks.' Mr Sheridan took a bite and the sandwich was gone. He took another. 'I suppose you didn't hear of a beastly accident that happened today?' he said.

'My dear,' said Mrs Sheridan, holding up her hand, 'we did. It nearly ruined the party. Laura insisted we should put it off.'

'Oh, mother!' Laura didn't want to be teased about it.

'It was a horrible affair all the same,' said Mr Sheridan. 'The chap was married too. Lived just below in the lane, and leaves a wife and half a dozen kiddies, so they say.'

An awkward little silence fell. Mrs Sheridan fidgeted with her cup. Really, it was very tactless of father ...

Suddenly she looked up. There on the table were all those sandwiches, cakes, puffs, all un-eaten, all going to be wasted. She had one of her brilliant ideas.

'I know,' she said. 'Let's make up a basket. Let's send that poor creature some of this perfectly good food. At any rate, it will be the greatest treat for the children. Don't you agree? And she's sure to have neighbours calling in and so on. What a point to have it all ready prepared. Laura!' She jumped up. 'Get me the big basket out of the stairs cupboard.'

'But, mother, do you really think it's a good idea?' said Laura.

Again, how curious, she seemed to be different from them all. To take scraps from their party. Would the poor woman really like that?

'Of course! What's the matter with you today? An hour or two ago you were insisting on us being sympathetic, and now –'

Oh well! Laura ran for the basket. It was filled, it was heaped by her mother.

'Take it yourself, darling,' said she. 'Run down just as you are. No, wait, take the arum lilies too. People of that class are so impressed by arum lilies.'

'The sterns will ruin her lace frock,' said practical Jose.

So they would. Just in time. 'Only the basket, then. And, Laura!' – her mother followed her out of the marquee – 'don't on any account –'

'What mother?'

No, better not put such ideas into the child's head! 'Nothing! Run along.'

It was just growing dusky as Laura shut their garden gates. A big dog ran by like a shadow. The road gleamed white, and down below in the hollow the little cottages were in deep shade. How quiet it seemed after the afternoon. Here she was going down the hill to somewhere where a man lay dead, and she couldn't realize it. Why couldn't she? She stopped a minute. And it seemed to her that kisses, voices, tinkling spoons, laughter, the smell of crushed grass were somehow inside her. She had no room for anything else. How strange! She looked up at the pale sky, and all she thought was, 'Yes, it was the most successful party.'

Now the broad road was crossed. The lane began, smoky and dark. Women in shawls and men's tweed caps hurried by. Men hung over the palings; the children played in the doorways. A low hum came from the mean little cottages. In some of them there was a flicker of light, and a shadow, crab-like, moved across the window. Laura bent her head and hurried on. She wished now she had put on a coat. How her frock shone! And the big hat with the velvet streamer – if only it was another hat! Were the people looking at her? They must be. It was a mistake to have come; she knew all along it was a mistake. Should she go back even now?

No, too late. This was the house. It must be. A dark knot of people stood outside. Beside the gate an old, old woman with a crutch sat in a chair, watching. She had her feet on a newspaper. The voices stopped as Laura drew near. The group parted. It was as though she was expected, as though they had known she was coming here.

Laura was terribly nervous. Tossing the velvet ribbon over her shoulder, she said to a woman standing by, 'Is this Mrs Scott's house?' and the woman, smiling queerly, said, 'It is, my lass.'

Oh, to be away from this! She actually said, 'Help me, God,' as she walked up the tiny path and knocked. To be away from those staring eyes, or to be covered up in anything, one of those women's shawls even. I'll just leave the basket and go, she decided. I shan't even wait for it to be emptied.

Then the door opened. A little woman in black showed in the gloom.

Laura said, 'Are you Mrs Scott?' But to her horror the woman answered, 'Walk in, please, miss,' and she was shut in the passage.

'No,' said Laura, 'I don't want to come in. I only want to leave this basket. Mother sent –'

The little woman in the gloomy passage seemed not to have heard her. 'Step this way, please, miss,' she said in an oily voice, and Laura followed her.

She found herself in a wretched little low kitchen, lighted by a smoky lamp. There was a woman sitting before the fire.

'Em,' said the little creature who had let her in. 'Em! It's a young lady.' She turned to Laura. She said meaningly, 'I'm 'er sister, miss. You'll excuse 'er, won't you?'

'Oh, but of course!' said Laura. 'Please, please don't disturb her. I – I only want to leave –'

But at that moment the woman at the fire turned round. Her face, puffed up, red, with swollen eyes and swollen lips, looked terrible. She seemed as though she couldn't understand why Laura was there. What did it mean? Why was this stranger standing in the kitchen with a basket? What was it all about? And the poor face puckered up again.

'All right, my dear,' said the other. 'I'll thenk the young lady.'

And again she began, 'You'll excuse her, miss, I'm sure,' and her face, swollen too, tried an oily smile.

Laura only wanted to get out, to get away. She was back in the passage. The door opened. She walked straight through into the bedroom where the dead man was lying.

'You'd like a look at 'im, wouldn't you?' said Em's sister, and she brushed past Laura over to the bed. 'Don't be afraid, my lass,' – and now her voice sounded fond and sly, and fondly she drew down the sheet – ' 'e looks a picture. There's nothing to show. Come along, my dear.'

Laura came.

There lay a young man, fast asleep – sleeping so soundly, so deeply, that he was far, far away from them both. Oh, so remote, so peaceful. He was dreaming. Never wake him up again. His head was sunk in the pillow, his eyes were closed; they were blind under the closed eyelids. He was given up to his dream. What did garden parties and baskets and lace frocks matter to him? He was far from all those things. He was wonderful, beautiful. While they were laughing and while the band was playing, this marvel had come to the lane. Happy . . . happy . . . All is well, said that sleeping face. This is just as it should be. I am content.

But all the same you had to cry, and she couldn't go out of the room without saying something to him. Laura gave a loud childish sob.

'Forgive my hat,' she said.

And this time she didn't wait for Em's sister. She found her way out of the door, down the path, past all those dark people. At the corner of the lane she met Laurie.

He stepped out of the shadow. 'Is that you, Laura?'

'Yes.'

'Mother was getting anxious. Was it all right?'

'Yes, quite. Oh, Laurie!' She took his arm, she pressed up against him.

'I say, you're not crying, are you?' asked her brother.

Laura shook her head. She was.

Laurie put his arm round her shoulder. 'Don't cry,' he said in his warm, loving voice. 'Was it awful?'

'No,' sobbed Laura. 'It was simply marvellous. But, Laurie –' She stopped, she looked at her brother. 'Isn't life,' she stammered, 'isn't life –' But what life was she couldn't explain. No matter. He quite understood.

'*Isn't* it, darling?' said Laurie.

§ *A Reworking of this Story* Ihimaera (2)

MARY URSULA BETHELL (1874–1945)

Pause

When I am very earnestly digging
I lift my head sometimes, and look at the mountains,
And muse upon them, muscles relaxing.

I think how freely the wild grasses flower there,
5   How grandly the storm-shaped trees are massed in their
      gorges
And the rain-worn rocks strewn in magnificent heaps.

Pioneer plants on those uplands find their own footing;
No vigorous growth, there, is an evil weed:
All weathers are salutary.

10   It is only a little while since this hillside
Lay untrammelled likewise,
Unceasingly swept by transmarine winds.

In a very little while, it may be,
When our impulsive limbs and our superior skulls
15   Have to the soil restored several ounces of fertilizer,

The Mother of all will take charge again,
And soon wipe away with her elements
Our small fond human enclosures.

§ *Ambivalent settlement* Fairburn (1), Curnow (1, 2)

R. A. K. MASON (1905–71)

On the Swag*

His body doubled
    under the pack
    that sprawls untidily
    on his old back
5   the cold wet dead-beat
    plods up the track.

---

* Swag: bundle (of possessions).

The cook peers out:
   'oh curse that old lag –
here again
10   with his clumsy swag
made of a dirty old
turnip bag.'

'Bring him in cook
from the grey level sleet
15   put silk on his body
slippers on his feet,
give him fire
and bread and meat.

Let the fruit be plucked
20   and the cake be iced,
the bed be snug
and the wine be spiced
in the old cove's night-cap:
for this is Christ.'

§ *Itinerant swagmen* Aus: Lawson (1), Baynton

A. R. D. FAIRBURN (1904–57)

1: Imperial

In the first days, in the forgotten calendars,
came the seeds of the race, the forerunners:
offshoots, outcasts, entrepreneurs,
architects of Empire, romantic adventurers;
5   and the famished, the multitude of the poor;
crossed parallels of boredom, tropics
of hope and fear, losing the pole-star, suffering
world of water, chaos of wind and sunlight,
and the formless image in the mind;
10   sailed under Capricorn to see for ever
the arc of the sun to northward.

They shouted at the floating leaf,
laughed with joy at the promise of life,
hope becoming belief, springing

15 alive, alight, gulls at the masthead crying,
    the crag splitting the sky, slowly
    towering out of the sea, taking
    colour and shape, and the land
    swelling beyond; noises
20 of water among rocks, voices singing.

    Haven of hunger; landfall of hope;
    goal of ambition, greed and despair.

    In tangled forests under the gloom
    of leaves in the green twilight,
25 among the habitations of the older gods
    they walked, with Christ beside them,
    and an old enemy at hand, one whose creed
    flourished in virgin earth. They divided the land;
    some for their need, and some
30 for aimless, customary greed
    that hardened with the years, grew taut
    and knotted like a fist. Flower and weed
    scattered upon the breeze
    their indiscriminate seed; on every hillside fought
35 God's love against the old antagonist.
    They change the sky but not their hearts who cross the seas.

    These islands;
    the remnant peaks of a lost continent,
    roof of an old world, molten droppings
40 from earth's bowels, gone cold;
    ribbed with rock, resisting the sea's corrosion
    for an age, and an age to come. Of three races
    the home: two passing in conquest
    or sitting under the leaves, or on shady doorsteps
45 with quiet hands, in old age, childless.
    And we, the latest: their blood on our hands: scions
    of men who scaled ambition's
    tottering slopes, whose desires
    encompassed earth and heaven: we have prospered greatly,
50 we, the destined race, rulers of conquered isles,
    sprouting like bulbs in warm darkness, putting out
    white shoots under the wet sack of Empire.

§ *Ambivalent settlement* Bethell, Curnow (1, 2)

2: Tapu*

To stave off disaster, or bring the devil to heel,
　　or to fight against fear, some carry a ring or a locket,
but I, who have nothing to lose by the turn of the wheel,
　　and nothing to gain, I carry the world in my pocket.

5　For all I have gained, and have lost, is locked up in this
　　　　　thing,
　　this cup of cracked bone from the skull of a fellow long
　　　　　dead,
with a hank of thin yellowish hair fastened in with a ring.
For a symbol of death and desire these tokens are wed.

The one I picked out of a cave in a windy cliff-face
10　　where the old Maoris slept, with a curse on the stranger
　　　　　who moved,
in despite of tapu, but a splinter of bone from that place.
The other I cut from the head of the woman I loved.

§ *Response to Maori culture* Hyde, Baxter (3)

ROBIN HYDE (1906–39)

The Last Ones

But the last black horse of all
Stood munching the green-bud wind,
And the last of the raupo huts
Let down its light behind.
5　Sullen and shadow-clipped
He tugged at the evening star,
New-mown silvers swished like straw
Across the manuka.

As for the hut, it said
10　No word but its meagre light,
Its people slept as the dead,
Bedded in Maori night.
'And there is the world's last door,
And the last world's horse,' sang the wind,

---

* **Tapu**: the sacred or forbidden.
3 raupo: bulrush.

8 manuka: common New Zealand shrub, usually
known as tea-tree.

15   'With little enough before,
      And what you have seen behind.'

§ *Elegies for Aboriginality* Ihimaera (1); Aus: Kendall, Oodgeroo; Can:
Armstrong

ALLEN CURNOW (1911–)

1: House and Land

       Wasn't this the site, asked the historian,
       Of the original homestead?
       Couldn't tell you, said the cowman;
       I just live here, he said,
5   Working for old Miss Wilson
       Since the old man's been dead.

       Moping under the bluegums
       The dog trailed his chain
       From the privy as far as the fowlhouse
10   And back to the privy again,
       Feeling the stagnant afternoon
       Quicken with the smell of rain.

       There sat old Miss Wilson,
       With her pictures on the wall,
15   The baronet uncle, mother's side,
       And one she called The Hall;
       Taking tea from a silver pot
       For fear the house might fall.

       People in the *colonies*, she said,
20   Can't quite understand . . .
       Why, from Waiau to the mountains
       It was all father's land.

       She's all of eighty said the cowman,
       Down at the milking-shed.
25   I'm leaving here next winter.
       Too bloody quiet, he said.

       The spirit of exile, wrote the historian,
       Is strong in the people still.

He reminds me rather, said Miss Wilson,
30   Of Harriet's youngest, Will.

The cowman, home from the shed, went drinking
With the rabbiter home from the hill.

The sensitive nor'west afternoon
Collapsed, and the rain came;
35   The dog crept into his barrel
Looking lost and lame.
But you can't attribute to either
Awareness of what great gloom
Stands in a land of settlers
40   With never a soul at home.

§ *Ambivalent settlement* Bethell, Fairburn (1), Curnow (2)

2: Landfall in Unknown Seas

*The 300th Anniversary of the Discovery of New Zealand
by Abel Tasman, 13 December, 1642*

I
Simply by sailing in a new direction
You could enlarge the world.
                    You picked your captain,
Keen on discoveries, tough enough to make them,
5   Whatever vessels could be spared from other
More urgent service for a year's adventure;
Took stock of the more probable conjectures
About the Unknown to be traversed, all
Guesses at golden coasts and tales of monsters
10   To be digested into plain instructions
For likely and unlikely situations.

All this resolved and done, you launched the whole
On a fine morning, the best time of year,
Skies widening and the oceanic furies
15   Subdued by summer illumination; time
To go and to be gazed at going
On a fine morning, in the Name of God
Into the nameless waters of the world.

O you had estimated all the chances

20 Of business in those waters, the world's waters
    Yet unexploited.
                        But more than the sea-empire's
    Cannon, the dogs of bronze and iron barking
    From Timor to the Straits, backed up the challenge.
25 Between you and the South an older enmity
    Lodged in the searching mind, that would not tolerate
    So huge a hegemony of ignorance.
    There, where your Indies had already sprinkled
    Their tribes like ocean rains, you aimed your voyage;
30 Like them invoked your God, gave seas to history
    And islands to new hazardous tomorrows.

    II
    Suddenly exhilaration
    Went off like a gun, the whole
    Horizon, the long chase done,
35 Hove to. There was the seascape
    Crammed with coast, surprising
    As new lands will, the sailor
    Moving on the face of the waters,
    Watching the earth take shape
40 Round the unearthly summits, brighter
    Than its emerging colour

    Yet this, no far fool's errand,
    Was less than the heart desired,
    In its old Indian dream
45 The glittering gulfs ascending
    Past palaces and mountains
    Making one architecture.
    Here the uplifted structure,
    Peak and pillar of cloud –
50 O splendour of desolation – reared
    Tall from the pit of the swell,
    With a shadow, a finger of wind, forbade
    Hopes of a lucky landing.

    Always to islanders danger
55 Is what comes over the sea;
    Over the yellow sands and the clear
    Shallows, the dull filament
    Flickers, the blood of strangers:
    Death discovered the Sailor
60 O in a flash, in a flat calm,

A clash of boats in the bay
And the day marred with murder.
The dead required no further
Warning to keep their distance;
65 The rest, noting the failure,
Pushed on with a reconnnaissance
To the north; and sailed away.

III

Well, home is the Sailor, and that is a chapter
In a schoolbook, a relevant yesterday
70 We thought we knew all about, being much apter
    To profit, sure of our ground,
No murderers mooring in our Golden Bay.

But now there are no more islands to be found
And the eye scans risky horizons of its own
75 In unsettled weather, and murmurs of the drowned
    Haunt their familiar beaches –
Who navigates us towards what unknown

But not improbable provinces? Who reaches
A future down for us from the high shelf
80 Of spiritual daring? Not those speeches
    Pinning on the Past like a decoration
For merit that congratulates itself,

O not the self-important celebration
Or most painstaking history, can release
85 The current of a discoverer's elation
    And silence the voices saying,
'Here is the world's end where wonders cease.'

Only by a more faithful memory, laying
On him the half-light of a diffident glory,
90 The Sailor lives, and stands beside us, paying
    Out into our time's wave
The stain of blood that writes an island story.

§ *Ambivalent settlement* Fairburn (1), Curnow (1); *'Discovery' of 'new' worlds*
Aus: McAuley; Can: MacEwen, King

JAMES BAXTER (1926–72)

1: On the Death of Her Body

It is a thought breaking the granite heart
Time has given me, that my one treasure,
Your limbs, those passion-vines, that bamboo body

Should age and slacken, rot
5   Some day in a ghastly clay-stopped hole.
They led me to the mountains beyond pleasure

Where each is not gross body or blank soul
But a strong harp the wind of genesis
Makes music in, such resonant music

10   That I was Adam, loosened by your kiss
From time's hard bond, and you,
My love, in the world's first summer stood

Plucking the flowers of the abyss.

2: Jerusalem Sonnet, I

The small grey cloudy louse that nests in my beard
Is not, as some have called it, 'a pearl of God' –

No, it is a fiery tormentor
Waking me at two a.m.

5   Or thereabouts, when the lights are still on
In the houses in the pa, to go across thick grass

Wet with rain, feet cold, to kneel
For an hour or two in front of the red flickering

Tabernacle light – what He sees inside
10   My meandering mind I can only guess –

A madman, a nobody, a raconteur
Whom He can joke with – 'Lord,' I ask Him,

---

6 pa: Maori camp or village.

'Do You or don't You expect me to put up with lice?'
His silent laugh still shakes the hills at dawn.

3: The Ikons

Hard, heavy, slow, dark,
Or so I find them, the hands of Te Whaea

Teaching me to die. Some lightness will come later
When the heart has lost its unjust hope

5   For special treatment. Today I go with a bucket
Over the paddocks of young grass,

So delicate like fronds of maidenhair,
Looking for mushrooms. I find twelve of them,

Most of them little, and some eaten by maggots,
10   But they'll do to add to the soup. It's a long time now

Since the great ikons fell down,
God, Mary, home, sex, poetry,

Whatever one uses as a bridge
To cross the river that only has one beach,

15 And even one's name is a way of saying –
'This gap inside a coat' – the darkness I call God,

The darkness I call Te Whaea, how can they translate
The blue calm evening sky that a plane tunnels through

Like a little wasp, or the bucket in my hand,
20 Into something else? I go on looking

For mushrooms in the field, and the fist of longing
Punches my heart, until it is too dark to see.

§ *Response to Maori culture* Fairburn (2), Hyde

---

2 **Te Whaea**: the Mother.

HONE TUWHARE (1922–)

Speak to Me, Brother

Brother!
Brother, don't push past me as if
I got the bad sores or something.
What's the rush: you on a promise?
5   You just finished night-shift? I see.
Funny how the City life cuts us down
the middle, brother. Seems like
the day and the night don't belong to
one another anymore. No, wait!

10   Look, if you was really going somewhere
you wouldn't go past me like I was a
kehua, see?
I want to talk: *korero* brother. It's the
old way: still good. So what the hell
15   if we're both late, eh?

You just joined up? I'll be damned.
You passed your medical: next week they
stick you in a uniform
Tell me brother, how does it make you
20   feel? Like Superman?
I see: You just like to feel the gun kick
in your hands, like: POW! POW! POW! POW!
You're *porangi* alright.

Hell I'd rather feel a woman buck and
25   twist –
Dominate? That's a big word, brother.
You lie it against a big hill: a fat storm
maybe?
Is *that* right.
30   You don't want them to dominate us?

Like, they're going to paddle down here on
the wooden sampans, eat all our pork-bones
and puha: fork out ninety cents for a
mutton-bird.

---

12 **kehua**: ghost.   13 **korero**: conversation; debate.
23 **porangi**: demented.   33 **puha**: edible wild green; sow-thistle.
34 **mutton-bird**: sooty shearwater; long-winged seabird.

35 Hell, you think those farmers are sick of
growing rice?

Look here, those rice farmers have got a
big feeling for their own land: their own
food: their own gods. Listen:
40 (sing) *Planting rice is not much fun*
If you have to carry a gun
When they come down out of the blue
Then you have to plant them too

Taihoa, brother, *taihoa*.
45 Like, it's a crime to knock the wood-pigeon
out of the trees: big fine if you're caught,
right?
No crime though, if you're a soldier. They
pay you good money to blast the farmer and
50 his wife and kids out of the bush: put his
straw house up in smoke. Great you know.

Windy? Hell brother, I'm shit scared

Defend the 'Free World?'
That holy Cow and Sheep College never taught
55 you much.
Help the 'Stars and Stripes'?
Fuck-sake, man: they can BUY and SELL us.
And don't wave *that* flag at me. You're chasing
a bad dream: a bad dream, brother.

60 Turn around.
See the sun come up? Bang on, eh?
That's the kind I want to see every morning,
come up. Not the kind they make with the
flash bomb, the steak and mushrooms.

65 See the mountain, brother?
You know as well as me our old people gave
that big heap of scoria a name, right?
That makes the mountain real: real, like us,
see?
70 And if you have to salute somebody, salute
the mountain, brother.

---

44 *taihoa*: wait.

If you have to take your *potae* off to someone,
let it be to the mountain, like the proverb
tells us

75   You speak, brother

§ *Language usage* Af: Ngugi (2); Carib: Braithwaite (3), Bloom; SEA:
Mohamad Bin Haji Salleh

FRANK SARGESON (1902–82)

I've Lost My Pal

It was early summer, shearing time. Tom and me went into the country and
we got a job picking up fleeces in a big shed. After we'd pulled the bellies
off the fleeces we had to roll them up and put them in the press. It was a
good job. We liked it. We had to work hard and we got covered in sheep
grease, but I'll tell you a thing about sheep grease. It comes off best in cold
water. And that saves a lot of bother.

I could tell you a lot of things about that shed. You know a lot of lambs
are beggars for not sitting still when you're shearing them. There was a
shearer who used to go maggoty[1] if a lamb wouldn't sit still. He'd heave it
back into the pen. But it's not about the shed I want to tell you. I want to
tell you about how I lost my pal Tom.

The shearers used to get tireder than Tom and me did. Evenings they
were done in. And most evenings they drank beer and that helped to make
them sleepy. All except one. His name was George and he was the one who
used to heave the lambs back into the pen. He'd come outside with Tom
and me, and we'd sit on the woodpile and smoke cigarettes and tell yarns.
Another thing, he'd stand in a tub and wash himself, then he'd dress up.
Yes, he'd put on a stiff collar and a go-to-Jesus[2] tie. All to come and sit on
the woodpile with Tom and me. We used to think it was funny. He liked
himself, we thought. He used to wash himself in the tub in front of everybody, and he was pleased at the things we used to say about the different
parts of him. He had a corker body anyhow.

Well, we used to sit on that woodpile just about every night. I don't know
why. It was hot in the kitchen anyhow, and nice and cool out on the woodpile. And of course we were just a couple of kids, and I suppose we felt a
bit shy among all those shearers. George used to come and sit there and tell
us a lot of yarns. He'd spend a lot of time filing his nails too, and running
a comb through his hair. He always wanted to know if he looked nice, and

---

72 **potae**: head-cover.
1 Get angry. 2 (Fit for) church-going.

we'd tell him he looked nice as pie. Sometimes he'd go maggoty because one of the dogs would start barking. He said it got on his nerves. He said that was his only trouble in life. His nerves. He said he could stand anything except things that got on his nerves. If anything got on his nerves, well, look out! He said if the dog got on his nerves too much he'd do it in, and he sounded at the time like as if he meant it.

Gosh, I'll never forget those nights on that woodpile. There was a bosker[3] moon too. We were too tired for anything except smoking one cigarette after another, and telling yarns. At least Tom and me were tired. George mightn't have been. I remember he said a bit about how tough he was, and about how no work could ever get him tired. But he said sometimes he sort of got tired inside. It was when he sort of felt everybody he met was too silly to talk to, wouldn't understand him if he did talk. Then, George said, it was the same with him as when anything got on his nerves. So let anybody who made him feel tired like that just look out.

It began this way. George told a yarn about how he'd been stuck up by the police over that old man that was found dead in a swamp. You know, the papers were full of it. There was a bootmark in some mud. George said how the police had looked at his boots but there was nothing doing. He said he had an alibi anyhow. It was the way he told us about it that got Tom narked. Tom reckoned he was making out he did the old man in. Or if he didn't he knew who did. George pretended to get hot under the collar, but you could see he was really pleased the way he'd got Tom thinking things.

Well, the next night George got Tom narked again. Maybe there always was a sort of goody-goody streak in Tom. He told George not to sling off at things so much. It was because George asked him if he wore a white flower on Mother's Day. Tom said he didn't.

Well, I don't either, George said, but if I did I'd have to wear a red one.

And when Tom asked him why, he said it was because he never had a mother. Tom didn't like him saying that. He told him he ought to have more respect for his mother even if she wasn't married. Then George said how he hadn't much time for getting married or regular jobs or anything like that. He said you might as well be dead as work at a regular job and have to keep a nagging wife. He certainly did sling off a lot. Then he wound up by saying he wasn't too shook on women anyhow.

Why not? Tom said. Give me a girl who's on for a cuddle and oh boy!

Right enough, George said, but when I was a kid a joker had me for a pet. See?

Was he a scoutmaster? I asked.

Oh, near enough, George said. He was a Sunday school teacher.

That got Tom narked. He told George he ought to be ashamed of himself for telling things like that.

Righto, kid, George said, forget it. I remember he did a big yawn. It made

---

3 Fine.

me think of what he'd said about some people making him feel tired inside. Then he got up off the woodpile and went inside. But first he heaved a few chunks of firewood in the direction of that dog. Off and on it was barking a treat.

Of course I told Tom he was silly to get narked over a thing like that. Just because a fellow told you straight-out about himself there wasn't any need to get hot under the collar. And didn't it take all sorts to make a world, anyhow? I told him he'd get on George's nerves, and hadn't George said look out? And of course Tom argued the point. Mind you, I felt sorry for Tom. He was all the time hoping for a steady job so he could get married. He was a good-looking young chap, Tom was, and mighty fond of loving. Very much so. And naturally he expected everyone to be pretty much like himself. So he didn't like George saying straight-out how he wasn't too shook on women, and how a Sunday school teacher once had him on for a pet. Well, Tom kept on arguing the point, so what with the dog barking fit to get on anyone's nerves I heaved a few more chunks of wood at it and left Tom sitting on the woodpile.

So the next day Tom didn't speak to me much. And this was a day when the lambs that George was shearing were no good at all at sitting still. He kept heaving them back into the pen. One he heaved so far it went whack on the side of the woolshed and fell down whop on the floor. Tom said, For Christ's sake! and George heard him say it. He sort of looked pleased like he had looked that other time when he had Tom thinking things about the old man that was found dead in the swamp. And the next lamb he sheared Tom and I saw him rip the poor little beggar right across the belly. Well, maybe it was an accident, but you sort of felt that George was a bit pleased. Tom went outside and he stayed outside longer than he ought, but I didn't blame him. I didn't blame George either. Well, I did a bit, but you can't expect a shearer to pick up a lamb in his arms and nurse it. Can you now?

As I've said Tom didn't speak to me much that day and I just left him alone. I fancied he didn't want me sitting out on the woodpile with him either, so when one of the shearers asked me to play him whisky poker I said I would. But when I got sick of that I went outside to find Tom. He wasn't on the woodpile, but George was. The dog was barking a treat too, worse than ever before. George was running his comb through his hair and he asked me if he looked nice. I said he did, and he began filing his nails. Then he began crooning a Bing Crosby, but he left off doing that to swear at the dog and heave a few chunks of firewood over that way. I asked him where Tom was and he said he knew but he wasn't splitting.

Well, it looked to me like as if Tom and George had been having another argument. I sat down on the woodpile and talked to George, and he said how Tom didn't know life, but he believed I did. He told me a lot. Oh, he knew life all right. Maybe he knew too much. At anyrate I could have sat and listened to a chap like that all night if it hadn't been for the way the damned dog was barking. Talk about getting on your nerves! And I thought I ought to be having a look for Tom. I guessed he'd be feeling pretty sore what with me rousing on to him the night before for being silly, and now having another argument with George. So I said I was going to look for him, and George said, O.K. brother. But I hadn't got up off the woodpile before George began walking over to the dog. It barked blue murder the nearer he got to it, and if it didn't do the maddest dance you ever saw on the end of its chain! How George managed to get in on it I don't know, but he did. There was a bosker moon, like I've said, and I just sat on that woodpile and watched George strangle the dog. I couldn't move. I couldn't. You see I knew then what had happened to Tom. For the life of me I couldn't move.

Of course George is going up for it. You'll see about it in the papers. And they're trying to blame him for the old man that was found in the swamp. Maybe he did it but he says he didn't. And he doesn't make any bones about doing Tom in. I don't know. I'm sore at losing Tom. I am that. But I have to admit that he'd sometimes get on your nerves and make you feel tired by arguing silly. Haven't you ever felt like that with anyone? Own up. I bet you have.

§ *Mateship* Aus: Gordon, Lawler, Seymour

JANET FRAME (1924–)

From Faces in the Water

Based on Janet Frame's own experiences in psychiatric hospitals, *Faces in the Water* questions the demarcation lines that separate 'sanity' and 'madness' and tacitly provides an indictment of the 'care' offered by such institutions. Here, in the second chapter of the novel, the protagonist Istina Mavet's fear of electric shock therapy is compounded by the feeling that it will result in a further loss of her individuality.

I was cold. I tried to find a pair of long woolen ward socks to keep my feet warm in order that I should not die under the new treatment, electric shock therapy, and have my body sneaked out the back way to the mortuary. Every morning I woke in dread, waiting for the day nurse to go on her rounds and announce from the list of names in her hand whether or not I was for shock treatment, the new and fashionable means of quieting people and of making them realize that orders are to be obeyed and floors are to be polished without anyone protesting and faces are made to be fixed into smiles and weeping is a crime. Waiting in the early morning, in the black-capped frosted hours, was like waiting for the pronouncement of a death sentence.

I tried to remember the incidents of the day before. Had I wept? Had I refused to obey an order from one of the nurses? Or, becoming upset at the sight of a very ill patient, had I panicked, and tried to escape? Had a nurse threatened, 'If you don't take care you'll be for treatment tomorrow?' Day after day I spent the time scanning the faces of the staff as carefully as if they were radar screens which might reveal the approach of the fate that had been prepared for me. I was cunning. 'Let me mop the office,' I pleaded. 'Let me mop the office in the evenings, for by evening the film of germs has settled on your office furniture and report books, and if the danger is not removed you might fall prey to disease which means disquietude and fingerprints and a sewn shroud of cheap cotton.'

So I mopped the office, as a precaution, and sneaked across to the sister's desk and glanced quickly at the open report book and the list of names for treatment the next morning. One time I read my name there, Istina Mavet. What had I done? I hadn't cried or spoken out of turn or refused to work the bumper with the polishing rag under it or to help set the tables for tea, or to carry out the overflowing pig-tin to the side door. There was obviously a crime which was unknown to me, which I had not included in my list because I could not track it with the swinging spotlight of my mind to the dark hinterland of unconsciousness. I knew then that I would have to be careful. I would have to wear gloves, to leave no trace when I burgled the crammed house of feeling and took for my own use exuberance depression suspicion terror.

As we watched the day nurse moving from one patient to another with the list in her hand our sick dread became more intense.

'You're for treatment. No breakfast for you. Keep on your nightgown and dressing gown and take your teeth out.'

We had to be careful, calm, controlled. If our forebodings were unwarranted we experienced a dizzy lightness and relief which, if carried too far, made us liable to be given emergency treatment. If our name appeared on the fateful list we had to try with all our might, at times unsucessfully, to subdue the rising panic. For there was no escape. Once the names were known all doors were scrupulously locked; we had to stay in the observation dormitory where the treatment was being held.

It was a time of listening – to the other patients walking along the corridor for breakfast; the silence as Sister Honey, her head bowed, her eyes watchfully open, said grace.

'For what you are about to receive the Lord make you truly thankful.'

And then we heard the sudden cheerful clatter of spoons on porridge plates, the scraping of chairs, the disconcerted murmur at the end of the meal when the inevitably missing knife was being searched for while the sister warned sternly, 'Let no one leave the table until the knife is found.' Then further scraping and rustling following the sister's orders. 'Rise, Ladies.' Side doors being unlocked as the patients were ordered to their separate places of work. Laundry, Ladies. Sewing room, Ladies. Nurses' Home, Ladies. Then the pegging footsteps as the massive Matron Glass on her tiny blackshod feet approached down the corridor, unlocked the observation dormitory and stood surveying us, with a query to the nurse, like a stockman appraising head of cattle waiting in the saleyards to go by truck to the slaughterhouse. 'They're all here? Make sure they have nothing to eat.' We stood in small groups, waiting; or crouched in a semi-circle around the great locked fireplace where a heap of dull coal smouldered sulkily; our hands on the blackened bars of the fireguard, to warm our nipped fingers.

For in spite of the snapdragons and the dusty millers and the cherry blossoms, it was always winter. And it was always our season of peril: Electricity, the peril the wind sings to in the wires on a gray day. Time after time I thought, What safety measures must I apply to protect myself against electricity? And I listed the emergencies – lightning, riots, earthquakes, and the measures provided for the world by man's Red Cross God Safety to whom we owe allegiance or die on the separated ice floe, in double loneliness. But it would not come to my mind what to do when I was threatened by electricity, except that I thought of my father's rubber hip boots that he used for fishing and that stood in the wash house where the moth-eaten coats hung behind the door, beside the pile of old Humor Magazines, the Finest Selections of the World's Wit, for reading in the lavatory. Where was the wash house and the old clothes with spiders' nests and wood lice in their folds? Lost in a foreign land, take your position from the creeks flowing towards the sea, and your time from the sun.

Yes, I was cunning. I remembered once a relationship between electricity and wetness, and on the excuse of going to the lavatory I filled the admission bath and climbed in, wearing my nightgown and dressing gown, and thinking, Now they will not give me treatment, and perhaps I may have a secret influence over the sleek cream-painted machine with its knobs and meters and lights.

Do you believe in a secret influence?

There had been occasions of delirious relief when the machine broke down and the doctor emerged, frustrated, from the treatment room, and Sister Honey made the welcome proclamation, 'You can all get dressed. No treatment today.'

But this day when I climbed in the bath the secret influence was absent, and I was given treatment, hurried into the room as the first patient, even before the noisy people from Ward Two, the disturbed ward, were brought in for 'multiples,' which means they were given two treatments and sometimes three, consecutively. These excited people in their red ward dressing gowns and long gray ward stockings and bunchy striped bloomers which some took care to display to us, were called by their Christian names or nicknames, Dizzy, Goldie, Dora. Sometimes they approached us and began to confide in us or touch our sleeves, reverently, as if we were indeed what we felt ourselves to be, a race apart from them. Were we not the 'sensibly' ill who did not yet substitute animal noises for speech or fling our limbs in uncontrolled motion or dissolve into secret silent hilarity? And yet when the time of treatment came and they and we were ushered or dragged into the room at the end of the dormitory all of us whether from the disturbed ward or the 'good' ward uttered the same kind of stifled choking scream when the electricity was turned on and we dropped into immediate lonely unconsciousness.

It was early in my dream. The tracks of time crossed and merged and with the head-on collision of hours a fire broke out blackening the vegetation that sprouts a green memory along the side of the track. I took a thimbleful of water distilled from the sea and tried to extinguish the fire. I waved a small green flag in the face of the oncoming hours and they passed through the scarred countryside to their destination and as the faces peered from the window at me I saw they were the faces of the people awaiting shock treatment. There was Miss Caddick, Caddie, they called her, bickering and suspicious, not knowing that she would soon die and her body be sneaked out the back way to the mortuary. And there was my own face staring from the carriageful of the nicknamed people in their ward clothes, striped smocks and gray woolen jerseys. What did it mean?

I was so afraid. When I first came to Cliffhaven and walked into the dayroom and saw the people sitting and staring, I thought, as a passerby in the street thinks when he sees someone staring into the sky, If I look up too, I will see it. And I looked but I did not see it. And the staring was not, as it is in the streets, an occasion for crowds who share the spectacle; it was an occasion of loneliness, of vision on a closed, private circuit.

And it is still winter. Why is it winter when the cherry blossom is in flower? I have been here in Cliffhaven for years now. How can I get to school by nine o'clock if I am trapped in the observation dormitory waiting for E.S.T.? It is such a long way to go to school, down Eden Street past Ribble Street and Dee Street past the doctor's house and their little girl's dollhouse standing on the lawn. I wish I had a dollhouse; I wish I could make myself small and live inside it, curled up in a matchbox with satin bed curtains and gold stars painted on the striking side, for good conduct.

There is no escape. Soon it will be time for E.S.T. Through the veranda windows I can see the nurses returning from second breakfast, and the sight of them walking in twos and threes past the border of snapdragons granny's bonnets and the cherry blossom tree brings a sick feeling of despair and finality. I feel like a child who has been forced to eat a strange food in a strange house and who must spend the night there in a strange room with a different smell in the bedclothes and different borders on the blankets, and waken in the morning to the sight of a different and terrifying landscape from the window.

The nurses enter the dormitory. They collect false teeth from the treatment patients, plunging them in water in old cracked cups and writing the names on the outside in pale blue ink from a ballpoint pen; the ink slips on the impenetrable china surface, and spreads, blurring from itself, with the edges of the letters appearing like the microfilm of flies' feet. A nurse brings two small chipped enamel bowls of methylated spirits and ethereal soap, to 'rub up' our temples in order that the shock will 'take.'

I try to find a pair of gray woolen socks for if my feet are cold I know that I shall die. One patient is careful to put on her pants 'in case I kick up my legs in front of the doctor.' At the last minute, as the feel of nine o'clock surrounds us and we sit in the hard chairs, our heads tipped back, the soaked cotton wool being rubbed on our temples until the skin tears and stings and the dregs of the spirits run down into our ears making sudden blockages of sound, there is a final outbreak of screaming and panicking, attempts by some to grab leftover food from the bed patients, and as a nurse calls 'Lavatory, Ladies,' and the dormitory door is opened for a brief supervised visit to the doorless lavatories, with guards set in the corridor to prevent escape, there are bursts of fighting and kicking as some attempt to get past, yet realizing almost at once that there is nowhere to run to. The doors to the outside world are locked. You can only be followed and dragged back and if Matron Glass catches you she will speak angrily, 'It's for your own good. Pull yourself together. You've been difficult long enough.'

The matron herself does not offer to undergo shock treatment in the way that suspected persons to prove their innocence are sometimes willing to take the first slice of the cake that may contain arsenic.

Floral screens are drawn to conceal the end of the dormitory where the treatment beds have been prepared, the sheets rolled back and the pillows placed at an angle, ready to receive the unconscious patient. And now everybody wants to go again to the lavatory, and again, as the panic grows, and the nurse locks the door for the last time, and the lavatory is inaccessible. We yearn to go there, and sit on the cold china bowls and in the simplest way try to relieve ourselves of the mounting distress in our minds, as if a process of the body could change the distress and flush it away as burning drops of water.

And now there is the sound of an early morning catarrhal cough, the springing squeak of rubber-soled shoes on the polished corridor outside, syncopated with the hasty ping-pong steps of cuban-heeled duty shoes, and Dr. Howell and Matron Glass arrive, she unlocking the dormitory door and standing aside while he enters, and both passing in royal procession to join Sister Honey already waiting in the treatment room. At the last minute, because there are not enough nurses, the newly appointed Social Worker who has been asked to help with treatment comes leaping in (we call her Pavlova).

'Nurse, will you send up the first patient.'

Many times I have offered to go first because I like to remind myself that by the time I am awake, so brief is the period of unconsciousness, most of the group will still be waiting in a daze of anxiety which sometimes confuses them into thinking that perhaps they have had treatment, perhaps it has been sneaked upon them without their being aware of it.

The people behind the screen begin to moan and cry.

We are taken strictly according to 'volts.'

We wait while the Ward Two people are 'done.'

We know the rumors attached to E.S.T. – it is training for Sing Sing[1] when we are at last convicted of murder and sentenced to death and sit strapped in the electric chair with the electrodes touching our skin through slits in

---

1 Prison with notoriously strict regime in Ossining, New York State.

our clothing; our hair is singed as we die and the last smell in our nostrils is the smell of ourselves burning. And the fear leads in some patients to more madness. And they say it is a session to get you to talk, that your secrets are filed and kept in the treatment room, and I have had proof of this, for I have passed through the treatment room with a basket of dirty linen, and seen my card. Impulsive and dangerous, it reads. Why? And how? How? What does it all mean?

It is nearly my turn. I walk down to the treatment room door to wait, for so many treatments have to be performed that the doctor becomes impatient at any delay. Production, as it were, is speeded up (like laundry economics – one set of clothes on, one set clean, one in the wash) if there is a patient waiting at the door, one on the treatment table, and another being given a final 'rub-up' ready to take her place at the door.

Suddenly the inevitable cry or scream sounds from behind the closed doors which after a few minutes swing open and Molly or Goldie or Mrs. Gregg, convulsed and snorting, is wheeled out. I close my eyes tight as the bed passes me, yet I cannot escape seeing it, or the other beds where people are lying, perhaps heavily asleep, or whimperingly awake, their faces flushed, their eyes bloodshot. I can hear someone moaning and weeping; it is someone who has woken up in the wrong time and place, for I know that the treatment snatches these things from you leaves you alone and blind in a nothingness of being and you try to fumble your way like a newborn animal to the flowing of first comforts; then you wake, small and frightened, and the tears keep falling in a grief that you cannot name.

Beside me is the bed, sheets turned back pillow arranged where I will lie after treatment. They will lift me into it and I shall not know. I look at the bed as if I must establish contact with it. Few people have advance glimpses of their coffin; if they did they might be tempted to charm it into preserving in the satin lining a few trinkets of their identity. In my mind, I slip under the pillow of my treatment bed a docket of time and place so that when and if I ever wake I shall not be wholly confused in a panic of scrabbling through the darkness of not knowing and of being nothing. I go into the room then. How brave I am! Everybody remarks on my bravery! I climb on to the treatment table. I try to breathe deeply and evenly as I have heard it is wise in moments of fear. I try not to mind when the matron whispers to one of the nurses, in a hoarse voice like an assassin, 'Have you got the gag?'

And over and over inside myself I am saying a poem which I learned at school when I was eight. I say the poem, as I wear the gray woolen socks, to ward off Death. They are not relevant lines because very often the law of extremity demands an attention to irrelevancies; the dying man wonders what they will think when they cut his toenails; the man in grief counts the cups in a flower. I see the face of Miss Swap who taught us the poem. I see the mole on the side of her nose, its two mounds like a miniature cottage loaf and the sprout of ginger hair growing out the top. I see myself standing in the classroom reciting and feeling the worn varnished desk top jutting against my body against my belly button that has specks of grit in it when I put my finger in; I see from the corner of my left eye my neighbor's pencil case which I coveted because it was a triple decker with a rose design on the lid and a wonderful dent thumb-size for sliding the lid along the groove.

'Moonlit Apples,' I say. 'By John Drinkwater.'

> At the top of the house the apples are laid in rows
> And the skylight lets the moonlight in and those
> Apples are deep-sea apples of green.

I get no further than three lines. The doctor busily attending the knobs and switches of the machine which he respects because it is his ally in the struggle against overwork and the difficulties depressions obsessions manias of a thousand women, has time to smile a harassed Good Morning before he gives the signal to Matron Glass.

'Close your eyes,' Matron says.

But I keep them open, observing the secretive signal and engulfed with helplessness while the matron and four nurses and Pavlova press upon my shoulders and my knees and I feel myself dropping as if a trap door had opened into darkness. I imagine as I fall my eyes turning inward to face and confound each other with a separate truth which they prove without my help. Then I rise disembodied from the dark to grasp and attach myself like a homeless parasite to the shape of my identity and its position in space and time. At first I cannot find my way, I cannot find myself where I left myself, someone has removed all trace of me. I am crying.

A cup of sweet tea is being poured down my throat. I grasp the nurse's arm.

'Have I had it? Have I had it?'

'You have had treatment,' she answers. 'Now go to sleep. You are awake too early.'

But I am wide awake and the anxiety begins again to accumulate.

Will I be for treatment tomorrow?

§ *Outsider figures* Hulme; *Women and 'madness'* Af: Head

WITI IHIMAERA (1944–)

1: The Whale

He sits, this old kaumatua,[1] in the darkness of the meeting house. He has come to this place because it is the only thing remaining in his dying world.

In this whanau,[2] this old one is the last of his generation. All his family,

---

1 Elder. 2 Family; extended family group.

they have died: parents, brothers, sisters, relations of his generation, all gone. Ruia, his wife, she's been dead many years. His friends, there are none. Children, mokopuna, yes, there are many of those. But of his time, only he and this meeting house remain.

The meeting house . . .

This old one, he sighs, and the sound fills the darkness. He looks upon the carved panels, the tukutuku[3] reed work, the swirling red and black and white kowhaiwhai[4] designs, and he remembers he awoke to life here. That was long ago, another world ago, when this meeting house and whanau, this village, brimmed over with happiness and aroha.[5] Always he has lived here. This meeting house has been his heart, his strength. He has never wished to leave it. In this place lie his family and memories. Some are happy, others are sad. Some are like dreams, so beautiful that they seem never to have existed. But his dreams died long ago. With each tangi, each funeral, they have died. And he is the last of the dreamers.

This kaumatua, his eyes dim. In this falling afternoon he has come to visit the meeting house for the last time. He knows it is the last time. Just as the sun falls and the shadows lengthen within the meeting house, so too is his life closing. Soon his photograph will be placed along the wall with those of his other friends, relations and tipuna – his ancestors. He will be glad to join them there. The world has changed too much and it is sad to see his world decaying.

This village was once a proud place, ringing with joy. Its people were a proud people, a family. One great family, clustered around this meeting house. Ae, they quarrelled sometimes, but it is only the happiness that this old one remembers.

But now many of the houses lie deserted. The fields are choked with weeds. The gorse creeps over the graveyard. And the sound of children laughing grows smaller each year.

Even the aroha, it is disappearing from this place. That is the most heart-breaking thing of all. Once the manawa, the heart, throbbed with life and the whanau gave it life. But over the years more and more of its children left and the family began to break apart. Of those that went few returned. And the heart-beat is weaker now.

He sighs again, this kaumatua. He will be glad to die, yet sad to leave. His people they will weep for him. Hera, his niece, she will cry very much. But in the end, she will remember . . . .

– Hera, don't you be too sad when I'm gone. If you are, you come to this meeting house. I'll be here, Hera. You come and share your aroha with me. You talk to me; I will listen.

He'd told her that when she was a little girl. Even then the world had been changing. Hera, she'd been one of the few of his mokopuna who'd

---

3 Form of wall decoration.   4 Golden-flowered tree.   5 Love; compassion.

been interested in the Maori of the past. The rest, they'd felt the pull of the Pakeha[6] world, like fish too eager to grab at a dangling hook. Only in Hera had he seen the spark, the hope that she might retain her Maoritanga.[7] And he had taught her all he knew.

– Hera, this is not only a meeting house; it is also the body of a tipuna, an ancestor. The head is at the top of the meeting house, above the entrance. That is called the koruru. His arms are the maihi, the boards sloping down from the koruru to form the roof. See the tahuhu, ridgepole? That long beam running from the front to the back along the roof? That is the backbone. The rafters, the heke, they are the ribs. And where we are standing, this is the heart of the house. Can you hear it beating?

And Hera, she had listened and heard. She had clutched him, afraid.

– Nanny! The meeting house, it lives!

– The meeting house, it won't hurt you, Hera, he had told her. You are one of its children. Turi Turi now.

And he had lifted the veils from the photographs of all her family dead and told her about them.

– That's your Nanny[8] Whiti. He was a brave man. This is my Auntie Hiria, she was very beautiful, ay? She's your auntie too. This man, he was a great rangatira[9]. . . .

Later, they had sat in the middle of the meeting house, he on a chair, she sitting on the floor next to him, and he had told her its history.

– This meeting house, it is like a book, Hera. All the carvings, they are the pages telling the story of this whanau. The Pakeha, he says they're legends. But for me they are history.

And page by page, panel by panel, he had recounted the history.

– That is Pau, coming from Hawaiki on the back of a giant bird. He brought the kumara[10] to Aotearoa.[11] This is Paikea, riding a whale across the sea to Aotearoa. He was told not to let the whale touch the land. But he was tired after the long journey, and he made the whale come to shore. It touched the sand, and became an island. You can still see it, near Whangara . . . See the tukutuku work on the walls? All those weavings, they represent the stars and the sky . . .

And Hera, her eyes had glistened with excitement.

– Really, Nanny, really?

– Ae, Hera. You remember . . . .

This old one, he closes his eyes to try to keep the sadness away. But closed eyes cannot hide the memory that even Hera had changed as she grew older. She too, like many of the other young people, had gone away to the city. And when she had returned for a visit, this old one could see that the Pakeha life had proved too strong for her. He had tried to lead her back to his world, and she had quarrelled with him.

---

6 White New Zealander; originally 'stranger'. 7 Maoriness. 8 Grandpa. 9 Chief; notable person. 10 Edible root; 'sweet potato'. 11 The shining land; old name for New Zealand.

– Don't, Nanny! The world isn't Maori any more. But it's the world I have to live in. You dream too much. Your world is gone. I can't live it for you. Can't you see?

But he had been stubborn, this kaumatua. He'd always been stubborn. If she would not come back to his world, then she would take it to the city with her.

– Come, Hera, I want to show you something.

– No, Nanny . . . .

– These books, in them is your whakapapa,[12] your ancestry. All these names, they are your family who lived long ago, traced back to the Takitimu canoe. You take them with you when you go back.

– Nanny . . . .

– No, you take them. And see this space? You put my name there when I die. You do that for me. You keep this whakapapa safe. And don't you ever forget who you are. You're Maori, understand? You are Maori . . . .

His voice had broken with grief then. And Hera had embraced him to comfort him.

– Nanny, you gave me too much love, she had whispered. You taught me too well to be Maori. But you didn't teach me about the Pakeha world . . . .

He opens his eyes, this old one, but he still hears his Hera's whisper. Ae, he had taught her well. And one day her confusion would pass and she would understand why. He'd known his world had died. But the spirit of his people, he didn't want to die too. That's why he had taught her well. That's why.

For a moment he mourns to himself, this old one. Sadly he recalls an ancient saying. How old it is he does not know. Perhaps it had come with the Maori when he journeyed across the sea to Aotearoa. From Hawaiki. From Tawhiti-roa, Tawhiti-nui, Tawhiti-pamamao, the magical names for the first home of the Maori. No matter . . . . Even before the Pakeha had come to this land, his coming had been foretold.

> *Kei muri i te awe kapara he tangata ke,*
> *mana te ao, he ma.*
> Shadowed behind the tattooed face a stranger stands,
> he who owns the earth, and he is white.

And with his coming, the tattooed face had changed. That was the way of things, relentless and unalterable. But the spirit of the Maori, did that need to change as well? Ae, even in his own day, Maoritanga had been dying. But not the spirit, not the joy or aroha. Now . . . .

He cannot help it, this kaumatua, but the tears fall.

---

12 Genealogy; family-tree.

The Maori language has almost gone from this whanau. The respect for Maori customs and Maori tapu,[13] that too was disappearing. No more did people take their shoes off before coming into this meeting house. The floor is scuffed with shoe-marks. The tukutuku work is pitted with cigarette burns. And even the gods and tipuna, they have been defaced. A name has been chipped into a carved panel. Another panel bears a deep scratch. And a paua[14] eye has been prised from a carved figure, a wheku.

This meeting house, it had once been noble. Now, the red ochre is peeling from the carvings. The reed work is falling apart. The paint is flaking from the swirling kowhaiwhai designs. And the floor is stained with the pirau, the beer, for even that has been brought into this meeting house.

So too have the Maori fallen from nobility. They do not come to this meeting house with respect, nor with aroha. They look with blind eyes at the carvings and do not see the beauty and strength of spirit which is etched in every whorl, every bold and sweeping spiral. They too are the strangers behind the tattooed face.

This old one, he has seen too many of his people come as strangers. The Maori of this time is different from the Maori of his own time. The whanau, the family, and the aroha which binds them together as one heart, is breaking, slowly loosening. The children of the whanau seek different ways to walk in this world. Before, there was a sharing of aroha with one another. No matter how far away some of the children went there was still the aroha which bound them closely to this meeting house and village. But the links are breaking. The young grow apart from each other. They look with shame at their meeting house and this village because it is decaying. They walk away and do not come back. That is why the manawa[15] beats so loud with agony, that is why this meeting house is dying. When Maori aroha dies, when the Maori walks away into another life, the meeting house weeps . . . .

– Aue! Aue![16]

This kaumatua, he fills the meeting house with the sound of his grief.

– Aue! Aue!

And from his grief springs a memory which adds to his despair. Of a time not long ago, when people from all Aotearoa gathered at this meeting house to celebrate the wedding of a child of this whanau.

The visitors, they had come from the Taranaki, from the Waikato, from the many parts of Te Ika a Maui,[17] even from Te Waipounamu – the South Island. They had arrived for the hui throughout the day. By car, by bus, by train they had come, and the manawa of this whanau had beaten with joy at their gathering together.

It had been like his own time, this old one remembers. The children laughing and playing around the meeting house. The men and women renewing

---

13 The sacred or forbidden. 14 Seashell, used to decorate the eyes of human figures represented on the *poupou* (carved panels on meeting-house walls). 15 Heart. 16 Expression of dismay. 17 Literally 'Maui's fish'; the North Island of New Zealand, supposedly fished out of the ocean by the hero Maui.

their friendships. The laughing and the weeping. The sweet smell of the hangi,[18] and the sudden clouds of steam as the kai[19] was taken from the earth. The girls swaying past the young men, eyeing the ones they wanted. The boys standing together, both bold and shy but hiding their shyness beneath their jokes and bantering. The kuias[20] gossiping in the cookhouse. The big wedding kai, and the bride and groom pretending not to hear the jokes about their first night to be spent together. The singing of the old songs . . . the cooks coming into the hall in their gumboots and old clothes to sing with the guests . . .

> *Karangatia ra! Karangatia ra!*
> *Pohiritia ra, nga iwi o te motu*
> *Ki rungo o Turanga. Haere mai!*
> Call them! Call them!
> Welcome them, the people of the land
> Coming onto this marae, Turanga. Welcome!

Ae, it had indeed been like the old times. The laughter and the joy had sung through the afternoon into the night. And he had sat with the other old men, watching the young people dancing in the hall.

Then it happened. Late in the night. Raised voices. The sound of quarrelling.

– Nanny! Come quick!

A mokopuna had grabbed his hand and pulled him outside, along the path to the dining room. More visitors had arrived. They had come from the Whangarei, and they were tired and hungry. He saw their faces in the light. But people of his whanau, they were quarrelling with the visitors. They would not open the door to the storeroom. It was locked now. There would be no kai for these visitors. They had come too late. Heart was locking out heart.

He had been stunned, this old one. Always there was food, always aroha, always open heart. That was the Maori way. Aroha.

And he had said to his mokopuna:

– Te toki. Homai te toki . . . the axe. Bring me the axe . . .

The crowd had heard his whispered fury. They parted for him. His tokotoko, his walking stick, it supported him as he approached the door. The music stopped in the hall. The kanikani, the dancing, stopped. People gathered. His fury gathered. The axe in his hand. He lifted it and . . . .

Aue . . . .

The first blow upon the locked door.

Aue . . . .

His tears streaming from his face.

Aue . . . .

The wood splintering beneath the blade.

---

18 Food cooked in a traditional Polynesian earth oven.　19 Food.　20 Old women.

Aue . . . .

His heart splintering too.

He gave his anger to the axe. He gave his sorrow to the blows upon the door. The axe rose and fell, rose and fell, and it flashed silver from the light. And people began to weep with him.

Then it was done. The door gave way. Silence fell. Weeping, he turned to the visitors. His voice was strained with agony.

– Haere mai, e te manuhiri. Haere mai. Haere mai. Come, visitors, Come. Enter.

He had opened his arms to them. Then, trembling, he had pointed at the splintered door.

– Ka nui te whakama o toku iwi ki a au. Anei ra toku whakama . . . . My people shame me. See? This is my shame . . . .

Then he had walked away, not looking back. Away from the light into the darkness. His heart, it was breaking. And he wished only to die and not see the shame.

This kaumatua, the memory falls away from him. He sees the darkness gathering quickly in the meeting house. How long has he been here, mourning? A long time. He sighs. Better to die than to see this changing world. He is too old for it. He is stranded here.

This old one, he grips his tokotoko and stands. Aue, he has lingered too long. One last look at this meeting house. The carved panels glint in the darkness. The kowhaiwhai designs flash with the falling sun. The evening wind flutters the black veils which hang upon the photographs of his dead. Soon he will join them. Soon his name will fill a space in the whakapapa of this whanau. Soon. . . .

So still he stands, this kaumatua, that he seems to merge into the meeting house and become a carved figure himself. Then his lips move. One last whisper to this meeting house, and he turns and walks away.

– No wai te he?

He walks along the dusty road, through the village. The houses are clustered close together, but closed to one another. Some are deserted, lifeless. A truck speeds past him, and he coughs with the choking dust.

– No wai te he?

He hears a gramophone blaring loudly from one of the houses. He sees into a lighted window, where the walls are covered with glossy pictures that have been carefully cut out of magazines. A group of young people are gathered around another house, laughing and singing party songs. They wave the pirau at him, and beckon him to come and join them. He turns away.

– No wai te he?

Down the path from the village he goes, to where his own house lies on the beach, apart from the village. Through the manuka,²¹ down the cliff to

---

21 Common shrub; 'tea-tree'.

the sand he walks. The sea is calm, the waves softly rippling. And far away the sun is setting, slowly drowning in the water.

– No wai te he?

Then he sees a cloud of gulls blackening the sky. Their guttural screams fill the air. They dive and swoop and cluster upon a dark mound, moving feebly in the eddying water.

And as the old one approaches, he sees that it is a whale, stranded in the breakwater, threshing in the sand, already stripped of flesh by the falling gulls. The water is washed with red, the foam flecked with blood.

He cries out then, this kaumatua.

The gulls shriek and wheel away from him. And in their claws they clasp his shouted words, battling and circling against one another with a flurry of black wings.

– No wai te he . . . Where lies the blame . . . the blame.

Where lies the blame, the blame . . . .

And the whale lifts a fluke of its giant tail to beat the air with its dying agony.

§ *Elegies for Aboriginality* Hyde; Aus: Kendall, Oodgeroo; *Maori experience* Grace

2: This Life is Weary

'This Life is Weary' is taken from *Dear Miss Mansfield*, a collection of short stories in which Witi Ihimaera pays 'tribute' to his New Zealand precursor, Katherine Mansfield, by providing his own alternative versions of some of her stories, versions which in many cases offer a very different viewpoint on the subject-matter of the original stories. 'This Life is Weary' responds to 'The Garden Party'.

1

The little cottages were in a lane to themselves at the very bottom of a steep rise. At the top was the house that the children called *The Big House* – everybody called it that because it was oh so lovely with its lovely house and gardens lived in by its lovely owners – like another world really, one much nicer than down here below the broad road which ran between. But Dadda would always laugh whenever the children were too filled to the brim about the goings on up there, and he would remind them that 'We are all equal in the sight of God' or 'Remember – the lilies of the field – ' This was Dadda's way of saying that no envy should be attached to *The Big House*, nor malice against its gilded inhabitants.

The children loved their Dadda so much, especially Celia the eldest, who thought he was the most wonderful, most handsome, most perfect man in the whole world. Truth to tell, Celia was not far wrong about him – Jack Scott was a fine man. His face was strong and open and was topped with

blond curly hair. His shoulders were broad and, altogether, he was a fine figure of a man. But Dadda was more than physically attractive – he possessed
a sense of goodness and wholeness, as if his physical beauty merely reflected
an inner purity untouched by coarseness. 'When I grow up, Dadda,' Celia
would say, 'I shall marry someone just like you.' To this Jack Scott would
laugh again – her dear, laughing Dadda – and caution Celia that beauty
or handsomeness faded with years and, 'Oh, my sweet Celia, follow your
heart and, wherever it leads, to ugly plump thin or brown, there lie you
down.'

This kind of simple honesty was what made Dadda so greatly loved in
this land of chocolate-brown houses. Although the very smoke coming out
of the chimneys might be poverty-stricken – not at all like the great silvery
plumes that uncurled from *The Big House* – one could hear the larks sing
whenever the carter, Jack Scott, was around. ' 'ere you, Old Faithful,' the
washerwomen would call as Dadda whistled past. ' 'ow come you're always
so 'appy of a mornin'?' Dadda would answer, 'God has given us another
beautiful day, ladies, and there are so many beautiful things in it.' And the
washerwomen would blush, for they took his remarks as declarations of
romance and they loved him all the more – not lasciviously, mind, because
they were decent women and beyond the age of temptation. 'Oh my, Jack
Scott,' they would call, 'you 'ave a way with the words, but be off with
you!' Ah yes, and the men loved Dadda too because of his uprightness and
fairness. 'You're a good lad, Jack,' the old pensioners would tell him whenever he was able to spare them some victuals. 'Yes, you're a good mate,' the
young men agreed. There was not a finer friend to the young men than
Dadda.

He was not old, was Dadda, being only twenty-nine, and his responsibilities as a good husband and father had not brought weariness to him. In the
case of Mam, though, Celia could see that life's travails had changed her
greatly from the little slip of a thing whom Dadda had met on the ship
bringing settlers from England. Romance had blossomed below decks
between Jack and Em – and Em's parents had not put a stop to it, for they
could tell that Jack would make honest passage through the world and, given
his good head for business, a profitable one. Nobody could want better for
a daughter of fifteen years. So, on arrival in Wellington, Jack and Em had
become man and wife, and they had fulfilled God's commandment to be
fruitful by producing Celia, Margaret and Thomas within the first three years
of marriage. The doctor had cautioned Jack, saying, 'Give Em some peace
now, lad, and let her body recover from the childbearing.' Dadda had laughed
and said, 'It's not for my want of trying, Doctor, but the babies just seem
to come and, if it is God's will' – And God willed that there should be two
more, the babes Matthew and Mark.

The Big House was regarded with simple awe by many who lived in the
little cottages below. Others were not so awestruck, looking upon *The Big
House* with a sense of grievance, for it represented everything that they had
hoped to escape from when they had left England. Even Dadda was not

untouched by the angry murmurs of the working men at meetings of an evening. But above all else, he truly believed that Work and Self-improvement would win the changes that all strived for.

Dadda went to work every morning before dawn. He would slip out of bed and creep with candle up into the loft to see his little ones. 'Blessed be the new day,' he would whisper, 'and God keep you all safe and well.' Then he would be gone, often not returning until long after dark. Mam had the babes to tend to and, whenever she could, she took small mending work from *The Big House* – she had artistic fingers for embroidery. As for the children, they went off to school during the week. Mam was very firm about this and did not want them swarming in the little crowded lanes like many of the other children who were kept at home.

However, Saturday afternoons were free for the children to do as they pleased and, without fail, this meant going up to *The Big House*, crossing quickly over the broad road between, to watch the house and the comings and goings of the lovely people who lived or visited there. Celia had found a special place – you had to slip between the rose bushes and under the karaka trees to get to it – right by the tennis court. Under the trees was an old wrought-iron loveseat, just ideal for the children. The seat had obviously been thrown out many years ago but it was comfortable enough – once you wiped away the birds' droppings – and perfect to observe from. There was the house, side on to the sun, gleaming like a two-storeyed dolls' house. The driveway was at the front with a circle of green in the middle. Oh, what excitement was occasioned whenever the front gateway opened and a carriage came in! There was a back gateway also and, there, the delivery vans and storemen would enter, bringing the groceries, meat and other supplies to Cook. Once, the children had seen the familiar figure of Dadda himself, and that night they couldn't wait to tell him, 'Dadda, oh Dadda! We saw you at *The Big House* today!' – as if grace and divinity had been suddenly bestowed on him. The house was surrounded with broad swathes of bright green lawn bordered by daisy plants. Just beyond the borders were the roses – hundreds and hundreds of glorious dark red roses of the kind that the children had seen on chocolate boxes.

It was Celia, of course, who thought of keeping notebooks on *The Big House*. Celia had always been an imaginative child and it only seemed natural that simple observation should lead to something more formal – like setting it all down in writing. Dadda and Mam were amused at first but grew to be thoroughly approving. 'Better that the children should be constructive,' Mam would say, 'than down here wasting their lives away.' And Dadda had said, 'Who knows? Some of what they see might rub off on them!' So it soon became part of the Saturday routine for Mam to sharpen pencils and, when the children became more serious about keeping notebooks, to let them take a simple lunch – a crust of bread each and a bottle with water in it – with them. 'Be back before dark!' Mam would cry as the children scampered off. 'We will, Mam, we will!' Celia would reply – because telling Mam and Dadda, right after supper, about what they had seen at *The Big*

House became part of the Saturday excursions also. And the children knew that Mam and Dadda welcomed their reports, taking them as signs that their children would do better than they had to make good lives for themselves.

Although Celia had never been to any theatre, watching *The Big House* was just as she imagined a play would be. Like all theatrical settings, the weather was always ideal up there and the days perfect and made to order. The backdrop was windless and warm, with a light blue sky flecked with gold. It was all so unlike the dark and dirty eyesore which cluttered the area the children came from. Indeed, sometimes it was difficult for the children to accept that this world was as real as their own – it really was as if they had paid a penny to go to His Majesty's Royal Theatre for a few hours of a drab Saturday afternoon. But what fun! Naturally, the house itself was the main stage prop, particularly the verandahs, top and bottom, and the french doors on to the verandahs. From out of these doors would come the lovely people of *The Big House*, the main actors of every Saturday afternoon performance. Head of the Household was Mr Sheridan, who worked in the city and never seemed to be around very much. He generally slept late on Saturdays, sometimes not appearing until 2 p.m., all hairy and drumming his chest after a wash. Mistress of the House was Mrs Sheridan, prone to sitting on a chair off the main bedroom and fanning herself like a lady in a magazine. Once, so Margaret swore, Mrs Sheridan actually waved to the children where they sat. 'Impossible,' Celia replied. Her version appeared that night, after supper, when she produced a sketch of Mrs Sheridan trying to swat at something going bbbzzzz – Mam and Dadda thought that was very funny, but Margaret was cross.

Mr and Mrs Sheridan had three daughters, Meg, Jose and Laura, and a son, Laurie – and it was on these four fascinating golden creatures that the children focused all their attention. Celia would scribble like mad in her notebook as Margaret and Thomas described every appearance: 'Meg has just washed her hair,' Margaret would say, in awe, because washing one's hair in the afternoon was the prerogative of the wealthy. 'Oh, look, there's Jose! She has put on her lovely silk petticoat and the kimono jacket.' And Thomas would reflect, 'Do you think she got the jacket from the Chinamen who play pakapoo?' To which Celia, the expert on fashion, would say, 'Kimonos come from Japan, Thomas, not China.' But Margaret might interrupt, 'Oh, quick, here comes Meg again! Doesn't she look pretty? I'll bet a beau is coming to call.' And sure enough, half an hour later, the gateway would open and a fine hansom would deposit a grave but hopeful young man. 'Oh, he's not right for Meg,' Celia would say. 'Pooh, no!' Thomas and Margaret would agree, for they knew that without doubt Meg was going to be a famous pianist. Her life was not to be squandered away on silly young men! Wasn't it true that every afternoon Meg practised the piano and showed signs of improving? – why, only four mistakes in the 'Für Elise' last Saturday! As for Jose, oh dear, she would just have to give up any thought of an operatic career. While her voice was strong enough, alas, her sense of timing was woeful. Worse still, she could never hold the tune. Apart from which, nobody could sing 'This Life is Weary' better than Dadda –

This Life is *Wee*-ary,
A Tear – a Sigh.
A Love that *Chan*-ges,
This Life is *Wee*-ary,
A Tear – a Sigh.
A Love that *Chan*-ges.
And then . . . Good-bye!

No, Jose would be better off receiving silly young men herself. In this manner, the children would observe, ponder, dream and hope that the characters whom they had come to love would grow, prosper and make the right decisions.

The children's main interest was in the heroine of the Sheridan family, the one whom they thought was most like themselves – Laura. Her every entrance was greeted in the same way as a diva by a star-struck audience – with a hushed indrawn breath, moment of recognition, long sigh of release and joyous acclamation. Laura was Celia's age – at least, that's what Celia insisted – and could do no wrong. She was the one whom the children most wanted to have as a friend, if class would ever allow it. Their notebooks were filled, positively to the very margins, with anecdotes, drawings and notes about Laura in all her moods. To even get a good likeness was difficult enough, for Laura was always flying in and out, here and there, to and fro. Often the children would have to compare their drawings for accuracy and, 'No, she didn't look like that,' Celia would say, 'she looked like this.' Then Margaret would interject, 'But she wasn't wearing the blue pinafore, she was wearing the yellow one with the tiny wee apron.' To which Thomas would respond, 'Well, she was just perfect as she was, a perfect little princess.' This was, in fact, patently inaccurate, because perfect little princesses were not tomboys – and there was a streak of this in Laura. Perfect little princesses did not do cartwheels on the front lawn or thumb their noses at beaux they didn't like. Oh, she was such a character sometimes! 'I wonder what her bedroom is like?' Margaret would wonder. 'Does it have a huge bed and are all her dolls propped up on the pillows?' Interrupting, Thomas would venture, 'And would there be a rockinghorse?' To which Celia would purse her lips and say, 'Perhaps. Rockinghorses are really for boys but – yes, Laura is bound to have one.'

On most occasions, the appearances by the Sheridans were seen from afar. There was one magical moment, however – the children had to pinch themselves to make sure they weren't dreaming – when Hans, one of the servants, brought a small table and four chairs on to the tennis court right in front of the children. Laura appeared with three of her dolls, placed them on chairs and proceeded to have afternoon tea with cakes and biscuits. 'Lady Elizabeth,' Laura said, 'would you care for some milk? Sugar? One lump or two?' Then, with a laugh, 'Oh, quite, Countess Mitzi, quite.' And Celia almost fainted away with pleasure when, turning to the third doll, Laura said, 'Princess Celia, how was your last visit to Paris?' For the rest of the afternoon the children were just transported, bursting with ecstasy – and they could hardly wait to tell Mam and Dadda. 'Oh, slow down, lovey,' Mam said to Celia. 'Do slow down!' And that put the seal on the entire afternoon, for it was exactly the sort of comment that the children were constantly passing about Laura herself.

2

One day, the children came running back from an afternoon watching *The Big House* with the news 'Oh, Mam! Dadda! There's going to be a garden-party! At *The Big House*! We heard Mrs Sheridan reminding Cook! Next Saturday! Oh, can we go for the whole day? With our notebooks? In the morning? So many people have been invited! Please, Mam! Please, Dadda!' As it happened, Em had hoped the girls would mind the babes while she visited her parents but, 'Let the little ones go,' Dadda said, adding with a wink, 'and I shall try to come home early in the afternoon, eh, Em love?' Trying not to blush, Em said, 'All right, children, you may go,' and the children clapped their hands together with glee. Then a thoughtful, twinkling look came into Mam's eyes and she suddenly left the kitchen to rummage in the glory box in the bedroom. When she came back she had some velvet and other material in her arms. 'Come here, Celia lovey,' Em said. 'My, you've grown – ' and her eyes sparkled with sadness, mingled with pride, at the thought of her eldest daughter growing into womanhood. 'What are you doing, Mam?' Celia asked. 'Why, measuring you, your sister and brother, of course,' Mam said. 'You can't go to a garden-party in your everyday clothes.' And Margaret said, 'But Mam, we're not invited – ' To which Em said, 'Hush, child. We can dream, can't we?' And Jack came to hold Em close and kiss her. 'That we can, Em love,' he said, 'that we can.'

The children could hardly contain themselves. All that week they conjectured about the garden-party – who would come, what food would be served, what Laura would wear, would there be a band, how many waiters – and they were so fidgety that Mam had to say, 'Do keep still, Margaret, or else your dress will not be ready in time!' Then Margaret would stay very still indeed, hardly drawing breath, because green velvet was her favourite colour and she wanted to look her very best – and Mam even made a green bow for her hair! Thomas, reluctant at first, also got into the swing of things. He knew that he was going to look a proper guy – and how was he going to get up to *The Big House* and back without the other swarming children seeing him – but, oh, there was such a delicious silky feeling to the new shirt! As for Celia, she had determined, 'Mam, I can make my own dress and hat.' So while Mam stitched costumes for Margaret and Thomas, Celia worked on a cloth that had once been a curtain. When Celia completed her dress Mam trimmed it with a lace ribbon she had been saving for herself.

Then, when all the stitching and sewing was completed, didn't the children look just lovely, parading in front of Dadda and Mam that Friday night before the garden-party? Hardly a wink was slept, so that when Dadda came to wake them, why, the children were already dressed and waiting! And wasn't Dadda the most perfect man? He had transformed the cart into a carriage and placed cushions on the seats. Then, bowing, he handed the children up, saying, 'Lady Margaret, if you would be so kind – Princess Celia, charmed – Sir Thomas, delighted – 'And Mam, trying not to laugh too much, came from the doorway with a hamper of cordial, sandwiches and a dear wee cake. 'Oh, Mam. Oh, Dadda,' was all that Celia could say because the words got caught in her throat. 'Have a lovely time, children,' Mam said. 'And Thomas, don't worry – your Dadda will pick you all up before dark from the gateway of *The Big House*. Byeeee – ' And she blew a kiss as they left.

And after all the weather was ideal. When the dawn came creeping across the sky, the children knew it was going to be a perfect day for the Sheridans' garden-party. From their position under the trees they saw the garden-party from beginning to end. They saw the Maori gardener already at work mowing the lawns and sweeping them. 'Oh, he's missed a piece!' Margaret wailed but, joy, he returned to sweep the swathe so that the lawn looked all combed the same way – not a lick out of place. 'Nothing must go wrong,' Celia nodded. Then the children saw movement in *The Big House* and knew that Mr and Mrs Sheridan, Meg, Jose, Laura and Laurie were at breakfast. Mr Sheridan came out the front door with a BANG to go through the gateway. At the same time the men came to put up the marquee. And who else but Laura, the little princess herself, should appear to give the men their instructions! 'Oh, she's so pretty! Thomas said, 'and look, she's eating bread and butter – just like we do.' The next few moments, though, were anxious ones for the children because at one point, Laura pointed to the tennis court. Yes, it was certainly the most appropriate place for the marquee but, 'It will spoil our view,' Celia whispered. And, why, Laura must have heard, because the workmen set the marquee near the karaka trees instead!

'Message, Laura!' a voice cried from the house, and away the little princess skimmed. But what was happening at the back door? Why, the florist had arrived and just look at the pots and pots of canna lilies – so radiant and frighteningly alive on their bright crimson stems! And then, from the drawing room, was that Meg on the piano? Pom! Ta-ta-ta Tee-ta! Oh dear, was Jose really going to embarrass herself by singing at the garden-party? There she was, warming up – 'This Life is *Wee*-ary, A Tear – a Sigh' – Oh dear, dear, dear. But now look! Someone else had arrived at the back door. Surely it was the Godber van, clattering into the yard, bringing lovely cream puffs! And there was the man from Godbers talking to Cook, and –

Suddenly the sky was filled with a soft radiance and it was almost like – like a shooting star, in the daytime though, going UP into the sky – and Celia felt such sweet pain that she wanted to weep. Her heart was so full, so overflowing, so brimming over, and in that same instant she thought of her Dadda.

Strange really, but for a while after that the house fell into silence. Laura's voice could be heard piping and alarmed. 'What is happening now?' Margaret asked. 'I'm not sure,' Celia said. 'Perhaps it is lunchtime already.' Indeed it was – hadn't time passed quickly? So Margaret opened the hamper, Celia laid the food out, and Thomas said, 'Lady Margaret, would you care for some wine?' Margaret clapped her hands together and, 'Thank you, Sir Thomas,' she said as Thomas poured some cordial into her glass. And you, Princess Celia?' Celia inclined her head. And oh, it was so much fun to be sitting there sipping wine on the perfect day.

Lunch in *The Big House* was over by half past one. The green-coated bandsmen arrived and established themselves right next to the children near the tennis court. The man on the tuba saw them and gave a cheery wave. Would he tell? No – he was too jolly to do that. Soon after, the guests began coming in streams – one carriage after the other – the women so lovely, oh so *lovely*. The band struck up. The hired waiters ran from the house to the marquee. Wherever the children looked there were couples strolling, bending to the flowers, greeting, and gliding across the lawn. The children were enchanted, transported, transformed – in Heaven – by it all. There in the shadows they imitated the movements of the guests, and sometimes when the band played, Sir Thomas first asked Lady Margaret and then Princess Celia to dance with him, on and on and on. The man on the tuba smiled when he saw them dancing and, oh goodness, when the waiters came to offer the band refreshments he must have pointed out the children! Over came one of the waiters with a tray of delicious cakes and cream puffs, and he bowed gravely, saying, 'Mesdames? Monsieur?' And always, far away in the sunlight was dear, darling Laura. Something was bothering her, but she was so gracious, wasn't she? 'Oh, I must sketch her,' Celia cried. And the perfect afternoon slowly ripened, slowly faded, slowly its petals closed. And soon it was all over.

The children were in ever such an excited state as they waited for their Dadda to pick them up. They had stayed beneath the trees until the very end when the last bandsman had packed his instrument and left. The man with the tuba had given a very cheery wave. By the time the children reached the gateway it was almost dark. 'Wasn't it wonderful when –' the children would reminisce to one another. They wanted to savour every minute of the garden-party and, 'Oh, write that one down, Celia,' Margaret would cry. 'We forgot about that moment.' So for a while they sat scribbling away in the gathering darkness. 'Weren't the guests all so lovely?' Margaret whispered. On and on the children chattered.

The darkness deepened. The children couldn't wait for Dadda to arrive so that they could get home quickly and tell him and Mam about the garden-party. When the night fell like a cloak, Celia said, 'Dadda must be delayed. Come along, let's go on home. Like as not we'll meet him coming up the hill.' Thomas was so happy that he didn't even think to be embarrassed should they meet any swarming children. Down, down, down into the sordid lanes the children descended. The lights were on in some of the houses. People were like silent wraiths slipping into and out of the light. All of a sudden someone came running from behind the children, passing them and turning the corner. When the children rounded the corner themselves, they saw a young man with a girl. The girl was pressed against him and she looked as if she was crying. Celia overheard the young man say, 'Was it awful?' The girl shook her head – and there was something terribly familiar in the motion – but it was so dark, so dark.

Then the children were in sight of their own house and they started to run towards it. But what was this? Lamps were shining in the front parlour. A dark knot of people stood outside. Women in shawls and men in tweed caps were gathered there. Without knowing why, Celia felt an awful feeling inside her heart. She saw Gran, Mam's mother, sitting in a chair beside the gate. As the children approached, Gran gave a cry. The knot loosened and voices came out of the darkness at the children, 'Oh, the poor wee children.' Gran kissed the children and held them tight. 'What's wrong, Gran?' Celia asked. 'There's been an accident, Celia dear,' Gran answered. 'Your father –' Celia pulled Margaret and Thomas quickly through the crowd and into the house. Auntie May was there in the passageway, but Celia didn't want *her*.

'Mam? Dadda?' Celia called. 'Mam?' Then another woman was there. Her face was all puffed up and red, with swollen eyes and swollen lips. 'Mam?' Celia whispered, because it was indeed her mother. But she looked so – so – *awful*.

'Your Dadda's gone,' Mam said. 'He's gone.'

Margaret started to wail and Thomas bit his lip and screwed up his eyes. The two children ran to the comfort of their mother's arms. But Celia just stood there. *Oh, Dadda, was that you, that soft radiance? Was that your soul coming to say goodbye before going to Heaven?* Then, in the corner, Celia noticed a basket of fruit – the fruit looked so lovely, oh so very lovely – and she remembered the garden-party. 'I must tell Dadda,' Celia thought. Her heart was breaking into a thousand pieces. 'Where's Dadda?' she asked. Mam motioned toward the bedroom.

For a moment Celia was too frightened to go in. She didn't want to *know*. She didn't want to see. All of a sudden, she felt a fleeting sense of unfairness that *The Big House*, with its gilded life, should be so impervious to all the ills of the world. But no, she shouldn't think like that. Dadda wouldn't want her to think like that, would he? 'Dadda?' she called from the doorway. 'Dadda?' She took a step and, why, there he was in his bed, and she had caught him asleep! There he was, glowing in the light of the smoky lamp, her handsome laughing Dadda. And fast asleep he was, sleeping so soundly that he didn't even stir when she knelt beside him. Curly headed Dadda, deeply, peacefully sleeping.

'Oh Dadda,' Celia whispered. She put her head against his, and the first glowing tear dropped down her cheek like a golden sun. 'It was a lovely garden-party, Dadda, just *lovely*,' she said.

§ *Reworking of 'The Garden Party'* Mansfield

ALBERT WENDT (1939–)

1: A Resurrection

Tala Faasolopito died at 2.30 p.m. yesterday at Motootua Hospital: we heard about it over the radio. He died, so the doctors have diagnosed, of coronary thrombosis. He also died one of the most respected and saintly pastors of the Congregational Church (and of the whole nation therefore).

He was born in the Vaipe, oldest son of Miti and Salamo Faasolopito, both now deceased, and a brother to three sisters and two brothers, whose names I've forgotten. However, the Vaipe has not seen Tala for over forty years, ever since he walked out of it in 1920, at the age of nineteen. I never knew him. What I know about him I have gained from my father and other Vaipe people who knew him. Or, let me say, the Tala I know is a resurrection, a Lazarus resurrected from the memory-bank of the Vaipe.

Tala did not kill the man who had raped his sister, he walked out of the Vaipe and into Malua Theological College to become an exemplary man of God. He never again set foot in the Vaipe. Not even when his father deserted his mother, not even when his mother died of a broken heart (so my mother has concluded) four years later, not even when his brothers and sisters disappeared one by one from the Vaipe in an attempt to escape his (Tala's) disgrace which had become *their* disgrace. The Vaipe was his cross, and he never wanted to confront it again. I once read an article about him in the 'Bulletin', 12th September, 1959: his place of birth, the Vaipe, was never once mentioned in that article. Tala became, for most of our extremely religiously-minded countrymen, a symbol of peace and goodwill, a shining example of virtuous, civilised and saintly living. But to most Vaipe people he was still Tala, the nineteen-year-old who had refused to become a man, their type of man sprung free like elephant grass from fertile Vaipe mud. Not that they did not become proud of him when he became a 'saint' (my father's description). They forgave him. But I believe that Tala never forgave himself. His choice not to avenge his sister's (family) honour determined the course of his life, the very sainthood he grew into. And he regretted that choice.

I possess copies of three of his now nationally-quoted sermons. The sermons are not very original: they reveal little of their composer or the heart of the religion he believed in; they are the usual-type sermons you hear over 2AP every Sunday night without fail. However, I also have the originals of two sermons which he composed a few months before he died and which he never made public. (My father, who grew up with Tala, got the originals from Tala's wife, Siamomua.)

The first sermon, dated Monday, 27th October, 1968, and written in an elaborate and ornate longhand (Tala went to Marist Brothers' School famous for such handwriting) on fragile letter-writing paper, is entitled: 'A Resurrection of Judas'. The second sermon, a typewritten script forty pages in length, is more a private confession than a sermon. It is dated 25th December, 1968, and under the date is this title printed in pencil: 'On the Birthday of Man'. A public perusal of these two sermons would have reduced Tala, in the fickle minds of the public, from saint to madman. For instance, in 'A Resurrection of Judas', Tala offers us a compellingly original but disturbing conclusion: 'Judas Iscariot was the Christ. He did not betray Jesus. Jesus betrayed Judas by not stopping him from fulfilling the prophecy.'

I think that the key to the door into the endless corridors that were Tala's life was his choice not to avenge his family's honour.

As a child I used to play under the breadfruit trees surrounding the fale[1] which belonged to Tala's family; this was after Tala had left the Vaipe for good. Tala's mother, who was a big woman with five chins (or so it seemed then) and long black hair streaked with grey, and an uncontrollable cough (they said she had TB), and ragged dresses that hung down her like animal skins, sometimes invited me into the main fale to play with her children. They were much older than me but they condescended to play hopscotch, sweepy, and skipping with me. I sometimes ate with them, mainly boiled bananas and sparse helpings of tinned herrings. (They were poor, so my parents told me.) I really enjoyed those times. The fale and shacks are still there today, reminding me, every time I pass them, of a contented childhood, but the people (distant relatives of the Faasolopitos) who now occupy them are strangers to me.

I often ran over the muddy track, leading over the left bank of the Vaipe from the ageless breadfruit trees, to the home of the family of the man, Fetu, who, by raping Tala's sister, became the springboard of Tala's life. The track is still there, like a string you can use to find your way out of a dense forest, but Fetu is dead, he has been dead for a long time – he died in prison, stabbed to death by another prisoner who could have been Tala twenty years before because Tala should have killed Fetu but didn't.

Tala and his ill-fated family, and Fetu, and this whole section of the Vaipe are anchored into my mind and made meaningful by the memory of that awesome deed which Tala did not commit; by the profound and unforgettable presence of the ritual murder which Tala and his family and most of the inhabitants of the Vaipe committed in their hearts, and which has become a vital strand of my heritage of memories – a truth which Tala, by avoiding it, had to live with all his life.

'We are what we remember: the actions we lived through or should have lived out and which we have chosen to remember.' Tala has written this in his sermon, 'On the Birthday of Man', page five.

Tala's ordeal, his first real confrontation with the choice that separates innocence from guilt, occurred the night of 3rd March, 1920.

---

1 Samoan house.

Behind the Vaipe, stretching immediately behind Tala's home up to Togafuafua and Tufuiopa and covering an area of a few uninhabited square miles, is a swamp. An area, into which a number of fresh water springs find their way turning the soil into mud and ponds, alive with crabs and shrimps and watercress and waterlily and wild taro[2] and taamu[3] and tall elephant grass and the stench of decay and armies of mosquitoes. Scene of children's war games: cowboys and Indians, massacres and ambushes and mudfights. Tala, so my father has told me, was the most skilful and adept crab and shrimp hunter in the Vaipe. His father (still remembered and referred to in the Vaipe as 'that spineless, worthless failure') was incapable of supporting his large family. He despised work of any type or form. So the burden of feeding and clothing and keeping the family together was left to Miti and Tala. She worked as a house-servant for expatriates, while Tala, who had left school at standard four, stayed home during the day to care for the younger children, and to forage for food. The swamp became a valuable source of food: succulent crabs and shrimp, taro and taamu. Sometimes he sold these at the market to get money to buy other essentials, such as kerosene for the lamp, matches, sugar, salt and flour.

The children always looked clean and healthy and happy, so I've been told. (When I came on the scene five years after Tala's departure, the Faasolopito children I played with were dirty, unkempt and spotted with yaws.) 'There was enough love and laughter and food to go around then', my father tells me. The eldest girl (and her name is of no importance to this story), a year younger than Tala, was extremely beautiful: a picture of Innocent Goodness, some Vaipe elders have described her to me.

The youth who emerged from the swamp that evening as the cicadas woke in a loud choral chant was on his way to meet a saint, a destiny he wasn't aware of yet. He was tired and covered with mud after a whole afternoon of digging for crabs; but now the thought of a cool shower and a hot meal and the smell and warmth of his family was easing his aching, as he went through the tangled bamboo grove on to the track that led to his home ahead – behind clumps of banana trees he had planted the Christmas before. Something brushed against his forehead, a butterfly? He looked up and saw through the murmuring bamboo heads a sky tinted with faint traces of red; the sun was setting quickly. Tomorrow there would be rain. As he moved past the banana trees the broad leaves caressed his arms and shoulders like the cool feathery flow of spring water. He saw the fale, oval and timeless in the fading light. (He took no notice of the group of people in the fale.) He veered off towards the kitchen fale expecting, at any moment, his youngest brother to come bursting out of the fale to greet him and inspect his catch. But no one came. He looked at the main fale again, at the silent group gathered like a frightened brood of chickens round the flickering lamp. Knew that something was terribly amiss. He dropped the basket of crabs and ran towards the light; towards the future he would avoid – to attain a sainthood that he would, on

---

2 Edible root. 3 Giant taro.

confronting the reality of old age, deny – in order to *be* Judas.

Tala walked – more a shuffle than a walk – towards Fetu's fale, trying to overcome the feeling of nausea which had welled up inside him the moment he had pulled the bushknife out of the thatching of the kitchen fale. The bushknife, now clutched firmly in his right hand, was a live, throbbing extension of his humiliation and anger and doubts and fear of the living deed which he had to fulfil in order to break into the strange, grey world of men. His whole life was now condensed into that cross-shaped piece of violent steel, a justification for Fetu's murder; 'my murder', Tala has written in 'On the Birthday of Man'. Fetu's imaginary murder was also his own murder, Tala believed. 'There is no difference between an *imagined* act and one actually committed'.

He stopped in the darkness under the talie[4] trees in front of Fetu's house – a small shack made of rusting corrugated iron and sacking. The clinking of bottles and glasses and the sound of laughter were coming from the shack. (Fetu operated what is known in the Vaipe as a 'home-brew den'; he had already served two prison terms for the illegal brewing of beer.) Tala had never been in the shack before, even when he had been sent by his mother to fetch his father, who sometimes came to Fetu's den to get violently drunk. He knew Fetu quite well, as well as he knew most of the other men in the Vaipe. He went up the three shaky steps and into the shack.

At the far corner, under the window and partly covered by shadow, squatted an old man, still as an object. In the middle of the room three youths were drinking at the only table. He knew them and they knew him, but they said nothing, they just stopped drinking and watched him. Tala saw no one else in the room. He went up and stopped in front of the three youths. The mud had dried on his skin and it felt like a layer of bandages through which blood had congealed. All the walls of the room were covered with pictures clipped randomly from newspapers and magazines, and the one light-bulb that dangled from the middle rafter gave the pictures a dream-like quality, ominous and unreal. A few empty beer bottles lay scattered across the floor, glistening in the harsh light.

'Are you looking for him?' one of the youths asked. Tala nodded. (Fetu and his family lived in the dark room, but no sound came from that room.)

'He isn't here,' the same youth said.

'I . . . have . . . I have to,' but he couldn't say it; it was too difficult and final a step to take into the unknown.

'To *kill* him?'

'Yes,' he said.

'Yes, you *have* to kill him,' the other two youths said. It was as if the youths (and the Vaipe) had resolved that he should kill Fetu, or die trying.

Tala turned slowly and left the shack. He told himself that he wasn't frightened.

---

4 Tropical almond.

No one in the Vaipe knows what happened next, for there was no one there to observe what Tala did before leaving the Vaipe forever. To the rich-blooded inhabitants of the Vaipe, a tale without an exciting (preferably violent) climax, no matter how exaggerated and untrue that climax may be, is definitely *not* a tale worth listening to. A yarn or anecdote especially concerning courage, must, in the telling, assume the fabulous depths and epic grandeur of true myth. And, being a Vaipean to the quick of my honest fingernails, I too cannot stop where actual fact ends and conjecture (imagination) begins; where a mortal turns into maggot-meat and the gods extend into eternity, as it were. So for Tala's life, for my Lazarus resurrected, let me provide you with a climax.

Tala waited under the talie trees until the youths had left the shack and the light had been switched off; until he glimpsed someone (Fetu?) slipping into the back of the shack; until he thought that Fetu had fallen asleep; then, without hope (but also without fear), he groped his way round the shack to the back room and up into the room which stank of sweat and stale food.

A lamp, turned quite low, cast a dim light over everything. Two children lay near the lamp, clutching filthy sleeping sheets round their bodies. On the bed snored Fetu; beyond him slept his wife. Tala moved to the bed and stood above Fetu. He raised the bushknife. He stopped, the bushknife poised like a crucifix above his head. Mosquitoes stung at the silence with their incessant drone.

'Forgive me,' he said to the figure on the bed which, in the gloom, looked like an altar. Carefully, he placed the bushknife across Fetu's paunch, turned, recrossed the threshold and went out into the night and towards an unwanted sainthood in our scheme of things.

In 'On the Birthday of Man', page forty, second to last paragraph, Tala writes: 'I believe now that to have killed then would have been a liberation, my joyous liberation.'

My father, a prominent deacon in the Apia[5] Congregational Chruch, is getting dressed to go to Tala's funeral service. (Tala's wife wants him to be one of the pallbearers.)

I'm not going to the funeral.

It is only a saint they are burying.

§ *Christianity in the Pacific* Hau'ofa

2: Towards a New Oceania

1. A Rediscovery of Our Dead

> 'These islands rising from wave's edge –
> blue myth brooding in orchid,
> fern and banyan, fearful gods
> awaiting birth from blood clot
> into stone image and chant –
> to bind their wounds, bury
> their journey's dead, as I
> watched from shadow root, ready
> for birth generations after . . . .'
>   (from 'Inside Us the Dead'[1])

I belong to Oceania – or, at least, I am rooted in a fertile portion of it – and it nourishes my spirit, helps to define me, and feeds my imagination. A detached/objective analysis I will leave to the sociologist and all the other 'ologists who have plagued Oceania since she captivated the imagination of the *Papalagi*[2] in his quest for El Dorado, a Southern Continent, and the Noble Savage in a tropical Eden. Objectivity is for such uncommitted gods. My commitment won't allow me to confine myself to so narrow a vision. So vast, so fabulously varied a scatter of islands, nations, cultures, mythologies and myths, so dazzling a creature, Oceania deserves more than an attempt at mundane fact; only the imagination in free flight can hope – if not to contain her – to grasp some of her shape, plumage, and pain.

I will not pretend that I know her in all her manifestations. No one – not even our gods – ever did; no one does (UNESCO 'experts and consultants' included); no one ever will because whenever we think we have captured her she has already assumed new guises – the love affair is endless, even her vital statistics, as it were, will change endlessly. In the final instance, our countries, cultures, nations, planets are what we imagine them to be. One human being's reality is another's fiction. Perhaps we ourselves exist only in one another's dreams.

In our various groping ways, we are all in search of that heaven, that Hawaiki, where our hearts will find meaning; most of us never find it, or, at the moment of finding it, fail to recognise it. At this stage in my life I have found it in Oceania; it is a return to where I was born, or, put another way, it is a search for where I was born:

> One day I will reach the source again
> There at my beginnings
> another peace
> will welcome me
> (from 'The River Flows Back', Kumalau Tawali: Manus, PNG[3])

---

1 By Wendt himself. 2 White man; person of European ancestry. 3 Papua New Guinea.

Our dead are woven into our souls like the hypnotic music of bone flutes: we can never escape them. If we let them they can help illuminate us to ourselves and to one another. They can be the source of new-found pride, self-respect, and wisdom. Conversely they can be the *aitu*[4] that will continue to destroy us by blinding us to the beauty we are so capable of becoming as individuals, cultures, nations. We must try to exorcise these aitu both old and modern. If we can't do so, then at least we can try and recognise them for what they are, admit to their fearful existence and, by doing so, learn to control and live honestly with them. We are all familiar with such aitu. For me, the most evil is racism: it is the symbol of all repression.

> Chill you're a bastard . . .
> You have trampled the whole world over
> Here your boot is on our necks, your spear
> into our intestines
> Your history and your size make me cry violently
> for air to breathe
> (from *The Reluctant Flame*, John Kasaipwalova: Trobriands, PNG)

Over the last two centuries or so, that most fearful chill, institutionalised in colonialism, was our perpetual cross in Oceania:

Kros mi no wandem yu	Cross I hate you
Yu kilim mi	You are killing me
Yu sakem aot ol	You are destroying
We blong mi	My traditions
Mi no wandem yu Kros	I hate you Cross

(from 'Kros', Albert Leomala: New Hebrides)

The chill continues to wound, transform, humiliate us and our cultures. Any real understanding of ourselves and our existing cultures calls for an attempt to understand colonialism and what it did and is still doing to us. This understanding would better equip us to control or exorcise it so that, in the words of the Maori poet Hone Tuwhare, 'we can dream good dreams again', heal the wounds it inflicted on us and with the healing will return pride in ourselves – an ingredient so vital to creative nation-building. Pride, self-respect, self-reliance will help us cope so much more creatively with what is passing or to come. Without this healing most of our countries will remain permanent welfare cases not only economically but culturally. (And cultural dependency is even more soul-destroying than economic dependency.) Without it we will continue to be exploited by vampires of all colours, creeds, fangs. (Our home-grown species are often more rapacious.) Without it the tragic mimicry, abasement, and humiliation will continue, and we will remain the often grotesque colonial caricatures we were transformed into

---

4 Spirits.

by the chill. As much as possible, we, mini in size though our countries are, must try and assume control of our destinies, both in utterance and in fact. To get this control we must train our own people as quickly as possible in all fields of national development. Our economic and cultural dependency will be lessened according to the rate at which we can produce trained man-power. In this, we are failing badly.

> In a flash he saw in front of his eyes all the wasted years of carrying the whiteman's cargo.
> (from 'The Crocodile', Vincent Eri: Papua, PNG)

If it has been a waste largely, where do we go from here?

> My body is tired
> My head aches
> I weep for our people
> Where are we going mother
> (from 'Motherland', Mildred Sope: New Hebrides)

Again, we must rediscover and reaffirm our faith in the vitality of our past, our cultures, our dead, so that we may develop our own unique eyes, voices, muscles, and imagination.

2. Some Questions and Possible Answers

In considering 'the Role of Traditional Cultures in Promoting National Cultural Identity and Authenticity in Nation-Building in the Oceanic Islands' (whoever thought up this mouthful should be edited out of the English language!) the following questions emerged:

(a) Is there such a creature as 'traditional culture'?
(b) If there is, what period is the growth of a culture is to be called 'traditional'?
(c) If 'traditional cultures' do exist in Oceania, to what extent are they colonial creations?
(d) What is authentic culture?
(e) Is the differentiation we usually make between the culture(s) of our urban areas (meaning 'foreign') and those of our rural areas (meaning 'traditional') a valid one?

Are not the life-styles of our towns simply developments of our traditional life-styles, or merely sub-cultures within our national cultures? Why is it that many of us condemn urban life-styles (sub-cultures) as being 'foreign' and therefore 'evil' forces contaminating/corrupting the 'purity of our true cultures' (whatever this means)?

(f) Why is it that the most vocal exponents of 'preserving our true cultures' live in our towns and pursue life-styles which, in their own
terminology, are 'alien and impure'?

(g) Are some of us advocating the 'preservation of our cultures' not
for ourselves but for our brothers, the rural masses, and by doing
this ensuring the maintenance of a status quo in which we enjoy
privileged positions?

(h) Should there be ONE sanctified/official/sacred interpretation of
one's culture? And who should do this interpreting?

These questions (and others which they imply) have to be answered satisfactorily before any realistic policies concerning cultural conservation in
Oceania can be formulated. The rest of this section is an attempt to answer
these questions.

Like a tree a culture is forever growing new branches, foliage, and roots.
Our cultures, contrary to the simplistic interpretation of our romantics, were
changing even in pre-papalagi times through inter-island contact and the
endeavours of exceptional individuals and groups who manipulated politics,
religion, and other people. Contrary to the utterances of our elite groups,
our pre-papalagi cultures were not perfect or beyond reproach. No culture
is perfect or sacred even today. Individual dissent is essential to the healthy
survival, development, and sanity of any nation – without it our cultures
will drown in self-love. Such dissent was allowed in our pre-papalagi cultures; what can be more dissenting than using war to challenge and over-
throw existing power – and it was a frequent occurrence. No culture is ever
static and can be preserved (a favourite word with our colonisers and romantic elite brethren) like a stuffed gorilla in a museum.

There is no state of cultural purity (or perfect state of cultural 'goodness')
from which there is decline: usage determines authenticity. There was no
Fall, no sun-tanned Noble Savages existing in South Seas paradises, no
Golden Age, except in Hollywood films, in the insanely romantic literature
and art by outsiders about the Pacific, in the breathless sermons of our elite
vampires, and in the fevered imaginations of our self-styled romantic revo-
lutionaries. We, in Oceania, did not/and do not have a monopoly on God
and the ideal life. I do not advocate a return to an imaginary pre-papalagi
Golden Age or utopian womb. Physically, we are too corrupted for such a
re-entry! Our quest should not be for a revival of our past cultures but for
the creation of new cultures which are free of the taint of colonialism and
based firmly in our own pasts. The quest should be for a new Oceania.

Racism is institutionalised in all cultures, and the desire to dominate and
exploit others is not the sole prerogative of the papalagi. Even today, despite
the glib tributes paid to a Pacific Way, there is much racial discrimination
between our many ethnic groups, and much heartless exploitation of one
group by another. Many of us are guilty – whether we are aware of it or not
– of perpetuating the destructive colonial chill, and are doing so in the avowed
interest of 'preserving our racial/cultural purity' (whatever this means).

Maintaining the status quo using this pretext is not only ridiculous but dangerous. The only valid culture worth having is the one being lived out now, unless of course we attain immortality or invent a time machine that would enable us to live in the past or future. Knowledge of our past cultures is a precious source of inspiration for living out the present. (An understanding also of other peoples and their cultures is vital.) What may have been considered 'true' forms in the past may be ludicrous now: cannibalism and human sacrifice are better left in the history books, for example. Similarly, what at first may have been considered 'foreign' are now authentic pillars of our cultures: Christianity and the Rule of Law, for instance. It won't do to over-glorify the past. The present is all that we have and we should live it out as creatively as possible. Pride in our past bolsters our self-respect which is necessary if we are to cope as equals with others. However, too fervent or paranoid an identification with one's culture – or what one deems to be that culture – can lead to racial intolerance and the like. Hitler too had a Ministry of Culture! This is not to claim that there are no differences between cultures and peoples. Or to argue that we abolish these differences. We must recognise and respect these differences but not use them to try and justify our racist claims to an imaginary superiority.

All of us have individual prejudices, principles, and standards by which we judge which sub-cultures in our national cultures we want to live in, and those features of our national cultures we want conserved and those we want discarded. To advocate that in order to be a 'true Samoan', for example, one must be 'fully-blooded Samoan' and behave/think/dance/talk/dress/and believe in a certain prescribed way (and that the prescribed way has not changed since time immemorial) is being racist, callously totalitarian, and stupid. This is a prescription for cultural stagnation, an invitation for culture to choke in its own body odour, juices, and excreta.

Equally unacceptable are outsiders (and these come in all disguises including the mask of 'adviser' or 'expert') who try to impose on me what they think my culture is and how I should live it and go about 'preserving' it. The colonisers prescribed for us the roles of domestic animal, amoral phallus, the lackey, the comic and lazy and happy-go-lucky fuzzy-haired boy, and the well-behaved colonised. Some of our own people are trying to do the same to us, to turn us into servile creatures they can exploit easily. We must not consent to our own abasement.

There are no 'true interpreters' or 'sacred guardians' of any culture. We are all entitled to our truths, insights, and intuitions into and interpretations of our cultures.

No national culture is homogenous. Even our small pre-papalagi cultures were made up of sub-cultures. In Polynesia, for instance, the life-styles of priests and ariki/ali'i[5] were very different from those of the commoners, women, and children. Contact with papalagi and Asian cultures (which are made up of numerous sub-cultures – and we, in Oceania, tend to forget this)

---

5 Titled people.

has increased the number of sub-cultures or life-styles within our cultures. Many urban life-styles are now just as much part of our cultures as more traditional ones.

To varying degrees, we as individuals all live in limbo within our cultures: there are many aspects of our ways of life we cannot subscribe to or live comfortably with; we all conform to some extent, but the life-blood of any culture is the diverse contributions of its varied sub-cultures. Basically, all societies are multi-cultural. And Oceania is more so than any other region on our sad planet

3. Colonialism: the Wounds

Let me take just two facets of our cultures and show how colonialism changed us.

(a) Education

'Kidnapped'

I was six when
Mama was careless
She sent me to school
alone
five days a week

One day I was
kidnapped by a band
of Western philosophers
armed with glossy-pictured
textbooks and
registered reputations
'Holder of B.A.
and M.A. degrees'

I was held
in a classroom
guarded by Churchill and Garibaldi
pinned up on one wall
and
Hitler and Mao dictating
from the other
Guevara pointed a revolution
at my brains
from his 'Guerilla Warfare'

Each three-month term
they sent threats to
my Mama and Papa

Mama and Papa loved
their son and
paid ransom fees
each time

Each time
Mama and Papa grew
poorer and poorer
and my kidnappers grew
richer and richer
I grew whiter and
whiter

On my release
fifteen years after
I was handed
(among loud applause
from fellow victims)
a piece of paper
to decorate my walls
certifying my release

(Ruperake Petaia: Western Samoa)

This remarkable poem aptly describes what can be called the 'whitefication' of the colonised by a colonial education system. What the poem does not mention is that this system was enthusiastically welcomed by many of us, and is still being continued even in our independent nations – a tragic irony!

The basic function of Education in all cultures is to promote conformity and obedience and respect, to fit children into roles society has determined for them. In practice it has always been an instrument for domesticating humankind. The typical formal educational process is like a lobotomy operation or a relentless life-long dosage of tranquillisers.

The formal education systems (whether British/ New Zealand/ Australian/ American/ or French) that were established by the colonisers in our islands all had one main feature in common: they were based on the arrogantly mistaken racist assumption that the cultures of the colonisers were superior (and preferable) to ours. Education was therefore devoted to 'civilising' us, to cutting us away from the roots of our cultures, from what the colonisers viewed as darkness, supersitition, barbarism, and savagery. The production of bourgeois papalagi seemed the main objective; the process was one of castration. The missionaries, irrespective of whatever colonial nationality or brand of Christianity they belonged to, intended the same conversion.

Needless to say, the most vital strand in any nation-building is education but our colonial education systems are not programmed to educate us for development but to produce minor and inexpensive cogs, such as clerks/ glorified office boys/ officials/ and a few professionals, for the colonial administrative machine. It was not in the colonial interests to encourage industries in our countries: it was more profitable for them that we remained exporters of cheap raw materials and buyers of their expensive manufactured goods. So the education was narrowly 'academic' and benefitted mainly our traditional elite groups who saw great profit in serving our colonial masters who, in turn, propped them up because it was cheaper to use them to run our countries. The elitist and 'academic' nature of this education was not conducive to training us to survive in our own cultures.

Colonial education helped reduce many of us into a state of passivity, undermined our confidence and self-respect, and made many of us ashamed of our cultures, transformed many of us into Uncle Toms and revenants and what V.S. Naipaul has called 'mimic men', inducing in us the feeling that only the foreign is right or proper or worthwhile. Let us see how this is evident in architecture.

(b) Architecture

A frightening type of papalagi architecture is invading Oceania: the super-stainless/super-plastic/super-hygenic/super-soulless structure very similar to modern hospitals, and its most nightmarish form is the new type tourist hotel – a multi-storied edifice of concrete/ steel/ chromium/ and air-conditioning. This species of architecture is an embodiment of those bourgeois values I find unhealthy/ soul-destroying: the cultivation/ worship of mediocrity, a quest for a meaningless and precarious security based on material possessions, a deep-rooted fear of dirt and all things rich in our cultures, a fear of death revealed in an almost paranoiac quest for a super-hygienic cleanliness and godliness, a relentless attempt to level out all individual differences in people and mould them into one faceless mass, a drive to preserve the status quo at all costs, and ETC. These values reveal themselves in the new tourist hotels constructed of dead materials which echo the spiritual, creative, and emotional emptiness in modern man. The drive is for deodorised/sanitized comfort, the very quicksand in which many of us are now drowning, willingly.

What frightens me is the easy/unquestioning acceptance by our countries of all this without considering their adverse effects on our psyche. In my brief lifetime, I have observed many of our countries imitating what we consider to be 'papalagi culture' (even though most of us will swear vehemently that we are not!). It is just one of the tragic effects of colonialism – the aping of colonial ways/ life-styles/ attitudes and values. In architecture this has led and is leading to the construction of dog-kennel-shaped papalagi houses (mainly as status symbols, as props to one's lack of self-confidence). The change from traditional dwelling to box-shaped monstrosity is gathering momentum: the mushrooming of this bewildering soulless desert of shacks and boxes is erupting across Oceania because most of our leaders and style-setters, as soon as they gain power/wealth, construct opulent dog-kennels as well.

Our governments' quest for the tourist hotel is not helping matters either; there is a failure to understand what such a quest is bringing. It may be bringing money through the middle-aged retired tourist, who travels from country to country through a variety of climates, within his cocoon of air-conditioned America/ Europe/ N.Z./ Australia/ Molochland, but it is also helping to bring these bourgeois values, attitudes, and life-styles which are compellingly attractive illnesses that kill slowly, comfortably, turning us away from the richness of our cultures. I think I know what such a death is like: for the past few years I have watched myself (and some of the people I admire) dying that death.

In periods of unavoidable lucidity, I have often visualised the ultimate development of such an architecture – air-conditioned coffins lodged in air-conditioned mausoleums.

4.   Diversity, a Valued Heritage

The population of our region is only just over 5 million but we possess a cultural diversity more varied than any other in the world. There is also a multiplicity of social, economic, and political systems all undergoing different stages of decolonisation, ranging from politically independent nations (Western Samoa/ Fiji/ Papua New Guinea/ Tonga/ Nauru) through self-governing ones (the Solomons/ the Gilberts/ Tuvalu) and colonies (mainly French and American) to our oppressed aboriginal brothers in Australia. This cultural, political, social, and economic diversity must be taken into account in any overall programme of cultural conservation.

If as yet we may not be the most artistically creative region on our spaceship, we possess the potential to become the most artistically creative. There are more than 1200 indigenous languages plus English, French, Hindi, Spanish, and various forms of pidgin to catch and interpret the Void with, reinterpret our past with, create new historical and sociological visions of Oceania with, compose songs and poems and plays and other oral and written literature with. Also numerous other forms of artistic expression: hundreds of dance styles: wood and stone sculpture and carvings; artifacts as various as our cultures; pottery, painting, and tattooing. A fabulous treasure house of traditional motifs, themes, styles, material which we can use in contemporary forms to express our uniqueness, identity, pain, joy, and our own visions of Oceania and earth.

Self-expression is a prerequisite of self-respect.

Out of this artistic diversity has come and will continue to come our most worthwhile contribution to humankind. So this diversity must be maintained and encouraged to flourish.

Across the political barriers dividing our countries an intense artistic activity is starting to weave firm links between us. This cultural awakening, inspired and fostered and led by our own people, will not stop at the artificial frontiers drawn by the colonial powers. And for me, this awakening is the first real sign that we are breaking from the colonial chill and starting to find our own beings. As Marjorie Crocombe of the Cook Islands and editor of *MANA* Magazine has written:

> Denigrated, inhibited and withdrawn during the colonial era, the Pacific people are again beginning to take confidence and express themselves in traditional forms of expression that remain part of a valued heritage, as well as in new forms and styles reflecting the changes within the continuity of the unique world of our Island cultures . . . The canoe is afloat . . . the volume and quality increase all the time.

One of the recent highlights of this awakening was the 1972 South Pacific Festival of Arts during which we came together in Fiji to perform our expressive arts; much of it was traditional, but new voices/new forms, especially in literature, were emerging.

Up to a few years ago nearly all the literature about Oceania was written by papalagi and other outsiders. Our islands were and still are a goldmine for romantic novelists and film makers, bar-room journalists and semi-literate tourists, sociologists and Ph.D. students, remittance men and sailing evangelists, UNO 'experts', and colonial administrators and their well-groomed spouses. Much of this literature ranges from the hilariously romantic through the pseudo-scholarly to the infuriatingly racist; from the 'noble savage' literary school through Margaret Mead and all her comings of age, Somerset Maugham's puritan missionaries/drunks/saintly whores and James Michener's rascals and golden people, to the stereotyped childlike pagan who needs to be steered to the Light. The Oceania found in this literature is largely papalagi fictions, more revealing of papalagi fantasies and hang-ups, dreams and nightmares, prejudices and ways of viewing our crippled cosmos, than of our actual islands. I am not saying we should reject such a literature, or that papalagi should not write about us, and vice versa. But the imagination must explore with love/ honesty/ wisdom/ and compassion; writers must write with *aroha/aloha/alofa/loloma*, respecting the people they are writing about, people who may view the Void differently and who, like all other human beings, live through the pores of their flesh and mind and bone, who suffer, laugh, cry, copulate, and die.

In the last few years what can be called a South Pacific literature has started to blossom. In New Zealand, Alistair Campbell, of Cook Island descent, is acknowledged as a major poet; three Maori writers – Hone Tuwhare (poet), Witi Ihimaera (novelist), and Patricia Grace (short stories) have become extremely well-known. In Australia, the aboriginal poets Kath Walker and Jack Davis continue to plot the suffering of their people. In Papua New Guinea, *The Crocodile* by Vincent Eri – the first Papuan novel to be published – has already become a minor classic. Also in that country poets such as John Kasaipwalova, Kumalau Tawali, Alan Natachee, and Apisai Enos, and playwrights like Arthur Jawodimbari are publishing some powerful work. Papua New Guinea has established a very forward-looking Creative Arts Centre, which is acting as a catalyst in the expressive arts movement, a travelling theatre, and an Institute of Papua New Guinea Studies. *KOVAVE* Magazine, put out by a group of Papua New Guinea writers, is already a respected literary journal.

MANA Magazine and MANA Publications, established by the South Pacific Creative Arts Society (owned/operated by some of us), have been a major catalyst in stimulating the growth of this new literature, especially in countries outside Papua New Guinea. Already numerous young poets, prose writers, and playwrights have emerged; some of them, we hope, will develop into major writers. One thinks of Seri, Vanessa Griffen, and Raymond Pillai of Fiji; of Eti Sa'aga, Ruperake Petaia, Sano Malifa, Ata Ma'ia'i, and Tili Peseta of Western Samoa; of Albert Leomala and Mildred Sope of the New Hebrides; of Celestine Kulagoe of the Solomons; of Maunaa Itaia of the Gilberts; of Makiuti Tongia of the Cook Islands; of Konai Helu Thaman of Tonga. I am proud to be also contributing to this literature. Most of us know one another personally; if we don't, we know one another's work well. Our ties transcend barriers of culture, race, petty nationalism, and politics. Our writing is expressing a revolt against the hypocritical/exploitative aspects of our traditional/commercial/and religious hierarchies, colonialism and neo-colonialism, and the degrading values being imposed from outside and by some elements in our societies.

> But they cannot erase my existence
> For my plight chimes with the hour
> And my blood they drink at cocktail parties
> Always full of smiling false faces
> Behind which lie authority and private interests
> > (from 'Uncivil Servants', Konai Helu Thaman: Tonga)

> As I walk this rich suburb
> > full of white and black chiefs
> I hear the barking of a dog
> I listen to its calls
> > knowing I am that dog
> > picking what it can
> > from the overflowing rubbish tins.

> I say to you chiefs
> > bury the scraps you can't eat
> So no hungry dog will come to eat
> > at your locked gate.

> Chiefs, beware of hungry
> > dogs!
> ('Beware of Dog', Makiuti Tongia: Cook Islands)

In the traditional visual arts there has been a tremendous revival, that revival is also finding contemporary expression in the work of Maori artists such as Selwyn Muru, Ralph Hotere, Para Matchitt, and Buck Nin; in the work of Aloi Pilioko of Wallis and Futuna, Akis and Kauage of Papua New Guinea, Aleki Prescott of Tonga, Sven Orquist of Western Samoa, Kuai of the Solomons, and many others.

The same is true in music and dance. The National Dance Theatres of Fiji and The Cook Islands are already well-known throughout the world.

This artistic renaissance is enriching our cultures further, reinforcing our identities/self-respect/and pride, and taking us through a genuine decolonisation; it is also acting as a unifying force in our region. In their individual journeys into the Void, these artists, through their work, are explaining us to ourselves and creating a new Oceania.

§ *Other South Pacific texts* Wendt (1), Hau'ofa, Subramani; *Tradition and modernity* Grace; Af: Achebe (1, 2, 3), Soyinka, Okot

KERI HULME (1947–)

From The Bone People

The Bone People explores the interaction of three outsiders in New Zealand society: the central figure, Kerewin Holmes, who lives alone in a tower, the widower Joe Gillayley and his autistic 'son', Simon, whom he subjects to physical abuse. Through this trinity of characters, Hulme works towards an unconventional and challenging view of human relationships, partly grounded in Maori custom and myth. In this section from the early part of the novel, Kerewin encounters Simon for the first time.

. . . It is still dark but she can't sleep any more.

She dresses and goes down to the beach, and sits on the top of a sandhill until the sky pales.

Another day, herr Gott, and I am tired, tired.

She stands, and grimaces, and spits. The spittle lies on the sand a moment, a part of her a moment ago, and then it vanishes, sucked in, a part of the beach now.

Fine way to greet the day, my soul . . . go down to the pools.
Te Kaihau,[1] and watch away the last night sourness.

And here I am, balanced on the saltstained rim, watching minute navy-blue fringes, gill-fingers of tubeworms, fan the water . . . put the shadow of a finger near them, and they flick outasight. Eyes in your lungs . . . neat.

---

1 Literally the windeater; wanderer or idler.

The three-fin blenny swirls by . . . tena koe, fish. A small bunch of scarlet and gold anemones furl and unfurl their arms, graceful petals, slow and lethal . . . tickle tickle, and they turn into uninteresting lumps of brownish-jelly . . . haven't made sea-anemone soup for a while, whaddaboutit? Not today, Josephine . . . at the bottom, in a bank of brown bulbous weed, a hermit crab is rustling a shell. Poking at it, sure it's empty? Ditheringly unsure . . . but now, nervously hunched over his soft slug of belly, he extricates himself from his old hutch and speeds deftly into the new . . . at least, that's where you *thought* you were going, e mate? . . . hoowee, there really is no place like home, even when it's grown a couple of sizes too small. . . .

There is a great bank of Neptune's necklaces fringing the next pool.

'The sole midlittoral fuccoid,' she intones solemnly, and squashes a bead of it under the butt of her stick. 'Ahh me father he was orange and me mother she was green,'[2] slithers off the rocks, and wanders further away down the beach, humming. Nothing like a tidepool for taking your mind off things, except maybe a quiet spot of killing. . . .

Walking the innocent stick alongside, matching its step to hers, she climbs back up the sandhills. Down the other side in a rush, where it is dark and damp still, crashing through loose clusters of lupins. Dew sits in the centre of each lupin-leaf, hands holding jewels to catch the sunfire until she brushes past and sends the jewels sliding, drop by drop weeping off.

The lupins grow less; the marram grass diminishes into a kind of reedy weed; the sand changes by degrees into mud. It's an estuary, where someone built a jetty, a long long time ago. The planking has rotted, and the uneven teeth of the pilings jut into nowhere now.

> It's an odd macabre kind of existence. While the nights away in drinking, and fill the days with petty killing. Occasionally, drink out a day and then go and hunt all night, just for the change.

She shakes her head.

> Who cares? That's the way things are now. (I care.)

She climbs a piling, and using the stick as a balancing pole, jumps across the gaps from one pile to the next out to the last. There she sits down, dangling her legs, stick against her shoulder, and lights a cigarillo to smoke away more time.

Intermittent wheeping flutes from oystercatchers.

The sound of the sea.

A gull keening.

When the smoke is finished, she unscrews the top of the stick and draws out seven inches of barbed steel. It fits neatly into slots in the stick top.

'Now, flounders are easy to spear, providing one minds the toes.'

Whose, hers or the fishes', she has never bothered finding out. She rolls

---

2 Protestant and Catholic colours.

her jeans legs up as far as they'll go, and slips down into the cold water. She steps ankle deep, then knee deep, and stands, feeling for the moving of the tide. Then slowly, keeping the early morning sun in front of her, she begins to stalk, mind in her hands and eyes looking only for the puff of mud and swift silted skid of disturbed flounder.

All this attention for sneaking up on a fish? And they say we humans are intelligent? Sheeit. . .

and with a darting levering jab, stabbed, and a flounder flaps bloodyholed at the end of the stick.

Kerewin looks at it with slow smiled satisfaction.

Goodbye soulwringing night. Good morning sinshine, and a fat happy day.

The steeled stick quivers.

She pulls a rolledup sack from her belt and drops the fish, still weakly flopping, in it. She hangs the lot up by sticking her knife through the sackneck into a piling side.

The water round the jetty is at thigh-level when she brings the third fish back, but there has been no hurry. She guts the fish by the rising tide's edge, and lops off their heads for the mud crabs to pick. Then she lies down in a great thicket of dun grass, and using one arm as a headrest and the other as a sunshade, falls quietly asleep.

It is the cold that wakes her, and clouds passing over the face of the sun. There is an ache in the back of her neck, and her pillowing arm is numb. She stands up stiffly, and stretches: she smells rain coming. A cloud of midge-like flies blunders into her face and hair. On the ground round the sack hovers another swarm, buzzing thinly through what would seem to be for them a fog of fish. The wind is coming from the sea. She picks up the sack, and sets off for home through the bush. Raupo[3] and fern grow into a tangle of gorse: a track appears and leads through the gorse to a stand of wind warped trees. They are ngaio.[4] One tree stands out from its fellows, a giant of the kind, nearly ten yards tall.

Some of its roots are exposed and form a bowl-like seat. Kerewin sits down for a smoke, as she nearly always does when she comes this way, keeping a weather eye open for rain.

In the dust at her feet is a sandal.

For a moment she is perfectly still with the unexpectedness of it.

Then she leans forward and picks it up.

It can't have been here for long because it isn't damp. It's rather smaller than her hand, old and scuffed, with the position of each toe palely upraised in the leather. The stitching of the lower strap was coming undone, and the buckle hung askew.

'Young to be running loose round here.'

---

3 Bulrush.   4 Coastal tree.

She frowns. She doesn't like children, doesn't like people, and has discouraged anyone from coming on her land.

'If I get hold of you, you'll regret it, whoever you are. . . .'

She squats down and peers up the track. There are footprints, one set of them. Of a sandalled foot and half an unshod foot.

> Limping? Something in its foot so that's why the sandal is taken off and left behind?

She rubs a finger inside the sandal. The inner sole was shiny and polished from long wearing and she could feel the indentation of the foot. Well-worn indeed . . . in the heel though there is a sharpedged protrusion of leather, like a tiny crater rim. She turns it over. There is a corresponding indriven hole in the rubber.

'So we jumped on something that bit, did we?'

She slings the sandal into the sack of flounders, and marches away belligerently, hoping to confront its owner.

But a short distance before her garden is reached, the one and a half footprints trail off the track, heading towards the beach.

Beaches aren't private, she thinks, and dismisses the intruder from her mind.

The wind is blowing more strongly when she pushes open the heavy door, and the sky is thick with dark cloud.

'Storm's coming,' as she shuts the door, 'but I am safe inside . . . .'

The entrance hall, the second level of the six-floored Tower, is low and stark and shadowed. There is a large brass and wood crucifix on the far wall and green seagrass matting over the floor. The handrail of the spiral staircase ends in the carved curved flukes of a dolphin; otherwise, the room is bare of furniture and ornament. She runs up the stairs, and the sack drips as it swings.

'One two three aleary hello my sweet mere hell these get steeper daily, days of sun and wine and jooyyy,'

the top, and stop, breathless.

'Holmes you are thick and unfit and getting fatter day by day. But what the hell . . . .'

She puts the flounders on bent wire hooks and hangs them in the coolsafe. She lights the fire, and stokes up the range, and goes upstairs to the library for a book on flatfish cooking. There is just about everything in her library.

A sliver of sudden light as she comes from the spiral into the booklined room, and a moment later, the distant roll of thunder.

'Very soon, my beauty, all hell will break loose . . .' and her words hang in the stillness.

She stands over by the window, hands fistplanted on her hips, and watches the gathering boil of the surf below. She has a curious feeling as she stands there, as though something is out of place, a wrongness somewhere, an uneasiness, an overwatching. She stares morosely at her feet (longer second toes still longer, you think they might one day grow less, you bloody were-wolf you?) and the joyous relief that the morning's hunting gave, ebbs away.

'Bleak grey mood to match the bleak grey weather,' and she hunches over to the nearest bookshelf. 'Stow the book on cooking fish. Gimme something escapist, Narnia or Gormenghast or Middle Earth,[5] or,'
it wasn't a movement that made her look up.

There is a gap between two tiers of bookshelves. Her chest of pounamu[6] rests inbetween them, and above it, there is a slit window.

In the window, standing stiff and straight like some weird saint in a stained gold window, is a child. A thin shockheaded person, haloed in hair, shrouded in the dying sunlight.

The eyes are invisible. It is silent, immobile.

Kerewin stares, shocked and gawping and speechless.

The thunder sounds again, louder, and a cloud covers the last of the sunlight. The room goes very dark.

If it moves suddenly, it's going to go through that glass. Hit rock-bottom forty feet below and end up looking like an imploded plum....
She barks,
'Get the bloody hell *down* from there!'

Her breathing has quickened and her heart thuds as though she were the intruder.

The head shifts. Then the child turns slowly and carefully round in the niche, and wriggles over the side in an awkward progression, feet ankles shins hips, half-skidding half-slithering down to the chest splayed like a lizard on a wall. It turns round, and gingerly steps onto the floor.

'Explain.'

There isn't much above a yard of it standing there, a foot out of range of her furthermost reach. Small and thin, with an extraordinary face, highboned and hollowcheeked, cleft and pointed chin, and a sharp sharp nose. Nothing else is visible under an obscuration of silverblond hair except the mouth, and it's set in an uncommonly stubborn line.

Nasty. Gnomish, thinks Kerewin. The shock of surprise is going and cold cutting anger comes sweeping in to take its place.

'What are you doing here? Aside from climbing walls?'

There is something distinctly unnatural about it. It stands there unmoving, sullen and silent.

'Well?'

In the ensuing silence, the rain comes rattling against the windows, driving down in a hard steady rhythm.

'We'll bloody soon find out,' saying it viciously, and reaching for a shoulder.

Shove it downstairs and call authority.

Unexpectedly, a handful of thin fingers reaches for her wrist, arrives and

---

5 Alluding to works by C. S. Lewis, Mervyn Peake and J. R. R. Tolkien. 6 Greenstone; New Zealand jade.

fastens with the wistful strength of the small.

Kerewin looks at the fingers; looks sharply up and meets the child's eyes for the first time. They are seabluegreen, a startling colour, like opals.

It looks scared and diffident, yet curiously intense.

'Let go my wrist,' but the grip tightens.

Not restraining violence, pressing meaning.

Even as she thinks that, the child draws a deep breath and lets it out in a strange sound, a groaning sigh. Then the fingers round her wrist slide off, sketch urgently in the air, retreat.

Aue. She sits down, back on her heels, way back on her heels. Looking at the brat guardedly; taking out cigarillos and matches; taking a deep breath herself and expelling it in smoke.

The child stays unmoving, hand back behind it; only the odd sea-eyes flicker, from her face to her hands and back round again.

She doesn't like looking at the child. One of the maimed, the contaminating. . . .

She looks at the smoke curling upward in a thin blue stream instead.

'Ah, you can't talk, is that it?'

A rustle of movement, a subdued rattle, and there, pitched into the open on the birdboned chest, is a pendant hanging like a label on a chain.

She leans forward and picks it up, taking intense care not to touch the person underneath.

It was a label.

1 PACIFIC STREET

  WHANGAROA

PHONE 633Z COLLECT

She turns it over.

SIMON P. GILLAYLEY

  CANNOT SPEAK

'Fascinating,' drawls Kerewin, and gets to her feet fast, away to the window. Over the sound of the rain, she can hear a fly dying somewhere close, buzzing frenetically. No other noise.

Reluctantly she turns to face the child. 'Well, we'll do nothing more. You found your way here, you can find it back.' Something came into focus. 'O there's a sandal you can collect before you go.' The eyes which had followed each of her movements, settling on and judging each one like a fly expecting swatting, drop to stare at his bare foot.

She points to the spiral stairs.

'Out.'

He moves slowly, awkwardly, one arm stretched to touch the wall all the way down, and she is forced to stop on each step behind him, and every time she stops, she can see him tense, shoulders jerking.

Lichen bole; glow-worms' hole; bonsai grove; hell, it seems like 15 miles rather than 15 steps . . . .

She edges round him at the livingroom door, and collects his sandal from the hearth. It is coated with silvery flounder slime.

'Yours?'

There is a barely perceptible nod. He stares at her unblinking.

'Well, put it on, and go.'

The rain's still beating down. She shrugs mentally. Serve him right.

He looks at the sandal in her hand, glances quickly at her face, and then, heart thumping visibly in his throat, sits down on the bottom step.

O you smart little bastard.

But she decides it is easiest to put the sandal on. Then push him out, bodily if need be.

'Give us your foot.'

With the same fearful stareguarded care he has affected throughout, he lifts his foot five inches off the ground. Kerewin stares at him coldly, but bends down and catches his foot, and is halted by a hiss. It, sssing through his closed teeth, bubbles of saliva spilling to his lips.

She remembers the strained walk, and looks more closely, and in his heel, rammed deep, is something; and the little crater in the sandal comes back to mind. She shuts her eyes and, all feeling in her fingertips, grazes her hand light as air over the protrusion. It was wooden, old wood, freshbroken, hard in the soft child-callous. Already the flesh round it is hot.

'We jumped on something that bit,' her voice mild as milk, and opens her eyes. The brat is squinting at her, his mouth sloped in a shallow upturned U.

'I suppose I can't expect you to walk away on that,' talking to herself, 'but what to do about it?'

Incongruously, he grins. It is a pleasant enough grin, but before it fades back into the considering U, reveals a gap bare of teeth on the left side of his jaw. The gap looks odd, and despite herself, she grins back.

'I can take it out before you go, if you want.'

He sucks in his breath, then nods.

'It'll probably hurt.'

He shrugs.

'Okay then,' hoping she has taken the tenor of the shrug rightly.

She gets bandage from the coffee-cupboard, a pair of needlenosed pliers from the knife-drawer, disinfectant from the grog cupboard.

'You better ahh tell your parents to get you a tetanus shot when you get home,' picking up his foot again, conscious of the eyes, very conscious of paleknuckled fingers gripping her step.

She sets the pliers flush with the end of the splinter, carefully so as not to pinch skin. There's an eighth inch gap between the jaws when they're closed on the wood. she holds it a moment, setting aside every sensation beyond splinter, pliers, her grip, and then presses hard and pulls down in one smooth movement. An inch of angular wood slides out.

The child jerks but might be pulling against a fetter for all the effect it

has. She scrutinises the hole before it closes and fills in bloodily. No dark
slivers, clean puncture, should heal well; and becomes aware of the hissing
and twisting and sets the foot free. The marks of her grip are white on his
ankle.

'Sorry about that. I forgot you were still on the end of it. The foot I
mean.' With the careless suppleness of the young, he has his foot nearly on
his chest. He broods over it, thumb on the splinter hole.

'Give it here again.'

She swabs the heel with antiseptic, bandages some protective padding over
it.

Sop for your conscience, Holmes me love. He can limp away easy into
the rain.

She stands, gesturing towards the door.

'On your way now, Simon P. Gillayley.'

He sits quite still, clasping his foot. Then he sighs audibly. He puts the
sandal on, wincing, and stands awkwardly. He brushes away the long fringe
of hair that's fallen over his eyes, looks at her and holds out his hand.

'I don't understand sign language,' says Kerewin coolly.

A rare kind of expression comes over the boy's face, impatience compounded with o-don't-give-me-that-kind-of-shit. He takes hold of his other
hand, shakes it, waves tata in the air, and then spreads both hands palms up
before her. Shaking hands, you get what I mean? I'm saying goodbye, okay?

Then he holds out his hand to her again.

Ratbag child.

She's grinning as she takes his hand, and shakes it gently. And the child
smiles broadly back.

'You come here by yourself?'

He nods, still holding onto her hand.

'Why?'

He marches the fingers of his free hand aimlessly round in the air. His
eyes don't leave her face.

'Meaning you were just wandering round?'

He doesn't nod, but makes a downward gesture with his hand.

'What does that mean?'

He nods, repeating the gesture on a level with his head.

'Shorthand for Yes?' unable to repress a smile.

Yes, say the fingers.

'Fair enough. Why did you come inside?'

She takes her hand away from his grasp. He has finely sinewed, oddly dry
hands. He points to his eyes.

Seeing, looking, I suppose.

She feels strange.

I'm used to talking to myself, but talking for someone else?

'Well, in case no-one ever told you before, people's houses are private and sacrosanct. Even peculiar places like my tower. That means you don't come inside unless you get invited.'

He's looking steadily at her.

'Okay?'

The gaze drops. He takes out a small pad and pencil from his jeans pocket and writes.

He offers the page to her.

In neat and competent capitals . . . how old are you, urchin? I KNOW I GET TOLD SP

'And you keep on doing it? You're a bit of a bloody hard case, boy.'

He is staring straight ahead now, eyes on the level of her belt buckle.

He gets told, meaning he must do it frequently . . . unholy, he's a bit young to be a burglar, maybe he's just compulsively curious?

'Well, there's a couple of cliches that fit in neatly here. One, curiosity killed the cat. Two, it takes all sorts to make a world. You want some lunch before you go? It might stop raining in the meantime. . . .'

He looks up abruptly, and she is startled to see his eyes fill with tears.

What in the name of hell have I said that would make it cry?

§ *Changing roles of women* Aus: Garner, Grenville; Can: Thomas, Marlatt, van Herk; *Outsider figures* Frame

PATRICIA GRACE (1937–)

From Potiki

Potiki is about a Maori community that finds its way of life threatened by property developers. This section is the Prologue which, with its stress on the ancestral activities of wood-carving and storytelling and the importance of humility and a respectful attitude towards the natural world, establishes the context for the challenge to traditional values which follows in the main part of the novel.

From the centre,
From the nothing,
Of not seen,
Of not heard,

There comes
A shifting,
A stirring,
And a creeping forward,

There comes
A standing,
A springing,
To an outer circle,

There comes
An intake
Of breath –
Tihe Mauriora.[1]

There was once a carver who spent a lifetime with wood, seeking out and exposing the figures that were hidden there. These eccentric or brave, dour, whimsical, crafty, beguiling, tormenting, tormented or loving figures developed first in the forests, in the tree wombs, but depended on the master with his karakia[2] and his tools, his mind and his heart, his breath and his strangeness to bring them to other birth.

The tree, after a lifetime of fruiting, has, after its first death, a further fruiting at the hands of a master.

This does not mean that the man is master of the tree. Nor is he master of what eventually comes from his hands. He is master only of the skills that bring forward what was already waiting in the womb that is a tree – a tree that may have spent further time as a house or classroom, or a bridge or pier. Or further time could have been spent floating on the sea or river, or sucked into a swamp, or stopping a bank, or sprawled on a beach bleaching among the sand, stones and sun.

It is as though a child brings about the birth of a parent because that which comes from under the master's hand is older than he is, is already ancient.

When the carver dies he leaves behind him a house for the people. He leaves also, part of himself – shavings of heart and being, hunger and anger, love, mischief, hope, desire, elation or despair. He has given the people himself, and he has given the people his ancestors and their own.

And these ancestors come to the people with large heads that may be round or square, pointed or egg-shaped. They have gaping mouths with protruding tongues; but sometimes the tongue is a hand or tail coming through from behind the head, or it is formed into a funnel or divided in two, the two parts pointing in different directions. There will be a reason for the type of head or tongue the figures have been given.

The carved ancestors will be broad-shouldered but short in the trunk and legs, and firm-standing on their three-toed feet. Or their bodies may be long and twisting and scaly, swimmers, shaped for the river or sea.

After the shaping out of the heads, bodies and limbs, the carver begins to smooth the figures and then to enhance them with fine decoration. The final touch is the giving of eyes.

---

1 Breath of life.   2 Sacred chants; prayers.

The previous life, the life within the tree womb, was a time of eyeless-
ness, of waiting, swelling, hardening. It was a time of existing, already
browed, tongued, shouldered, fingered, sexed, footed, toed, and of waiting
to be shown as such. But eyeless. The spinning, dancing eyes are the final
gift from the carver, but the eyes are also a gift from the sea.

When all is finished the people have their ancestors. They sleep at their
feet, listen to their stories, call them by name, put them in songs and dances,
joke with them, become their children, their slaves, their enemies, their
friends.

In this way the ancestors are known and remembered. But the carver may
not be known or remembered, except by a few. These few, those who grew
up with him, or who sat at his elbow, will now and again remember him
and will say, 'Yes, yes, I remember him. He worked night and day for the
people. He was a master.' They may also add that he was a bit porangi[3] too,
or that he was a drunk, a clapmouth, a womaniser, a gambler or a bullshit
artist.

Except that he may have been a little porangi, and that he certainly
became a master, none of these words would apply to the carver of this
chapter of our story. He was a humble and gentle man.

He was the youngest child of middle-aged parents who, because he was
sickly as a baby, decided that he should not go to school.

Before the parents died, and when the boy was ten years old, they
wrapped him in scarves and put him at the elbow of a master carver who
was just at that time beginning the carvings for a new house. This man had
no woman. He had no children of his own.

The boy sat and watched and listened and, until he was fourteen, he barely
moved except to sweep shavings and smooth and polish wood.

Then one day the master shaped out a new mallet from a piece of rimu[4]
and carved a beaky head at the tip of the handle, and gave the head two
eyes. He handed the mallet to the boy and said, 'Unwrap yourself from the
scarves, son, and begin work. Remember two things,' he said. 'Do not carve
anyone in living memory and don't blow on the shavings or your wood will
get up and crack you.'

The boy let the scarves fall at his feet, and took the mallet in his hand.
At the same time he felt a kicking in his groin.

He never went back into scarves. He dropped them in the place where
he had sat at the elbow of his tutor and never went back for them. Later
in life he, in turn, became master of his craft. There was no one to match
him in his skill, and many would have said also that there were none who
could match him as a great storyteller and a teller of histories.

Near the end of his life the man was working on what he knew would
be the last house he would ever carve. It was a small and quiet house and
he was pleased about that. It had in it the finest work he had ever done.

There were no other carvers to help him with his work but the people

---

3 Demented.   4 A conifer, sometimes called red pine.

came every day to cook and care for him, and to paint patterns and weave panels and to help in every possible way. They came especially to listen to his stories which were of living wood, his stories of the ancestors. He told also the histories of patterns and the meanings of patterns to life. He told of the effects of weather and water on wood, and told all the things he had learned at the elbow of his tutor, all the things he had spent a lifetime learning.

At the time when he was about to begin the last poupou[5] for the new house he became ill. With the other poupou, the ones already completed, much discussion, quarrelling and planning had taken place. The people were anxious to have all aspects of their lives and ancestry represented in their new house. They wished to include all the famous ancestors to which they were linked, and also to include the ancestors which linked all people to the earth and the heavens from ancient to future times, and which told people of their relationships to light and growth, and to each other.

But the last poupou had not been discussed, and the people, to give honour to the man, said, 'This one's yours, we'll say nothing. It's for you to decide.'

The man knew that this would be the last piece of work that he would do. He knew that it would take all of his remaining strength and that in fact he would not complete the work at all.

'If I don't finish this one,' he said, 'it is because it cannot yet be finished, and also because I do not have the strength. You must put it in your house finished or not. There is one that I long to do but it cannot yet be completed. There is no one yet who can carry it forward for me because there is a part that is not yet known. There is no one yet who can complete it, that must be done at some future time. When it is known it will be done. And there is something else I must tell you. The part that I do, the figure that I bring out of wood, is from my own living memory. It is forbidden, but it is one that I long to do.' The people did not speak. They could not forbid him. They went away quietly as he turned towards the workshop.

He decided that he would leave himself hollow for this last work, that he would not bring out this final figure with his eyes or his mind, but only with his hands and his heart. And when he spoke to the wood he only said, 'It is the hands and the heart, these hands and this heart that will bring you out of the shadows, these hands and this heart before they go to earth.'

In his old age his eyes were already weak, but he covered the workshop window to darken the room, and his hands and his heart began their work.

The boy at his elbow asked no questions and no one else came near.

After several weeks the carver pulled the cloth from the workshop window. He called the people in and told them that the top figure was done. 'I'll tell you the story,' he said, 'but the lower figure must be left to a future time, for when it is known.

'This is the story of a red-eyed man, who spent his life bent in two, who

---

5 Carved panels on side-walls inside a meeting-house.

had no woman and no children of his own. He procreated in wood and gave knowledge out through his elbow. At this elbow of knowledge there is a space which can be left unfilled, always, except for this pattern of scarves. It is like a gap in the memory, a blind piece in the eye, but the pattern of scarves is there.

'His head is wide so that it may contain the histories and sciences of the people, and the chants and patterns, and knowledge concerning the plants and the trees. His forehead is embellished with an intricate pattern to show the status of his knowledge. His eyes are small because of the nearness of his work and because, before my time, he worked in a dim hut with a lantern at night, and worked many hours after dark.

'His tongue is long and fine and swirling, the tongue of a storyteller, and his neck is short so that there is no great distance from his head to his arms. His head and his hands work as one.

'The rounded back and the curve of the chest tell of his stoopiness and his devotion. The arms are short because of the closeness to his work. He has come to us with six fingers on each hand as a sign of the giftedness of his hands.

'The mallet in his right hand rests on his chest, and the mallet is another beating heart.

'His left hand grasps the chisel, and he holds the chisel against his pelvis. The long blade of the chisel becomes his penis thickening to the shape of a man. And this chisel-penisman resembles himself, like a child generated in wood by the chisel, or by the penis in flesh.

'The eyes of the man and the eyes of the penis-child contain all the colours of the sky and earth and sea, but the child eyes are small, as though not yet fully opened.

'There is no boldening of the legs, and they are not greatly adorned, but they are strong and stand him strongly to his work. And between and below his three-toed feet there is an open place. It is the space for the lower figure, but there is none yet to fill that place. That is for a future time.

'All about the man you can see the representations of his life and work, but with a place at the elbow which will remain always empty except for the pattern of scarves.

'A man can become master of skills in his lifetime but when he dies he may be forgotten, especially if he does not have children of his own. I give him to you so that he will not be forgotten. Let him live in our house.

'"A life for a life" could mean that you give your life to someone who has already given his to you. I was told not to call out anyone in living memory, but it is done. I was told not to give breath to wood but . . . "A life for a life" could mean that you give your life to someone who has already given you his own.'

When the people had gone and he had sent the boy away the carver closed the workshop door. He put his face close to the nostrils of the wood face, and blew.

The next morning the people lifted the poupou from off him and dressed him in fine clothes.

§ *Maori/Aboriginal experience* Ihimaera (1); Aus: Oodgeroo, Mudrooroo, Davis, Morgan; Can: King, Armstrong; *Tradition and modernity* Wendt (2)

EPELI HAU'OFA (1939–)

The Seventh and Other Days

When Jehovah created the Universe in six days and rested on the Seventh, He said it was good and that Man must so regulate his periods of work and rest. The children of Abraham observed the rule, and Christians everywhere do likewise; everywhere, that is, except in the little land of Tiko, notwithstanding its strict Sabbatarian laws. This doesn't mean that Tiko works seven days or even five days a week. No. In order to know its ways of doing things one has to find out first in which direction the Good Lord moves and then think of the opposite of that movement. The Lord moves one way, followed by Christians everywhere, and Tiko goes in the opposite direction, all on its own. Thus if the Lord works six days and rests on the Seventh, Tiko rests six days and works on the Seventh.

'And that's the truth,' said Manu with a firm nod of his heavy head. 'Our people work so hard on Sunday it takes a six-day rest to recover.'

'That's not true!' cried the ancient preacher. 'Nobody works or even plays on Sunday; it's against the law!'

Not wishing to argue with an obstinate octogenarian, Manu told the preacher about his great relative, Sione Falesi.

Sione is a Most Important Person who holds high positions in both the secular and the spiritual affairs of the realm. Sione stands six feet tall, weighs well nigh three hundred pounds, and looks every ounce a great Polynesian aristocrat, as Satusi, his wife of twenty-five years, puts it. Indeed, Sione is a true Polynesian chief, a practising Christian, and a self-confessed sinner who goes to church every Sunday mainly to ask God's forgiveness for his many, many errors.

Sione's house stands not too far from his local church, which has a huge bell. At precisely four-thirty every Sunday morning the big bell booms. Yes, it booms; the bells of Tiko don't peal like those elsewhere. Furthermore the bell at Sione's church booms simultaneously with thousands of other bells throughout the realm, wherein are four times as many churches as all other public establishments combined.

At the first sound of the great boom Sione bounces off his wife and crashes on to the floor stark awake. Satusi also bounces, falls on him, and is very cross because of the interruption. Their sixteen children spring up making nary a noise lest they receive the end of the broom. Everyone in the country jumps up at the same time as Sione and his family. And the bells stop booming only when everyone has gone to church. There is no other way of getting those bells to stop, which explains the almost one hundred per cent church attendance in the realm. Everyone goes to church; everyone, that is, except Manu, who owns the only pair of ear-plugs in the country. And Manu stays fast asleep.

That's how Sunday begins in tiny Tiko; and there is a long day ahead. Every two hours the big bells boom, and every two hours everyone but Manu goes to church. Everyone prays, everyone sings, everyone confesses; on their seats, on their feet, and on their knees. And throughout the Seventh Day the Lord is praised, the Lord is flattered, and the Lord is begged. Though perhaps the Lord doesn't hear if it's His day off.

The final act of piety takes place at 10.00 p.m. when each family gathers to say the family prayer before it retires to a well-earned six-day rest and recovery period.

Sione has sixteen children, none of whom was born on a Sunday. His wife is pregnant again and it is absolutely certain that the child will enter this world on any day but the Seventh. Indeed no one in the realm has ever been conceived or born from sunrise to midnight on a Sunday, on account of the bells which keep people inside the churches. It's impossible to commit sin of any kind on the Seventh Day. Babies could be born on Sundays, say the doctors at the National Hospital, only if their makers had sinned on this day. But no one does, not even Sione, although he is a Most Important Person.

'The Seventh is the Day of the Lord; every other day belongs to Satan,' Manu explained. And Satan, as Teachers of Sunday School say, does nothing but lead people into Temptation. Thus the six days that belong to Satan are not only a period of rest and recovery, but also of Temptation and much, much sin.

Yet notwithstanding their pious demeanour and assertions to the contrary, Sione and his friends would have it no other way. So through rest and oh such awful sin during the six days after the Seventh, Sione has sired sixteen children, with more yet to come. Sione firmly believes that by raising a large family he is doing the Almighty a handsome favour. Didn't Jehovah tell Abraham to produce as many issue as there are grains of sand on earth or stars in the firmament? Yes, Jehovah did, said Sione, and there aren't yet as many people in Tiko as there are grains in even a handful of sand.

So Sione inevitably opposes the Family Planning Association (FPA) and what it represents. When the Association talked of the population explosion, Sione retorted that there aren't any explosions in Tiko except from behinds of members of the FPA. When the Association reasoned that if people rest less they will procreate less, Sione countered that rest and procreation are God's gifts to Man and have, therefore, nothing to do with the FPA. When the Association appealed to the clergy to lighten the Sunday burden so that people would not spend so much time resting at home on other days, the clergy would not countenance the suggestion, proclaiming that only when their flocks go to Heaven will they rest on a Sunday. Their flocks, said the clergy, may rest as much as they want on other days. And rest they do: at home, in the bush, on chairs, everywhere.

Sione, for example, drives every morning from Monday to Friday to his office to loaf on the chair behind his desk. At three o'clock every day from Monday to Friday he hurries home to spend the rest of the day on his wife.

None of this does any good whatever for National Development, said the Wise Men at the Thinking Office. These Men of Wisdom once hired an Overseas Expert to look into the feasibility of making Tikongs work on weekdays.

The expert, a certain Mr Merv Dolittle from the Department of Aboriginal Affairs, Canberra, Australia, interviewed half a dozen Very Important Persons, the last being Sione Falesi. Mr Dolittle arrived at Sione's office an hour earlier than had been arranged and found him playing cards with his secretary, Ana Taipe.

'Well, come in, come in, Mr Dolittle. You're rather early aren't you?' Sione greeted his guest with no sign of embarrassment. 'Would you like to play five hundred with us? No? What a pity. Take a seat, then. We're just having our morning-tea break.'

'Morning-tea break?' queried Mr Dolittle, glancing at his watch. It was nine o'clock. His eyes scanned the office for teacups.

'You won't see anything, Mr Dolittle. We have no money for tea so we kill the allotted time playing cards. If you can't feed your face you may as well fiddle with your fingers. That's what I always say. Ana, clear the desk and take the cards with you. Good girl. We'll resume at lunch-time.'

The secretary left the office and Sione turned to the expert. 'Nice girl that one. She's the sharpest card player in Tiko. That's why I hired her. She's not much good at anything else though. All our good ones are in New Zealand.'

'What does Ana do?'

'All sorts of things, Mr Dolittle. She and I play cards at morning-tea time and at lunch-time. Every so often we get into the spirit of things and play on. What's two hours here and there, I ask you?'

'What else does she do?'

'All sorts of things, like I said,' said Sione, racking his brain for Ana's positive attributes. 'She's a damn good masseuse. I've got this slipped disc you see, and she's been fixing it for five years now. Every day, in fact. She's tremendous; you must try her sometime.'

'Is your work-load heavy, Mr Falesi?'

'Oh yes, very heavy indeed. You should see me on Sundays when I work eighteen hours non-stop for God. Life's a burden, an enormous burden,' said Sione, sighing heavily. 'But one must do one's bit for the Almighty. He's been very good to Tiko; you can see it all around. . . .'

'What about the other days?' Mr Dolittle cut in.

'What? Oh, yes. The other days, of course. Well, you see, Mr Dolittle . . . .' Sione stopped as if something had suddenly struck him. Then a wide grin creased his face. 'Incredible!' he ejaculated. 'How about that?'

'How about what?'

'Your name. Dolittle. It's so beautiful! Heavens above, you must be one of us! Ana! Ana! Bring the cards back in!'

'I must say that I've never, in all my life . . .' Mr Dolittle began to protest, then thought better of it, rose, excused himself, and beat a hasty exit. The incident was more than sufficient to enable him to grasp the nature of the problem. He wound up his tour that very day, called a press conference, and declared that this lot of natives, like the Aborigines, had an enormous untapped potential for work; but that His Excellency's Government must first import the Protestant Ethic, two little words hitherto unheard of in the realm, although most Tikongs are Protestants. When Radio AP2U broadcast and explained the full meaning of the said ethic, the entire population suddenly turned deaf.

'And deafness comes from too much rest,' Manu proclaimed.

When one rests too much one grows too many hairs inside one's ears, blocking out all sounds except the voice of flattery. That's why people of the common order, the vast majority of Tikongs, are the most adept flatterers in the Pacific: they have spent so much time practising it. And to many Important Persons, the so-called Sitters-on-Chairs, Wise Men, Traumatised Experts, Devious Traders, and assorted Pulpit Poops, flattery is sweeter than ice cream.

One of these Sitters-on-Chairs is, of course, Manu's gigantic relative Sione, nemesis of the Family Planning Association and father of sixteen children. One Monday morning Sione was sitting behind the desk of his office. The desk top was shining clean with nothing on it except a copy of *Penthouse* magazine confiscated from a visiting American yacht.

Sione's foreign-aid adviser, to whom he has delegated all his work, entered the office on this lovely Monday morning to announce that their agency was on the verge of bankruptcy. Sione sat motionless staring through the window; not a muscle moved. He heard nothing, he saw nothing; he was in deep repose as always on the first day after the Seventh.

The foreign-aid adviser nevertheless perceived that as soon as he opened his mouth the three-inch hairs protruding from Sione's ears began to bunch up, blocking the ear-holes as effectively as Manu's ear-plugs. The adviser mumbled a profanity, stalked out in disgust, and lost his way, eventually finding himself, as usual, slumped over the bar of the Tiko Club.

Immediately afterwards the underpaid agency cleaner, Lea Fakahekeheke, crept into the office, insinuated himself behind Sione, and whispered thus into his ear: 'Most Respected Sir, the New Zealand Air Delegation which came last Friday told me you're the wisest and most handsome man in the whole world.'

Even before Lea moved his lips the hairs in Sione's ears, as if anticipating what was coming, disentangled themselves and conducted the honeyed words swiftly into his brain. He suddenly came alive, breaking into a smile, yelling and hugging Lea.

Then he unlocked the agency safe, pulled out two five-dollar bills, and pressed them into Lea's half-unwilling hands, ordering him to take the day off. Lea slithered away well satisfied.

Every second week for over fifteen years Lea has gone to the office to whisper nice things into Sione's ear, and the Great Man has never failed to reward him each time with no less than ten dollars, which is considerably more than his fortnightly earnings.

'And who leads whom in Tiko?' Manu asked, never for a moment expecting a reply.

§ *Christianity in the Pacific* Wendt (1)

BILL MANHIRE (1946–)

From South Pacific

This is the central section of a longish short story, which offers a playful treatment of the manufacturing of cultural identities and history.

. . . London was cold – grey and puzzling. People bumped into one another on the footpaths, they clustered in shivering groups around map-books. Black rubbish bags were stacked against shopfronts, taxis nudged their way along the streets. He had found a small hotel a few blocks from the British Museum. His room was on the top floor, with a view of roofs and chimney pots. Mary Poppins stuff.

The roof of the building opposite was buried in rubble – timber, plasterboard, lumps of plumbing and splintered brick. Men lowered it all through scaffolding to a skip below. A sign on the front of the building said *Prestige Office Space*. Along the road another sign said *Superior Office Space*.

His first act had been to get out the South Pacific board. He put New Zealand in place, in the picture, then propped the game on top of the dressing table. Evidence of home. On the calendar above his bed he circled the departure date – making sure he was sure of it. There was something wrong with the calendar. The legend read, 'March – the Gardens at Crathes Castle, Grampian'. But the picture was of Ben Nevis, snow-clad, against a background of cloud.

He woke with a start at three in the morning. In the thin light from the bedlamp he searched for the book Jean had given him. The *Envoy from Mirror City*.[1] It was part of the life story of Janet Frame, the New Zealand writer. It was about the time she had spent overseas – a suitable gift for travellers.

He leafed through the pages. Janet Frame was in Andorra, in the Pyrenees. She had become engaged to an Italian, El Vici Mario, who lodged in the same house as she did. They had walked together in the mountains, and he

---

1 The third volume of Frame's autobiography, 1985.

had said to her, *'Voulez-vous me marier, moi?'* El Vici could speak three languages. He had a blue-and-white bicycle, picked grapes and had fought against the fascists. Janet Frame did not say yes but she did not say no either. She did not know how to. She told El Vici that she had to go to London before the marriage, that there were 'things to see to'. She would be back soon. She bought a return ticket – but she never meant to return.

Allen marked his place; he yawned.

Deep in Andorra, deep in Allen's sleep, El Vici waited patiently for Janet Frame. He whispered to himself in French, Spanish and Italian. He was a tall, stooped figure with two-toned shoes, and he wheeled his blue-and-white bicycle along the roads of Europe, road after road, until one day, there he was, wheeling his bicycle through the small arcade behind New Zealand House. El Vici gazed into the window of Whitcoulls' little bookshop. He saw a display of books by Janet Frame. He shivered in the cold.

Allen had just finished serving a customer when El Vici pushed open the shop door.

'Prego, ' said El Vici. He was holding the South Pacific board. *'Dov'è Nuova Zelanda?'*

El Vici's nicotine-stained finger hovered above the expanse of blue. Allen felt sorry for him. Another traveller lost in a foreign city.

He took El Vici's finger and dipped it in a jar of Vegemite.

'Taste that,' he said. 'Go on, try it.'

A man in the trade section at New Zealand House said to him across a desk that he should really have made some sort of preliminary appointment before he left home. He seemed pleased to be talking, though. He introduced himself as Mike Bekeris. He drummed his fingers on the game board.

'Lots of blue,' he said. 'South Pacific, eh?'

'Well, the real game mostly takes place in the players' consultations and so on.' Allen felt he had to offer something. 'It's a role-playing game, really. The board's as much a matter of focus as anything. Every time you discover a new country you can place it on the board, physically put it there. So while you have to work with given names, you can build up the map as you go along. We've tried to mimic the actual conditions of exploration. In fact, you could play a whole game through without even discovering New Zealand.'

A girl put her head around the door and said, 'That's all right about Martin Crowe.'[2]

Mike Bekeris said to Allen: 'Not quite my sort of thing, personally, board games. But then your problem isn't going to be selling it to me.'

'No,' said Allen.

'I'll be straight with you, Mr Douglas.' Mike Bekeris leant across the desk like an actor in a play. 'A lot of people come in here in your position – cottage industry sort of thing – and there isn't a great deal of return for any-

2 New Zealand cricketer.

one on the time put in. In any case, my hands are tied. I can give you, oh, half an hour, but then you have to decide just how serious you want our involvement to be. '

'Fair enough,' said Allen.

'Now I take it you aren't in production yet – well you can't be, or you'd have something more finished to show me. So what are your options? I'd say you can try and market direct, or you can pass the whole thing across to one of the big companies.'

'How do you mean?'

'Well, you would license Waddingtons, let us say, to produce and market the game in certain territories. I won't be telling you anything new there. Your problem is that Waddingtons might not see much future for a game like this in Europe or North America and they might want to sell back into Australasia. If they want to see you at all.'

'We thought we would try to do our own marketing at home,' said Allen.

'So: direct marketing. But remember that over here you'd be chasing your tail inside a huge market looking for the specialist market. You'd certainly need someone on the ground, so you'd be looking at a fairly big outlay in the first instance. So maybe that means you have to go after sponsorship.'

'You mean here?' said Allen. 'Or at home?'

'Actually, the thing you have to decide,' said Mike Bekeris, 'is whether you want us to come any further down the track with you. We've moved on to a firm cost-recovery system these days: I don't come free on the tax-payer. So if you'd like us to do a bit of preliminary work – e.g. try to set up appointments with game manufacturers – then you have to commit your-self to a bit of expenditure. However you go, you can still write off 60 per-cent of your trip as product development.'

Allen stared at a wall poster – 'Auckland: City of Sails'. The blue slashed with sheets of white. He felt that Mike Bekeris was daring him to do some-thing quite outrageous. But what, exactly?

'Why don't you think about it,' said Mike Bekeris, 'and give me a call over the next few days?'

The cold ate into everything. Sheets of paper flapped slowly down the Haymarket. Allen walked up through Soho, past restaurants and sex shops. It was mid-afternoon, a respectable time of day, and Soho seemed more dis-creet, more muted than he remembered. There were no posters outside the cinemas he passed. No one called softly from the mouths of hostess bars.

Sex was more prominent in the Virgin Games Shop in Oxford Street. At least, he found himself noticing the sex games first. Libido, Foreplay, Dr Ruth's Game of Good Sex. They seemed to be versions of strip poker, over-laid with questions of the Trivial Pursuit kind. Dr Ruth promised 'interac-tive cards'.

The fantasy games bred among themselves at the back of the shop. Dungeons and Dragons, Talisman, Runequest, Call of Cthulhu, Thieves' World, Star Trek, Sorcerer's Cave . . . Near them were the history games.

You could fight every campaign of the American Civil War, you could join battle with Napoleon across the map of Europe. Among the World War II games, one called Pacific War caught his eye. But it turned out to involve America and Japan fighting the battles of 1941– 45.

He asked an assistant if the shop had any travel or exploration games and was pointed to a display of a game called Capital Adventure – 'a travel game for people going places'. Some skill seemed to be involved in choosing the best air route between one capital city and the next. 'Take calculated risks,' said the box, 'and face the dangers that every global traveller meets.'

But there was no overlap with South Pacific.

He looked for the assistant again and described South Pacific, pretending it was a game he had read about somewhere and would be interested to buy.

'Sounds interesting,' said the assistant. It was the sort of thing they would want to have in stock, but he had never seen it. Did Allen know who made it?

'A New Zealand company, I think.'

'Ah, well.'

'If I get the details,' said Allen, 'I could drop you a note.'

'We'd surely appreciate it. We try to be comprehensive. I *think* there used to be something called Columbus. Discover America sort of thing.'

Back at the hotel Allen pushed open the door of the tiny guest lounge. A wall heater beamed its warmth on a Bengali family who sat in front of the television. One of them, an elderly woman, held a badminton racquet across her knees. Allen watched for a few minutes – Tottenham and Arsenal in extra time – then went up to his room.

His bed had been made, the cover turned back. Two hairclips lay on the pillow. He stared at them, at the shiny insect legs. He felt for his wallet in his pocket.

He looked out Monika's number and went down to the coinbox in the hall. She answered the telephone herself. She had been expecting to hear, she said. Jean had sent a letter: they must get together.

'I'm afraid it wouldn't work for you to come round here,' she said. 'But I wonder if we mightn't do something on Saturday? I can bring Lark. We can make a bit of a day of it. The thing is, I haven't got all that much money at the moment.'

They met under an AIDS billboard outside the London Dungeon. Allen insisted on buying the tickets. Lark was half-price, in any case.

'I'll write you off as a business expense,' he said.

'I hope you don't mind starting off here,' Monika said as they walked through the clinical half darkness. 'Lark's been wanting to come for ages. I'm sure it'll be dreadful. Like the Chamber of Horrors.'

She had a green jewelled stud in the side of her nose. It glinted, catching the candlelight as they moved around.

'Are we under the river?' asked Lark. 'Bet we are.' She ran ahead.

They strolled among the unconvincing horrors of tourist London, passing from a scene of Druid sacrifice to a life-size model of St George, who was strapped to an X-shaped cross and bled where his flesh had been scraped by jagged combs. Further on, blood poured from the neck of Mary Queen of Scots like water from a playground drinking fountain. Behind a window live rats scurried about a skull.

'Poor things,' said Lark. 'Aren't they cute?'

'It's a *plague* display,' said Allen. 'You're supposed to be frightened.'

Beside the skull was a bowl filled with grain. He could just make out the lettering of the word DOG on the bowl's surface.

They paused in front of Sawney Beane, the Scottish cannibal. He and his family had lived for 25 years in a cave near Edinburgh. They killed unsuspecting passers-by, cutting up their bodies and pickling them. They chuckled horribly over their evening meal. After they had been captured, the men were castrated; their arms and feet were cut off, and they were left to bleed to death. The notice said that the women 'were burned in three fires'.

'Why?' said Lark. 'Why did they do that to the women?'

'Witch paranoia,' said Monika. 'They thought the women had all the real power.'

'Your father would know,' said a woman, tugging a small boy after her. But she was talking about something else.

They sat in a cafeteria at the Barbican.

'I thought it would be *frightening*,' said Lark.

Monika fingered the bone pendant which Allen had brought her from Jean.

'It's designed not to be,' said Monika. 'You're supposed to get a taste of terror but without the reality.'

She looked at Allen as if to indicate that she was saying one thing to Lark and another to him.

'Listen,' said Lark. She read out a witch's spell from one of the postcards Allen had bought.

'To win the love of a woman who does not want you, thread a needle with her hair and run it through the fleshiest limb of a dead man.'

She looked at her mother's cropped hair.

'You're safe, Mummy. No one would ever get your hair through the needle. It's far too short.'

'First find your dead man,' said Monika. 'Then we'll see.'

Allen remembered her taking his hand in a Greek restaurant in Camden Town, years ago. She had long hair then. Jean was there. His fingers were clenched up inside his palm. She unbent his fingers, one by one, then placed his hand flat, palm down, on the table. 'That's advice,' she said, 'not a proposition.'

'I think you should send your children the scariest ones,' said Lark.

Outside it was snowing. The snow fell into a long rectangular pond of water. There were ducks on the water, and beyond it was the 16th-century church of St Giles-without-Cripplegate where, said the guidebook, Oliver Cromwell had been married.

Lark went out to stand in the snow. She waved at them through the window. But the snow wasn't going to settle.

'Eight years old,' said Allen. 'Amazing.'

'Jean hasn't seen her since she was five weeks old.'

Lark waved through the window.

'But she had to go back,' said Allen. 'We went back together. She'll be across on the next trip. If this game works out.'

'South Pacific,' said Monika.

'South Pacific,' said Allen.

A pale leaflet lay on the floor outside his bedroom door.

'Rubber: the fantasy; Love Potions; Pillow Talk; The Mistress: I'm waiting to talk to you!' There were drawings of girls in lingerie, and a list of names, each with a telephone number. *Saucy Girls!*

He folded the sheet and tucked it into his pocket. A souvenir.

Next day, Sunday, he walked in the City, drifting through anaemic sunshine. At St Paul's he bought a tiny crystal bell for Jean. There was a gift-shop just inside the main entrance.

In his hotel bedroom he played a game of South Pacific. But his mind failed to concentrate. Player A discovered Samoa but failed to control his crew, who introduced the native population to alcohol, then a few moves later gave them syphilis. Player B drifted in the blue.

Allen lay on the bed and masturbated. He would not call Mike Bekeris.

He tried to imagine the voice of a saucy girl but could only imagine silence. But it was all right. The light caught the jewel in the side of Monika's nose as she lowered her head towards him and her hair, long, abundant, fell forward, shielding her face.

He spent his last two days staying with one of his father's cousins, Margaret. Margaret's house lay directly beneath the flight-path at Gatwick. She could tell one kind of aircraft from another by the engine noise as they came in to land. On top of the television she kept a photograph of her late husband.

It was an amiable duty visit. Allen gave news of home, and Margaret was happy to leave him largely to himself. He went for walks, jotted down notes for a possible game on Antarctic exploration, glanced at a chapter from the Janet Frame book. He would leave the book with Margaret.

There was news of a ferry disaster. A boat had capsized sailing out of a Belgian harbour.[3] As many as 200 were feared drowned. Margaret settled in her chair in front of the television, holding the remote control, flicking between channels.

Allen rang a saucy girl. He pressed the phone close to his ear.

---

3 The *Herald of Free Enterprise* ferry disaster in Zeebrugge harbour on 4 March 1987.

A voice welcomed him to International Celebrity Line. He was through to Erica Croft.

Erica Croft explained that as a top model she visited many exciting places. Today she was on location in the South Pacific.

'We're shooting one of those chocolate bar commercials – you know, the desert island bit where you discover the treasure chest full of chewy bars. It's lovely out here, with the bleached golden sands and palm trees and gently rippling waves.'

She said that since they had a break in shooting, she would say something about some of the other countries she had been to.

'Once I went to shoot a calendar with a few other girls in North Africa. We were hoping to get a lovely tan and come back with great stories and lovely pictures, but the whole trip was an absolute disaster. There were sandstorms on the beach and it poured with rain. All the girls got bitten by insects.

'Another trip I went on earlier this year was to Cyprus, to shoot a commercial for babies' nappies. There were 25 babies plus all the parents plus all the lighting plus the cameraman – all in one tiny room which was actually a ballet school. Well you can imagine the chaos in there. That was another trip that turned out to be a bit of a disaster. But they managed to make the commercial in the end, it came out looking ever so good.

'Before I go, let me just tell you today's secret. I'd really like to learn to fly.'

Allen pressed the receiver to his ear. 'Don't forget to call tomorrow when I'll be revealing even more about myself,' said Erica Croft. Then there was music, then the line went dead.

§ *Constructed national/regional identities* Curnow (2), Wendt (2); TransC: Ondaatje (1)

SUBRAMANI (1947–)

Marigolds

I can hear the gurgle in the toilet, and water rushing to fill the cistern. In a moment the toilet door will unlatch. Dharma will be in the kitchen again. And I'm clinging hopelessly to this Sunday morning, afraid of the waves of depression that hit us about 2 P.M.

Throughout the night I dribbled copiously like a baby; in the morning, woke up with the dreadful sensation that my hair had turned crimson, and flesh dissolved into a vegetable curd. In spite of countless experiments with digestive habits, especially after they diagnosed a cancerous growth at the lower end of my alimentary canal, I still have those dreams. I must have struck the iron of the bed with my left arm. It flapped at my side like a broken wing as I limped to the balcony to warm my bones. Dharma, up earlier than usual, had slipped out in the dark for her Sunday ritual. My wife is a sun-worshipper. She pours cold tap water from a brass lota[1] on a Tulsi[2] plant as the sun rises, chanting some obscure Sanskrit mantra, which I'm sure she does not understand. She pulls the orhini[3] over her head when she discovers I'm watching.

There used to be such a pleasant chirping of birds in the trees when we had just built the house. Now the bush is gone, leveled by squatters. Our house is a bit ungainly. Dharma was elated when it was finished. She has kept some marigold seeds in a bottle. She said she'll have a garden. We don't have a garden yet. Except the dried-up flower bed in front which carries Dharma's Tulsi plant.

The sun is a shimmering disc. I can feel it soaking up the moisture from the grass. Lord, the incurable distress of a vacant, bright Sunday! Each time there's a scrunch of wheels on the gravel, my attention is automatically drawn to the street, expecting to be rescued from this self-made prison. Dharma inevitably gravitates toward the kitchen. My fingers begin to twitch nervously on my lap as I wait for the prattling in the kitchen: it will fall like an avalanche down from the crevices of my head, tearing my nerves to shreds. I'm relieved she's standing in the middle of the kitchen, staring vacantly at the smoke-stained walls. She sighs ruefully. I watch her rouse herself and walk into the passage. She throws a quick evasive look into the lounge and slinks into the bedroom. I can picture her flexing the muscles of her toes, studying her fingernails or gazing emptily at the bare walls.

Last week my mother left our house. One morning, she flew up in a rage, accusing me of wanting her out of the way. She starting flinging everything I had given her at me: blankets, medicine, tobacco. She called a neighbor and had her things removed to the destitute home. I went to fetch her in a taxi after school. She refused to see me. 'Mother,' I pleaded, 'I have come to take you home. Why are you playing these games? You know I want you back, Mother.' For a second I thought she was going to scratch my face. 'Aach!' she shrieked, trying to control herself, and turned away from me.

She'll come back. Out of spite. To humiliate me, accuse me of ingratitude, and taunt me with her craziness. She'll mutter away in Hindi: 'My little nigger who wanted to fly. So she has clipped your wings. You are a disgrace like your father. Treating a poor, ailing woman who is your mother like this. . . . You can't treat me like this, you know! I will tell the magistrates. I will let the whole world know. . . . So Cheta is ashamed of his illiterate relatives because he is a big man with a post. . . . You are nothing, I tell you. Nothing.' She'll spit her phlegm in a tin half-filled with red mud which she keeps by her bedside. When she is calmer, I'll listen to all her complaints about her ailments and give her tobacco money. Her limbs are crabbed and gnarled by rheumatism. She seldom sleeps when the night is cold. She sits in the dark smoking homemade cigars. Her skin has become dismal like the cigars she smokes.

---

1 Mug.   2 Basil, used in *puja* (or worship).   3 Headcloth; veil.

As a rule, Dharma has absolute reverence for convention. However, she is most un-Hindu in her contempt for trespassers (trespassers destroy our equilibrium!). She despises my mother, above all, who she swears is a demented witch come to destroy our house. The old grimalkin pampers her in that belief. All day she plays strange tricks with Dharma, and laughs ghoulishly when the latter is not watching.

Sometimes I amble along to Mr. Rangaswamy's house. I can see the postal clerk squatted in a semi-lotus position on his porch, reading.

'Unclaimed trash filched from the Post Office,' I quipped once to impress Dharma. Mr. Rangaswamy's two passions, his only weaknesses he claims, are yogic breathing and politics. He offers me the disemboweled car seat, mounted on a board and pushed against the wall, to sit on. I listen to his bleating South Indian voice, hoping to be affected by some of his enthusiasm, as he unearths the issues and hidden trends in government, and belches intermittently to emit stale, sour wind from his chest. The wisps of gray hair on the sides of his balding head quiver as he becomes increasingly eloquent. Abruptly he relapses into silence, nodding toward my house. 'She has been on the balcony twice.' And I totter back, my brain inflamed. The lurking beast inside the cage of my ribs lifts its head like a pre-historic monster. Once in the lounge, however, all my rage is doused. Dharma, almost disappearing in the bedroom, waits for me to react, then skulks inside. More than anything else she resents the reproaches that I never make. Silence is my secret weapon.

There's an unhappy, sullen doll on my bookcase. Dharma bought it to decorate the lounge. Like my wife, she watches all my thoughts from some secret vantage point. One weekend I broke her head. I can see a film of tears in her glassy eyes.

After my visit to Mr. Rangaswamy one Sunday, I was slicing cucumber in the lounge. I shuffled into the kitchen for some salt. Dharma turned with a start, and cringed with fear when she saw the knife in my hand. She howled like a crazy woman, bolted outside, and hid behind a hedge. All afternoon there was a trapped, threatening air in the house. It was then I realized how our life had gradually slipped beyond the margin of security. She stole inside after dark, and locked herself in the bedroom.

Each time Cecil returns from Australia he seems darker, swarthier, older. The Australian climate doesn't seem to agree with him. He stays at our house during his brief vacation. He brings his daughters, two of the most secretive and unpleasant children I know, to show them the island of his birth. He rarely goes out even when the weather is fine. When he is tired of sitting in the lounge, he takes a mat behind the house and sprawls under the mango tree in his t-shirt and slacks. Tremors of brotherly love ooze from the depths of my flesh when I watch him lying there under the mango tree, waiting for a soft breeze. There are so many things I want to know and discuss. But Cecil has always been the quiet one. All I know about him is he's a dentist in Sydney, has two houses, and his wife Dorothea is a nurse.

The children, wrapped in coarse woolen clothes in spite of the stinging heat, are always in the passage, whispering in each other's ears and throwing furtive glances at us. They aren't like real children, soft and innocent, but unhealthy looking and adult-like in their demeanor. I tried to take the younger one in my arms. She wriggled out crying, 'You smell like an old man!'

In the bathroom, I peeled off my clothes, and stood, naked, in front of the mirror and sniffed my body. Sure enough, the dried-up hide that encased my limbs emitted a fetid smell – the odor of death. I paced like a trapped animal in the lounge making loud shuffling noises until Mr. Rangaswamy came out on his porch, spectacle in hand, and peered quizzically at my behavior. I bought some lotion on the way home from school and splattered myself with the stuff. Dharma's cold, frowning eyes told me she didn't approve. She felt pleasantly tormented by the thought that she had somehow been betrayed. I hid the lotion in a cupboard.

Once again my attention turns to the diurnal sounds that signal the passing of hours: the change of radio music; the squatters chatting softly under the growing shadows of houses after their siesta; the children out in the yard with their kites. The air of torpor has slowly vanished. There's no longer the frightening noonday stillness which had invaded the huts. The kites glide like tiny machines against the glistening blue vault. Imperceptibly the afternoon, now a shade cooler, is wearing on. I have seen the wind steal behind the house; the leaves of the mango tree are astir. Dharma is urinating noisily: she has left the toilet door ajar.

At precisely 9 P.M. each night Dharma is in the bedroom, dusting the sheets and pillows, pulling down the mosquito net. By 9:30 she's in her clumsy nightwear on her side of the bed. From there she gauges my actions by the movement of my slippers. She knows exactly when I'm fumbling with the strings of my pajamas, turns briefly to see I'm settled in, then pulls the cord to switch the light off.

I toss and turn feeling for a soft, comfortable place on the pillow. With my eyes shut I muse about the marigolds, groping through a labyrinth which is now a crater, now a tomb, waiting for the deliriously happy state of being suddenly afloat. Abruptly, without much effort, without losing breath, I'm flung upward like a billowing parachute. I propel myself higher with my elbows – it's one skill I'm sure of – into a vast, open field of heavy-blowing marigolds. Acres of succulent plants, the size of sunflowers, blazing maddeningly in the sun, still straining for growth.

The latter part of the dream is less pleasurable, more threatening. The voices of children, forever on the fringe of audibility, lead me through a meandering pattern to the stone altar under a crumbling thatch, smelling of goat dumpings on the sides, where I suffer reproaches from the shadow. I do not know who I am or where I am. I squirt my eyes open. Then begins the agonizing effort to push myself afloat again. Slowly light walls up, and the familiar surrounding slides into place.

I brought a sprig of marigold for Dharma's hair: the stunted flower was glowing like a jewel in the school garden. She left it in the lounge. When she came back for it, I had taken the flower in my mouth.

For years I looked after the school garden. Until they made me the deputy head. Now I virtually run the school. And feel quietly superior. The head is an odious fellow, seen hurrying in the corridor, jangling a bunch of keys and giving everyone a formal nod like the previous head. He has an infuriating habit of peeking into the staff room and flicking his tongue between his lips that are burned by alcohol. He pretends he is seeking Mrs. Sharma for consultation. (Mrs. Sharma already looks peeved and ready to burst into his office.) Meanwhile, his snout is turned toward Hina. Hina tilts her face in query, and fumbles into her handbag for a handkerchief to blow her pretty nose. Her mouth opens in youthful laughter, as soon as he moves away, revealing all the slippery membranes inside. Yes, I have allowed my eyes to roll on their youthful limbs. But mainly for the pleasure of catching them in a coarse, unguarded gesture. Each morning for some obscure reason I expect a slight limp in their erect torsos. I had to pay dearly for my surreptitious action. I dropped behind Hina in the staff room one morning: she was hopelessly smothering a giggle at the mention of a wad of cotton wool to prevent the yellow discharge in my right ear. Since then she has taken instructions with averted eyes.

I haven't picked up any of the urban smartness. Still, I can see through all the blatherings and boastings in the staff room, all the desultory conversation about their precocious children who are studying medicine or law, their new-fangled houses (on stilts) in Beach Estate, and the relative performances of their shiny cars. Sufficient to drive anyone distraught! Most of them ignore me, behave as if I do not exist. I'm not game enough to be asked to their Friday night drinking parties. I have struck up a friendship with Eroni, the physical education instructor. The Fijian lad is the only person who takes me seriously, calls me 'Mr. Chetram' politely, even though he regards me as a member of the desperate, money-grubbing fraternity which he despises but secretly hopes to emulate. He shakes his head at my frugal lunch, and smiles pitifully. Eroni affirms the historical basis of my existence.

It takes me a little longer each morning to dispel the clouds from my head and arrange my thoughts before I enter the classroom. The students no longer take seriously all the postures I assume for their benefit: my magnanimity, my cheerfulness, my warmth. Instead they ridicule my blustering ways, and snigger with a criminal leer on their faces when they find me in disarray. Encouraged, of course, by the blush of anger on my face when I grope for words or silence the amused chuckle in the back.

Standing alone in the staff room toilet in front of the gushing water in the bowl, after the Friday morning session, I saw clearly how my whole existence has been in bad faith. The lies I had lived in order to hold, to maintain serenity, accepting countless humiliations without rebelling, suppressing all aggression out of fear of creating new situations which I might not be able to control, where my tolerance was just a mask to preserve my inner freedom and weakness, my reticence an empty posture to cover my defects and avoid censure, had warped everything that was wholesome and fine in my life. Now the certainty on Dharma's face stabbed me like mockery.

I did not return wearily to 21 Yala Street that Friday afternoon with my satchel and umbrella. At noon I slipped away from the agitated staff and their provocative pupils toward Suva. All my life I had lived according to other people's expectations. Now I wanted a life of my own to start a new road. The passengers smiled strangely at me on the bus: I was the lost member of a tribe just returned to the fold. I strode in the swirling crowd on the pavement remembering the faces, odors, and cravings which had slowly been obscured in my memory. Again the city was the mela of my childhood where lost amid the tents, stalls, and games, I roamed like a free spirit. The splash of color were myriads of marigolds. The warm fragrance of the unseen flower suddenly pervaded the air. I waited for the sense to snap open.

Afterward the stalls, the tents, the games were all washed by rain.

I cannot distinguish, having become a prey to so many delusions, how much of what happened that night was real, how much simply a dream. I recall feeling that all the unlit streets and alleys, vacant rooms and parks were so many empty and unillumined realms of my existence. The boisterous, good-humored taxi driver steered me into a bar which smelled of urine and sweat. I told myself I shouldn't have taken so much alcohol. I detached myself from the drinkers and headed toward the toilet. The bowl overflowed on the greasy floor, and bits of newspaper and cigarette butts swirled in the pool of water. I waddled outside to clear my head.

The dingy metal cage inched upward from a subterranean depth. It seemed like a slow drift into the air from the labyrinth of my dream. I could have remained there all night but for the wiry creature in a hippie blouse who stared strangely at me, coughed nervously when our eyes met, and dropped his gaze involuntarily on the spent match which he rolled with his toe. When the gate slid open I broke into a run. He followed me to the pavement like a shadow in a dream.

The taxi driver surfaced again and lumbered along by my side. Like kindred spirits we marched into a restaurant. My companion ordered several Chinese dishes and beer. I watched him in the wall mirror, totally enthralled by the vigor of his conversation and his appetite, as he chomped his food in a ravenous fit. 'Damn it,' he cried, swigging from a bottle. 'It's so easy to be happy. So damn easy.' There were drunken tears in his eyes. His face gleamed with perspiration.

And then the drunken ride through the resisting darkness. The streets were washed by rain. The car stopped at the desolate end of the city. My companion shot out in the rain with his coat over his head, and disappeared into what looked like a run-down bungalow. I waited with spluttering desires; was relieved when there were no catcalls or jeers from the neighborhood. I trudged laboriously up the short flight of stairs, egged on by my companion, almost stumbling on a cat which purred persistently against my legs. My breath became loud and phlegmy. I felt a curious weakening of the knees. I must have been sick afterward. There was vomit in my shoes. The mattress smelled of child's urine.

Dharma didn't sniff me all over or taunt me with questions as she is wont to do. She sat on the sofa in her crumpled nightgown, brutally quiet. I ignored her and staggered into the bathroom. When I came out she was sobbing quietly, her head between her knees. 'Stop it!' I cried, feeling anger welling inside my head. 'Stop it this minute!' She looked up fiercely, trembled, and bawled. A light suddenly appeared on Mr. Rangaswamy's porch. I struck her across the mouth. She gulped and reeled back, emitting a stifled shriek. I clutched a braid of tangled hair and reached for her throat. She struggled, knocking the doll onto the floor. I struck the doll aside, and hit her again, and kicked her in the groin, and left her in a heap. I locked the bedroom door and crawled into bed.

The serenity has gone from the day. There is turmoil in the sky where heavy black clouds are lit up by wafts of red like blood. Our world is shrinking. There's a hopeless gulf between the lounge and the kitchen. After the futile gesture, my pathetic freedom, what was I to do? A slow anguish grips my heart, the anguish of being unsupported. Everything, history and customs, had prepared me for this impasse. There is no alternative life: a hundred years of history on these islands has resulted in wilderness and distress.

In a moment I'll shift to the balcony. The kites are fluttering in the eddies.

§ *Hindu acculturation* Carib: Naipaul (2); SEA: Maniam

Part VI

SOUTH ASIA

India

MULK RAJ ANAND (1905–)

From Untouchable

Along with R. K. Narayan and Raja Rao, who also first came to the fore in the 1930s, Anand is known as one of the 'Big Three' of Indo-Anglian fiction. His first novel, *Untouchable*, describes a day in the life of Bakha, a sweeper, and in so doing mounts a sharp attack on the caste system, which excluded 'untouchables' from virtually all areas of Indian life. The two extracts included here, both from the early part of the novel, illustrate its use of naturalism to register social protest. In the final section of the novel Bakha listens to three speakers who offer possible solutions to the problem of 'untouchability': an Englishman who suggests he turn to Christianity; Mahatma Gandhi, who tells a public meeting that the caste system is the bane of Hinduism; and a Muslim advocate of the modern flush toilet. He returns home, particularly impressed by the last two.

The outcastes' colony was a group of mud-walled houses that clustered together in two rows, under the shadow both of the town and the cantonment, but outside their boundaries and separate from them. There lived the scavengers, the leather-workers, the washermen, the barbers, the water-carriers, the grass-cutters and other outcastes from Hindu society. A brook ran near the lane, once with crystal-clear water, now soiled by the dirt and filth of the public latrines situated about it, the odour of the hides and skins of dead carcasses left to dry on its banks, the dung of donkeys, sheep, horses, cows and buffaloes heaped up to be made into fuel cakes. The absence of a drainage system had, through the rains of various seasons, made of the quarter a marsh which gave out the most offensive smell. And altogether the ramparts of human and animal refuse that lay on the outskirts of this little colony, and the ugliness, the squalor and the misery which lay within it, made it an 'uncongenial' place to live in.

At least, so thought Bakha, a young man of eighteen, strong and able-bodied, the son of Lakha, the Jemadar[1] of all the sweepers in the town and the cantonment, and officially in charge of the three rows of public latrines which lined the extreme end of the colony, by the brook-side. But then he

---

1 Foreman.

had been working in the barracks of a British regiment for some years on probation with a remote uncle, and had been caught by the glamour of the 'white man's' life. The Tommies had treated him as a human being and he had learnt to think of himself as superior to his fellow-outcastes. Otherwise, the rest of the outcastes (with the possible exception of Chota, the leather-worker's son, who oiled his hair profusely, and parted it like the Englishmen on one side, wore a pair of shorts at hockey and smoked cigarettes like them; and Ram Charan, the washerman's son who aped Chota and Bakha in turn) were content with their lot.

Bakha thought of the uncongeniality of his home as he lay half awake in the morning of an autumn day, covered by a worn-out, greasy blanket, on a faded blue carpet which was spread on the floor in a corner of the cave-like, dingy, dank, one-roomed mud-house. His sister slept on a cot next to him and his father and brother snored from under a patched, ochre-coloured quilt, on a broken string bed, on the other side.

The nights had been cold, as they always are in the town of Bulandshahr, as cold as the days are hot. And though, both during winter and summer, he slept with his day clothes on, the sharp, bitter wind that blew from the brook at dawn had penetrated to his skin, past the inadequate blanket, through the regulation overcoat, breeches, puttees and ammunition boots of the military uniform that clothed him.

He shivered as he turned on his side. But he didn't mind the cold very much, suffering it willingly because he could sacrifice a good many comforts for the sake of what he called 'fashun', by which he understood the art of wearing trousers, breeches, coat, puttees,[2] boots, etc., as worn by the British and Indian soldiers in India. 'Ohe, lover of your mother,' his father had once abusively said to him, 'take a quilt and throw away that blanket of the goras;[3] you will die of cold.' But Bakha was a child of modern India. The clear-cut styles of European dress had impressed his naïve mind. This stark simplic-ity had furrowed his old Indian consciousness and cut deep, new lines where all the considerations which made India evolve a skirty costume as best fit-ted for the human body, lay dormant. Bakha had looked at the Tommies, stared at them with wonder and amazement when he first went to live at the British regimental barracks with his uncle. He had had glimpses, during his sojourn there, of the life the Tommies lived: sleeping on strange, low canvas beds covered tightly with blankets; eating eggs, drinking tea and wine in tin mugs; going to parade and then walking down to the bazaar with cig-arettes in their mouths and small silver-mounted canes in their hands. And he had soon become possessed with an overwhelming desire to live their life. He knew they were white sahibs. He had felt that to put on their clothes made one a sahib too. So he tried to copy them in everything, to copy them as well as he could in the exigencies of his peculiarly Indian circumstances. He had begged one Tommy for the gift of a pair of trousers. The man had given him instead a pair of breeches which he had to spare. A Hindu sepoy,[4]

---

2 Strip of cloth wound round leg from ankle to knee.   3 White men.   4 Indian soldier (in colonial period).

for the good of his own soul, had been kind enough to make an endowment of a pair of boots and puttees. For the other items he had gone down to the rag-seller's shop in the town. He had long looked at that shop. Ever since he was a child he had walked past the wooden stall on which lay heaped the scarlet and khaki uniforms discarded or pawned by the Tommies, pith sola topis, peak caps, knives, forks, buttons, old books and other oddments of Anglo-Indian life. And he had hungered for the touch of them. But he had never mustered up courage enough to go up to the keeper of the shop and to ask him the price of anything, lest it should be a price he could not pay and lest the man should find from his talk that he was a sweeper-boy. So he had stared and stared, stealthily noticing the variety of their queer, well-cut forms. 'I will look like a sahib,' he had secretly told himself. 'And I shall walk like them. Just as they do, in twos, with Chota as my companion. But I have no money to buy things.' And there his fantasy would break down and he would walk away from the shop rather crestfallen. Then he had had the good luck to come by some money at the British barracks. The pay which he received there had, of course, to be given to his father, but the baksheesh which he had collected from the Tommies amounted to ten rupees, and although he couldn't buy all the things in the rag-seller's shop he wished to, he had been able to buy the jacket, the overcoat, the blanket he slept under, and had a few annas left over for the enjoyment of 'Red-Lamp' cigarettes. His father had been angry at his extravagance, and the boys of the outcastes' colony, even Chota and Ram Charan, cut jokes with him on account of his new rigout, calling him 'Pilpali[5] sahib'. And he knew, of course, that except for his English clothes there was nothing English in his life. But he kept up his new form, rigidly adhering to his clothes day and night and guarding them from all base taint of Indianness, not even risking the formlessness of an Indian quilt, though he shivered with the cold at night. . . .

TAN-NANA-NAN-TAN, rang the bells of a bullock-cart behind him as, like other pedestrians, he was walking in the middle of the road. He jumped aside, dragging his boots in the dust, where, thanks to the inefficiency of the Municipal Committee, the pavement should have been but was not. The fine particles of dust that flew into his face as he walked and the creaking of the cart-wheels in the deep ruts seemed to give him an intense pleasure. Near the gates of the town were a number of stalls at which fuel was sold to those who came to burn their dead in the cremation ground a little way off. A funeral procession had stopped at one of these. They were carrying a corpse on an open stretcher. The body lay swathed in a red cloth painted with golden stars. Bakha stared at it and felt for a moment the grim fear of death, a fear akin to the terror of meeting a snake or a thief. Then he assured himself by thinking: 'Mother said, it is lucky to see a dead body when one is out in the streets.' And he walked on, past the little fruit-stalls where

---

5 Imitation.

dirtily clad Muhammadans with clean-shaven heads and henna-dyed beards cut sugar cane into pieces, which lay in heaps before them, past the Hindu stall-keepers, who sold sweetmeats from round iron trays balanced on little cane stools, till he came to the betel-leaf shop, where, surrounded by three large mirrors and lithographs of Hindu deities and beautiful European women, sat a dirty turbaned boy smearing the green heart-shaped betel leaves with red and white paint. A number of packets of 'Red-Lamp' and 'Scissors' cigarettes were arranged in boxes on his right and whole rows of biris[6] on his left. From the reflection of his face in the looking-glass, which he shyly noticed, Bakha's eyes travelled to the cigarettes. He halted suddenly, and, facing the shopkeeper with great humility, joined his hands and begged to know where he could put a coin to pay for a packet of 'Red Lamp'. The shopkeeper pointed to a spot on the board near him. Bakha put his anna there. The betel-leaf seller threw some water over it from the jug with which he sprinkled the betel leaves now and again. Having thus purified it he picked up the nickel piece and threw it into the counter. Then he flung a packet of 'Red-Lamp' cigarettes at Bakha, as a butcher might throw a bone to an insistent dog sniffing round the corner of his shop.

Bakha picked up the packet and moved away. Then he opened it and took out a cigarette. He recalled that he had forgotten to buy a box of matches. He was too modest to go back, as though some deep instinct told him that as a sweeper-boy he should show himself in people's presences as little as possible. For a sweeper, a menial, to be seen smoking constituted an offence against the Lord. Bakha knew that it was considered a presumption on the part of the poor to smoke like the rich people. But he wanted to smoke all the same. Only he felt he should do so unobserved while he carried his broom and basket. He caught sight of a Muhammadan who was puffing at a big hubble-bubble[7] sitting on a mattress, spread on the dust at one of the many open-air barbers' stalls that gaudily flanked the way.

'Mian ji, will you oblige me with a piece of coal from your clay fire-pot?' he appealed.

'Bend down to it and light your cigarette, if that is what you want to do with the piece of coal,' replied the barber.

Bakha, not used to taking such liberties with anybody, even with the Muhammadans, whom the Hindus considered outcastes and who were, therefore, much nearer him, felt somewhat embarrassed, but he bent down and lit his cigarette. He felt a happy, carefree man as he sauntered along, drawing the smoke and breathing it out through his nostrils. The coils of smoke rose slowly before his eyes and dissolved, but he was intent on the little white roll of tobacco which was becoming smaller every moment as its dark grey and red outer end smouldered away.

Passing through the huge brick-built gate of the town into the main street, he was engulfed in a sea of colour. Nearly a month had passed since he was last in the city, so little leisure did his job at the latrines allow him, and he

---

6 Local tobacco.   7 Rudimentary form of hookah, Asian tobacco-pipe.

couldn't help being swept away by the sensations that crowded in on him from every side. He followed the curves of the winding, irregular streets lined on each side with shops, covered with canvas or jute awnings and topped by projecting domed balconies. He became deeply engrossed in the things that were displayed for sale, and in the various people who thronged around them. His first sensation of the bazaar was of its smell, a pleasant aroma oozing from so many unpleasant things, drains, grains, fresh and decaying vegetables, spices, men and women and asafoetida.[8] Then it was the kaleidoscope of colours, the red, the orange, the purple of the fruit in the tiers of baskets which were arranged around the Peshawari fruit-seller, dressed in a blue silk turban, a scarlet velvet waistcoat embroidered with gold, a long white tunic and trousers; the gory red of the mutton hanging beside the butcher who was himself busy mincing meat on a log of wood, while his assistants roasted it on skewers over a charcoal fire, or fried it in the black iron pan; the pale-blond colour of the wheat shop; and the rainbow hues of the sweetmeat stall, not to speak of the various shades of turbans and skirts, from the deep black of the widows to the green, the pink, the mauve and the fawn of the newly-wedded brides, and all the tints of the shifting, changing crowd, from the Brahmin's white to the grasscutter's coffee and the Pathan's swarthy brown.

§ *Differing approaches of 'Big Three' to writing a novel in English* Narayan, Rao

R. K. NARAYAN (1907-)

From The Man-Eater of Malgudi

Like several of Narayan's novels, *The Man-Eater of Malgudi* focuses on a South Indian small businessman, whose traditional way of life is upset by the advent of an alien force. Here Nataraj, a printer, has the peace of his daily existence shattered when a bullying taxidermist, Vasu, moves into his premises and both through the exercise of his profession and his general behaviour violates many of the values that the Tamil Brahmin Nataraj holds sacred. At first sight the novel appears to be a social comedy, in which a submissive 'little man' is dominated by a character who is his polar opposite. However, as several commentators have noted, it is also a Hindu fable, in which Vasu occupies the mythic role of a *rakshasa* (or demon). This is hinted at from the moment when he makes his first appearance, here in Chapter 2, with hair 'like a black halo'.

Sastri had to go a little earlier than usual since he had to perform a *puja*[1] at home. I hesitated to let him go. The three colour labels (I prided myself on the excellence of my colour-printing) for K.J.'s aerated drinks had to be

---

8 Resinous plant gum, used medicinally.   1 Act of worship.

got ready. It was a very serious piece of work for me. My personal view was that the coloured ink I used on the label was far safer to drink than the dye that K.J. put into his water-filled bottles. We had already printed the basic colour on the labels and the second was to be imposed today. This was a crucial stage of the work and I wanted Sastri to stay and finish the job.

He said, 'Perhaps I can stay up late tonight and finish it. Not now. Meanwhile will you . . .' He allotted me work until he should be back at two o'clock.

I had been engrossed in a talk with the usual company. On the agenda today was Nehru's third Five-Year Plan; my friend Sen saw nothing but ruin in it for the country. 'Three hundred crores – are we counting heads or money?' His audience consisted of myself and the poet, and a client who had come to ask for quotations for a business card. The discussion was warming up, as the client was a Congressman who had gone to prison fourteen times since the day Mahatma Gandhi arrived in India from South Africa. He ignored for the time being the business that had brought him and plunged into the debate, settling himself inexorably in a corner. 'What's wrong with people is they have got into the habit of blaming everything on the Government. You think democracy means that if there is no sugar in the shops, Government is responsible. What if there is no sugar? You won't die if you do not have sugar for your morning coffee some days.' Sen disputed every word of the patriot's speech.

I listened to the debate until I noticed Sastri's silhouette beyond the curtain. Sastri, when there was any emergency, treated me as a handy-boy, and I had no alternative but to accept the role. Now my duty would be to fix the block on the machine and put the second impression on all the labels and spread them out to dry, then he would come and give the third impression and put the labels out to dry again.

He explained some of the finer points to me, 'The blocks are rather worn. You'll have to let in more ink.'

'Yes, Mr Sastri.'

He looked at me through his small silver-rimmed glasses and said firmly, 'Unless the labels are second-printed and dry by three o'clock today, it's going to be impossible to deliver them tomorrow. You know what kind of a man K.J. is . . .'

What about my lunch? Sastri did not care whether I had time for food or not – he was a tyrant when it came to printing labels, but there was no way of protesting. He would brush everything aside. As if reading my mind he explained, 'I'd not trouble you but for the fact that this *satyanarayana puja* must be performed today in my house; my children and wife will be waiting for me at the door . . .' As it was he would have to trot all the way to Vinayak Street if his family were not to starve too long.

Wife, children. Absurd. Such encumbrances were not necessary for Sastri, I felt. They were for lesser men like me. His place was at the type-board and the treadle. He produced an incongruous, unconvincing picture as a family man. But I dared not express myself aloud. The relation of employer and employee were reversed at my press whenever there was an emergency.

I accepted the situation without any fuss. According to custom my friends would not step beyond the curtain, so I was safe to go ahead with the second impression. Sastri had fixed everything. I had only to press the pedal and push the paper on to the pad. On a pale orange ground I had now to impose a sort of violet. I grew hypnotized by the sound of the wheel and the dozen kinks that were set in motion by the pressure I put on the pedals. Whenever I paused I could hear Sen's voice, 'If Nehru is practical, let him disown the Congress . . . Why should you undertake projects which you can't afford? Anyway, in ten years what are we going to do with all the steel?' There was a sudden lull. I wondered if they had been suddenly struck dumb. I heard the shuffling of feet. I felt suddenly relieved that the third Five-Year Plan was done with.

Now an unusual thing happened. The curtain stirred, an edge of it lifted, and the monosyllabic poet's head peeped through. An extraordinary situation must have arisen to make him do that. His eyes bulged. 'Someone to see you,' he whispered.

'Who? What does he want?'

'I don't know.'

The whispered conversation was becoming a strain. I shook my head, winked and grimaced to indicate to the poet that I was not available. The poet, ever a dense fellow, did not understand but blinked on unintelligently. His head suddenly vanished, and a moment later a new head appeared in its place – a tanned face, large powerful eyes under thick eyebrows, a large forehead and a shock of unkempt hair, like a black halo.

My first impulse was to cry out, 'Whoever you may be, why don't you brush your hair?' The new visitor had evidently pulled aside the poet before showing himself to me. Before I could open my mouth, he asked, 'You Nataraj?' I nodded. He came forward, practically tearing aside the curtain, an act which violated the sacred traditions of my press. I said, 'Why don't you kindly take a seat in the next room? I'll be with you in a moment.' He paid no attention, but stepped forward, extending his hand. I hastily wiped my fingers on a rag, muttering, 'Sorry, discoloured, been working . . .' He gave me a hard grip. My entire hand disappeared into his fist – he was a huge man, about six feet tall. He looked quite slim, but his bull-neck and hammer-fist revealed his true stature. 'Shan't we move to the other room?' I asked again.

'Not necessary. It's all the same to me,' he said. 'You are doing something? Why don't you go on? It won't bother me.' He eyed my coloured labels. 'What are they?'

I didn't want any eyes to watch my special colour effects, and see how I achieved them. I moved to the curtain and parted it courteously for him. He followed me. I showed him to the Queen Anne chair, and sat down at my usual place, on the edge of my desk. I had now regained the feeling of being master of the situation. I adopted my best smile and asked, 'Well, what can I do for you, Mr . . . ?'

'Vasu,' he said, and added, 'I knew you didn't catch my name. You were saying something at the same time as I mentioned my name.'

I felt abashed, and covered it, I suppose, with another of those silly smiles. Then I checked myself, suddenly feeling angry with him for making me so uneasy. I asked myself, 'Nataraj, are you are afraid of this muscular fellow?' and said authoritatively, 'Yes?' as much as to indicate, 'You have wasted my time sufficiently; now say quickly whatever you may want to say.'

He took from his inner pocket a wad of paper, searched for a hand-written sheet and held it out to me. 'Five hundred sheets of note-paper, the finest quality, and five hundred visiting cards.'

I spread out the sheet without a word and read, 'H. Vasu, M.A., Taxidermist'. I grew interested. My irritation left me. This was the first time I had set eyes on a taxidermist. I said, assuming a friendly tone, 'Five hundred! Are you sure you need five hundred visiting cards? Could you not print them one hundred at a time? They'd be fresh then.'

'Why do you try to advise me?' he asked pugnaciously. 'I know how many I need. I'm not printing my visiting cards in order to preserve them in a glass case.'

'All right. I can print ten thousand if you want.'

He softened at my show of aggressiveness. 'Fine, fine, that's the right spirit.'

'If you'd like to have it done on the original Heidelberg[2] . . .' I began.

'I don't care what you do it on. I don't even know what you are talking about.'

I understood the situation now; every other sentence was likely to prove provocative. I began to feel intrigued by the man. I didn't want to lose him. Even if I wanted to, I had no means of getting rid of him. He had sought me out and I'd have to have him until he decided to leave. I might just as well be friendly. 'Surely, whatever you like. It's my duty to ask, that's all. Some people prefer it.'

'What is it anyway?' he asked.

I explained the greatness of Heidelberg and where it was. He thought it over, and suddenly said, 'Nataraj, I trust you to do your best for me. I have come to you as a friend.' I was surprised and flattered. He explained, 'I'm new to this place, but I heard about you within an hour of coming.' He mentioned an obscure source of information. 'Well, I never give a second thought to these things,' he said. 'When I like a man, I like him, that's all.'

I wanted to ask about taxidermy, so I asked, looking at his card, 'Taxidermist? Must be an interesting job. Where is your er . . . office or . . .'

'I hope to make a start right here. I was in Junagadh – you know the place – and there I grew interested in the art. I came across a master there, one Suleiman. When he stuffed a lion (you know, Junagadh is a place where

---

2 Printing press – in this case owned not by Nataraj, but by his neighbour.

we have lions) he could make it look more terrifying than it would be in the jungle. His stuffings go all over the world. He was a master, and he taught me the art. After all we are civilized human beings, educated and cultured, and it is up to us to prove our superiority to nature. Science conquers nature in a new way each day; why not in creation also? That's my philosophy, sir. I challenge any man to contradict me.' He sighed at the thought of Suleiman, his master. 'He was a saint. He taught me his art sincerely.'

'Where did you get your M.A.?'

'At Madras, of course. You want to know about me?' he asked.

I wonder what he would have done if I had said, 'No, I prefer to go home and eat my food.' He would probably have held me down.

He said, 'I was educated in the Presidency College. I took my Master's degree in History, Economics and Literature.' That was in the year 1931. Then he had joined the civil disobedience movement against British rule, broken the laws, marched, demonstrated and ended up in jail. He went repeatedly to prison and once when he was released found himself in the streets of Nagpur. There he met a *phaelwan*[3] at a show. 'That man could bear a half-ton stone slab on his check and have it split by hammer strokes; he could snap steel chains and he could hit a block of hard granite with his fist and pulverize it. I was young then, his strength appealed to me. I was prepared to become his disciple at any cost. I introduced myself to the *phael-wan*.' He remained thoughtful for a while and continued, 'I learnt everything from this master. The training was unsparing. He woke me up at three o'clock every morning and put me through exercises. And he provided me with the right diet. I had to eat a hundred almonds every morning and wash them down with half a *seer* of milk; two hours later six eggs with honey; at lunch chicken and rice; at night vegetables and fruit. Not everyone can hope to have this diet, but I was lucky in finding a man who enjoyed stuffing me like that. In six months I could understudy for him. On my first day, when I banged my fist on a century-old door of a house in Lucknow, the three-inch panel of seasoned teak splintered. My master patted me on the back with tears of joy in his eyes, "You are growing on the right lines, my boy." In a few months I could also snap chains, twist iron bars, and pulverize granite. We travelled all over the country, and gave our shows at every market fair in the villages and in the town halls in the cities, and he made a lot of money. Gradually he grew flabby and lazy, and let me do everything. They announced his name on the notices, but actually I did all the twisting and smashing of stone, iron, and what not. When I spoke to him about it he called me an ungrateful dog and other names, and tried to push me out. I resisted . . . and . . .' Vasu laughed at the recollection of this incident. 'I knew his weak spot. I hit him there with the edge of my palm with a chopping movement . . . and he fell down and squirmed on the floor. I knew he could perform no more. I left him there and walked out, and gave up the strong

---

3 Wrestler; strong man.

man's life once and for all.'

'You didn't stop to help him?' I asked.

'I helped him by leaving him there, instead of holding him upside down and rattling the teeth out of his head.'

'Oh, no,' I cried, horrified.

'Why not? I was a different man now, not the boy who went to him for charity. I was stronger than he.'

'After all he taught you to be strong – he was your guru,' I said, enjoying the thrill of provoking him.

'Damn it all!' he cried. 'He made money out of me, don't you see?'

'But he also gave you six eggs a day and – how much milk and almonds was it?'

He threw up his arms in vexation. 'Oh, you will never understand these things, Nataraj. You know nothing, you have not seen the world. You know only what happens in this miserable little place.'

'If you think this place miserable, why do you choose to come here?' I was nearest the inner door. I could dash away if he attempted to grab me. Familiarity was making me rash and headstrong. I enjoyed taunting him.

'You think I have come here out of admiration for this miserable city? Know this, I'm here because of Mempi Forest and the jungles in those hills. I'm a taxidermist. I have to be where wild animals live.'

'And die,' I added.

He appreciated my joke and laughed. 'You are a wise guy,' he said admiringly.

'You haven't told me yet why or how you became a taxidermist,' I reminded him.

'H'm!' he said. 'Don't get too curious. Let us do business first. When you are giving me the visiting cards? Tomorrow?' He might pulverize granite, smash his guru with a slicing stroke, but where printing work was concerned I was not going to be pushed. I got up and turned the sheets of a tear-off calendar on the wall. 'You can come tomorrow and ask me. I can discuss this matter only tomorrow. My staff are out today.'

At this moment my little son Babu came running in crying 'Appa!'[4] and halted his steps abruptly on seeing a stranger. He bit his nails, grinned, and tried to turn and run. I shot out my hand and held him. 'What is it?' I asked. He was friendly with the usual crowd at my press, but the stranger's presence somehow embarrassed him. I could guess why he had come; it was either to ask for a favour – permission to go out with his friends, or cash for peppermints – or to bring a message from his mother.

'Mother says, aren't you coming home for food? She is hungry.'

'So am I,' I said, 'and if I were Mother I wouldn't wait for Father. Understand me? Here is a gentleman with whom I am engaged on some important business. Do you know what he can do?' My tone interested Babu and he looked up expectantly.

---

4 Daddy.

Vasu made a weary gesture, frowned and said, 'Oh, stop that, Mr Nataraj. Don't start it all again. I don't want to be introduced to anyone. Now, go away, boy,' he said authoritatively.

'He is my son . . .' I began.

'I see that,' Vasu said indifferently, and Babu wriggled himself free and ran off.

Vasu did not come next day, but appeared again fifteen days later. He arrived in a jeep. 'You have been away a long time,' I said.

'You thought you were rid of me?' he asked, and, thumping his chest, 'I never forget.'

'And I never remember,' I said. Somehow this man's presence roused in me a sort of pugnacity.

He stepped in, saw the Queen Anne chair occupied by the poet, and remarked, half-jokingly, 'That's my chair, I suppose.' The poet scrambled to his feet and moved to another seat. 'H'm, that's better,' Vasu said, sitting down. He smiled patronizingly at the poet and said, 'I haven't been told who you are.'

'I'm I'm . . . a teacher in the school.'

'What do you teach?' he asked relentlessly.

'Well, history, geography, science, English – anything the boys must know.'

'H'm, an all-rounder,' Vasu said. I could see the poet squirming. He was a mild, inoffensive man who was unused to such rough contacts. But Vasu seemed to enjoy bothering him. I rushed in to his rescue. I wanted to add to his stature by saying, 'He is a poet. He is nominally a teacher, but actually . . .'

'I never read poetry; no time,' said Vasu promptly, and dismissed the man from his thoughts. He turned to me and asked, 'Where are my cards?'

I had a seasoned answer for such a question. 'Where have you been this whole fortnight?'

'Away, busy.'

'So was I,' I said.

'You promised to give me the cards . . .'

'When?' I asked.

'Next day,' he said. I told him that there had been no such promise. He raised his voice, and I raised mine. He asked finally, 'Are we here on business or to fight? If it's a fight, tell me. I like a fight. Can't you see, man, why I am asking for my cards?'

'Don't *you* see that we have our own business practice?' I always adopted 'we' whenever I had to speak for the press.

'What do you mean?' he asked aggressively.

'We never choose the type and stationery for a customer. It must always be the customer's responsibility.'

'You never told me that,' he cried.

'You remember I asked you to come next day. That was my purpose. I never say anything without a purpose.'

'Why couldn't you have mentioned it the same day?'

'You have a right to ask,' I said, feeling it was time to concede him something. The poet looked scared by these exchanges. He was trying to get out, but I motioned him to stay. Why should the poor man be frighened away?

'You have not answered my question,' said Vasu. 'Why couldn't you have shown me samples of type on the first day?'

I said curtly, 'Because my staff were out.'

'Oh!' he said, opening his eyes, wide. 'I didn't know you had a staff.'

I ignored his remark and shouted, 'Sastri! Please bring those ivory card samples and also the ten-point copper-plate.' I told Vasu grandly, 'Now you can indicate your preferences, and we shall try to give you the utmost satisfaction.'

Sastri, with his silver-rimmed glasses on his nose, entered, bearing a couple of blank cards and a specimen type-book. He paused for a second, studying the visitor, placed them on the table, turned and disappeared through the curtain.

'How many are employed in your press?' Vasu asked.

The man's curiosity was limitless and recognized no proprieties. I felt enraged. Was he a labour commissioner or something of the kind? I replied, 'As many as I need. But, as you know, present-day labour conditions are not encouraging. However, Mr Sastri is very dependable; he has been with me for years . . . ' I handed him the cards and said, 'You will have to choose. These are the best cards available.' I handed him the type-book. 'Tell me what type you like.'

That paralysed him. He turned the cards between his fingers, he turned the leaves of the type-book, and cried, 'I'm damned if I know what I want. They all look alike to me. What is the difference anyway?'

This was a triumph for me. 'Vasu, printing is an intricate business. That's why we won't take responsibility in these matters.'

'Oh, please do something and bring me my cards,' he cried, exasperated.

'All right,' I said, 'I'll do it for you, if you trust me.'

'I trust you as a friend, otherwise I would not have come to you.'

'Actually,' I said, 'I welcome friends rather than customers. I'm not a fellow who cares for money. If anyone comes to me for pure business, I send them over to my neighbour and they are welcome to get their work done cheaper and on a better machine – original Heidelberg.'

'Oh, stop that original Heidel,' he cried impatiently. 'I want to hear no more of it. Give me my cards. My business arrangements are waiting on that, and remember also five hundred letter-heads.'

§ *Differing approaches of 'Big Three' to writing a novel in English* Anand, Rao; *Passivity and engagement* Desai

RAJA RAO (1908–)

From Kanthapura

Narrated by a grandmother whose voice is a repository of the oral tradition, *Kanthapura* tells how a South Indian village's revolt against a domineering plantation owner comes to be informed by the Gandhian ideal of non-violence. The novel is, however, far removed from social realism and owes much to the belief in Vedantic philosophy which underlies all Rao's writing. Its Foreword stresses the extent to which legend penetrates everyday Indian life and discusses the problems of writing this kind of novel in English. In the passage which follows, the narrator establishes the central context for the story she is about to tell, by describing 'our village'.

Foreword

My publishers have asked me to say a word of explanation.

There is no village in India, however mean, that has not a rich sthala-purana, or legendary history, of its own. Some god or godlike hero has passed by the village – Rama[1] might have rested under this pipal-tree,[2] Sita[3] might have dried her clothes, after her bath, on this yellow stone, or the Mahatma himself, on one of his many pilgrimages through the country, might have slept in this hut, the low one, by the village gate. In this way the past mingles with the present, and the gods mingle with men to make the repertory of your grandmother always bright. One such story from the contemporary annals of my village I have tried to tell.

The telling has not been easy. One has to convey in a language that is not one's own the spirit that is one's own. One has to convey the various shades and omissions of a certain thought-movement that looks maltreated in an alien language. I use the word 'alien', yet English is not really an alien language to us. It is the language of our intellectual make-up – like Sanskrit or Persian was before – but not of our emotional make-up. We are all instinctively bilingual, many of us writing in our own language and in English. We cannot write like the English. We should not. We cannot write only as Indians. We have grown to look at the large world as part of us. Our method of expression therefore has to be a dialect which will some day prove to be as distinctive and colourful as the Irish or the American. Time alone will justify it.

After language the next problem is that of style. The tempo of Indian life must be infused into our English expression, even as the tempo of American or Irish life has gone into the making of theirs. We, in India, think quickly, we talk quickly, and when we move we move quickly. There must be something in the sun of India that makes us rush and tumble and run on. And our paths are paths interminable. The Mahabharatha *has 214,778 verses and the* Ramayana

---

1 Hero of *Ramayana*, one of the two great Sanskrit epics. 2 Large Indian fig-tree, related to banyan.
3 Heroine of *Ramayana*.

48,000. Puranas there are endless and innumerable. We have neither punctuation nor the treacherous 'ats' and 'ons' to bother us – we tell one interminable tale. Episode follows episode, and when our thoughts stop our breath stops, and we move on to another thought. This was and still is the ordinary style of our story-telling. I have tried to follow it myself in this story:

It may have been told of an evening, when as the dusk falls and through the sudden quiet, lights leap up in house after house, and stretching her bedding on the veranda, a grandmother might have told you, newcomer, the sad tale of her village.

Our village – I don't think you have ever heard about it – Kanthapura is its name, and it is in the province of Kara. High on the Ghats[4] is it, high up the steep mountains that face the cool Arabian seas, up the Malabar coast is it, up Mangalore and Puttur and many a centre of cardamom and coffee, rice and sugarcane. Roads, narrow, dusty, rut-covered roads, wind through the forests of teak and of jack,[5] of sandal and of sal,[6] and hanging over bellowing gorges and leaping over elephant-haunted valleys, they turn now to the left and now to the right and bring you through the Alambè and Champa and Mena and Kola passes into the great granaries of trade. There, on the blue waters, they say, our carted cardamoms and coffee get into the ships the Red-men bring, and, so they say, they go across the seven oceans into the countries where our rulers live.

Cart after cart groans through the roads of Kanthapura, and on many a night, before the eyes are shut, the last lights we see are those of the train of carts, and the last voice we hear is that of the cart-man who sings through the hollows of the night. The carts pass through the Main Street and through the Potter's Lane, and then they turn by Chennayya's Pond, and up they go, up the passes into the morning that will rise over the sea. Sometimes when Rama Chetty or Subba Chetty have merchandise, the carts stop and there are greetings, and in every house we can hear Subba Shetty's 350-rupee bulls ringing their bells as they get under the yoke. 'Ho,' says Subba Chetty, 'hè-ho,' and the bulls shiver and start. The slow-moving carts begin to grind and to rumble, and then the long harsh monotony of the carts' axles through the darkness. And once they are on the other side of the Tippur Hill the noise suddenly dies into the night and the soft hiss of the Himavathy rises into the air. Sometimes people say to themselves, the Goddess of the River plays through the night with the Goddess of the Hill. Kenchamma is the mother of Himavathy. May the goddess bless us!

Kenchamma is our goddess. Great and bounteous is she. She killed a demon ages, ages ago, a demon that had come to ask our young sons as food and our young women as wives. Kenchamma came from the Heavens – it was the sage Tripura who had made penances to bring her down – and she waged such a battle and she fought so many a night that the blood soaked and soaked into the earth, and that is why the Kenchamma Hill is all red.

---

4 Mountains. 5 Fruit-tree. 6 Tree yielding timber and resin.

If not, tell me, sister, why should it be red only from the Tippur stream upwards, for a foot down on the other side of the stream you have mud, black and brown, but never red. Tell me, how could this happen, if it were not for Kenchamma and her battle? Thank heaven, not only did she slay the demon, but she even settled down among us, and this much I shall say, never has she failed us in our grief. If rains come out, you fall at her feet and say 'Kenchamma, goddess, you are not kind to us. Our fields are full of younglings and you have given us no water. Tell us, Kenchamma, why do you seek to make our stomachs burn?' And Kenchamma, through the darkness of the sanctum, opens her eyes wide – oh! if only you could see her eyelids quicken and shiver! – and she smiles on you a smile such as you have never before beheld. You know what that means. That every night, when the doors are closed and the lights are put out, pat-pat-pat, the rain patters on the tiles, and many a peasant is heard to go into the fields, squelching through the gutter and mire. She has never failed us, I assure you, our Kenchamma.

Then there is the smallpox, and we vow that we shall walk the holy fire on the annual fair, and child after child gets better and better – and, but for that widow of a Satamma's child, and the drunkard Dhirappa's brother's son, tell me, who ever has been taken away by smallpox? Then there was cholera. We gave a sari and a gold trinket to the goddess, and the goddess never touched those that are to live – as for the old ones, they would have died one way or the other anyway. Of course, you will tell me that young Sankamma, Barber Channav's wife, died of it. But then it was not for nothing her child was born ten months and four days after he was dead. Ten months and four days, I tell you! Such whores always die untimely. Ramappa and Subbanna, you see, they got it in town and our goddess could do nothing. She is the Goddess of Kanthapura, not of Talassana. They ought to have stayed in Talassana and gone to Goddess Talassanamma to offer their prayers.

'O Kenchamma! Protect us always like this through famine and disease, death and despair. O most high and bounteous! We shall offer you our first rice and our first fruit, and we shall offer you saris and bodice-cloth for every birth and marriage, we shall wake thinking of you, sleep prostrating before you, Kenchamma, and through the harvest night shall we dance before you, the fire in the middle and the horns about us, we shall sing and sing and sing, clap our hands and sing:

> Kenchamma, Kenchamma,
> Goddess benign and bounteous,
> Mother of earth, blood of life,
> Harvest-queen, rain-crowned,
> Kenchamma, Kenchamma,
> Goddess benign and bounteous.

And when the night is over, and the sun rises over the Bebbur Mound, people will come from Santur and Kuppur, people will come from the Santur Coffee Estate and the Kuppur Cardamom Estate, from coconut gardens and sugarcane fields, and they will bring flowers and fruit and rice and dal[7] and sugarcandy and perfumed sweetmeats, and we shall offer you all, dancing and singing – the bells will ring, the trumpets tear through the groves, and as the camphor rises before you, we shall close our eyes and hymn your praise. Kenchamma, Great Goddess, protect us! O Benign One!'

Our village had four and twenty houses. Not all were big like Postmaster Suryanarayana's double-storied house by the Temple Corner. But some were really not bad to look at. Our Patwari Nanjundia had a veranda with two rooms built on to the old house. He had even put glass panes to the windows, which even Postmaster Suryanarayana could not boast of. Then there were the Kannayya-House people, who had a high veranda, and though the house was I know not how many generations old, it was still as fresh and new as though it had been built only yesterday. No wonder that Waterfall Venkamma roared day and night against Rangamma.

'Why should a widow, and a childless widow too, have a big house like that? And it is not her father that built it,' said she. 'It's my husband's ancestors that built it. I've two sons and five daughters, and that shaven widow hadn't even the luck of having a bandicoot to call her own. And you have only to look at her gold belt and her dharmawar sari. Whore! And so, night and day did she howl, whenever she met Temple Lakshamma or Bhatta's wife Chinnamma coming back from the river. To tell you the truth, Venkamma's own house was as big and strong as her sister-in-law's. But she said it was not large enough for her family. Besides, she could not bear the idea that it was occupied by Rangamma's father and mother, and when the vacations came Rangamma had all her younger brothers, and the children of the elder one from Bombay – 'all those city-bred fashionable idiots,' – to spend the summer. 'Tell me,' said Venkamma one day to Akkamma, bringing forward her falling sari over her shaven head, 'why should our family feed theirs? If her parents are poor, let them set fire to their dhoti[8] and sari and die. Oh, if only I could have had the courage to put lizard-poison into their food! Well that will come too.' She would clap her hands and go into her house leaving Front-House Akkamma to hurry up her steps.

Akkamma had people come to visit them. You know, Coffee-Planter Ramayya is a cousin of her sister-in-law, and when he is on his way to Karwar he sometimes drops in to see them – and even spends a night there. He left his Ford on the other side of the river, for the ferry did not ply at night, and he came along. Today he is there and people are all busy trying to see him. For midday meal he will have a vermicelli *paysama*[9] and Patwari Nanjundia and his son-in-law are both invited there. There are others coming too. The Temple people and the Fig-Tree-House people, and Dorè, the

---

7 Lentils.   8 Traditional Indian male attire, covering body from waist to ankle.   9 Sweet made with thickened milk.

'University graduate,' as they call him. He had lost his father when still young and his mother died soon after, and as his two sisters were already married and had gone to their mothers-in-law, he was left all alone with fifteen acres of wet land and twenty acres of dry land. And he said he would go to the city for 'higher studies' and went to a University. Of course, he never got through the Inter even – but he had city-ways, read city-books, and even called himself a Gandhi-man. Some two years ago, when he had come back from Poona, he had given up his boots and hat and suit and had taken to dhoti and khadi,[10] and it was said he had even given up his city habit of smoking. Well, so much the better. But, to tell you the truth, we never liked him. He had always been such a braggart. He was not like Corner-House Moorthy, who had gone through life like a noble cow, quiet, generous, serene, deferent and brahmanic,[11] a very prince, I tell you. We loved him, of course, as you will see, and if only I had not been a daughterless widow, I should have offered him a granddaughter, if I had one. And I know he would have said: 'Achakka, you are of the Veda Sastra Pravina Krishna Sastri's family, and is it greater for you to ask something of me, or for me to answer "Yea"?' He's the age my Seenu is, and he and Seenu were as, one would say, our Rama and brother Lakshamana. They only needed a Sita to make it complete. In fact, on that day, as everybody knew, Coffee-Planter Ramayya had come to offer his own daughter to Moorthy. But the horoscopes did not agree. And we were all so satisfied . . .

Till now I've spoken only of the Brahmin[11] quarter. Our village had a Pariah[12] quarter too, a Potters' quarter, a Weavers' quarter, and a Sudra[13] quarter. How many huts had we there? I do not know. There may have been ninety or a hundred – though a hundred may be the right number. Of course, you wouldn't expect me to go to the Pariah quarter, but I have seen from the streetcorner Beadle Timmayya's hut. It was in the middle, so – let me see – if there were four on this side and about six, seven, eight that side, that makes some fifteen or twenty huts in all. Pock-marked Sidda had a real *thothi*[14] house, with a big veranda and a large roof, and there must have been a big granary somewhere inside, for he owned as much land as Patwari Nanjundia or Shopkeeper Subba Chetty, though he hadn't half Kanthapura as Bhatta had. But lately, Sidda's wife went mad, you know, and he took her to Poona and he spent much money on her. Bhatta, of course, profited by the occasion and added a few acres more to his own domain. Clever fellow this Bhatta! One day he was sure to become the Zamindar[15] of the whole village – though we all knew him walking about the streets with only a loin-cloth about him.

The Potters' Street was the smallest of our streets. It had only five houses. Lingayya and Ramayya and Subbayya and Chandrayya owned the four big

---

10 Homespun cloth, sometimes worn as a sign of traditional simplicity.   11 Pertaining to the highest of the four classical Hindu castes: of priests and scribes.   12 Member of low caste or no caste at all.   13 Fourth and lowest of the four classical Hindu castes; traditionally labourers, fishermen and servants.   14 Inner court-yard.   15 Landlord.

houses, and old Kamalamma had a little broken house at the end of the street where she spent her last days with her only son. Formerly, they say, the Potter's Street was very flourishing, but now, with all these modern Mangalore tiles, they've had to turn to land. But Chandrayya still made festival-pots, and for Gauri's festival we've always had our pots done by him. He makes our images too and he even sold them at the Manjarpur fair. The rest of the Potters were rather a simple, quiet lot, who tilled their lands and now and again went out to the neighbouring villages to help people to make bricks.

Now, when you turned round the Potters' Street and walked across the Temple Square, the first house you saw was the nine-beamed house of Patel Rangè Gowda. He was a fat, sturdy fellow, a veritable tiger amongst us, and what with his tongue and his hand and his brain, he had amassed solid gold in his coffers and solid bangles on his arms. His daughters, all three of them, lived with him and his sons-in-law worked with him like slaves, though they owned as much land as he did. But then, you know, the Tiger, his words were law in our village. 'If the Patel says it,' we used to say, 'even a coconut-leaf roof will become a gold roof.' He is an honest man, and he has helped many a poor peasant. And heavens! What a terror he was to the authorities!

The other sudras were not badly-fed householders and they had as usual two or three sons and a few daughters, and one could not say whether they were rich or poor. They were always badly dressed and always paid revenues due and debts after several notices. But as long as Rangé Gowda was there, there was no fear. He would see them through the difficulties. And they were of his community.

The Brahmin Street started just on the opposite side, and my own house was the first on the right.

Between my house and Subba Chetty's shop on the Karwar Road was the little Kanthapurishwari's temple. It was on the Main Street Promontory, as we called it, and became the centre of our life. In fact it did not exist more than three years ago, and to tell you the truth, that's where all the trouble began. Corner-House Narsamma's son, Moorthy – our Moorthy as we always called him – was going through our backyard one day and, seeing a half-sunk linga, said, 'Why not unearth it and wash it and consecrate it?' 'Why not!' said we all, and as it was the holidays and all the city boys were in the village, they began to put up a little mud wall and a tile roof to protect the god. He was so big and fine and brilliant, I tell you, and our Bhatta duly performed the consecration ceremony. And as Rangamma said she would pay for a milk and banana libation, and a dinner, we had a grand feast. Then came Postmaster Suryanarayana and said, 'Brother, why not start a *Sankara-jayanthi*?[16] I have the texts. We shall read the *Sankara-Vijaya*[17] every day and somebody will offer a dinner for each day of the month.' 'Let the first

---

16 Birth anniversary of Sankara (AD 788–820), founder of most influential school of Vedanta. 17 Text written by four early disciples of Sankara.

be mine,' said Bhatta. 'The second mine,' said Agent Nanjundia. 'The third must be mine,' insisted Pandit Venkateshia. 'And the fourth and the fifth are mine,' said Rangamma. 'And if there is no one coming forward for the other days, let it always be mine,' she said. Good, dear Rangamma! She had enough money to do it, and she was alone. And so the *Sankara-jayanthi* was started that very day.

It was old Ramakrishnayya, the very learned father of Rangamma, that said he would read out the *Sankara-Vijaya* day after day. And we all cried out 'May the Goddess bless him,' for there was none more serene and deep-voiced than he. We always went to discuss Vedanta with him in the afternoons after the vessels were washed and the children had gone to school. And now we gathered at the Iswara's temple on the Promontory, instead of on Rangamma's veranda. How grand the *Sankara-jayanthi* was! Old Ramakrishnayya read chapter after chapter with such a calm, bell-metal voice, and we all listened with our sari fringes wet with tears. Then they began to lay leaves for dinner. And one boy came and said, 'I shall serve, aunt!' And another came and said, 'Can I serve *paysam*, aunt?' And another came and said, 'I shall serve rice, aunt,' and this way and that we had quite a marriage army and they served like veritable princes. Then, when we had eaten and had washed our hands, the younger women sang, and we discussed the *maya-vada*,[18] and after that we went home. We hastily pushed rice on to the leaves of the young and came back for the evening prayers. There used to be bhajan.[19] Trumpet Lingayya with his silver trumpet was always there, and once the music was over, we stayed till the camphor was lit, and throwing a last glance at the god, we went home to sleep, with the god's face framed within our eyes. It was beautiful, I tell you – day after day we spent as though the whole village was having a marriage party.

Then sometimes there used to be *Harikathas*.[20] Our Sastri is also a poet. You know, the Maharaja of Mysore had already honoured him with a Palace Shawl, and Sastri had just sent His Highness an epic on the sojourn of Rama and Sita in the Hill country. They said he would soon be honoured with a permanent place in the court. And he is a fine singer, too. But he is an even grander *Harikatha*-man. When he stood up with the bells at his ankles and the cymbals in his hands, how true and near and brilliant the god-world seemed to us. And never has anyone made a grander *Harikatha* on Parvati's winning of Siva. He had poetry on his tongue, sister. And he could keep us sitting for hours together. And how we regretted the evening the *Sankara-jayanthi* was over. The air looked empty.

But by Kenchamma's grace it did not end there. The next morning Moorthy comes to us and says, 'Aunt, what do you think of having the Rama festival, the Krishna festival, the Ganesh festival? We shall have a month's bhajan every time and we shall keep the party going.'

---

18 The philosophy of *maya* or the illusory nature of experience.   19 Hindu devotional song.   20 Legendary stories told to the accompaniment of music and verse.

'Of course, my son,' say we, 'and we shall always manage each to give a banana libation if nothing else.'

§ *Different approaches of 'Big Three' to writing a novel in English* Anand, Narayan; *Language usage*; Das, Bhatt; AF: Ngugi (2); Carib: Brathwaite (3)

ATTIA HOSAIN (1913–)

Gossamer Thread

He came back late from the office and went straight to his room. He wanted to shake off the oppressive silence of the streets with their abandoned trams and buses scattered like toys tired children had forgotten to put back in their places. Quiet people walked warily, conscious of armed policemen, and stared at his car with hostility as he drove past them.

His wife heard him come in, told the servant to prepare tea and bring it to the sitting-room, and went there to wait for him. When he came into the room, she felt, with the sensitiveness of timidity, his silence spiked with ill humour.

'You look worried; is anything wrong?' she asked diffidently.

'No, nothing. I'm just tired,' and he began reading the evening paper, not wishing to encourage conversation. Every problem that drove branching wedges into his mind was filtered by hers to a simplification that irritated him. If he explained his disquiet, it would become composite of trite sentiments: 'Everything is wrong; the world is wrong.'

She poured him a cup of tea, and as she sipped her own her thoughts scattered and danced, resting fleetingly on the children, the servants, the house, herself, then converging on him who was the constant focus.

She said: 'I'm afraid dinner will be late. The cook had to walk from the bazaar because the strike started without warning. It's most disturbing.'

Her simplification enraged him. There might very well be bloodshed if the strikers decided to defy the ban against the meeting, and all she could think of was that dinner would be late. He thought it easier to pretend he had not heard her.

She attempted another approach.

'Ali phoned.'

He looked up with interest. 'Did he? When did he get here?'

'This morning. He should ring again any minute.'

'Did he say how long he'd be here?'

'Two or three days. I asked him to come here this evening, but he's busy and said he would ring you.'

He had turned to the paper again before she could finish the sentence, but his mind had wandered from its menaces down the lifeline between the mentioned name and the secure remembered past.

There had then been no urgent problems but those that were subjective, without external impositions, and with basic physical origins. His ambition – of which he was conscious without admission; and his snobbery – of which he was unconscious – dominated his thoughts and steered his actions. As a student he was extremely popular, possessed all the right attributes, was good at games and successful with women, passed tiresomely necessary examinations with the minimum effort required, and was derisive of those who turned to intellectual and artistic activities because, he maintained, they were eccentric or weaklings. This, he felt, was the general opinion. His material well-being and his generous allowance from home he accepted as unquestioningly as the fact of being alive.

'Have you,' he asked his wife suddenly, 'any idea where my college albums are kept?'

'Oh yes, of course. Shall I get them out?'

'Not now, but I wish you would keep them handy. I might want to show them to my friends and I cannot ask you each time to search for them.'

'I don't need to; but it's so long since you asked for them; they gather dust lying . . . .' but she realised it was useless continuing.

When he had returned home, he found it irksome conforming to restrictions which he had outgrown during his years abroad. It was a release when he joined a firm and was posted to a city modern enough to enable him to live as he wished. With his charm and his means he soon became a favourite of the smart social set. For some time he was able to preserve himself, physically and mentally, as near an image as possible of the popular undergraduate, cushioned against the jarring impact of external problems by his personal interests. The first shock came when his father died and he had to face financial facts of which he had no previous awareness. Responsibility added new layers to his mind, just as soft living had covered his athletic body with flesh. He changed perceptibly.

'There is an invitation,' she said, 'to the reception next week. Shall I accept it?'

'God! they are a bore.' He did not look up from the paper.

'I'll refuse it then.'

He felt irritated by her literal mind and said sharply: 'We might as well go. There is no point in offending people.'

As a concession to his mother's importunity, and seeking refuge in professed cynicism, he had consented to marry the simple, immature girl she had chosen for him. She was decorative enough and submissive enough to increase his self-confidence. But from under the strong seal of his personality portions of her own escaped waxlike with visible, uneven edges of which both were conscious. It increased her diffidence and his domination.

'I forgot to tell you, they phoned from the bookshop that the books you ordered should be in by tomorrow's mail.'

He looked up with interest. 'Did they? I've waited long enough,' then added with a persuasive smile: 'Will you please go round and get them for me? They are so inefficient, they are sure not to send them for days.'

'Of course. I was wondering if the car . . .' but she found herself addressing the newspaper and accepted the relapse into silence.

He was justifiably proud of his collection of progressive – he stressed the word on suitable occasions – literature. His conversion to interests he had once derided as pseudo-intellectual exhibitionism appeared sudden to most of his old friends, but in his mind there had been an unrest for a considerable period of time, and its canalisation in these particular channels seemed natural to him who prided himself on his inherent good sense and judgment. It had started after six years of youthful, thoughtless living.

He had come to an age as uncomfortable as early adolescence. His years had not yet pushed him towards older men, and the younger ones whose company he sought disapproved of him.

It was a generation which personified a new spirit of urgent seriousness that found no time for his way of living except to express contempt or worse. He found himself suddenly in a void.

Splintering the brittle silence, she said:

'I wonder where Arun is?'

He looked up frowning: 'What made you suddenly think of him?'

'I was thinking of dinner, and what the cook said, and if there's trouble Arun will be with the strikers and he might get hurt.' She said it as simply as a child talking.

'Good God! All you can think of is dinner or a man being hurt. Do you understand what this strike signifies?' He worked himself up to rhetorical frenzy: 'The naked struggle of progress and reaction.' Then he stopped suddenly, shrugging his shoulders.

She looked at him wide-eyed.

'I know I cannot understand. All the words you use confuse me. I don't understand everything Arun says, but I admire him, he is so good and I hate to think he may be hurt.'

There was no response, but she had not expected one and went out of the room to see the cook.

In his search for mental anchorage he found in Arun an assured guide. He provided the link absent hitherto between him and the new generation, being his own age, yet with their outlook. Arun's profound knowledge had given him good guidance, and he spoke with the assurance of one who had learned his lessons well. There was a happy expansion of interests for him; he read a great deal, attended meetings, joined societies, worked on committees. He succeeded in securing a prominent place for himself in this new world; and in the old it was too secure to be lost.

She came back agitated: 'The cook says there has been trouble, firing . . .'

'Must you get information from the servants?' He was coldly disapproving.

She stood looking at him with worried eyes. 'Isn't it awful if it's true? I was right to worry about Arun.'

'You cannot surely believe in kitchen rumours,' he said irritably. She sat and stared at him, her brows still wrinkled with worry.

He admired Arun even though he was used as an example by those who said his own manner of living contradicted his professions, pointing out Arun's ascetic self-denial, born as he was to the same standards of wealth and comfort. He coupled his defence with attack by admitting he lacked courage, that he had to think of his wife and children, but that dramatic, individual gestures were of little real value, and what mattered was to think on the right lines and not obstruct progress.

She said sadly: 'Now everything will be upset for tomorrow. Do you think we should put it off?'

'Put what off?'

'Our party. Have you forgotten?'

'Oh for heaven's sake, don't worry about unimportant things.'

His wife's detachment from the problems to which he attached supreme importance was of little consequence to him. From her he required no mental recognition, but merely an acceptance of those patterns of social behaviour which he put before her. She poured tea as gracefully for a prince as a professor, a ruler as a revolutionary. They lived, entertained and were entertained as always; there had been merely an additional trimming for a new type of guest. Arun had never been able to adjust himself to their way of life, but he himself was convinced that intolerant, puritanical fervour harmed the cause of winning over new supporters. It had sharp thorns that probed too deep. For that reason he preferred Arun's friend, a young mechanic whose convictions were free of all complexes, so integrated that he was at ease anywhere and with anyone. He considered it an attribute of sincerity that they had both reached the same point from opposite directions.

'Will you please,' asked his wife, 'hurry back from the meeting tomorrow in time for the party?'

'Meeting? Which meeting?'

'I thought . . .'

'Oh that one. I've changed my mind,' he said, and getting up, walked out of the room. He did not wish to expose his inquietude. Once again he had to face a mental conflict, this time between convictions and action. It was no longer possible for a man to straddle across two worlds in ideological conflict; the drift apart was swift and a man could not tear himself apart, but must jump to one side.

The telephone rang sharply and she called out: 'You had better answer it. It must be Ali.'

She heard his first hearty greeting change to a note of nervous hesitation. The conversation was very brief and when he returned she was alarmed by the look in his eyes.

'Who was it? Is anything wrong?'

He did not answer her questions but said quietly: 'Will you please see to it that no one comes here? Tell the servants we do not wish to be disturbed.'

She nodded in silent bewilderment, and left the room. When she came back, he was walking nervously up to the outside door and back, but she did not ask questions, knowing they would be unwelcome. He seemed to be waiting for the knock which, when it came, gentle and insistent, made him start and hurry to open the door.

She exclaimed in surprise, 'Arun.'

Arun smiled at her, weary. His thin face was pale and he was breathing rapidly. Her husband shut the door without a word.

Arun said: 'I couldn't say much over the phone. I had to know whether you were alone so I took the risk of going into the restaurant.' He added simply: 'The police are looking for me.'

'The police,' she gasped and put her hand to her mouth.

Her husband looked nervously at the door and said: 'What can I do to help you?'

'Let me stay here tonight.'

'Here?' His voice struck a sharp high note.

'I must stay; I have to stay. It does not matter if they find me tomorrow night, but for one day I must be free. There is so much to be done. Everything depends on it. You've always helped, you must do it now.'

'But,' he stammered, 'they know we are friends, they know me; they may come here to look for you.'

'It is because they know you they will not come here,' Arun said coldly.

He flushed: 'But the servants may see you; there is no place to hide you from them.'

Arun pleaded: 'It's only for a short while, there must be some place. You don't seem to realise how much depends on it – I came to you because I believed you were the one who would understand best.'

He said in agitation: 'I'll do anything else you ask. If you need money to help you get away. You must understand too . . .'

He could not continue, frozen by the cold reproachful eyes that looked at him from the ascetic face.

'I understand,' Arun said, as he walked slowly towards the door.

She called out softly, 'Arun,' and as he turned his dead face to her, she said, 'Don't go away.'

§ *Politics and private lives* Sahgal, Arasanayagam, Selvadurai; SEA: Ee Tiang Hong (2), Wong Phui Nam, Thumboo, Jeyaretnam.

NISSIM EZEKIEL (1924–)

1: Background, Casually

I

A poet-rascal-clown was born,
The frightened child who would not eat
Or sleep, a boy of meagre bone.
He never learnt to fly a kite,
5   His borrowed top refused to spin.

I went to Roman Catholic school,
A mugging Jew among the wolves.
They told me I had killed the Christ,
That year I won the scripture prize.
10   A Muslim sportsman boxed my ears.

I grew in terror of the strong
But undernourished Hindu lads,
Their prepositions always wrong,
Repelled me by passivity.
15   One noisy day I used a knife.

At home on Friday nights the prayers
Were said. My morals had declined.
I heard of Yoga and of Zen.
Could I, perhaps, be rabbi-saint?
20   The more I searched, the less I found.

Twenty-two: time to go abroad.
First, the decision, then a friend
To pay the fare. Philosophy,
Poverty and Poetry, three
25   Companions shared my basement room.

II

The London seasons passed me by.
I lay in bed two years alone.
And then a Woman came to tell
My willing ears I was the Son
30   Of Man. I knew that I had failed.

In everything, a bitter thought.
So, in an English cargo-ship
Taking French guns and mortar shells
To Indo-China, scrubbed the decks.
35 And learned to laugh again at home.

How to feel it home, was the point.
Some reading had been done, but what
Had I observed, except my own
Exasperation? All Hindus are
40 Like that, my father used to say,

When someone talked too loudly, or
Knocked at the door like the Devil.
They hawked and spat. They sprawled around.
I prepared for the worst. Married,
45 Changed jobs, and saw myself a fool.

The song of my experience sung,
I knew that all was yet to sing.
My ancestors, among the castes,
Were aliens crushing seed for bread
50 (The hooded bullock made his rounds).

III
One among them fought and taught,
A Major bearing British arms.
He told my father sad stories
Of the Boer War. I dreamed that
55 Fierce men had bound my feet and hands.

The later dreams were all of words.
I did not know that words betray
But let the poems come, and lost
That grip on things the worldly prize.
60 I would not suffer that again.

I look about me now, and try
To formulate a plainer view:

---

49 crushing seed: Bene Israel tradition has it that their ancestors took to oil pressing soon after arrival in India.
Hence *Shanwar teli*, Saturday oil-pressers, i.e. those who did not work on Saturdays. [author's note.]

The wise survive and serve – to play
The fool, to cash in on
65   The inner and the outer storms.

The Indian landscape sears my eyes.
I have become a part of it
To be observed by foreigners.
They say that I am singular,
70   Their letters overstate the case.

I have made my commitments now.
This is one: to stay where I am,
As others choose to give themselves
In some remote and backward place.
75   My backward place is where I am.

§ *Diverse cultural inheritances/borderline protagonists* Aus: Malouf; Carib: Walcott (2); SEA: Somtow

2: The Patriot

I am standing for peace and non-violence.
Why world is fighting fighting,
Why all people of world
Are not following Mahatma Gandhi
5   I am simply not understanding.
Ancient Indian Wisdom is 100% correct.
I should say even 200% correct.
But Modern generation is neglecting –
Too much going for fashion and foreign thing.

10   Other day I'm reading in newspaper
(Every day I'm reading Times of India
To improve my English Language)
How one goonda fellow
Throw stone at Indirabehn.
15   Must be student unrest fellow, I am thinking.
Friends, Romans, Countrymen, I am saying
    (to myself)
Lend me the ears.
Everything is coming –
Regeneration, Remuneration, Contraception.
20   Be patiently, brothers and sisters.

---

13 goonda: rogue.   **14 Indirabehn**: Indira Gandhi, literally 'Sister Indira'.

You want one glass lassi?
Very good for digestion.
With little salt lovely drink,
Better than wine;
25 Not that I am ever tasting the wine.
I'm the total teetotaller, completely total.
But I say
Wine is for the drunkards only.

What you think of prospects of world peace?
30 Pakistan behaving like this,
China behaving like that,
It is making me very sad, I am telling you.
Really, most harassing me.
All men are brothers, no?
35 In India also
Gujaraties, Maharashtrians, Hindiwallahs
All brothers –
Though some are having funny habits.
Still, you tolerate me,
40 I tolerate you,
One day Ram Rajya is surely coming.

You are going?
But you will visit again
Any time, any day,
45 I am not believing in ceremony.
Always I am enjoying your company.

§ *Language usage* Rao, Das, Bhatt

DOM MORAES (1938–)

Sinbad

Winds sniffed, the graves
Of each sea identified,
Numbered, still the tickled waves
Fumbling, toss of the dead.

5 Sinbad, your trips!
Diamonds clawed by vultures!

---

41 Ram Rajya: the rule, or kingdom, of Rama.

Flying over defunct countries
You need raw colours for new maps.

Old friends folding up in strange places.
10 New friends holding out hearts.
Bronze breasts iced in white lace:
Cold cups of kindness.

Choose your rock, seamate, stay with it.
Lose your shadow, it's of no use.
15 The last bronze bird puts you down,
Tidier than a horse, final.

Ashes and marred walls deface you.
Where is this wind from,
Sinbad, defining its own course?
20 Some of us never know home.

§ *Mythical migrants* Bhatt, Haq; Carib: Walcott (4)

A. K. RAMANUJAN (1929–93)

Small-Scale Reflections on a Great House

Sometimes I think that nothing
that ever comes into this house
goes out. Things come in every day

to lose themselves among other things
5 lost long ago among
other things lost long ago;

lame wandering cows from nowhere
have been known to be tethered,
given a name, encouraged

10 to get pregnant in the broad daylight
of the street under the elders'
supervision, the girls hiding

behind windows with holes in them.

Unread library books
15   usually mature in two weeks
and begin to lay a row

of little eggs in the ledgers
for fines, as silverfish
in the old man's office room

20   breed dynasties among long legal words
in the succulence
of Victorian parchment.

Neighbours' dishes brought up
with the greasy sweets they made
25   all night the day before yesterday

for the wedding anniversary of a god,

never leave the house they enter,
like the servants, the phonographs,
the epilepsies in the blood,

30   sons-in-law who quite forget
their mothers, but stay to check
accounts or teach arithmetic to nieces,

or the women who come as wives
from houses open on one side
35   to rising suns, or another

to the setting, accustomed
to wait and to yield to monsoons
in the mountains' calendar

beating through the hanging banana leaves.

40   And also, anything that goes out
will come back, processed and often
with long bills attached,

like the hooped bales of cotton
shipped off to invisible Manchesters
45   and brought back milled and folded

for a price, cloth for our days'
middle-class loins, and muslin
for our richer nights. Letters mailed

have a way of finding their way back
50 with many re-directions to wrong
addresses and red ink marks

earned in Tiruvalla and Sialkot.

And ideas behave like rumours,
once casually mentioned somewhere
55 they come back to the door as prodigies

born to prodigal fathers, with eyes
that vaguely look like our own,
like what Uncle said the other day:

that every Plotinus we read
60 is what some Alexander looted
between the malarial rivers.

A beggar once came with a violin
to croak out a prostitute song
that our voiceless cook sang

65 all the time in our backyard.

Nothing stays out: daughters
get married to short-lived idiots;
sons who run away come back

in grandchildren who recite Sanskrit
70 to approving old men, or bring
betelnuts for visiting uncles

who keep them gaping with
anecdotes of unseen fathers,
or to bring Ganges water

75 in a copper pot
for the last of the dying
ancestors' rattle in the throat.

And though many times from everywhere,

---

59 **Plotinus**: Neo-Platonist philosopher of 3rd century AD.

60 **Alexander**: Alexander the Great, Macedonian conqueror of 4th century BC.

recently only twice:
80   once in nineteen-forty-three
from as far away as the Sahara,

half-gnawed by desert foxes,
and lately from somewhere
in the north, a nephew with stripes

85   on his shoulder was called
an incident on the border
and was brought back in plane

and train and military truck
even before the telegrams reached,
90   on a perfectly good

chatty afternoon.

§ *House as symbol* Alexander, Wijenaike, Hashmi; Af: Dangarembga; Can: Atwood (4); Carib: Walcott (1), Naipaul (2)

JAYANTA MAHAPATRA (1928–)

Grandfather

(Starving, on the point of death, Chintamani Mahapatra embraced Christianity during the terrible famine that struck Orissa in 1866.)

The yellowed diary's notes whisper in vernacular.
They sound the forgotten posture,
the cramped cry that forces me to hear that voice.
Now I stumble in your black-paged wake.

5   No uneasy stir of cloud
darkened the white skies of your day; the silence
of dust grazed in the long afternoon sun, ruling
the cracked fallow earth, ate into the laughter of your flesh.

For you it was the hardest question of all.
10   Dead, empty trees stood by the dragging river,
past your weakened body, flailing against your sleep.
You thought of the way the jackals moved, to move.

Did you hear the young tamarind leaves rustle
in the cold mean nights of your belly? Did you see

15   your own death? Watch it tear at your cries,
break them into fits of hard unnatural laughter?

How old were you? Hunted, you turned coward and ran,
the real animal in you plunging through your bone.
You left your family behind, the buried things.
20   the precious clod that praised the quality of a god.

The imperishable that swung your broken body,
turned it inside out? What did faith matter?
What Hindu world so ancient and true for you to hold?
Uneasily you dreamed toward the centre of your web.

25   The separate life let you survive, while perhaps
the one you left wept in the blur of your heart.
Now in a night of sleep and taunting rain
my son and I speak of that famine nameless as stone.

A conscience of years is between us. He is young.
30   The whirls of glory are breaking down for him before me.
Does he think of the past as a loss we have lived, our own?
Out of silence we look back now at what we do not know.

There is a dawn waiting beside us, whose signs
are a hundred-odd years away from you, Grandfather.
35   You are an invisible piece on a board
whose move had made our children grow, to know us,

carrying us deep where our voices lapse into silence.
We wish we knew you more.
We wish we knew what it was to be, against dying,
40   to know the dignity

that had to be earned dangerously,
your last chance that was blindly terrifying, so unfair.
We wish we had not to wake up with our smiles
in the middle of some social order.

§ *Grandfather poems* Can: Purdy (1), Mandel, Bowering; TransC: Ghose (2)

KAMALA DAS (1934–)

An Introduction

I don't know politics but I know the names
Of those in power, and can repeat them like
Days of week, or names of months, beginning with
Nehru.   I am Indian, very brown, born in
5 Malabar, I speak three languages, write in
Two, dream in one.   Don't write in English, they said,
English is not your mother-tongue.   Why not leave
Me alone, critics, friends, visiting cousins,
Every one of you?   Why not let me speak in
10 Any language I like?   The language I speak
Becomes mine, its distortions, its queernesses
All mine, mine alone.   It is half English, half
Indian, funny perhaps, but it is honest,
It is as human as I am human, don't
15 You see? It voices my joys, my longings, my
Hopes, and it is useful to me as cawing
Is to crows or roaring to the lions, it
Is human speech, the speech of the mind that is
Here and not there, a mind that sees and hears and
20 Is aware.   Not the deaf, blind speech
Of trees in storm or of monsoon clouds or of rain or the
Incoherent mutterings of the blazing
Funeral pyre.   I was child, and later they
Told me I grew, for I became tall, my limbs
25 Swelled and one or two places sprouted hair.   When
I asked for love, not knowing what else to ask
For, he drew a youth of sixteen into the
Bedroom and closed the door.   He did not beat me
But my sad woman-body felt so beaten.
30 The weight of my breasts and womb crushed me.   I shrank
Pitifully.   Then . . . I wore a shirt and my
Brother's trousers, cut my hair short and ignored
My womanliness.   Dress in sarees, be girl,
Be wife, they said.   Be embroiderer, be cook,
35 Be a quarreller with servants.   Fit in.   Oh,
Belong, cried the categorizers.   Don't sit
On walls or peep in through our lace-draped windows.
Be Amy, or be Kamala.   Or, better
Still, be Madhavikutty.   It is time to
40 Choose a name, a role.   Don't play pretending games.
Don't play at schizophrenia or be a

Nympho.   Don't cry embarrassingly loud when
Jilted in love . . . . I met a man, loved him.   Call
Him not by any name, he is every man
45   Who wants a woman, just as I am every
Woman who seeks love.   In him . . . . the hungry haste
Of rivers, in me . . . . the oceans' tireless
Waiting.   Who are you, I ask each and everyone,
The answer is, it is I.   Anywhere and,
50   Everywhere, I see the one who calls himself
If in this world, he is tightly packed like the
Sword in its sheath.   It is I who drink lonely
Drinks at twelve, midnight, in hotels of strange towns,
It is I who laugh, it is I who make love
55   And then, feel shame, it is I who lie dying
With a rattle in my throat.   I am sinner,
I am saint.   I am the beloved and the
Betrayed.   I have no joys which are not yours, no
Aches which are not yours.   I too call myself I.

§ *Language usage* Rao, Ezekiel, Bhatt

KEKI DARUWALLA (1937–)

Death of a Bird

Under an overhang of crags
fierce bird-love:
the monals mated, clawed and screamed;
the female brown and nondescript
5   the male was king, a fire-dream!
My barrel spoke one word of lead:
the bird came down, the king was dead,

or almost dying:
his eyes were glazed, the breast still throbbed.
10   We tucked him pulsing as he was in our rucksack.
The female rose, in terror crying!
With bird-blood on our hands we walked,
and as the skies broke into rags
of mist, why did our footsteps drag?

15   The cumulus piled on the crags.
We smote the pony on its shanks

---

3 monals: type of pheasant.

to hurry him; around a bend
he swivelled and went down the flank
of rock a thousand feet below
20   to where the roaring river flowed.

His scream
climbed up the gorge, a nightmare fang
which ploughed my blistered dreams and sowed
begging children.
25   Depressed a bit we took the road;
walking like ciphers disinterred
from some forgotten code.

Dusk caught up with us, and bears;
my terror-gun spat at the shades
30   but missed each time.
When jackals howled, sniffing my ribs
trembling she asked if they were wolves?
I simply held her hand in mine
and walked on further to a cave
35   hemmed in by pine we would have missed
but for a growling *bhotia* dog
the resin-tappers left behind
to guard their cans and beaded ichor
pimpling like a spray of cysts.
40   Just yards off an escarpment wrote
hieroglyphs on a scroll of mist.

And as she crumpled with a chill
I lit a fire of turf and peat
and rubbed her clotted sides and feet
45   and found her waking in my hands
(this shadow-pair of quickening hands)
like embers in a shadow-net.
In the wet lanes of her body
we, apprehensive, met.

50   And as we rose to the final kill –
two electric saws meeting on a hill
in the narrowing bones of a fractured tree –
each of us thought the other was free
of the pony's scream and the monal's wings
55   and the prowling bears in the firelight-rim.

---

36 *bhotia*: large sheep-dog found in mountain regions.

Her head on my heartbeat, hair locked in my fingers
she purred into sleep; the night seemed to flower
late with our dreams
for the moon came out just for an hour or two
60   and the monal-wings came feathering down
in a passion of dusky gold and blue.
And the wolves, with the mist, went over the cliff –
but for the wind we both would have dreamt
the very same dream of quiescence and love;
65   but the wind was a thorn in the flesh of the night
and moaned aloud like a witch in the flue.

I broke my gun in two across the back
of an ash-grey dawn. A brown bird left the crags
flying strongly, and as its shadow crossed us
70   it shrieked with fear and turned to stone
dropping at our feet.
'It's the queen-monal! We are accursed!' she said.
'Just watch its eyes!' For though the bird was near dead
its eyes flared terror like bits of dripping meat!

NAYANTARA SAHGAL (1927–)

Martand

Martand took his lean length out of the comfortable depths of our best arm-chair and said reluctantly, 'I'd better be going.'

Naresh, my husband, did not reply.

I looked up at Martand but he was not looking at me. He never did, eye-to-eye, except when we were alone, and then hungrily, as if each time were going to be the last – as it easily might have been.

I got up, too. I wanted to cry out every time he left me, to hear my own voice wailing like a lost child's. We had been talking politics, if the chaos caving into everyday life could be called that. Strain and suspense had become part of office and home. There was no getting away from it. Crying would have been a release from that as well.

Refugees glutted the district, and more and more kept straggling in. Not one big flood with an end to it. This was an endless, haggard human sea of people who knew with profound instinct that there was no going back. They were here to stay. And here, food and medicine were short. Space was getting harder to squeeze out. There had been little enough before. And time was running out.

'In other countries men can dream,' Martand had said earlier in the evening, 'but our dreams remain food and shelter, shelter and food, year after year. We've never had enough for ourselves and now we have to provide for these extra God knows how many.'

'We *know* how many,' said Naresh bitterly. 'Millions. Why beat about the bush? It's going to get desperate, wait and see, unless the refugees ease off.'

It was clear that a serious crisis, the worst yet, might soon be upon us. Martand had agreed.

'It already is,' Naresh had said with harsh finality. 'We should have sealed the frontier long ago.'

'And let them die,' lay unspoken between us.

'Well it's not our problem,' Naresh threw at us defiantly, as though either of us had protested.

'Isn't it?'

Martand had looked at my husband consideringly, compassionately as he said it, and I at the wall. I was caught between fact and vision, between the two men, belonging mind and body to each. I loved and believed in them both, but Martand, I knew, was trying to do the more difficult thing. He kept trying to hold a tide at bay, by turning it off its dreadful course, if he could, with the tone of his voice, the look in his eyes – such instruments as human beings are left with when hardly any other resource remains. Inner religion pitted against destruction. For Martand still had visions of a good world. For months Naresh and I had shared them, here in this very room till late into the night. Now, only I did.

We had talked all evening about the refugee crisis, but what a nerve-racking thing our own three-cornered companionship had become. What a lot of gaiety I needed simply to get through each day without continual mention of disaster. Disaster was always there. Was there ever a time it had not been? But now ordinary everyday happiness had become part of it. I felt happy only when I was near Martand and then I would have to be careful not to let it show. That was how it had become, the once easy natural give and take between the three of us. Now only its outer crust remained, a paper-thin but sheltering wall that hid my private torment. I have lived inside it these six months, ever since we had met Martand soon after our Kashmir holiday.

Martand is the Kashmiri name for the Sun God and there is a temple to him in Kashmir – miles of drive past brilliant young green rice, in the earth's most beautiful valley flanked with tall straight poplars, fringed with feathery willows, under serene expanses of sky. I had needed to go to Kashmir quite apart from the pilgrimage I wanted to make to the temple. I had longed to get away from the frantic, teeming district in Naresh's charge to clean open space, Kashmiri space. There were other nearer hill stations but I couldn't bear the thought of any other. And then, incredibly, Naresh had got his leave. With every Government officer so heavily overworked we had hardly expected it.

Naresh had grumbled goodnaturedly about the distance. 'What a prejudiced lot you Kashmiris are, convinced there's no place like Kashmir.' But he had given in.

There isn't, of course. Kashmir is unique. I did not want the rationed beauty of other places, a glimpse of hill and cloud. I wanted a pageant of it, the immense incomparable valley unravelling as we drove through it. I wanted to surrender to something bigger than necessity, and I had to visit the Martand shrine. Where science had failed, faith might work.

The temple was off the motor road. It was thirteen hundred years old, a massive burnt-out saga of ruined glory with a broken Grecian colonnade surrounding it. When we got there, it seemed afire under the late afternoon sun, a tiger gold, its energy rippling visibly through it carvings. Then the light changed and softened before our eyes, sinking deeply into the stone, leaving it flesh-warm and pulsating. I put the flat of my hand on a lovely broken column, leaned my forehead against it and felt it all taken into me.

'Have you had enough?' Naresh asked indulgently.

He was sitting against one of the columns smoking his pipe.

'How's that going to get you a child, granted Martand is the fount of fertility?' he asked.

Reluctantly I gave my hand's contact with the stone and came to him with my answer.

'Now? Here?' he protested.

'Why not,' I pleaded, 'there's no one for miles around.'

'But the village is less than a mile away. Anyone could come along.'

'Please, we're wasting time.'

And we wasted no more. The gold fire in me caught up with Naresh as he pulled me down beside him.

Martand, when we first met him just after that holiday, reminded me of that ruined splendour. He looked descended from an ancient, princely lineage. I felt a shock of recognition and betrayal.

'You look frightened,' were the first personal words he said to me.

I was. I should have waited for him. But I couldn't tell him that. Instead I told him he had an unusual name and asked him about his ancestry, and Martand laughed.

'If I tried awfully hard,' he said, 'I suppose I could find out my great-grandfather's name.'

I must have looked scandalized.

'Is that very dreadful?' he had teased. 'No, there's no blue blood in my veins. I come from solid middle class stock. Scholarships all through medical college. But there's romance in the ordinary. Romance isn't the heights. It's what a passing stranger recognizes. It could even be in working in an inferno like this, and learning to love it.'

Naresh saw Martand out of his car and came back into the room. He was bone tired and irritable.

'He never knows when to leave. I've got an early meeting tomorrow. He probably has to be up at the crack of dawn too.'

I said, to take his mind off Martand, 'When do you think this refugee business will let up?'

'On Doomsday,' he said violently. 'That's when any problem in this country is going to let up.'

He went into the bedroom to put away the whisky bottle while I rinsed out the glasses. A lot of whisky got drunk whenever Martand came.

Naresh came back. 'He drinks like a fish, too,' he said, helping me with the glasses.

Naresh was angry, but not about the drinking. He was angry with Martand for still having dreams, and with me for being enmeshed in them.

When we were in bed he said, 'How long are we going to make excuses for not being able to meet targets, not having enough to feed and clothe people and make life livable for them? And now with this ghastly deluge going on and on, we'll never have enough of anything in our lifetime. Have you thought of that? I want to get out of this hell-hole and live a decent life somewhere where people have *enough* of everything. It doesn't seem too much to ask. Let's get out for a year or so.'

I felt paralysed.

'I'm making some enquiries, he went on, 'I could ask for a temporary posting at one of our missions abroad. Just for a breath of fresh air. I've had a bellyful here.'

I lay in bed, trying to empty my mind of thinking. A lot of whisky had got drunk – by all of us. Martand had once said, 'It helps to numb feelings. One can't watch all this unprotected and remain human.' It was one of the few times he had admitted to strain. 'Do you agree we should get out then, darling?' Naresh mumbled, his hand on my breast for comfort.

And he fell asleep without waiting for an answer.

There was a crowd as usual outside Martand's clinic next morning, looking torpidly, dully at me as I walked through. Flies, dust, heavy, hopeless heat. Another day of learning to love it, I thought, and another minute till I open that door to Martand.

He was sitting at his desk, his sleeves rolled up, his feet in slippers, his stethoscope still around his neck. He had forgotten to take it off, like he sometimes forgot to eat, and continually forgot the huge dishevelment around him. He asked his assistant to bring some coffee.

'Sorry the cup isn't very elegant,' he said when it came.

He was always saying things like that. Sorry, when he repaid a debt, about handing me grubby-looking change or a tattered note. Sorry that we could not see the hills from his window – there were none to see. There was only a grim growing mass of humanity, almost machine-like in its menacing immobility as it waited. I couldn't see these people as individuals any more. It was It. Waiting for cholera shots, for rations, for clothes, for space, for air, for life, for hope, as if it could do nothing, nothing for Itself. A monster robot seeking succour, devouring the pitifully little we had.

'Do you think the kingdom of heaven is a germ-free place?' asked Martand, giving me his smile over his coffee cup.

I put mine noisily down, spilling coffee. I felt a rush of hysteria and horror at all the sights and smells of suffering interminably around us. How could he stay so untarnished at the heart of them?

'Who cares? It's here in this mess we have to live. Oh Martand, I can't bear to stay or to go away. I can't bear anything any more.'

'You must,' he warned, no longer smiling. 'There's a very long road ahead of us yet. Don't lose your nerve now.'

He meant the refugee crisis, as well as the time span left to him and me to find our way to each other on the dangerous, joyful, heart-breaking road we were travelling together. He got up to go into the dispensary and carry on his work, and I remembered why I had come.

'I found these peaches in the bazar. There hasn't been any good fruit for such a long time, I had to bring them for you. I'm taking some home for us, too.'

'Then take these with you. I'll come and eat them at your house. I'll come to dinner,' he said.

'No don't. Naresh won't like it. He was very irritable last night.'

'Was he? Why?'

There was that untouched *innocence* about Martand, a purity without which I could no longer live. That was why I couldn't give him up, however long we had to wait for this to work out. There was so little time to talk about personal problems, and when we were alone together we did not talk.

At the door to the dispensary Martand turned around to say. 'Let me speak to Naresh about us.' It is not the first time he had urged this.

'No!' I cried.

'He is too good a man to deceive.'

'Don't you know anything about human nature?' Panic made me shrill.

'All right, all right,' said Martand softly, 'I must go now, my love. Take care, won't you, as you drive home. It's a bad day today. Some of my staff are giving trouble and refusing to work. And thank you for the peaches.'

I left his share on the table. For my cheap ideas of safety – my safety – I would deprive myself of the sight of him and the sound of his voice this evening. Safety in a mad world did not make much sense, and I was not made for living a double life. My endurance was wearing thin. One of these days I would throw myself on Naresh's mercy and tell him. One of these days, but not today.

At home I washed the peaches and put them on the dining table. When I came back into the dining room with plates and cutlery, Naresh was standing there staring at them.

'You're home early,' I said and I knew in a flash it was time – at once – to tell him about Martand.

Naresh was waiting, a queer stricken look on his face of half-knowing, fearing, unbelieving, and the tension grew intolerable. I went up to him and he put his arms around me.

'Then you hadn't heard,' he said. 'That's why I came – to tell you –'

I looked up at him, all my terrors realized.

'Martand was stabbed,' he said, 'less than half an hour ago. Not by a refugee, by one of his own assistants. They sent for me immediately. I was with him when he died.'

Naresh sobbed while I stood holding him, deadly calm, as if I had known this would happen. I still had my sight and hearing, but that was all. Nothing could move me any more.

'We'll go away,' he wept, 'we'll go away.'

Yes, I thought, to a place where there was enough of everything and charity could be a virtue, not a crime. We would go where my child could be born in safety, and where a man would not be murdered for loving mankind. As we clung together I knew we had both changed invisibly beyond recall. Naresh, mourning Martand, had found his faith in goodness again, while I, surely as I breathed, knew that everywhere within hand's reach was evil.

§ *Politics and private lives* Hosain, Arasanayagam, Selvadurai; SEA: Ee Tiang Hong (2), Wong Phui Nam, Thumboo, Jeyaretnam; *Kashmir* Agha Shahid Ali

ANITA DESAI (1937–)

From In Custody

In Custody dramatizes a conflict which is central to several of Desai's novels: that between a passive, reflective mode of existence and a more outward and passionately engaged life. Here the timid protagonist Deven, a college lecturer, finds his world turned upside down when he becomes involved with one of Delhi's leading poets, the mercurial Nur, a figure he has previously idolized. The conflict between the two modes of existence is also played out on another level, with the 'safe comfortable' language of Hindi, the subject Deven teaches, being contrasted with the passionate outpourings of Nur's Urdu verse. In the first of the two passages extracted here, Deven is commissioned by his friend Murad, a magazine editor, to interview Nur; in the second he goes to do so.

. . . 'Everybody thinks it an easy thing to bring out a magazine,' he went on. 'Nobody knows of the cost involved. Every month there is a crisis – the printing press refusing to print unless past bills are cleared, the distributor refusing to pay for last month's supplies of copies, the telephone bill, the postage . . . Such expenses. What can you know about it?' he challenged Deven aggressively. 'Worries, worries, worries. And where are the readers? Where are the subscriptions? Who reads Urdu any more?'

'Murad, your magazine must be kept alive for the sake of those who do still read it,' Deven said fervently.

'That is what I am doing,' Murad glared at him. 'Now I am planning a special issue on Urdu poetry. Someone has to keep alive the glorious tradition of Urdu literature. If we do not do it, at whatever cost, how will it survive in this era of – that vegetarian monster, Hindi?' He pronounced the last word with such disgust that it made Deven shrink back and shrivel in his chair, for Hindi was what he taught at the college and for which he was therefore responsible to some degree. 'That language of peasants,' Murad sneered, picking his teeth with a matchstick. 'The language that is raised on radishes and potatoes,' he laughed rudely, pushing aside the empty plates on the table. 'Yet, like these vegetables, it flourishes, while Urdu – language of the court in days of royalty – now languishes in the back lanes and gutters of the city. No palace for it to live in the style to which it is accustomed, no emperors and nawabs to act as its patrons. Only poor I, in my dingy office, trying to bring out a magazine where it may be kept alive. That is what I am doing, see?' He threw another proud and angry look at Deven and spat out a small piece of chewed matchstick in his direction.

'I know, I know, Murad,' Deven sighed. 'How happy I would be to join you on the staff, work for you, for the journal. But I can't give up my job here. I had to take it when it was offered. I was married, Sarla was expecting, you know . . .'

'How could I know,' Murad said. 'Am I supposed to be responsible for that?' He laughed crudely.

Deven pretended not to hear. He went on trying to win Murad's sympathy. 'I could not have supported even myself by writing in Urdu, let alone Sarla and a child. I can write Urdu now only as my hobby.'

'Only your hobby,' mocked Murad. 'Can you serve a language by taking it up "only as your hobby"? Doesn't it deserve more? Doesn't it deserve a lifetime's dedication – like mine?' he demanded.

Deven lifted both hands in the air with a helpless gesture of accepting all Murad had to say, accepting and admitting defeat.

Then Murad unexpectedly barked at him, 'So, what about sending me something for my special number on Urdu poetry, hunh?'

Deven's hands fluttered on to his knees as he melted at the suggestion and felt a glow creep through him at the thought of writing something in the language which had been his first language when he was a child in the half-forgotten, unsubstantial city of childhood, and which was still his first love. The glow was also caused by pride, of course, at being asked to contribute a piece by the editor of what he took to be a leading Urdu journal. That was what Murad had assured him it was and he was happy to believe it. 'Will you print my poems if I send them to you – the remaining ones in the sequence?'

'No. Who wants to read your poems?' Murad said at once, abruptly. 'I have enough poems for the issue already. As soon as I sent out the circular announcing it, contributions started pouring in. Poems, poems, poems. Everybody writes them, I tell you,' he complained, plucking at his hair in mock distress. 'I had to stop them. I had to pick and choose. Only the best, I said. Firaq, Faiz, Rafi, Nur . . .'

'Nur? He has sent you some poems?'

Murad looked evasive and shrugged. 'Poor man, he is very old and ill. I have said I will only publish new work, not excerpts from old collections, and he has written nothing new. He is finished.'

'But no special issue on Urdu poetry would be complete if it did not have some verse by Nur,' exclaimed Deven, scandalized. 'Old, new, it doesn't matter – you must have Nur.'

'Of course I must have Nur,' responded Murad, looking suddenly smug. 'Nur will be the star of the issue. The light that blazes in the centre and sends its rays to all corners of the world where his verse is known – in Iran, Iraq, Malaysia, Russia, Sweden – do you know, we have sent his name to the Nobel Prize Committee for its award for literature once again?'

Deven nodded. They did this every year, he knew. He himself was convinced that one day the response would come from Stockholm, and shake the literary world of India to its foundations. He felt it beginning to shake already, under his feet. The two o'clock bus from Moradabad roared by. When it had passed and he could make himself heard, he asked, 'So you will print some of the old poems after all? The great Rose poems, or the Winter ones? You know – ' and he made ready to declaim his favourite lines, the ones that contained all the enchantment and romance he had ever experienced in his life.

But Murad cut him short by leaning forward on his elbows and speaking almost into his ear. 'No, I won't, Deven. I don't print stale old stuff in my journal. Even if I have to wait two, three, four months before I get all the material I want, I get it – then I print. I want a full feature on Nur – Nur in his old age, the dying Nur before he is gone, like a comet into the dark. I want you to do that feature.'

'I?' breathed Deven, so overcome that he quite forgot for the time the noisy surroundings, the empty plates, even the foul breath from Murad's mouth so close to his face. It was the comet he was seeing, swift and pale in the dark like a bird of the night.

'You go and see Nur,' Murad continued. 'You know his work well – oh, as well as anyone, I suppose. You wrote a book about him once, didn't you?'

'A monograph, yes. Will you publish it?' Deven asked breathlessly, thinking that when a comet appeared all kinds of strange happenings might occur. For a moment he became confused and thought it was not Nur who was the comet but Murad who had come from Delhi to visit him, to show him a light: he was willing to believe anything.

But Murad snapped crossly, 'No, I won't. Of course not. I don't want to become bankrupt. I want to bring out my journal. That is what I'm talking about, idiot. Try and listen. Be serious. I want you to track him down in his house in Chandni Chowk – '

'Oh, they say he does not like visitors,' Deven said quickly. The comet was something to be feared, he just remembered, it was a bad omen, not lucky. He could not have said why but he was frightened.

'Look, will you do this feature for me or not?'

'Of course I will, Murad.' He became meek. He hung his head, looking at his fingers clutching the edge of the table. On each fingernail a pale cuticle loomed bleakly.

'Then do as I say. Find him. Go to him and interview him. Discuss the Urdu scene with him. Ask him for his new work. He must have some, dammit, and I want it. I need it for the special issue see?' . . .

If it had not been for the colour and the noise, Chandni Chowk might have been a bazaar encountered in a nightmare; it was so like a maze from which he could find no exit, in which he wandered between the peeling, stained walls of office buildings, the overflowing counters of shops and stalls, wondering if the urchin sent to lead him through it was not actually a malevolent imp leading him to his irrevocable disappearance in the reeking heart of the bazaar. The heat and the crowds pressed down from above and all sides, solid and suffocating as sleep.

With the accuracy of his malevolence, the boy suggested 'Cold drink?' at a stall where poison-green and red sherbets in bottles topped with lemons and carrot juice in damp, oozing earthen jars were in great demand.

Deven shook his head contemptuously and they walked on down the sari lane where lurid Japanese nylon saris covered with octopi and spiders of flower patterns and nets of gold and silver embroidery flashed from doorways like gaudy but shimmering prostitutes propositioning the passers-by, while the rich soft traditional silks were folded and stacked in sober, matronly bales at the back. Shopkeepers eyed them casually but did not rise from their bolsters or cease to pick their toes, in order to attract their attention; they were so obviously not worth any.

They turned into the food lanes where there was little custom at this hour and flies were allowed to nuzzle the pyramids of crystallized fruit undisturbed and milk steamed and bubbled in drowsy pans.

They walked past shady-looking and evil-smelling shops where herbal medicines and panaceas were being wrapped in paper packets by men who looked too ostentatiously like quacks, past booths in which astrologers and palmists and soothsayers had spread out the exotic tools of their trade – elaborately illustrated scrolls, mynah birds in cages, birthstones and gems in open boxes – and pavement stalls where scarves and handkerchiefs and underwear were heaped in mounds of starched cotton, or thick glasses and enamel plates balanced on each other in precarious display, and came out into a circle lined with silversmiths and jewellery shops.

Here Deven halted in despair. He knew he could not be near the poet's residence in this pullulating honeycomb of commerce. Spreading out his arms, he told the boy, 'We must be lost. This is not the right place. It is no use to go further. I'm not going on.' His desperation made the blood beat in his ears so that he didn't hear the frantic ringing of a bicycle bell and was very nearly run over by a cycle rickshaw heavily loaded with parcels heading for the railway station. Its driver, acrobatic as a monkey with a red cap, managed to swerve in time, doing no more than running over Deven's foot, but his parcels slid off the slippery rexine seat and were scattered over the street. Deven was so dazed by this near-accident that it took him a while to realize he was being accused of having caused it, and abused filthily and loudly. The boy was helping the rickshaw driver collect the parcels but when Deven bent to help, he was shoved aside by a blow from his elbow and forced to move on. Breathlessly they hurried down a narrow lane that was lined with nothing but gutters and seemed to serve as a latrine for the entire neighbourhood. The high green walls that threw it into deep shadows belonged to a hospital of *ayurvedic*[1] medicine. It was as gloomy as a prison.

Deven broke into a hobble in order to get to the end of it without inhaling the sickly air there. The boy pursued him, panting, 'Cup of tea? Here's a teashop – have a cup of tea at least, sahib.'

'No, no tea,' Deven hissed at him. 'I want to get to Nur Sahib's house by three o'clock. Where is it? Do you know where it is or not?'

'Very far,' said the boy, gazing back at him steadily and standing firm outside the tea stall where packets of tea and baskets of eggs dangled in the sooty doorway in invitation. 'It will be better to have some tea and a rest first.'

'*No* rest, *no* tea,' Deven bawled at him, bending down to bare his teeth in the boy's face.

The boy shrugged but his expression did not change. Stepping over a flowing gutter, shoving aside a great humped bull that was quietly munching paper bags from an open dustbin that lay on its side, spilling its contents across the gutter so that it was blocked and had begun to flood, he turned a corner into another lane. On one side of it stretched the high wall of the gloomy green hospital and along the other was a row of small, tightly shut wooden doors set into straight, faded walls. There was no signboard on any of them but the boy went up to one and beat on it with the palms of his hands till, after a long interval, it was opened.

Then Deven knew it was not the familiar nightmare because if it was, the door would have remained shut.

Before he could make out who had opened the door and now stood behind it, he heard an immense voice, cracked and hoarse and thorny, boom from somewhere high above their heads: 'Who is it that disturbs the sleep of the aged at this hour of the afternoon that is given to rest? It can only be a great fool. Fool, are you a fool?'

And Deven, feeling some taut membrane of reservation tear apart inside him and a surging expansion of joy at hearing the voice and the words that could only belong to that superior being, the poet, sang back, 'Sir, I am! I am!'

There was an interval and then some mutters of astonishment and horror at this admission. In that quiet pause, pigeons were heard to gurgle and flutter as if in warning from the wings.

'Shall I let him in?' called the opener of the door, still hidden behind it. It was a female voice, high-pitched and frayed with irritation.

'Bring him then,' moaned the poet in the upper reaches of the building

---

1 Traditional Indian system of medicine.

which rose in tiers around a small inner courtyard where a tap dripped, a broken bicycle lay and a cat slept.

'I have been dreaming of fools,' the voice above went on muttering. 'I am surrounded by fools. Fools will follow me, pursue me and find me out and capture me so that in the end I myself will join their company. Bring him up then, bring him up,' and again Deven felt another warm, moist tide of jubilation rise and increase inside him at being recognized, named and invited into the presence of a man so clearly a hero. On tiptoe, trembling a little, he stepped over the high threshold into the house, then stopped, remembering the boy who had brought him here and the need to dismiss him. Surely he ought to be rewarded for his part in what had turned out to be a gloriously successful pursuit. His face lit to a radiance, he smiled at the boy and thrust the folded newspaper wrapping into his hands with benign absent-mindedness, then turned back into the house and, rejoicing, obeyed the wave of the henna-painted hand from behind the door and began to run up flight after flight of wooden stairs from which dust rose at every step.

It was to him as if God had leaned over a cloud and called for him to come up, and angels might have been drawing him up these ancient splintered stairs to meet the deity: so jubilantly, so timorously, so gratefully did he rise. This, surely, was the summons for which he had been waiting all these empty years, only he had not known it would assume this form. In his mortal myopia and stupidity, he had expected it to come from Sarla when he married her, or from the head of the department at his college who alone could promote and demote and alter his situation in life, or even from Murad who, after all, lived in the metropolis and edited a magazine. The poetry he had read and memorized lay beneath all these visible tips of his submerged existence, and he had thought of it more as a source of comfort and consolation than as a promise of salvation. He had never conceived of a summons expressed in a voice so leonine, splendid and commanding, a voice that could grasp him, as it were, by the roots of his hair and haul him up from the level on which he existed – mean, disordered and hopeless – into another, higher sphere. Another realm it would surely be if his god dwelt there, the domain of poetry, beauty and illumination. He mounted the stairs as if sloughing off and casting away the meanness and dross of his past existence and steadily approaching a new and wondrously illuminated era.

Although there were no angels singing 'Hallelujah! Hallelujah!' in accompaniment, the pigeons cooed loudly with agitation and the old man could be heard muttering incredulously, 'Fool, says he's a fool – hah!' and Deven took that as sufficient invitation to enter.

The room in which the poet lay resting, like a great bolster laid on a flat low wooden divan, was in semi-darkness. Not only were the bamboo screens hanging in every doorway let down to keep out the sun that beat upon the top floor of the building most fiercely, but the walls were lined with dark green tiles that added to the shadowy gloom. The few pieces of furniture –

a single armchair with elongated arms that seemed designed for some earlier, larger species of man, a small gate-legged table piled with very shabby books, a revolving bookcase with more of them, several solid cushions and bolsters cast upon the cotton mats on the floor, were like objects carved out of this murkiness, heavy and palpable with gloom.

In the midst of all the shadows, the poet's figure was in startling contrast, being entirely dressed in white. His white beard was splayed across his chest and his long white fingers clasped across it. He did not move and appeared to be a marble form. His body had the density, the compactness of stone. It was large and heavy not on account of obesity or weight, but on account of age and experience. The emptying out and wasting of age had not yet begun its process. He was still at a moment of completion, quite whole. This gave him the power and the dignity to be able to say to the intruding stranger, in a murmur, 'Who gave you permission to disturb me?'

'Sir,' croaked Deven, fumbling in his shirt pocket for Murad's letter, 'I have a letter here – '

'Couldn't it wait?' sighed the old man in a fading voice. Was he drifting back into sleep? There was an age, after all, when the difference between sleep and waking became very faint and could be crossed at ease, continually.

'Sir, I have come to Delhi only for one day. I must return to my college in Mirpore,' Deven stammered. 'I have a letter here from Murad Beg – editor of *Awaaz* – '

'Can't you see, it is too dark for me to read? I am resting. I don't know where my spectacles are. Read it to me. Now that you have ruined my sleep you might as well read it to me.'

Deven unfolded the letter, trying to hush the loud crackling made by the sheets of paper, and then tried to read audibly and smoothly Murad's floridly written letter of introduction. It flustered him to have to read the flattering names Murad had called him, just as the wheedling, begging tone of his request for an interview made him uncomfortable. A poet of such godlike magnitude ought to have been presented with a prayer or a petition but not with flattery or bribes.

It made the old man on the bed curl up his lips and make a spitting sound through his beard. He unclasped his thin fine fingers with their pale, fish-like skin and fish-like spattering of the brown freckles of age, and waved them dismissively. 'That joker – he should paint his face, wear a false nose, and perform in a travelling circus,' he said derisively. 'Are you a part of his circus?'

'No, no, sir,' Deven protested, still standing stooped over the letter in his hand, not quite read to the end. 'I sometimes – he sometimes asks me to contribute to his magazine. He has asked me to interview you for the special issue on Urdu poetry. It is a great honour for me, sir, a great privilege. I mean, if you allow me – ' he added quickly, looking anxious.

Should he have told the poet about the monograph he had written on him and that still awaited publication? Or would the poet consider that presumptuous rather than flattering? He hesitated.

The house was very still, miraculously silent. The tall hospital walls cut it off from the hubbub of the bazaar, Deven supposed. All he could hear were the pigeons complaining to and consoling each other up on the dusty ledges of the high skylights, and the laboured sound of the poet's breath, snarled in his throat with some elderly phlegm.

'Urdu poetry?' he finally sighed, turning a little to one side, towards Deven although not actually addressing himself to a person, merely to a direction, it seemed. 'How can there be Urdu poetry when there is no Urdu language left? It is dead, finished. The defeat of the Moghuls by the British threw a noose over its head, and the defeat of the British by the Hindi-wallahs tightened it. So now you see its corpse lying here, waiting to be buried.' He tapped his chest with one finger.

'No, sir, please don't talk like that,' Deven said eagerly, perspiration breaking out on his upper lip and making it glisten. 'We will never allow that to happen. That is why Murad is publishing his journal. And the printing press where it is published is for printing Urdu books, sir. They are getting large orders even today. And my college – it is only a small college, a private college outside Delhi – but it has a department of Urdu – '

'Do you teach there?' A wrinkled eyelid moved, like a turtle's, and a small, quick eye peered out at Deven as if at a tasty fly.

Deven shrank back in apology. 'No, sir, I teach in – in the Hindi department. I took my degree in Hindi because – '

But the poet was not listening. He was laughing and spitting as he laughed because he did it so rustily and unwillingly. Phlegm flew. 'You see,' he croaked, 'what did I tell you? Those Congress-wallahs[2] have set up Hindi on top as our ruler. You are its slave. Perhaps a spy even if you don't know it, sent to the universities to destroy whatever remains of Urdu, hunt it out and kill it. And you tell me it is for an Urdu magazine you wish to interview me. If so, why are you teaching Hindi?' he suddenly roared, fixing Deven with that small, turtle-lidded eye that had now become lethal, a bullet.

'I studied Urdu, sir, as a boy, in Lucknow. My father, he was a schoolteacher, a scholar, and a lover of Urdu poetry. He taught me the language. But he died: He died and my mother brought me to Delhi to live with her relations here. I was sent to the nearest school, a Hindi-medium school, sir,' Deven stumbled through the explanation. 'I took my degree in Hindi, sir, and now I am temporary lecturer in Lala Ram Lal College at Mirpore. It is my living, sir. You see I am a married man, a family man. But I still remember my lessons in Urdu, how my father taught me, how he used to read poetry to me. If it were not for the need to earn a living, I would – I would – 'Should he tell him his aspirations, scribbled down on pieces of paper and hidden between the leaves of his books?

'Oh, earning a living?' mocked the old man as Deven struggled visibly

---

2 Members of the ruling Congress party.

with his diffidence. 'Earning a living comes first, does it? Why not trade in rice and oil if it is a living you want to earn?'

Crushed, Deven's shoulders sagged. 'I am – only a teacher, sir,' he murmured, 'and must teach to support my family. But poetry – Urdu – these are – one needs, I need to serve them to show my appreciation. I cannot serve them as you do – '

'You don't look fit to serve anyone, let alone the muse of Urdu,' the old man retorted, his voice gaining strength from indignation. Or perhaps he was wider awake now; he sounded upright even if he was still reclining. 'Sit down,' he commanded. 'There, on that stool. Bring it closer to me first. Close. Here, at my side. Now sit. It seems you have been sent here to torment me, to show me to what depths Urdu has fallen. All right then, show me, let me know the worst.' He rolled out the syllables, in a lapidarian voice, as if he were inscribing an epitaph. 'I am prepared for suffering. Through suffering, I shall atone for my sins.' He groaned. 'Many, many sins,' and shifted on the wooden bed as if in pain.

Deven, to his astonishment, heard himself repeat the poet's familiar words as he had heard his father recite them to him when he had sat beside him on the mat in the corner of the verandah of the old house. '*Through suffering I shall atone for my sins.*' He repeated it twice, and then, as if unwinding a kite's thread from the spool that his memory still held, he went on reciting that great poem of Nur's that his father had loved to recite and that he still read, ceremoniously, whenever he felt sad or nostalgic and thought of his father and his early childhood and all that he had lost. It rose above him into that upper realm occupied by poetry and hovered over their heads, an airborne kite.

'Many sins, and much suffering; such is the pattern.
Fate has traced on my tablet, with blood . . . .'

His voice grew steadier as he found his memory not failing him but flooding in confidently and carrying him along on its strong current. He could almost feel the smoothness of his father's reed pens which he played with while he listened, and smell the somewhat musty, but human and comforting, odour of his father's black cotton coat with the missing buttons and the torn pockets, thickly darned at the corners. A tender, almost feminine lilt entered his voice with those memories and the poet listened engrossed, now and then joining in with his own cracked voice as if he had forgotten the lines and was happy to be reminded.

'My body no more than a reed pen cut by the sword's tip,
Useless and dry till dipped in the ink of life's blood.'

He broke off, chuckling. 'Your pronunciation is good. Very clean, chaste. Do you remember more?' and Deven, swaying upon the stool, recited on and on in a voice that grew increasingly sing-song. As he continued, he began to be overcome by the curious sensation that he was his own mother, rocking back and forth on her heels as she half-sang, half-recited a story in the night, and that the white bolster-like figure on the bed beside him was a child, his child, whom he was lulling to sleep. He understood completely, in these minutes, how it must feel to be a mother, a woman. He had not known before such intimacy, such intense closeness as existed in that dark and shaded room where his voice merged with those of the pigeons to soothe the listening, lulled figure before him. He was also aware, with the welling up of a drop of sadness that now rose and trickled through him, moistly, that this moment that contained such perfection of feeling, unblemished and immaculate, could not last, must break and disperse.

§ *Passivity and engagement* Narayan; *Delhi* Ahmed Ali

EUNICE DE SOUZA (1940–)

1: Marriages Are Made

My cousin Elena
is to be married.
The formalities
have been completed:
5 her family history examined
for T.B. and madness
her father declared solvent
her eyes examined for squints
her teeth for cavities
10 her stools for the possible
non-Brahmin worm.
She's not quite tall enough
and not quite full enough
(children will take care of that)
15 Her complexion it was decided
would compensate, being just about
the right shade
of rightness
to do justice to
20 Francisco X. Noronha Prabhu
good son of Mother Church.

§ *Arranged marriage* Hosain, Seth, Fernando

---

11 non-Brahmin: low-caste; perceived as impure (by orthodox brahmins).

2: Women in Dutch Paintings

> The afternoon sun is on their faces,
> they are calm, not stupid,
> pregnant, not bovine.
> I know women like that
> 5   and not just in paintings –
> an aunt who did not answer her husband back
> not because she was plain
> and Anna who writes poems
> and hopes her avocado stones
> 10   will sprout in the kitchen.
> Her voice is oatmeal and honey.

§ *South Asian women's roles* Hosain, De Souza (1), Alexander, Wijenaike

SALMAN RUSHDIE (1947–)

From Midnight's Children

As its opening, the first of the two passages included here, indicates, *Midnight's Children* is centred on the comic analogy that the narrator, Saleem Sinai, born at the exact moment of India's Independence, draws between his own life-story and that of the young nation. The book brings together a number of non-realist narrative modes, among them traditional Hindu and Islamic storytelling, magic realism, Western metafiction and the hybrid cinematic style of the 'Bombay talkie', to explore the difficulties of constructing a history. The second passage here (from the middle of the novel) suggests that the magical powers of the 1,001 midnight's children born during the same night as Saleem and India represent the multiple possibilities that Independence offered the country, possibilities which Saleem feels have been extinguished during the next three decades.

I was born in the city of Bombay . . . once upon a time. No, that won't do, there's no getting away from the date: I was born in Doctor Narlikar's Nursing Home on August 15th, 1947. And the time? The time matters, too. Well then: at night. No, it's important to be more . . . On the stroke of midnight, as a matter of fact. Clock-hands joined palms in respectful greeting as I came. Oh, spell it out, spell it out: at the precise instant of India's arrival at independence, I tumbled forth into the world. There were gasps. And, outside the window, fireworks and crowds. A few seconds later, my father broke his big toe; but his accident was a mere trifle when set beside what had befallen me in that benighted moment, because thanks to the occult tyrannies of those blandly saluting clocks I had been mysteriously handcuffed to history, my destinies indissolubly chained to those of my country. For the next three decades, there was to be no escape. Soothsayers had prophesied me, newspapers celebrated my arrival, politicos ratified my authenticity. I was left entirely without a say in the matter. I, Saleem Sinai, later variously called Snotnose, Stainface, Baldy, Sniffer, Buddha and even Piece-of-the-Moon, had become heavily embroiled in Fate – at the best of times a dangerous sort of involvement. And I couldn't even wipe my own nose at the time.

Now, however, time (having no further use for me) is running out. I will soon be thirty-one years old. Perhaps. If my crumbling, over-used body permits. But I have no hope of saving my life, nor can I count on having even a thousand nights and a night. I must work fast, faster than Scheherazade,[1] if I am to end up meaning – yes, meaning – something. I admit it: above all things, I fear absurdity.

And there are so many stories to tell, too many, such an excess of intertwined lives events miracles places rumours, so dense a commingling of the improbable and the mundane! I have been a swallower of lives; and to know me, just the one of me, you'll have to swallow the lot as well. Consumed multitudes are jostling and shoving inside me; and guided only by the memory of a large white bedsheet with a roughly circular hole some seven inches in diameter cut into the centre, clutching at the dream of that holey, mutilated square of linen, which is my talisman, my open-sesame, I must commence the business of remaking my life from the point at which it really began, some thirty-two years before anything as obvious, as *present*, as my clock-ridden, crime-stained birth.

(The sheet, incidentally, is stained too, with three drops of old, faded redness. As the Quran tells us: *Recite, in the name of the Lord thy Creator, who created Man from clots of blood*.). . .

Understand what I'm saying: during the first hour of August 15th, 1947 – between midnight and one a.m. – no less than one thousand and one children were born within the frontiers of the infant sovereign state of India. In itself, that is not an unusual fact (although the resonances of the number are strangely literary)[2] – at the time, births in our part of the world exceeded deaths by approximately six hundred and eighty-seven an hour. What made the event noteworthy (noteworthy! There's a dispassionate word, if you like!) was the nature of these children, every one of whom was, through some freak of biology, or perhaps owing to some preternatural power of the moment, or just conceivably by sheer coincidence (although synchronicity on such a scale would stagger even C. G. Jung), endowed with features, talents or faculties which can only be described as miraculous. It was as though – if you will permit me one moment of fancy in what will otherwise be, I promise, the most sober account I can manage – as though history, arriving at a point of the highest significance and promise, had chosen to sow, in that instant, the seeds of a future which would genuinely differ from anything the world had seen up to that time.

---

1 Narrator of *The 1001 Nights*, who tells stories to delay her death. 2 Particularly suggestive of *The 1001 Nights*.

If a similar miracle was worked across the border, in the newly-partitioned-off Pakistan, I have no knowledge of it; my perceptions were, while they lasted, bounded by the Arabian Sea, the Bay of Bengal, the Himalaya mountains, but also by the artificial frontiers which pierced Punjab and Bengal.

Inevitably, a number of these children failed to survive. Malnutrition, disease and the misfortunes of everyday life had accounted for no less than four hundred and twenty of them by the time I became conscious of their existence; although it is possible to hypothesize that these deaths, too, had their purpose, since 420 has been, since time immemorial, the number associated with fraud, deception and trickery. Can it be, then, that the missing infants were eliminated because they had turned out to be somehow inadequate, and were not the true children of that midnight hour? Well, in the first place, that's another excursion into fantasy; in the second, it depends on a view of life which is both excessively theological and barbarically cruel. It is also an unanswerable question; any further examination of it is therefore profitless.

By 1957, the surviving five hundred and eighty-one children were all nearing their tenth birthdays, wholly ignorant, for the most part, of one another's existence – although there were certainly exceptions. In the town of Baud, on the Mahanadi river in Orissa, there was a pair of twin sisters who were already a legend in the region, because despite their impressive plainness they both possessed the ability of making every man who saw them fall hopelessly and often suicidally in love with them, so that their bemused parents were endlessly pestered by a stream of men offering their hands in marriage to either or even both of the bewildering children; old men who had forsaken the wisdom of their beards and youths who ought to have been becoming besotted with the actresses in the travelling picture-show which visited Baud once a month; and there was another, more disturbing procession of bereaved families cursing the twin girls for having bewitched their sons into committing acts of violence against themselves, fatal mutilations and scourgings and even (in one case) self-immolation. With the exception of such rare instances, however, the children of midnight had grown up quite unaware of their true siblings, their fellow-chosen-ones across the length and breadth of India's rough and badly-proportioned diamond.

And then, as a result of a jolt received in a bicycle-accident, I, Saleem Sinai, became aware of them all.

To anyone whose personal cast of mind is too inflexible to accept these facts, I have this to say: That's how it was; there can be no retreat from the truth. I shall just have to shoulder the burden of the doubter's disbelief. But no literate person in this India of ours can be wholly immune from the type of information I am in the process of unveiling – no reader of our national press can have failed to come across a series of – admittedly lesser – magic children and assorted freaks. Only last week there was that Bengali boy who announced himself as the reincarnation of Rabindranath Tagore[3] and began

---

3 Bengali writer, winner of the 1913 Nobel Prize for Literature.

to extemporize verses of remarkable quality, to the amazement of his parents; and I can myself remember children with two heads (sometimes one human, one animal), and other curious features such as bullock's horns.

I should say at once that not all the children's gifts were desirable, or even desired by the children themselves; and, in some cases, the children had survived but been deprived of their midnight-given qualities. For example (as a companion piece to the story of the Baudi twins) let me mention a Delhi beggar-girl called Sundari, who was born in a street behind the General Post Office, not far from the rooftop on which Amina Sinai had listened to Ramram Seth, and whose beauty was so intense that within moments of her birth it succeeded in blinding her mother and the neighbouring women who had been assisting at her delivery; her father, rushing into the room when he heard the women's screams, had been warned by them just in time; but his one fleeting glimpse of his daughter so badly impaired his vision that he was unable, afterwards, to distinguish between Indians and foreign tourists, a handicap which greatly affected his earning power as a beggar. For some time after that Sundari was obliged to have a rag placed across her face; until an old and ruthless great-aunt took her into her bony arms and slashed her face nine times with a kitchen knife. At the time when I became aware of her, Sundari was earning a healthy living, because nobody who looked at her could fail to pity a girl who had clearly once been too beautiful to look at and was now so cruelly disfigured; she received more alms than any other member of her family.

Because none of the children suspected that their time of birth had anything to do with what they were, it took me a while to find it out. At first, after the bicycle accident (and particularly once language marchers had purged me of Evie Burns), I contented myself with discovering, one by one, the secrets of the fabulous beings who had suddenly arrived in my mental field of vision, collecting them ravenously, the way some boys collect insects, and others spot railways trains; losing interest in autograph books and all other manifestations of the gathering instinct, I plunged whenever possible into the separate, and altogether brighter reality of the five hundred and eighty-one. (Two hundred and sixty-six of us were boys; and we were outnumbered by our female counterparts – three hundred and fifteen of them, including Parvati. Parvati-the-witch.)

Midnight's children! . . . From Kerala, a boy who had the ability of stepping into mirrors and re-emerging through any reflective surface in the land – through lakes and (with greater difficulty) the polished metal bodies of automobiles . . . and a Goanese girl with the gift of multiplying fish . . . and children with powers of transformation: a werewolf from the Nilgiri Hills, and from the great watershed of the Vindhyas, a boy who could increase or reduce his size at will, and had already (mischievously) been the cause of wild panic and rumours of the return of Giants . . . from Kashmir, there was a blue-eyed child of whose original sex I was never certain, since by immersing herself in water he (or she) could alter it as she (or he) pleased. Some of us called this child Narada, others Markandaya, depending on which old fairy story of sexual change we had heard . . . near Jalna in the heart of the parched Deccan I found a water-divining youth, and at Budge-Budge outside Calcutta a sharp-tongued girl whose words already had the power of inflicting physical wounds, so that after a few adults had found themselves bleeding freely as a result of some barb flung casually from her lips, they had decided to lock her in a bamboo cage and float her off down the Ganges to the Sundarbans jungles (which are the rightful home of monsters and phantasms); but nobody dared approach her, and she moved through the town surrounded by a vacuum of fear; nobody had the courage to deny her food. There was a boy who could eat metal and a girl whose fingers were so green that she could grow prize aubergines in the Thar desert; and more and more and more . . . overwhelmed by their numbers, and by the exotic multiplicity of their gifts, I paid little attention, in those early days, to their ordinary selves; but inevitably our problems, when they arose, were the everyday, human problems which arise from character-and-environment; in our quarrels, we were just a bunch of kids.

One remarkable fact: the closer to midnight our birth-times were, the greater were our gifts. Those children born in the last seconds of the hour were (to be frank) little more than circus freaks: bearded girls, a boy with the fully-operative gills of a freshwater mahaseer trout, Siamese twins with two bodies dangling off a single head and neck – the head could speak in two voices, one male, one female, and every language and dialect spoken in the subcontinent; but for all their marvellousness, these were the unfortunates, the living casualties of that numinous hour. Towards the half-hour came more interesting and useful faculties – in the Gir Forest lived a witch-girl with the power of healing by the laying-on of hands, and there was a wealthy tea-planter's son in Shillong who had the blessing (or possibly the curse) of being incapable of forgetting anything he ever saw or heard. But the children born in the first minute of all – for these children the hour had reserved the highest talents of which men had ever dreamed. If you, Padma, happened to possess a register of births in which times were noted down to the exact second, you, too, would know what scion of a great Lucknow family (born at twenty-one seconds past midnight) had completely mastered, by the age of ten, the lost arts of alchemy, with which he regenerated the fortunes of his ancient but dissipated house; and which dhobi's[4] daughter from Madras (seventeen seconds past) could fly higher than any bird simply by closing her eyes; and to which Benarsi silversmith's son (twelve seconds after midnight) was given the gift of travelling in time and thus prophesying the future as well as clarifying the past . . . a gift which, children that we were, we trusted implicitly when it dealt with things gone and forgotten, but derided when he warned us of our own ends . . . fortunately, no such records exist; and, for my part, I shall not reveal – or else, in appearing to reveal, shall falsify – their names and even their locations; because, although such evidence would provide absolute proof of my claims, still the children of

---

4 Laundry-man's.

midnight deserve, now, after everything, to be left alone; perhaps to forget; but I hope (against hope) to remember . . .

Parvati-the-witch was born in Old Delhi in a slum which clustered around the steps of the Friday mosque. No ordinary slum, this, although the huts built out of old packing cases and pieces of corrugated tin and shreds of jute sacking which stood higgledy-piggledy in the shadow of the mosque looked no different from any other shanty-town . . . because this was the ghetto of the magicians, yes, the very same place which had once spawned a Hummingbird whom knives had pierced and pie-dogs had failed to save . . . the conjurers' slum, to which the greatest fakirs and prestidigitators and illusionists in the land continually flocked, to seek their fortune in the capital city. They found tin huts, and police harassment, and rats . . . Parvati's father had once been the greatest conjurer in Oudh; she had grown up amid ventriloquists who could make stones tell jokes and contortionists who could swallow their own legs and fire-eaters who exhaled flames from their arseholes and tragic clowns who could extract glass tears from the corners of their eyes; she had stood mildly amid gasping crowds while her father drove spikes through her neck; and all the time she had guarded her own secret, which was greater than any of the illusionist flummeries surrounding her; because to Parvati-the-witch, born a mere seven seconds after midnight on August 15th, had been given the powers of the true adept, the illuminatus, the genuine gifts of conjuration and sorcery, the art which required no artifice.

So among the midnight children were infants with powers of transmutation, flight, prophecy and wizardry . . . but two of us were born on the stroke of midnight. Saleem and Shiva, Shiva and Saleem, nose and knees and knees and nose . . . to Shiva, the hour had given the gifts of war (of Rama, who could draw the undrawable bow; of Arjuna and Bhima; the ancient prowess of Kurus and Pandavas[5] united, unstoppably, in him!) . . . and to me, the greatest talent of all – the ability to look into the hearts and minds of men.

But it is Kali-Yuga;[6] the children of the hour of darkness were born, I'm afraid, in the midst of the age of darkness; so that although we found it easy to be brilliant, we were always confused about being good.

There; now I've said it. That is who I was – who we were.

Padma is looking as if her mother had died – her face, with its opening-shutting mouth, is the face of a beached pomfret. 'O baba!' she says at last. 'O baba! You are sick; what have you said?'

No, that would be too easy. I refuse to take refuge in illness. Don't make the mistake of dismissing what I've unveiled as mere delirium; or even as the insanely exaggerated fantasies of a lonely, ugly child. I have stated before that I am not speaking metaphorically; what I have just written (and read aloud to stunned Padma) is nothing less than the literal, by-the-hairs-of-my-mother's head truth.

---

5 Mythic warriors in the Sanskrit epics. 6 The Age of Darkness, in which humanity is currently living; last of the four ages which make up a day in the life of Brahma.

Reality can have metaphorical content; that does not make it less real. A thousand and one children were born; there were a thousand and one possibilities which had never been present in one place at one time before; and there were a thousand and one dead ends. Midnight's children can be made to represent many things, according to your point of view: they can be seen as the last throw of everything antiquated and retrogressive in our myth-ridden nation, whose defeat was entirely desirable in the context of a modernizing, twentieth-century economy; or as the true hope of freedom, which is now forever extinguished; but what they must not become is the bizarre creation of a rambling, diseased mind. No: illness is neither here nor there.

'All right, all right, baba,' Padma attempts to placate me, 'Why become so cross? Rest now, rest some while, that is all I am asking.'

§ *Alternative histories* Aus: Davis; Can: Wiebe; Carib: Reid, Walcott (3); *National identities/Partition* Seth, Sidhwa; Rushdie also in TransC

AMITAV GHOSH (1956–)

From The Shadow Lines

Like *Midnight's Children*, *The Shadow Lines* is centred on the experience of a family, which can be seen as a microcosm for a broader national (or international) experience. The lives of the family have been irrevocably changed as a result of the Partition of Bengal. The 'shadow lines' of the title are the borders drawn by politicians that separate people, and the text shows the arbitrariness of cartographical divisions. 'Shadow lines' are, however, more than just this: they are also the lines of demarcation that separate colonized and colonizer, present and past, self and other. These two passages (from the middle and end of the novel) illustrate these concerns, as the family plan a journey across the border to Dhaka and as the narrator's second cousin, Robi, tells his niece, Ila and the narrator himself about the death of his older brother Tridib on this visit to Dhaka.

. . . A few weeks later, at dinner, my father, grinning hugely, pushed an envelope across the table to my grandmother. That's for you, he said.

What is it? she said, eyeing it suspiciously.

Go on, he said. Have a look.

She picked it up, opened the flap and peered into it. I can't tell, she said. What is it?

My father burst into laughter. It's your plane ticket, he said. For Dhaka – for the third of January, 1964.

That night, for the first time in months, my grandmother seemed really excited. When I went up to see her, before going to bed, I found her pacing around the room, her face flushed, her eyes shining. I was delighted. It was the first time in my eleven-year-old life that she had presented me with a response that I could fully understand – since I had never been on a plane myself, it seemed the most natural thing in the world to me that the prospect of her first flight should fill her with excitement. But I couldn't help worrying about her too, for I also knew that, unlike me, she was totally ignorant about aeroplanes, and before I fell asleep that night I resolved that I would make sure that she was properly prepared before she left. But soon enough it was apparent to me that it wasn't going to be easy to educate her: I could tell from the direction of the questions she asked my father that, left to herself, she would learn nothing about aeroplanes.

For instance, one evening when we were sitting out in the garden she wanted to know whether she would be able to see the border between India and East Pakistan from the plane. When my father laughed and said, why, did she really think the border was a long black line with green on one side and scarlet on the other, like it was in a school atlas, she was not so much offended as puzzled.

No, that wasn't what I meant, she said. Of course not. But surely there's something – trenches perhaps, or soldiers, or guns pointing at each other, or even just barren strips of land. Don't they call it no-man's land?

My father was already an experienced traveller. He burst out laughing and said: No, you won't be able to see anything except clouds and perhaps, if you're lucky, some green fields.

His laughter nettled her. Be serious, she snapped. Don't talk to me as though I were a secretary in your office.

Now it was his turn to be offended: it upset him when she spoke sharply to him within my hearing.

That's all I can tell you, he said. That's all there is.

My grandmother thought this over for a while, and then she said: But if there aren't any trenches or anything, how are people to know? I mean, where's the difference then? And if there's no difference, both sides will be the same; it'll be just like it used to be before, when we used to catch a train in Dhaka and get off in Calcutta the next day without anybody stopping us. What was it all for then – Partition and all the killing and everything – if there isn't something in between?

I don't know what you expect, Ma, my father retorted in exasperation. It's not as though you're flying over the Himalayas into China. This is the modern world. The border isn't on the frontier: it's right inside the airport. You'll see. You'll cross it when you have to fill in all those disembarkation cards and things.

My grandmother shifted nervously in her chair. What forms? she said. What do they want to know about on those forms?

My father scratched his forehead. Let me see, he said. They want your nationality, your date of birth, place of birth, that kind of thing.

My grandmother's eyes widened and she slumped back in her chair.

What's the matter? my father said in alarm.

With an effort she sat up straight again and smoothed back her hair. Nothing, she said, shaking her head. Nothing at all.

I could see then that she was going to end up in a hopeless mess, so I took it upon myself to ask my father for all the essential information about flying and aeroplanes that I thought she ought to have at her command – I was sure, for example, that she would roll the windows down in mid-air unless I warned her not to.

It was not till many years later that I realised it had suddenly occurred to her then that she would have to fill in 'Dhaka' as her place of birth on that form, and that the prospect of this had worried her in the same way that dirty schoolbooks worried her because she liked things to be neat and in place – and at that moment she had not been able quite to understand how her place of birth had come to be so messily at odds with her nationality.

My father could see that she was worrying over something. But Ma, he said, teasing her; why are you so worried about this little journey? You've been travelling between countries for years. Don't you remember – all those trips you made in and out of Burma?

Oh *that*, my grandmother laughed. It wasn't the same thing. There weren't any forms or anything, and anyway travelling was so easy then. I could come home to Dhaka whenever I wanted.

I jumped to my feet, delighted at having caught her out – she, who'd been a schoolmistress for twenty-seven years.

Tha'mma, Tha'mma! I cried. How could you have 'come' home to Dhaka? You don't know the difference between coming and going!

I teased her with that phrase for years afterwards. If she happened to say she was going to teach me Bengali grammar, for example, I would laugh and say: But Tha'mma, how can you teach me grammar? You don't know the difference between coming and going. Eventually the phrase passed on to the whole family and became a part of its secret lore; a barb in that fence we built to shut ourselves off from others. So, for instance, when we were in our teens, often, when Ila was in Calcutta and we happened to meet an acquaintance who asked: When are you going back to London? we would launch into a kind of patter: But she has to go to Calcutta first; Not if I'm coming to London; Nor if you're coming to Calcutta . . . And at the end of it, sobbing hysterically with a laughter which must have seemed as affected as it was inexplicable to those who heard it, I would say: You see, in our family we don't know whether we're coming or going – it's all my grandmother's fault. But, of course, the fault wasn't hers at all: it lay in language. Every language assumes a centrality, a fixed and settled point to go away from and come back to, and what my grandmother was looking for was a word for a journey which was not a coming or a going at all; a journey that was a search for precisely that fixed point which permits the proper use of verbs of movement.

. . . But Robi didn't hear me. He was leaning towards Rehman-shaheb, gripping the table, his knuckles white.

I remember it because my brother was killed there, he said. In a riot – not far from where my mother was born. Now do you see why I remember?

Rehman-shaheb leapt to his feet, his face red with embarrassment.

Robi stood up, pushed his way past us and went out.

Oh, I'm so . . . Rehman-shaheb said to Ila. I didn't mean . . . I really didn't.

Don't worry, Ila said quickly. It's not your fault. I know you didn't mean it. It's mine – I shouldn't have brought up the subject.

Ila snatched up her coat, gave Rehman-shaheb's arm one last pat and whispered: It's all right, don't worry. Then she followed me out of the restaurant.

He was gone by the time we were out. It was a while before we saw him, in the distance, as he passed a lamp-post. He was striding fast down the Clapham Road, towards Stockwell. We began to run.

When we caught up with him we tried to fall in step, but his strides were so long we virtually had to run to keep up. We walked past the fast-food shops on the Clapham Road, beneath the railway bridge and the underground station at Clapham North. At length Robi came to a halt. He shook his arms free and said: I need to sit somewhere. Just for a minute.

There was an overgrown garden to our left, and within it a derelict white church, with a short flight of steps in front. Robi led us through the gate and up to the steps. Clearing a space for himself among the leaves on the stairs, he sat down and lit a cigarette.

It's a dream, you know, he said, blowing a plume of smoke at his feet. I only get it about twice a year now, but it used to be once a week, when I was younger – in college, for instance. But I learnt to control it – I often know when it's coming, and on nights like that I try not to sleep. It always begins with our car going around a corner. There's a muddy kind of field on one side, a very small one, but it's got a crooked goalpost stuck in the mud. We turn the corner and there they are, ahead of us, strung out across the road. Sometimes it's a crowd, sometimes just a couple of men. I know their faces well now, better than I know my friends'. There's one with a very thin face and a wispy moustache and a crooked mouth. He's always in it. The odd thing is, that no matter how many men there are – a couple, or dozens – the street always seems empty. It was full of people when we went through it – a bazaar, all the shops open, people going in and out, rickshaws, thela-garis,[1] vendors, donkeys. And there were people in the houses above the shops too, looking down at us, from the windows and balconies. But all the shops are shut now, barricaded, and so are the windows in the houses. There's no one on the balconies. The street's deserted, but for those men. I can see little details sometimes: a green coconut, for instance, lying in the middle of the road, wobbling when the breeze catches it; a slipper on the pavement – not a pair, just a single rubber slipper, lying there abandoned.

There's a grinding kind of noise somewhere inside the car, and it lurches, throwing everyone forward, so that I almost bang my head against the dash-

---

1 Push-carts.

board. Someone in the back seat, I think it's my mother, but I've never been sure, cries: Don't stop, go on.

And the car does go on, in fact the driver had merely changed gears without declutching properly. It's moving forward again now – not steadily, but in short jerks, because the driver's so scared he's lost control of his right foot. His cap's fallen off, and he's sitting hunched over the wheel, with sweat dripping down his face. The security guard, sitting beside me, in the front seat, is looking ahead, fingering his shirt.

Then the men begin to move towards us – they're not running, they're gliding, like skaters in a race. They fan out and begin to close in on us. It's all silent, I can't hear a single thing, no sound at all.

The security guard pushes me down and reaches back to make sure our doors are locked. I can only see his blue uniform now, from where I am. I can't see his face and I can't look outside. I see him reaching under his shirt, and when he pulls out his hand there's a revolver in it, a very small one. It's got an odd colour, sort of slate-grey. I can see it in detail because it's right next to my face.

Then the car veers away, and suddenly there's a huge thump on the bonnet, and somebody screams at the back. I look up then, lifting my head just a little, until it's level with the bottom of the windscreen, and there's a face there, on the other side of the glass, the nose flattened, the eyes looking in. It's the man with the crooked mouth; he's lying flat on the bonnet, and he's seen me. He raises his arm and swings it back; there's something in it, but I don't know what it is, I can never see it. His arm comes swinging down, over his head in an arc, and suddenly the windscreen clouds over and crashes in. When I look up at the driver there's a cut across his face, and he's clutching a flap of skin trying to hold it in place, on his cheek. He doesn't have either hand on the steering wheel. The car lurches, rolls forward, and stalls, with its front wheel in a gutter.

The security guard pushes me down again, and then he throws the door open and jumps out, with the revolver ready in his hand. He shouts something, I don't know what, and then he shouts again, and there's a crash, and I know he's fired a shot. I look out then, out of the window, and I see the men, circling around us, drawing back, and the sound of the shot is still echoing off those closed windows and empty balconies.

There's a moment of absolute quiet as they watch us and we watch them. It's so still I can hear the sound of the driver's blood dripping on the steering wheel. And then the silence is broken: there's a creak somewhere behind us – it's a small sound, but in the quiet it sounds like a thunderclap. We all turn: we in the car, they outside. And do you know what it is? It's the rickshaw – Khalil's rickshaw – with the old man, our grand-uncle, whom we'd gone to rescue, sitting at the back, all dressed up in his lawyer's coat.

And as I watch, the rickshaw begins to grow. It becomes huge, that rickshaw, it grows till it's bigger than the shops and the houses; so big that I can't see the old man sitting on top. But those men are running towards it, as fast as it grows, they're scrambling up its wheels, up its poles, along the sides. They've forgotten us now; there's no one around us – they're all busy climbing up the rickshaw. The security guard jumps in, grinning, and shouts something to the driver: he's telling him to start the car and get going while he can – to think about his face later. And they're shouting at the back too, telling the driver to be quick, to get going. The driver reaches for the key, he's stretched his arm all the way out, as far as it'll go, but it doesn't reach, no matter how hard he tries. And while he's straining to reach the key, somebody gets out at the back; I hear the door slamming shut. When I look around I see May: she's tiny, shrunken, and behind her is that rickshaw, reaching heavenwards, like a gigantic anthill, and its sides are seething with hundreds of little men.

May is screaming at us; I can't hear a word, but I know what she's saying. She's saying: Those two are going to be killed because of you – you're cowards, murderers, to abandon them here like this.

The door opens again, and I know in my heart that Tridib is going to get out too. I stretch out a hand to pull him back into the car, but my hand won't reach him; I try to shout, but I have no voice left, I cannot make a single sound.

And that is when I wake up, gagging, trying to scream.

Robi shook another cigarette out of his pack and tried to strike a match. The first match broke, and he threw it away and struck another, held it steady and lit his cigarette.

I've never been able to rid myself of that dream, he said. Ever since it first happened. When I was a child I used to pray that it would go away: if it had, there would have been nothing else really, to remind me of that day. But it wouldn't go; it stayed. I used to think: if only that dream would go away, I would be like other people; I would be free. I would have given anything to be free of that memory.

He laughed, looking at the glowing tip of his cigarette.

Free, he said laughing. You know, if you look at the pictures on the front pages of the newspapers at home now, all those pictures of dead people – in Assam, the north-east, Punjab, Sri Lanka, Tripura – people shot by terrorists and separatists and the army and the police, you'll find somewhere behind it all that single word; everyone's doing it to be free. When I was running a district I used to look at those pictures and wonder sometimes what I would do if it were happening in my area. I know what I'd have to do; I'd have to go out and make speeches to my policemen, saying: You have to be firm, you have to do your duty. You have to kill whole villages if necessary – we have nothing against the people, it's the terrorists we want to get, but we have to be willing to pay a price for our unity and freedom. And when I went back home, I would find an anonymous note waiting for me, saying: We're going to get you, nothing personal, we have to kill you for our freedom. It would be like reading my own speech transcribed on a mirror. And then I think to myself, why don't they draw thousands of little lines through the whole subcontinent and give every little place a new name? What would it change? It's a mirage; the whole thing is a mirage. How can anyone divide a memory? If freedom were possible, surely Tridib's death would have set me free. And yet, all it takes to set my hand shaking like a leaf, fifteen years later, thousands of miles away, at the other end of another continent, is a chance remark by a waiter in a restaurant.

He shrugged, threw away his cigarette, and stood up.

I suppose we should be going, he said.

Then Ila, who had been sitting beside him, stood up too and put an arm around his shoulders and another around mine, and held us together. We stood a long time like that, on the steps of that derelict church in Clapham, three children of a free state together, clinging.

§ *National identities/Partition* Rushdie, Sidhwa; *Cartographies* Can: Birney (2), Reaney; Aus: Tranter; TransC: Ondaatje (1)

VIKRAM SETH (1952–)

From A Suitable Boy

A Suitable Boy has been compared with classics of nineteenth-century European social realism. Similar in scope to a novel such as *Middlemarch*, it offers a wide-ranging anatomy of a society – in this case that of post-Independence India – by concentrating on the intertwined lives of four families. As in many Victorian novels, marriage provides a central focus for a consideration of social mores, but the context here is altogether different. A brief extract cannot give a sense of the complexities of the novel, since the effect relies on a slow, cumulative build-up. However, this early section from the account of a wedding illustrates its technique and relates to the central theme, the attempt to find 'a suitable boy' for Lata Mehra, here seen reflecting on the arranged marriage of her sister.

It was a little untraditional, Lata couldn't help thinking, that Pran hadn't ridden up to the gate on a white horse with a little nephew sitting in front of him and with the groom's party in tow to claim his bride; but then Prem Nivas was the groom's house after all. And no doubt if he had followed the convention, Arun would have found further cause for mockery. As it was, Lata found it difficult to imagine the lecturer on Elizabethan Drama under that veil of tuberoses. He was now placing a garland of dark red, heavily fragrant roses around her sister Savita's neck – and Savita was doing the same to him. She looked lovely in her red-and-gold wedding sari, and quite subdued; Lata thought she might even have been crying. Her head was covered, and she looked down at the ground as her mother had doubtless instructed her to do. It was not proper, even when she was putting her garland round his neck, that she should look full in the face of the man with whom she was to live her life.

The welcoming ceremony completed, bride and groom moved together to the middle of the garden, where a small platform, decorated with more white flowers and open to the auspicious stars, had been erected. Here the priests, one from each family, and Mrs Rupa Mehra and the parents of the groom sat around the small fire that would be the witness of their vows.

Mrs Rupa Mehra's brother, whom the family very rarely met, had earlier in the day taken charge of the bangle ceremony. Arun was annoyed that he had not been allowed to take charge of anything. He had suggested to his mother after the crisis brought on by his grandfather's inexplicable actions, that they should move the wedding to Calcutta. But it was too late for that, and she would not hear of it.

Now that the exchange of garlands was over, the crowd paid no great attention to the actual wedding rites. These would go on for the better part of an hour while the guests milled and chattered round the lawns of Prem Nivas. They laughed; they shook hands or folded them to their foreheads; they coalesced into little knots, the men here, the women there; they warmed themselves at the charcoal-filled clay stoves placed strategically around the garden while their frosted, gossip-laden breath rose into the air; they admired the multicoloured lights; they smiled for the photographer as he murmured 'Steady, please!' in English; they breathed deeply the scent of flowers and perfume and cooked spices; they exchanged births and deaths and politics and scandal under the brightly-coloured cloth canopy at the back of the garden beneath which long tables of food had been laid out; they sat down exhaustedly on chairs with their plates full and tucked in inexhaustibly. Servants, some in white livery, some in khaki, brought around fruit juice and tea and coffee and snacks to those who were standing in the garden: samosas, kachauris,[1] laddus,[2] gulab-jamuns,[3] barfis[4] and gajak[5] and ice-cream were consumed and replenished along with puris[6] and six kinds of vegetables. Friends who had not met each other for months fell upon each other with loud cries, relatives who met only at weddings and funerals embraced tearfully and exchanged the latest news of third cousins thrice removed. Lata's aunt from Kanpur, horrified by the complexion of the groom, was talking to an aunt from Lucknow about 'Rupa's black grandchildren', as if they already existed. They made much of Aparna, who was obviously going to be Rupa's last fair grandchild, and praised her even when she spooned pistachio ice-cream down the front of her pale yellow cashmere sweater. The barbaric children from rustic Rudhia ran around yelling as if they were playing pit-thu[7] on the farm. And though the plaintive, festive music of the shehnai[8] had now ceased, a happy babble of convivial voices rose to the skies and quite drowned out the irrelevant chant of the ceremonies.

Lata, however, stood close by and watched with an attentive mixture of fascination and dismay. The two bare-chested priests, one very fat and one fairly thin, both apparently immune to the cold, were locked in mildy insistent competition as to who knew a more elaborate form of the service. So,

---

1 Small *puri*-like savoury with spicy filling.   2 Lentil-based yellow sweet.   3 Fried brown sweet with white inside, served in a rosewater syrup.   4 Solidified milk sweets.   5 Sweet made from sesame and sugar or jaggery.   6 Deep-fried bread.   7 Game played with seven pieces of tiles.   8 A wind instrument, particularly associated with weddings.

while the stars stayed their courses in order to keep the auspicious time in abeyance, the Sanskrit wound interminably on. Even the groom's parents were asked by the fat priest to repeat something after him. Mahesh Kapoor's eyebrows were quivering; he was about to blow his rather short fuse.

Lata tried to imagine what Savita was thinking. How could she have agreed to get married without knowing this man? Kind-hearted and accommodating though she was, she did have views of her own. Lata loved her deeply and admired her generous, even temper; the evenness was certainly a contrast to her own erratic swings of mood. Savita was free from any vanity about her fresh and lovely looks; but didn't she rebel against the fact that Pran would fail the most lenient test of glamour? Did Savita really accept that Mother knew best? It was difficult to speak to Savita, or sometimes even to guess what she was thinking. Since Lata had gone to college, it was Malati rather than her sister who had become her confidante. And Malati, she knew, would never have agreed to be married off in this summary manner by all the mothers in the world conjoined.

In a few minutes Savita would relinquish even her name to Pran. She would no longer be a Mehra, like the rest of them, but a Kapoor. Arun, thank God, had never had to do that. Lata tried 'Savita Kapoor' on her tongue, and did not like it at all.

The smoke from the fire – or possibly the pollen from the flowers – was beginning to bother Pran, and he coughed a little, covering his mouth with his hand. His mother said something to him in a low voice. Savita too looked up at him very quickly, with a glance, Lata thought, of gentle concern. Savita, it was true, would have been concerned about anyone who was suffering from anything; but there was a special tenderness here that irritated and confused Lata. Savita had only met this man for an hour! And now he was returning her affectionate look. It was too much.

Lata forgot that she had been defending Pran to Malati just a short while ago, and began to discover things to irritate herself with.

'Prem Nivas' for a start: the abode of love. An idiotic name, thought Lata crossly, for this house of arranged marriages. And a needlessly grandiloquent one: as if it were the centre of the universe and felt obliged to make a philosophical statement about it. And the scene, looked at objectively, was absurd: seven living people, none of them stupid, sitting around a fire intoning a dead language that only three of them understood. And yet, Lata thought, her mind wandering from one thing to another, perhaps this little fire was indeed the centre of the universe. For here it burned, in the middle of this fragrant garden, itself in the heart of Pasand Bagh, the pleasantest locality of Brahmpur, which was the capital of the state of Purva Pradesh, which lay in the centre of the Gangetic plains, which was itself the heartland of India ... and so on through the galaxies to the outer limits of perception and knowledge. The thought did not seem in the least trite to Lata; it helped her control her irritation at, indeed resentment of Pran.

'Speak up! Speak up! If your mother had mumbled like you, we would never have got married.'

Mahesh Kapoor had turned impatiently towards his dumpy little wife, who became even more tongue-tied as a result.

Pran turned and smiled encouragingly at his mother, and quickly rose again in Lata's estimation.

Mahesh Kapoor frowned, but held his peace for a few minutes, after which he burst out, this time to the family priest:

'Is this mumbo-jumbo going to go on for ever?'

The priest said something soothing in Sanskrit, as if blessing Mahesh Kapoor, who felt obliged to lapse into an irked silence. He was irritated for several reasons, one of which was the distinct and unwelcome sight of his arch political rival, the Home Minister, deep in conversation with the large and venerable Chief Minister S.S. Sharma. What could they be plotting? he thought. My stupid wife insisted on inviting Agarwal because our daughters are friends, even though she knew it would sour things for me. And now the Chief Minister is talking to him as if no one else exists. And in my garden!

His other major irritation was directed at Mrs Rupa Mehra. Mahesh Kapoor, once he had taken over the arrangements, had set his heart on inviting a beautiful and renowned singer of ghazals[9] to perform at Prem Nivas, as was the tradition whenever anyone in his family got married. But Mrs Rupa Mehra, though she was not even paying for the wedding, had put her foot down. She could not have 'that sort of person' singing love-lyrics at the wedding of her daughter. 'That sort of person' meant both a Muslim and a courtesan.

Mahesh Kapoor muffed his responses, and the priest repeated them gently.

'Yes, yes, go on, go on,' said Mahesh Kapoor. He glowered at the fire.

But now Savita was being given away by her mother with a handful of rose-petals, and all three women were in tears.

Really! thought Mahesh Kapoor. They'll douse the flames. He looked in exasperation at the main culprit, whose sobs were the most obstreperous.

But Mrs Rupa Mehra was not even bothering to tuck her handkerchief back into her blouse. Her eyes were red and her nose and cheeks were flushed with weeping. She was thinking back to her own wedding. The scent of 4711 eau-de-Cologne brought back unbearably happy memories of her late husband. Then she thought downwards one generation to her beloved Savita who would soon be walking around this fire with Pran to begin her own married life. May it be a longer one than mine, prayed Mrs Rupa Mehra. May she wear this very sari to her own daughter's wedding.

She also thought upwards a generation to her father, and this brought on a fresh gush of tears. What the septuagenarian radiologist Dr Kishen Chand Seth had taken offence at, no one knew: probably something said or done by his friend Mahesh Kapoor, but quite possibly by his own daughter; no one could tell for sure. Apart from repudiating his duties as a host, he had

---

9 Popular form of love-poem or song, particularly in Urdu; derived from Persian.

chosen not even to attend his granddaughter's wedding, and had gone furiously off to Delhi 'for a conference of cardiologists', as he claimed. He had taken with him the insufferable Parvati, his thirty-five-year-old second wife, who was ten years younger than Mrs Rupa Mehra herself.

It was also possible, though this did not cross his daughter's mind, that Dr Kishen Chand Seth would have gone mad at the wedding had he attended it, and had in fact fled from that specific eventuality. Short and trim though he had always been, he was enormously fond of food; but owing to a digestive disorder combined with diabetes his diet was now confined to boiled eggs, weak tea, lemon squash, and arrowroot biscuits.

I don't care who stares at me, I have plenty of reasons to cry, said Mrs Rupa Mehra to herself defiantly. I am so happy and heartbroken today. But her heartbreak lasted only a few minutes more. The groom and bride walked around the fire seven times, Savita keeping her head meekly down, her eyelashes wet with tears; and Pran and she were man and wife.

After a few concluding words by the priests, everyone rose. The newlyweds were escorted to a flower-shrouded bench near a sweet-smelling, roughleafed harsingar[10] tree in white-and-orange bloom; and congratulations fell on them and their parents and all the Mehras and Kapoors present as copiously as those delicate flowers fall to the ground at dawn.

Mrs Rupa Mehra's joy was unconfined. She gobbled the congratulations down like forbidden gulab-jamuns. She looked a little speculatively at her younger daughter, who appeared to be laughing at her from a distance. Or was she laughing at her sister? Well, she would find out soon enough what the happy tears of matrimony were all about!

Pran's much-shouted-at mother, subdued yet happy, after blessing her son and daughter-in-law, and failing to see her younger son Maan anywhere, had gone over to her daughter Veena. Veena embraced her; Mrs Mahesh Kapoor, temporarily overcome, said nothing, but sobbed and smiled simultaneously. The dreaded Home Minister and his daughter Priya joined them for a few minutes, and in return for their congratulations, Mrs Mahesh Kapoor had a few kind words to say to each of them. Priya, who was married and virtually immured by her in-laws in a house in the old, cramped part of Brahmpur, said, rather wistfully, that the garden looked beautiful. And it was true, thought Mrs Mahesh Kapoor with quiet pride: the garden was indeed looking beautiful. The grass was rich, the gardenias were creamy and fragrant, and a few chrysanthemums and roses were already in bloom. And though she could take no credit for the sudden, prolific blossoming of the harsingar tree, that was surely the grace of the gods whose prized and contested possession, in mythical times, it used to be.

§ *Arranged marriage* Hosain, De Souza (1), Fernando

---

10 Tree *Nyctanthes arbor tristi* and its flower.

AGHA SHAHID ALI (1949–)

1: Postcard from Kashmir

Kashmir shrinks into my mailbox
my home a neat four by six inches.

I always loved neatness. Now I hold
the half-inch Himalayas in my hand.

5   This is home. And this the closest
I'll ever be to home. When I return,
the colors won't be so brilliant.
the Jhelum's waters so clean
so ultramarine. My love
10   so overexposed.

And my memory will be a little
out of focus, in it
a giant negative, black
and white, still undeveloped.

§ *Kashmir* Sahgal

2: A Wrong Turn

In my dream I'm always
in a massacred town, its name
erased from maps,
no road signs to it.
5   Only a wrong turn brings me here

where only the noon sun lives.
I'm alone, walking among the atrocities,
guillotines blood-scorched,
gods stabbed at their altars,
10 dry wells piled up with bones,
a curfew on ghosts.

Who were these people?
And who finished them to the last?
If dust had an alphabet, I would learn.

15 I thrust my hand
into the cobwebbed booth
of the town's ghost station,

the platform a snake-scaled rock,
rusted tracks waiting for a lost train,
20 my ticket a dead spider
hard as stone.

SUJATA BHATT (1956–)

A Different History

1
Great Pan is not dead;
he simply emigrated
            to India.
Here, the gods roam freely,
5 disguised as snakes or monkeys;
every tree is sacred
and it is a sin
to be rude to a book.
It is a sin to shove a book aside
10   with your foot,
a sin to slam books down
            hard on a table,
a sin to toss one carelessly
            across a room
15 You must learn how to turn the pages gently
without disturbing Sarasvati,
without offending the tree
from whose wood the paper was made.

2
Which language
20 has not been the oppressor's tongue?
Which language
truly meant to murder someone?
And how does it happen
that after the torture,
25 after the soul has been cropped

---

1 Pan: Greek god of flocks and herds.   16 Sarasvati: Hindu goddess of wisdom, who among other things presides over libraries.

with a long scythe swooping out
of the conqueror's face –
the unborn grandchildren
grow to love that strange language.

§ *Language usage* Rao, Ezekiel, Das; *Mythical migrants* Moraes, Haq; Carib:
Walcott (4)

MEENA ALEXANDER (1951–)

House of a Thousand Doors

This house has a thousand doors
the sills are cut in bronze
three feet high
to keep out snakes,
5   toads, water rats
that shimmer in the bald reeds
at twilight
as the sun burns down to the Kerala coast.

The roof is tiled in red
10   pitched with a silver lightning rod,
a prow, set out from land's end
bound nowhere.
In dreams
waves lilt, a silken fan
15   in grandmother's hands
shell coloured, utterly bare as the light takes her.

She kneels at each
of the thousand doors in turn
paying her dues.
20   Her debt is endless.
I hear the flute played in darkness,
a bride's music.
A poor forked thing,
I watch her kneel in all my lifetime
25   imploring the household gods
who will not let her in.

§ *House as symbol* Ramanujan, Wijenaike, Hashmi; Carib: Walcott (1),
Naipaul (2); *South Asian women's roles* Hosain, De Souza (1, 2), Wijenaike

GITHA HARIHARAN (1954–)

The Remains of the Feast

The room still smells of her. Not as she did when she was dying, an over-ripe smell that clung to everything that had touched her, sheets, saris, hands. She had been in the nursing home for only ten days but a bedsore grew like an angry red welt on her back. Her neck was a big hump, and she lay in bed like a moody camel that would snap or bite at unpredictable intervals. The goitred lump, the familiar swelling I had seen on her neck all my life, that I had stroked and teasingly pinched as a child, was now a cancer that spread like a fire down the old body, licking clean everything in its way.

The room now smells like a pressed, faded rose. A dry, elusive smell. Burnt, a candle put out.

We were not exactly room-mates, but we shared two rooms, one corner of the old ancestral house, all my twenty-year-old life.

She was Rukmini, my great-grandmother. She was ninety when she died last month, outliving by ten years her only son and daughter-in-law. I don't know how she felt when they died, but later she seemed to find something slightly hilarious about it all. That she, an ignorant village-bred woman, who signed the papers my father brought her with a thumb-print, should survive; while they, city-bred, ambitious, should collapse of weak hearts and arthritic knees at the first sign of old age.

Her sense of humour was always quaint. It could also be embarrassing. She would sit in her corner, her round, plump face reddening, giggling like a little girl. I knew better than ask her why, I was a teenager by then. But some uninitiated friend would be unable to resist, and would go up to my great-grandmother and ask her why she was laughing. This, I knew, would send her into uncontrollable peals. The tears would flow down her cheeks, and finally, catching her breath, still weak with laughter, she would confess. She could fart exactly like a train whistling its way out of the station, and this achievement gave her as much joy as a child might get when she saw or heard a train.

So perhaps it is not all that surprising that she could be so flippant about her only child's death, especially since ten years had passed.

'Yes, Ratna, you study hard and become a big doctor madam,' she would chuckle, when I kept the lights on all night and paced up and down the room, reading to myself.

'The last time I saw a doctor, I was thirty years old.'

'Your grandfather was in the hospital for three months. He would faint every time he saw his own blood.'

And as if that summed up the progress made between two generations, she would pull her blanket over her head and begin snoring almost immediately.

I have two rooms, the entire downstairs to myself now, since my great-grandmother died. I begin my course at medical college next month, and I am afraid to be here alone at night.

I have to live up to the gold medal I won last year. I keep late hours, reading my anatomy textbook before the course begins. The body is a solid, reliable thing. It is a wonderful, resilient machine. I hold on to the thick, hard-bound book and flip through the new-smelling pages greedily. I stop every time I find an illustration, and look at it closely. It reduces us to pink, blue and white, colour-coded, labelled parts. Muscles, veins, tendons. Everything has a name. Everything is linked, one with the other, all parts of a functioning whole.

It is poor consolation for the nights I have spent in her warm bed, surrounded by that safe, familiar, musty smell.

She was cheerful and never sick. But she was also undeniably old, and so it was no great surprise to us when she took to lying in bed all day a few weeks before her ninetieth birthday.

She had been lying in bed for close to two months, ignoring concern, advice, scolding, and then she suddenly gave up. She agreed to see a doctor.

The young doctor came out of her room, his face puzzled and angry. My father begged him to sit down and drink a tumbler of hot coffee.

'She will need all kinds of tests,' the doctor said. 'How long has she had that lump on her neck? Have you had it checked?'

My father shifted uneasily in his cane chair. He is a cadaverous looking man, prone to nervousness and sweating. He keeps a big jar of antacids on his office desk. He has a nine to five accountant's job in a government-owned company, the kind that never fires its employees.

My father pulled out the small towel he uses in place of a handkerchief. Wiping his forehead, he mumbled, 'You know how these old women are. Impossible to argue with them.'

'The neck,' the doctor said more gently. I could see he pitied my father.

I think it was examined once, long ago. My father was alive then. There was supposed to have been an operation, I think. But you know what they thought in those days. An operation meant an unnatural death. All the relatives came over to scare her, advise her with horror stories. So she said no. You know how it is. And she was already a widow then, my father was the head of the household. How could he, a fourteen-year-old, take the responsibility?'

'Hm,' said the doctor. He shrugged his shoulders. 'Let me know when you want to admit her in my nursing home. But I suppose it's best to let her die at home.'

When the doctor left, we looked at each other, the three of us, like shifty accomplices. My mother, practical as always, broke the silence and said, 'Let's not tell her anything. Why worry her? And then we'll have all kinds of difficult old aunts and cousins visiting, it will be such a nuisance. How will Ratna study in the middle of all that chaos?'

But when I went to our room that night, my great-grandmother had a sly look on her face. 'Come here, Ratna', she said. 'Come here, my darling little gem.'

I went, my heart quaking at the thought of telling her. She held my hand and kissed each finger, her half-closed eyes almost flirtatious.

'Tell me something, Ratna,' she began in a wheedling voice.

'I don't know, I don't know anything about it,' I said quickly.

'Of course you do!' She was surprised, a little annoyed. 'Those small cakes you got from the Christian shop that day. Do they have eggs in them?'

I was speechless with relief.

'Do they?' she persisted. 'Will you,' and her eyes narrowed with cunning, 'will you get one for me?'

So we began a strange partnership, my great-grandmother and I. I smuggled cakes and ice cream, biscuits and samosas, made by non-Brahmin[1] hands, into a vegetarian invalid's room. To the deathbed of a Brahmin widow who had never eaten anything but pure, home-cooked food for almost a century.

She would grab it from my hand, late at night after my parents had gone to sleep. She would hold the pastry in her fingers, turn it round and round, as if on the verge of an earthshaking discovery.

'And does it really have egg in it?' she would ask again, as if she needed the password for her to bite into it with her gums.

'Yes, yes,' I would say, a little tired of midnight feasts by then. The pastries were a cheap yellow colour, topped by white frosting with hard, grey pearls.

'Lots and lots of eggs,' I would say, wanting her to hurry up and put it in her mouth. 'And the bakery is owned by a Christian. I think he hires Muslim cooks too.'

'Ooooh,' she would sigh. Her little pink tongue darted out and licked the frosting. Her toothless mouth worked its way steadily, munching, making happy sucking noises.

Our secret was safe for about a week. Then she became bold. She was bored with the cakes, she said. They gave her heartburn.

She became a little more adventurous every day. Her cravings were varied and unpredictable. Laughable and always urgent.

'I'm thirsty,' she moaned, when my mother asked her if she wanted anything. 'No, no, I don't want water, I don't want juice.' She stopped the moaning and looked at my mother's patient, exasperated face. 'I'll tell you what I want,' she whined. 'Get me a glass of that brown drink Ratna bought in the bottle. The kind that bubbles and makes a popping sound when you open the bottle. The one with the fizzy noise when you pour it out.'

'A Coca-Cola?' said my mother, shocked. 'Don't be silly, it will make you sick.'

---

1 Impure (from a high-caste brahmin point of view).

'I don't care what it is called,' my great-grandmother said and started moaning again. 'I want it.'

So she got it and my mother poured out a small glassful, tight-lipped, and gave it to her without a word. She was always a dutiful grand-daughter-in-law.

'Ah,' sighed my great-grandmother, propped up against her pillows, the steel tumbler lifted high over her lips. The lump on her neck moved in little gurgles as she drank. Then she burped a loud, contented burp, and asked, as if she had just thought of it, 'Do you think there is something in it? You know, alcohol?'

A month later, we had got used to her unexpected, inappropriate demands. She had tasted, by now, lemon tarts, garlic, three types of aerated drinks, fruit cake laced with brandy, bhel-puri[2] from the fly-infested bazaar nearby.

'There's going to be trouble,' my mother kept muttering under her breath. 'She's losing her mind, she is going to be a lot of trouble.'

And she was right, of course. My great-grandmother could no longer swallow very well. She would pour the coke into her mouth and half of it would trickle out of her nostrils, thick, brown, nauseating.

'It burns, it burns,' she would yell then, but she pursed her lips tightly together when my mother spooned a thin gruel into her mouth. 'No, no,' she screamed deliriously. 'Get me something from the bazaar. Raw onions. Fried bread. Chickens and goats.'

Then we knew she was lost to us. She was dying.

She was in the nursing home for ten whole days. My mother and I took turns sitting by her, sleeping on the floor by the hospital cot.

She lay there quietly, the pendulous neck almost as big as her face. But she would not let the nurses near her bed. She would squirm and wriggle like a big fish that refused to be caught. The sheets smelled, and the young doctor shook his head. 'Not much to be done now,' he said. 'The cancer has left nothing intact.'

The day she died, she kept searching the room with her eyes. Her arms were held down by the tubes and needles, criss-cross, in, out. The glucose dripped into her veins but her nose still ran, the clear, thin liquid trickling down like dribble on to her chin. Her hands clenched and unclenched with the effort and she whispered, like a miracle, 'Ratna.'

My mother and I rushed to her bedside. Tears streaming down her face, my mother bent her head before her and pleaded, 'Give me your blessings, Paati. Bless me before you go.'

My great-grandmother looked at her for a minute, her lips working furiously, noiselessly. For the first time in my life I saw a fine veil of perspiration on her face. The muscles on her face twitched in mad, frenzied jerks. Then she pulled one arm free of the tubes, in a sudden, crazy spurt of strength, and the I.V. pole crashed to the floor.

---

2 A sour-sweet and pungent mixture of various ingredients.

'Bring me a red sari,' she screamed. 'A red one with a big wide border of gold. And,' her voice cracked, 'bring me peanuts with chilli powder from the corner shop. Onion and green chilli bondas[3] deep-fried in oil.'

Then the voice gurgled and gurgled, her face and neck swayed, rocked like a boat lost in a stormy sea. She retched, and as the vomit flew out of her mouth and her nose, thick like the milkshakes she had drunk, brown like the alcoholic coke, her head slumped forward, her rounded chin buried in the cancerous neck.

When we brought the body home – I am not yet a doctor and already I can call her that – I helped my mother to wipe her clean with a wet, soft cloth. We wiped away the smells, the smell of the hospital bed, the smell of an old woman's juices drying. Her skin was dry and papery. The stubble on her head – she had refused to shave her head once she got sick – had grown, like the soft, white bristles of a hairbrush.

She had had only one child though she had lived so long. But the skin on her stomach was like crumpled, frayed velvet, the creases running to and fro in fine, silvery rivulets.

'Bring her sari,' my mother whispered, as if my great-grandmother could still hear her.

I looked at the stiff, cold body that I was seeing naked for the first time. She was asleep at last, quiet at last. I had learnt, in the last month or two, to expect the unexpected from her. I waited, in case she changed her mind and sat up, remembering one more taboo to be tasted.

'Bring me your eyebrow tweezers,' I heard her say. 'Bring me that hair-removing cream. I have a moustache and I don't want to be an ugly old woman.'

But she lay still, the wads of cotton in her nostrils and ears shutting us out. Shutting out her belated ardour.

I ran to my cupboard and brought her the brightest, reddest sari I could find: last year's Diwali[4] sari, my first silk.

I unfolded it, ignoring my mother's eyes which were turning aghast. I covered her naked body lovingly. The red silk glittered like her childish laughter.

'Have you gone mad,' my mother whispered furiously. 'She was a sick old woman, she didn't know what she was saying.'

She rolled up the sari and flung it aside, as if it had been polluted. She wiped the body again to free it from foolish, trivial desires.

They burnt her in a pale-brown sari, her widow's weeds. The prayer beads I had never seen her touch encircled the bulging, obscene neck.

I am still a novice at anatomy. I hover just over the body, I am just beneath the skin. I have yet to look at the insides, the entrails of memories she told me nothing about, the pain congealing into a cancer.

She has left me behind with nothing but a smell, a legacy that grows fainter every day. For a while I haunt the dirtiest bakeries and tea-stalls I

---

3 Green chillis deep-fried in batter. 4 Hindu festival of lights held in October or November and celebrating Lakshmi, goddess of prosperity.

can find. I search for her, my sweet great-grandmother, in plate after plate of stale confections, in needle-sharp green chillies, deep-fried in rancid oil. I plot her revenge for her, I give myself diarrhoea for a week.

Then I open all the windows and her cupboard and air the rooms. I tear her dirty, grey saris to shreds. I line the shelves of her empty cupboard with my thick, newly-bought, glossy-jacketed texts, one next to the other. They stand straight and solid, row after row of armed soldiers. They fill up the small cupboard quickly.

Sri Lanka

PATRICK FERNANDO (1931–82)

The Fisherman Mourned by His Wife

When you were not quite thirty and the sun
Had not yet tanned you into old-boat brown,
When you were not quite thirty and not begun
To be embittered like the rest, nor grown
5   Obsessed with death, then would you come
Hot with continence upon the sea,
Chaste as a gull flying pointed home,
In haste to be with me!

Now that, being dead, you are beyond detection,
10   And I need not be discreet, let us confess
It was not love that married us nor affection,
But elders' persuasion, not even loneliness.
Recall how first you were so impatient and afraid,
My eyes were open in the dark unlike in love,
15   Trembling, lest in fear, you'll let me go a maid,
Trembling on the other hand, for my virginity.

Three months the monsoon thrashed the sea, and you
Remained at home; the sky cracked like a shell
In thunder, and the rain broke through.
20   At last when pouring ceased and storm winds fell,
When gulls returned new-plumed and wild,
When in our wind-torn flamboyante
New buds broke, I was with child.

My face was wan while telling you, and voice fell low,
25   And you seemed full of guilt and not to know
Whether to repent or rejoice over the situation.

---

22 flamboyante: flame-tree.

You nodded at the ground and went to sea.
But soon I was to you more than God or temptation,
And so were you to me.

30   Men come and go, some say they understand,
Our children weep, the youngest thinks you're fast asleep:
Theirs is fear and wonderment.
You had grown so familiar as my hand,
That I cannot with simple grief
35   Assuage dismemberment.

Outside the wind despoils of leaf
Trees that it used to nurse;
Once more the flamboyante is torn,
The sky cracks like a shell again,
40   So someone practical has gone
To make them bring the hearse
Before the rain.

§ *Arranged marriage* Hosain, De Souza (1), Seth

YASMINE GOONERATNE (1935–)

1: Big Match, 1983

Glimpsing the headlines in the newspapers,
tourists scuttle for cover, cancel their options
on rooms with views of temple and holy mountain.
'Flash point in Paradise.' 'Racial pot boils over.'
5   And even the gone away boy
who had hoped to find lost roots, lost lovers,
lost talent even, out among the palms,
makes timely return giving thanks
that Toronto is quite romantic enough
10   for his purposes.

Powerless this time to shelter or to share
we strive to be objective, try to trace
the match that lit this sacrificial fire,
the steps by which we reached this ravaged place.
15   We talk of 'Forty Eight' and 'Fifty Six,'

---

15 'Forty . . . Six': dates of Sri Lankan independence and election of S. W. R. D. Bandaranaike's nationalist government.

of freedom and the treacherous politics
of language; see the first sparks of this hate
fanned into flame in Nineteen Fifty Eight,
yet find no comfort in our neat solutions,
20   no calm abstraction, and no absolution.

The game's in other hands, in any case,
these fires ring factory, and house, and hovel,
and Big Match fever, flaring high and fast,
has both sides in its grip and promises
25   dizzier scores than any at the Oval.

In a tall house dim with old books and pictures
calm hands quiet the clamouring telephone.
'It's a strange life we're leading here just now,
not a dull moment. No one can complain
30   of boredom, that's for sure. Up all night keeping watch,
and then as curfew ends and your brave lads
dash out at dawn to start another day
of fun, and games, and general jollity,
I send Padmini and the girls to a neighbour's house.

35   Who, me? – Oh, I'm doing fine. I always was
a drinking man, you know, and nowadays
I'm stepping up my intake quite a bit,
the general idea being that when those torches
come within fifty feet of his house, don't you see,
40   it won't be my books that go up first, but me.'

A pause. Then, steady and every bit as clear
as though we are neighbours still as we had been
in 'Fifty Eight,' 'Thanks, by the way, for ringing.
There's nothing you can do to help us, but
45   it's good to know some lines haven't yet been cut.'

Out of the palmyrah fences of Jaffna
bristle a hundred guns.
Shopfronts in the Pettah, landmarks of our childhood,
curl like old photographs in the flames.
50   Blood on their khaki uniforms, three boys lie dying:
a crowd looks silently the other way.
Near the wheels of his smashed bicycle
at the corner of Duplication Road a child lies dead
and two policemen look the other way

---

46 palmyrah: palm with fan-shaped leaves.   **46** Jaffna: Tamil stronghold in north of Sri Lanka.

55 as a stout man, sweating with fear, falls to his knees
beneath a bo-tree in a shower of sticks and stones
flung by his neighbour's hands.
The joys of childhood, friendships of our youth
ravaged by pieties and politics,
60 screaming across our screens, her agony
at last exposed, Sri Lanka burns alive.

§ *Post-independence Sri Lanka* Wikkramasinha, Wijesinha, De Zoysa, Selva-durai; Gooneratne also in TransC

2: This Language, This Woman

Beware how you insult her
in your ignorance, accident of your birth,
goaded by the jealous fury of your own girl
who still resents, it seems, that old flirtation.
5 Reproaching her forever with your dearth
you miss the loveliness of her
unfolding in perpetual renewal
of suppleness still, her generosity.

If you should try to take her from me
10 I'd launch no thousand ships to bring her back
the *braggadocio* of the imperial theme
that shielded her being now a derelict wreck.
I'd sail some paper boats that bear her name
as this one does, till you grant credit to
15 my confidence in a fidelity
greater than Helen's.   She would not go,
being truer than a mother, sister, wife,
dearer than life.

No more an Empress's daughter, with a bribe
20 locked in her purse,
the clerks, the merchants, and their hireling tribe
long since dispersed,
gone the protectors who, while pampering her,
lined their own coffers:
25 her menfolk falter in a far country,
their vigour ended,
she wanders here alone and unbefriended,
herself at last, and nothing else to offer.

---

56 **bo-tree**: sacred pipal tree; tree under which the Buddha's enlightenment occurred.

So do not call her slut, and alien,
30   names born of envy and your own misuse
that whisper how desire in secret runs.
She has known greatness, borne illustrious sons,
her mind's well-stored, her lovely nature's rich,
filled with these splendid warm surprises which,
35   now the distorting old connection's done,
fit her to be your mistress, and my Muse.

§ *Myth reworked* Haq; Carib: Lamming (2), Walcott (4); SEA: Somtow; Gooneratne also in TransC

PUNYAKANTE WIJENAIKE (1933–)

From Giraya

Giraya is a Gothic novella centred on the unease felt by its narrator, Kamini, the young wife of the son of an upper-class Sri Lankan family, whose past and present are both shrouded in mystery. The old family house, presided over by Kamini's mother-in-law Adelaine, is a symbol of the social world into which Kamini has married. When it yields up its secrets in a powerful, melodramatic climax, where Adelaine is murdered and Kamini's husband Lal is revealed to be homosexual, this world is effectively destroyed. Kamini discovers that its relationships were very different from what she had assumed and for the first time feels sympathy for the dead Adelaine, whom she now sees as having tried to preserve her family in a 'house of corruption'. The opening section, included here, establishes the sense of menace and mystery that dominates *Giraya*.

The Walauwe, the old manor house, waits in silence. Is it awaiting death with courage? Why must anyone need courage to face death? Surely death is but another change and are we not accustomed to that in life as well? The walauwe may be pulled down, brick by brick, and then it will rise again with new bricks and new tiles. It will live again under a new name, a new coat of paint and a new way of life. Already blue-prints for the new house are spread on the dining table by the new mistress of the house. She must have had the plans ready a long time ago; perhaps a year ago, when my story begins.

Yes, a house retains its personality only so long as its inmates live within its walls. When they die, or run away, the house must change. If it is not pulled down, it must at least assume a second personality. It must be reborn. Like a human being a house must die before taking life again. The old ebony furniture will be sold as valuable antiques and the yellowed lace curtains pulled down. The old walauwe will die, but the house will live on. To fear death then must be a foolish thing. And yet there are those who cling to the old life and old ways as a frightened, reluctant babe clings to its mother's womb at birth. Ah, birth and death could be hard moments!

The Giraya, the arecanut-slicer,[1] lies motionless, its steel damascened legs spread wide open, its hands clasped in perpetual worship. Its face is stern, contemptuous with straight nose and firm chin. Its knot of hair is low at the nape of the neck. The blacksmith who created it must have had a certain woman in mind. Why did he make a giraya in the shape of a woman? The body has a beautiful bird design worked upon it. It is truly a work of art. Yet it should not lie immobile merely to please the eyes. The blade which grips the arecanut and cuts it now lies as motionless as the face.

The betel leaf which plays a manifold role in our lives should, at the approach of a New Year, become a symbol of peace and goodwill. Once fresh and green from the vine in the courtyard they now lie shrivelled like bitter old women upon the betel tray, along with the cardamoms, cloves, and the white chunam[2] in the *killotaya*, the silver circular box, gleaming richly ornate and attractive in the moonlight filtering in through the iron bars of the window. The betel wallet, the *hambiliya*, with the bunch of silver household keys attached to it once jingled when she walked. Now they too lie as still as the giraya, the arecanut-slicer. Dare I touch any one of them? What would the daughter of the walauwe say? At the thought of her my heart begins to pound. Here is the large bag that was her mother's – the betel bag in which she used to carry everything she required for a chew of betel, whenever she went on inspection tours of the estate; the betel leaves in a box, the wallet, the chunam box and the giraya.

The moonlight touches its rich, proud but faded embroidery, sprawled over the cloth like dead spiders. The moonlight also touches the tassels that pull its wide mouth together. But it cannot reach the womb, the inside of the bag, lined in soft, white silk like the underskirts she used to wear. Everything about her was white and soft and expensive, even the underskirts trimmed with lace made by the devoted Lucia Hamy. I could almost see her now, seated over there by her mistress's bed, on the low hard stool permitted her, working on the pillow lace. The bobbins of thread would swing back and forth turning out a ribbon of lace, fine and white, lilke a web.

Beneath the table on which the giraya and its companions lie, stands the *padikkama*, the brass spittoon, its mouth a dark hungry hole. I shudder as I look away. But the gleam of the giraya draws my eyes again. What strange power it has over me! And yet what further power could it have, lying there still and cold as its dead mistress upon her bed. Need I take its hard unyielding body into my hands again? Do I want to take it, now that Lal, my husband, is no longer here?

A tremor goes through me. It begins in my neck and goes down to my toes. The giraya's hands are clasped like hers in death. But across its cold

---

1 Slicer for astringent nut from a type of palm-tree, used for betel-chewing; also used as a weapon by exorcists. 2 Substance derived from limestone or equivalents to add flavour in betel-chewing.

hard neck there is no soft white chiffon scarf to hide the grotesque scars of death. How strange it is that it had to be the hands of faithful Lucia Hamy that put an end to the power of the giraya in this house. She who had nurtured and waited upon it like a devoted slave, throughout the many years . . . she who used to tenderly rub a little eau-de-cologne with a piece of cotton wool, whenever a mosquito dared sting the soft flesh of her mistress.

No, I no longer need to touch the giraya. It has no further power to break the new evil hanging over me. Maybe I should hire a *kattadiya*, an exorcist, and in his hands the giraya might be endowed with new power . . .

My poor child lies in innocent sleep in his cot in my room. Ah my son! Because of you, how I have changed! And yet you lie asleep unmindful of me and the whole world. You are not concerned with the future, only the present. You leave the future trustingly in my hands. Soon you will wake and cry because you are hungry, and I will have to answer that need too. You are childhood itself, innocent, hopeful, content . . . Yes, I was like you once, so long ago that it seems another life. But now I am an adult and a mother, some one who must worry and struggle, regardless of what is right or wrong. A mother must forget herself and think of her child.

Yes, my son, there are only three of us left in the house today. You, your father's sister Manel and I. But soon, tomorrow perhaps, there will be a fourth. But it will not be your father, my son, oh no. He has run away, deserted us in our time of need. Tomorrow there will be another man in the house.

There is a belief among us that the period between the death of a year and the birth of another should be observed in idleness. Until the sun travels to its new position of power in the sky it will be an unpropitious period. Yes, you do well to sleep then. I am so weary too but I dare not sleep. I can only watch and wait and yes, I can read over the diary I have kept of the dying year.

I turn its pages. I have not made entries daily. There have been days when I have waited like today, and watched and hoped. I have been afraid as I am afraid now. Now I am afraid of the birth of a New Year. I cling to the Old Year as it struggles with its death pangs. Even though the dying year has been an unpleasant one, I cling to it. This then must be what we fear in death. The unknown new life. When we have gone from this life, whither shall we fly? Without a clear vision where could we go? If we knew, we would feel no fear.

My mind brings up a picture from my past. As a child I had gone on a long, weary journey to Adam's Peak.[3] Seated in a hired car my eyes were on each hill as it loomed at the turn of the road. Bigger and bigger they seemed to grow, each seeming like a giant wearing a devil's mask with protruding eyeballs and hanging red tongues. Child that I was, I wished the car to halt, but

---

3 Site of pilgrimage in Sri Lanka's Central Highlands, with footprint-shaped imprint claimed as Buddha's by Buddhists, Shiva's by Hindus, Adam's by Muslims and St. Thomas's by Christians; a.k.a. Sri Pada.

on and on it went, twisting and turning while each mile brought us closer and closer to fearful devils. I closed my eyes and when I opened them I cowered, expecting to see the most terrifying creature of all. But instead there was nothing but another stretch of grey road. I relaxed and laughed. The devils were a thing of the past then. And suddenly my laughter ceased. A new, unknown hill loomed larger than ever before me . . .

And now as I read my diary the face of Manel appears larger than the rest. How could this be? The once pale lips seem to have lost their trembling uncertainty. They are not like the thin hard lips of Adelaine, my mother-in-law.

BAK (April) 13th

On Bak 13th, twelve months ago, the rusty iron gates of the walauwe opened slowly. Throughout the year the gates remained closed and padlocked by old Loku, the gardener. Anyone who wished to come in or go out had to call out to old Loku to open them. It is not easy to call old Loku. I do not yet know whether he is slightly deaf or it is a peculiarity of his nature not to come when called. He will come when you are least expecting him, silently as a ghost.

From my position near the door leading out into the open verandah I can see the procession of people in bright New Year clothes, carrying children and trays of sweet-meats and milk-rice and fruits, coming up the drive to the walauwe steps. Even the barking of the two Alsatians, confined to their kennels, seems to blend with the joyous drumming in the village beyond the estate.

My mother-in-law sits erect upon her ebony throne in the verandah. The chair having been brought out for the occasion from the dark drawing room within, is richly carved and upholstered in a faded, red brocade.

Before her is a table of immense beauty. It stands upon a single rounded leg but its circular surface is an opened flower whose petals are of Ceylon's best timbers. A petal of teak next to a petal of mahogany, then a *nadun*[4] strip and a dark, burning ebony. Between each petal runs a delicate line of ivory. Upon this table lies the betel tray, the *bulath heppuwa*, with the cardamoms and cloves, chunam and tobacco. The uncut arecanut and the giraya lie on top. Each guest will cut his or her own arecanut the way he or she wishes, into fine fragrant slices or hard small pieces. This is the only time of the year when the giraya will be handled by anyone other than old Lucia Hamy. She is not happy about this. She hovers about the betel tray like a jealous mother over a new-born child.

The villagers come ever closer, gathering round the circular lawn ornamented with a bird bath of chipped marble, a stone seat covered with fungus and a few rose bushes struggling bravely against overpowering weeds. They

---

4 Highly prized orange-brown wood used for furniture, etc.; from tree endemic to the wet zone of Sri Lanka.

come up steps flanked by cement pots with drooping ferns and begonias on to the cool old-fashioned tiled verandah, each in turn, to greet the lady of the walauwe.

My in-laws still hold a prominent place in the village as one of the oldest but now dying, aristocratic families. As my mother-in-law greets her visitors, my husband, Lal, and his sister, Manel, spring dutifully to their places on either side of her.

She is a small-made woman, my mother-in-law. Dainty and fair of skin with finely set features over delicate bone. The lips are thin and pale, the eyes dark brown and set in hollowed shadows, the eyebrows faint above them. She wears a pale grey cotton saree. The folds are gathered and held over the left shoulder with an amethyst brooch. In her tiny ears are amethyst earrings and she wears a bracelet of the same stone. Her jacket is of grey, old, imported lace. The sleeves are puffed and there is lace at the neck. She never wears any colour except grey or white. She has said that she would mourn her children's father's death until her own. And so, though the colour for the New Year is red, she wears her cloth of grey, so steadfast is she in her duty. Her hair, at the age of sixty-four is only faintly streaked with silver, and her teeth are small and firm and even. She reads her sermon book without glasses. In her knot of hair set low at the nape of the neck is thrust a jewelled hair ornament. She wears no make-up save for a dusting of a pale pink powder and a dab of eau-de-cologne. I can imagine her faithful hand-servant Lucia Hamy patting on the powder with a large long handled puff in the private places of her body. . . .

She sits proudly, with a look of pious tolerance on her cold, pale face. Her palms are clasped together like the hands of the giraya as she receives the homage of her many subjects. When she addresses them her voice is thin, imperious, falling like raindrops upon a poor parched earth. She expects those who hear it to drink it in, for it would have to last them until the next year when once more the gates of the Maha Walauwe will be open to the public.

But this is undoubtedly one of her good moments. Those who hear her voice do not know that it can twist and turn, coiling with fury like a snake when roused.

She accepts the gifts of betel and sweetmeats, fruit and milk-rice with traditional goodwill, handing out small sums of money in return. These people, these villagers and labourers, belong to a class far below herself and her family. I could see her placing them unconsciously among the mammoties, weeding forks, sickle knives, handcarts and road rollers of her estate. They exist only to keep her estate and her family going. She ignores the changing world defiantly.

My husband Lal stands beside her, a few steps ahead of his sister, as the only son of the family. He smiles nervously like a child unsure of itself. He says nothing but only nods briefly whenever someone presents him with betel. He takes the sheaves awkwardly into his hands. I think of our son, Sugath, his and mine, asleep in the cot in our room. He is but two months old and yet I have seen in his sleeping face traces of a man's firmness, of maturity that is so lacking in his father.

Manel is a flower by name only. She has never blossomed bodily or mentally. At the age of thirty she stands a few paces behind her brother who is thirty-five. Occasionally I see her throw a nervous, uncertain glance at the estate Superintendent who waits among the crowd to offer his betel to his employers.

I watch old Lucia Hamy next. She takes the round *bulath heppuwa*, the betel tray, into her hands and offers it roughly and reluctantly to the waiting visitors. She does this to show her position in the walauwe ... and because she cannot bear to have anyone touch the giraya of her mistress. . . .

While old Loku brings out benches, and mats from the kitchen quarters, the children, frank in their curiosity, begin to wander freely about the place. One little thing in a pink nylon dress with a sash, runs barefoot up the verandah and into the inner hall. I see my mother-in-law look at old Lucia who puts down the betel tray on the petal-shaped table and goes after the daring child. I see the gleam of the giraya in her hand. I turn and follow the child swiftly. Lucia limps furiously behind me. Her left leg is shorter than her right, and her mouth is twisted to a side. She covers the floor far more quickly than I anticipate, but I reach the little girl first. I put a steady hand on her shoulder. I bend down and whisper to her and discourage her wide-eyed interest in the family portraits on the table, the old carved but uncomfortable furniture with the brocade upholstery. The old, worn English carpet is not meant for her little bare and dusty feet to stand upon. The china from the continent, a dainty doll and a Dresden shepherdess are not for her. I lure her away before she can touch them. Instead I point out to her the remote paintings upon the faded walls; an English cottage set in a garden of roses, an ice-capped peak with a mist round it, a painted basket of apples, grapes and pears; the mosaic tile half way up the wall bearing upon its surface the family crest. . . .

Lucia Hamy's hot breath fans my neck while I talk to the child, her hand firm in mine. Though I have lived in the walauwe now for a year I cannot yet control the tremor that enters my body each time Lucia Hamy is near me. Apart from her twisted mouth her eyes roll violently like the sea in a storm. The whites are like foam and the pupils are dark waters that rage. Her hair is wild and wispy about her dark, ugly face, her body short yet brutal in its strength. Her nipples are visible just below the hem of her loose jacket, for she looks upon the brassiere as a modern evil. If one believes in devils one can well believe that Lucia Hamy possesses one within her.

She thrusts a sudden hand forward and grasps the child by its hair. Lucia Hamy has the strength of an untamed bull in her bones. Now she uses this strength against a child who cries in terror. She pushes the little thing roughly back onto the verandah regardless of me. It is an ugly, unnecessary scene. A silence falls upon the crowd. The spirit of goodwill vanishes. The mother of the child looks with open hostility at the lady of the walauwe seated unmoved in her chair. The villagers believe that Lucia Hamy is mad. Is the 'mad' woman not going to be put away? Is she going to be permitted to ill-treat a child?

The child is crying. The father takes her in his arms and glares at Lucia Hamy. Out of courtesy he says nothing to her. But his face is dark and sullen. Then I hear the Superintendent say a few words of consolation. . . .

My mother-in-law, Adelaine rises like a queen after holding court. She goes into the house followed by her son and daughter and old Lucia carrying the betel tray and giraya. From the watching crowd I hear a snigger, then a laugh. It is both bold and rude. Lucia Hamy closes the doors of the walauwe. For those within, the New Year festivities are over. I linger on the verandah, watching the crowd disperse. In the labourers' homes and in the village too, the drum-playing, the bursting of crackers, the friendly exchange of betel leaves, the giving of milk-rice and sweet-meats go on. . . . The temple will be crowded with white-clad worshippers, and the playground filled with the sound of children's laughter. . . . But within the closed doors of the walauwe silence reigns.

§ *House as symbol* Ramanujan, Alexander, Hashmi; Carib: Walcott (1), Naipaul (2); *South Asian women's roles* De Souza (2), Alexander; *Gothic SEA:* Lee Kok Liang

LAKDASA WIKKRAMASINHA (1941–78)

Don't Talk to Me about Matisse

Don't talk to me about Matisse, don't talk to me
about Gauguin, or even
the earless painter van Gogh,
& the woman reclining on a blood-spread . . .
5 the aboriginal shot by the great white hunter Matisse

with a gun with two nostrils, the aboriginal
crucified by Gauguin – the syphilis-spreader, the yellowed
      obesity.

Don't talk to me about Matisse . . .
the European style of 1900, the tradition of the studio
10 where the nude woman reclines forever
on a sheet of blood.

772 • *Jean Arasanayagam*

Talk to me instead of the culture generally –
how the murderers were sustained
by the beauty robbed of savages: to our remote
15 villages the painters came, and our white-washed
mud-huts were splattered with gunfire.

§ *Art and social commitment* Gooneratne (2), Arasanayagam, Wijesinha, De
Zoysa; Af: Achebe (2)

JEAN ARASANAYAGAM (1940–)

Passages

I should be dead by now or thought of as some
New migrant poet shaking the dust off my feet
And kissing foreign soil but, I am neither,
Trying out, instead of chartering
5   Some new route to safety or escape, new dance
Steps for a phantom costume ball wearing those
Clothes, heavy with their mothball scent that once
Belonged to youthful summers, unrehearsed those shrouds
That wrap our spectres, put new meat upon these
10   Bones so starkly marionette in stance and gesture,
Stepping out in fancy dress we wore to tread
In stately minuettes, move as ghost through mirrored
Walls that float their bubble images to burst and
Disappear, fleshless as time, waltzing through
15   A spectral world in crinolined skirts fichued in
Tulle, a sprig of orchids at our breast;

That was no time to mourn, then how do we remember
Joy, only a single thread snarled between the
Interstices of those ruined pillars
20   Leaves its brilliant silk caught between
The edge of teeth that bite on memory
Trapped like kingfisher
In snaring net;

That I am still alive makes my return, time's
25   Ghost, to lift the stones off from the breast of
Martyrdom to speak for all whose breath is

Less than vapour in a misty dawn, whose
Bodies no enchanted herb can bring to life
Yet whose flesh and blood transubstantiates
30 Our thought to make us new converts,
Communicants who once more lift the chalice,
Break the bread and celebrate the suffering
Of the Cross;

Watch violence through the telescope of years, feel
35 My life flat, a trampled shadow as the hobnailed
Boots tramp over and over again covering new terrain
Freshly conquered; know fear chill as a clammy toad
Perched on my belly feel the gnaw of night rats
In my sleep, the quiet louse that feeds within the armpit,
40 Have thought of exile, dig many times over
My own grave hearing the thump fall of heavy sod
Tumbling in its quick descent within the pit;

Yet all these years those strangers at my gate
With whom I had no kinship either of flesh or tongue
45 Stood outside those half closed windows watching us
At our strange charades as we gravely danced to
Music each step taking us further and further
Back into deepening shadow away from curious eye.

We were birds of a feather, yes, flocking in that
50 Closed sanctuary, thought that no one would displace
Us, our lives pulled out in secret like those
Hidden gifts from Christmas stockings full of strange
Surprises, snowballs and nuts, apples and books
With gilded pages, searched deep to find whether
55 Our lives could see reflections in other lives
And faces, however humdrum, walk into
Country cottages or manor house or cowslip meadows;

Outside those walls the deep drains filled with
Blood from abattoirs, the huge clay pots simmered
60 With meats slipped off the hooks, black rugs of
Tripe, rallipallams of entrails and intestine,
Bloodied heads and hearts and slaughtered flanks
Of beasts while we sat down and feasted
– With starched white damask napkins
65 Spread upon our knees and silver forks and knives
That cut those silvery slivers into delicate morsels
To whet our finicky appetites – grasped in our fingers.

---

61 **rallipallams**: coloured ruffles of cloth or crêpe paper used in traditional Kandyan decorations.

One hears now, yet one has always heard, death
Rattles in the throat of those who die, those of our
70 Kin and gently as they breathe their last we feel
That peace, their peace since they no longer suffer;

It is the end for them, for us the wait begins
This time for our own selves, ancestral dreams
Now haunt us and we study curious as a bunch
75 Of sight seers come back to visit colonies of lost
Empires the flagstones of old churches slabbed
With ancient tombstones, plaques, memorial tablets
Names, dates, epochs of conquest that have gone
To sleep sunk in the comfort of four-posters,
80 Rust-banks, stretched out beside a wall
Where lizards creep on ratanned chaise-longues;

Here then, we stop short, take breath and
Wonder what records our bitter, nameless
Silence leaves behind as we join that vast
85 Concourse of sated worms fed with rich
Sermons from a predikanten's mouth.

§ *Politics and private lives* Hosain, Sahgal, Selvadurai; SEA: Ee Tiang Hong
(2), Wong Phui Nam, Thumboo, Jeyaretnam

RAJIVA WIJESINHA (1954–)

From Days of Despair

Days of Despair revives characters from Wijesinha's earlier novel *Acts of Faith* in a
mythic narrative set 'sometime in the future'. It deals with political events in 'Ceylon'
and the island's relationship with its powerful northern neighbour, 'Hind'. Here, in
the first part of the opening chapter, the author offers a playful treatment of events in
the recent history of Hind's ruling dynasty, associating himself with his namesake,
Rajiv Gandhi.

Our hero will be called Rajiv, suggesting to the minds of the more cynical
of our readers the suspicion that this novel will be about me. They, indeed
you, need not worry. This is intended to be a conventional novel, and

---

86 predikanten: minister of Dutch Protestant church.

our hero therefore must be great. I unfortunately have not as yet achieved greatness, whereas this Rajiv was not only born great, he also had greatness thrust upon him, when his brother fell out of the sky for instance.[1]

There are, this being a sordid world, those who say that his brother's wife, the ravishing Swedish air hostess Brunnhilde, pushed him out and then tried to thrust herself upon Rajiv. On this story we offer no comment. Suffice it for the moment to say that as our story opens Rajiv is still unmarried, even if Brunnhilde does live, not exactly with him, but in a separate section of his state mansion in the heart of old Delhi. Together with her, perhaps to act as chaperones, live several of her brothers and her cousins and her aunts. Rumour has it that with their help through commissions and omissions, blind eyes usually, she is amassing a tremendous fortune. For our part we can confidently assert that Rajiv has no share in this. He does not require that sort of greatness as well.

That he was destined for greatness was known from the start, long before Brunnhilde appeared on the scene, known if not to everyone at least to his mother and his grandfather, who used to suckle him himself too in accordance with the awareness that was developing in him that he would come in time absolutely to symbolize Mother India. For the old man what made Rajiv special, in preference to his elder brother, were the incipient breasts that, on top of his undoubted masculinity, suggested how readily he would fit into any role his nation demanded of him: keen for a return to old values, he saw in his grandson the modern equivalent of all those divinely androgynous figures who had always caught his fancy in the pages of the Mahabharata.[2]

Rajiv's mother, the Widow[3] as she became soon after he was conceived, did not share her father's feelings. For her the position of the stars was enough, and with those behind him she felt Rajiv had no need of his breasts. Before he reached adolescence she had them removed. Her father was distraught. But then, soon afterwards, Mother India herself was dismembered, with pieces removed to left and to right,[4] and the name of the trunk that remained was cut short to Hind. The old man's[5] faith in his grandson was restored. At the same time, taking control as he now had to do of a smaller area than he had dreamed of while he read the Mahabharata in his prison cell, he was not pleased.

He realized there was no point in holding Rajiv responsible. But day after day, for a year and longer, he did not cease to heap reproaches upon his daughter for the callous and hasty action that had made partition inevitable. All he got in reply was a shrug of the shoulders and a charge of superstition. Now however we can judge that his words did have their effect. From the time the Widow succeeded her father, the final aim of all her actions was to make her country whole again; and, being a thorough sort, she was

---

1 Rajiv Gandhi, former prime minister of India; his brother Sanjay died in a plane crash in 1980.   2 One of the two great Sanskrit epics.   3 Indira Gandhi.   4 Alluding to the Partition of India, with the creation of West and East (subsequently Bangladesh) Pakistan in 1947.   5 Jawaharlal Nehru, first prime minister of India after Independence.

concerned not only with the breasts that had been removed, but also with all the other little bits and pieces that must once have belonged to the main body. Of course as far as she knew Rajiv had lost nothing else during his adolescence. But she noticed that he developed hair on his body only very late in life, after the storming of Goa[6] (it was much later that it occurred to her that it was her worries about that deficiency that had provoked her father's action in retaking what was an integral part of the Motherland). And it was after the great Mongol invasion some time later that she saw that Rajiv's high forehead was growing higher, and that his baldness was really very astonishingly premature. It was then that she began to look wistfully at the lands beyond the Himalayas to the north.

And perhaps it was for connected reasons that, unlike most mothers in Hind, she did not make sure that Rajiv married soon after he came of age. The usual explanation is that Brunnhilde proved too much for her, and she wanted to keep Rajiv at least safely under her control. But that explanation will not suffice. There were other ways of achieving that aim. Rather, it seems to me clear that she was worried that Rajiv would not feel comfortable in marriage, not at any rate until she had done something about the little island that lay detached off the south of India in the Ocean she wanted freed from all other influences; so that it might be entirely, not of course hers, but under the control of the land she so satisfactorily represented and that her son too would represent in time even more fittingly.

From all this our readers, swiftly or not, would have gathered that this is meant to be a political novel. At the same time there is much else that is vital, not only what might be called the obvious such as the psychological, but also the spiritual and, in this day and age especially, the structural. This last I should confess fits in with my own predilections. For me the most powerful of the indications that Rajiv was certain to succeed was his name.

It means Blue Lotus. I discovered this when I was thirteen and he was thirty, in the year his mother defended the Muslim Martyrs of the East against the Menace of the West, unquestionably her most signal success, though it brought for the moment no actual material gains. Rajiv himself may have been more impressed by her acquisition of the little mountain kingdom of Sackem, after which the growth on his face became so luxuriant that no one afterwards except in jest could call him a beardless boy. Coincidentally, it was about that very time that my own moustache began to flourish; but from the point of view of the country it must be clear that the creation of Easthind out of Westhind was the greatest step forward. Indeed, I would even go so far as to suggest that Rajiv, and even his generally farsighted mother, were being selfish in erecting a fence to separate Easthind from Hind proper, at the time when mammary tissue began to collect again and another minor operation was required.

---

6 By the Indian army in 1961.

Yet I can also sympathize with him (which is why it seems to me better in the end to achieve greatness than to be born great, or to have it thrust upon one, in so many embarrassing ways). I still remember my embarrassment when I discovered what my name meant, embarrassment enhanced by the fact that I was at the time at a public school supposed to be built on British lines, and in the tropics of course everything happens much more quickly. Yet one can recover from anything; and now I am emphatically proud, as there is no doubt our hero is, and should be in spite of passing irritations.

For the fact is, there can be no name more appropriate for our ancient subcontinent. The lotus part stands for Buddhism, the most spiritual of religions, showing how purity can spring from the dungheap, the many concentric petals unfolding to the perceptive mind such as your own the shadowy cycle of life at the very heart of which lies the final solution, the annihilation of the self (at this point I have to confess they lose me, but then I am still immature, and you can find a much more thorough account in any good book on the subject). The colour blue is that of Vishnu, the most beloved of the Hindu gods, the Preserver, who comes down to earth whenever he is needed, as Krishna for instance in the Mahabharata, and also as Rama when he had a whole book devoted to his exploits, (though for the moment at any rate the plot of the Ramayana is a sensitive subject, concerned as it is with the invasion of Ceylon by a massive army from Great Hind).[7]

But there is no need to be diverted here. Let us simply acknowledge now that the name Blue Lotus typifies all that is best in the ancient cultures of the east, that it brings together two nations that have the same interests at heart, two religions that should never have been considered separate, springing as they did from the self-same soil. It is this community of the spirit that makes clear that, when the two nations which through the centuries have been the spiritual homes of Buddhism and Hinduism are brought together, it will be through peaceful negotiation not with the bloodshed and animosity that will be required to make Mother India whole again as far as the other missing pieces are concerned. As far as external appearances go, of course, the other parts may seem much more important; the world will concentrate on the cavortings in Easthind and Westhind of Tweedledum and Tweedledee, as they try to resist the inevitable; but the perceptive will by now have realized that the essential connection to be made is that with the island that lies to the south, at that point on the map which the old traditional systems of medicine showed to be the source of all strength for all humankind. It is not only a matter of politics: for our hero, and the subcontinent for which he stands, to be fulfilled psychologically, spiritually, indeed structurally, he must bridge the gap, and do so without inflicting any wounds.

---

7 In the *Ramayana* Rama leads an expedition to recover his beloved Sita from Ravana, the demon-king of Lanka.

Of course the cynical may claim that history shows this is impossible to do. Even Rama came only temporarily, to take back what he had lost. But that is a start, if one is seeking for inspiration. And there is always a first time for anything, as Brunnhilde said on that fateful day when her husband took her up in his aeroplane.

§ *Post-independence Sri Lanka* Gooneratne (1), Wikkramasinha, De Zoysa, Selvadurai

RICHARD DE ZOYSA (1958–90)

Apocalypse Soon*

The child plays in the fire
scattering sparks.
When suddenly the street erupts
in waves of flaming hate
5   and splintered flying glass
shattering old amities and sharding bonds
forged (so we thought) proof
against heat.

After sharp showers the street boys play in mud
10   when suddenly a flood of enmity
thicker than blood
descends
and to the singing of the lead
khaki and gunmetal and iron tread
15   advance and take their vantage at the corner.

Hot August night
with pustulating stars burning like sores
above.
Love is a sweat
20   and intercourse in shadows will beget
lust only for the frenzies of a rape
of sluttish cul-de-sacs and bottlenecks.

The bottlenecks are broken; jagged ends
pierce the vitals of a nation.
25   Death words are spoken, old familiars

---

* The poem appeared in 1981 at a time of ethnic disturbances.

fall silent and retreat to roots.
The junction stations soon will fill
with seething hordes like ants before the rain
fear-breathing herds hard-ridden to the kill
30   and on the concrete platforms hob-nailed boots
drown out the thunder of the train.

Divide and rule. And pendulous to the North
hangs Jambudvipa, stained with her own blood
bleeding heart red as ripe pomegranate
35   and bitter as the damson. All the fruits of hate
quivering she holds. Waiting to drop
into our gaping mouths.

Dark faces on the city pavements pale
beneath the mysteries of holy ash
40   what of the roots spread wide and deep
and far beyond the limestone of the North?
A wind blows through the halls of high commerce
the brilliant trembles at the flare of nostril
flames falter in the sacred lamps of brass
45   in dwellings on the arcades of Colombo.

71
was lots of fun
we had our curfew parties.

58
50   was not so great
and now . . .
      What happens now?

Will, out of blackened streets and rubble ruins
caravans ride forth into the blazing
55   deserts of isolation, where the crack
of lonely snipers' rifles fill the air
and Brahmins hover, flickering in the haze
of heat-filled sky?
Has the Fifth Horseman come again to raise
60   his banner, and wreak havoc on the land?

§ *Post-independence Sri Lanka* Gooneratne (1), Wikkramasinha, Wijesinha,
Selvadurai

---

46 & 49: 71 . . . 58: dates of earlier ethnic clashes.   **57 Brahmins:** upper-caste Hindus.

SHYAM SELVADURAI (1965–)

From Funny Boy

Sub-titled 'a novel in six stories', *Funny Boy* is about the experiences of Arjie, a Tamil boy growing up in an affluent Colombo family and, as in so many novels of child-hood, discovering himself and the world around him. In this case his most important discoveries concern his sexuality – he realizes that he is a 'funny boy' – and the racial conflicts of his society. Gradually the war going on in the Jaffna peninsula begins to encroach on the family's hitherto insulated life. In the extract included here, from the fourth of the 'six stories', Arjie's father has taken Jegan, the son of a friend from his own schooldays, into his family and business. Jegan is from Jaffna and has told Arjie that he was once a 'Tiger'.

We came home from school one day to find Amma[1] and Neliya Aunty sitting on the verandah, looking alarmed.

'What happened?' Diggy asked.

'The police were here,' Amma said.

'The police!' I said. Amma and I looked at each other, remembering our last encounter with the police.

'What did they want?' Diggy asked.

'They wanted to speak to Jegan,' Neliya Aunty said.

'Why?' I asked, feeling suddenly afraid.

They both shrugged.

'Anyway,' Amma said. 'I called the office. Jegan and your Appa[2] should be here soon.'

We went to put away our schoolbags. As we walked down the hall, Sonali took my arm and asked what I thought was happening. I shook my head. I couldn't help remembering that conversation Jegan and I had on the beach. I wondered if the police visit was connected to his having been a Tiger.[3]

When my father and Jegan arrived home, I was surprised to discover that my father was thinking along the same lines I was. Once Amma told them what had happened, my father turned to Jegan and said, 'I've never asked you this, son, but I need to know. Were you or are you connected with the Tigers?'

Jegan was silent for a moment. Then he nodded. My parents looked at him, appalled. 'But not any more,' Jegan said hurriedly, trying to reassure them.

'Are you sure, son?' my father said gravely. 'This is not the time to hide anything from us.'

'I'm sure, Uncle,' Jegan replied.

'But what do the police want, then?' Amma asked anxiously.

My father telephoned a friend of his who was high up in the police and

---

1 Mother. 2 Father. 3 Tamil Tiger insurgent.

explained the situation to him. Then he just listened and nodded for what seemed like a long time. When he put down the phone, Amma asked what the man had said.

'He'll look into it,' my father said.

'Meanwhile, what do we do?' she asked.

'He advised us to go to the police station without waiting for them to come to us. That way they'll know we're innocent.'

'Is that the best thing to do?' Amma asked.

'I'm afraid so.'

Amma and I looked at each other doubtfully.

My father stood up. 'Better put on a fresh shirt and tie,' he said to Jegan. 'Things like that are always important.'

Jegan nodded but didn't get up. He looked very frightened.

My father patted him on the back. 'Don't worry, son,' he said. 'You are innocent, so what can they do?' As an afterthought he added, 'Anyway, it's best not to mention this Tiger business.'

That evening, we sat around on the front verandah and waited for my father and Jegan to return. Even though the next day was a school day, neither Amma nor Neliya Aunty forced us to go inside and do our homework. I glanced at Neliya Aunty and Amma, and I was reminded of that terrible morning when we had sat on the verandah, waiting for the police to come and take them to identify Daryl Uncle's body. As the hours passed, Amma and Neliya Aunty got up from time to time to do little tasks, but they always returned to the verandah. Gradually the darkness obliterated the red glow of the sky.

Finally, we heard my father's car outside, and Amma sent me to open the gate. The glare of the headlights prevented me from seeing into the car; it was only when it had passed me on the way to the garage that I saw that Jegan was not inside.

I closed the gates and went up the driveway. Amma had come down the verandah steps, and she saw the expression on my face.

'Only Appa came back,' I said.

She drew in her breath. My father had closed the garage door and was walking towards us.

'What happened?' Amma called out to him. 'Where is he?'

'Oh, they just kept him for the night,' my father said. He was trying hard to sound casual.

'What!' Amma cried.

'Just routine stuff.'

'How can it be routine to keep someone in jail overnight?'

By now Neliya Aunty, Sonali, and Diggy had joined us.

My father looked at Amma, irritated. 'They just wanted to ask him a few questions, that's all.'

'Couldn't he have gone back tomorrow morning?'

My father shrugged.

'You didn't say anything?'

'I did, but under the Prevention of Terrorism Act they have the right to keep him.'

'But he's not a terrorist!'

My father was silent for a moment. His face looked suddenly tired. 'Don't be too sure about that,' he said. We stared at him.

'Evidently they spotted him at the Ministry of Sports grounds chatting with two men whom they later arrested. The men were planning to assassinate a prominent Tamil politician because he is considered a traitor by the Tigers.' I gasped involuntarily. Everyone turned to look at me.

'Wait a minute. You go jogging with him, no?' Amma said to me.

'Did you see him talk to these men?' Neliya Aunty asked.

I nodded.

'Son,' my father said gravely, 'tell us exactly what you saw.'

I told them all that I had seen. How Jegan had recognized the men and how they had chatted briefly while they were jogging and later as well when we sat on the grass. I also told them about Jegan's decision afterwards to change sports grounds, a decision which now made sense to me.

'He's innocent,' Amma said, once I was finished. 'How could he have been involved in the assassination plan?'

'How do you know he's innocent?' my father asked. 'We can't be a hundred per cent sure.'

'You mean you honestly think he's guilty?' Amma asked, astonished.

My father was silent. We all stared at him, angry and hurt that he would really believe this.

'Look,' my father eventually said, 'the best thing is to get as little involved as possible. If they find out that Jegan is connected to the assassination attempt, we could be accused of harbouring a terrorist.'

'Nonsense,' Amma said. 'Why would they accuse us?'

'These days, every Tamil is a Tiger until proven otherwise.'

'So you're just going to leave Jegan there?'

My father turned to her, impatient how. 'You forget, Nalini, that I have a business to maintain. There are many Sinhalese in this city who would love to see me go under. I have to be very careful.'

The next morning, I was awakened by the sound of my father calling to Amma. Just from the tone of his voice I could tell something had happened. I hurriedly knotted my sarong and went out into the hall. Amma and my father were leaning over the newspaper on the dining table. I came up to them and looked at the column they were reading. The heading read, KEY SUSPECT IN ASSASSINATION PLOT DISCOVERED.

'See that!' my father said to Amma, jabbing his finger at a line in the article. 'The suspect, Jegan Parameswaran, resides with a well-known Tamil hotelier.'

He groaned and pushed his hair back from his forehead. He and Amma regarded each other for a long moment.

The phone rang then, and Amma went to pick it up. 'Oh, hello, Mala,' she said.

I could hear Mala Aunty's excited voice on the other end of the line. 'Yes, we saw the article,' Amma said wearily.

For the rest of the morning the phone rang constantly.

My father came home very late for lunch that day. We had already returned from school when he arrived. He looked grim as he sat down at the table. We waited for him to speak, but he didn't say anything until he had dished out some food onto his plate.

'The office staff have read Jegan's name in the paper,' my father said to Amma. 'Some were sympathetic, but others said nothing. It's only a matter of time before the hotel staff finds out.' He took a mouthful of food. 'You won't believe what I found on my desk this morning.'

We waited for him to continue.

'A hate note,' he said bitterly. 'Accusing me of being a Tiger.'

'But how did the note get on your desk?' Amma asked.

'How else do you think? A staff member put it there.'

We stared at him, shocked. I had been in my father's office many times and I knew all his employees. It was impossible to think that any of them was capable of such maliciousness.

My father pushed his plate away. 'And the filthy phone calls both for Sena and me. Poor Mrs. Wickramasinghe, our receptionist, was in tears by lunchtime.'

He shook his head and sighed. 'I don't know if I'll ever be able to live this down.'

§ *Politics and private lives* Hosain, Sahgal, Arasanayagam; *Childhood discovery* Sidhwa; Af: Gurnah; Carib: Lamming, Senior; SEA: Maniam

Bangladesh

KAISER HAQ (1950–)

A Myth Reworked

His father bought him a kite, a kite in Tri-colours,
with paper frills and paper cut-out of a man
pasted on. It was a man with gold buttons on his sleeves
and wings of a bat. 'Batman! Batman!' he cried and capered
5   as the kite had just time enough to lift off and see-saw once
before he was dragged away to be washed for school.

School was an old, fat, ugly man
and a lady, not young, not old, and full.
He told them in a voice deep as God's
10   of clever Daedalus who fashioned wings
with bird feathers and wax
to escape from prison with his son, his stupid son,
Icarus, who didn't listen to dad
and flew too close to the sun,
15   so the wax melted, scattering the feathers –
served him right, the feather-brained son:
he plunged into the sea and drowned.

The lady's backside jiggled when she walked,
her breasts bounced like a yoyo when she sat down,
20   and swung like a left hook when she turned
from the black-board and caught his eyes escaping
through the window to climb a string to the bright red
and black square of a kite pasted high in a corner,
like a stamp, on the blue envelope of the sky.

25   She piped like an alto saxophone
stern words that warned and cajoled,
words, words, words that exploded about his ears,
stories of reckless boys plummeting earthward
because their kites wouldn't buoy them up

30 when they lost their footing on the cornice.
    He mustn't be one of those foolish ones,
    he owed it to his family, his nation,
    his own sense of responsibility, etc.,
    etc., and then the bell

35 rang, emptying his ears and mind of all
    save thought of kite and wind and sky.
    Creeping away to the rooftop after tea
    he tossed his friend up to feel the breeze
    letting string slide smoothly from the spool,
40 Thinking of Icarus and unlucky kite-fliers
    he lifted himself gingerly over the parapet
    to the cornice, holding on with one hand
    for support – he wouldn't fall, he was sure,
    he was a wise Icarus. The kite shot up,
45 up, up as ah! ohms of sweet sensations shot
    through the nerves. The world became a million
    million strings of electric guitars.
    He hummed in accompaniment;
    but just a snatch,

50 stopped short
    by a brick coming off in his hand,
    The cornice hit his head, the string snapped
    and Batman swayed drunkenly downward to earth.
    He bounced off and slid through leaves
55 that rustled merrily and didn't moan,
    a stump of branch stabbed his ribs,
    the clothesline wished it were strong enough
    to slice through his young flesh.
    And when he came to rest
60 he didn't know himself
    from the soft,
    cold earth,
    poor boy,
    one more hapless Icarus.

§ *Myth reworked* Bhatt, Gooneratne (2); Carib: Lamming (2), Walcott (4);
SEA: Somtow

Pakistan

AHMED ALI (1910–94)

From Twilight in Delhi

Set in the early years of this century, *Twilight in Delhi* tells the story of a marriage between lovers from different sections of the city's Muslim community. However, the novel is first and foremost an elegy for an older Islamic world, as can be seen in the references to the departed 'glory' of Mogul India in this, the opening passage. The text's frequent use of poetry both contextualizes the present-day situation of its Muslim characters and also stresses the mutability and transience of existence. Ahmed Ali was a Delhi-born writer who migrated to Pakistan after the Partition of the Indian sub-continent.

Night envelopes the city, covering it like a blanket. In the dim starlight roofs and houses and by-lanes lie asleep, wrapped in a restless slumber, breathing heavily as the heat becomes oppressive or shoots through the body like pain. In the courtyards, on the roofs, in the by-lanes, on the roads, men sleep on bare beds, half naked, tired after the sore day's labour. A few still walk on the otherwise deserted roads, hand in hand, talking; and some have jasmine garlands in their hands. The smell from the flowers escapes, scents a few yards of air around them and dies smothered by the heat. Dogs go about sniffing the gutters in search of offal; and cats slink out of narrow by-lanes, from under the planks jutting out of shops, and lick the earthen cups out of which men had drunk milk and thrown away.

Heat exudes from the walls and the earth; and the gutters give out a damp stink which comes in greater gusts where they meet a sewer to eject their dirty water into an underground canal. But men sleep with their beds over the gutters, and the cats and dogs quarrel over heaps of refuse which lie along the alleys and cross-roads.

Here and there in every mohallah[1] the mosques raise their white heads towards the sky, their domes spread out like the white breasts of a woman bared, as it were, to catch the starlight on their surfaces, and the minarets point to heaven, indicating, as it were, that God is all-high and one . . . .

---

1 Locality.

But the city of Delhi, built hundreds of years ago, fought for, died for, coveted and desired, built, destroyed and rebuilt, for five and six and seven times, mourned and sung, raped and conquered, yet whole and alive, lies indifferent in the arms of sleep. It was the city of kings and monarchs, of poets and story tellers, courtiers and nobles. But no king lives there today, and the poets are feeling the lack of patronage; and the old inhabitants, though still alive, have lost their pride and grandeur under a foreign yoke. Yet the city stands still intact, as do many more forts and tombs and monuments, remnants and reminders of old Delhis, holding on to life with a tenacity and purpose which is beyond comprehension and belief.

It was built after the great battle of Mahabharat by Raja Yudhishtra in 1453 B.C., and has been the cause of many a great and historic battle. Destruction is in its foundations and blood is in its soil. It has seen the fall of many a glorious kingdom, and listened to the groans of birth. It is the symbol of Life and Death, and revenge is its nature.

Treacherous games have been played under its skies, and its earth has tasted the blood of kings. But still it is the jewel of the eye of the world, still it is the centre of attraction. Yet gone is its glory and departed are those from whom it got the breath of life. Where are the Kauravs and the Pandavas?[2] Where are the Khiljis and the Saiyyeds?[3] Where are Babur and Humayun and Jahangir?[4] Where is Shah Jahan[5] who built the city where it stands today? And where is Bahadur Shah[6], the tragic poet and the last of that noble line? Gone they are, gone and dead beneath the all-embracing earth. Only some monuments remain to tell its sad story and to remind us of the glory and splendour – a Qutab Minar or a Humayun's Tomb, the Old Fort or the Jama Mosque, and a few sad verses to mourn their loss and sing the tale of mutability:

> I'm the light of no one's eye,
> The rest of no one's heart am I.
> That which can be of use to none
> Just a handful of dust am I.

And, as if to echo the poet king's thoughts, a silence and apathy of death descended upon the city, and dust began to blow in its streets, and ruin came upon its culture and its purity. Until the last century it had held its head high, and tried to preserve its chastity and form. Though the poet who sang its last dirges while travelling in a bullock-cart to Lucknow, city of the rival culture, managed to keep silent and, to preserve the chastity of his tongue, did not indulge in conversation with his companion yet when he reached that other town and sat in the crowd to be asked to recite his verse no one extended to him the invitation. For no one knew him, until, seeing his plight, one man asked him where he hailed from, and thus he replied:

> Why do you ask my native place,

---

2 Warring families in the Sanskrit epic, the *Mahabharata*. 3 Direct descendants of the Prophet Mohammed. 4 Mogul emperors. 5 Mogul emperor, famed for his architectural achievements which included the building of the Taj Mahal. 6 Last of the Mogul emperors, who ruled under the British and who after the Indian Mutiny was deported to Rangoon.

O dwellers of the East,
Making mock of me for the poor plight I am in?
Delhi, which was once the jewel of the world,
Where dwelt only the loved ones of fate,
Which has now been ruined by the hand of Time,
I'm a resident of that storm-tossed place . . . .

But gone are the poets too, and gone is its culture. Only the coils of the
rope, when the rope itself has been burnt, remain, to remind us of past
splendour. Yet ruin has descended upon its monuments and buildings, upon
its boulevards and by-lanes. Under the tired and dim stars the city looks
deathly and dark. The kerosene lamps no doubt light its streets and roads;
but they are not enough, as are not enough the markets and the gardens, to
revive the light that floated on the waters of the Jamuna or dwelt in the
heart of the city. Like a beaten dog it has curled its tail between its legs,
and lies lifeless in the night as an acknowledgment of defeat.

Still a few shops of the milk-sellers are open, and someone comes and
buys a couple of pice worth of milk, drinks it, and throws the earthen cup
away to be licked by cats who steal out of dark corners. And still a beggar
or two goes by singing in a doleful voice his miserable song, tap-tapping the
slab-paved streets with his bamboo stick, or whining in front of doors:

'Give in the name of God, mother, and may thy children live long.'

Or a belated flower-vendor sells jasmines in a sing-song voice putting one
hand on his ear, holding the basket to his side with the other, shouting in
resonant tones: 'Buy the flowers of jasmine.'

But the city lies indifferent or asleep, breathing heavily under a hot and
dusty sky. Hardly anyone stops the flower-vendor to buy jasmines or opens
a door to satisfy the beggar. The nymphs have all gone to sleep, and the
lovers have departed.

Only narrow by-lanes and alleys, insidious as a game of chess, intersect
the streets and the city like the deep gutters which line them on either side,
and grow narrower as you plunge into them, giving a feeling of suffocation
and death, until they terminate at some house front or meet another net of
by-lanes as insidious as before.

Such a net of alleys goes deep into the bowels of the city shooting from
Lal Kuan, and going into Kucha Pandit turns to the right and terminates at
Mohallah Niyaryan, which has a net of by-lanes of its own. One branch of
it comes straight on, tortuous and winding, growing narrower like the road
of life, and terminates at the house of Mir Nihal. As you look at it only a
wall faces you, and in the wall a door. Nothing else. As you enter the house
through the vestibule you come into an inner courtyard. Right in front is a
low kotha[7] and under it two small rooms. On the left is an arched veranda
opening on to a raised platform made of brick and behind it a long room.
On either side of the veranda and the platform are small rooms, and by the
side of the entrance is the lavatory, a narrow bathroom, then the kitchen

---

7 An upper-storey house.

black with smoke. In the centre of the courtyard an old date palm tree raises its head up towards the sky, and its long leaves clustering together conceal a part of the sky from view, and its trunk, curved and sagged in the middle, looks ugly and dark. At the foot of the date palm a henna tree is growing, and sparrows have built their nests in its branches. Two earthen dishes hang from it, one full of water the other of grain for the sparrows and wild pigeons who have built their nests in the cornices of the veranda and in the thick red and white curtains hanging above the arches.

By the wall of the kotha are flat wooden couches with a red cloth covering them; and on the platform and in the courtyard are beds covered with white bed sheets which glow in the dim light of a kerosene lantern.

An old lady in her fifties is lying on one of the beds in the courtyard with her head-cloth lying near her. On another bed are Mehro Zamani, her youngest daughter, a girl of fourteen, healthy and plump, and Masroor, a young boy of about thirteen, her nephew, a cousin's son.

'It must be eleven o'clock, and your father has not come back yet,' Begam Nihal says to her daughter. 'You'd better go to sleep. It is very late.'

'No, mother,' her daughter says to her, ' the story you were telling us was so good. I am not sleepy. Tell us another.'

The old lady fanned herself and said:

'You have heard enough for today.'

'But, aunt, do tell us the story of the king who had turned into a snake,' said Masroor turning on his stomach and looking at his aunt expectantly.

'We have heard that,' said Mehro Zamani as she fanned herself. 'Amma, tell us what happened in the Mutiny. You were once telling us how the Farangis[8] had turned all the Mussalmans out of the city. Why did they do that?'

'It's a long story. I will tell you some other day,' the old lady replied. 'Your father will be coming soon. And the heat is so oppressive. . . .'

The young folk feel disappointed. It is late and they are sleepy.

Mehro lies on her bed and looks up at the stars, and vague thoughts come into her mind, thoughts of kings and princes and soldiers. She thinks of a man far away whose proposal has come for her hand. What can he be like? She wonders. She has never seen him. They are extremely rich people, she has heard; and Meraj – that is his name – is very fond of shooting. And she associates him with the Prince in the story with whom the Princess was in love. But the thought of leaving the home, her father and mother, brothers and relations, comes into her mind. She heaves a sigh, and feeling dejected and downcast closes her eyes.

Masroor has already gone to sleep.

Begam Nihal sits up, draws her dome-shaped paan[9]-box, puts lime and katha[10] on a betel leaf, then adds finely-cut areca nut,[11] some cardamom, a little tobacco, rolls it up and puts it in her mouth. Then she lies down again

8 Foreigners. 9 Betel-leaf with nuts in it. 10 Astringent and narcotic vegetable eaten in betel-leaf. 11 Astringent nut, used for betel-chewing.

and begins to fan herself, occasionally fanning her daughter too . . . .

'Hai, hai, what has happened to my fan? Bi Anjum, are you awake ? Have you seen my fan?' comes a voice from the kotha.

'What do I know of your fan? the other voice replies. 'It must be on your bed.'

'It is not here.'

'Then it must have fallen down. . . .'

Then a silence descends upon the house. A gust of hot wind blows, and the leaves of the date palm rustle. The lantern flickers, but the flame steadies again.

§ *Delhi* Desai

BAPSI SIDHWA (1938–)

From Ice-Candy-Man

Like *The Shadow Lines*, *Ice-Candy-Man* shows the impact of Partition on individual lives. At the beginning of the novel the Parsee narrator Lenny is a small child afflicted with polio, growing up in Lahore. Her eighteen-year-old Ayah, Shanta, takes her to the park where they encounter Ayah's various admirers, who represent a varied range of occupations and communities. As Independence and Partition loom, people become increasingly obsessed with communal divisions, while the innocent Lenny asks 'Can one break a country?' The extracts included here are from the first half of the novel and introduce the 'shady' figure of Ice-candy-man, who will subsequently betray Ayah into prostitution. When Gandhi visits Lahore in the second of the three extracts, Lenny is struck by the 'ice lurking deep beneath [his] hypnotic and dynamic femininity'.

. . . We no longer use the pram to visit Godmother's house: it is a short ten minute walk. But when Ayah[1] takes me up Queens Road, past the YWCA, past the Freemasons' Lodge, which she calls 'The Ghost Club', and across the Mall to the Queen's statue in the park opposite the Assembly Chambers, I'm still pushed in a pram. I love it.

Queen Victoria, cast in gunmetal, is majestic, massive, overpowering, ugly. Her statue imposes the English Raj in the park. I lie sprawled on the grass, my head in Ayah's lap. The Fallettis Hotel cook, the Government House gardener, and an elegant, compactly muscled head-and-body masseur sit with us. Ice-candy-man is selling his popsicles to the other groups lounging on the grass. My mouth waters. I have confidence in Ayah's chocolate chemistry . . . lank and loping the Ice-candy-man cometh . . .

I take advantage of Ayah's admirers. 'Massage me!' I demand, kicking the handsome masseur. He loosens my laces and unbuckles the straps gripping

---

1 Nanny; nursemaid.

my boots. Taking a few drops of almond oil from one of the bottles in his cruet set, he massages my wasted leg and then my okay leg. His fingers work deftly, kneading, pummelling, soothing. They are knowing fingers, very clever, and sometimes, late in the evening, when he and Ayah and I are alone, they massage Ayah under her sari. Her lids close. She grows still and languid. A pearly wedge gleams between her lips and she moans, a fragile, piteous sound of pleasure. Very carefully, very quietly, I manoeuvre my eyes and nose. It is dark, but now and then a dart of twilight illuminates a subtle artistry. My nose inhales the fragrance of earth and grass – and the other fragrance that distils insights. I intuit the meaning and purpose of things. The secret rhythms of creation and mortality. The essence of truth and beauty. I recall the choking hell of milky vapours and discover that heaven has a dark fragrance. . . .

Gandhijee visits Lahore. I'm surprised he exists. I almost thought he was a mythic figure. Someone we'd only hear about and never see. Mother takes my hand. We walk past the Birdwood Barracks' sepoy[2] to the Queens Road end of Warris Road, and enter the gates of the last house.

We walk deep into a winding, eucalyptus-shaded drive: so far in do we go that I fear we may land up in some private recess of the zoo and come face to face with the lion. I drag back on Mother's arm, vocalising my fear, and at last Mother hauls me up some steps and into Gandhijee's presence. He is knitting. Sitting cross-legged on the marble floor of a palatial veranda, he is surrounded by women. He is small, dark, shrivelled, old. He looks just like Hari, our gardener, except he has a disgruntled, disgusted and irritable look, and no one'd dare pull off his dhoti![3] He wears only the loin-cloth and his black and thin torso is naked.

Gandhijee certainly is ahead of his times. He already knows the advantages of dieting. He has starved his way into the news and made headlines all over the world.

Mother and I sit in a circle with Gita and the women from Daulatram's house. A pink-satin bow dangling from the tip of her stout braid, Gita looks ethereal and content – as if washed of all desire. I notice the same look on the faces of the other women. Whatever his physical shortcomings, Gandhijee must have some concealed attractions to inspire such purified expressions.

Lean young women flank Gandhijee. They look different from Lahori women and are obviously a part of his entourage. The pleasantly plump Punjabi women, in shalwar-kamizes and saris, shuffle from spot to spot. Barely standing up, they hold their veils so that the edges don't slip off their heads as they go to and from Gandhijee. The women are subdued, receptive; as when one sits with mourners.

Someone takes Mother's hand, and hand in hand we go to Gandhijee. Butter wouldn't melt in our mouths. Gandhijee politely puts aside his knitting and uncreases his disgruntled scowl; and with an irrelevance I find alarm-

---

2 Indian soldier (in colonial period). 3 Traditional Indian male garment, covering body from waist to ankle.

ing, says softly, 'Sluggish stomachs are the scourge of the Punjabis . . . too much rich food and too little exercise. The cause of India's ailments lies in our clogged alimentary canals. The hungry stomach is the scourge of the poor – and the full stomach of the rich.'

Beneath her blue-tinted and rimless glasses Mother's eyes are downcast, her head bowed, her bobbed hair – and what I assume is her consternation – concealed beneath her sari. But when Gandhijee pauses, she gives him a sidelong look of rapt and reverent interest. And two minutes later, not the least bit alarmed, she earnestly furnishes him with the odour, consistency, time and frequency of her bowel movements. When she is finished she bows her head again, and Gandhijee passes his hand over her head: and then, absently, as if it were a tiresome after-thought, over mine.

'Flush your system with an enema, daughter,' says Gandhijee, directing his sage counsel at my mother. 'Use plain, lukewarm water. Do it for thirty days . . . every morning. You will feel like a new woman.

'Look at these girls,' says Gandhijee, indicating the lean women flanking him. 'I give them enemas myself – there is no shame in it – I am like their mother. You can see how smooth and moist their skin is. Look at their shining eyes!'

The enema-emaciated women have faint shadows beneath their limpid eyes and, moist-skinned or not, they are much too pale, their brown skins tinged by a clayish pallor.

Gandhijee reaches out and suddenly seizes my arm in a startling vice. 'What a sickly-looking child,' he announces, avoiding my eye. 'Flush her stomach! Her skin will bloom like roses.'

Considering he has not looked my way even once I am enraged by his observation. 'An enema a day keeps the doctor away,' he crows feebly, chortling in an elderly and ghoulish way, his slight body twitching with glee, his eyes riveted upon my mother.

I consider all this talk about enemas and clogged intestines in shocking taste: and I take a dim and bitter view of his concern for my health and welfare. Turning up my nose and looking down severely at this improbable toss-up between a clown and a demon I am puzzled why he's so famous – and suddenly his eyes turn to me. My brain, heart and stomach melt. The pure shaft of humour, compassion, tolerance and understanding he directs at me fuses me to everything that is feminine, funny, gentle, loving. He is a man who loves women. And lame children. And the untouchable sweeper – so he will love the untouchable sweeper's constipated girl-child best. I know just where to look for such a child. He touches my face, and in a burst of shyness I lower my eyes. This is the first time I have lowered my eyes before man.

It wasn't until some years later – when I realised the full scope and dimension of the massacres – that I comprehended the concealed nature of the ice lurking deep beneath the hypnotic and dynamic femininity of Gandhi's non-violent exterior.

And then, when I raised my head again, the men lowered their eyes. . . .

There is much disturbing talk, India is going to be broken. Can one break a country? And what happens if they break it where our house is? Or crack it further up on Warris Road? How will I ever get to godmother's then?

I ask Cousin.

'Rubbish,' he says, 'no one's going to break India. It's not made of glass!'

I ask Ayah.

'They'll dig a canal . . .' she ventures. 'This side for Hindustan and this side for Pakistan. If they want two countries, that's what they'll have to do – crack India with a long, long canal.'

Gandhi, Jinnah, Nehru, Iqbal, Tara Singh, Mountbatten[4] are names I hear. And I become aware of religious differences.

It is sudden. One day everybody is themselves – and the next day they are Hindu, Muslim, Sikh, Christian. People shrink, dwindling into symbols. Ayah is no longer just my all-encompassing Ayah – she is also a token. A Hindu. Carried away by a renewed devotional fervour she expends a small fortune in joss-sticks, flowers and sweets on the gods and goddesses in the temples.

Imam Din and Yousaf, turning into religious zealots, warn Mother they will take Friday afternoons off for the Jumha prayers. On Fridays they set about preparing themselves ostentatiously. Squatting atop the cement wall of the garden tank they hold their feet out beneath the tap and diligently scrub between their toes. They wash their heads, arms, necks and ears and noisily clear their throats and noses. All in white, check prayer scarves thrown over their shoulders, stepping uncomfortably in stiff black Bata shoes worn without socks, they walk out of the gates to the small mosque at the back of Queens Road. Sometimes, at odd hours of the day, they spread their mats on the front lawn and pray when the muezzin[5] calls. Crammed into a narrow religious slot they too are diminished: as are Jinnah and Iqbal, Ice-candy-man and Masseur.

Hari and Moti-the-sweeper and his wife Muccho, and their untouchable daughter Papoo, become ever more untouchable as they are entrenched deeper in their low Hindu caste. While the Sharmas and the Daulatrams, Brahmins like Nehru, are dehumanised by their lofty caste and caste-marks.

The Rogers of Birdwood Barracks, Queen Victoria and King George are English Christians: they look down their noses upon the Pens who are Anglo-Indian, who look down theirs on the Phailbuses who are Indian-Christian, who look down upon all non-Christians.

Godmother, Slavesister, Electric-aunt and my nuclear family are reduced to irrelevant nomenclatures – we are Parsee.

What is God?

All morning we hear Muccho screeching at Papoo. 'I turn my back; the bitch slacks off! I say something; she becomes a deaf-mute. I'll thrash the wickedness out of you!'

---

4 Leaders of various communities and groups prior to Independence. 5 Muslim crier who calls people to prayer.

'I don't know what jinn's[6] gotten into that women,' says Ayah. 'She can't leave the girl alone!'

I have made several trips to the back, hanging around the quarters on some pretext or other, and with my presence protecting Papoo.

Papoo hardly ever plays with me now. She is forever slapping the dough into chapatties, or washing, or collecting dung from the road and plastering it on the walls of their quarters. The dried dung cakes provide fuel.

In the evening she sweeps our compound with a stiff reed *jharoo*,[7] spending an hour in a little cloud of dust, an infant stuck to her hip like a growth.

Though she looks more ragged – and thin – her face and hands splotched with pale dry patches and her lips cracked, she is as cheeky as ever with her mother. And forever smiling her handsome roguish smile at us.

Late that evening Ayah tells me that Muccho is arranging Papoo's marriage.

I am seven now, so Papoo must be eleven.

My perception of people has changed.

I still see through to their hearts and minds, but their exteriors superimpose a new set of distracting impressions.

The tuft of *bodhi*[8]-hair rising like a tail from Hari's shaven head suddenly appears fiendish and ludicrous.

'Why do you shave your head like that?' I say disparagingly.

'Because we've always done so, Lenny baby, from the time of my grandfather's grandfathers . . . it's the way of our caste.'

I'm not satisfied with his answer.

When Cousin visits that evening I tell him what I think. 'Just because his grandfathers shaved their heads and grew stupid tails is no reason why Hari should.'

'Not as stupid as you think,' says Cousin. 'It keeps his head cool and his brain fresh.'

'If that's so,' I say, challenging him, 'why don't you shave your head? Why don't Mother and Father and Godmother and Electric-aunt and . . .'

Cousin stops my mouth with his hand and as I try to bite his fingers and wiggle free, he shouts into my ears and tells me about the Sikhs.

I stop wiggling. He has informed me that the Sikhs become mentally deficient at noon. My mouth grows slack under his palm. He carefully removes his hand from my gaping mouth and, resuming his normal speaking voice, further informs me: 'All that hair not only drains away their grey-matter, it also warms their heads like a tea-cosy. And at twelve o'clock, when the heat from the sun is at its craziest, it addles their brains!'

It is some hours before I can close my gaping mouth. Immediately I rush

---

6 Spirit. 7 Broom. 8 Tufted.

to Imam Din and ask if what Cousin says is true.

'Sure,' he says, pushing his hookah away and standing up to rake the ashes.

'Just the other day Mr Singh milked his cow without a bucket. He didn't even notice the puddle of milk on the ground . . . It was exactly two seconds past twelve!'

Cousin erupts with a fresh crop of Sikh jokes.

And there are Hindu, Muslim, Parsee, and Christian jokes.

I can't seem to put my finger on it – but there is a subtle change in the Queen's Garden. Sitting on Ayah's crossed legs, leaning against her chocolate softness, again the unease at the back of my mind surfaces.

I fidget restlessly on Ayah's lap and she asks: 'What is it, Lenny? You want to do soo-soo?'

I nod, for want of a better explanation.

'I'll take her,' offers Masseur, getting up.

Masseur leads me to the Queen's platform. Squatting beneath the English Queen's steely profile, my bottom bared to the evening throng, I relieve myself of a trickle.

'Oye! What are you gaping at?' Masseur shouts at a little Sikh boy who has paused to watch. His long hair, secured in a top-knot, is probably already addling his brain.

Masseur raises his arm threateningly and shouts: 'Scram!'

The boy flinches, but returning his eyes to me, stays his ground.

The Sikhs are fearless. They are warriors.

I slide my eyes away and, pretending not to notice him, stand up and raise my knickers. As Masseur straightens the skirt of my short frock I lean back against his legs and shyly ogle the boy.

Masseur gropes for my hand. But I twist and slip away and run to the boy and he, pretending to be a steam-engine, 'chook-chooking' and glancing my way, leads me romping to his group.

The Sikh women pull me to their laps and ask my name and the name of my religion.

'I'm Parsee,' I say.

'O *kee*? What's that?' they ask: scandalised to discover a religion they've never heard of.

That's when I realise what has changed. The Sikhs, only their rowdy little boys running about with hair piled in top-knots, are keeping mostly to themselves.

Masseur leans into the group and placing a firm hand on my arm drags me away.

We walk past a Muslim family. With their burka-veiled[9] women they too sit apart. I turn to look back. I envy their children. Dressed in satins and high heels, the little Muslim girls wear make-up.

---

9 Muslim woman's enveloping garment.

A group of smooth-skinned Brahmins and their pampered male offspring form a tight circle of supercilious exclusivity near ours.

Only the group around Ayah remains unchanged. Hindu, Muslim, Sikh, Parsee are, as always, unified around her.

I dive into Ayah's lap.

As soon as I am settled, and Ayah's absorption is back with the group, the butcher continues the interrupted conversation:

'You Hindus eat so much beans and cauliflower I'm not surprised your yogis levitate. They probably fart their way right up to heaven!' He slips his palm beneath his armpit and, flapping his other arm like a chicken-wing, generates a succession of fart-like sounds.

I think he's so funny I laugh until my tummy hurts. But Ayah is not laughing. 'Stop it,' she says to me in a harsh sombre whisper.

Sher Singh, who had found the rude sounds as amusing, checks himself abruptly. I notice his covert glance slide in Masseur's direction and, looking a little foolish, he suddenly tries to frown.

I twist on Ayah's lap to look at Masseur. He is staring impassively at the grinning butcher: and Butcher's face, confronted by his stolid disfavour, turns ugly.

But before he can say anything, there is a distraction. A noisy and lunatic holyman – in striking attire – has just entered the Queen's Garden. Thumping a five-foot iron trident with bells tied near its base, the holyman lopes towards us, shouting: '*Ya Allah!*' A straight, green, sleeveless shift reaches to his hairy calves. His wrists and upper arms are covered with steel and bead bangles. And round his neck and chest is coiled a colossal hunk of copper wiring. Even from that distance we can tell it's the Ice-candy-man! I've heard he's become Allah's telephone!

A bearded man, from the group of Muslims I had noticed earlier, goes to him and deferentially conducts him back to his family. As Ice-candy-man hunkers down, I run to watch him.

A woman in a modern, grey silk burka whispers to the bearded man, and the man says, 'Sufi Sahib, my wife wants to know if Allah will grant her a son. We have four daughters.'

The four daughters, ranging from two to eight, wear gold high-heeled slippers and prickly brocade shirts over satin trousers. Frightened by Ice-candy-man's ash-smeared face and eccentric manner, they cling to their mother. I notice a protrusion in the lower half of the woman's burka and guess that she is expecting.

His movements assured and elaborate, eyeballs rolled heavenwards, Ice-candy-man becomes mysteriously busy. He unwinds part of the wire from the coil round his neck so that he has an end in each hand. Holding his arms wide, muttering incantations, he brings the two ends slowly together. There is a modest splutter, and a rain of blue sparks. The mad holyman says 'Ah!' in a satisfied way, and we know the connection to heaven has been made. The girls, clearly feeling their distrust of him vindicated, lean and wiggle against their mother, kick their feet up, and whimper. Their mother's hand darts out of the burka, and in one smart swipe, she spanks all four. Nervous eyes on Ice-candy-man, the girls stick a finger in their mouths and cower quietly.

Holding the ends of the copper wire in one hand, the holyman stretches the other skywards. Pointing his long index finger, murmuring the mystic numbers '7 8 6', he twirls an invisible dial. He brings the invisible receiver to his ear and waits. There is a pervasive rumble; as of a tiger purring. We grow tense. Then, startling us with the volume of noise, the muscles of his neck and jaws stretched like cords, the crazed holyman shouts in Punjabi: 'Allah? Do You hear me, Allah? This poor woman wants a son! She has four daughters . . . one, two, three, four! You call this justice?'

I find his familiarity alarming. He addresses God as 'tu', instead of using the more respectful 'tusi'. I'm sure if I were the Almighty I'd be offended; no matter how mad the holyman! I distance myself from him mentally, and observe him stern faced and rebuking.

'Haven't You heard her pray?' Ice-candy-man shouts. Covering the invisible mouthpiece with his hand, in an apologetic aside, he says: 'He's been busy of late . . . You know; all this Indian independence business.' He brings the receiver to his ear again.

Suddenly he springs up. Thumping his noisy trident on the ground, performing a curious jumping dance, he shouts. 'Wah Allah! Wah Allah!' so loudly that several people who have been watching the goings-on from afar, hastily get up and scamper over. Sikhs, Hindus, Muslims form a thick circle round us. I notice my little Sikh friend. I can tell from the reverent faces around me that they believe they are in the presence of a holyman crazed by his love of God. And the madder the mystic, the greater his power.

'Wah, Allah!' shouts Ice-candy-man. 'There is no limit to your munificence! To you, king and beggar are the same! To you, this son-less woman is queen! Ah! the intoxication of your love! The depth of your compassion! The ocean of your generosity! Ah! the miracles of your cosmos!' he shouts, working himself into a state. And, just as suddenly as he leapt up to dance before, he now drops to the ground in a stony trance. Our ears still ringing from his shouts, we assume his soul is in communion with God.

The woman in the burka, believing that the holyman has interceded successfully on her behalf, bows her body in gratitude and starts weeping. The bearded man fumbles in the gathers of his trousers and places two silver rupees – bearing King George's image – at the holyman's entranced toes.

§ *National identity/Partition* Ghosh; TransC: Ghose (2); *Childhood discovery* Selvadurai; Af: Gurnah; Carib: Lamming, Edgell, Senior; SEA: Maniam

ALAMGIR HASHMI (1951–)

1: So What If I Live in a House Made by Idiots?

So what if I live in a house made by idiots?
In the last one, holes were filled with toothpaste;
was so airtight breathing became a task.
Its bomb-shelters were excellent and made
5 you feel ready.
This has the walls wet (from tears it causes)
and sloughs every three months.
The floors are the best thing in it, get cleaned;
for the monsoon might blow off the roof,
10 yet can you imagine a house without a floor?
The lawn now has a few flowers to its credit.
But the grass keeps debiting. The municipal waters
give it further lease, and the insects introduce you minute
by minute to a part of yourself.
15 The sun can kiss the face and the back of its neck
at the same time. I call it a place to live.

§ *House as symbol* Ramanujan, Alexander, Wijenaike: Af: Dangarembga;
Can: Atwood (4); Carib: Walcott (1), Naipaul (2)

2: Inland

1
West Aliquippa, Pennsylvania,
is said to be
the only inland town in the U Ess
that can be entered or left
5 in just one direction.
. So that going in

and out of is all one thing,
a quality of feeling;
with the scenery first going
10 backwards, then forwards.

2
I was born in a place so
far inland of Asia
that only the mountains,
of Himalayan attitude,

15 could reach up
to the open air.
Then, so high, one
couldn't have breathed.

The gay sea breezes
20 only crashed down
there. The new geographers
call this Vale of Tears
a monsoon.
Urdu, optimist's algebra,
25 dubs it *Moon Soon*,
as if it were only
a matter of time.

3
Now I live in a country
where each town is inland
30 the moment you are out of town;
the sea having shied away
more than a glacier's age ago
and granted a conical tundra
of obese rocks
35 rising above ancient railway
stations.

Take Zurich, with its *Sackbahnhof*
swallowing trains by the minute
without a burp.
40 Then, the Moby Dick disgorges.
The flying eels
are frisky, with the thousands
in the body of steel.

4
Take this, my train. It leaves reverentially,
45 on back feet,
twitching
on each hairpin bend
to bite its own tail.
Inside, they smoke.
50 I suffocate.

---

37 *Sackbahnhof*: a station.

At the fifth kilometer,
a blue neon
says AIRGATE.
I can breathe now; wish
55   to leave by the other side
while the current lasts.

5
Yes, I can leave this train
for that shunting there: *ausserorts,*
agora, Ausland.
60   One of these two, painted green,
will arrive. I can still
board it at any junction.
After all, it is not the train
of thought.

§ *Mental geographies* Ghosh, Sidhwa; Aus: Malouf; TransC: Ondaatje (2)

---

59 *Ausland*: abroad; foreign countries.

Part VII

SOUTH-EAST ASIA

Malaysia

LLOYD FERNANDO (1926–)

From Scorpion Orchid

Scorpion Orchid is set in pre-Independence Singapore at a time of conflict and race riots during the anti-colonial struggle. In this troubled atmosphere, four undergraduates attempt to sustain their friendship, which can be seen as a microcosm of the ideal of a multiracial community since each represents one of the main ethnic groups of the region: Malays, Chinese, Indians and Eurasians. As can be seen in the second chapter, included here, Fernando's novel undermines Eurocentric historiography by inserting Malay intertexts into his narrative of recent historical events.

'There he is.'

'Where?'

'Talking to Huang.' Guan Kheng waved and shouted, 'Hey, Sabran!' He turned to Peter and said, 'Come on.'

'No, let him finish. No point going into that crowd.'

They stood to one side and watched the Chinese, Indians and Malays jostle out of the ground, unendingly it seemed. The lorries, neatly arranged in files, began to fill up. Banners of white cloth with slogans in English, Malay and Chinese crudely written in red and black ink began to unfurl and were held aloft on poles at each end. The men squatting in one lorry began to cheer and their applause was taken up by others. Singing broke out, ragged and out of tune, but soon gained tempo. They might have been football partisans returning from a rousing game.

'Look at those banners,' Peter said. ' "British Realty is sucking our blood", there, that one. If I were the governor I'd line them up and shoot the bloody lot of them.'

'Sabran too?'

'Sabran is a fool to get mixed up in this.' Peter was angry that they could not have the good times they had had when they first entered the university. 'Just wait and see when he starts looking for a job.'

Sabran saw them at last and dodged through the lorries which were grinding out, to the accompaniment of bursting firecrackers. It was the eve of the Chinese New Year. He wore a shirt with rolled up sleeves and crumpled trousers. He was trying to force himself to stop breathing hard. When Guan

Kheng asked, 'How did it go?' he said, 'Fine. Fine.'

Guan Kheng, impassive behind his rimless spectacles, asked, 'What does that mean? Joint union or no joint union?'

Sabran blinked momentarily. 'Of course we're going to join. You should have seen the men. I was doubtful at first. First, we introduced Thian, the President of the Prosperity Union. Thian spoke in Mandarin. Huang translated into English. Then I translated that into Malay. Then, Rassidi, the President of the Co-operative Union, spoke. I translated my translation into Mandarin. It was going so slow I was worried. Then Thian got up again and tried to speak in Malay. It was so funny the crowd laughed. I think that did it. After that it was all cheering.'

It was then that they found at the point of the headland a rock lying in the bushes. The rock was smooth, about six feet wide, square in shape, and its face was covered with a chiselled inscription. But although it had writing, this was illegible because of extensive scouring by water. Allah alone knows how many thousands of years old it may have been. After its discovery crowds of all races came to see it. The Indians declared that the writing was Hindu but they were unable to read it. The Chinese claimed that it was in Chinese characters. I went with a party of people, and also Mr Raffles[1] and Mr Thomson, and we all looked at the rock. I noticed that in shape the lettering was rather like Arabic, but I could not read it because, owing to its great age, the relief was partly effaced.

Many learned men came and tried to read it. Some brought flour-paste which they pressed on the inscription and took a cast, others rubbed lamp-black on it to make the lettering visible. But for all that they exhausted their ingenuity in trying to find out what language the letters represented, they reached no decision.

. . . Mr Coleman was then engineer in Singapore and it was he who broke up the stone; a great pity, and in my opinion a most improper thing to do, prompted perhaps by his own thoughtlessness and folly. He destroyed the rock because he did not realise its importance . . . As the Malays say, 'If you cannot improve a thing at least do not destroy it.'[2]

'I don't know what there is to cheer about,' Peter said gloomily. 'It means you are going to have a showdown with Realty. And that means trouble.'

'No. Just wait and see.'

'Let's go and get a bite,' Guan Kheng said.

'Sure. I'm hungry.' Sabran looked around. 'I thought you said Santi has come back from the Federation.'

'Yeah, he's back. He's somewhere here.'

'The bugger looks exhausted,' Peter said. 'Hollow eyes, and thin as a stick. Must have screwed all the female rubber tappers from Johore to Perlis.'

They saw him sitting on a bench at a vendor's stall outside the grounds,

1 Thomas Stamford Raffles, East India Co. administrator responsible for the acquisition of Singapore in 1819.
2 Like the italicized passage at the end of this extract, this quotation is from the *Hikayat Abdullah* (1849), autobiography of Abdullah bin Abdul Kadir Munshi, often regarded as the father of modern Malay literature.

eating a plate of fried *mee*,[3] Indian style. He looked up, his face streaming with perspiration. 'Your meeting okay?' he asked Sabran.

'Yeah. The committees of the two unions are going to meet next week. They are going to plan joint action. You want to come?'

'What, me?'

'Yes.'

'What for?'

'You could translate for the Indian workers.'

Santinathan kept his eyes on Sabran as he drained a glass of pink syrup. 'You're in for trouble if you don't look out, my boy,' he said at last.

'That's what I say,' Peter put in. 'You don't think the police are going to stand by and watch the country go to ruin, do you?'

'Don't be crazy, man,' Guan Kheng said.

'I'm not crazy. Just look at all those rumours, too many people are getting jittery.'

'You mean our unions must not join together because of the rumours?' Sabran looked steadily at Peter.

'No, man, I don't mean that. But if you have too many people excited all together with all kinds of rumours flying about, there's sure to be trouble. Stands to reason.'

Guan Kheng said, 'You better stop that kind of talk, Peter. Or you'll get us all into trouble.'

Peter lowered his voice. 'I have a cousin in the Police Force. He says they're really worried about Tok Said. They think he is the cause of all the wild talk that's going about. And until the talk stops, they're not keen about public meetings, rallies, marches and so on. That's all I'm trying to say.'

The four of them had been sixth-formers together and were now undergraduates in their third year at the university. They had moved in a group as young men who are contemporaries and enjoy company do, but the bond of their young manhood was wearing off and they were not fully aware of it yet.

The car park outside the grounds was nearly deserted, the dusk had deepened and the vendors were preparing to leave.

'We're going to get something to eat,' Guan Kheng said to Santinathan. A single cracker explosion out on the road punctuated his speech. From another part of the city the sound of the crackers was continuous, like distant gunfire.

Santinathan lit a cigarette and inhaled deeply. No smoke appeared when he breathed out. 'Who's paying? You? Okay I'll join you. This bugger's *mee* was not so good today.'

'I have a message for you from Miss Turner,' Peter said as they got into the car which Guan Kheng had hired for the evening. 'Next Wednesday you must bring out the five essays you missed during your Federation orgy, or else –'

---

3 Noodles.

Santinathan blew smoke out with a loud whiz this time. 'That bitch needs to be bedded with a gorilla.' As they drove through the streets he lowered his gaze from the unmoving black high up, down to the dirt-stained buildings below. A huge coloured wheel spun continuously against one wall and it seemed they drove on the rim of the wheel, moving in a vast circle while the coloured lights played on them like a kaleidoscope continually changing the colour of their faces, and the smoke from the exploding crackers smothered them so that they looked like refugees in flight.

The shutters were up in the street as they entered, but from several upper windows of the derelict houses there snaked long dark writhing lines whose ends, a few feet from the road, sparked and snapped continuously like snorting dragons. They did not speak. It seemed as if they were moving on a cloud of smoke. Guan Kheng drove slowly through the winding alley cluttered with hawkers' barrows. Their journey seemed endless. It was as if they had got into a rut as deep as the dark houses that lined the street, and could do nothing but follow its unknown course.

A paraffin lamp finally appeared at the end of the road where a dingy wall rose square in front of them, up into the blackness. Guan Kheng swung the car round until it nosed against a dustbin. The edge of the road streamed wet and bits of cast-off food glistened near the tables. A little boy moved forward as if in a trance and placed tiny saucers at the table where they sat. Behind them a lone Chinese violin scraped.

'Practically the only place you can get a meal anywhere tonight,' Guan Kheng said.

'I wonder if Sally will be here tonight,' Peter said.

'She'll be here. She's got no people in Singapore.'

'Santi, did you see the Thaipusam last week?' Guan Kheng asked. 'In Tank Road.'

'No. Why?'

'So many fellows carrying the *kavadi*.[4] You know how many? Over three hundred. Including Chinese. There was a real traffic jam I can tell you. I swear there was a fellow carrying one that looked like you.'

They laughed.

'Can you lend me ten dollars?' Santinathan's face shone with perspiration. 'For ten dollars I – I'll carry a *kavadi*. Ten dollars. It's cheap.'

'*Ka* – What's that?' Peter mockingly hummed Santinathan's up and down Tamil intonation.

'Do you know it was nearly the same for the fire-walking ceremony in Yio Chu Kang last year?' Guan Kheng continued. 'Nearly two hundred and fifty people.'

Sabran said, 'Same thing in Pulau Besar, off Malacca. Crowds visiting the *keramat*[5] of the seven Muslim saints. They cross in boats, make offerings and pray.' He stopped. 'Looks like a whole lot of people want to cleanse themselves.'

---

4 Decorated arch, carried on shoulders as an act of penance.   5 Sacred place; place of pilgrimage.

'Let's begin with a bath for Santi,' Peter said. 'He badly needs one.'

'I need ten dollars,' Santinathan said.

Sabran spoke to Peter. 'Ay, you don't know what is a *kavadi*?'

Guan Kheng was polishing his glasses. 'I bet you a hundred you'll never carry one.'

'Why should he know what a *kavadi* is? This is not his country,' said Santinathan. 'He's going back "home" – to England. Aren't you, Peter? Only with a name like his, I wonder whether they'll let him in. D'Almeida. Peter D'Almeida.' He whizzed out smoke rapidly.

'And what about you? If you ever go back to India, they'll put you in the Andamans,[6] that's certain.'

'What about it, Santi? Hundred.'

Sabran looked at Guan Kheng. 'Do you think it's because of Tok Said?'

'Maybe.'

'Well, what are the police worried about if that's what he's making people do?'

'It's too unusual, man, that's what,' Peter joined in. 'Usually there are about half a dozen – or at most a dozen at these ceremonies. Something funny is going on. It's like a scare. And the crowds – they're far bigger than in previous years.'

'Well let everybody repent – if that's what Tok Said wants them to do. And the police had better be grateful.'

There was a lull in the explosions. Now they sounded in single bangs behind which headless urchins lurked or darted.

'Ay, Santi look,' Guan Kheng suddenly leaned forward to point at something, and the loose wooden table top tilted up at him and fell back. The others turned to look. A figure dressed in white trousers and white shirt was approaching. In the smell and darkness of the alley it cut an incongruous figure.

'A freshie.'

'Yeh, the one we ragged last week.'

'Tell him to get lost,' Santinathan said. 'No, wait. Ask him to come here. If he can lend me ten dollars, I'll let him go.'

Guan Kheng got up and shouted, 'Hey, bastard. Come here. Come here.' The dim white shirt and trousers at the end of the street stopped moving. 'Come here, I say.'

'What do you want ten dollars for? For Sally?'

Santinathan puffed three or four times at the cigarette end. It was so short he held it carefully between finger and thumb, his cheeks puffed out and his eyes almost closed in the effort to avoid the smoke from the stub. At last he threw it away. He said seriously, 'You see, it's like this. My father is dead. My mother is sick and bedridden. I am the sole breadwinner of the family. We are four months in arrears of rent, and we have had nothing to eat but bread and water –'

---

6 Group of islands in the Bay of Bengal, formerly a penal settlement.

'Balls to you,' D'Almeida said conversationally. The white shirt had reached them, a tie knotted in front of it. Above it was a face whose youthfulness shone even in the paraffin light. The voice was nervous. 'Good evening.'

Santinathan lit another cigarette. D'Almeida's face straightened as though into a rectangle. Through tight lips he said, 'You haven't learnt yet, have you? Down.'

'Good evening, reverend sires.'

'Down.'

The youth stood still.

'I said down.'

'You can't do this to me outside.'

They laughed heartily. The urchins who had been exploding single crackers at a time stopped and approached, to enjoy the spectacle. D'Almeida caught hold of the tie and tugged three or four times. 'Down,' he said kindly.

When the youth was spread-eagled on the wet road face down, 'What are you doing here?' Guan Kheng asked him.

'I live in this street,' said the youth from the road surface.

They went through the routine, trying to think of new things to make the youth do, since the old things were not satisfying, nor even funny anymore. Or they said it was funny and didn't laugh. They made the youth 'pump' until he could no longer support himself on his arms and lay oblivious, panting on the filth at the side of the road. Then he had to slither up to Santinathan who put his foot on him saying, 'Stoop, villain, stoop! . . . er . . . what? Lie prostrate on the low disdainful earth, and be the footstool of great Tamburlaine,[7] that I may rise and go for my –' He broke off and asked, 'Where's Sally?'

Then Guan Kheng asked him to go and urinate in the monsoon drain. The youth got up and stood by the drain but there was no sound, and was called back again. Guan Kheng pushed a glass of water at him. 'Here, drink this, it might help. No, wait. This will speed the action up a bit.' He poured half a bottle of black sauce into the water. The youth closed his eyes and drank it, then went back to the edge of the drain.

Santinathan wasn't looking. The food had arrived and he began to eat, his eyes steady on the girl who had brought it. Her lips were smudged with red and her long hair, though combed, looked like dry coconut fibre. She wore a sleeveless white blouse and a cheap-looking satin skirt with a glittering brooch at the waist. She moved among them as old friends, before sitting down next to Guan Kheng.

Santinathan said, 'Ay, Sally. You don't love me anymore?'

'What for to love you? You got no money.'

They laughed.

'All right. Love Guan Kheng for his money. But love me for myself alone.'

---

7 An allusion to Marlowe's *Tamburlaine the Great*, Part 1, Act IV, Scene 2.

He put his hand on his heart.

Laughing, she said, 'I love Peter for himself alone. But you – not even for money. I think you better pray to God to change your luck.'

'We want him to carry a *kavadi*. That will change his luck,' said Guan Kheng.

'I know what,' said Peter. 'Let's all subscribe and send him to Tok Said. Sally, you agree?'

The smile left Sally's face. She fumbled with her brooch and looked away.

A brief silence caught them unawares. Peter broke it, saying heartily, 'I love you too, Sally. But right now I want a beer; what about you chaps?'

Guan Kheng removed his arm lingeringly from her shoulders and she went away. 'Why doesn't she go home – at least for the New Year,' he said, staring after her.

'Now don't start that,' Sabran said. 'It's like the first question a man asks a woman in bed. "What's a nice girl like you doing in a joint like this?" '

'But how many girls can you find like her?'

'Hundreds,' said Santinathan.

'You're wrong.'

Peter said suddenly, 'Did she get angry because I mentioned Tok Said just now?'

Guan Kheng waved a hand dismissively. 'Ah, come on, man, don't imagine things.'

Santinathan turned to the freshman. 'Have you got ten dollars?'

The freshman was beginning to feel that he had had enough. 'Ye-es . . . but . . . you can't –'

'Uh-huh. You want to use it yourself. Well, go and find your own whore. Go on, get out of here.'

'Hey, wait a minute.' D'Almeida got up sucking his teeth loudly, and called the freshman back. The figure returned disconsolately.

'Santi, you want to go?' Guan Kheng passed him a couple of notes. Santinathan got up and walked towards the staircase in the shadow.

Peter said, 'Freshie. Bastard. I'm talking to you, man. Do a war dance round this table.'

The street was deserted now. Even the urchins had gone, and only the burst of a firecracker now and then broke the stillness. It was the eve of the New Year, the time of the gathering of the clans, the time when old injuries are forgiven, and new beginnings made, a time of sadness for the loss of the passing years, and of hope for the future, a time when deep in the consciousness is the realisation of the appalling flow of time and the strange disturbing changes that make newer universes stare into existence.

The dingy shutters of the worn three-storeyed shophouses that cramped the street on either side were up; hardly a pedestrian appeared. Against the leaden-blue glare of the street lamp at the end of the alley, the three friends

---

8 Shadow puppet-play (see overleaf).

sat round their table, lean silhouettes in a modernistic *wayang kulit*,[8] while a fourth figure danced round them Red Indian fashion.

'Higher,' shouted Guan Kheng. 'Pull those knees higher. Stop!' The youth stopped and stood awkwardly. 'What, you haven't seen cowboy films? You haven't seen Red Indians dance, ah?' He turned to the others. 'What am I saying? He probably sees no other films. All right, come on, once again. And whoop louder.'

The majority of the female slaves were Balinese and Bugis. They were brought up by men of all races, Chinese, Indians, Malays, who took them to wife and whose numerous progeny are here to the present day. There were also Malay boats bringing slaves from Siak. A great number of them came from the hinterland of Siak, from Menangkabau and from Pekan Baharu. They were all being herded into Singapore, driven along the road and beaten with canes like goats being taken to the market. That is how slaves were sold during those days both in Malacca and in Singapore, like a cattle market. I went back to the town and told Mr Raffles about what I had seen. He replied, 'That business will not last much longer for the English are going to put a stop to it. It is a wicked thing and many people have gone and made reports about it to Parliament in England demanding that the slave trade shall cease.' And he added, 'It is not only here that this sinful business goes on. To England too boatloads are brought from other countries, and thousands of the black men are turned into slaves. Then they are put up like goods for sale in all the countries of Europe. If we live to be old we may yet see all the slaves gain their freedom and become like ourselves.'

§ *Federation* Carib: Bennett; *Alternative histories* Aus: Davis; Can: Wiebe; Carib: Reid, Walcott (3); SA: Rushdie

LEE KOK LIANG (1927–92)

Five Fingers

When I went into the room, he was sitting in his favourite chair, staring at the rows of books lined up in the shelves. He did not turn his head. He was always like that. But I knew he knew I was here.

I walked up, and drawing up a stool, sat opposite him, with the Chinese chessboard between us. We played quietly.

After a while, I said, 'Old Fellow, your mind is keen today. Perhaps that's why you make such a lot of money. You are not a fool like I am. Feeding four children is no fun, even if I have youth on my side. You are a wise chap, Old Fellow. That's why you don't marry. Why don't you marry, Old Fellow.'

As I spoke, he stopped looking at the chessboard. He sat up taut. He looked for a long time at me in silence, hardly breathing at all. With a quick motion he stood up; I thought he was going to strike me. But, instead, he gripped hard at my shirt. Without paying any attention to my protests he dragged me from my seat and pulled me after him with surprising vigour. We half ran through a narrow corridor, and upon coming to a small doorway at the far end, he turned to me.

'Come, don't be surprised. I have something I would like to show you.'

He went in and knelt down, while he fitted a key to a dusty chest in the far corner. He took out a box and handed it to me.

'Look into it, my child. Look.'

It was a beautiful lacquered box, about the size of a small volume, richly embossed with dragons, dark red in colour, with silver strips running along its borders. A bird, finely carved, having small dots of jade where the eyes should have been, perched, wings outstretched, on the top of its cover. I grasped at one of the wings and tilted the cover. I looked inside.

There, lying on the velvet bottom, was a hand. A female hand, embalmed. It was cut off above the wrist where the flesh appeared to be mutilated and dark brown.

'Look, my child, at the fingers. They once belonged to a girl hardly younger than you. The girl lived in a city a hundred and twenty miles from here. She studied at a private school. One day a boy came to the class. The boy was like you. Only younger. He was from a poor family. He loved her. He knew that she loved him too. He felt it. But they did not speak. No, good boys and girls never spoke to each other in those days. So they loved in silence.

'Then one day he found out that they had the same surname, just by chance, when the teacher called out their full names at the annual examination. No, now he could never marry her. Not even hope to. He should not continue to love her. He could not sin. He was not born to sin. But still his heart was hers.

'War started. The city was threatened and all the citizens had to evacuate. Their families moved to a village and happened to stay at the same old house. Their families did not know each other but because of their same surname, they shared the clan house together in time of stress. So they occupied two adjoining rooms, the only ones that did not leak, on the east side. There were no beds, no benches, no mattresses. All had to sleep on the floor. The boy's family took the first room. The second was taken by the girl's family.

'One night, the boy who had been sleeping on the hard floor next to the wall, discovered that some of the bricks at the foot of the wall were loose. He had no pillow. So he cautiously took them out, praying at the same time he might not disturb the spirits of this ancient building, and arranged the bricks so that he would be able to rest his head on them comfortably. The hole made in the wall was about a palm's width. He was about to sleep when he heard a rustling noise among the loose sand in the hole.

'Maybe it was only a rat, he thought. He turned over on his side and plunged his hand into the hole. He suddenly grasped at a thing. Soft and warm. Five of them. They were all wriggling in his palm. They struggled to escape. But he held tight. They moved to the left and right. Suddenly he knew. He knew and he trembled. The wriggling had stopped; and the imprisoned five, with twitching movements, lay in his palm. He slowly pulled the thing out. The wriggling started.

'But when he placed his face against the thing, the wriggling paused, and, somewhat nervously, the thing lay quivering on his face; the five explored. At first, with much hesitation but soon they gained confidence and with feather-duster strokes they played compassionately on his face. They ran over his eyes with cool steps. His eyes full of tears rubbed against them. Like a sponge they sucked up the wetness and bathed his whole face. He felt comfortable and happy. But they would not keep still. The mouth, the ear, the nose. To each one they talked. Sometimes gently, sometimes mischievously, giving hope and sympathy, but always with love.

'Night after night they came. At the approach of dawn they rushed back into cover. He got only a fleeting glimpse of whiteness and shapeliness. He dared not stop them or entrap them, for he knew that they were shy. Any bold move would have frightened them.

'One day the news came that the city had fallen, and the soldiers were fast approaching the village. That night, while the boy lay waiting, they crept out of the hole with slow mournful steps. They stood still, glowing at the tips, as the moonlight shone on them. They combed his hair, the five of them, with anxious and reluctant strokes. All of a sudden they pulled hard at his hair. They leapt full upon his cheeks and wrenched the flesh like the teeth of a trap. They went back to his hair. They returned to his face. The movements grew feverish. The boy sensed that all was not well.

'He lay still and listened to what they had to tell him. The message was simple. The soldiers were coming. They must leave him. The soldiers were coming. All this while the movements grew convulsive. He could stand it no more. They must not leave him. They must not. He had to tell. He put them between his teeth. He bit. The hysterical movements stopped. The five lay quiet and dazed by his violence. He placed his lips against the marks made by the teeth. One by one, his mouth pleaded with them, entreated them to stay longer, even for a night. His mouth pressed reasons and arguments on them.

'The next morning, the boy's mother told him that the family next door would stay for a few days longer than was at first intended. The girl suddenly refused to follow her family. For no reason, she regarded that day as an evil day and would not go. As it was mainly for her safety that the family had evacuated, they had to linger on. Dragging her away would not be possible, as silence and stealth were needed to slip through the sentries. When he heard it, he felt a great happiness.

'Towards evening, as he sat on the floor, he heard the sound of heavy, tramping feet. The soldiers. They knocked down the massive front door. He heard screams, pleading, helpless screams, from the next room. He rushed out; but a soldier smashed him down with the butt of the rifle. When he recovered they had all gone.

'The old house was silent: He went from hall to hall, room to room. There was no one. His mother and father, where were they? And she? He walked painfully across the idol hall to the backyard. And found her. Lifeless. Spattered with blood. It was all his fault. All his. He had to go away. But no. In a daze he went to the kitchen and took from the table a butcher's knife. He returned to her. He held the knife high up. It came down and he laughed.'

§*Gothic relationships* SA: Wijenaike

EE TIANG HONG (1933–90)

1: Heeren Street, Malacca

I
Gharry and palanquin are silent.
The narrow street describes
Decades of ash and earth.

Here in the good old days
5   The *Babas* paved
A legend on the landscape.

And sang their part –
God Save The King
In trembling voices,

10   Till the Great Wars came,
And the glory went, and the memories
Grave as a museum.

Ah, if only our children
On the prestige of their pedigree
15   Would emulate their fathers,

Blaze another myth,
Mediating in every wilderness
Of this golden peninsula.

---

1 Gharry: Indian carriage.
5 *Babas*: Straits-born Chinese.

1 palanquin: covered litter, usually carried by a number of men.

II
Newcomer urchin strides the gutter
20   Reeking cockroach, rat and faeces.
On *charpoy jaga* fast asleep.

Under antique lanterns
The *Babas*, comfortable on old benches,
Gaze at Fords and Mercedes

25   While swallows shrill
Shriek in the twilight
Stealing over the obscurity of eaves.

§ *Elegy for older ways* Wong Phui Nam; NZSP: Hyde

2: Arrival

And this is the terminus of truth?
Objective of the dreams and all
The speculations we saved up
A lifetime and paid for?
5   This dust and this laterite?

And this the welcome awaits us,
The glossy pamphlets promised
During the long hours to console
A tedious journey?
10   This dust on a barren ground?

Are we really arrived, have we
Really reached as the smooth guide says
The great and beautiful city?
Where the perennials thornless and lovely
15   Bear only fragrant thoughts and men
Open as flowers, pure as sky?

Dust grits my eye.

§ *Politics and private lives* Wong Phui Nam, Thumboo, Jeyaretnam; SA:
Hosain, Sahgal, Arasanayagam, Selvadurai

---

21 *charpoy*: rope bed.   21 *jaga*: guard.

WONG PHUI NAM (1935–)

Prospect in Spring

At the death of great houses
the waste of cities
the land returns to desolation
of its rivers   and its hills:
5   the high walls under a mild sun
lie fissured
           opened in great wounds
to the ravening tide of spring.
These flowers that well up from the ground
10   are tears   I will weep
against adversity.
    I think of you my children. My fear
darkens around this chirruping
of sparrows
15   fighting beneath the walls.
The skies these nights are louring   red
with beacon fires
          built for the invasion.
I would there were news from home.
20   Daily the comb slips more easily through my hair.
Of little use my passions   held
this hair-pin in my fingers
which will not catch then falls
from the hair against the palm.

§ *Politics and private lives* Ee Tiang Hong (2), Thumboo, Jeyaretnam; SA: Hosain, Sahgal, Arasanayagam, Selvadurai; *Elegy for older ways* Ee Tiang Hong (1)

MOHAMAD BIN HAJI SALLEH (1942–)

Do Not Say

do not say my people are lazy
because you do not know.
you are only a critic, an onlooker.
you cannot know or judge,
5   passing the kampong in your car,
staring at economic data.

---

5 **kampong**: Malay village.

do not think my people are weak
because they are gentle,
because they do not build skyscrapers.
10 have you ever worked in a ladang,
or danced the ronggeng?
can you sing the dondang sayang?
do not think that we have only music
because we love life.

15 do not write that we have no literature, culture.
have you ever listened to the sajak or pantun
stayed a night at the bangsawan?
have you read the epic shairs
or the theological theses?
20 how many times have you wondered about history in
the blade
and ancestry in the handle of the keris,
or felt the pattern of the songket?
have you lived in a kampong?

do not condemn us as poor
25 because we have very few banks.
see, here the richness of our people,
the brimful hearts that do not grab or grapple.
we collect humanity from sun and rain and man,
transcending the business and the money.

30 do not tell us how to live
or organise such nice associations and bodies.
our society was an entity
before the advent of political philosophy.

do not say –
35 because you do not know.

§ *Language usage* Carib: Brathwaite (3), Bloom; NZSP: Tuwhare

---

10 **ladang**: clearing for non-irrigated farming.
12 **dondang sayang**: a type of serenade in which both members of a couple sing verses alternately.
17 **bangsawan**: Malay opera.
21 **keris**: traditional Malay dagger.
22 **songket**: hand-woven cloth, shot with gold or silver thread.

11 **ronggeng**: dance for couples, sometimes accompanied by song.
16 **sajak**: form of modern Malay verse.
18 **shairs**: literary form in which the language is rhythmic.

K. S. MANIAM (1942–)

From The Return

The Return is about the experiences of a Malaysian Hindu community in the period before and after Independence in 1957. Events are seen through the eyes of a growing boy, gradually discovering himself and the world around him and moving away from his origins. Here, in the opening chapter, the focus is on his grandmother, who illustrates Hinduism adapting itself and changing in a new context, a process which is subsequently accelerated. Political events, such as the Japanese Occupation and the Emergency provide a backcloth to the action, further disturbing links with the ancestral past.

My Grandmother's life and her death, in 1958, made a vivid impression on me. She came, as the stories and anecdotes about her say, suddenly out of the horizon, like a camel, with nothing except some baggage and three boys in tow. And like that animal which survives the most barren of lands, she brooded, humped over her tin trunks, mats, silver lamps and pots, at the junction of the main road and the laterite trail. Later she went up the red, dusty path, into the trees and bushes, the most undeveloped part of Bedong. The people of this small town didn't know how she managed, but they saw her before a week passed, a settled look on her face, a firm gait to her walk.

A bit of land had been cleared beside the infrequently trodden path to the Hindu cemetery. From salvaged planks, no one knew from where, she nailed the first shelter among the many she was to design. Her three sons cowered in there most of the time.

'They were like chickens afraid of slaughter,' a man who had known my grandmother when she first got to Malaysia, said, laughing.

'She was a great walker in those days. She trudged to the estates, sometimes ten miles away, a load of saris she had brought from India on her shoulders. They were soon gone. Then Letchumunan, the textile merchant, gave her a cut for peddling his goods. But your grandmother wanted to light her own lamp! And her boys had become wild fowl, dust of all Bedong on their feet,' the man said, his eyes glazed with searching the past for my grandmother's image.

But she had become a tinker, the white flour sack of tools bulging on her back. The women who came to answer her calls, thought, having run out of initiative, that she had come to beg. My grandmother shook her head, refusing the glass of water or tea – she wanted work. Day after day she squatted in the common yard (the shared ground of Indian habits?) of several houses, her equipment set up. The children heralded her arrival with:

'The camel is coming! The hump is here!'

Under the ringing nickname, she bent proudly to her task. The white sack yielded a tiny stove, anvil, hammer, spatulas, rolls of copper, silver foil, aluminium, lead, and a husky bellows. The children wouldn't go away, hushed and crowded round her, waiting for a miracle.

'Bring out the pot we wanted to throw away last year!' some man jok-
ingly called one day.

My grandmother smiled to herself and fanned the coal fire with the bellows. She held the pot handed to her against the sky.

'It was like looking at stars on a lonely night,' she told me, when she
recalled, in snatches, her early days.

They crowded round her, jostling each other, to witness this pale woman,
head always covered with a sari border, fumble at the job. The bellows
husked, the coals danced blue, the tiny hammer and spatulas flashed, crossing the morning sunlight into a mysterious pattern. A knob-like steel rod
pressed and cajoled. The pot hovered, light in her hands, like a delicate butterfly over the flames. When she handed the pot back the man received it
reverently. My grandmother chuckled, recalling the man's surprise.

The Indian families in Bedong, within three months, had nothing to offer
except the respectful glass of tea. She ended her tinker's career and once
more stood, characteristically, at the cross-roads, contemplating a new job.
All her Indian skills and heritage had been depleted.

'It was like treading Indian soil once more,' she commented reflectively,
when she sat later on the *thinnai*[1] of her newly-built, first real house.

For a time, she said, she went around casting away the 'evil eye' from ailing children. I saw her at work, some years later, her reputation still undi-
minished. She would fast a whole day, then, travelling sometimes on rickety
bicycles, sometimes in rattling private cars, she alighted at the house of the
stricken, often in remote rubber estates. The older women in the family
sometimes did the job, but didn't possess the special 'touch' my grandmother
had. The victim of evil forces, usually emaciated, was led into the only bedroom the family shared. Under my grandmother's gentle hands the boy
squatted, trembling, on the floor. To the dust the family had collected from
the four corners of the house, she added certain leaves, extracting them from
her embroidered pouch. I don't know whether it was her mere presence or
the ritual itself which was effective, but the boy followed us to the door,
unaided, when we left. The handful of chillies, dirt, salt and leaves my grandmother had thrown into the kitchen fire crackled furiously, a sign that the
possessing spirit had to flee unceremoniously!

Another event interrupted her new development. The Japanese
Occupation put a stop to free movement. She reverted to farming, tending
her maize, tapioca and vegetable plots. She sold the surplus, accepting bags
of the almost-worthless Japanese currency. Years later our house in the hospital compound was broken into by thieves; they carted away a whole trunk
of what they assumed to be hoarded Malaysian notes. The moonlight must
have played a ghastly joke on them as they dug their hands into piles of the
banana tree bills.[2] We discovered the trunk abandoned a hundred yards away,
'our treasure' intact!

My grandmother barely survived the Japanese Occupation but already she

---

1 Raised cement verandah. 2 Currency used during Japanese occupation.

had become Periathai, the Big Mother. Even her grandchildren addressed her by that name. If they didn't, they were admonished by any Indian within earshot.

I was already attending school when Periathai built that real house of hers. It had a large, cool hall, a small room and an old-fashioned, Indian cooking place. We, her grandchildren, enjoyed more the colourful entrance to this house. A double-pillared affair, it had strange stories carved on its timber faces. The carver, a man who had come from India hopeful of a well-paid job, readily accepted the small fee and lodgings Periathai offered. His trudging through a series of rejections had made him a perpetual wanderer, a dependent on his story-creating chisel. He must have put all his disappointments, nostalgia and dreams into those four pillars. The walls, thinnai and even the *kolam*[3]-covered yard appeared insignificant. Some of the Ramayana[4] episodes stood out with palpable poignancy: Rama challenged, bow and arrow at the ready, yet his brows lined with anxiety for the missing Sita. The sculptured, fold-like flames envelope Ravana's palace and threaten to engulf Sita's tender, shapely limbs and breasts. One pillar carried the creation of the Ganges, the cascading water stilled, another the typical, rustic look of the Indian village.

Some Fridays, when Periathai said elaborate prayers, the grandchildren were invited. We waited for her, seated on the thinnai, observing the other houses, hemmed in by hibiscus hedges, isolated by a life of their own. The rowdier among us sprawled on the unclinging, plastered soil of the compound. Then the light dimmed and Periathai arrived with her hand-cart. She never said a word but we knew every gesture and movement of the ritual she enacted on such evenings. Preceding her to the communal bathshed, we washed ourselves reverently, then returned to the thinnai, a hushed lot.

Periathai forfeited her customary warm bath. Instead, she punished herself with cold water; we heard the slap of the water on her body resounding through the mysterious dusk. When she finally emerged she was dressed in simple, white garments, her face rubbed over with saffron paste. Her hair, let down completely, fell tapering to her knobbly waist. She was almost shy then, hardly daring to look at us. But inside the house – we had been instructed to witness, even to participate – she assumed an absorbed, impenetrable air. The complex series of events gave her no time to think.

Periathai opened one of the two tin trunks she had brought from India. Handling every object gently, she took out a statue of *Nataraja*, the cosmic dancer[5] ringed by a circle of flame, a copper tray, a hand-woven silver-and-gold sari, bangles and a *thali*.[6] These were laid out, Nataraja raised in the centre, on an earthen dais on the wall niche. Then she drew forth bronze tier lamps and, pouring oil from a clay container, she set them, three in number, alight. The sari, the jewelry and the idol glowed now, creating a

---

3 Intricate designs in courtyards. 4 One of the two great Sanskrit epics, in which the hero, Rama, rescues his beloved, Sita, from Ravana, the demon king of Lanka. 5 God responsible for the creation of the universe. 6 Sacred yellow thread worn by Hindu wives.

kind of eternity around them. Periathai sat cross-legged, hair wet and in unadorned clothes before the holy niche and entered a deep contemplation. Perhaps Nataraja spoke to her of the original spirit, and her personal articles of the home she had left behind. It was a re-immersion, a recreating of the thick spiritual and domestic air she must have breathed there, back in some remote district in India.

The spell broke the moment she turned and smiled at us. We scrambled for places on the large, iron bedstead beside which were ranged clay and copper vessels holding strange delights. There was a kind of dried, sour meat that tasted like stringy jelly. There were balls of puffed rice with just the right pinch of chillie, and from another long-necked jar came snaky bits cooked in thick treacle. We were only given two-tooth bites of these tasty morsels, more as an appetiser for the main meal on the thinnai. There, *vadais*,[7] left over from the day's sales, dhal curry filled with brinjals,[8] potatoes, pumpkin cubes, tomato slices and *avarakai* (Indian legumes), were served with rice. Those of us who had 'behaved' received a teaspoonful of home-brewed ghee[9] to flavour the spread. Then, with only a tier lamp placed in the centre of the most complicated kolam in the cowdung-plastered compound, Periathai told us stories. Her voice transformed the kolams into contours of reality and fantasy, excitingly balanced. I felt I stood on the edge of a world I may have known.

But this feeling came crashing down with the proclamation of Emergency rule over certain parts of the country. We lived under the regimented, dark sky of curfew land. The roads looked deserted even at the times they were opened to the public. An unshakable darkness fell over us, every night, at eleven when all lights had to be extinguished. During the first few weeks, strange apparitions appeared just inside the closed door, boisterous activities sounded in the bathroom and tins rattled. I dreamed always of a blood-covered figure suddenly confronting me with a blood-stained *parang*,[10] asking for sanctuary. We lived, officially, in what was termed a 'black area'. This designation covered small towns and remote kampungs[11] close to jungle fringes and foothills, perfect hiding places for communist terrorists. An English estate manager had been gorily stabbed to death in his lonely bungalow, only a few miles from Bedong. The other British planters, the handful who remained, went to their Club in Sungai Petani, escorted by the military in jeeps. Sungai Petani, my schooltown, was a 'white area', that is, a communist-free region.

Periathai's carved columns and kolams were neglected. She only spent the occasional night at home. Her adopted daughter, Pakiam, merely guarded the house against thefts. Determined to keep her vadai business going, she slept on a cramped, wooden platform at the back of a provision shop. The vadais would be ready, cooked on a make-shift stove, before the town was opened to the public for two hours in the morning. Then the siren went. Periathai hurried back to the Indian provision shop to wait for the two hours

---

7 Round dhal (or lentil) cakes. 8 Aubergines. 9 Clarified butter. 10 Long-bladed knife. 11 Villages.

of business in the afternoon. Grieved by the separation from me, she made me keep her company for a day or two. People used to look quizzically at her and a few bought her wares out of charity.

'Never let anything break your spirit,' she told me, though I didn't understand her.

On rainy days the streets were even more desolate, the nights completely dark, when only phantom figures squelched on the soft ground outside the window. I learned to live within prison conditions, danger massing beyond in the familiar surroundings, freedom only a dozen miles away. During the long, sleepless nights I thought sparingly; morning was a release, not an expansion. The darkness, the siren wail and an occasional gunshot built into a monstrous fear depriving me of normal behaviour. If curfew hours were reduced, as happened sometimes, to commemorate some national event, I didn't know what to do with the extra time. Used to seeing armed men at checkpoints, I panicked when there were none.

Periathai died when the curfew was lifted for good and the military disappeared from the scene in 1958. Her fortunes reached pre-Emergency prosperity, but the lump she had always had on her shoulder had grown to the size of a clenched fist. She tried to incise it but it never 'ripened'. Her sons took her first to the Group Hospital and later to the District Hospital in Sungai Petani. The doctor shook his head: it was terminal cancer. Periathai shrugged the diagnosis off and continued to occupy her place at the pawnshop pillar.

Her sons had their own families, so she expanded her house, adding to it two more rooms, and bought her adopted daughter jewelry. But some inner preoccupation robbed her walk of its customary jauntiness and her expression, this-world consciousness. These spells were, initially, fleeting, isolated incidents. It was when the Town Council officials got to her that she began to lose weight. She divided her time between her vadai hand-cart and the Town Council Office, appealing for land ownership on the grounds that she had occupied that bit of land long enough to be its rightful heir.

'My many spirits roam it,' she told me. 'When I die I'll never stop haunting the place.'

But she had no papers, only a vague belief and a dubious loyalty. The houses around hers were already being pulled down. Rafters, fallen beams and charred remains gaped like a death larger than Periathai's approaching demise whenever I went – and these occasions had grown fewer – to visit her. She refused to leave the house for fear that it might be demolished during her absence. Her customers sometimes placed special orders with which she kept herself busy.

The Town Council men sent her an eviction notice.

She covered her vadai hand-cart, stood it at the foot of the large bedstead, and didn't get up for almost a week. Her body began to waste away; her sons, their wives, and her grandchildren were constantly in the house. But she lay, her back turned against them, the fist-like tumour straining her blouse.

The weeks that followed emaciated her. Periathai soon lay, hardly rustling, like a wrinkled bamboo stem on the voluminous sheets. The Town Council sent her another official letter: she could stay in the house until her death. Periathai managed a smile when I got to a strangely deserted house that evening. She held out the envelope to me. When I finished reading the 'reprieve' she said:

'Lift me.'

I hesitated. She hadn't moved from the bed for more than a month.

'Lift me,' she repeated.

I took her by the arm-pits for she was light enough, but once on the floor she shook my hands off. Moving with great effort she wobbled towards the shrine-niche. Pakiam trailed behind and, obeying Periathai's unspoken commands, pulled out the tin trunk from under the bedstead. She took out the wedding sari, *thundu*[12] – all mildewed – and the thali. Laying them out on a copper tray, she placed it before Nataraja. Under her trained fingers the several wicks of the tier lamps sprang into life almost at once. Periathai knelt down painfully. The incense and camphor Pakiam burned filled the room with thick smoke. But somehow Nataraja glowed dully. The light that fell from the tier lamps didn't throw the tin trunk, mats, lamps and hand-cart into solid relief as it had on Periathai's ritual Fridays.

From then on she sank fast. Our parents warned us not to go near her. But we had to edge close to her to catch what she was saying. She talked with obvious effort, but talk she did, with a vague premonition, of all that her eyes had seen, her ears had heard, and to whatever her spirit had responded.

We moved in to listen to the saffron-scented, death-churned memories, stories, experiences and nostalgia. She was a child, a young girl, a new bride and a widow. There was rasping wind in her voice, cold fear, romance exalting strength and devastation. She blubbered most about the sea, crooning to it, beseeching for a safe passage with her tin trunks. Some mornings she was a freshly harvested field, smelling of stalks and turned earth. We forgot our parents' warning not to breathe in her fluid words too closely. We forgot and leaned against the curve of the land she built, now with desolating winds, now with a dark and humid soil and filled with abundant fruit. Yet it was also a land haunted by ghosts, treaded lightly by gods and goddesses, violated by murderers, where a widow went through the fire to reach a dead husband.

And now the town came to her, unable to face the empty pawnshop pillar. They streamed in continuously, stood silently at the large bedstead, stared at the covered hand-cart and, stirring themselves suddenly, went out to the kitchen, to a cup of warm tea and a plate of vadais. While she sank, while her body fluids dried up, a flow of noise and chatter built up around her. She looked out of gaunt eyes, now at this man, now at that woman, and they remembered the deft hands that had danced to a certain rhythm as she

---

12 Woven white cloth.

wrapped their vadais. If her body diminished, her eyes never lost their vitality. And on the morning she died, speechless, her eyes never spoke a farewell.

§ *Hindu acculturation* Carib: Naipaul (2); NZSP: Subramani; *Childhood* Af: Gurnah; Carib: Lamming, Edgell, Senior; SA: Selvadurai

SHIRLEY GEOK-LIN LIM (1943–)

1: Christmas in Exile

Christmas is coming and I think of home:
A colonial Christmas and second-hand nostalgia
As simple as home-made cottonwool snow,
Paste holly and a cheap plastic conifer.
5   Where Christ is born in odd conditions,
To customary churches and celebration.
O silent, holy night, we sing, beneath
The clear hot equatorial sky.
Where, as everywhere, even to the hour of birth,
10   Soldiers keep watch. Frivolity
Is circumscribed by birth, by death.

§ *Cultural colonization* Af. Dangarembga

2: On Reading Coleridge's Poem*

'Alone on a wide wide sea!' he wrote;
And we, reading this, wonder if he'd known
What it was all about. How then could he
With this passion live, frightening
5   Every stranger, the strange old sea-dog?
Or else made passionate monologue,
Out of harm's way, harmless, trusting
To construct passing and indestructible,
Word upon word, felicity?
10   Remembering too, the wished-for return,
The forgiving priest, the willing pilot,
The throng by the harbour, curious, appalled –
We could hope this was true; but know here
Like the passing stranger, only pity, fear.

§ *Responses to European texts* Lee Tzu Pheng, Somtow; Af: Coetzee; Carib: Lamming (2), Walcott (4), Gilkes

---

* 'The Ancient Mariner'.

Singapore

EDWIN THUMBOO (1933–)

Gods Can Die

I have seen powerful men
Undo themselves, keep two realities
One for minor friends, one for the powers that be,
The really powerful. Such people take a role
5 Supporting managers of state. And late
Accept some essential part, in some distant project.
But after a bit of duty,
That makes them fester with intentions,
They play the major figure to old friends.
10 We understand and try to seek a balance in the dark
To know the private from the public monument,
To find our way between the private and the public argument
Or what *can* be said or if a thing is meant
Or meant to make amends? is generous or mean?

15 The casual word, the easiness, the quick straight answer,
The humane delay, the lack of cautiousness
That gave simple laughter to our evenings
Are too simple for these days of power
Whose nature is to hint not state.
20 So when one has a chance to talk the conversation
Hesitates on the brink of momentous things;
He ponders . . .
Suggesting by some unremark
There was much more to be said.

25 It's a pity: good men who seek to serve
Blind themselves unto a cause,
Then use the fate of nations as a rationale
To take their friends aside,
To lead themselves into some history.
30 We gain uncertain statesmen: many lose a friend.

But I am glad that others are powerful with compassion,
Who see before we do what troubles us
And help in kindness, take ignorance in tow.
If not for such we lose our gods
35 Who lived but now are dying in our friends.

§ *Politics and private lives* Ee Tiang Hong (2), Wong Phui Nam, Jeyaretnam;
SA: Hosain, Sahgal, Arasanayagam, Selvadurai

LEE TZU PHENG (1946 –)

Excluding Byzantium: On Objections to Living Near a Home for the Elderly Sick

'That is no country for old men.'
The aging poet meant another place,
the body contemptible, incompatible
with the passions of the mind:

5   it is easier, somehow, to bear such ostracism;
art has the compensation of its own realities;
art can mould pain into singing birds,
and scarecrows image saints in holy fires.

Outside of art, what consolations thrive?
10 Decrepitude may push you to the side of life.
Sickness can make a stranger of the best-loved face.
Mortality's a monster, some think better
relegated to a hidden place.
Hospices and nursing homes may reek
15 of worse than age; a lingering pall
sour the taste of all human endeavour.
It takes much more than empathy, perhaps,
to receive the aged sick into our midst
without protest, even unvoiced, while
20 life points us to our expected end.

How many will have art to keep them safe?
How many, art to house our grim reminders?
We know we but banish ourselves to claim
'this is no country for old men'.

§ *Responses to European texts* Lim (2), Somtow; Af: Coetzee; Carib: Lamming
(2), Walcott (4), Gilkes

---

1 'That ... men.': cf. Yeats' 'Sailing to Byzantium', to which subsequent lines of the poem also allude.

PHILIP JEYARETNAM (1964–)

Making Coffee

On waking my thoughts are of the jungle, that half-hour before first light, shoulders numbly hunched over damp rifle, awaiting the dawn, air moist, bones cold. In the bathroom it is as if I have not shaved or showered for a week. I splash water onto my face with the eagerness of a young soldier back in camp after a week's patrolling. At least it has resisted the flab to which my friends have succumbed.

The maid has coffee ready downstairs, and Weixian packed and ready to meet the school bus. She's past the age when she might welcome a hug from her father, so I just smile and tell her to have a good day. I ask Nina if the mistress is up yet. She's not, so I open the newspaper and take a sip of coffee. I'm never fully awake till I've had my coffee.

Another day of meetings awaits me. The older I get the less real work I seem to do, the more it's just networking, pumping hands, that's what gets the business. There are always youngsters to keep the wheels turning, eager and bright, convinced that their big break is just around the corner. At four o'clock golf with the Minister. Mutual back-scratching, cooperation between government and business essential for the greater good of the nation. I tell him what the industry needs, he listens, adopts what he can, and projects to the public an image of assured competence. I am a man with connections, a man who gets things done.

On the green one often hears the crackle of small arms fire. I imagine young green bodies darting through the undergrowth, up, four seconds, down, cover, aim, fire, up, four seconds, on and on until nausea grips you in the pit of the stomach. Today the Minister is in a good mood, expansive, he tells stories of constituency dinners, when the garlands weigh him down like rubber tyres and he's introduced by some community worthy who keeps calling him Minster. He laughs at every story I offer, then nods solemnly when I say we really need more leadership if we are ever truly to go regional. 'We're all small businessmen. Comfortable making the easy money, scared of taking risks. Government must take the initiative. Break the old mind-set.'

Beers in the clubhouse turn into dinner. Without the Minister of course, he's off for some function or other. I eat with others who joined us over drinks, impressed not only by my nonchalant manner with the Minister, but also by the way I was on first-name terms with his bodyguard.

By the time I reach home Weixian is asleep. Shirley is awake in her room, watching TV. I enter, peck her on the lips, and after fielding the essential, dutiful questions retire to a glass of scotch. No massage interrupted my busy schedule today and my loins burn for a woman, even Shirley, but I leave it, knowing that I will only be rebuffed. One reaches a stage when things are too comfortable to risk any attempt at making things better.

This is not of course how it always was. Those were feverish days when I first met Shirley, a different faculty at the U but the same year, and so some three years my junior. I didn't feel comfortable with her at all, not at all. She was so good-looking, effortless in her movements, lively and charming. I felt leaden and dull beside her, old beyond my years . . . and challenged. I pursued her with a dogged single-mindedness, and when she finally consented to date me I did not stop until I held her naked in my arms. Touching the blood on the sheets I told her that now at last she was no longer a child, and now at last she was mine. She cried, and could not stop crying, though in between her sobs she told me how much she loved me. How good life felt in those days, to have a woman, to be doing well in studies, to have the world before me. Or even earlier, in Officer Cadet School, my whole life focused on graduating, obtaining a commission, not just for me, but for each and every member of my platoon. We were cadets together, striving for excellence, breathing duty, honour, country as we ran together, singing of our nation.

Life has gone well. A pretty wife, a healthy daughter, a house my parents could never have dreamed of owning. My middle-aged unease is really the purest self-indulgence. What more surely could I ask for?

The next day I visit my parents. I am always gratified by mother's fuss. Father is gruff, as usual. He hardly speaks. No doubt he resents the impotence of old age, the dependency into which my success has thrust him. Looking at those tough hands that once wielded ever so readily a stout bamboo cane I cannot resist a certain satisfaction. This quickly passes however, for I want his approval more than his resentment. I know he is disdainful of the fact that Shirley has not accompanied me, that she would never tend me as mother does him. He cannot understand that it is a different world, that no woman, at least no worthwhile woman, can devote herself to a man in the way that once was universal. They want their own lives, their own identities, and Shirley does a lot of good in the community, with charities and women's groups, though sometimes I wish she'd spend more time with Weixian (but who of course am I to talk?). Mother gives me *bak chang*[1] to take home, as if even after all these years away from her she must still make sure I'm properly fed.

She would certainly agree with the sentiments of the latest campaign to persuade people to marry younger and have kids earlier, that children bring purpose and direction to one's life, that one should live for one's children. The sentiments are noble ones, and yes I do love Weixian. When she's ill I ache inside at my powerlessness. But the campaign's message is fatally flawed, for if one human being lacks meaning, can find no purpose within his own life, how does it help, how does it supply that missing meaning, to bring another lost and lonely person into the world?

I wonder if Shirley's loins have welcomed other men since we married. She would be statistically anomalous if they had not, for she remains slim

---

1 Glutinous rice dumpling filled with meat and wrapped in leaf.

and pretty, and God knows what little sex we do have can hardly satisfy her. I marvel at my equanimity, my dispassionate contemplation of such matters, for it was only what some fifteen years ago when I had that fight, if one can call it that, with Dennis. He had been making passes at her, I'm sure of it, though she insisted it was only a matter of friendship. The bugger had not demurred when I accused him of dishonourable motives, nor put up any resistance to the two slaps I had given him, palm open, across his right cheek. These days I'd probably be glad if some man showed an interest in her. A welcome diversion, an amusement for her.

With the first person I pursued after our marriage I made the mistake of courting her, of pretending grand passions as in the days before I met Shirley, when I wanted a woman's body but not her heart, but knew one had to approach the average undergraduate, her head filled with romantic notions, from inside out as it were. I didn't realise the same rule does not apply to women who have broken free from adolescence, and so scared her into a kind, compassionate refusal of my advances. I did not make the same mistake again, and have enjoyed numerous desultory dalliances since.

I am interrupted in my early afternoon reverie, my usual eyes-open, day-dreaming nap, by Meng. He's one of my most enthusiastic young engineers. The sort of fellow who can be counted on for at least one useful incremental improvement to the production process every month, still young enough to enjoy the grand illusion that one of these days he'll come up with something really big, an idea or invention that will make him truly rich, and more importantly earn him universal fame and respect.

He needs my go-ahead on a proposal on which he sent me a memo a week ago. I can't remember having seen it until my secretary digs it out and reminds me that I'd KIVed it the week before. Ah yes, I rush to say, a very interesting suggestion, but it really needs to be passed through Ong and his team. Meng objects, he feels any delay is just a waste of money, but I silence him by asking him whose money is he talking about, and doesn't he understand the need to follow procedures in any organisation. He crawls away like a dejected puppy. My secretary raises her eyebrows at me, and I wonder if the two of them are having an affair for her to be so obvious about her sympathies.

I go home early for dinner, feeling the need to spend time with the family, only to find that Weixian has gone to stay at a friend's place, and Shirley's playing bridge at the Club. I watch TV, then read for a while. Nina comes by to ask if I need anything, and for a moment, idly turned towards her, I admire her curves, apparent despite the unshapely house dress, then quickly shut the door on such dangerous thoughts, the sort of thing that can ruin a man forever, and say no, thank you Nina, I can manage.

I think of my sisters, both overseas, one married to a Canadian doctor, another to an English lawyer. Both their husbands floated through Singapore sometime ago and were really blessed with remarkable good fortune in meeting and marrying my sisters. They were always devoted to me, and I am envious of their husbands, who have taken them away, so far from me.

They, and mother, were always on my side. No matter that I had tracked mud through the flat, they would happily clean it up before father's return. When he stood over me with report card in one hand, cane in the other, they were there to plead on my behalf. He probably felt his position undermined, his supremacy usurped, a long long time ago, long before I started work at twice the salary he had retired on.

Shirley comes home late. I hear her in the kitchen and go downstairs. There's alcohol, cognac I think, on her breath, and her eyes are a little wild. Where were you I ask, knowing what she will say, and that it will not be the truth. Playing bridge. The girls suggested a drink after. I nod, and help her with the coffee maker. We cooperate on the filter paper, the scoops of ground coffee, the water, and I think of late nights in the hostel, instant coffee then of course, nights of yearning before the net I cast had captured her, I think of stripping and assembling rifles, my section of cadets in one line, moving faster and faster with each practice until our fingers are rubbed sore, I think of late nights working through calculations, poring over designs, those early days of work. I kiss her hard on the lips, and then more gently, my tongue thrusting between her parted lips, her body giving as she leans back against the countertop. I taste the cognac, taste her and someone else, and feel myself harden against her. The coffee smells great in my nostrils as I stand here, enfolding my wife, mourning those days of grand illusion.

§ *Politics and private lives* Ee Tiang Hong (2), Wong Phui Nam, Thumboo; SA: Hosain, Sahgal, Arasanayagam, Selvadurai

The Philippines

NICK JOAQUIN (1917–)

From The Woman Who Had Two Navels

The Woman Who Had Two Navels is a classic study of fragmented consciousness, brought about by colonialism. Set mainly in Hong Kong, the novel is centred on the figure of the Filipina Connie Escobar, whose claim that she has two navels can be seen to embody the cultural confusion in which her country has been left as a consequence of its double colonization, by Spain and the United States. Connie's sense of anatomical abnormality and her desire to keep it secret also suggests a culturally engendered inability to accept her body. Here in the opening chapter she seeks help from a Hong Kong Filipino horse-doctor. He suggests that the root of her problems is not physical and she embarks on a quest for psychic wholeness, which results in her eventually accepting that she has only one navel.

When she told him she had two navels he believed her at once; she seemed so urgently, so desperately serious – and besides, what would be the point in telling a lie like that, he asked himself, while she asked him if he could help her, if he could arrange 'something surgical,' an operation.

'But I'm only a horse-doctor,' he apologized: to which she retorted that well, if he could fix up horses . . . And she cried that it was urgent: her whole life depended on it.

He inquired how old she was, and noting – while she replied that she was thirty – how her eyes turned cagey for the first time since she came into the room he wondered, putting on his spectacles, if she might be knocking off a few years, but could not tell, for the stylized face with the black hat pulled low over it recorded no time in years, only in hours.

'But does my age matter?' she asked, turning coy.

'And are you married?' he primly pursued.

She nodded and, slipping off a glove, displayed her left hand, the thread of metal round the third finger not more polished than the flesh it bound.

' – with children?'

'No.' Again she sounded cautious. 'But I've not been married long,' she quickly added; and more quickly still, defiantly, 'The truth is,' she rapped out, 'I was married only this morning.'

His face went blank, and she began to tell him about her life.

'When I was a little girl I thought everybody else had two navels . . . Oh, *you* smile – you've never had to face a fact that was yours only, not general data. You were a nice boy – weren't you, Doctor? – and lovingly sheltered. I can see that. You've always lived in the world where people have the right number of navels. But I shared – or thought I shared – that world only when I was very little. I was the Eve of the apple at five years old: that was when I found out.

'I was walking with my doll one hot day in our garden and we came to a pond with goldfish in it. I decided that Minnie – Minnie was my doll – that she wanted a wash. So we sat down by the pond and I discovered that she had only one navel. I felt so sorry I cried, rocking her naked little body in my arms, trying to comfort her, and promising not to throw her away like the others. And then I became thoughtful. The day was growing dark all around me, it was going to rain. But who was I sorry for? Which of us was wrong? I sat very still by that pond, my tears flowing and the raindrops starting to fall. I carefully examined Minnie again and when I found that she had other parts missing I grew calmer – but I had grown crafty too. Nobody must know that I suspected. Poor Minnie would have to be sacrificed because I had torn her clothes off and could not put them back again. I hardly noticed the thunderstorm as I hunted around for a string and a big stone. I tied the stone to Minnie, kissed her for the last time, and dropped her into the pond. I threw in my bracelet too. Then I ran home soaking wet and told the grown-ups that a thief had grabbed me and had stolen my bracelet and doll. They didn't believe me, of course – there are always armed guards planted all over our house: if you pushed a chair you bruised a detective – but everybody pretended to believe; nothing happened to me; except that night, in my dreams, the goldfish ate up poor Minnie, and I was there in the pond, watching, and was not sorry. After that I was like Eve after the apple. I was very careful about keeping myself well covered up, especially when there were other children around being careless. I found out about them, they never found out about me.'

'How about your family?' he asked.

She said she was an only child. 'Mother knows, of course. I don't know about Father. When Mother or the maids gave me a bath they put on such matter-of-fact faces I was often tempted to point at myself and giggle. I knew that they knew that I knew, but we all pretended that I didn't and that *they* didn't. The set-up was perfect for blackmail: I never had to threaten them aloud. If you beget a monster of a child it could prove you were rather monstrous yourself. I did what I pleased and was never punished. Can you imagine what kind of a childhood it was? If it was a childhood at all . . .'

But once past the teens – 'When you know how just one pimple can be such a torment, so think what I went through' – she had become indifferent. She had realized it was silly to squander thought and tears on so trivial an oddity; she stopped worrying. 'My one big scare was when it became stylish to bare the midriff. Imagine! They would have been like pig's eyes peering out . . .' But she had taken ill and had stayed in bed until the style staled. She had fallen in love with several boys who wanted to marry her but she had always drawn back: she dreaded a husband's eyes on her secret. 'He might be horrified – I could never have stood that – or he might say I had cheated.' So she had put off and put off marrying – until, suddenly, she was thirty, and she turned frantic.

'I could see myself getting older, painting myself thicker – a regular hard-boiled veteran, up to my neck in clubs and charities – having affairs with younger and ever younger men and sneaking off on 'combined-business-and-pleasure' trips abroad . . . Ugh! That sort of freelancing may be slick but it's not everybody's bowl of rice. So I swept a most eligible man off his feet – and married him, this morning.'

It was quite a wedding, the way she described it. She assured him it would be in all the papers – 'and not on the society page either. On the *front* page.'

'Are your people important?' he asked.

'Father's one of the sacred elders in the government, Mother's a famous beauty, and my husband has four or five generations of sugar money behind him. But that's not why. About the front page, I mean. "Bride of the Season Marches Off the Scene Too Soon." ". . . *Running up the stairs in her charming Paris gown, the bride then laughingly hurled the bouquet at her husband's face, to the astonishment of a cosmopolitan crowd . . ."*'

'Did you?' he asked uneasily, and she laughed at him.

'No – of course not. We were having a very noisy breakfast at my house afterwards, with all those cosmopolitan people, and he looked at me and I looked at him and he said shouldn't we run over to his apartment and start packing because we were going off on an American honeymoon. I hadn't slept for nights worrying over that moment. I thought: he'll uncover and discover and everything will be over. And I remembered the little girl crying by the pond and Minnie naked and all the world suddenly dark . . . But I smiled bravely and said yes to him, only I would have to run up and change first. So I ran up and changed and slipped down the back way and into a taxi and off to the airport where I took a plane. And here I am.'

'Here' was Hong Kong, in midwinter, on Kowloon side.

And why *here*? wondered Pepe Monson, removing bewildered eyes from her face and looking rather dazedly around the room; feeling the room's furniture hovering vaguely – the faded rug on the floor; the sofa near the doorway, against the wall; the two small Filipino flags crossed under a picture of General Aguinaldo; the bust of the Sacred Heart upon the bookshelf, between brass candlesticks; the tamaraw[1] head above each of the two shut windows . . .

Fog bulged against the windowpanes, as though elephants were wedging past. Hawkers, four stories below, sounded miles away, or whispering half-heartedly. Pepe Monson was grateful for the elephants and hushed hawkers but would have preferred the usual view at the window – of the harbor, gay with junks and ferryboats; of the downtown buildings standing up in white

---

1 Small buffalo, peculiar to Mindanao.

ranks across the water, in the noon sun, the island's rock delicately ostentatious behind them, with toylike houses necklacing the various peaks or stacked like steps up the slopes or snuggling into private shelves and niches down the sides. But there was a fog and no view, and the lights were on in the cold room, but the cold was only a mist her mouth made to the woman sitting before his desk insulated in black furs to her ears, her hat's brim cutting an angle of shadow across her face, and pearls gleaming at her throat when she leaned forward.

'But what on earth made you come here to me?' he asked. 'Had you heard about me?'

' – from Kikay Valero. She said you did a wonderful job on her horse. So I thought I would look you up. Besides, you're a fellow countryman. You are, aren't you?'

'My father is a Filipino, and so was my mother. I suppose I am too, though I was born over here and have never been over there.'

'Did you never want to go?'

'Oh, most awfully. I wanted to study there but my father wouldn't let me. I went to England instead – and then to the Argentine, for the cattle stuff.'

He understood her careless glance around the room. When she caught his eye, she flushed and he smiled.

'At home,' she hurried to explain, 'you would have an office that showed you had been abroad.'

'Maybe I will, when I go there.'

'Why wouldn't your father let you?'

'He was in the revolution against Spain and in the resistance against the Americans, and when both uprisings failed he came and settled here and swore not to go home, neither himself nor his sons, until it was a free country again.'

'Well, it is now.'

'And he did go back, last year. But he didn't stay long. Now we're trying to persuade him to make another visit.'

'But why wouldn't he stay? Was he frightened?'

She had leaned forward and the pearls gleamed.

Her face blurred before him as, growing sad, he thought of his father in the next room, sitting in an armchair, a shawl around his shoulders and his feet propped up on a stool and no hope at all in the quiet eyes fixedly staring ahead . . .

The girl's eyes were fixedly staring ahead too, and he drew back – though there was all the table between them – rather alarmed by the intensity of her regard and having fleetingly felt how odd that there should be in this room with him, making its furniture hover; that there should be seated before his desk, making its papers uneasy – in black furs and a black hat, with gray gloves on her hands and pearls at her throat – a woman who had two navels. But her eyes stopped short of him; the pause was hers alone; she had forgotten her question and was not awaiting the answer that he (the room having organized itself again around his old desk) was about to speak when she suddenly shivered and came to.

Sitting up and blinking away the tears while she fetched out her cigarette case, she remarked that her mother was in Hong Kong, too.

'Oh, does she live here?'

'No – just over on business.'

§ *Competing ancestries* Aus: Morgan; Carib: Walcott (2), Williams, Brodber

Thailand

S. P. SOMTOW (1952–)

From Jasmine Nights

Jasmine Nights is a novel about the coming-of-age of Little Frog, an upper-class Thai boy, who refuses to accept his nationality or Thai culture, calls himself Justin and speaks only English. The opening chapter, 'Death of a Chameleon', sketches in Little Frog's chameleon-like existence as 'a creature of two worlds' who, while living in the enclosed environment of his family's estate in Bangkok, fashions an alternative fantasy-life for himself from Western discourses as varied as Greek mythology and Hollywood cinema.

It is January of the year 1963 and I am a creature of two worlds. In one of these worlds I am a child. The world is circumscribed by high stucco walls topped with broken glass. By day the sun streams down and the mangoes glisten in the orchard behind the blue Gothic mansion with its faux Corinthian columns, the house of my three grandmothers and of our familial patriarch. Evenings, the jasmine bushes bloom, and the night air sweats the choking sensuality of their fragrance. Three other houses stand on the estate: my bachelor uncle's, uncompromisingly Californian in its split-level ranch style and adobe brick walls; the wooden house of my three maiden aunts, whom I call the three Fates, with its pointed eaves, backing out on to a pavilion above the pond, where I live among intimate strangers; and last, the ruined house, which is the entrance to my other world.

In my other world I am not a child. I am what I choose to be. I speak the language of the wind. I have synthesized this world out of images in history books and story books and books of poetry and from half-remembered scenes of England. It is cool in this world. A balustrade can be a stepladder to Olympus where I stand and look into the eyes of Zeus, who bears a remarkable resemblance to Finlay Currie, the white-maned St Peter from *Quo Vadis*.[1] A marble foyer draped with cobwebs is the Roman Senate, and from behind the arras I can hear Hamlet whispering to his mother and Clytemnestra pleading with Orestes for her life.[2] There is a room with as many books as there are stars. There is an attic where I have fought the

---

1 l951 film set in Nero's Rome, directed by Mervyn Le Roy.   2 The central action in the Choëphoroe, the second part of Aeschylus's *Oresteia* trilogy.

Trojan War a thousand times over, fine-tuning the outcome with my fellow Olympians. There are more rooms in the ruined house than I have ever counted. There are tapestries and busts of forgotten people and cobras that slither through century-old piles of laundry.

I have lived inside the walled universe for almost three years. Travel in and out of the universe is accomplished by means of a silver-green Studebaker driven by a man in a khaki uniform, whose name I have still not learned. I am an alien here. I sweat like a pig all the time. I forget to bathe. I have never uttered a word of the language; my tongue will not form the words, even though over the years I have begun to grasp their meaning. My numerous relations do not know I understand them, and they address me in a stilted Victorian English which I refer to as 'eaughing', since it so frequently makes use of the phoneme 'eaugh'. Some of the servants have begun to realize I am not deaf; they regard my refusal to speak Thai as an eccentricity, one of the many inscrutabilities of the privileged. They call me Master Little Frog. My secret name is Justin.

I have not seen my parents in three years. There is a photograph of them beside my bed. They are standing in front of a snowbank. It is England, or perhaps Canada. They are waving to me. It is a smudgy photograph, taken with a Kodak Brownie from the steps of a Caravelle jet plane. The frame is exquisite – black lacquer inlaid with Vietnamese mother-of-pearl, with an intagliate rendition of our family crest, a design of mating nagas. I am not entirely sure what has caused me to be separated from them, and why I have been shipped to the walled universe. Sometimes I think I am to blame. Sometimes I think they are on a secret mission in Russia, spying on an atom bomb plant under the guise of mink-farming Siberian peasants. Sometimes I think they have gone to Mars, where they are doing reconnaissance work for the American president. I have written a poem, over two hundred stanzas long and still unfinished, in which I enumerate all the places where they might be; I keep the poem inside a box of blue marble whose lid is a three-dimensional reproduction of Botticelli's *Venus*. One of the three Fates brought it back from Italy last summer. The marble box is my most precious possession, along with a portable Hermes typewriter that once belonged to Rupert Murdoch.[3]

Here's a slide:

A closeup of a set of false teeth, floating in a glass of water on a shelf next to the bathroom sink. They belong to Samlee, my nanny, my secret beloved. Samlee sleeps on a straw mat at the foot of my bed. Before she goes to sleep she sits and fans me with a bamboo fan, and she tells me stories about disembodied heads that crawl along the garden paths at night, dragging their slimy guts behind them. She does not know how frightened I am because she does not think I understand.

The beauty of this nanny is not easy to describe. She is not quite sane,

---

3 Australian-born newspaper magnate.

and she is middle-aged, and I have seen her sleepwalk into the garden sometimes, and stand in the moonlight unkempt and half-clad, her visage white as death from the perfumed powder with which she paints her face each night. On such occasions she mutters to herself in a dialect I cannot understand. Perhaps it is because she has left her teeth behind.

The glass of water is empty all day long. But in the small hours, as she snores, her betelnut breath mingling with the jasmine that wafts in through the wire mosquito netting of the windows and the disquieting odour, a little like *nam pla*,[4] that arises from her cotton *panung*[5] somewhere to the south of her silver belt-chain . . . in the small hours when I creep into the bathroom for my late-night date with Homer or Euripides, I often look up from the *Harvard Classics* and see the false teeth glimmering in the half-light. The bathroom is also the residence of my pet chameleon. The Homer is bound in a red so bright he cannot quite accomplish the transformation. I let him run up and down my leg while I accomplish the ostensible purpose of my visit to the bathroom. A *tukae*[6] barks in the distance.

My chameleon too is Homer, though he's too stupid to know his own name. I pick him up and drop him on a twig in the terrarium. Banana leaves brush against the bathroom window. I don't dare open the window to get a banana because I'm afraid of letting in the mosquitoes.

I tiptoe to bed and wrap myself around my side pillow. I close my eyes. The false teeth dance in my head. They chatter. The walls of Troy are crumbling.

They are crumbling in the ruined house. I have wound a silk curtain around my skinny shoulders, and I rage up and down the stairs. I am the fire sweeping through King Priam's palace.[7] I am the wooden horse ramming the Cyclopean walls. I run down corridors, brandishing the plastic sword I received from my father Zeus.

I'm in the temple where Priam prays with his withered arms embracing the altar. The Greeks are charging. Their bronze boots smash against the flagstones. A sword flashes. The king's head flies through the air. What sacrilege! What gross impiety! I am the flame that follows the head as it rolls downhill, the furious flame, the eater of cities. Homer, on my shoulder, holds on for dear life.

But now the fire is out of control. I do not know where I am. I have turned a corner, opened a door that has always been locked before. I freeze. Troy fades. I am not alone.

This room is not like the others. An electric fan stands in one corner, swivelling from side to side, dragging the cobwebs with it. Silk curtains are tightly drawn, permitting no light save that of a naked bulb that sways a little. There is a low table surrounded by triangular cushions, and on the table are a mortar and pestle and a silver *phaan*[8] piled with leaves and betelnuts.

---

4 A fish sauce. 5 Cloth garment wrapped around hips. 6 Large lizard. 7 Like other references in this passage, an allusion to Homer's *Iliad*. 8 Presentation platter.

There is an enormous leather armchair in the room. It rocks. It faces away from me. Poking up from behind the chair's high back is a tuft of silvery hair.

There is someone there. The lightbulb sways. My shadow sways. The cobwebs sway in the wind from the electric fan.

I have seen *Psycho*[9] fifteen times. I have visited the fruit cellar of the Bates house in my dreams. I know what is to be found in leather armchairs in abandoned houses. I feel my heart stop beating.

Will the armchair suddenly whip round to reveal the mummified corpse of Norman Bates's mother? I step back. My Homeric drapery slides to the floor.

'Who is there?' The chair has not moved. The voice is as ancient and gravelly as the stones of Troy. It speaks in Thai. 'Come on, who is it?'

Before I can stop myself, I say, 'It's me, Norman.'

The tuft of silver hair shifts. The chair rocks. The room is black and white. Black and white. I have seen *Psycho* fifteen times but I have never seen it quite this close before. I step back, slam the door, run down the corridor, stand at the top of the stairs breathing in spasms and clutching my breast with my eyes squeezed tight shut.

When I open my eyes again there's colour. The floor of the foyer is pink marble. The weeds in the cracks are a ferocious shade of green. A celadon vase, taller than me, leans against the wall, which is luridly wallpapered with red and gold leaf. I blink a couple of times to make sure I've left the Hitchcockian universe far behind.

It was a fantasy, I tell myself. I put Homer on the lip of the vase and wait to see if he will turn the cold blue-green of the worn glaze.

Another slide:

The first day of the funeral. I do not know whose funeral it is. Every car on the estate has been commandeered for our convoy. It is an important funeral, because Aunt Ning-nong, the eldest of the three Fates, has personally supervised my bath, squatting on the toilet seat and barking out directions to Samlee as she applies the sponge. I never remove my underwear when I am being bathed by women, but when the moment comes for Samlee to hand me the sponge so that I can take care of my aubergine (as she coyly calls it) my aunt does not avert her eyes as does Samlee, thrusting the sponge at me and casting her gaze down at the floor as she kneels beside the tub, a pose that is not dissimilar to the picture of the nymph Europa about to be ravished by Zeus in the form of a bull in *Every Child's Picture Book of Greek Mythology*, whose every colour plate I have committed to memory; but I digress since I was actually talking of my aunt, who stares fixedly at me as I attempt to stuff the sponge down my underwear and take a few halfhearted swipes . . .

---

9 Classic 1960 Hitchcock thriller, which like *Hamlet* and the *Oresteia* involves a tormented mother–son relationship.

Yes indeed, it is an important funeral. We will be in and out of it for seven days. A new suit has been ordered for me from the tailor, a white suit with long trousers that will chafe my ankles all week long, and a black arm-band. I wear black patent leather shoes.

I share the front seat of the Studebaker with Samlee and the nameless driver. We move sedately through the gates, crossing the *klong*[10] by way of a creaky bridge, threading our way through the labyrinth of *sois*[11] toward the funeral site, some temple. My three aunts are in the back seat; despite being dressed in mourning, each has managed a dazzling display of décolletage.

Ning-nong stares out of the window at a water buffalo. Their facial similarity does not escape me. I sit glumly between the two servants, my hand in my pocket and Homer in my hand.

Nit-nit, the number two, says, 'Well, this has certainly cast a pall on the New Year. By the time it's all right to throw a party, no one will be doing the mashed potato[12] any more.'

'You never could do it anyway,' says Noi-noi, the youngest. 'You always step on everyone's feet.'

'At least it's not the Madison,'[12] Nit-nit muses.

'Yes,' says Ning-nong, whose thirty-one years give her pronouncements an unassailable authority, 'you really made a fool of yourself at the American ambassador's Christmas party.'

'You're all so boring,' I say, 'with your dances. I wish you'd left me at home.'

'Eaugh!' the three of them exclaim in uncanny unison. Ning-nong adds, 'Show some respect, Little Frog. It's not every day someone as important as' – at this point she mumbles the name and titles of the deceased, which go on for some time – 'passes away.'

'Yes, but why are we going for seven days?'

'Because, my recalcitrant nephew, the Visoksakuls are going for *six* days, and if we don't go for *seven* people won't realize that we are more closely related to the dearly departed, even though it *is* only through the female line . . . '

'But we're just going to be sitting around listening to a bunch of monks chanting for hours and *hours* . . . '

'Oh, nonsense, Little Frog. The food'll be good.'

The food is astoundingly good. On the first day of the funeral I never get anywhere near the place of honour, or the golden cone in which the body of whoever-it-was has been encased. We are ushered directly to a banquet-in-progress.

We proceed to a vast canvas pavilion that has been erected in a meadow inside the temple compound. The dinner tables are so long that one cannot see to the end of them. The repast is a twenty-course *toh chiin*,[13] so our

---

10 Canal.   11 Narrow alleys.   12 1960s dance crazes.   13 Banquet (of many courses).

showing up *in medias res* is unlikely to leave us hungry by the end of the evening. As we arrive they are just bringing on the suckling pigs, thirty or forty of them, on silver platters, each one with electric lights in its eyes. If there is any chanting of mantras going on, it is somewhere in the distance, submerged in the gossiping of relatives; I am only subliminally aware that this is a sacred place. There are children running around everywhere. I resist the temptation to join them. I am afraid that when challenged I will not be able to speak.

I take the first vacant seat and find myself surrounded by the inhabitants of our family estate; it is as if I have never left the house. At the head of the table sits the patriarch of our family, my honoured grandfather, or, strictly speaking, great-uncle, who is only spoken of in whispers. To his left is Vit, my bachelor uncle, who was recently sent down from Cambridge but has managed to set up a gynaecological clinic on Sathorn Road. Opposite him are my three grandmothers (I should say one grandmother and two great-aunts, the one a sister of the patriarch, the other a number three wife going on two) who are methodically dissecting one of the suckling pigs.

The three Fates have not deigned to sit at the table; they are milling around, protesting about their diets, and Nit-nit is botching the twist. Where is Samlee? I wonder. But I know she may not enter this pavilion; there is another pavilion, conveniently out of sight but within summoning range, for the various attendants, chauffeurs and spear-carriers.

Uncle Vit expounds learnedly on the wonders of the female anatomy, and everyone at the table is spellbound. He is the only person not wearing one of these tailor-made white suits; on the other hand, he is a doctor, practically a holy man; his cowlick, five-o'clock shadow and hornrimmed spectacles are the sigils of his sanctitude. I find him immensely boring, and I cannot follow his Thai, because he rarely utters a word that contains fewer than seven syllables.

I sit in silence for a while. I can be a very solemn child sometimes. Although I have no emotional connection with the deceased, I do not feel that levity is called for. After all, I reflect, the funeral of Hector was a grave affair, taking up the entire last book of the *Iliad*. Trying to disguise my greed behind the appearance of fastidiousness, I toy with my ivory chopsticks for about five minutes before allowing them to plummet toward the pig like a pair of Cruise missiles.

I stop short barely in time. Homer is resting on the suckling pig's back, nestled between two squares of crispy skin. For once, he has taken on the exact coloration of his environment. Furtively, I look for a way of directing my chameleon unobtrusively into my pocket. He starts to climb up my chopstick. All you can see is a head, because his torso has blended chimerically with the pig's.

'My goodness,' says one of the grandmothers, glancing my way, 'isn't that a *jingjok*?'[14]

---

14 Small lizard.

'It most certainly is not!' I say. 'That's Homer, my pet chamele – ' but I have no chance to finish because Homer has scampered off the edge of the tablecloth. Quickly I duck under the table.

It is another world. It's dark. White fumes curl up from a dozen dishes where coils of anti-mosquito incense smoulder. Here and there, an aluminium spittoon punctuates the row of legs – stately shapely columns that terminate in black stilettos. Grass peers through holes in the straw mats. A scrawny temple dog scratches and waits for alms. Where is Homer? There, there . . . weaving in and out of the forest of legs . . . I crouch down on all fours. I cup my hands over where I think he'll leap. I don't call his name. Chameleons never listen.

He's resting beside a shoe, about a size eight, shiny and black. A spiked crocodile-skin heel nuzzles the size eight. I creep closer. I almost have him. I hold my breath. Don't move, don't move.

Then, abruptly, there is music – a jangling heterophony of xylophones and gongs and wailing oboes. The size eight begins to tap in time to the music. It's going to descend on Homer. It's going to crush him. I make a grab. His tail comes away in my hand. His torso has been impaled on the crocodile spike. Before my grief can register, the leg has swung and hurled my chameleon into a spittoon.

I fly after it. My hand reaches into the spittoon and clasps the body of my chameleon. Homer expires. My hand touches something else, something hard and clanky. The smoke clears a little and I see what it is. I recognize it at once, for it is achingly familiar to me from my long nights of immersion in the ancient classics. It is a set of dentures.

It is *the* set of dentures – for have I not memorized every rill, every ridge, every cusp and molar? I clutch the dentures and the dead lizard to my bosom. A feeling of utter desolation steals over me. My stomach is tying itself in knots and I am on the verge of tears. I have never felt so alone.

At that moment, my sense of smell tells me Samlee is near. It's that heady smell of jasmine and *nam pla* that issues nightly from her nether garments. How is it that my true love has come to me here, in this secret world walled off by lace-trimmed tablecloths? I look up and there she is. She is on her knees, and her arms are clasped firmly around the legs of Uncle Vit, whose trousers have somehow fallen about his ankles. Samlee, elder goddess of my secret pantheon, has her eyes closed and bobs her head up and down, and her lips are tightly wrapped around my uncle's gnarled and rampant aubergine.

An unholy terror seizes me. Fifteen viewings of *Psycho* have not prepared me for so outlandish a ritual. I am a castaway in an alien kingdom, my only friend in two pieces in my clenched fists. I cannot breathe. The mosquito incense chokes me. I'm drowning in the humid air. Desperate, I claw my way out between the legs of one of my grandmothers. For a second, glasses tinkle, lights dazzle, conversations buzz. My uncle is still holding forth on the virtues of gynaecology. Does he not know that my nanny has bewitched him, that she's sucking the life force from him like a *phii krasue*, a spirit of the night?

I duck through a canvas flap and suddenly I am in a curtained-off inner pavilion. Women in black dresses sit on the mats in various poses of reverence. There is a single chair in the room, and on it sits a woman ancient and skeletal. A tuft of silver-white hair adorns her head. I know that hair. I look around. This is not black-and-white. This is not a movie.

I'm standing there with my dead chameleon in my hands. Oh God, I start to cry. It is the most appalling moment of my life. So far.

The ancient woman speaks. 'Norman Bates, is it not?'

'I – I – '

'Come now. Come to me. you don't have to crawl if you don't want to. Are you surprised that I, too, withered as I am, have seen *Psycho*? Ah, but I was a spry eighty-nine when it came out. I could still get to the cinema.' She coughs and then commands, with an imperious wave, 'Betelnut *woay*!'[15]

A servant scurries up to her with a tray.

'Come closer, Little Frog. You're the one who refuses to speak Thai, is it not?' She does not say '*Thai*' but '*bhasa khon*' – the language of human beings. 'Ah, but you wince when I call you Little Frog. By what name do you call yourself?'

'Justin.'

She cackles like the Wicked Witch of the West.[16] 'Justin! Now I've heard everything.' She has switched to English. I become bolder. I approach her on my hands and knees, for it seems to be the custom. She wipes away my tears with a fold of her silken handkerchief. 'Now tell your great-grandmother why you are crying.'

'Homer is dead.'

'Delicious! My, my, what a refined sensibility you have, my dear! But don't you think three thousand years is a long time still to be in mourning?'

I start to laugh. 'No, no, Great-grandmother! I mean my pet chameleon.' And I show her Homer's gory remnants. Seeing him like this sets me weeping again. 'And furthermore, I've found out that my nanny is a *phii krasue*.'

'A very tragic day indeed,' she says with due solemnity. 'But you must bring his body over to the ruined house, next time you come, and you and I will have a proper cremation. Otherwise his spirit will wander the earth, unable to be reborn into the cycle of karma.'

'Oh, Great-grandmother, you *do* understand.' I'm still weeping, but they are tears of pleasure as well as bereavement.

She spits her betel into a Ming spittoon. She takes my face between her palms, smoother than calfskin, and she says, 'Little Frog, Little Frog . . . you must *give* a little moore. You are so unbending. Here you are, twelve years old, and you do not even know your own name! And you have only one

---

15 An expression of contempt. 16 Another cinematic reference: to *The Wizard of Oz* (1939).

year left. One year to find out who you are.' She picks at the gold threads in her *jongkabaen*.[17]

'What do you mean, Great-grandmother?'

'You mean they haven't told you yet? That you're being sent to Eton when you turn thirteen?'

'Eton?' – I have heard of Eton. Eton is in my other world. The cold world. England. The place of the Olympians and the Norse Gods and the ancient Romans. My geography, you will note, is much of a piece with my perception of time. Suddenly I can feel the wind and the snow. I shiver.

'Now listen to me, my child. Contrary to what you may have led yourself to believe, you are not English. I know you are a creature of two worlds' – I gasped at the millennial sagacity of one so able to divine these secret truths about me – 'but the path you must take lies between them. Think of your chameleon. Perhaps his death is a sign. Perhaps it is you who must absorb his spirit now, my child, you who must learn to change your colour as you change your habitat . . . without changing the colour of your soul. If you don't learn this, I promise you that you will spend the rest of your life adrift, clinging to planks, without ever catching sight of land.'

'So how is it, Great-grandmother, that you know so much? I don't think I've ever even met you before, and yet . . . '

'Well, Little Frog,' she says, 'we do have the same taste in movies.' And, plucking the betelnut pestle from the tray, she begins to stab at the air and shriek '*Wheet! wheet! wheet!*' I begin laughing and soon I'm bawling again, but this time it is sheer joy.

Another slide: I'm dozing off in the Studebaker on the ride home. I hear the three Fates whispering.

'So, Samlee, you're being transferred to the brick house then?'

'So what is it you've done to attract the attention of the *khun phuchai*?[18] You're not even pretty.'

'Oh, but she has talents.'

'Oh, shut up! That's nasty.'

A slide: I wake up in the night. She is sitting on the bed. She is idly rubbing my back, not knowing that I'm awake. She mumbles toothlessly to herself and to me: 'Oh, Master Little Frog . . . oh, Samlee's angel . . . how I'm going to miss you . . . oh, it's terrible to be born into this world a lowly *khiikhaa* like me . . . oh, you can't know . . . life is suffering.'

I open one eye. I quickly shut it again before she can see me. A single still after-image lingers behind sealed eyelids.

In the moonlight, in the jasmine-scented breeze, my beloved nanny weeps.

§ *Responses to European texts* Lim (2), Lee Tzu Pheng; Af: Coetzee; Carib: Lamming (2), Walcott (4), Gilkes

---

17 A brocaded trouser-like garment. 18 Master of the house.

Part VIII

TRANS-CULTURAL WRITING

LOUISE BENNETT (1919–)

Colonisation in Reverse

Wat a joyful news, Miss Mattie,
I feel like me heart gwine burs'
Jamaica people colonizin
Englan in reverse.

5   By de hundred, by de t'ousan
From country and from town,
By de ship-load, by de plane-load
Jamaica is Englan boun.

Dem a-pour out o' Jamaica,
10   Everybody future plan
Is fe get a big-time job
An settle in de mother lan.

What a islan! What a people!
Man an woman, old an young
15   Jusa pack dem bag an baggage
An tun history upside dung!

Some people don't like travel,
But fe show dem loyalty
Dem all a-open up cheap-fare-
20   To-Englan agency.

An week by week dem shippin off
Dem countryman like fire,
Fe immigrate an populate
De seat o' de Empire.

25   Oonoo see how life is funny,
Oonoo see de tunabout,
Jamaica live fe box bread
Outa English people mout'.

For wen dem catch a Englan,
30   An start play dem different role,
Some will settle down to work
An some will settle fe de dole.

---

25 Oonoo: you all.

Jane say de dole is not too bad
Because dey payin' she
35 Two pounds a week fe seek a job
Dat suit her dignity.

Me say Jane will never find work
At the rate how she dah-look,
For all day she stay pon Aunt Fan couch
40 An read love-story book.

Wat a devilment a Englan!
Dem face war an brave de worse,
But I'm wonderin' how dem gwine stan'
Colonizin' in reverse.

§ *Carib in Britain/Language usage* Selvon, Johnson, Dabydeen, D'Aguiar, Phillips; Carib: Selvon, Agard, Bloom; Bennett also in Carib

SAM SELVON (1923–94)

Working the Transport

One time a fellar name Small Change get a work with London Transport. Small Change not really his name, but that is how all the boys know him as. I mean, you could know a fellar good, owe him money, or he owe you, go all about with him, and the both of you good, good friends, and yet if a day don't come when it really necessary to know what his true name is, he would dead and you still calling him Small Change.

Small Change hail from Barbados. You know where Barbados is? You don't? Well that is your hard luck. Anyway you must be read in the papers about how London Transport send men down there in the West Indies to get fellars to work on the tube and bus, and it look as if they like Barbadians, because they didn't go to any other islands: they just get some of the boys from Little England – that is what they call Barbados down there – and bring them up to work the transport.

At the time Small Change was working on a barge what used to go out to the big ships and bring in goods. He used to handle a oar so big that two–three fellars had to handle one oar.

When Small Change get the wire that they recruiting fellars to go to England and work, he left the barge same time and went home and put on some clean clothes and went to the office where they was recruiting these fellars.

'Can you drive?' they ask Change.

'Me? Drive?' Change smile and try to make his face look like he driving bus ever since he born. 'I was born behind a wheel.'

'Have you got your licence?'

'Yes, but not right here. I could go back home for it, though, if you want.'

'Driving in London isn't like driving in Barbados, you know.' The Englishman lean back in his chair, smoking a Lighthouse, which is the Barbadian equivalent to a Woods.[1]

Change didn't deign to say anything to that, he just wait.

'How about your education?'

'Codrington College,' Change say. Change never went to school, but he call the name of one of the best college in that part of the world, and hope for the best.

'Have you got any recommendations?'

Change wasn't sure what the word mean, so he say quickly: 'No, but I could get some if you want.'

Well in the end Change find himself on a ship going to England. I mean, when you have ambition you have to play boldface and brazen, otherwise you get no place at all. It have fellars who get to the top only playing bold-face, telling people they could do this and that when they don't know Adam from Eve. Change was always like that from small, only, he more boldface than ambitious, that's why he was only rowing them big barge instead of holding down a smart work in the island.

Anyway, Change come to London city, with Alipang, All-Fours, Catch-as-Catch-Can, Jackfish and a set of other fellars what get work with London Transport. (I sure you must be see All-Fours already – he have a work conducting in a bus, he only have eight fingers in all.)

Coming up on the ship, Change get the other fellars to gen him up on addition and subtraction, and he rig up a contraption like a car, with steering wheel and gear and clutch and brakes, and all the time the ship coming to England Change sitting there behind the wheel learning from one of the boys how to drive.

Of course, when the ship reach England it wasn't long before they find out that Change don't know anything about driving. In the garage a test[2] tell him to move a bus, and Change get in as cool as anything, sit down, start the engine, press the clutch, race the engine, and throw in a reverse gear by mistake and back the bus up against the wall and give it a big dent right where it had an advertisement for binoculars, besides breaking up the glass in the back window where does have the names of the places where the bus going to.

Afterwards Jackfish tell him: 'Man, I warn you all the time I teaching you on the ship, that these buses in London funny. And you mean you don't know how to put in a reverse?'

'The buses really funny,' Change say. 'Upstairs and downstairs, and I don't too like the view when you sit down in the driver seat.'

Jackfish say: 'You better try conducting old man.'

So Change say he prefer to conduct instead of drive, and they put him

---

1 Woodbine cigarette. 2 Man.

on a course to learn the ropes. Everything they teach Change went in one ear and out the other. Change not paying any particular attention: he studying a little thing that he get in with down by the Elephant,[3] where he living. When Change get in with this thing she ask him: 'Can you rock 'n' roll?'

'Can I rock 'n' roll!' Change repeat. 'Child, that dance out of fashion where I come from, we used to do that two years ago. The latest thing now is hip 'n' hit. You mean to say is only now you all doing rock 'n' roll in London?'

'Hip 'n' hit?' the blonde say, puzzled. 'What's that?'

'I'll show you Saturday night, when we go dancing,' Change say.

So while the transport people trying to learn Change how to conduct, Change studying some kind of newfangle step, and when elevenses come he went to the other boys and tell them how he have to invent a new dance else the West Indies would be let down.

Catch-as-Catch-Can who used to lime out regularly at all the dances it have in Barbados, tell Change to take it easy.

'You want to learn some new steps?' Catch say. 'Give me a beat.'

So Change sit down on the platform on a bus and start to beat the side, and Alipang finish drinking tea and hitting the empty cup with the spoon, while Jackfish keeping time on the bar it have what you does hold on to when you going in the bus. And Catch dancing some fancy steps, a kind of Gene Kelly mixup with some mambo and samba and some real carnival 'break-away', which is what they call the dancing the people dance in the islands when is carnival time.

'This bus have a good tone,' Change say, looking up to see what number bus it is, as if the number make a difference.

'You watching?' Catch say. 'See if you could manage that.'

So Change get up and start to do as Catch was doing, and Catch saying no, not that way, and showing him how.

Them other English fellars gather around enjoying the slackness, because you know how they themselves cargoo, they don't know how to shake a leg or how to get hep, until the fellar who was in charge finish his tea and come and say: 'All right fellows, break it up.'

Change get a 196 bus to conduct, from Tufnell Park in the north to Norwood Junction in the south. The first morning he went to work, the bus get about a quarter-mile from the garage before Change realise that he left all his tickets behind. He had was to ring the bell and stop the bus and go out and tell the driver what happen. This time so all them people hustling to get to work and want to know what happening: in the end they had to get out and wait for another bus while the driver drive back to the garage for Change to collect the tickets.

Meantime he learning all the teddy boys and teddy girls in the Elephant to dance hip 'n' hit, until it become a real craze south of the river.

---

3 The Elephant and Castle (in South London).

It was ruction in the town when the teddies start up on this new dance that Change introduce, and pretty soon everybody forget about 'rock 'n' roll' and start to concentrate on 'hip 'n' hit', and the old Change figuring out if he can't make something on the side by giving lessons after work.

Meantime, too, he get tired of running up and down the stairs in the bus to punch ticket, and having to work the old brains hard to figure out how much change to give, two and a half, tenpence, one and four, and all them funny ways the English have with money, instead of a flat dollar and cents.

One evening in a rush hour he surprise to pick up Alipang by Waterloo station.

'What happening boy, which part you working?' Change ask.

'Underground, boy,' Alipang say.

'Underground! In the tubes and them?'

'Yes. I guarding at one of the stations.'

'Alipang, is a hard work boy? It hard as conducting bus?'

'Easy as kissing hand, man. All you have to do is say mind the doors, right, all change, and so on.'

'I tired with this bus work, man. I think I going to ask for a transfer to the tubes and them. Where you going?'

'Norwood Junction. That is one and two?'

'It used to be. Is one and four now, papa,' Change say, punching two tickets, one for the one and the other for the four.

'L.T.[4] bleeding money in this country,' Alipang observe.

Two months later Change was working in the underground, patrolling the platform in a station and calling out 'Mind the doors!' and 'Right!' Things look like they was going all right, until they move Change from the station where he was and put him Marble Arch to work, on the Central Line. Well somehow or other Change get the idea that is 'all change' at the Arch for every train that pass, and the first morning he on duty he call out 'All change!' for a train that was going through to Liverpool Street, and cause big confusion in the tube station when everybody come off the train and stand up waiting for the other one. In fact, what Change do was he cause a dislocation of the schedules of all the trains on the Central Line, from West Ruislip to Ongar, and how he didn't get fire that time was a wonder. When L.T. ask him for an explanation, Change beg for another chance. 'This country so cold,' Change say, 'I can't think properly. But I will get accustom soon.'

'This is your last chance,' L.T. warn him, and put him to work collecting tickets. Change like that too bad. He sitting down on top an escalator all day long and collecting tickets, and sometimes when things dullish he clipping the tickets for passengers going down.

Well, it ain't have a lot more episode to tell you about Change, except how he lose the work at last. I mean L.T. really try with that test.

At this stage Change was settling down nicely to punching ticket at the

4 London Transport.

top of the escalator, but something had to spoil it, and you know what – woman. As soon as a man start to prosper a little and catch himself in this world, woman come in and cause misery. All over the world is the same thing, even in London. And as soon as they come they start to make bassa-bassa, which is to say, anything they touch they put blight on it and cause trouble.

Was the little blonde what Change learn to do the hip 'n' hit. The girl behind Change all the time, and won't leave him in peace. And climax come one afternoon. Things was dullish, and a smart chick was coming up the escalator, and Change stop the thing and begin to talk, trying to make a date. Well little Blondie come up same time and start to make big noise, asking Change if that is what he does be doing behind her back, trying to date other women, and she start to tussle with the chick, and poor Change trying to part them and soothe things. In the scramble Change cap fall on the escalator and begin to go down, and Change start after it. Well same time, as the gods would have it, a L.T. inspector coming up on the other side, and he see all what happening.

This time they didn't ask Change for an explanation. They just fire him.

'Never mind, they are taking on workers in King's Cross,' Blondie tell Change afterwards.

But Change give she a clout behind she head and went to mourn to the other boys about what happen.

§ *Carib in Britain/Language usage* Bennett, Johnson, Dabydeen, D'Aguiar; Carib: Selvon, Agard, Bloom

RUTH PRAWER JHABVALA (1927–)

Myself in India

I have lived in India for most of my adult life. My husband is Indian and so are my children. I am not, and less so every year.

India reacts very strongly on people. Some loathe it, some love it, most do both. There is a special problem of adjustment for the sort of people who come today, who tend to be liberal in outlook and have been educated to be sensitive and receptive to other cultures. But it is not always easy to be sensitive and receptive to India: there comes a point where you have to close up in order to protect yourself. The place is very strong and often proves too strong for European nerves. There is a cycle that Europeans – by Europeans I mean all Westerners, including Americans – tend to pass through. It goes like this: first stage, tremendous enthusiasm – everything Indian is marvellous; second stage, everything Indian not so marvellous; third stage, everything Indian abominable. For some people it ends there, for others the cycle renews itself and goes on. I have been through it so many times that now I think of myself as strapped to a wheel that goes round and round and sometimes I'm up and sometimes I'm down. When I meet other Europeans, I can usually tell after a few moments conversation at what stage of the cycle they happen to be. Everyone likes to talk about India, whether they happen to be loving or loathing it. It is a topic on which a lot of things can be said, and on a variety of aspects – social, economic, political, philosophical: it makes fascinating viewing from every side.

However, I must admit that I am no longer interested in India. What I am interested in now is myself in India – which sometimes, in moments of despondency, I tend to think of as my survival in India. I had better say straightaway that the reason why I live in India is because my strongest human ties are here. If I hadn't married an Indian, I don't think I would ever have come here for I am not attracted – or used not to be attracted – to the things that usually bring people to India. I know I am the wrong type of person to live here. To stay and endure, one should have a mission and a cause, to be patient, cheerful, unselfish, strong. I am a central European with an English education and a deplorable tendency to constant self-analysis. I am irritable and have weak nerves.

The most salient fact about India is that it is very poor and very backward. There are so many other things to be said about it but this must remain the basis of all of them. We may praise Indian democracy, go into raptures over Indian music, admire Indian intellectuals – but whatever we say, not for one moment should we lose sight of the fact that a very great number of Indians never get enough to eat. Literally that: from birth to death they never for one day cease to suffer from hunger. *Can* one lose sight of that fact? God knows, I've tried. But after seeing what one has to see here every day, it is not really possible to go on living one's life the way one is used to. People dying of starvation in the streets, children kidnapped and maimed to be sent out as beggars – but there is no point in making a catalogue of the horrors with which one lives, *on* which one lives, as on the back of an animal. Obviously, there has to be some adjustment.

There are several ways. The first and best is to be a strong person who plunges in and does what he can as a doctor or social worker. I often think that perhaps this is the only condition under which Europeans have any right to be here. I know several people like that. They are usually attached to some mission. They work very hard and stay very cheerful. Every few years they are sent on home leave. Once I met such a person – a woman doctor – who had just returned from her first home leave after being out here for twelve years. I asked her: but what does it feel like to go back after such a long time? How do you manage to adapt yourself? She didn't understand. This question which was of such tremendous import to me – how to adapt oneself to the differences between Europe and India – didn't mean a thing to her. It simply didn't matter. And she was right, for in view of the things she sees and does every day, the delicate nuances of one's own sensibilities are best forgotten.

Another approach to India's basic conditions is to accept them. This seems to be the approach favoured by most Indians. Perhaps it has something to do with their belief in reincarnation. If things are not to your liking in this life, there is always the chance that in your next life everything will be different. It appears to be a consoling thought for both rich and poor. The rich man stuffing himself on pilao can do so with an easy conscience because he knows he has earned this privilege by his good conduct in previous lives; and the poor man can watch him with some degree of equanimity for he knows that next time round it may well be *he* who will be digging into that pilao while the other will be crouching outside the door with an empty stomach. However, this path of acceptance is not open to you if you don't have a belief in reincarnation ingrained within you. And if you don't accept, then what can you do? Sometimes one wants just to run away and go to a place where everyone has enough to eat and clothes to wear and a home fit to live in. But even when you get there, can you ever forget? Having once seen the sights in India, and the way it has been ordained that people must live out their lives, nowhere in the world can ever be all that good to be in again.

None of this is what I wanted to say. I wanted to concentrate only on myself in India. But I could not do so before indicating the basis on which everyone who comes here has to live. I have a nice house, I do my best to live in an agreeable way. I shut all my windows, I let down the blinds, I turn on the airconditioner; I read a lot of books, with a special preference for the great masters of the novel. All the time I know myself to be on the back of this great animal of poverty and backwardness. It is not possible to pretend otherwise. Or rather, one does pretend, but retribution follows. Even if one never rolls up the blinds and never turns off the airconditioner, something is bound to go wrong. People are not meant to shut themselves up in rooms and pretend there is nothing outside.

Now I think I am drawing nearer to what I want to be my subject. Yes, something is wrong: I am not happy this way. I feel lonely, shut in, shut off. It is my own fault. I should go out more and meet people and learn what is going on. All right, so I am not a doctor nor a social worker nor a saint nor at all a good person; then the only thing to do is to try and push that aspect of India out of sight and turn to others. There are many others. I live in the capital where so much is going on. The winter is one round of parties, art exhibitions, plays, music and dance recitals, visiting European artistes: there need never be a dull moment. Yet all my moments are dull. Why? It is my own fault, I know. I can't quite explain it to myself but somehow I have no heart for these things here. Is it because all the time underneath I feel the animal moving? But I have decided to ignore the animal. I wish to concentrate only on modern, Westernised India, and on modern, well-off, cultured Westernised Indians.

Let me try and describe a Westernised Indian woman with whom I ought to have a lot in common and whose company I ought to enjoy. She has been to Oxford or Cambridge or some smart American college. She speaks flawless, easy, colloquial English with a charming lilt of an accent. She has a degree in economics or political science or English literature. She comes from a good family. Her father may have been an I.C.S.[1] officer or some other high-ranking government official; he too was at Oxford or Cambridge, and he and her mother travelled in Europe in pre-war days. They have always lived a Western-style life, with Western food and an admiration for Western culture. The daughter now tends rather to frown on this. She feels one should be more deeply Indian, and with this end in view, she wears handloom saris and traditional jewellery and has painted an abnormally large vermilion mark on her forehead. She is interested in Indian classical music and dance. If she is rich enough – she may have married into one of the big Indian business houses – she will become a patroness of the arts and hold delicious parties on her lawn on summer nights. All her friends are there – and she has so many, both Indian and European, all interesting people – and trays of iced drinks are carried round by servants in uniform and there is intelligent conversation and then there is a superbly arranged buffet supper and more intelligent conversation, and then the crown of the evening: a famous Indian maestro performing on the sitar. The guests recline on carpets and cushions on the lawn. The sky sparkles with stars and the languid summer air is fragrant with jasmine. There are many pretty girls reclining against bolsters; their faces are melancholy for the music is stirring their hearts, and sometimes they sigh with yearning and happiness and look down at their pretty toes (adorned with a tiny silver toe-ring) peeping out from under the sari. Here is Indian life and culture at its highest and best. Yet, with all that, it need not be thought that our hostess has forgotten her Western education. Not at all. In her one may see the best of East and West combined. She is interested in a great variety of topics and can hold her own in any discussion. She loves to exercise her emancipated mind, and whatever the subject of conversation – economics, or politics, or literature, or film – she has a well-formulated opinion on it and knows how to express herself. How lucky for me if I could have such a person for a friend! What enjoyable, lively times we two could have together!

In fact, my teeth are set on edge if I have to listen to her for more than five minutes – yes, even though everything she says is so true and in line with the most advanced opinions of today. But when she says it, somehow, even though I know the words to be true, they ring completely false. It is merely lips moving and sounds coming out: it doesn't mean anything, nothing of what she says (though she says it with such conviction, skill, and charm) is of the least importance to her. She is only making conversation in the way she knows educated women have to make conversation. And so it is with all of them. Everything they say, all that lively conversation round the buffet table, is not prompted by anything they really feel strongly about but by what they think they ought to feel strongly about. This applies not only to subjects which are naturally alien to them – for instance, when they

---

1 Indian Civil Service.

talk oh so solemnly! and with such profound intelligence! of Godard[2] and Becket and ecology – but when they talk about themselves too. They know Modern India to be an important subject and they have a lot to say about it: but though they themselves *are* Modern India, they don't look at themselves, they are not conditioned to look at themselves except with the eyes of foreign experts whom they have been taught to respect. And while they are fully aware of India's problems and are up on all the statistics and all the arguments for and against nationalisation and a socialistic pattern of society, all the time it is as if they were talking about some *other* place – as if it were a subject for debate – an abstract subject – and not a live animal actually moving under their feet.

But if I have no taste for the company of these Westernised Indians, then what else is there? Other Indians don't really have a social life, not in our terms; the whole conception of such a life is imported. It is true that Indians are gregarious in so far as they hate to be alone and always like to sit together in groups; but these groups are clan-units – it is the family, or clan-members, who gather together and enjoy each other's company. And again, their conception of enjoying each other's company is different from ours. For them it is enough just to *be* together; there are long stretches of silence in which everyone stares into space. From time to time there is a little spurt of conversation, usually on some commonplace everyday subject such as rising prices, a forthcoming marriage, or a troublesome neighbour. There is no attempt at exercising the mind or testing one's wits against those of others: the pleasure lies only in having other familiar people around and enjoying the air together and looking forward to the next meal. There is actually something very restful about this mode of social intercourse and it certainly holds more pleasure than the synthetic social life led by Westernised Indians. It is also more adapted to the Indian climate which invites one to be absolutely relaxed in mind and body, to do nothing, to think nothing, just to feel, to *be*. I have in fact enjoyed sitting around like that for hours on end. But there is something in me that after some time revolts against such lassitude. I can't just *be*! Suddenly I jump up and rush away out of that contented circle. I want to do something terribly difficult like climbing a mountain or reading the *Critique of Pure Reason*.[3] I feel tempted to bang my head against the wall as if to wake myself up. Anything to prevent myself from being sucked down into that bog of passive, intuitive being. I feel I cannot, I must not allow myself to live this way.

Of course there are other Europeans more or less in the same situation as myself. For instance, other women married to Indians. But I hesitate to seek them out. People suffering from the same disease do not usually make good company for one another. Who is to listen to whose complaints? On the other hand, with what enthusiasm I welcome visitors from abroad. Their physical presence alone is a pleasure to me. I love to see their fresh complexions, their red cheeks that speak of wind and rain; and I like to see their

---

2 The film director, Jean-Luc Godard.   3 Best-known work of Immanuel Kant.

clothes and their shoes, to admire the texture of these solid European materials and the industrial skills that have gone into making them. I also like to
hear the way in which these people speak. In some strange way their accents,
their intonations are redolent to me of the places from which they have
come, so that as voices rise and fall I hear in them the wind stirring in English
trees or a mild brook murmuring through a summer wood. And apart from
these sensuous pleasures, there is also the pleasure of hearing what they have
to say. I listen avidly to what is said about people I know or have heard of
and about new plays and restaurants and changes and fashions. However,
neither the subject nor my interest in it is inexhaustible; and after that, it
is my turn. What about India? Now they want to hear, but I don't want to
say. I feel myself growing sullen. I don't want to talk about India. There is
nothing I can tell them. There is nothing they would understand. However, I do begin to talk, and after a time even to talk with passion. But
everything I say is wrong. I listen to myself with horror; they too listen with
horror. I want to stop and reverse, but I can't. I want to cry out, this is
not what I mean! You are listening to me in entirely the wrong context!
But there is no way of explaining the context. It would take too long,
and anyway what is the point? It's such a small personal thing. I fall
silent. I have nothing more to say. I turn my face and want them to go
away.

So I am back again alone in my room with the blinds drawn and the airconditioner on. Sometimes, when I think of my life, it seems to have contracted to this one point and to be concentrated in this one room, and it is
always a very hot, very long afternoon when the airconditioner has failed. I
cannot describe the *oppression* of such afternoons. It is a physical oppression
– heat pressing down on me and pressing in the walls and the ceiling and
congealing together with time which has stood still and will never move
again. And it is not only those two – heat and time – that are laying their
weight on me but behind them, or held within them, there is something
more which I can only describe as the whole of India. This is hyperbole, but
I need hyperbole to express my feelings about those countless afternoons
spent over what now seem to me countless years in a country for which I
was not born. India swallows me up and now it seems to me that I am no
longer in my room but in the white-hot city streets under a white-hot sky;
people cannot live in such heat so everything is deserted – no, not quite, for
here comes a smiling leper in a cart being pushed by another leper; there is
also the carcase of a dog and vultures have swooped down on it. The river
has dried up and stretches in miles of flat cracked earth; it is not possible
to make out where the river ceases and the land begins for this too is as
flat, as cracked, as dry as the river-bed and stretches on for ever. Until we
come to a jungle in which wild beasts live, and then there are ravines and
here live outlaws with the hearts of wild beasts. Sometimes they make raids
into the villages and they rob and burn and mutilate and kill for sport. More
mountains and these are very, very high and now it is no longer hot but terribly cold, we are in snow and ice and here is Mount Kailash on which sits

Siva the Destroyer wearing a necklace of human skulls. Down in the plains they are worshipping him. I can see them from here – they are doing something strange – what is it? I draw nearer. Now I can see. They are killing a boy. They hack him to pieces and now they bury the pieces into the foundations dug for a new bridge. There is a priest with them who is quite naked except for ash smeared all over him; he is reciting some holy verses over the foundations, to bless and propitiate.

I am using these exaggerated images in order to give some idea of how intolerable India – the idea, the sensation of it – can become. A point is reached where one must escape, and if one can't do so physically, then some other way must be found. And I think it is not only Europeans but Indians too who feel themselves compelled to seek refuge from their often unbearable environment. Here perhaps less than anywhere else is it possible to believe that this world, this life, is all there is for us, and the temptation to write it off and substitute something more satisfying becomes overwhelming. This brings up the question whether religion is such a potent force in India because life is so terrible, or is it the other way round – is life so terrible because, with the eyes of the spirit turned elsewhere, there is no incentive to improve its quality? Whichever it is, the fact remains that the eyes of the spirit *are* turned elsewhere, and it really is true that God seems more present in India than in other places. Every morning I wake up at 3a.m. to the sound of someone pouring out his spirit in devotional song; and then at dawn the temple bells ring, and again at dusk, and conch-shells are blown, and there is the smell of incense and of the slightly overblown flowers that are placed at the feet of smiling, pink-cheeked idols. I read in the papers that the Lord Krishna has been reborn as the son of a weaver woman in a village somewhere in Madhya Pradesh. On the banks of the river there are figures in meditation and one of them may turn out to be the teller in your bank who cashed your cheque just a few days ago; now he is in the lotus pose and his eyes are turned up and he is in ecstasy. There are ashrams[4] full of little old half-starved widows who skip and dance about, they giggle and play hide and seek because they are Krishna's milkmaids. And over all this there is a sky of enormous proportions – so much larger than the earth on which you live, and often so incredibly beautiful, an unflawed unearthly blue by day, all shining with stars at night, that it is difficult to believe that something grand and wonderful beyond the bounds of human comprehension does not emanate from there.

I love listening to Indian devotional songs. They seem pure like water drawn from a well; and the emotions they express are both beautiful and easy to understand because the imagery employed is so human. The soul crying out for God is always shown as the beloved yearning for the lover in an easily recognisable way ('I wait for Him. Do you hear His step? He has come'). I feel soothed when I hear such songs and all my discontentment falls away. I see that everything I have been fretting about is of no impor-

---

4 Spiritual retreats.

tance at all because all that matters is this promise of eternal bliss in the Lover's arms. I become patient and good and feel that everything is good. Unfortunately this tranquil state does not last for long, and after a time it again seems to me that nothing is good and neither am I. Once somebody said to me: 'Just see, how sweet is the Indian soul that can see God in a cow!' But when I try to assume this sweetness, it turns sour: for, however much I may try and fool myself, whatever veils I may try, for the sake of peace of mind, to draw over my eyes, it is soon enough clear to me that the cow *is* a cow, and a very scrawny, underfed, diseased one at that. And then I feel that I want to keep this knowledge, however painful it is, and not exchange it for some other that may be true for an Indian but can never quite become that for me.

And here, it seems to me, I come to the heart of my problem. To live in India and be at peace one must to a very considerable extent become Indian and adopt Indian attitudes, habits, beliefs, assume if possible an Indian personality. But how is this possible? And even if it were possible – without cheating oneself – would it be desirable? Should one want to try and become something other than what one is? I don't always say no to this question. Sometimes it seems to me how pleasant it would be to say yes and give in and wear a sari and be meek and accepting and see God in a cow. Other times it seems worth while to be defiant and European and – all right, be crushed by one's environment, but all the same have made some attempt to remain standing. Of course, this can't go on indefinitely and in the end I'm bound to lose – if only at the point where my ashes are immersed in the Ganges to the accompaniment of Vedic hymns, and then who will say that I have not truly merged with India?

I do sometimes go back to Europe. But after a time I get bored there and want to come back here. I also find it hard now to stand the European climate. I have got used to intense heat and seem to need it.

§ *Psychology of migration* Ghose (1), Rushdie, Mistry; *'West' in South Asia* Ranasinghe

ZULFIKAR GHOSE (1935–)

1: This Landscape, These People

I

My eighth spring in England I walk among
    the silver birches of Putney Heath,
    stepping over twigs and stones: being stranger,
    I see but do not touch: only the earth
5   permits an attachment. I do not wish
    to be seen, and move, eyes at my sides, like a fish.

And do they notice me, I wonder, these
Englishmen strolling with stiff country strides?
I lean against a tree, my eyes are knots
10   in its bark, my skin the wrinkles in its sides.
I leap hedges, duck under chestnut boughs,
and through the black clay let my swift heels trail like
     ploughs.

A child at a museum, England for me
is an exhibit behind a glass case.
15   The country, like an antique chair, has a rope
across it. I may not sit, only pace
its frontiers. I slip through ponds, jump ditches,
through galleries of ferns see England in pictures.

II
My seventeen years in India I swam
20   along the silver beaches of Bombay,
pulled coconuts from the sky, and tramped
red horizons with the swagger and sway
of Romantic youth; with the impudence
of a native tongue, I cried for independence.

25   A troupe came to town, marched through villages;
began with two tight-rope walkers, eyes gay
and bamboos and rope on their bare shoulders;
a snake charmer joined them, beard long and grey,
baskets of cobras on his turbaned head;
30   through villages marched: children, beating on drums, led

them from village to village, and jugglers
joined them and swallowers of swords, eaters
of fire brandishing flames through the thick air,
jesters with tongues obscene as crows', creatures
35   of the earth: stray dogs, lean jackals, a cow;
stamping, shouting, entertaining, making a row

from village to village they marched to town:
conjurers to bake bread out of earth, poets
to recite epics at night. The troupe, grown
40   into a nation, halted, squirmed: the sets
for its act, though improvised, were re-cast
from the frames of an antique, slow-moving, dead past.

India halted: as suddenly as a dog,
barking, hangs out his tongue, stifles his cry.
45   An epic turned into a monologue
of death. The rope lay stiff across the country;
all fires were eaten, swallowed were all the swords;
the horizon paled, then thickened, blackened with crows.

Born to this continent, all was mine
50   to pluck and taste: pomegranates to purple
my tongue and chillies to burn my mouth. Stones
were there to kick. This landscape, these people –
bound by a rope, consumed by their own fire.
Born here, among these people, I was a stranger.

III
55   This landscape, these people! Silver birches
with polished trunks chalked around a chestnut.
All is fall-of-night still. No thrush reaches
into the earth for worms, nor pulls at the root
of a crocus. Dogs have led their masters home.
60   I stroll, head bowed, hearing only the sound of loam
at my heel's touch. Now I am intimate
with England; we meet, secret as lovers.
I pluck leaves and speak into the air's mouth;
as a woman's hair, I deck with flowers
65   the willow's branches; I sit by the pond,
my eyes are stars in its stillness; as with a wand,

I stir the water with a finger until
it tosses waves, until countries appear
from its dark bed: the road from Putney Hill
70   runs across oceans into the harbour
of Bombay. To this country I have come.
Stranger or an inhabitant, this is my home.

§ *South Asian diaspora* Ghose (2), Naipaul, Mukherjee, Gooneratne,
Rushdie, Mistry; Af: Vassanji; Carib: Naipaul (2); NZSP: Subramani; SEA:
Maniam

2: The Attack on Sialkot

Grandfather, eighty now, his pilgrimage
to Mecca over, still lives there, at peace
with his Muslim conscience. At our last meeting
he sat in the courtyard of a mosque, still

5   as an idol, while I stood outside, garish
as a poster against the whitewashed wall
in my mohair suit and corduroy hat,
advertising my patient secularism.

Gunfire made Sialkot a kiln to fire
10   Pakistan's earthen-pot faith. I listened
to the news hour after hour the whole month
and saw maps in newspapers, an arrow
pointed at Sialkot. Grandfather's breastplate
of Islam had become fragile as china
15   in the intruding heresy of tanks.
I see that arrow still: aimed at grandfather.

It was a messy, a child's pudding plate
of a town during my first seven years.
I pulled at grandfather's beard and dragged down
20   his turban when he carried me to school.
He turned five times a day towards Mecca, bowed
low in prayer and at night swung me round
the bed so that my feet did not insult
the holy direction, the one truth he knew.

25   From the east and southeast the tanks, from the air
the jets converged all month on Sialkot
in a massive pilgrimage, bloodier than
the annual sacrifice of goats and sheep.
Grandfather, the landmarks are falling, which
30   way will you turn now? Islam, Islam, that's
all you cared for, stubborn as a child, while
I had gone westward, begun to eat pork.

Grandfather, if the old house falls, if you
die where you built and Sialkot collapses,
35   I shall have no Mecca to turn to, who
admire cathedrals for their architecture.
Religion is irrelevant to grief:
you will not agree, nor will Pakistan,
finding in this war the old Islamic
40   pride rise like a congregation in a mosque.

§ *Grandfather poems*: SA: Mahapatra; Can: Purdy (1), Mandel, Bowering;
Partition of sub-continent SA: Ghosh, Sidhwa

V. S. NAIPAUL (1932–)

From A Way in the World

Described by Naipaul as 'a sequence', *A Way in the World* is a work which dissolves boundaries between fact and fiction and history and autobiography, by interspersing fragmentary accounts of episodes from the author's own life with 'unwritten stories', two of them fictionalized dramatizations of episodes in Trinidadian history which Naipaul had previously treated in *The Loss of El Dorado*. The book propounds a view of history as a layered site, illustrating the extent to which cultures are built 'on the middens of their predecessors' and thus repudiating cultural essentialism. Here in the Prelude, the story of Leonard Side introduces the text's concern with the problematics of mixed, trans-cultural origins.

I left home more than forty years ago. I was eighteen. When I went back, after six years – and slowly: a two-week journey by steamer – everything was strange and not strange: the suddenness of night, the very big leaves of some trees, the shrunken streets, the corrugated-iron roofs. You could walk down a street and hear the American advertising jingles coming out of the Rediffusion sets in all the little open houses. Six years before I had known the jingles the Rediffusion sets played; but these jingles were all new to me and were like somebody else's folksong now.

All the people on the streets were darker than I remembered: Africans, Indians, whites, Portuguese, mixed Chinese. In their houses, though, people didn't look so dark. I suppose that was because on the streets I was more of a looker, half a tourist, and when I went to a house it was to be with people I had known years before. So I saw them more easily.

To go back home was to play with impressions in this way, the way I played with the first pair of glasses I had, looking at a world now sharp and small and not quite real, now standard size and real but blurred; the way I played with my first pair of dark glasses, moving between dazzle and coolness; or the way, on this first return, when I was introduced to air-conditioning, I liked to move from the coolness of an air-conditioned room to the warmth outside, and back again. I was in time, over the years, and over many returns, to get used to what was new; but that shifting about of reality never really stopped. I could call it up whenever I wished. Up to about twenty years ago whenever I went back I could persuade myself from time to time that I was in a half-dream, knowing and not knowing. It was a pleasant feeling; it was a little like the sensations that came to me as a child when, once in the rainy season, I had 'fever'.

It was at a time like that, a time of 'fever', during a return, that I heard about Leonard Side, a decorator of cakes and arranger of flowers. I heard about him from a school teacher.

The school she taught at was a new one, beyond the suburbs of the town, and in what had been country and plantations right up to the end of the war. The school grounds still looked like a piece of a cleared sugar-cane or coconut estate. There wasn't even a tree. The plain two-storey concrete building – green roof, cream-coloured walls – stood by itself in the openness and the glare.

The teacher said, 'The work we were doing in those early days was a little bit like social work, with girls from labouring families. Some of them had brothers or fathers or relations who had gone to jail; they talked about this in the most natural way. One day, at a staff meeting in that very hot school with the glare all around, one of the senior teachers, a Presbyterian Indian lady, suggested that we should have a May Day fair, to introduce the girls to that idea. Everybody agreed, and we decided that the thing to do would be to ask the girls to make flower displays or arrangements, and to give a prize to the girl who did the best display.

'If you had a prize you had to have a judge. If you didn't have a good judge the idea wouldn't work. Who was this judge to be? The people we taught were very cynical. They got it from their families. Oh, they were very respectful and so on, but they thought that everybody and everything was crooked, and in their heart of hearts they looked down on the people above them. So we couldn't have a judge from the government or the Education Department or anybody too famous. This didn't leave us with too many names.

'One of the junior teachers, very young, a country girl herself, fresh from the GTC, the Government Training College, then said that Leonard Side would make the perfect judge.

'Who was Leonard Side?

'The girl had to think. Then she said, "He work all his life in flowers."

'Well. But then somebody else remembered the name. She said Leonard Side gave little courses at the WAA, the Women's Auxiliary Association, and people there liked him. That was the place to find him.

'The Women's Auxiliary Association had been founded during the war and was modelled on the WVS in England. They had a building in Parry's Corner, which was in the heart of the city. There was everything in Parry's Corner, a garage for buses, a garage for taxis, a funeral parlour, two cafés, a haberdashery and dry-goods shop, and a number of little houses, some of them offices, some of them dwelling-places; and the well-known Parry family owned it all.

'It was easy for me to go to Parry's Corner, and I offered to go and talk to Leonard Side. The WAA was in a very small building from the Spanish time. The flat front wall – a thick rubble wall, plastered and painted, with rusticated stone slabs at either end – rose up directly from the pavement, so that you stepped from the narrow pavement straight into the front room. The front door was bang in the middle of the pavement wall, and there was a little curtained window on either side. Door and windows had yellow-brown jalousies, linked wooden cross slats you could lift all at once and use an iron pin to close.

'A brown woman was sitting at a desk, and on the dusty wall – dust catching on the unevenness of the plastered rubble wall – were Information Office posters from England. The Tower of London, the English countryside.

'I said, "They tell me I could find Mr Side here."

' "He over there, across the road," the woman at the desk said.

'I crossed the road. As always at this time of day, the asphalt was soft and black, as black as the oil-stained concrete floor of the big shed of a garage where the Parry buses were. The building I entered was a modern one, with grey-washed decorated concrete blocks mimicking chipped stone. It was a very clean and plain kind of place, like a doctor's office.

'I said to the girl sitting at the table, "Mr Side?"

'She said, "Go right in."

'I went through to the inner room, and there I could hardly believe what I saw. A dark Indian man was doing things with his fingers to a dead body on a table or slab in front of him. I had gone to Parry's Funeral Parlour. It was a famous place; it advertised every day on the radio with organ music. I suppose Leonard Side was dressing the body. "Dressing" – I just knew the word. I had had no idea what it meant. I was too frightened and shocked to say anything. I ran out of the room, and the front room, and got out into the open again. The man ran out after me, calling in a soft voice, "Miss, miss."

'And really he was quite a good-looking man, in spite of the hairy fingers I had seen dressing the dead body on the table. He was very pleased to be asked to judge the girls' flower competition. He even said he wanted to give the first prize. He said that if we allowed him he would make a special posy. And he did, too. A little posy of pink rosebuds. Our May Day fair was a great success.

'A year passed. Fair time came again, and I had to go again and look for Leonard Side. This time I wasn't going to forget: I wasn't going to the funeral parlour. The only place I was going to meet Leonard Side was the Women's Association. I went there late one afternoon after school, about five. The little Spanish-style house was full of women, and in the inside room Leonard Side was doing things with dough, using those hairy fingers to knead dough. Using those fingers to work in a little more milk, then a little more butter.

'He was teaching the women how to make bread and cake. After he had finished doing the dough, he began to teach them how to ice a cake, forcing with those hairy fingers coloured icing out of the special cones or moulds he had. He pressed on and then into the moulds with his hairy fingers, and out came a pink or green rosebud or a flower, which he then fixed with icing-flecked fingers on to the soft iced cake. The women said ooh and aah, and he, very happy with his audience and his work, worked on, like a magician.

'But I didn't like seeing those fingers doing this kind of work, and I liked it less when, at the end, with those same fingers he offered the women little things he had iced, to eat on the spot, as a treat. He liked offering these little treats. They were offered almost like a wafer in church, and the women, concentrating, ate and tasted with a similar kind of respect.

'The third year came. This time I thought I wouldn't go to Parry's Corner to meet Leonard Side. I thought I would go to his house instead. I had found out where he lived. He lived in St James, quite near where I lived. That was a surprise: that he should have been so close, living that life, and I shouldn't have known.

'I went after school. I was wearing a slender black skirt and a white shirty top and I was carrying a bag with school books. I blew the horn when I stopped. A woman came out to the front gallery, bright in the afternoon light, and she said, "Come right in." Just like that, as though she knew me.

'When I went up the steps to the front gallery she said, "Come in, Doctor. Poor Lenny. He so sick, Doctor."

'Doctor – that was because of the car and blowing the horn, and the bag, and the clothes I was wearing. I thought I would explain later, and I followed her through this little old St James wood house to the back room. There I found Leonard Side, very sick and trembling, but dressed for a meeting with the doctor. He was in a shiny brass fourposter bed with a flowered canopy, and he was in green silk pyjamas. His little hairy fingers were resting on the satin or silk spread he was using as a coverlet. He had laid himself out with great care, and the coverlet was folded back neatly.

'There were crepe-paper flowers in a brass vase on a thin-legged side table or vase-stand, and there were satiny cushions and big bows on two simple cane-bottomed bent-wood chairs. I knew at once that a lot of that satin and silk had come from the funeral parlour, and was material for the coffins and the laying out of the bodies.

'He was a Mohammedan, everyone knew. But he was so much a man of his job – laying out Christian bodies, though nobody thought of it quite like that – that in that bedroom of his he even had a framed picture of Christ in Majesty, radiating light and gold, and lifting a finger of blessing.

'The picture was centrally placed above the door and leaned forward so much that the blessing of the finger would have seemed aimed at the man on the bed. I knew that the picture wasn't there for the religion alone: it was also for the beauty, the colours, the gold, the long wavy hair of Christ. And I believe I was more shocked than when I saw him dressing the body and later when I saw him using the same fingers to knead dough and then to squeeze out the terrible little blobs of icing.

'It was late afternoon, warm still, and through the open window came the smell of the cesspits of St James, the cesspits of those dirt yards with the separate little wood houses, two or three to a lot, with runnels of filth from the latrines, runnels that ran green and shiny and then dried away in the dirt; with the discoloured stones where people put out their washing to bleach; with irregular little areas where the earth was mounded up with dust and sand and gravel, and where fruit trees and little shrubs grew, creating the effect not of gardens but of little patches of waste ground where things grew haphazardly.

'When I looked at those hairy fingers on the coverlet and thought about the house and the woman who had called me in – his mother – I wondered about his life and felt sorry and frightened for him. He was sick now; he wanted help. I didn't have the heart to talk to him about the girls and the May Day fair, and I left the house and never saw him again.

'It was his idea of beauty that upset me, I suppose. That idea of beauty had taken him to the job in the funeral parlour, and had got him to deck out his bedroom in the extravagant way he had. That idea of beauty – mixing roses and flowers and nice things to eat with the idea of making the dead human body beautiful too – was contrary to my own idea. The mixing of things upset me. It didn't upset him. I had thought something like that the very first time I had seen him, when he had left his dead body and run out after me to the street, saying, "Miss, miss," as though he couldn't understand why I was leaving.

'He was like so many of the Indian men you see on the streets in St James, slender fellows in narrow-waisted trousers and open-necked shirts. Ordinary, even with the good looks. But he had that special idea of beauty.

'That idea of beauty, surprising as it was, was not a secret. Many people would have known about it – like the junior teacher who had brought his name up at the staff meeting, and then didn't know how to describe him. He would have been used to people treating him in a special way: the women in the classes clapping him, other people mocking him or scorning him, and people like me running away from him because he frightened us. He frightened me because I felt his feeling for beauty was like an illness; as though some unfamiliar, deforming virus had passed through his simple mother to him, and was even then – he was in his mid-thirties – something neither of them had begun to understand.'

This was what I heard, and the teacher couldn't tell me what had happened to Leonard Side; she had never thought to ask. Perhaps he had joined the great migration to England or the United States. I wondered whether in that other place Leonard Side had come to some understanding of his nature; or whether the thing that had frightened the teacher had, when the time of revelation came, also frightened Leonard Side.

He knew he was a Mohammedan, in spite of the picture of Christ in his bedroom. But he would have had almost no idea of where he or his ancestors had come from. He wouldn't have guessed that the name Side might have been a version of Sayed, and that his grandfather or great-grandfather might have come from a Shia Muslim group in India. From Lucknow, perhaps; there was even a street in St James called Lucknow Street. All Leonard Side would have known of himself and his ancestors would have been what he had awakened to in his mother's house in St James. In that he was like the rest of us.

With learning now I can tell you more or less how we all came to be where we were. I can tell you that the Amerindian name for that land of St James would have been Cumucurapo, which the early travellers from Europe turned to Conquerabo or Conquerabia. I can look at the vegetation and tell you what was there when Columbus came and what was imported later. I can reconstruct the plantations that were laid out on that area of St James. The recorded history of the place is short, three centuries of depopulation followed by two centuries of resettlement. The documents of the resettlement are available in the city, in the Registrar-General's Office. While the documents last we can hunt up the story of every strip of occupied land.

I can give you that historical bird's eye view. But I cannot really explain the mystery of Leonard Side's inheritance. Most of us know the parents or grandparents we come from. But we go back and back, forever; we go back all of us to the very beginning; in our blood and bone and brain we carry the memories of thousands of beings. I might say that an ancestor of Leonard Side's came from the dancing groups of Lucknow, the lewd men who painted their faces and tried to live like women. But that would only be a fragment of his inheritance, a fragment of the truth. We cannot understand all the traits we have inherited. Sometimes we can be strangers to ourselves.

§ *Origins* Can: Wiebe, Kroetsch (1); Naipaul also in Carib

ANNE RANASINGHE (1925–)

At What Dark Point

Every morning I see him
Sitting in the speckled shade
Of my blossom laden araliya tree
Which I planted many years ago
5   In my garden, and the branches now
Have spread into our lane.
Under my tree in a shadow of silence
He sits, and with long skeletal hands
Sorts strands from a tangle of juten fibres
10   And twisting, twisting makes a rope
That grows. And grows. Each day.

Every morning I pass him. He sits
In the golden-haze brightness under
The white-velvet fragrance of
15   My tree. Sits
On the edge of his silence twisting
His lengthening rope and
Watching
Me.

20   And seeing him sit day after day,
Sinister, silent, twisting his rope

---

3 araliya: frangipani.

To a future purpose of evilness
I sense the charred-wood smell again,
Stained glass exploding in the flames
25   (A fireworks of fractured glass
Against the black November sky)
The streets deserted, all doors shut
At twelve o'clock at night,
And running with animal fear
30   Between high houses shuttered tight
The jackboot ringing hard and clear
While stalking with the lust for blood
I can still hear
The ironed heel – its echoing thud –
35   And still can taste the cold-winter-taste
Of charred wood midnight fear.
Knowing
That nothing is impossible
That anything is possible
40   That there is no safety
In words or houses
That boundaries are theoretical
And love is relative
To the choice before you.

45   I know
That anything is possible
Any time. There is no safety
In poems or music or even in
Philosophy. No safety
50   In houses or temples
Of any faith. And no one knows
At what dark point the time will come again
Of blood and knives, terror and pain
Of jackboots and the twisted strand
55   Of rope.
And the impress of a child's small hand
Paroxysmic mark on an oven wall
Scratched death mark on an oven wall
Is my child's hand.

§ *War/holocaust* Kogawa; *'West' in South Asia* Jhabvala

---

23 I . . . again: alluding to the holocaust from which Anne Ranasinghe fled just before the outbreak of World War II.
44 To . . . you: 'sometimes in the concentration camps fathers preferred to kill their sons rather than let them fall into the hands of the Nazis' [author's note].

26 November: Ranasinghe and and her mother fled from their flat in Essen on 9 November 1938; her father was taken to Dachau.

JOY KOGAWA (1935–)

From Obasan

Obasan is about the dispossession of Japanese-Canadians in the aftermath of Pearl Harbour. After the attack, the narrator Naomi Nakane's family are moved from their home in Vancouver, first to the interior of British Columbia and then to Alberta. The novel suggests the bigotry underlying this supposed security measure and in so doing questions Canadian commitment to cultural diversity. Naomi's Aunt Emily devotes her life to exposing the cover-up of her community's treatment in World War II, while her other aunt, Obasan, remains silent and apparently resigned, a symbol of more traditional Japanese values. *Obasan* mixes documentary-like collage with more poetic passages which suggest that there is a 'silence' which has yet to be explained. In Chapters 37 and 38, included here, Naomi finally learns the full horror of her mother's fate which has been kept from her.

Chapter 37

There are only two letters in the gray cardboard folder. The first is a brief and emotionless statement that Grandma Kato, her niece's daughter, and my mother are the only ones in the immediate family to have survived. The second letter is an outpouring.

I remember Grandma Kato as thin and tough, not given to melodrama or overstatement of any kind. She was unbreakable. I felt she could endure all things and would survive any catastrophe. But I did not then understand what catastrophes were possible in human affairs.

Here, the ordinary Granton rain slides down wet and clean along the glass, leaving a trail on the window like the Japanese writing on the thin blue-lined paper – straight down like a bead curtain of asterisks. The rain she describes is black, oily, thick, and strange.

'In the heat of the August sun,' Grandma writes, 'however much the effort to forget, there is no forgetfulness. As in a dream, I can still see the maggots crawling in the sockets of my niece's eyes. Her strong intelligent young son helped me move a bonsai tree that very morning. There is no forgetfulness.'

When Nakayama-sensei reaches the end of the page, he stops reading and folds the letter as if he has decided to read no more. Aunt Emily begins to speak quietly, telling of a final letter from the Canadian missionary, Miss Best.

How often, I am wondering, did Grandma and Mother waken in those years with the unthinkable memories alive in their minds, the visible evidence of horror written on their skin, in their blood, carved in every mirror they passed, felt in every step they took? As a child I was told only that Mother and Grandma Kato were safe in Tokyo, visiting Grandma Kato's ailing mother.

'Someday, surely, they will return,' Obasan used to say.

The two letters that reached us in Vancouver before all communication ceased due to the war told us that Mother and Grandma Kato had arrived safely in Japan and were staying with Grandma Kato's sister and her husband in their home near the Tokyo Gas Company. My great-grandmother was then seventy-nine and was not expected to live to be eighty but, happily, she had become so well that she had returned home from the hospital and was even able on occasion to leave the house.

Nakayama-sensei opens the letter again and holds it, reading silently. Then, looking over to Stephen, he says, 'It is better to speak, is it not?'

'They're dead now,' Stephen says.

Sensei nods.

'Please read, Sensei,' I whisper.

'Yes,' Aunt Emily says. 'They should know.'

Sensei starts again at the beginning. The letter is dated simply 1949. It was sent, Sensei says, from somewhere in Nagasaki. There was no return address.

'Though it was a time of war,' Grandma writes, 'what happiness that January 1945 to hear from my niece Setsuko, in Nagasaki.' Setsuko's second child was due to be born within the month. In February, just as American air raids in Tokyo were intensifying, Mother went to help her cousin in Nagasaki. The baby was born three days after she arrived. Early in March, air raids and alarms were constant day and night in Tokyo. In spite of all the dangers of travel, Grandma Kato went to Nagasaki to be with my mother and to help with the care of the new baby. The last day she spent with her mother and sister in Tokyo, she said they sat on the tatami[1] and talked, remembering their childhood and the days they went chestnut picking together. They parted with laughter. The following night, Grandma Kato's sister, their mother, and her sister's husband died in the B-29 bombings of March 9, 1945.

From this point on, Grandma's letter becomes increasingly chaotic, the details interspersed without chronological consistency. She and my mother, she writes, were unable to talk of all the things that happened. The horror would surely die sooner, they felt, if they refused to speak. But the silence and the constancy of the nightmare had become unbearable for Grandma and she hoped that by sharing them with her husband, she could be helped to extricate herself from the grip of the past.

'If these matters are sent away in this letter, perhaps they will depart a little from our souls,' she writes. 'For the burden of these words, forgive me.'

Mother, for her part, continued her vigil of silence. She spoke with no one about her torment. She specifically requested that Stephen and I be spared the truth.

In all my high school days, until we heard from Sensei that her grave had been found in Tokyo, I pictured her trapped in Japan by government regu-

---

1 Japanese mat.

lations, or by an ailing grandmother. The letters I sent to the address in Tokyo were never answered or returned. I could not know that she and Grandma Kato had gone to Nagasaki to stay with Setsuko, her husband, who was a dentist, and their two children, four-year-old Tomio and the new baby, Chieko.

The baby, Grandma writes, looked so much like me that she and my mother marveled and often caught themselves calling her Naomi. With her widow's peak, her fat cheeks and pointed chin, she had a heart-shaped face like mine. Tomio, however, was not like Stephen at all. He was a sturdy child, extremely healthy and athletic, with a strong will like his father. He was fascinated by his new baby sister, sitting and watching her for hours as she slept or nursed. He made dolls for her. He helped to dress her. He loved to hold her in the bath, feeling her fingers holding his fingers tightly. He rocked her to sleep in his arms.

The weather was hot and humid that morning of August 9. The air-raid alerts had ended. Tomio and some neighborhood children had gone to the irrigation ditch to play and cool off as they sometimes did.

Shortly after eleven o'clock, Grandma Kato was preparing to make lunch. The baby was strapped to her back. She was bending over a bucket of water beside a large earthenware storage bin when a child in the street was heard shouting, 'Look at the parachute!' A few seconds later, there was a sudden white flash, brighter than a bolt of lightning. She had no idea what could have exploded. It was as if the entire sky were swallowed up. A moment later she was hurled sideways by a blast. She had a sensation of floating tranquilly in a cool whiteness high above the earth. When she regained consciousness, she was slumped forward in a sitting position in the water bin. She gradually became aware of the moisture, an intolerable heat, blood, a mountain of debris, and her niece's weak voice, sounding at first distant, calling the names of her children. Then she could hear the other sounds – the faraway shouting. Around her, a thick dust made breathing difficult. Chieko was still strapped to her back, but made no sound. She was alive but unconscious.

It took Grandma a long time to claw her way out of the wreckage. When she emerged, it was into an eerie twilight formed of heavy dust and smoke that blotted out the sun. What she saw was incomprehensible. Almost all the buildings were flattened or in flames for as far as she could see. The landmarks were gone. Tall columns of fire rose through the haze and everywhere the dying and the wounded crawled, fled, stumbled like ghosts among the ruins. Voices screamed, calling the names of children, fathers, mothers, calling for help, calling for water.

Beneath some wreckage, she saw first the broken arm, then the writhing body of her niece, her head bent back, her hair singed, both her eye sockets blown out. In a weak and delirious voice, she was calling Tomio. Grandma Kato touched her niece's leg and the skin peeled off and stuck to the palm of her hand.

It isn't clear from the letter but at some point she came across Tomio, his legs pumping steadily up and down as he stood in one spot not knowing where to go. She gathered him in her arms. He was remarkably intact, his skin unburned.

She had no idea where Mother was, but with the two children, she began making her way toward the air-raid shelter. All around her people one after another collapsed and died, crying for water. One old man no longer able to keep moving lay on the ground holding up a dead baby and crying, 'Save the children. Leave the old.' No one took the dead child from his outstretched hands. Men, women, in many cases indistinguishable by sex, hairless, half clothed, hobbled past. Skin hung from their bodies like tattered rags. One man held his bowels in with the stump of one hand. A child whom Grandma Kato recognized lay on the ground asking for help. She stopped and told him she would return as soon as she could. A woman she knew was begging for someone to help her lift the burning beam beneath which her children were trapped. The woman's children were friends of Tomio's. Grandma was loath to walk past, but with the two children, she could do no more and kept going. At no point does Grandma Kato mention the injuries she herself must have sustained.

Nearing the shelter, Grandma could see through the grayness that the entrance was clogged with dead bodies. She remembered then that her niece's father-in-law lived on a farm on the hillside, and she began making her way back through the burning city toward the river she would have to cross. The water, red with blood, was a raft of corpses. Farther upstream, the bridge was twisted like noodles. Eventually she came to a spot where she was able to cross and, still carrying the two children, Grandma Kato made her way up the hillside.

After wandering for some time, she found a wooden waterpipe dribbling a steady stream. She held Tomio's mouth to it and allowed him to drink as much as he wished though she had heard that too much water was not good. She unstrapped the still unconscious baby from her back. Exhausted, she drank from the pipe, and gathering the two children in her arms, she looked out at the burning city and lapsed into a sleep so deep she believed she was unconscious.

When she awakened, she was in the home of her niece's relatives and the baby was being fed barley water. The little boy was nowhere.

Almost immediately, Grandma set off to look for the child. Next day she returned to the area of her niece's home and every day thereafter she looked for Mother and the lost boy, checking the lists of the dead, looking over the unclaimed corpses. She discovered that her niece's husband was among the dead.

One evening when she had given up the search for the day, she sat down beside a naked woman she'd seen earlier who was aimlessly chipping wood to make a pyre on which to cremate a dead baby. The woman was utterly disfigured. Her nose and one cheek were almost gone. Great wounds and pustules covered her entire face and body. She was completely bald. She sat in a cloud of flies, and maggots wriggled among her wounds. As Grandma watched her, the woman gave her a vacant gaze, then let out a cry. It was my mother.

The little boy was never found. Mother was taken to a hospital and was expected to die, but she survived. During one night she vomited yellow fluid and passed a great deal of blood. For a long time – Grandma does not say how long – Mother wore bandages on her face. When they were removed, Mother felt her face with her fingers, then asked for a cloth mask. Thereafter she would not take off her mask from morning to night.

'At this moment,' Grandma writes, 'we are preparing to visit Chieko-chan in the hospital.' Chieko, four years old in 1949, waited daily for their visit, standing in the hospital corridor, tubes from her wrist attached to a bottle that was hung above her. A small bald-headed girl. She was dying of leukemia.

'There may not be many more days,' Grandma concludes.

After this, what could have happened? Did they leave the relatives in Nagasaki? Where and how did they survive?

When Sensei is finished reading, he folds and unfolds the letter, nodding his head slowly.

I put my hands around the teapot, feeling its round warmth against my palms. My skin feels hungry for warmth, for flesh. Grandma mentioned in her letter that she saw one woman cradling a hot-water bottle as if it were a baby.

Sensei places the letter back in the cardboard folder and closes it with the short red string around the tab.

'That there is brokenness,' he says quietly. 'That this world is brokenness. But within brokenness is the unbreakable name. How the whole earth groans till Love returns.'

I stand up abruptly and leave the room, going into the kitchen for some more hot water. When I return, Sensei is sitting with his face in his hands.

Stephen is staring at the floor, his body hunched forward motionless. He glances up at me, then looks away swiftly. I sit on a stool beside him and try to concentrate on what is being said. I can hear Aunt Emily telling us about Mother's grave. Then Nakayama-sensei stands and begins to say the Lord's Prayer under his breath. 'And forgive us our trespasses – forgive us our trespasses,' he repeats, sighing deeply, 'as we forgive others . . .' He lifts his head, looking upward. 'We are powerless to forgive unless we first are forgiven. It is a high calling, my friends – the calling to forgive. But no person, no people is innocent. Therefore we must forgive one another.'

I am not thinking of forgiveness. The sound of Sensei's voice grows as indistinct as the hum of distant traffic. Gradually the room grows still and it is as if I am back with Uncle again, listening and listening to the silent earth and the silent sky as I have done all my life.

I close my eyes.

Mother, I am listening. Assist me to hear you.

Chapter 38

Silent Mother, you do not speak or write. You do not reach through the night to enter morning, but remain in the voicelessness. From the extremity of much dying, the only sound that reaches me now is the sigh of your remembered breath, a wordless word. How shall I attend that speech, Mother, how shall I trace that wave?

You are tide rushing moonward pulling back from the shore. A raft rocks on the surface bobbing in the dark. The water fills with flailing arms that beckon like seaweed on the prow. I sit on the raft begging for a tide to land me safely on the sand but you draw me to the white distance, skyward and away from this blood-drugged earth.

By the time this country opened its pale arms to you, it was too late. First, you could not, then you chose not to come. Now you are gone. Tonight, Aunt Emily has said a missionary found your name on a plaque of the dead. A Canadian maple tree grows there where your name stands. The tree utters its scarlet voice in the air. Prayers bleeding. Its rustling leaves are fingers scratching an empty sky.

There is no date on the memorial stone. There are no photographs ever again. 'Do not tell Stephen and Naomi,' you say. "I am praying that they may never know.'

Martyr Mother, you pilot your powerful voicelessness over the ocean and across the mountain, straight as a missile to our hut on the edge of a sugar-beet field. You wish to protect us with lies, but the camouflage does not hide your cries. Beneath the hiding I am there with you. Silent Mother, lost in the abandoning, you do not share the horror. At first, stumbling and unaware of pain, you open your eyes in the red mist and, sheltering a dead child, you flee through the flames. Young Mother at Nagasaki, am I not also there?

In the dark Slocan night, the bright light flares in my dreaming. I hear the screams and feel the mountain breaking. Your long black hair falls and falls into the chasm. My legs are sawn in half. The skin on your face bubbles like lava and melts from your bones. Mother, I see your face. Do not turn aside.

Mother, in my dreams you are a maypole. I dance around you with a long paper streamer in my hand. But the words of the May Day song are words of distress. The unknown is a hook that pierces the bone. Thongs hang down in the hot prairie air. Silence attends the long sun dance.

Grandma sits at a low table in a bombed country writing words she does not intend me to hear. 'The child,' she writes, 'is not well.' She does not declare her own state of health. The letters take months to reach Grandfather. They take years to reach me. Grandfather gives the letters to Aunt Emily. Aunt Emily sends letters to the Government. The Government makes paper airplanes out of our lives and files us out the windows. Some people return home. Some do not. War, they all say, is war, and some people survive.

No one knows the exact day that you die. Aunt Emily writes and receives no replies. All that is left is your word, 'Do not tell . . . .'

Obasan and Uncle hear your request. They give me no words from you. They hand me old photographs.

You stand on a street corner in Vancouver in a straight silky dress and a light black coat. On your head is a wide-brimmed hat with a feather and your black shoes have one strap and a buckle at the side. I stand leaning into you, my dress bulging over my round baby belly. My fat arm clings to your leg. Your skirt hides half my face. Your leg is a tree trunk and I am branch, vine, butterfly. I am joined to your limbs by right of birth, child of your flesh, leaf of your bough.

The tree is a dead tree in the middle of the prairies. I sit on its roots still as a stone. In my dreams, a small child sits with a wound on her knee. The wound on her knee is on the back of her skull, large and moist. A double wound. The child is forever unable to speak. The child forever fears to tell. I apply a thick bandage but nothing can soak up the seepage. I beg that the woundedness may be healed and that the limbs may learn to dance. But you stay in a black-and-white photograph, smiling your yasashi smile.

Gentle Mother, we were lost together in our silences. Our wordlessness was our mutual destruction.

Nakayama-sensei is still praying softly, a long long prayer.

'Father, if your suffering is greater than ours, how great that suffering must be,' he is saying. 'How great the helplessness. How we dare not abandon the ones who suffer, lest we again abandon You.' His voice rises and falls as it did when he was praying at Grandma Nakane's funeral in Slocan. 'We are abandoned yet we are not abandoned. You are present in every hell. Teach us to see Love's presence in our abandonment. Teach us to forgive.'

Obasan's eyes are closed and her hands are moving back and forth across the gray cardboard folder – to erase, to soothe.

I am thinking that for a child there is no presence without flesh. But perhaps it is because I am no longer a child I can know your presence though you are not here. The letters tonight are skeletons. Bones only. But the earth still stirs with dormant blooms. Love flows through the roots of the trees by our graves.

§ *War/holocaust* Ranasinghe; *Critique of Canadian multiculturalism* Mistry

DAPHNE MARLATT (1942–)

Arriving at Shared Ground Through Difference

It wasn't sharing but difference in a multiplicity of ways i felt first as a child in Malaya where i was taught the King's (it was then) English, to mind my P's & Q's, to behave and speak 'properly,' when all the while i was surrounded by other languages that were not proper at all for a white colonial child, but which nevertheless i longed to understand, filled as they were with laughter, jokes, calls, exclamations, comfort, humming. Sometimes rocked to sleep, sometimes teased or scolded, sometimes ignored by the sounds of Cantonese, Malay, Thai, i stood on the fringe and longed to know what the stories were that produced such laughter, such shakings of the head. When my Amahs[1] spoke only English, they knew and i knew it was not the same, it meant we had to be 'proper.' O the complexities of the power dynamic between colonial children and their mother-substitutes, these women who had given up the possibility of families for themselves but who nevertheless led other lives, barely heard between the lines proper to their servant roles, and who illicitly imparted some of that culture, some of that life-experience to their Mem's[2] children. I grew up loving the emotive sound of women's voices and distrustful of a system that dismissed women's experience in general, and some women's more than others', depending on the colour of their skin and the language(s) they spoke – and many spoke more than the single-minded ruling one.

Then there was my mother's mother tongue: English English with its many intensifiers, its emphatic sentence pitches, its ringing tones of boarding-school elocution lessons. Learning to speak properly – 'Don't drawl like that, it sounds so dreadfully American. Why can't you pronounce the ends of your words?' The trouble was i had become embarrassed by the language i spoke which branded me as both excessive (those intensifiers) and excessively polite in Canadian schoolyards. My speech sounded exaggerated: 'Wha'd ya mean "awfully sorry"' You're not awful are you?' It sounded pretentious: 'listen, *nobody* walks on the *grawss*.' At first 'wanna,' and 'movies' and 'you guys' sounded funny in my mouth, as if i were trying to speak counterfeit words. But imitation cut both ways: there was now a whole new level of my own vocabulary, words that sounded false on the street: cinema, rubbish, being sent to Coventry, not to mention that give-away, Mummy, a world away from Mom. And so i engaged in long battles with my mother, each of us trying to correct the other, she correcting for purity of origin, while i corrected for common usage – each of us with different versions of 'the real thing.' The struggle over reality is a deadly one that cuts to the root of being. Words were always taken seriously in my house because they

---

1 Nannies; nursemaids. 2 Memsahibs; European ladies.

were the weapons of that struggle. But a woman's sense of herself in the language she speaks can only be denied so long before it transforms into a darker (side of the moon), a more insistent ir-reality, not unreal because its effects are felt so devastatingly in its subject and those around her. Her words, her very style of speaking derided by her own children, her colonial manners and English boarding-school mores dismissed as inappropriate by Canadianized daughters who denied any vestige of them in their own behaviour and speech, she withdrew into chronic depression and hypochondria. 'Unbalanced.' 'Loony.' But to deny: to completely say no to. A powerful mechanism. A form of colonialism at work within the family.

§ *Psychology/language of migrancy* Ondaatje (2), D'Aguiar, Philip, Mistry; Marlatt also in Can

BHARATI MUKHERJEE (1940–)

Loose Ends

She sends for this Goldilocks doll in April.

'See,' she says. The magazine is pressed tight to her T-shirt. 'It's porcelain.'

I look. The ad calls Goldilocks 'the first doll in an enchanting new suite of fairy tale dolls.'

'*Bisque* porcelain,' she says. She fills out the order form in purple ink. 'Look at the pompoms on her shoes. Aren't they darling?'

'You want to blow sixty bucks?' Okay, so I yell that at Jonda. 'You have any idea how much I got to work for sixty dollars?'

'Only twenty now,' she says. Then she starts bitching. 'What's with you and Velásquez these days? You shouldn't even be home in the afternoon.'

It's between one and two and I have a right, don't I, to be in my Manufactured Home – as they call it – in Laguna Vista Estates instead of in Mr. Vee's pastel office in the mall? A man's mobile home is his castle, at least in Florida. But I fix her her bourbon and ginger ale with the dash of RealLemon just the way she likes it. She isn't a mail-order junky; this Goldilocks thing is more complicated.

'It makes me nervous,' Jonda goes on. 'To have you home, I mean.'

I haven't been fired by Mr. Vee; the truth is I've been offered a raise, contingent, of course, on my delivering a forceful message to that greaser[1] goon, Chavez. I don't get into that with Jonda. Jonda doesn't have much of a head for details.

'Learn to like it,' I say. 'Your boyfriend better learn, too.'

---

1 Hispanic American (derogatory).

She doesn't have anyone but me, but she seems to like the jealousy bit. Her face goes soft and dreamy like the old days. We've seen a lot together.

'Jonda,' I start. I just don't get it. What does she want?

'Forget it, Jeb.' She licks the stamp on the Goldilocks envelope so gooey it sticks on crooked. 'There's no point in us talking. We don't communicate anymore.'

I make myself a cocktail. Milk, two ice cubes crushed with a hammer between two squares of paper towel, and Maalox. Got the recipe from a Nam[2] Vets magazine.

'Look at you.' She turns on the TV and gets in bed. 'I hate to see you like this, at loose ends.'

I get in bed with her. Usually afternoons are pure dynamite, when I can get them. I lie down with her for a while, but nothing happens. We're like that until Oprah[3] comes on.

'It's okay,' Jonda says. 'I'm going to the mall. The guy who opened the new boutique, you know, the little guy with the turban, he said he might be hiring.'

I drop a whole ice cube into my Maalox cocktail and watch her change. She shimmies out of khaki shorts – mementoes of my glory days – and pulls a flowery skirt over her head. I still don't feel any urge.

'Who let these guys in?' I say. She doesn't answer. He won't hire her – they come in with half a dozen kids and pay them nothing. We're coolie labor in our own country.

She pretends to look for her car keys which are hanging as usual from their nail. 'Don't wait up for me.'

'At least let me drive you.' I'm not begging, yet.

'No, it's okay.' She fixes her wickedly green eyes on me. And suddenly bile pours out in torrents. 'Nine years, for God's sake! Nine years, and what do we have?'

'Don't let's get started.'

Hey, what we have sounds like the Constitution of the United States. We have freedom and no strings attached. We have no debts. We come and go as we like. She wants a kid but I don't think I have the makings of a good father. That's part of what the Goldilocks thing is.

But I know what she means. By the time Goldilocks arrives in the mail, she'll have moved her stuff out of Laguna Vista Estates.

I like Miami. I like the heat. You can smell the fecund rot of the jungle in every headline. You can park your car in the shopping mall and watch the dope change hands, the Goldilockses and Peter Pans go off with new daddies, the dish-washers and short-order cooks haggle over fake passports, the Mr. Vees in limos huddle over arms-shopping lists, all the while gull guano drops on your car with the soothing steadiness of rain.

Don't get me wrong. I liked the green spaces of Nam, too. In spite of the consequences. I was the Pit Bull – even the Marines backed off. I was

---

2 Vietnam.   3 Oprah Winfrey, talk-show hostess.

Jesse James hunched tight in the gunship, trolling the jungle for hidden wonders.

'If you want to stay alive,' Doc Healy cautioned me the first day, 'just keep consuming and moving like a locust. Do that, Jeb m'boy, and you'll survive to die a natural death.' Last winter a judge put a vet away for thirty-five years for sinking his teeth into sweet, succulent coed flesh. The judge said, *when gangrene sets in, the doctor has no choice but to amputate.* But I'm here to testify, Your Honor, the appetite remains, after the easy targets have all been eaten. The whirring of our locust jaws is what keeps you awake.

I take care of Chavez for Mr. Vee and come home to stale tangled sheets. Jonda's been gone nine days.

I'm not whining. Last night in the parking lot of the mall a swami with blond dreadlocks treated us to a levitation. We spied him on the roof of a discount clothing store, nudging his flying mat into liftoff position. We were the usual tourists and weirdos and murderous cubanos. First he played his sinuses OM-OOM-OOMPAH-OOM, then he pushed off from the roof in the lotus position. His bare feet sprouted like orchids from his knees. We watched him wheel and flutter for maybe two or three minutes before the cops pulled up and caught him in a safety net.

They took him away in handcuffs. Who knows how many killers and felons and honest nut cases watched it and politely went back to their cars? I love Miami.

This morning I lean on Mr. Vee's doorbell. I need money. Auguste, the bouncer he picked up in the back streets of Montreal, squeezes my wind-breaker before letting me in.

I suck in my gut and make the palm trees on my shirt ripple. 'You're blonder than you were. Blond's definitely your color.'

'Don't start with me, Marshall,' he says. He helps himself to a mint from a fancy glass bowl on the coffee table.

Mr. Vee sidles into the room; he's one hundred and seventy-five pounds of jiggling paranoia.

'You look like hell, Marshall,' is the first thing he says.

'I could say the same to you, Haysoos,'[4] I say.

His face turns mean. I scoop up a mint and flip it like a quarter.

'The last job caused me some embarrassment,' he says.

My job, I try to remind him, is to show up at a time and place of his choosing and perform a simple operation. I'm the gunship Mr. Vee calls in. He pinpoints the target, I attempt to neutralize it. It's all a matter of instrumentation and precise coordinates. With more surveillance, a longer lead time, a neutral setting, mishaps can be minimized. But not on the money Mr. Vee pays. He's itchy and impulsive; he wants a quick hit, publicity, and some sort of ego boost. I served under second looies[5] just like him, and

4 Jesus. 5 Lieutenants.

sooner or later most of them got blown away, after losing half their men.

The story was, Chavez had been sampling too much of Mr. Vee's product line. He was, as a result, inoperative with women. He lived in a little green house in a postwar development on the fringes of Liberty City, a step up, in some minds, from a trailer park. By all indications, he should have been alone. I get a little sick when wives and kids are involved, old folks, neighbors, repairmen – I'm not a monster, except when I'm being careful.

I gained entry through a window – thank God for cheap air conditioners. First surprise: he wasn't alone. I could hear that drug-deep double-breathing. Even in the dark before I open a door, I can tell a woman from a man, middle age from adolescence, a sleeping Cuban from a sleeping American. They were entwined; it looked like at long last love for poor old Chavez. She might have been fourteen, brassy-haired with wide black roots, baby-fat-bodied with a pinched, Appalachian face. I did what I was paid for; I eliminated the primary target and left no traces. Doc Healy used to teach us: torch the whole hut and make sure you get the kids, the grannies, cringing on the sleeping mat – or else you'll meet them on the trail with fire in their eyes.

Truth be told, I was never much of a marksman. My game is getting close, working the body, where accuracy doesn't count for much. We're the guys who survived that war.

The carnage at Chavez's cost me, too. You get a reputation, especially if young women are involved. You don't look so good anymore to sweatier clients.

I lean over and flick an imaginary fruit fly off Haysoos Velasquez's shiny lapel. Auguste twitches.

'What did you do that for?' he shrieks.

'I could get you deported real easy.' I smile. I want him to know that for all his flash and jangle and elocution lessons so he won't go around like an underworld Ricky Ricardo, to me he's just another boat person. 'You got something good for me today?'

A laugh leaks out of him. 'You're so burned out, Marshall, you couldn't fuck a whore.' He extracts limp bills from a safe. Two thousand to blow town for a while, till it cools.

'*Gracias, amigo.*' At least this month the trailer's safe, if not the car. Which leaves me free to hotwire a newer model.

Where did America go? I want to know. Down the rabbit hole, Doc Healy used to say. Alice knows, but she took it with her. Hard to know which one's the Wonderland. Back when me and my buddies were barricading the front door, who left the back door open?

And just look at what Alice left behind.

She left behind a pastel house, lime-sherbet color, a little south and a little west of Miami, with sprinklers batting water across a yard the size of a badminton court. In the back bedroom there's a dripping old air conditioner. The window barely closes over it. It's an old development, they don't have outside security, wire fences, patrol dogs. It's a retirement bungalow like they used to advertise in the comic pages of the Sunday papers. No one was around in those days to warn the old folks that the lots hadn't quite surfaced from the slime, and the soil was too salty to take a planting. And twenty years later there'd still be that odor – gamey, fishy, sour rot – of a tropical city on unrinsed water, where the blue air shimmers with diesel fumes and the gray water thickens like syrup from saturated waste.

Chavez, stewing in his juices.

And when your mammy and pappy die off and it's time to sell off the lime-sherbet bungalow, who's there to buy it? A nice big friendly greaser like Mr. Chavez.

Twenty years ago I missed the meaning of things around me. I was seventeen years old, in Heidelberg, Germany, about to be shipped out to Vietnam. We had guys on the base selling passages to Sweden. And I had a weekend pass and a free flight to London. Held them in my hand: Sweden forever, or a weekend pass. Wise up, kid, choose life, whispered the cook, a twenty-year lifer with a quarter million stashed in Arizona. Seventeen years old and guys are offering me life or death, only I didn't see it then.

When you're a teenage buckaroo[6] from Ocala, Florida, in London for the first time, where do you go? I went to the London Zoo. Okay, so I was a kid checking out the snakes and gators of my childhood. You learn to love a languid, ugly target.

I found myself in front of the reticulated python. This was one huge serpent. It squeezed out jaguars and crocodiles like dishrags. It was twenty-eight feet long and as thick as my waist, with a snout as long and wide as a croc's. The scale of the thing was beyond impressive, beyond incredible. If you ever want to feel helpless or see what the odds look like when they're stacked against you, imagine the embrace of the reticulated python. The tip of its tail at the far end of the concrete pool could have been in a different county. Its head was out of water, resting on the tub's front edge. The head is what got me, that broad, patient, intelligent face, those eyes brown and passionless as all of Vietnam.

Dead rabbits were plowed in a corner. I felt nothing for the bunnies.

Then I noticed the snakeshit. Python turds, dozens of turds, light as cork and thick as a tree, riding high in the water. Once you'd seen them, you couldn't help thinking you'd smelled them all along. *That's* what I mean about Florida, about all the hot-water ports like Bangkok, Manila and Bombay, living on water where the shit's so thick it's a kind of cash crop.

Behind me, one of those frosty British matrons whispered to her husband, 'I didn't know they *did* such things!'

'Believe it, Queenie,' I said.

That snakeshit – all that coiled power – stays with me, always. That's what happened to us in the paddyfields. We drowned in our shit. An

---

6 Young male.

inscrutable humanoid python sleeping on a bed of turds: that's what I never want to be.

So I keep two things in mind nowadays. First, Florida was built for your pappy and grammie. I remember them, I was a kid here, I remember the good Florida when only the pioneers came down and it was considered too hot and wet and buggy to ever come to much. I knew your pappy and grammie, I mowed their lawn, trimmed their hedges, washed their cars. I toted their golf bags. Nice people – they deserved a few years of golf, a garden to show off when their kids came down to visit, a white car that justified its extravagant air conditioning and never seemed to get dirty. That's the first thing about Florida; the nice thing. The second is this: Florida is run by locusts and behind them are sharks and even pythons and they've pretty well chewed up your mom and pop and all the other lawn bowlers and blue-haired ladies. On the outside, life goes on in Florida courtesy of middlemen who bring in things that people are willing to pay a premium to obtain.

Acapulco, Tijuana, Freeport, Miami – it doesn't matter where the pimping happens. Mr. Vee in his nostalgic moments tells me Havana used to be like that, a city of touts and pimps – the fat young men in sunglasses parked at a corner in an idling Buick, waiting for a payoff, a delivery, a contact. Havana has shifted its corporate headquarters. Beirut has come west. And now, it's Miami that gives me warm memories of always-Christmas Saigon.

It's life in the procurement belt, between those lines of tropical latitudes, where the world shops for its illicit goods and dumps its surplus parts, where it prefers to fight its wars, and once you've settled into its give and take, you find it's impossible to live anywhere else. It's the coke-and-caffeine jangle of being seventeen and readier to kill than be killed and to know that Job One is to secure your objective and after that it's unsupervised play till the next order comes down.

In this mood, and in a Civic newly liberated from a protesting coed, I am heading west out of Miami, thinking first of driving up to Pensacola when I am sideswiped off the highway. Two men get in the Civic. They sit on either side of me and light up cigarettes.

'Someone say something,' I finally say.

They riffle through the papers in the glove compartment. They quickly surmise that my name is not Mindy Robles. 'We know all about this morning. Assault. Grand theft auto.'

'Let's talk,' I say.

I wait for the rough stuff. When it comes, it's an armlock on the throat that cuts air supply. When they let me speak, I cut a deal. They spot me for a vet; we exchange some dates, names, firefights. Turns out they didn't like Mindy Robles, didn't appreciate the pressure her old man tried to put on the police department. They look at our names – Robles and Marshall – and I can read their minds. We're in some of these things together and no one's linked me to Chavez – these guys are small time, auto-detail. They keep the car. They filch a wad of Mr. Vee's bills, the wad I'd stuffed into my wallet. They don't know there's another wad of Mr. Vee's money in a secret place. And fifty bucks in my boots.

Instead of an air-conditioned nighttime run up the Gulf coast, it's the thumb on the interstate. I pass up a roadside rest area, a happy hunting ground for new cars and ready cash. I hitch a ride to the farthest cheap motel.

The first automobile I crouch behind in the dark parking lot of the Dunes Motel is an Impala with Alabama license plates. The next one is Broward County. Two more out-of-staters: Live Free or Die and Land of Lincoln. The farther from Florida the better for me. I look in the windows of the Topaz from New Hampshire. There's a rug in the back seat, and under the rug I make out a shiny sliver of Samsonite. Maybe they're just eating. Clothes hang on one side: two sports jackets for a small man or an adolescent, and what looks to me like lengths of silk. On the rear-view mirror, where you or I might hang a kid's booties or a plastic Jesus and rosaries, is an alien deity with four arms or legs. I don't know about borrowing this little beauty. These people travel a little too heavy.

The Dunes isn't an absolute dump. The pool has water in it. The neon VACANCY sign above the door of the office has blown only one letter. The annex to the left of the office has its own separate entrance: SANDALWOOD RESTAURANT.

I stroke the highway dust out of my hair, so the office won't guess my present automobileless state, tuck my shirt into my Levis and walk in from the parking lot. The trouble is there's nobody behind the desk. It's 11:03; late but not late enough for even a junior high jailbait[7] nightclerk to have taken to her cot.

Another guest might have rung the bell and waited, or rung the bell and banged his fist on the counter and done some swearing. What I do is count on the element of surprise. I vault into the staff area and kick open a door that says: STRICTLY PRIVATE.

Inside, in a room reeking of incense, are people eating. There are a lot of them. There are a lot of little brown people sitting cross-legged on the floor of a regular motel room and eating with their hands. Pappies with white beards, grammies swaddled in silk, men in dark suits, kids, and one luscious jailbait in blue jeans.

They look at me. A bunch of aliens and they stare like I'm the freak.

One of the aliens tries to uncross his legs, but all he manages is a backward flop. He holds his right hand stiff and away from his body so it won't drip gravy on his suit. 'Are you wanting a room?'

I've never liked the high, whiny Asian male voice. 'Let's put it this way. Are you running a motel or what?'

The rest of the aliens look at me, look at each other, look down at their food. I stare at them too. They seem to have been partying. I wouldn't mind

---

7 Under-age young woman.

a Jack Daniels and a plate of their rice and yellow stew stuff brought to me by room service in blue jeans.

'Some people here say we are running a "po-tel".' A greasy grin floats off his face. 'Get it? My name is Patel, that's P-A-T-E-L. A Patel owning a motel, get it?'

'Rich,' I say.

The jailbait springs up off the floor. With a gecko-fast tongue tip, she chases a gravy drop on her wrist. 'I can go. I'm done.' But she doesn't make a move. 'You people enjoy the meal.'

The women jabber, but not in English. They flash gold bracelets. An organized raid could clean up in that room, right down to the rubies and diamonds in their noses. They're all wrapped in silk, like brightly-colored mummies. Pappy shakes his head, but doesn't rise. 'She eats like a bird. Who'll marry her?' he says in English to one of his buddies.

'You should advertise,' says the other man, probably the Living Free or Dying.[8] They've forgotten me. I feel left out, left behind. While we were nailing up that big front door, these guys were sneaking in around back. They got their money, their family networks, and their secretive languages.

I verbalize a little seething, and when none of the aliens take notice, I dent the prefab wall with my fist. 'Hey,' I yell. 'I need a room for the night. Don't any of you dummies speak American?'

Now she swings toward me apologetically. She has a braid that snakes all the way down to her knees. 'Sorry for the inconvenience,' she says. She rinses gravy off her hands. 'It's our biggest family reunion to date. That's why things are so hectic.' She says something about a brother getting married, leaving them short at the desk. I think of Jonda and the turbaned guy. He fired her when some new turbaned guy showed up.

'Let's just go,' I say. 'I don't give a damn about reunions.' I don't know where Jonda ended up. The Goldilocks doll wasn't delivered to Laguna Vista Estates, though I had a welcome planned for it.

This kid's got a ripe body. I follow the ripe body up a flight of outdoor stairs. Lizards scurry, big waterbugs drag across the landings.

'This is it,' she says, She checks the air conditioning and the TV. She makes sure there are towels in the bathroom. If she feels a little uneasy being in a motel room with a guy like me who's dusty and scruffy and who kills for a living, she doesn't show it. Not till she looks back at the door and realizes I'm not carrying any bags.

She's a pro. 'You'll have to pay in cash now,' she says. 'I'll make out a receipt.'

'What if I were to pull out a knife instead,' I joke. I turn slightly away from her and count the balance of Haysoos's bills. Not enough in there, after the shakedown. The fifty stays put, my new nest egg. 'Where were you born, honey? Bombay? I been to Bombay.'

'New Jersey,' she says. 'You can pay half tonight, and the rest before you

---

8 The owner of the Topaz from New Hampshire: from the motto on the state's car licence plates.

check out tomorrow. I am not unreasonable.'

'I'll just bet you're not. Neither am I. But who says I'm leaving tomorrow. You got some sort of policy?'

That's when I catch the look on her face. Disgust, isn't that what it is? Distaste for the likes of me.

'You can discuss that with my father and uncle tomorrow morning. She sashays[9] just out of my reach. She's aiming to race back to the motel room not much different than this except that it's jammed with family.

I pounce on Alice before she can drop down below, and take America with her. The hardware comes in handy, especially the kris. Alice lays hot fingers on my eyes and nose, but it's no use and once she knows it, Alice submits.

I choose me the car with the Land of Lincoln plates. I make a double switch with Broward County. I drive the old Tamiami Trail across the remains of the Everglades. Used to be no cars, a narrow ridge of two-lane concrete with swamps on either side, gators sunning themselves by day, splattered by night. Black snakes and mocassins every few hundred yards. Clouds of mosquitoes.

This is what I've become. I want to squeeze this state dry and swallow it whole.

§ *South Asian diaspora* Ghose (1, 2), Naipaul, Gooneratne, Crusz, Rushdie, Mistry; Af: Vassanji; Carib: Naipaul (2); NZSP: Subramani; SEA: Maniam

YASMINE GOONERATNE (1935–)

Bharat Changes His Image

Originally a separately published short story, 'Bharat Changes His Image' is a central chapter in *A Change of Skies*, Yasmine Gooneratne's satirical novel about a Sri Lankan couple who migrate to Australia. The narrator Navaranjini/Jean's ingenuous description of a key episode in their assimilation into Australian life illustrates the extent to which the novel's irony is itself trans-cultural, cutting both ways.

We have lived quite a long time in Australia now, but even during our first five years here my husband and I discovered many, many fascinating things about this country, its landscape, its wildlife and its people.

One thing *I* learned is, that while Australia is very rich in unusual species of bird, beast and fish, there are some varieties of Australian wildlife which should be carefully avoided. 'Australia, the most dangerous country in the world,' said the brochure the Rentokil man left in our letter box when he came round to spray the foundations of our house against funnel-web spiders and redbacks. Those are creatures every newcomer to Australia is warned

---

9 Walks casually.

about. And when I told Christina Dory how much I was looking forward to practising my swimming skills in the summer, she looked very concerned and told me to beware of jellyfish off Australian beaches in January, and sharks and stonefish all the year round.

'Better watch out for stonefish, they're poisonous, and very very dangerous,' Christina said. 'One encounter with a stonefish can be fatal.'

Another thing I found out about Australia is, that like the Australian stonefish, which lies on the bottom of the ocean floor like a harmless piece of rock until you step on it, Australian people can be endlessly surprising. One surprising thing about them is, that deep, very deep, a long way down, Australians are true Orientals at heart.

Of course, like many Asian visitors to this country, I didn't find that out at first, because Australians hide their sensitive souls under a rough exterior. I was fooled, just like everyone else. Just like my husband.

From the moment we arrived in Australia, my husband started having problems with his image. Before we came to Australia, I'd no idea he *had* an image, apart from his reflection in the bedroom mirror or his shadow on the grass. But now it seemed he'd acquired one, and with it he'd acquired problems: problems connected, as far as I could make out, with the various aspects in which, he felt, he appeared to the Australians around us.

My Hindu mind couldn't grasp at first what these problems could possibly be. There are images of Lord Shiva in temples all over Sri Lanka, and the whole point about Shiva, surely, *is* that He appears in various aspects, and we can worship Him in any of them. Everyone knows *that*. My mother taught me to worship Lord Shiva in my husband. I've always tried to follow her instructions, especially when my husband is under strain. So I listened very, very carefully as he told me all about these problems.

But he saw how puzzled I was, and he clicked his tongue impatiently. 'Look,' he told me. '*We're* Asians. *They're* Australians. When Australians meet us, that's what they notice first. Difference.'

'But we're not "Asians" here,' I said. 'When Australians say "Asians" they don't mean *real* Asians, like us. They're talking about –'

My husband looked very hard at me, and I stopped myself, just in time. 'I've told you a hundred times, Baba, *don't say that word*,' my husband said crossly. 'And Australians can't make fine distinctions between one kind of Asian and another, stupid. Australians never had an empire.'

Now, I wouldn't call myself an intellectual person (though it's something I would very much like to be). But never once, before we came to Australia, did my husband ever call me 'stupid'. Things of quite minor importance which had seemed perfectly all right at home, and were part of our normal everyday existence there, are apparently all wrong here. Or so my husband appeared to think. It just shows, I told myself, trying not to care that he had just called me 'stupid', how much under strain he is.

You see, at home in Sri Lanka, and I suppose in India too, which is the centre, after all, of the *real* Asian world, we always called Far Eastern people 'Ching-Chongs'. My husband says it's a racist way of speaking, that we

learned racism from the British in our colonial days, and must discard it
totally now that we are free. But coming from such a Westernised family as
his, he just doesn't understand. There's nothing racist about saying . . . that
word; racism's unknown in India and Sri Lanka. Race and caste and colour
just have their appointed places there in a divine scheme of things, in which
everything moves in a beautifully regulated order. Everyone knows *that*.

Though it's a concept Westerners find hard to grasp, and so, sadly, do
westernised Asians like my husband.

Being so westernised, for instance, my husband is only semi-vegetarian.
Unlike me. And so, naturally, many of his ideas too are only, so to speak,
semi-Asian. Unlike mine. I do a lot of cooking, now that we live in Australia
and have no servants in the house, so my thoughts about living here do tend
to get a bit mixed up, sometimes, with my herbs and spices. And it was
while I was cooking some prawns for my husband one day, which we'd
bought at the Pyrmont Fish Markets, that it suddenly struck me that people like us, *real* Asians, must have been created as a kind of human Golden
Mean, cooked golden brown and just right.

I'm not racist, of course, as that nice Australian on talk-back radio keeps
saying all the time, but it does seem to me that Westerners and . . . Far
Easterners really do look rather alike – so pale and . . . well, sallow – a bit
like the way raw shellfish look, before they're curried, and get some colour
and taste into them. Not too appetising, really.

My husband says we Asians are racist about colour. Well, he couldn't be
more wrong. Our people aren't racist about colour, they just honour a very
ancient and holy tradition that has clear rules about what's beautiful and
what's not. The marriage ads at home rate complexions according to that
tradition, and I've always been pleased that my own complexion happens to
be the exact shade they rate highest. I notice that manufacturers of suntan
creams here call it Natural Tan, and Australian women seem to kill themselves every summer trying to acquire it.

Well, no wonder, for personally – and I'm being quite objective about it
because, of course, you're born the colour you are, you don't invent it, do
you – personally, I like the way I look. And I should add that never, here
or at home, have I met anyone – well, never a man, anyhow – who hasn't
made it perfectly clear *he* likes the way I look, too. 'Golden Delicious' my
husband used to call me during those romantic first weeks when everything
about Australia was new and delightful.

How soon he had become unhappy! It occurred to me that he might be
a good deal happier living in this foreign country if we both learned to speak
the language. That very week, I went to the School of Languages at Southern
Cross University, and asked if I could be enrolled as a student of Australian.
But it didn't work out. There were rows of Japanese students queueing up
to learn English, and rows of Australian students queueing up to learn
Japanese. Nobody seemed interested in teaching, or studying, Australian. I
was very disappointed.

But I often have the radio on while I'm in the kitchen, and while I was listening to talk-back radio one day, I thought I would help my husband in a positive way by improving my Australian vocabulary.

So I bought myself a notebook, placed it beside the radio in the kitchen, and whenever I heard an unfamiliar word, or heard someone say that he represented seventy-five per cent or eighty-five per cent or ninety-five per cent of all Australians, I jotted down whatever he had to say. That way I came across a lot of really interesting new words and phrases.

Some I found quite surprising. Like this very ancient Australian word which begins with a 'b' and rhymes with 'custard', which I first heard used – at a party! – by one of my husband's colleagues at the university. I consulted our host, who told me to my surprise that Australians use this word as a term of affection.

Professor Dory told me a story about an Australian academic he knew who had apologised to an English don for using this word freely at a Cambridge sherry party. (Professor Dory is an Australian, of course, but he went to Yale for his PhD, my husband says, so he has to put on this really broad Aussie accent when he tells stories about Australians abroad.)

'Sorry, mate,' the Australian had said. 'I oughter've warned yer. Back in Oz, yer know, we call everyone a bastard.'

The Englishman had gazed at him in mild astonishment. 'And why ever not?' he had asked.

Professor Dory's stories were often about well-meaning Australians getting what he calls 'the warm sherry welcome' in Britain, and he's an expert linguist, my husband says, so I'm sure he's right in saying that Australians call people names when they really like them very much. He laughed heartily as he told me this story, so I laughed too. But I wasn't at all happy about it, not really. We Asians respect genealogy and well-established family lines, and that word means . . . Well, there's just no way I'd have called anyone a bastard, however affectionate I might have been feeling at the time.

Except Ronald Blackstone. I'd have called *him* any number of good Australian names any time, with no affection at all in any of them. Ronald Blackstone is a sociology professor from the University of Woop-Woop who started up all our problems when he nicknamed a Sydney suburb 'Vietnamatta' because it was full, so he said, of Asians. (Far Easterners, he'd meant, of course.)

'Asians,' he'd said on radio, 'pollute the air with the fumes of roasting meat. And we Australians,' he'd added, 'must be alert to the dangers involved for our society if we allow Asians in who cannot assimilate and accept our customs.'

Well, for weeks afterwards, the newspapers printed letters praising Professor Blackstone for speaking out on Australia's immigration policy. That was when my husband started having problems with his image, and I started listening carefully to talk-back radio, and watching television, and working hard on my Australian vocabulary. My notebook, which was filling up with new phrases on a range of different topics, gave me confidence. Whenever I got my husband alone, I tried out my new vocabulary on him. I felt this would give him confidence too.

One day, as he came in the door, I said, 'G'day, darl. I've come to terms with my sexuality.'

He looked alarmed to hear this, and I had the distinct impression that he avoided me for the rest of the evening. So the following day, I tried again with some new words and phrases I'd heard on talk-back radio that morning.

'Why should you care what Blackstone says?' I asked. 'Your eyes aren't slits and your head doesn't slope. It's obvious he doesn't mean *you*.'

My husband just looked depressed. 'Want to bet?'

Seeking ways to assimilate, we discovered the time-honoured Australian custom of name swapping. Professor Dory says it dates back to convict days, and had a new vogue after war was declared in 1939 and hundreds of German immigrants anglicised their names practically overnight in Australia. And though there's no war on now that I know anything about, it seems the grandfather of one of my husband's graduate students found that his family name of Michalakis was bad for business, so he swopped his name for a Scottish one. For two generations now they've belonged to the Australian branch of the Clan Mackenzie.

My husband's family name, which is mine too now, of course, had been conferred on one of his ancestors in the fourteenth century. It had been an honour bestowed on that victorious general of the Southern Kingdom at a royal wedding which had followed a long and bloody battle. (The battle had been fought against Tamil invaders from the Kingdom of Jaffna – among whom, as a matter of fact, there had probably been some of my own ancestors, since Amma's family belongs to the warrior caste of the North. In our ancestral home in Jaffna there are still some ancient spears, and swords rusty with blood stains.)

My husband's family name of Mangala-Davasinha poetically combines words meaning 'Wedding Day' with a complimentary description of his ancestor as an all-conquering lion. When our friend Mr Koyako advised us to retain, if possible, something of the past when we changed our name, I suggested to my husband that we simply shorten our surname to 'Sinha'.

Mr Koyako approved of this idea. That way, he said, the name would still mean 'lion', but most important of all, it would indicate identity with my husband's community, the Sinhalese.

'Too much like 'Singh',' my husband said. 'They'll think I carry a dagger in my turban, like the Sikhs on London Transport.'

'But you don't *wear* a turban, dear,' I reminded him. And I added playfully, 'Sikh transit gloria mundi, darl. Remember?'

This was one of my husband's 'Sikh' jokes, invented when he was travelling by bus to do his PhD research at the British Museum, and bought his ticket most days from a turbanned conductor. I had thought the memory would make my husband smile. However, he just looked irritated. So for the moment I abandoned the idea of cheering him up, and in spite of the long and glorious history of his name, we looked for a user-friendly model to replace it.

It didn't take long to find one.

'I had the name on my door in the School changed today,' my husband told me a few days later. 'We'll be calling ourselves 'Mundy' from now on. 'Mangala-Day', Mun-Dy, get it? I'm told it's a highly respected Australian name.'

Well. I'd have liked some warning. After all, it's my name, too. But though I couldn't help hoping at the start that Professor Blackstone would soon find himself up shit creek without a paddle, I've become quite accustomed to 'Mundy' now. It's certainly much easier to say 'Mrs Mundy here' when I ring someone to fix things when the Dishlex or the Hoover's on the blink. Nobody asks me now to spell my name for them, or says 'Hey, come again? Bit hard to get my tongue round *that* one!', clowning around the way Aussies love to do.

Next we traded in our first names. This was a really hard thing to do. For me because, besides being my own personal name, Navaranjini has a really auspicious meaning in Sanskrit. My husband's name, Bharat, means 'India' in just about every Indian language there is. But it meant something more to us, for my husband had been named Bharat to commemorate his grand-father's scholarship in Indian languages. And now, having come to know Grandfather Edward through his travel journal, giving up Bharat seemed to us to be a betrayal of everything he had stood for.

Ah, well, never mind. What's it matter? Following Professor Blackstone's radio talk, those Oriental names and their meanings were among the first things we dumped, as if they'd been run-down cars.

So now we're Jean and Barry Mundy! True blue, fair dinkum[1] Aussies. Well, maybe not *very* fair, but certainly blue-blooded. And probably dinkum, too. Mind you, it took time getting used to our new names. There are problems attached to waking up with Barry when you've gone to bed with Bharat.

But as I told myself firmly throughout that difficult time, that's the mar-vellous thing about life, you can make yourself believe anything if you work at it really hard.

I recalled, in fact, not having liked my old name much, and having always wanted to change it – maybe it was a premonition, and I was sensing even then, when I was only six and sulking in silence when anyone called me Navaranjini at home, that I was bound for Botany Bay.

Next we swapped our Austin for a Holden, and moved to another suburb.

'A great big ugly bugger of a house,' said the ad in the real estate agent's window. 'No respecter of persons. Newly built, still unshaven around the walls. Needs a woman to bring him into line. Just a softy, really.'

Above this was a colour photograph of the house, and the price.

It was expensive all right, but houses are places to live in all your life, and leave to your children. My notebook told me the agent's calling the house this word (the one that begins with a 'b' and rhymes with 'rugger')

---

1 Real; genuine.

showed the house was lovable in a very Australian way. So I prepared myself to love it.

Until Barry said we'd make a thumping profit on it when we next moved, since Vaucluse is such a prestigious suburb.

Life now became one surprise after another. The next thing I knew, Barry scrapped his spectacles, and went in for contact lenses. That certainly was a good move: Barry has nice eyes, with really terrific lashes, and now you could see them properly. He seemed much happier as a result of all these changes, and instead of standing about at parties with a glass of orange juice in his hand, sulking and reading insults into everyone's innocent remarks, he'd have a really beaut time.

'Goodonya, Barry!' I said to him one evening. We were on our way to a reception at the university Lodge. 'Your image is in such great shape now, mate, that one of these days you'll be trading-in your wife.'

Barry gave the tiniest little start, but of course he knew it was only my little joke. On the whole I didn't think we'd come too badly out of all the trade-ins we'd been doing to advance Australia fair. Especially when a tall silver-haired Australian, who'd been looking appreciatively across the room all evening at my flame-coloured silk sari and the matching *tilak* on my forehead, came over and asked whether I'd like some champagne.

'However did you know I just love champagne?' I said.

'Because you've had two already,' he said. 'I've been watching you.'

Well, it was a fun party. By this time, too, my Australian vocabulary had improved out of sight. In the company of Barry's colleagues – that very intellectual Francesca Sweetlips, for instance, and Professor Doubleton-Trout, who's a sweet old dear but whose conversation is so full of Anglo-Saxon attitudes and allusions that half the time one can't make out what he's saying, and even Red Kodd – though I must say Red always does his best to put me at my ease by reading his *vers libre* compositions to me – I had sometimes felt a bit like a fish out of water. But by this time I felt much more at home, now that I could twig what people around me were on about.

And another thing – I found, as I learned to speak their language, that Australians didn't seem so unappetising any more, somehow. Not at all. Especially in their appearance. When we first came to Australia, I saw every Australian, especially the men, as red-faced and yellow-haired. Or else white-faced and brown-haired. As I got to know them better, I began to take in details. And some of the details that I noticed were not unappetising at all. Quite the opposite, in fact.

He was back in a flash to refill my glass. 'I'm Ron Blackstone,' he said.

While he took the bottle back to the bar, I turned to Barry. Barry wasn't there. Perhaps he'd slipped out for a breath of fresh air. I wished he hadn't, I felt I was moving into dangerous waters, and needed his support.

My companion returned, bearing a newly frothing beer for himself .

'Professor Blackstone,' I said. 'I've been looking forward so much to meeting you. For weeks, really, I've been thinking of nothing else.'

He seemed pleased to hear this. For what seemed a long time he gazed at me as if mesmerised. I find I have this effect on Australian men, especially mature ones who know the real world.

'How extraordinarily nice of you to say so,' he said.'I take it you're a student here?'

For a moment I was filled with real regret. Close up, I'd noticed his eyes crinkled delightfully at the corners. Like Paul Newman's. But the moment soon passed. As I gazed up into the deceitful blue eyes of this pleasantly smiling ratbag, the events of three miserable months crashed in my ears like the war drums of the North that had called my ancestors to battle in centuries past.

'I'm not a student, Professor Blackstone,' I said. 'I'm someone whose life you have personally made a hell on earth.'

He had been bending over me, listening attentively, his eyes fixed on mine, but now he stepped back rather quickly.

'I'm also,' I went on, 'a *wife*. The wife of someone whose personality you have utterly destroyed.'

He looked concerned. 'Are you quite sure,' he said, 'that you're feeling all right?'

I took a deep breath, visualised the relevant pages of my vocabulary notebook, and uttered a silent prayer to Shiva. 'Of course I'm not feeling all right,' I replied. 'How can I be feeling all right when I find myself in the company of blackguards and brutes? Of scabs and scumbags? Is there,' I asked – and here I turned to the other people in our little group (Jennifer Coquelle was there, I remember, and Bragge Groper, and Professor Ling from Chinese Literature, and Jeff and Patricia Tailor) and I drew them into our discussion, just as I had been taught to do at the finishing school I attended in Delhi – 'Is there another such shit-stirrer in the universe? Another dog's dinner named Ronald Blackstone?'

The conversation in the room died suddenly. Of course, I hadn't spoken softly, in my natural voice. The elocution teacher at that finishing school always insisted that if we found ourselves speaking a foreign language, we must remember to treat that language with respect. 'Enunciate each word, gels,' she would say, 'clearly and precisely. So that there cannot be any doubt or confusion about what you are saying.'

And that was how I spoke to Professor Blackstone, in Australian.

In the silence around us I became aware, behind Professor Blackstone's startled face, of another face with a very different expression on it.

'Barry!' I called, and waved.

But Barry unaccountably disappeared again, so I turned back to Professor Blackstone. 'Yes,' I said contemptuously. '*Barry*. Do you know what "Barry" means in Sinhala? Let me tell you, Professor Blackstone. In Sinhala, the word *bari* means "incapable". It means "impotent". And it was *you* who made my husband trade in Bharat for a name like *Barry*.'

I gave him the withering look Rukmani Devi gives the villain in that marvellous Sri Lankan film, *Broken Promise*. 'You are a yahoo[2] and a wrinkly,

---

2 Brute in human shape: from species in *Gulliver's Travels*, Book IV.

Professor Blackstone,' I said, 'a shithead and a stinker.'

People were looking round at us nervously. My vocabulary was standing up well, but I suppose my voice *was* getting a shade out of control. As well it might. I was filled with anger, but the man I'd just called a stinker seemed to think it was due to the champagne, because he stopped a passing waitress and urged me to help myself to a sausage roll from her tray.

This was too much. 'How *dare* you!' I said furiously. '*You*, a so-called sociologist who should know that *real* Asians would *die* before they touched charred pig meat, *you*, polluting the air with meat fumes from your filthy, smelly barbie in your weed-ridden backyard . . .'

The waitress quickly withdrew her tray, and vanished. I continued. '*You* have the impudence to offer *me* a *sausage roll*, you ignorant, non-vegetarian racist? I am a Tamil, Professor Blackstone, and a Hindu. Pure veg, and proud of it. What do you take me for? A pork-eating Ching-Chong?'

And then I remembered the new words I'd learned from representative Australians on talk-back radio, and added, 'A slit-eyed slope-head?'

The barbarian I was addressing seemed to emerge from a deep trance. 'Madam,' he said. 'You call me a racist. I am forced to tell you this: You, madam, have put me completely to shame.'

Well. I'll admit I was stunned. He'd said he was ashamed! And he'd apologised, just like that! Which just shows you mustn't judge people too hastily. As I told Barry in the car going home that evening, this experience showed that Australians *can* be civilised. If you go about it tactfully.

I looked with new respect, even affection, at this racist I'd just reformed. And then I thought – why, if he can be gracious, I can be gracious too! For it had struck me that I should encourage him in his reformed way of thinking by demonstrating how well *real* Asians of culture and good will assimilate to the Australian way of life.

'Professor Blackstone,' I said smiling, and bringing my palms together I bowed to him as Lord Krishna bowed to the noble enemy He defeated on the battlefield of Kurukshetra.[3] 'I'm afraid I have to leave now, but I'm so glad we met. Goodbye, you bastard.'

It seemed that my affectionate Australian farewell had left him speechless with surprise and pleasure. And that's how I learned that, deep in their hearts, Australians are true Orientals: like us, they feel so deeply, so intensely, that words aren't always adequate to express their emotions. How, I thought fondly, can I let this good man know, in true Oriental fashion, that I wish him well? And then the right auspicious words came floating into my mind from where I'd written them on page five of my notebook.

'May all your chooks[4] turn into emus, Professor Blackstone,' I said, 'and kick your flaming dunny[5] down.'

§ *South Asian diaspora* Ghose (1), Naipaul, Mukherjee, Crusz, Rushdie, Carib: Naipaul (2); NZSP: Subramani; SEA: Maniam; Gooneratne also in SA

---

3 Scene of the battle between the Kurus and the Pandavas in the Sanskrit epic of the *Mahabharata*; modern Panipat in north India. 4 Domestic fowl. 5 Outdoor toilet.

RIENZI CRUSZ (1925–)

Roots

What the end usually demands
is something of the beginning,
and so
I conjure history from a cup
5   of warm Portuguese blood
from my forefathers,
black diamond eyes, charcoal hair
from my Sinhalese mothers;
the beached catamaran,
10 gravel voices of the fishermen,
the catch still beating like a heart
under the pelting sun;
how the pariah dogs looked urgent
with fish meal in their brains,
15 the children romped, sagged,
then melted into the sand.

A Portuguese captain holds
the soft brown hand of my Sinhala mother.
It's the year 1515 A.D.,
20 when two civilizations kissed and merged,
and I, burgher of that hot embrace,
write a poem of history
as if it were only the romance
of a lonely soldier on a crowded beach
25 in Southern Ceylon.

§ *South Asian diaspora* Ghose (1, 2), Naipaul, Mukherjee, Gooneratne, Ondaatje (1), Rushdie, Mistry; Carib: Naipaul (2); NZSP: Subramani

MICHAEL ONDAATJE (1943–)

1: *From* Running in the Family

In *Running in the Family*, the Canadian-based writer Michael Ondaatje undertakes a journey back to his Sri Lankan origins. The book is, however, far more than a travel journal. It is also a family album, which describes the eccentricities of his privileged

---

21 burgher: descendant of Dutch or Portuguese colonists of Sri Lanka.

middle-class 'historical relations' during the late colonial period, and a meditation on Sri Lanka more generally. It employs an eclectic mixture of modes, among them reported dialogues, photography, poetry – both ancient and modern – by Ondaatje and others and imaginative reconstructions of episodes in his family's history. This section, 'Tabula Asiae', reflects on the mapping of Sri Lanka by the Western imagination, as an exotic, 'other', feminized space.

Tabula Asiae

On my brother's wall in Toronto are the false maps. Old portraits of Ceylon. The result of sightings, glances from trading vessels, the theories of sextant. The shapes differ so much they seem to be translations – by Ptolemy, Mercator, François Valentyn, Mortier, and Heydt – growing from mythic shapes into eventual accuracy. Amoeba, then stout rectangle, and then the island as we know it now, a pendant off the ear of India. Around it, a blue-combed ocean busy with dolphin and sea-horse, cherub and compass. Ceylon floats on the Indian Ocean and holds its naive mountains, drawings of cassowary[1] and boar who leap without perspective across imagined 'desertum' and plain.

At the edge of the maps the scrolled mantling depicts ferocious slipper-footed elephants, a white queen offering a necklace to natives who carry tusks and a conch, a Moorish king who stands amidst the power of books and armour. On the south-west corner of some charts are satyrs, hoof deep in foam, listening to the sound of the island, their tails writhing in the waves.

The maps reveal rumours of topography, the routes for invasion and trade, and the dark mad mind of travellers' tales appears throughout Arab and Chinese and medieval records. The island seduced all of Europe. The Portuguese. The Dutch. The English. And so its name changed, as well as its shape, – Serendip, Ratnapida ('island of gems'), Taprobane, Zeloan, Zeilan, Seyllan, Ceilon, and Ceylon – the wife of many marriages, courted by invaders who stepped ashore and claimed everything with the power of their sword or bible or language.

This pendant, once its shape stood still, became a mirror. It pretended to reflect each European power till newer ships arrived and spilled their nationalities, some of whom stayed and inter-married – my own ancestor arriving in 1600, a doctor who cured the residing governor's daughter with a strange herb and was rewarded with land, a foreign wife, and a new name which was a Dutch spelling of his own. Ondaatje. A parody of the ruling language. And when his Dutch wife died, marrying a Sinhalese woman, having nine children, and remaining. Here. At the centre of the rumour. At this point on the map.

§ *Cartographies* Can: Birney (2), Reaney; Aus: Tranter; SA: Ghosh; *Sri Lankan diaspora* Gooneratne, Crusz

---

1 Large, flightless bird.

2: *From* In the Skin of a Lion

In the Skin of a Lion comes closer to the form of a conventional novel than any of Ondaatje's earlier works, but still suggests the necessarily fragmentary nature of conceptions of identity and nationality. Set in Toronto in the inter-war years, it is about the lives of immigrant workers, such as Nicholas Temelcoff, building a downtown bridge. In telling their stories, Ondaatje suggests diverse provenances for the city and by implication for Canada. Consequently the novel can be viewed a text which shows multiculturalism as central to the Canadian experience long before it became official policy in the 1970s and which foregrounds the trans-cultural nature of national cultures.

. . . Nicholas Temelcoff is famous on the bridge, a daredevil. He is given all the difficult jobs and he takes them. He descends into the air with no fear. He is a solitary. He assembles ropes, brushes the tackle and pulley at his waist, and falls off the bridge like a diver over the edge of a boat. The rope roars alongside him, slowing with the pressure of his half-gloved hands. He is burly on the ground and then falls with terrific speed, grace, using the wind to push himself into corners of abutments so he can check driven rivets, sheering valves, the drying of the concrete under bearing plates and padstones. He stands in the air banging the crown pin into the upper cord and then shepherds the lower cord's slip-joint into position. Even in archive photographs it is difficult to find him. Again and again you see vista before you and the eye must search along the wall of sky to the speck of burned paper across the valley that is him, an exclamation mark, somewhere in the distance between bridge and river. He floats at the three hinges of the crescent-shaped steel arches. These knit the bridge together. The moment of cubism.

He is happiest at daily chores – ferrying tools from pier down to trestle, or lumber that he pushes in the air before him as if swimming in a river. He is a spinner. He links everyone. He meets them as they cling – braced by wind against the metal they are rivetting or the wood sheeting they hammer into – but he has none of their fear. Always he carries his own tackle, hunched under his ropes and dragging the shining pitons behind him. He sits on a coiled seat of rope while he eats his lunch on the bridge. If he finishes early he cycles down Parliament Street to the Ohrida Lake Restaurant and sits in the darkness of the room as if he has had enough of light. Enough of space.

His work is so exceptional and time-saving he earns one dollar an hour while the other bridge workers receive forty cents. There is no jealousy towards him. No one dreams of doing half the things he does. For night work he is paid $1.25, swinging up into the rafters of a trestle holding a flare, free-falling like a dead star. He does not really need to see things, he has charted all that space, knows the pier footings, the width of the cross-walks in terms of seconds of movement – 281 feet and 6 inches make up the central span of the bridge. Two flanking spans of 240 feet, two end spans of 158 feet. He slips into openings on the lower deck, tackles himself up to bridge level. He knows the precise height he is over the river, how long his ropes are, how many seconds he can free-fall to the pulley. It does not matter if it is day or night, he could be blindfolded. Black space is time. After swinging for three seconds he puts his feet up to link with the concrete edge of the next pier. He knows his position in the air as if he is mercury slipping across a map.

A South River parrot hung in its cage by the doorway of the Ohrida Lake Restaurant, too curious and interested in the events of the night to allow itself to be blanketed. It watched the woman who stood dead centre in the room in darkness. The man turned on one light behind the counter. Nicholas Temelcoff came over to the bird for a moment's visit after getting the drinks. 'Well, Alicia, my heart, how are you?' And walked away not waiting for the bird's reply, the fingers of his left hand delicately holding the glasses, his arm cradling the bottle.

He muttered as if continuing his conversation with the bird, in the large empty room. From noon till two it was full of men, eating and drinking. Kosta the owner and his waiter performing raucous shows for the crowd – the boss yelling insults at the waiter, chasing him past customers. Nicholas remembered the first time he had come there. The dark coats of men, the arguments of Europe.

He poured a brandy and pushed it over to her. 'You don't have to drink this but you can if you wish. Or see it as a courtesy.' He drank quickly and poured himself another. 'Thank you,' he said, touching his arm curiously as if it were the arm of a stranger.

She shook her head to communicate it was not all right, that it needed attention.

'Yes, but not now. Now I want to sit here.' There was a silence between them. 'Just to drink and talk quietly. . . . It is always night here. People step in out of sunlight and must move slow in the darkness.'

He drank again. 'Just for the pain.' She smiled. 'Now music.' He stood up free of the table as he spoke and went behind the counter and turned the wireless on low. He spun the dial till there was bandstand. He sat down again opposite her. 'Lot of pain. But I feel good.' He leaned back in his chair, holding up his glass. 'Alive.' She picked up her glass and drank.

'Where did you get that scar?' He pointed his thumb to the side of her nose. She pulled back.

'Don't be shy . . . talk. You must talk.' He wanted her to come out to him, even in anger, though he didn't want anger. Feeling such ease in the Ohrida Lake Restaurant, feeling the struts of the chair along his back, her veil tight on his arm. He just wanted her there near him, night all around them, where he could look after her, bring her out of the shock with some grace.

'I got about twenty scars,' he said, 'all over me. One on my ear here.' He turned and leaned forward so the wall-light fell onto the side of his head. 'See? Also this under my chin, that also broke my jaw. A coiling wire did that. Nearly kill me, broke my jaw. Lots more. My knees. . . .' He talked on. Hot tar burns on his arm. Nails in his calves. Drinking up, pouring her another shot, the woman's song on the radio. She heard the lyrics underneath Temelcoff's monologue as he talked and half mouthed the song and searched into her bright face. Like a woman with a fever.

This is the first time she has sat in a Macedonian bar, in any bar, with a drinking man. There is a faint glow from the varnished tables, the red checkered tablecloths of the day are folded and stacked. The alcove with its serving counter has an awning hanging over it. She realizes the darkness represents a Macedonian night where customers sit outside at their tables. Light can come only from the bar, the stars, the clock dressed in its orange and red electricity. So when customers step in at any time, what they are entering is an old courtyard of the Balkans. A violin. Olive trees. Permanent evening. Now the arbour-like wallpaper makes sense to her. Now the parrot has a language.

He talked on, slipping into phrases from the radio songs which is how he learned his words and pronunciations. He talked about himself, tired, unaware his voice split now into two languages, the woman hearing everything he said and trying to remember it all. He could see her eyes were alive, interpreting the room. He noticed the almost-tap of her finger to the radio music.

The blue eyes stayed on him as he moved, leaning his head against the wall. He drank, his breath deep into the glass so the fumes would hit his eyes and the sting of it keep him awake. Then he looked back at her. How old was she? Her brown hair so short, so new to the air. He wanted to coast his hand through it.

'I love your hair,' he said. 'Thank you . . . for the help. For taking the drink.'

She leaned forward earnestly and looked at him, searching out his face now. Words just on the far side of her skin, about to fall out. Wanting to know his name which he had forgotten to tell her. 'I love your hair.' His shoulder was against the wall and he was trying to look up. Then his eyes were closed. So deeply asleep he would be gone for hours. She could twist him around like a puppet and he wouldn't waken.

She felt as if she were the only one alive in this building. In such formal darkness. There was a terrible taste from that one drink still on her tongue, so she walked behind the zinc counter, turning on the tap to wash out her mouth. She moved the dial of the radio around a bit but brought it back securely to the same station. She was looking for that song he had half sung along with earlier, the voice of the singer strangely powerful and lethargic. She saw herself in the mirror. A woman whose hair was showing, caught illicit. She did what he had wanted to do. She ran her hand over her hair briefly. Then turned from her image.

Leaning forward, she laid her face on the cold zinc, the chill there even past midnight. Upon her cheek, her eyelid. She let her skull roll to cool her forehead. The zinc was an edge of another country. She put her ear against the grey ocean of it. Its memory of a day's glasses. The spill and the wiping cloth. Confessional. Tabula Rasa.

At the table she positioned the man comfortably so he would not fall on his arm. *What is your name?* she whispered. She bent down and kissed him, then began walking around the room. This orchard. Strangers kiss softly as moths, she thought.

§ *Canadian multiculturalism* Kogawa, Philip, Mistry

LINTON KWESI JOHNSON (1952–)

Doun de Road

heavy heavy terror
on the rampage
o dont you worry
it is so near . . .
5   fatricide is only
the first phase . . .

yes, the violence of the oppressor runnin wild;
them pickin up the yout them fe suss;
powell prophesying a black, a black, a black conquest;
10   and the National Front is on the rampage
making fire bombs fe burn we.

terror fire terror fire reach we:
such a suffering we suffering
in this burning age of rage;
15   no place to run to get gun
and the violence damming up inside.

so in the heat
of the anguish
you jus turn:
20   turn on your brother

---

8 **fe suss:** on suspicion.

9 **powell:** Enoch Powell, politician noted for his controversial anti-immigration speeches.

           an yu lick him
           an yu lash him
           an stab him
           an kill him

25   and the violence damming up inside.

       O that history should take such a rough route,
       causing us this bitterness and pain on the way,
       is a room full of a fact you cant walk out;

       fatricide is only the first phase,
30   with brother fighting brother stabbing brother:
       them jus killing off them one another,
       but when you see your brother blood jus flow;
       futile fighting; then you know
       that the first phase must come to an end
35   and time for the second phase to show.

§ *Carib in Britain/Language usage* Bennett, Selvon, Dabydeen, D'Aguiar;
Carib: Selvon, Agard, Bloom; *Nation language* Carib: Brathwaite (3)

DAVID DABYDEEN (1956–)

Two Cultures

       'Hear how a baai a taak
       Like BBC!
       Look how a baai a waak
       Like white maan
5   Caak-hat pun he head, wrist-watch pun he haan!
       Yu dadee na Dabydeen, plant gyaden near Blackbush Pass?
       He na cut wid sickle an dig wid faak?
       He na sell maaket, plantain an caan?
       An a who pickni yu rass?
10   Well me never see story like dis since me baan!

       E bin Inglan two maaning, illegal,
       Eye-up waan-two white hooman,
       Bu is wha dem sweet watalily seed
       Go want do wid hungrybelly Blackbush weed
15   Like yu, how yu teet yella like dhall

---

1 **baai**: boy.   9 **pickni**: child.
9 **yu rass**: contraction of 'your arse'; a swear-word.   15 **dhall**: lentils.

An yu tongue black like casrip!
Dem should a spit, vamit pun yu, beat yu rass wid whip!
Is lungara like yu spoil dem good white people country,
Choke an rab, bruk-an-enta, tief dem people prapaty!

20   So yu tink yu can come hey an play big-shat,
Fill we eye wid cigarette, iceapple an all dat?
Aweh po country people bu aweh ga pride:
Jess touch me gyal-pickni, me go buss yu back-side.'

§ *Carib in Britain/Language usage* Bennett, Selvon, Johnson, D'Aguiar:
Carib: Selvon, Agard, Bloom

SALMAN RUSHDIE (1947–)

From Imaginary Homelands

. . . England's Indian writers are by no means all the same type of animal. Some of us, for instance, are Pakistani. Others Bangladeshi. Others West, or East, or even South African.

And V. S. Naipaul, by now, is something else entirely. This word 'Indian' is getting to be a pretty scattered concept. Indian writers in England include political exiles, first-generation migrants, affluent expatriates whose residence here is frequently temporary, naturalized Britons, and people born here who may never have laid eyes on the subcontinent. Clearly, nothing that I say can apply across all these categories. But one of the interesting things about this diverse community is that, as far as Indo-British fiction is concerned, its existence changes the ball game, because that fiction is in future going to come as much from addresses in London, Birmingham and Yorkshire as from Delhi or Bombay.

One of the changes has to do with attitudes towards the use of English. Many have referred to the argument about the appropriateness of this language to Indian themes. And I hope all of us share the view that we can't simply use the language in the way the British did; that it needs remaking for our own purposes. Those of us who do use English do so in spite of our ambiguity towards it, or perhaps because of that, perhaps because we can find in that linguistic struggle a reflection of other struggles taking place in the real world, struggles between the cultures within ourselves and the influences at work upon our societies. To conquer English may be to complete the process of making ourselves free.

But the British Indian writer simply does not have the option of rejecting English, anyway. His children, her children, will grow up speaking it,

---

16 casrip: casareep, a cassava-based cooking syrup.   19 **Choke an rab**: 'choke-and-rob'; mug.
18 **lungara**: trash.

probably as a first language; and in the forging of a British Indian identity the English language is of central importance. It must, in spite of everything, be embraced. (The word 'translation' comes, etymologically, from the Latin for 'bearing across'. Having been borne across the world, we are translated men. It is normally supposed that something always gets lost in translation; I cling, obstinately, to the notion that something can also be gained.)

To be an Indian writer in this society is to face, every day, problems of definition. What does it mean to be 'Indian' outside India? How can culture be preserved without becoming ossified? How should we discuss the need for change within ourselves and our community without seeming to play into the hands of our racial enemies? What are the consequences both spiritual and practical, of refusing to make any concessions to Western ideas and practices? What are the consequences of embracing those ideas and practices and turning away from the ones that came here with us? These questions are all a single, existential question: How are we to live in the world?

I do not propose to offer, prescriptively, any answers to these questions; only to state that these are some of the issues with which each of us will have to come to terms.

To turn my eyes outwards now, and to say a little about the relationship between the Indian writer and the majority white culture in whose midst he lives, and with which his work will sooner or later have to deal:

In common with many Bombay-raised middle-class children of my generation, I grew up with an intimate knowledge of, and even sense of friendship with, a certain kind of England: a dream-England composed of Test Matches at Lord's presided over by the voice of John Arlott, at which Freddie Trueman bowled unceasingly and without success at Polly Umrigar;[1] of Enid Blyton and Billy Bunter, in which we were even prepared to smile indulgently at portraits such as 'Hurree Jamset Ram Singh', 'the dusky nabob of Bhanipur'.[2] I wanted to come to England. I couldn't wait. And to be fair, England has done all right by me; but I find it a little difficult to be properly grateful. I can't escape the view that my relatively easy ride is not the result of the dream-England's famous sense of tolerance and fair play, but of my social class, my freak fair skin and my 'English' English accent. Take away any of these and the story would have been very different. Because of course the dream-England is no more than a dream.

Sadly, it's a dream from which too many white Britons refuse to awake. Recently, on a live radio programme, a professional humorist asked me, in all seriousness, why I objected to being called a wog. He said he had always thought it a rather charming word, a term of endearment. 'I was at the zoo the other day,' he revealed, 'and a zoo keeper told me that the wogs were best with the animals; they stuck their fingers in their ears and wiggled them about and the animals felt at home.' The ghost of Hurree Jamset Ram Singh walks among us still.

---

1 English fast bowler and Indian batsman in their heyday in the 1950s. 2 Stereotypical upper-class Indian of Greyfriars School in Frank Richards's Billy Bunter stories.

As Richard Wright found long ago in America, black and white descriptions of society are no longer compatible. Fantasy, or the mingling of fantasy and naturalism, is one way of dealing with these problems. It offers a way of echoing in the form of our work the issues faced by all of us: how to build a new, 'modern' world out of an old, legend-haunted civilization, an old culture which we have brought into the heart of a newer one. But whatever technical solutions we may find, Indian writers in these islands, like others who have migrated into the north from the south, are capable of writing from a kind of double perspective: because they, we, are at one and the same time insiders and outsiders in this society. This stereoscopic vision is perhaps what we can offer in place of 'whole sight'.

There is one last idea that I should like to explore, even though it may, on first hearing, seem to contradict much of what I've so far said. It is this: of all the many elephant traps lying ahead of us, the largest and most dangerous pitfall would be the adoption of a ghetto mentality. To forget that there is a world beyond the community to which we belong, to confine ourselves within narrowly defined cultural frontiers, would be, I believe, to go voluntarily into that form of internal exile which in South Africa is called the 'homeland'. We must guard against creating for the most virtuous of reasons, British-Indian literary equivalents of Bophuthatswana or the Transkei.

This raises immediately the question of whom one is writing 'for'. My own, short, answer is that I have never had a reader in mind. I have ideas, people, events, shapes, and I write 'for' those things, and hope that the completed work will be of interest to others. But which others? In the case of *Midnight's Children* I certainly felt that if its subcontinental readers had rejected the work, I should have thought it a failure, no matter what the reaction in the West. So I would say that I write 'for' people who feel part of the things I write 'about', but also for everyone else whom I can reach. In this I am of the same opinion as the black American writer Ralph Ellison, who, in his collection of essays *Shadow and Act*, says that he finds something precious in being black in America at this time; but that he is also reaching for more than that. 'I was taken very early,' he writes, 'with a passion to link together all I loved within the Negro community and all those things I felt in the world which lay beyond.'

Art is a passion of the mind. And the imagination works best when it is most free. Western writers have always felt free to be eclectic in their selection of theme, setting, form; Western visual artists have, in this century, been happily raiding the visual storehouses of Africa, Asia, the Philippines. I am sure that we must grant ourselves an equal freedom.

Let me suggest that Indian writers in England have access to a second tradition, quite apart from their own racial history. It is the culture and political history of the phenomenon of migration, displacement, life in a minority group. We can quite legitimately claim as our ancestors the Huguenots, the Irish, the Jews; the past to which we belong is an English past, the history of immigrant Britain. Swift, Conrad, Marx are as much our literary forebears as Tagore or Ram Mohan Roy. America, a nation of immigrants, has created great literature out of the phenomenon of cultural transplantation, out of examining the ways in which people cope with a new world; it may be that by discovering what we have in common with those who preceded us into this country, we can begin to do the same.

I stress this is only one of many possible strategies. But we are inescapably international writers at a time when the novel has never been a more international form (a writer like Borges speaks of the influence of Robert Louis Stevenson on his work; Heinrich Böll acknowledges the influence of Irish literature; cross-pollination is everywhere); and it is perhaps one of the more pleasant freedoms of the literary migrant to be able to choose his parents. My own – selected half consciously, half not – include Gogol, Cervantes, Kafka, Melville, Machado de Assis; a polyglot family tree, against which I measure myself, and to which I would be honoured to belong.

There's a beautiful image in Saul Bellow's latest novel, *The Dean's December*. The central character, the Dean, Corde, hears a dog barking wildly somewhere. He imagines that the barking is the dog's protest against the limit of dog experience. 'For God's sake,' the dog is saying, 'open the universe a little more!' And because Bellow is, of course, not really talking about dogs, or not only about dogs, I have the feeling that the dog's rage, and its desire, is also mine, ours, everyone's. 'For God's sake, open the universe a little more!'

§ *Psychology/language of migrancy* Marlatt, Ondaatje (2), Mistry, Philip; Rushdie also in SA

FRED D'AGUIAR (1960–)

Letter from Mama Dot

I
Your letters and parcels take longer
And longer to reach us. The authorities
Tamper with them (whoever reads this
And shouldn't, I hope jumby spit
5   In dem eye). We are more and more
Like another South American dictatorship,
And less and less a part of the Caribbean.
Now that we import rice (rice that used
To grow wild!), we queue for most things:

---

4 jumby: malevolent spirit.

10 Flour, milk, sugar, barley, and fruits
You can't pick anymore. I join them
at 5 a.m. for 9 o'clock opening time,
People are stabbing one another for a place
And half the queue goes home empty-handed,
15 With money that means next to nothing.
Every meal is salt-fish these days; we even
Curry it. Send a box soon. Pack the basics:
Flour, for some roti; powdered milk;
And any news of what's going on here.
20 No luxuries please, people only talk, shoes
Can wait till things improve (dey bound
Fe improve cause dem cawn get no worse!)
Everybody fed-up in truth; since independence
This country hasn't stopped stepping back;
25 And if you leave you lose your birthright.
With all the talk of nationality we still hungry.
Neil has joined the forces against all advice.
He brings home sardines saved from his rations
For our sunday meal; he wears the best boots
30 In town. The fair is full of prizes
We threw out in better days and everyone wins
Coconuts. I wouldn't wish this on anyone,
But it's worse somehow without you here.
Write! We feast on your letters.

II
35 You are a traveller to them.
A West Indian working in England;
A Friday, Tonto, or Punkawallah;
Sponging off the state. Our languages
Remain pidgin, like our *dark, third,*
40 *Underdeveloped,* world. I mean, their need
To see our children cow-eyed, pot-bellied,
Grouped or alone in photos and naked,
The light darkened between their thighs.
And charity's all they give: the cheque,
45 Once in a blue moon (when guilt's
A private monsoon), posted to a remote
Part of the planet they can't pronounce.
They'd like to keep us there.
Not next door, your house propping-up
50 Theirs; your sunflowers craning over

---

18 roti: Indian bread.

37 A ... Punkawallah: Man Friday, Lone Ranger's partner or Indian fan-attendant: all suggestive of a compliant colonial attitude.

The fence, towards a sun falling
On their side; begonias that belong
To them shouldering through its tight
Staves; the roots of both mingling.
55 So when they skin lips to bare teeth
At you, remember it could be a grimace
In another setting: the final sleep
More and more of us meet in our prime,
(Your New Cross fire comes to mind);
60 Who dream nowadays of peace.
You know England, born there, you live
To die there, roots put down once
And for all. Drop me a line soon,
You know me. *Neva see come fo see.*

§ *Carib in Britain/Language usage* Bennett, Selvon, Johnson, Dabydeen; Carib: Selvon, Agard, Bloom

M. NOURBESE PHILIP (1947–)

She Tries Her Tongue; Her Silence Softly Breaks

All Things are alter'd, nothing is destroyed
Ovid, *The Metamorphoses* (tr. Dryden)

the me and mine of parents
the we and us of brother and sister
the tribe of belongings small and separate,
when gone . . .
5 on these exact places of exacted grief
i placed mint-fresh grief coins
sealed the eyes with certain and final;
in such an equation of loss tears became
a quantity of minus.
10 with the fate of a slingshot stone
loosed from the catapult pronged double with history
and time on a trajectory of hurl and fling
to a state active with without and unknown
i came upon a future biblical with anticipation

§ *Psychology/language of migrancy* Marlatt, Ondaatje (2), Mistry

---

59 New Cross: fire in South London on 18 January   64 *Neva . . . see:* a creole proverb.
1981, in which thirteen young black people died.

CARYL PHILLIPS (1958–)

From Crossing the River

Crossing the River contains four separate stories spanning 250 years, each about an aspect of the African diaspora. Yet the book is as much a novel as a story-collection: the four narratives complement one another and are framed by short opening and closing sections (included in their entirety here) which link them. The main characters are Nash, a black American who goes to Liberia as a missionary in the nineteenth century; Martha, who travels to the American Wild West; Captain Hamilton, skipper of an eighteenth-century slave ship; and Joyce, a Yorkshirewoman, who marries Travis, a black American G.I. posted to her village during World War II. Together they form 'the chorus of a common memory' and in the final section, which links them with numerous other African diaspora experiences, they reverse the cycle of guilt and betrayal begun by the Middle Passage.

A desperate foolishness. The crops failed. I sold my children. I remember. I led them (two boys and a girl) along weary paths, until we reached the place where the mud flats are populated with crabs and gulls. *Returned across the bar with the yawl,[1] and prayed a while in the factory chapel.* I watched as they huddled together and stared up at the fort, above which flew a foreign flag. *Stood beneath the white-washed walls of the factory, waiting for the yawl to return and carry me back over the bar.* In the distance stood the ship into whose keep I would soon condemn them. The man and his company were waiting to once again cross the bar. We watched a while. And then approached. *Approached by a quiet fellow.* Three children only. I jettisoned them at this point, where the tributary stumbles and swims out in all directions to meet the sea. *Bought 2 strong man-boys, and a proud girl.* I soiled my hands with cold goods in exchange for their warm flesh. A shameful intercourse. I could feel their eyes upon me. Wondering, *why?* I turned and journeyed back along the same weary paths. *I believe my trade for this voyage has reached its conclusion.* And soon after, the chorus of common memory began to haunt me.

For two hundred and fifty years I have listened to the many-tongued chorus. And occasionally, among the sundry restless voices, I have discovered those of my own children. My Nash. My Martha. My Travis. Their lives fractured. Sinking hopeful roots into difficult soil. For two hundred and fifty years I have longed to tell them: Children, I am your father. I love you. But understand. There are no paths in water. No signposts. There is no return. To a land trampled by the muddy boots of others. To a people encouraged to war among themselves. To a father consumed with guilt. You are beyond. Broken-off, like limbs from a tree. But not lost, for you carry within your bodies the seeds of new trees. Sinking your hopeful roots into difficult soil. And I, who spurned you, can blame only myself for my present misery. For

---

1 Jolly-boat.

two hundred and fifty years I have waited patiently for the wind to rise on the far bank of the river. For the drum to pound across the water. For the chorus to swell. Only then, if I listen closely, can I rediscover my lost children. A brief, painful communion. A desperate foolishness. The crops failed. I sold my children.

. . . I hear a drum beating on the far bank of the river. A breeze stirs and catches it. The resonant pounding is borne on the wind, carried high above the roof-tops, across the water, above the hinterland, high above the tree-tops, before its beat plunges down and into the interior. I wait. And then listen as the many-tongued chorus of the common memory begins again to swell, and insist that I acknowledge greetings from those who lever pints of ale in the pubs of London. Receive salutations from those who submit to (what the French call) neurotic inter-racial urges in the boulevards of Paris. ('No first-class nation can afford to produce a race of mongrels.') But my Joyce, and my other children, their voices hurt but determined, they will survive the hardships of the far bank. Only if they panic will they break their wrists and ankles against Captain Hamilton's instruments. *Put 2 in irons and delicately in the thumbscrews to encourage them to a full confession of those principally involved. In the evening put 5 more in neck-yokes.* Survivors all. In Brooklyn a helplessly addicted mother waits for the mist to clear from her eyes. They have stopped her benefit. She lives now without the comfort of religion, electricity, or money. A barefoot boy in São Paulo is rooted to his piece of the earth, which he knows will never swell up, pregnant, and become a vantage point from which he will be able to see beyond his dying *favela.*[2] In Santo Domingo, a child suffers the hateful hot comb, the dark half-moons of history heavy beneath each eye. A mother watches. Her eleven-year-old daughter is preparing herself for yet another night of premature prostitution. Survivors. In their diasporan souls a dream like steel. *I praise His holy name that I was fortunate enough to be born in a Christian country, amongst Christian parents and friends, and that you were kind enough to take me, a foolish child, from my parents and bring me up in your own dwelling as something more akin to son than servant. Truth and honesty is great capital, and you instilled such values in my person at an early age, for which I am eternally grateful to you and my Creator.* Enduring cities which whisper falsehoods through perfectly shaped wooden lips. *A dream began to wash through her mind. Martha dreamed that she had traveled on west to California, by herself, and clutching her bundle of clothing. Once there she was met by Eliza Mae, who was now a tall, sturdy colored woman of some social standing. Together, they tip-toed their way through the mire of the streets to Eliza Mae's residence, which stood on a fine, broad avenue.* For two hundred and fifty years I have listened. To voices in the streets of Charleston. (The slave who mounted this block is now dying young from copping a fix on some rusty needle in an Oakland project.) I have listened. To reggae rhythms of

---

2 Brazilian shack or slum.

rebellion and revolution dipping through the hills and valleys of the Caribbean. I have listened. To the saxophone player on a wintry night in Stockholm. A long way from home.[3] For two hundred and fifty years I have listened. To my Nash. My Martha. My Travis. *Joyce. That was all he said. Just, Joyce. I could see now the gap in the middle of his teeth. At the bottom. And then he reached out and pulled me towards him. I couldn't believe it. He'd come back to me. He really wanted me. That day, crying on the platform, safe in Travis's arms.* For two hundred and fifty years I have listened. To the haunting voices. Singing: Mercy, Mercy Me. (The Ecology.) Insisting: Man, I ain't got no quarrel with them Vietcong. Declaring: Brothers and Friends. I am Toussaint L'Ouverture,[4] my name is perhaps known to you. Listened to: Papa Doc. Baby Doc.[5] Listened to voices hoping for: Freedom. Democracy. Singing: Baby, baby. Where did our love go?[6] Samba. Calypso. Jazz. Jazz. Sketches of Spain in Harlem. In a Parisian bookstore a voice murmurs the words. Nobody Knows My Name.[7] I have listened to the voice that cried: I have a dream[8] that one day on the red hills of Georgia, the sons of former slaves and the sons of former slave-owners will be able to sit down together at the table of brotherhood. I have listened to the sounds of an African carnival in Trinidad. In Rio. In New Orleans. On the far bank of the river, a drum continues to be beaten. A many-tongued chorus continues to swell. And I hope that amongst these survivors' voices I might occasionally hear those of my own children. My Nash. My Martha. My Travis. My daughter. Joyce. All. Hurt but determined. Only if they panic will they break their wrists and ankles against Captain Hamilton's instruments. A guilty father. Always listening. There are no paths in water. No signposts. There is no return. A desperate foolishness. The crops failed. I sold my beloved children. *Bought 2 strong man-boys, and a proud girl.* But they arrived on the far bank of the river, loved.

§ *African disapora/Atlantic crossings* Carib: Brathwaite (1, 2, 3), Nichols

ROHINTON MISTRY (1952–)

Squatter*

Whenever Nariman Hansotia returned in the evening from the Cawasji Framji Memorial Library in a good mood the signs were plainly evident.

---

3 Title of Jamaican-American Claude McKay's 1937 autobiography. 4 Haitian patriot and leader in the Haitian revolution. 5 François Duvalier and his son, Claude, twentieth-century Haitian dictators. 6 1960s recording by the Supremes. 7 1961 volume of essays by James Baldwin. 8 Most famous speech of Civil Rights activist Martin Luther King, delivered in 1963.
* 'Squatter' originally appeared without annotations or glossary and the footnotes included here have been provided by the editor and advisers.

First, he parked his 1932 Mercedes-Benz (he called it the apple of his eye) outside A Block, directly in front of his ground-floor veranda window, and beeped the horn three long times. It annoyed Rustomji who also had a ground-floor flat in A Block. Ever since he had defied Nariman in the matter of painting the exterior of the building Rustomji was convinced that nothing the old coot did was untainted by the thought of vengeance and harassment, his retirement pastime.

But the beeping was merely Nariman's signal to let Hirabai inside know that though he was back he would not step indoors for a while. Then he raised the hood, whistling 'Rose Marie,' and leaned his tall frame over the engine. He checked the oil, wiped here and there with a rag, tightened the radiator cap, and lowered the hood. Finally, he polished the Mercedes star and let the whistling modulate into the march from *The Bridge On The River Kwai*.[1] The boys playing in the compound knew that Nariman was ready now to tell a story. They started to gather round.

'*Sahibji, Nariman* Uncle,' someone said tentatively and Nariman nodded, careful not to lose his whistle, his bulbous nose flaring slightly. The pursed lips had temporarily raised and reshaped his Clark Gable moustache. More boys walked up. One called out, 'How about a story, Nariman Uncle?' at which point Nariman's eyes began to twinkle, and he imparted increased energy to the polishing. The cry was taken up by others, 'Yes, yes, Nariman Uncle, a story!' He swung into a final verse of the march. Then the lips relinquished the whistle, the Clark Gable moustache descended. The rag was put away, and he began.

'You boys know the great cricketers: Contractor, Polly Umrigar, and recently, the young chap, Farokh Engineer.[2] Cricket *aficionados*, that's what you all are.' Nariman liked to use new words, especially big ones, in the stories he told, believing it was his duty to expose young minds to as shimmering and varied a vocabulary as possible; if they could not spend their days at the Cawasji Framji Memorial Library then he, at least, could carry bits of the library out to them.

The boys nodded; the names of the cricketers were familiar.

'But does any one know about Savukshaw, the greatest of them all?' They shook their heads in unison.

'This, then, is the story about Savukshaw, how he saved the Indian team from a humiliating defeat when they were touring in England.' Nariman sat on the steps of A Block. The few diehards who had continued with their games could not resist any longer when they saw the gathering circle, and ran up to listen. They asked their neighbours in whispers what the story was about, and were told: Savukshaw the greatest cricketer. The whispering died down and Nariman began.

'The Indian team was to play the indomitable MCC as part of its tour of England. Contractor was our captain. Now the MCC being the strongest

---

1 'The Colonel Bogey March', from David Lean's 1957 film with music by Malcolm Arnold; 'Colonel Bogey', was originally a World War I whistling tune. 2 Indian test-match batsmen of the 1950s and 1960s.

team they had to face, Contractor was almost certain of defeat. To add to Contractor's troubles, one of his star batsmen, Nadkarni, had caught influenza early in the tour, and would definitely not be well enough to play against the MCC. By the way, does anyone know what those letters stand for? You, Kersi, you wanted to be a cricketer once.'

Kersi shook his head. None of the boys knew, even though they had heard the MCC mentioned in radio commentaries, because the full name was hardly ever used.

Then Jehangir Bulsara spoke up, or Bulsara Bookworm, as the boys called him. The name given by Pesi *paadmaroo*[3] had stuck even though it was now more than four years since Pesi had been sent away to boarding-school, and over two years since the death of Dr Mody. Jehangir was still unliked by the boys in the Baag,[4] though they had come to accept his aloofness and respect his knowledge and intellect. They were not surprised that he knew the answer to Nariman's question: 'Marylebone Cricket Club.'

'Absolutely correct,' said Nariman, and continued with the story. 'The MCC won the toss and elected to bat. They scored four hundred and ninety-seven runs in the first inning before our spinners could get them out. Early in the second day's play our team was dismissed for one hundred and nine runs, and the extra who had taken Nadkarni's place was injured by a vicious bumper that opened a gash on his forehead.' Nariman indicated the spot and the length of the gash on his furrowed brow. 'Contractor's worst fears were coming true. The MCC waived their own second inning and gave the Indian team a follow-on, wanting to inflict an inning's defeat. And this time he had to use the second extra. The second extra was a certain Savukshaw.'

The younger boys listened attentively; some of them, like the two sons of the chartered accountant in B Block, had only recently been deemed old enough by their parents to come out and play in the compound, and had not received any exposure to Nariman's stories. But the others like Jehangir, Kersi, and Viraf were familiar with Nariman's technique.

Once, Jehangir had overheard them discussing Nariman's stories, and he could not help expressing his opinion: that unpredictability was the brush he used to paint his tales with, and ambiguity the palette he mixed his colours in. The others looked at him with admiration. Then Viraf asked what exactly he meant by that. Jehangir said that Nariman sometimes told a funny incident in a very serious way, or expressed a significant matter in a light and playful manner. And these were only two rough divisions, in between were lots of subtle gradations of tone and texture. Which, then, was the funny story and which the serious? Their opinions were divided, but ultimately, said Jehangir, it was up to the listener to decide.

'So,' continued Nariman, 'Contractor first sent out his two regular openers, convinced that it was all hopeless. But after five wickets were lost for just another thirty-eight runs, out came Savukshaw the extra. Nothing mattered any more.'

---

3 Pesi the farter.   4 Garden, but here referring to an apartment building.

The street lights outside the compound came on, illuminating the iron gate where the watchman stood. It was a load off the watchman's mind when Nariman told a story. It meant an early end to the hectic vigil during which he had to ensure that none of the children ran out on the main road, or tried to jump over the wall. For although keeping out riff-raff was his duty, keeping in the boys was as important if he wanted to retain the job.

'The first ball Savukshaw faced was wide outside the off stump. He just lifted his bat and ignored it. But with what style! What panache! As if to say, come on, you blighters, play some polished cricket. The next ball was also wide, but not as much as the first. It missed the off stump narrowly. Again Savukshaw lifted his bat, boredom written all over him. Everyone was now watching closely. The bowler was annoyed by Savukshaw's arrogance, and the third delivery was a vicious fast pitch, right down on the middle stump.

'Savukshaw was ready, quick as lightning. No one even saw the stroke of his bat, but the ball went like a bullet towards square leg.

'Fielding at square leg was a giant of a fellow, about six feet seven, weighing two hundred and fifty pounds, a veritable Brobdingnagian, with arms like branches and hands like a pair of huge *sapaat*,[5] the kind that Dr Mody used to wear, you remember what big feet Dr Mody had.' Jehangir was the only one who did; he nodded. 'Just to see him standing there was scary. Not one ball had got past him, and he had taken some great catches. Savukshaw purposely aimed his shot right at him. But he was as quick as Savukshaw, and stuck out his huge *sapaat* of a hand to stop the ball. What do you think happened then, boys?'

The older boys knew what Nariman wanted to hear at this point. They asked, 'What happened, Nariman Uncle, what happened?' Satisfied, Nariman continued.

'A howl is what happened. A howl from the giant fielder, a howl that rang through the entire stadium, that soared like the cry of a banshee right up to the cheapest seats in the furthest, highest corners, a howl that echoed from the scoreboard and into the pavilion, into the kitchen, startling the chap inside who was preparing tea and scones for after the match, who spilled boiling water all over himself and was severely hurt. But not nearly as bad as the giant fielder at square leg. Never at any English stadium was a howl heard like that one, not in the whole history of cricket. And why do you think he was howling boys?'

The chorus asked, 'Why, Nariman Uncle, why?'

'Because of Savukshaw's bullet-like shot, of course. The hand he had reached out to stop it, he now held up for all to see, and *dhur-dhur, dhur-dhur* the blood was gushing like a fountain in an Italian piazza, like a burst water-main from the Vihar-Powai reservoir, dripping onto his shirt and his white pants, and sprinkling the green grass, and only because he was such a

---

5 Thin-soled slippers.

giant of a fellow could he suffer so much blood loss and not faint. But even he could not last forever; eventually, he felt dizzy, and was helped off the field. And where do you think the ball was, boys, that Savukshaw had smacked so hard?'

And the chorus rang out again on the now dark steps of A Block: 'Where, Nariman Uncle, where?'

'Past the boundary lines of course. Lying near the fence. Rent asunder. Into two perfect leather hemispheres. All the stitches had ripped, and some of the insides had spilled out. So the umpires sent for a new one, and the game resumed. Now none of the fielders dared to touch any ball that Savukshaw hit. Every shot went to the boundary, all the way for four runs. Single-handedly, Savukshaw wiped out the deficit, and had it not been for loss of time due to rain, he would have taken the Indian team to a thumping victory against the MCC. As it was, the match ended in a draw.'

Nariman was pleased with the awed faces of the youngest ones around him. Kersi and Viraf were grinning away and whispering something. From one of the flats the smell of frying fish swam out to explore the night air, and tickled Nariman's nostrils. He sniffed appreciatively, aware that it was in his good wife Hirabai's pan that the frying was taking place. This morning he had seen the pomfret she had purchased at the door, waiting to be cleaned, its mouth open and eyes wide, like the eyes of some of these youngsters. It was time to wind up the story.

'The MCC will not forget the number of new balls they had to produce that day because of Savukshaw's deadly strokes. Their annual ball budget was thrown badly out of balance. Any other bat would have cracked under the strain, but Savukshaw's was seasoned with a special combination of oils, a secret formula given to him by a *sadhu*[6] who had seen him one day playing cricket when he was a small boy. But Savukshaw used to say his real secret was practice, lots of practice, that was the advice he gave to any young lad who wanted to play cricket.'

The story was now clearly finished, but none of the boys showed any sign of dispersing 'Tell us about more matches that Savukshaw played in,' they said.

'More nothing. This was his greatest match. Anyway, he did not play cricket for long because soon after the match against the MCC he became a champion bicyclist, the fastest human on two wheels. And later, a pole vaulter – when he glided over on his pole, so graceful, it was like watching a bird in flight. But he gave that up, too, and became a hunter, the mightiest hunter ever known, absolutely fearless, and so skilful with a gun he could have, from the third floor of A Block, shaved the whisker of a cat in the backyard of C Block.'

'Tell us about that,' they said, 'about Savukshaw the hunter!'

The fat ayah, Jaakaylee, arrived to take the chartered accountant's two children home. But they refused to go without hearing about Savukshaw the

---

6 Holy man.

hunter. When she scolded them and things became a little hysterical, some other boys tried to resurrect the ghost she had once seen: 'Ayah *bhoot*! Ayah *bhoot*!'[7] Nariman raised a finger in warning – that subject was still taboo in Firozsha Baag; none of the adults was in a hurry to relive the wild and rampageous days that Pesi *paadmaroo* had ushered in, once upon a time, with the *bhoot* games.

Jaakaylee sat down, unwilling to return without the children, and whispered to Nariman to make it short. The smell of frying fish which had tickled Nariman's nostrils ventured into and awakened his stomach. But the story of Savukshaw the hunter was one he had wanted to tell for a long time.

'Savukshaw always went hunting alone, he preferred it that way. There are many incidents in the life of Savukshaw the hunter, but the one I am telling you about involves a terrifying situation. Terrifying for us, of course; Savukshaw was never terrified of anything. What happened was, one night he set up camp, started a fire and warmed up his bowl of chicken-*dhansaak*.'[8]

The frying fish had precipitated famishment upon Nariman, and the subject of chicken-*dhansaak* suited him well. His own mouth watering, he elaborated: 'Mrs Savukshaw was as famous for her *dhansaak* as Mr was for hunting. She used to put in tamarind and brinjal,[9] coriander and cumin, cloves and cinnamon, and dozens of other spices no one knows about. Women used to come from miles around to stand outside her window while she cooked it, to enjoy the fragrance and try to penetrate her secret, hoping to identify the ingredients as the aroma floated out, layer by layer, growing more complex and delicious. But always, the delectable fragrance enveloped the women and they just surrendered to the ecstasy, forgetting what they had come for. Mrs Savukshaw's secret was safe.'

Jaakaylee motioned to Nariman to hurry up, it was past the children's dinner-time. He continued: 'The aroma of savoury spices soon filled the night air in the jungle, and when the *dhansaak* was piping hot he started to eat, his rifle beside him. But as soon as he lifted the first morsel to his lips, a tiger's eyes flashed in the bushes! Not twelve feet from him! He emerged licking his chops! What do you think happened then, boys?'

'What, what, Nariman Uncle?'

Before he could tell them, the door of his flat opened. Hirabai put her head out and said, '*Chaalo ni*,[10] Nariman, it's time. Then if it gets cold you won't like it.'

That decided the matter. To let Hirabai's fried fish, crisp on the outside, yet tender and juicy inside, marinated in turmeric and cayenne – to let that get cold would be something that *Khoedaiji*[11] above would not easily forgive. 'Sorry boys, have to go. Next time about Savukshaw and the tiger.'

There were some groans of disappointment. They hoped Nariman's good spirits would extend into the morrow when he returned from the Memorial Library, or the story would get cold.

---

7 Nursemaid, ghost! 8 A favourite Parsee food item. 9 Aubergine. 10 Let's go. 11 God.

But a whole week elapsed before Nariman again parked the apple of his eye outside his ground-floor flat and beeped the horn three times. When he had raised the hood, checked the oil, polished the star and swung into the 'Colonel Bogie March,' the boys began drifting towards A Block.

Some of them recalled the incomplete story of Savukshaw and the tiger, but they knew better than to remind him. It was never wise to prompt Nariman until he had dropped the first hint himself, or things would turn out badly.

Nariman inspected the faces: the two who stood at the back, always looking superior and wise, were missing. So was the quiet Bulsara boy, the intelligent one. 'Call Kersi, Viraf, and Jehangir,' he said, 'I want them to listen to today's story.'

Jehangir was sitting alone on the stone steps of C Block. The others were chatting by the compound gate with the watchman. Someone went to fetch them.

'Sorry to disturb your conference, boys, and your meditation, Jehangir,' Nariman said facetiously, 'but I thought you would like to hear this story. Especially since some of you are planning to go abroad.'

This was not strictly accurate, but Kersi and Viraf did talk a lot about America and Canada. Kersi had started writing to universities there since his final high-school year, and had also sent letters of inquiry to the Canadian High Commission in New Delhi and to the U.S. Consulate at Breach Candy. But so far he had not made any progress. He and Viraf replied with as much sarcasm as their unripe years allowed, 'Oh yes, next week, just have to pack our bags.'

'Riiiight,' drawled Nariman. Although he spoke perfect English, this was the one word with which he allowed himself sometimes to take liberties, indulging in a broadness of vowel more American than anything else. 'But before we go on with today's story, what did you learn about Savukshaw, from last week's story?'

'That he was a very talented man,' said someone.

'What else?'

'He was also a very lucky man, to have so many talents,' said Viraf.

'Yes, but what else?'

There was silence for a few moments. Then Jehangir said, timidly: 'He was a man searching for happiness, by trying all kinds of different things.'

'Exactly! And he never found it. He kept looking for new experiences, and though he was very successful at everything he attempted, it did not bring him happiness. Remember this, success alone does not bring happiness. Nor does failure have to bring unhappiness. Keep it in mind when you listen to today's story.'

A chant started somewhere in the back: 'We-want-a-story! We-want-a-story!'

'Riiiight,' said Nariman. 'Now, everyone remembers Vera and Dolly, daughters of Najamai from C Block.' There were whistles and hoots; Viraf nudged Kersi with his elbow, who was smiling wistfully. Nariman held up his hand: 'Now now, boys, behave yourselves. Those two girls went abroad for studies many years ago, and never came back. They settled there happily.

'And like them, a fellow called Sarosh also went abroad, to Toronto, but did not find happiness there. This story is about him. You probably don't know him, he does not live in Firozsha Baag though he is related to someone who does.'

'Who? Who?'

'Curiosity killed the cat,' said Nariman, running a finger over each branch of his moustache, 'and what's important is the tale. So let us continue. This Sarosh began calling himself Sid after living in Toronto for a few months, but in our story he will be Sarosh and nothing but Sarosh, for that is his proper Parsi name. Besides, that was his own stipulation when he entrusted me with the sad but instructive chronicle of his recent life.' Nariman polished his glasses with his handkerchief, put them on again, and began.

'At the point where our story commences, Sarosh had been living in Toronto for ten years. We find him depressed and miserable, perched on top of the toilet, crouching on his haunches, feet planted firmly for balance upon the white plastic oval of the toilet seat.

'Daily for a decade had Sarosh suffered this position. Morning after morning, he had no choice but to climb up and simulate the squat of our Indian latrines. If he sat down, no amount of exertion could produce success.

'At first, this inability was no more than mildly incommodious. As time went by, however, the frustrated attempts caused him grave anxiety. And when the failure stretched unbroken over ten years, it began to torment and haunt all his waking hours.'

Some of the boys struggled hard to keep straight faces. They suspected that Nariman was not telling just a funny story, because if he intended them to laugh there was always some unmistakable way to let them know. Only the thought of displeasing Nariman and prematurely terminating the story kept their paroxysms of mirth from bursting forth unchecked.

Nariman continued: 'You see, ten years was the time Sarosh had set himself to achieve complete adaptation to the new country. But how could he claim adaptation with any honesty if the acceptable catharsis continually failed to favour him? Obtaining his new citizenship had not helped either. He remained dependent on the old way, and this unalterable fact, strengthened afresh every morning of his life in the new country, suffocated him.

'The ten-year time limit was more an accident than anything else. But it hung over him with the awesome presence and sharpness of a guillotine. Careless words, boys, careless words in a moment of lightheartedness, as is so often the case with us all, had led to it.

'Ten years before, Sarosh had returned triumphantly to Bombay after fulfilling the immigration requirements of the Canadian High Commission in New Delhi. News of his imminent departure spread amongst relatives and friends. A farewell party was organized. In fact, it was given by his relatives in Firozsha Baag. Most of you will be too young to remember it, but it was a very loud party, went on till late in the night. Very lengthy and heated arguments took place, which is not the thing to do at a party. It started like this: Sarosh was told by some what a smart decision he had made, that his whole life would change for the better; others said he was making a mistake, emigration was all wrong, but if he wanted to be unhappy that was his business, they wished him well.

'By and by, after substantial amounts of Scotch and soda and rum and Coke had disappeared, a fierce debate started between the two groups. To this day Sarosh does not know what made him raise his glass and announce: "My dear family, my dear friends, if I do not become completely Canadian in exactly ten years from the time I land there, then I will come back. I promise. So please, no more arguments. Enjoy the party." His words were greeted with cheers and shouts of hear! hear! They told him never to fear embarrassment; there was no shame if he decided to return to the country of his birth.

'But shortly, his poor worried mother pulled him aside. She led him to the back room and withdrew her worn and aged prayer book from her purse, saying "I want you to place your hand upon the *Avesta*[12] and swear that you will keep that promise."

'He told her not to be silly, that it was just a joke But she insisted: "*Kassum kha*[13] – on the *Avesta*. One last thing for your mother. Who knows when you will see me again?" and her voice grew tremulous as it always did when she turned deeply emotional. Sarosh complied, and the prayer book was returned to her purse.

'His mother continued: "It is better to live in want among your family and your friends, who love you and care for you, than to be unhappy surrounded by vacuum cleaners and dishwashers and big shiny motor cars." She hugged him. Then they joined the celebration in progress.

'And Sarosh's careless words spoken at the party gradually forged themselves into a commitment as much to himself as to his mother and the others. It stayed with him all his years in the new land, reminding him every morning of what must happen at the end of the tenth, as it reminded him now while he descended from his perch.'

Jehangir wished the titters and chortles around him would settle down, he found them annoying. When Nariman structured his sentences so carefully and chose his words with extreme care as he was doing now, Jehangir found it most pleasurable to listen. Sometimes, he remembered certain words Nariman had used, or combinations of words, and repeated them to himself, enjoying again the beauty of their sounds when he went for his walks to the Hanging Gardens[14] or was sitting alone on the stone steps of C Block. Mumbling to himself did nothing to mitigate the isolation which the other boys in the Baag had dropped around him like a heavy cloak, but he had grown used to all that by now.

Nariman continued: 'In his own apartment Sarosh squatted barefoot.

---

12 Parsee holy book.   13 Swear an oath.   14 The Pherozeshah Gardens on Malabar Hill in Bombay; called 'the Hanging Gardens', because they are built on top of a series of reservoirs.

Elsewhere, if he had to go with his shoes on, he would carefully cover the seat with toilet paper before climbing up. He learnt to do this after the first time, when his shoes had left telltale footprints on the seat. He had had to clean it with a wet paper towel. Luckily, no one had seen him.

'But there was not much he could keep secret about his ways. The world of washrooms is private and at the same time very public. The absence of feet below the stall door, the smell of faeces, the rustle of paper, glimpses caught through the narrow crack between stall door and jamb – all these added up to only one thing: a foreign presence in the stall, not doing things in the conventional way. And if the one outside could receive the fetor of Sarosh's business wafting through the door, poor unhappy Sarosh too could detect something malodorous in the air: the presence of xenophobia and hostility.'

What a feast, thought Jehangir, what a feast of words! This would be the finest story Nariman had ever told, he just knew it.

'But Sarosh did not give up trying. Each morning he seated himself to push and grunt, grunt and push, squirming and writhing unavailingly on the white plastic oval. Exhausted, he then hopped up, expert at balancing now, and completed the movement quite effortlessly.

'The long morning hours in the washroom created new difficulties. He was late going to work on several occasions, and one such day, the supervisor called him in: "Here's your time sheet for this month. You've been late eleven times. What's the problem?" '

Here, Nariman stopped because his neighbour Rustomji's door creaked open. Rustomji peered out, scowling and muttered: '*Saala*[15] loafers, sitting all evening outside people's houses, making a nuisance, and being encouraged by grownups at that.'

He stood there a moment longer, fingering the greying chest hair that was easily accessible through his *sudra*,[16] then went inside. The boys immediately took up a soft and low chant: 'Rustomji-the-curmudgeon! Rustomji-the curmudgeon!'

Nariman held up his hand disapprovingly. But secretly, he was pleased that the name was still popular, the name he had given Rustomji when the latter had refused to pay his share for painting the building. 'Quiet, quiet!' said he. 'Do you want me to continue or not?'

'Yes, yes!' The chanting died away, and Nariman resumed the story.

'So Sarosh was told by his supervisor that he was coming late to work too often. What could poor Sarosh say?'

'What, Nariman Uncle?' rose the refrain.

'Nothing, of course. The supervisor, noting his silence, continued: "If it keeps up, the consequences could be serious as far as your career is concerned."

'Sarosh decided to speak. He said embarrassedly, "It's a different kind of problem. I . . . I don't know how to explain . . . it's an immigration-related problem."

---

15 Term of abuse, literally 'wife's brother'. 16 Muslin vest worn by Parsee men.

'Now this supervisor must have had experience with other immigrants, because right away he told Sarosh, "No problem. Just contact your Immigrant Aid Society. They should be able to help you. Every ethnic group has one: Vietnamese, Chinese – I'm certain that one exists for Indians. If you need time off to go there, no problem. That can be arranged, no problem. As long as you do something about your lateness, there's no problem." That's the way they talk over there, nothing is ever a problem.

'So Sarosh thanked him and went to his desk. For the umpteenth time he bitterly rued his oversight. Could fate have plotted it, concealing the western toilet behind that shroud of anxieties which had appeared out of nowhere to beset him just before he left India? After all, he had readied himself meticulously for the new life. Even for the great, merciless Canadian cold he had heard so much about. How could he have overlooked preparation for the western toilet with its matutinal demands unless fate had conspired? In Bombay, you know that offices of foreign businesses offer both options in their bathrooms. So do all hotels with three stars or more. By practising in familiar surroundings, Sarosh was convinced he could have mastered a seated evacuation before departure.

'But perhaps there was something in what the supervisor said. Sarosh found a telephone number for the Indian Immigrant Aid Society and made an appointment. That afternoon, he met Mrs Maha-Lepate at the Society's office.'

Kersi and Viraf looked at each other and smiled. Nariman Uncle had a nerve, there was more *lepate* in his own stories than anywhere else.

'Mrs Maha-Lepate was very understanding, and made Sarosh feel at ease despite the very personal nature of his problem. She said, "Yes, we get many referrals. There was a man here last month who couldn't eat Wonder Bread – it made him throw up."

'By the way, boys, Wonder Bread is a Canadian bread which all happy families eat to be happy in the same way; the unhappy families are unhappy in their own fashion by eating other brands.' Jehangir was the only one who understood, and murmured: 'Tolstoy,' at Nariman's little joke. Nariman noticed it, pleased. He continued.

'Mrs Maha-Lepate told Sarosh about that case: "Our immigrant specialist, Dr No-Ilaaz, recommended that the patient eat cake instead. He explained that Wonder Bread caused vomiting because the digestive system was used to Indian bread only, made with Indian flour in the village he came from. However, since his system was unfamiliar with cake, Canadian or otherwise, it did not react but was digested as a newfound food. In this way he got used to Canadian flour first in cake form. Just yesterday we received a report from Dr No-Ilaaz. The patient successfully ate his first slice of whole-wheat Wonder Bread with no ill effects. The ultimate goal is pure white Wonder Bread."

'Like a polite Parsi boy, Sarosh said, "That's very interesting." The garrulous Mrs Maha Lepate was about to continue, and he tried to interject: "But I – " but Mrs Maha-Lepate was too quick for him: "Oh, there are so many interesting cases I could tell you about. Like the woman from Sri Lanka – referred to us because they don't have their own Society – who could not drink the water here. Dr No-Ilaaz said it was due to the different mineral content. So he started her on Coca-Cola and then began diluting it with water, bit by bit. Six weeks later she took her first sip of unadulterated Canadian water and managed to keep it down."

'Sarosh could not halt Mrs Maha-Lepate as she launched from one case history into another: "Right now, Dr No-Ilaaz is working on a very unusual case. Involves a whole Pakistani family. Ever since immigrating to Canada, none of them can swallow. They choke on their own saliva, and have to spit constantly. But we are confident that Dr No-Ilaaz will find a remedy. He has never been stumped by any immigrant problem. Besides, we have an information network with other third-world Immigrant Aid Societies. We all seem to share a history of similar maladies, and regularly compare notes. Some of us thought these problems were linked to retention of original citizenship. But this was a false lead."

'Sarosh, out of his own experience, vigorously nodded agreement. By now he was truly fascinated by Mrs Maha-Lepate's wealth of information. Reluctantly, he interrupted: "But will Dr No-Ilaaz be able to solve my problem?"

' "I have every confidence that he will," replied Mrs Maha-Lepate in great earnest. "And if he has no remedy for you right away, he will be delighted to start working on one. He loves to take up new projects." '

Nariman halted to blow his nose, and a clear shrill voice travelled the night air of the Firozsha Baag compound from C Block to where the boys had collected around Nariman in A Block: 'Jehangoo! O Jehangoo! Eight o'clock! Upstairs now!'

Jehangir stared at his feet in embarrassment. Nariman looked at his watch and said, 'Yes, it's eight.' But Jehangir did not move, so he continued.

'Mrs Maha-Lepate was able to arrange an appointment while Sarosh waited, and he went directly to the doctor's office. What he had heard so far sounded quite promising. Then he cautioned himself not to get overly optimistic, that was the worst mistake he could make. But along the way to the doctor's, he could not help thinking what a lovely city Toronto was. It was the same way he had felt when he first saw it ten years ago, before all the joy had dissolved in the acid of his anxieties.'

Once again that shrill voice travelled through the clear night: 'Arré Jehangoo! Muà,[17] do I have to come down and drag you upstairs!'

Jehangir's mortification was now complete. Nariman made it easy for him, though: 'The first part of the story is over. Second part continues tomorrow. Same time, same place.' The boys were surprised, Nariman did not make such commitments. But never before had he told such a long story. They began drifting back to their homes.

As Jehangir strode hurriedly to C Block, falsettos and piercing shrieks

---

17 An exclamation, literally 'dead'.

followed him in the darkness: '*Arré* Jehangoo! *Muà* Jehangoo! Bulsara Bookworm! Eight o'clock Jehangoo!' Shaking his head, Nariman went indoors to Hirabai.

Next evening, the story punctually resumed when Nariman took his place on the topmost step of A Block: 'You remember that we left Sarosh on his way to see the Immigrant Aid Society's doctor. Well, Dr No-Ilaaz listened patiently to Sarosh's concerns, then said, "As a matter of fact, there is a remedy which is so new even the IAS does not know about it. Not even that Mrs Maha-Lepate who knows it all," he added drolly, twirling his stethoscope like a stunted lasso. He slipped it on around his neck before continuing: 'It involves a minor operation which was developed with financial assistance from the Multicultural Department. A small device, *Crappus Non Interruptus*, or CNI as we call it, is implanted in the bowel. The device is controlled by an external handheld transmitter similar to the ones used for automatic garage door-openers – you may have seen them in hardware stores." '

Nariman noticed that most of the boys wore puzzled looks and realized he had to make some things clearer. 'The Multicultural Department is a Canadian invention.[18] It is supposed to ensure that ethnic cultures are able to flourish, so that Canadian society will consist of a mosaic of cultures – that's their favourite word, mosaic – instead of one uniform mix, like the American melting pot. If you ask me, mosaic and melting pot are both nonsense, and ethnic is a polite way of saying bloody foreigner. But anyway, you understand Multicultural Department? Good. So Sarosh nodded, and Dr No-Ilaaz went on: "You can encode the handheld transmitter with a personal ten digit code. Then all you do is position yourself on the toilet seat and activate your transmitter. Just like a garage door, your bowel will open without pushing or grunting." '

There was some snickering in the audience, and Nariman raised his eyebrows, whereupon they covered up their mouths with their hands. 'The doctor asked Sarosh if he had any questions. Sarosh thought for a moment, then asked if it required any maintenance.

'Dr No-Ilaaz replied: "CNI is semi-permanent and operates on solar energy. Which means you would have to make it a point to get some sun periodically, or it would cease and lead to constipation. However, you don't have to strip for a tan. Exposing ten percent of your skin surface once a week during summer will let the device store sufficient energy for year-round operation."

'Sarosh's next question was: "Is there any hope that someday the bowels can work on their own, without operating the device?" at which Dr No-Ilaaz grimly shook his head: "I'm afraid not. You must think very, very carefully before making a decision. Once CNI is implanted, you can never pass a motion in the natural way – neither sitting nor squatting."

'He stopped to allow Sarosh time to think it over, then continued: "And

---

18 Canada pioneered multiculturalism in the 1970s; it was proclaimed as federal government policy in 1971.

you must understand what that means. You will never be able to live a normal life again. You will be permanently different from your family and friends because of this basic internal modification. In fact, in this country or that, it will set you apart from your fellow countrymen. So you must consider the whole thing most carefully."

'Dr No-Ilaaz paused, toyed with his stethoscope, shuffled some papers on his desk, then resumed: "There are other dangers you should know about. Just as a garage door can be accidentally opened by a neighbour's transmitter on the same frequency, CNI can also be activated by someone with similar apparatus." To ease the tension he attempted a quick laugh and said, "Very embarrassing eh, if it happened at the wrong place and time. Mind you, the risk is not so great at present, because the chances of finding yourself within a fifty-foot radius of another transmitter on the same frequency are infinitesimal. But what about the future? What if CNI becomes very popular? Sufficient permutations may not be available for transmitter frequencies and you could be sharing the code with others. Then the risk of accidents becomes greater." '

Something landed with a loud thud in the yard behind A Block, making Nariman startle. Immediately, a yowling and screeching and caterwauling went up from the stray cats there, and the *kuchrawalli*'s[19] dog started barking. Some of the boys went around the side of A Block to peer over the fence into the backyard. But the commotion soon died down of its own accord. The boys returned and, once again, Nariman's voice was the only sound to be heard.

'By now, Sarosh was on the verge of deciding against the operation. Dr No-Ilaaz observed this and was pleased. He took pride in being able to dissuade his patients from following the very remedies which he first so painstakingly described. True to his name, Dr No-Ilaaz believed no remedy is the best remedy, rather than prescribing this-mycin and that-mycin for every little ailment. So he continued: "And what about our sons and daughters? And the quality of their lives? We still don't know the long-term effects of CNI. Some researchers speculate that it could generate a genetic deficiency, that the offspring of a CNI parent would also require CNI. On the other hand, they could be perfectly healthy toilet seat-users, without any congenital defects. We just don't know at this stage."

'Sarosh rose from his chair: "Thank you very much for your time, Dr No-Ilaaz. But I don't think I want to take such a drastic step. As you suggest, I will think it over very carefully."

' "Good, good," said Dr No-Ilaaz, "I was hoping you would say that. There is one more thing.The operation is extremely expensive, and is not covered by the province's Health Insurance Plan. Many immigrant groups are lobbying to obtain coverage for special immigration-related health problems. If they succeed, then good for you."

'Sarosh left Dr No-Ilaaz's office with his mind made up. Time was run-

---

19 Woman who collects garbage.

ning out. There had been a time when it was perfectly natural to squat. Now it seemed a grotesquely aberrant thing to do. Wherever he went he was reminded of the ignominy of his way. If he could not be westernized in all respects, he was nothing but a failure in this land – a failure not just in the washrooms of the nation but everywhere. He knew what he must do if he was to be true to himself and to the decade-old commitment. So what do you think Sarosh did next?'

'What, Nariman Uncle?'

'He went to the travel agent specializing in tickets to India. He bought a fully refundable ticket to Bombay for the day when he would complete exactly ten immigrant years – if he succeeded even once before that day dawned, he would cancel the booking.

'The travel agent asked sympathetically, "Trouble at home?" His name was Mr Rawaana, and he was from Bombay too.

' "No." said Sarosh, "trouble in Toronto."

' "That's a shame," said Mr Rawaana. "I don't want to poke my nose into your business, but in my line of work I meet so many people who are going back to their homeland because of problems here. Sometimes I forget I'm a travel agent, that my interest is to convince them to travel. Instead, I tell them: don't give up, God is great, stay and try again. It's bad for my profits but gives me a different, a spiritual kind of satisfaction when I succeed. And I succeed about half the time. Which means," he added with a wry laugh, "I could double my profits if I minded my own business."

'After the lengthy sessions with Mrs Maha-Lepate and Dr No-Ilaaz, Sarosh felt he had listened to enough advice and kind words. Much as he disliked doing it, he had to hurt Mr Rawaana's feelings and leave his predicament undiscussed: "I'm sorry, but I'm in a hurry. Will you be able to look after the booking?"

' "Well, okay," said Mr Rawaana, a trifle crestfallen; he did not relish the travel business as much as he did counselling immigrants. "Hope you solve your problem. I will be happy to refund your fare, believe me."

'Sarosh hurried home. With only four weeks to departure, every spare minute, every possible method had to be concentrated on a final attempt at adaptation.

'He tried laxatives, crunching down the tablets with a prayer that these would assist the sitting position. Changing brands did not help, and neither did various types of suppositories. He spent long stretches on the toilet seat each morning. The supervisor continued to reprimand him for tardiness. To make matters worse, Sarosh left his desk every time he felt the slightest urge, hoping: maybe this time.

'The working hours expended in the washroom were noted with unflagging vigilance by the supervisor. More counselling sessions followed. Sarosh refused to extinguish his last hope, and the supervisor punctiliously recorded "No Improvement" in his daily log. Finally, Sarosh was fired. It would soon have been time to resign in any case, and he could not care less.

'Now whole days went by seated on the toilet, and he stubbornly refused to relieve himself the other way. The doorbell would ring only to be ignored. The telephone went unanswered. Sometimes, he would awake suddenly in the dark hours before dawn and rush to the washroom like a madman.'

Without warning Rustomji flung open his door and stormed: 'Ridiculous nonsense this is becoming! Two days in a row, whole Firozsha Baag gathers here! This is not Chaupatty beach, this is not a squatters' colony, this is a building, people want to live here in peace and quiet!' Then just as suddenly, he stamped inside and slammed the door. Right on cue, Nariman continued, before the boys could say anything.

'Time for meals was the only time Sarosh allowed himself off the seat. Even in his desperation he remembered that if he did not eat well, he was doomed – the downward pressure on his gut was essential if there was to be any chance of success.

'But the ineluctable day of departure dawned, with grey skies and the scent of rain, while success remained out of sight. At the airport Sarosh checked in and went to the dreary lounge. Out of sheer habit he started towards the washroom. Then he realized the hopelessness of it and returned to the cold, clammy plastic of the lounge seats. Airport seats are the same almost anywhere in the world.

'The boarding announcement was made, and Sarosh was the first to step onto the plane. The skies were darker now. Out of the window he saw a flash of lightning fork through the clouds. For some reason, everything he'd learned years ago in St Xavier's about sheet lightning and forked lightning went through his mind. He wished it would change to sheet, there was something sinister and unpropitious about forked lightning.'

Kersi, absorbedly listening began cracking his knuckles quite unconsciously. His childhood habit still persisted. Jehangir frowned at the disturbance, and Viraf nudged Kersi to stop it.

'Sarosh fastened his seat-belt and attempted to turn his thoughts towards the long journey home: to the questions he would be expected to answer, the sympathy and criticism that would be thrust upon him. But what remained uppermost in his mind was the present moment – him in the plane, dark skies lowering lightning on the horizon – irrevocably spelling out: defeat.

'But wait. Something else was happening now. A tiny rumble. Inside him. Or was it his imagination? Was it really thunder outside which, in his present disoriented state, he was internalizing? No, there it was again. He had to go.

'He reached the washroom, and almost immediately the sign flashed to "Please return to seat and fasten seat-belts." Sarosh debated whether to squat and finish the business quickly, abandoning the perfunctory seated attempt. But the plane started to move and that decided him; it would be difficult now to balance while squatting.

'He pushed. The plane continued to move. He pushed again, trembling with the effort. The seat-belt sign flashed quicker and brighter now. The plane moved faster and faster. And Sarosh pushed hard, harder than he had ever pushed before, harder than in all his ten years of trying in the new land. And the memories of Bombay, the immigration interview in New Delhi, the farewell party, his mother's tattered prayer book, all these, of their own accord, emerged from beyond the region of the ten years to push with him and give him newfound strength.'

Nariman paused and cleared his throat. Dusk was falling, and the frequency of B.E.S.T. buses plying the main road outside Firozsha Baag had dropped. Bats began to fly madly from one end of the compound to the other, silent shadows engaged in endless laps over the buildings.

'With a thunderous clap the rain started to fall. Sarosh felt a splash under him. Could it really be? He glanced down to make certain. Yes, it was. He had succeeded!

'But was it already too late? The plane waited at its assigned position on the runway, jet engines at full thrust. Rain was falling in torrents and take-off could be delayed. Perhaps even now they would allow him to cancel his flight, to disembark. He lurched out of the constricting cubicle.

'A stewardess hurried towards him: "Excuse me, sir, but you must return to your seat immediately and fasten your belt."

' "You don't understand!" Sarosh shouted excitedly. "I must get off the plane! Everything is all right, I don't have to go any more. . ."

' "That's impossible, sir!" said the stewardess, aghast. "No one can leave now. Takeoff procedures are in progress!" The wild look in his sleepless eyes, and the dark rings around them scared her. She beckoned for help.

'Sarosh continued to argue, and a steward and the chief stewardess hurried over: "What seems to be the problem, sir? You *must* resume your seat. We are authorized, if necessary, to forcibly restrain you, sir."

'The plane began to move again, and suddenly Sarosh felt all the urgency leaving him. His feverish mind, the product of nightmarish days and torturous nights, was filled again with the calm which had fled a decade ago and he spoke softly now: "That . . . that will not be necessary . . . it's okay, I understand." He readily returned to his seat.

'As the aircraft sped down the runway, Sarosh's first reaction was one of joy. The process of adaptation was complete. But later, he could not help wondering if success came before or after the ten-year limit had expired. And since he had already passed through the customs and security check, was he really an immigrant in every sense of the word at the moment of achievement?

'But such questions were merely academic. Or were they? He could not decide. If he returned, what would it be like? Ten years ago the immigration officer who had stamped his passport had said, "Welcome to Canada." It was one of Sarosh's dearest memories and thinking of it, he fell asleep.

'The plane was flying above the rainclouds. Sunshine streamed into the cabin. A few raindrops were still clinging miraculously to the windows, reminders of what was happening below. They sparkled as the sunlight caught them.'

Some of the boys made as if to leave, thinking the story was finally over.

Clearly, they had not found this one as interesting as the others Nariman had told. What dolts, thought Jehangir, they cannot recognize a masterpiece when they hear one. Nariman motioned with his hand for silence.

'But our story does not end there. There was a welcome-home party for Sarosh a few days after he arrived in Bombay. It was not in Firozsha Baag this time because his relatives in the Baag had a serious sickness in the house. But I was invited to it anyway. Sarosh's family and friends were considerate enough to wait till the jet lag had worked its way out of his system. They wanted him to really enjoy this one.

'Drinks began to flow freely again in his honour: Scotch and soda, rum and Coke, brandy. Sarosh noticed that during his absence all the brand names had changed – the labels were different and unfamiliar. Even for the mixes. Instead of Coke there was Thums-Up, and he remembered reading in the papers about Coca-Cola being kicked out by the Indian Government for refusing to reveal their secret formula.

'People slapped him on the back and shook his hand vigorously, over and over, right through the evening. They said: "Telling the truth, you made the right decision, look how happy your mother is to live to see this day;" or they asked: "Well, bossy, what changed your mind?" Sarosh smiled and nodded his way through it all, passing around Canadian currency at the insistence of some of the curious ones who, egged on by his mother, also pestered him to display his Canadian passport and citizenship card. She had been badgering him since his arrival to tell her the real reason: "*Saachoo kahé*,[20] what brought you back?" and was hoping that tonight, among his friends, he might raise his glass and reveal something. But she remained disappointed.

'Weeks went by and Sarosh found himself desperately searching for his old place in the pattern of life he had vacated ten years ago. Friends who had organized the welcome-home party gradually disappeared. He went walking in the evenings along Marine Drive, by the sea-wall, where the old crowd used to congregate. But the people who sat on the parapet while waves crashed behind their backs were strangers. The tetrapods were still there, staunchly protecting the reclaimed land from the fury of the sea. He had watched as a kid when cranes had lowered these cement and concrete hulks of respectable grey into the water. They were grimy black now, and from their angularities rose the distinct stench of human excrement. The old pattern was never found by Sarosh; he searched in vain. Patterns of life are selfish and unforgiving.

'Then one day, as I was driving past Marine Drive, I saw some one sitting alone. He looked familiar, so I stopped. For a moment I did not recognize Sarosh, so forlorn and woebegone was his countenance. I parked the apple of my eye and went to him, saying, "Hullo, Sid, what are you doing here on your lonesome?" And he said, "No no! No more Sid, please, that name reminds me of all my troubles." Then, on the parapet at Marine Drive, he told me his unhappy and wretched tale, with the waves battering away at

---

20 Are you telling the truth?

the tetrapods, and around us the hawkers screaming about coconut-water and sugar-cane juice and *paan*.

'When he finished, he said that he had related to me the whole sad saga because he knew how I told stories to boys in the Baag, and he wanted me to tell this one, especially to those who were planning to go abroad. "Tell them," said Sarosh, "that the world can be a bewildering place and dreams and ambitions are often paths to the most pernicious of traps." As he spoke, I could see that Sarosh was somewhere far away, perhaps in New Delhi at his immigration interview, seeing himself as he was then, with what he thought was a life of hope and promise stretching endlessly before him. Poor Sarosh. Then he was back beside me on the parapet.

' "I pray you, in your stories," said Sarosh, his old sense of humour returning as he deepened his voice for his favourite *Othello* lines'[21] – and here, Nariman produced a basso profundo of his own – ' "When you shall these unlucky deeds relate, speak of me as I am; nothing extenuate, nor set down aught in malice: tell them that in Toronto once there lived a Parsi boy as best as he could. Set you down this; and say, besides, that for some it was good and for some it was bad, but for me life in the land of milk and honey was just a pain in the posterior." '

And now, Nariman allowed his low-pitched rumbles to turn into chuckles. The boys broke into cheers and loud applause and cries of 'Encore!' and 'More!' Finally, Nariman had to silence them by pointing warningly at Rustomji-the-curmudgeon's door.

While Kersi and Viraf were joking and wondering what to make of it all, Jehangir edged forward and told Nariman this was the best story he had ever told. Nariman patted his shoulder and smiled. Jehangir left, wondering if Nariman would have been as popular if Dr Mody was still alive. Probably, since the two were liked for different reasons: Dr Mody used to be constantly jovial, whereas Nariman had his periodic story-telling urges.

Now the group of boys who had really enjoyed the Savukshaw story during the previous week spoke up. Capitalizing on Nariman's extraordinarily good mood, they began clamouring for more Savukshaw: 'Nariman Uncle, tell the one about Savukshaw the hunter, the one you had started that day.'

'What hunter? I don't know which one you mean.' He refused to be reminded of it, and got up to leave. But there was loud protest, and the boys started chanting, 'We-want-Savukshaw! We-want Savukshaw!'

Nariman looked fearfully towards Rustomji's door and held up his hands placatingly: 'All right, all right! Next time it will be Savukshaw again. Savukshaw the artist. The story of the Parsi Picasso.'

§ *Canadian multiculturalism* Kogawa, Ondaatje (2); *South Asian diaspora* Gooneratne, Naipaul, Mukherjee, Rushdie; Carib: Naipaul (2); NZSP: Subramani

---

21 Alluding to *Othello*, v 2 341ff.

Further Reading

This is a select bibliography of guides, literary histories, works about specific genres or aspects of post-colonial literatures, and works on post-colonial theory. Space has made it impossible to include author listings, but works mentioned here will help in the location of further materials on particular writers.

Achebe, Chinua, *Hopes and Impediments*, London: Heinemann, 1988.

Adam, Ian and Tiffin, Helen, eds., *Past the Last Post: Theorizing Post-Colonialism and Postmodernism*, Hemel Hempstead: Harvester Wheatsheaf, 1991.

Ahmad, Aijaz, *In Theory: Classes, Nations, Literatures*, London and New York: Verso, 1992.

Ashcroft, Bill, Griffiths, Gareth and Tiffin, Helen, *The Empire Writes Back: Theory and Practice in Post-Colonial Literatures*, London and New York: Routledge, 1989.

Ashcroft, Bill, Griffiths, Gareth and Tiffin, Helen, eds., *The Post-Colonial Studies Reader*, London and New York: Routledge, 1995.

Atwood, Margaret, *Survival: A Thematic Guide to Canadian Literature*, Toronto: Anansi, 1972.

Banham, Martin, Hill, Errol and Woodyard, George, *The Cambridge Guide to African and Caribbean Theatre*, Cambridge: Cambridge University Press, 1994.

Baugh, Edward, ed., *Critics on Caribbean Literature*, London: Allen and Unwin, 1978.

Benson, Eugene and Connolly, Lloyd W., eds., *The Routledge Encyclopedia of Post-Colonial Literatures in English*, 2 vols., London and New York: Routledge, 1994.

Bhabha, Homi, *The Location of Culture*, London and New York: Routledge, 1994.

Bhabha, Homi, ed., *Nation and Narration*, London and New York: Routledge, 1990.

Boehmer, Elleke, *Colonial and Postcolonial Literature: Migrant Metaphors*, Oxford and New York: Oxford University Press, 1995.

Booth, James, *Writers and Politics in Nigeria*, London: Hodder and Stoughton, 1981.

Brown, Lloyd, *West Indian Poetry*, Boston: Twayne, 1978.

Brydon, Diana and Tiffin, Helen, eds., *Decolonising Fictions*, Aarhus: Dangaroo, 1992.

Coetzee, J. M., *White Writing: On the Culture of Letters in South Africa*, Johannesburg: Radix, 1988.

Dance, Daryl Cumber, ed., *Fifty Caribbean Writers*, Westport, Conn.: Greenwood, 1986.

Davies, Carol Boyce and Fido, Elaine, *Out of the Kumbla: Caribbean Womanist Perspectives on Caribbean Literature*, Trenton, NJ: Africa World Press, 1990.

Durix, Jean-Pierre and Carole, *An Introduction to the New Literatures in English*, Paris: Longman France, 1993.

Frye, Northrop, *The Bush Garden*, Toronto: Anansi, 1971.

Gelder, Ken and Salzman, Paul, *The New Diversity: Australian Fiction, 1970–88*, Ringwood, Vic.: Penguin, 1989.

Gérard, Albert, *European-Language Writing in Sub-Saharan Africa*, 2 vols., Budapest: Akadémia Kiadó, 1986.

Gikandi, Simon, *Reading the African Novel*, London: James Currey, 1987.

Gilkes, Michael, *The West Indian Novel*, Boston: Twayne, 1981.

Gilroy, Paul, *The Black Atlantic: Modernity and Double Consciousness*, London and New York: Verso, 1993.

Goodwin, Ken, *Understanding African Poetry*, London: Heinemann, 1982.

Goodwin, Ken, *A History of Australian Literature*, London: Macmillan, 1986.

Gurnah, Abdulrazak, ed., *Essays on African Writing, 1: A Re-Evaluation*, London: Heinemann, 1993.

Harrex, S.C., *The Fire and the Offering: The English-Language Novel in India, 1935–70*, 2 vols., Calcutta: Writers Workshop, 1977.

Harris, Wilson, *The Womb of Space: The Cross-Cultural Imagination*, Westport, Conn.: Greenwood, 1983.

Heath, Jeffrey M., ed., *Profiles in Canadian Literature*, 6 vols., Toronto: Dundurn Press, 1980–6.

Herdeck, Donald, ed., *Caribbean Writers: A Bio-Bibliographical Sourcebook*, Washington: Three Continents, 1979.

Hergenhan, Laurie, ed., *The Penguin New Literary History of Australia*, Ringwood, Vic.: Penguin, 1988.

Howells, Coral Ann, *Private and Fictional Words: Canadian Women Novelists of the 1970s and 1980s*, London: Methuen, 1987.

Huggan, Graham, *Territorial Disputes: Maps and Mapping Strategies in Contempoary Canadian and Australian Fiction*, Toronto: University of Toronto Press, 1994.

Hutcheon, Linda, *The Canadian Postmodern: A Study of Contemporary English-Canadian Fiction*, Toronto: Oxford University Press, 1988.

Iyengar, K. R. Srinivasa, *Indian Writing in English*, New Delhi: Sterling, rev. edn, 1984.

Keith, W. J., *Canadian Literature in English*, London: Longman, 1985.

Killam, G. D., *The Writing of East and Central Africa*, London: Heinemann, 1984.

King, Bruce, *The New English Literatures*, London: Macmillan, 1980.

King, Bruce, *Modern Indian Poetry in English*, New Delhi: Oxford University Press, 1987.

King, Bruce, ed., *West Indian Literature*, London: Macmillan, 1979.

Klinck, Carl and New, W. H. *Literary History of Canada: Canadian Literature in English*, 2nd edn, Toronto: University of Toronto Press, 1990.

Kramer, Leonie, ed., *The Oxford History of Australian Literature*, Melbourne: Oxford University Press, 1981.

Kroetsch, Robert, *The Lovely Treachery of Words*, Toronto: Oxford University Press, 1989.

Mukherjee, Meenakshi, *The Twice-Born Fiction*, London: Heinemann, 1971.

Mukherjee, Meenakshi, *Realism and Reality: The Novel and Society in India*, New Delhi: Oxford University Press, 1985.

Naik, M. K., *A History of Indian Writing in English*, New Delhi: Sahitya Akademi, 1981.

Neumann, Shirley and Wilson, Robert, *Labyrinths of Voice: Conversations with Robert Kroetsch*, Edmonton, Alberta: NeWest Press, 1983.

New, W. H., *A History of Canadian Literature*, London: Macmillan, 1989.

Ngugi wa Thiong'o, *Decolonising the Mind: The Politics of Language in African Literature*, London: James Currey and Heinemann, 1986.

Ramchand, Kenneth, *The West Indian Novel and Its Background*, London: Faber, 1970.

Ramchand, Kenneth, *An Introduction to the Study of West Indian Literature*, London: Nelson, 1976.

Rushdie, Salman, *Imaginary Homelands: Essays and Criticism, 1981–1991*, London; Granta, 1991.

Rutherford, Anna, ed., *From Commonwealth to Post-Colonial*, Aarhus: Dangaroo, 1992.

Said, Edward, *Orientalism: Western Conceptions of the Orient*, London: Routledge, 1978.

Sharrad, Paul, ed., *Readings in Pacific Literature*, Wollongong: University of Wollongong New Literatures Research Centre, 1993.

Singh, Kirpal, *The Writer's Sense of the Past: Essays on Southeast Asian and Australasian Literature*, Singapore: Singapore University Press, 1987.

Slemon, Stephen and Tiffin, Helen, eds., *After Europe: Critical Theory and Post-Colonial Writing*, Aarhus: Dangaroo, 1989.

Soyinka, Wole, *Myth, Literature and the African World*, Cambridge: Cambridge University Press, 1976.

Spivak, Gayatri Chakravorty, *The Post-Colonial Critic: Interviews, Strategies, Dialogues*, ed. Sarah Harasym, London and New York: Routledge, 1990.

Stead, C.K., *In the Glass Case: Essays on New Zealand Literature*, Auckland: Auckland University Press, 1981.

Sturm, Terry, ed., *The Oxford History of New Zealand Literature*, Oxford: Oxford University Press, 1991.

Subramani, *South Pacific Literature: From Myth to Fabulation*, Suva: University of the South Pacific Press, 1985.

Suleri, Sarah, *The Rhetoric of English India*, Chicago: Chicago University Press, 1992.

Tiffin, Chris, ed., *South Pacific Images*, St. Lucia, Qld.: University of Queensland Press, 1978.

Toye, William, ed., *The Oxford Companion to Canadian Literature*, Toronto: Oxford University Press, 1983.

Wilde, William H., Hooton, Joy and Andrews, Barry, *The Oxford Guide to Australian Literature*, Melbourne: Oxford University Press, 1985.

Williams, Patrick and Chrisman, Laura, eds., *Colonial Discourse and Post-Colonial Theory*, Hemel Hempstead: Harvester Wheatsheaf, 1993.

Author Index

Title Index